Premiere of the
WORLD'S GREATEST AIR SPECTACLE
HELL'S ANGELS
EARLY IN MAY AT THE
GEO. M. COHAN Theatre
42nd ST. AND B'WAY, NEW YORK
Produced by ~ ~
Howard Hughes
AT A COST OF FOUR MILLION DOLLARS

HOWARD HUGHES:

HELL'S ANGEL

by Darwin Porter

ISBN 0-9748118-1-5
All Rights Reserved
Copyright 2005, Blood Moon Productions, Ltd.

302A West 12th Street, #358
New York, NY 10014
www.BloodMoonProductions.com

First Edition published April 2005
Cover Art by Outboxx.com
Photos courtesy of Photofest (www.photofestnyc.com)
and The Haggart Collection
Corporate logo by Ed Husser

Blood Moon Productions

(www.BloodMoonProductions.com) originated in 1997 as the Georgia Literary Association, a radical press established by Danforth Prince and staffed by journalists with links to *The Frommer Guides*.

Its product list focuses on literary treatments of hard-core revelations about the history of Hollywood, always with an abiding respect for the creative talent that fueled Hollywood's Golden Age. Upcoming titles include a radical new look at Marlon Brando, available in November of 2005.

Howard Hughes, Jr., in his "lucky fedora," late 1930s or early 1940s.

**This book is dedicated to Stanley Mills Haggart,
wherever he might be.**

Acknowledgments

This biography is compiled mainly from personal reminiscences of men and women who knew Howard Hughes, Jr. Some loved him at one point or another during their relationship. Some hated him intensely from the very beginning. Ultimately, most of the intimates felt betrayed, usually after they were dumped and Hughes moved on to other conquests.

My first exposure to the complicated legacy of Howard Hughes was during the late 1940s, on the set of *Slattery's Hurricane,* where my mother was working as an assistant to two of its co-stars, Linda Darnell and Veronica Lake. Each of them thought that my blond curls were "cute." One day, I overheard them indiscreetly "comparing notes" about their separate experiences dating Howard Hughes. That night, salaciously, I wrote down everything I heard them say. Hughes sounded fascinating, especially since my mother had just joined the local HUGHES FOR PRESIDENT Club, scores of which were being organized at that time across America. Since it appeared likely that Hughes would become America's next president, I began a journal. As the decades passed, my notes grew to the point where they filled a large wooden trunk.

Over the years in New York, Hollywood, Mexico, San Francisco, Chicago, London, Miami, Nassau, Virginia, and other places, hundreds of people contributed to my portrait of Hughes. Sometimes, I culled a paragraph or two from someone who knew him only casually. Other revelations were more extensive, as in the case of silent film star Blanche Sweet. But regardless of its source, each bit of information was like a piece of a puzzle, always providing some insight—major or minor—into this enigmatic figure.

Seemingly everyone who ever came into contact with Hughes, fleetingly or intimately, had at least one anecdote. As was to be expected, some sources were more helpful than others. To each of those who contributed, living or dead, I am profoundly grateful. **May the departed rest in peace.**

In Memoriam:

Without the pioneering research of **Richard Bennett** and **Rebecca Stroud**, I could never have written so extensively and intimately about Hughes's early days and his school years. Richard and Rebecca never completed a draft of the book they planned, *Young Hughes,* but they did manage to compile a pithy collection of research. Reared in Houston, and familiar with that city's legend and lore, they knew Hughes's mother, Allene Gano Hughes; his aunt, Annette Gano Lummis; Dudley Sharp, Hughes's boyhood friend; and Dudley's mother, Estelle Sharp. They were familiar with young Hughes's private schools and summer camps. And as dyed-in-the-wool Houstonians, they knew Ella Rice Hughes and her entourage, gathering the most intimate details I have ever read about Hughes's disastrous first marriage. Through Ella, they met James Overton Winston, her early beau, her final husband, and her only true love.

They had originally intended to publish their book in 1938, capitalizing on Hughes's newfound cult status as an American aviation hero. But for reasons never sufficiently explained, but which might have derived from potential reprisals from Hughes himself, they abandoned their project prior to the completion of a first draft, leaving their research notes under the stewardship of New York literary agent **Bertha Klausner**. In the 1960s, envisioning a refocused and updated biography of Howard Hughes, Ms. Klausner obtained permission for me to draw upon the research material left behind by Richard and Rebecca.

Another major source of information about Hughes was extracted from **Johnny Meyer**, Hughes's publicist and pimp. No one knew more about Hughes's sexual dalliances than Meyer.

I was introduced to Johnny Meyer by the late New York literary agent **Jay Garon**, who is best remembered for having launched the career of the best-selling novelist John Grisham. In the mid-1970s, Garon negotiated long and hard with Meyer for the production of a personalized memoir about his involvement with the mysterious Mr. Hughes. In exchange for his revelations, Meyer expected a very large advance. Before agreeing to such an advance, Garon insisted that Meyer be "vetted" as a means of seeing what he had to reveal. I was hired to attend the vetting sessions, taking notes, confirming, and cross-checking his statements with what I already knew about the grimy underbelly of Hollywood. Despite my enthusiastic role as note taker and scribe, Garon did not offer me the job of crafting Meyer's memoirs. Instead, he planned to entrust its ghost-writing to James Kirkwood, a well-established novelist and playwright who eventually won a Pulitzer Prize for his contributions to the Broadway musical, *A Chorus Line.*

When Garon had extracted enough information from Meyer for the compilation of a book proposal, he began tough negotiations with publishers for a stiff advance on what he hoped would become an explosive bestseller. But suddenly, perhaps under threat of reprisals, Meyer abruptly withdrew from the project. The deal was abandoned. Later, Meyer mysteriously died. Perhaps he knew too much.

My enduring thanks go to **Stanley Mills Haggart** for the reams of information he gathered, sometimes compulsively, during his many years as a writer, actor, and artist in early Hollywood. He was an inside operator, a man-about-town during an era when a handsome, charming, and debonair newcomer could meet virtually anyone, long before high-security clearances and meddling publicists made casual access to movie stars virtually impossible. Because of his huge contribution to my understanding of Howard Hughes and his entourage, he almost deserves credit for co-authorship of this biography.

Stanley and I formed a 20-year writing partnership that produced more than 50 titles, many of which were renewed at annual intervals, and published by houses that included Simon & Schuster and Arbor House. With an attention to chronology and detail that evoked the style of Marcel Proust, Stanley almost obsessively dictated his memoirs about love, sex, ambition, filmmaking, and scandal in early Hollywood. For years prior to his death in 1980, he worked on drafts of those memoirs. Although they've never been published, I've drawn upon them extensively.

Stanley Haggart both lived with and worked for **Cary Grant** and **Randolph Scott** during a period of their affair when Hughes was a frequent visitor to their home. Stanley's insights into the dynamics of this strange trio are deeply appreciated.

The information that Stanley gathered from **Noah Dietrich** was invaluable. Stanley first met Dietrich when he worked at Hughes's headquarters at 7000 Romaine Street in the 1940s, a job secured for him by his very close friend at the time, Randolph Scott. Dietrich compiled, through a ghost-writer, a slim and uncontroversial volume of his own memoirs, *Howard: the Amazing Mr. Hughes,* long after he'd been ousted from his lofty role as majordomo of the Hughes empire. Published in 1972, four years before Hughes's death, it's as noteworthy for what it doesn't reveal as it is for what it does. Dietrich's discretion was probably motivated by fear of a libel suit from Hughes. In years gone by, the head honcho of the Hughes empire had purchased many a Hughes biography only to supress it. Dietrich himself feared the same fate for his memoirs.

I also drew extensively upon the journals of Stanley's indomitable and news-conscious mother, **Maria Jane Haggart**, who migrated to Hollywood early in the 20th century, when its population numbered only four thousand people. Mrs. Haggart, with her young son, lived next door to the fabled Hollywood journalist and columnist, **Adela Rogers St. Johns**, who knew a lot about everyone and everything in town. (Detractors claimed that she knew every time that a rat crossed Hollywood Boulevard.) As the decades passed, and as her friendship with Mrs. Haggart deepened, Ms. St. Johns became particularly skilled at figuring out which star had murdered which victim.

The roots of this Hughes biography also evolved from a provocative but unheralded collection of mini-biographies that Stanley and I once co-authored. Entitled *Where Are They Today?,* the book, alas, never found a publisher. It documented the indiscretions and pathos associated with movie stars of early Hollywood, mainly those from the 20s and 30s, many of whom never successfully made the transition from Silent Films to Talkies. Although we didn't always invoke his name as part of our interview process, Hughes's role in the lives of many of the people we interviewed was often mentioned as a vital part of their recollections. Some of the actresses we interviewed, and at least one of the male stars (**Ralph Graves**), admitted to having had affairs with the aviator. Perhaps *Where Are They Today?* was too potentially libelous to have found a publisher, or perhaps its anecdotes were recited merely as a means for retired actors to vengefully settle old scores. After reviewing the manuscript, Random House's publisher Bennett Cerf scribbled a note to our literary agent Bertha Klausner, "Who wants to read about a lot of broken-down hags and has-beens?"

Times have changed. Blood Moon Productionshas imposed upon me the importance of salvaging and transcribing these insights before it's too late.

For an understanding of how this book was compiled, the extensive contributions of two Hollywood agents, **John Darrow** and **Henry Willson**, must also be cited. John Darrow, a once-handsome romantic actor who transformed himself into a Hollywood agent and talent scout, was part of the original cast of *Hell's Angels.* From a foothold as Hughes's lover during his early career, he eventually introduced Hughes to other male lovers after his affair with Hughes had cooled. Later, the task of procuring male partners for Hughes was transferred to another Hollywood agent and talent scout, Henry Willson, who was never shy about demanding sexual favors from wannabe actors he auditioned. Willson brought Hughes together with two of the most important figures of his life: Jack Buetel (costar of *The Outlaw*) and Faith Domergue, who—when she was only fifteen—became Hughes's live-in mistress.

Dozens of friends, enemies, lovers, business associates, directors, and fellow actors contributed to this book's anecdotes about Errol Flynn, Robert Taylor, and Tyrone Power. Many discarded associates, mostly male, of those stars have written unpublished memoirs about their sexual involvements with these matinee idols. At least some of those manuscripts were submitted to Jay Garon's literary agency. Each provided insights into the closeted lives of Taylor, Flynn, and Power. My appreciation is extended to Garon for allowing me to read these unpublished works, from which I extracted valuable information, especially about the relationship of Hughes to each of those stars.

A special tribute is extended to my friend, actor **Robert Francis**, who died tragically and early, in ways described within this biography. I met him for the first time when he was part of a publicity campaign sweeping through South Florida, when I requested an interview as a reporter for *The Miami Herald.* He gave me lengthy insights into his involvement in the lives of both Spencer Tracy and Hughes.

Many of Hughes's breakthroughs in aviation were enabled by **Glenn Odekirk**, a brave and brilliant aviation engineer who, it was said, could make virtually anything fly. He demanded to be paid for every interview he ever granted. Upon learning that he expected a fee, most reporters turned him down, yet for only $2,000, he was willing to review his entire experience—both private and professional—with Hughes. In most cases, he was the only source who knew the behind-the-scenes story of several of Hughes's pioneering breakthroughs in aviation. My thanks go to **Elizabeth Talbot-Martin** for hooking Stanley and me up with Glenn, whom she respected as a friend and neighbor. Thanks also go to **Albert Belkstein**, who talked candidly about Odekirk and Hughes as well.

Remarkable material emerged from **Albert ("Cubby") Broccoli** and his cousin, **Pat DeCicco**, both of them longtime friends of Hughes. Cubby was privy to many of Hughes's secrets. Pat knew even more, and frequently talked openly and freely after a final and particularly bitter falling-out with his former patron.

I owe thanks to **Senator Ralph Owen Brewster**, with whom I once dined in Maine during the research for the first edition of what became *Frommer's Guide to New England*. The deposed senator's insights into his epic and widely publicized conflict with Hughes were most enlightening.

Material about self-described former lovers of Hughes, including **Terry Moore** and **Gloria Vanderbilt,** were drawn from sources that included their own published revelations.

The contribution of **William ("Billy") Haines**, movie star turned decorator, was immense. Stanley Haggart's dossier on **Nazimova** and her relationship with Howard Hughes, Sr., was most useful. I knew the silent screen star, **Mae Murray**, during the final years of her life, and owe her a debt for relaying information about her experiences with Hughes, Sr., and also for tales of her heady days as queen of MGM. Former child actor **Philippe De Lacy** generously shared his trunk of memorabilia about **Barbara LaMarr**, including a copy of a letter that she once wrote to a lovesick young Hughes.

For helping me craft the early portrait of Hughes himself, I extend a special bouquet to **Eleanor Boardman**, who lived up to her long-standing reputation as the most outspoken woman in Hollywood. I also thank **Madge Bellamy** (a junkyard dealer when I met her, but once the *Darling of the Twenties);* **Ingrid Bergman** (whom I interviewed at her summer home on an island off the western coast of Sweden during a trip I made there for The Frommer Guides); the British actress **Lilian Bond** (who said that before Hughes, she'd never met a rich man who was handsome); **Russell Birdwell** (a marvelous source about how *The Outlaw* was really made); **Joan Blondell** (my longtime friend and for one happy summer, housemate); **Evelyn Brent** (star of Hughes's *The Mating*

Call); the doomed actress **Marie Prevost** (material about her was supplied by silent screen star **Lila Lee** over drinks at her son's home in Key West); **Jack Buetel** (during an encounter in Oregon, he was very guarded in his disclosures); cowboy star **Johnny Mack Brown** (who was even more guarded in *his* disclosures); **Bruce Cabot** (for insights into the love affairs of Errol Flynn); **Nancy Carroll** (who related scandals about virtually everybody); **Igor** and **Oleg Cassini** (my material was gleaned from their own published revelations—not from personal interviews); **Mae Clarke** (after she recovered from the grapefruit that James Cagney squashed into her face); aviatrix **Jacqueline Cochran** (thanks to an introduction that was arranged in Miami by photojournalism's Wilson Hicks); **Claudette Colbert** (in Barbados); **June Collyer** (Hughes found that her face practically glowed); **Jeanne Craine** (who gave valuable insights into Hughes's marriage with Jean Peters); **Joan Crawford** (who found Hughes creepy and who steadfastly refused to associate with him); **Richard Cromwell** (who was married, briefly and disastrously, to Angela Lansbury); director **Preston Sturges** (whose patrician upbringing might have helped him not be afraid of Hughes); **George Cukor** (who was especially helpful in his recollections about Katharine Hepburn and Cary Grant); **Alexander d'Arcy** (a close friend of Hughes during the 1930s); **Faith Domergue** (who shed light on her tortured and underaged relationship with Hughes); screenwriter **Ben Hecht; Hedy Lamarr** (as amusing as she was shocking); **Alice Faye** (for her memories of Tyrone Power); director/actor **Mel Ferrer** (for behind-the scenes stories about the filming of *Vendetta)* **Victor Mature** (in Miami, he told more than he should have); **Patricia Peardon** (whose photograph appeared on the cover of *Life* Magazine for her Broadway role as *Junior Miss)* for her inside knowledge about Hughes's affairs with her longtime friends Katharine Hepburn and *debutante* Brenda Frazier; director **Howard Hawks** (he was especially strong about tales of *The Outlaw); * **Ava Gardner** (in London, she was both candid and cynical about Hughes, her own allure, and her screen career in general); **George Raft** (who knew a lot about the making of *Scarface* and Hughes's relationship with Humphrey Bogart and Billie Dove); **Bette Davis** (almost vengefully candid in her dotage); **Corrine Griffith** (a surprising mixture of self-enchantment and greed); **Ralph Graves** (who outed himself as a bisexual); **Jane Greer** (as adorable as she was revealing); **James Hall** (for his recollections about Jean Harlow and the making of *Hell's Angels); * **Hedda Hopper** (Stanley Haggart's close friend); **Uncle Rupert Hughes** (who was violently critical of his nephew during the division of the Hughes family estate); **Barbara Hutton** (for her indiscreet diaries and for her invitation to that party in Marrakesh); actor **John Ireland**; agent **Ilse Lahn** (for her insights into the death of Paul Bern, husband of Jean Harlow); **Dorothy Jordan** (*Funny Face,* the beautiful and friendly belle from Tennessee); **Greta Keller** (the continental *chanteuse,* my housemate, who provided revelations about her murdered husband, David Bacon, and his troubled relationship with Hughes); **Lana Turner** (who grew increasingly revelatory as she aged); **Peter Lawford** (for his deadly but accurate comments); **Janet Leigh** (whose oral reports sometimes differed from what had been published about her); **Ida Lupino** (bitterly outspoken); **Kenneth MacKenna** (a close friend of both Stanley Haggart and Humphrey Bogart); an ill and aging **Guy Madison** (who remembered much about Hughes and his own ill-fated wife, Gail Russell); **Anna Magnani** (rich with anecdotes about Ingrid Bergman, Hughes, and Roberto Rossellini); **Gummo Marx** (for material about Faith Domergue and Jack Buetel); actress **Patsy Kelly** (for insights into the death of Thelma Todd); agent **Johnny Maschio** (who knew a whole lot about everybody); **Virginia Mayo** (the Hughes romance that never got airborne); lawyer **Neil McCarthy**; actors **Adolphe Menjou** and **Pat O'Brien** (for tales about the making of *The Front Page); * actor/director **Burgess Meredith** (for stories about everybody); **Una Merkel** (for Ramon Novarro anecdotes); director **Lewis Milestone** (for memories about Hughes's earliest days in film); photographer **Rod St-Just** (for hot memoirs about Hollywood's sexual underground); **Ann Miller** (for information about the tragic life of her friend, Linda Darnell); **Brian Aherne** (for stories about *Sylvia Scarlett)*; *Miami Herald* reporters **George Mills** and **Jane Wood Reno** (for information about Hughes's mysterious disappearance for several panicky months during the closing months of World War II); **Robert Mitchum**; silent screen star **Colleen Moore**; **Audie Murphy** (the much-decorated war hero who relayed his undying hatred of Hughes); **Marshall Neilan** (a friend of Stanley Haggart and a former husband of Blanche Sweet); **David Niven; Ramon Novarro**; **Floyd Odlum** (who was especially helpful about Hughes and his near-destruction of RKO); **Louella Parsons** (perpetually indiscreet and perpetually haunted by weak kidneys); **Joe Petrali**; **Dick Powell; Vincent Price** (for "precious gossip," delivered at the Plaza Hotel in Rome, about practically everybody); The outrageous **Pussy-Katt**; **Fay Wray** (who revealed the exact whereabouts of Hughes when the world press believed he was with Katharine Hepburn); **Gene Tierney; Irene Mayer Selznick** (she once told the author and **Tennessee Williams** that Hughes had once even proposed marriage to her); **Stewart Granger** (some surprisingly candid confessions, including thoughts of murder); **Robert Stack** (for his material on young JFK); actor **Chester Morris** (for memories of Hughes, Billie Dove, and *Cock of the Air); * **Charles Starrett** (for more memories of Billie Dove, Hughes, and the early Talkie, *The Age for Love); * **Tallulah Bankhead** (for an outrageous, albeit drunken, confession about an encounter between Marlene Dietrich, Hughes, and "*moi, dah-ling"), * **Gloria Swanson, Franchot Tone** (a Hughes-hater); **James Whale**; director **Irwin Willat** (also a to-the-death Hughes-hater; Stanley Haggart had a bit role in his last film); **Faye Emerson; Roddy McDowall** (for a charming account of Hughes's unsuccessful pursuit of his best friend, Elizabeth Taylor); "Mr. Acapulco," **Teddy Stauffer** (for revelations about Hughes and his relationship with Tyrone, Lana, Hedy, Faith, and James Dean); **Barbara** ("How'd ya like to sleep with a movie star?") **Payton**;

one-time studio head **Peter Rathvon** (for information about Hughes's feud with Dore Schary and his disastrous takeover of RKO); **Fritz Lang** (for stories about *Rancho Notorious* and *Clash by Night);* and **Ben Lyon** (a close friend of Stanley Haggart, he contributed greatly to memories of Hughes, the filming of *Hell's Angels,* and material about his "discoveries," Jean Harlow and Marilyn Monroe.)

To all these people—dead or alive—and to many others not mentioned, I extend my heartfelt thanks for the contributions that helped in the unveiling of that remarkable personality, Howard Hughes, Jr.—an American original.

Author's Note

In the pages ahead, the source of each individual bit of information is positioned very close to the spot where the information actually appears. Also, within the pages ahead, direct quotations have been transcribed "as they were remembered" by the people who originally heard the remarks. They're presented in the same format, and in the same phraseologies, that were used when those remarks were originally transmitted to either Stanley or me. If the exact wording and phraseologies of any individual quotation are *not* accurately presented, the author hopes that the points being made, and the impressions being relayed, have nonetheless been rendered as accurately as possible.

Throughout this biography, I sincerely hope that I have transmitted and preserved the essence of once-fabled lives, including that of Mr. Hughes himself. He inhabited a Golden Age that will never come again.

Darwin Porter
New York City
January, 2005

CHAPTER ONE
Hollywood, 1921

Party-loving Hollywood was setting out to put the roar in the Roaring Twenties.

With his wife and son safely tucked away in Houston, Texas, Howard Hughes Sr., or "Big Howard" as he was called, sat looking up at the mauve-colored sky over Los Angeles. But not for long.

Female screams around the swimming pool quickly diverted his eye. Milling about the pool, or else splashing in it, was a bevy of beautiful, long-limbed showgals better looking than any he'd seen in the fleshpots of Chicago or New York.

Hughes was not a handsome man but he was secure in his belief that before the evening ended he could snare any of these big-breasted chorines. Not bad for a Missouri farm boy who had been born dirt poor in 1869.

He was rugged and tall; a man of rough-hewn, roguish looks who'd wandered across the dusty plains of Oklahoma and between the snow-capped mountains of Colorado, seeking to strike it rich by buying and selling leases on silver and zinc mines. He'd also been a regular aboard the gambling showboats that steamed up and down the Mississippi, each of them loaded with wild and wanton women whose charms were usually available for one gold dollar. Whiplashed by the booms and busts of the Robber Baron Age, he sometimes flaunted his bundles of cash to entrap the shapeliest and most glamorous of women and occasionally, a virginal teenage girl.

From boomtown to boomtown, he'd been a wildcatter, coping with a string of broken dreams, but still hoping to acquire "all the pots of gold at the end of the rainbow."

He'd wanted a wife who "acted and looked like a queen" and he found her one Christmas Day in Dallas in 1902 as he came into the ballroom of the Gaiety Hall for a Yuletide Cotillion. Allene Stone Gano, born in 1883, was only nineteen when he was introduced to her. Clad in a pink lace gown, she'd stunned him with her flowing brunette hair, high cheekbones, and liquid brown eyes— an ascetic appearance of enormous appeal to a thirty-two year-old roustabout who'd spent most of his sexual life suckling at the breasts of prostitutes. She was in the Social Register, daughter of a prominent Texas judge and granddaughter of a famous general in the Confederate army.

He was happy that he'd dressed up that night in his Brooks Brothers, charcoal gray, pin-striped suit, with white spats, a black bowler hat, and a diamond stickpin.

1

Her eyes had seemed to dance as he'd gazed into them. She'd stood before him, tall and reed-thin, a young filly of charm and grace.

From the beginning, he'd viewed her as ideal wife material, the kind of woman he could impregnate, stash away in a fine home somewhere, visit on occasions, and continue to lead the wild bachelor life he'd always had. Wife or no wife, Howard Sr. valued his freedom above all.

In spite of his wild living, he was an educated man, having been born the son of a Missouri lawyer. Hughes Sr. had graduated from Harvard, had earned his law degree from the University of Iowa, and for a time had practiced law with his father in Keokuk, Iowa. His courtship of Allene had been brief. After his proposal under a full Texas moon in March of 1903, the couple were married only a few weeks later, on May 24, at the home of her parents on Masten Street in Dallas.

When Howard Sr. had met Allene Gano, he'd been mesmerized by her charm and her taste in clothing. Although her French Huguenot family had urged her to marry a multi-millionaire, she'd fallen for Hughes Sr. At the time he had exactly fifty-thousand dollars in the bank, and on their 1904 honeymoon in Britain and the Continent, he managed to spend $49,100 of that treasure, something that even the Gilded Age scions of the Rockefellers, Vanderbilts, and Astors didn't exceed during their spendthrift tours across Europe.

Even if he had a wife and son, he'd need to be able to run away at a moment's notice, perhaps to mud-dirt Texas towns like Goose Creek or Pierce Junction where he might strike it rich in the oil business. Back then, he'd known that such rip-roaring towns would be only stations along the way for him, places to join local riggers hunting for the black gold that lurked in the bowels of the earth.

Allene had not only married him, but stood by him, even as he neared the age of forty and still hadn't hit pay dirt. And then there came a sudden reversal of fortune.

He'd had no great success as a wildcatter, but he had nevertheless struck it rich with his "rock eater," a drill with 166 cutting edges that could pierce through granite. "Or drill through Hell itself," Hughes claimed.

Up until then, oilmen had used the standard "fishtail" bit with two cutting edges that blunted whenever they hit hard rock.

Even though he lied and wasn't the sole inventor, as he'd later maintain, he'd acquired two U.S. patents on August 10, 1909. He'd made many improvements to the bit, but the invention itself had been purchased for $150 from Granville A. Humason, a young Mississippi millwright.

Hard rock, once thought impenetrable, could be pierced by his "rock bit" and the precious oil reserves tapped. The rock drill had forever changed the way men pursued oil deposits.

Years later, Hughes Jr. was asked if his father's tool company had a monopoly. "Of course not!" he replied. "People who want to drill for oil and not use the Hughes bit can always use a pick and shovel."

By the time Hughes Sr. arrived in Hollywood in 1921, word had spread through the movie colony that "the richest oilman in Texas" was in town. With his drill plowing for oil in countries around the world, and his bank account growing fatter and fatter by the day, Hughes felt he deserved some pleasure.

The Hollywood party to which he'd been invited was getting wilder. Already six bathing beauties had pulled down the tops to their suits and jumped into the pool.

He was trying to pick his favorite for the

Howard Hughes Sr.

evening when he was overcome with the smell of a strangely scented, over-perfumed cigarette.

Looking around, he spotted his hostess—attired in a flamboyant peacock dress of emerald green and royal blue—gliding toward him with a long cigarette holder. She was the grand empress of the estate, the Garden of Alla, with its swimming pool in the shape of the Black Sea of her homeland.

"Howard, darling," she called out to him in a Russian-accented voice.

He rose from his chaise longue to stand in front of her. Since she was a virtual midget, he towered over her. Her head of frizzy hair hardly came to his navel, yet this petite little bird was the Queen of Hollywood.

The exotic Alla Nazimova herself.

She extended her mauve-colored gloved hand to him for it to be kissed.

***

Nazimova artfully seated herself in a peacock chair across from Hughes, as an Amazon-like maiden wearing a breast plate arranged her gown. Standing over her was a Nubian slave in a pink-colored, bulging loincloth gently fanning her, as she continued to smoke her Turkish cigarette. She motioned for the Nubian to offer Hughes one of the cigarettes, which he accepted.

"You Hollywood stars sure like drama," he said.

With her pumpkin-shaped head and gunboat feet, Nazimova confronted him. "My whole life is devoted to drama. In fact, I don't think I'm capable of doing anything that's not dramatic."

As he inhaled deeply on the cigarette, he leaned back and more closely studied the image of Nazimova. Her beauty was but an illusion, yet she was the highest paid actress in Hollywood, earning $13,000 a week. He respected women who earned their own money and didn't depend on a man to keep them like chattel.

3

When a tall, handsome man came over to shake Hughes' hand, Nazimova introduced him as Charles Bryant. She called him "the Rosebud of my life."

Bryant quickly departed. Nazimova moved closer to Hughes, her face coming into the spotlight. He noticed that heavy rice powder covered the pockmarks of some childhood illness.

"Charles is not really my husband," she said. "He's actually my beard. He's a bad actor, really just a bit player. I bring him out to show him off anytime the press wants an interview." She gazed toward the beauties in the pool. "Otherwise, I prefer my tender young maidens."

"I hope we won't be fighting for the same pussies tonight," Hughes said to her.

"Not at all," she said. "I've arranged very special entertainment for you."

"Can't wait," he said.

"Mr. Hughes," she said rather abruptly. "You and I have much in common. I am dangerously seductive because of my beauty and charm. In spite of your rather plain looks, you are also dangerously seductive because of your money. You and I ruthlessly pursue glamorous women. But, unlike yourself, I prefer a man from time to time. Not for sexual pleasure of course, but because I want to know how to relate to them on the screen. How to make passionate love to them like I did to Rudolph Valentino in *Camille*."

"You're one hell of an emotionalist," he said.

"Emotionalist," she repeated, mulling that over a moment. "I've been called many things—never that. Noticing how intently he was scrutinizing her, she must have mistaken his interest. "I must warn you," she cautioned him. "Don't fall in love with me the way Valentino's wife, Jean Acker, did. I'm exactly as I am on the screen. I betray lovers as ruthlessly as men have always betrayed women. I would only break your heart. Shatter it into so many pieces you'd never be able to put it together again."

"I've never been in love, Nazimova, and I never will be," he said. "I take momentary pleasures in bodies presented to me. But when that short-lived pleasure is over, I move on. I prefer to sleep alone. *Love!* Men who fall in love never succeed in this world. They are mere lovesick fools—nothing more."

"A man after my own heart," Nazimova said. "The only thing I've ever loved is that incredible image of my flickering face on the screen."

The cigarette was making him feel

Nazimova

4

drugged—almost but not quite like getting too drunk. He knew that Nazimova hadn't invited him to her Garden of Alla to admire his physique, and he was anxious to finish their business so that he could pursue the intrigues of the night. "Assuming I want to go into the business of making movies, and I'm just flirting with the idea, just how much money do you need to make *Salome*?"

"I need another $100,000," she said matter-of-factly. "I'm putting up $300,000 of my own money, and that's all I have in the bank. It's what I've saved from what my accountants call a lifestyle lashed with extravagances."

"I know the Biblical story," he said, "but what kind of costume epic are we talking about here?"

"*Salome* will be the most artistic film ever made in the history of Hollywood."

"Artsy-fartsy," he said. "Will it have sex and plenty of it?"

"Beyond anything that's ever made it to the screen," she promised. "In tribute to Oscar Wilde's drama, I'm demanding that my entire cast be homosexual, and very scantily dressed. It will have beautiful slave boys, and a Syrian captain of the palace guard fitted in black tights with a natural pouch showing, a beaded necklace placed over his chest before a fishnet hood is draped over his body and his nipples painted purple. The black male slaves will be selected for their physiques and will wear white wigs with curls like those of Mary Pickford. Each will be clad in a silver lamé loincloth. The handsome Roman soldiers will appear in sleeveless armor to better show off their muscles. They'll wear metallic skirts ending just below their crotches, and they'll each be bare-legged. The black executioner will be played by a stunning Mandingo wearing a fully packed satin loincloth. His string of white beads will be as big as ostrich eggs matching the size of his testicles, with will be outlined in all their male glory."

"And the young gals?" Hughes asked. "What about them?"

"I'm selecting the most beautiful women in Hollywood to play the ladies of Herod's court," she said. "Except they won't be women, but men dressed as women and sporting wigs."

"I see," Hughes said. "Let me think it over tonight, and I'll give you my answer tomorrow morning at nine o'clock."

"As you desire," she said, standing up, as her hand-maiden rushed to help her.

"And my party favor for tonight?" he said, having tired of Nazimova's film talk. *Salome* was not his dream fantasy.

"She's already waiting at the front of the Garden of Alla," she said provocatively. "Waiting to take you in her arms for a night of exquisite pleasure unlike what you've ever known before."

"I can't wait!" Hughes said, getting up and kissing Nazimova's gloved hand once more. "Your film sounds exciting, and I can tell you one thing right now: I think I'm going to back it—maybe back the whole thing so that you won't have to put up one red cent."

"Oh, Howard darling, that would make me the happiest goddess in Hollywood."

***

Nazimova paled in comparison to what was waiting for Hughes at the entrance to the Garden of Alla. A sleek canary yellow Rolls-Royce stood ready to whisk him away into the night. Because of the car's darkened glass, he could make out only the shadowy figure of the woman seated in the rear.

Upon his approach, two liverymen in pink uniforms rose in their white boots from the box of the limousine where they were waiting patiently. The one on the right opened the door handle to the rear compartment. To Hughes, the handle looked like real gold.

The moment he peered into the vehicle he recognized its occupant. It was Mae Murray, "the girl with the bee-stung lips," who was rapidly replacing Nazimova as the Queen of Hollywood.

Never in his life had Hughes seen such a stunning beauty. All in white satin and ermine, she wore an elaborate headdress of feathers as befits the ex-Follies showgirl that she was. She beckoned him to sit beside her in the midnight blue patent leather interior. Her perfumed aroma evoked a field of gardenias, and her gold gown was studded with white pearls. A dazzingly large marquis diamond was glued to her forehead, sparkling in the night.

She giggled as Hughes took the seat beside her. He'd heard that Murray had a husband, Robert Leonard, stashed somewhere, but obviously he was not in the picture for tonight.

Mae Murray

"Miss Murray," he said, reaching out to kiss her extended hand the way he'd paid homage to Nazimova. "I'm your greatest fan!"

"You flatter me, sir!" she said, signaling her chauffeur, also clad in a pink uniform, to drive forward into the night, wherever they were going.

"I'm the one who is flattered," Hughes told her. "I couldn't believe it when Nazimova told me that one of the biggest stars in Hollywood wanted to spend the night with me."

"*The* biggest," she corrected him.

"I'm just a plain man," he said.

"Not to worry," she said. "I'll supply the beauty for both of us."

He noticed her gold purse. "Is it true that you actually carry little bags of gold in that purse?" he asked. "Or is that just newspaper gossip?"

"It is absolutely true, Mr. Hughes." She giggled again and opened her purse.

He peered inside to discover small bags of actual gold dust. "Don't that beat all!"

"If you stay in Hollywood long enough," she said, "you'll discover many strange phenomenon."

At her mansion, a Spanish-styled hacienda, on Adelaide Drive, one of the pink-clad footmen opened the door and offered his arm to Hughes. Brushing aside such a feminine gesture, Hughes made his way out of the Rolls on his own, and then reached back, extending his arm to Murray to assist her from her chariot.

Lined up in a row, the two footmen and the chauffeur stood at military attention to await their instructions for the evening.

Murray looked first at Hughes and then at her servants. "Boys," she said, gazing once again at Hughes, "I'm sure the gentleman here will spend the night, so I'll have no further need of you until morning."

Taking her by the arm, Hughes followed one of the footmen who opened a side gate that led into a secret garden. Wandering into it with her, he'd never seen a garden in such full bloom and one so beautiful. It overpowered him with the smell of gardenias. That was obviously her favorite flower.

The garden pathway was paved with yellow brick. To his astonishment, he spotted a dead body lying in their pathway. She giggled as he bent to examine the corpse. It was "Gloria Swanson," or a good facsimile of her. In a beaded dress of silver lamé, the Swanson dummy lay sprawled across the bricks, her dress riding indecently high, revealing red silk bloomers.

Murray giggled again as he took her arm and stepped over Swanson.

"Charlie Chaplin" was propped up drunk on a wrought-iron park bench ten feet away. In the middle of an oleander bush, a soggy "Mary Pickford" was so inebriated she was holding onto the shrub for support.

"I see your friends have lost the battle of the booze," he said.

She steered him down another yellow brick pathway that led to her menagerie where she introduced him to her favorite, a caged leopard cub named Night Fever. She also showed him a cage containing seven monkeys and an aviary of tropical birds, including birds of prey. As they moved toward the house, a Great Dane and a St. Bernard rushed up to greet them, followed at a more leisurely pace by at least a dozen white and black "showcats."

A doorman welcomed them into her greenhouse-like foyer and into the baroque parlor where Murray ordered bootleg hooch for the both of them. She just assumed that Hughes was a drinking man.

Tossing her ermine aside, she sat across from him on her red satin sofa. "I believe in leading an electric life. High voltage!"

"My kind of gal!" he said.

"You're looking at me like you're this great big boa constrictor, and I'm a pheasant in the wild. Like you're about to devour me."

"Do you think it's possible for a man to fall madly in love with a woman on first sight?" he asked.

"If that woman is Mae Murray, I believe it is not only possible but highly probable."

"Would you scream and call the police if I got up from this lonely chair and came to join you on that tempting sofa?" he asked.

"Mr. Hughes, Mae Murray is not among the faint-of-heart. They call me self-enchanted—but that's wrong. My talent in life involves enchanting others. Please, come hither."

On wobbly knees, he rose slowly from his chair. "Keep in mind, I'm a mere mortal—not some Greek God down from Olympus."

"But tonight, I'll make you feel like a God."

Her bee-stung lips beckoned for him to taste them.

***

Texas 1905-1916

The tombstone of Howard Robard Hughes Jr. lists his date of birth as December 24, 1905. Like so much of the Howard Hughes legend, that was a lie. For reasons of her own, his mother, Allene, always insisted during her short life that the date she gave birth to her baby, the child who would become America's first billionaire, was Christmas Eve. Her beloved Sonny, as she erroneously claimed, was born on "the same night as the Christ child."

No birth certificate has survived, and most sources and books list Allene's fictional date as the actual birth of Howard Hughes Jr., a young man who would be called "The Huck Finn of American Industry."

It was in 1910 that James Lawlow, owner of Houston's Rice Hotel, reported that Hughes Sr. and Allene dined with him on Christmas Eve in 1905. There was no way she could have been in a hospital giving birth on that night. Lawlow recalled that he'd sat with Mr. and Mrs. Hughes in his dining room, having awarded them the best table in the house. He even remembered the menu of roast Christmas turkey with chestnut dressing along with "Santa Claus potatoes" and candied Jersey sweets. For dessert, he'd ordered his chef to make them festive hot mince pie. Ironically, only a few months earlier, Lawlow had tossed Mr. and Mrs. Hughes out on the street because of their unpaid hotel bill. Since Hughes had recently acquired some money and had finally paid the bill, all was forgiven on the night of the Christmas Eve banquet.

While these Yuletide festivities were being celebrated, Sonny was already three months old and in the care of a nanny back at the Hughes's home,

It was actually during the late summer of 1905, one of the longest and hottest in the history of Texas, that Allene had carried her pregnancy to term. In spite of her claims to the contrary, her son had been born on September 14, 1905, as the first winds of autumn had begun to stir the dust on the sun-baked and unpaved streets of Houston. Stagnant water stood in ditches on the sides of these roads, breeding mosquitoes. Those autumnal winds also had brought the smell of decaying carcasses from the stockyards and the reek of oil "filled the air, painted the houses, choked the lungs, and stained men's souls."

Later in his life, every day that Howard Hughes Jr. spent with his mother, he would be reminded of that fictional date of Christmas Eve when she allegedly brought him into the world when she was twenty-two years old.

When she was angry at him, she would shout at him, "My body's wasted! I'm in constant pain day and night because my guts were all torn up pushing you from my body. All because I gave birth to an ungrateful son."

Dr. Oscar Norsworthy had told her that she could never have another child. Howard Robard Hughes Jr. would never know a brother or sister.

Although the date she assigned to her son's birth was a lie, her extraordinary ordeal had been real. She had endured "nine hours of hell," as she put it, giving birth to her son. Even the doctors at Houston Baptist Hospital had called hers the most difficult birth the hospital staff had ever witnessed.

On the night of the birth, Dr. Norsworthy had reported to Hughes that his wife of eighteen months was hemorrhaging badly. "With the life of your wife fading," Dr. Norsworthy had said, "there is virtually no way to save the baby. Prepare yourself for the worst. I fear Mrs. Hughes will not live to greet the dawn."

Two hours later, a miracle happened. Shortly before dawn on the morning of September 24, Dr. Norsworthy and a team that included two other surgeons had stemmed the flow of blood in Allene. The surgeons had to give her four blood transfusions.

Hughes had been forced to wait in the corridor for thirty minutes before Dr. Norsworthy finally emerged with the good news that he was the father of a robust baby boy.

His wife had been hauled to the recovery room, where it had appeared that it was still unlikely that she'd pull through.

Hughes Sr. had burst into tears when informed of his wife's greatly diminished state. "Money doesn't matter at a time like

Howard Hughes Jr.

this," he'd told the doctor. "Do anything, get any specialist. The best in the land."

With his wife sleeping peacefully the following night, Hughes had gone to one of his favorite hangouts, the poker table at Houston's Fire Station Number Eight. With him, he'd brought the fanciest of Havana cigars and the best of French brandy to celebrate the birth of his son. The fire captain, Edgar H. Davis, had ordered the ringing of the giant brass chimes of the firehouse.

Residents, mostly the families of oil workers, had heard the shrill echo of these pealing chimes and had poured anxiously into the streets, which were lit by newly installed electric lights, casting an amber-colored glow. When they'd learned that it wasn't a life-threatening emergency, like the town burning down, but a celebration, they had descended on the firehouse.

Hearing them coming, Hughes had sent word to McDuffy's Tavern to deliver all the kegs of beer he had in his cellar.

The neighbors were celebrating but hadn't been sure why. They were drinking up all the beer. Many of the younger men were also purchasing cocaine from the peddlers working the crowd. In those days, bags of cocaine were just as readily available as a glass of beer in one of the taverns.

Finally, Hughes Sr. had emerged from the firehouse to address the beer-guzzling crowd. "Tonight my son was born," he'd told his cheering audience. "A big healthy boy and a true Texan. He'll be a bigger figure than his old man will ever be. I predict he'll become the most famous and richest man in America. Not only that, but no doubt president of the United States one of these days."

At least two of three of Hughes's predictions would come true.

***

Years after his death, later day psychiatrists, such as Dr. Raymond Fowler, digging into the long-hidden dossiers and documents in the possession of the Howard Hughes estate, concluded that young Howard's relationship with his beautiful mother, Allene, was "emotionally incestuous."

Dr. Fowler's conclusion, after working for three years on a psychological profile of Howard for the Hughes estate, concluded that Allene was a "phobic, hysterical overseer" of her son.

It was true that Sonny was of a "delicate constitution," not gaining weight as he should, and "being of a nervous disposition." Using the pretense of possible ill health, she virtually didn't let the boy out of her sight until he was eight years old.

From the beginning, Allene believed that her Sonny was special, and she wanted the world to take notice of that. She didn't want her beloved boy to be like the other rough-and-tumble boys growing up in the frontier oil town of Houston. To set her son apart, she began to purchase clothing for him that made him look like a Texas version of Little Lord Fauntleroy.

She dressed him in frilly, heavily starched, and elaborately pressed white shirts with ruffles. His knickerbockers, as she more formally called his "knickers," were made of black velvet. She bought only black MaryJane shoes for him, and rather sheer white hosiery that came right up to his kneecaps, as she wanted very little skin showing.

When Allene drove him to school, Sonny stood out from the other kids. With all his shyness and tendency to be embarrassed, that was the last thing he wanted. Even though he pleaded with his mother to let him "blend in with the other boys," Allene refused to change his dress code.

Looking like a dandy in a frontier town, Sonny had to endure the taunts of his hell-raising classmates, who mocked him for "dressing like a girl." They called him "a sissy." In those days sissies were not called faggots.

At night, far from the critical eyes of his schoolmates, she discarded the flannel gowns that many young boys of his age wore to bed. She insisted instead on dressing him in delicate silk undergarments imported from Paris and intended for use by young girls. When Sonny objected to wearing this frilly lingerie, she refused to let him take off the garments. "This lingerie is the most expensive money can buy," she told him. "Intended for the prettiest little girls in the world. You are the prettiest boy in the world. If it's good enough for these spoiled little ladies, it's good enough for my son."

When Hughes Sr. was home, which he rarely was, Allene assigned him a separate bedroom. In the master bedroom, she slept with Sonny in a four-poster bed draped in delicate lace. When Sonny couldn't go to sleep, which was often the case, she pulled down her nightgown and allowed him to suckle at her breasts, long after her milk had dried up.

When she woke Sonny in the morning, she insisted on putting him through an elaborate ritual of ablutions, once employed in upper-class Victorian

Howard, Jr. and Allene Hughes

homes in Britain. In her bathroom, she inspected him from head to toe. First she checked his hair for lice, and then he was forced to open his mouth wide while she peered into his throat. After an inspection of his ears, she would begin an intense examination of his body, lingering for a long time in the area of his genitals. Since he was uncircumcised, she would pull back the glans of his small penis, looking for any spot or blotch. Later, she would demand that he turn his back to her and spread his cheeks. Greasing her finger with oil, she would insert it in his anus, ostensibly in a search for hemorrhoids.

Only after this inspection was over would she allow him to use the toilet. She stood by his side as his bowels moved. She inspected his stool, looking for tapeworms, as she claimed. Only then did she allow him to flush. The inspection was followed by a bath in very hot water, using a harsh lye soap to kill germs. Before departing for school, she gave him a heavy dose of Mrs. Rokamov's Russian Mineral Oil.

11

At night he had to down Epsom salts, endure another precise physical examination, and another bath in lye soap before she'd dress him in frilly lingerie for sleep in her all-protective arms.

"I will always be there for you," she'd whisper in his ear. "You'll never have need of another woman."

***

Not all the boys at the Episcopal parish school of Christ Church Cathedral made fun of Sonny. After the first week, he'd made friends with Dudley Sharp. Dudley was destined to become one of the most important relationships of young Howard's life.

As Sonny's uncle, Rupert Hughes, once remarked, "My nephew, Howard Jr., had only two friends in his life—young Dudley Sharp, whom he betrayed, and Cary Grant, whom he didn't."

Dudley was the type of boy Hughes Sr. wanted his own son to be. Tall and rail-thin, Sonny had a ghostly pale pallor and looked sickly. Dudley was the physical opposite. With a swimmer's build, he was healthy, robust, sun-tanned, surprisingly masculine for one so young, and strikingly handsome. None of the bullies at school called him a "sissy." If they did, it would be the last time that they would do so.

Just as Sonny "lived within his own shell," Dudley was very gregarious, making friends, talking to both adults and children with poise, and blessed with a winning personality that attracted both boys and girls to him.

From the first day in kindergarten, Sonny and Dudley became instant friends.

Dudley was the only boy in Sonny's school to win the approval of Allene. For years, Dudley's father, Walter Sharp, had been a partner in the Sharp-Hughes Tool Company. Like "Big Howard," Sharp had been a fellow wildcatter. A tall, rangy man, not unlike a young Gary Cooper, he in time became one of the founders of Texaco. Together with another partner, Edward Prater, Hughes Sr. and Walter Sharp had founded the amusingly named Moonshine Oil Company, forerunner of Hughes Tool Company.

When Sonny was out of school, Allene devoted all her time to him. When her boy was in class, she spent leisurely hours with Estelle, Walter Sharp's wife who had become her best friend. Privately, in spite of her fondness for Allene, Estelle expressed her reservations to Walter about Allene's "attempt to keep Sonny in the womb," as she so graphically put it. When she learned her own son liked Sonny, she encouraged the relationship, feeling that it would be good for young Howard to be "weaned a bit from his mother's tit." Estelle probably had no knowledge of how accurate her breast comparison was.

Looking back years later, Dudley, even as a young boy, had been aware of Allene's unnaturally close ties to her son. He once said, "They shared a bond so powerful and so intense that I'd never seen anything to match it—before or since."

Also enrolled in the parish school, Ella Rice was a beautiful little girl from a socially prominent family in Texas. Two years older than Sonny, she was the daughter of David Rice. Her uncle, William, had founded Rice Institute, which in time became Rice University.

Even before he was six years old, Sonny was telling Dudley that when he grew up he was going to marry Ella Rice. Howard Hughes Jr. must have been the only six-year-old in Houston plotting his future marriage.

Dudley, as he recalled years later, told Sonny that he not only didn't like girls, but felt that they were silly things. He claimed when they weren't playing with dolls, they liked to pester boys, and he didn't want to have anything to do with them. Sonny persisted in his daydreaming about Ella, and when Valentine's Day came around, he bought Ella the biggest card in all of Houston, presenting it to her with a mammoth, heart-shaped box of chocolates. Even as a child, Sonny was given ten dollars a week spending money, an unheard-of weekly stipend for a child in those days. Sonny rarely spent the money but instead stashed it in the attic of his home.

When Sonny presented Ella the box of chocolates in the schoolyard, she giggled, took it and the card, and ran over to the corner of the playground where she was joined by three of her playmates. She opened the card and read its message of love before instructing one of her little friends to return it to Sonny. "Tell him I don't love him," she told her messenger, "and never will." Ella kept the box of chocolates, however, and shared them freely with her playmates.

Stunned by the rejection and mocked by Ella's friends, Sonny retreated from the playground with Dudley by his side. Dudley would remember that day forever. He claimed that Sonny's face was twisted with anger at his humiliation. "I'll get even with that Ella Rice if it's the last thing I ever do," he told Dudley.

It was a vow he'd keep.

***

With his pal, Dudley, Allene's beloved Sonny entered Prosso School at the age of eight. Run by Dr. James Richardson for children of elite Houston parents, it was the city's best private school. Hughes Sr. was delighted, telling Dudley's father, Walter, that at last his son "could escape from the boa constrictor grip" of Allene.

Sonny was not a good student and from the beginning showed erratic behavior. Dr. Richardson told his parents that "the boy doesn't seem to fit in." He spent his free time on the playground talking only to Dudley, although casting a fascinated eye at a beautiful eight-year-old classmate, Margaret Cullinan. Ella Rice would be put in mothballs for a number of years. It was obvious

Sonny had become smitten with Margaret, who went out of her way to ignore him.

Two months into the school term, Sonny smuggled some of Allene's most precious jewelry from her bedroom and showed up on the playground with it. He put on a pair of his mother's diamond earrings and fastened on her favorite diamond-and-ruby necklace. In front of an astonished Margaret, he approached her, removed the jewelry, and offered the gems to her as a gift. She gleefully accepted.

This was the first known incident when young Howard had presented jewelry to a girl, and it would become a lifelong addiction. In time he would present jewelry to everybody from Katharine Hepburn to Ava Gardner. Those two stars returned the sparklers, although dozens of starlets accepted, and kept, Hughes's jewelry and wanted more.

Mrs. Cullinan, Margaret's mother, arrived at the Hughes's home around six o'clock that evening and forced her daughter to return the jewelry. Instead of exploding with anger, Allene advised Sonny to give away only the tiniest of her gems—not her most valuable diamonds.

Sonny would take jewelry from Allene's treasure chest only one more time. He stole a gold ring, studded with rubies and diamonds, and presented it to Dudley as a friendship ring. When Estelle Sharp discovered her son wearing Allene's ring, she demanded that he return it.

When Dudley brought it over to the Hughes's home and attempted to give it back, Sonny burst into tears and threatened to jump out of an upstairs window. Instead of accepting the return of the jewelry, Allene graciously told Dudley he could keep the ring. He would wear the ring eight more years until he was forced to hock it when he was strapped for cash.

When Sonny was only ten years old, Allene became determined that he be crowned king of the May Day Fête at Christ Church Cathedral, which she and Big Howard attended when her husband wasn't riding the rails in his private car with fancily dressed prostitutes guzzling French champagne.

His paid companions entertained him when he wasn't sitting at table playing poker for high stakes with oilmen to whom he was hawking his new drill bit.

Allene wrote to her church rector, claiming "Sonny is both tall and well-mannered and would make a most excellent King of the May Day Fête. I'm enclosing a check for one thousand dollars to ensure your event will be a big success!" The grateful rector responded that Sonny would definitely rule over the festivities.

For the event, Allene had his costume custom-tailored. He was a vision in green velvet with gold piping, wearing a lace shirt with puffed, gathered sleeves and a white lace collar. Attached to his lean shoulders was a gold cape with a crimson-colored satin lining.

Dudley was rather contemptuous of the honor, claiming that "the other boys

14

Howard Jr. at age 16

at the school thought being king was just for sissies." That point of view led to an argument, and Sonny struck at Dudley. The much stronger Dudley punched Sonny in the face, blooding his nose.

Fearing that Allene would not let him see Dudley again if she heard of this violence, Sonny told her he fell off his bike. She put him to bed for three days and demanded that her doctor appear at ten every morning. Three days later when Sonny was allowed to return to school, he made up with his friend.

Later in life, Dudley said, "Being king was real important to Sonny, even if his crown were made of paper. He told me that he was thrilled when he surveyed the other forty-two boys and girls. His 'subjects' were dressed in white togas. Sonny said it was at that May Day thing that he decided he wanted to rule over other people and never take orders from anyone again—except his mother."

Two weeks after the May Day event, Sonny's dentist, Dr. Walter Scherer, reported seeing the boy, along with Dudley, enter Mabel's Luncheonette for a sandwich. Sonny ordered a chicken salad sandwich, Dudley opting for a chocolate milkshake. "When Howard was served the sandwich, he took one bite out of it and declared the mayonnaise rancid. He pushed his plate right off the table and onto the floor. The boy was a real pistol!"

Sonny continued to take his promotion to royalty seriously. In spite of his soft-spoken manner, suggesting humility, Howard Hughes Jr. in time became imperious. His future aide, Noah Dietrich, labeled him "a despot," sometimes behind his back calling his boss "Howard the Arrogance."

It was while enrolled at Prosso that Sonny began to break his strong bond with his mother. In the past she had always arrived ten minutes before school let out to retrieve her son. She would not let him out of her sight until it was time for classes to begin the following morning.

Somehow Sonny prevailed on Allene to allow him to spend his late afternoons with Dudley at a workshop that Walter Sharp had constructed for his son behind their home at the intersection of Eagle and Main Streets. With its beautiful landscaping and old oak trees, the Sharp home resembled Twelve Oaks in the yet-to-be-made film, *Gone With the Wind.*

Both Sonny and Dudley weren't interested in school books, but in mechanics, or anything electronic. The boys built a ham radio set, lifting some of the parts from the Sharp family doorbell. They were among the first government-licensed ham radio ham operators, with the call letters of *5CY*. With their transmitter, Dudley and Sonny began to broadcast their own show, mainly comments

15

about the hot weather. Neighbors within a sixteen-block radius of their work-shop began tuning in to their show.

With his wireless broadcasting set, Sonny could communicate with ships in the Gulf of Mexico. When he discovered that the bleeps and dashes from these vessels were really Morse Code, he taught himself the code. "Within a week, he was talking to these ships," Dudley claimed. "It was amazing. Unlike me, my best friend was a genius."

Sonny convinced Dudley they should learn to play music so they could entertain their listeners. At first Sonny tried to play the ukulele but quickly switched to the saxophone, convincing Dudley that he should learn the instrument too. Dudley, after less than a month, decided "my mama didn't raise no saxophone player" and abandoned his lessons. A determined Sonny, however, stuck to the saxophone, driving Allene crazy with the noise, which she described as "Sonny's tootlings."

He would continue to play the saxophone, with utterly no tune, in lonely hotel rooms for years to come.

**

Tragedy struck the Sharp family on November 28, 1912 when Walter Sharp died of a heart attack at the age of forty-two, leaving Dudley and his mother, Estelle, bereft. That afternoon Dudley came by the Hughes household to tell Allene and Sonny the sad news.

Sonny tightly embraced Dudley as the young boy sobbed at the loss of his father. As Allene witnessed the scene, she was sympathetic to a point. But, apparently, she felt the embrace had gone on too long. Very gently she pried Sonny from Dudley's arms and suggested that he'd better go back to the Sharp home to comfort Estelle.

The next week the reality of the situation dawned on Estelle, as she found herself in partnership with Big Howard and his profligate spending habits. Among other items, he was billing the tool company for his wardrobe, as he wanted to be known as the best dressed man in America. So lavish was his wardrobe that when he traveled, he rented a separate rail car with a valet just for his clothing and shoes.

Without telling Allene, Estelle also discovered that her partner was charging "entertainment" costs to the company, including jewelry he purchased for his prostitutes.

Unable to tolerate this behavior, she sold her shares in the tool company for $65,000 to Ed Prather, one of the biggest mistakes a woman ever made in America's booming Edwardian age. With the new drill bit, the company would one day be worth billions.

Prather, too, tried to control the lavish spending of Big Howard but to no avail. To show him who was really the boss, Big Howard changed the name of

16

the company to the Hughes Tool Company on February 3, 1915.

When Prather could take it no more, he sold out to Big Howard. Since most of this buy-out was in cash and under the table, the exact sum was not disclosed. But it can be assumed that Prather sold his interest in the company for a fraction of its worth.

Hoping to loosen Sonny from his mother's skirttails, Big Howard prevailed upon Allene to send their son to Camp Teedyuskung in the Pocono Mountains of northeastern Pennsylvania. It was the summer of 1916. The head master of the camp was Daniel Carter Beard, who six years earlier had been one of the founders of Boy Scouts of America.

He was known for taking "silver-spooners"—young boys born to rich families—and turning them into rugged Buckskin Men after a summer of hiking, camping, canoeing, tent living, and flapjack frying in the mountain wilds.

Only after extreme urging on the part of her husband did Allene agree to escort Sonny to the camp, with the understanding that after she deposited him at the camp, she'd stay in New York City for an extended visit. Once she reached the Poconos, she received endless assurances from Beard that her son's health, including his stools, would be carefully monitored. Sonny was enrolled in a "stockade" (a rustic communal dormitory) on June 28.

Only a week after her return to New York City, Allene was overcome with panic as she read news articles of the spread of infantile paralysis in Brooklyn and elsewhere in the United States. She'd heard that one of the Buckskin boys had a "flu like virus," and she feared that he might spread polio to her son. Beard wrote back and reassured her that Sonny was gaining weight and growing healthier by the day, and that the boy with the flu would be placed in quarantine until he was well again.

Throughout the coming weeks, Allene continued to bombard Beard with letters, each one of which was answered with the scoutmaster's reassurances that her little Sonny was doing very well. "And, yes, his bowels are just fine," Beard added as a postscript, "although I don't relish the job of inspecting them every day."

When Allene could no longer stand the separation from Sonny, she arrived at camp on August 21 and abruptly checked him out, in spite of Beard's pleadings to let him remain.

Sonny's fellow Buckskin Men made fun of him when Allene appeared on the scene in a chauffeur-driven black limousine, complete with maid and eight large trunks. She personally packed Sonny's Russian mineral oils, the patent medicines she'd insisted he take to camp, and his elaborate wardrobe, all of which he'd never worn since the day he enrolled.

With Sonny beside her, Allene fled to Cleveland to wait out the summer polio scare at the home of Felix, her husband's younger brother and a teacher of light opera.

From Cleveland, she wrote Big Howard that she'd rescued "my little chick." During the rest of the summer, Allene lectured Sonny on the dangers he'd face if he came down with polio and how his life would be ruined. In graphic and vivid detail, she described the horrors of "any and all" diseases that he would suffer if he came into contact with germs. At times, according to her brother-in-law, Allene reduced Sonny to tears. He would run screaming in fear to his room.

Thus, the phobia to germs that would haunt the rest of his life was instilled in him during that summer of 1916, if not before.

The other fear she had was that Sonny was growing so fast that his feet might not fit his shoes. She insisted on measuring his feet every morning and then examining the fit of his shoes. She warned Sonny that if this weren't done, he might wake up and not be able to walk. "One morning," she told him in front of Felix, "I'll be able to get up. But when I look back at you, both your feet and legs will be paralyzed. You'll never be able to walk again in your life and will be totally dependent on me." As she delivered that lecture to Sonny, he sobbed in fear.

Allene very tenderly would wipe away his tears and assure him, "If that horrible day ever comes when you can't walk, I'll become your legs."

In light of events to come, it was as if she were an eerie prophet.

***

Although Sonny begged his mother to be allowed to return to Camp Teedyuskung the following summer, she refused. Big Howard had just acquired a sixty-foot yacht, *Rollerbit*, which he claimed he'd had equipped "Vanderbilt and Astor style" with brass railings, teakwood floors, mahogany trim, and even real gold fixtures in the green marble-clad bathrooms.

With a crew, Big Howard took Allene, Sonny, and Dudley on several cruises in the Gulf of Mexico.

Although his mother demanded that he sleep with her in her cabin, Sonny defied her, perhaps for the first time. He wanted his own cabin, to which he invited Dudley to share his bed.

One morning when Allene entered her son's cabin without knocking, she found Sonny and Dudley asleep in each other's arms. After she'd ordered Dudley from the cabin, she gave Sonny the most thorough inspection he'd ever endured, claiming she was looking for "telltale clues." Later in the day, she complained bitterly to Big Howard, who assured her that nothing was wrong. "All boys go through a stage like that—even myself." He told her that she would either let Dudley continue to sleep with Sonny or else, "as captain of this vessel, I'll have you walk the plank."

Back in Houston, Sonny continued to lobby to go to Camp Teedyuskung, and Allene consistently refused.

With Dudley back in his own home, Allene resumed sleeping with her son.

18

One night he woke her up, crying out that "my body is hurting all over. I'm in pain. Help me, mother!"

In the middle of the night, Allene summoned her doctor who could find nothing wrong with the boy. Sonny continued to cry out in pain. He told the doctor that he needed the bracing air of lake and mountain at the camp and reminded him how much healthier he was when he'd returned from camp last summer.

Allene steadfastly refused to let him go until Big Howard returned from one of his trips. Seeing what bad shape Sonny was in, his father made arrangements for the boy to be sent by train to the Poconos, with a black chauffeur, named "Jonnie Johnson," accompanying him. In spite of Allene's objections, Sonny prevailed upon his father to let Dudley go with him.

Allene warned her husband that he was making a "big mistake," as she'd begun to fear Sonny's attachment to Dudley. She couldn't quite articulate her concerns other than saying, "Dudley is old for his age—much too mature for such a young boy. It's like he's three or four years older than Sonny—not the same age at all."

She fired off a letter to the camp's director, Beard, telling him that he had to continue to inspect Sonny's stool every morning, measure his shoe size, and see that he takes his Russian mineral oil. She added a postscript. "Sonny is forbidden to eat the camp's flapjacks which are bad for his health. While I'm on the subject, I also forbid you to feed flapjacks to Dudley too."

Before Beard had a chance to respond, Allene had written him another letter, warning him that Sonny was "overly sensitive," and that none of the "camp bullies" should be allowed to taunt him.

Beard began to write completely contradictory letters to Allene and Big Howard. After Sonny had been to camp for two weeks, Beard hailed his progress to Allene, citing his bird studies and his scout-crafting skills.

To Big Howard, he painted a different portrait. "Dudley Sharp virtually seems to own your son, protecting him day and night and not letting him mingle with the other boys. They share the same stockade and seem inseparable and will not indulge in activities that don't involve each other. Howard's favorite counselors from last year have joined the Army and your boy is not getting along with the new gang."

As Allene was later to learn, Dudley and Beard had conflicted several times over "exactly who is Howard's boss—you or me?"

In late July, Beard wrote a private and confidential letter to Big Howard. In the letter, not intended for Allene's eyes, he told Hughes Sr. that he'd walked into Howard's stockade and had caught the two boys masturbating each other.

"We just can't allow this at camp," Beard said. "As a founder of the Boy Scouts, I have instilled in our platform our motto of good, clean living. The Boy Scouts cannot—and will not—tolerate even the suggestion of deviant behavior."

On the same day, Beard wrote Allene that "Both boys are doing fine and are enjoying camp life to its fullest."

Since Big Howard was away on one of his trips, Allene read both letters, including the one just for the eyes of her husband.

She became hysterical and called Estelle Sharp to tell her of what she'd learned. Like Big Howard had done, Estelle assured her that "it was just a phase," and that Allene would make it worse by "making a Federal case out of it."

Not listening to Estelle's advice, Allene packed her clothes that day and boarded a train for New York. From there, she planned to have a chauffeur drive her to Camp Teedyuskung where she was going to forcibly remove Sonny from the camp, leaving Dudley to get home however he might.

She did not warn her husband of her impending arrival and headed directly for the lavish suite the two of them occupied at the Vanderbilt Hotel whenever they were in New York together.

Ordering the bellhops to bring up her luggage, she went to the suite and was let in by the assistant manager, Frank Gargan, who knew her well from previous visits.

Inside the darkened living room, she headed for the master bedroom to wake up Big Howard. Turning on the light to confront him, she found him lying naked in bed with one of the most beautiful teenage girls she'd ever seen.

"Okay, okay," Big Howard said angrily, sitting up sleepily on white satin pillows. The shapely beauty awoke at the same time, rubbing sleep from her eyes.

"You've caught me," he told Allene. "I can't lie." He looked at the beautiful girl. "I might as well introduce the two of you. Allene, this is Eleanor Boardman. Eleanor, this is my wife."

Allene ran screaming from the bedroom threatening to kill herself by jumping from one of the windows of the suite's living room. The scene was eerily evocative of her son's earlier threat to jump to his death from their home.

Dudley and Sonny were allowed to stay at camp until it closed for the summer. Beard had tried to transfer Dudley to another stockade until Sonny threatened to run away if he did. Relenting, Beard gave in and let the two boys continue to sleep together.

He figured it was up to Big Howard to send instructions after reading his letter. To his surprise, Beard never received any reply from Big Howard. Also to his amazement, he never received any more letters from Allene either, and she'd been bombarding him with mail all summer.

Three days before the camp closed, Allene wrote him that she'd be sending her black driver, Jonnie, to pick up both Dudley and Sonny. He would drive them to New York where all three of them would then board the train back to Houston.

What Sonny didn't know, and would not know for several years, was that his mother had been given a far greater problem than Dudley.

She was having to expand the boundaries of her marriage to accommodate the stunning teenage girl, Eleanor Boardman, a model for Eastman Kodak.

***

Montecito, California, 1985

One of the grand divas of silent pictures, and eventually, the wife of director King Vidor, Eleanor Boardman today is a largely forgotten figure. Her role in the lives of Howard Hughes Senior and Junior has never before been fully revealed.

Inside her Spanish-style home in Montecito, California in the 1980s, Eleanor was still statuesque, patrician, and sophisticated, evoking a character from F. Scott Fitzgerald's "Lost Generation."

Still candid in her remarks, she lived up to her long-standing reputation as "The Most Outspoken Woman in Hollywood."

With the passage of time, and with most of her films turned to dust, Eleanor had remained very down-to-earth, rather realistic in her appraisals, and devoid of the theatricality that encapsulated many other stars of her era. In speaking of "Big Howard" and his son, she had a bittersweet tone in her voice.

She first met Big Howard in 1916 in the lobby of the Vanderbilt Hotel in New York where he was staying in a suite with his wife. Eleanor was lodged at the same hotel with her fiercely religious and overprotective mother.

"Mother and I were sitting across from Mr. and Mrs. Hughes having tea," Eleanor recalled as if it were yesterday. The Philadelphia-born beauty said she recognized Hughes because his picture had recently appeared in the New York papers, although she couldn't recall why. "I couldn't help but notice that, in spite of his wife's disapproval, he was staring at me as if I were a chocolate fudge sundae and he hadn't eaten in days. He was making me uncomfortable, but exciting me at the same time. Even in those days I had a wisecrack for every occasion. When he kept staring and staring, I up and told him, 'If you keep looking for one more minute, you'll have to pay admission.'"

She remembered him flushing red with embarrassment. He immediately apologized, stood up, and said, "You ought to be in pictures." She leaned back in her chair in her courtyard in Montecito and laughed. " Remember, this was 1916. That cliché line wasn't so old back then. Like the true gentleman he was, he came over and introduced himself. Mother nodded politely. When introduced, I smiled my best model portfolio smile at Allene Hughes. From that moment, both of us just knew we were natural-born enemies."

After the introductions, Hughes had eyes only for Eleanor, telling her that he was a talent scout for his brother, Rupert Hughes, in Hollywood. Rupert was already a celebrated writer in his day. One of his movies, *Gloria's Romance*, which he'd co-written with his second wife, Adelaide Manola, was doing big box office. It starred Miss Billie Burke, "that apostle of happiness."

"Hughes wasn't the prettiest man I'd ever met, but I'd heard he was a very rich oilman from Texas," Eleanor said. "His son Howard turned into a great beauty. Those looks came from his mother's side of the family. Initially, I was impressed with Big Howard's diamond cufflinks and his diamond stickpin. But Allene also wore diamonds, even though it was the afternoon."

Eleanor claimed that Big Howard's words were "like an explosion of dreams inside my head. More than anything I wanted to be a film actress, although mother thought films were wicked, even though she didn't mind me being a model for Kodak. Right away, I figured Hughes was my meal ticket to Hollywood—how wrong I was! I'd heard stories about how beautiful young girls like me screwed their way to the top, and I was ready and raring to surrender my virginity to the right man who came along."

When Hughes handed Eleanor his business card, his broad, rough hand caressed her more delicate porcelain one and lingered a bit too long. Their bonding was interrupted by Allene, who complained of a headache and demanded to be taken up to her suite.

The actress claimed that when Allene returned to Texas three days later, Hughes called her right after he'd escorted his wife to Grand Central. "He invited me over that night to a champagne dinner at his suite," Eleanor said. "I made up some lie for mother. Big Howard was very courtly. As I fully expected, the dirty deed happened that night in the same bed where he'd made love to his wife. When I told him I was a virgin, he at first didn't believe me. But when I convinced him, he became so excited he could hardly control himself. He was very gentle with me and actually taught me how to make love to a man."

Eleanor remembered how in the weeks ahead, their love-making grew more robust as she became more experienced. "I refused oral sex, however. He told me most nice gals, including his wife, said no to that. He said it was okay with him because plenty of prostitutes were always available for that."

Before he left New York, Hughes had confessed that he loved his wife but not in a sexual way, claiming that she was frigid. "He said that Allene was really in love with their son, and he didn't know what to do about that—'except get our boy out of her clutches as often and as soon as possible.'"

"Today in a more enlightened age," Eleanor said, "we'd call both father and son 'child molesters'—and so they were. I was a bit old for Big Howard at the time, having just turned eighteen. He told me that he and his fellow oilmen often slept with girls sixteen or even younger. He said that some of his best sex was with a beautiful thirteen-year-old girl. Since I'd grown up in an era where old men often married teenage gals, I didn't find that a particularly strange custom."

When Eleanor was forced to say good-bye to Hughes, who was returning to Texas, she broke down and cried. Her hurt feelings were soothed somewhat when he presented her with a pair of diamond earrings.

Hughes later told her that wherever he went in America, he saw the picture of her as "The "Kodak Girl," plastered on billboards, in drug stores, and in train stations. Eleanor was posed in a homemade black-and-white striped dress, standing in a field of daisies with a camera thrown over her shoulder.

"Young women I was meeting in the theater—when mother finally left me in an all-girl hotel—told me that Hughes was very promiscuous and that he'd never call me again."

That was hardly the case. "He'd left a standing order that I was to be delivered fresh American Beauty roses every day," Eleanor said. "Within two weeks of checking out of the Vanderbilt, he was calling me to arrange another rendezvous."

With complete candor, Eleanor claimed that during the short life of Howard Hughes Sr., she was his only long-time mistress. "With all the other floozies," she said, "it was strictly one-night stands. I think for a while he was actually in love with me, and often spoke of divorcing his wife and marrying me. But the star-launch he'd promised with Rupert Hughes was a long time coming. Howard Sr. looked like a stern-faced Presbyterian deacon, but was a fantastic lover. I was enthralled with him until one afternoon when he unceremoniously dumped me. But that was in the early Twenties, before I became a star. It's a story for another day."

✝✳✳

Houston, 1916

The exact details of the agreement that was formulated between Big Howard and Allene on the train back to Houston will never be known. But by the time Sonny had finished summer camp, the new rules around the Hughes home had become apparant.

In the aftermath of Allene catching her husband in bed with Eleanor Boardman, she informed him that he'd be denied any conjugal visits. In addition, Allene was granted complete control over her offspring, telling Howard Sr. that he would not be allowed to interfere in the rearing of her son.

At the end of the summer, when Dudley and Sonny arrived from camp at the train station in Houston, Allene was there to meet her boy. She warmly embraced him but didn't speak to Dudley, who was rescued by his own mother, Estelle. En route home, Allene informed Sonny that he was not to speak to "the Sharp boy ever again."

Outwardly, Sonny agreed to her demands. But privately, he had no intention of obeying her and would continue his very intimate friendship with Dudley for years to come. He simply defied his mother, but in secret.

For the new school term, he was enrolled at Houston's Montrose School, which was close to the elegant Beaconfield Apartments where Big Howard had installed his family in a lavish duplex suite with three bedrooms. He had agreed to sell their house after Allene had decided that she preferred apartment living instead of life within a house and garden. At the Beaconfield, Big Howard was assigned a room down the hall from his wife.

Since he had been ostracized from his wife's bedroom, Big Howard in time became an accomplice of Sonny's in circumventing his mother's rigid demands. After Allene refused to go, Howard Sr. took his son yachting in the Gulf of Mexico. He occasionally invited him on special train rides across the country. On each of these trips, he arranged for Dudley to go along too. Allene never found out about this deception, although Dudley's mother, Estelle, was privy to what was happening.

Big Howard didn't want to know the exact nature of any personal intimacies between Sonny and Dudley. What impressed him more was that Sonny was defying Allene. Without knowing the exact details of his wife's relationship with his boy, he instinctively sensed that it was an unhealthy detour.

His father promised Sonny that as soon as he was old enough, he would send him to school back East.

"I might be pulling up stakes in Texas myself," Big Howard told Sonny. "Relocating in Los Angeles." Sonny's romance-writing uncle, Rupert, was dazzling his brother with possibilities of "endless sexual conquests among the most beautiful girls in the world." Rupert claimed that the cream of America's young women, often still in their teens, were arriving daily at Los Angeles' Union Station, and most of them were "available for plucking—that's plucking, but it also sounds like something even better."

The only person privy to the private relationship of Allene and Sonny was Dudley himself, who later claimed that "Sonny told me everything that was going on." Dudley only betrayed young Howard's confidence when their personal relationship broke up and he was bitterly rejected.

Based entirely on what Dudley later revealed, we know that Allene was not at all severe during her talks to her son about what she'd learned from Beard at summer camp. "I recognize that you are growing up and have the needs of all young men entering puberty," Allene reportedly said. "It's only natural."

"You aren't mad at me?" Sonny asked.

"Not at all," she responded. "But we must change the rules somewhat. What you did with Dudley is wrong and must never be repeated. Women were put on the face of the earth to satisfy such needs in a man. One day you'll marry some fine woman right here in Houston. Since you're young and your judgment might be questionable, I'll pick her out for you myself. In the meantime, I will find a way to cope with your growing needs."

After his return from summer camp, according to Dudley, Sonny was no longer dressed at night in the lingerie that Allene had attired him in when he was younger. He now started to sleep naked in the same bed with his mother, although Allene insisted that she wear a nightgown.

"I get a hard-on when she touches me real intimate," Sonny confided to Dudley. "Sometimes at night, she holds me so tight I can hardly breathe. One

24

night she played with me. She told me it would provide some relief to me. I began to like it and sometimes I let her play with me three or four times a night. It does cut down on my being so nervous."

Sonny once heard one of the boys at school talk about what he'd gotten a girl to do with his penis, claiming she'd taken it in her mouth and "swallowed my seed." That night Sonny begged Allene to do that to him, but she adamantly refused.

"Instead she brought out a pink porcelain bowl," Sonny told Dudley. "Mother would approach me with the bowl and play with me even when I didn't want it. But I always came through for her—so to speak."

During the course of her masturbatory relationship with her son, Allene refused to allow him to touch himself, claiming that privilege for herself.

And then the relationship with her son took an even more bizarre turn. After months of masturbating her son, she suddenly cut off the practice, claiming it was a "nasty thing to do." She told him he was never to masturbate himself again. Sonny got around that restriction by slipping off to see Dudley where they continued to ocassionally indulge in mutual masturbation.

One night when Sonny came home, Allene had a servant prepare his favorite dinner of steak and peas. She told him that she had a big surprise waiting for him in her bedroom where she wanted to retire to bed with him quite early that evening.

An hour later, upstairs in the privacy of their shared bedroom, Allene ordered Sonny to remove all his clothing so she could bathe him.

Instead of her usual lye soap, she brought out a delicately perfumed lavender soap. After bathing him, she toweled him dry but for some reason did not indulge in her usual examination of his body parts.

She put a big towel around him and led him into the dressing room that adjoined her master bedchamber.

There, laid out on a silk-upholstered divan were four lavishly tailored dresses. "I want you to imagine you're a model and try on each of these for me. I think when you're in them, you'll look even more beautiful than you already are."

"Do I have to, mother?"

"You must do it for me, son," she said, kissing him gently on the lips.

"But why?" he protested.

"It has taken me a long time to face the truth. But I've come to realize that you are a lovely girl who's trapped in a boy's body."

CHAPTER TWO
Hollywood, 1917

It was one of those blistering hot afternoons that Texans by August 23, 1917 had learned to endure.

Slipping out of his house, Sonny had told Allene he was going for a ride on his bicycle. That was true. He was also planning a forbidden visit with Dudley.

As the afternoon broiled, Sonny and Dudley seemed to be the only life moving on the block. Still dressed in their uniforms from Camp Teedyuskung, with their pointed caps, the boys retired to their workshop.

There they indulged in a ritual common to boys in a pre-AIDS era. It was Sonny who proposed that he delicately slice his wrist with a sharp knife and that Dudley do the same. That way their bloods could mingle into a bond of friendship that would last always. At first reluctant, Dudley agreed to go along with his best friend.

Big Howard had raised Sonny's allowance from ten dollars a week to twenty dollars a week, an amount that was considered a very good paycheck at the time. Since he didn't need the money, Sonny gave Dudley ten dollars a week from his allowance. That allowed Dudley "to buy anything I wanted at the store," as he later put it.

Sonny cut his wrist until it was bleeding profusely, and cut even deeper into Dudley, which brought tears to the boy's eyes. As Dudley later recalled, "our blood flowed together. From that day on, until I began to interpret things differently, Sonny and I were bonded at the hip like Siamese twins."

As Dudley bandaged Sonny's wrist, before tending to his own, Sonny told him that he was going to tell Allene that he fell off his bicycle and cut his wrist on a piece of glass.

Fully bandaged, the two boys walked into the wilting family garden. In the cauldron-like heat, Sonny looked up at the sky and said the he would pray "that ten thousand angels would weep crocodile tears and cool off the damn place."

His wish wasn't granted. If anything, the already fiery hot day was heating up dangerously in another part of the town, only three miles away.

Unknown to him at the time, Sonny's life would forever be altered by events that would occur later on that infamous day.

***

In another part of town, the 24th Infantry Division of the Third Battalion was a tightly knit, supremely macho, all-black section of the National Guard.

Shortly before the United States declared war on Germany, its members were sent by train from their regimental encampment at Columbus, New Mexico, to Houston. They were assigned to guard the military installation being constructed by white laborers at Camp Logan. From the day of their arrival, the black men were subjected to racial slurs from the camp laborers.

On the second day after their arrival, the guardsmen were visited by the police chief of Houston. He told them he didn't know or care where they came from. "But as long as you're in Houston, you're to act like good niggers and behave yourself—or else! We can even regulate which water fountain you Ubangi boys can slurp from."

On the afternoon of August 23, two white policemen arrested a black guardsman when he attempted to interfere with their beating of a drunken black woman. When Corporal Charles Baltimore, one of a dozen military policemen assigned to the division, went to the local police station to inquire about the soldier's arrest, he got into a fight with another policeman assigned to the division and was hit over the head with a rifle. When he attempted to flee, two policemen chased him and found him in an unoccupied house where he was shot in the shoulder.

Taken to a local hospital, Baltimore ultimately survived. But word reached his fellow guardsmen that he'd been killed. The men of the 24th division were sweating in overheated barracks and their tempers rose with the temperature outside.

Their anger raging, the guardsmen, under the supervision of their sergeant, a muscular black man named Vida Henry, who'd been a boxer, hastily organized a vigilante party. At seven o'clock the division marched into the San Felipe section of Houston where Baltimore had been shot.

Seeing the marching men, Houston Police Captain Joseph Mattes defiantly confronted them from his open car. He ordered the march to halt. Henry shot and killed him and his two fellow officers.

From that point on, all eyewitness reports differ from each other. What is known is that the 24th went on a rampage, killing white men, women, and even children, on sight and without provocation.

The riot raged for three hours, causing panic throughout the city. White men, fearing attack, broke into local stores, stealing rifles and ammunition. Each man claimed that he was going to protect his family "at all costs."

The governor of Texas, James Ferguson, summoned white Army reinforcements stationed in Galveston. Hundreds of self-appointed vigilantes took control of the streets, with vaguely defined orders to shoot *all* black men on sight.

Before the night was over, sixteen white men, women and children had been killed, along with four black men. Another twelve were seriously wounded.

Retreating with his men back to their sweltering barracks, Sergeant Henry committed suicide by firing a bullet into his head.

28

Military tribunals later indicted 118 of the enlisted men and found 110 of them guilty. Nineteen of the mutinous soldiers were hanged, and another 63 received life sentences. No white officers or civilians were brought to trial.

***

When Sonny at the Sharp house heard about the riot, he quickly bicycled back home "to protect my mother from the niggers." The exact details of what happened that night in the Hughes household will never be known. Years later, Dudley tried to reconstruct the events based on what Sonny had told him.

Back at the Hughes household, Sonny couldn't find his mother or her two black servants.

Finally, he heard sobs coming from her bedroom. In the room, he searched for her, finding her cowering under the bed, her clothing ripped. She was sobbing so hysterically he couldn't understand what had happened to her.

With the help of a neighbor, he was able to get her moved from the bedroom and transported to the hos-

Howard Jr., at age 14

pital. There a doctor told Sonny that his mother claimed that three of the black MPs had broken in on her and brutally raped her at gunpoint. Supporting her allegations was the fact that Allene's body was severely bruised, and she had cuts on her face and arms.

When Hughes Sr. rushed back to Houston two days later, he found his wife "serenely calm—almost bizarrely so." Her doctor told Big Howard that there were no signs of his wife having been raped, and that he suspected her cuts and bruises were self-inflicted. Allene was referred to as "a sexual hysteric."

In the weeks ahead, Allene kept Sonny close to her protective arms. No longer talking about germs, she filled his head with fears that black men not only rape women but pretty white boys as well. She told him that their penises were three times the size of a white man's and that when they raped young boys they often caused permanent damage to their guts, similar to what her body had suffered while giving birth to him.

In the years ahead, Howard maintained that he had been caught "right in the middle of the race riot." At times, he also claimed that he was struck in the head with the rifle butt of a black guardsman, permanently damaging his hearing. In reality, he was completely unharmed and never encountered one of the rampaging guardsmen.

The overheated events of that August night in Houston, combined with Allene's horrific stories of her brutal alleged rape, would have a profound affect on Howard for the rest of his life.

**

Las Vegas, 1968

On April 4, 1968, in his Las Vegas office, an older Howard Hughes Jr. sat listening to his television broadcast news about the assassination of Martin Luther King Jr. During the nation-wide turmoil that followed the assassination, memories of that August night in Houston must have been evoked.

He called in an assistant and dictated this memo:

I can summarize my attitude about employing more Negroes very simply. I think it's a wonderful idea for somebody else, somewhere else. I know this is not a very praiseworthy point of view, but I feel that Negroes have already made enough progress in the last century, and there is such a thing as overdoing it.

Howard Hughes

**

Houston, 1918-19

Allene never forgave Big Howard for being out of town when the race riots exploded. In vivid detail, she continued to describe her assault from "those slimy, smelly niggers."

Believing that all black men carried venereal disease, she journeyed to her doctor in Houston for any sign of infection. Even though several doctors diagnosed her as "out of harm's way," Allene was convinced that she had "latent syphilis," which could not be detected by doctors but which might burst out at any minute and destroy her delicate but otherwise healthy body.

As a concession to Allene, Big Howard agreed to erect a big and "secure" two-floor house for his family in the exclusive Montrose district of Houston "where the elite resided." A Georgian styled brick residence with marble floors, five bedrooms, and a garage large enough for two long limousines, it was a respectable addition to the neighborhood. The address was 3921 Yoakum Street, north of Rice Institute, and Big Howard brought his wife and son to live there in the summer of 1918.

Dan Beard seemed to have survived his ordeal of catching Dudley and Sonny masturbating and invited both of them back to Camp Teedyuskung. The director even promised that the newer recruits at camp—called "Buckskin Tenderfoots"—would address Sonny as "Sir" and that as a sign of his seniority, Allene's boy would wear three red stripes on his shirt.

But when she learned that Dudley had already signed up for another summer, Allene steadfastly refused to allow her boy to return to camp. In 1918, mother and son jointly weathered another fiery summer together in Houston.

***

Sonny's interest quickly shifted from bikes to America's new fascination— the automobile. Without telling his parents, at the age of fourteen, young Howard descended on The Stutzy Automobile Purchasing Agency in downtown Houston where the newly arrived 1920 version of the latest Bearcat caught his eye.

As salesman, Jack Horner, later reported, "I didn't pay much attention to the boy, thinking he had just come to admire the cars. In fact, I didn't even get up to greet him. The boy had to come over to me. Finally, he did. He said, 'I'm Howard Hughes Jr. I want to buy that Bearcat. I don't care what it costs. Send it over today.' He scribbled his address on a sheet of paper, handed it to me, and walked out of the showroom."

Horner thought it might be some sort of prank. On an impulse, he went and called Hughes Sr. at his tool company, reporting that his son wanted the latest Bearcat even though it bore a staggering price tag of seven- thousand dollars. "I told Hughes that it was the fastest thing on the road and could go at the then-incredible speed of ninety miles an hour."

"Did my son say he wanted it?" Hughes Sr. asked.

"Yeah, he wants it delivered to your house," Horner said.

"If that's what my boy said, you'd better haul ass and get it over there."

Once the Bearcat was delivered, Sonny immediately set about taking it apart and reassembling the roadster piece by piece.

When he'd done that, he invited Big Howard and Allene for a drive in the country.

Without a lesson, he'd taught himself how to drive.

In spite of Allene bursting into screams two or three times, the ride went smoothly. Eventually, Howard Hughes Jr. would become a natural and intuitive pilot of any vehicle on land or in the air.

***

One day in early May 1919, Sonny overheard his mother pleading with his father on the telephone. Somehow, she'd learned that Big Howard wasn't in New York, as he had told her, but had taken the train to Philadelphia, the home town of Eleanor Boardman. He had checked into the

Eleanor Boardman

31

city's best hotel, where he was entertaining the beautiful young Kodak model and her dreams of movie stardom.

Sonny heard Allene threatening to divorce his father if he didn't abandon his new love. Allene must have know of her husband's dalliances with other women, but this romance with Eleanor threatened her more than any of the others.

Sonny did not hear the rest of the conversation because he retreated upstairs to bed for the rest of the day. When Allene discovered him there, she offered to call the family doctor. But Sonny claimed it wasn't necessary.

Growing taller and with his body filling out, he had recently taken up basketball at the YMCA. He was also becoming skilled at diving and swimming. Claiming that all this vigorous physical exercise had tested his endurance, he demanded total rest for the remainder of the day.

He also insisted that she black out the room with draperies, an eerie evocation of a demand that he would repeatedly make to his Mormon attendants throughout the final decades of his life.

She arose early the following morning. Although she called for him to get up several times, there was no answer. Sensing that something was wrong, she ran back to the bedroom.

"Mother!" he shouted at her. "My legs! I can't move them."

Screaming hysterically, Allene tore the covers from him and began to massage his legs but to no avail. Her worst nightmare had come true. Sonny was paralyzed. On the phone to their doctor, Frederick Lummis, she demanded that he come at once. "Sonny has polio!"

Doctor Lummis arrived to examine Sonny that morning, and informed Allene of what she already knew. Her son had all the signs of infantile paralysis. A wheelchair was summoned for him later that day.

On the phone from Philadelphia, Big Howard promised to take the next train to Houston.

That night, Allene held Sonny in her arms. He seemed strangely relieved, as he would later relate to Dudley. "Now—maybe—you and father won't get a divorce. I'll need both of my parents to take care of me now."

Within two days, Big Howard arrived back in Houston. He immediately telephoned the director of the Rockefeller Institute for Medical Research in New York, wanting only the best for his son.

Dr. Simon Flexner, the country's greatest expert on polio and meningitis research, could not come to Houston but agreed to send his most trusted associate, Dr. H. T. Chickering.

What transpired next became a secret between Dr. Chickering and Sonny.

Howard Hughes Jr. would spend the rest of his life "buying people." Testing the power of money, the first person he "bought" was Dr. Chickering.

***

Mackinac Island, 1919

After six weeks as Howard Jr's private physician in Houston, Dr. Chickering agreed to accompany the wheelchair-bound Sonny and Allene to one of the most prestigious hotels of the Robber Baron Age, the Grand Hotel on Mackinac Island. Standing on 500 acres of lawns and gardens overlooking the Straits of Mackinac, between the upper and lower peninsulas of Michigan, midway between Lakes Huron and Michigan, it was one of the most stylish midsummer venues in America at the time. Guests fanned themselves on a 600-foot pillared verandah (according to the *Guinness Book of Records*, it's the longest open-air verandah in the country), while seated in upholstered rocking chairs. Modern audiences might remember the hotel as the setting for *Somewhere in Time,* starring Christopher Reeve in his prime and Jane Seymour.

As part of the pomp and circumstance of their arrival, Allene had arranged for them to be picked up at the local railway station by three horse-drawn surreys that carried them, along with massive quantities of luggage and medical equipment, up to the hotel.

From the very first, as Dr. Chickering was to record in his medical journal, he knew that Sonny was perfectly healthy when he initially examined him in Houston. But his boss, Dr. Flexner, had told him that he could interpret his sojourn in Texas and on Mackinac Island as a well-deserved vacation. For his efforts, Chickering drew a high salary, with all his expenses paid, and Flexner was particularly grateful for the ten-thousand dollar check that the Rockefeller Institute had received from Big Howard.

Week after week, Dr. Chickering hovered over Sonny as protectively as Allene had done. He lifted him in and out of his wheelchair, tested his blood, and examined him thoroughly every day. Allene also conducted her own examinations.

Dr. Chickering didn't record this, but he later admitted that Sonny paid him five thousand dollars, which he'd accumulated from unspent allowances, as part of a conspiracy to keep his secret.

Every afternoon in Houston, the doctor had wheeled Sonny down Yoakum Boulevard in the Montrose section. Allene had been told it was for the fresh air. Actually the doctor was taking Sonny to Dudley's house.

Once in Dudley's backyard, Sonny would rise unassisted from his wheelchair and disappear into the workshop with Dudley for perhaps an hour and a half before being wheeled back to the Hughes home.

This charade continued from their suites at the Grand Hotel on Mackinac Island. Every afternoon Sonny would be wheeled into the park. Allene never accompanied them because of her "deadly fear of wild animals and winged creatures."

As Allene enjoyed afternoon tea on the verandah of the resort, Dr. Chickering would disappear with Sonny, still in his wheelchair.

Sonny had met a twenty-three-year-old man who worked as a waiter in the resort's grand dining room. Phil Arthur had a wife stashed away somewhere back in Virginia, but he was meeting Sonny secretly every afternoon.

The young man was well-muscled and extraordinarily handsome. In spite of the difference in their ages, Sonny seemed enthralled to be in his presence.

When the doctor and his patient had moved away from the sightlines of the verandah, Sonny would rise from his wheelchair and race toward the lake where he had a rendezvous with Phil in the boathouse.

As Dr. Chickering later reported to Dr. Flexner, "Howard Hughes Jr. is a homosexual." He suspected that Sonny was paying Phil to have sex with him.

Allene had reported to the manager the theft of one-thousand dollars from her purse, blaming one of the maids. Although two maids were fired, Dr. Chickering believed that Sonny stole the money and was slowly distributing it to Phil for favors rendered.

At the end of their stay at the Grand Hotel, when they were leaving the next day, Allene was having her afternoon tea on the hotel's verandah. Suddenly, from across the wide porch, Sonny walked toward her, accompanied by Dr. Chickering. There was no wheelchair in sight.

Allene practically screamed when she spotted her son walking upright and raced to embrace him. He told her that the doctor, like some faith-healer, had miraculously cured him and that his legs felt fine. Overjoyed, Allene burst into tears.

The next morning Dr. Chickering was "richly rewarded" before his return to the Rockefeller Institute, his vacation over.

Back in Houston, Big Howard was overjoyed, marveling at his son's recovery. Abandoning Eleanor Boardman back East, he and Allene had a reconciliation.

There was more. Big Howard invited both Allene and Sonny for a yachting trip to Coronado Island off the coast of California.

After a few days on the West Coast, Sonny told both his parents that he had fallen in love with California that late summer and that he planned to live there for the rest of his life. He begged to be enrolled in school in California, claiming that his parents could come and visit him whenever they wanted to.

Allene steadfastly refused, telling him that he was to return to South End Junior High, the public school in Montrose where they lived. Although Sonny threw a temper fit, the passion that was associated with his California quest was not lost on Big Howard. But it would have to wait for another day.

***

Houston, 1920

In Houston, Sonny spent a disappointing year enrolled at the South End Junior High School, where his grades were "lackluster." He had no interest in books and couldn't wait for the school day to end so that he could slip off with Dudley.

Big Howard knew that his son's "unnatural attachment" to his former partner's son was continuing. Unlike Allene, he didn't feel that forcibly cutting off the relationship was the way to handle it.

One afternoon, Big Howard invited both Dudley and his son to the Hughes Tool Company where he had set up a worktable for them. Even though Allene protested that she didn't rear "my son to be a garage mechanic," she reluctantly allowed him to work at the company. Big Howard challenged the boys to "invent something."

Within Howard's first week back from school, he and Dudley plotted to invent a "motorcycle." A few months previously, both Big Howard and Allene had refused to purchase a motorcycle for him, even though his father had bought a roadster for him in spite of the fact that he was under aged. Like many parents, Big Howard felt that his son would be safer driving a car than a motor-cycle.

In the shop, Dudley and Howard attached a small gasoline engine and a newly developed automobile self-starter to a standard pedal-driven bicycle. The boys were assisted in no small part by Big Howard's chief engineer, Matt Boehm.

Although the contraption couldn't go very fast, Dudley and Howard offered neighborhood kids a ride on their motorized bike for a nickel. Having never seen such a machine, concerned mothers were horrified when they spotted their offspring riding along the streets atop such a strange vehicle. Their fear was that the gasoline tank would explode and burn their children alive. It never did. In fact, it proved to be a fairly reliable vehicle until Howard abandoned it, pre-ferring to drive around town in his roadster instead.

Howard never bothered to get a driver's license, but told Dudley that he always kept two- hundred dollars in cash in the vehicle's glove compartment in case a patrolman stopped him. "All cops can be bought," Howard told Dudley, and during the decades that followed, events would prove how right he was.

The fame of the motorbike grew and on June 10, 1920, *The Houston Post* headlined the story: 14-YEAR-OLD INVENTS LIGHTER AND CHEAPER MOTORCYCLE. Dudley's contribution wasn't mentioned. This would be but the first of thousands of headlines in the years to come, announcing young Howard's inventiveness to the world.

***
West Newton, Massachusetts, 1920-21

One night, during a dialogue with a fellow oilman on a train, after a visit to Eleanor Boardman in Philadelphia, Big Howard learned of the exclusive Fassenden School in West Newton, Massachusetts. The school was founded in 1903 in the rolling hills of one of Boston's oldest suburbs. It even had a nine-hole golf course, a game to which Sonny was becoming addicted. Golf would later become one of his lifetime passions.

Intrigued with the prospect of sending Sonny to this school, he came to real-ize that he could gracefully break up the relationship his son had with Dudley and at the same time free his boy from the clutches of Allene. He also wanted to send Sonny to Harvard, following in his own footsteps, and felt that at Fassenden Sonny might take his education more seriously.

In spite of his agreement with Allene not to interfere, Big Howard decided, in his own words to his brother Rupert, "To take the bull by the horns—and just do it. After all, what can Allene possibly do to prevent it?"

When Allene learned about Big Howard's plans for Sonny, she took to her bed where she "lay in agony" for three weeks, administered to daily by Dr.

Frederick Lummis, a family friend who would eventually marry her sister, Annette.

Ignoring her protests, Big Howard boarded the train to Boston with his fourteen-year-old son, heading for Fessenden. On the way there, he couldn't help but notice the admiring glances from young women that his son received. Painfully shy, Sonny had blossomed into an exceptionally handsome young man at six feet, three inches.

"When I take you to Hollywood and my brother Rupert gets a look at the fine man you've become, I bet he'll turn you into a film star for sure. My boy, Sonny!"

It was at that point that his son informed his father that he didn't want to be known as Sonny any more and that he had "no interest whatsoever in the flickers."

Big Howard confessed that, in contrast, he himself was very interested in breaking into pictures as a financial backer. He claimed that Rupert was stepping up the pressure for him to relocate to Hollywood, maintaining that there was "big money" to be made in pictures, citing his own successful writing career as an example of that.

"Rupert told me that if I come to Hollywood, instead of '*Samuel Goldwyn Presents*', signs will say '*Howard Hughes Presents*.'"

Although Big Howard would continue to flirt with the idea of backing films, mainly as a pretense to seducing the likes of Mae Murray and Eleanor Boardman, it would ultimately be his son who would inspire the mantra "*Howard Hughes Presents.*"

***

It was aboard a long East-bound train ride that Big Howard explained to his son about the conflicting natures that almost genetically ran through the Hughes's bloodstreams. "The Hughes siblings are a weird mixture of the practical and the flighty, the mechanical and the artistic. My two brothers and my sister became all artsy-fartsy, and I became the engineer, the inventor, the mechanic. In you, Sonny, I believe that both sides of nature exist. You'll be a great artist of some sort—and I don't mean a Sunday painter—and you'll also be a great engineer like your old man. I just know it. I can feel it in you."

The romantic streak in the Hughes family had come from Jean Amelia Summerlin, a beautiful, delicate, and sensitive woman who loved literature, art, "and all things beautiful." She wrote poetry, was a talented musician, and read at least one potboiling romantic novel a day.

At the end of the Civil War, she'd married Felix Turner Hughes in the small Missouri town of Memphis. Felix had fought with the Missouri Militia on the side of the Union against the Confederacy. Jean on the other hand denied that she'd been born in Iowa and claimed to have been born in Virginia, site of her ancestors, because she believed that coming from the South "sounded more romantic than being born in the cornfields with pigs."

It still remains a mystery why this romantic and frequently daydreaming woman married Felix Hughes, whom she later called "the most practical man on earth." Schoolteacher. Lawyer. American patriot. Stern disciplinarian. The mayor of Keokuk, Iowa, from 1894 to 1896. Later judge of the superior court in the same town.

Near the end of the 19th century, he conceived the idea of a mile-long dam across the Mississippi River to Illinois. At the time of its completion in 1913, the dam harnessed water power and stopped the flooding that had previously threatened the area. Even *The New York Times* called it "the engineering marvel of the world."

In time Felix and Jean became parents of a daughter, Greta, born June 4, 1866, a year after the Civil War. She was followed on September 9, 1869 by their oldest son, Howard Robard Hughes, a name that he and, eventually, his own son eventually would carry. A third child, Rupert, was born on January 31, 1872. In some ways, Rupert was the rarest of all, having rested in the womb for eleven months. "I don't think I wanted to face the world," Rupert later said. "At least I was born with a full head of hair."

Another son, named after his father, Felix, was born on October 1, 1874. Yet another son, Reginald, was born in 1876, but he died in 1881.

A girl, Jean, named after her mother, was born in 1880 but died a few months later. A final male child, "Baby Hughes," was born in 1883, but died before he could be named.

As her children were growing up in Iowa, a hot summer day would find the mother, Jean (who was sometimes identified as "Mimi"), sitting in a towering cherry tree among the branches, composing her romantic plots, spinning entire novels in her head. Young Felix and Greta took an interest in music, both studying opera in Paris. Rupert would fulfill his mother's dreams by pursuing a career as a writer, recording tales of "the glamorous life" in New York and Hollywood.

The oldest boy, Howard Sr., showed no interest in art at all. He was more fascinated by timepieces, which he would take apart to see what made them tick. He'd do the same thing with an automobile, taking it apart piece by piece and then reassembling it.

Early in his life he showed entrepreneurial skill. Since his own stern father, the judge, refused to give his brood an allowance, Howard Sr. earned his pocket money by staging cockfights for the men of the town who liked that sport's combination of violence and gambling. When he wasn't doing that, he was getting into brawls with the bullies in Keokuk, Iowa.

In 1895, Howard Hughes, Sr. left Iowa and set out on what he claimed was "my grand adventure in a frontier land of discovery: America itself."

***

At the Fessenden School in West Newton, Howard Jr. was alone for the first time, his life brightened by daily letters from Allene that were filled with outpourings of her love. More restrained was a weekly letter from Dudley, pledging "my friendship always."

After the first ten days at school, a shipment arrived from Houston containing grapefruits the size of small melons, and large blood-red oranges. Howard ate what he wanted and sold the other pieces of citrus to his classmates at a nickel apiece.

He didn't need the money. Before leaving the Boston area, Big Howard gave in to Little Howard and granted him "unlimited expense money." To appease his son, Big Howard signed a letter of credit where "the sky's the limit." Even among the sons of wealthy men who attended Fessenden, this was an unheard-of concession.

Fellow students reported that young Howard was shy and reclusive, even refusing to attend school dances, although several pretty girls had more or less maneuvered themselves into a position where he might ask them out for a date. One of his fellow classmates claimed that Howard showed no interest whatsoever in girls, even though "that's all that the rest of us could talk about that year."

His growing deafness was already becoming a problem, and he asked his instructors to allow him to sit in the front row in spite of his shyness. He blamed his bad hearing on a damaged eardrum caused by a swimming pool accident when he was eight years old. In reality, it may have been congenital. His two uncles, Felix and Rupert, and his grandfather on his father's side, all suffered from poor hearing.

When Howard wasn't in class, he was often spotted on the prep school's nine-hole golf course. Later in life, it was said that his main interest in Katharine Hepburn was not in her "bony physique with no breasts," but in her great game of golf.

For the first time in his life, Howard paid attention to his school assignments. When the other students slept, he studied his books until the early hours of morning. He found a way to sneak out of his bleak and lonely dormitory room by climbing through a window in the basement of the school gym.

One of the school's professors found him at three o'clock one morning on the tennis courts. His fists balled in determination, he was shouting at the walls of the gym, "You can make it! I know you can. Just do it!"

Petulantly, he wrote to Allene complaining of the "crushing load of homework that is destroying my health." Immediately she fired off a letter to the headmaster, F. J. Fessenden, demanding that he ease up on the boy. He wrote her back that "nothing is expected of your son that isn't expected of any other boy here."

For the Thanksgiving holidays, Allene demanded that her son come home, but he wrote her that he couldn't make it all the way back to Texas in so short a time. She wrote back that she and her husband would meet him in New York instead. He then claimed that he was doing poorly in school and wanted to stay on campus and catch up on his studies. Allene reluctantly agreed to that.

Howard left his dormitory early one morning and headed for Boston by himself. He was gone for ten days, notifying the headmaster that he'd been stricken "with some very bad virus" and was under a doctor's care at a clinic in Boston. He warned Fessenden not to alert his mother, because she became hysterical at the slightest sign of illness and would withdraw him from school. "Finishing the term at Fessenden is more important to me that anything," Howard wrote, "and I'll be well soon and back in class." Although it was

38

against school rules, Fessenden agreed.

The next week Howard showed up in class, looking less nervous than ever and in the prime of health. In fact, he looked as if he'd been on a slow cruise to Bermuda. He was a lot friendlier with his classmates, more outgoing, and more willing to participate in school activities. To thank Fessenden for allowing him to recover without parental interference, he donated $1,500 for new uniforms and equipment for the basketball team.

Only two or three of his classmates figured out what brought about this remarkable transformation in Howard.

Somewhere during his absence from campus, he had acquired a new best friend as a replacement for Dudley.

***

Even to this day, Victor Sachel remains a complete mystery. Had Howard's classmates not encountered him with Sachel, his name would not be known. He was described as a young man, perhaps in his mid-twenties, who was extraordinarily good looking with a strong masculine appeal. He was about as tall as Howard but far more muscular.

When introduced to someone, he usually didn't have anything to say and looked as if he wanted to escape. His only interest in life seemed to revolve around Howard. Sachel had dinner with him every evening, and Howard continued to slip out of his dormitory at night to run away, presumably to have a rendezvous with Sachel, who had taken a small apartment near the school.

What is known is that Howard managed to spend the then staggering sum of $25,000 from his line of credit during the school term, and not on any purchases for himself. When the school term was over, he left with his same clothes and possessions.

However, Sachel was seen driving around West Newton in a shiny new car, and he always appeared finely dressed in the latest styles—in fact, he was a bit of a dandy.

At the local shops, Howard appeared frequently with Sachel, at one point demanding that a shoe salesman order expensive alligator shoes shipped up from Florida for Sachel.

At Lenny's Steak House, young Howard always demanded that the owner reserve the best steaks for Sachel and himself and rewarded him with frequent ten-dollar bills for doing just that. Steak was the only main course that Sachel and Howard were ever known to eat—never chicken, fish, or pork.

Toward the end of the school term, Sachel seemed to disappear just as mysteriously as he'd arrived. A rumor was spread that Sachel had impregnated a sixteen-year-old girl from a prominent family in West Newton. The speculation was that Sachel had to leave town overnight under threat from the impregnated girl's father.

In the final weeks of school, Howard appeared despondent and took no more interest in his school work. He dropped out of all activities and spent lonely hours in his dormitory room resting on an uncomfortable cot with a thin mattress.

The headmaster wrote Big Howard that "something might be wrong with your boy."

In New York at the time, Big Howard took the train to Boston for a long overdue reunion with his son.

***

Arriving at Fessenden for the weekend, Big Howard invited his son to New London, Connecticut, to watch the boat races between Yale and his alma mater, Harvard. His son was clearly bored but went along anyway to please his father. Perhaps he feared that Big Howard would confront him about the thousands of dollars spent from his line of credit, but no mention was made of it.

Big Howard was such an avid fan of his alma mater, Harvard, that he promised young Howard anything he wanted if Harvard emerged victorious in the boat race. When the Harvard team won, young Howard immediately presented his father with a demand.

Walking down to the site of the Thames River races, he'd spotted an entrepreneur advertising "sky rides for five bucks" per passenger in a Curtiss Seaplane. Although he'd made a promise to give his son whatever he wanted if Harvard won, Big Howard refused the request to go for a ride, fearing it would endanger the boy's life. The plane looked none too safe. Finally, when young Howard created a scene by breaking down and crying, his father relented.

Buckled in, and piloted by Captain Horace Hudson, who kept the small craft airborne for twelve minutes, father and son flew into the sky. Big Howard later admitted that he had been terrified.

Young Howard wasn't frightened to be up in the clouds at all. When Big Howard gratefully put his feet on solid earth, he was shaking. Clutching his stomach, he vomited. But his son told him, "I was born to fly like the birds. I've never known such a thrill in my life. When I finish school, I'm going to become a great pilot."

That short flight did indeed mark a turning point in the life of Howard Hughes Jr. In the decades to come, no beautiful woman, no handsome man, no business deal, would ever generate as much passion in him as when he was manning the controls of an airplane—big or small.

***

Howard ended his school year and headed back to Houston to spend the summer with Allene and to reunite with Dudley Sharp.

His school records at Fessenden mysteriously disappeared one day, but the headmaster announced that he had cleared the equivalent of the eighth grade "with distinction." Big Howard told his brother Rupert in Los Angeles that, "I've taken the first step in weaning my son from Allene's tit!"

His classmates at Fessenden were just as baffled by Howard when he graduated as when he'd first enrolled. One of his classmates, Percy Williams, who'd roomed with Howard briefly until the boy demanded his own room, asked him to sign his yearbook. Howard found the page where students were to list their ambitions. He signed *yegg* as his intended profession. That was a slang word at the time meaning thug or gangster.

In that same yearbook, the class prophet wrote, "Howard Hughes Jr. has a big ranch in Texas where he raises toothless cows." Writing in the same yearbook, the class historian said, "Howard Robard Hughes Jr. comes from just where you'd expect: Texas. But we're not certain just where he's going."

***

Houston 1921

It was a different household that awaited Howard on his return to the blistering heat of Houston. Allene arrived at the railway station in a long, black, chauffeur-driven limousine to pick him up. Although she embraced him warmly, he sensed a change in her mood toward him.

She seemed less desperate, less possessive, less concerned with his well-being. Their nine-month separation had made an enormous difference in their relationship, even though he wasn't certain how.

Dudley Sharp was waiting for him in the living room of the house on Yoakum Drive. Howard embraced his best friend, even though he noticed a chill between them.

He was obviously shocked to see Dudley being invited as a guest into their home. At first he viewed his friend's presence as a major compromise on Allene's part. Perhaps she'd decided that Dudley wasn't such a bad influence after all, and had rescinded her command that her son could no longer associate with him.

Howard wondered about the new relationship between Allene and Dudley. He didn't question either of them about it, but Dudley seemed to have acquired an intimate familiarity with the Hughes household, knowing the layout of the rooms and where everything was better than Howard himself.

He'd obviously spent a lot of time there.

Howard was even more surprised when Dudley showed him upstairs to his newly decorated bedroom. For the first time in his life, Howard was going to get a bedroom of his own with a lock on the door. No more sleeping in the master bedroom with Allene.

As Dudley helped Howard with his luggage, Howard went to the door to lock it. He moved toward Dudley, wanting to embrace and kiss him like he'd done on the day he'd told him good-bye before heading East. Dudley backed away and extricated himself from Howard's embrace.

"What's wrong?" Howard asked.

"That was kid's stuff," Dudley said, seemingly embarrassed. "I've given up shit like that. I'm dating girls now. We were just boys then. We're men now."

Howard must have been stunned at this sudden rejection. As with Ella Rice, the young girl at school, he'd wait long and patiently for his revenge on Dudley.

Seemingly without emotion, Howard Jr. stiffly embraced Allene at Houston's railway station. Instead of an embrace, he shook Dudley's hand. Big Howard had already said his good-bye to Allene and was already on board waiting for Little Howard in the family's private rail car.

He was taking his son to Los Angeles to a new life.

Instead of sending Howard to one of the East Coast prep schools, Big Howard had enrolled his boy in the exclusive Thacher School, a boarding school, in Ojai, California. That way he could be closer to Howard since he was spending more time at the offices of Hughes Tool Company in Los Angeles than in Houston.

At his "fantasy home" on Los Feliz Boulevard in Los Angeles, Rupert Hughes awaited the arrival of his brother and his nephew. Unlike the tall, lean, ruggedly handsome Big Howard, Rupert was short and plump. His cherubic features and manner were often compared to those of a pixie.

Such an unlikely man was to become the Hollywood role model for young Howard.

A novelist, screenwriter, and director, Rupert had once written to his arts-conscious mother, Jean Hughes, whom he called "Mimi," that, "My brother has no prospects to speak of. He is already thirty-six years old and has not kept a steady job. The only gold he finds is fool's gold. He's better with a deck of cards like a Mississippi riverboat gambler than he is in striking it rich in the oil fields."

That long-ago observation, however, had become ancient history. As the Santa Fe Zephyr sped westward from Texas to Los Angeles, Big Howard could have bought out Rupert in a minute, even though his chubby little brother was one of the most successful entrepreneurs in the emerging Hollywood.

Only the week before, Rupert had written to his mother, Mimi, with a very different impression. "With that damn drill bit, Big Howard has made me eat my words—chew them up and spit them out. He's rich beyond the wildest dreams of any wildcatter. I'm rich myself. But he's so rich it's vulgar. I predict your oldest boy will become America's first billionaire, whereas dear old me will probably die with no more than fifty-thousand dollars in the bank. When Little Howard inherits all that money one day, I'll become a postscript, the poor uncle of a rich nephew, all my contributions forgotten and eclipsed by HH Sr. and Jr."

In spite of the envy he felt for his brother, Rupert had set out to "live a thousand years and a thousand lives."

He would instill that same philosophy into young Howard.

In New York Rupert had become celebrated for his short stories about the glamorous life of the pre-World War I era. In many ways, he was fulfilling the long-suppressed dreams of his beloved mother Mimi, who spent her entire life fantasizing about "what could never be." Her fondness for romantic novels fueled her fantasy of herself as a heroine being swept away by a dashing knight

in shining armor who would arrive on a white stallion. In reality, she was growing more and more discontented with her husband, Felix, and they bickered
constantly. She confessed to Rupert that she and Felix had not slept together
since the death of their last child.

A graduate of Yale, Rupert had become a literary celebrity as early as 1903.
He'd survived an ugly divorce in New York from Syracuse-born Agnes Wheeler
Hedge. In a story that appeared on the front page of *The New York Times*, she'd
accused Rupert of having "a dozen lovers" since the beginning, in 1897, of their
six-year marriage. He'd fired back with the very same accusation hurled at her.
In 1921 Rupert had remarried, this time to a beautiful actress, Adelaide Manola
Bissell, whom young Howard had never met.

For his reunion with his relatives at Los Angeles' Union Station, Rupert
arrived in a chauffeur-driven purple limousine, which he'd borrowed from the
silent screen star, Francis X. Bushman. Hoping to impress his older brother,
Rupert had attired himself in a green suit with a sunflower yellow tie. "To go
Hollywood," he'd also purchased a pair of shoes which had been gilded with
real gold. His wife, Adelaide, called them "your fairy slippers—all you need is
a magic wand."

Getting off the train, Big Howard spotted his younger brother and called to
him. But Rupert's eye was immediately riveted to his nephew, whom he hadn't
seen in many a year. He was astonished at how tall and handsome the young
Howard had become. It was then and there that Rupert decided he was going
to make Howard Hughes Jr. the reigning male star of the silent screen.

The tall and dashing young man who appeared at the station with his father
was dressed like a romantic airplane pilot. Impulsively Rupert decided that
he'd write an aviation picture for Howard and direct it himself.

Even as he rushed in his "fairy slippers" to embrace his brother and his
nephew, Rupert had come up with the title of his new flicker: HELL'S
ANGELS.

***

At the dawn of the Twenties, Rupert had become one of Hollywood's most
successful writers and one of its most gossiped-about celebrities. The Sunday
brunches he hosted at his gabled, Gothic mansion had become legendary,
attracting the elite of Hollywood.

The producer, Samuel Goldwyn, had lured Rupert to the West Coast to
write the screenplays for silent films. The shrewd Goldwyn had failed with
many writers, but not with Rupert. He was pulling in a phenomenal paycheck
of $125,000 a year, far more than he made when he was an editor in a dull job
at *Encyclopedia Britannica*.

Rupert continued to urge his brother to invest some of his drill bit revenues
"into the flicker business." To impress both his father and his nephew, Rupert
had carefully arranged for the biggest names in Hollywood to attend his Sunday
brunch the following day. "All the greatest stars, even Mary Pickford and
Douglas Fairbanks, will be there," Rupert gleefully told both Howards. "All
the big producers and directors. Cecil B. DeMille. Goldwyn himself."

On the Saturday night before his party, Rupert called William Desmond Taylor, the director, to make certain that he'd attend. "Wait until you see my nephew," he told the director. "He's more gorgeous than Wallace Reid and a hell of a lot prettier than your boy, Antonio Moreno."

Taylor assured Rupert that he'd be there tomorrow "to get a look at this new piece of male flesh."

***

Rupert had found an architect who'd designed the entrance to his home in the style of an *Arabian Nights* fantasy. Through the gateway the following Sunday morning paraded a spectacularly dressed bevy of stars, directors, and producers.

Taking Howard by the hand, Rupert led his nephew into the garden for personal introductions to some of the world's most celebrated people. "Think of this as your debutante party," Rupert said.

"I'm no god damn debutante," Howard countered, insulted that his uncle would use a term on him reserved for girls. "I'm a man now!"

"Good to hear that," Rupert said. "Allene's not dressing you up in girl's clothing anymore?"

"How in hell did you learn about that?" Howard asked.

Before the all-knowing Rupert could answer, Howard was being introduced to the most famous couple on earth: the recently married Mary Pickford and Douglas Fairbanks, Sr.

In 1918, in Houston, Howard had gone with Dudley to see *Johanna Enlists*, based on a story by Rupert and his co-writer, the also famous Frances Marion. In this comedy-romance, Pickford had played a young girl living on her father's backwoods farm. The picture had been directed by William Desmond Taylor, to whom Howard had been promised an introduction later in the day.

To young Howard, the Fairbanks duo

Loving couple: Douglas Fairbanks, Sr., and Mary Pickford

44

were a dazzling, golden pair. Both of them had worldwide fame, lots of money, and also physical beauty. They were the true Queen and King of Hollywood.

In Rupert's view, Howard immediately made a serious blunder. "Someday I'm going to be more famous than either of you—and a lot richer."

Taken aback, Pickford was the first to recover. "I'm sure you will," she assured him. 'You've got the money and money translates into power. How can you lose?"

"And Mary could have added, you've got the looks, too," Fairbanks said. "Just like my boy, Doug, Jr. I want you to meet him. He's a bit younger than you but mature for his age. I think you two guys will hit it off."

"You *are* a beauty," Pickford told Howard. "Doug worries that his son will go into the movies too. If that happens, and you, too, become a movie star, Doug here will no longer be the screen's most beautiful male animal." Sensing her husband's upset, she hastily added, " Of course, in my eyes Doug will always be the handsomest man on the planet."

After meeting Hollywood's two crowned heads, the introductions were coming so fast and furious for Howard that he couldn't keep the names and faces straight. He'd never heard of some of Rupert's guests. Others, his uncle assured him, were very important even if he didn't know who they were.

'The big thing," Rupert said, "is that *I* know who they are. My paycheck depends on it."

Sometimes as he was moving with young Howard across the garden, Rupert had time to whisper an intimate detail before approaching a celebrity for an introduction. Such was the case with Viola Dana, the beautiful actress whose political views were somewhere to the right of Attila the Hun.

The press at the time protected her and didn't publish any of her more out-rageous comments, including her often expressed opinion, "that all the niggers in America should be rounded up and shipped back to Africa where they belong."

Her extreme rightwing views, however, didn't extend to sex. Before approaching her, Rupert whispered to Howard, "So the story goes, she's laid everything in Hollywood except the linoleum."

Howard was surprised when Dana immediately kissed him on the mouth, even extending a flicker of her fast-moving pink tongue. No woman, other than Allene, had ever kissed him on the mouth before. As he later told Rupert, "I liked it a lot. Gave me a hard-on."

Howard towered over the diminutive actress. "Big boy, my lips come up to your belt," Dana said. "That's gonna make it real convenient when I have a few more drinks and get you off."

That was the first come-on Howard had ever received from a film actress. It would be followed in the years to come by literally thousands of roughly equivalent propositions from women.

"Did she mean that?" Howard eagerly asked Rupert just before Dana spot-ted her latest lover, Buster Keaton, coming into the garden. She turned to Howard for one final kiss on the lips. "See you later, stud."

When she was out of hearing range, Rupert said to Howard, "Viola likes two things—teenage boys like yourself and, strangely enough, comedians.

She's carrying on affairs right now with both Keaton and Fatty Arbuckle. Where she finds Fatty's little dickie underneath all that blubber, I don't know."

Rupert's eagle eye was diverted to two men talking in the far corner of his garden near a splashing fountain. "See those men over there?" Rupert asked Howard. "Sam Goldwyn and Cecil B. DeMille. I'm sure you saw *We Can't Have Everything.* Cecil's brother, William de Mille and I wrote that with Cecil directing."

"I saw it," Howard said.

"My soapy mother-love melodrama, *The Old Nest*—Reginald Barker directed it—brought in a million big ones for Sammy baby." As Rupert guided Howard closer to the men, Rupert confided, "Cecil doesn't like to fuck women. He likes to jerk off while sucking a woman's toes."

"That's more than I need to know," Howard whispered as he approached DeMille and Goldwyn. Goldwyn appeared ordinary in a dark blue business suit. The bald but more flamboyant DeMille wore perfectly tailored elephant gray riding breeches and gleaming brown leather boots.

After introductions were made and hands were shaken, both DeMille and Goldwyn showed little interest in Howard. Rupert, however, knew how to interest an audience. He confided to the two impresarios that Big Howard was also a guest, and he was in Hollywood seeking film properties in which to invest.

Suddenly, it was apparent that both DeMille and Goldwyn had "big pictures" in need of financing.

They quickly excused themselves and headed toward Big Howard, who was talking with the actress, Blanche Sweet.

"Sorry for the brush-off," Rupert apologized to Howard. "You've got to prove yourself in Hollywood before you can impress those vultures. But here comes a big director who will give you his undivided attention."

Howard looked across the lawn as a handsome older man approached him with an extended right hand.

"Hello," he said in an educated and well-modulated voice. "You must be the person Rupert described as the most beautiful boy in Hollywood, where the competition for that title is rough. I'm William Desmond Taylor."

Tentatively, Howard extended his hand to Taylor who held it for so long, even clasping his left hand over it, that he didn't think he'd be able to retrieve it any time soon.

***

New York, 1983

One of the leading ladies of the Nickelodeon era, Chicago-born Blanche Sweet, opened the door to her modestly furnished apartment in the Murray Hill section of New York City. Her lodgings were a very far cry from the mansion that Norma Desmond occupied in *Sunset Boulevard.* The year was 1983, and the actress who waited at the door to the apartment in Murray Hill had reached the peak of her film career between 1910 and 1914, arguably making her the first real film star.

Deep into her third drink, she invited this reporter "to hurry up and catch up with *self* so we can be on the same wave length." She had a habit of speaking of herself as "self" or "myself." A small woman with a dazzling, almost Cupid-like smile, she still possessed "eyes as blue as any sky that ever blanketed southern California," in the fan magazine words of her long-faded era.

At times she appeared like a China doll of delicate porcelain, not a real woman at all. She was heavily made up and wearing extremely long eyelashes. A militant left-winger, and once a member of the Communist Party, she sat on her frayed sofa beside an autographed picture of Cuba's Fidel Castro.

"Why would anyone be interested in *myself?*" she asked. "Most of my films are but celluloid turned to dust." Nonetheless, she began a long recitation of her illustrious career, beginning when she was eighteen-months-old in 1897 and was carried onto the stage in a melodrama called *Blue Jeans*.

"My God, *self* broke into films in 1909, and by 1911, I was playing heroines for D.W. Griffith," she said. "A great director, a genius really, but a shit. At least he had the good taste to let me succeed Mary Pickford at Biograph. In *The Lonedale Operator*, I virtually invented the cinema's first independent heroine. But do you think anyone's honoring my contribution to film today? It's Chaplin this, Mary Pickford that. As if *self* didn't exist!" Holding up an empty glass, she commanded, "Make yourself useful and get me another drink, sugar."

"My God, baby," she said when her fourth drink was presented, "I'm Mother Courage. I've survived it all. Even the god damn San Francisco earthquake of 1906. Yes, even that."

Her famous temperament flared only when the subject of Howard Hughes, Senior and Junior, came up. "Is that what *self* has become? Some postscript to two filthy rich, cold-hearted beasts? Their hearts were as black as the oil they pumped from the ground."

She recalled in vivid detail the Sunday brunch at Rupert's house where she'd first met Howard Hughes, Jr. back in 1921.

"Even though my director, Marshall Neilan, was vowing eternal devotion," Blanche said, "I was making out like a bandit with Howard Sr. He was promising me the world, claiming he was going to produce A-list motion pictures and make me the biggest star in Hollywood. Later I found out the blowhard was using the same shit line on Mae Murray, Eleanor Boardman, and who knows how many others."

"From time to time, I helped him get his rocks off, but he didn't finance one of *myself's* dreams," Blanche said. "I did

Blanche Sweet

get a diamond bracelet and a big ruby ring out of the deal, though. I was forced to hock both of them when I fell on bad days. By 1958 the great Blanche Sweet was a clerk in a god damn department store. So much for screwing around with billionaires."

She remembered Big Howard bringing "Junior" over to meet her at the Sunday brunch in Rupert's garden. "God, he was tall for his age. A bit skinny for my tastes but very handsome. If I hadn't been making it with his dear old dad, *self* would have kidnapped him. I saw that old queen, William Desmond Taylor, standing nearby in the garden making jealous eyes at *myself*."

Blanche even remembered what she wore. "*Myself* had dressed entirely in white that day—white hat, a white lace veil, white dress, white stockings, and white shoes."

She recalled that sometime during Rupert's afternoon brunch, Big Howard asked her if she'd accompany Howard Jr. to a night club that evening. His chauffeur-limousine was already parked outside Rupert's Arabian Fantasy gate.

"I got into the car and sat between Senior and Junior," Blanche said. "Junior complimented me on my film, *The Unpardonable Sin*, which I'd made in 1919, with Marshall Neilan, my future husband, directing. It had been based on a novel written by Rupert. Junior then said something rather strange. 'I always like to see a flicker where a beautiful woman gets debased by German soldiers.' I think Junior was a bit kinky even back then. Then Big Howard told his driver to take us to the Ambassador Hotel, where he'd rented a suite, probably to escape from the burden of being Rupert's house guest. Howard Sr. told Howard Jr. and *self* that he'd be gone for about an hour and that we were to wait together in the back seat of the limousine. Big Howard also said that he wanted to check up on an illegal shipment of bourbon. He'd found some bourbon that he said had been aging since 1915, and he seemed hell-bent on cornering the world supply for his future parties. I took out a cigarette," Blanche recalled. "Mabel Normand had taught me how to smoke. Junior graciously lit it for *myself*. We sat there in silence as I smoked. From the limousine's bar, Junior poured us both a drink of daddy's bourbon, even though I thought he was a bit young to be hitting the bottle. After I crushed out my cigarette, he impulsively leaned over and kissed *myself* on my scarlet red mouth. He had no manners or grace at all. A very awkward boy. With his tongue down my throat, he reached inside my low-cut dress and grabbed my left tit and squeezed it. Fortunately for him, I was a wild and reckless *tamale* in those days. You might call me the first women's libber. As a way of playing along, I grabbed his balls." She paused, having almost finished her fourth drink. "I couldn't believe it. I felt something like a sledgehammer in his pants. I'd gone to bed with Big Howard several times, and he was a good lover if you like the missionary position. He was built like a normal male, nothing to write home about. But after groping Junior, I decided that their nicknames were wrong. Big Howard should have been called Little Howard, and Little Howard should have been called Big Howard."

Blanche admitted that *self* didn't know what overcame her. She said she unbuttoned Junior's trousers for a closer inspection. "In a town where men were known for having whoppers, Junior measured right up there with the best of them. I don't want to provide you with the clinical details, but right there in the back seat of his daddy's limo, I went down on Howard Hughes Jr."

"When I finished, he wanted to know if I'd swallowed it," she said. "He told me that he had a friend in Texas, Dudley, I think it was—who always spat it out and that my way was much better. I figured that this wasn't his first blow-job, but perhaps the first time a woman had gone down on him. Apparently, he liked it a lot. He returned for some repeat performances, but the kid and I never had intercourse. I think I was the first woman to introduce Junior to what became one of the great passions of his life—having beautiful women go down on him. It became his lifetime addiction, many other equally beautiful women like *myself* have told me."

In New York in the 80s, the interview with Blanche Sweet stretched late into the night. Even when she could no longer articulate properly, she still wanted to remember the past, revealing a litany of stories that, as an ensemble, could inspire a virtual rewrite of the social history of Hollywood in the Teens and Twenties.

Finally, during her fond *adieu*, she stood on wobbly legs at the door to her apartment. "Don't tell me that *self* is going to go down in film history, not as one of the great Griffith actresses, but as the bitch who gave Junior his first blow job from a woman?"

No answer was expected.

She remembered to add something to that night she went on the town with Senior and Junior. "We were at a club somewhere," Blanche said. "Big Howard was at a distant table talking to someone he knew from Texas. Junior turned to me and said, 'I guess after what we did in the limo, I'll have to marry you.' Isn't that the cutest thing any boy could say to a woman?"

Blanche Sweet slammed the door, as if that act alone would blot out a troubled past.

***

Los Angeles, 1921

Howard presumed that Blanche Sweet spent the night with Big Howard at the Ambassador Hotel the following evening. Rupert and his second wife, Adelaide, had been invited to a dinner party at Samuel Goldwyn's house. Rupert referred to the producer by his original name of "Goldfish." Big Howard had mysteriously disappeared.

That left Howard Jr. all alone for the evening, but an incoming call from the director, William Desmond Taylor, soon changed all that. Taylor was full of talk about casting Howard as the lead in his next motion picture, and he promised that he'd meet soon with Rupert to write "the perfect script" for Howard's film debut.

Taylor said that he'd come to Rupert's house at eight o'clock that night to take him out for a night on the town. "You're a fully grown man now and don't need personal supervision any more."

Before ringing off, Taylor told him, "I hope you don't mind. I'm bringing along Rod St. Just. He's a famous photographer of the Hollywood underground—and a lot of fun. With his mannerisms, he's off-putting at first, but when you get to know him he's a real swell bloke."

As Howard would later write to Dudley in Houston, "I felt like a real man getting invited out on the town by an important director who wants to make me a bigtime star. Hollywood is my kind of town. I don't think I'll ever live anywhere else. I'll dread it when I have to go to Ojai to school."

All of Los Angeles seemed like one vast playground, as he informed Dudley in his letter. "I've already seduced my first movie star. Blanche Sweet."

***

Right on time, William Desmond Taylor's chauffeur-driven car arrived to pick up Howard. Sitting in the back seat was Rod St. Just, who let out a whistle when he spotted Howard. "Your reputation has preceded you," Rod said. "You're beautiful. I must photograph you."

Rod St. Just introduced himself as "the world's greatest still photographer." A veteran of the boudoirs and back alleys of Hollywood, he specialized in photographing private parties. In addition to that, many stars, both male and female, had posed nude for him, wanting to capture their bodies at the peak of their youth and beauty. Rumor had it that Francis X. Bushman, Mabel Normand, and Rudolph Valentino, among many others, had already faced Rod's hawkeye and his camera.

Rod was the most effeminate man Howard had ever encountered. Men like that were beaten up and run out of Houston, but Howard seemed strangely amused by the photographer. Rod explained that Taylor had preceded them, asking to be dropped off earlier in the evening at a well-known dive, Fruitfly, a gay bar that flourished in Hollywood in the early Twenties before the police shut it down. On the way there, Rod filled Howard in on all the gossip about William Desmond Taylor. "This lothario is the lover of both Mabel Normand and Mary Miles Minter. He's even fucking little Mary's mother, Charlotte Shelby."

"More power to him."

"That's not all he fucks," Rod said enigmatically.

"What's this club, Fruitfly?" Howard asked.

"It's a queer meeting den of guys and gals with strange tastes. Forbidden fruit attracting fruitflies. The men can act as effeminate as they want or the women as manly. In fact, many of the gals arrive dressed in kimonos—the fashion of the moment. The staff of gorgeous boys and girls wheel around drugs—opium, morphine, marijuana—on tea carts. Even heroin if you want it. Ever had drugs?"

"Once back in Houston," Howard said. "My friend Dudley and I bought some cocaine one night. We got real stupid. I liked it."

At the time of Howard's meeting with William Desmond Taylor, the director was one of the most gossiped-about men in Hollywood. He was said to have been a student in Dublin, a Klondike miner, a construction engineer, a British soldier, and a London stage actor. His father, a stern and unforgiving colonel in the British army, had banished his son to a farm in Harper, Kansas, and then accidentally "re-discovered" him on stage in London.

In Hollywood, Taylor had directed *The World Apart*, with Wallace Reid, Tinseltown's handsomest male actor, moving on to direct both Mary Pickford and her brother Jack, allegedly seducing both of them.

At Fruitfly, a club where only members were allowed inside, a young Mexican boy parked Rod's car. A doorman led Howard and Rod down a long and dimly lit corridor that smelled strangely of urine. In the outer foyer, after gaining clearance, Rod shelled out fifty dollars for the two of them to enter. No club in America at that time charged such an outrageous cover, but since the Fruitfly "is so special," in Rod's words, the manager could get away with "this grand larceny."

Howard was ushered into the rear, a room so dark he could hardly make out the faces of the patrons until his eyes adjusted. The smoke was like a London fog, but the smell was not of regular tobacco. The aroma was strange to Howard's nostrils. The place was what he might have conjured up as an opium den.

Rod assured Howard that a lot of famous people were in attendance that night: Jack Pickford, Mabel Normand, Wallace Reid, Tom Ince, the famous director, and Bobby Harron, the handsome but fading D.W. Griffith star. "I've staked out Bobby for the evening," Rod assured Howard. Howard recalled having seen Bobby play "The Boy" in Griffith's *Intolerance*.

Rod ushered Howard into one of the private rooms in back where he encountered the august presence of William Desmond Taylor for the second time. Taylor had already launched his evening of debauchery before their arrival. He appeared drunk to Howard but was holding his liquor and/or drugs like the stately British gentleman he was.

A masculine-looking Chinese woman in a red kimono stood in the corner near a tea cart from which Taylor was making a selection of opium and marijuana cigarettes. Seeing Howard, Taylor beckoned him to enter a room lit by only two red lights. "Come in, my dear boy," Taylor said. "My oh my, aren't we the most beautiful sight in Hollywood."

Soon Howard was seated on floor cushions facing the director. Rod, Taylor, and Howard lit up their marijuana cigarettes in colored paper after the Chinese peddler disappeared.

The dialogue that took place between Taylor and Howard that night was later revealed in the notorious underground memoirs of Rod St. Just, circulated in 1936 in private editions throughout Hollywood.

Taylor reached for Howard's hand and kissed it the way he might do with Mary Pickford. "My big, strapping, darling man," Taylor said in a low voice. "My camera will capture your youth and beauty to perfection. I can't wait until we start filming."

As Rod recalled, Howard had little to say that night. Taylor did most of the talking. The marijuana had made him mellow.

"I've lived a varied and rich life," he said to Howard, virtually ignoring the presence of Rod. "Since I'm called upon to reproduce real life on film, I draw upon my past experiences. A story can't be presented on screen in a human, gripping manner unless the director has been in contact with the situation depicted."

"Surely your life can't have covered all the plots you've got to film?" Howard asked.

"I've seen it all," Taylor assured him. "For instance, I never thought that being marooned for an entire winter in the backwoods of Alaska would be one of the most valuable things that could have happened to me. It was a terrible period for me. I had only sled dogs for company. But it was being alone with those dogs so constantly that gave me a love for animals in my pictures. I learned how to handle them. They say I'm very successful when I use animals in my pictures. If that's so, it is entirely due to the six months I spent alone with those dogs."

"I've seen two or three of your pictures," Howard said. "I like the way you focus on the smallest detail. Even a doorknob in one of your pictures becomes fascinating. I'd be honored to star in your next picture."

At this point, Taylor placed a firm hand on Howard's leg and didn't remove it for quite a while, at least not until he needed to light up another marijuana cigarette.

Rod's drug of choice for the night was cocaine, which he invited Howard to share with him. Howard almost gleefully indulged.

Leaning back with his second marijuana cigarette, this one wrapped in a kind of chartreuse-colored paper, Taylor continued what eventually became more or less of a monologue.

"How would a man act if he were about to be killed by a crazed fool—or in danger of death from any other source?" he asked. "Once in the Klondike my cabin was entered by a man who calmly announced that he was going to kill me. He quoted passages from the Bible as authority. I took the Bible from him and showed him he was wrong—and he forgot all about killing me. But for a moment there I faced death. Some of the stars in my films face death, and I'm able to convey to them the emotions I felt back in the Klondike."

His hand was back on Howard's leg, but this time, placed much closer to his crotch. "All the technical assistants in the world won't help a director if he doesn't know life as it really is."

"What are you going to do with me?" Howard asked, as Rod looked on silently like a voyeur. Noticing the placement of the director's hand, he quickly added, "I mean, on the screen."

Taylor leaned over to Howard and kissed his right ear, inserting his tongue. "I'm going to do something revolutionary for a flicker. I'm going to photograph you like you were a beautiful girl. I'm going to have the camera caress you— your face, your eyes, your eyelids, that succulent mouth. That gorgeously ripe male body about to explode into full bloom. Up to now, directors have concentrated on only female beauty on the screen. But most of any movie-going audience is female. I want women to enjoy the same excitement in watching a film as a man does, perhaps a man who's seeing Theda Bara up there vamping for dear life."

"I won't go nude," Howard protested, moving away from Taylor.

In his counterattack, the director grabbed the drugged Howard and crushed him into his strong muscled body, inserting his tongue in Howard's mouth.

After a mild protest, Howard gave in. When Taylor broke away, it was only to lick at Howard's neck and place gentle bites along the curvature of his neck.

Rod couldn't help but notice that Taylor's roving hand had settled on its target for the evening. He was obviously arousing some strong sexual feelings in Howard.

Only once did Howard break away. "Rupert told me that you were a real ladies' man—one of the most notorious in Hollywood."

"Your uncle got that right," Taylor said. "There are two things I adore more than all others on earth. A woman's young vagina and boy's young ass, both of which I eat before fucking. I can't get enough of either, and I like them both equally. Don't you find that in ice cream, it's hard to determine if you like strawberry or peach better? Both are wonderful."

Suddenly, as Rod noted, Taylor had become aware of his presence. "Rod, I want you to go out and chase Bobby Harron the rest of the night. As for young Howard Hughes Jr. here, I have plans for him. I'm going to acquaint him with every erogenous zone in his body."

Rod staggered to his feet and looked at Howard before leaving. The young man seemed in another world, not in control of what was happening to him.

"And lock the door on your way out," Taylor said as a final command.

Howard Hughes Jr.

CHAPTER THREE
Ojai, California, 1921

Set on 200 acres of beautiful landscaping, the Thacher School stood on the site of a failed orange and avocado ranch. Having flopped as a rancher, the stern headmaster, Sherman Day Thacher, was a former quarterback for the Yale football team. At first, he didn't have an opening for Howard. Nor was he impressed with his academic background. But after Hughes Sr. agreed to put up the money for a new gymnasium, Thacher found room for Howard after all.

He was assigned to a sparsely furnished dormitory room, which he shared with three other boys, within a three-story, Spanish Mission-style building. To ease his son's loneliness, Big Howard purchased the finest black stallion he could find in the San Fernando Valley and had it shipped by box car freight to Ojai. Howard immediately fell in love with the horse and, for some reason, named it "Coon." In time, he developed a passion for horseback riding that would rival his devotion to golf. He could be seen early every morning riding through the sagebrush, exploring the lonely ravines filled with scrub oak.

A lackluster student, Howard wanted the term to end before it had even begun. Instead of algebra, he daydreamed of his two ambitions in life: To become a bigtime movie star and to pilot his own private plane.

From Houston, "mother hen" letters started arriving from Allene, reminding Howard to take his Russian mineral oil. She constantly inquired about his health. When he mentioned casually that he'd developed a boil on his left hand, Allene hastily summoned Dr. Chickering once again from the Rockefeller Institute. Arriving in Ojai, the doctor found that Howard's boil had almost healed, so he indulged himself in another vacation at Big Howard's expense.

All of a sudden, the concerned letters from Allene abruptly ended. Howard wrote Dudley to inquire about his mother. Dudley wrote back that Allene was extremely agitated and wasn't sleeping at night. Often, late at night, she could be seen wandering up and down Yoakum Boulevard.

It was weeks later that Howard found out the truth. Allene had learned that Big Howard was keeping Eleanor Boardman in high style at a lavish suite at the Ambassador Hotel in Los Angeles. Not only that, but Rupert planned to star her in a film, *Souls for Sale.*

After mulling it over for a month, Allene decided to take the train from Houston to Los Angeles where she planned to arrive unexpectedly at her husband's suite, the way she'd once done in New York.

In Los Angeles, she went directly to Big Howard's suite and was let in by a bellhop. She didn't find her husband there and saw no telltale signs of Eleanor. What Allene didn't know was that Big Howard and Eleanor had gone down to Mexico for a two-week vacation while Rupert stayed in Los Angeles working on the script for her film debut.

Taking advantage of the superior medical facilities in Los Angeles, Allene consulted three specialists, each of whom gave her the same bad news. She was pregnant. It was a tubular pregnancy, the fetus developing outside the uterus. Doctors in Texas had warned her that she could never have another child—and now she found herself in this extremely dangerous condition.

Decades later, Eleanor said that Big Howard learned of his wife's pregnancy when they returned from their vacation in Mexico. He told Eleanor that he hadn't slept with his wife in two years and hadn't a clue as to who the father was.

Because of his own rampant infidelities, Big Howard decided not to confront his wife about the probability of a lover in her life. "Frankly, I'm sort of relieved," he confided to Eleanor. "It takes the heat off of me."

In a bizarre and seemingly erratic change of mood, Allene then decided to leave Los Angeles on a train back to Houston before Big Howard arrived back from his holiday in Mexico with Eleanor.

With his wife safely back in Houston, he felt free to move Eleanor into the suite with him since he didn't expect a return visit.

Little did he know at the time that the Hughes household, dysfunctional as it was, was about to experience a total collapse.

***

Los Angeles, Winter 1921-22

Sometime after Howard's fifteenth birthday, he started to lead his life at the Thacher School virtually as an adult, coming and going as he wished. Classmates reported that Howard was often missing from school, taking long weekends in Los Angeles and returning with dazzling tales of piloting small airplanes and "near fatal crashes."

It isn't known what compromise the school's headmaster, Thacher, made with either Big Howard or "Junior" himself, but years later, Eleanor Boardman claimed that Big Howard had resigned himself to the fact that his son "was not Harvard material," and more or less gave him free rein to do as he pleased.

One of the most mysterious periods in young Howard's life began in the winter of 1921. Blanche Sweet is the only person who ever spoke convincingly about this period of the boy's life, and even she had to speculate, as she wasn't completely aware of what was going on.

What she did know was that William Desmond Taylor continued to pursue young Howard. Taylor and Rupert came into conflict over a suitable script for

Howard's film debut. Taylor was enthusiastically promoting Howard as an ingenue in a script called *The Ideal Boy*, whereas Rupert still wanted to feature Howard as a dashing young pilot in an aviation movie. Naturally, Howard opted for the aviation film, although he deferred to Taylor's judgment as well. Howard promised both Rupert and Taylor that he'd star in each of their epics.

It is not known when, but at some point Taylor introduced Hughes to Spanish-born Antonio Moreno (né Antonio Garrido Monteagudo y Moreno), the first Spanish-speaking star in the history of American motion pictures. The Antonio Banderas of his day, he'd been frequently cast, pre-Valentino, as a Latin lover at a time when all Hispanic men on screen were portrayed as scoundrels. Until Moreno burst into view, no hero in films was allowed to be Hispanic. Even in his early pictures, Valentino himself was cast as a villain.

Blanche Sweet, starring in *Judith of Bethulia* in 1913, the first full-length silent film, had met Moreno, who had appeared in the film as an extra, and had become his friend. Although it was rumored that they were lovers, they were not. Blanche claimed that Moreno "was a closeted homosexual and we were just sisters."

William Desmond Taylor had also met Moreno and had become enchanted with the beautiful young man. Taylor learned that Moreno had been discovered on a Spanish beach by two American tourists, Benjamin Curtis and Enrique de Cruzat Zantetti. Charmed and intrigued by the handsome and well-built Spaniard, the two men had brought

Antonio Moreno

him to America. Once in New York, Moreno pursued a career—first in the theater, where he was hampered by a Spanish accent, and later in films.

By the time Taylor introduced him to Howard, Moreno had already starred in such early pictures as *Two Daughters of Eve* in 1912, with Lillian Gish, and *So Near, Yet So Far Away* in the same year, starring Mary Pickford.

Blanche later revealed that she'd dined several times with Taylor, Moreno, and Howard. "Everybody was so terribly discreet back in those days, but it was obvious to me that my friends were having a three-way. Considering Howard's age, it would be called child molestation today. But I don't think Howard was being taken advantage of. Let's face it: Years later, Howard became a child molester himself. He was a very determined and ambitious boy back then. I remember him telling me one time that 'above all else, I want to be the most famous man in the world. And I don't care by what means I become famous, as long as the fame comes.'"

He also confided to Blanche that money was of no concern to him. "I'll never have to worry about where my next buck is coming from," the teenager said. "Father has promised me that his tool company will continue to make money for me even if I live to be one-hundred and ten."

Perhaps Taylor made a mistake in introducing his two handsome friends, Moreno and Howard, to each other. In Blanche's view, "Antonio and Howard formed a much closer bond than young Howard had with the older Taylor. Taylor's main appeal involved his continual promises of stardom for Howard," Blanche said. "Perhaps that was enough to intrigue the boy."

At this point in his career, Moreno was being promoted as a male sex symbol, although the term had not come into vogue at the time. Instead of a sex symbol, Moreno was labeled "spicy," which meant the same thing in the vernacular of the day.

Ramon Novarro

Blanche said that when Moreno was not sleeping with Howard, he was sleeping with Ramon Novarro, a former nude Mexican model who was struggling to gain a foothold in motion pictures. Novarro was also having an affair with Valentino.

"I don't know this for a fact," Blanche later recalled, "but I suspect that Taylor was being edged out of the picture. I think Howard, Ramon, and Antonio started sleeping together without Taylor directing the scene. I never really understood the bedtime mathematics with those boys, but there was a lot of fucking and sucking going on. In various combinations, Howard would bring them by my house on weekends. I don't know when he ever attended classes because he was in Los Angeles—or so it seemed—all the time. I was still carrying on with Big Howard, although Eleanor Boardman had already started to ease me out the door ever so gently. It didn't really matter, since I was beginning to fall in love with Mickey Neilan."

At some point, and without Big Howard's knowledge, Junior began to take flying lessons. Moreno—but not Novarro—also wanted to be a pilot, and would go with Howard on his daredevil airplane rides over the local buttermilk clouds.

"Whenever we were together," Blanche said, "all Howard spoke about was flying."

One California pilot, Ralph Seiter, said that he later learned that Howard was taking flying lessons from three different schools at the same time. "He came to me and said he'd never flown before. But the moment I took him up in the air, I knew he was a liar. The kid knew how to fly as well as I did. I felt he was picking my brain. Pretending he didn't know anything so he could learn all my theories about how to fly before discarding me and going on to the next pilot. I think he also liked to be complimented about what a quick learner he was, pretending he'd mastered aviation on his first time up. Whatever his reasons, I knew back then that the boy was a natural born aviator. Moreno wasn't any good, though. Once when we were having engine problems, he panicked and threw up in my plane."

Blanche said that as a young man about Hollywood, Howard had not yet evolved into the eccentric that he later became in life. "He was shy and retiring, but I sensed great intelligence there. He tended to hang out with older people, absorbing everything about them like a sponge. Later on, he became notorious for his bad dressing, even wearing dirty sneakers to confront a judge in court. But in those early days he was a neat dresser, showing up at my house in white shirt, tie, and a well-fitted tailored suit made from the best of British fabrics. At the time, Big Howard was the best-dressed man in America, and I think he selected his boy's suits."

Sometimes Howard would invite Blanche to go flying with him. A pilot, Glenn Martin, had taken her flying in 1913, and she'd become addicted to it. Miller was a stunt pilot, and Blanche later introduced him to Howard.

"Glenn involved Howard in some very dangerous stunts," Blanche said. "Glenn was completely reckless. Howard wasn't afraid at all, but I later learned that both of them were nearly killed one afternoon over the skies of Santa Barbara. Afterwards, neither of them wanted to talk about it."

Martin later said that one of Howard's airborne passions was to get on the trail of a train heading East at about sixty miles an hour and race along with it overhead in a single-engine craft. "He was fiercely competitive in the air, even back then," Martin claimed.

When Blanche moved into her house at Camden Drive and Franklin Boulevard in Beverly Hills, Martin and Howard would fly over her rear garden, dipping the plane's wings at the sight of her sunning herself nude by her pool. "I didn't care if I put on a show for them," she said. "If they wanted a free look, they got one."

Although she confessed to having an affair with the handsome Glenn Martin, she said that Howard never saw her in the nude "up close and personal" on the ground.

"Oh, he still liked those blow-jobs, and I was willing to administer them, but I swear there was never any intercourse between us. As for vaginal penetration, in that department, I honestly believe Howard was still a virgin, at least with women. He was to make up for it years later, of course."

The actress recalled that Howard, Jr., would always arrive at her doorstep with an expensive present. "The gifts from Big Howard, however, were always much bigger and grander than those from Howard, Jr., but I continued to see both of them until they found other romantic outlets and I entered into my ill-fated marriage to Mickey Neilan."

Blanche spoke with regret about not having married Big Howard. "I might have had a chance with him," she speculated. "That way, Junior and I would have ended up as co-owners of that god damn tool company. I wouldn't be living in this crummy apartment in New York City, but in a big mansion on Sunset Boulevard in Los Angeles. The grandest of them all. But what the hell! It's too late to think about that now. I'll soon be dead anyway, and it won't matter any more."

At her New York apartment in 1983, the aging actress had grown too tired and too drunk to carry on. She invited this reporter back for another night and some final revelations, but cautioned that to gain entrance the following night, two large bottles of Chivas Regal would be the price of admission.

***

Sometimes Rupert would send a long black limousine to Ojai to haul Howard to Rupert's home in Los Angeles for one of his Sunday afternoon garden parties. It was at these parties that Howard began meeting key players in the film industry, many of whom would have pivotal, but momentary, roles in his life.

Howard's life would be altered by tragic events that occurred in February and March of 1922. But when he arrived one January weekend at his uncle's house, both the house and garden reeked of gaiety. As Howard walked across the garden to greet Blanche, she was in the middle of a story she was relating to Gloria Swanson, Hughes Sr., Mickey Neilan, and Rupert.

Since Cecil B. DeMille had turned down Rupert's invitation that afternoon, and wasn't at the party, Blanche was using the occasion to tell embarrassing stories about the director. "I first met Cecil in 1915 when he directed me in *The Captive*. You know, the one about the Balkan War between Turkey and Montenegro. That fool Cecil had real ammunition put into the soldiers' rifles. One of the actor's guns went off. The bullet entered the head of an actor in back of him, and blew his brains out. I'll never forget looking at all that gray matter splattered about. Cecil didn't seem unduly concerned. 'It's one of the hazards of making a film,' he told me. That is, when his mouth was free from sucking my toes." She turned to Swanson. "You've worked with him. Did he suck on your toes, too?"

Swanson, at least at parties and in public, was more ladylike and well-mannered than Blanche. "Mr. DeMille and I have enjoyed only the finest of professional relationships. You're a very wicked girl to be telling these stories in front of everybody. Soon they'll be all over Hollywood." Lavishly dressed, even though it was still mid-afternoon, the diminutive Swanson withdrew from the circle, heading deeper into the garden.

Big Howard followed her with young Howard behind him.

"Gloria, I want you to meet my boy, Howard, Jr.," Big Howard said. "I'm right proud of him."

Swanson looked up at him. "I'm making a film with an actor who I under-

60

stand is your dearest friend. Antonio Moreno."

Howard flushed with embarrassment. "I know him."

"The film is called *My American Wife*," Swanson said. "I've become good friends with another actress working with me, Aileen Pringle. She doesn't think much of your friend. Claims he's never had an idea above the waist."

With that remark, Swanson headed for the living room trailed by Big Howard, who looked hopelessly back at his son as if to signal that this new actress in his life couldn't be controlled.

A little later, Rupert revealed what Howard Jr. must have suspected all along. Big Howard was having an affair with Little Gloria.

"What about Eleanor Boardman?" Howard asked.

"She and many others are still in the picture." Rupert told his nephew. "My brother (your father) is quite the ladies' man."

Before the end of the party, Rupert had told Howard a lot more.

Swanson had a husband, Herbert K. Somborn, stashed away somewhere. Yet she was sleeping with both Big Howard and the director, Mickey Neilan, on the side. Even so, her press agents had Swanson issuing statements to newspapers "that the marriage contract is the strongest tie in the world even if love goes out the window."

When he wasn't with Swanson, Big Howard spent time with either Blanche or Eleanor. There was another complication: Blanche had fallen in love with Mickey Neilan.

"Whatever this Mickey Neilan has," Howard told Rupert, "you should bottle it. It looks like he's the biggest competition in town."

"You'll have a chance to judge that for yourself," Rupert said. "He's been invited today."

By six o'clock, Mickey showed up drunk and late for Rupert's party. Swanson had already departed, as had Blanche.

After giving his son a warm handshake, Big Howard left for his suite at the Ambassador Hotel. Howard could only ponder what his father's evening would be like.

Howard was also getting ready to leave, when Rupert hurried across the garden to fetch him. "Mickey's here!" he said.

"God's Anointed," Howard said sarcastically.

In the twilight of a fading day, Mickey Neilan staggered across the garden with his hand outstretched.

Mickey looked up at young Howard. "The word around town is that William

Rupert Hughes

61

Desmond Taylor has fallen madly in love with you, tossed Antonio Moreno aside, and is going to cast you as the star of his next film."

Howard was stunned at such a spontaneous drunken comment in front of his uncle and quickly tried to excuse himself.

Realizing belatedly how sensitive the teenage boy was, Mickey desperately tried to make amends.

"I'm a numerologist," he said. "Give me the date of your birth and some other figures and I can predict the future in Hollywood for Howard Hughes Jr."

"Sorry, I've got to go," Howard said, eager to escape from Mickey.

"Surely, you want to know what's going to happen to your future," Mickey said. "Ask Rupert how good I am."

"I don't really believe in that shit, but everything Mickey predicted about me has already come true," Rupert said.

"Okay, I guess, I can wait around a bit," Howard said.

"There's more," Mickey promised. "I want to take you tonight to meet William Randolph Hearst. He's a dear friend. Actually, I'm closer to Marion Davies than I am to Hearst. But she's not in town. Hearst will love you."

***

Later that evening, in a limousine en route to Hearst's party in Santa Monica, accompanied by Rupert, Blanche Sweet, and Howard Jr., Mickey predicted three things about Howard, based on the numbers that he had supplied: (1) He'd grow up to become the greatest film producer in the world; (2) He'd become America's richest man; and (3) He'd fall in love with a thousand people. Significantly, Mickey said "people" instead of women.

Howard Jr. later told Rupert that he'd been disappointed with Mickey's numerology. "I wanted him to tell me that I was also going to become the world's greatest aviator."

***

It must have been hard for a teenager like Howard not to have been intimidated by a baron like William Randolph Hearst. He had wealth beyond most kingdoms, and the beach house in Santa Monica was appropriately lavish. But with young Howard, he appeared kindly, genuine, and natural.

The rotund Hearst took time out to greet Howard personally, ushering Rupert, Mickey, and Blanche into his walnut-lined library before releasing them to join the other guests.

Howard had heard all the stories about Hearst's ruthlessness and shrewdness, but in front of his guests he possessed a certain impish boyishness, especially with that high-pitched voice of his. A visit to him was like calling on a king. There was a rumor back then that he "owned most of Mexico," or at least held deeds to vast tracts of land there.

A waiter came in and took drink orders, although Hearst personally interceded and asked him to bring Howard a glass of cold milk. "We have to watch over our growing boy here."

"He's already grown big enough," an already intoxicated Blanche quipped.

Settling down in a large Queen Anne armchair, Hearst dominated the conversation. His tone was very confidential, and it was obvious that he had been pained by the recent rumors that Charlie Chaplin was having an affair with his mistress, Marion Davies.

He seemed to want some kind of revenge against Marion, and was using this invited audience to get it. "Everybody thinks I'm faithful to Marion." His eyes twinkled. "But that is hardly the case. I still have my roving eye, the same eye that attracted me to showgals in the first place. Once a man has that roving eye, he doesn't get rid of it easily. Even in old age."

"You don't look old at all," Rupert said, trying to flatter him. Actually Hearst did look old. "You appear to have more vim and vigor than men half your age."

That remark seemed to impress Hearst. He ordered his servant to put on some music. As Hearst slowly rose to his feet, Rupert and the other guests detected a charming gaucheness in the press baron. To Howard's utter surprise, he began to dance a wild Charleston that years from that date would have rivaled that of Joan Crawford in *Our Dancing Daughters*.

Hearst invited Howard and the others to join in. Howard declined but Blanche eagerly accepted. Howard seemed entranced watching the two of them dance the Charleston.

When the music ended, W.R. collapsed into his armchair, seemingly exhausted. "I'm also a wild tap-dancer," he said to Howard between breaths. "Do you want me to demonstrate my tap-dancing talents?"

"You'd better not," Howard said, sipping the cold milk that had been served to him.

As Hearst chatted with his guests, even though they were eager to join the party, Howard, as he later told Rupert, sensed a terrible loneliness in the chief. He couldn't imagine why he'd be lonely, since he could summon anybody, even the President of the United States, to wherever he was.

"I miss Marion," he said. "She's supposed to be in Florida with her sisters but I've not been able to get in touch with any of them."

"I hope there's nothing wrong," Mickey said.

Hearst leaned forward in his chair. "There's plenty wrong! Where in hell is Chaplin? He's out of town too. I've not been able to get in touch with him, either. He's a disgusting pervert. Some day he's going to get into big trouble. Maybe end up in jail."

Bounding out of his chair again, Hearst invited his guests to see some of his recent art acquisitions, including a painting by Sir Joshua Reynolds. He moved closer to Howard and Blanche. "Don't tell anybody, but some of the pieces within my fabled collection are fake. So far, no one has figured out which of them aren't real, and I've had art experts here to dinner."

"Your dinner parties are fabulous," Mickey chimed in.

"As soon as Marion returns, I'll invite you," Hearst said to Howard, ignoring the drunken Mickey.

Hearst directed his guests to his terrace even though the evening was chilly. Howard gallantly took off his jacket and placed it around Blanche's nude shoulders.

The sky was still bathed in a pinkish glow left by the recently set sun. "I'm building a castle north of here. I'm going to have my own zoo. There will be tigers, apes, rare birds, reptiles, lions, bears, and orangutans. I plan to stock the land around the castle with ewes, elks, buffaloes, and deer, all of them roaming around more or less in the wild."

"That sounds fabulous," Howard said. "I can't wait to see it."

"I'll invite you many times," Hearst promised.

And so it came to be. Hearst was a man of his word.

***

In the early morning of February 1, 1922, William Desmond Taylor was shot to death in his fashionable bungalow at 404-B South Alvarado Street in Los Angeles. Details about what took place in that bungalow before the police arrived will never be fully known.

The only source of information that this writer had about the involvement of Howard Jr. and Antonio Moreno in the Taylor murder was Blanche Sweet, and she was not completely in the loop. But she had many well-informed things to say about one of the most famous—and still unsolved—murders in the history of Hollywood.

William Desmond Taylor

For several weeks before his death, Taylor had been tantalizing Howard with predictions of future stardom. "If you stay with me, I'll make you into the biggest male film star in Hollywood. Bigger than Wallace Reid. More alluring than Valentino. You photograph beautifully, far more appealingly than Antonio himself. Your sex appeal is appreciated by both men and women. I don't know anyone who has ever met you who doesn't want to take off your trousers. I think your special appeal will be picked up by the camera."

Howard giddily shared Taylor's predictions about his future stardom with Rupert, Blanche, and Moreno.

Several weeks before his murder, Taylor had ordered his favorite photographer, Rod St. Just, to take intimate pictures of Howard. "Photograph him as you would the prettiest girl who ever got off the train in Los Angeles." St. Just later admitted that Howard agreed to pose nude for Taylor's private collection. Taylor already possessed nude photos of Ramon Novarro, Moreno, Mary Miles Minter, and Mabel Normand, among others.

A call came into Howard's dormitory at the Thacher School in Ojai at three o'clock that fatal morning. On the other end of the phone, Moreno told him that Taylor had been fatally shot. From his own home, Moreno had been talking with Taylor on the phone when the bullet was fired.

Moreno told Howard that he had immediately driven to Taylor's bungalow, where he examined the body in the director's study, finding him dead. His fear was that someone might have seen him enter the bungalow and would finger him as the assailant. He had to flee. But before he did, as he told Howard, he removed any incriminating evidence that Taylor had on both of them, including the nude photographs taken by St. Just.

Howard thanked him profusely and told him that he'd leave at once for Los Angeles. When Howard got to Moreno's house, as Blanche later learned, Moreno surrendered the compromising photographs to Howard, along with the uncompleted film script, with Taylor's notations, for Howard's screen debut.

Howard later told Blanche that Moreno "wanted some remuneration for my troubles." Going to his father, Howard asked for ten thousand dollars in cash. He told Big Howard that he'd gotten a young girl in Ojai into trouble and wanted to arrange for an abortion.

As he later reported to Blanche, Big Howard seemed right proud of his son. "I think he viewed my impregnating this imaginary girl as my initiation into manhood," Howard said. "He told me that he, too, had had to arrange a few abortions in his time."

Although no one was ever convicted of William Desmond Taylor's murder, Moreno, according to Blanche Sweet, went to his grave believing that Taylor was murdered that night by a minor Hollywood personality named Charlotte Shelby. Shelby was the domineering mother of ingénue actress Mary Miles Minter, who at the time was rapidly overtaking Mary Pickford as America's cinematic sweetheart. According to Moreno, as related years later to this reporter by Blanche Sweet, Taylor, at the time of his murder, was courting and having sexual relations with both Shelby and her daughter, Mary Miles Minter. On the night of the murder, he broke off his affair with the mother in preparation for his (potentially lucrative) marriage to the daughter.

Adding injury to the mother's insult, after his marriage to the daughter, the director intended to take over the management of Minter's blossoming career, including the control of her highly lucrative purse, effectively cutting Shelby off from the source of her income.

According to Moreno, on the night of the murder, Shelby, after a violent argument with Taylor, disguised herself as a man, returned a few hours later to Taylor's bungalow, and shot him with a revolver. Later, Shelby paid a veteran movie character actor, Carl Stockdale, $100,000, which she'd stolen from her daughter, to testify in court that he had been playing cards with Shelby at her apartment at the time Taylor was shot. Years later, Stockdale admitted to friends that in direct contradiction with his official testimony, he had been alone at home that night, reading a novel and listening to the radio.

In the wake of the public scrutiny that followed Taylor's murder, the career of Mary Miles Minter was destroyed, even though there was no direct evidence that she had been involved in the actual slaying of her favorite director and husband-to-be. Also ruined in the aftermath of the murder was the career of Mabel Normand, whose earlier affair with William Desmond Taylor was made public as part of the investigation. Ironically, despite the general pain the scandal caused to virtually everyone associated with it, no one was ever officially charged or convicted of Taylor's murder, which continues to be defined even today as one of the most important unsolved mysteries in Hollywood.

Secretly, Howard attended Taylor's funeral, arriving late, standing in the rear, and leaving before the services were over.

A British flag was draped around the open casket, and the February sun shone brightly through the windows, even though the winds that day kept the air chilled. A stray beam of sunlight found its way through a piece of ruby-stained glass in the chancel window. It bathed the bier in a mist of shimmering colored light.

Howard returned early to the back seat of his rented limousine. Curtains blacked him out. After about thirty minutes, after the ceremony ended, he was joined by Blanche Sweet and Antonio Moreno.

The sight and sound of Scottish bagpipers in full regalia emerged from the site of the funeral. Three volleys were fired by a British military squad in honor of Taylor's past service record. Then the bugler placed his instrument to his lips and sounded taps.

Both Moreno and Blanche asked Howard if he planned to continue his plans for a movie career. "While waiting for you in the car, I decided that was a dream to be dreamed," Howard told them. "I don't want to be a star. I'm going to produce films instead. That way, I can be the boss."

En route to the Ambassador Hotel, Howard asked for the lifetime silence of both Blanche Sweet and Antonio Moreno about his own involvement in the life and death of William Desmond Taylor. Both of them agreed to keep quiet about what they knew. Moreno went to his death in 1967 without revealing his own role at the murder site. Blanche, however, remained silent until 1983, when she decided, "What the hell!"

Houston, 1922

At Ojai on the afternoon of March 29, 1922, Howard spent the sunny hours horseback riding with Moreno, who had driven up from Los Angeles to be alone with his friend, and to keep him abreast of all the revelations in the wake of the death of William Desmond Taylor.

The sun was burning brightly in Ojai but was positively scorching the streets of Houston even though it was still only March. Allene had gone shopping with her younger sister, Annette Gano, who had been living with her at the Hughes household on Yoakum Boulevard since 1919. A graduate of Wellesley College, Annette was a tall and imposing woman, who had served as a Red Cross volunteer in France during World War I, distributing coffee and doughnuts to the embattled Yankee soldiers.

The purpose of the sisters' shopping expedition involved ordering Annette's bridal gown. Annette was already thirty-one at the time, which was a bit old back then for a woman to still be in the marriage market. But a Houston doctor, friend, and distant relative of the Hughes family, Frederick Rice Lummis one of several doctors who had attended over the years to the medical needs of either Allene or Sonny, had asked for her hand in marriage. His practice was flourishing, and he was kind and gentle to her. Allene urged her sister to marry him "sooner than later."

Annette was well aware of her sister's sexual involvement with young Dudley Sharp. Although she disapproved, she also went to great care to protect her sister's secret and to keep Big Howard from learning about the involvement.

Big Howard, as Annette later learned, knew of his wife's pregnancy, but he never found out that Dudley was her lover. Annette saw that he didn't.

Understandably, Allene never wanted her son to know that she was sexually and emotionally involved with his best friend. Eventually, however, Annette revealed the story to Rupert, and he gossiped about it to his friends in Hollywood, which is the only way this liaison ever became known. Otherwise, it would have remained one of the many dark and murky secrets of the Hughes family.

According to Annette, her sister

Howard Hughes Jr.

was in the dressing room of a department store in Houston, trying on a green silk dress from Paris, when she doubled over and clutched at her stomach. She cried out to Annette, "My guts are on fire!"

In her hysteria, Annette ran over to the department store manager, Don R. Riddle, and pleaded with him to summon an ambulance at once. In less than twenty minutes, Allene was seen by customers being carried out of the store on a stretcher. She had begun to hemorrhage.

At the hospital, she was immediately given an emergency examination by Dr. Gavin Hamilton. Seeing her condition and determining that she was pregnant, he immediately ordered a *curettage* – he used the word curettement—a medical procedure that involved the scraping of the uterus.

As Allene was hauled into the operating room, Annette sent a telegram to Big Howard at the Ambassador Hotel in Los Angeles. An hour later when Hughes Sr. was delivered the telegram, he kissed Eleanor good-bye and rushed to take the next train to Texas, not even bothering to pack any personal belongings. He decided not to alert his son that his mother might be dying.

Although some accounts place Big Howard at the hospital as his wife went into surgery, such was not the case. He only learned about what had happened to his wife after his train pulled into Houston.

Dr. Hamilton administered gas anesthesia to Allene before performing the emergency surgery. He had determined that her pregnancy was life threatening and had to be terminated. But after the gas entered her system, Allene's heart stopped beating. Dr. Hamilton abandoned his operation and announced to his assistants that the patient was dead.

Allene's body had already been delivered to the morgue by the time Big Howard arrived in Texas.

Dr. Hamilton later claimed that Big Howard "was not visibly shaken by the news of Allene's death at the age of thirty-nine. He was mainly concerned that word not leak out that his wife had been pregnant."

After his conference with Dr. Hamilton, Big Howard did a strange thing. He sent two telegrams, the first to Rupert in Los Angeles, informing him of Allene's death.

The other telegram was dispatched to his son at Ojai. In that telegram, Big Howard wrote: "Your mother is gravely ill. Return to Houston at once. Go first to Los Angeles where Rupert will see you off on the train back to Texas. Come at once!! Love, Father."

Back at the mansion on Yoakum Boulevard, his sister-in-law, Annette, gave Big Howard a letter from Allene. She'd written it a month previously, as if she had a premonition of her upcoming death. In the letter, she wrote that she forgave her husband for his "fondness" for Eleanor Boardman and also forgave him "your many other transgressions."

She made one final request. Upon her death, she wanted the family home on Yoakum Boulevard to go to her sister, Annette. She also requested that fifty percent of her share in the Hughes Tool Company go to her relatives, with the remaining fifty percent of her shares going to her son, Howard.

Still jolted by the news of his wife's death and her farewell letter, Big Howard was in for yet another surprise. At seven o'clock Estelle Sharp sent word to him that her son, Dudley, had attempted suicide by slashing his wrists. Dudley had lost a lot of blood, and his young life was in jeopardy.

Having no idea about why Dudley would try to kill himself, Big Howard told Annette that he was going to the hospital to comfort Estelle and that he would remain there until Dr. Hamilton "assures me that the boy is out of danger."

Still sobbing from the loss of her sister and horrified at this latest tragedy, Annette could not bring herself to tell her brother-in-law why Dudley might have tried to do himself in. All she could manage to say, as Big Howard left his residence, was "Lightning strikes twice."

***

Los Angeles, 1922

There are two accounts of what happened next at Ojai. Sherman Thacher, the headmaster at Howard's school, later claimed that Rupert arrived in the middle of the night in a black limousine and took Howard out of school, demanding that his driver take them at once to his home in Los Angeles.

But later, Rupert stated in an article that appeared in *American Magazine* that he was "merely standing by to comfort Howard when he was driven down from Ojai." In the magazine interview, Rupert said that he did not, at first, tell Howard "the bitter truth," but expressed his sympathy and assured him that Allene would recover. He went on to say that he'd booked Howard a first-class seat on the next train to Houston, and that he also reserved the seats both in front and in back of Howard so that he'd have greater privacy.

But the account that Rupert related to his friends and associates in Hollywood differed from what he had told the reporter from American Magazine. Rupert told his boss, Samuel Goldwyn, such friends as Eleanor Boardman and Blanche Sweet, and members of the extended Hughes family a somewhat different story. En route to the railway station, Rupert summoned his courage, faced young Howard, and said, "Your father is too heart-broken to tell you the truth, and I'm sorry that the task has fallen to me. I want you to be brave when I tell you what I must. You're going to find out sooner or later. Allene died on the operating table."

Rupert later expressed his amazement at Howard's reaction. Knowing of Howard's legendary closeness to his mother, Rupert feared that the boy might become hysterical. "There was absolutely no emotion on his face when I told him the news," Rupert later said. "His face was entirely blank. I couldn't believe my own eyes. Howard looked stern most of the time. If his expression changed at all, it was because of a faraway look that come into his eyes, like he wasn't even listening to my words but had entered some state of serenity all his own. I put my hand on his shoulder and even reached out to embrace him. But he pulled away as if stung by my touch."

On the platform of the rail station, Rupert later maintained that he—not Howard—had been the one fighting back tears. He told Howard good-bye and wished him well. "Once again I tried to embrace the boy, but he preferred to give me a cold handshake instead."

Up to that point, Howard had not spoken one word since hearing of the news of Allene's death. Before climbing the metal steps onto the train, Howard stood on the platform and gave Rupert a steely look. "For the first time in my life, I'm free," Howard said. "No one will ever again tell me what to do."

***

Houston, 1922

When he got to Houston, Howard Jr. discovered his father sitting and staring vacantly at the antiques, the crystal, and the Georgian silver in the living room of the Yoakum mansion. Upstairs a servant was packing his bespoke tailored suits and his handmade dress shirts, along with his platinum watches and diamond or ruby rings.

Instead of telling his son that he was sorry that he'd lost his mother, Big Howard said that he was leaving the house because it "held too many memories" of Allene. Even her favorite perfume, jasmine, seemed to linger in the air. Big Howard was a man of his word. In the short time he had left on this earth, he would book the best suite at the Rice Hotel whenever he had business in Houston.

Both Big Howard and Little Howard seemed eager to place Annette's body in the ground just as soon as possible so that they could resume their private lives once again in Hollywood. Before leaving Houston, Big Howard secured Annette's promise that she would postpone her marriage to Dr. Frederick Rice Lummis for one year and become a "substitute mother" to look after his son. Dr. Lummis himself only reluctantly agreed to that. Actually, Big Howard had originally demanded that Annette remain single and devote the rest of her life to being a mother to Howard. She thought that demand totally preposterous and adamantly refused.

In their black mourning suits, Big Howard and Little Howard stood with Dr. Lummis and Annette listening to a preacher say the final words over Allene. Only Annette cried at her sister's too early departure from life.

Dudley was too weak and too devastated to attend the funeral, although his brother, Bedford Sharp, was among the pallbearers who carried the fantastically expensive and intricately carved rosewood coffin—lined in white satin—to its final resting place in the family burial plot at the shaded and immaculately groomed Glenwood Cemetery.

70

***
Los Angeles, 1922

Back in Los Angeles, Howard confided to Rupert that he didn't think his father was mourning the death of Allene, but that he was overcome with guilt for having cheated on her so early and so frequently within the marriage.

Howard returned only briefly to the Thacher School at Ojai. His father wanted him to drop out of school and come to live in Los Angeles. That was what Howard wanted too. Headmaster Thacher argued bitterly with Big Howard, claiming he was "ruining the boy's life by taking him out of school," but Big Howard, who had all the money, and most of the power, prevailed.

Early one Saturday morning, Howard told his classmates good-bye, got into the back seat of a sleek black limousine, and headed for a new life in Los Angeles.

It was later revealed that Howard had developed a particularly intimate relationship with Owen McBride, his physics professor at Thacher. The boy often went riding with McBride and was seen having private dinners with him at off-campus restaurants. When Howard checked out of Thacher for the last time, McBride began sobbing hysterically and had to be excused from conducting his classes for almost two weeks.

The limousine deposited Howard at a Spanish colonial-style bungalow on the luxuriant and flowery grounds of Vista Del Arroy, a plush vacation retreat in Pasadena, often a favorite nest for wealthy polo players. Even though he was married to Mary Pickford at the time, the dashing Douglas Fairbanks Sr. was often seen on the grounds and was said to be carrying on a clandestine affair "with a girl too beautiful."

In his deluxe suite at the Ambassador Hotel, Big Howard had become the major party-giver in Los Angeles. "Wine, women, and illegal hooch flowed," Rupert told Nazimova, who maneuvered to get herself invited to "this wholesale debauchery."

Somehow Big Howard decided that instead of being an actual presence in his son's life, he would lavish expensive gifts and money on the teenager from afar. Hughes Sr. sent flowers to adorn the bungalow occupied by Annette and Howard. The best of British tailors, with their expensive fabrics in hand, paid house calls at the bungalow to outfit young Howard with the finest wardrobe in Los Angeles, rivaled only by that of Big Howard himself. He also arranged for tailors to make his son outfits for tennis, golf, and horseback riding. Big Howard at one point even ordered three dozen pairs of handmade leather shoes crafted for his son, one pair made in part with pure gold and another pair in a shockingly gaudy alligator green.

Bribing some members of the administration at the California Institute of Technology with a total payout of fifty thousand dollars, Big Howard won a coveted enrollment for his son as an uncredited pupil. "Howard didn't even have a high school diploma," Annette later revealed. "But some of the top engineers at Cal Tech were tutoring him. Oh, the power of money!" Many of these engineers reported to Annette that they felt that Howard was a budding genius despite of his lack of formal education.

Ordering his son to come to the Ambassador in his limousine, the boy found Big Howard, assisted by a crew of tuxedo-clad musicians, entertaining Gloria Swanson at a lavish dinner in his private suite. "The champagne flowed and the caviar filled a big crystal bowl," Howard later told Annette. Although she had been rather rude to him at the time of their first meeting, Swanson was at her most gracious during the dinner.

"All of us wear masks, darling," she told young Howard. "Our only decision is how we choose to deceive the world."

"Do I look like I'm wearing a mask?" Howard asked.

"Of course, you're wearing a mask," Swanson said. "You're pretending to be this shy, awkward boy. Very unassuming. But it's a mask to conceal your real personality. You are more ambition-crazed than I am. You want fame and glory even more than I do. You want the world worshipping at your feet the same as I do. In fact, you and I are made from the same bolt of lightning. Only I'm more flamboyant on the surface, and you burn with a fiery flame internally."

Howard, as he later told Antonio Moreno and Blanche Sweet, wasn't impressed with Swanson, finding her too florid for his simpler tastes. But his father seemed enthralled with her, in spite of her many other romantic involvements.

On that night, and right in front of Swanson, Big Howard informed his son that he was taking away his allowance. At first the boy started to express his grave disappointment until his father told him that he was replacing the allowance with an unlimited letter of credit. "The town is yours," Big Howard said in front of the gossipy Swanson, who later told "everybody," even Louella Parsons. Howard was so excited at the news that he jumped up and embraced his father, practically lifting him off the floor. That was the only known time, at least in front of a witness, that Howard hugged his father.

Almost as if to "apply gilt to the lily," as Swanson later said, "he told the boy that a long, black Duesenberg limousine was waiting downstairs for him." It turned out that Big Howard had hired three different chauffeurs, outfitting each of them in elephant gray uniforms with large black fedoras. These men were to work on three back-to-back shifts of eight hours each so that Howard would have a limo at his disposal 24 hours a day.

Before his son left in rapture that night, Big Howard confided that he had chartered three railroad cars to take more than a dozen "oil cronies" to the Kentucky Derby. After that, he was traveling by private rail car from Kentucky to New York, where his mammoth yacht was waiting to take him on a sail to the West Indies. Once he toured Jamaica and Havana, he was going to sail through the Panama Canal, returning to Los Angeles in three months.

Back in Pasadena, Annette had summoned Howard's favorite cousin, Kitty Callaway, from Dallas, to come to the bungalow to keep her company since Howard was gone most of the day and night.

Kitty and Howard immediately picked up the thread of their solid friendship, and she often accompanied the boy on chauffeur-driven trips to the movie palaces in Hollywood. Some days, as Annette later reported, "Kitty and Howard saw three flickers in six hours."

Regardless of what his plans were for the evening, Howard nearly always dined by the pool near their bungalow with both Kitty and Annette. Lavish dinners were prepared for Annette and Kitty, with Howard preferring a steak and a plate of very small peas. He consumed the same meal every night. Perhaps taking a cue from his father, Howard often hired out-of-work musicians in Pasadena to serenade them while they dined.

After dinner, Howard would disappear into his black limousine and go off into the Los Angeles night to amuse himself. He never told Kitty or Annette where he was going or what he did, and neither woman asked him, perhaps out of fear. "I am my own man now," Howard told Annette one day, "and I'll go where I please and do what I please."

Shortly after arriving in Pasadena, Annette incurred Howard's wrath, and she didn't want to provoke him again. With her, she'd brought a letter from Allene, which she'd written two months before her death, perhaps sensing that something might go wrong with her delicate condition.

Howard took the letter from her and ripped it to shreds. "Don't ever mention the name of Allene to me again!"

***

One morning a call came in from Rupert, who was filming *Souls for Sale*, starring Eleanor Boardman. Howard was aware that Eleanor was the favorite of his father's mistresses. Rupert invited Howard to come to the set on Monday morning to see how movies were made.

Vastly intrigued, the sixteen-year-old skipped his classes at Cal Tech and set out in his limousine toward Rupert's film studio. His uncle had made the invitation even more intriguing when he said that Charlie Chaplin would be joining them for lunch. The Little Tramp was appearing in a cameo in Rupert's film and had specifically asked to meet young Howard.

Chaplin at the time was the most famous man in the world, and that invitation thrilled him. But Rupert always liked to add "something to sweeten the pot," as he was fond of saying. "Mae Busch plays the second lead, and the third lead is played by the most beautiful girl in all the world. You'll love her. More to the point, she'll go crazy when she sees a handsome young devil like you."

"And who is this stunning woman?" Howard asked.

"The one, the only, Barbara LaMarr."

On the set of *Souls for Sale*, which Rupert was directing, Eleanor was heading an all-star cast with such major players as Mae Busch, Barbara LaMarr, and Richard Dix in secondary roles. Not only that, but he had assembled some of the biggest names of the silent screen—both actors and directors—to appear in cameos. In addition to Chaplin himself, the all-star cast included ZaSu Pitts, Dagmar Godowsky, Bessie Love, June Mathis, Anna Q. Nilsson, Florence Vidor, King Vidor, Patsy Ruth Miller, Erich von Stroheim, and Claire Windsor. The film also had roles for Howard's long-standing friend, Blanche Sweet, and his new numerology-loving acquaintance, Marshall (Mickey) Neilan. Although Mickey had recently married Blanche, he was still romancing Big Howard's mistress, Gloria Swanson. The only person missing at a big luncheon that Rupert had thrown for the cast was the mysterious Barbara LaMarr.

Howard was guest of honor at the luncheon, his major introduction to *le tout* Hollywood. As he wrote Dudley Sharp back in Houston, "For the first time in my life I felt like a man in my own right—not a boy living in my father's shadow."

Rupert had placed his boyishly shy nephew at the head of the table with Eleanor on his left and Chaplin on his right. In years to come, both Chaplin and Howard himself would become known as child molesters because of their fondness for fifteen-year-old girls. Even though Howard was a child himself when he met Chaplin, he immediately bonded with him.

Although Blanche said she was seated eight places away between Fred Niblo and William Haines, and was not privy to what was being said at the head of the table, she recalled decades later that she felt Chaplin was a bit taken by Howard's good looks and striking presence.

"The world didn't know Charlie's secret at the time," Blanche said. "but Charlie Chaplin, the great womanizer, occasionally liked young boys on the side. I must say he had good taste. Whenever Charlie did decide to go for some boy-ass, he picked young ones so beautiful they looked better than us gals. I did see Charlie engaging in animated conversation with both Eleanor and Howard, and occasionally I heard the name Mary Pickford. Chaplin was dining out on stories about Little Mary Sunshine. He was as witty and clever off-screen as he was on. A shit, but a talented one. The highlight of the dinner came when someone from wardrobe brought Chaplin a blonde curly wig and a Little Miss Rebecca of Sunnybrook Farm gingham dress. He stood up, turned from us, and put on the wig and slipped on the dress. Parading around the table, he performed history's most devastating impersonation of Pickford. If she had seen it, I don't think she'd have the courage to ever face a camera again. He captured her silly mannerisms in astonishing detail. As I said, he was a shit but there's never been a star like him."

As amused as he was by Chaplin, Howard seemed to have eyes only for the beautiful Eleanor.

Years later she admitted that "the boy obviously was smitten with me from the very first time he took my hand. When I extended my hand to him, he bowed and kissed it. I was flattered. How many sixteen-year-old American boys do you know who go in for hand-kissing, then and now? I thought at the time that maybe boys are attracted to the same type of woman that lures their dear old dads."

In the comfort of her Montecito home and looking back over the decades, she confessed, "When Charlie was parading around the table as Mary Pickford, I slipped Howard my phone number and told him to call me later in the evening. He was just a kid, but I was a wild and impulsive thing in those days, especially when I got together for a night on the town with my dear gay friend, William Haines. We didn't call boys like Billy gay in those days, however. I heard that Big Howard was two-timing me with the Swanson bitch, and I think I wanted to get even. At any rate, that darling boy said he'd call me later."

Eleanor noted that before the luncheon ended, Chaplin also slipped Howard his phone number. "I didn't know what that was about at the time, although I found out later what The Little Tramp was up to."

Eleanor said that she was amused when her pal, Billy Haines, followed Howard to the men's room after lunch. "Billy had just a small part in the film. He played a character appropriately named Pinkey. Don't you love that name for a gay actor? Later Billy confided to me what happened in the men's room."

"He took the urinal next to Howard," Eleanor said, "and was very impressed. 'He looked as big as Chaplin, who was a notorious exhibitionist,' Billy told me. 'In spite of his small stature, there was nothing little about The Little Tramp.'"

"So what did you do?" the outspoken Eleanor asked Billy.

"I looked down at it and then I looked into those brown eyes. I decided to come right out with it. I said to him, 'First, I'd like to suck on that lollipop, then I'd like to spend an hour rimming you, and, finally, I'd like to plow into you for the rest of the night.'"

Billy admitted that Howard didn't seem taken back at all. The actor already knew of Howard's sexual involvement with Antonio Moreno and Ramon Novarro. As he told Eleanor, "I figured that after

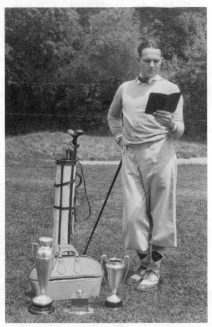

William Haines

75

those two, I had a chance and he wasn't going to punch me out."

"What did he say, for God's sake?" Eleanor asked.

"He was okay about my first offer to plunge down on him," Billy said. "He wasn't certain about the second offer, claiming he didn't know what rimming was. And he nixed the idea of me plowing him, claiming he didn't go that route."

In a series of interviews conducted at his beautiful antique-filled home in the 1970s, Billy Haines, in the presence of his longtime lover, Jimmie Shields, said that, "It was the beginning of a beautiful friendship between Howard and me. It would last for two decades, and would be conducted primarily in homosexual hangouts to which Howard became addicted. After we got the obligatory blow-job behind us two weeks later, Howard and I decided we'd become friends—not lovers. I've always been a top and that wasn't Howard's scene. He was more the oral type."

On the third interview, Billy made an astonishing confession over dinner at a restaurant in Los Angeles. "I was the first to tell Howard that his uncle, Miss Rupert, was one of Hollywood's most closeted homosexuals. Howard was shocked and completely unaware of that. I'll always remember a strange look on his face that day when he learned the news. In some way, he seemed delighted at learning what I told him. I also told him that Rupert had given me a number of blow-jobs—in fact, that's how I got the part in *Souls for Sale*, minor though it was. It was as if possessing this tantalizing bit of information about Rupert, Howard suddenly had power over his uncle. I didn't know at the time what Howard was going to do with this secret, although that became much more clear later on."

Back at the urinal in 1922, and after both Billy and Howard had buttoned up, the two young men agreed to get together. As they walked out of what Billy called "the crapper," he recalled seeing Howard's face light up when he saw Eleanor approaching. "Howard confided to me that he had a date with her later that evening," Billy said. "I was astonished since Eleanor and I were confidantes. I knew she was balling Howard's old man. I felt I had to warn the young boy about that—and I did."

"Howard looked at me with those brown eyes that could melt frozen butter," Billy said. "'I'm well aware of that,' he told me, 'and it'll make taking her all the sweeter.'"

***

Montecito, 1985

Living up to her reputation of making shockingly candid comments, Eleanor always claimed that she was the first woman to have seduced Howard Hughes Jr. "First the father, then the son," she said in her later years. "At least I kept it in the family."

She'd heard from Blanche that Howard Jr. and that actress had already had "some hanky-panky in the back seat of a limo, but I don't think they got beyond the lick-the-lollipop stage."

Eleanor always remembered her first night "breaking in Howard," although she hardly recalled it as a passionate experience. "I was seven years older than the boy, but had about two decades more sexual experience. After all, I'd been broken in by Howard's old man himself."

With amusement, she called young Howard "the Minuteman." Smiling, she said, "actually it was more like thirty seconds. Those people who warn women against seducing virginal teenaged boys know what they're talking about. Howard was embarrassed, and I felt like a fool to be in bed with a young kid. We never repeated the experience, although, amazingly, he developed a crush on me and wanted to. I turned him down."

She claimed that somehow Big Howard found out about his son's dalliance with her. "I thought he'd be furious and would threaten to disinherit the boy. Not at all. He actually seemed pleased and encouraged me to launch an affair with his kid. 'Howard will be very, very rich one day,' his old man told me. 'You could do much worse. The boy will grow up to keep some woman in diamonds and ermine.'"

Eleanor said that she later learned why Big Howard was eager to get rid of her. "He'd fallen madly in love with Gloria Swanson, although I didn't know that at the time. But I got my revenge. After Big Howard rather unceremoniously dumped me, he was given his walking papers by Miss Gloria. Back in those days when it came to men, she had a short attention span."

"Don't feel sorry for me," she cautioned. "Of course, my marriage to King Vidor, the womanizer, didn't work out, but so what? I managed to seduce some of the most famous men in the world, including F. Scott Fitzgerald when King and I sailed transatlantic with Zelda and him to Paris. I even carved a notch on my belt for Ernest Hemingway, whom I met in Paris. I struck out with James Joyce—he was blind as a bat anyway—but I seduced Pablo Picasso one night in the south of France. Talk about kinky!"

After making *Souls for Sale*, Eleanor continued to see Rupert, and they would work together again when he directed her in the 1924 picture, *True As Steel*.

Eleanor claimed that "Rupert once told me that young Howard cheated his family out of millions of dollars and was completely ruthless and that he hated both his mother and father, rejoicing in their early deaths. So much for an uncle's love for his nephew!"

Eleanor said that she remembered encountering Howard one final time at a party that Marion Davies gave in Santa Monica. "He came onto me really strong," she said, "and frankly I was tempted to give it another try. I'd heard all these stories about his seductions of Hollywood's most beautiful women, and I assumed he had had a lot more experience since our ill-fated encounter."

She claimed that he told her he wanted to drive her home but that he had an errand to run first and would be back within an hour.

"I remember sitting there waiting for him for two hours," she said. "He never came back to the party, and I went home alone. I never saw Howard Hughes again, and I never benefited financially from having known either the father or the son."

She looked around her living room in Montecito as if she wanted to redesign it. "God damn it, I should have been an architect instead of a movie star. I hate Hollywood!"

***

Catalina Island, 1922

Beginning in the 1930s, with occasional exceptions that included Cary Grant, to whom he could confide almost anything, Howard never discussed his private life with anybody But while still a teenager, and "sowing his oats," as Big Howard put it, the young man shared news about his conquests with any number of people.

As a close friend of Barbara LaMarr's, Billy Haines was all too eager to hear about Howard's fateful meeting with the screen goddess. In Billy's case, he heard both Howard's version and Barbara's side, concluding that it was pretty much the same story.

Howard had not met Barbara on the set of *Souls for Sale*, and had gone off with Eleanor instead. Two nights later, after he'd finished having dinner with his "guardians," Kitty and Annette, beside the pool of his residence at Vista del Arroyo, he remained by the water, contemplating a midnight swim.

As he later told Billy Haines, "a young woman who looked like a goddess came out of one of the bungalows across the courtyard." As he was to learn later, it was Barbara LaMarr. She wore a white robe, but dropped it around her ankles when she neared the edge of the pool. She was nude. Apparently, she was unaware of Howard's presence, since he was concealed in shadows.

He recalled how incredibly beautiful the girl was. Her body was perfect enough to be sculpture. Suddenly, she dived into the pool.

Impulsively Howard removed all his clothes and dived in with her. Swimming up close to her, he claimed that he thought she might scream or flee to the edge of the pool and escape.

But she seemed too self-assured for that. She had a tiny waist with voluptuous hips. Instead of fleeing from Howard, she pressed her body against his. He later related to Billy that the moment her breasts pressed against his naked chest, he got an immediate erection under the water. He had to touch and feel her to see if she were real.

Where Howard left off in detail, Barbara later supplied the missing data to Billy. She said that within a half hour she and Howard were in her bungalow,

78

which was being paid for by Douglas Fairbanks Sr. for his private dalliances with the emerging star.

"Howard was the most awkward lover I've ever known," Barbara confided to Billy. "But it was his very boyishness that appealed to me. I decided to take him under my wing and teach him all I knew."

Since they couldn't enjoy privacy at Vista Del Arroyo, Howard before dawn proposed to her that he commandeer Big Howard's yacht and crew and sail with her to Catalina Island.

In those days, Barbara was almost the impulsive kid that Howard was. She was delighted at the idea. Fleeing in Howard's limo at three o'clock in the morning, she didn't write a good-bye note to Fairbanks and failed to let Rupert know that she wasn't going to show up for work on the

Barbara LaMarr

set. Likewise, Howard didn't write a good-bye note to either Annette or Kitty.

Howard easily took command of his father's ocean-going yacht, although he did leave a note informing his father that he had "borrowed" the vessel for two weeks.

It was in the bright dawn of a new day that Howard for the first time saw the depth and beauty of Barbara's eyes. "They were like no other eyes I'd ever seen," he later told Billy. "Green like a river I'd once seen in New England and sprinkled with flecks of purple." That was about as poetic as Howard ever got in describing anything. He almost never was that effusive.

Under black, wavy hair, which hung down to her porcelain-like shoulders, Barbara had skin as smooth as baby flesh.

As Howard got to know her in the days ahead, she told him that her real name was Reathe and that she'd grown up in the Imperial Valley of California. Later, she learned that she had been a foster child. She said she used to day-dream about the identity of her real parents, imagining that she had been born some fairy princess who was sent into exile so that a wrongful heir could inherit a kingdom that rightfully belonged to her.

He told her that he would one day come into a kingdom of his own, one of vast riches and power. He promised her that when he took over his father's company, he would lavish jewelry and other precious things on her. "You'll have everything you could possibly desire—and more!"

She related that she dreamed of being swept off her feet one day by a handsome prince on a beautiful white horse. "Something almost like that actually did happen to me." She told him that "the handsomest cowboy who ever lived," a young rancher named Jack Little, spotted her one afternoon and became so mesmerized by her beauty that he began to stalk her, sitting in his saddle on his horse outside her house until two or three o'clock in the morning, rain or shine. "One day he just lifted me up from the ground onto his horse and rode off into the desert with me. Jack and I were soon married. But in only seven months, he came down with pneumonia and died. I was a widow at sixteen."

Once they reached the island, they lived on the yacht and explored Catalina by day. Mostly they stayed in the yacht's master suite making love to each other.

"I had to teach him to bathe with a woman," Barbara told Billy when she returned to Hollywood. "Even how to handle a woman's breasts, especially the delicate nipples. I taught him how to hold back and pleasure a woman with his God given assets, including his tongue. Howard was my eager pupil. Our sex life started without much hope, although he was certainly blessed with the right equipment. But by the time that yacht sailed back to Los Angeles, Howard Hughes Jr. was an accomplished lover. Well, almost. Only time can bring the refinement."

On Catalina Island, Howard could sit for two or three hours with Barbara, not saying a word. He seemed content to listen to the ocean pound against the shore. Sometimes she would light up a cigarette, smoking it only half way before she flicked the butt toward the water's edge as if to express her own scorn of the turbulent water.

She was much more articulate than he was, and confided in him that she was actually a poetess. "In my heart I'll always be a poetess," she told him. "Writing is my passion, even more than sex, although sex is very important to me."

During her early debut in Hollywood, since there was no market for her poetry, she had turned to script and novel writing. She was able to sell her first novel to Fox, who filmed it under the title of *The Mother of His Children*, starring Gladys Brockwell.

Emboldened by her success, she continued to write scripts, and one day she was introduced to Mary Pickford and her love, Douglas Fairbanks Sr. "Mary told me, 'My dear, you are far too beautiful to be working behind the camera. Your vibrant personality and great beauty should be shared with film audiences.'"

Barbara told Howard that Fairbanks didn't make a comment on her beauty but he must have been enthralled with her, because he cast her in his film, *The Nut*. Pleased with her work, he then gave her the coveted role of Milady de Winter in *The Three Musketeers*.

"Somewhere along the way, he fell madly in love with me and installed me in Pasadena," Barbara confided. "When not making love to Mary, he comes to my bungalow and makes love to me."

"Did Ramon Novarro also fall in love with you when you were making *The*

Prisoner of Zenda?" Howard provocatively asked, already knowing the answer.

"From what Billy Haines tells me, Ramon is in love with you—not me," she said. "But we're great friends. In the film, each of us competes with the other to see who can be photographed as the most beautiful."

Over dinner that night Barbara shared her dreams with Howard. By then, he'd fallen madly in love. "Theda Bara was the vampire of the early silent films. But I'll be the vamp--modern and American--for the Twenties. Theda was exotic, claiming to have been born in Egypt. Cincinnati was more like it. I believe that our home-grown vamps will be the equal of any foreign vamps— maybe much more alluring."

"You're a vamp!" he told her. "You've stolen my heart. I can't go back to my life. I want to take this yacht and sail with you around the world."

She promised that she'd give up her stardom and accompany him. "There will be no need for marriage," she told him. "Our love will bind us together."

His romantic dream ended in the cold light of a new day when he woke up the following morning and discovered that she had gone. The writer in her had left him a letter, a copy of which later cropped up within her estate and was widely circulated as part of Hollywood memorabilia.

My Darling Howard,

This has been the most idyllic two weeks of my life, as we hid out from the world.

I'll sail to the romantic ports of the world but only in my imagination. Dreams to be dreamed are more enticing than reality itself.

Your love-making was young and tender, whereas I've only known brutal men before. Lovers intent on satisfying their own passion—not mine. Although it pains my heart to write this, I must confess that I want to sample so many more men in this world, brutal or not. I cannot confine myself to just one man. In my heart I know I have but a short time on this earth. It is my destiny to know many of the world's most beautiful men and to take them as my lovers.

In you, I have met Prince Charming. But I also know that the world is filled with Prince Charmings. In fact, we bring from the lavender wrappings of our memories all of those ideals we have of the man our Prince Charming is to be. We then drape those lavender wrappings over the man before us. I have done that with you. I will always carry the memory of you with me. I know this note will break your heart. Unfortunately, I am fated to break men's hearts. That's why they call me the girl too beautiful. I can't help it!

I will love and treasure you always, even if always is a shorter time frame than I ever realized. Until I met you, I always thought that rich men were ugly. I believed that those qualities that men possess to make them rich also make them incapable of being loved. I was wrong.

Your devoted angel,
Barbara LaMarr

***
Los Angeles, 1922

Howard was indeed heart-broken and vowed that he'd never give his love to another woman...or man.

When he arrived back at Vista Del Arroyo after an absence of more than two weeks, he confronted a hysterical Kitty and Annette, both of whom feared that he'd been kidnapped.

After consoling them, he knocked on the door of Barbara's bungalow. There was no answer. Later he learned from management that she'd hurriedly moved out, leaving no forwarding address.

Billy Haines tried to distract him by taking him from one wild Hollywood party to another. Howard remained sullen in spite of the temptations thrown at him.

On several occasions, Paul Bern joined Billy and Howard on their rounds of such clubs as That Old Black Magic. Bern had been born a Jew in Germany, emigrating to America in 1909, and living in a tenement flat in Manhattan. Graduating from the American Academy of Dramatic Arts in 1911, he worked on Broadway as an actor for a while, and was also employed by a film company in Toronto. Sometime before 1920, he arrived in Hollywood, where he became a film cutter and a script editor before eventually being appointed as the assistant to Irving Thalberg at MGM.

He was known for developing crushes on some of Hollywood's most beautiful women, although he usually turned to men for sexual satisfaction. Billy told Howard that Bern's penis was "so small it's like that of a stud mouse. He can't have intercourse with a woman. It's physically impossible."

Employed at the time as a scenarist, Bern was well-educated and soft spoken. Even though he was still young, his hairline had already started to recede.

Howard barely tolerated Bern, disliking his pedantic mannerisms. When Bern started going "out on the town" with Barbara and Billy, Howard asked not to be included in their all-night romps. He was still carrying a torch for Barbara and resented Bern for taking her out.

He was especially infuriated to learn from Billy that Bern had proposed marriage to Barbara. When she turned him down at a night club, he retreated to the men's room. It was there that Billy found him, putting his face in a toilet bowl and flushing it several times, trying to drown himself. Billy forced him to get up and called an attendant to dry off the lovesick fool.

Later, Billy told Howard, "I don't think Paul really meant to drown himself. He just wanted to attract Barbara's attention—that's all."

Howard could not reconcile Billy's stories about Bern's impotence with published exploits of his dalliances with some of the industry's major stars such as Mabel Normand.

In time Bern's name would even be linked to fan dancer Sally Rand and Joan Crawford, neither of whom had much tolerance for impotent men.

Billy attempted in vain to explain it: "All those women spend their lives running from wolves. Paul courts their minds—not their bodies. Having been complimented on their tits all their lives, they are flattered that a member of the male species would even recognize that they have a mind."

Howard continued to pump Billy for news about Barbara, since the actor was continuing to party with both Howard and the goddess, only not at the same time. Billy was also friends with actress Elsie Ferguson, who was being seen on screens around the nation in *Sacred and Profane Love*.

He had secured a copy of the rough draft of an article that Elsie was writing about Barbara for a magazine. The article was subsequently revised before printing, but Howard got to read the first version.

In her article, Elsie wrote:

Barbara LaMarr is a lovely panther—graceful, silky, forever quiescent, yet with a primitive look of warning in the back of her lovely eyes that change colors with her volatile emotions. That look fascinates and attracts, even while it warns of the danger of arousing her and bringing a realization that beneath all this velvety like softness are the claws of a panther. Claws that can kill. The primitive heart of a sleek jungle animal lurks in Barbara LaMarr's heart. It is the secret of her timeless appeal.

If a man looks into the eyes of Barbara LaMarr, he will lose himself there. Her second husband, Lawrence Converse, testified in court that the first time he met her, he found her beauty so startling that it obliterated from his mind the fact that he was already married. He claimed emotional amnesia.

He testified in court that Barbara's beauty caused a blood clot creating pressure on his brain. To remove the clot, doctors in Los Angeles operated on him. Before he was hauled off to that fatal operating table, his final words were, "Tell Barbara that I will love her through eternity."

***

From the set of *Souls for Sale*, Howard received a call one afternoon from Billy, telling him that Barbara had seriously injured herself during filming. Her back was in such great pain that she was carried off the set on a stretcher, screaming in agony.

Doctors at the studio administered drugs which in time proved addictive. In the weeks ahead, and long after her back pain had subsided, Barbara continued to take the drugs. When combined with alcohol, which she consumed in lethal doses, the drugs over a period of months led to a rapidly deteriorating physical condition.

To make matters even worse, the actress began to stay up virtually all night on a round of party-going that was considered appalling even by Hollywood standards.

By the time she'd turned twenty-eight, she was already announcing to the press that she was "world-weary." Fan magazines had taken to calling her "a modern day Cleopatra." "I never sleep more that two hours a day," she told the press. "I have better things to do. Chief among those things to do is taking lovers like roses. That is, by the dozen!"

By 1925, she was suffering from tuberculosis, and could hardly finish her last film, *The Girl from Montmartre*. That winter she left Hollywood, a train taking her fragile body back to her home town of Altadena, California.

There on January 30, 1926, she died. On hearing the news, a saddened Howard sent a thousand American beauty roses. But he turned down Billy's invitation to go with him to Barbara's funeral. Among the 40,000 mourners was Louis B. Mayer, who remained enamored of Barbara even in death. When another stunning beauty—this one from Austria—arrived at Metro-Goldwyn-Mayer, Mayer ordered that her name be changed from Hedy Kiesler to Hedy Lamarr in honor of Barbara.

After the funeral, Howard told Billy, "Barbara made thirty films, had four-hundred lovers, including me, and died at the age of twenty-nine. But she lived seven decades of life in three decades. I'll do the same! I'll be dead at thirty but what a life I will have lived!"

***

Three messages came in from Charlie Chaplin, but when Howard returned the calls, The Little Tramp was busy or otherwise occupied on the set. He and Howard never connected, and Howard couldn't figure out why the actor comedian wanted to see him. "I'm only a kid," Howard said to Annette. "Maybe he wants you to play in his next movie," Annette said. Howard assured her that he didn't do comedy.

A call came in from Douglas Fairbanks Sr. At first Howard feared that he had learned that he'd taken Barbara to Catalina Island. When he eventually got back to Fairbanks Sr. on the phone, it was to hear an invitation to come to Pickfair on Saturday afternoon and play tennis with his son, Douglas Fairbanks Jr. Their tennis pro who'd supervise their games would be Big Bill Tilden, the athlete who dominated the world of tennis in the Twenties.

As tempting as that was, Howard never got around to actually setting a date. He was too busy making plans. Through Big Howard's manipulations, he'd been accepted at Rice University, in spite of his lack of a high school diploma. Obviously Big Howard had bribed someone in the administration once again.

As the train pulled out of the station at Pasadena, Howard vowed he'd return. On the platform with Annette and Kitty, he stood six feet three inches tall, watching Pasadena fade away. He vowed, "I'll be back. And when I do, I'm going to become the king of Hollywood."

CHAPTER FOUR
Houston, 1923

When Annette Gano's year of babysitting for Howard finally came to an end, she began formulating her plans to marry the incredibly patient Dr. Frederick Rice Lummis.. Big Howard had urged her to postpone the marriage and to continue to look after his son, but she refused. In a kind of compromise, however, Annette, after an exchange of cash, acquiesced to Big Howard and agreed to move with her new husband and Howard Jr., into the mansion on Houston's Yoakum Boulevard, with the intention of functioning as guardian and chaperone for Howard during his upcoming term at Rice University.

As an important part of the wedding ceremony, Howard Sr. had promised to take the train to Houston to give the bride, his sister-in-law, away. But on the day of the wedding, he didn't show up.

Howard rarely saw his father, who always had more pressing appointments in Los Angeles, New York, cruising Bahamian waters, or elsewhere. Howard did not hear that any one woman had replaced Eleanor Boardman or Gloria Swanson. According to Uncle Rupert, Big Howard had become a serial "seducer of showgals."

Howard's boyhood friend, Dudley Sharp, was debating whether to go to Princeton or Cornell. Dudley wanted Howard to go with him to an Ivy League school in the East, but Howard adamantly refused. Annette, however, never believed that Howard was serious about attending Rice.

After Howard Jr.'s return to Houston, he spent most of his time on the golf course of the Houston Country Club. He found a new golfing partner in the unlikely candidate of Superior Court Judge Walter Montieth, a legal figurehead whose advice and friendship would later serve Howard well.

In later years, following his break with Howard, Dudley had some harsh appraisals of his former friend. "He wanted to prove himself as Howard Hughes without the Junior attached. He really resented bearing his father's name, even

Eleanor Boardman

though Big Howard was the source of his wealth and the man who made incredible things possible for Howard. He hated Houston, and I never found out why he returned in the first place, since he wasn't taking his studies too seriously. He kept telling me that he was going to become even bigger in the world than his dad. I repeatedly asked him in what did he want to excel. All he would say was, 'I want to become the biggest fish in three of the biggest ponds.'"

Once, when Howard Sr. returned from one of his mysterious trips, he arrived in a big way. Sailing into Sylvan Beach on his yacht, he rented the entire dance pavilion for Howard, complete with a sixty-piece band. His father had invited all the leading debutantes from Houston to attend. It was his way of launching his son into high society, Texas style.

One of those debutantes was Ella Rice.

***

Dubbed the "most sought-after debutante in Houston," the beautiful, dark-haired Ella Rice was the exact opposite of Barbara LaMarr, a promiscuous Jazz Age baby of Hollywood. With her genteel Southern manners and regal bearing, Ella more closely resembled the character of Melanie in the film, *Gone With the Wind*, that would be made in years to come. No one could ever accuse her of being a budding Scarlett O'Hara.

The society matrons of Houston noted that Ella was a "dead ringer" for Howard's late mother, Allene. In the community, Ella stood as a virginal pillar of virtue with gold-plated credentials that got her invited to all the finest homes in Texas, even the governor's mansion. She had been born the grandniece of William Marsh Rice, for whom Rice Institute—later Rice University—was named.

"Ella's family had all the social pedigree that a girl could ever hope for," said Betty Mayfield, one of her acquaintances. "The only thing they didn't have was the one thing the Hughes family possessed in great abundance—and that was money."

Although Howard and Ella had first met in school, when Sonny was five years old and Ella an "older woman" of seven, their paths had rarely crossed since that time. Dudley estimated that since school days, Ella had seen Howard no more than six times, all of which were at large parties in Houston. "I doubt if they had exchanged more than a few sentences with each other over the years."

On the night of Big Howard's bash, Ella was "practically engaged" to James Overton Winston, a strikingly handsome and rather dashing young financier who was known for "setting many a girl's heart fluttering," in the words of Betty Mayfield.

To borrow again from Margaret Mitchell's yet-to-be-created set of characters, James was Ashley Wilkes, with Howard being more the rogue like Rhett

Butler. Big on physical beauty, James was short on cash. When he first met Ella on a blind date arranged by a school friend, he had exactly $15.67 in his bank account.

At the dance, Howard, looking more handsome than he'd ever looked in his life, in the full bloom of youth, approached Ella and asked her to dance with him. Even though it was expected in those days that a young woman would always grant one dance to the host of the party, if asked, Ella turned him down. That was not typical of her behavior, as she was known for her impeccable social grace and manners. She stood next to James who extended his hand. At first Howard was reluctant to shake it, but he finally did.

Even James urged Ella to accept Howard's invitation to dance, but she refused. "I've promised all my dances to James," she told Howard. "We're madly in love and plan to get married as soon as James builds up a nest egg."

Perhaps remembering his long-ago rejection on the playground in school, Howard turned and walked away.

An hour later, when Big Howard was talking in the corner with Dudley, his son came over to join them. "I've hauled out the prettiest gals in Texas for you tonight," his father said. "I didn't invite any Dallas gals because everybody in Texas knows the women of Houston are prettier. See any filly you'd like to brand?"

Howard looked across the pavilion. "There is one. *Ella Rice.*"

"But she's practically engaged to James," Dudley protested.

"It doesn't matter," Howard said.

Big Howard studied the dancing figure of Ella, as she whirled around the floor with James. "As I live and breathe, and if I didn't know better, I'd swear that Allene had come back to life. You've got good taste, boy. That Ella gal is the spitting image of your mother."

***

Big Howard returned home to celebrate Christmas with his son. Instead of staying at the Yoakum mansion, he booked his now familiar suite at the Rice Hotel.

On his first day back, he summoned Howard to the hotel and told him he had some bad news. Rupert's second wife, Howard's Aunt Adelaine, had hanged herself in Haiphong harbor in French Indochina. Accompanied only by her nurse, she was on an around-the-world trip. "When Rupert heard the news," Big Howard said, "he was in bed with this two-bit actress, Elizabeth Dial. She had a part in *Souls for Sale.*"

His Aunt Adelaine meant very little to Howard, and he didn't appear to be shaken by the news at all.

But Howard's new uncle, Dr. Lummis caught him later in the evening in what looked like an attempt to hang himself. Howard angrily denied that he was contemplating suicide as his aunt had done. Somewhere he'd read where a bow-knot in a rope could be fixed so that a person would appear to be hanging. But at the last minute, the knot could be untied to prevent strangulation. His uncle ordered Howard never to attempt such a foolish experience again.

The brother, Tom Hepburn, of Howard's future girlfriend, Katharine Hepburn, had hanged himself in such a way.

For Christmas dinner at the Rice Hotel, Big Howard invited his son as guest of honor along with Annette and Dr. Lummis, Dudley, and his mother, Estelle. Howard was resentful that his father had also invited Sheryl Steele, a Broadway chorine, to this event.

A big-busted woman with bleached hair, Sheryl was obviously intoxicated even before she arrived at the dinner. Her vulgar manners so shocked Annette that she left the dinner early with her husband.

After they'd gone, Sheryl called them "bluenoses" and claimed that she could now speak more candidly. She advised Estelle to find herself another man before it was too late for her. She told Howard and Dudley that at their age they should sleep with "whores in Niggertown who'd teach them everything they needed to know about women. That way, when you get married one day, both of you studs will really know how to satisfy your wives."

She then announced at table that when she first met Big Howard, she could "feel hot peppers up my thighs."

That comment was a bit much, even for her admirer, Big Howard. He angrily ordered her to return to his suite. Seemingly embarrassed, he rushed through his dessert and excused himself. Before that, however, he signaled the waiter to bring in his expensive Christmas gifts for Dudley and his mother—a gold watch for Dudley and a mink coat for Estelle. To his son, he presented the papers for a new Duesenberg, even though Howard's vehicle at the time was only a year old.

When Big Howard left the table to join Sheryl in his suite, Dudley asked Howard why he'd looked so disappointed getting the new car. "Damn it, if somebody gave me a Duesenberg, I'd be jumping up and down with joy."

Howard's face was a mask of bitterness. "For weeks, I'd been begging my father to buy me my own small plane. I thought I'd broken down his resistance. Guess I'll have to wait until I'm older and can buy my own."

On that resentful and gloomy note, the Christmas dinner at the Rice Hotel came to an end.

Hoping to rescue the holiday season, Dudley and Estelle sent invitations to both Howard and his father, as well as Annette and Dr. Lummis, for a champagne celebration at their home on New Year's Eve. She pointedly didn't invite Sheryl Steele.

Dudley recalled that Big Howard arrived almost two hours late. On his arm, he was accompanied by Sheryl, even though she hadn't been invited. Nonetheless, Estelle graciously received the couple, inviting them into her living room where Howard and Dudley had already finished off two bottles of bootleg champagne. Dr. Lummis and Annette confined their drinking to sipping sherry.

As Annette poured champagne for her newly arrived guests, she couldn't help but notice that the chorine was wearing an exactly similar style of mink coat that Big Howard had presented to her a week before.

Sheryl was also flashing a diamond and ruby ring from Cartier Jewelers in New York and a diamond necklace. Big Howard proudly showed off diamond cufflinks and a wristwatch which he claimed Sheryl had purchased for him. At the time of his death, the bill at Cartier Jewelers for the cuff links and wristwatch had never been paid.

Fueled by the champagne, Howard confronted his father once again about the airplane. In front of Dudley and his mother, he said that he could understand why his father didn't want him to own his own plane, but that he wanted him to agree to let him take flying lessons. The flying lessons he'd taken in Los Angeles were apparently unknown to Big Howard.

"Planes will be flying all over this country one day," Howard predicted, "carrying both passengers and cargo from coast to coast."

Big Howard saw no future in commercial aviation. "It's a quick way to die in a crash if that's what you want. If you want to cut short your life, you won't do it while I'm in control. I stupidly agreed to go up in the air with you once. That's the last time I'll do that. You belong with your feet solidly on the ground. Not daydreaming about flying high in the sky."

Sheryl chimed in, "Who'd want to fly anyway? If God had wanted us to fly, we'd been born with wings."

Usually, at least during his early days, Howard was deferential and courtly around women. But he turned with a fury on Sherry and ordered her to shut up.

That led to a violent confrontation between father and son, Dudley later reported, "I'd never known them to have a dog fight before. This was perhaps their first. It was all about aviation."

Dudley later said that he was a little too drunk to remember what exact words were exchanged. "Everything that had been swept under the carpet for years was exposed, like Big Howard's cheating on his wife with actresses and cheap chorus girls. Howard accused him of neglecting him and not being a decent father. Big Howard countered that his son would never amount to anything and was a spoiled little rich brat who turned vicious when he didn't get his way. "You'll waste your life as a playboy spending money you didn't earn."

Annette later reported that she feared Big Howard was on the verge of striking his son, and she urged her husband to intervene.

"Big Howard was so furious that I felt he wanted to deliver some fatal blow to his son, yet was hesitant to strike him in the face," Annette later claimed. "Finally, he ordered Sheryl to get up and leave the house. He stormed out after her. But he had one final, chopping blow to his son. He turned to look back at the boy. I've never seen such disgust on a man's face. In front of everybody, he said, 'How do you think *I* feel? Just like your Uncle Rupert, you're nothing but a queer!'"

Annette recalled that after Big Howard slammed the door, Howard burst into tears. "Dudley reached up to comfort him and gently escorted him up the steps to his own bedroom, where Howard remained for the next two weeks, refusing to return to the Yoakum mansion."

During the rest of his time in Houston, Big Howard never called him or returned to the Sharp residence. He told Annette and Estelle that he planned to disinherit the boy unless he changed his ways—and soon.

On January 11, 1924, he began to consult with his lawyers about changing his will.

***

Houston, 1924

Eager to leave Houston and return to the fleshpots of Los Angeles, Big Howard awoke early on the morning of January 14. He was still troubled by his break with his son, as he'd told Sheryl over champagne the night before, but this particular morning his mind was preoccupied with other thoughts.

As Sheryl languished sleepily in the suite's luxurious bed, Big Howard admired his physique in a full-length mirror. He was proud that at the age of fifty-four he was still in such good shape and could satisfy the sexual demands of a lusty twenty-year old chorine, who was used to having much younger men make love to her.

Today was his big day for opening up frontiers for his rapidly expanding Toolco, his nickname for the Hughes Tool Company. For lunch, he'd invited six important oil barons from Southern California, where new wells were being drilled almost daily.

After going for a brisk ten-block walk to keep in shape, he told R.C. Kuldell, his right-hand man in Houston, that, "I've never felt better in my life." Before retiring to his suite to write his luncheon speech, he confided several smutty details to Kuldell about his relationship with the chorus girl.

Kuldell went back to Toolco's office but returned to the Rice Hotel at five minutes to twelve to accompany his boss to the luncheon. A former Army colonel, Kuldell was a tough, weather-beaten man with a reputation for womanizing. Big Howard was completely dependent on him to run his cash cow while he was conducting sales conferences, or gallivanting, in New York, Los Angeles, or The Bahamas.

At his luncheon speech, where he'd ordered the best of Texas prime rib for his honored guests, Big Howard revealed that his new roller bit for 1924 would be self-lubricating, an enormous breakthrough in engineering that would revolutionize the oil industry. To please his guests, he also announced plans for the opening of a Toolco office in San Diego so that the oil barons wouldn't have to commute all the way to Los Angeles. He also informed the men that Toolco was currently marketing 150 drills in various shapes, sizes, and types, or "species," as Big Howard called his bits. To inject a little humor into the luncheon, Big Howard made some crude joke that "the tool at Toolco and the tool in my trousers are just great. One earns me a fortune and the other ensures that I'll have a good time with the money."

Later Kuldell pronounced the luncheon "the most successful Howard had even given. He already controlled Texas. Now he was going to become the big wheel in Southern California."

By two-thirty that afternoon, Big Howard had returned alone to his offices in the Humble Building. There, as he sat behind a large oak desk, a gift which his late wife, Allene, had purchased for him, he met privately with S.T. Brown, the sales manager for Toolco.

"My roller bit will dominate oil exploration around the world," Big Howard predicted to Brown, who would later recall in vivid detail that fateful day. "Southern California will be just another stepping stone for me with new markets opening up all the time. Alaska. Europe. The Middle East. The dinosaurs left a lot of oil in the ground and before I die my roller bit will go after most of it. When I'm laid to rest, the world will have to come up with another energy source, because I don't plan to leave anything in the ground. Brown, my boy, I'm going to become America's first billionaire."

As he looked into his own future, Big Howard became more and more animated, getting up from his desk and pacing furiously around the room as if he was overcome with how big his future was going to be.

All of a sudden, Big Howard stopped ranting and clutched at his heart, his face convulsed with pain. "His whole head just seemed to turn purple like he was choking," Brown later revealed. "His neck seemed to swell up real big. After a few seconds, he held onto his desk for support. His legs just seemed to give way. He was in spasms when he hit the floor. I rushed over and loosened his tie but I feared the worst."

Brown told the Houston police that "loosening some god damn tie wasn't going to save his life." He immediately called C.M. Aves, Big Howard's family doctor. Fortunately, Dr. Aves was nearby and rushed at once to the Humble Building, entering Big Howard's private office.

Examining the patient on the floor, he could discover no heart beat. "He's dead!" he announced to Brown. Rising to his feet, the doctor ordered Brown to call the officers of Toolco and to place another emergency call to Annette Lummis. "It's her job to tell Sonny."

As an afterthought, Dr. Aves advised that Brown had also better call the Houston police chief. "When men as rich as Howard Hughes die suddenly," he said, "foul play is always suspected."

Earlier that day young Howard had told Annette that he'd be playing golf at the Houston Country Club with Judge Walter Montieth. Not wanting to break the bad news to the boy on the phone, Annette decided to drive over to the golf course.

First, she called her husband, Dr. Lummis, to ask him to make funeral arrangements. Her husband already knew of Big Howard's death, as he'd just received a phone call from Dr. Aves. Hughes's doctor suspected that the sudden heart attack was a result of an embolism, which is when the normal flow of blood to the heart is impeded by the presence of a foreign object, such as an air bubble, in the blood stream.

At the golf course, Annette interrupted Howard's game of golf with the judge and told him about his father's sudden death. She would tell the press that the boy was "overcome with grief and had to be assisted off the course."

Later, she wrote a different version of that afternoon to Rupert in Los Angeles. "Howard showed no remorse at all," she claimed. "He actually insisted on finishing his game of golf, even though the judge warned him that such behavior might not be appropriate."

After the game was over—Howard lost to the judge—he refused to ride back to the Yoakum mansion with Annette. "He went into the clubhouse and placed a call to Frank Andrews, the family attorney."

"I want to read my father's will," he informed Annette before driving off in his 1924 white Duesenberg with its red leather upholstery.

***

In the office of attorney Frank Andrews, the just orphaned Howard was presented with two wills from Big Howard, one written eleven years previously and the other drafted the week before. In the first will, Big Howard left half his estate to Allene, one-fourth going to his son, and the remaining one-fourth to be divided equally among his parents, Jean (Mimi) and Felix T. Hughes Sr., with their other son, Felix T. Hughes Jr. cut in for part of his parents' share. Big Howard did not leave any money to his other brother, Rupert. Frank Andrews told young Howard that at the time the will was drawn up, Big Howard had maintained that Rupert was making plenty of money "writing Hollywood junk and could take care of himself."

In that will, Big Howard stated that, "I desire and request that my son Howard be given as good an education as possible."

He also suggested that the Houston Land & Trust Company be appointed guardian of his estate until his son turned twenty-one. The *de facto* guardian of Howard was still Annette Lummis, who wanted him to continue at Rice University until he was graduated.

To Howard's utter dismay, Andrews also read the more recent will, the one that had been drafted following their blow-up at the Sharp house on New Year's Eve. Howard immediately became embittered when he read the second will, in which Big Howard had diminished his son's share of the estate to less than

94

half. But he was delighted to see that this second will had neither been signed nor witnessed and was therefore invalid.

In front of Andrews, Howard ripped the second will to shreds. "It's a piece of shit! How dare he betray me like this and give away what's rightfully mine." Andrews later recalled that he was shocked at Howard's explosion of anger, considering how generous his father had been to him in life.

But that day in Houston, however, Andrews held his tongue. With his best client dead, he was eager to curry favor with the new heir. "My father never asked me what I wanted. He decided what I was to do and then forced me to do it whether I wanted to or not. No one will make me do anything I don't want to ever again. Both of my parents tried to control me. They can't control me from the grave."

Andrews chose not to point out to his new and suddenly rich client that many parents try to direct their children's lives. He did inquire if Howard planned to resume his education at Rice, as he was certain that Annette and other members of the Hughes clan would want that. "I've spent my last day on a college campus," Howard announced rather arrogantly to the attorney.

Even as funeral preparations were being made, the staff at Andrews' office was busy tallying up Big Howard's assets. Appraised for tax purposes, the value of the entire estate came to $871,518 in property, notes, stocks and bonds. Company assets were appraised at $750,000 of that amount. This figure was kept deliberately low for tax purposes. Even at the time, the market value of Toolco would have been at least $8 million—maybe a lot more.

Big Howard had run up personal bills totaling $258,000, and that amount would have to be deducted from the estate. These bills ranged from $2 for a Ludwig whistle from the Parker Music Company of Houston to $515 from James Bell & Son tailors in New York. Howard had charged but not paid for two tuxedos and four black velvet waistcoats.

Big Howard's funeral was conducted in the library of the Yoakum mansion, with Peter Gray Sears presiding. He was the pastor at Christ Church and had also officiated at Allene's funeral.

The house was virtually filled with large floral arrangements, most of them sent by Texas oil barons. Even the Houston police sent Lilies of the Valley to drape over the elephant-gray casket studded with gold fittings and lined in crimson satin.

In attendance were Ella Rice and her beau, James Winston. Ella's mother, Mattie Rice, was related to Annette's husband, Dr. Lummis, so there was some distant family relationship.

Howard did not follow the mournful funeral procession to Glenwood Cemetery. Once there, Big Howard, the errant and wandering husband, at last was joined to his long-suffering wife in tree-shaded twin graves.

Big Howard and Allene had left behind an emotionally shattered eighteen-year-old, who was haunted by a fear of germs and overly concerned with his health. He told Dudley that he feared an early death such as his parents had experienced.

During the final burial rites at the cemetery, Howard remained alone in his bedroom, playing with his ham radio as he attempted to contact ships at sea, as he had done as a child.

That night when Annette, along with Dr. Lummis, returned to the Yoakum mansion, Howard had disappeared. She assumed that he had gone on a country drive since his car was missing. "He needs to think things out alone," she told Dr. Lummis.

It was later learned that Howard spent the night in his father's suite at the Rice Hotel, no doubt in the arms of his father's former mistress, Sheryl Steele. On a tantalizing note, it was later learned that Howard invited Dudley to join Sheryl and himself on the second night.

After having disappeared for so long, Howard reappeared at the Yoakum mansion with no explanation as to where he'd been or what he'd done. He immediately went into the library, where his father's burial services had been conducted, and placed an urgent call to Frank Andrews. The attorney later recalled "the fierce determination in the boy's voice."

"I don't want to own seventy-five percent of Toolco," Howard shouted into the phone. "I want to own one-hundred percent so I'll not have to report to anyone. I'm leaving for New York tomorrow, and I'm going to London and Paris. When I return, I want you to have bought out my grandparents and my uncle."

"But you're still a minor?" Andrews protested.

"Yeah, since you brought that up," Howard said. "That's the second problem for you to solve. My golfing partner, Judge Montieth, told me there's a loophole in Texas law. Investigate that. The judge said there's a way I can be declared a legal adult even though I'm not twenty-one."

"I've never heard of such a precedent," Andrews said.

"Find out about it," Howard ordered. "You can talk confidentially to the judge about this. He's a very close friend of mine. Maybe some money will have to change hands. The judge wouldn't be the first of his breed to take some money under the table." Before ringing off, Howard had a final reminder for his attorney. "Drop the Junior from my name. My old man's dead. I'm the *Senior* now in the Hughes family."

The next morning he boarded a Chicago-bound train with Estelle Sharp and her son, Dudley. Once in Chicago, they would change trains for New York. From the port of New York, they would sail to London together.

Once aboard the ship and still in New York harbor, Howard sent a final telegram to Andrews back in Houston. "When I get back to Texas, I want to see some real progres (sic) made on my requests. If I find you haven't moved forward, please be aware that there are many other lawyers in the great State of Texas who'd just love to have a rich young man like me as a client."

96

England, 1924

Estelle, still billing herself as Mrs. Walter Sharp, had impulsively decided that she wanted to go on a trip to London and Paris, staying at all the deluxe hotels. In the wake of his father's death, when Howard graciously agreed to finance the trip for her and Dudley, she demanded that he, along with her son, be one of her two male escorts. Still disturbed by Big Howard's death, Annette agreed to the trip, although she had misgivings.

Much of the European jaunt is still cloaked in mystery, although some details have leaked out over the years. Howard booked one stateroom for Estelle and another for Dudley and himself, where they pursued their friendship and romance. Presumably, Estelle knew what was going on, but seemed to have no objections whatsoever. In that sense, she was more of a modern woman than most other daughters of the Edwardian age.

Estelle wrote to Annette that the boys were taking beautifully to crossing the Atlantic and that they dressed up "like fine young gentlemen every night for dinner." She also noted that Howard and Dudley "were the showstoppers of all the young men aboard, and were eagerly sought out as dancing companions." She concluded, "What Howard needs right now, more that anything, is to escape from lawyers and greedy, grasping relatives trying to suck blood money from him, money he's entitled to. Big Howard should have left him in one-hundred percent control and not placed him in financial jeopardy by having to deal with that Hughes clan. They know I sold my interest in the tool company too cheaply, and I fear they are not going to let that happen with Howard. I predict a big family battle ahead. In fact, this battle over the estate will probably break up the Hughes family into warring factions."

In London, Howard escorted his friends to the theater, swanky night clubs, pubs, cruises on the Thames, whitebait dinners in Greenwich, and even the British Museum. At the latter he decided that in spite of their riches he was not a museum-goer.

Leaving Estelle in the clutches of a handsome young guide, who'd just been graduated from Oxford, he ordered a chauffeur in a limousine to drive Dudley and him to some airfield in East Anglia, the exact location unknown. Dudley later remembered the airfield being somewhere near Cambridge.

After money exchanged hands, Howard persuaded the pilot that he was an ace aviator. The teenager was allowed to fly a small craft over the fens, marshes, and bucolic Constable landscapes of East Anglia and out over the North Sea. Dudley, often terrified, went along for the ride.

One afternoon, after landing and refueling somewhere, Howard flew over the Yorkshire Moors. On their return to London, after having been away for five nights, Howard assured Dudley that flying over a country "is the only way to sightsee."

Back in London after a farewell dinner at the Café Royale, where Estelle demanded to be seated in Oscar Wilde's old booth, both Howard and Dudley persuaded her to make their first commercial air flight from London to Paris. Such flights were "the rage of the age."

Estelle was terrified to make such a journey. But Howard assured her it was not only the fastest way to get there, but the safest. Sensing his determination, she reluctantly agreed to go along, even though predicting "this will be the death of all of us."

The flight went smoothly in spite of some heavy winds over the English Channel. Estelle later told Annette that she'd never "seen such joy on a boy's face" as she'd witnessed on Howard's when he was flying over the Channel. Normally not a talkative person, Howard couldn't stop talking about the unlimited future of commercial aviation.

Although Howard at that point in his young life didn't know the means by which he'd achieve his goal, he stated his determination to become a major player in the world of commercial aviation in the years ahead.

"One day," he predicted to both Estelle and Dudley, as the craft began to swoop down onto Paris, "I'm going to own my own god damn airline."

***

Paris, 1924

The trip took a turn for the worse in Paris where Howard had booked two suites at the prestigious Hotel Crillon on the Place de la Concorde in the heart of the city.

The exact details will never be known, since all the participants are dead, but at some point one night at Le Dôme in Montparnasse Dudley confessed that he'd had an affair with Allene in the months preceding her early death.

Perhaps it was that extra bottle of wine he shouldn't have ordered, but Dudley confessed to his lover and his own mother. The reaction of Estelle to the news is not known. Whatever inner turmoil Howard felt upon hearing the confession wasn't manifested immediately. It would take many months before his true reaction would be revealed in his rejection of Dudley.

At that moment, Howard, in his stoic way, seemed to show no emotion at all, in spite of what must have been deep personal antagonism at the news, especially since he was sleeping with and making love to the same young man who'd made love to his mother. But such a virtually incestuous tie with Allene was hardly foreign to him.

When this news leaked out in Houston, and became the subject of cruel gossip, many insiders felt that both Howard and Estelle knew about the relationship between Dudley and Allene before Dudley finally admitted it.

"What could Estelle be thinking when she let her boy go and spend night after night in Allene's house?" asked local gossip, Betty Mayfield. "Allene's excuse for having Dudley at her home was her fear that someone would break in on her and rape her. She still maintained that myth about the rape from all those army black men, even though everybody, including the Houston police, knew she was a liar about that night."

When Howard, returning to Houston from his boarding school in California, discovered that Dudley knew his way around the Yoakum mansion better that he did, he had to suspect that there was some intimacy between his mother and his best friend.

"I would see Allene and Dudley out together at restaurants," Mayfield said. "He was always there to escort her wherever she wanted to go in Big Howard's absence, which was most of the time. Everybody was talking about this unnatural relationship between a young boy and an old woman. Just by the way they acted around each other, you could tell that those two were love birds in spite of the difference in their ages."

The next day in Paris, and in the weeks to come, Howard continued to treat Dudley in the same way he always had, in spite of any personal misgivings he might have had about his best friend. It wasn't until he got back to Houston that Howard began to make some of his antagonism known, although not in any confrontational way.

Howard never actually promised it, but Dudley assumed that he was the heir apparent to Howard's "old" buttercup yellow Duesenberg now that Big Howard had presented his son a more luxurious 1924 model. Dudley had even told friends of his that he'd soon be riding around in the swanky vehicle after his return from the Continent.

After having dinner with Estelle every night in Paris, Dudley and Howard would go "on the town," sampling some of the city's famous night life. They were enthralled when they attended the Folies Bergère. As two handsome young men, with seemingly endless money to spend, Howard and Dudley were also solicited by both male and female prostitutes.

Their favorite night club was called Caméléon, near Place Clichy. After two o'clock in the morning, the decadent audience was treated to various exhibitions behind closed doors. Guests, providing they put up the francs, could pay for whatever scene they wanted. Sometimes the patrons requested a black man, perhaps from French Algeria, with a blonde German woman. One favorite act at the time was with two sixteen-year-old male twins, performing sixty-nine on each other. Women with women were also requested. On one occasion, Dudley and Howard witnessed an orgy of off-duty French sailors who hired out their services to make extra money performing.

Sometimes dawn would be breaking across Paris as Howard and Dudley walked along the Seine, too filled with excitement to go back to the Crillon.

The world at the time seemed bathed in the same pink light as the early morning landscapes of Paris. Howard talked endlessly about his hopes and dreams when he'd become chief of Toolco.

Without so much as an invitation, Dudley, too, thought he'd be a part of a future as rosy as the sky over Paris that morning, as they hailed a taxi back to their hotel.

***

When Howard rose from his bed at one o'clock the following afternoon, he reached over for Dudley but found a missing space. On the night table was a note from Dudley, saying that he was accompanying Estelle to the Louvre that afternoon and promising to be back at the hotel at five o'clock.

When Dudley and Estelle returned to the Crillon at the appointed time, they found Howard had done another one of his disappearing acts.

Unknown to Estelle and Dudley, Mickey Neilan had arrived in Paris. Rupert had told him that young Howard was now in charge of Toolco and would soon be coming to Hollywood to make movies. Mickey wanted to get to him before any other producer or director did.

He already knew that Howard was not immune to homosexual liaisons. The womanizing Mickey had plenty of heterosexual credentials. They included Gloria Swanson, who called him "my wild Irish love," and his new wife, Blanche Sweet, both of whom had fallen madly in love with him. But like so many other Hollywood male players at the time, Mickey always said that he didn't object to homosexuals making love to him, providing it was from the waist down and that they didn't "use any weapon more probing than their tongues."

But since he had never actually courted a homosexual before, he didn't know how to go about it, other than employing the same technique he used on seducing women such as Swanson. In fact, the way he choreographed his courtship of Howard more or less paralleled his romancing of Swanson in the same city of Paris in 1922.

Howard was astonished to find three vases filled with roses when he woke up and wandered into the living room of his suite. There was a note from Mickey, inviting him to a "wild party" in a château south of Paris. Without waiting for acceptance, Mickey promised he'd be at the Crillon to pick Howard up at four-thirty that afternoon. That way, they'd have time to arrive at the party before sunset.

Perhaps at that moment, Howard decided to begin his payback to Dudley for that revelation about seducing Allene. Without leaving a note to either Estelle or Dudley, Howard

Gloria Swanson

called Mickey's hotel and accepted the invitation.

Although Howard's initial impression of a drunken Mickey had not been favorable, he became fascinated by the director during the three short days and longer nights they spent together in Paris. Born to a life of privilege, Howard was intrigued by the rough and tumble existence that Mickey had experienced as a kid.

A school drop-out at the age of eleven when his father died, the boy supported himself and his mother by doing odd jobs. While still a teenager, he worked as a juvenile in a stock company before coming to Hollywood where he was hired as a chauffeur for D.W. Griffith, then a director at Biograph.

Griffith found the charming young man "dashingly handsome" and cast him in some small parts. By 1913, Mickey was directing his first picture for the American Film Company. In years to come he would drift between directing and acting. In 1917, he directed Mary Pickford in *Rebecca of Sunnybrook Farm* long before anyone ever heard of Shirley Temple. He also had an affair with Pickford, since her marriage to Owen Moore was on the rocks.

At the time of his Paris rendezvous with Howard, Mickey had directed his wife, Blanche, in *Tess of the D'Urbervilles*, based loosely on the famous novel by Thomas Hardy. If Howard had any misgivings about running off with Mickey, the husband of his friend, Blanche, he kept them to himself.

Always animated and eager to party, Mickey was distinguished by his curly, sandy-colored hair. He wore glasses but they did not detract from his raw masculinity and sex appeal.

Swanson found him "dashing, brilliant, and a madcap." Howard knew from personal experiences that Hearst held Mickey in distain, but that was because he was rumored to be having an affair with his mistress, Marion Davies.

It was said that Mickey had an inner radar that directed him to "the best dames and the best booze." Mickey always said he didn't like to indulge in anything that wasn't either "illegal or immoral." Young Howard eagerly listened to his advice, especially when he told him, "Don't give a god damn what the stinking world thinks of you. Follow your own desires and have a great life—and fuck everybody else!"

Fully dressed in tuxedos, Mickey and Howard, on the night following their château party, descended on Maxim's for three bottles of the best champagne. That was followed by a long dinner at La Rose de France, a long-gone Montmartre restaurant frequented in part by "ladies" who really weren't that under their gowns. Reportedly, Howard was vastly amused when a bevy of transvestites solicited Mickey and him.

Dinner was followed by a retreat to a jazz club, Blue Note, in Montparnasse. By two o'clock in the morning, Mickey himself had taken the star spotlight, playing New Orleans jazz and the latest Broadway showtune hits. The mixed crowd of homosexuals and heterosexuals adored him and demanded repeated encores. Before dawn they descended on Les Halles for a bowl of the famous French

101

onion soup at Le Pied de Cochon. They were joined by the mink-clad flotsam of the night.

The third night, they didn't go out at all, but ordered a champagne and caviar supper at Mickey's hotel suite. Whatever happened between the two men that night will never be known. Years later, Blanche claimed that Mickey was very vague on the details of their final night together in Paris.

Later, when Howard started producing movies, and Mickey came to him with the nucleus of a screenplay, *Everybody's Acting*, Howard bought it and filmed it.

Back in Hollywood, Mickey told Blanche some of the details of his experiences with Howard in Paris. Years later, she recalled being more amused at the episode than jealous.

One can only speculate what Howard told Estelle and Dudley about his three-day disappearance when he finally returned to his suite at the Hotel Crillon. His going away obviously didn't cause a permanent break in his friendship, because three days later Estelle, Howard, and Dudley were spotted at a plush casino in the environs of Brussels.

The man who one day would "buy" Las Vegas got his first taste for gambling in Belgium, although in the years ahead he preferred to gamble on life, not at tables.

Starting out cautiously at the roulette table with a five-dollar bet, Howard steadily built up a winning pile of plaques, switching from red to black and back again. Before the night was over, he'd won a staggering ten thousand dollars.

Suddenly, he told Dudley, "I fear Lady Lucky is jilting me." Cautiously he placed only a five-dollar bet and lost. Once he'd done that, he reached out and swooped up the remaining $9,995 worth of plaques and cashed them. Estelle was impressed at his self-control.

Taking a ferryboat across the English Channel, the trio arrived in London for two final nights. From London, they took the train to Southampton for their ocean voyage back to New York.

By then, if he already didn't know it, Howard had learned that "money talks." He objected to the size of the first-class cabin he'd be sharing with Dudley.

Howard refused the cabin and went directly to the captain. Perhaps the teenage boy bribed him—that's not known. What is known is that Howard and Dudley were assigned the finest stateroom on board, even though the U.S. Ambassador to Great Britain had to be bumped into the smaller cabin Howard objected to.

From that point on, and for every night of the voyage, Estelle, Howard, and Dudley dined at the captain's table. As he stood on the deck watching New York harbor come into view, Howard told Dudley and Estelle that "my whole future depends on how clever I can be in the next few months."

Houston, 1924

Wanting desperately to hold onto his newly minted millionaire clientele, attorney Frank Andrews had been working overtime to force Howard's grandparents and uncle to sell their stock in Toolco. Felix Sr., then eighty-five, and his wife Jean (Mimi), eighty-two, had moved from the cold winters of Keokuk to Rupert's sunny estate in Los Angeles. The remaining member of the Toolco stockholders, Felix Jr., had been invited to Los Angeles, but had not yet moved west.

Howard was deeply disappointed to learn that his grandmother, Mimi, had actually laughed at his proposal for a buy-out of her Toolco stock. She said that Howard was "an infant" in the eyes of the law and couldn't enter into any legal agreement anyway. Besides, his grandmother also claimed that she and her aging husband needed the income derived from Toolco not only to support themselves but to leave a financial legacy to pass on to their remaining children, including Rupert who'd been excluded from Big Howard's will.

That news was disappointing to Howard, but Andrews had confirmed that under Texas law if a nineteen-year-old minor could convince the court that he was capable of handling his business affairs without adult supervision, he could be declared "legally responsible." Howard wanted to press for such a hearing, and he also wanted the case to come before his friend and golfing partner, Judge Walter Monteith.

Within one month after his return to Texas, Judge Monteith played a game of golf with Howard—as always, the judge won even though he was a poor player—and had lunch as Howard's guest at the clubhouse. After lunch, both of them went into the sauna and subsequently enjoyed massages from two expert masseurs. Later they retired into the slumber chamber for rest and relaxation. During this session, which lasted about an hour, the judge quizzed Howard about several details regarding Toolco. Later, Montieth told his legal assistants that "the boy answered every single question put to him."

Of course, the judge knew nothing about the machinations of running a tool company and wouldn't have known if Howard's answers were right or wrong.

Annette objected to Howard's legal maneuvering but had no real power over him. She told friends in Houston that he was "just possessed to be declared an adult."

***
Los Angeles, 1924

Unable to get his relatives to sell their stock, Howard invited himself to Rupert's estate in Los Angeles to meet with his grandparents.

Learning of her favorite son's death, Mimi had donned a black dress that she'd wear for the rest of her life. "Life is so cold and dark," she told her grandson when he came into the living room to greet her. "I'm so desolate. My life is finished. There is nothing left."

At first Felix Sr. and Mimi welcomed Howard warmly as part of the family mourning ritual. Later, she told her husband and Rupert that she secretly believed that Howard was relieved to have his father "out of the picture."

But in the first few days, Mimi befriended Howard and discussed future plans with him, including the continuation of his education. Howard even convinced Mimi to sell her expensive car, claiming that he feared that she'd become too old to drive. Regrettably he pocketed the money generated by the sale of the vehicle and never gave it to her.

It didn't take long for Mimi and Felix Sr. to become painfully aware of why Howard had come to see them. It wasn't to mourn the death of his father, but to persuade them to sell their stock to him. At one point the negotiations became so bitter that Mimi agreed to sell her share and that of her husband's for only ten dollars.

She wasn't completely serious about the offer but hoped to shame her grandson, not realizing that at the time that he was virtually without shame.

The dispute with his grandparents grew so bitter that Howard finally denounced both of them. "I want you out of my life!" he shouted at them. "Both of you are so old you should have died a long time ago."

After that outburst, Mimi retreated to her bedroom and announced she didn't want to see Howard any more. The aging, sensitive, and artistically inclined woman would speak only once more to her grandson, and that would be on the phone. Still rather spry and well versed in the law, Felix Sr. threatened to bring a lawsuit against his grandson.

Matters became even more complicated when Howard's other uncle, Felix Jr., arrived and immediately demanded $250,000 for his share of the stock. In the midst of a divorce, Felix Jr. was eager to acquire a lot of cash—and soon. Negotiations between Felix Jr. and Howard became so hostile that Felix Jr. slapped the boy's face real hard, knocking him down. Not known for violence, Howard did not strike him back.

As for Rupert, who'd been cut out of everything, he was secretly negotiating to have himself declared Howard's guardian. Although he had no business experience with the tool company, he plotted to take over the assets of the company until Howard turned twenty-one.

Even though appalled by Rupert's manipulations behind the scenes, Howard maintained the pretense of a great loving trust for Rupert. With no sincerity at all, Howard told Rupert, "With my father out of the way, you've become the Big Guy in my life." Rupert fell for this flattery. Actually, Howard was like a hungry cat waiting to devour an overweight rodent.

Suddenly, Howard was going to the Los Angeles Athletic Club for workouts and steambaths with Rupert, for long drives along the southern California coast, and for late night dinners. At one point Rupert rented them a house in Santa Monica for an escape from the pressures and prying eyes of Hollywood. Rupert did not invite either of his parents or his live-in girlfriend, Elizabeth Dial, on any of these holiday breaks.

Having learned of Rupert's homosexual streak, Howard was determined to take advantage of it.

Many Hollywood writers, including Mart Martin, have known that Rupert seduced the teenage boy at one point, although details are sparse. It probably occurred at the Santa Monica beach house. Martin, in fact, lists Howard's first sexual experience as being with Rupert, to whom he is said to have lost his virginity at the age of fifteen. Martin and the other writers were almost on target, except for the fact that Howard was eighteen at the time, and he didn't lose his virginity to Rupert, having surrendered it several years prior to that.

Back in Houston, Dudley and Estelle learned only bits and pieces of what was happening in Los Angeles. What is known is that once Rupert had performed oral sex on Howard on several occasions, the teenager then used that molestation to blackmail his paternal uncle.

Howard knew that Rupert had great influence over Mimi. Threatened with exposure of his own secret streak of homosexuality, Rupert, although furious, gave in to Howard's demands. After several long sessions with his parents, Rupert finally forced Mimi to cave in, albeit with great reluctance. Her husband went along with her.

With Rupert appearing to have taken Howard's side, Mimi agreed to accept $75,000 for her share and that of Felix Sr. for their stock. Felix Jr. held out and got his first asking price of $250,000. His uncle told Howard, "It is my first and final offer. If you don't give me the money, and even if Mimi and Dad sell to you, I'll still be one of the shareholders of Toolco, and I'll make your life living hell if you don't cough up the money."

On May 28, 1924, Toolco became Howard's exclusive property when Frank Andrews informed him that he now controlled one-hundred percent of the stock. The total cost of the buy-out had been $325,000.

To raise that kind of money, Howard had to drain Toolco of all its operating capital. But it was a gamble he was willing to chance.

Considering the millions the tool company would make in the years ahead, this sellout price was viewed even at the time as "highway robbery," in Mimi's bitter words.

Her last words to her grandson came in a phone call he'd placed to her. Detesting the atmosphere at Rupert's mansion, Howard had moved on and was occupying the same suite at the Ambassador Hotel where his father had had dalliances with Eleanor Boardman and Gloria Swanson. With Billy Haines and other Hollywood friends, Howard was entertaining as lavishly as Big Howard once did.

"You're too irresponsible to run my son's company," Mimi charged over the phone.

"Just you wait and see," Howard angrily countered. "I'm a responsible adult! In fact, I'm returning to Houston to run the company. I'm going to settle down and get married."

"Just who are you marrying?" she asked.

"Ella Rice," he said before slamming down the phone forever on the old woman.

Rupert had to go to New York on a picture deal. Even though he'd been instrumental in forcing Mimi to agree to the buy-out, Rupert was still bitter as reflected in his letter to "Blessed Mimi," which he'd written from New York's Biltmore Hotel.

I never in my life heard of such bald robbery as he attempted and carried out. It was an astounding display of grasping—dishonorable ungenerous selfishness. He actually robbed you and Felix of what Howard willed you. He pretended to be generous to his darling Mimi and offered you as a gift about a quarter of what your own son wished you to have. When he yielded he yielded only to compulsion, yielded with the worst possible grace, lied flatly again and again and altogether behaved outrageously. He is a miser and a selfish little beast.

Your loving son,
Rupert

Although Howard never wanted anything to do with Mimi and his grandfather, or Felix Jr. for that matter, and although he despised Rupert, he still maintained a cordial relationship with his uncle.

"Why don't you tell the son of a bitch to go fuck himself?" Dudley suggested in a letter from Houston.

"Not yet," Howard said. "That day will come. In the meantime, I'm going into the movie business and dear old cocksucking Uncle Rupert will be very useful to me."

In time, when he no longer needed him, Howard would also drop Rupert and even refuse to attend his funeral. His grandparents would never forgive him, especially Mimi. Shortly before her own death, she spoke of her "bitterness toward *that* boy." Signing her own Last Will and Testament right before she died in 1928, she left her estate to be divided among Rupert and Felix Jr. She wrote, "I mention the name of my grandson, Howard R. Hughes Jr., to show that I have not forgotten him and that I purposely have not given him anything in this my Last Will and Testament."

Even though he wasn't legally an adult, Howard nonetheless assumed charge of Toolco in the summer of 1924. At the company, he made an astonishing confession to Frank Andrews. "It was my father's business—not mine," Howard told his attorney. "The only interest I have in Toolco is how much money I can make from it every month. I'm going to pursue far bigger games than my father ever did, only I need financing. I want you to meet with the managers of the company about how much money I can expect to haul in every month. After all, it's *my* company and *my* money. I can do what I want with it now."

Howard didn't waste a day after legally becoming nineteen, appearing in Superior Court on December 26, 1924, the first business day after Christmas.

The nineteen-year-old came before his friend, Judge Montieth, who declared Howard "legally an adult" two years before he turned twenty-one. The judge had only one admonition for Howard. He suggested that he return to his studies at Rice University.

Howard promised the judge that he would enroll at Princeton University during the next semester, attending classes with his best friend, Dudley.

He had no intention of keeping that promise.

Later, as Betty Mayfield claimed, "It was rumored throughout Houston society that Montieth accepted ten thousand dollars in cash from the boy. Others claimed he took as much as twenty five thousand under the table."

Once the judge's decree had come through, Howard never again invited Montieth for a game of golf in spite of repeated calls from the judge, who could not understand the sudden rejection since Howard had been granted everything he'd asked for in court.

Howard had accomplished what no other teenager in America—or adult for that matter—had ever done. He'd sowed the seed by which he would turn himself into America's first homegrown billionaire.

With his relatives safely emasculated, he could now turn his attention to winning the hand of Ella Rice in marriage.

But, first, he had to eliminate James Winston as his competition.

***

Houston, 1925

For thirty-two years, Noah Dietrich ran Hughes's vast industrial empire, and was—to some degree—one of Howard's confidants. He knew far more about his client's personal adventures than he related in *Howard: The Amazing Mr. Hughes*, published in 1972. Of course, Howard and several key players were still alive at the time of publication, and Dietrich showed great restraint in his rather short volume, at times not even giving the name of the party, such as actress Billie Dove, that he was writing about.

Dietrich's spin on the Ella Rice/Howard Hughes marriage was so simplistic that it was ridiculous. Dietrich claimed that Howard won Ella's hand by feigning illness. According to the story, Howard's doctor called Ella, informing her that his patient was in a coma and kept calling out her name.

Dropping everything, Ella was said to have rushed to the stricken Howard's bedside where the teenage millionaire then experienced a miraculous recovery. In the next sentence, Dietrich has Ella and Howard married within three weeks.

No woman as smart and as sophisticated as Ella Rice would have fallen for such a ploy. Nor would she have abandoned "the man of my dreams," James Winston, because an acquaintance of hers, Howard, was sick. Actually, Howard wasn't sick at all.

The actual story, as best as can be pieced together, is far more complicated than the Dietrich version. Over the years Dudley and others have shed more light on what actually happened.

In Dudley's version, Howard set out to woo James away from Ella. Of course, the way to do that was with money. It is not know how Howard got in touch with James, but soon the handsome young man was seen driving Howard's buttercup yellow Duesenberg around Houston, much to the chagrin of Dudley, who had wanted the vehicle for himself.

Just as Howard used to disappear for long weekends with Dudley, he now took James as his companion. Ella was furious at James for deserting her, and at first she didn't fully comprehend the unlikely relationship of James and Howard. "They are rivals for my hand," Ella protested to Annette, who was far more knowledgeable about such matters than Ella. However, Annette, at least at the beginning, did not intervene.

Eventually the inevitable showdown came between James and Ella, with Howard present. It was at the Yoakum mansion. James confronted Ella and told her he was not a rich man and could not provide for her. "He actually urged me to marry Howard instead of him," Ella later confided to Annette, who wrote Rupert with all the details.

Infuriated, Ella denounced James. From her bedroom on the second floor, Annette could hear Ella screaming at James in the foyer of the Hughes home. "He's bought you like he buys everybody else," she shouted at him. Normally she rarely raised her voice. She told James she never wanted to see him again. Turning on Howard, she also denounced him for corrupting James. Before storming out of the house, Ella told Howard she never wanted to see him again either.

This was hardly a prelude to marriage, but Howard was very persistent and won Ella over in a very short time. Dudley claimed it was easy getting rid of James. "A seduction, a yellow Duesenberg, and twenty-five thousand dollars did the trick."

Disillusioned with her former beau, Ella was very vulnerable when she finally agreed to marry Howard. Howard implored Annette to try to persuade Ella to go through with the marriage. In those days, as now, women often married for money, or "for home and hearth," wanting security more than romance.

The most persuasive argument came from Libby Rice Farish, Ella's older sister, who was "pushing forty." Libby pointed out that Howard Hughes Jr. was the most desirable and sought after bachelor in the State of Texas. She predicted that Howard and Ella, a male beauty and a female beauty, would no doubt produce a remarkable son who one day would become President of the United States.

Ella did agree to start dating Howard. It can never be fully understood, but his boyish charm eventually broke down her barriers. "When Howard wanted to woo someone," Estelle Sharp said, "he could be formidable, even at an early age. To be tall, dark, and handsome, and to shower a young girl with flowers, expensive presents, even jewelry, and offer to make her the Queen of Hollywood sharing his throne as the King of Hollywood, was pretty heady stuff in those days. At one point, I think Howard even threatened to slit his wrists if Ella didn't give in."

Behind the scenes, Ella's mother, Mattie Rice, may have been Howard's best secret weapon. At that time, Mattie had tremendous influence over her daughter. Although the Rice family was influential, Ella's branch was the poor relations. Mattie wanted wealth and prestige for her daughter. Annette had already persuaded "Aunt Mattie" that she couldn't send Howard to Los Angeles "with all those vampire movie people ready to rob him blind."

The *coup de grâce* came when Howard showed up at Aunt Mattie's door and showed her a will he'd drawn up. In the will he left, among other bequests, ten thousand dollars to Dudley Sharp. But "to my wife," he'd written even before the marriage, "Ella Rice Hughes, I bequeath the sum of five hundred thousand dollars in first class, high grade securities, to be delivered to her by my Executors as soon after my death as can conveniently be arranged." He also granted his wife-to-be a lifetime annuity of $50,000 a year.

The wedding was announced for the evening of June 1, 1925 since Ella claimed, "I've always dreamed of a June wedding." Significantly, Howard's ten-page will that contained the provisions for Ella noted above was signed on May 30, 1925.

The night before the wedding Ella lost her nerve and protested to her mother that she "didn't love Howard and couldn't go through with the wedding."

"My darling dear," Mattie told her, "how many women who have been married in the State of Texas actually went to their honeymoon bed in love with their husbands? If love for a man is to come, it will come only after many years of facing the joy and the pain of life together. What matters is that as Mrs. Howard Hughes Jr., you're going to be in a position to help your family. With this marriage, our rich relatives will no longer look down their noses on us. We'll be walking taller and prouder that any other family in Houston."

***

June 1 dawned steamy and hot, the kind of day in Texas where all you could do was sit on the front porch with a gasping hound dog, drink lemonade, and fan yourself. Dudley was dressed in a white linen suit. As he recalled years later, "I had to change my underwear three times before the day was over. My drawers were soaking wet and were clinging to my crotch."

A local florist, William J. Billings, said, "I think we had to round up every flower in Texas for these nuptials. You'd think the President of the United States had been assassinated."

Ella's older sister, Libby, had married William S. Farish, chairman and founder of Standard Oil, and the wedding was held at their stylish mansion on Remington Lane, one of Houston's most fashionable addresses.

"There were so many garlands of flowers and feathery ropes of blossoms that it looked like a May Day parade gone haywire," Billings said.

When he later arrived in Hollywood, Howard joked with Billy Haines. "I was so fucking nervous I had to get sucked off by Dudley to calm my nerves before the ceremony."

A vision in apple-green chiffon and her grandmother's creamy antique lace, Libby was matron of honor. Dudley was Howard's best man.

Tout Houston showed up in all their finery. Missing from the ceremony were Rupert and Howard's grandparents.

Libby had learned of the wedding march played at the nuptials of Britain's Queen Victoria when she wed her "beloved" Albert, and had demanded that the orchestra she'd hired play the same march.

Even though the day had dawned hot and bright, threatening clouds suddenly appeared in the sky as the wedding march began, followed by thunder and lightning. Perhaps symbolic of the marriage, an ominous storm roared over the barren Texas plains toward the city of Houston.

Officiating at the ceremony was the Rev. Peter Gray Sears, who had presided over the funerals of both of Howard's parents.

A visible sigh rose from the women in the audience when Howard in a cream-colored linen suit and a navy blue tie appeared. "I'd never seen him look so handsome," Dudley said. "All the women who attended movies were raving about how glorious Wallace Reid looked on screen. But Howard had any movie star beat in those days."

Maybelle Webb, a reporter for *The Houston Chronicle*, went rhapsodic in print about the beautiful bride and her white chiffon gown with lace the color of flowers in a potpourri. "Her tulle veil was held in place by a cap of rose point lace and creamy seed pearls, adjusted with just-picked orange blossoms and white gardenias that smelled of enchanted gardens. In her porcelain arms she held a bridal shower of Lilies of the Valley."

110

After the wedding, and before embracing Dudley in private, Howard confided, "I feel I've married a stranger. You should never have let me go through with the ceremony. Ella will never mean as much to me as you do."

***

En Route to Chicago, 1925

On the train ride to Chicago, as their private rail car crossed the great American plains, the newly married Ella Rice Hughes lost her virginity to Howard.

The details of that night will never be known except for one tantalizing clue.

On the beach in Southampton, Long Island, on his honeymoon, Howard wrote Dudley a letter of distress. "The marriage is a disaster! Ella and I are not sexually compatible."

CHAPTER FIVE

Los Angeles, 1925

Word of the arrival of Mr. and Mrs. Howard R. Hughes, Jr., of Houston, Texas, at Union Station in Los Angeles spread like the wildfires that often deforested the Hollywood Hills.

Like touring royalty, they were seen along the streets as they drove to the Ambassador Hotel in their open Phaeton, a luxury model that was usually associated with film gods and goddesses. A pair of Rolls-Royce Silver Clouds, one for each of them, had already been shipped from New York.

Two hotel limos from the Ambassador had to be sent to collect their Parisian leather trunks filled with expensive clothing. At the beginning of his marriage, and in contrast to his sloppy dress in later life, Howard set out to become America's best dressed man, following in the elegant footsteps of Big Howard.

The gardens of the Ambassador smelled of orange blossoms and gardenias when Howard and Ella arrived at the entrance. At first, some of the other guests thought they were movie stars. Even before being shown to their suite by a bevy of well-tailored bellboys, Howard received messages from Douglas Fairbanks Sr., Charles Chaplin, and Marion Davies, the mistress of William Randolph Hearst, each asking him to call.

From the Vanderbilt Hotel in New York, Howard had sent a telegram notifying the manager of the Ambassador to cancel his reservation of the honeymoon suite for Ella and himself. In Los Angeles, he preferred a suite with separate bedrooms instead.

The first person Howard telephoned in Hollywood was Billy Haines. The actor asked, "Are you a staid old married man now or can we go out on the town and raise hell?"

"I'm smothering," Howard confided in him. "After that god damn honeymoon, I've decided my marriage is going to be in name only. Let's go out tonight and have fun."

Leaving Ella to her own devices in the Ambassador suite, Howard went night clubbing with Billy and his friends, not returning to the room until eight o'clock the next morning. At this early stage in his life, Howard had developed a taste for transvestite night clubs. Apparently, Ella asked her new husband where he'd been all night. But her question was met with such hostility that she was afraid to inquire about his comings and goings from that day forth.

The night before, she'd written a bitter note to Annette in Houston, complaining about her marriage to Howard. "It was as much a mistake for him as it was for me. We have absolutely nothing in common. Nonetheless, I'm determined to make a go of it. I won't be the only woman in America enduring a loveless, sexless marriage."

***

When he awoke that afternoon, Howard began interviewing personnel who'd answered his advertisement for an executive assistant. The most promising was Noah Dietrich, a tough-minded accountant who knew the oil business and was viewed as a genius about corporate financing. With revenues from Toolco coming in at the then astonishing rate of five thousand dollars a day, Howard needed someone to manage his money and to collect enough cash to finance his dreams in Hollywood.

A former prize fighter, Dietrich was only thirty-six years old. During the interview Howard asked Dietrich complicated questions. How does a battleship find its target? How does an internal combustion engine work? Finally, the most important question of the day, what did Dietrich think about investing in motion pictures?

Dietrich's response to that was so negative that it almost ended his association with Howard before it begun. "Investing in Hollywood is the fastest way a sucker can be parted with his money."

Howard made Dietrich wait for three weeks before he called him again, offering him the job of business manager of his empire at a salary of ten thousand dollars a year.

The next day he rented an adjoining suite for Dietrich at the Ambassador. In his memoirs, Dietrich discreetly recalled that Howard and Ella were sharing "a bedroom with twin beds." In truth, they were sharing a suite with two different bedrooms.

In the immediate years ahead, a smart manager like Dietrich could have made Howard a billionaire long before he actually became one. But instead he had to divert a constant stream of funds from the tool company to finance whatever reckless scheme Howard thought up that day.

Following the demands of his young new boss, Dietrich operated with an almost military precision in doing what he was asked to. One of Howard's demands involved the development of a steam-powered automobile that could travel from Los Angeles to San Francisco on a single tank of water.

At Cal Tech, engineers, after many a month, actually came up with such a vehicle. The car, Dietrich informed Howard, would cost a buyer more than half a million dollars, maybe a lot more.

Howard took only one drive with Dietrich in the five-passenger open touring vehicle before discovering its fatal flaw. If any of the vehicle's radial tubing was punctured during a crash, the passengers would be scalded to death. Howard commanded that the steam-powered vehicle be returned to the factory where he ordered it sold as junk, "the type Louis B. Mayer used to sell before he became a Hollywood big shot."

As junk, the half-million dollar vehicle brought twenty-one dollars.

In his first few years with Howard, Dietrich, following the orders of his boss, managed to lose five million dollars speculating on worthless Wall Street stocks.

***

Accepting Douglas Fairbanks Senior's invitation to Pickfair, Howard was happy to meet Doug's son, Fairbanks Jr., who was four years younger than Howard. Once both young men discovered they were saxophone players, the friendship was sealed.

Mary Pickford, Howard soon learned, didn't really like her stepson all that much. But whenever she invited the teenager to one of her dinners at Pickfair, she graciously included Howard as well, although never extending an invitation to Ella.

One night at Pickfair, Howard might be seated next to the Duchess of Alba or perhaps Henry Ford and his wife, Clara. He might even turn around at table and find himself staring into the ugly but mischievous face of Albert Einstein. The queen of Siam might be in the bathroom refreshing herself, or else Howard found himself in the steam room sitting buck naked with the likes of the Duke of Windsor, wondering if small penises were a genetic flaw in the British royal family.

Both young Doug and Howard were thrilled when they learned that Bill Tilden, the greatest tennis player of all time, would arrive the following afternoon to teach them the secrets of the game.

Douglas Fairbanks Jr.

The next day, Doug Jr. showed up on the courts looking like a prepubescent Ganymede in clinging blue seersucker briefs. Until that day Howard had seen players wear only white. Tilden focused most of his attention on young Doug instead of Howard. "I couldn't help but notice the glimmer in Tilden's eye," Howard later told Billy Haines.

"No wonder," Billy said. "Tilden's a child molester."

Fairbanks Sr. later came out to the court, and Tilden beat "d'Artagnan's musketeer" so badly he retreated back into the house to join Pickford.

That night Howard, along with Doug, was invited to dinner at Pickfair. After a lavish meal, over which Mary Pickford presided, the guests retired to the living room for parlor games. Howard was finding that he had very little to say to Lord and Lady Mountbatten, and almost nothing to say to the Duke and Duchess of Sutherland.

Suddenly Fairbanks Sr. flew into a rage at his Japanese valet. He screamed, shouted and denounced the servant in front of his stunned guests. Grabbing the lightweight valet by the heels, Fairbanks picked him up and swung him into the air, as the boy spun around Fairbanks' head.

Lady Mountbatten regarded it with cold-faced detachment, perhaps assuming that this is how American movie stars behave at home. The Duchess of Sutherland screamed in fright. But when Fairbanks finally let the boy come out of orbit, seemingly unharmed, the other guests were told he was a trained acrobat and that it was only a stunt to amuse them.

The following week, Howard arrived for his regular tennis game with Doug, only to find Fairbanks, Sr. beating up on Tilden who lay sprawled on the court, not fighting back or even putting up the slightest resistance. Howard raced to pull Fairbanks off the tennis pro. "Get that pansy asshole off my grounds," Fairbanks yelled at Howard. "*Now.*" He turned in anger and disgust, heading back to the house. Fairbanks was one of the first in Hollywood to use the word "pansy" to refer to a homosexual. The word would not come into general usage until 1929.

Without saying anything or even looking back, Tilden picked himself up from the courts and headed for his car.

Howard invited Doug, Jr., for a drive in his silver Rolls. Seeing them head out, Fairbanks came down from the porch and raced over. He leaned into the car and pointed a finger at his son. "Just let me catch you doing that one more time, and you won't have a weenie to play with. I'll cut it off." He slapped Howard's arm. "Thanks, kid. At least there's someone in Hollywood who can be trusted with my son."

Howard said nothing, but drove Doug in silence, delivering him to the home of his mother, Beth Sully Fairbanks.

Before getting out of the car, Doug invited Howard to visit him on location in Arizona where he was going to shoot Zane Grey's *Wild Horse Mesa*.

"I play Billie Dove's kid brother," he told Howard. "She's the most beautiful woman in the world, and I'm madly in love with her. But she's married."

Before driving on, Howard gave the younger boy some advice. "Never let a husband stand in the way of a love affair."

***

When Howard agreed to meet Chaplin for dinner, he expected that The Little Tramp would have invited at least a dozen other guests. Not so. Chaplin was sitting alone at a choice table for two in the elegant restaurant at the Ambassador Hotel.

At first Howard suspected that there might be an attempt to seduce him, since Billy Haines had already told him about Chaplin's fondness for teenage boys and girls. "But you're a bit long in the tooth for Chaplin," Billy had told Howard. "Usually he doesn't like his meat aged."

Nervous as he was, Howard was immediately put at ease by Chaplin's grace, intellect, wit, and charm, all of which he possessed in abundance.

With cunning instinct, Howard knew not to tell Chaplin how much he loved his films. The entire world had seen all of Chaplin's movies, and he was probably tired of hearing that. At first Howard was astounded to find that the most important film star on earth didn't have a retinue of bodyguards and studio chiefs following him around.

Howard later reported the entire evening in great detail to Billy.

"Being the star that he was, Chaplin immediately took over the conversation," Howard later said. Stars, he'd already learned, were rarely interested in anybody other than the face staring back at them in the mirror.

Chaplin surveyed the dining room, many of its tables filled with the great stars of the silent era. "This whole place is like wandering around in one of your dreams," he said. "It was built on a dream and has become a dream factory. One day all the beauty that's here will be swept away."

"Before it disappears, I want in on the action," Howard said.

"Tell me you want to be a producer, maybe even a director—but not an actor," Chaplin said.

"I'm no actor," Howard said. "I've had offers. But I'm not outgoing enough."

"With your good looks, of course, you'd be a natural cast as a handsome leading man," Chaplin said. "Many male stars today are like wooden figures. Take Norman Kerry, for example. When he isn't panting after Valentino or getting drunk, he appears in films. All he has to do is stand still and let his leading lady do all the emoting." He sighed and waved limply in the direction of Norma Talmadge's table. "If only the man who originally developed Hollywood could see it now."

"I don't know how this place got started," Howard said.

"Back in 1883 a real-estate developer, Horace Henderson Wilcox, owned all this land. It was a ranch eight miles northwest of Los Angeles. He wanted to subdivide the land and create a Utopia here. A place where Methodism reigned. He was dead set against alcohol. Anybody who drank liquor was barred from Hollywood. Can you imagine? The way Wilcox saw it, Hollywood was to be a Christian community dedicated to clean living."

"It's just as well Horace can't see it now."

With a twinkle in his eye, Chaplin sampled his blood-rare steak. Howard moved more timidly toward his, and then called the waiter back and rejected the green peas as too large. He demanded that the waiter return with a bowl of only the smallest peas in the kitchen.

While he ate, Chaplin didn't say much. Howard was the same way. After devouring his steak, Chaplin signaled the waiter to remove the plate at once. He couldn't stand to sit at a table with a dirty plate. Again, he surveyed the room. "The whole world knows who I am. I'm famous in some places that have never heard of Jesus Christ. I've become so famous that it's getting harder and harder for me to lead a private life."

"You must be pursued by fans wherever you go."

"They give me no peace," Chaplin said. "I dislike the press intensely. What I want the world to have is on the screen. I don't feel I owe my fans the intimate details of my private life."

"Look what details about the divorce of Francis X. Bushman did for his career," Howard said. "America doesn't like its screen heroes to be wife-beaters."

"Francis had it coming," Chaplin said. "He's such an exhibitionist. He's always at the athletic club walking around nude showing off his stuff. I'm told that Elmo Lincoln has something even bigger. What a lot of people don't know is that 'The Little Fellow' isn't so little. Most of my growth went to my dick. After Lincoln and Bushman, I take third prize. A lot of young women I bed complain about my size but I plunge in anyway."

Howard was mildly surprised at the sudden turn in the conversation. Sex was the last thing he'd associate with the screen image of Charles Chaplin.

"Let's skip dessert and have our real treat upstairs in a suite I've reserved," Chaplin implored.

"I like you a lot," Howard said. "But I don't see you and me as a romantic couple."

Chaplin laughed. "No, no dear boy, you read me wrong. I've had this public dinner with you in front of Hollywood—no doubt they'll think I'm giving you advice about breaking into motion pictures. Our dining together masks my real plans for the evening. I already have a stunning creature waiting for me upstairs. Not only that, but I have a surprise for you as well."

"I'm not sure I want to go along with this," Howard said.

With his canny sense of people, Chaplin delivered the line that would capture Howard's attention. "She was your father's most glamorous mistress."

***

In the second best suite at the Ambassador Hotel—Howard and Ella already occupied the finest one—Chaplin opened the door for Howard. There on a satin sofa sat America's most famous mistress, the blonde-haired film actress and ex-Follies girl, Marion Davies. She did not get up to greet Howard, but extended her hand to him, a hand-kissing custom he found awkward and would soon abandon. Chaplin planted a wet kiss on Marion's bee-stung, scarlet-painted lips.

Howard looked around for his surprise, finding no other woman. Chaplin was content to skip dessert, letting Marion be his warm tart for the evening. But Howard actually requested the missing dessert. Marion wanted dessert, too.

Both the actress and the young Texas millionaire quickly agreed that ice cream was their favorite treat. "I can eat more ice cream than any man or woman in Los Angeles," Marion boasted. "I'm still eating when the other suckers turn green." Howard preferred banana, but she vetoed that, claiming that the best ice cream in the world was made with blood-red California oranges.

"You mean, orange sherbet?" Howard asked.

"No, baby, real oranges for ice cream," Marion told him. "The chef at the Ambassador makes it specially for me. You've got to try it. It's like pussy, baby. Once a man tries it, he can't get enough of it."

In later life, Howard would have another girl friend addicted to orange ice cream: Miss Ava Gardner, a tarheel from North Carolina.

The following day, Howard would report to Billy Haines about his "historic night at the Ambassador." Davies would give a highly edited report to W.R. Hearst, claiming that she and her sister had encountered Howard having dinner in the hotel restaurant.

As Marion was to tell Louella Parsons the following day, "I found Howard big, awkward, overgrown, a real country boy who's almost too polite and a little hard of hearing. I liked him a lot. I'm going to see to it that W. R. invites him to all our parties at San Simeon."

"When I do invite you to San Simeon," Marion told Howard, "I prefer you to keep this little rendezvous I'm having with Charlie a secret."

"The boy's very discreet," Chaplin assured his mistress.

"Please don't think I'm a whore," the intoxicated Marion said, pouring herself some more bootleg gin. "Charlie and I have this harmless flirtation. After all, I have to have some fun in my life. I'm young and living with a man thirty-four years my senior. He's away from me a lot, and he has no intention of divorcing his Catholic wife. She was a chorus gal like me before she got all grand."

"I'm not one to judge," Howard hastily added. "I'm not devoted to my bride either."

"Kindred spirits," Chaplin added.

"All the men in Hollywood are afraid to get near me," Marion complained. "They dare not risk the wrath of W.R. and what his newspapers could do to their careers. One actor had a kissing scene with me. He was so afraid of angering W.R. that his knees were shaking. After he'd kissed me like a Presbyterian deacon, he went whoosh when the director yelled cut. W.R. has spies everywhere."

"But why isn't Charlie afraid?" Howard asked.

"With Charlie, the danger is part of the attraction," Marion claimed. "Besides, Charlie is too big a fish in Hollywood for W.R. to fry."

Later, Chaplin and Marion told hilarious stories about the filming of her movie, *Zander the Great*, in which she'd starred. "I play an orphan gal, and I had to get in the cage with this god damn lion. There was a protective wall of glass, but I was so afraid I nearly pissed my pants. Louis B. Mayer wanted me to get so close that it looked like I was kissing the beast. The director promised me the lion was toothless. But when it smelled me, it roared, and I saw big fangs. I went crazy, trying to crawl out of that cage screaming bloody murder. I just knew he was going to eat me for lunch."

"I wasn't in the picture, but I happened to arrive on her set that day," Chaplin said. "I quickly agreed to fill in for her. Marion took me to her dressing room, and I put on one of her dresses and a blonde wig. I did the scene with the lion in two takes, with Marion coming in only for the close-ups."

There was a sudden knock on the door. The agile Chaplin rose to his feet to answer the rap. Throwing open the double doors, he announced, "Lady and young gentleman, may I present the screen's leading vamp of yesterday, Miss Theda Bara."

At first taken back, Howard soon realized that it wasn't Theda Bara at all, but the leading screen vamp of the 1920s, Miss Gloria Swanson, who had dumped Big Howard as her lover. She was dressed up, however, as Theda Bara.

"My young man," she said, walking toward Howard. "We meet again."

Long before she became a living caricature of *Sunset Boulevard's* Norma Desmond during the last two decades of her life, a younger Swanson was more fun loving, and, in Marion's words, a prankster at heart. That's why she'd readily agreed to dress up like Theda Bara to greet Howard.

The four of them, each to become a Hollywood legend in the decades ahead, spent an enjoyable hour drinking and telling outrageous stories.

Both Chaplin and Swanson recalled their first meeting at Essanay, a leading film studio in the days of the early silents. "I remember my first day there," Chaplin said. "Miss Louella Parsons was head of the scenario department. I was very rude to her when she gave me a script. I told her I write my own scenarios. Later I was trying to find a pretty young girl to cast as the lead in my first film there. They sent me an actress who had no reaction at all. I turned her down." He moved his hand toward Swanson as if directing her to take over the story. "May I present that young girl tonight. Still young. And even more beautiful. Miss Gloria Swanson."

Swanson laughed, displaying Chiclet white teeth. "I was deliberately bad that day because I didn't want to get cast in a slapstick comedy with Charlie. Of course, he would have stolen the picture from me."

At some point in the evening, Chaplin took a drunken Marion by the hand

120

and directed her into one of the bedrooms, after bidding good night to Swanson and Howard.

By the time Chaplin woke up the next morning to go to the studio—Marion was still sleeping—he discovered a note from Swanson and Howard in the living room.

"One hell of an evening," Howard wrote. Swanson added an enigmatic postscript. "Little Howard has now become Big Howard."

The following evening at the Tiger Club with Billy, Howard related in vivid detail his evening with this Hollywood trio. In spite of Billy's prodding, he never revealed if he'd bedded Swanson or not.

Years later, Billy recalled, "That evening, Howard's face looked more boyish than ever. He was like a little boy who'd brought home a report card with all A's."

"Billy," Howard said, "I've been accepted by Hollywood royalty. Charlie Chaplin. Gloria Swanson. Marion Davies. Even old man Hearst likes me, or so Marion claims. I'm one of them, and I didn't have to work my way up to the top. Invitations to Pickfair. To San Simeon. I'm on my way. Only problem is, I've got to get rid of Ella and send her back to Texas. I can't go back to the Ambassador every night and face the guilt she's piling on me. God took away my parents, but I've saddled myself with another burden."

***

Ella Rice Hughes

Noah Dietrich, Howard's business guru, was much kinder in his memoirs than he needed to be. He remembered that "before he had married Ella," his employer had begun to audition a series of beautiful young women, some of them teenagers. Actually, this custom of Howard's was to last for decades, and it began to occur shortly *after* his marriage to the Texas debutante.

Howard hired a local procurer, known only as "Jimmy the Greek," to station himself during the day at Union Station in Los Angeles. Once there, he was instructed to seek out only the shapeliest of the new female arrivals, most of them traveling west by train with dreams of becoming the next Norma Talmadge, Constance Bennett, Mae Murray, Pola Negri, or Gloria Swanson.

But before she spent a night with Howard, Jimmy saw to it that the young woman picked up at the station was delivered to a spa where she was thoroughly scrubbed, her skin cleaned, her nails manicured, her hair styled, and her body

121

subjected to endless steam baths to "drain out any impurities," as Howard put it.

Even at this early age, he had become adept at oral sex, and he wanted his women immaculately groomed and sweet smelling. Although in time he wouldn't bathe as frequently as he should, and was rather unaware of his own body odor, he could not tolerate "a woman who smells," as he told Jimmy the Greek. Jimmy didn't just work for Howard, but also procured for Francis X. Bushman, Samuel Goldwyn, Mack Sennett, Tom Mix, and Sessue Hayakawa, the latter preferring young men instead of young women.

Jimmy the Greek wasn't the only one on his payroll. Howard also hired Hal Connon as his late-night driver. During the day, Connon, a pug-nose former prize fighter, also drove for the Los Angeles Police Department. In his memoirs, Dietrich discreetly calls Connon "Bruce Davis," so as not to identify him.

Connon's job was to deliver young women to a room at the Ambassador Hotel. Unknown to Ella in the Hughes family suite, Howard kept a spare room on the ground floor in which he'd entertain the young women selected by Jimmy the Greek. Chaplin maintained similar quarters for the same purposes. Howard did not always approve of his procurer's selection for the night, and sometimes quickly sent the woman on her way. During Howard's sessions with the women, which never lasted long, Connon was always waiting behind the wheel of a limousine to cart her off into the night after Howard was finished.

One particular favorite was red-haired "Toffee" Fairmont, who admitted to Howard that that wasn't her real name but the *nom de plume* she planned to use when she became "the next Laura La Plante." The honey blonde with a rather large bust claimed that she had been raised as the daughter of "aristocratic" tobacco planters near Winston-Salem, North Carolina.

Judging by her speech and manners, Howard concluded she was Southern white trash. But she was good at giving and receiving oral sex, and she was extremely clean.

It isn't known what happened, but one night Howard and Toffee became embroiled in a bitter dispute. Apparently, he requested that she engage in an act she called "perverted," which of course, was something other than oral sex.

Although nude, she grabbed a black mink coat he'd given her earlier that evening, wrapped it around her body, and fled down the hallway, out onto the grounds and into the parking lot where Connon waited in the limousine. She demanded to be taken back to her apartment at once.

Even though blinding rain was coming down, and Connon warned her how dangerous driving conditions were, she insisted that he leave at once. If not, she threatened to call the police and expose Howard in the press.

Driving through almost hurricane-force winds, Connon, who had been drinking bootleg hooch while waiting for Toffee, skidded at the intersection of Beverly Street and First Street. He slammed into a telephone pole. In the back seat at the time of the accident, Toffee was thrown through the front window and died instantly, her throat cut on the shattered glass.

When two Los Angeles patrolmen arrived on the scene, they found Connon lying unconscious on the ground. Apparently, the impact had knocked him from the driver's seat. Toffee lay sprawled on the hood, dead, her black mink coat open to reveal her nude body underneath.

Since he was "one of our own," the Los Angeles police believed Connon's story that he had seduced the girl in a motel and was driving her home. When asked where her clothes were, and how he could afford to buy her a mink coat on his salary, he must have answered something convincingly, but his response was not recorded.

The case was ruled an accidental death, and no charges were filed, in spite of the fact that Connon was driving drunk.

When Dietrich reported the incident to Howard the next day, he appeared unconcerned, telling his right-hand man to handle it in whatever way he thought best.

No pay-off was offered to Connon at the time. However, two weeks later, when he consumed a quart of illegal bourbon one night, and in a drunken rage slashed his wife's right arm with a knife, he was arrested, booked, and jailed. Instead of calling a lawyer, Connon called Dietrich, pleading with him to intervene with Howard to get the charges dropped. The next morning when Connon's wife had "calmed down," she was reluctant to press charges.

Dietrich secured his release and even found a job for Connon that paid fifty dollars a week. That wasn't enough. Connon soon began cajoling Dietrich, demanding a thousand dollars in cash. Dietrich called Howard, who agreed to pay it. A month later, Connon demanded five thousand dollars.

"You deal with it, Noah," Howard said.

Dietrich claimed that he called Connon into his office and warned him that he could have him back in jail on a blackmail charge. "This time you might get five years—even more," Dietrich warned.

Connon soon learned that he wasn't going to get any more money. Dietrich did agree that he would give him a ticket to Kansas City, Missouri, where Connon's parents lived on the outskirts on a farm. Dietrich provided a "nest egg" of five hundred dollars for Connon to purchase a caterpillar tractor. It was suggested that the former police driver take up farming like his parents, earning extra money by renting out his tractor to other farmers. Connon was never heard of again.

This would be one of dozens of attempts to blackmail Howard in the years ahead. He would not always get off so easily, and in at least one case, a considerable fortune would exchange hands.

Ralph Graves

123

***

On the grounds of the Wilshire Country Club golf course, Howard had ordered a film crew to shoot his game of golf under the pretense that he thought that by watching himself in action he could improve his playing.

As he was about to hit the ball, he looked up as a handsome, strapping young man, muscle bound like a boxer, walked across the greens to shake his hand. Normally, Howard avoided hand-shaking if at all possible, but he warmly clasped the hand of matinee idol Ralph Graves, a close friend of Big Howard's and a fellow Houstonian.

The two young men stood seemingly checking each other out. Standing only an inch shorter than Howard, Ralph was a charming Ohio-born actor who'd been in Hollywood since 1917, working with D.W. Griffith, Lillian Gish, Mack Sennett, and Gloria Swanson.

Big Howard had been especially fond of Ralph, and had at one time placed him on Toolco's payroll when the actor was out of work. Ralph, however, was never required to perform any services for Toolco.

Ralph had often attended Big Howard's wild parties at the Ambassador Hotel. Howard remembered his father telling him, "Some day after I'm gone, and only if it's economically feasible, I want you to help out Ralph Graves if he ever needs anything. He's a talented and a faithful friend. Two rare combinations."

Over lunch at the country club, Ralph did indeed need something. He pitched a script he'd written, in which he wanted to star and direct. "I fear I won't always look as sexy as I do today," Ralph told Howard. "I'd better take up directing."

No one had ever pitched a movie plot to Howard before, and he was fascinated by Ralph's scenario about a Bowery bum who adopts a baby. "It'll make a hell of a movie," Ralph assured Howard, claiming he could bring in the entire film for forty thousand dollars.

Before the afternoon ended, Ralph had his check for forty thousand dollars and a dinner date to go night-clubbing with Howard. Howard had a previous date with Billy Haines but called to cancel.

"Right from the first, Howard and Graves hit it off," Billy recalled years later. "Frankly, I think Ralph was just hustling Howard the way he'd done with other big shots in the movies, but I kept my wisecracking mouth shut for once in my life."

During the entire time that *Swell Hogan* was being shot, Howard spent all his evenings with Ralph and never with Ella, much to her bitter annoyance. As part of their initial agreement, Ralph allowed Howard to sit on the sidelines watching how movies were made. Of almost anyone connected with *Swell Hogan*, Howard asked highly technical questions, but didn't interfere in production, the way he'd do in so many of his future films.

Before shooting ended, expenditures had mushroomed to eighty thousand dollars. Howard kept supplying the checks, ten thousand dollars at a time.

Louella Parsons had called Ralph's screen personality "up and at 'em," although the actor demonstrated little of that emotion on film. His speaking voice was flat and colorless but that didn't matter since talking pictures had yet to burst onto the American screen.

At long last, production on *Swell Hogan* came to an end, and Howard requested that he see it alone in a studio screening room. After the first showing, he asked the projectionist to show it again and again, finally leaving the studio at six o'clock the following morning.

With no experience in film, Howard the following afternoon attempted to save the movie by re-editing it with the help of a highly skilled film editor whose name is lost to history. Hollywood rumor has it that she was Dorothy Arzner, a strong-willed former waitress, ambulance driver, and stenographer, who later became the most prominent female film director in the studio system of the 1920s and 1930s, directing such stars as Howard's future girlfriend, Katharine Hepburn. Arzner later became one of the poster girls of the lesbian movement. In spite of the talent of this woman, whose cutting of the 1922 Valentino film, *Blood and Sand*, was hailed as brilliant, *Swell Hogan* could not be rescued.

In its newly edited version, Howard invited Rupert to come to the studio to see it. After sitting impatiently through the film, his uncle gave an immediate review. "It's nothing. No plot. No build up. No character development. The acting stinks. Destroy the film. If anybody sees it, you and that homo, Graves, will be the laughing stock of Hollywood. Before leaving the studio, Rupert warned Howard, "If you continue to make films, you'll squander the fortune my brother left you."

The next day Howard ordered the projectionist to destroy all footage, and *Swell Hogan*, regrettably, is lost to Hollywood history.

"I've spent enough on this shitty film," Howard told the projectionist. Amazingly, he was to spend even more. Noah Dietrich later found out that Howard had heard that producer Harry Cohn planned to use the sets of *Swell Hogan*, paid for by Howard, for another film he was going to shoot. Using sets left over from a previous film was common practice in those days.

Howard was determined that Cohn wasn't going to benefit from his misfortune. For three thousand dollars, Howard had all the sets destroyed at Universal Service Studios, where *Swell Hogan* had been shot.

Not surprisingly, the collapse of *Swell Hogan* came at the same time as the collapse of Howard's friendship with Ralph.

Ralph Graves survived the bad press on *Swell Hogan*, and continued to work in the film industry, in spite of having no acting talent, ending up in farewell performances in the 1949 version of *Batman and Robin* and also, made in the same year, *Joe Palooka in the Counterpunch*.

Santa Barbara, 1972

Interviewed at his Santa Barbara home in the early 1970s, Ralph Graves was deep into alcoholism, consuming more vodka in an afternoon than an average drinker could down in an entire week. Yet he was still able to articulate.

Even though he still called gay men "fairies," he also outed himself before that term became fashionable. Claiming he was "essentially a man for the ladies," he did admit that he'd had affairs with such notables as W. Somerset Maugham and Noël Coward.

Months later, in an interview with veteran reporter Anthony Slide, author of *Silent Players*, Ralph admitted to having had a homosexual affair with Mack Sennett in the early 1920s. "Mabel Normand was nowhere in sight when Mack and I lived together for two years. He wanted me every night. A lot of those famous womanizers of Hollywood in the Twenties and Thirties, including Mack, did it as a cover-up of their true feelings."

That remark led to the inevitable questions about Howard Hughes. "His reputation is that he bedded a lot of the most beautiful gals in Hollywood. It's also known to a few hundred people in the industry that he also bedded a lot of beautiful guys, too, including me. From the very beginning, I knew Howard was a homo. I was a great friend of the boy's father since I too was a Houstonian. Papa Hughes was definitely no fairy—I can swear by that. But he knew his son was a cocksucker."

Continuing to drink, Ralph admitted, "I hustled the kid, calling him the sucker with the money. I got him to finance *Swell Hogan*. It was a bomb. I brought the picture in for about fifty thousand dollars and pocketed another thirty for myself. I deserved it. Hell, I was the director and the star. If it had been a hit, Howard and I would have gone on to make other films together."

After the fifth hour, Ralph wanted to talk for several more days, claiming "I have a lot of stories to tell."

The next day, he didn't seem to want to talk much about Howard, but about Hollywood in general. "Speaking of fairies, did you know that D.W. Griffith had this thing for his juvenile lead, Bobby Harron? He liked me a lot in those days, too, and cast me in *Scarlet Days* and *The Greatest Question*. I also starred with Carol Dempster in *Dream Street* in 1921. D.W. would call me in to 'discuss script' but would spend more time kissing me than he did on script. Isn't it a hoot that the first film I ever made, back in 1918, was called *Men Who Have Made Love to Me*."

On the third day of interviewing, Ralph said, "You should be writing a book about me and early Hollywood—not about that faggot Hughes. I know where all the ghosts are buried. Take that dyke, Barbara Stanwyck. You name 'em. I've got dirt. Colleen Moore, Bessie Love, Blanche Sweet. Mabel Normand.

Frank Capra. Harry Cohn. Irving Thalberg. Mildred Harris...you know, Chaplin's bitch was having a three-way with Lillian and Dorothy Gish."

On a parting note, Ralph said, "One more thing about baby-faced Howard with the brown eyes. Even though I fucked him in more ways than one, he was quite gentlemanly about the end of our affair. He called my acting and directing in *Swell Hogan* ludicrous, but as a parting gift, he sent me a brand new Duesenberg. I never saw him again."

Ralph Graves died in obscurity on February 18, 1977, no doubt from drinking himself into the grave.

***

Los Angeles, 1925

In 1925 even the wildest of imaginations could not have predicted that the rather barren and badly equipped Mines Field in Inglewood would one day become the Los Angeles International Airport. It was here that Howard went every weekend to meet J.B. Alexander, one of California's most skilled pilots, who gave Howard flying lessons in his newly pur-

chased Waco aircraft. Alexander at one point told Noah Dietrich that Howard "can fly better than I can, but if he still wants to keep spending money on lessons, it's fine by me." Howard was paying Alexander one hundred dollars a day, although the pilot would have gladly done it for a twenty dollar bill.

Accompanied by his new friend, Douglas Fairbanks Jr., Howard attended the U.S. National Air Show one Sunday, watching daring army pilots perform death-defying stunts. One cocky pilot flew past the grandstand at an altitude of fifty feet— upside down. Many of the spectators screamed in horror.

Later Howard was introduced to the pilots, including the German ace, Ernst Udell, and the handsome, young American aviator, Charles A. Lindbergh.

The meeting of Howard Hughes Jr. and Charles Lindbergh, both of whom were destined to become the most famous aviators of the 20th century, went off uneventfully. "Lindy" extended his hand to Howard, who didn't shake it, complaining he'd injured his wrist. Actually, he was afraid of germs. Lindy just turned and walked away. Little did Howard know at the

Billie Dove

time that he would become more jealous of Charles A. Lindbergh than he
would be of any other man on the planet.

Married: Douglas Fairbanks, Jr.
and Joan Crawford

***

Arizona, 1925

In his Waco, Howard flew to
Arizona to visit Douglas Fairbanks Jr.
on the set of his latest film, *Wild Horse
Mesa*. It once again teamed him with
the beautiful Billie Dove, on whom
Doug had developed a very serious
crush. Not revealing it to Doug,
Howard had also developed a crush on
Billie. The actress was married at the
time to the director of the film, the
handsome but dreaded Irwin Willat, who over the years became known for his
psychotic outbursts.

On the set, Doug offered to introduce Howard to Billie and her husband, but
he declined, preferring to view her from afar, not knowing at the time what
important roles both Willat and Billie would play in his immediate future.

Bunking together in a dreary motor court, Doug confessed his "fear of flying" to Howard, telling of a traumatic experience he'd had while filming *The
Air Mail*, which also starred Billie Dove, along with Warner Baxter in the male
lead.

Only fourteen at the time, but looking mature for his age, Doug was called
upon by the director, who was also Willat, to make a parachute jump from a
mail plane. Although a stunt man could have been used, Doug bravely insisted
on doing the daring feat himself.

With a camera attached to the side of the pilot's cockpit, the flier was
instructed to clamp the joystick between his knees while he hand-cranked the
camera to film Doug's jump. Fighting fear at every dangerous step, Doug made
it through howling winds to the tip of the wing. Once there, he became paralyzed with fear and began to sob hysterically. "Thinking I was going to die, I
crawled back inch by inch into the cockpit, still crying my eyes out," Doug said.
"Willat was stone silent when we landed and called for my double. 'Your father
takes incredible risks in the making of his films,' Willat told me. 'You're nothing but a coward!'"

Even though he was the movie's director, Willat never spoke to Doug again
for the rest of the filming, but relayed instructions to him through an assistant.

128

"He must have hated it when I was assigned to him again," Doug said.

Howard didn't meet Billie Dove, but he was introduced to Zane Grey. *Wild Horse Mesa* was adapted for the screen from one of his novels, the best-selling books ever written about the old American West. Doug posed with Grey, Howard did not. He was more concerned with escaping temperatures that rose that day to 103 degrees F.

The next afternoon in the vicinity of the Painted Desert, Howard and Doug watched six young Navajo braves, clad only in breechclouts, with their waist-length black hair waving in the desert wind, race each other. It was a memorable sight and should have been captured on film, but wasn't.

Doug was mesmerized by the young braves going through a ritual their ancestors had performed long before the Europeans arrived to conquer the continent.

Howard was so impressed with the Navajos riding bareback that he vowed on the spot to make a Western one day.

And so he would.

***

Before flying back to Los Angeles, Howard had promised to be with Douglas Fairbanks, Jr., as soon as he returned from location. But Howard would never call him again. An invitation was waiting from Rupert that would lead to Howard meeting a new male friend who would make him forget all about Doug.

In his highly selective memoirs, *The Salad Days*, Doug mentions Howard but gives no indication of their brief emotional involvement. (As regards the reams of material that Doug left out of his memoirs, Brownell Davidson, a literary critic, defined *The Salad Days* as "the hors d'oeuvres, but not the main course.")

In his book, Doug states that he never invited Howard to one of the many parties that he and Joan hosted, and always resented Howard's "money will buy anything" attitude. One of the anecdotes related within the autobiography recites how, on a movie set, Doug learned that Howard had asked a third party if he could "get a date with Joan Crawford," even though she was married at the time to Doug. Doug claims that Howard, in his quiet Texas drawl, boasted that if she accepted, he might offer Joan a "very big present." Howard wasn't talking mink coats and jewelry this time, but was referring to the size of his penis.

Even after Joan Crawford had divorced Doug and was "dating and marrying other men," she would continually refuse Howard's requests for a date. When Billy Haines, her closest friend, asked why, she bluntly replied, "I adore homosexuals, but not in my bed after midnight."

Tired of the Ambassador Hotel and feeling cramped in the suite he shared with Ella, Howard ordered Dietrich to find a house to rent. Ella wanted to move to Pasadena, "where all the good and decent people live," but Howard refused.

As Dietrich searched for an acceptable house, Howard forged ahead with the formation of a movie corporation. Since he felt he was spending far too much money setting up corporations "and making lawyers rich," he took an existing subsidiary of Toolco (Caddo Rock Drill Company, which was based in Louisiana) and converted that into Caddo Productions. After Dietrich had set that up, Howard announced that he was now officially a motion picture producer and would start interviewing stars and reviewing scripts.

Madge Bellamy

Dietrich recalled that Howard was constantly getting into trouble with starlets, and that he kept his newly hired Los Angeles lawyer, Neil McCarthy, "busy putting out brushfires." The attorney was usually able to buy off these beautiful young women with a mink coat, perhaps sable, definitely some jewelry—diamonds or rubies, or a combination of both—and cash. "It was a town where money talked," Dietrich later said, "and at Toolco the green stuff sprouted up every day, with Howard controlling one hundred percent of the stock."

With his wife stashed in a hotel suite, Howard in quick succession embarked on three separate affairs—two with women who were among the most beautiful to appear on the silver screen in the Twenties, and the third with a young actor slated to become one of the biggest names in the history of Hollywood.

***

Before finding another man in his life to replace Doug, Howard first discovered a woman who had already been hailed in Hollywood—the feisty but incredibly lovely Madge Bellamy, a fellow Texan with brunette hair and big brown eyes, who was six years his senior. He met her at Pickfair.

She'd made her stage debut at the age of nine playing a slave in *Aïda* in a production staged in Denver. Her debut led to the arrest of the theater manager who was charged with violating child labor laws.

Arriving in Hollywood, she immediately earned a reputation as an actress who refused to "put out" for a role. She made that clear when Howard at the Pickfair dinner table started to flirt with her. "I'll go out with you, Mr. Hughes, but like a girl with a boy on a date—not as an actress trying to get a part in your next film."

When Howard first met her, Madge had scored her biggest hit in the 1922 silent film, *Lorna Doone*, which is perhaps the only reason she's still remembered today—that and for her appearance in John Ford's *The Iron Horse*.

Mary Pickford had personally chosen her to co-star with her brother, Jack, in the 1923 *Garrison's Finish*. Pickford and Madge were said to be sharing beauty secrets with each other and were frequently seen together when Fairbanks Sr. was engaged in various affairs with other stars. Pickford and Madge were, in fact, so close that Howard suspected lesbianism, which didn't bother him at all.

At the dinner table at Pickfair, Madge entertained the guests by telling them why she'd turned down the role of Esther in the MGM epic, *Ben-Hur*. "Too many horses," she informed an astonished Louis B. Mayer.

On their first date together, Madge seriously infuriated Howard with a remark for which he never forgave her. "I've heard you've already had *Ben-Hur*," she said, a reference to a brief affair he had had with Ramon Novarro. "Why not sample the actress who turned down the picture?"

She was the first actress to note Howard's paranoia, which would grow worse year by year. "He wouldn't sit out on my side porch overlooking the garden because he feared spies might be lurking there. He wouldn't talk personal things on the phone, because he said someone might be listening in. Several times when he was driving, he took a lot of diversionary tactics trying to shake off some car he said that was following us. I thought he was a bit crazy. Later on, I found out that men were actually following him around, although for what purpose I hadn't a clue. Maybe industrial spies. Perhaps Ella Rice had hired them for all I know. Howard was still a baby when I met him—a kid, really—but he had more problems than any middle-aged adult should have been saddled with."

Interviewed decades later when she was running a junkyard, having squandered all her money, Madge asked, "What red-blooded gal wouldn't have fallen for Howard Hughes? He was boyishly handsome—no, not that—he was gorgeous. He used to come over late at night to visit me at my *palazzo*." Amid her piles of rusting metal, Madge in a blonde curly wig evoked Bette Davis as she appeared in *Whatever Happened to Baby Jane?*

At the peak of her career, and long before falling on bad days, Madge lived in a building in Los Angeles known as "The Cedars," a *faux* replica of a Castilian castle.

"Our romance lasted for all of three weeks, maybe not even that long," Madge said. "He was breathing hot and heavy for me, but then, all of a sudden, I couldn't get him on the phone. Only later did I learn that that gold-digging bitch, Constance Bennett, had dug her scarlet-painted claws into him."

After Howard jilted her, Madge married a stockbroker, Logan Metcalf, in 1928, but four days later she demanded a divorce. "After Howard, Logan felt like a pin prick. I couldn't feel anything."

Logan Metcalf, at the time of her inaugural meeting with Howard, loomed in her future. But on the evening of her first meeting with Howard, she amused dinner guests at Pickfair with equivalent outrageous comments.

It's fortunate that Madge never married Howard after his divorce from Ella. Madge's reaction to lovers who strayed was violent. In 1943 she made headlines around the world when she shot her millionaire lover, A. Stanford Murphy, for jilting her. The two-timing Murphy survived his gunshot wound, and Madge got only five days in prison before she was placed on probation.

She died at the age of 89 on January 24, 1990 in Upland, California, having never completed her memoirs, first entitled *I Was Madge Bellamy* and later renamed *Darling of the Twenties*.

At the age of 87, Madge gave her final interview. "I always avoided romantic mush all my life and maybe missed out on the ultimate human experience. But then I've always been my own person, and how many of the bastards and floozies who sold themselves in Hollywood can say that?"

***

Houston, 1925

Howard put Ella back on the train to Houston in the fall of 1925. His excuse was that she was needed to prepare the Yoakum mansion in time for the Thanksgiving, Christmas, and New Year's holidays. Actually, he didn't care about any of those holidays. Instead, he perceived her presence in his life as too inhibiting.

Ella protested, but Howard won out in the end. Loaded with thirty-two trunks filled with the latest Paris *couture*, along with an assortment of furs, Ella arrived back in Houston and was welcomed home by Annette and Dr. Lummis.

The moment Ella walked into the Yoakum household, she realized that everything was in perfect shape. Howard's staff of servants had seen to that. There was nothing for her to do.

After only four nights, Ella left the gloomy house and went to stay with her sister, Libby Farish, in the posh residential section of River Oaks. Libby was well aware that Houstonian society was gossiping that Howard planned to divorce his wife. But as she made the social rounds, Ella held her head high. No one actually confronted her with these rumors.

At the approach of Thanksgiving, and still no Howard, Ella began to send telegrams, pleading with him to come back to Texas. He didn't actually answer any of these urgent messages, ordering Dietrich to draft a response. "What do you want me to say?" the bewildered Dietrich asked. "Oh, make up something," Howard said impatiently before heading out the door.

Thanksgiving came and went, and Ella still had no word from Howard. By December 21, she sent two cables. In one, she wrote: "I miss you something awful. Please come back. We'll make this marriage work."

Howard didn't even give that telegram to Dietrich for a response.

Facing Christmas Eve without Howard, Ella sent another urgent telegram. "Can't understand why I haven't heard from you. Am counting on you leaving L.A. tomorrow."

When Christmas Eve came and still no word from Howard, Ella sent him birthday wishes, not knowing he'd been born in September. "I'm thinking of you every minute. Happy Birthday!"

Howard not only didn't send Ella a Christmas gift, he forgot to have Dietrich deposit money into her bank account, which meant that she not only didn't have funds to give the servants presents, but she couldn't even pay their salaries.

Finally, on the day after Christmas, Howard cabled, "Still busy. No chance of leaving."

Ella didn't respond to Howard's latest delay, but his stern aunt, Annette, blasted off a reply. She could be very blunt and to the point. "You have a wife in Houston who needs you. Get home immediately!"

That did the trick. Howard sent word that he'd be arriving in Houston in time for New Year's. Unknown to Ella, he'd be accompanied by Dietrich and a new set of golf clubs, a gift from Constance Bennett.

As Dietrich would later recall, Howard hardly spoke to Ella when he arrived at the Yoakum mansion. "After all that time had passed, he didn't even embrace her," Dietrich said, "and she looked stunning. Beautifully dressed and made up. Any man would be proud to possess her."

Ella had accepted invitations for them to attend a number of end-of-the-year society parties, to which she asked Howard to accompany her. "He did-n't say no, but he didn't say yes either," Dietrich said. He suspected that Ella wanted to arrive with Howard on her arm to show Houstonians that her marriage was still intact.

Annette later claimed that Howard never went to one party. When Ella did go, she was accompanied by her sister.

Avoiding the Toolco offices, Howard spent every day at the Houston Country Club.

"Howard's return to Houston wasn't a conjugal visit," Dietrich claimed. Howard had a bed placed in the same wood-paneled library

Constance Bennett

where his father's funeral services had been conducted. He also ordered a locksmith to put a lock on the door. Howard was given the only key. Even the servants weren't allowed in to clean the room.

***

Los Angeles, 1926

Billy Haines had made three friends while appearing in *Sally, Irene and Mary*: Joan Crawford, whom he'd nicknamed "Cranberry," the beautiful Constance Bennett, and the film's director, Edmund Goulding. Billy was eager to share all three of "my new delights" with Howard.

Only Crawford balked, perhaps having already heard rumors about Doug Fairbanks Jr. (her future husband) and Howard. Goulding was most eager to invite Howard to one of his parties, the most notorious in Hollywood. Constance Bennett pronounced Howard "the man of my dreams" before even meeting the rich Texan.

Constance and Billy Haines eventually become lifelong friends. Constance bluntly told the homosexual actor: "I want to marry a millionaire, and Howard Hughes, Jr. is the one." When Billy said, "He's already married," she informed him, "Darling, everybody's married at some time or the other, even me. Marriage means nothing. A contract meant to be broken. Otherwise, why would there be divorce courts? Now, be a lamb and set up a meeting with this cowboy. I'll house-break him."

At least a year older than Howard (Constance would never admit her real age), she was a sophisticated New Yorker. She was the oldest of three daughters of Richard Bennett, an old-fashioned stage trouper whose acting style was often compared to John Barrymore's. Constance's sister, Joan Bennett, would eventually eclipse her older sister's fame as a movie star.

Spoiled and headstrong, Constance specialized in glamour, with her strong jaw—inherited from her father—her high cheekbones, and large eyes called "china blue" in the fan magazines. Arguably, she was the best dressed woman in Hollywood—a real fashion plate, characterized by her marcelled blonde bob.

At the time Howard met her, she'd just completed nine films, all within one year, and was at the peak of her career. In ways that evoked the character she'd played in *Sally, Irene and Mary*, Constance was seeking a sugar daddy. But he didn't have to be old, like most sugar daddies. A millionaire her own age would do just fine.

Howard didn't have to pursue Constance. She chased after him. Soon they were seen at all the major parties in Hollywood. When anyone asked Howard where his wife was, he always claimed she was indisposed that evening. Actually, she was in fine health, sitting alone at the Ambassador Hotel with a closet filled with the latest Parisian fashions, begging Howard to take her out. He had allowed her to return to Los Angeles in January of 1926.

To explain why he was out with Constance, he said that he was considering putting her under contract to be the star of his next three films. Secretly, he would have preferred to be with Billie Dove, instead of Constance, but Billie would have to wait for a more opportune time.

On their first date, Howard took Constance to an afternoon tea dance at the Cocoanut Grove, right at the Ambassador Hotel where he lived. These dances were legendary for attracting Hollywood's most voracious wolves, promising movie contracts to the most shapely of the young hopefuls, male and female, who showed up here waiting to be discovered.

A long, leisurely dinner followed at the Brown Derby Restaurant, across from the Ambassador. Lines of autograph seekers waited patiently for hours to assault their favorites for signatures. When Howard showed up with Constance, "the dream of all shopgirls," a position she'd eventually have to relinquish to her rival, Joan Crawford, a near-riot ensued

At the time, none of those screaming girls knew who Howard Hughes was, and he was pushed aside. He later told Edmund Goulding, "One fat monster of a girl actually pushed me, shouting, 'Get out of my way—you're a nobody!'"

The very fact that Howard would escort Constance to such a swank and highly visible eatery as the Brown Derby was proof enough that he didn't even care about his marriage to Ella anymore. He did have some rationale, however, for being seen with almost any Hollywood beauty, married or not. He was the head of a new film production studio, and he planned to make movies and cast beautiful women in the roles. All his "dates," at least according to Howard, were "for business purposes only."

Howard related the story of Constance's seduction of him to Billy. Significantly, he called it her seduction of him instead of his seduction of her.

Dietrich had looked at almost thirty rental properties in the Greater Los Angeles area before deciding on an elegant mansion in the Hollywood Hills that he thought would be suitable for Ella and Howard.

That afternoon he'd given Howard the key after Howard had announced that he wanted to inspect the property after dark, because the nighttime view over the city was spectacular. But instead of his wife, he invited Constance to look at the property with him.

Howard was notorious for always losing his keys. Back in Houston, Annette Lummis remembered having to pay for glass in French doors every week. Forgetting his key, Howard would frequently break the windows of the doors to gain entrance.

At the Hollywood mansion, he realized that he had once again forgotten the appropriate key. Picking up a rock from the flower garden, he smashed his way into the property. Taking Constance Bennett by the hand, he entered the large living room where the oak antiques were covered in white sheeting. With the full moon streaming in, the property had a ghostly look.

Howard took Constance in his arms and kissed her deeply. He managed to remove her silk gown and all of her lingerie while still fully clothed himself. "Take off every stitch!" she ordered. He removed his clothing and stood tall, gangly and naked before her.

"The wristwatch, too," she commanded. Dudley had given him the wristwatch in Paris and he'd worn it ever since, even though some men at the time considered wristwatches on men effeminate.

As he mounted her, she sunk her teeth into his lower lip as his weight came down on her.

"Fuck Gilbert Roland out of me!" she shouted.

He knew he was hard of hearing, but her words baffled him. Who…? Wha…?

"My last lover, you bastard! Ride me cowboy, or else I'll tear that big thing off you." She clawed into his back, drawing blood, locking her legs around him. Fearing her teeth would sink into his throat, he locked his chin against his chest.

"I rode her from one end of the room and back again," he later confided to Billy. "If I hadn't, I truly believe that she would have killed me."

When it was over, she said, "I came again and again. No one has ever given me so many orgasms."

"What are you talking about?" he demanded to know. "Only men can have an orgasm."

"Don't they teach you little boys anything down in Texas?" she asked, rising from the floor and standing by the large windows overlooking the garden, as the moon illuminated her ravished body. "You're still a greenhorn, boy." She burst into laughter.

He was humiliated.

Incidentally, Howard never rented the house of seduction. He turned it down, telling Dietrich, "It's too gloomy."

***

Feeling he'd been mocked during his lovemaking with Constance, Howard set out to improve his technique and to learn more about women. Barbara LaMarr obviously hadn't taught him everything he needed to know.

He approached the subject scientifically, the way he'd go about equipping an airplane for an around-the-world flight in years to come.

He wisely figured out that the best place to improve his technique was Maude's House. The unofficial name of this bordello, with its red-velvet upholstery, four-poster beds draped in lace, and scarlet-colored wallpaper, was "The House of a Thousand and One Delights."

Many of the top male stars of the era went there secretly. Maude, a large, buxom lesbian, had a specialty: she hired young women who were look-alikes of the leading stars of silent pictures: Marion Davies, Gloria Swanson, Pola

Negri, Mae Murray, Colleen Moore, Eleanor Boardman, and, yes, Constance Bennett.

An obvious choice for Howard would have been the Constance Bennett carbon copy. But he delayed seducing her until he'd learned all the tricks that could be taught him from the other "inmates." By the time he bedded "Constance Bennett," he was a more skilled lover. After that, the real Constance Bennett began to tell her friends that Howard's love-making had improved considerably, crediting herself as the cause of that.

During their brief courtship, the stunningly beautiful Constance and the strikingly handsome Howard were true Jazz Age Babies, hitting the hot spots and dancing the nights away at Montmartre or the Cocoanut Grove. Louella Parsons and others spread the word that Howard would soon announce his divorce from Ella Rice to marry Constance, who proudly showed off jewelry Howard had given her. Rupert cautioned Howard that he had to be more discreet, because he was giving Ella dangerous ammunition to use against him in their eventual divorce.

Howard told Rupert, Noah Dietrich, Billy Haines and others, that he had no intention of divorcing Ella. "A wife's a pain in the ass," he always said, "but I find it convenient to have one stashed away somewhere."

His obvious reason in saying that was because a bona-fide wife protected him from gold-diggers, of which Constance was the major prospector. Constance urged him to file for divorce. Or, as she put it to her sister, Joan Bennett, "I told him to pay the Texas cow off and send her back to the Houston stockyards."

At one point during their whirlwind romance, Constance and Howard attended an orgy. When Edmund Goulding had directed Constance in *Sally, Irene and Mary*, she'd learned that Goulding invited both men and women to participate in his all-night debaucheries, which had become one of the leading scandals of Hollywood.

Paul Bern, various movie stars such as John Gilbert, and the best-looking men and women at various studios—especially MGM—attended these orgies where women with women could be seen making love—men with men, even women and men. Bern himself never participated, as he was always the voyeur. That night Constance and Howard were also voyeurs, attending the sex romp like "sightseers."

The host of the all-night orgy, Edmund Goulding, was born near London, the son of a butcher, in the twilight of the Victorian era. In addition to being a director, he was also an actor, playwright, novelist, singer, composer, and screenwriter. On the night Constance, with Howard on her arm, arrived at Goulding's spacious house, he was dressed as a stern British nanny. At these events, Goulding was always willing to deliver corporal punishment for those in need of his services. He was fond of saying, "You don't sodomize an ass until you've spanked it red."

In Hollywood, Goulding was known as a great woman's director before the advent of George Cukor, who eventually would strip him of the title. During a chat with Constance and Howard, Goulding said, "On the screen I specialize in tasteful, cultured dramas. Off-screen, my specialties are promiscuity and voyeurism." Appraising Howard from head to toe, he said, "I hear you're going to become a producer. Before you buy any other furniture for your new office, purchase a casting couch. And, remember, a boy or girl can't be too young. Not too long ago fourteen-year-old boys were taking a bride and heading West to tame the wilderness."

Goulding introduced John Barrymore to Howard. Although it was not his usual custom, Howard lost his steely self-control and shook the hand of The Great Profile. As he later said laughingly to Goulding and Constance, "It was better than shaking something else." At the time, Barrymore was completely nude. He had nothing to say to Howard, his attention diverted to two beautiful young starlets on Goulding's lavish sofa.

When Constance went "to powder my nose," Howard encountered his sometimes friend, Ramon Novarro. This former nude model at a Los Angeles art school informed Howard that he was going to allow himself to be auctioned off that night in the nude. "Wait till Louis B. Mayer hears what his *Ben-Hur* is up to," Howard told him.

"I want the world to see my body," Novarro said. "After all, I'm prettier than any woman in Hollywood. One reviewer said that I'm too beautiful to be taken seriously."

"That's not a compliment," Howard warned him.

"My hour has come," Novarro said. "I represent sexual ambiguity on the screen."

Later in the evening when Novarro's nude body was auctioned off, bidding was low. Secretly, through Goulding, Howard raised the ante to five hundred dollars, which brought loud clapping from the audience. Later, Novarro was terribly disappointed when the highest bidder did not come forward to claim his body. Not knowing that Howard had been the actual bidder, Novarro complained to him. In response, Howard replied, "Oh, Ramon, put on your clothes and go home."

At these orgies, Goulding supplied the handsome hunks, rounded up at various studios, but Mickey Neilan often rounded up most of the beautiful young women. "Mickey didn't mind putting on a show at these parties," Billy Haines recalled. "He was a real exhibitionist, like Barrymore and Ramon. A true rake like the type who flourished in the 18th century. He would often say to a starlet, 'Wouldn't you like to find out about the secret weapon that drives Gloria Swanson and Blanche Sweet crazy?'"

Howard was delighted to encounter Mickey again, whom he hadn't seen since Paris, in spite of the director's attempts to get in touch with Howard through Noah Dietrich.

In this most unlikely of settings, as Howard sat with a clothed Mickey watching two young starlets make love, the director pitched his latest screen treatment. Maybe Howard's judgment was clouded, or else he was too diverted by the scene taking place only feet from him, but before the two women approached a "thunderous orgasm," Howard purchased the script of *Everybody's Acting*, agreeing to hire Mickey as director.

A week or two after the orgy, Adela Rogers St. Johns, the columnist, knew all the details about it, as she had a pipeline to every sewer in Hollywood. Goulding's orgies were events she could never report on, however. Through one of her contacts, the exact source not remembered, St. Johns learned what to her was an even more tantalizing bit of information about Howard. Somehow she found out that he was visiting Maude's at least four times a week, where he would request the services of "Constance Bennett."

Encountering the real Constance at a party thrown by Norma Talmadge, St. Johns could not keep this juicy tidbit to herself. The journalist told the movie queen the truth about Howard.

"Constance went almost insane," St. Johns recalled from her nursing home in Arroyo Grande, California, decades later.

That same night as the Talmadge party, which Howard for some reason did not attend, Constance confronted him later when he paid a midnight visit to her residence. Although he wasn't there, Dietrich later reported that it turned into "the battle of the century."

Enraged, Constance threw a vase at Howard, injuring the left side of his face. This was eerily reminiscent of a violent future assault Howard would suffer from another movie queen: Ava Gardner.

"When you could have had me, you turned to a fucking substitute," Constance is alleged to have screamed at Howard.

It was all too much for her. She left Howard that night, but didn't give up her pursuit of a gold-plated millionaire.

Only weeks later, she found what she'd been looking for in the person of Phillip Plant, heir to a steamship and railroad fortune. During their brief marriage, Constance became "the darling of Continental society." Howard made attempts to resume their relationship, but she rebuffed him.

Later, trapped in a loveless marriage, Constance divorced Plant but not until "he left me with a fortune—I'm fixed for life," as she told St. Johns. Returning to pictures, she pursued another married rich man, Joseph Kennedy, when he wasn't dating Gloria Swanson. When Swanson was with Kennedy, Constance went after her husband, Henri Marquis de la Falaise de la Coudray, and eventually won this dubious gigolo prize.

As for Howard, he still paid visits to Maude's. But one night he dumped "Constance Bennett" for a much hotter number. Maude assured Howard, "I've tried this filly out myself." She ushered Howard into her best private room, where on the bed lay the woman of his dreams and the actress called "the world's most beautiful."

It was "Miss Billie Dove" herself, or at least in Howard's appraisal, "the best damn look-alike I've ever seen. My God, it has to be Billie's twin sister."

***

For the cast of his comedy, *Everybody's Acting*, Mickey Neilan assembled a rather lackluster cast: Betty Bronson, Ford Sterling, Louise Dresser, and Henry B. Walthall.

The plot spun around five bachelors, all of them actors, who adopt an orphaned baby girl who grows into a beautiful young woman as played by Betty Bronson. For his services, Howard paid Mickey $20,000, and the film was budgeted at $150,000, eventually making a $75,000 profit when it was released by Adolph Zukor and Jesse Lasky under the banner of Paramount.

A deal with Louis B. Mayer was out of the question, because the MGM chief hated Mickey's guts, ever since he'd loudly said, "Oh, shit!" in the middle of Mayer's lengthy speech to studio workers. Along with most of the cast of *Tess of the D'Urbervilles*, Mickey had stormed out of the auditorium that day, loudly proclaiming, "I've got a picture to make." Mayer never forgave him and had even gone so far as to call Howard, warning him not to hire Mickey. As a harbinger of what was to come in his future battles with the Hollywood elite, Howard slammed down the phone on the powerful studio czar.

Unlike his behavior during the filming of his later movies, Howard did not interfere in production, adopting a hands-off policy instead. "But he watched us like a bird of prey about to devour a fat canary," Betty Bronson later recalled in her retirement in Altadena, California. "He was taking in every move on the set with a clinical eye. I know that all the ladies in Hollywood were crazy about him, but I found him frightening. It wasn't like he was just learning about filmmaking. It was like he was stealing Mickey's directorial brains for himself."

Critics dismissed *Everybody's Acting* as a piece of insignificant fluff, but Howard was content that it made a profit, which he gleefully reported to Rupert. His uncle neither condemned the film, nor congratulated Howard. Obviously jealous of his nephew, Rupert was far more interested in touting his own success. At some point he invited Howard to the studio where *The Winning of Barbara Worth*, directed by Henry King, was being shot. Rupert's official position, as later listed in the credits for that movie, was "titler."

"I want you to see how a real movie is made!" Rupert told his nephew.

***

In marked contrast to the low-budget nature of Howard's film, the western, *The Winning of Barbara Worth*, had been acquired by Samuel Goldwyn for $125,000. As a novel, written by Harold Bell Wright, it had sold an astonishing three million copies. It was the epic tale of the reclamation of the Imperial Valley by harnessing the Colorado River.

Most of the film was to be shot on location in what was becoming the town of Barbara Worth, Nevada, in the midst of Black Rock Desert, where daytime temperatures hovered around 100 degrees F. On one occasion, the thermometer reached 130 degrees F, although temperatures dropped to freezing that night.

The female star of the film was Vilma Banky, Samuel Goldwyn's exotic hothouse flower, who spoke in a grating blend of pidgin English and "back street Budapest." When she didn't open her mouth, she vied with Billie Dove for the title of most beautiful actress on the silver screen.

Gary Cooper

The director, Henry King, was shooting interiors in the studio as outdoor sets were being completed in Nevada. Rupert excused himself to talk to King.

At that point, Howard spotted Rod St. Just, his photographer friend. Rod was racing with two cups of coffee to a dressing room and invited Howard to come along with him "to meet my new discovery."

Within the privacy of the dressing room, an extraordinarily handsome young man of twenty-four stood up, towering one inch over Howard, and extended his broad hand. "Name's Frank Cooper. But these Hollywood boys have changed it to Gary Cooper. I recognize you from your pictures in the paper. You're Howard Hughes, that rich guy from Texas."

As Rod could obviously see, Howard was a bit mesmerized by this rugged young actor who wore blue jeans but no shirt. He had chiseled if irregular features under a mop of dark brown hair and was decidedly macho before that term had come into vogue. Soft-spoken, he was trim and leggy. His piercing blue eyes bore in on Howard's brown ones. As Rod later noted, "Howard held Gary's hand a little longer than most. Hell, what am I saying. It was a triumph to get Howard to shake anybody's hand. So I assumed Howard didn't mind getting germs from Gary."

Howard looked on as Rod, who was also a make-up artist, took a tube of lipstick and painted a scarlet Cupid's bow mouth on Gary.

Such a mouth would have been more appropriate on MGM screen goddess Mae Murray, and even then it had become old-fashioned, mocked by many directors, especially Erich von Stroheim. Rod then applied heavy eye shadow to Gary, before taking a tube of hair cream and plastering down his dark brown hair like some Valentino clone.

"Hey, what are you doing to this man of the Old West?" Howard asked, not disguising his horror.

141

"The studio wants me to make him look like Valentino," Gary said. "He's dead and the studios are looking for a replacement for a new round of Sheik roles."

Howard told Rod how ridiculous that was. Nonetheless, Howard accompanied Gary and Rod to the site of the photo shoot. Assuming a Valentino mask, Gary posed with half-drooping eyelids.

During the shoot, Gary informed Howard that he'd been cast as a dispatch rider, Abe Lee, in the Barbara Worth film. The role had originally been awarded to actor Harold Goodwin, but he couldn't make it, having been delayed in the filming of *The Honeymoon Express*, directed by Ernst Lubitsch.

The producer, Samuel Goldwyn, had been reluctant to give the role to an inexperienced actor like Gary. But the Montana-born actor won the part by default.

"I told Henry King I'd give my left ball for the part," Gary said. "He told me he'd give me the part and let me hang on to my balls at the same time." He winked at Howard. "King seems to think I'll need both my balls in Hollywood."

Rod told Howard that the plot calls for him to die in Ronald Colman's arms. "I told that British fluff that if he decides to kiss me, no tongue!" Gary said with a smile. He confessed, "I'd much rather do the scene with Vilma Banky. I think I've fallen in love with her."

"Forget it!" Rod warned him. "I've told you she's a lesbian."

"I could convert her," Gary boasted. "I've already slept with her husband-to-be. Why not the wife?"

Howard looked astonished. "Who is this husband to be?"

"Rod La Rocque," Rod said. "Yes, Hollywood has two Rods. But he's a star and makes all the money."

"You'll meet the other Rod later," Gary said.

"Only if I have to," Howard replied.

After the shoot, Rupert appeared with Frances Marion, the resident screenwriter on the set of *Barbara Worth*. Drawing a salary of three thousand dollars a week, she was the highest paid screenwriter in Hollywood and the most famous. Noticing Gary, she remarked to Howard. "That's my kind of man. He could walk through a market and start all the melons vibrating."

After they'd gone, Howard stood alone on the set. On the way back to the dressing room, Gary stopped by and handed him a piece of paper with his telephone number on it. "I'm free tonight. I've made this screen test and I want you to see it. It cost me sixty-five dollars. Every last plug nickel I had."

"I'm not free tonight, but I'll cancel what I had planned. I'd like to see your screen test."

When Gary had gone to the dressing room, Rod came up to Howard, who reported the invitation.

"Go for it!" Rod urged. "You're in for the biggest surprise of your life.

142

Gary's called The Montana Mule."

"I don't know," Howard said cautiously. "Our bodies are too similar. It might not work."

"You won't find a better lover or any male in Hollywood more beautiful."

"Perhaps," Howard said, still unsure. "I don't know if we'll hit it off."

"Gary is utterly charming," Rod said. "And he'll drop his pants for anybody in Hollywood, male or female, who he thinks is loaded. That Montana cowpoke loves money, and especially loves people who are rich. Go for it and call me tomorrow and tell me every detail, regardless of how sordid."

***

Rod St. Just would eventually arrive at some conclusions about the relationship of Howard Hughes and Gary Cooper based on what both parties told him: Over dinner at the Ship Café, Howard learned that Rod La Rocque had been supporting Gary financially, but that they had conflicted recently because La Rocque had refused to buy him a car, which Gary badly needed.

According to Gary, as related to Rod St. Just, the upcoming union between Rod La Rocque and Vilma Banky would be purely a marriage of convenience. After the wedding, La Rocque would discreetly continue to date boys, and Vilma would be free to pursue her lesbian lady friends.

Howard had made it a point to review a copy of Gary's one-minute screen test. Over dinner, Howard congratulated Gary on how well he photographed, which was true, but later, he complained to Rod St. Just that the screen test was "dull and dreary, and he's wearing too many cosmetics."

The short movie clip shows Gary riding a tired steed down the wide main street of a western town, eerily evoking a setting from his future classic, *High Noon*. Gary quickly dismounts by jumping off the horse. He then removes his ten-gallon Stetson and wipes his brow, as his face turns to the camera, his mouth widening into a shit-eating grin. He turns to let the camera capture first his left and then his right profile.

Gary Cooper eventually became known throughout America as a man of few words, but over dinner at the Ship Café, Howard found him talkative and amusing. Gary told him that he'd appeared briefly with Lightnin', the Super Dog, in *Lightnin' Wins*. At the time, Lightnin' was the screen rival of Rin-Tin-Tin. Howard also learned that originally Gary wanted to be a cartoonist, not an actor. At one time, to earn badly needed money, he worked as a baby photographer, going around his home town of Helena, Montana, in the dead of a frigid winter, asking housewives if he could take pictures "of their brats."

Gary's inaugural movie roles weren't particularly auspicious: When he appeared briefly in a by now largely-forgotten film, *Tricks*, the director said he looked like a string bean and made him wear five extra shirts so he wouldn't look so skinny. In another flick, he had to catch cowboy star Tom Mix as he fell off a horse. The following week, on another picture, he got to pet Rin-Tin-Tin.

According to Rod St Just, Gary met Rod La Rocque one night while both he and La Rocque were cruising a pick-up park in downtown Los Angeles. In a description by Gary that was later reported by Rod St Just, "You not only get to bring a guy home for sex, but you get to experience the thrill that he might murder you at any minute."

Rod St Just later complained that neither of the players ever related many details about what happened on the night of Howard's first date with Gary Cooper. "But then some very interesting things happened very suddenly. In almost no time at all, Gary told Rod La Rocque that he didn't need any more of his money. Then he moved into an apartment that had been arranged and paid for by Howard through Noah Dietrich. Then, Gary got his car, a brand-new roadster the color of butternut squash that Howard said reminded him of the color of the plains of Montana. Soon after retrieving the car, Gary disappeared for a few days, revealing later that he'd stayed at a beach house in Santa Monica that Howard had rented for the week."

As the years passed, both Gary and Howard would each have many other lovers, mainly women. But according to Rod St Just, a bond was formed between them at that beach house in Santa Monica that would last for another three years until suddenly they seemed to tire of each other.

Dozens of biographies and books on Hollywood have taken note of the persistent rumors that Gary Cooper had a sugar daddy during his lean early days in Hollywood. Some rumors claimed that Gary's benefactor was a shipbuilder with a mansion outside San Diego. Other rumors credited him with being an important movie producer, or perhaps a famous actor of the silent screen, with suspicion centering on John Gilbert. It was even gossiped about that Gary Cooper's man of mystery was a prince of one of the royal families of Europe, exiled to America because of his homosexuality.

But based on what both Howard and Gary had told him, Rod St. Just and a few other Hollywood insiders would arrive at the conclusion that Gary's benefactor was younger than Gary himself:

It was Howard Hughes, Jr.

CHAPTER SIX
Los Angeles, 1927

At last Noah Dietrich came up with a home that Howard found suitable. It was a mansion at 211 Muirfield Drive in the exclusive Hancock Park section of Los Angeles. Ella continued to hold out for Pasadena, "where my true friends are," but Howard turned a deaf ear to her request. That deaf ear was both symbolic and real, since he had noted even more deterioration in his hearing during the previous months.

The thing that most appealed to Howard was that the house abutted the Wilshire Country Club. Regardless of his schedule, he was still determined to become the world's greatest golfer. "His playing was fantastic," Dietrich later recalled. "I mean, he was really good. But regardless of how well he played, he always heard of a championship golfer who was even better. Howard was just too distracted to put in the training needed to become the world's leading golfer."

A widow, Eva K.J. Fudger, wanted a thousand dollars a month rent—a staggering sum in those days—for the house. When Hughes showed up at her door, looking disheveled and unshaven from having been up all night, she was horrified. She later told Dietrich that his client looked like a hobo.

She'd never heard of Howard and his tool company. Before she'd trust him to live in her house with its antiques and art objects, she demanded that he pay her six-thousand dollars in advance, thinking that he would not be able to come up with the money. He did and moved in with Ella as the widow moved out.

Much later, Howard would order Dietrich to purchase the Spanish mission style house. The widow wanted $115,000 for the house and $35,000 for the furnishings. When Dietrich pleaded for more time to negotiate, Howard demanded that he wanted the house now. Even though Dietrich protested, he agreed to carry out the commands of his boss. "That widow made a killing," Dietrich said. Years later, when Howard sold the house, it brought only $60,000.

Ella told her friends that she wanted to have an heir for the Hughes fortune. She hoped that the birth of a son would rein in Howard. But when Howard locked himself off in a separate wing, and never came to her brocaded chamber, she knew how impossible that would be.

For his own private quarters, Howard chose the elegant study that opened onto the gardens in back. The room had a private entrance so he could come and go without any of the servants in the main house seeing him. Ella took the master bedroom on the second floor.

Howard almost never spoke to Ella during her stay at Muirfield. If she gave a dinner party for her friends from Pasadena, he would deliberately occupy himself that night in another part of town. Sometimes she would go out on the golf course to see if he were all right, but he'd order her off the greens, charging that "you're ruining my game."

Dietrich estimated that Howard took Ella out only three times after they moved into Muirfield. Each occasion was to a Hollywood party.

A popular actor of the time, Ben Lyon, invited "Mr. and Mrs. Howard R. Hughes Jr.," and was amazed when the invitation to his Santa Monica beach house was accepted. Lyon, a soft-spoken and handsome actor from Atlanta, Georgia, was four years older than Howard and had been appearing in films since 1918. Within three short years, he would marry and form a lifelong association with one of the leading vamps of the silent screen, Bebe Daniels.

But when Howard met Ben, he was playing the field. Howard was impressed with his rumored list of seductions, such legendary names of stage and screen as Jeanne Eagels, Pola Negri, Gloria Swanson, and Big Howard's former mistress, Eleanor Boardman. He also was said to have had affairs with Howard's former flames, Blanche Sweet and Barbara LaMarr. At the time Howard met him, Ben was having an affair with Mary Astor—"a terrific actress. You've just got to cast her as the lead in your next film."

Amazingly, Howard took the advice of his new acquaintance. At the time Howard met Ben, he was starring in *For the Love of Mike*, which turned out to be Claudette Colbert's only silent movie.

"I had been wanting to get cast in one of Howard's films—and I would eventually—so I invited him to my party hoping to suck up," Ben recalled years later when he was appearing in London. "I didn't think he would show up at my Santa Monica beach house, but, surprise of surprise, he did. I think he was impressed with my reputation as the Lothario of Hollywood."

Ben claimed, "We hit it off beautifully right from the beginning. His wife, Ella, was very shy and retiring. She appeared well-mannered and well brought up, and she was definitely the best dressed woman there, with the most expensive jewelry, although there were a lot of big stars in attendance, like Aileen Pringle, May McAvoy, and Lois Wilson. I'd invited Billie Dove, but she canceled on me at the last minute. Otherwise, Howard would have met Billie Dove long before he actually did."

"If I recall, and I do, Howard spent most of the evening talking to me," Ben said. "We became fast friends. When I married Bebe in June of 1930, Howard was one of the ushers. Can you imagine? It was probably the only time Howard was a damn usher in his entire life. If I'd been smart, I would have made him my best man."

"My friendship with Howard began the very next day," Ben said. "He called me and invited me for a game of golf at the Wilshire Country Club. Later we had lunch. Then he took me over to a small house he'd rented a block from his mansion in Hancock Park. He called it Angelo, and I soon figured out it was a lovers' hideaway. Howard just bluntly asked me if I could arrange a few private parties for him at Angelo. In those days, I had more girls than I could shake a stick at, and I gladly volunteered. I guess you might say I became a pimp for him. I thought he'd be great for my career."

In Howard's first weeks at Angelo, it wasn't a parade of Hollywood beauties seen going in and out of Angelo, but a tall and lean actor, Gary Cooper. He was making an aerial picture called *Wings*, and he wanted Howard to come and look at it being shot, since he was so interested in aviation.

Not knowing at the time that it would change his life, Howard accepted the invitation to visit the set of *Wings*.

***

Wings billed itself as "a drama of the skies," and it became the first ever Oscar winner for best picture. A Paramount release, it starred Clara Bow, with whom Gary Cooper had launched a tumultuous affair. The co-stars were two "incredibly handsome" actors, Richard Arlen and Charles (Buddy) Rogers, who would go on to marry Mary Pickford.

In the film, Buddy and Richard vie for the hand of the same young woman, as played by Jobyna Ralston. Richard won out in real life, as he married her after the picture was wrapped.

Clara Bow was cast as the girl-next-door who joins the medical corps as an ambulance driver. She hated the part, claiming it was "a man's picture and I'm just the whipped cream on top of the pie."

Gary had given Howard a copy of the script, which he'd read. He wasn't impressed, finding the human drama "sudsy." He told Gary that he really was interested in seeing how the director would stage the scenes of aerial combat.

Howard Hughes was an original, but if he had a role model for the next two or three years, it was William Wellman, the twenty-nine-year old rookie director of the two-million dollar epic, the most expensive picture Paramount had ever made. "Wild Bill," as he was called, was a Hollywood maverick.

In 1917, he'd joined the French Foreign Legion, where he'd learned to fly, becoming an ace fighter pilot with the celebrated Lafayette Flying Corps. He survived a near-fatal airplane crash with injuries that left the limp he'd have for the rest of his life. As the years went by, he exaggerated that limp, claiming that it attracted women to his bed.

Making only $250 a week, the director had to marshal a cast and equipment that included 3,500 army personnel, 165 planes, and 65 pilots.

In 1970 in Los Angeles, five years before his death of leukemia, Wellman recalled his first meeting with Howard. "God damn it, I wasn't able to direct when he was on the set. He shot questions at me—really informed questions—

with such rapid fire that he tested the breadth of my knowledge about flying. At one point, he even pleaded with me to cast him as one of the pilot extras. Fool that I was, I turned him down. Maybe that's why he didn't ask me to direct his own epic, *Hell's Angels.*"

Wellman always took credit for the discovery of Gary Cooper. With a slight smirk on his face, he'd always say, "Actually Howard was the first man to discover Coop's hidden talents!"

He was directing Clara Bow around the time she became celebrated as "The *It* Girl." "Clara had *It*," Wellman said, "but Coop was definitely the *It boy.* He was like catnip to both men and women. I think he was born with *It.* In time, Gable with his big ears would have *It.* In spite of his lisp, Bogie had *It.* It takes chemistry and *It* to become a top star and make millions."

"On the other hand," Wellman continued, "Howard Hughes didn't have *It.* Handsome as the Devil and richer than God, this Texan lacked personality. With Howard, it was *Me! Me! Me!* He never gave of himself to anybody else, male or female. I felt he just expected me to teach him how to make a film about aviation. He seemed to think it was his divine right. I should have charged the fucker for my time!"

On the set of *Wings*, Gary went to enjoy a breakfast of beer and pretzels. Wellman then introduced Howard to Richard Arlen, who had been a pilot for the Canadian Royal Flying Corps during World War I.

Suddenly, just as they started to talk about flying, Brooklyn-born Clara Bow herself appeared. Wellman made the introductions, but Howard's eye was diverted to the menagerie of animals behind her. A fat black maid was trying to restrain seven chow dogs and a frisky monkey, each of the animals dyed a flaming red to match Clara's own hair.

Only when the animals settled down did Howard take in Clara Bow herself, whom the press was proclaiming both "the bee's knees" and "the cat's pajamas."

What he saw was a sexy tart with bobbed hair, saucer-like eyes, perky lips, and a personality so vivacious it made him nervous. "I hear you can take the snap out of a gal's garters," this jazz-age baby said to Howard.

"I understand we have something in common Miss Bow," Howard said. He obviously wasn't going to reveal that what they had in common was Gary Cooper.

"And what might that be?" Clara asked. "Certainly not bank accounts."

"We share the same attorney, Neil McCarthy," he said.

"Yeah, I just got a big bill from him," she said, "and don't know how I'm gonna pay it."

He looked her up and down, as if appraising livestock. "I'm sure you'll find a way. Neil told me that he got Paramount in your contract to relinquish its non-negotiable morals clause. Good thinking in your case!" He turned and walked away.

Wellman claimed that Clara was so furious she practically spat at Howard's back.

Taking all this turmoil in was a minor actress, Hedda Hopper, appearing in an uncredited part in *Wings*. She was storing up ammunition for the day when she'd become the second leading gossip maven of Hollywood.

Later in the day, Clara would tell her, "Gary's hung like a horse and he can go all night. I've named him Studs."

Gary's part in the picture lasted less than two minutes. He played veteran flier Cadet White, a tough flight instructor who is lecturing two green air cadets, Buddy and Richard. Gary dresses them down, telling them they need to show more guts if they want to fly the way he does. He appears in dusty infantry shoes, leggings, beat-up khakis, and leather flying helmet.

He's handed a Cadbury chocolate candy bar and takes a bite of it but tosses the remainder aside before gallantly leaving for a test flight. On the mission, he is killed. Wellman dramatically focuses the eye of the camera on the unfinished piece of candy.

Later Gary claimed that he was picking his nose during the scene and pleaded with Wellman to reshoot it. The director refused, claiming it was a perfect take. Later, Gary told Howard, "My fucking career is ruined."

Even after Gary was no longer needed on the picture, Howard remained fascinated by the filming of *Wings,* which took a full year to shoot in an era when a picture was often made in less than three weeks.

Without an invitation, Howard flew to Kelly Field, outside San Antonio, Texas, to watch the film being made. He learned that the War Department had lent millions of dollars worth of equipment and uniforms.

"Had I known the bastard was a spy," Wellman later said, "picking up valuable data for his own picture, I would have kicked him off my set."

Howard was mesmerized to see cameras attached to each plane to catch the action and was especially impressed that Wellman demanded clouds for the aerial combat scenes. Once, he waited eighteen days in a row for fluffy clouds to appear. In the months to come, Howard would wait much longer for those clouds during the shooting of *Hell's Angels*.

James Hall and Ben Lyon in
Hell's Angels

While sitting around waiting, the actors had plenty of time on their hands during their stay at the St. Anthony Hotel in San Antonio.

In his memoirs, Wellman claimed that the hotel "became the Armageddon of a magnificent sexual Donnybrook." He noted that by the time their hotel stay was over, a total of nine months, every one of the elevator operators was pregnant—"each and every one."

149

He also claimed that Clara did her part to keep the actors and crew entertained, enjoying dalliances not only with Richard and Buddy, but with director Victor Fleming, who was shooting a Western nearby. "And there must have been at least a dozen others," Wellman recalled in an interview. "Clara's excuse was that it took a dozen men to satisfy her now that Gary was out of the picture."

When at last *Wings* was released, Gary generated more fan mail than either Richard or Buddy. The actor himself was modest about his performance, claiming, "Some critics thought I gave my best performance as a piece of chocolate."

Back in Hollywood, Howard vowed that he would make a much more dramatic—"and hell of a lot better"—picture about aviators in aerial combat.

He ordered Noah Dietrich to start rounding up all the World War I footage that he could, depicting aerial combat. Locked away in his study at Muirfield, Howard would play this newsreel footage over and over. He told Dietrich, "I'm going to make the greatest aviation movie of all time, using my own money—and you're going to help me finance it with profits from Toolco."

"How much?" Dietrich asked.

"At least two million," Howard said.

"When Howard said two million," Dietrich recalled, "I knew that I could just double that figure" and get a more realistic account of the actual funds that would be needed.

In the meantime, Howard's Caddo Productions was going ahead with the job of churning out movies.

***

News reached Howard that the famous Moldova-born director, Lewis Milestone, was leaving Hollywood for self-imposed exile in Europe. The hot-tempered, feisty director had recently been fined $200,000 by the California courts in the wake of a lawsuit with Warner Brothers, which he had lost.

After learning that he had filed for bankruptcy Howard decided that here was a golden opportunity to snare a major director at a reasonable price. Within the week, he'd met with Milestone and had signed him to a three-year contract with Caddo pictures. The director's launch film was *Two Arabian Knights*.

An adventure comedy about World War I, it was a rip-off of director Raoul Walsh's highly successful *What Price Glory?*, which in 1926 had co-starred Victor McLaglen and Edmund Lowe as the memorable Sergeant Flagg and Captain Quirt. Howard even went so far as to hire James T. O'Donohue, one of the scenarists on *What Price Glory?*, to work on the script. Milestone "looked like he'd been run over with a steam-roller" when Howard presented him with a budget of $500,000 in a day when even first-class films were made for far less.

For the two battling American soldiers, Milestone cast the "incredibly handsome" William Boyd—later to become famous and rich playing Hopalong Cassidy—as Private W. Dangerfield Phelps. For his "almost poetically ugly" cohort—Milestone's words—the director cast German-born Louis Wolheim as Sergeant Peter McGaffney.

Years later, Milestone would once again cast Wolheim, this time as one of the stars of his legendary *All Quiet on the Western Front*. Wolheim died tragically shortly after the release of what was to become a classic film.

Escaping from a German prison, the American doughboys disguise themselves as Arabs and book passage on a ship sailing for Jaffa. The beautiful Mary Astor is improbably cast as Mirza, an Arab girl. Both men fall in love with her, and, as it turns out, she is the daughter of the Emir of

Louis Wolheim and William Boyd in
Two Arabian Knights

Jaffa, a role played by Michael Vavitch. A pre-*Frankenstein* Boris Karloff was cast as the purser.

With its completely improbable plot, *Two Arabian Knights* ended up with an Academy Award at the first-ever ceremonies held in the Blossom Room of the Hollywood Roosevelt Hotel on May 16, 1929. Milestone beat out Chaplin and won for best director for a comedy. Director Frank Borzage won for best director for drama because of his stewardship of *Seventh Heaven*. That was the only time there were two awards for director, one for comedy and the other for drama. In the future, these two categories would be combined into only one Oscar.

Although writer Ben Hecht still dubbed Howard "the sucker with the money," *Two Arabian Knights* went on to make more than $650,000. Howard was elated at this triumph over Rupert, who, in spite of all his films, had never won an Academy Award. "I'm no longer the rich kid playing around with movies," Howard told his uncle.

Later he confided to Milestone, "It was only because Rupert predicted my failure that I stayed in the business—just to show him." At this point in their relationship, Howard and his uncle were barely on speaking terms. The fight over Big Howard's estate had left permanent scars.

During the making of the film, Howard did not interfere with Milestone's direction but was a shadowy and silent presence on the set, hawk-eying every move the director made. Continuing that pattern, Howard did not interfere with Milestone's final cut of the film.

When he was finished, Milestone drove to Lake Arrowhead for some much needed rest and relaxation, Someone whose identity is unknown then confronted Milestone with the news that Howard was at the studio recutting his film. Abandoning his vacation, Milestone drove back to Los Angeles where he came raging back into the studio to find that Howard, with film all around him, was indeed re-editing *Two Arabian Knights.*

As co-producer John W. Considine Jr., later said, "You could hear Milestone's screams all the way back in the Ukraine."

In a "calm-down-Milly-ride," Howard invited the director for a spin in his Stanley Steamer. Milestone later recalled, "That god damn Texas fool went a hundred miles an hour with me no longer screaming about cutting the film, but with me begging for my life. Finally, I promised to calm down."

"Hughes came to an abrupt stop and nearly threw me through the windshield," Milestone claimed. "He carefully explained that my version of the film had already been shipped to New York for distribution. He said he was taking apart the film and going over it carefully because he wanted to learn how the final version of a movie was put together. It was a self-taught classroom—nothing more."

With the success of *Two Arabian Knights*, Howard launched production plans for "the mother of all pictures," to be known as *Hell's Angels.* Since it would take so long for this picture about World War I aviators, evocative of *Wings*, to come to the screen, he would also produce other films in the meantime.

Howard would later deny it, but Rupert practically on his deathbed was still claiming that the original idea and plot for the picture was his. The proposed scenario had been pitched to Howard when Rupert at the time was promoting the handsome young Texan as a potential matinee idol.

For the rest of his life, Rupert would proclaim that *Hell's Angels* was the "picture my bastard nephew stole from me with the same cold heart he robbed my parents of my brother's bequest to them."

There is a trio of films that won the Academy Award that cannot be viewed today, including *Two Arabian Knights*. Two of them (*The Way of All Flesh*—best actor—and *The Patriot*—best screenplay) are believed to have been lost, probably forever. *Two Arabian Knights,* however, does exist and is owned by the Howard Hughes Estate, which has not made it available. It is said to be housed "in a hidden location," gathering dust.

***

Woodland Hills, California, 1985

Mary Astor in her autobiographical *My Story* is a bit off in recalling Howard's film career, writing that *Two Arabian Knights* was his first venture into film-making. Because Howard was earning a reputation as a seducer of beautiful women, word quickly spread along Hollywood and Vine that Howard and Mary Astor were having a torrid affair. As a WAMPAS Baby Star and beauty contest winner at the age of fourteen, Mary would have certainly qualified as an ample sexual challenge for Howard.

In 1985 at the Motion Picture Country Home in Woodland Hills, California,

Mary flatly denied those long-ago rumors. "It was the affair that never happened," she claimed. In failing health and suffering a heart condition, she was a lonely, forgotten star, refusing to see fans and giving almost no interviews except through "divine intervention" or on the recommendation of old friends.

"Actually, I wasn't dazzled by Hughes at all," Mary said. "I heard that he found me a cool cucumber. Behind his back I called him *Faunt* as in *Little Lord Fauntleroy*, because every day he showed up on the set in another outfit. Each one looked as if it still had the price tag on it. Years later, future lady friends such as Ava Gardner would ridicule his sloppy wardrobe. But when I knew him, he was still a dandy with a fondness for argyle socks if I remember."

"If Howard had given me the eye, I might have said yes," Mary said. "I was a bit wild in those days. Actually, I was very much in love with Ken." Her reference was to director Kenneth Hawks. She would marry him in 1928, a union that ended in his death in an airplane crash three years later. Kenneth was the brother of Howard Hawks, who would direct future pictures for Howard.

"Rumors about my so-called affair with Hughes quickly died down," Mary said. "A juicier story was making the rounds. Instead of shacking up with poor me, Hughes was hopping on Hopalong, although we didn't call William Boyd that in those days."

Apparently, Howard had misjudged Mary. She turned out to be a woman of violent passions with a high sex drive. Before meeting Howard, she'd already been clutched to the manly breasts of Douglas Fairbanks Sr. and John Barrymore, both on and off the screen.

Of *Two Arabian Knights*, she mostly remembered being "half-drunk, half-frozen, and half-nauseated" by the taste and smell of oil and salt water during scenes shot in San Pedro Harbor. She ridiculed Hughes as a producer, citing an example of his coming onto an indoor movie set and asking, "Where's the fourth wall?"

Howard watched in dismay in 1936 when Mary became involved in a court battle with her second husband, Dr. Franklyn Thorpe, over the custody of her daughter As evidence that she was an unfit mother, he introduced her private diary.

In it, she revealed many details about her affairs, none more notable than with the married George S. Kaufman. Snippets of the diary were released to the press. One passage, referring to Kaufman, read:

It was wonderful to fuck the sweet afternoon away. I don't know where George got his staying power. He must have cum three times in an hour.

She also wrote of other lovers including Clark Gable and Ronald Colman.

The diary was eventually impounded by the court and kept locked until 1952, when the courts ordered that it be burned. The public never got to read the full revelations.

"If I still kept a diary, Humphrey Bogart would have definitely made it," she said, alluding to a brief affair she had with him during the making of *The Maltese Falcon* in 1941, in which she played the cool, ruthless, and beautiful Brigit O'Shaughnessy, opposite Bogie's Sam Spade. "He called me Baby long before Bacall. He always related to me like I had no clothes on."

She had kind memories of Howard during the humiliation and exposure she suffered with her diary. "He called me and, to my surprise, volunteered his help if I needed him, and that included money."

In the retirement home, Mary had survived alcoholism, three divorces, an attempted suicide, and a national sex scandal. And she was still here.

In saying good-bye, she said she'd be remembered for these immortal lines, which in time were used by dozens of other actresses:

There are five stages in the life of an actress: Who's Mary Astor? Get me Mary Astor. Get me a Mary Astor type. Get me a young Mary Astor. Who's Mary Astor?

***

Los Angeles, 1927

Right before his involvement with a woman destined to become the world's most famous platinum blonde, Jean Harlow, another blond entered Howard's life.

William Boyd.

Howard told both Billy Haines and Rod St. Just that he found Boyd "very, very handsome." The actor had already been discovered and cast in films by Cecil B. DeMille long before he played the lead in *Two Arabian Knights.*

Before he rode off into the sunset as Hopalong Cassidy, William Boyd was considered "a hell-raising sex maniac in Hollywood," Adela Rogers St. Johns said privately, not in print.

His fellow co-star, Louis Wolheim, long before he played the lead in *Two Arabian Knights,* once confided, "Bill was basically heterosexual. Although he preferred women, he wasn't averse to letting a man service him if he felt it would advance his career. He takes sex wherever he finds it. He and Gary Cooper have a lot in common."

One of five children, Boyd had run away from home at the age of seventeen and had supported himself as best he could in jobs that required "more brawn than brains." Sometimes that was as a nude model or even a male prostitute for both men and women.

DeMille was fond of quoting Boyd on his

William Boyd

past. According to the director, the actor once told him, "If you've got a broad chest, blond hair, a big cock, and are devastatingly handsome, you can always find something, 'cause a pretty boy never has to go hungry.'"

Intriguingly, and there is no more information available, Boyd confided to his intimates that he used to "perform" at private parties for one hundred dollars a night.

When Howard first met Boyd, the actor was ten years older than he was, but his interest was piqued. The first weekend he had free, he invited Boyd for a sail to Catalina Island.

Only some of the details of that trip have been revealed. But somewhere in the reddish light of a fading Catalina sun on a long-ago afternoon, Howard had a close encounter with his golden boy with hair so blond it was almost gray.

Their idyllic time together—an off-the-record weekend—might have gone unnoticed except for one event. Howard invited Boyd to go with him to one of Richard Arlen's notorious all-nude male parties being held that same weekend at a secluded cove.

These parties hosted by the handsome bisexual actor were not a secret, but gossiped about among the innermost circles. Depending on the weekend, guests included Douglas Fairbanks Jr., Gary Cooper, Joel McCrea, Billy Haines, Buddy Rogers, Ramon Novarro, Edmund Goulding, and such lesser known actors as Kenneth MacKenna and Anderson Lawler.

Many future writers would label Howard "the bashful billionaire." Actually, he wasn't that shy and had little concern about showing off his body. He was, in fact, rather proud of his endowment, and would spend virtually the last twenty years of his life in the nude.

Howard's infamous weekend on Catalina Island only became known all over Hollywood because somehow, someway, a photographer managed to take nude pictures of the guests, including Howard and Boyd.

"Within the week," Rod St. Just recalled, "copies of those photographs were bringing top dollar in Hollywood. Many of the stills exist today in private collections. I just wish I had taken them. The studios worked overtime trying to suppress the incident."

Rod claimed that he personally bought the negatives to the pictures of Boyd and Howard. "Howard gave me ten thousand dollars but told me to start negotiating at two thousand. I had to part with all the money before I could buy the negatives. Photographs of Cooper and some other stars were practically sold on Hollywood & Vine. I think every queen in Hollywood who wanted pictures got them."

Many of these photographs later appeared in "underground" publications with limited circulation.

Rod was vague about the course of the Hughes/Boyd affair and wasn't certain about when it actually ended. "Maybe three weeks of white heat, then a sometimes thing," was his best estimation.

***

On May 21, 1927, Howard stayed glued to his radio set, listening in fury at the news of the history-making voyage of Charles A. Lindbergh on his non-stop transatlantic flight to Paris. He rode alone in a twin-engine plane, the *Spirit of St. Louis*. Had that little engine given out, he would have gone to a watery grave. All the commentators were hailing a new American hero, a handsome daredevil of amazing courage. The adulation sickened Howard.

House servants at the Muirfield mansion could hear the rage of their boss as he shouted back at the radio. Even the thick locked doors of his library couldn't drown out his voice. "I'll beat the bastard's record. So help me!" His bellowing vow was heard by the gardener, Robert Quantrill, who was planting new gardenia bushes outside Howard's window.

The next day, Howard continued to barricade himself in his library, not sending out for food or drink. He listened to the news of Lindbergh's tumultuous reception by the Parisians, who shouted *Vive Lindbergh!* in the streets. Upon the aviator's return to New York, an even greater welcome awaited him before he'd go on to be celebrated throughout the United States.

In the months ahead, whenever there was major news about Lindbergh, Howard abandoned all his plans for the day to sit by his radio. On June 13, 1927, he heard a broadcast about Lindbergh's triumphant return to New York. The largest crowd of well-wishers in the city's history, an estimated 4½ million New Yorkers, turned out, and some eighteen tons of paper were dumped on the streets from skyscraper windows.

An enraged Howard, in a phone call to Dietrich, predicted that one day New Yorkers would give him an even more enthusiastic hero's welcome.

Perhaps in a last desperate attempt to save her rapidly deteriorating marriage, Ella announced that she was going on a summer vacation in New England with her sister, Libby Farish. At least that's one point of view. Other more cynical observers noted that the much abused Ella might have embarked on a mission of revenge to pay Howard back for all his philandering.

After taking a train all the way to Boston, Libby and Ella journeyed by limousine to the summer resort of Pecketts-on-Sugar-Hill at Franconia, New Hampshire. Once there, Ella sent word to Howard that she and Libby were driving to Manchester, New Hampshire, a distance of ninety miles, to welcome Lindbergh to that city along with thousands of others.

On his victory tour of America, women were "throwing themselves at the aviator hero," in the words of one radio announcer. A Manchester newspaper reporter wrote, "Married or not, it was all the same wherever Lindy went. Women swooned over him greater than they did over Valentino." He cited an example of a matronly woman approaching Lindbergh in a local restaurant to look inside his mouth to see what he was eating for lunch, discovering it was a pimento cheese sandwich. While all this was going on, some maid was stealing

156

Lindy's dirty underwear from his hotel suite as a souvenir.

A ten thousand dollar check to the city's parks department had already assured Ella of a seat at the chief banquet table honoring Lindbergh that night.

Although it is known that Ella met with and talked to Lindbergh that night, the rest of the evening will forever remain a mystery. When Libby returned to Houston, she very discreetly dropped the word that the aviator "had been enchanted with the lovely Ella. He was completely mesmerized."

By the time word traveled along Houston's gossip circuit, the scoop was that Ella and Lindy were having a torrid affair. Libby later confided to Annette Lummis that Ella and Lindy spent the night together in his hotel suite. In time, this news got back to Howard, no doubt via Rupert, who apparently was gleeful at hearing the story from Annette.

Howard's reaction to the possible affair has not been recorded, as he apparently confided in no one, not even Dietrich.

On hearing this news about his wife and his arch rival, he immediately fired off a wire to Ella: "Were you able to see Lindberg?" Howard never learned to spell the hero's name correctly. "Did he live up to your fantasy?"

Usually it was Howard who didn't respond to Ella's telegrams. This time she chose not to answer him but to leave him guessing and simmering in his jealous stew.

It didn't help matters when Marion Davies phoned him the next month. Dietrich later claimed that Howard "almost had a stroke" when Marion dropped a bit of tantalizing news. Her benefactor, William Randolph Hearst, had met secretly with Lindbergh. The aviator had been offered half a million dollars, plus ten percent of the profits, if he'd appear in a picture produced by Hearst about aviation.

Marion reported to Howard that Lindbergh was seriously tempted by W.R.'s offer and had even gone so far as to sign a contract. Later, Lindbergh learned that W.R. had designated Marion to be his co-star in the film.

The household staff at Muirfield would later report that Howard "burst into an insane rage." He was not a hunter but often took a gun along to shoot at pigeons flying too close to his yacht, while making the crossing to Catalina Island. After slamming down the phone, Howard took his gun and went into the gardens of Muirfield, shooting blindly into the air. The gardener, Quantrill, was able to restrain him.

It was Rupert himself who had first proposed that Howard be the star of a movie about aviation. Nothing came of that, but Howard had gone ahead with his own plans to produce—not star in—his own picture about pilots. He told Dietrich he feared that if the Lindbergh picture were made, audiences would flock to that film and stay away from his own movie.

Lindbergh did not take up W.R.'s offer, and pleaded with him to tear up the contract, which the newspaper czar reluctantly did. Another producer later offered Lindbergh a guaranteed five-million dollars if he'd sign a movie contract to star as a dashing leading man in pictures. He turned that one down too. However, he did accept a far more limited series of testimonials and endorsements which capitalized off his fame.

When Howard learned that Lindbergh had turned down all movie offers, he was seriously tempted to contact him and offer him the lead in *Hell's Angels*. But he thought better of it, fearing that Lindbergh's fame was so great that it would detract from his own celebrity as producer.

Howard also had to disappoint Gary Cooper when he came to Muirfield to meet with Howard. Gary made a pitch that he and Clara Bow be cast as the stars of *Hell's Angels*. Howard had to turn Gary down, fearing that using the same stars who had appeared in *Wings* would be detrimental to his own movie. "I don't want it to look like I'm making a sequel," he told Gary.

In the years ahead, Howard avidly read any news of Lindbergh that he could, and was mesmerized by the saga of the kidnapping and subsequent death of the Lindbergh baby. When Lindbergh, on the eve of the U.S. entry into World War II, urged America to stay out of the global conflict, Howard denounced his rival as a Nazi sympathizer. Howard claimed that unlike himself, Lindbergh was not a true American patriot.

At one point, Dietrich was ordered to see if Howard could purchase the *Spirit of St. Louis*. Howard's motive, apparently, was not to preserve it as a memorial to Lindbergh, but to tear it apart and sell the aircraft as junk.

Dietrich filed Howard's request in the top of his desk drawer and never brought up the subject again with Howard. No second order ever came in from Howard. He always contemptuously referred to the historic plane as "that sweet little thing."

Howard later criticized Lindbergh's history-making flight to Paris, claiming that if he had been the pilot, he would have flown *Spirit* all the way to Rome. "Then the god damn Pope would have lifted his skirts and raced across the airfield to kiss me!"

***

While plotting the upcoming production of his epic, *Hell's Angels,* Howard quickly produced two more films and continued a series of not-very-serious nor very long affairs. He was just months from launching himself into his greatest love affair and his most famous motion picture. In the meantime, he kept himself busy until the real thing came along.

Their past misunderstandings cleared up, Howard once again turned to Lewis Milestone to direct a gangster movie, a crime film-noir called *The Racket*. Character actor Louis Wolheim was called back in the supporting role of Nick Scarsi, a bootleg racketeer based on the life of gangster Al Capone.

The lead role of the dedicated cop, Captain McQuigg, went to Thomas Meighan, a strikingly handsome leading man of the silent screen whose star was fading near the end of the Twenties. Rugged and strong-jawed, he had piercing blue eyes and stood six feet tall with the build of an athlete.

Meighan was known for seducing his leading ladies, including Mary Pickford with whom he appeared in a Western drama, *M'Liss*, and Norma Talmadge with whom he'd co-starred in *The Forbidden City*.

He was rumored to have had an affair with Big Howard's former mistress, Gloria Swanson, during the filming of DeMille's *Male and Female*, which also starred the beautiful Lila Lee.

In retirement, Lila Lee lived in Key West in a home provided by her gay son, James Kirkwood, who'd won the Pulitzer Prize as co-author of the Broadway musical, *A Chorus Line*. Ever since they'd appeared in *Male and Female*, she and Thomas Meighan had remained close friends—"never lovers," she was quick to point out.

She visited her favorite actor several times on the set during the filming of *The Racket*. "Everyone in the know, including Milestone himself, was predicting that Hughes would swoon over Tommy," Lila said. "In reality, Hughes found two other cast members more to his liking—beautiful Marie Prevost and a dashingly handsome blond actor, John Darrow. It wasn't a casting couch thing, though, because John and Marie had already been cast in their parts before meeting Hughes."

She recalled Meighan taking her to see *The Racket*. Critics agreed that Howard had come up with another winner. "There was even talk that it might be best picture of the year," Lila said, "but it lost out."

"The Hughes affair with Marie, and I talked to her about it myself, lasted for only a weekend," Lila recalled. "It took place at a Santa Monica beach house, either owned or rented by Ben Lyon."

"I saw Marie a week after the seduction," Lila said. "She claimed she was madly in love with Hughes. I remember her exact words. 'Why is Clara Bow raving about Gary Cooper's equipment? She should audition Howard Hughes. But if she does, I'll scratch the eyes out of the bitch.'"

Relaxing in her living room in Key West, Lila went on, "Howard Hughes was a fairly unknown commodity in Hollywood in those days. The way he treated women was still a bit of a secret. Poor Marie had a lot to learn. She thought Hughes would continue the affair. Apparently, the lying bastard had told her that he was in love with her. He might have said that on a Saturday night. By Monday morning, it was back to business for Hughes. On the set of *The Racket,* he practically ignored the poor girl after the Santa Monica episode. It really broke her heart. She was emo-

Marie Prevost

159

tionally fragile as it was."

Born in Canada and seven years older than Howard, Marie Prevost was the first in Howard's series of doomed girl friends. A Mack Sennett bathing beauty, she was seduced by the bisexual director. Howard had first seen her on the screen in F. Scott Fitzgerald's *The Beautiful and the Damned.* He had been impressed by her looks, and had gone once again to see her in the Ernst Lubitsch film, *The Marriage Circle.* Lubitsch had succeeded in bringing out the beautiful seductress side of Marie, erasing the last remaining trace of her convent school education in Montréal. Howard may have suggested to Milestone to give her the lead in *The Racket*, in which she played a torch song night club singer.

Beginning in 1926, her life had taken a tragic turn when her mother, to whom she was very close, died in an automobile accident in Florida. The news took a devastating toll on Marie, and she began to drink heavily.

"She and Hughes initially bonded by talking about the early deaths of their mothers," Lila claimed. "In time Hughes often seduced women by talking about their mothers, or, in many cases, such as Ginger Rogers, actually inviting the mother out on a date, making it a threesome. Of course, I don't mean sexually."

"Before she realized she'd been dumped," Lila said, "Marie told me that Hughes had liberated her sexually. I think that meant teaching her the joys of oral sex. Until then, Marie had presumably had sex only in the missionary position, including with that prissy right-winger, Adolphe Menjou. God, I detested that stuffed shirt."

Following *The Racket*, the professional and personal life of Marie went on a downward spiral, as her alcoholism increased. Because of her weight gain, she was no longer offered star roles, but appeared in very minor parts, most often playing a wise-cracking, gum-chewing blonde floozy.

"Real second banana parts," Lila said. Even so, Marie appeared with some of the leading stars of the Thirties, including Joan Crawford, Barbara Stanwyck, Clark Gable, and Howard's own discovery, Jean Harlow.

Lila remembered encountering Marie on Hollywood Boulevard in the mid-Thirties. "I think she was surviving on one bottle of Scotch and one grapefruit a day. She looked awful and was penniless. She told me she'd recently engaged in a to-the-death drinking bout with John Gilbert. He won. How could either of them have known that they each had only months to live at that time?"

"Marie told me that she'd made four attempts to get in touch with Hughes, begging him for money," Lila said. "She was living in this run-down cockroach palace on Cahuenga Boulevard."

"The same year she'd filmed *The Racket*, she'd also made *A Blonde for the Night,*" Lila said. "That more or less sums up Marie's involvement with Hughes."

Howard never returned Marie's calls and instructed Dietrich to turn down her repeated requests for money. A few months later Marie was found dead in

160

her seedy apartment, her corpse decomposing. She'd been dead for several days.

Her body was discovered on January 21, 1937, by neighbors because of the incessant barking of her dachshund. To survive, the pathetic animal had made mincemeat of her body. After her death, Nick Lowe, the songwriter, penned a song, "Marie Provost" (sic). In it, he sung of Marie becoming "the doggie's dinner."

Like Mozart, the faded beauty was buried in an unmarked pauper's grave in Los Angeles. Amazingly, she still had a fan club until 1958, when its last aging member, still paying homage to one of the great beauties of the silent screen, died.

***

With the handsome young actor, John Darrow, frequently at his side, Howard launched into pre-production work on *Hell's Angels,* still vowing to make the greatest movie of all time.

John had become a live-in guest at Howard's secret hideaway, Angelo, now that Gary Cooper and William Boyd no longer came to call.

Mickey Neilan is credited with giving Howard the story for *Hell's Angels*, although Rupert still said that he originated the concept when he wanted his nephew to star in a film about aviation.

Howard wisely hired Harry Behn to write the script along with Howard Estabrook. As a producer, Howard had been impressed with Behn's work on

John Darrow

The Racket, and the screenwriter had also penned MGM's *The Big Parade*, starring John Gilbert, in his biggest hit.

As Behn and Estabrook labored over the script, Mickey and Howard plotted the most brutal aerial combat scenes ever to be staged in front of a motion picture camera. The initial planning for *Hell's Angels* was done at Metropolitan Studios at Cahuenga Avenue and Romaine Street in Hollywood.

Rupert did everything he could to persuade Howard not to go ahead with *Hell's Angels*, claiming that the public was sick of the gore of World War I and wanted its "mud and blood forgotten." Howard differed, citing the success of such films as *The Big Parade, Wings,* and *What Price Glory?* When Howard wouldn't listen to him, Rupert predicted that "you'll lose your shirt on this one."

Howard remained convinced that his aerial sequences could capture the romance of flying, even if the pilots were engaged in combat. "There's a romanticism about pilots battling in the air." He compared it to dueling knights during the Age of Chivalry. Mickey dismissed all this talk of "knighthood in the sky," denouncing it as "bullshit" behind Howard's back.

Not listening to any dire warnings, Howard pursued his dream, turning his back on any devil's advocate. That included Dietrich, who'd been instructed to raid Toolco's bank reserves, which he did, looting Houston of one million dollars, with millions more to come.

After the first few weeks, Mickey decided he couldn't tolerate any more interference from Howard. When he'd directed *Everybody's Acting*, Mickey had total artistic control, although Howard observed his every move. But for *Hell's Angels*, Howard demanded that he be included in every decision, regardless of how minor. Despite his status as the film's director, Mickey suffered the indignity of having nearly every one of his orders countermanded.

When he could take no more, Mickey shouted at Howard, "I want out of this fucking zoo. Find yourself another director." He stormed out of Metropolitan, and for the rest of his life retained a burning hatred of Howard, a man whom he'd originally courted.

Howard replaced him with Luther Reed, a Wisconsin native who'd written about aviation for five years for the *New York Herald*. He'd become a director, turning out such forgettable flickers as *New York* and *Evening Clothes*, both in 1927. After only two months, Reed too could no longer stand Howard's interference. "Find yourself another god damn director," Reed shouted at Howard in front of cast and crew when he countermanded his latest directive. "Direct the picture yourself, cocksucker!"

"That's exactly what I'll do, you incompetent shithead!" Howard shouted at Reed's back as he stormed across the stage toward the exit sign.

Weak on plot, *Hell's Angels* is the story of two brothers attending Oxford. They enlist in the RAF when World War I breaks out. They also fall in love with the same girl, who appears rather indifferent to them both. The brothers volunteer for a suicide mission in a captured German bomber.

On October 31, 1927, Howard began the principle shooting of the interiors of *Hell's Angels* at General Service Studios in Hollywood. Since meeting Ben Lyon, on loan from Warner Brothers, Howard had become increasingly friendly with this handsome star, much to the annoyance of John Darrow, who did not conceal his hostility on the set.

Ben was cast in the lead, playing opposite another popular actor, James Hall. As much as he liked Ben, Howard detested James Hall, finding him prudish off screen and wooden on screen. But since he'd signed a contract, Howard continued with James Hall playing Ben's brother.

As Howard's favorite young man of the moment, and that was obvious to the cast, John Darrow was cast as the dashing Karl Armstedt, a member of the German Zeppelin crew. Other than his catching the eye of Howard, John had few acting credentials at the time, having appeared in such fluff as the 1927 *High School Hero,* characterized only by its boring scenario.

For the female lead, Howard originally wanted the very sexy Dorothy Mackaill, with her blonde bob, great legs, and generous lower lip. But she had other commitments, including five other films to make in 1927. Mackaill would one day compete and lose to Jean Harlow the role in *Red Dust* opposite Clark Gable.

Howard's second choice was Greta Nissen, one of the era's reigning blonde beauties of the screen. Almost immediately Howard regretted his decision, clashing several times with Greta who spoke in a heavy Norwegian accent. No romantic sparks were generated between Howard and Greta. Behind her back, he mockingly referred to her as Brunhild. "The fucking bitch should wear a breast plate and sing opera." He told Harry Behn that "this Nissen creature makes me nervous. Thank God the picture is silent. That's the worst voice since Vilma Banky opened her pussy-licking mouth."

One of the Hollywood personalities who began to intrigue Howard was Ben Lyon, whose reputation as a womanizer and sexual athlete was widespread throughout Hollywood. Ben had had a famous and much publicized affair with Marilyn Miller, "the toast of New York" and one of the reigning stars in Broadway musicals. Their affair followed her messy divorce from Jack Pickford, brother of Mary. On the side, Ben was dating silent screen vamp, Bebe Daniels, whom he would eventually marry.

Born of Irish descent, Ben Lyon was touted as the all-American equivalent of Latin lovers Ramon Novarro and Antonio Moreno. With his dark hair and blue eyes, he had a clean-cut all-American look. If a director were shooting a script about a college football team, he might cast Ben as the captain.

According to Harry Behn, Ben joined Howard in a string of seductions of young starlets, most of which had been arranged by Ben himself. These off-the-record romances would mark the pattern of Howard's life for the immediate decades to come.

Ben was eager to take to the skies with Howard and his boss began to instruct him as a pilot even though Howard would not obtain his own pilot's license until January 7, 1928. Ben and Howard often flew off together on week-ends.

James Hall later remembered Ben bragging in his dressing room that he and Howard had booked three beautiful starlets into three different rooms within the same hotel in San Diego, where they kept "the ladies satisfied, and none of the gals was the wiser."

On some occasions, if we can trust Hall's memory, Ben and Howard stayed in the same room with two of the various starlets they "auditioned," often seducing them on the same bed at the same time. "I put on quite a show for Howard," Hall quotes Ben as having said. "I think he's a *voyeur*."

Details are sketchy, but at some point Howard seduced the good-looking and very masculine actor Ben Lyon. James Whale in his pre-*Frankenstein* days knew Ben quite well when they worked together on *Hell's Angels*. Whale confirmed that Ben indeed did have an affair with Howard. "Ben was one of the biggest ladies men in the world," Whale later said. "He was also boyishly cute and very athletic, the kind of likable and charming man Hughes went for. I guess if you're an actor, and even though a bona-fide heterosexual, you might drop your trousers if the richest man in the world—and your producer—makes such a request. Since Hughes was known at the time for his expertise in

Ben Lyon and Greta Nissen

giving oral sex, Ben didn't have it so bad. One day I overheard John Darrow having a big fight with Hughes over Ben, and I knew this other little cutie had found out."

"For God's sake, did any of these boys—or did any of the Hughes women—think that this Texas alley cat would remain faithful to them?" Whale asked. "In those days and for years to come, Howard Hughes was a tiger burning bright and lusting after anything in the night, male or female. His only requirement: His prey had to be gorgeous."

Many fans remember Ben the way he looked when he got older and was married to Bebe Daniels. Like so many actors, he went through a baby-face period. "When he smiled at me with that schoolboy look, my heart would melt but he was out of my league," Whale confessed. "I saw him nude several times in his dressing room and he had quite an athletic build and was rather well-endowed, the way Hughes liked. He did tell me one time that Louis B. Mayer found him too scrawny for *Ben-Hur* and he lost out on that big part. So what did Mayer up and do? Give it to that Mexican girl, Ramon Novarro. What a lady she was, prancing around as *Ben-Hur.*"

"Ben did confide one big secret to me about Howard in bed," Whale said in a conspiratorial tone. He quotes Ben as saying, "While he was making love to me, and doing all the work, I might add, he wanted me to talk at the same time, describing what it was like screwing Billie Dove when we made *The Tender Hour* together in 1927. It was obvious to me that Billie Dove was going to be Howard's next big conquest."

***

A letter arrived from his boyhood friend, Dudley Sharp, asking Howard to be the best man at his upcoming wedding in Houston. Dudley had been the best man at the wedding of Ella Rice to Howard.

Although Howard ignored most requests such as that, he did send a telegram to Dudley in which he congratulated him on his upcoming marriage. "Too busy with *Hell's Angels,*" Howard wrote. "Can't make it. Sorry."

"Very short of money," Dudley answered Howard with another request. He wanted to bring his new bride to meet Howard and stay with him for two weeks in the roomy mansion at Muirfield.

"That won't be possible," was Howard's terse reply. "San Diego, however, is nice this time of year."

"The friendship was over after that second telegram," Dudley later said. At the same time, he revealed that he had requested money from Howard in the autumn of 1925 and had also been rejected. His mother, Estelle Sharp, could no longer afford his tuition or an allowance for him to continue at Princeton. She had urged Dudley to contact his boyhood friend. "After all, if Big Howard hadn't gotten me to sell Daddy's shares, we'd be part owner of Toolco today."

Not wanting to ask for an out-and-out loan, Dudley met with the officials of the Alloy Steel Corporation in Dayton, Ohio. They agreed to pay him a kick-back of twelve-thousand dollars if he would convince Toolco to order metal from them. Howard turned down the proposal, even though it would not have cost him any money, and ordering steel on Alloy's terms would have saved him fifty-thousand dollars in one year alone.

Howard told Dietrich, "Don't mention the name of Dudley Sharp to me again. If he ever tries to correspond with me again, file the letter unopened."

Without Howard's help, Dudley went on to enjoy a successful career. An Eisenhower Republican, he in time would become secretary of the U.S. Air Force.

***

Los Angeles, 1928

Even as he moved forward with *Hell's Angels,* Howard produced another film, *The Mating Call,* directed by James Cruze. Howard had seen the director's *The Covered Wagon* in 1923 a total of three times and had been impressed with Cruze's take-charge style of handling a difficult picture.

Although Mormons would later become the menacing guards at the door of the reclusive and dying Howard Hughes, Utah-born Cruze may have been the first Mormon Howard ever met.

The Mating Call was filmed during the twilight of silent pictures, but it did have a musical score. Budgeted at $400,000, it would barely make a profit in spite of the top-grade talent engaged in its production.

Because he was almost completely absorbed by *Hell's Angels,* Howard did not try to direct *The Mating Call*, giving Cruze more or less a free hand. Howard did show up frequently on set, however, but that may have been because of his romantic interest in two of the female cast members.

The film was based on a novel by Rex Beach, a popular writer of his day. One of Beach's novels, *The Spoilers*, was made into five different films, including a 1942 version starring Marlene Dietrich.

Herman J. Mankiewicz wrote the titles for *The Mating Call*, for its release as a silent movie. By 1941 he'd co-authored the screenplay with Orson Welles for *Citizen Kane,* which would win them a co-Oscar for writing. Based on the life of William Randolph Hearst, Citizen Kane is still considered the greatest motion picture ever made. It contains an unflattering portrait of Marion Davies, the press tycoon's mistress. If Welles had followed Mankiewicz's original wish, *Citizen Kane* would have been based on the life of Howard Hughes—not Hearst.

To write the scenario of *The Mating Call*, Howard hired William Axt and David Mendoza, the two hottest writers in Hollywood. They had scored big with such successes as *The Big Parade* in 1925, *Ben-Hur*, also in 1925, and *Don Juan* the following year.

Howard once again cast Thomas Meighan as his leading man. Meighan and Howard had a somewhat formal—actually, a chilly—relationship, and Howard would never use him again. He told Cruze after two weeks of shooting, "I've misjudged Meighan and shouldn't have hired him again. His star is fading."

Howard was much more enchanted by the film's two leading ladies, Renée Adorée and Evelyn Brent, both beauties.

When signed to do the movie, in which she played a Russian immigrant impounded on Ellis Island, Renée was at the peak of her career. She'd scored big opposite John Gilbert in *The Big Parade*. When Gilbert wasn't resting in the arms of Greta Garbo, Gilbert and Renée would become on-and-off again lovers for three more years and would remain close friends after that.

At the time Howard met her, Renée spoke a little English but with a heavy French accent. With the coming of talkies, she would improve her English so that her voice recorded better.

Renée had performed in the circus since she was five years old and later became a dancer at the Folies-Bèrgere in Paris. Around five feet tall, her petite stature, sensuous beauty, and penetrating eyes attracted Howard. She told Cruze that she thought Howard "is the handsomest American

Renée Adorée

man I've ever seen, even better looking than John Gilbert."

When news reached Louella Parsons that Howard had cast Renée in *The Mating Call*, the gossip maven pronounced her "one of the sexiest leading ladies in film today." That column piqued Howard's sexual curiosity.

In an interview given shortly before his death in Los Angeles in the summer of 1942, Cruze said, "Hughes just had to have Renée, at least for one night. He put about as much emotion into the affair as purchasing a gold bracelet for a starlet for the night. But he must have promised Renée the world. A big career. Marriage. God only knows. At any rate, she fell for him—and big."

Renée had once been married to actor Tom Moore, the former brother-in-law of Mary Pickford during her ill-fated marriage to Owen Moore. "After Howard," Renée told Cruze, "Tom doesn't even count. Not even as a distant memory."

In ill health, Cruze tried to remember as best he could what happened during the filming of *The Mating Call*. "Renée had had experience with Hollywood wolves, but she was still naïve. Back in those days, Hughes's reputation wasn't as ingrained as it later became. The gals actually fell for his line. When he lost interest in Renée—maybe after a shack-up that lasted no more than forty-eight hours, he just didn't know her. She was crushed."

"I watched her career slowly fade and even saw her last picture, *The Singer from Seville,*" Cruze said. "It was released in 1930. Renée never made it in Talkies and became one of the doomed ladies of the silent screen."

She died early in her life on October 5, 1933 of tuberculosis. Upon her death, John Gilbert said he regretted that "so many bullies and bastards remain in Hollywood while a sweet decent girl like Renée has to fill the graveyards."

"Renée told me that she wanted to continue the affair with Hughes," Cruze said. "But she was simply abandoned. Howard had already seen her female co-star and decided that instead of Renée he wanted Evelyn Brent."

***

Although he still owned his Waco, Howard, on the advice of Noah Dietrich, purchased a Boeing P-4. He had it rebuilt by Douglas Aircraft at Clover Field. On several occasions he ordered that work be completely redone. Costs mounted, as he demanded one new safety feature after another, until the final bill ran up to $75,000.

The Boeing had originally cost less than $50,000. Refusing to pay for the overhaul, he eventually got the bill down to $15,000, which meant that Douglas Aircraft lost thousands on the deal. The president of the company, Donald Douglas, vowed "never to do business with the son of a bitch ever again."

Although concerned with the safety features on the Boeing P-4, Howard was reckless in piloting other planes. "He'd just jump aboard and start flying one of those fuckers, with no concern for its safety features, much less his own life," Dietrich recalled.

Having heard about this, Evelyn Brent, the co-star of *The Mating Call,* was at first afraid to fly with him when he invited her to come aboard for the revamped Boeing's inaugural flight to San Diego.

From her modest apartment in Westwood Village in 1974, Evelyn recalled her strange, brief relationship with her producer. "When Hughes first asked me out, I thought he meant dinner—maybe dancing. Instead, we ended up in San Diego where he'd rented a suite."

Over dinner and on a sardonic note, Evelyn and Howard talked about Mormons. As an actress, she'd come into prominence in two British features, both released in 1922. One, *Trapped by Mormons,* was followed by its sequel, *Married to a Mormon.* These films, even in their day, were viewed as lurid and incendiary, documenting "the menace of the Mormon church and its teachings," especially about polygamy.

As later life demonstrated, Howard did not share Evelyn's distaste for Mormons. He often selected them as "palace guardsmen," and he liked

Evelyn Brent

the fact that none of the Mormons on his staff smoked or drank.

Evelyn amused Howard with her stories about the director of the anti-Mormon pictures, H.B. Parkinson, who believed that virginal English girls were being lured to Utah, where in his view they were forced into sexual slavery by men who had many other wives.

Howard was already familiar with the career of Parkinson. At a private showing with Marion Davies and Charlie Chaplin, he'd seen Parkinson's *The Life Story of Charles Chaplin.* Much of the film was true, especially the part that revealed The Little Tramp's fascination with pubescent girls. Chaplin was furious and somehow got the film suppressed. Pirated copies were released, however, and the film was frequently shown at Hollywood parties in 1926 and 1927.

Chaplin told Howard, "Some day you'll become as famous as I am, and some asshole will make a movie of your life. Don't let them. Suppress it!" Later Howard took Chaplin's advice, when he secretly paid Orson Welles fifty-thousand dollars for him and Herman Mankiewicz to base the subject of *Citizen Kane* not on him but on William Randolph Hearst instead.

Initially, if only for a weekend, Howard was attracted by Evelyn's beauty. She had porcelain white skin, a Cupid mouth, and curly brunette hair. On and off the screen she evoked a smoldering intensity. On screen, playing exotic and dangerous characters, she always had a hint of mystery about her, a screen char-

168

acterization that would soon become the hallmark of Marlene Dietrich. It is said that her director, Josef von Sternberg, originally created the screen persona of Marlene by experimenting with Evelyn in two of his films, *Underworld* in 1927 and *The Dragnet* in 1928. In his pre-Marlene days, Von Sternberg was so intrigued with Evelyn that he also cast her in his 1928 *The Last Command.*

Six years older than Howard, and born in Tampa, Florida, Evelyn was the daughter of an Italian woman who was only fourteen years old at the time of Evelyn's birth. Her Irish-American father was all of seventeen. On their first date in San Diego, Evelyn aroused Howard's sympathy by speaking of her terrible upbringing. Orphaned by the time she was fourteen herself, she was forced to support herself, drifting into show business. When she'd saved up five hundred dollars, she went to London and managed to get cast in British films, including those two pictures about the Mormons. Back in the States, she was hailed as "the British beauty," not revealing her true origins.

When interviewed in 1974 in her apartment in Westwood, California, a year before her death, Evelyn recalled, "That bastard Hughes promised me everything that night in San Diego. He claimed he was going to sign me to a personal contract and star me in five major motion pictures, paying me one-hundred thousand dollars per picture. Of course, that was before he met that whore, Billie Dove. He actually carried through on the movie deal, but with Dove, and not with me. Fool that I was, I fell for his line."

Even when dumped by Howard, Evelyn still had a contract with Paramount and starred in *Interference* in 1929, one of that studio's first talkies. Regrettably, her first talking pictures were dismal failures at the box office, even though she had a pleasant speaking voice. Her future roles between 1930 and 1950 grew smaller and smaller, and she eventually retired from the screen to become a talent agent.

"I was an actor's agent in the 1950s, and I pitched several deals toward Hughes when he owned RKO," Evelyn claimed. "But he never went for anything. It was like writing to a stone wall. I never got a response."

She vividly remembered that night in San Diego back in 1928 when Howard took her to his hotel suite after dinner. "Yes, he did make love to me. I have to be perfectly frank. I didn't know myself in those days. I really believed that sex was something a woman had to endure, not a source of pleasure. While Howard was making love to me, I looked into his eyes. He wasn't even there. It was like he had drifted into some far and distant place."

Waking up the following Sunday morning around ten o'clock, she said, "I thought Hughes was still in bed with me. But while I was sleeping, he'd gotten up and slipped out of the suite and flew back to Los Angeles in his new plane. The jerk didn't even pay the hotel bill. I had taken only ten dollars in my purse. Mad money. That's all I had. The hotel manager wouldn't let me leave until the bill was paid. I called Caddo in Los Angeles, and I think at one point even Noah Dietrich got involved. Finally, an agreement was reached with Caddo, and they were billed for our weekend. Fortunately, I had a girlfriend who lived in San Diego, and she agreed to drive me back to Los Angeles. The next week when I saw Hughes on the set, he didn't even acknowledge me. Men!"

In time, Evelyn gave up all men, having divorced three husbands. In her Westwood apartment, her live-in lover was the actress Dorothy Conrad.

At the time of her death of a heart attack on June 4, 1975, Evelyn had not appeared on the screen in twenty-five years.

***

Many of the nation's leading stunt pilots, especially Paul Mantz and Roscoe Turner, began assembling in January of 1928 at Mines Field at Inglewood (now the Los Angeles International Airport). These pilots were hand-picked by J. B. Alexander, Howard's former flight instructor. Most of the pilots—many World

Dogfight scene from *Hell's Angels*

War I aces—earned their living by performing dangerous stunts at country fairs around the nation.

A few months earlier, Frank Tomick, had been signed by Howard to search the country for a fleet of planes—German, American, British, and French. Many of these aircraft, which had seen actual combat, had been shipped to the United States after World War I. Tomick found planes in "mothballs" in such states as Virginia and especially New Jersey.

170

When not enough planes were located in the United States, Tomick purchased aircraft from France, Germany, and England, finding them at partially abandoned airfields in England's East Anglia, or dusty, giant warehouses in the suburbs of Paris or Berlin.

He bought several Fokker D. VIIIs, the top killer of World War I, along with Nieuports, S.E.5s, and DeHavillands, but he didn't always find what he wanted.

Back in California, a crew of thirty-five mechanics, along with members of Howard's prop department, converted Curtiss Jennies into what looked like British Avros. Since an intact German Gotha bomber could not be found, Sikorskys were disguised to look like the Kaiser's fabled craft that had once caused panic in London.

In the San Fernando Valley, Howard purchased a cow pasture and turned it into Caddo Field, named after his production company. Howard himself flew the antiquated and dangerous Spads he'd purchased along with the RAF's former "Sopwith Camels."

The armada quickly became known as the Howard Hughes Air Force in Hollywood. It was the largest private air force ever assembled, some eighty-seven private planes, although press reports claimed more than one hundred aircraft.

The fired director, Mickey Neilan, contemptuously dismissed Howard's efforts. "That god damn Texas bastard is going to restage World War I." At the time, Mickey accurately predicted to the press that several stunt pilots would die. "I knew his original plans. Life doesn't mean anything to him. If those pilots are fools enough to follow his command, they deserve to die!"

Dietrich watched in horror as costs mounted. He repeatedly fought with Toolco executives as he raided their diminishing cash time and time again. Dozens of protests arrived from Houston, but the officers had no choice but to release the money. "It's my god damn money, and I'll spend it however I wish," Howard angrily informed Dietrich.

Howard hired more than one thousand extras, along with a cast of thirty-five and a crew that at various times numbered anywhere from 101 to 167.

Although barred, Louella Parsons defiantly came onto the set one hot afternoon. In an article entitled, "The Man Nobody No's," she commented, "I remember watching the picture being made and even I was appalled at the way Hughes spent money. At one time he had twenty-four cameramen shooting battle scenes. He was creating his own war, and it was almost as expensive as the real one."

It was a bit of an exaggeration, but Dietrich at the time might have agreed with Parsons. He'd already spent five hundred thousand dollars on "worthless junk in the skies."

During the early stages of the film, Howard showed the stamina of the twenty-three-year old that he was by working long stretches at a time, twenty or even thirty hours at a stretch. He expected his crew to do the same. He thought nothing of calling one of his cast at three o'clock in the morning if a new idea occurred to him.

He had long ago thrown away the wristwatch that Dudley Sharp had given him and would never wear one again.

Ella was an almost forgotten figure. He never responded to any of her messages which she slipped under the door of his study at Muirfield. Even though they often slept under the same roof, she might as well have been back in Houston as far as Howard was concerned.

Long work sessions were followed by reckless partying when Howard chose to escape the tension. He once disappeared—no one was quite sure where—for forty-eight hours with John Darrow. During his absences, *Hell's Angels* virtually ground to a halt. Sometimes Howard would vanish for about the same amount of time with Ben, leaving John to silently fume at Howard's hideaway, Angelo. When he did show up, Howard never told John where he'd gone or what he did with Ben.

James Whale later recalled Howard shouting at John. "For Christ's sake, you're not my wife! I think I still have one of those, and I don't want another."

***

On the set of *Hell's Angels* the next day, Howard ordered his staged dogfights between "German" and "British" pilots to be filmed by cameras mounted inside airplanes, a revolutionary technique in its day. This method of filming greatly improved on what Howard had witnessed when director William Wellman photographed *Wings*.

One night Howard stayed awake until dawn dreaming up his most dangerous stunt. By seven o'clock that morning, he ordered Frank Clarke to come to the runway where Howard stood beside a Thomas Morse S4C Scout. Clarke was one of the most daredevil pilots on Howard's crew, and he'd personally selected him for the dangerous shot.

Still chewing on a bread roll, Clarke listened with growing apprehension as Howard ordered him to perform "a banked take-off." To the pilot's astonishment, Howard asked him to dive toward the earth but "jerk back" when he reached an altitude of only two-hundred feet.

"You're out of your mind," Clarke bluntly told him, daring to challenge his director. "If the plane goes lower than a thousand feet, the Morse will crash."

"A good flier could do it," Howard said sarcastically.

"I'm not going to do it, and I'm not going to let one of my boys do it, even one of the crazy ones."

Howard wasn't used to having his commands defied.

Clarke warned him that the Morse had a rotary engine. "If sharply banked in the same direction as the rotation, the plane will spin dangerously out of control as it nears the ground."

Howard's face flushed with anger. "You're a shithead!" he shouted. He was using that word with greater frequency. "A coward to boot." Turning to face the astonished crew, who had assembled around the plane, he yelled, "If Sissy Boy here can't do the job, I can!"

Clarke backed away from the plane. "It's a graveyard stunt. Go up in the air and kill yourself!"

Ignoring him, Howard called for his chief cameraman, Harry Perry, to whom he gave last minute instructions about angles. Then, in front of the stunned pilots, Howard leaped into the cockpit, wearing a leather jacket, argyle socks, an argyle sweater, and a pair of russet-red corduroy breeches. He looked like an overgrown schoolboy as he sat contemptuously in the cockpit. Once the engine was started, he tested his instruments and had a graceful take-off into the wild blue yonder.

He circled the field at Inglewood at least a dozen times, learning to maneuver his craft. He had agreed with Perry on some signal before he was to make his plane plunge toward the earth.

"Hughes was a total fool at this point," Perry later recalled. "He was more interested in getting the shot than in saving his skin. When the plane was about a thousand feet over the tarmac, I heard this awful screech. It sounded like a hundred big fat crows singing a mocking chorus. Suddenly, when he was no more than eight hundred feet above the ground, even this crazed daredevil must have known he was in trouble."

Watching Howard's dive, stunt pilot Paul Mantz said, "I knew at this point that Hughes could not pull out of the dive. The Morse was racing directly toward the ground. It looked like curtains for Hughes. I stood with my mouth hanging open looking at his upcoming death. There was nothing I could do."

As the plane plunged to a point only one hundred feet from the tarmac, Mantz could see Howard in the cockpit. He tossed off his leather helmet and braced his feet against the dashboard. "It was all over for Hughes," Mantz said.

The Morse went into a tailspin and nose-dived into the tarmac. The impact was heard for miles around. The left wing folded first.

"I'll never forget the sound of the propellers digging into the macadam," Mantz said. "It was a gruesome screech of death." The wings were torn from the fuselage, and the landing gear splintered like brittle wood.

"There goes our god damn meal ticket," Clarke said to the other stunt pilots. "I warned the fool."

After impact, Reginald Callow was the first member of the crew to run toward the wreckage to pull Howard out. "As I yanked him out, he was covered in blood," Callow recalled in a 1975 interview. "He was dazed. Didn't know what in hell he was saying. I remember he said, 'That's another par hole I made. I shot a four on that one.' He was babbling. I guess he thought he was on the Wilshire golf course."

Others have claimed that Howard was thrown from the plane and was found propped up against the hangar. Callow disputed that. "I should know. I was the one who pulled my boss from the cockpit."

As Callow heard the sirens of the ambulance arriving on the airfield, he thought Howard "was a goner. I didn't see how any doctor could save him at this point. His skull looked crushed in."

Callow later said he wanted to resign from the picture before any more lives were lost. "At that point, I thought Hughes was crazy." However, he stuck through until the bitter end, witnessing the deaths of several other stunt pilots. He went on to become one of the best assistant directors in Hollywood, holding that position during the filming of *Gone With the Wind.*

When Noah Dietrich arrived at the Inglewood Hospital, he confronted Dr. Monroe Campbell. "Give it to me straight and in layman's lingo," Dietrich ordered.

"There's a crack in his skull," Dr. Campbell said. "It runs from the top of his head to just over his left eyelid. There are lacerations and injuries at the top of his spinal cord. Brace yourself. There may even be brain damage. We think he's lost the sight in his right eye."

The next day, with almost reckless disregard for the actual circumstances, Louella Parsons and other newspaper reporters claimed that Howard walked away from the wreckage without a scratch. One commentator wrote that he "waved his lucky Stetson at the ground crew before brushing the soot and grime off his breeches."

In Houston a day later, from the home of her wealthy sister, Libby Farish, where she was living, Ella heard about Howard's crash. Furious that Dietrich hadn't personally notified her, she took the next train to Los Angeles.

Once she reached the Inglewood Hospital, Howard denounced her for returning. "You want a son?" Two nurses heard Howard shout at Ella. "Well, I'm giving birth to something that means more to me than any snot-nosed kid. I'm birthing *Hell's Angels.* I'm not going to let some god damn airplane crash stand in my way. Now get the hell out of here!"

In what Dietrich later viewed as a miracle, Howard was soon back on the set, defying the orders of his doctors. "I'm fully recovered," he falsely claimed.

It is believed that Howard suffered lasting brain damage in the wake of this accident, the first of others to come. Only when an autopsy was performed by doctors upon his corpse in Texas did they discover a shard of metal still lodged in his skull from the long-ago accident.

Following this crash, he would suffer from blinding migraines for the rest of his life. Not only that, but he would also suffer from lapses in memory, which would grow more frequent as the years drifted by.

Not one of the sanest people before the accident, he would become more and more irrational with each passing year.

Dietrich later blamed it on the plane crash, but Howard signed a contract with a Shanghai movie star known as "the Mary Pickford of China." "Butterfly" Wu was the most famous and most beautiful star of her country.

Born to a Cantonese family in either 1906 or 1908, she counted fluent Mandarin as one of her language skills. When Chinese pictures started to talk, her knowledge of both Mandarin and Cantonese made her top box office. She would, in fact, star in the first Chinese talkie ever made.

She would go on to star in both Mandarin and Cantonese films up until the Japanese invasion of her homeland. In post-war Shanghai and Hong Kong, she would make a comeback.

"Why Howard ever signed her, I haven't a clue," Dietrich said. "Since there was nothing for her to do, Butterfly returned to Shanghai."

Somehow Ben Lyon told Howard about the "glories" of Asian girls, and had even misinformed Howard, as part of a rather juvenile misconception, about "how their plumbing is constructed different from Caucasian gals."

Apparently, the engineer in Howard had to find this out for himself. If he were going to be "dating Chinese," he only wanted the best and most famous. He moved in on Butterfly when she visited Hollywood.

"Apparently he promised her that he would lay all of Hollywood at her feet," Dietrich later confided.

The details of the so-called romance between Howard and Butterfly have long ago disappeared from radar, except for this tantalizing comment.

Noah Dietrich said he asked Howard what it was like making love to this Chinese beauty.

"Noah," Howard replied, "have you ever fucked a log that fell in the forest twenty years ago?"

***

During Howard's frequent "disappearances," John Darrow wasn't sitting around his cottage knitting. He had met Russell Gleason, a handsome and intelligent young juvenile actor who was three years younger than Howard.

He was the son of the famous character actor, James Gleason, most often cast as a tough-talking, hard-boiled urbanite, known for roles that included a detective, a marine sergeant, a gambler, and a boxer's manager. He'd married Lucille Webster, a minor actress, whose career never equaled her husband's.

Rail-thin, Oregon-born Russell had appeared on stage with his parents in some of their productions. He'd made his film debut in the 1929 *The Sophomore,* and had also been cast as third lead in *The Flying Fool,* a film that co-starred two of Howard's cast-off lovers, Marie Prevost and William Boyd. Russell's only A-List picture would be the Oscar-winning *All Quiet on the*

Western Front.

Although he worked steadily after making that classic, he was for the rest of his career cast only in B pictures.

Russell appeared with his parents in a series of Higgins family comedies for Republic in the late 30s and early 40s, but his career was going downhill fast. Although he tried a few times, Russell never developed that touch of Damon Runyon-style New Yorkness that had made his father such a success, especially when he'd received an Oscar nomination for his role of Max Corkle in *Here Comes Mr. Jordan* in 1941.

Eventually, Russell married Cynthia Lindsay, a radio and screen actress best known today for her affectionate memoir, *Dear Boris*, published in 1975 and devoted to the Gleason's family friend, Boris Karloff.

John Darrow was emotionally involved with Howard in the hopes that he would boost his film career. But there is evidence, mainly from James Whale, that John "fell hopelessly in love with young Gleason," and that Howard learned about it. "Although Hughes was cheating on John left and right, he still wanted to pay back his sometimes lover for his (perceived) betrayal."

Russell Gleason

"Through means of his own, Hughes set up a secret date with Russell, and the kid accepted," Whale claimed. "I mean, after all, we're talking Howard Hughes here. What struggling young actor wouldn't accept such an invitation?"

The inevitable happened. Russell fell in love with Howard and dropped John, who received a "Dear John" note. Although furious, John never confronted Howard with this betrayal because he didn't want to alienate such a powerful ally in the film industry.

Howard would continue into the Thirties with an involvement on some level with both Russell and John. "I don't even know whether his relationship with Russell remained sexual or not," Whale said. "I doubt that it did. I do know what happened with John Darrow. When he lost his boyish good looks, he still stayed in Hughes's good graces. By that time, he'd learned what type of

176

young man Hughes liked. He took up pimping for Hughes instead."

Mystery still surrounds the death of Russell Gleason on Christmas Day in 1945. He'd been drafted into the Army and had completed his basic training. During this grueling period, he wrote Howard at least fifteen letters, desperately pleading with him to intercede for him and get him out of the Army. Perhaps Howard had the power to do that because of his government connections—perhaps not. The point was that Russell thought Howard had such power.

When Howard refused even to take Russell's calls, the aging "juvenile" threatened Howard with blackmail. He was going to expose Howard's private life to the press if his former lover didn't give him twenty five thousand dollars and obtain an exemption for him from military service.

On Christmas Day, 1945, only twenty-four hours before Russell was to ship out for active duty, he died in a fall from a Manhattan hotel window. The New York police ruled that it was an accident and that Russell had fallen from the hotel window. In those days before air conditioning, New York City hotel windows were open for ventilation. But a four and a half foot wall separated the window from the floor. It would have been almost impossible for Russell to fall out the window, unless he was leaning dangerously out of it, and even then he would have almost needed to jump.

Some newspaper reporters speculated that Russell Gleason's death was actually a suicide leap. One reporter moronically wrote that Russell killed himself "to avoid being sent into combat."

There was no combat. Hostilities had ceased with the Japanese surrender in September after Harry Truman had ordered the dropping of two atomic bombs on the island empire.

Up until his death at Woodland Hills, California, on April 12, 1959, James Gleason always insisted to all who would lend an ear, "Howard Hughes had my son murdered!"

**

Suffering from lack of sleep, Howard took over the German Zeppelin sequences, wanting them to be among the most dramatic scenes in *Hell's Angels*. His special effects department had devised two sixty foot models of the dreaded Kaiser Zeppelin.

The climax of the scene comes with the Zeppelin's fiery descent toward earth. Dietrich totaled up the cost at nearly half a million dollars. Mickey Neilan, the fired director, told the press that he made his best movies on far less money than that. He predicted inaccurately that the picture would end up costing eight million dollars if Howard continued on "his mad quest."

It was for one of the close-ups of the Zeppelin airship that Howard became the laughing stock of Hollywood, ridiculed as "One Hundred Takes Hughes." According to the script, the pilots of the Zeppelin were hoping to escape back to the Continent in the wake of its raid on London.

As the script indicated, the dirigible was rapidly losing altitude. The pilot ordered that all ballast must be jettisoned, including several members of the crew, to cut down on the craft's weight.

German aviators, again according to the plot, were asked to volunteer to jump to their deaths for the Fatherland. As large wind machines billowed smoke to evoke clouds, more than three dozen sturdy stuntmen jumped out of the *faux* Zeppelin onto thick padding concealed below out of camera range. Never satisfied, Howard ordered take after take until the stuntmen had jumped out of the Zeppelin more that one hundred times.

James Whale later said that he thought each take looked authentic, but Howard kept ordering another shot. In Whale's words, "Before a shot finally pleased Hughes, the poor men could hardly walk, much less jump. If I remember correctly, and I do, I took the prettiest and most muscular stuntman home for an in-depth massage that night."

Remembering how William Wellman wouldn't shoot mock aerial battles for *Wings* unless he had the right cloud formations, Howard followed his mentor's example. In his private plane, he roamed the smog-free blue skies over Los Angeles looking for what he called "buttermilk," meaning billowing, cumulous clouds. When he couldn't find what he wanted, he'd fly back to base. A grip would post a sign: NO WAR TODAY! NO CLOUDS! REPORT BACK TOMORROW!

Stunt scene from *Hell's Angels*

Howard eventually found that the clouds over Oakland tended to be thick and fluffy. He ordered that his entire air force be moved to Oakland where aerial combat photography went on for another grueling four months.

The film was running up bills of five thousand dollars a day, much of it absorbed waiting for the clouds to roll in. As costs soared, Dietrich and Toolco officials protested but to no avail. When Howard was determined, he wouldn't listen to objections from anyone, including the most skilled of his stunt pilots.

Reginald Callow recalled that Howard had many bitter fights with Frank Clarke about the safety of the antiquated World War I aircraft he'd purchased. Howard falsely claimed that his mechanics had put all his planes in mint condition. Clarke shot back, "They're flying coffins."

"In the middle of their heated argument," Callow said, "the motor dropped out of a Fokker. End of argument. Clarke won the argument but Howard won the war. Shooting continued. After all, Howard was the sucker with the big bucks. But perhaps the real suckers were the stunt pilots."

Roscoe Turner was the best stunt pilot working on *Hell's Angels*. Howard had devised one of the most dramatic scenes in the film, depicting a converted German Gotha bomber—once the most deadly weapon in the arsenal of the Luftwaffe, portrayed in this incident by a retro-fitted Sikorsky— hit by British ground fire. The plot calls for the craft to lurch dangerously before it spins out of control and hurdles to the earth, where it crashes into a fiery furnace of death and destruction.

Knowing that Turner would be risking his life for the filming of the scene, Howard offered him five thousand dollars. As much as he wanted the money, this daredevil said no. He and Howard argued for an hour. Howard pleaded his case, claiming that he wanted Turner to fly the Sikorsky to the highest altitude possible, then nosedive toward the ground. If he couldn't pull it out of this stall, he was to jump out and parachute to safety.

Stubbornly rejecting all offers, Turner stormed away. Howard immediately went to see Dick Grace, Hollywood's most famous "crash pilot." Howard had remembered the daring stunts Grace had performed for director William Wellman during the shooting of *Wings*.

Instead of five thousand dollars, Howard, for reasons known only to himself, offered Grace only two hundred and fifty dollars to perform the same stunt. Grace came back with a counter offer. "I'll do it for ten thousand."

Howard turned down that offer and went to yet another stunt pilot, Al Wilson, who said he could pull it off. "Name your price," Howard said.

"A thousand dollars," Wilson said.

"It's a deal," Howard agreed.

To accompany Wilson during his dangerous stunt, Howard hired "grease monkey" Phil Jones, assigning him to ride in the rear of the plane, releasing smoke bombs to simulate that the craft was on fire. If Wilson couldn't get the plane out of its stall, then Jones was told to parachute to safety. He was willing to perform this risky stunt because he had recently contacted syphilis and needed money for treatments.

The daring feat was performed as both Wilson and Jones flew to the highest possible altitude and then plunged the plane into its stall. As Howard had feared, his pilot couldn't pull it out of the plunge. As Howard looked up to the sky, he saw Wilson jumping out of the cockpit and parachuting to earth.

He searched for Jones's parachute but saw nothing. The "Gotha bomber" crashed into an orange grove from a height of seven thousand feet and exploded, killing Jones. It was never determined why the young mechanic didn't bail out. There was speculation that he was unable to because he'd been knocked unconscious.

There were other deaths. The first fatality had occurred when stunt pilot Al Johnson hit high-tension wires flying from Glendale Airport to Mines Fields. His plane got tangled in the electric power lines, and he was badly burned. Amazingly, he survived and was rushed to the nearest hospital. Howard paid him a visit but the pilot never regained consciousness. Death came to Johnson eighteen hours after Howard's visit.

Yet another aviator, C.K. Philips, was flying a SE-5 to a location in Oakland. Carelessly, he hadn't checked his fuel before taking off. Running out of gas at one thousand feet over the earth, he was forced into a "deadstick landing," meaning without the motor running. Philips was killed instantly upon impact.

Wilson must have been the stunt pilot with nine lives, as soonafter, he was involved in yet another crash. Flying a Fokker D.VIII this time, he was in his cockpit as his propeller suddenly dropped off, falling through the air until it hit Hollywood Boulevard. It rolled and bounced down the street, sending cars off to the side of the road. Startled pedestrians scampered to safety, and no one was killed. The pilot-less plane crashed about two blocks from Grauman's Chinese Theatre. Again, no one was injured.

Wilson had bailed out, landing by parachute in the Olympic-sized swimming pool of movie tycoon Joe Schenk, who was conducting "a nude aquatic audition" with a hopeful young blonde starlet. The pilot's landing at such an inopportune time became the fodder for gossip at Hollywood parties for at least two more months.

***

It was the last banquet.

Tout Hollywood was shocked to receive an unusual invitation from Howard and Ella Hughes for a proper sit-down dinner at their Muirfield estate at Hancock Park. Ella had returned to Los Angeles after the Lindbergh encounter in New Hampshire, and had planned the gala as if she wanted to present a united front to Hollywood, showing this world that her marriage to Howard was still intact.

Every day as she made lavish preparations, she posted a sign on Howard's library door, reminding him of the Saturday night event. She'd purchased him a hand-tailored tuxedo that even such a fancy dresser as Big Howard would have been proud to wear.

For the fête, Ella had ordered a two-thousand dollar *couture* gown "in creamy peach" from Paris, and had adorned herself with her most expensive jewelry, including a diamond and ruby brooch.

In a daring move, she invited Howard's associates in the film world as well as her Pasadena society crowd. In real life, these two groups, always contemptuous of each other, never mingled socially.

The event was scheduled for the last Saturday in 1928. At the designated hour of seven o'clock, custom-made cars, such as that driven by Gloria Swanson's chauffeur, began to arrive in the driveway, along with silver, purple, or black Rolls-Royces; sleek, streamlined Packards, showy Hispano-Suizas, and custom-made Duesenbergs, some with scarlet-red upholstery and many painted in crayon colors.

For the illegal martinis, Ella ordered many cases of bootleg gin, much of it imported from Britain, which had been stashed away at the Ambassador Hotel and sent over to Muirfield.

Swanson was determined to be the best dressed woman there, and in a "black swan gown," she succeeded, although the competition was tough. Years later, she recalled that some of the show business contingent wasn't as well-dressed as the Pasadena society crowd, and the two groups didn't mingle, standing on opposite sides of the living room. She remembered one particularly obnoxious man with a cigar who wore a sports jacket in lime green and lemon yellow.

Ella gracefully glided between the two antagonistic cabals, assuring each of them that Howard was making two movies at the same time and must have been unavoidably detained at the studio.

"Lillian Gish in her greatest closeup didn't put on such a brave, courageous smile as Ella Rice did that night," Swanson claimed.

At eight-thirty, when her head chef insisted that he could not hold dinner any longer, Ella gave the command for the party to move into the dining room, out of which tables overflowed into the courtyard.

"The dinner party was almost over before Howard arrived," Blanche Sweet would later recall. "I think it was almost nine-thirty. He was dressed like a bum, and his white shirt was stained like he had dripped soup on it. He wore a pair of corduroy slacks in some ghastly shade of cowshit brown. He wore no stockings but the dirtiest pair of tennis shoes ever seen. They looked like they had been at a hog-calling contest in Mississippi."

"Without even acknowledging Ella, Howard sat down at his reserved seat at the head of the table and announced to the head waiter—hired for the evening and formally dressed—that he was hungry enough to eat a horse," Blanche said.

"Ella had served the grandest meal I'd ever seen in all my days in Hollywood," Ben Lyon recalled. "Lobster medallions heaped with dollops of the rarest of caviar. Sautéed foie gras. Roast suckling pig from a chef she'd hired who had cooked for the King of Spain. It was spectacular. Howard rejected everything and ordered a little steak—seared on the outside, blood-red on the inside—along with a small salad and some green peas. Instead of all the fancy wine, Howard asked for a glass of water with two ice cubes. When served, he gobbled his steak but took time to separate the big peas from the little peas, pushing the big peas aside and refusing to touch them."

At the end of the meal, Howard wiped his mouth on Ella's precious imported Madeira linen, dropping the napkin on the floor as he stood up and pushed back his upholstered chair. "If you good people will excuse me, I'm going to bed." Without saying another word, he turned his back on the dinner party and headed to the library where he proceeded to bolt the door.

"I don't think there was an actress in Hollywood, with the possible exception of myself, who could have pulled off the next scene," Swanson later said. "Ella Rice was a patrician. She held her head high and got through the rest of the evening. At the door, she personally thanked each guest, even the vulgarian in the sports coat, for coming."

When all the guests were gone, Ella ordered her maid to follow her to her upstairs bedroom. Once there, she began to pack all her clothing and possessions. It took until nearly five o'clock the next morning.

By six o'clock she was heading for the train station in Pasadena in a chauffeur-driven limousine, trailed by another van with all her luggage.

When Howard awoke at ten o'clock, a servant told him that his wife had left Muirfield and was heading back to Houston on the train.

"Let me see the note?" Howard demanded.

"She left no note, sir."

***

In the exciting year to come, most thoughts of Ella were forgotten.

New lovers, both male and female, were on the horizon. Three of the lovers waiting in the wings—two actresses and one actor—would in time become Hollywood legends.

CHAPTER SEVEN
Los Angeles, 1929

One morning, a sleep-deprived Howard stormed into Noah Dietrich's office and announced, "*Hell's Angels* is going to talk." Disoriented, Dietrich learned that the previous night, Howard had seen a private showing of Al Jolson's *The Jazz Singer*, which had actually been released many months before, in October of 1927, its use of sound creating a nation-wide sensation.

"Chaplin lied to me," Howard claimed. "He told me that talking pictures were a fad that would go away in a few months. I think sound has raised its ugly voice, and it's here to stay." Although he was never known for his skill as a mimic, he gave a very bad rendition of Jolson bellowing, "Wait a minute, folks, wait a minute—you ain't heard nothin' yet!"

Fearing that Howard was planning to reshoot the whole picture, on which he'd already spent an astronomical two million dollars, Dietrich protested, but to no avail. He urged him to release the film as it was, since silent flickers were still playing across the country. What he didn't say was that the silents were still being screened, but often to empty houses as the public rushed to hear recorded voices in "the talkies" instead.

To prove that he was right and Dietrich wrong, Howard staged a sneak preview of *Hell's Angels* in Pasadena. His aerial combat scenes and his dogfights were largely ignored by the inattentive audience. They seemed bored with Howard's multi-million-dollar extravaganza. Ben Lyon, James Hall, and Greta Nissen opened and closed their mouths soundlessly on the screen as the audience squirmed in their seats.

At the end of the showing, Howard's increasingly annoying uncle, Rupert, predicted that the film would be a financial disaster. After all the loss of life, the millions spent, and the months of grueling work by the cast and crew, Rupert in the lobby of the theater told Howard that he should put the film in mothballs like he'd done with *Swell Hogan*. "Or else destroy it!" Rupert added. That last remark earned Rupert a punch in the nose, a rare violent act on the part of Howard, who rarely struck anyone.

Dietrich issued an inaccurate warning. "*Hell's Angels* will drive Toolco to financial ruin." But Howard went ahead with his plans to reshoot most of the film anyway.

He'd determined that much footage of the expensive drama could be saved, especially the combat scenes. He'd add sound to his dogfights in the sky. "My god damn air force will be noiseless no more," he told James Whale.

All of the interior scenes, however, would have to be reshot. The voices of his two male stars, Ben Lyon and James Hall, recorded well. The problem was the thick Norwegian accent of Greta Nissen. This blonde looked stunningly beautiful, but her voice was the doom of her career.

The poet, Joseph Moncure March, was hired away from MGM to write dialogue for a new script. Whale began to rehearse the actors in their new speaking parts. The director urged Howard to come up with a female star—and soon—but he stalled, telling Whale "to work around the gal until I find her."

In and out of Metropolitan Studios paraded a bevy of young beauties, mostly blonde, for screen tests. Howard could not agree on the right girl. He even hired two projectionists and would summon one of them to the studio at two or three o'clock in the morning to look at the previous films of female contenders who might be right for the part of Helen.

His fellow Houstonian, the sleek and elegant blonde, Ann Harding, was recommended to him. She was photographed in a very dignified, almost refined matter. Howard pronounced her "too genteel," claiming that "the part calls for a whore in spite of her fancy airs."

Harding survived the rejection, shortly thereafter signing for *Holiday* which brought her an Oscar nomination. Regrettably, Harding's *Holiday* has been doomed to obscurity, replaced eight years later with another version, which starred Katharine Hepburn, Howard's future girlfriend.

One myth that circulated through Hollywood was that Howard was seeking an unknown for the lead role because he couldn't afford a "name" actress. Such gossip was ridiculous. He was prepared to spend another two million dollars, and possibly more, to make *Hell's Angels* a talkie. That budget could easily have covered the salary of any of the biggest female stars in Hollywood, even one who commanded one hundred thousand dollars per picture. Most stars he could have had for one-fourth of that salary.

Although she didn't print it in her column, gossip maven Louella Parsons told Marion Davies and W.R. Hearst that Howard was a casting couch director. This legend began at the time of his recasting of *Hell's Angels*. In a sense, it was true. But a casting couch usually suggests that an actor or actress goes to bed with a producer or director in whom they have no sexual interest. Or, as Ben Lyon so bluntly put it, "they fuck to get the part."

Howard auditioned both established actresses and unknown ones. He never insisted that these women lie on his casting couch. "Many of the girls wanted to bed this shy, rich, and handsome Texan, even if they didn't get the damn part," Ben said. "Howard never forced himself on any of them. The ladies seduced him, and I was there to see much of the action up close and personal."

One day Whale approached Howard on the set. "I've found our Helen," he said. "She's blonde. She's beautiful. Tarty yet with a certain vapid elegance. I've cast her in *Angels* in an uncredited part as a girl selling kisses. Want to meet her?"

"Who is this wonder?" Howard asked.

"You'll fall for her," Whale predicted. "She's going to become one of the biggest stars in Hollywood. What Mae Murray was to your father, Marian Marsh is going to become to you."

***

Howard was continuing to see actor Russell Gleason, and he too raved about Marian Marsh, having met her in *The Sophomore*. Marian had been right under Howard's nose all along but he'd paid no attention to her until Whale and Russell sang her praises.

Born in British-controlled Trinidad in 1913, Marian was a leading lady in films from the early 30s until 1942. If she's remembered at all today, it's for her appearance playing Trilby to John Barrymore's *Svengali* in 1931. Trilby's fabled nude scene in that film was actually shot with a double who wore a body stocking.

Howard was initially intrigued with her, and they dated several times but no serious romance developed. Marian, however, is still included in the round-up of "the usual suspects" among Howard's girlfriends.

Whale, and he was only guessing, claimed that he felt Howard's relationship with Marion was "merely platonic." They were seen together on a number of occasions. During the time they were dating, he seemed to undergo a tremendous change of character from the shy Texas millionaire in the late Twenties to a more self-assured young man about town in the early 1930s. Perhaps it was Howard who got Marian interested in aviation. In time, the fading star would marry Cliff Henderson, a promoter and spokesperson for the aviation industry, and general manager of the National Air Races from their inception in 1928 until 1939. Henderson was also the founder of the City of Palm Desert.

Marian could successfully bat her saucer-blue eyes while charming a potential husband in real life, but in films she remained rather expressionless, like her portrayal of Trilby in *Svengali*. Howard was initially attracted by her doll face, but after a screen test, he decided he could do very little with her. Even the fabled director Josef von Sternberg, who succeeded so magnificently in his direction of Marlene Dietrich, failed to get much from her when

Marian Marsh

he directed her in *Crime and Punishment* in 1935.

Nonetheless, Howard liked Marian, and they had an easy relationship. It was with a certain sadness that her fans watched her career drift into obscurity. This reporter's attempts to track her down to her Palm Desert lair to hear about her side of her friendship with Howard were not successful.

Dietrich later claimed that Howard flew Marian in his Sikorsky across the broad plains of America to Chicago and New York but there was "no real chemistry there."

As was his way, Howard soon became distracted by other beautiful actresses vying for his attention.

"It seemed that every actress in Hollywood wanted the part of Helen," Whale said. "So many, in fact, that Howard found that these women were taking up too much of his time. At one point, he refused to see all "but the most beautiful and the sexiest."

"He was like a kid in a candy store," Whale further claimed. "Some of the most gorgeous women in the world were making themselves available to him. His male beauty had faded a bit after plastic surgery, but his face had assumed a more manly character. Of course, all of these women were a little too much, and every now and then he liked to escape to the arms of a Gary Cooper type—that is, when Gary himself wasn't available. I personally believed that he continued to see Coop long after the insider crowd thought it was over. In that, I suppose, I remain an opinion of one."

***

Throughout the shooting of *Hell's Angels,* Howard was fuming at another director, also named Howard. Howard Hawks, shooting *The Dawn Patrol,* was already touting it as "the greatest air epic ever!" In Howard's view, he himself was shooting the greatest air epic ever.

Howard was already familiar with the picture's two male stars, the more prominently featured of which was Richard Barthelmess. Lillian Gish had called him "the most beautiful face of any man who ever went before the camera." Although no longer on the best of terms with Howard, the picture's costar was Douglas Fairbanks Jr.

Throughout his life Howard both admired the success of Hawks as a director and also resented that acclaim. He was also jealous of Charles Lindbergh's heroic breakthroughs in aviation.

Growing increasingly paranoid, Howard became convinced that Hawks was stealing material from *Hell's Angels* to use in *The Dawn Patrol*, including some of the ideas behind Howard's unique aerial combat scenes. At least some of these ideas came from Elmer Dyer, reputedly the best aerial cameraman in Hollywood, who had worked for, and advised Howard, in *Hell's Angels,* and who was now working for Hawks on *Dawn Patrol.*

Actor Neil Hamilton, once famous as the "Arrow Collar Man" when he was a model, was overheard making a remark in a nightclub. Sharing third billing in *The Dawn Patrol,* he told friends that Hawks was rushing to have his picture released before *Hell's Angels* "so that he can sweep the market first."

When reported to Howard, Hamilton's remark drove him into a rage. That afternoon he secretly hired five members of Hawks's crew to spy on the filming of *The Dawn Patrol*, promising each of them five hundred dollars if they would supply him with revealing information.

To retaliate against Hawks, Howard also hired some of the director's best stunt pilots, offering them more money if they came to work for *Hell's Angels*. Hawks later revealed, "I had pilots under 'exclusive' contract, and Hughes also had the same pilots under 'exclusive' contract."

Even when Howard had finished his scenes involving airplanes, he ordered Dietrich to continue to buy up World War I craft so that they would not be available to Hawks. There was a sudden demand for Spads and Camels, which prior to that had been rusting in mothballs.

Finally, when he could take it no more, Howard showed up early one Sunday morning, after a sleepless night, at Hawks's doorstep for a confrontation.

No one will ever know exactly what words transpired between the two combative directors. Hawks was a notorious liar and could never be trusted. He later gave a rather sanitized version of the encounter to the press. However, on the set of *The Dawn Patrol,* he told Doug Fairbanks Jr. and Richard Barthelmess "what really happened," or so he claimed.

"I woke up one morning with the mother of all headaches," Hawks said. "I'd just gotten in at four that morning after a night of drinking and fucking Thelma Todd. We must have finished off two bottles. My head was pounding like someone was in there with a sledgehammer. I suddenly woke up with a start realizing an intruder was also persistently ringing my doorbell. It wasn't even six o'clock."

Wrapping a towel around his nude body, Hawks stumbled to the door, planning to bludgeon to death the unwanted guest. "I threw open the door to confront Howard Hughes. His blood vessels were popping out of his skin. That was one mad Texas boy, but I wasn't afraid of him at all."

George O'Brien

187

"Howard Hughes here," he said.

Hawks was contemptuous. "As if I didn't know who you are. My worst nightmare."

"I'm making an air epic," Howard said, standing in the doorway and not invited in. "And I'm told you're making a pale imitation of it."

"We'll battle it out at the box office," Hawks said.

"You've got a scene in your shitty picture where a guy is hit by a bullet of a German aircraft," Howard said. "He's shown spitting up blood. You stole that from me."

"Like hell I did!" Hawks countered. "I wrote that scene myself. It's original. In case you didn't know, I stole the incident directly from World War I. Pilots were shot. They vomited blood. That happened to hundreds of pilots. You don't own the concept. Now get the fuck off my doorstep, or I'm calling the police."

"I want you to take that god damn scene out of your picture," Howard demanded. "Or else!"

"Listen, Hughes, you're a rich Texan," Hawks said. "Oil or something. You're in the movie business on a lark. A hobby for you. I'm a filmmaker. I shoot films for a living. The scene stays in!"

"I'll sue your ass!"

Hawks slammed the door in Howard's face.

"I stumbled back into my kitchen and made a sure-fire cure for a hangover," Hawks said. "Four-fifths tomato juice. One-fifth hot pepper sauce. But as I was to find out later, I didn't get rid of Hughes so easily by slamming the door in the fucker's face!"

Receiving no satisfaction from his one-on-one with Hawks, Howard came up with a scheme that afternoon. He had to obtain a copy of the script of *The Dawn Patrol*, hoping to bring an injunction before Hawks could release his epic.

He summoned his assistant director, Reginald Callow, and his screen writer, Joseph Moncure March, to Muirfield. The unholy trio conceived a scenario whereby they would approach Hawks's secretary with a bribe.

"Wine and dine her," Howard ordered. "Hell, fuck her if you have to. If that doesn't work, give her five hundred dollars."

Amazingly, the secretary accepted a dinner invitation from both men, which rather surprised them. Callow was a bit suspicious. "It looks too easy," he said, "like taking candy from a baby."

Over dinner the secretary agreed to obtain a copy of the script and illegally hand it over to them. She told them that if they came by her apartment the following evening around eight o'clock, she'd be there with a copy of the script.

The next evening Callow and March showed up at her apartment at the appointed time. After they counted out the five hundred dollars, the secretary handed them the script.

188

Just as they were telling her goodnight, two Los Angeles detectives emerged from the bedroom with handcuffs for both Marsh and Callow. They were taken to the local police station and booked.

By midnight, Howard learned of their arrest. He called Dietrich at once and demanded that he do something "to get Joe March out of jail. He's got important work due on my script." "What about Reggie?" Dietrich asked. "Fuck him!" Howard said. "I don't need him so much. He can rot in jail for all I care."

In the middle of the night, Dietrich approached a friend of his who was a superior court judge. After accepting a bribe, the judge agreed to hold a hearing at five o'clock that morning when no members of the press were around.

At a three-minute hearing, the judge released the men without bail.

For some reason, Hawks never followed up with charges against the script thieves. The case was dropped.

Not grateful for that act of conciliation, Howard called Neil McCarthy, his attorney. "I want you to sue the hell out of Howard Hawks."

June Collyer

"What's the charge?" McCarthy asked.

"How the hell do I know?" Howard asked. "Copyright infringement, whatever. Why do I pay you all the money I do? For you to come up with the fucking charges." He slammed down the phone on the attorney.

***

Beverly Hills, 1965

In his search for an actress to play Helen, Howard ordered his projectionist to screen for him a copy of the silent film, *East Side, West Side*. Made in 1927, it starred June Collyer and George O'Brien.

Howard was immediately impressed with June and ordered a screen test for her right away. Apparently, he was also physically attracted to George O'Brien and filed his name away in his little black book, hoping to have someone arrange a future encounter with this exceptionally handsome actor, who was known for stripping down any time a photographer such as Rod St. Just wanted a nude shot.

When he met June, a New York native who had been born one year after himself, Howard was immediately impressed with how photogenic her face was. He told Whale, "Her face practically glows. Call it luminous if you will. And no actress ever had such fantastic dimples."

At her home in Beverly Hills, three years before her death in 1968 of bronchial pneumonia, June remembered Howard with both generosity and a tinge of regret bordering on bitterness.

"You'd hardly call our first meeting romantic," June said. "Just as I appeared, some of his rambunctious crew was pulling a big stunt on Hughes. Because he was so young, they jokingly called him 'the kid' or 'boy' behind his back, as I was to learn later. Hughes had gone to the privy to take a crap I guess. While he was in this makeshift outhouse, as flimsy as a piece of cardboard, a stunt pilot turned on the propeller of his plane. The wind gusts blew the outhouse down. Hughes came running out of the wreckage with his trousers down as he desperately tried to pull up his underwear. I've heard of *coitus interruptus*, but I don't know what you'd call the state Hughes was in." She laughed at her own memories.

Whale later added more information to Howard's running battle with his stunt pilots. The engineer in him got even, and he constructed a hydraulic device that shot water through a pipe and into the bottom of a septic tank. As the pilots went in to defecate, the waste from below was shot upwards onto their exposed buttocks. The one-upmanship games continued throughout the shoot. One pilot drilled a trio of holes into a wooden partition for the insertion of a penis. The largest one was marked for pilot Frank Clarke, with another pilot, Frank Tomick, getting the average sized one. The smallest hole for the smallest penis went to Howard, which infuriated the hell out of him as he was proud of his large endowment.

Thelma Todd

"And so began our hot, torrid affair which lasted about as long as it takes a candle to burn down," June said. "It was fun, though. But somewhere along the way I realized Hughes was just toying with me. He had no intention of casting me in the role of Helen."

She recalled that on their first date that same evening, he took her back to Muirfield. "I'd heard that he was married to some Texas broad, but she was nowhere to be seen. I guess she'd gone back to Houston or something."

Astonishingly, after a dinner prepared by some of his servants, June claimed that Howard took her into his study

190

to show her some films. "I just assumed they were previews of some of the dogfights in *Hell's Angels*, because that's all he talked about through dinner."

He began to screen some badly photographed pornographic movies that starred Joan Crawford. "I remember one of them was called *Bosom Buddies*, and it involved a lesbian scene," June said. "I recall Hughes saying, 'Wait until Fairbanks Jr. gets a look at these.' For some reason, he seemed to have a great resentment against Crawford and young Fairbanks—I don't know why. Maybe they had done something bad to him. He was enjoying the fact that Crawford was being humiliated by having these movies shown at Hollywood parties. I had never seen pornography before or since. Frankly, I thought that Crawford was better in *Mildred Pierce* than she was in those stinking movies. I once talked to Humphrey Bogart, who told me that he'd seen these blue films at Texas Guinan's speakeasy in New York back in the late Twenties."

Years later, Howard was still screening these so-called blue movies for some of his guests, as actress Terry Moore confessed in her bittersweet memoirs, *The Beauty and the Billionaire*.

***

Los Angeles, 1929

From the moment he met her, Howard was mesmerized by the blonde-haired comedienne, Thelma Todd, who signed her notes, cards, and letters "Hot Toddy." The wise-cracking bombshell, who had wanted to be a schoolteacher until she became Miss Massachusetts of 1925, was a hard-drinking Jazz Age baby. Normally, Howard didn't like actresses who were lushes, but Thelma amused him in a way that none of his previous girlfriends had done.

Unknown to Howard at the time, Thelma was also a pill-popper, desperately trying to keep her weight down in spite of her heavy drinking. Thelma called her drinking "tippling."

The tall blonde with the "Baby Blues," before her tragic early ending, was known as a custard-pie comedienne under the tutelage of tough-minded producer, Hal Roach.

Over the years, she was cast opposite the Marx Brothers, Jimmy Durante, Buster Keaton, Laurel and Hardy, Wheeler and Woolsey, and Joe E. Brown. Gary Cooper had taken Howard to see the western, *Nevada*, in 1927, in which Thelma had appeared.

From his first night with her, Howard felt she had the talent to rise above slaphappy roles, and he wanted to give her the chance to play Helen in his serious drama of *Hell's Angels*. She was so delighted that such an important producer would take an interest in her that she virtually told him she'd do "anything for him," or so her frequent co-star, Patsy Kelly, later claimed.

Thelma's confidante, Brooklyn-born Patsy Kelly, years later when she was a guest of Tallulah Bankhead, said "Hughes and Thelma hit it off. I think they

191

had known each other for only four hours before they wanted to make whoopee."

The same age as Howard, Thelma, a New England born bundle of talent, called Patsy the next day and told her, "I not only got the part but I've got myself a new boyfriend."

Howard laughed at her observations when he took her to the Plantation Café, which was managed at the time by Fatty Arbuckle, the disgraced comedian. Tuxedoed, Fatty greeted them in a very personable way and showed them to a table near one occupied by Buster Keaton sitting with Charlie Chaplin. At a faraway table, John Gilbert sat alone, drinking himself to death and perhaps lamenting the coming of sound to movies.

At table where illegal booze was served, Thelma told Howard, "Men are always chasing after me, and I don't run very fast."

As the evening grew serious, at least according to Patsy Kelly, Thelma came to believe that Howard had seen through her façade and sensed a serious actress waiting to escape.

For one week, Thelma announced to everybody that "My lead role in *Hell's Angels* is all but wrapped up. The contract is being drawn up now. It's the part I've waited for all my life. When the contract's signed, I'll take off a few pounds. Howard wants me thinner. Right now, I'm cute and bouncy, but Howard will want me leaner and meaner for the part."

Called a few days later to a dinner meeting at the Brown Derby, Thelma gleefully went, finding movie mogul Joe Schenck and Howard Hughes there, along with her agent, Roland West, who had also become her lover. West was aware that she was "two-timing" him with Howard, but he had previously encouraged her to "fuck your way to the top."

With dangling diamond earrings and a white beaded gown similar to one worn in a film by Clara Bow, Thelma faced the triumvirate. Out of nervousness, she immediately apologized for putting on a few extra pounds, claiming she could take them off in three weeks.

Schenck, who had agreed to distribute *Hell's Angels* for Howard, was concerned that Thelma might run into a contractual problem with her producer, Hal Roach.

She assured both Howard and Schenck that she was certain "Hal would let me go because I have a free-lance clause in my contract." She also assured the men that she also had a "potato clause" in that same contract, so there was no way that she'd be putting on any more weight.

As Thelma later told Patsy, "the four of us sat there getting stinking, dirty, rotten drunk. Even Howard, though I'd been told he never drank. Maybe a cocktail or two and that was it. We stayed there until midnight. I kissed Roland good-bye and went home to Muirfield with Howard. My promised night of love-making didn't happen, though. It was midnight when we got there, and he passed out in the living room. There was nothing I could do to revive him."

The next day, when Thelma was filming a three-reel musical, *High C's*, she broke at lunch to go to Hal Roach's office. But instead of giving his consent for the freelance role,

192

he attacked her for going to Howard without consulting him first.

"There's no way I'll ever let you take that part in *Hell's Angels*," he said, threatening her. "If you even attempt it, you'll never work again in Hollywood. I've devoted time and money building you up as a comedienne the country loves. The role in *Hell's Angels* calls for a whore. The blonde bitch sleeps with all the pilots. It will destroy your image."

There was more verbal abuse to come. Thelma stood and took it.

"My lawyers studied your contract this morning," he said. "It clearly states that I have to approve any free-lance roles you're offered. And I don't approve of the part in *Hell's Angels*. You're out of the picture before you even got into the damn thing. Besides, Hughes is a nut. He'll never finish that god damn film."

Carole Lombard

That night, without Howard or Roland West, Thelma went on a drinking spree and piled up her car at two o'clock in the morning. Fortunately, she didn't injure anyone. She fled from the scene of the accident, and later told the police that her car had been stolen. No charges were ever filed.

Two days later, after Roland negotiated furiously but unsuccessfully with Roach, he placed an early morning call to Thelma. "You're out of the picture," he gloomily reported.

"That god damn Roach," she shouted into the phone. "I could strangle the bastard."

"It's not Roach," Roland said. "It's Hughes. He found himself another blonde."

"Oh, shit!"

In spite of the rejection, Thelma would once again re-enter the life of Howard Hughes.

After a trip East to recover, Thelma confronted reporters when she arrived back in Hollywood. She was asked how it felt to lose such an important role.

"No big deal, fellahs," she said. "A blonde, even a bleached one, is a blonde and a part is a part. Who in the hell cares? In my next movie, *Corsair*, I'm changing my name to Alison Loyd—a whole new image for me—and winning the Oscar. No more custard pies in the kisser!"

She did just that. Only she didn't win an Oscar. The film flopped.

She came back again as the comedienne, Thelma Todd.

Without knowing it, she'd embarked on the road to disaster, becoming another one of Howard's doomed ladies.

"I've slept with Joseph Kennedy, so why not Howard Hughes?"

Before Howard stood a Hollywood original, Miss Carole Lombard, still in the process of inventing herself.

He looked startled, as if he hadn't heard her correctly. This former pie-in-the-face Mack Sennett cutie had come over at James Whale's request to make a screen test for the role of the still uncast Helen. Time was running out on the schedule of *Hell's Angels*, and Howard needed to find a replacement…and soon.

Until he met and fell in love with Ava Gardner, he would never meet such a potty-mouth as Lombard.

When he didn't respond to her Kennedy line, she seemed to work overtime figuring out ways to shock him. "Ben Lyon tells me you like a gal with tits." Right in front of him, she manipulated her dress to expose her left breast. "You're not entitled to look at the right one until you've signed me to play Helen. Then you can have whatever you want. It's all yours, baby!"

"The part calls for a woman to be a bit of a slut," Howard said, standing up from his desk. "At least you qualify for that."

Carole Lombard, who in those days called herself "A Scotch-English lass," was actually born Jane Alice Peters in Fort Wayne, Indiana. She was three years younger than Howard.

Directed by James Whale, her screen test was scheduled for that afternoon. Intrigued with her, although not especially drawn to "talk dirty" women, Howard invited her to dinner that night.

"Some dinner!" she later told Whale. "I got a stale baloney sandwich at midnight. Some studio grip brought it to us when I told Howard I was starving to death and would have to suck semen from him for protein if he didn't get me something to eat soon."

Instead of dinner at the Brown Derby as he'd originally promised, Howard took her to 7000 Romaine Avenue in Hollywood where he showed her his staff's experiments in color film. "I missed out on the coming of sound," he said, "but I'm convinced that in the future, all films will be shot in color. They'll talk and have color, too."

Before his experiments, films had been hand-painted to add a bit of color. This tinting, often blue of scenes after dark, or sepia for turbulent skies, wasn't very effective.

Technicolor was under way, but the drawback was costs. Howard's company, employing at least two scientists from Cal Tech, as well as a skilled engineer from Toolco headquarters in Houston, was called Multicolor. Howard laboriously explained the process to a bored Lombard, who'd dressed for an evening on the town.

Although Howard was correct in his assessment of color in pictures, his timing was wrong. Before he abandoned the experiment, he'd spent nearly two-million dollars.

Carole Lombard would go on to grace the screen and become a Hollywood legend, especially when she married Clark Gable, king of the box office. But the world would remember her face on the silver (black and white) screen, not in Technicolor.

Carole confided to Whale that after her stale sandwich, Howard drove her high into the Hollywood Hills "for a long talk." There, he told her about his plane accident and how he'd never liked his face since surgery.

She confided that she had experienced equivalent feelings during events that had begun with an automobile accident.

On a date with Harry Cooper, son of the vice president of Security First National Bank of Los Angeles, she was riding in the passenger seat when his Bugatti roadster crashed. The windshield was shattered, a shard of glass slicing through the right side of her face, slitting it open from the corner of her nose to her cheekbone.

The doctor told her that during surgery, the use of an anesthetic would make her facial muscles relax in ways that would reduce the possibility that her face would be restored to what it had been before. She bravely informed him that if that were the case, she would endure the four-hour operation without anesthesia. In agonizing pain, and fully conscious, she lasted through each of the sixteen stitches required.

In the aftermath, plastic surgery was eventually required anyway. And even after that, the scar was never completely erased and had to be covered over with makeup.

She told Howard, "I went through it all, because I wanted to be a god damn fucking movie star."

He seemed to identify with her plight, perhaps because of his own disfigurement. The next afternoon, he viewed her screen test with great concentration, demanding that it be run a total of fourteen times. Making no comment until the final showing, Howard abruptly stood up and signaled to his projectionist to go home.

"I've seen all I want to see," he said to Whale.

"Is she in or out?" Whale asked.

"I'll let you know tomorrow," he said, leaving the studio without another word.

When Whale met with Howard the following morning, he got the impression that Howard had spent the night with Carole, although he revealed nothing. "I've called my attorney," he said to the director. "Lombard is Helen. Start rehearsing her at once. Since this is a talking picture, be careful what she says. She talks like a sailor's parrot. Every tenth word is 'fucking.'"

Lombard could be very blunt about her sexual liaisons. When she learned that Ben Lyon was Howard's friend in more ways than one, she kidded him without mercy during evenings on the town. Often Howard invited both Ben and Carole as his guests for the night. Since Ella Rice Hughes seemed to have permanently left, he moved Carole into Muirfield.

"I can give him something you can't," Carole mockingly told Ben one night at the Zulu Club, with its African motif.

"And what might that be?" Ben asked, repeating the dialogue to James Whale the next day.

"I found out Howard's favorite type of sex with a woman," Carole allegedly said. "And I had to look it up in the dictionary. Intermammary intercourse, it's called."

"You mean sticking it between a woman's breast?" Ben said. "Hell, I've been doing that for years. But it's not my favorite thing."

On the day before she was to go before the cameras on *Hell's Angels*, Carole arrived at Muirfield to find her luggage packed and a limousine waiting to take her back to her real home. In desperation, she called Whale at the studio to find out what happened, since Howard wouldn't come to the phone.

"I've been trying to get in touch with you," he said. "I've got bad news! This morning Hughes cast Jean Harlow as Helen."

To this day it isn't known exactly why Howard dumped Carole so abruptly. In a confidential talk with Louella Parsons, Marion Davies at San Simeon offered the best reason. "The night I introduced Howard to Billie Dove—and he'd been urging me to do that for weeks—I knew it was curtains for Lombard." Forbidden to print that story, Louella proceeded to spread the gossip across Hollywood.

Randolph Scott

After her marriage to Clark Gable in 1939, Carole encountered Howard on at least two occasions, once at a dinner party. Apparently, no mention was ever made about why he gave her the part in *Hell's Angels*, then abruptly snatched it away.

Miriam Hopkins, the only actress in Hollywood who Bette Davis hated more than Joan Crawford, once said that she sat across from Carole and Howard at a party in Beverly Hills. "Hughes was there with Ginger Rogers that night," Miriam recalled. "I'd heard that Carole and Hughes had had an affair. But he had not one word to say to her, focusing all his attention on Ginger instead. It was like he'd never met Carole."

Later, when Miriam was in the powder room with Carole, she said the actress did deliver a one-liner about Howard. "He's got Clark beat by four inches, but Hughes has no soul."

It would actually be another Howard (Hawks) who would do more for Carole's career than most. She was his second cousin. Meeting her after years

196

had gone by, he was taken with her image at a Hollywood party as she held a gin and tonic in her hand. Her laughter and off-color remarks intrigued Hawks, who cast her opposite John Barrymore in Columbia's *Twentieth Century* in 1934. That film liberated the on-screen Carole Lombard and made her a big star.

A Transcontinental and West Air luxury airplane (TWA), of which Howard Hughes Jr. was the kingpin, crashed near Las Vegas on January 16, 1942, killing all eighteen passengers aboard, including Carole Lombard and her mother.

The day before, Carole had sold more than two million dollars worth of war bonds. At the time of her death, she was earning half a million dollars a year, making her the highest paid female star in Hollywood.

For Carole's funeral, Howard sent Clark Gable a large wreath of red American Beauty roses. He signed it: "In loving memory, H. Hughes."

***

One of the most ambitious men ever to set foot in California arrived at Howard's studio with a letter of introduction from his family back East. From Orange County, Virginia, Randolph Scott claimed that Big Howard had been a friend of his own father, whom he'd known from their wildcatter days.

Taking one look at this strapping, handsome, soft-spoken Southerner, Howard didn't even bother to read the letter of introduction. "He fell for six feet four inches of hard, tanned muscle," James Whale recalled. With a rather horsey face, Randolph had a gracious manner about him, rather courtly in fact. Square-jawed, he stood with a regal stance, and had a lazy, swinging walk that evoked another lanky actor, Gary Cooper.

Actually Randolph Scott hadn't come to Hollywood to be an actor. He'd studied engineering and was applying for a position with Toolco.

When Howard learned that Randolph knew how to play golf, he immediately invited him to the local country club. On the golf course, both men got acquainted with each other and even found that they shared some prejudices in common, including a dislike of Jews and blacks. After the game, the two handsome young men went in to take a shower together, and apparently Howard liked what he saw of Randolph, who had been a nude model in Washington, D.C., before riding the westbound train to Los Angeles.

Before the day was over, Howard had invited him to Muirfield where he found out that he was sexually compatible with this athletic young man.

Howard soon convinced Randolph that he should give up engineering and pursue a career as a matinee idol. Howard promised that until he had a starring part for him, he would get Randolph work as an extra, which he proceeded to do, securing him a bit part in the film, *The Far Call*.

After their first week of living together and sleeping together every night, Howard became convinced that Randolph was a cold and calculating individual "with the soul of an adding machine," he told Whale. That cold heart didn't bother Howard at all, especially when Randolph agreed to do whatever Howard wanted in bed. A natural top, he became a bottom for Howard, even though he found that role both painful and humiliating. Howard, however, seemed to enjoy his dominance over this rugged athlete.

"To get ahead, Randolph would screw anything or get screwed," Whale said. "Just look what he'd do in the years ahead. I mean, look at that rich Marion DuPont scarecrow he married for money. He set out to become as rich as Howard Hughes. In that he didn't succeed, but he did become the richest actor in Hollywood."

By the second week, Howard had already put Randolph on a back burner in his life, as he ardently pursued affairs with two actresses. Randolph painfully learned that he wasn't going to become Howard's boy and share in Toolco's riches, but would only be a sometime toy.

Left alone for most nights of the week and hungry for sex, he wandered one night into Griffith Park in Los Angeles. That was the major meeting place for homosexual pickups. But it was extremely dangerous because homosexuality was illegal and arrests were frequent. Handsome young men were hired as vice cops to work undercover to entrap homosexuals in the park. Once one of these cops was propositioned by a man, the victim would be immediately arrested.

Randolph was the victim of such a fate on his first and last visit to the park. Booked at a local precinct, Randolph immediately called Howard to bail him out. Howard phoned his attorney, Neil McCarthy, who could get anybody off on any charge, including murder, or so his legend went. In those days, bribery was an accepted custom with the Los Angeles police. After securing Randolph's release and parting with three thousand dollars in crisp bills, McCarthy drove Randolph back to Muirfield where Howard greeted him with a stern lecture. In the years to come, Howard would always credit himself for having saved Randolph's career.

In the weeks ahead, whenever Howard didn't come home, Randolph still pursued young men, but in more discreet ways. It was only when he met Cary Grant that he would flaunt his homosexuality.

Not wanting to get arrested again, Randolph began to "make the lavender rounds," as Billy Haines called it. Howard had introduced Randolph to Billy and had asked his friend to show Randolph around Hollywood.

After seducing him, Billy did just that. "First, it was *moi*," Billy said. "Then Ramon Novarro. Nils Asther (that affair lasted for only one night). Ben Lyon (maybe two nights at the most). James Whale (Randolph submitted to a blow-job). Joel McCrea (Randolph found him hotter than he found Howard). And, then, the second love of his life, Gary Cooper. Grant was always *numero uno*."

In the weeks ahead, when Randolph wasn't seen with Howard, he was out with Gary Cooper. Sometimes they would go away on weekends together.

"Those two taciturn gentlemen never said more than three words to each other, or so I bet, on a weekend, but I just know that there was plenty of action under the bedsheets," Billy said.

Randolph had been introduced to Gary when he was hired to help the Montana-born actor with his lines in *The Virginian*, which was a talkie. Rather proud of his endowment, Gary often received guests in his dressing room "buck ass naked," as he put it. Randolph was pleasantly stunned when Gary opened the door and invited him in.

It seems that somewhere during their conversation, the telephone rang. Some woman—perhaps that Mexican spitfire, Lupe Velez—was on the other end of the phone, telling Gary what she was going to do to him later that night.

Randolph later told Billy. "There I sat watching Gary rise to the height of Mt. Everest. I was impressed—even bigger than Howard."

His association with Gary Cooper and Howard didn't make Randolph rich overnight. "The only thing I got from Gary," he later told Whale, was "Lupe Velez. I inherited her when Gary dumped her."

Adela Rogers St. Johns, the newspaper columnist, claimed that Velez was being passed around in those days from one celebrity to another, "like a Christmas fruit cake that no one wants. First, Jack Dempsey. Then John Gilbert, followed by Randolph Scott. She ended up marrying Tarzan, however." The columnist was referring to Johnny Weissmuller.

Although Randolph's romance with Gary would be short lived, Cooper's legacy lived on throughout Randolph's career. In spite of his millions, the Western star eventually became known as "the poor man's Gary Cooper."

"Regardless of his other lovers in the years ahead, male or female—and that includes Cary Grant—Randolph Scott came running if Howard ever called him to 'come fly with me,'" Billy said. "If there's one thing that Virginia boy respected, it was money, and Howard Hughes had more of that stuff than he could count."

***

Arriving from Kansas City, Missouri, Jean Harlow was only eighteen years old when she met Howard Hughes, who still had not cast the role of Helen in *Hell's Angels*. Actually, the actress, who wasn't even an actress at the time, had borrowed her screen name from her mother, whose maiden name had been Jean Harlow. The blonde bombshell's actual given name at the time of her birth was Harlean Carpenter.

Many men, including Ben Lyon, claimed that they had discovered Jean and introduced her to Howard. The actual introduction, however, was made by James Hall, who had enjoyed a brief affair with Jean before they drifted apart. James had first met Jean when he co-starred with Clara Bow in *The Saturday Night Kid*, with Jean appearing in an uncredited role.

Married at sixteen to stockbroker Charles (Chuck) McGrew, Jean was fresh from affairs with actor Gilbert Roland, bandleader Roy Fox, and Joel McCrea, with whom she'd made a lackluster screen test. Jean's career was going nowhere at this point, and once again she was appearing in an uncredited role, in spite of her striking looks.

One day on a Hollywood set, his arm linked with Jean's, Hall introduced her to Howard and suggested he order a screen test. Her hair was referred to unattractively as "albino blonde." Howard took in her figure, showcased in a sexy, revealing, bias-cut dress that had been designed by Edith Head for Clara Bow. Bow had given it to Jean when she'd grown too fat to wear it.

Focusing on her breasts, Howard said, "You don't wear a bra."

"I read that women in ancient Egypt didn't wear bras, so why should I?" she asked.

"Why indeed?" he said before turning and walking away.

This was the unlikely meeting of two future Hollywood legends who would be forever linked.

Even though Howard told Hall he wasn't impressed with Jean, he ordered Tony Gaudio, his cameraman, to make a three-minute test of her. David Marx, a crew member of *Hell's Angels*, later confirmed in an interview that it was Hall, not Ben Lyon who brought Jean to meet Howard for the first time.

That day Howard had ordered his projectionist to screen two bit parts of Jean's for him, her appearance with Charlie Chaplin in *City Lights* and her appearance with Laurel and Hardy in *Double Whoopee*. After viewing the two segments, he told James Whale, "Harlow lacks the magic it takes to be a star."

The next day after Howard, with Whale, viewed her screen test, he still remained unimpressed yet almost inexplicably, he decided to negotiate a contract with her agent anyway. Under that albino hair, he found that her face "was puffy and sulky and her head photogenically wrong for her body. She's got great tits, though."

Joe Angel, the former president of Metro Pictures, who was booted out of his job by Louis B. Mayer, also watched the test with Howard. He found her Missouri accent "so thick it sounds like a bar maid screaming for the brewmaster to open a fresh keg for the boys." Later, when the name Jean Harlow became a household word, Engel claimed that he'd discovered Jean, and that he was the one who had introduced her to Howard.

The scriptwriter, Joseph Moncure March, who should have had a better choice of words, compared Jean's figure to a dust pan, making one wonder what dust pans looked like at his house.

To the surprise of all his crew, even Hall, Howard impulsively announced that "Harlow gets the part. Get her agent over here if she even has an agent."

Since no one was ever able to penetrate the mind of Howard Hughes, there is only speculation about why he cast her in such a pivotal role when he clearly found her unsuitable.

That morning, Howard told Ben Lyon that he'd had a major fight with Carole Lombard and had broken off relations with her.

Years later, James Hall said he knew why Howard didn't cast a major star in the role. "He wanted to take an unknown actress and make her a star. We'd heard rumors that he had a bet with Rupert that he could take a sow's ear and turn it into a silk purse. He planned to sign a gal of his creation to a five-year contract to take advantage of her peak earning period and her greatest beauty— and he wanted her to sign before she became famous so he could get her to work for peanuts. He also wanted a woman who would be putty in his hands." In lieu of a better explanation, Hall's assessment will have to stand.

By six o'clock that evening, Harlow's agent Arthur Landau showed up to negotiate with Howard. He would later claim that it was he who had introduced Jean to Howard.

Landau was never reliable with the truth. He told interviewers that he discovered Jean on the set of *Double Whoopee* and brought her that very day to see Howard, forgetting that the picture had already been released before Jean showed up on the set of *Hell's Angels.*

Standing less than five feet tall, Landau was short and thin with a thick streak of sentimentality. Citing the fact that Greta Nissen pulled in $2,500 a week, he offered Jean to Howard for $1,500 a week with a six-month minimum.

Howard laughed in his face. "She gets only $1,500 for the whole six weeks. Take it or leave it!" As he threatened to break off negotiations, Landau caved in and accepted these humiliating terms for his new client, who was already three months in arrears on her rent.

In trying to pitch her to Howard, Landau claimed, "She looks like a whore on her first day in a brothel. Still willing to do anything and not dried up inside."

Before dismissing Landau, Howard told him to see that Jean showed up for work with her hair even whiter. "And never say albino blonde in front of me again. From now on, we're going to bill her as platinum blonde." That term, of course, became Jean Harlow's trademark and the basis of her fame.

When Jean was asked by reporters how she got cast as the female star on *Hell's Angels,* she said, "I guess Howard Hughes got tired of looking at all the blondes in Hollywood and went for me."

Ben Lyon

***

201

As shooting began on *Hell's Angels*, James Whale noted that Harlow could not work long in front of the camera before she had to excuse herself and race to her dressing room. At first the director thought she had weak kidneys. She later told him that she had to disappear to rub her nipples with ice cubes. "That makes them erect in front of the camera."

Reginald Callow was horrified that Howard had cast her as Helen. "She's the world's worst actress."

Inexperienced and in her first major role, she and Whale had several clashes. When given a line that had been written by Howard himself, Jean claimed she couldn't say it. "It's the corniest god damn line in the history of movies."

She was so adamant that Howard had to be called to the set to force her to utter the line.

Appearing before Ben Lyon in a particularly revealing evening gown, Jean asks, "Would you be shocked if I put on something more comfortable?" It became the most famous line in the movie and part of the Jean Harlow legend. Howard was right.

Whale exploded on the set one day and denounced Jean in front of the crew, forcing her to run away in tears. Believe it or not, the actress, who throughout most of the Thirties would be known for sex on the screen, wasn't playing a scene with Ben with enough allure. The next day, Whale demanded she perform the scene again and again. Nothing she did satisfied him. "Tell me what you want me to do," she pleaded with him. "My dear girl," Whale told her, "I can tell you how to be an actress but I can't tell you how to be a woman."

After the first week of shooting, Whale went to Howard to demand that Jean be replaced with Carole Lombard, his original choice. "Keep the cameras rolling," Howard ordered. "Teach her what she needs to know and don't bother me with this. Maybe that damn platinum hair will carry the day for her. No one will notice her acting. Only her tits!"

As a reward for the humiliations she endured, Jean received the absolute minimum paycheck the Screen Actors' Guild allowed. Making things worse, she came down with an affliction of "Klieg eyes," or burnt eyeballs. Her Multi-Colored segments required massive floodlighting, and she was sometimes exposed to these harsh lights sixteen hours a day. A studio doctor confirmed that her conjunctiva had been burned."

Howard was on the set when he heard Whale ridicule Jean. "You're not only giving a bad performance, but a ridiculous one. I predict audiences will boo you when they're not falling out of their seats convulsed with laughter."

Instead of defending an already insecure star-to-be, Howard felt that the solution to the problem involved dressing her even more provocatively. With a designer, he helped create a backless gown. Originally, the gown showed the upper two inches of "the crack in her ass," as Whale put it. Her bodice was cut so low it had to be held up by rhinestone-studded straps like those used by strippers. Whale called for restraint, but Howard demanded that Jean's "come-hither negligée" be opened even wider. "Make it so wide the audience can see all the way to Honolulu."

Eventually, the gown had to be modified, since Jean was practically nude on camera. Still, Howard demanded that his cameraman emphasize Jean's bustline, as he would do in a later film, *The Outlaw*, starring Jane Russell.

William Heller, publicist for the picture, said, "Howard personally directed the stills showing Harlow with a plunging décolletage." Howard, at least according to Heller, said, "I've tested those breasts personally, and that's what I'm selling to the American public. Harlow's tits—not her acting!"

Somewhere during the shooting of *Hell's Angels,* Howard began an affair with Jean Harlow that would go through many vicissitudes.

***

There has been a slew of biographies claiming that Jean Harlow and Howard Hughes never had an affair, as if that could really be determined. Of all the biographers, only Peter Harry Brown and Pat H. Broeske got it right, writing accurately about a sexual relationship.

Ben Lyon, who was actually on the scene and still a confidant of Howard's at the time, claimed that "sexual sparks were ignited between Howard and Jean Harlow after the first week. She wasn't really his type, and he regarded her as a whorish slut. People have cited that as evidence that they didn't connect sexually."

"Let's not forget that Howard occasionally visited whorehouses, even though claiming he detested sluts," Ben said. "Maybe he did. But he still patronized them for reasons of his own. Not all his conquests were with prim and proper ladies like Ella Rice. His attraction to Jean was a love/hate thing. He wanted to put her in bondage, but Jean was far too free-spirited for any kind of slavery, except, perhaps, to her mother."

Howard confessed to longtime agent Johnny Maschio that Jean both excited him and turned him off at the same time. "She's not my type," Howard is quoted as having said as if echoing Ben's words. "A little too coarse and vulgar for my tastes." Nonetheless, Maschio claims that the two lovers disappeared once for four days during the shooting of *Hell's Angels*. They went just over the U.S./Mexican border to Agua Caliente, which stars frequented in those days, sometimes for off-the-record weekends.

Maschio also claimed that Howard took Jean on a gambling expedition aboard a cruise ship in international waters off the coast of California, where he played roulette and blackjack. The captain of the vessel, Utah-born Alfred Harrison, later revealed that, "Miss Harlow and Mr. Hughes shared the same cabin and same bed. That doesn't mean they had an affair, but I doubt if they were in there engaged in Bible reading."

Joan Crawford, out with Billy Haines (strictly platonic) for a night on the town, remembered seeing Howard and Jean together in a padded booth at the Cocoanut Grove. "He was practically playing with her tits, which were on ample display," Crawford said.

Adela Rogers St. Johns reported seeing Jean enter Howard's bedroom after midnight one weekend at San Simeon. W.R. Hearst had a rule that no unmarried couple could share the same bedchamber, although that hardly applied to the press baron and his mistress, Marion Davies.

Marion, however, always giggled at the indiscretions going on, reminding her favored guests that "W.R. goes to bed early, and when the cat is away the mice will play." Love-making between unmarried couples was all right by her. Since she was herself sleeping with another woman's husband, she could hardly object on moral grounds.

Howard informed Noah Dietrich that he was having an affair with his leading lady. For reasons of his own, Dietrich claimed in his memoirs that Jean was not an *inamorata* of Howard's, yet he privately admitted to friends and other biographers that he knew about Howard's relationship with Jean.

Yet Dietrich had no restraint about protecting the reputation of the long-dead Jean Harlow in his memoirs. He claimed that she offered to sleep with him if he'd have Toolco pay off a fifteen-hundred dollar bill for clothing she'd acquired when Howard sent her on the road to publicize *Hell's Angels*. Dietrich even claimed that she pulled "me down on my office couch" in an attempt at seduction. He said that it took all his will power, which was put to a strenuous test, to resist her.

When Jean reached New York, at least according to Dietrich, she "pulled the same act," in his words, on Howard's representative there. Dietrich sadly cites how that dalliance ruined the rep's life. He was an Irish Catholic with a wife and four children, but was prepared to give it all up for Jean.

"Harlow's promise to marry him didn't mean a damn thing," Dietrich later said. "I suspect the blonde bombshell had forgotten all about the hopeless lovesick fool by the time her train reached Chicago heading west again."

Howard also confessed to Billy Haines that he was "fucking Harlow, a lousy cocksucker but a great lay if you like the missionary position."

Ben quoted Jean as saying, "I like sex as much as the next gal, except it's so messy. Talk about messy! Howard is a real pervert. He wants things done to him that no self-respecting gal would do. For that, he should go to a whorehouse. I hear the gals there do everything."

To the press, including writer Anita Loos, Jean made this statement: "Howard's got a lot of charm in his own funny way. But he never mixes business with pleasure."

That comment must have been met with utter cynicism by Loos, who knew that Howard always mixed business with pleasure.

"As far as I'm concerned," Jean said, "I might be another airplane. The nearest Howard ever came to making a pass at me was offering me a bite of his cookie."

In today's lingo, such a statement would have been met with a *"Yeah, right!"*

Later, during a drive to Palm Springs for a weekend retreat, Jean told George Raft, Humphrey Bogart, and director Rowland Brown that she suspected that Howard liked boys more than girls. "When he took me to bed, he had three autographed photos of Randolph Scott in his room. When he was fucking me, I got the impression that he kept looking at those pictures to keep himself hard."

One of Howard's attempts at intercourse failed miserably, at least according to Jean. "He just couldn't get it up," she confessed to Raft. "I tried everything and it stayed limp."

In another decade, Bette Davis would face the same problem with Howard. But, like the Duchess of Windsor with her Duke, Bette would be far more clever than Jean in improvising.

Jean would be the first woman to ever talk about Howard's impotence. In the years to come, it would become an increasing problem for him even in the presence of some of the world's most sought-after women.

***

As Gloria Swanson in white chiffon glided by Howard on the dance floor of the Biltmore Hotel's Starlight Ballroom, Marion Davies took Howard by the arm. At long last she was going to take him across the floor to meet Miss Billie Dove, the reigning film star of the silent screen. For weeks, Howard had been beseeching her to introduce him to one of her best friends. She'd warned him that Billie was a Venus's flytrap and he should avoid her at all costs, but he was insistent. She also put him on alert that her husband since 1923, the bull-necked director, Irwin Willat, was jealous, possessive, and "perhaps psychotic."

On the way to Billie Dove's table, Marion encountered Corrine Griffith, sitting at the head of a table that included Pola Negri, Lowell Sherman, and Nita Naldi. Howard ignored Marion's introduction to all these other stars, concentrating his focus entirely on Corrine.

A fellow Texan from Texarkana, and eleven years older than Howard, Corrine had been starring in films since 1916. She mesmerized people who encountered her face for the first time. The "Orchid Lady of the Screen," as she was called, was hailed as the most beautiful woman in silent pictures. It was a contradiction, but across the room sat Corinne's rival, Billie Dove, acclaimed as the most beautiful woman—not only in pictures—but in the world.

Howard gazed into Corinne's blue eyes and almost seemed to want to fondle her lovely brown hair. He looked at her hair so longingly, she smiled and said, "It's my natural color, and no other actress in pictures can say that." Her entourage laughed.

Standing silently before her, Howard finally found his tongue. He made a remark that was completely uncharacteristic of him. He almost never engaged in flattery. "The close-up was invented to capture the beauty of your face."

Again, the table laughed, but Howard didn't seem to hear the mockery. All he managed to say was, "I'll call you tomorrow," before Marion urged him on across the room to meet the room's other reigning beauty.

Unknown to Howard at the time, Corrine wasn't eager to meet with him at all. After this social event, she had an off-the-record midnight date with a handsome young extra named Clark Gable who had appeared briefly in her 1925 film, *Declassée*. Corrine considered Clark "too raw" to introduce to the social elite of Hollywood.

"Keep your tongue from hanging out," Marion warned Howard as they approached Billie Dove's table. Like Corrine, Billie was surrounded by her entourage, some eight guests that notably included Ben Lyon, Norma Talmadge, and Charlie Chaplin.

After weeks of seeing Billie from afar, once in the presence of Douglas Fairbanks Jr., Howard was awkward and shy when introduced to this sophisticated screen star. Billie later confided to Ben, "I thought I was meeting an overgrown Texas schoolboy. I felt he couldn't really be the multi-millionaire, Howard Hughes, that everybody was talking about."

Once Billie had shaken his hand, Howard had absolutely nothing to say to her. To him, she must have appeared like a Dresden doll in a champagne-colored satin gown. This classic American beauty was not only a bigtime movie star, but was widely regarded by directors as the epitome of female perfection on camera.

Speaking through pouty lips painted a scarlet red, she said, "Good evening, Mr. Hughes. Are those oil wells still pumping in Texas?" He did not bother to correct her to inform her he made his money not through oil but through a drill bit.

Her large hazel eyes seemed to draw him nearer to her, yet they warned him to stay back at the same time. He took in her flawless and creamy complexion and smelled her perfume, which was appropriately called "Seduction."

Howard's thoughts on meeting Billie will never be known. He'd read all he could about her, including how she'd launched herself in 1919 as one of Flo Ziegfeld's bevy of Follies beauties that at one time had included Marion Davies herself. Finally, he was able to speak in front of the table. "Is it true that Irving Berlin wrote *A Pretty Girl Is Like A Melody* for you?"

"It would be immodest of me to answer that," she said.

"I see all of your films," he said. At the time of their meeting, Billie was one of the biggest attractions in cinema, ranking up there with the two reigning box-office champions, Colleen Moore and Clara Bow. Billie Dove's films, at the time of their meeting, surpassed those of Greta Garbo, Mary Pickford, and Gloria Swanson in box-office receipts.

He held her hand for a long moment, looking into her large expressive eyes. He seemed to focus on her sensitive mouth, perhaps imagining the pleasure it could give him. Born of Swiss immigrants, she was two years older than Howard, but as Marion later noted, she seemed so much more worldly that Howard could almost pass for her son.

As he continued to absorb her soft, voluptuous femininity, he told her that she looked glorious in Technicolor. She had appeared in this new two-colored film process, and was rumored to have had an affair with Douglas Fairbanks Sr. when they made a color version of *The Black Pirate* in 1926.

"I've been doing some experimenting in color myself, and getting nowhere," he told her.

From Ben, Howard learned that Billie's marriage to Willat was in serious trouble. He knew that behind Willat's back, she played the field. Ben had confessed to having an affair with her in 1927 when they co-starred in *The Tender Hour* directed by George Fitzmaurice.

Howard's meeting with Billie was brief. Back at Marion's table, Howard told her that he wanted to know where Billie was going to appear every night. He planned to show up at the same gatherings.

True to his word, Howard appeared the next night at the Montmartre Café, a vision in white, from his tie to his suit and including his white wing-tipped shoes. Billie too was dressed entirely in white when Howard first spotted her. She was dancing around the floor in the arms of Billy Haines. On a signal from Howard, the male Billy delivered the female Billie into the presence of Howard.

"We meet again, Mr. Hughes," she said in front of Billy. "Are you following me?"

"A mere coincidence," Howard responded.

"I'm sure that's not true." Blowing a kiss to Billy, she took Howard's hand and walked with him to an open-air terrace. As Billie Dove would report to Billy Haines the next day, "It was a full California moon and either the garden was scented or else it was my perfume. But I kissed him. I also said, 'Mr. Hughes, is it true that I'm the only star in Hollywood that you have not deflowered?'"

"My reputation is greatly exaggerated," he reportedly told her. Without hesitation, he took her in his arms and kissed her deeply.

Unknown to either of them, a young Irish private eye, Pat O'Casey, had excused himself from his date for the evening to oversee what was happening on the terrace between the married Howard and much-married Billie Dove.

Howard was not aware that Willat was gathering evidence to use against Billie in his upcoming divorce from her. Willat's career as a director was fading, and he wanted as much of her savings as he could get.

"I'll give Billie up," Willat was quoted as saying, "but here's my big chance to set myself up real pretty for life. I'm not going to waste such a golden opportunity. Let them have their fun, but what costly fun it'll be for the both of them."

Willat was not a man known for making idle threats.

With Randolph Scott moved out of Muirfield and into an apartment, Howard still turned to him for the occasional satisfaction of his homosexual desires. And Jean Harlow was still under contractual bondage to him.

With virtually no one's knowledge, Howard contacted Corrine Griffith almost daily, hoping to get her to go out with him. She consistently turned him down, even when he offered her a startling $17,000 a week if she'd sign a contract with his Caddo film studio. He was tenacious in his pursuit of her and would continue to go after her until the prize was his, even if it took years.

In spite of all these entanglements, Howard pursued Billie Dove like a hungry wolf lusting for a cuddly, tasty sheep. It seems doubtful that she was the love of his life, as so many biographers have claimed, even Howard himself. Both Howard and Billie during the white heat of their affair were still embroiled with other lovers, and with spouses lurking in the background.

In time, the world would learn that Howard was not faithful to Billie. He was never faithful to anyone, male or female. What was not known is that Billie had other men on the side even during the most intense passion of her affair with Howard. It was this lusting after other men that would eventually destroy their relationship.

***

Although he was not prepared for a total commitment to Billie, Howard began to bombard her with expensive presents, all paid for by checks signed by Noah Dietrich. First a diamond bracelet to be followed by a diamond-and-ruby tiara. He practically purchased every red American Beauty rose in southern California until he found out that she preferred only white roses.

The rarest of orchids, the sweetest-smelling gardenias, along with those white roses, were delivered daily to Billie. "No presidential funeral ever got so many flowers as that white lady," to quote Billie's housekeeper. The most expensive perfumes in Hollywood were delivered to Billie's home in large decanters. When she went to her dressmaker, she learned that her bill, previously in arrears, had been paid in full. Not only that, but twenty-five thousand dollars had been deposited into her account for the order of future *couture*.

When Marion Davies and Billie Dove invited Norma Talmadge, Carol Dempster, and her New York banker friend, Edwin S. Larsen, for a picnic, a plane suddenly appeared overhead, buzzing the site. Coming in for a landing, Howard emerged in his helmet and leather jacket. Though not invited, he joined the picnickers.

Unknown to Billie, two detectives had been hired by Willat to trail his wife to get evidence on her. Willat hired yet another detective to trail Howard as well. Like something from a Mack Sennett comedy, Howard had also hired two detectives to trail Billie. Presumably, Howard and Billie were the most spied upon lovers in Hollywood.

The detectives always lost their trail when Billie began to fly with Howard in his private plane on weekends. Perhaps they'd fly to the vineyards in Sonoma County or else head south for Big Howard's once-favorite resort, the Coronado Hotel in San Diego. Once he flew her to the Grand Canyon.

When not wooing Billie, Howard faced a massive three million feet of film to cut. For the final cut of *Hell's Angels,* he could use only one percent of it. To Dietrich's horror, the budget on the film was rapidly approaching four-million dollars.

Like Big Howard before him, Howard took to the sea, determined to become a grand yachtsman. He ordered Dietrich to negotiate for the purchase of a 175-foot craft, the *Hilda,* anchored at Santa Barbara and requiring a crew of eighteen to operate.

The *Hilda* had been owned by the multimillionaire New York steel magnate, Charles Boldt, and his wife, Hilda, had been granted the yacht in a divorce settlement. Ironically, the boat had previously been named *King Vidor*, in honor of the husband of Eleanor Boardman, Big Howard's former mistress.

For three straight weekends in a row, he sailed away with Billie as his sole guest on Friday night, returning the following Monday, presumably as part of a series of "test drives" to determine if he really wanted to buy the yacht. When he tried to borrow the *Hilda* a fourth time, its owner Hilda Boldt, rebelled, claiming that he'd tested it enough. "I want to see $450,000 in cash or else no dice." Shocked at the price, Dietrich negotiated it down to $350,000.

Dietrich was certain if he held out long enough, he could get this widow of a steel magnate to come down yet another $100,000. But Howard had already made plans with Billie to go sailing and told Dietrich to buy it. After Dietrich failed to talk him into waiting, he went ahead and paid Mrs. Boldt her asking price.

In full possession of the *Hilda* for the first time, Howard ordered his crew to prepare a romantic moonlit champagne supper for Billie and him on the aft deck. At the appointed time, Billie appeared on the moonlit deck looking like a goddess to him. She was barefoot and dressed in baggy white sailor shorts studded with gold stars. A thin halter top exposed most of her milky breasts.

Dinner was delayed as she ordered a foot rub. As he massaged one of her feet, she used the other one to rub against his burgeoning crotch. Soon his massage progressed from her feet to her calves, and then her thighs, as he removed her sailor pants.

In the single most pornographic passage ever written in a movie star memoir, a future flame of Howard's, actress Terry Moore, in her book, *The Passions of Howard Hughes*, described his seduction of Billie in graphic detail, including how he pulled off his trousers to reveal an erect penis to Billie and the fact that he wore no underwear.

As they progressed with their foreplay, Billie ordered him to, "Get the champagne and pour it over my feet and up my legs and onto my pussy." Those exact words appear in Terry's memoirs, followed by this page-scorching description. "He started kissing her toes, then he licked off her calves, and as he reached her thighs, she reached down and began stroking his erection."

The only misstatement in the memoirs is that Terry claimed that this was Howard's first oral sex with a woman. That was hardly the case, as it was his preferred form of seduction with both men and women.

Terry has Billie "moaning, wailing, almost sobbing as she writhed against him, pulling and pushing his head, and then she let loose with a scream from deep within her as her entire body convulsed around him."

Terry got the sex play between them right, and she wasn't even one year old when this happened. One can only speculate that he must have told Terry the lurid details one night during pillow talk.

The same description of this oral sex act on Billie more or less matched the report that the young Irish detective, Pat O'Casey, gave to Irwin Willat. O'Casey had hired himself out as a member of the eighteen-member crew of the *Hilda*. He was spying on Billie and Howard every chance he got.

Once the *Hilda* reached shore, he would provide a detailed written report to Willat, who was "still planning to rob both the lovebirds blind."

Decades later Willat confirmed that O'Casey made such a report to him, confirming what Terry Moore described in her book.

As Howard later told Ben Lyon, "Billie can give oral sex as good as she likes to receive it."

"I know, my dear boy, Ben told him. "Remember, I broke her in for you."

***

Only the night before, May 31, 1929, Louella Parsons had gushed that the union of Howard Hughes and Billie Dove was "divine fate." But on the morning of June 1, Howard was thinking only of himself as the sweat rolled down his body. He staggered into the entrance of his Muirfield estate, collapsing on the terrazzo floors in the foyer. He'd been working for thirty-six hours straight cutting *Hell's Angels*.

Two male servants rushed to pick him up and carry him upstairs to the master bedroom. A call was immediately placed to Noah Dietrich, who summoned Dr. Verne Mason to Muirfield. The doctor had attended to Howard after his plane crash on the set of *Hell's Angels*.

When Dr. Mason and Dietrich reached Muirfield, Howard's resident housekeeper, Beatrice Dowler, rushed to the door to greet them. "Mr. Hughes is dying," she said. "He's unconscious and sweating blood."

Upstairs, Dr. Mason discovered a patient that he suspected was dying of spinal meningitis. In 1929 before the introduction of antibiotics, that disease was often fatal.

For two days and nights, Dietrich and Dr. Mason never left Muirfield, leaving the master bedroom only for meals in Howard's sanitized kitchen. His condition seemed to worsen by the hour. "I don't think Mr. Hughes is going to make it through another night," Dr. Mason told Dietrich. "Better call his wife, although I fear by the time she gets here it'll be time for the funeral."

There had been no communication between Howard and Ella since early March. Nonetheless, Dietrich wired Ella at the Ambassador Hotel in New York. That following morning she was set to sail on the French Liner, *Normandie*, to France with her sister, Libby, and Libby's husband, W.S. Farish.

"Howard's dying," Dietrich's cable said. "Return immediately to Los Angeles."

Initially, Ella was suspicious, thinking that Howard was feigning illness as he had so often done before. But on reconsideration, she felt it was a genuine plea for reconciliation. Accompanied by her protesting sister, who continually denounced Howard as a "whoremonger," Ella boarded the train heading for Chicago. She cabled Dietrich to inform her in Chicago about Howard's condition.

When Ella's train was only one hour from its approach into Chicago, Dr. Mason was sitting in an armchair by Howard's bed nodding off. He was suddenly awakened by movement under the bedcovers and the moans of his patient, who was coming to life for the first time since his collapse in his foyer. Howard was not only regaining consciousness but trying to kick off his covers. Weakly he tried to sit up. "What in god damn hell is going on here?" were his first words.

Dr. Mason attended to him at once and summoned Dietrich to the room. "I'm starving," Howard told Dietrich. "Order me a steak the way I like it."

As he gobbled his breakfast, even eating the big peas as well as the little peas, something he never did, he learned news that infuriated him. Dietrich informed Howard that he had summoned Ella from New York and that her train would soon be in Chicago.

"Why in the fuck did you send for her?" Howard demanded to know. "You know I don't want her here. It's all over between us."

Even though weakened, Howard immediately swung into action, placing a call to Michael McCloud, the head of the office of Chicago Western Union. He dictated a cablegram to Ella, demanding that it be sent to her on the train. It read: "Just heard you had left. Why didn't you let me know first? My temperature is down to one-hundred today." [He didn't actually know that but it was later confirmed by Dr. Mason to have been accurate.] "I do not know why Dietrich wired you, but it is nothing serious. It is ridiculous for you to spend three days on the train so please go back to New York and call me from there. By all means, don't come. Don't come until you talk to me on the phone."

Traveling with her sister, Libby, Ella received the cablegram on her train but chose to ignore its message. In Chicago, Libby and Ella changed trains, boarding the Santa Fe Limited headed for Pasadena.

Howard rested, thinking that Ella had taken the train from Chicago back to New York to continue with plans for her ocean voyage to France. That afternoon he called Billie, telling her that he had recovered and asking her to come and stay with him at Muirfield, to which she agreed.

On a sunny day, Howard was resting in the master bedroom, still recovering, and Billie was taking a luxurious bubble bath. A woman servant came to tell her that Ella Hughes had just arrived in the driveway.

"I jumped out of my bath, and I think I was stark naked as I darted out the back door and into the garden," Billie later told Ben Lyon. "A servant had to fetch some clothes for me before I could flee the grounds."

As Billie had gone out the back door, Ella and Libby entered through the front entrance. Ella rushed immediately to the master bedroom where she confronted an astonished Howard, who thought she was in New York. "Get out!" he shouted at her. "Get out of my house. I never want to see you again. I loathe you. You're nothing but a cud-chewing Texas cow!"

Ella burst into tears. Before fleeing the room, she spotted Billie's mauve pelisse with a matching feather boa resting on an armchair. As she ran down the steps, she knew all those rumors about Howard and Billie Dove were true. Louella Parsons was practically broadcasting news of the affair.

Ella was in the house for no more than five minutes, just enough time to confer with Dr. Mason. He told her that he had made the wrong diagnosis. Instead of spinal meningitis, Howard had come down with a bad case of influenza.

Dietrich was having breakfast in Howard's garden when Beatrice Dowler alerted him that Ella had arrived at Muirfield but was leaving at once with her sister in a limousine. Rushing around the side of the mansion, Noah confronted Ella as she was getting into the back of the long, shiny vehicle. She stuck her head out and said, "Noah, inform Howard that as soon as I reach Houston, I'm filing for divorce."

For some reason, in his memoirs Dietrich wrote that Ella and Libby stayed at Muirfield for around two weeks, although he knew that wasn't true. But he never believed in full disclosure. He didn't even identify the "beautiful actress leaving by the back entrance" as Billie Dove.

In the weeks to come, Dietrich would negotiate the divorce settlement with Ella's Texas attorneys. Howard's fortune at the time was estimated at thirty million dollars, and, according to Texas law, Ella was entitled to half of it. Amazingly she agreed to settle for only $1,250,000. Not only that, but Howard was given liberal payment terms: five annual installments of $250,000.

"He got away with murder on that deal," Dietrich later said. "If only his luck would have held out against all the other blood-suckers waiting for him in the years ahead."

***

Even though Howard was professing his devotion for Billie Dove and Ben Lyon was publicizing his undying passion for actress Bebe Daniels, the two men frequently left "the loves of their lives" behind as they dashed down to Agua Caliente in Mexico for off-the-record weekends.

For those two closeted bisexuals, Mexico was where they found their freedom as they went on wild sprees, indulging their sexual fantasies either with young boys or younger girls.

Back in Los Angeles, Howard was still seeing both Randolph Scott and "the Adonis," John Darrow, he'd cast in *Hell's Angels*. How he found time to do all this and still keep up a grueling work schedule is still baffling, but he would manage to pull off such stunts for the rest of his salad years.

The only embarrassment from Agua Caliente came in the form of a blackmail photograph. Ben would drink heavily and Howard would imbibe occasionally. But when he did drink heavily in those days, he often became what he himself admitted was "a bit insane."

On one of those reckless nights, when he'd finished off four bottles of champagne with Ben, he put on a dress he'd bought that day and asked a Mexican photographer to take a picture of him sitting in Ben's lap, kissing him on the lips. It was supposed to have been all in fun.

When Dietrich opened the envelope delivered to Caddo studios, he noted not only the photograph but a demand for ten thousand dollars from the photographer. Realizing how damaging the photograph could be to his reputation in Hollywood, Howard immediately dispatched Dietrich to Agua Caliente where he managed to buy back the negative for two thousand dollars. He'd taken the extra eight thousand dollars "just in case." Although he admitted to bootlegging for Howard and other tawdry tasks, Dietrich left this incident out of his "tell-all" memoirs.

Another candid photograph, taken in jest, also caused Howard grief. He'd photographed Ben seated on a log with a sawed-off branch emerging between his legs, evoking a mammoth erect penis. As a joke, he had his publicity department send out this picture to Ben's female fans.

Regrettably, one of these fans, Caroline Black, of San Bernardino, was only fourteen. When she showed the picture to her father, he reacted violently and set out on a campaign "to destroy Caddo films." First he sent a petition to all the women's clubs of southern California, asking them to boycott any film released by Howard. He also turned the picture over to the district attorney of San Bernardino County, asking him to bring a case against both Ben and Howard, charging them with an attempt to corrupt a minor. Finally, he filed a one million dollar lawsuit against Ben and Howard, which Neil McCarthy settled out of court after Black was offered one hundred thousand dollars to drop the charges.

There was more trouble ahead.

***

Black Thursday dawned on October 29, 1929. It was the day of the Wall Street crash. On that doomed morning, men were killing themselves over their sudden losses.

Dietrich rushed to the studio where Howard was still working on *Hell's Angels*. "You've lost five million dollars in the last hour!" he shouted at his boss.

Amazingly, Howard didn't say a word but continued cutting his film as if he didn't want to hear of this disaster.

Ben Lyon came to him that afternoon, pleading with him to lend him money to cover margin payments on his own stocks.

Howard adamantly refused. "I don't lend money!" he shouted at Ben, who retreated from the studio.

Their relationship all but ended that day. The old camaraderie, the wild sex parties, the procuring of virile pilots or mechanics for him, the weekend escapades came tumbling down like the stocks on Wall Street.

Howard was about to enter a strange new period of his life, characterized by daredevil risks and behavior patterns that were almost pathological.

***

After his recovery, Howard sailed with Billie aboard the *Hilda* to Catalina Island. The trip, as Howard later told Randolph Scott, was almost like a honeymoon now that he no longer had Ella's shadow lurking behind him.

Howard detested the name *Hilda* and had rechristened his yacht, *Rodeo*, based on the name of a character, "Rodeo West," that Billie had played in her talkie, *The Painted Angel*, adapted from a Fannie Hurst story. Since her co-star, Edmund Lowe, was a notorious Hollywood homosexual, Howard had no reason to be jealous of Billie's leading man.

Aboard the yacht, as it anchored in the port of Avalon, Howard carefully planned his most romantic dinner. Even a full moon cooperated with him. As a soft breeze was blowing in the candlelight, his on-ship butler arrived with a gold-colored florist box with a ribbon made of pure spun gold.

After gently opening it, Billie discovered a dozen white orchids inside surrounded by fresh gardenias. In the center rested a red-velvet jewel box. Opening it, she discovered a huge diamond engagement ring.

"I want you to become the next Mrs. Howard Hughes," he said to her.

Almost in tears, she immediately accepted. But when he went to kiss her, she drew back. "Marrying me won't be so easy."

She'd postponed her bad news until now. Before embarking for Catalina, she had had a confrontation with Irwin Willat, who was threatening to name

214

Howard as a correspondent in a very messy and very public divorce proceeding. With his own divorce with Ella not yet finalized, Howard feared that he could not afford such bad publicity.

Although Ella had tentatively agreed to Dietrich's divorce settlement, she had not signed any documents. Howard feared that a highly publicized divorce between Billie and Willat would tarnish Ella's own name. She was very sensitive about what Houston society thought about her.

Billie detonated her bomb. Willat was demanding to let her go peacefully for $350,000. Dietrich would later claim it was $325,000, but in an interview granted shortly before he died Willat put the figure at $350,000.

Despondent, Howard paced the deck all night. By morning, when Billie found him shooting at sea gulls soiling his deck, he told her he was going to agree to the blackmail demand.

"Money is the easiest way to buy our way out of this," he told her. "That is, if Black Thursday left me with any cash at all."

She relayed a final request from Willat. Even if Howard agreed to pay the extortion, Willat wanted to meet with him at the bungalow where he lived. Howard didn't understand why, but told Billie that he would agree to that rather odd request. "You're worth it. To have you, I'd meet with the Devil himself."

As they sailed back to Santa Barbara, that meeting came close to never happening. Billie almost drowned.

She was crossing the deck, heading back to the stateroom, when a Pacific swell, seemingly coming out of nowhere, churned up waves of twenty-five feet. These waves without warning swept across the deck of the *Rodeo*. The powerful surge from the sea knocked her down. "I felt someone had me by the legs and was dragging me overboard," she later told Howard.

At the last minute, the ship's captain spotted her and ran to save her. Grabbing her by her delicate ankles with his big, strong hands, he pulled her back on deck only seconds before she'd have been swept into the turbulent sea.

Howard was down below tinkering with the ship's engine when told of what happened. He raced to the stateroom where he found the ship's captain and his first mate wrapping a "wet rat" Billie in blankets.

He quickly knelt down by her side, finding her trembling and in tears. "You could have been swept overboard," he told her, stating what was obvious. "It took that swell to teach me how much I love you. Without you, I would die. I'll never leave you."

These are the most romantic lines that Howard would ever be known to utter to any woman. Had he stopped there, it would have been fine, as she reached out to embrace him warmly. He burst into tears and buried his head in her lap. "I'll always love you, my darling Allene."

Up until that embarrassing and revealing moment, he had not uttered the name of his mother since her untimely death.

Shortly after his return to Muirfield from his sailing trip, Howard drove himself to Willat's bungalow. The meeting was private and Howard never discussed the minute details of what was said between the director and himself.

Later, it was learned that Willat had a far greater demand than the $350,000 he wanted for an uncontested divorce. Originally, he had Howard trailed to learn the details of his romancing of his wife.

In doing that, his detectives, especially Pat O'Casey, had learned other intimate details about Howard's private life. Willat found out about Howard's clandestine affairs with John Darrow and Randolph Scott. He also discovered that Howard had paid handsome young hustlers to service him as well.

Howard was visibly shaken when he left Willat's bungalow. Although he'd demanded that Willat tell him how much more money he wanted, the director refused. "There will be time for that later, after the divorce."

Howard was forced to admit this latest extortion attempt to Dietrich, who would be in charge of making the blackmail payments.

Dietrich was horrified at yet another blackmail attempt. "There's nothing we can do," he said, "except wait for the other shoe to fall."

"Tomorrow morning he wants $350,000 in cash," Howard said. "Take it across town to him. In increments of one thousand dollar bills."

"Even if you make the second ransom payment," Dietrich said, "and God only knows how much that will be, Willat might have you by the balls for life."

"In that case, we'll just have to have him done away with," Howard said. "There's a limit to how far I'll be pushed."

***

On December 9, 1929, a Houston judge granted Ella her divorce on grounds of "excesses and cruel treatment." She also charged that Howard had steadily neglected her and that he was "irritable, cross, critical, fault-finding, and inconsiderate." Howard did not contest the divorce.

In time Ella would marry the "true love of my life," James Overton Winston. It was no longer a question of his lack of money and inability to support her in a style to which she was accustomed. Howard's money was enough for the both of them.

Two years later in Houston on Toolco business, Dietrich encountered Ella at a society party. He started to tell her the latest news about Howard but she interrupted him. "Why should I be interested in news about someone I've never heard of?" She turned and walked away.

With his divorce behind him, Howard began contemplating his next marriage. "As soon as her divorce comes through, I'm marrying Billie," he later told Dietrich. "She's the only woman I've ever loved."

CHAPTER EIGHT
Nevada, 1929

With his own divorce about to be finalized, and without any protests from Ella about the settlement, Howard turned his attention to freeing Billie from the marital clutches of Irwin Willat. Howard's lawyer, Neil McCarthy, told him that a divorce would be granted more quickly in Nevada than in California. All that Billie had to do was establish a residency for six weeks.

Howard concocted an scheme where they could live in Nevada and escape press scrutiny. Riding in economy seats, he took Billie on the train to Nevada. They were disguised as farmers and introduced themselves to the homesteaders there as brother and sister.

Floyd and Arlene Struck owned a one hundred and fifty acre spread, and they gladly welcomed the handsome stranger, "George Johnson," and his stunningly lovely sister, "Marion." The Strucks never drove into town to see a movie and they never read a newspaper, so they didn't have a clue that their guests were a world famous pair, Howard Hughes and Billie Dove.

Wearing a blue and white checked gingham dress with a flowered bonnet, "the world's most beautiful woman" helped out at household chores, while Howard tended the fields with the local farmer. At night Howard and Billie slept in a corrugated metal hut with a dirt floor and an opening for a window with no glass panes.

Billie recalled years later that she felt that Howard, the richest man in America, was the happiest he'd ever been in his life, living this rustic, cornseed existence and toiling in the fields like a day laborer for exactly one dollar a day, plus room and board.

It was never explained to Billie exactly why they had to pretend to be farmers' helpers to speed up the divorce process. She didn't understand why she couldn't live somewhere in Nevada in luxury until the residency requirement was met. "It was all part of Howard's madness at the time, and I went along with it," she said. "In many ways, it was fun. I even learned to can pickles. I guess I never realized before they were made from cucumbers."

After doing some research, McCarthy notified Howard that the hut on a Nevada farm would not qualify as a legal residence. By that time, Howard had grown bored with farm work. He ordered Dietrich to send a limousine.

To the astonishment of the farmer and his wife, a black Duesenberg promptly arrived to drive Howard and Billie back to California, where she would seek a divorce from Willat through regular channels. To the farmer's further astonishment, Howard handed him ten one hundred dollar bills and thanked him for the hospitality and graciousness shown to him and to his "sister."

His career as a field hand over, Howard would do manual labor only once again in his life.

Billie Dove

***

Los Angeles, 1929

Back in Los Angeles, Howard began to behave erratically. He'd dropped Ben Lyon from his list of friends, but he continued to meet for private sessions with both John Darrow and Randolph Scott. He began to suspect that Billie, on the nights he wasn't with her, was also seeing another man. In a pattern that would be repeated throughout the rest of his romantic life, he hired detectives to follow her, just as Irwin Willat had done.

Within two weeks, Howard received the first of two reports on Billie's activities. The star had resumed her old romance with George Raft, with whom she'd had an affair when she was a Follies beauty for Ziegfeld in New York. The part-time actor, part-time gangster, had come to Hollywood to break into films.

Howard's detectives reported that Raft was down on his luck—actually he was broke—and was forced to room with an actor he'd known from his speakeasy days in New York. It was Humphrey Bogart, a minor Broadway juvenile who'd also come to Hollywood, like Raft, to break into films.

Howard was familiar with Bogart's name, as Rupert had written the actor's first screen role. Shot in 1928, the movie was called *The Dancing Town* and had starred Helen Hayes. A short instead of a full-length feature, the 20-minute film in some releases had also been named *Prancing Prune*.

Howard was informed that Billie was heading for the Raft/Bogart apartment, and he decided to trail her. His agent had already secured a duplicate of the key to the apartment for only one hundred dollars.

Howard asked his favorite photographer, Rod St. Just, to accompany him to the rendezvous. After a certain amount of time had passed, Howard, along with

218

his two detectives and Rod, entered the apartment surreptitiously to have the couple photographed, presumably as they made love.

Breaking in on people and photographing them in *flagrante delicto* was a common custom in those days. What Howard planned to do with this photographic evidence is not known.

The scene that ensued was like a silent screen comedy about marital infidelity. Rod St. Just years later tried to piece together exactly what happened:

"Billie Dove went to Bogart's apartment all right," he recalled. "But not to have sex with Raft. She'd already done that and while going at it, sampling the actor's legendary 'Blacksnake', she lost an earring that Howard had given her. Only Raft's roomie, a then relatively unknown Bogart, was at the apartment when she came on her Easter egg hunt to retrieve the jewelry that had been lost two nights before. Raft was down in San Diego that night with one of his gangster pals, no doubt Owney Madden."

Rod remembered that one of the two detectives turned the key to Bogart's apartment and slipped in, trailed by another detective, Howard, and himself.

"There was no sound at first," Rod remembered. "Then we heard the sound of a struggle coming from the bedroom. Dove screamed at Bogart. On a cue from Howard, I rushed in and snapped a picture of the scene. Bogart was jaybird naked and struggling with a fully clothed Dove. I caught him in all his uncut glory. She looked like she'd just emerged fresh from her *toilette*. Bogart may have stripped down and was hoping to accost her for some fun and games as soon as her Ladyship emerged from the crapper. I never thought Dove went to the apartment to have sex with Bogart. But horny boy that he was, he decided to take advantage of the situation. How many hot-blooded men ever get a chance to be alone in an apartment with the world's most beautiful women? If I went in for that stuff, I couldn't blame him."

When Billie rushed into the living room, she confronted Howard. He hurled some accusations back at her. She shot back, "Fuck you, you impotent bastard. You god damn faggot!" She raced out the door.

"From that remark," Rod said, "I gathered that Howard had failed to get it up like he did with Harlow," Rod said. "But apparently, he had no trouble getting it up for Scott and Darrow."

After one of the burly detectives ordered Bogart to dress, he was ushered into his own living room to meet the unwelcome Howard.

"One of the detectives told Bogart he was going for a ride," Rod remembered. "To me, that meant only one thing. Howard was going to kill Bogart!"

***

Howard didn't want to kill Bogart—or perhaps he would have liked to if he thought he could get away with it. Instead he "wanted to put the fear of, if not God, then Howard Hughes, in the struggling young womanizer," as Rod St. Just later described.

Seated between two detectives, Bogart was driven to Mines Field, where aircraft used in the making of *Hell's Angels* rested. Bogart was strapped into the back seat of a two-seater plane and left with the engine idling for an hour, wondering what was going to happen to him. He'd heard that stunt pilots had died during the shooting of *Hell's Angels*, and he was genuinely frightened. He later told his friend, fellow actor Kenneth MacKenna, that he thought "Hughes was going to have his boys work me over."

Dressed in a leather jacket with a helmet, Howard appeared on the tarmac and got into the cockpit. Launching the airplane upward into the pinkish predawn sky, Howard had the errant Bogart at his complete mercy.

During the first fifteen minutes, it was smooth sailing among the clouds for both of them, as they had the sky over Los Angeles all to themselves except for some early rising birds.

All of a sudden Howard began to pilot the craft recklessly, as if recreating some of the ersatz dogfights that had been filmed in *Hell's Angels*. Propelling the plane like an air show stuntman, he put the craft into a somersault. Like a dangerous missile, the plane seemed to be going into a tailspin, hurtling to the earth. The rooftops of several residential buildings came into view.

Bogart started to scream. "Don't, you god damn fool," he shouted. "I don't want to die!"

At the last possible moment Howard brought the craft up from its freefall, sailing smoothly over the peaks of the buildings that could easily have become their joint burial ground. He headed into the clear sky once again as the sun came up over California. After a few more minutes, the plane landed smoothly on the tarmac.

After Howard got out of the cockpit and disappeared, the same pair of burly men who'd broken into his apartment came to unstrap Bogart from the back of the plane.

As he landed on his feet on the ground, he realized for the first time that he'd messed his pants.

Later, after he made emergency repairs in the toilet, the two "pieces of beef" directed him into Howard's office, where the Texan sat behind his desk with his feet up, most of his face concealed in the shadow of a Fedora.

Howard came right to the point. "Listen, Bogart, and listen good. I intend to marry Billie Dove. If you make any attempt to fuck her again, you'll be a footnote in Hollywood history—and definitely a soprano."

Bogart protested that it was "just a prank—you know, like in college."

Howard quickly reminded him that by tomorrow, he'd have a photograph of him with his dick hanging out.

"I'm gonna have that picture developed and maybe five thousand prints made of it. If you fuck with me at any time in the future, copies of that photograph are going to be mailed to every influential person in Hollywood. We're talking Mayer, Thalberg, Laemmle, the works."

"No need to do that," Bogart said. "I'll be a good boy. I really mean that."

"Of course, you will." Howard continued to study him intently. "As long as I have that picture, I can make you jump rope."

"Maybe I'm still a little shaky from that plane ride, but I don't get it," Bogart said.

"Once or twice a week, I need some smooth errand boy to do a job for me," Howard said.

"What kind of job?" Bogart asked with growing apprehension.

"No killing or stuff like that," Howard said. "When I need to have someone's joints realigned, I've got plenty of men to do that. Like those two guys who brought you to the plant. They're good at their work. No, I'm talking something else. Some of my errands call for one of you fast-talking New York actors. A guy who can wear a tux, look presentable, and perform certain tasks for me."

"I still don't get it," Bogart said.

"Why should you?" Howard asked. "There's nothing you need to know now. When I want you to perform a task for me, I'll get in touch with you and tell you exactly what it is I want done."

"I guess I won't learn about what you've got in mind until the time comes," Bogart said.

"You sound like a smart man. A wimp, but smart."

"Can I go now?" Bogart said. "I've got to report to the studio for a new picture I'm doing. It's with George O'Brien."

"I've seen his films," Howard said. "Mr. Body Beautiful. I hear he bats both ways in the ballpark."

"I haven't personally sampled the merchandise, but I can virtually assure you that's true."

"Good to know that," Howard said. "That bit of information might come in handy some day."

Bogart saw him scribble a note in the little book he kept in his breast pocket.

"I'm going to be late for work," Bogart said. "Can I go now?"

"Sure you can," Howard said, "because I'm through with you, at least for the moment and I don't want to see your ugly face again until I need you. I'll have someone contact you."

That was said like an ominous threat.

For some illogical reason, Howard seems to have blamed Bogart for all the trouble he'd been having with his lady love, and not the truly guilty parties, Billie and her sometimes lover, George Raft.

Bogart later told the complete story about his experience with Billie, and his demented airplane ride with Howard, to his close friend, actor Kenneth MacKenna.

***

Billie, who had been staying at Muirfield, engaged in a battle royal with Howard the moment he returned from Bogart's first and most harrowing airplane flight.

Muirfield's housekeeper, Beatrice Dowler, later reported hearing the sound of breaking crystal, screams, shouts, and recriminations, although she could not make out the exact words.

Later she heard Billie run screaming from the mansion and into the night. Howard did not follow after her, but Beatrice could still hear him shouting in rage.

Beatrice went to sleep but was awakened shortly before dawn that morning. "It sounded like explosions coming from the cellar," she told Dietrich in a panicky phone call.

Jumping into his car wearing only his pajamas and bathrobe, he drove frantically from the cozy bed he shared with his wife in Westwood Park, fearing Howard had aroused all the neighbors. Seeing no other lights on in the high-class neighborhood, he decided the cellar at Muirfield must be well-insulated.

In the cellar, he found Howard with the Thompson submachine gun that had been used in the shoot-out scenes from *Hell's Angels*. Howard had shot up the ceiling and shattered most of the expensive bottles of Big Howard's pre-Prohibition liquor, which had previously been stored in Houston and in Los Angeles at the Ambassador Hotel.

"There were many rare vintages," Dietrich later said. "Maybe with a market value of some one hundred thousand dollars. Howard had laid the bottles to waste. The whole cellar would reek of Scotch and bourbon for weeks to come."

Dietrich later recalled that he felt Howard was "in a bad state mentally." Actually his client was in the middle of a nervous breakdown.

With the help of two male servants, Dietrich managed to get Howard, still smelling of illegal booze, to bed. After he seemed to be resting, Dietrich hastily called Dr. Verne Mason to come and sedate his boss even further.

Shortly before dawn, Dr. Mason arrived in the driveway at Muirfield. "I don't know what he shot into Howard's arm, but the chief slept for two days and two nights in a row," Dietrich recalled. "At one point I feared he might have lapsed into a coma."

When Howard revived, he ordered Beatrice to have the kitchen staff prepare him three large steaks. He was famished.

His first call after his meal was to Billie, who tearfully claimed that when rushing out of Muirfield, she had tossed her large diamond engagement ring out the window.

Before the day ended, Howard had presented her with an even larger diamond. They re-committed themselves once again to their engagement, and

222

Howard told Dietrich he still planned to marry Billie as soon as her divorce came through. He hadn't heard from Willat about his blackmail threat, and he told Dietrich he was very uneasy. "The guy's a psycho," Howard said. "He could be plotting anything right now."

A few days later, Howard spent the night with John Darrow at his secret retreat, Angelo. Left alone, Billie decided to attend a Hollywood party. Louella Parsons was the guest of honor.

The next morning over his glass of milk, Howard read the headlines: "TERRIBLE CRUELTY ASSERTED BY INTERNATIONAL BEAUTY," shouted the *Examiner*. "BILLIE DOVE SAYS WILLAT SLUGGED HER." The headlines were true. In a call to Howard, Louella said she'd witnessed the entire incident. Willat had stormed into the party uninvited and had physically attacked her.

Howard immediately called Neil McCarthy, instructing him to get a restraining order against Willat and to have Billie file an assault-and-battery charge against her husband.

When Billie returned to Muirfield, she met privately in the library with Howard. Dietrich was not privy to this conversation. Billie urged Howard to stop all legal actions against Willat.

Earlier that same day, she'd met with Willat at his bungalow, and he'd shown her some items from his growing file of incriminating evidence about Howard's secret bisexual life. At that meeting, and after having already received $350,000 from Howard in exchange for the promise of an uncontested divorce, Willat demanded an additional $350,000 as a blackmail payoff.

Billie urged Howard to meet the latest demand.

Apparently, proof of Howard's bisexuality presented no significant problem for the worldly wise Billie. "Ever since I entered show business in New York, I've been surrounded by homosexual or bisexual men," she later told Dietrich. "I just assume that all men in Hollywood are like that, and I had already heard plenty of stories about Howard and Ben Lyon. How could I blame Howard? I, too, have had sex with Ben. But it's not the men in his life I'm jealous of. It's the women! Just don't ever let me catch him with another woman!"

Years later, Dietrich also asserted that Billie then demanded to know if Howard had been sleeping with Jean Harlow. Dietrich went on to say that he then lied to her and assured her that Howard didn't even like Jean.

"But if I ever catch the two of *them* together," Billie threatened, "I'll remove the last platinum strand from her head, leaving her platinum bald, and then I'll go for all the platinum short hairs. I'm told she bleaches herself down there, too."

***

Los Angeles, 1930

On January 2, 1930, Billie, in a black Chanel suit with pearl buttons and a black straw toque imported from Paris, made a stunning appearance before the judge in the Los Angeles Superior Court. She had arrived in Howard's longest, blackest, and sleekest limousine. Stepping out of the car, she faced a media circus, as reporters screamed their single question: "When are you and Hughes getting married?"

Like a graceful black swan, Billie eased herself into the witness box at exactly 9:07 a.m. At 10:12 a.m., Judge Henry R. Archbald granted her petition for divorce. Willat did not show up in court to contest it. Howard's attorney, Neil McCarthy, had done his job well. Perhaps the case had gone smoothly for them because Judge Archbald was a friend of Howard's. They had been frequently seen together on the eighteen-hole course of the Los Angeles Country Club.

Reporters expected Howard to show up at the proceedings to lend moral support to Billie, but although he remained in telephone contact with McCarthy, he had mysteriously disappeared.

Bogart later revealed to Kenneth MacKenna exactly where Howard was that day. Under threat of blackmail because of the damaging photographs taken of him, Bogart was only too willing to do Howard's bidding when he called to tell Bogart that he wanted him to arrange a meeting with one of Hollywood's most handsome hunks of beefcake, George O'Brien. Howard was well aware that at the time, O'Brien and Bogart were making a movie together, *A Holy Terror,* for Fox.

O'Brien was called "The Chest." At the time of his inaugural rendezvous with Howard, O'Brien had already had affairs with two famous bisexuals, actor Spencer Tracy and director John Ford. Howard had once ordered his projectionist to show him that epic western of the silent film, *The Iron Horse,* which O'Brien had starred in under the direction of Ford. O'Brien was even rumored to have had an affair with Rudolph Valentino when he appeared in a small part in The Sheik's 1922 *Moran of Lady Letty.*

Howard's long forgotten love, Antonio Moreno, had also told him that he'd once had an affair with O'Brien, so Howard knew the actor was "up for grabs," even though he was also an addicted ladies' man as well.

The details of what transpired when Bogart set up the Saturday night rendezvous between O'Brien and Howard will never be graphically known. But it was assumed to have been a successful romantic link because Howard took refuge in a beach house in Santa Monica with O'Brien on the day Billie went to court.

Rod St. Just, who knew both O'Brien and Hughes intimately, later claimed that "Romance never entered the picture. But they had great sex together. Although Howard had performed analingus sex on Billie Dove, he'd never done that to a man before, because he felt that men weren't clean back there. But George turned Howard on to that pleasure."

O'Brien was a virtual joke in Hollywood because of the obsessive care and attention he devoted to keeping a clean anus. He would tell anyone who was interested how clean he was, and even expose himself for their inspection if he detected interest. He felt that "dirty Rosebuds" led to infectious diseases and that all American homes and public buildings should install bidets.

His lecture on cleanliness appealed to germ-obsessed Howard. O'Brien maintained with complete seriousness that both men and women should keep their asshole kissing clean at all times in case they suddenly met someone who wanted to stick his or her tongue up there. "Always be prepared," he once told Bogart.

He claimed that his rosebud (and the rest of his skin as well) was as tender as a baby's ass because of his diet of three raw avocados a day. He suggested an avocado sandwich on white toast in the morning, an avocado with a bit of lemon juice for lunch, and a large helping of guacamole and a very rare steak at night.

"I can only assume that George and Howard discovered how immaculately clean each other's assholes were because during the next three months Howard was on that avocado diet," Rod claimed. "Their affair didn't last that long because I heard George was soon back in the arms of his best friend, Spencer Tracy."

***

Billie Dove had been invited to a party at the home of Jeanette MacDonald, honoring actor Kenneth MacKenna and movie diva Kay Francis. These two notorious bisexuals were planning to get married. Bogart too had been invited to the party. Oddly enough, although married at the time to Mary Philips, a Broadway actress, he was seen at the gathering with his first wife, another Broadway actress, Helen Menken.

While Bogart was giving his first-ever interview to Louella Parsons, Howard placed a call to him. One of his spies had just told him that Willat was on the way to the party for a post-divorce showdown with Billie, and he was ordered to remove her at once from the party without arousing suspicion.

While still under the threat of blackmail, Bogart had no choice but to do Howard's bidding.

Bogart's attempt to rescue Billie came a little too late. As he walked into the living room, filled with *le tout* Hollywood, Willat had already barged in to confront his former wife. He was shouting at her that "Hughes will never marry you, you tramp!"

Seeing Carole Lombard, he called her a slut and a bitch and falsely accused her of carrying on an affair with Howard at the time, even though the couple had broken up months before and she was with William Powell that night.

Moving toward Billie, Willat slapped her so hard she fell to the floor.

Powell and another actor, Charles Bickford, restrained the bull-necked director. The party's hostess, Jeanette MacDonald, rushed into her living room and ordered Willat out of the house.

The next morning, Louella Parsons would write, "Instead of the peace dove, the menace of a constant beating from her former husband, Irwin Willat, hovers over the head of pretty Billie Dove."

Arriving at Muirfield, Bogart turned Billie over to a concerned Howard, who ushered her upstairs to a bedroom, summoning his housekeeper, Beatrice, to tend to her, as her face was streaked with tears. Bogart discreetly did not tell Howard that Willat had attacked his wife once again.

A servant ushered Bogart into the library where he was surprised to find a good-looking trio of actors, Billy Haines, Ben Lyon, and Randolph Scott.

Before Bogart arrived with Billie, Howard had been discussing a script prepared by Ben Hecht, the best screenwriter in Hollywood. Called *Queer People*, it was based on a novel by two brothers, Carroll and Garrett Graham, and was a seething indictment of Hollywood. It was also the most viciously anti-Semitic scenario ever presented for possible filming until Joseph Goebbels would make such films in Berlin during the Nazi era.

Howard asked Bogart if he'd consider appearing in the upcoming film as a right-wing newspaper columnist, a character that was obviously based on Walter Winchell. Howard mentioned that he was going to ask Bogart's friend, Spencer Tracy, to play a role patterned on Louis B. Mayer in gross caricature.

The lead was intended for Billy Haines, playing a Hollywood reporter through whose eyes the story unfolds. Howard knew that Ben was under strain that night and didn't want to be in the same room with Randolph Scott, suspecting that his close friendship with Howard had been usurped by this good-looking Virginian. Ben viewed Randolph as a money-grubbing hustler out to use Howard.

Only an hour earlier, Ben had protested to Howard that he was desperate for another role. He claimed that after one hundred and five weeks of making both the silent and talking versions of *Hell's Angels,* his fan mail had dwindled from a thousand letters a week to only two dozen. "I've been off the screen for so long that my fans have forgotten me," he protested to Howard, who consented to cast him in *Queer People* as a scheming Hollywood agent.

Seated in the library, Billy read the script aloud. Bogart appeared to be dismayed by its anti-Semitic portraits, but Randolph clearly approved, since the scenario seemed to match his own belief that Jews were taking over Hollywood and destroying it. At one point, Randolph interrupted Billy's reading to tell Howard, "If anybody's got the balls to film this, you're the guy, Howard."

Howard told them that he wanted to cast Billie Dove and Ramon Novarro as a Hollywood couple, both big stars, trapped in a loveless marriage. Randolph would be cast as a handsome cowboy who arrives in Hollywood to become another Tom Mix. In the script, he falls for Billie, rescues her from her loveless marriage and from Hollywood itself, and all its "vicious Jews," and rides off into the sunset with her. Very little of this new script had anything to do with the original novel.

When Billy Haines finished reading the script, Howard thought the happy ending was a bit corny "but we can work on it," he assured the men.

For the next few months and up until the end of the summer of 1931, Howard would have the script revised time and time again, with a constantly changing plot. When word of its possible production leaked out, he received several death threats. A Jew, Joe Schenck, even threatened to sabotage distribution of *Hell's Angels* if Howard didn't abandon his plans to film *Queer People*.

Finally, Louis B. Mayer, accompanied by an unlikely ally, Joseph Kennedy, arrived at Muirfield for a private meeting with Howard. Beatrice later claimed that the conference went on for about an hour in Howard's library. She said she heard all three men shouting at each other. Finally, Kennedy and Mayer left. Beatrice did not know what threats Mayer and Kennedy made to Howard, but she said he was despondent for days.

Howard already hated Mayer. After that day, he would develop a lifelong hatred of Kennedy as well.

One morning Howard called his publicity department and told them to release a story to the press. In the release, he announced that "*Queer People* would have taken the public behind the scenes of Hollywood. I regret we were not allowed to make it."

Since he was one of the richest men in the world and an independent film producer, the release left reporters stunned. Who was responsible for pulling the plug?

The newsmen were never able to answer that one, and Howard refused to speak of the film ever again.

***

As Howard prepared for the gala opening of *Hell's Angels*, Noah Dietrich rushed into his office with the latest upset. Once in Howard's office with the door shut, Dietrich spread out a series of eight photographs.

They had been taken by photographer Edwin Bower Hesser. Five of them portrayed a seventeen-year-old Jean Harlow wearing only a diaphanous scarf that clearly revealed her breasts and her body. The other three were full frontal nudes without any cover-up.

Hesser himself was not the blackmailer. Someone had stolen the pictures from his studio and was attempting to use them to blackmail Howard on the eve of his release of *Hell's Angels*.

"Before you release *Hell's Angels*, we'll expose these pictures of your little blondie if you don't cough up fifty thousand dollars," the blackmail note said.

"We hear you've invested four million in your movie. Don't you think it's worth another fifty thousand bucks to save your star's reputation?" The note ended abruptly with a postscript that the blackmailers would soon be in touch with instructions about where the money was to be delivered.

Dietrich was in a quandary, wanting to save Howard's investment. In those days, nude pictures of a star could mean the death of a career. Howard seemed puzzled and confused, not knowing if he should give in to the blackmailers. He immediately called his attorney. Neil McCarthy asked that the pictures be delivered to him.

After viewing them, he called Howard and suggested that he pay the blackmailers off. "I don't like to give in to blackmailers. But you've lost millions and Toolco has almost run out of ready cash. *Hell's Angels* is your big gamble. Maybe you should pay and call it insurance on your film's release, and thereby avoid a scandal."

After days of trying to figure out what to do, Howard did nothing, ignoring the advice of McCarthy and Dietrich. Amazingly, he was right about this decision. Often, in his past, he had made the wrong choices. For some strange reason, the blackmailers never contacted him again, and left no instructions about how the money was to be delivered to them.

After Jean became a more established star, the blackmail pictures would surface one more time. But then, instead of involving Howard, the blackmailers approached Jean directly with a threat to destroy her career.

At the time Jean was having an affair with Abner ("Longy") Zwillman, who had just given her a shiny new red Cadillac. Once again, the blackmailers were asking for fifty thousand dollars.

As Howard learned, Jean secretly took the blackmail threat to Longy, asking his help. This time the blackmailers set up a secret rendezvous where the money was to be delivered. That meeting between Longy's men and the two blackmailers occurred in the middle of the night. The next morning, the blackmailers, both of them gangsters from New York, were found shot in the head, their bodies dumped onto a beach at Laguna. No arrests were ever made.

When Dietrich informed Howard of the killings, he said, "I think actual murder is carrying it a bit far. However, there are times, I suppose, when murder is the easiest way out. At least it doesn't cost much money to have someone bumped off." Considering what was going to happen to Howard in the years to come, Dietrich wondered if that afternoon was providing some insight into his own future dealings with blackmailers.

The nude pictures of Jean Harlow would surface after her death, and some of them would actually be published. At that point, their release could hardly harm a career that had gone to the grave.

Although Howard never got directly involved in the battle over the nude pictures of Harlow, he would later become intimately involved in another nude picture scandal of yet another blonde bombshell: Marilyn Monroe.

Hollywood, 1930

On the night of May 27, 1930, Grauman's Chinese Theatre on Hollywood Boulevard was the site of the world premiere of *Hell's Angels*. Tinseltown would never see the likes of such a gala opening again.

Working hand in hand with Howard, master showman Sid Grauman accepted forty thousand dollars in expenses to help stage the event. He secured the help of local police in blocking off a huge part of the boulevard for the gawking spectators. Only six hundred policemen were on hand that night to tame a crowd whose size ranged, by various estimates, anywhere from 15,000 to half a million.

Jean Harlow

A full mile of the boulevard was lit with 185 white arc lights, sending columns of light into the sky to compete with the moon and outdazzle the stars. At every intersection were cutouts of the Hughes Fighting Force—DeHavillands, Snipes, Grummans, Fokkers, and Zeppelins.

Klieg lights scanned the skies as if searching for enemy aircraft. When Howard's stunt pilots roared in, they were part of a friendly fighter squadron, dropping flares. They emitted ribbons of smoke colored patriotically in red, white and blue. Not only that, but Howard had hired stuntmen to parachute out of the planes and onto Hollywood Boulevard. Except for one pilot who landed on a jagged wrought-iron fence, and "ruined his married life," the stunt went off successfully.

Fan-shaped clusters of red, blue, and yellow lights were installed in the Hollywood Hills to shine down on the theater.

Caught in the biggest traffic jam the West had ever known, Howard, in his limousine with Billie Dove, arrived an hour late for the première. The curtain was held. Howard was dressed in a specially made tailored tuxedo that would have made Big Howard proud, and Billie had on a baby blue gown of satin and held a nosegay of violet-colored orchids.

But it was actually Jean Harlow, who was riding in the limousine in front, who received the loudest and most vocal reception when she arrived at the première. A large blowup of her, dressed in a sexy gown and illuminated in red, had enthralled the audience. But when the Duesenberg that contained her arrived at the entrance to the theater, the spectators were enthralled with the real thing.

Out stepped Jean Harlow, swathed in white fur, with startling platinum-colored hair that the press was still calling "flaxen." Actually in spite of her cool demeanor, she was shaking in fear, fully expecting that the audience would respond to her performance with boos and hisses.

Her porcelain skin was made even whiter by a scarlet slash of lipstick. Borrowed diamonds hung from the neck of this one hundred dollar a week mama. Her white satin gown, revealing her breasts, looked like it had been painted on. Both men and women screamed at the sight of her beauty. Ominously, her escort was Paul Bern, who would figure so violently in her future.

Even before the masses had seen the movie, it was evident that Hollywood had crowned a new goddess. Other actresses didn't know it at the time, but their own crowns had already slipped from their heads. Clara Bow, Corrine Griffith, Colleen Moore, Mary Pickford, Gloria Swanson, and even Billie Dove had each begun their respective declines into obscurity.

Ben Lyon and Bebe Daniels were met with less enthusiastic applause. John Darrow and James Hall, the other stars of the picture, arrived separately. John was furious that he couldn't ride in the same limousine as Howard. "I have as much right to him as that bitch, Dove," he complained to Hall.

In a string of other limousines, Hollywood royalty spilled out onto the red carpet, none more notable than Charlie Chaplin and Gloria Swanson. It was a gala night that brought out showman Florenz Ziegfeld and his wife, Billie Burke, along with Jerome Kern, Buster Keaton, Irving Berlin, Leslie Howard, Maurice Chevalier, Lionel Barrymore, Cecil B. DeMille, and Dolores del Rio.

As Howard, Billie, and Jean paraded into the theater to sit down, they received a standing ovation from the 1,024-member audience who had each paid eleven dollars a ticket, an alltime high price at the time. The actual scalper's price was fifty dollars a ticket. Howard had time only to take in the scarlet curtain onto which a picture of a Sopwith Camel had been painted.

Master of Ceremonies, Frank Fay, a big star at the time and known today as Barbara Stanwyck's first husband, opened at ten o'clock with the one-hour vaudeville show that preceded the actual presentation of the film. Mrs. Alice Vernon's Dancing Poodles led the way to the star act of the night, Captain Roscoe Turner and his pet lion cub, "Gilmore." Only two hours before, they had landed from New York on a transcontinental flight that had broken world records. In a few short years, Howard would break that record himself.

The curtain went up at eleven o'clock. The scenes of aerial combat mesmerized the audience who had never seen anything like it. With her atrociously bad acting, Jean escaped ridicule because of her stunning looks, although Mordaunt Hall of *The New York Times* dismissed her as "mediocre." Audiences giggled at Ben's overacting, especially at his hysteria in a scene where he is captured by Germans.

All in all, it was the grandest night Hollywood had ever seen, even though a bitter economic depression had come to the land about seven months before. At long last, Howard, the "sucker kid with the money," was a big name in the picture business. More films loomed in his future.

For the next nineteen weeks, the film played to capacity audiences. Howard and Billie attended the première in New York, where it opened simultaneously within two separate theaters. *Hell's Angels* was also a success in London, where audiences thrilled to the scenes of aerial combat, and didn't ridicule the so-called English accents of Ben Lyon, Jean Harlow, and James Hall.

In London, *The Daily Express* called it "the greatest masterpiece the screen has ever known." At home, the critical reaction was a bit harsher, although no one faulted the dogfight scenes. Jean's plunging neckline and her platinum hair thrilled audiences as much as did the aerial combat.

Critics weren't so sure. *The New Yorker* found Jean "just plain awful." As for her own performance, Jean defined it as "a bitch in heat."

Robert E. Sherwood, the Pulitzer Prize winning author, wrote: "The leading players include an obstreperously alluring young lady named Jean Harlow, of whom not much more is likely to be heard." How wrong he was. He also wrote that, "If the lamentable truth must be known, *Hell's Angels* is pretty much of a mess."

Dietrich later claimed that in spite of the picture's great success, it lost one and a half million dollars of its four million dollar investment. Actually, it didn't. *Hell's Angels* would play for twenty years, grossing eight million dollars, paying back its original cost and earning a four million dollar profit.

***

As movie audiences across the nation lined up to see *Hell's Angels* and Jean Harlow's breasts, Howard, along with Billie Dove, sailed to Europe on a vacation.

Aboard the *Europa*, Howard left New York harbor with Billie, her eight trunks of clothing (she was bringing Paris *couture* to Paris), her two boxes of jewelry (mostly gifts from Howard), and her two maids (one white, one black).

The trip was relatively uneventful as they acted and behaved like rich American tourists, visiting the usual haunts in London, Paris, and Venice.

As Howard was to tell Dietrich, his days abroad with Billie were to be the "most idyllic" of his life. In her, he'd found "both a mother and a girlfriend combined into one."

As Billy Haines privately joked back in Hollywood, "Howard carried out the incest that he'd contemplated but never really followed through with Allene Hughes."

During the first week of their serious dating, Billie had become aware of Howard's deafness problem. Exaggerating her words, she spoke while looking right into his face so he could read her lips even if he couldn't always hear her.

Through the completion of *Hell's Angels* and beyond, Howard continued to bombard her with proposals of marriage. She kept turning him down and continued to conduct secret affairs in spite of her being tailed by his spies. Every week or so she arranged to slip away from the private dicks and go up the freight elevator to a suite at the Ambassador Hotel. Once there, she received George Raft, resuming the love-making they had known since their early show business days in New York.

To Raft, she confessed that Howard had periods of impotence that lasted for days. "He bears a terrible burden," she told Raft who in turn told others. "He's known for his conquests of women—only the most beautiful of course—but it's not because of an overpowering sex drive. He wants the reputation for seducing the world's most beautiful women. But this is often mere myth."

From Vienna, Billie expressed a desire to see the beautiful city of Prague. But she had a motive other than seeing that city's fabled baroque architecture. Somehow she managed to get Howard's permission to have his hearing tested by Dr. Karl Bruner, one of the world's greatest specialists on hearing disorders.

After the tests, Dr. Bruner reported an astonishing hearing loss of 40% for Howard. He was also said to have developed tinnitus, subjecting him to a constant ringing in the ears. Not only that, but he suffered from otosclerosis, an abnormal growth of bone in the middle ear. The condition would only grow worse.

For some reason Howard did not attend the premiere of *Hell's Angels* at the London Pavilion. Had he, he would have met the Duke and Duchess of York, who during World War II were to rule as King George VI and Queen Elizabeth.

While abroad, Howard plotted the future direction of Billie's career. He wanted to be in complete charge.

Upon Howard's return to America, Noah Dietrich waited with some shocking news.

Hell's Angels and the Wall Street collapse had virtually bankrupted Howard, with Toolco's cash reserves dropping to less than one hundred thousand dollars.

At breakfast at Muirfield, Dietrich said, "This is a real secret and word must not get out. But to put it bluntly, you're broke. We've milked the cow too many times. She's gone dry on us."

His accountant showed him the bitter truth on paper. For the first time since 1912, Toolco was losing money. The depression that lay across the land had finally come to rest at Muirfield's door. It must have been humiliating for Howard to learn that a payment in the divorce settlement with Ella was due, and he would have to default.

"Howard, I hate to say it, but you can no longer afford Billie Dove," Dietrich said.

232

"What in hell do you mean, Noah?"

"You've spent a million and a half on her already. You paid Willat big bucks for the uncontested divorce. The *Rodeo* ate up $350,000. The trip to Europe cost $25,000. Neil McCarthy got another $25,000 for Billie's divorce. That doesn't include jewelry."

Worse news was yet to come. Stopping over in New York with Billie, Howard, acting on an "insider's tip," had purchased a significant number of blue-chip Chrysler bonds. The next day, the bottom fell out of Chrysler. The bonds were worthless. In one night, on a supposedly very safe investment in the bond market, Howard had lost another four million dollars.

To save the day, Dietrich desperately negotiated a loan from City Bank-Farmer's Trust Company for 2.7 million dollars. Howard agreed to cut his expenses to $250,000 a year. An agreement was reached with Ella's brother-in-law, William S. Farish, to stagger his divorce installments throughout the Thirties, with a final payoff scheduled for sometime in 1939.

Until she was paid in full, Ella was to hold in trust 25 percent of Toolco stock. In a humiliating concession, Howard agreed to obtain Ella's approval, in writing, for any expenditure greater than $100,000.

The final blow came when Howard agreed with his former brother-in-law not to make any more films until 1939, although he was allowed to go ahead with the five films which he'd already launched. He wanted those films to star his lady love, Miss Billie Dove.

***

Hollywood moguls did not know that Howard was broke, and rumors spread that he was about to purchase Paramount, United Artists, Fox, Warner Brothers, Universal, Metro-Goldwyn-Mayer, and First National. What he did instead was urge Billie to end her contract with First National and work exclusively with him. His Caddo films signed her to a very lucrative contract for five pictures.

Howard ignored putting a limitation on his spending and gave Billie *carte blanche* to redecorate Muirfield. In his garage, two shiny new vehicles appeared, a fashionable Duesenberg coupe and a Rolls Royce Silver Cloud. When the Los Angeles Public Library asked him for a $10,000 contribution, he turned them down but lavished another $25,000 on jewelry for Billie.

"When he was absent from her, he sent her jewelry," Dietrich later said. "That meant Billie got a lot of jewelry."

His other mistress, Jean Harlow, was kept in virtual poverty, as she was still under contract to him, working for less money than any star in Hollywood. He had no immediate plans for her, but was finding it lucrative to lend her out to other studios, taking the profits she reaped for himself.

Someone had written that Jean had a "slightly lazy sexual aggression," and

Howard agreed with that, or so he told Billy Haines in trying to explain why he kept having sex with his number one star. Nonetheless, they weren't always loving. Often they were fighting. Jean kept demanding more money, and Howard kept turning her down. She was trapped into a contract that had been negotiated before she'd become a star.

Executives at First National over the years spread conflicting stories about why they released Billie Dove from her contract. In her first talkie, "her voice had a silken quality and recorded well," said one executive. But others at the studio were more critical, finding her "voice too high and a bit shrill."

Part of this problem could be blamed on the primitive recording devices in use at the time. One publicist, Glenn Richards, said, "Frankly, we were glad to get rid of Billie. Although she was still box office dynamite when Hughes acquired her services, in reality her career was at an end. She would never regain the lofty position she held in silent pictures. The coming of sound meant twilight time for her. Audiences stayed away in droves from her talkies."

Seemingly unaware of that, Howard acquired the script for *The Age for Love* for her. Based on a novel by Ernest Pascal, the script was turned over to Robert E. Sherwood, who had so vehemently attacked the scenario of *Hell's Angels* in the press. "If he thinks he can come up with a great script, let the asshole try," Howard told director Frank Lloyd.

As it turned out, Sherwood was a better critic of movies than a scriptwriter. When the film was released, *Variety* proclaimed, "It takes 81 minutes to tell practically nothing."

Howard had cast Charles Starrett as Billie's leading man in this lukewarm melodrama of married life that was eventually razzed by audiences when it was presented at the Rivoli Theatre in New York.

Legend has it that Starrett as an actor came to Howard's attention while he was filming *Damaged Love* with June Collyer, with whom Howard had a brief flirtation. The film had been directed by Irvin Willat during the breakup of his marriage with Billie. The bullnecked director was a tarantula at any time, but was especially difficult during the filming of the appropriately named picture, *Damaged Love.* He became so tyrannical in his demands with Starrett that the former football player punched him in the nose, breaking it. When Howard heard the story, he told June Collyer, "Any enemy of an enemy of mine is a friend of mine. Starrett gets the part."

"Billie may or may not have known—she probably did know, it was that obvious—but Hughes fell for that strapping Charlie in a big way," Frank Lloyd later revealed. "It was obvious to the entire cast. But there was a real problem here. Charlie was strictly heterosexual. He complained to me that Hughes was in hot pursuit of him. He didn't want to anger such a powerful producer at the beginning of his career, but he didn't want to go to bed with him either."

When asked who won out, Lloyd confessed that Howard did. "I know for a fact that they flew away for three or four weekends together to God knows where. I don't know what sexual arrangement they finally made with each other, but I'd bet my left toe that Charlie never reciprocated. He probably let himself be serviced and that was it."

Although years later he ended up looking like a broken down old cowpoke riding off into the sunset, Charles Starrett, at the time of his casting in *The Age for Love*, was considered by some critics "as the handsomest man in movies." This good-looker had once been a member of the Dartmouth College football team, and had an athletic physique to go with a male beauty that caused women in the audience to swoon.

Charles Starrett and Billie Dove in *The Age for Love*

This six-foot two hunk of beefcake was just breaking into movies when Howard discovered him. Like Howard, he was the scion of a rich tool company, the Starrett Tool and Die Works of Massachusetts. Tall and self-assured, he projected romantic thrills onto the screen. Before meeting Howard, he'd had an affair with one of the actresses playing opposite him in *Fast and Loose*, Carole Lombard, and off-screen she'd sung praises about his prowess in the bedroom.

The actual star of *Fast and Loose* was the compulsively vivacious Miriam Hopkins, making her movie debut. The Georgia belle, who Tennessee Williams would one day call "our finest Southern actress" as a dig against Tallulah Bankhead, originally wanted to seduce Starrett, but the New England-born actor was not turned on by her soon-to-be famous gestures and endless chattering, which he called, "flim-flam." Carole easily made off with the linebacker stud.

As it turned out, Charles Starrett didn't need Howard to jump-start his career. After a lackluster beginning in films, he became one of the film industry's top Western stars playing *The Durango Kid*, beginning with a 1940 Columbia Western that took off at the box office. The hit led to a string of Durango Kid oaters that made Starrett one of the most popular Western heroes of the silver screen. What the character of Hopalong Cassidy did for William Boyd, *The Durango Kid* did for Charles Starrett.

Still athletic and handsome in his white Stetson, black shirt, and a long flowing scarf, Starrett remained a matinee idol until the early 1950s. His beautiful silk scarf, it was later learned, was actually a piece of silk taken from a nightgown which Rita Hayworth, a future lover of Howard's, once wore in a

235

movie.

Starrett, years later at his home in Laguna Beach, California, still remembered Howard with bitterness. "He had money and he had power, and he used both unwisely. He took advantage in very unfair and cruel ways."

Almost blind and in failing health, he refused to go into any more details. "I never meant to become a Western star," he said. "I really wanted to be a romantic lead. Hughes was going to do that for me. I'm sick of reading books about what a great ladies' man Hughes was. That wasn't the Hughes I knew back in the days when movies were learning to talk. Case closed!"

***

Rather pretty by normal standards, actress Lois Wilson, a close friend of Gloria Swanson, and a WAMPUS Baby Star of 1922, was also cast in *The Age for Love.* Up to then, her most notable film had been James Cruze's *The Covered Wagon*, in which she'd co-starred with the homosexual actor, J. Warren Kerrigan, leading to false reports of some big romance between them. Howard had been impressed with her interpretation of Daisy in the first version of F. Scott Fitzgerald's *The Great Gatsby* in 1926. That film is believed to be lost today.

During the making of *The Age for Love,* Lois was romantically linked with the steely eyed and square jawed Richard Dix, a former football and baseball player. Richard had been her co-star in the 1926 version of *Let's Get Married.*

Howard didn't interfere with Frank Lloyd's direction of *The Age for Love*, but appeared frequently on the set, as did Richard himself. The two men bonded, and Howard was further impressed when Richard won a best actor nomination for Edna Ferber's *Cimarron,* which was named best picture of the year in 1931.

Richard Dix

Usually when Howard was interested in someone, he invited the person, male or female, to "come fly with me." In the case of Richard and Lois, he often invited both of them to fly with him simultaneously, at one point taking them to San Francisco, where they shared a suite with two bedrooms. Perhaps by inviting them as a couple, he diverted the suspicions of Billie Dove.

Howard often talked about putting Richard Dix under personal contract, but nothing ever came of that. In 1927, Richard had been Paramount's top money-maker, earning an impressive salary of $4,500 a week.

Where was Billie Dove all this time? She was busy playing the lead in her first movie for Howard, and also avidly pursuing both golf and flying lessons. To teach her to fly, Howard hired J. B. Alexander, still one of the best pilots in California. And for her golf lessons, Howard hired a handsome young golf pro, Roy Wilde, known at the time as one of the best golf instructors in California. Standing six feet two inches and hailing from Lincoln, Nebraska, Wilde had blond hair, blue eyes, and what was called "the perfect physique." Actors, directors, and producers seemed to be constantly telling him that he "should be in pictures."

Both as a golf instructor and as a social ornament at their parties, Wilde was eagerly sought out by the Hollywood elite. Ever the sexual opportunist, Roy slept with both men and women. It is believed, but not known for certain, that Howard had an affair with Roy. They were often seen in the sauna and showering together, and Howard invited him to Muirfield for several weekends.

Billie Dove's busy schedule of movie-making, golf, and flying lessons left Howard more available for Lois and Richard. Howard never did much talking, but always seemed a fascinated listener as the stars told him of their early struggles in motion pictures. Lois was nine years older than Howard, and Richard was twelve years older.

Howard was particularly fascinated with stories about Rudolph Valentino, with whom Lois had co-starred in his 1924 flop, *Monsieur Beaucaire*. Lois always claimed that Valentino told her that he'd never slept with either of his two wives, Jean Acker and Natacha Rambova.

What intrigued Howard even more were tales about the battles Lois had with her director, Irwin Willat, at Paramount during the 1925 filming of *Rugged Water*. "He's a complete sadist," Lois told Howard. "Billie Dove was a fool to marry that monster." Although he'd heard such stories before, Howard was also amused at how Cecil B. DeMille, a foot fetishist, had worshipped Lois's toes in 1922 during the filming of *Manslaughter*.

Many years later, from the premises of her elegantly decorated Sutton Place apartment in New York City, Lois recalled Howard with both amusement and sadness. "I think he was a very lonely man," she claimed. "Believe it or not, he had a hard time forming a relationship with man or woman. At the time I met him, Richard and I were planning to be married. I'm sorry we didn't go through with it. Louella Parsons was always ranting that Billie was the love of Howard's life. But I had my suspicions. I noticed that he could have been with Billie a lot more frequently if he'd really loved her all that much. Although I'm sure they were lovers, they spent a lot of time away from each other during the so-called white heat of their affair. If Howard Hughes ever had a love of his life, it was Cary Grant. It was most definitely not Billie Dove. And certainly not Katharine Hepburn."

"I think Howard was physically attracted to me," Lois said. "He made that very obvious, time and time again, including one occasion in my dressing room when he made a clumsy attempt to seduce me. Frankly, I think he was more attracted to Richard than to me. Richard once admitted to me that in his early days in Hollywood, he'd had sex with men, although in the main he was a great ladies' man. Even so, he spent a few private weekends with Howard."

She recalled her final meeting with Howard after the wrap on filming for *The Age for Love*. "Richard and I were having a rather romantic evening at my place when the doorbell rang. Answering it, I was surprised to see Howard standing on the doorstep looking rather forlorn. Of course, I invited him in."

"Richard and I were planning a night with just the two of us, but Howard stayed and stayed, talking about anything, about nothing at all. Finally, when it was three o'clock in the morning, Richard asked him to leave. He looked very disappointed. It was like we hurt his feelings. Later that morning, Richard and I talked it over. Both of us believed that Howard had come over to join us in bed. He didn't exactly ask, but he made it obvious. I guess you might say we turned him down. He was insulted, because he never saw either one of us ever again."

***

Howard decided to humiliate Bogart once or twice again for his attempt to seduce Billie. Fearing trouble if he didn't respond, the young Bogart arrived at Muirfield mansion and was ushered into a garden-like living room by a male servant. Bogart later reported in detail the angry exchange he heard between Howard and Jean Harlow to his friend, Kenneth MacKenna.

As Bogart came into the room, he looked at Jean, who was dressed entirely in white, including her stockings and her shoes. Howard was seated serenely in a Queen Anne armchair, the wings evoking some heavenly throne. Both Jean and Howard just briefly acknowledged Bogart's presence.

"Bogart," Jean said, "I don't care if you hear this or not." A mask of contempt came across her slightly puffy albino face as she looked over at Howard. "I was just telling this fairy here that I'm god damn tired of working for one hundred dollars a week on a five-year contract. I want out!"

"I'm forced to lend you out to other studios," Howard said, "because I have nothing for you now. Any more movies I produce will call for a real actress. You can't act and you can't be directed. You're nothing but a one-dimensional vamp. You can wear low-cut gowns, seduce men, smoke, and drink—that's it."

"In *Hell's Angels*, I did everything you asked me to. I really suffered. Standing

Humphrey Bogart

238

under those bright lights sixteen hours a day until I got Klieg eyes. I lay around with burnt eyeballs for six weeks."

"During which you were sent a weekly paycheck from my office," Howard said. "Don't forget that."

"Who could forget your crummy little check," she shouted at him. "Not even enough to pay the grocery bill."

"It's enough for you to live on," he said. "But you're supporting your mother and that Wop lover of hers."

"Yeah, I've got a family to take care of—that's true," she said. "I'm also the biggest name in pictures. And the most underpaid. You found that out on that fucking train ride we took East. Big names were aboard that train. That French fairy, Maurice Chevalier. Miss Billie Dove, most beautiful woman on earth. And the richest man in America. Mr. Howard Hughes of Texas. But tell Bogart who the public turned out to see at every stop we made. Jean Harlow! I'll say it again, you deaf faggot. *Jean Harlow*. That's star power, baby, and don't you forget it!"

"Okay, okay," he said, growing impatient with her. "You're a fucking star. So what? Do you think you're the only star I've ever known? The only star I've ever fucked? I can sign up any star in Hollywood I want. I can fuck them too. When Howard Hughes calls, they come running."

"That's not because you're such a great lay, baby," she said. She glanced at Bogart who was already deep into his second drink.

"I've had better lays from gas jockeys I pulled into the back seat of my car while they were filling up my tank," she said. She looked at Howard. "Did I make you jealous? Little baby Howie here specializes in gas jockeys. It's his favorite form of amusement. I think the smell of gasoline on their sweaty male bodies is an aphrodisiac to him."

"Shut your fucking face, you bitch," Howard said.

"Because of the contract," she said to Bogart, "he keeps me chained to him. All he does is lend me out."

"At least you got to fuck both Johnny Mack Brown and Clark Gable in *The Secret Six*," Howard said. "There were some fringe benefits to that job."

"Yeah," she said in shrill contempt. "You'd kick Gable out after one night. What a disappointment. But Johnny boy is your type."

"I heard when you fucked up that shitty little boxing flick, *The Iron Man*, you even seduced Lew Ayres, and most of the time he's a pansy," Howard charged.

"Don't put Lew down," she said. "He might take it up the ass, but he can also get it up for a woman." She went over and placed her face right up against Howard's. "That's something no mere woman can count on Howard Hughes doing for her. The tall, rich Texan and his very unreliable erection."

Impulsively he slapped her face. She backed away from him, rubbing her cheek, and walked toward Bogart at the bar. "Impotent men like to beat up on

Lew Ayres

women. They figure if they can't fuck them, they can always beat the shit out of them."

Bolting down a drink, Jean stood on wobbly white high heels to look over at Howard. "I happen to know you got one thousand big ones a week for lending me out for *The Public Enemy.*"

"I also raised your salary to two hundred a week," he said. "But until you came along, I'd never heard the word tramp used on the screen before to describe a woman. Tramp used to mean Chaplin's *The Little Tramp.* But in your case, the word fits."

It was Jean who slapped Howard this time. He stood back from her but didn't strike her.

She burst into tears. "Please, Howard, allow Joe Schenck to transfer my contract over to Goldwyn. You have no roles for me, no future plans. It's obvious: we're going nowhere together as a team."

As if to pay her back for that slap, he looked at her cruelly. "Goldwyn's not interested. He's already turned you down. He also got a call from Darryl Zanuck at Warner's. He told Goldwyn you're the worst actress in Hollywood. He said directors have to cut many of your scenes because you simply can't act them out. Maybe Mayer will go for you." Suddenly, he grabbed Jean by her platinum hair. He yanked a strand, as if holding it up for Bogart to inspect. "What do you think?" he asked. "A woman whose fame lies in the color of her bleached hair."

"Hey, pal," Bogart said, "let's cut out the rough stuff."

Jean ran to the other side of the room where she seemed to summon her strength. She walked back to confront Howard. "So you won't give in to my demands." She placed her hand on her hip as she did in the movies. "If I'm gonna go work for Louis B. Mayer in the future, I'm gonna have to get used to dealing with bigger shits than you. I think you'd better listen to me." She lifted her chin up toward Howard's face and glared defiantly at him. "Or else…"

"What else?" he asked. "You think you can blackmail me? Others have tried. When you've got money, the whole world is trying to blackmail you. What are you going to do? Call Louella Parsons and tell her we had an affair. Parsons already knows that."

"No," she said. "I'm not calling any one columnist. Tomorrow morning, I'm calling a whole god damn press conference. I'm gonna announce to the world the fact that I'm pregnant. And…" She paused, looking at Howard with

240

a certain kind of glee. "And I'm telling all the boys who show up with their cameras that Howard Hughes is the father. On one of the few nights he could get it up for a woman, Hughes became the papa of my bastard baby. I'm carrying around little Howard Hughes Jr. in my gut."

"Wouldn't it be Howard Hughes the Third?" Bogart corrected her.

***

Howard called Dr. Verne Mason to sedate Jean for the night. Afterward, he ushered Bogart to an upstairs bedroom where Billie Dove waited impatiently. Beautifully dressed and made up, she hardly acknowledged Bogart but turned her immediate attention to Howard instead. "What have you decided to do?"

"I'm going to buy the bastard off," Howard said. "Not with the million dollars he's demanding, but with half a million. All in cash."

"Irwin, that prick, will be fixed for the rest of his life, and may he choke on it," she said.

As Bogart was to learn, Willat had already been paid $350,000 for allowing Billie to divorce him. But Willat was now making yet another, all-new demand for yet another payment, this one totaling $500,000. And Bogart, to his chagrin, was being coerced into accompanying Billie across town to Willat's bungalow to retrieve it.

"Bogart will take you there," Howard said to her. "Make sure you have all the evidence before you turn the money over to him. Also, my lawyers want him to sign a document. See that Bogart witnesses it."

"I know the bull-necked son-of-a-bitch very well," she said. "You're worried that he'll keep hitting you again and again. But I think this is it. Irwin got a total of $850,000 thanks to me, all in cash. It doesn't matter if he never directs another film. He's a lousy director anyway."

"You're turning out to be an expensive bauble," Howard said in a voice with a sharp bite.

She picked up a hairbrush from her vanity table and threw it at him. "I'm not a god damn bauble. Your first payoff to Irwin saved you a hell of a lot more money than it cost you. If Willat had contested his divorce from me, and named you as an adulterer, Ella Rice would have taken far more than a million dollars from you in that divorce settlement. And this payoff tonight has nothing to do with me. It's payment for your own mistakes. If my boyfriend, Mr. Howard Hughes, didn't have a fondness for plugging young men in the ass, he wouldn't be in the trouble he's in now."

Her words angered him so much he looked as if he wanted to strike her. Before storming out of the room, he turned to Bogart. "She'll tell you what to do."

In the middle of the night, Bogart drove Billie across town to Willat's bungalow where the blackmail money was paid. The director turned over all his evidence and never again pressed Howard for more cash.

***

In spite of the commercial failure of *The Age for Love*, Howard moved quickly forward with yet another picture, *Cock of the Air*, for Billie. Once again, he brought back Robert Sherwood to write the scenario. To save money on the aerial scenes, he planned to draw on the massive inventory of out-takes for *Hell's Angels*. Cast opposite Billie was Chester Morris playing a dashing young American aviator modeled to some degree on Howard himself. "Cock of the Air," Howard said smugly to Dietrich. "The story of my life."

Because of censorship issues, the steamy love scenes that Howard had arranged between Billie and her leading man largely ended up on the cutting-room floor.

Biographers have long speculated about why Billie Dove left Howard Hughes. The other "Billy," actor William Haines, who had come back into Howard's life and was seeing him regularly, had a strong opinion decades later.

"The great love affair between Billie Dove and Howard was exaggerated," Billy claimed. "But at least it was genuine, unlike all that phony baloney years later about his so-called hot affair with Katharine Hepburn."

"Before their break, Howard wasn't seeing a lot of Billie anyway," Billy claimed. "He was beginning to treat her like Ella Rice. Stash her away somewhere and then leave her for days at a time. Billie, however, wasn't submissive like Ella. Billie was a woman with a strong libido and a lust for action. When Howard was away for long periods with his boyfriend of the moment, Billie also had a boyfriend or two to pass the hours away."

Billie Dove and Chester Morris in "Cock of the Air."

Billy Haines claimed that Howard told him that his handsome golf pro, Roy Wilde, revealed to him one day that he'd come down with the clap. "That sure put an end to germ-obsessed Howard's involvement with that one. If there was one thing Howard was really afraid of, it was venereal disease."

A week later, Howard drove to the golf course unexpectedly. Billie had gone there earlier for a lesson from Roy, driving Howard's Rolls Royce Silver Cloud. "She took lessons from him all right," Billy claimed. "Howard found them in the back seat of his Rolls going at it like rabbits. No doubt Roy was sharing some of that clap with Billie. Howard never touched her again. I think he regarded her as unclean from that point onward. Tainted merchandise. Now you know why Billie Dove never told the press why she left Howard. Actually it was the other way around. He dropped her."

After some time had passed, Howard ordered his attorney, Neil McCarthy, to buy out his contract with Billie. He had dropped all plans to finish the other three pictures with her, even though she had a contract. McCarthy drew up an agreement that awarded Billie $255,000 for the unmade films. Privately, Dietrich let the matter rest for a few months, finally settling the matter with Billie's attorney for only $100,000. Dietrich claimed that Howard never mentioned the contract or the name of Billie Dove again.

The fatal blow to Billie's career came shortly thereafter. Even though she'd lost money for Howard in both of the films he'd made with her, William Randolph Hearst cast her in her final film, *Blondie of the Follies*, in which she co-starred with Marion Davies. Billie was cast as a gutsy showgirl competing with Marion for the love of a playboy, as played by Robert Montgomery.

Seeing the rushes, Hearst feared that Billie was stealing the picture from his beloved mistress, and ordered that her best scenes be cut. Billie later claimed that Hearst also ordered his cameraman to photograph her badly.

Billie Dove remained a pilot, a painter, and a poet, but said goodbye to Hollywood forever. After her affair with Howard ended, she married wealthy Bob Kenaston, a ranger and a real-estate investor. She even said no when David Selznick offered her the role of the bordello keeper, Belle Watling, in *Gone With the Wind*.

Born at the dawn of the 20th century, Billie Dove almost lived to see the millennium, dying of pneumonia on the last day of 1997 in Woodland Hills, California.

***

Still coerced into doing Howard's bidding because of his fear of exposure, Humphrey Bogart was ordered to drive Jean Harlow to Tijuana for an abortion. After Howard gave him five thousand dollars in cash, Bogart headed south with the pregnant blonde bombshell.

Bogart later told his closest friend at the time, Kenneth MacKenna, that out of compassion, and perhaps infatuation, for the star, he had proposed marriage to Jean sometime during the trip, promising that he'd maintain that he was the father of her soon-to-be-born child, and that he'd divorce the woman he was married to at the time, Broadway actress Mary Philips.

Although she appears to have led him on, Jean had no intention of ever marrying Bogart. Without warning, in the middle of the night, she impulsively left the bedroom of the hotel in Tijuana which she shared with Bogart and checked into a clinic in Tijuana to have the abortion, as she had always intended.

Two hours later, the distraught manager of the hotel pounded on the door of Bogart's room, informing him that the abortion of "your girl friend" had been botched. She was bleeding severely, and barely holding onto life.

At the hospital, after Bogart learned firsthand of her dangerous condition, he called Howard in Los Angeles. Within hours, Howard arranged the best medical assistance available for the stricken star, sending a large black limousine with curtained-off windows to pick her up in Tijuana, and to move her to the best hospital in San Diego, where he demanded that she check in under an assumed name. He then arranged to have Dr. Verne Mason flown to San Diego as her personal physician.

Bogart's role as messenger boy had come to an end. "You really fucked this one up, asshole." Howard told him on the phone before slamming down the receiver.

In one of Howard's rare acts of compassion, he stayed by Jean's bed in San Diego, renting the hospital room next to her, and buying the best medical care available in San Diego. To supplement the services of Dr. Mason, Howard then arranged for a widely reputed German-born specialist, Dr. Herbert Mueller, flown in from Los Angeles, for some additional "emergency repairs" on Jean, whatever that meant.

The details of Howard's next days with Jean, urging her on the road to recovery, were never recorded and will never be known. But Howard told Dietrich that her life at one point "hung by a very slender thread." Since Jean had wanted the baby, and since Howard had pressured her into having the abortion, he felt responsible for her disaster.

When she had recovered sufficiently to travel overland, Howard ordered the biggest limousine in Los Angeles and had it specially equipped for her comfort. With a skilled chauffeur to drive them and with Howard issuing orders to avoid bumps in the road, Howard rode all the way back to Los Angeles with her. Somewhere during that ride, he agreed that he would stop exploiting her by lending her out for fat fees while keeping her on her small salary and pocketing the difference.

"You're going to be a big star," he allegedly told her, "and you're entering your peak earning power. I'm not going to stand in your way."

He did not go back on his promise, as he had done with so many other young stars. When MGM offered Jean a promising contract with some of its best roles, Howard agreed to sell her contract to Louis B. Mayer for an astonishingly low forty thousand dollars. He told friends it was for sixty thousand dollars. In the next few years, when he watched her star rise to the highest level in Hollywood, he told Dietrich that he regretted his decision. "Never again will I let sympathy get in the way of a business decision."

Before leaving Jean off at the home of her overly protective mother and sleazy stepfather, Howard promised that "I'll be there for you if you ever get in trouble and need me." That was an offer she would take advantage of in her immediate future.

Howard watched intently from afar as her live appearances at movie houses drew record-breaking audiences across the country. And although he was no longer sleeping with her and wasn't really jealous, he still wanted to know the private details of her love life. His spies supplied him with ongoing lists of Jean's bedfellows. Among them were Lew Ayres, husband of Ginger Rogers, her stepfather and manager, Marino Bello, Clark Gable, Howard Hawks, William Powell, and James Stewart ("when it comes to kissing, Jean is the best"). Howard also learned at one point that she was having an affair with the long-winded North Carolina author, Thomas Wolfe. Howard had known of her attraction to gangsters, and it came as no surprise that she was also sleeping with his own friend, Benjamin (Bugsy) Siegel.

Extending a rare privilege to Jean, Howard would make himself available to receive calls through her upcoming marriages in the years ahead—first to Paul Bern, nicknamed "Small Dong," and then to cinematographer Harold Rosson, nicknamed "Long Dong."

Of her many future relationships, the Bern marriage was the most troubling for Howard. Through his long association with Billy Haines, Howard had met Bern when he first arrived in Hollywood. He called Jean and warned her not to marry him, claiming that Bern was basically a homosexual with "the smallest dick in Hollywood." Howard also claimed that Bern was completely impotent with both men and women. "Not only that," Howard added, "he's pot-bellied and practically bald."

Jean was known for her quick temper, and apparently she was furious at Bern on the day Howard called.

"I'll never marry that son-of-a-bitch," an angry Jean shouted back at Howard. "I hate Paul Bern. What an asshole!" Bern, in Jean's view, had been spending far too much time with Greta Garbo, Joan Crawford, and Norma Shearer. But with an almost child-like emotion, she quickly forgave Bern.

Howard, along with the rest of Hollywood, was shocked to read on July 3, 1932, of Jean's wedding to Paul Bern. Louis B. Mayer didn't attend, but Irving Thalberg, Norma Shearer, David and Irene Selznick, and John Gilbert showed up.

As Howard rightly predicted to Dietrich, "It'll be the most disastrous marriage in the history of Hollywood."

***

Los Angeles, 1931

With two Billie Dove flops and a broken romance in his very recent past, Howard continued to forge ahead making movies. He immediately began pouring his energies into *Sky Devils*, a lightweight melodrama about aviators and their love interests. Its production would be relatively inexpensive thanks to its ability to recycle some of the dogfight sequences from *Hell's Angels*.

Ironically, excess footage from *Hell's Angel* that wasn't used in *Sky Devils* would eventually be sold, as the years went by, to other film makers. They

245

included the producers of *The White Sister* in 1933 and the producers of *Army Surgeon*, produced as late as 1942 when America had entered yet another war.

Sky Devils was conceived by Edward Sutherland, who became the director. The very clever wit, Robert Benchley, was called in to help shape the script, and he was assisted by writers Carroll and Garrett Graham, authors of *Queer People*, who peppered the script with bisexual references.

For the lead, Howard wanted the up-and-coming stage actor, Spencer Tracy, who had recently arrived in Hollywood. Howard admired Tracy's acting ability but detested him personally, calling him "nothing but a cheap Irish drunk." These two Hollywood bisexuals didn't bond at all. What impressed Howard about Tracy was his seductions of beautiful women, which would become legendary, and his ability to capture some of the handsomest men in Hollywood, notably Lew Ayres, Johnny Mack Brown, and George O'Brien.

Sutherland initially thought that Howard and Spencer Tracy would have a lot in common. When asked, Tracy said, "I've got enough problems of my own. I don't want to look inside Hughes's head. That would make me drink even more than I do." One of the reasons that Tracy might have detested Howard was his objection to Howard's exploitation of his friend Bogart. Tracy and Bogart had recently become good friends, and Tracy had nicknamed him Bogie, which stuck, of course. Ironically, Tracy and Howard would become rivals in years to come, eventually vying for the affections of Katharine Hepburn.

For the "second banana" role in the film, Howard cast a Broadway actor, William Boyd, in the part. This was not the same "platinum blond" William Boyd (the future Hopalong Cassidy) who had co-starred in Howard's production of *Two Arabian Knights*. To distinguish between the two rival actors with the same name, the *Sky Devils* co-star was referred to in the press as William "Stage" Boyd, because of his extensive previous experience on Broadway.

Howard still had to cast the female lead in the film. Jean Harlow wanted the part but he turned her down because of her strong image associations with *Hell's Angels.*

In a very short time, Howard would cast the lithe and leggy Ann Dvorak as the star of *Sky Devils*. How they met became a Hollywood legend.

Early one evening at Muirfield, Howard called Joan Crawford, who had frequently rebuffed his advances in spite of frequent invitations. In the wake of the Billie Dove debacle, Howard had re-activated his pursuit of Crawford. To his surprise, she agreed to take his call one afternoon. Not only that, but she promised to visit him at Muirfield that upcoming Saturday night.

Unknown to Howard, Crawford had become intimate buddies with Dvorak. They were rumored to be lovers. Both women were bisexuals who sometimes shared their men. Hoping to get rid of Howard once and for all, Crawford called Dvorak and asked her if she'd go to Muirfield in her place. "He'll be expecting me, but he'll get you as a consolation prize," Crawford told the younger actress and chorus girl. In a spirit partly of fun, partly of adventure, and not

Ann Dvorak

having a date for the night, Dvorak, who wasn't more than nineteen at the time, agreed to show up that evening at Muirfield wearing "the sexiest dress I own."

At the appointed time, the teenager was ushered into Howard's living room by his housekeeper, Beatrice Dowler. Dvorak had a lean, sharp face that was not altogether pleasing to Howard, and he didn't like what he would later call "her New York nose."

In contrast, he was very impressed with her figure, showcased in a red silk gown, the only one she owned at the time. That dress clung to her like a Jean Harlow fit. He'd seen women who were more beautiful, but rarely one with such raw sex appeal. The cleavage of her gown extended virtually to her hips. With the wrong movement on her part, one of her bare breasts might pop out, as she wore no brassiere.

She sat across from Howard and ordered a Scotch from Beatrice. He didn't like his women to drink but said nothing. No mention was made about how he had been expecting Joan Crawford and not Ann Dvorak. He couldn't help but notice that her gown was split up to reveal a creamy thigh, and he was certain that she didn't have on a stitch of underwear. He practically wanted to seduce her on the spot. Howard was later to relate all these details to both Noah Dietrich and Billy Haines.

As he talked to her, he found her very direct and outspoken. Although still a teenager, she seemed worldly beyond her years, and he suspected that he was not the first man she had ever seduced.

"The way she kept lifting those creamy thighs gave me an immediate erection," Howard told Billy.

As the night wore on, Howard later claimed that Dvorak revealed a ferocity of ambition unequaled since Joan Crawford and her sometimes lover, Barbara Stanwyck, hit town.

She expressed her gratitude to Crawford. "When I was one of the hoofers in *Hollywood Revue of 1929*, I met Crawford and she helped my career a lot." Dvorak confided to Howard. "She told me a gal has to fuck both the director and the producer on a film."

Howard leaned back to study her more closely and get a better look up her dress. "In the case of my next film, and if you're looking for a part, you need to fuck only the producer."

"You're my kind of guy, and a handsome fucker at that," Dvorak said. "And I know from experience that guys built like you have big cocks." At least that is what Howard later claimed she said. Neither Dietrich nor Billy Haines were given any more details of that evening at Muirfield. Dvorak herself would later recall the romance. "On the first evening I met him, Hughes spent a lot of time telling me how, for five million dollars, he'd bought an amazing sixty-five movie houses in southern California, his native Texas, and redneck Oklahoma. All of this expansion was occurring at a time when millions of Americans were standing in bread lines or polishing red apples to sell on the street."

After her first night at Muirfield, Ann Dvorak emerged with the female lead in *Sky Devils.* Not only that, but Howard awarded her with a much-coveted exclusive contract as well.

***

Although he was hysterically busy launching motion pictures, Howard still found time to become Hollywood's party boy. As a bisexual, he lived in two entirely different worlds. One of those worlds was exceedingly macho. Howard became the leader of Hollywood's first "rat pack," hanging out with wolves who pursued young starlets, most often blonde.

In the early 1930s, his name was romantically linked to some fifty women. They included established actresses such as Ginger Rogers and Nancy Carroll, starlets, chorines, party girls, and East Coast debutantes. It is highly doubtful that he had sex with most of these beautiful young women, many of whom were just "arm candy" (today's term) for public show.

Meanwhile, Howard's homosexual universe centered around Billy Haines and the popular transvestite clubs of that era.

One of the key players in Howard's "rat pack" clique was Johnny Maschio, once an assistant director for Cecil B. DeMille, and later, a well-known Hollywood agent. Two other major players included yet another agent, the good-looking Pat DeCicco, and his charming, but relatively unattractive cousin, Albert Broccoli, nicknamed "Cubby."

Cubby later claimed that he first met Howard while he was sitting alone at the exclusive Colony Club, a members-only meeting place for the Hollywood elite. Cubby, to relieve his boredom, began to spin a silver dollar he'd won in Reno. "A tall, lean character was seated four bar stools along the counter," Cubby claimed. "He's watching me and the spinning dollar. 'Heads or tails?' he asks. 'Heads,' I say. I lost and he (Howard Hughes) took the silver dollar."

Several generations previously, in Italy, the ancestors of Cubby Broccoli had genetically engineered a new vegetable, broccoli, which they named after their family, by pollinating cauliflower with rabe. Before coming to Hollywood, Cubby worked as a coffin maker.

He is known to modern audiences as the man who brought James Bond to life on the big screen, producing seventeen box-office hits based on the British superspy's exploits, including *Octopussy, Live and Let Die, Diamonds are Forever, Thunderball, Goldfinger,* and *From Russia With Love.*

Cubby Broccoli's cousin, Pat DeCicco, is known today for marrying two famous women: the film actress, Thelma Todd in 1932, and heiress Gloria Vanderbilt in 1941. Both of these women were former girlfriends of Howard. Luckily for biographers, Cubby and Pat are both excellent off-the-record sources for information about many of Howard's sexual involvements during the Thirties.

Since Howard was shy with women, Pat began operating as his front man and pimp. The relationship between the two men grew extremely close, and there was widespread speculation in Hollywood about the degree of intimacy associated with their friendship. Pat was, at least as far as is known, heterosexual, but he was also exceedingly sexy and handsome, a combination which sometimes targeted him for homosexual propositions. And he was usually willing to do Howard's bidding, whatever the request.

"If Howard expressed an interest in a woman, Pat saw that he got her for his friend," actor Alexander d'Arcy once recalled. D'Arcy was a Johnny-come-lately to Howard's Rat Pack, having become a member in 1935. Born in Egypt, D'Arcy was usually awarded roles as a supporting player in Hollywood, often portraying "oily" types. He's best known today for appearing with Marilyn Monroe in *How to Marry a Millionaire.*

"Pat didn't have to work hard to get women for Howard," Cubby said. "For the most part, the women flocked to Howard. All Pat had to do was get their phone numbers and write down their names. For budding starlets at the time, bedding Howard Hughes was a feather in their cap. In later years, it was tantamount to a woman claiming she'd slept with John F. Kennedy."

Howard, often seen alone with Pat or else accompanying a beautiful young woman, was spotted at the most exclusive restaurants in Los Angeles. Pat and Howard were seen placing bets at both the Santa Anita and the Hollywood Park racetracks. Sometimes Pat went alone with Howard on cruises aboard his private yacht. At other times they were accompanied by starlets.

James Campbell, once assistant manager of the Hotel Del Coronado, a movie star hangout near San Diego, recalled that Pat and Howard would sometimes check into a suite alone at his posh hotel and not emerge for the rest of the weekend. "The staff just assumed they were lovers," Campbell claimed. "Many times they brought women down from Hollywood with them, but never anybody famous."

Pat's nickname for Howard was "Lambie."

D'Arcy later said that Pat was "the straightest man in Hollywood. He loved women as much as I did. But I wouldn't have put it past him to drop his trousers for Howard. Pat would fuck a rattlesnake if he thought it would advance his career. Don't get me wrong. I loved the guy. But he played a dangerous game, especially when he got mixed up with the mob. He may have been more involved in Thelma Todd's murder than the police thought at the time."

It was through Pat, a close friend of Lucky Luciano, that Howard began a history of acquaintances with various notorious gangsters, including Bugsy Siegel.

One woman he dated post-Billie Dove was June Lang, whom he met when he was escorting Marian Marsh to the Cocoanut Grove. June caught Howard's attention by tossing a sugar cube at his head. In minutes, he'd dumped Marian and was whirling June around the dance floor. She later commented on their so-called romance. "I found him sexless. He never even tried to kiss me." She dumped him after a few dates.

In 1939, June married Johnny Roselli, the gangster, although she allegedly did not know about his mob connections at the time she fell for him. He was passing himself off as an aspirant movie producer. When she did find out, she urged him to go legit. But he never really did. The scandal of her involvement with this gangster, whose decomposed body was found in 1976 in a 55-gallon steel drum floating in a bay off the coast of Florida, derailed her career, but she continued in minor roles until 1947.

***

On nights he wasn't with his macho buddies, Howard spent the evenings going with Billy Haines to such so-called "pansy clubs" as B.B.B.'s Cellar, operated by a flamboyant drag queen, Bobby Burns Berman. His revue of a dozen comely boys attired in women's gowns was the hottest show in town.

New arrivals from Germany, Josef von Sternberg and Marlene Dietrich, were among the frequent patrons of this club, as were Constance Bennett, Joan Crawford, Norma Talmadge, Edmund Lowe, and Lilyan Tashman. Even Greta Garbo was said to have made a mysterious appearance at B.B.B.'s Cellar.

One night Howard appeared with Billy Haines at Jimmy's Backyard on Ivar Street. It was operated by Thomas Gannon, who must have been paying off the Los Angeles Police Department to keep it open. Other "pansy clubs" opened and closed with distressing regularity. In the midst of the Depression, patrons of the club were having a gay old time.

Gannon hurried to greet Howard, informing him that the whitewashed walls of the club "are to suggest the moral purity of my clients." In contrast, Gannon noted the carpet. "It's in virgin's blood red, dear heart," he said to an amused Howard.

Howard spotted Humphrey Bogart sitting with Lilyan Tashman and her husband, Edmund Lowe. Rumors were circulating that Bogart, at the time a young Broadway actor, was a frequent houseguest of this notorious couple. Tashman was fresh from an affair with Greta Garbo, and Lowe was fresh from affairs "with every hot young male actor in Hollywood."

Seeing Howard, Bogart got up and quickly introduced him to Tallulah

Bankhead, the lover of his first wife, Helen Menken, from their Broadway days.

"Let's get together some night, dah-ling," Tallulah said to Howard in front of the table of guests, "and suck each other's cocks."

Hardly used to potty-mouthed women, despite his earlier contacts with Carole Lombard, Howard appeared shocked upon meeting Tallulah.

"You've got yourself a deal," Howard said jokingly, although embarrassed by her outrageousness.

"But, first, I've got to get over the clap," Tallulah said. "Got it from that divine Gary Cooper. I hope he doesn't give it to you, too."

"No fear of that," Howard said. "I don't go that route."

"Don't kid a kidder, dah-ling, like your old mama Miss Tallu of Alabama. *I know everything.*" She asked Howard to join her table, claiming that she was expecting the biggest star on Broadway. "She's just arrived in town, dah-ling," Tallulah said, "and I didn't have time to arrange an escort for her." Knowing Howard's fondness for dating big-name stars, she asked, "Since you're free, dah-ling, the pleasure shall be all yours."

"Is she really a big star or are you exaggerating a bit?" Howard asked.

"Trust me, angel, the biggest! Her grace, charm, and classic beauty would make a puppy dog out of a Tyrannasaurus Rex."

Howard agreed to go in his limousine, pick up this divine creature, and bring her back to Jimmy's.

An hour later all heads turned in the direction of the door. Howard was making his entrance with his date for the evening.

It was matronly Ethel Barrymore.

There was a silence in the room except for the demonic cackle of Tallulah herself.

***

In the backyard of Jimmy's Backyard, Bogart stood snorting cocaine with Howard. "I've been rough on you, Bogart, and I know it, but we'll call a truce. I just wanted to teach you a lesson. You won't be the first man—or the last—I need to teach a lesson to."

"So, I'm off the hook, pal?" Bogie asked.

"Absolutely," Howard said. "I'll destroy those pictures of you." Because you delivered George O'Brien to me, I owe you a favor."

"Not to mention the Harlow thing," Bogart said.

"Sorry you messed that up, and I'm sorry you brought up the subject," Howard said, snorting back more cocaine. "By the way, some accounting is in order. I gave you five thousand bucks, with the instructions that you were supposed to pay Harlow's medical expenses. But the way things worked out, I paid

251

most of the bills myself directly from L.A., and you've still got the money."

"I still have more than four thousand of what you gave me," Bogart said. "But I was hoping that since you have so much money, and I have so little, you might let me keep it."

Howard seemed to think a minute. "Considering that George O'Brien thing you brought to my door, I'll call it even."

"Hot damn!" Bogart said. "I'm gonna need the money. Fox is not gonna renew me. Perhaps you'll put me under personal contract."

"You're not my type," Howard said. "The only way you could get any more money out of me at this point is to come up with something better than George O'Brien.

"If I could top myself," Bogart said. "I mean, come up with the handsomest stud in Hollywood, do you think you could spare another five thousand? You see I'm going back to New York, and I hear ninety percent of the actors along Broadway are waiting in line at the soup kitchen."

"I don't think you could do it," Howard said. "O'Brien would be a tough act to follow."

"What about Johnny Mack Brown?"

Howard looked stunned. "You're bullshitting me. He's available?"

"I took the liberty of discussing you with him," Bogart said. "He's ready, willing and able. Just waiting for your call."

"You have Johnny Mack Brown delivered to my house on Saturday night and the five thousand bucks are yours."

"You've got yourself a deal, pal," Bogart said shaking his hand.

"The best thing about money is that it can buy the unobtainable," Howard said.

"Maybe we'd better be getting back to the party," Bogart said. "Tallulah might send a posse out looking for us. Or, knowing her, spread rumors that we've sneaked off together to have sex."

"You wish," Howard said. "Where I'm concerned, you can only dream. But as a consolation prize, I'm offering you an evening on the town with me and Ethel Barrymore."

"That's not so bad," Bogart said. "I'd love to get to know Ethel Barrymore. Maybe she'll cast me in a play with her. I need the work."

"Ethel it is for us tonight," Howard said, taking one final snort of cocaine before facing the crowd inside. "But the deal is, if Ethel demands that one of us fuck her tonight, you've got to do the honors."

CHAPTER NINE
Los Angeles, 1932

After three flops in a row (*Sky Devils* hadn't really prospered), the film industry had begun to view Howard as a has-been. To prove them wrong, Howard launched what would eventually be interpreted as two of the most prestigious pictures of the early talkies—*The Front Page* and *Scarface*.

The best writing team in the business, Ben Hecht and Charles McArthur, had scored a hit on Broadway with a zany play about the newspaper business, *The Front Page*. Howard bought the screen rights to the play for $125,000, an astonishing figure back then. A few years later, the rights to *Gone With the Wind* would sell for only $50,000. Hecht and MacArthur then demanded an additional $80,000 to write the scenario. Howard balked at this final demand, hiring two lesser known writers, Bartlett Cormack and Charles Lederer, instead.

For *The Front Page*, he brought back his favorite director, Lewis (Milly) Milestone, who had won an Oscar for his direction of *All Quiet on the Western Front*. The overriding fear was that *The Front Page*, a one-set film, would look like a Broadway play. Milestone overcame that hurdle by using a tracking camera to keep pace with the "machine-gun" dialogue on screen. The grotesquely ugly Louis Wolheim, who had played the lead in *Two Arabian Knights*, was cast as the lovably conniving newspaper editor, Walter Burns, but only three weeks after filming began, he collapsed on the set. He was taken to a Los Angeles hospital where a doctor informed Milestone that Wolheim was "eaten up with cancer." He died a few days later.

Adolphe Menjou, the dashing but sarcastic actor with a moustache evocative of a stage villain from a Victorian play, was cast subsequently as the lead.

Menjou and Howard detested each other on sight, in spite of their shared right-wing views. Behind Howard's back,

Adolphe Menjou and Pat O'Brien
in *The Front Page*

Menjou called him a "cocksucking pervert." Howard was kinder to the actor, suggesting that "he looks like a repainted Rolls Royce."

Howard in the twenties had followed the example of Big Howard, often appearing in bespoke tailoring. But by the time *The Front Page* was released, Howard had adopted his sloppy dress code for life. His suits looked like he'd slept in them, which he probably had. Menjou, on the other hand, was famous for his sartorial style. Thinking that Howard knew nothing of tailoring, the actor foolishly suggested that he could help Howard improve his wardrobe. Taking one cynical look at Menjou, Howard spoke not a word but walked away from the set, never to speak to the actor again.

Cast in the second lead, that of a newspaper reporter named Hildy Johnson, was the New York stage actor, Pat O'Brien. Milwaukee-born Irish, and a drunk much like his best friend, Spencer Tracy, O'Brien also didn't impress Howard, although he'd agreed to the casting.

When he met Howard for the first time, O'Brien tried to impress him to no avail. First, he told Howard that he'd seen a stage version of *The Front Page* performed by an all-black cast in Hoboken, New Jersey, for a tails-and-white tie crowd. Howard didn't reveal his distain for blacks, and said nothing. Trying to connect, O'Brien quipped, "California's a great place to live if you're an orange," a line he stole from comedian Fred Allen. Again, Howard wasn't impressed. Like his friend Spencer Tracy, O'Brien didn't click with Howard.

Milestone introduced him to his two leading ladies. Famous today for the way James Cagney smashed a grapefruit into her face, Mae Clarke was cast as a prostitute, and Mary Brian played Pat O'Brien's sympathetic girlfriend.

Howard was less than enthralled with Mary Brian. "She's a nice girl," he told Milestone. "A nice, open, honest face. Nice smile. Nice teeth. Nice blue eyes. She has the same emotion in every scene. *Nice*."

"But she's from Texas like yourself," Milestone said.

"She's not like any Texas broad I've ever met," Howard said before turning away.

Mary Brian would re-enter Howard's life unattractively once again several years later, when Howard's lover, Cary Grant, announced that he was going to marry her, angering Howard. In later life, her career over, Brian took up painting portraits as a hobby. One of her first paintings was of Howard, depicting him as a giant prick. She ultimately got her revenge on both Cary and Howard simply by outliving them, dying in the final hours of 2002.

Howard found the film's other leading lady, Mae Clarke, a bit more to his liking. "Clarke should always play whores," he said to Milestone. "Unhappy ones." In a way, he was right, as the role of the hooker in the 1931 version of *Waterloo Bridge* became one of her more memorable pictures until, nine years later, Vivien Leigh took over the role, making it her own. In Vivian Leigh's version of the film, she was cast opposite Howard's future boyfriend, Robert Taylor.

Howard was mildly titillated to learn from Milly Milestone that Clarke was a bisexual like himself. She'd had an affair with Barbara Stanwyck in New York in 1926 when they'd appeared together in the stage drama, *The Noose*.

Howard accurately predicted that both Clarke and O'Brien would be awarded with star parts for only a few more short years before fading. "This film belongs to the boys," Howard said to Milestone. "The ladies are just for window dressing. Any actress in Hollywood could play these parts."

Uncharacteristically, Howard didn't interfere in the production of *The Front Page*, letting the very talented Milestone direct as he saw fit.

Taking him at his word, the director arranged for the establishment of a bar, a few steps from the sound stage, where both crew and actors could take a drink whenever they wanted. That ran up a big bill for Howard. Milestone didn't like to get up before noon, so he scheduled his daily filmings to begin every afternoon at one o'clock. Often, after a dinner break, they would resume shooting until one o'clock the next morning. A genuine craps table was set up off set, and there was a continuous game going on throughout the entire shoot.

Almost from the moment the film was released, Howard knew he had a hit. *The Front Page* became the quintessential newspaper movie and inspired a host of other films, even remakes. Starring Rosalind Russell and Cary Grant, *His Girl Friday* did even better box office in 1940 than Howard's 1931 hit. The director of *His Girl Friday* was none other than Howard Hawks, Howard's on-again, off-again friend and sometimes rival.

Much to Rupert's green-eyed envy, *The Front Page* was nominated for Best Picture, Menjou for Best Actor, and Milestone for Best Director. The only sour note was the film's banning in Chicago. Local politicians didn't like the premise that they were crooks.

Milestone later recalled, "What's more interesting even than the casting of Pat O'Brien and Menjou in the lead roles was my original cast. Howard Hughes nixed both of the actors I wanted instead of O'Brien—James Cagney and Clark Gable."

***

On their first meeting, Clark Gable and Howard hit it off. In many ways, the ruggedly handsome and masculine star was Howard's type. Billy Haines had already told Howard that he'd "had" Gable back in 1925 when he was a struggling bit player. The almost aggressively heterosexual Gable had allegedly told Haines, "I'll do anything to become a star—and I mean *anything!*" Now that Gable's star was on the rise, Billy wondered out loud if that offer were still true.

Howard had already admitted to Billy that he was attracted to the actor's good looks and devilish grin, two characteristics that would eventually turn him into the most widely recognized male sex symbol of the Thirties.

Milestone arranged the meeting after learning that Gable was available and that he wanted the role of the newspaper reporter, Hildy Johnson, in *The Front*

Page.

The director later recalled the first encounter between Gable and Hughes: "Howard was not a talkative man but he was chattering away with Gable. They seemed to speak the same language. Whether the stories were true or not, Gable was spinning yarns about his days as an oil wildcatter that must have evoked memories of Big Howard for Howard Jr. Gable also claimed that he'd been a garage mechanic, and Howard had a long history of being attracted to men in that field. Then Gable claimed to have been both a lumberjack and a telephone lineman."

After they had been talking for about fifteen minutes, and again according to Milestone, Gable said, "Howard, you and I have the same goal in Hollywood."

"And what might that be?" Howard asked.

"To become the two biggest shits in Tinseltown and to fuck every big movie star out here."

From across the desk, Howard set down his glass of milk and smiled at Gable. "You're my kind of man, Clark."

Gable could not have been unaware of the intense scrutiny he was getting from Howard. For the occasion of their meeting, he had put on casual riding breeches and a battleship gray turtleneck sweater.

Finally, Howard called attention to Gable's looks. "I've seen you on screen before. You somehow look different. Like you've changed."

"I'm a new man," Gable said. He flashed a smile showing his teeth. "New dentures. Some faggot over at MGM insisted I part my hair on my left. He kept that natural cowlick I have. In photographs they let it break loose and dangle over my right eye. That's supposed to make women cream in their bloomers.

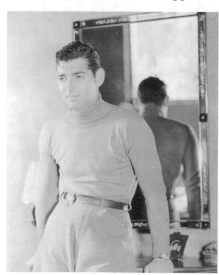

Clark Gable

They also plucked my eyebrows. I ain't Joan Crawford yet, but I'm getting there if they come at me with those tweezers again. I work out every day in the studio gym. The goal is broader shoulders and trim waistline. Women go for that."

"And others," Howard said quickly.

"What was that again?" Gable asked.

"Never mind."

"I've got a rival over at MGM," Gable said. "Johnny Mack Brown. He's about twenty-six or so. Irving Thalberg is pitting Johnny boy against me. They're giving him the big push with rugged he-man promotion like they're doing with me. He's a good-looking fucker like me and has a lot going for him. One of us is going to win out."

Totally left out of the conversation, Milestone hastily added, "It's going to be you, Clark. I know Johnny. He's got that languid southern drawl. You don't. Your voice will record better. I hear MGM is lining up all its big stars to appear with you. If you aren't bedding them now, you'll soon be starring opposite— on and off the screen—the usual suspects: Jean Harlow. Norma Shearer. Joan Crawford. Greta Garbo."

"I hear Garbo's pussy is so big that any man who fucks her falls in," Gable said. "Bring 'em on. I'll sleep with all of them, although any gal in bed with me isn't going to get much sleep. The gals don't have to be big name stars. Hash slingers or call gals, all pussies are dark at night. One woman is just like another to me. Love 'em and leave them. In some ways, and I'm sure Howard agrees, call gals are better. Unlike call gals, the good girls stick around and want a big romance. I want to keep moving. A different one every night will suit me fine. And despite my past or future marriages, I'll never be faithful to just one pussy."

"You do have a graphic way of speaking," Howard said. "You'd be perfect cast as a newspaper reporter."

Milestone claimed that Howard invited Gable to fly with him that weekend to San Francisco, and the actor accepted. He never learned any details of that trip. Howard never spoke to him about what happened.

But when Howard came back into his office the following Monday, he angrily announced to Milestone that Gable was not going to get the role. The director really wanted Gable for the part, but Howard would not hear of it. Finally Milestone asked why. "His ears are so big they make him look like a taxi with both doors wide open," Howard said. Milestone recalled Howard making a final enigmatic comment before dropping the subject. "Besides, his tits are too small."

Although he tried, Billy Haines never learned the details of that weekend. However, he told such pals as Joan Crawford and Ramon Novarro, plus countless others, what he suspected the problem was.

"Clark's the worst lay in Hollywood, and amazingly he'll admit that himself," Billy later said. "His foreskin is so tight it's difficult for him to draw it back over his glans. He also doesn't keep that little charger clean. Not only that, he's a premature ejaculator. Not Howard's cuppa!"

Before the end of the decade, when gossipy George Cukor was directing Gable as Rhett Butler in *Gone With the Wind*, he kidded his star about his involvements with Howard and Billy Haines. Vivien Leigh later claimed that Gable never spoke to Cukor again as long as he remained on the picture. Soon, partly because of Gable's lobbying, Cukor was replaced with director Victor Fleming.

With Gable not cast in *The Front Page*, Milestone called Darryl F. Zanuck and asked if James Cagney would be available. Zanuck said Cagney was available.

The next day, Cagney was ushered into Howard's office. Before the two men were introduced, Howard gave a fast appraisal of Cagney. "Throw this fucking little runt out of my office!" Howard shouted.

***

Its lifespan would be short, but Howard drifted into a quickie romance with the sexy screen vamp, Nancy Carroll, in the wake of his split from Billie Dove. "It was love on the rebound," as Louella Parsons claimed.

At the time, Nancy was in the dying throes of a romance with Joseph Kennedy, who had taken up with her after splitting from Gloria Swanson.

Bubbly and button-cute, Nancy was a red-haired former chorus girl who was making it big in the early sound era. In fact, as viewed by film historians today, she was the first movie star to emerge strictly from talking pictures. Stars whose voices recorded properly sometimes managed to rescue their careers. Others, whose voices were wrong, were replaced by actors imported from Broadway, where presumably they already knew how to speak.

At the time, Howard made it a point to see every major film released, and he was impressed with Nancy's singing and dancing in *Follow Thru*, a frothy 1930 musical shot in Technicolor that is remembered today only for introducing the hit song, "Button Up Your Overcoat." In the film, her hair came out a bit too fire engine red, but her skin photographed beautifully, a stunning peaches-and-cream complexion setting off the cuteness of her face. Her baby blues sparkled. It is said that no one in the history of Hollywood ever had eyes as blue as Nancy's. Howard's former "date," Ethel Barrymore, told her decorator, "I want draperies of a special shade of blue—the blue of Nancy Carroll's eyes."

Nancy Carroll

After seeing the film, *Abie's Irish Rose*, Howard told Noah Dietrich, "That's one pert nose on that Nancy Carroll. I think it's the sexiest nose in Hollywood. Even sexier that the nose of Myrna Loy."

"But you can't make love to a nose," Dietrich protested.

"There's a lot that can be done with a human nose," Howard mysteriously countered.

He had met Nancy at several Hollywood A-list parties. She was at the peak of her career when he was first introduced to her by Louella Parsons at the

Roosevelt Hotel. Howard had another date that evening, and so did Nancy. But they kept encountering each other. One night Nancy slipped him her telephone number, and he called her four days later.

At home with Cary Grant (left)
and Randolph Scott

At the time of their first date, Nancy, amazingly, was the most popular actress in pictures, but that lofty position would last only as long as it takes for a sickly butterfly to expire. She was proficient both as a sparkling comedienne and as an actress in melodrama. With her Cupid's bow mouth, she was the gamine darling of the Depression.

Her performance in the recently released *Devil's Holiday* had won her an Oscar nomination. In *Devil's Holiday*, Nancy had been cast as a gold-digging manicurist.

Ironically, at the time Howard asked Nancy out on their first date, she had been cast in *Hot Saturday* with two leading men—Howard's current lover, Randolph Scott, and his future lover, Cary Grant.

In 1963, two years before her death, the author of this biography was introduced to Nancy Carroll in the lobby of a Broadway theater. Introductions were made by Stanley Haggart, her old-time friend from the 1930s. They recalled some hilarious story about the two of them, along with four other actors and actresses, being in the same bed in some Beverly Hills home when the bed caught on fire.

Over dinner that night at Sardi's, Nancy was already a forgotten star of the Thirties. She was candid and outspoken and filled with many regrets, feeling that Hollywood had tossed her aside at her prime.

"Gloria Swanson, the bitch, always claimed that Howard never had any real interest in me," Nancy said, "but that he pursued me because I was the mistress of Joe Kennedy. If there was one man on the planet Howard hated, it was Joe

259

Kennedy. I never knew the reason for such hatred. But it was there and it was real. On our first date and after only a drink or two, Howard lit into Joe and attacked him viciously. Joe was a son of a bitch. But, as I was soon to learn, Howard was a son of a bitch too."

She admitted that her affair with Howard lasted for only three nights. "Unknown to me at the time, Howard suffered from constipation. Totally nude, he excused himself, picked up a magazine on aviation, and disappeared into the bathroom of the master bedroom at his Muirfield home. I had worn an expensive piece of black lingerie that night and was waiting for him in bed. On the previous two nights, he'd proven that he was a proficient lover. Unlike Joe Kennedy, Howard had the equipment to please a woman. In that bed, I waited and waited until an hour had gone by. I was always known for my hot Irish temper. When I could take this neglect no more, I got up, put on my evening gown, and stormed out of the house, driving off into the night."

What happened to her lover? Howard had sat and sat on the toilet. Engrossed in his reading, he completely forgot about the seductive star languishing in his boudoir.

"It wasn't quite the end of us," Nancy said. "A stunningly gorgeous diamond-and-ruby necklace arrived at my house, and I was willing to forgive Howard," the aging actress said at Sardi's. "In fact, I felt indebted to him after I accepted it. Actually, I found him very handsome and at times charming. When he called to invite me to go dancing with him at the Cocoanut Grove, I accepted."

George Raft

"But that evening was a disaster too," Nancy claimed, "and I swore off on Howard Hughes forever. At first things went swimmingly. I looked gorgeous as we danced around the floor together. The trouble came when I excused myself to go to the powder room. I left Howard talking in the corner with a very debonair George Raft. That surprised me somewhat because I thought Howard and George hated each other because of their mutual jealousy over Billie Dove. But I guess they had both recovered from Dove because Howard soon cast George in a star part in *Scarface*."

At this point, George Raft himself picks up the story. While working at a casino in London, he accepted an invitation for dinner from Stanley Haggart and the author and said he remembered that night at the Grove very well. "When Nancy went to the can, Hughes was talking *Scarface* with me. He said that Howard Hawks wanted me to play a secondary role. I told him I was interested, although the bastard was offering me only five hundred dollars for the part. Desperate for the role, I agreed to that measly bit."

Raft remembered that he detected Howard's attention being diverted. "He was no longer listening to me—that is, if the bastard could hear anything I said anyway. He kept staring at a blonde a few tables away. She had platinum hair, but not as white as Jean Harlow's, who I was fucking at the time. She was about twenty-one. Even from afar, I could tell this was one sassy dame—call it brassy. She sure commanded attention. She was escorted by her producer, Mervyn LeRoy. They were making *42nd Street* at the time. Most Hollywood wolves stayed away from her since she was out with LeRoy. Hughes headed for her table. The rest is Hollywood history."

"Don't tell us," said Stanley Haggart. "Ginger Rogers!"

"Who else?" was Raft's deadpan response.

When Nancy returned from the toilet, she asked Raft about what had happened to Howard. "Surely he's not gone to the toilet again. If so, we'll be here all night."

Raft merely nodded to the table where Howard sat talking to Ginger Rogers. "I remembered that hot-tempered little Irish lass storming out of there. Nancy never saw Hughes again."

The Nancy Carroll/Howard Hughes romance ended that night except for this final postscript: Ten days after the fiasco at the Cocoanut Grove, Howard received a call from Joe Kennedy. "I hear you've been seen out with Miss Nancy," he said in his mocking Bostonian voice. Howard later reported the details of the talk to Noah Dietrich.

At first Howard thought it was the call of a jealous lover, but at the time, he didn't understand the personality quirks of Joe Kennedy.

"Miss Nancy likes to play-act at being my naughty *Back Street* woman," Kennedy said. He was referring to a popular Fannie Hurst novel, *Back Street*. Released in 1932, this film is the classic tale of the "noble" mistress of a married man who must slip away from a wife he doesn't love for visits to his real love on the "back streets of life." Earlier, Nancy had tried out for the role of the mistress, losing it to Irene Dunne.

Before Howard could protest that their involvement was over, Kennedy said, "I want you to take the bitch off my hands. I've said *adieu* to Swanson, and now it's *adios* to Miss Nancy Carroll. You'll enjoy her if you like red pussy, and she's tighter than Gloria."

He abruptly hung up the phone on Howard.

At that 1960s dinner at Sardi's, Nancy said, "It's just as well that old Joe dumped me. I heard

Ginger Rogers

261

later that he went back for one final conjugal visit to Rose's bed. The fulfill-ment of that marital duty led to the birth of Edward Moore Kennedy. My money's on Teddy as the next president of the United States."

***

In Ginger Rogers, born Virginia Katharine McMath in Independence, Missouri, in 1911, Howard found an actress whose right-wing views made him look like a liberal. She was fast with the quip or the wisecrack.

When Ginger, a WAMPAS Baby Star of 1932, extended her hand to Howard at the Cocoanut Grove, he held it for a very long time, ignoring host Mervyn LeRoy's introduction to the rest of his table, which included his moth-er.

Gaining notice on the theater circuit in Texas and Oklahoma, Ginger, a fast-rising star, had toured with her act, "Ginger and the Redheads." At the time of her meeting with Howard, she had divorced her childhood sweetheart, Jack Pepper, whom she married in 1928 when she was seventeen years old. The mar-riage lasted only ten months during which time they toured together in an act entitled, "Ginger and Pepper." "Ain't that a cute name?" Ginger always asked anyone remotely interested.

Howard finally released the hand of this beautiful woman who was on the dawn of a celebrated film career with dancing partner Fred Astaire. She was decades away from taking a job, as she eventually did, as a fashion consultant for the J.C. Penney chain.

Ginger later wrote that during her night out at the Cocoanut Grove, which had one of the best orchestras in town, "I noticed a very tall gentleman on the dance floor looking at me. His face seemed stern, mask-like, almost as though he was trying to keep his feelings hidden. The severity of his expression was alleviated by a half-smile that played around his lips every time his glance caught mine."

That flirtatious beginning set the stage for one of Howard's longest and most enduring affairs with a Hollywood actress, although the romance would be on-again, off-again, and would even survive Howard's sexual attraction to her second husband, Lew Ayres.

Amazingly until she was told by LeRoy, Ginger didn't know who Howard was. Even though newspapers were constantly running his picture, she didn't recognize his face. Both LeRoy and Ginger thought Howard was a rich Texas oilman. As long as she dated him, she never knew the source of his wealth. As late as the 1950s, she was still referring to him as an oilman.

At the Cocoanut Grove on that long-ago night, Ginger remembered Howard approaching LeRoy's table of guests, getting a chair for himself, and just "squeezing in." Ignoring her, he launched into shop talk with LeRoy, claiming that he wanted him to direct a picture for him one day.

262

When the orchestra struck up the music after a fifteen-minute break, Howard rose to his feet and asked Ginger to a slow dance, cheek to cheek. Glancing at LeRoy for permission, Ginger agreed. Before Howard left the table, LeRoy warned Howard that he might not be able to keep up with Ginger. She, however, found his dancing quite passable. "At least he kept up with the beat."

Alhough she was supposedly "mad about the boy," meaning Mervyn LeRoy, Ginger still had a roving eye, later claiming that she found Howard "almost handsome" and also wondering "what he'd be like as a date."

After the dance, Ginger returned to table to find that the other guests of LeRoy's had stayed on the floor to dance a slow waltz, the second number. LeRoy had apparently disappeared, perhaps to go to the men's room. "Cigarette me, big boy," Ginger said to Howard. He didn't know it, but that was a soon-to-be famous line from her picture, *Young Man of Manhattan*. She'd appeared opposite Charles Ruggles, the star of the picture being the Parisian actress, Claudette Colbert. To her dying day, Ginger claimed that Colbert had made a pass at her during the making of that film.

At the time of her meeting with Howard, Ginger had been cast as the sassy, wisecracking, leggy chorine of *42nd Street* and would soon film the famous number, "Shuffle Off to Buffalo." Ginger played Anytime Annie ("the only time Anytime Annie said no, she didn't hear the question").

That night Ginger also told Howard that she'd been cast in *Gold Diggers of 1933*. "It's not typecasting," she said. "Ginger Rogers is no gold digger."

As she spoke to him, he found a slightly abrasive edge to her voice. "Everybody around you seems impressed with your money," she said. "Not me! I'm going to make it on my own in Hollywood without the aid of any man or his money. Men won't have to buy me. I'll buy them!"

"I like her a lot," Howard told Dietrich the following day. "I'm tired of women with blue eyes. Ginger has green eyes. She's a bit brittle, though."

At the time of her meeting with Howard, all the fan magazines were predicting that the wedding of Ginger to Mervyn LeRoy, the Warner Brothers director, was imminent. Ginger would later claim that it was on the night that she was dancing with Howard that she expected a marriage proposal from LeRoy later that evening. It never came.

What did come was a call from Louella Parsons a few days later, informing Ginger that LeRoy had called her and revealed his true plans. He was going to marry Doris Warner, daughter of his studio boss.

Ginger said she retreated to her bedroom to nurse her wounds. "If I weren't so damn mad at Mervyn, I would have had my heart broken."

It was the same bedroom that Ginger's mother, Lela Rogers, entered three days later. "Howard Hughes was just on the phone. Do you know him?"

Ginger told her that LeRoy had introduced him to her at the Cocoanut Grove. "He's calling with an invitation for you to attend the premiere of his movie, *Scarface*," Lela said. "He said he'd call back in five minutes to hear what your answer is."

The answer was yes. Although the premiere of *Scarface* was hardly the elaborate production that *Hell's Angels* was, she was excited by the invitation. It would be the first of many Hollywood premieres with various men that she'd attend.

The premiere would mark the beginning of one of the most important affairs in either of their lives.

On the night of the *Scarface* premiere, Howard arrived at the theater in a long black limousine. Before walking down the red carpet, he helped Ginger from the rear. She looked stunning, dressed in white satin with an ermine wrap.

A radio announcer, a harbinger of Joan Rivers, told the breathless world, "Ladies and gentlemen, Howard Hughes has just arrived. He's escorting the lovely Miss Billie Dove." An assistant whispered something into the announcer's ear. "Correction, ladies and gentlemen, Howard Hughes is escorting the lovely and vivacious Ginger Rogers tonight."

In subsequent weeks, Ginger would learn the full story of Howard's travails in bringing *Scarface* to the screen.

***

True to his promise, Bogart delivered companionship to Howard in the handsome frame of Johnny Mack Brown, one of the era's most sought-after leading men. As for the competition at MGM between Clark Gable and Johnny Mack Brown, Howard's opinion was expressed to Noah Dietrich. "For my money," he said, "I'm betting on Johnny boy. He's got sex appeal. Gable doesn't."

Perhaps Howard was motivated by competition with his sometimes mistress, Jean Harlow, knowing she'd enjoyed the charms of both actors during their collective filming of *The Secret Six*. The film's title brought a laugh to wicked Billy Haines. "In Gable's case, the film should have been retitled *The Secret Five*." Johnny Mack Brown had another suggestion. "If the film were about me, it should've been called *The Secret Nine*."

All-American Johnny Mack Brown was one of the greatest halfbacks ever to play for the Crimson Tide at the University of Alabama. Although he had been offered a career in professional football, he chose drama instead, hoping to become a romantic leading man in Hollywood. In 1928, Louis B. Mayer, impressed with his looks and his prowess on the gridiron, offered him a contract at MGM. But after seeing his lackluster screen test, the studio boss ordered him to take acting lessons immediately.

Evidently, the acting lessons helped, because soon Johnny was appearing in such films as *Our Dancing Daughters* with Joan Crawford, with whom he had an affair, followed by another affair with Norma Shearer. Those were relatively harmless compared to the affair he'd had with Marion Davies when they had co-starred together in *The Fair Co-Ed*. In those days, it was very risky for an actor to incur the ire of her patron, William Randolph Hearst.

Like many pre-code actors of his day, Johnny also had a homosexual streak in him. He had settled into a more or less ongoing relationship with the bisexual actor, Spencer Tracy. And Billy Haines had had sex with Johnny when they made *Slide, Kelly, Slide* together.

With his future at MGM in doubt, and Gable gaining on him almost weekly, Johnny had a good reason to meet Howard, even if he was being dangled as a meaty prize. He was hoping that Howard would sign him to a long-term contract and put him under personal management.

Arriving exactly on time one Saturday night at Muirfield, Johnny was shown inside by Beatrice Dowler and offered a drink. She told him that Howard would be notified that he was here and would join him shortly. After about an hour and no Howard, Johnny grew impatient. He went to see Beatrice, who told him, "Oh, Mr. Hughes is still out in the garage, tinkering with one of his engines."

"That's not very flattering," Johnny said, asking to be shown the garage.

Out back, Johnny went into the garage to find a pair of long, lanky legs sticking out from under a Duesenberg. In a slow but charming accent he'd been rehearsing since his birth on September 1, 1904, in Dothan, Alabama, Johnny introduced himself to Howard.

Howard must have been immediately intrigued with Johnny's masculine presence, charm, and good looks. At the time, Johnny was extraordinarily handsome, with a male beauty that would last for only a few short years.

A special dinner had been prepared for Johnny, all his favorite Southern dishes, although Howard stuck to his steak and peas. To Johnny's surprise, Howard's after-dinner entertainment involved taking Johnny into his private screening room where he ran the actor's 1930 film, *Billy the Kid*. "He [Hughes] was utterly fascinated by the character of Billy the Kid," Johnny said years later. "I told him that the great cowboy actor, William S. Hart, had personally trained me for the role. He was amazed that for added realism I used the actual pistols that were once owned by Billy the Kid."

In retirement in the early 1960s and obese beyond recognition, Johnny said, "I had no idea that Howard was picking my brain and was planning even back then to make his own film called *Billy the Kid*. Of course, the title was later changed to *The Outlaw*."

Johnny talked freely of his career, but refused to discuss any personal involvements with Howard or Marion Davies. "Hughes made a lot of promises about getting my career as a leading man launched, but he could have been talking to the Texas wind. He did nothing for me." The aging cowboy actor denied any romantic entanglements with either Howard or Marion. He did admit his suspicion that Hearst, believing "those god damn lies," sabotaged his career as a leading man at Metro, enlisting a powerful ally, his friend Louis B.

Mayer.

Johnny and Howard became instant companions after that first night at Muirfield. In the weeks to come, Howard used the airplane as his tool of seduction, as he would do time and time again with girlfriends and boyfriends. He flew Johnny to Arizona, to San Francisco, and even to Mexico for off-the-record weekends.

Beatrice Dowler remained convinced that Johnny had an affair with her boss. "I know for a fact that they slept naked in the same bed together at Muirfield."

The only other clue was provided by Billy Haines. At an all-male party at Muirfield, a drunken Johnny said to him about one of his foremost rivals, "After me, Howard will never speak of Charles Starrett ever again."

In Johnny, Howard found a certain wit. He always liked the way Johnny referred to John Wayne as "Marion" (his original name), and he took delight in revelations about Hollywood scandals. Johnny told Howard that Marion Davies had said that Hearst could no longer get an erection and had to satisfy her orally.

Two of Howard's lovers, both George O'Brien and Johnny, in separate dialogues, told Billy Haines that on very rare occasions—usually in the middle of the night—Howard would don a woman's gown and parade around the house. "I think it had to do with some hang-up with his late mother back in Texas," Billy said. "I heard she used to dress her son in girl's clothes. It's hard for me to picture Howard in a dress. With his long and lanky frame, he must have looked like a scarecrow. George told me he put on women's clothes with deadly seriousness and never in a spirit of fun. Also, Howard always insisted that I take him to the latest transvestite revues. He even went to bed with some of the more outrageous queens. During most of the 1930s, drag clubs remained a favorite of his. He was seen at the clubs so often that word quickly spread through the Hollywood grapevine that he was a homosexual. He wasn't. Bisexual would have been a better term because he did have a fascination with women's boobs."

When Gable knocked him out of the competition, Johnny searched for a new niche in Hollywood. In 1934, Mae West cast him opposite her in *Belle of the Nineties*. Before getting the part, he had to visit her apartment, where she told him "to drop drawers for a little inspection, and it had better not be little!"

After Mae, he drifted into "oaters" (low-budget Westerns) at Poverty Row studios as his career gradually wound down.

As Howard continued to collect trophy lovers, both male and female, he also launched himself aggressively into the making of *Scarface*, hoping for a hit to restore his tarnished reputation in Hollywood.

***

Howard bought the screen rights to the gangster novel, *Scarface,* from the novel's author Armitage Trail. For its adaptation to the screen, Howard hired screenwriter Ben Hecht, who added some very odd clauses to his contract.

Hecht demanded to be paid one-thousand dollars a day in cash and promptly at six o'clock every afternoon. Perhaps Ben had heard that Howard was strapped for cash. Surprisingly, Howard agreed to those demands.

He had read something about the Borgias, and decided he wanted the film to be based on Cesare Borgia's incestuous desires for his sister, Lucretia. "Incest is something I know about," Howard told Hecht. "My uncle, Rupert, had a long-term sexual relationship with his sister, Greta. My aunt."

To further confuse matters, Howard wanted the story updated to a Chicago setting depicting crime czars battling over bootleg liquor territory. The lead character, Tony Camonte, would obviously be based on gangster Al Capone. An assassin had once attempted to slice Capone's throat—hence the nickname "Scarface." Of course, not much of this had to do with the Borgias.

Hecht agreed to complete the script in only eleven days for a total price of $11,000, a great bargain for Howard since Hecht was one of the most highly paid scriptwriters in the business.

Two weeks later, a first draft of his script had fallen into the hands of Capone, who dispatched two of his most violent henchmen to call on Hecht in Los Angeles. Hecht remembered that the goons barged into his hotel room after midnight. In Hecht's words, they looked as ominous as "any pair of movie gangsters, their faces set in scowls and guns bulging in their coats."

"Is this stuff about Al Capone?" one of the hoods demanded to know.

Hecht assured him that the film was about another gangster he'd known in Chicago, Deanie O'Banion, "the last of the first-class killers."

"If this stuff ain't about Al, why are you callin' it *Scarface?*" the first henchman demanded. "Everybody will think it's Al."

"That's the reason," Hecht said. "Al is one of the most famous and fascinating men of our time. If we call the movie *Scarface*, everybody will want to see it, figuring it's about Al, which it isn't. That's called showmanship."

Believe it or not, the gangsters seemed to buy that, but demanded to know, "Who's this fella Howard Hughes?"

"The sucker with the money," Hecht said.

"Then to hell with him." The gangsters left Hecht's room and never showed up again.

Even though Howard was still in litigation with Howard Hawks, claiming that the director plagiarized his script of *Hell's Angels* in his competing aviation movie, *The Dawn Patrol*, he still wanted Hawks to direct *Scarface*, feeling he was the best in his field.

That lawsuit had caused a further rift between Howard and his uncle Rupert. *Dawn Patrol* had been written by John Monk Saunders, who was then married to Avis, Rupert's stepdaughter.

Howard reached Hawks when he was playing golf at the Lakeside Country Club. He asked to be allowed to come and play the game with Hawks, but the director refused. When Howard's lawyer, Neil McCarthy, called Hawks and agreed to drop the suit, Hawks agreed to play eighteen holes with Howard. Later, he claimed he beat Howard by shooting seventy-one. Before the end of the game, Hawks had agreed to direct *Scarface* for $25,000.

Hawks suggested James Cagney or Edward G. Robinson to play Tony Camonte. But Howard rejected the idea, since they were already associated with gangster movies, and he wanted *Scarface* to be more original than that type casting would suggest. Irving Thalberg wanted the role for his contract player, Clark Gable, but Howard nixed that idea. "I don't care to speak to Gable for the rest of my life."

Finally, the agent, Al Rosen, pitched the Austrian-born actor, Paul Muni, who had made a name for himself in the Yiddish Art Theatre in New York. At first, Muni turned down the idea, fearing he would be miscast. The choice of Muni was an odd one for both Howards, each of whom was anti-Semitic. Finally, Howard offered the actor $20,000 but he held out and got $27,000.

When Hawks actually met Muni and saw how thin he was, he told wardrobe to make him wear a padded suit for more bulk.

Paul Muni and Ann Dvorak in *Scarface*

For the role of the top gunman, Guino Rinaldo, Howard wanted George Raft, even though this part-time gangster, part-time actor, had been the lover of Billie Dove. If Howard had any doubts about casting a former rival in the film, it disappeared when Raft agreed to do the picture for only five hundred dollars. "He's perfect for the part, since he *is* a gangster," Howard told Hawks. "Let Billie and everybody else see Raft for the sleazeball he is." Raft was perfectly cast as the oily haired sidekick to Capone, tossing a nickel coin, an act that would become his trademark. The screen character was based on Frank Rio, Capone's bodyguard.

Scarface's crosstown rival, Gaffney, was to be played by Boris Karloff, the British actor generating excitement on the screen as *Frankenstein*.

For the female lead of Cesca Camonte, sister of the notorious Tony, both Howard and Hawks agreed that Ann Dvorak was the sexy choice, especially when they saw her dancing with Raft at a private party. At the party, Dvorak

268

wore a black silk gown almost cut down to her hips, with nothing on underneath it. Howard had already seduced her, as had Raft. She would soon be bedding Hawks himself.

With Ann Dvorak, Howard began a lifelong fascination with the penile measurements of his rivals in love. Often he would quiz women he was seducing about the exact measurements of his competitors.

He did that with Dvorak, demanding to know the size of Raft's legendary "Blacksnake," and how his own penis compared in size.

When he heard that she was sleeping with the director, he also wanted to know how Hawks measured up. On the golf course, Hawks had bragged to Howard about his "ten-inch pecker." But the director was such a liar Howard didn't believe him. He was more assured when Dvorak told him that Hawks had only an average sized penis and was often impotent. Howard must have been grateful that he'd always shown a certain sexual prowess around Dvorak and that she hadn't learned of his own occasional bouts of impotence.

Like a voyeur, Howard watched the rushes of a hot scene between Dvorak and Muni, playing her brother, over and over again until about three o'clock in the morning in his library at Muirfield. He became visibly moved by the scene, enough so that he drove his Rolls Royce over to the home of the actress. Once there, he demanded entry. Pulling off his clothes, he seduced her in her bed, then got up, put on his pants, and drove off. The next day, sanity prevailed. Even Howard knew that this brother-and-sister scene between Muni and Dvorak wouldn't pass the censors.

Hawks tried to chase Howard off the set every time he appeared. But one afternoon Howard arrived with two of his assistants carrying live ammunition. He demanded that Hawks use real bullets in the machine guns. At first Hawks objected, claiming one of the cast or crew might get killed, but Howard as producer prevailed.

"I want to see those machine guns spitting real bullets," Howard said. The decision that day was to have tragic consequences. Gaylord Lloyd, brother of screen comedian Harold Lloyd, visited the set two weeks later to see the action. Positioning himself where he was told not to stand, Gaylord came under attack. A bullet ricocheted dangerously, and he suffered the permanent loss of sight in one eye.

In talking pictures, Howard became the film industry's strongest advocate of sex and violence. He urged Hawks to put in more car chases (and crashes) and lots of machine gun fire. At one point Howard wanted to release the picture as *Blood and Bullets*.

After the film wrapped, Hawks told his Hollywood cronies that he flew to Chicago and personally showed *Scarface* to Al Capone himself following a lavish dinner in a Chicago hotel. "Capone loved it!" Hawks later claimed.

Such an event never happened. Capone was in Leavenworth Prison, having been convicted of income tax evasion.

***

In March of 1932 Howard had followed with keen interest the news events surrounding the kidnapping of the infant son of his aviator rival, Charles Lindbergh. Over the radio he'd heard the news that the baby was found murdered before the abductors specified how a fifty thousand dollar ransom payment was to be delivered.

Since he didn't have any children of his own, Howard himself began to fear that he might be kidnapped and held for ransom—possibly killed. For a while he ordered bodyguards for himself, and summoned in locksmiths to increase the security around Muirfield and to install extra gates for his protection.

Howard had been known for flashing a roll of money in night clubs throughout the city. Noah Dietrich every week sent him at least two thousand dollars in large and small bills. One Saturday when the money was delivered to Muirfield, Howard sent it back. Dietrich called for an explanation. "I'll no longer carry money on me," Howard said. "Not one cent!"

"How are you going to buy a cup of coffee or make a phone call?" the perplexed Dietrich asked.

"I'll borrow a quarter or even a dime from someone," Howard said. From that day forth, and as inconvenient as it often was, he no longer carried money on him, which often put him at the mercy of strangers.

"It was pathetic," his night-clubbing friend, Cubby Broccoli, said. "The world's richest man begging for a dime."

It was with this new sense of security that Howard accepted an invitation to spend an evening with Tallulah Bankhead at Marlene Dietrich's house. "We've all had the divine Gary Cooper, dah-ling," Tallulah said to Howard. "Let's get together and compare measurements."

Howard had met Marlene at several of the then notorious "pansy clubs," often when she was on the arm of her director, Josef von Sternberg. But Howard and Marlene never had a close encounter. He was eager to seduce the German beauty because he admired her style, her dress, and her glamour.

Howard arrived early at Marlene's house, with Tallulah being the tardy guest. He was shown into her living room where the beautifully gowned Marlene, a vision in pink, waited for him.

Miss Tallulah Bankhead

270

Howard had seen Marlene as Lola in *The Blue Angel* six times, and he'd confused the character with Marlene herself.

No one knows exactly what they talked about while waiting for Tallulah, but when the Alabama diva was shown into the living room, she found Marlene and Howard discussing what security precautions she'd taken in the wake of the kidnapping of the Lindbergh baby. Howard was inordinately interested in the subject.

She told him that in mid-May she'd received extortion letters threatening the life of her beloved daughter, Maria, if she didn't deliver ten thousand dollars. In a written threat, Marlene was told that "if you want to be a screen star, pay, and if you don't she'll be but a loving memory to you."

The threats to Marlene's daughter proved to be idle. But hearing about such a ransom note only intensified Howard's own fears. Marlene seemed to play on his anxieties, as she claimed that the press endangered his life by publishing story after story about how rich he was.

"I've never had to worry about that myself," Tallulah said. "The wolf is always at my door. I've never had a decent pot to piss in."

Marlene Dietrich

Hearing that remark and taking it literally, Howard the next day ordered a gold chamber pot made by Tiffany's for delivery to Tallulah. At her more outrageous parties, she used to bring out that pot for a public display of a "little tinkle-tinkle from your Aunt Tallu."

Back at Marlene's house, Tallulah tried to bring some gaiety to the party by talking about movies. "I always did want to get into Marlene's pants," she said, referring to being offered a role Marlene had turned down. "I ask you, Howard, who is the more *Tarnished Lady?* Marlene or me? And, dah-ling, the reason I'm introducing you to this enchanting creature tonight is to make up for my foul deeds in fixing you up with Ethel Barrymore."

"Miss Barrymore was very nice," Howard said gallantly.

He was mildly surprised that Tallulah and Marlene were friends, because he felt that Paramount was promoting a feud between them, as it hoped to turn Tallulah into "another Marlene" on the screen.

In his very undiplomatic way, he brought up this subject. Marlene quickly explained. "Paramount has made four million dollars with *Morocco*, *Dishonoured*, and *Shanghai Express.* If Paramount has yet another Marlene, the studio bosses figure they might make eight million dollars."

"Oh, forget all that silly talk, dah-ling," Tallulah said. "What utter nonsense, turning me into another Marlene, another Garbo. Hasn't it ever occurred to anyone that Miss Tallulah Bankhead is completely an American original and can only be herself?"

Sitting on the sofa next to Howard, she suddenly turned to him, placing her hand within striking distance of his crotch. "Enough of what Marlene thinks of herself, and what Tallulah thinks of herself. What do you, a Hollywood producer, think of these two scandalous pussies before you?"

Howard was not known for his insightful remarks. Perhaps inspired by the company he was keeping, he did deliver a rather accurate appraisal. "Both of you are great actresses. But I fear each of you will always be a supporting player to the two most mercurial personalities in Hollywood, Miss Bankhead and Miss Dietrich."

After that, all Marlene could say was, "Mr. Hughes, it is time the three of us climbed the stairs to hear our bedtime stories."

"I guarantee you we won't put you to sleep," Tallulah promised. "Instead of reading to you, we'll act out our beddie-poo stories."

"Indeed we will," Marlene said. "Mr. Hughes, you are about to become the luckiest man on the planet."

"I know you're not the type to write memoirs, but if you ever do, you could devote an entire chapter to this night," Tallulah said.

That night, Howard Hughes was seduced by both *Fraülein* Dietrich and that volatile bundle of overripe Alabama charm, Miss Tallulah Bankhead.

Marlene came right up to Howard and leaned toward him, giving his right ear a slight bath with her darting, serpentine tongue. "I've never been to bed with a Texan. Tonight I want to find out if it's true what they say about tall, lanky men from the Lone Star State."

"You won't be disappointed," Howard said, taking each woman by the arm and heading to the foyer and the steps beyond.

Looking up at the stairs and then at Howard, Tallulah kissed him lightly on the lips. "I'm sure your mama told you about the pot of gold at the end of the rainbow. Wait until you see what's waiting for you upstairs!"

The next day Tallulah told the story of her night with Howard and Marlene to her friend Billy Haines, who then told it to everyone. That

Howard Hughes Jr.

month it was the number one topic of conversation at parties, even making it to the dinner table at Pickfair.

***

From the very beginning of the *Scarface* shoot, Howard faced dire warnings from the censors, the Motion Picture Producers and Distributors, chaired by the grotesquely ugly, right-wing fanatic, Will Hays. When this former chairman of the Republican Party saw the first cut of the film, he demanded a new ending and at least thirty minutes of cuts, which virtually robbed the picture of its plot and integrity. He even demanded another title—*Shame of the Nation.*

Hawks urged Howard to defy the board, but he feared losing the Seal of Approval. With $800,000 of his own money invested in the film, he felt that he'd never earn his money back unless *Scarface* were allowed to be shown in all the cities of America.

Caving in to Hays's demands, Howard began to tamper with Hawks's cut, even agreeing to insert "a little sermon in the middle of the film lecturing against the evils of crime." William Randolph Hearst himself was selected as the actor to deliver that lecture.

When a final cut was made for release, Hawks was furious at Howard for allowing *Scarface* to be mutilated. But Howard was granted his Seal of Approval. Even so, the Censorship Board of New York banned the film for showing in that state. Aided by members of the press, including *The New York Herald-Tribune*, Howard attacked his political enemies who were trying to suppress his film. At the urging of Hays, Howard had opted to kill the more dramatic ending where Tony was mowed down by gunfire on the street, dying a "heroic" gangster's death. The substitute ending showed Tony turning "chicken-hearted" as he was hauled off to the gallows to be hanged.

When word reached Howard that Hays had vowed that "Scarface will never be shown on the screens of America," Howard swung into action. Hays said that he could never give his approval to a picture that glorified crime, even though in the past twelve months he had given the Seal of Approval to more than fifty gangster films.

Howard viewed the attempt to suppress his film as part of a conspiracy in Hollywood to destroy him as an independent filmmaker. This was no doubt accurate, and not just a reflection of Howard's paranoia.

Not all states, including Louisiana, had censorship boards, so Howard decided to open *Scarface* in New Orleans. Playing to a packed house, it premiered at Loews State Theatre in New Orleans. He accurately predicted that the film would get rave reviews. The momentum in both the press and word of mouth began to build. Even such powerful columnists as Walter Winchell were singing the praise of *Scarface* in print. Like a punch in the face of Will Hays, Wilton A. Barrett, executive secretary of the National Board of Review, endorsed *Scarface*.

Howard opted to show the uncut version of *Scarface* to the press at a special screening at Grauman's Chinese Theatre in Hollywood, where this unadulterated version met with rave reviews.

Eventually, the strait-laced Presbyterian, Will Hays, bowed to mounting pressure and granted the Seal of Approval to *Scarface*. His personal hatred and vendetta against Howard, however, would continue for the rest of his life.

Howard emerged from the fray with a hit picture and a public image as a warrior fighting against unreasonable censorship in America. But when he would return to making pictures, notably *The Outlaw*, he would face his biggest battle yet with the censors.

Although Howard viewed *Scarface* as his greatest achievement in film, even more than *Hell's Angels*, he would order it locked away in his private vaults for years at a stretch, even when a distributor offered him two million dollars for its re-release. The only way a whole new generation could see *Scarface* was mostly at clandestine screenings with 16mm bootleg copies.

In 1983, after Howard's death, the Hughes estate made a deal for a remake starring Al Pacino. The story was transferred from Chicago to Miami. Will Hays would have died a second death if he'd seen the new Al Pacino version, one of the most violent films ever made and riddled with obscene language.

In Hollywood Howard let it be known that "the pigheaded independent from Texas" was leaving films forever. He resigned from the Motion Picture Producers and Distributors of America, an organization which had treated him badly. He let his friends know that he was turning the industry over to the "king kikes," a racial slur on Louis B. Mayer, Harry Cohn, and Jack Warner.

Newlyweds: Paul Bern and Jean Harlow

"I'm taking to the skies and my freedom. No censorship there," Howard proclaimed to Noah Dietrich.

"All my time will be devoted to aviation," he told Billy Haines.

"What about sex?" his friend asked.

"I'll make time for it," Howard said.

***

Howard warned Jean Harlow not to marry Paul Bern, but his platinum-haired former star didn't heed his advice. Howard told his friends that the couple were the two most incompatible people in Hollywood.

Although generally liked by the movie colony, Bern had his enemies as well. Some of them called him "the creepy little man."

Bern married Harlow on July 2, 1932. Even though wed to what many men dreamed about at night, Bern continued to go out on the town for flings at bars frequented by homosexuals. According to Bern's friend, Billy Haines, he also continued to patronize male hustlers, usually out-of-work actors needing to pay the rent. One hustler known only as "Jack" became one of Bern's particular favorites.

"Paul wouldn't talk about Jean," Billy said, "but he didn't look like a very happy puppy after the marriage. His skin had become ghostly pale. He was really haggard and had lost weight. He was very distraught and had developed a nervous tick in his left eye."

The marriage didn't last long. On September 5, 1932, about two months after the wedding ceremony, Bern was dead. He'd been shot to death in a house he'd purchased for Jean, which she hated, set in the midst of five acres of grounds in Benedict Canyon in Beverly Hills. Bern's butler, John Carmichael, discovered the body in Jean's all-white boudoir. Bern was nude and lying sprawled on the floor in front of a full-length mirror. Before the shooting, his body had been drenched in Jean's favorite perfume, Mitsouko. He'd been shot in the head with a .38 caliber revolver, which was still in his hand.

Was it a suicide? Murder?

As in the death more than 30 years later of blonde bombshell, Marilyn Monroe, Bern's suicide or murder still remains one of the unsolved mysteries of Hollywood. Only one thing is certain. Virtually everybody associated with Bern's death, however remotely, lied. No one got the story straight, and, to make matters even more puzzling, some of the key participants changed their stories over the years, contradicting earlier testimony or claims.

Instead of calling the police, Carmichael alerted Whitey Hendry, head of security at Metro-Goldwyn-Mayer, where Bern was employed. Within the hour, Louis B. Mayer, accompanied by David O. Selznick and Irving Thalberg, arrived at the scene of the suicide/murder. Under Mayer's direction, they immediately began to rearrange the objects within the house, an action which appeared to involve tampering with evidence. Mayer was convinced that Jean had shot her husband in the head, and that his chief moneymaker had to be protected at all costs. He began to devise a possible scenario before the police arrived. Thirty minutes later, Howard Strickling, head of MGM publicity and known as "The Fixer," also arrived on the scene.

The son of a Presbyterian minister, Strickling knew "where all the bodies were buried," although he hated hearing himself characterized that way. If

Clark Gable, driving while drunk, ran over a pedestrian and killed him, Strickling was called in for damage control.

The details of what might have happened that night were supplied by Ilse Lahn, the *doyenne* of the German colony in Hollywood. Eventually, she became a famous literary agent and this author's representative for film property sales. On a rare visit to New York in the 1970s, she talked for hours about the death of Paul Bern, her once dear friend, and why she felt it was murder instead of suicide. At the time of Bern's death, Ilse was not an agent but was working as a dubbing supervisor at MGM.

"Everyone in the German colony in Hollywood at the time knew that Paul had been murdered," Ilse claimed, "and that the killer was Harlow herself. Clark Gable might have thought she was 'a good kid,' but I always detested the tramp and begged Paul not to marry her."

She remembered that when she became an agent years later, Strickling came to her house and wanted to seek her help in finding a writer to co-author a tell-all memoir about his behind-the-scenes role at MGM. "After spending a lifetime of keeping the secrets of the stars," Ilse said, "he seemed to want to unburden himself. Get it off his chest, so to speak."

In his proposed book, Strickling planned to devote an entire chapter to the Bern murder and the subsequent cover-up. Strickling claimed that he found no suicide note but discovered a strange entry in Bern's guest book, which had also been signed—on other pages—by such notables as Gary Cooper and his then girlfriend, actress Lupe Velez.

Dearest dear,
Unfortuately (sic) this is the only way to make good the frightful wrong I
have done you and to wipe out my humiliation.
I love you.
Paul.
You understand last night was only a comedy

The note trails off without a period at the end of the sentence as if Bern had meant to write something else. It was never clear to whom the note was written, much less what it was about. If indeed it were a suicide note, an entry in a guest book seemed an improbable place to leave it.

When Mayer was first shown the note by Strickling, he ordered that it be destroyed. Strickling, however, prevailed upon the studio chief to change his mind, claiming that the entry read like a suicide note and would establish suicide as the means by which Bern died instead of a possible murder.

Mayer finally agreed, and then wanted to go even further in establishing a motive. He decided that the note might suggest impotence as the reason Bern killed himself. "He couldn't do his duty as a man," Mayer told Strickling.

Bern's lack of sexual prowess had been the subject of much Hollywood gossip. The famous fan dancer and stripper, Sally Rand, once went on record as saying, "I can speak from experience. I know firsthand and can vouch for it, Paul wasn't impotent."

Yet another girlfriend, Barbara LaMarr, had gone to bed with Bern a year before her early death. She told columnist Adela Rogers St. Johns that Bern had no right to marry any woman. Apparently, in "graphic, technical, and explicit" detail she described how Bern's genitalia had never developed larger than those of a small boy.

In his notorious biography of Harlow, author Irving Shulman has Jean denouncing her husband for having "a dangle half the size of my pinkie."

"Harlow did not discover Paul's deficiencies on their wedding night as so many have assumed," Ilse claimed. "She'd gone to bed with him before and was well aware of his lack of endowment. She knew what she was getting before she married Paul."

Strickling maintained that Bern had told him that he had informed Jean before the marriage that sex would not be important in the relationship. "Instead of sex, I will give you undying love and respect," Bern is alleged to have told Harlow.

Mayer's theory of impotence prevailed and was flashed around the world. It did have one drawback, however. Bern died on September 5, 1932 and the Bern/Harlow marriage occurred more than two months previously, on July 2. Presumably, Bern's impotence would have long been revealed to Jean at that point, since they shared the same bed in the house on Easton Drive.

Although he did not specify the exact nature of his discovery, Strickling told Ilse that Mayer also ordered him to remove a batch of material deemed "lurid," including a dildo. To Strickling, that suggested that Bern might have had intercourse with his new wife via a dildo. "There were also certain photographs not meant for public consumption," Strickling claimed. When Ilse inquired about the whereabouts of the personal property removed from the dead man's house, Strickling said he didn't know where it was concealed.

Amazingly, although the body had been discovered that morning, it wasn't until 2:17 pm that Irving Thalberg actually called the police to come over. No one to this day knows who tipped off the press. But before two detectives arrived at Easton Drive, a Los Angeles newspaper had issued an EXTRA! about Bern's suicide, and it was already being hawked on the streets as a squad car pulled into the driveway.

"There were more cover-ups to come," Strickling told Ilsa. "At one point even Howard Hughes got involved."

***

The whereabouts of Jean Harlow on the night of her husband's murder or suicide remain unclear to this day. Beatrice Dowler, Howard's housekeeper, remembered a distraught Jean arriving in tears at the Muirfield estate to see Howard. He also confirmed to Noah Dietrich the next day that he'd seen Jean on the night of Bern's death.

Presumably for the first time, Howard in his library learned about "the other woman" in Bern's life. She was Dorothy Millette, Bern's common-law wife with whom he'd lived in New York and Toronto. Bern claimed that she had been in a coma for ten years. In spite of no marriage license, Bern always identified Dorothy, a struggling actress, as "Mrs. Paul Bern." For ten years, Dorothy was institutionalized. Her condition today would be diagnosed as schizophrenia. Bern paid for her upkeep in the asylum

Jean Harlow, Howard Hughes Jr.

and, when she was released, continued to send her a monthly check.

After her release, Dorothy wanted to come to Los Angeles and resume her life with Bern, pleading with him to divorce Jean. When Bern refused, she demanded fifty thousand dollars from him so that she could start a new life for herself. Bern agreed to meet with her in the house on Easton Drive. That night, he suggested that Jean spend the night with her mother, Mama Jean. Apparently, he told Jean all about Dorothy and claimed that he wanted to meet with her privately to resolve the question of their "triangle."

Jean later told Strickling that she did go to her mother's house but impulsively decided that her place was with her husband during his confrontation with Dorothy. Her fear was that if Dorothy claimed that she was married to Bern at the time Jean wed him, she'd be accused of bigamy, which might ruin her screen career.

Jean confided to Strickling that she drove back to Easton Drive. After parking her car, she was walking up the driveway when she heard a shot. She claimed she stood paralyzed in her tracks, afraid to go into the house. Jean went on to assert that she saw an unidentified woman fleeing through the front door. Having never seen Dorothy Millette before, she didn't know if this were Bern's "other wife."

Apparently, Jean revealed a different version to Howard, who told Dietrich that Jean said that she did enter the murder house. She claimed that after she entered the house, minutes after Dorothy had driven away, she discovered Bern shot in the head and lying nude on the floor. The gun, if the reports are to be believed, was lying five feet from his corpse. Jean then stated that she took the gun and placed it in Bern's hand to make it look like a suicide. She felt that if

Dorothy were arrested, the whole sordid story of her relationship with Bern would be exposed in the press along with ruinous bigamy charges. Fearing the consequences, she didn't want Dorothy to be found to talk to the police.

Jean also told Strickling she drove over to Muirfield to seek Howard's advice. "I had no one else to turn to," she claimed.

As Howard would later relate to Noah Dietrich, he didn't believe a word that Jean said. He felt that she was telling a lie, and that she had been the one who murdered Bern after a violent argument.

Isle Lahn agreed with Howard's assessment. She claimed that Bern told her that his marriage had been a grave mistake and that he was going to divorce Jean and return to Dorothy now that she was cured. "Dorothy needs me, Jean does not," Bern is alleged to have said.

"That haughty little darling, Miss Harlow, couldn't stand being dumped for another woman, and a rather ugly one at that," Isle said. "Harlow feared that if word got out that America's leading sexpot couldn't hold on to her man, she would be ridiculed in the press."

Whether he believed Jean's story or not, after hearing it, Howard swung into action. He told Jean to return to her mother's house, then summoned her doctor, Robert Kinnicott, and ordered him to scdate her heavily. That way, when the police came to question her, she would be in no condition to answer their questions.

District Attorney Buron Fitts issued a subpoena dated September 7 and had it delivered to Jean's house. Dr. Kinnicott notified the DA that Jean was "too ill for personal appearances." An inquest was held, concluding that Bern died from a self-inflicted gunshot wound. There was no attempt ever made to contact Dorothy Millette. The Paul Bern case was officially closed on September 12.

Friends other than Howard offered to comfort Jean. Clark Gable wanted to seduce her so that she could know what "a real man felt like." Actress Marie Dressler offered her comfort as well. The platinum bombshell turned down both offers.

Dorothy Millette herself come to a mysterious end. She rode the train from Los Angeles to San Francisco. From there, she boarded the *Delta Queen* for Sacramento. She was never seen alive again.

Her fate remains unknown to this date. A Japanese fisherman later discovered her badly decomposed body in the river. After an autopsy, a coroner's report labeled her death a suicide like Paul Bern's. She was known for keeping a diary but before her hotel room in San Francisco could be searched by the police, someone had entered and had stolen the diary.

Ilse blamed Howard Hughes for the mysterious death of Dorothy Millette. Her speculation was that he had hired one of his burly bodyguards to follow Millette when she boarded the ferryboat, and that he had then pushed her overboard where she drowned.

Strickling, during his conference with Ilse about his proposed book, disagreed with Ilse. He claimed that Jean had turned to another trusted friend, the gangster, Abner (Longy) Zwillman, and that two of this mobster's boys had done the dirty deed. Earlier, Longy had ordered the killing of two of Jean's blackmailers when they threatened to expose her nude photographs.

Right before his death, Noah Dietrich was pointedly asked his own theory about the death of Dorothy. "I wouldn't put it past Howard to do this as a favor for Harlow," he said. "Like many of Howard's schemes, this one wasn't thought out too carefully. If Dorothy did kill Bern, then she should have stayed alive. But with her out of the picture, and not able to testify, the blame for the murder might have focused entirely on Harlow, where it probably belonged all along. I'll go to my dying grave believing what I believe, and that is that Jean Harlow killed Paul Bern following a violent argument, when he told her that he was leaving her for Dorothy. What Harlow wanted with that no-dick creep I'll never figure out."

Over the years, speculation continued about Paul Bern's death. In a magazine article in November of 1960, Howard's former screenwriter, Ben Hecht, wrote:

Paul Bern, remembered for having committed suicide as the impotent bride groom of Jean Harlow, the great cinema sexpot, did no such thing. His suicide note, hinting that he was sexually impotent and had therefore "ended the comedy" was a forgery. Studio officials decided, sitting in a conference around his dead body, that it was better to have Paul dead as a suicide than as the murder victim of another woman. It would be less a black eye for their biggest moviemaking heroine, La Belle Harlow. It might crimp her box office allure to have her blazoned as a wife who couldn't hold her husband. It was a delicate point of the sort that is clear only to the front office theologians of a great studio.

The crime reporter, Hank Messick, had his own scenario as published in his book, *The Beauties and the Beasts*. He claimed that Longy Zwillman drove both Jean Harlow and Dorothy Millette in the same car to the home of Bern. The night turned into a disaster, and Dorothy fired the fatal shot after a bitter argument. Jean "watched in horror!" Then the cover-up began. Messick asserts that Longy then drove Jean to her mother's house and Dorothy to San Francisco, from which she embarked on that fatal ferryboat ride to Sacramento. Presumably, although this is not made clear, one of Longy's men had Dorothy pushed overboard into the river.

The Bern/Harlow house was later occupied by Jay Sebring, the premier men's hair stylist in Hollywood. Until she ditched him for her future husband, Roman Polanski, Sharon Tate, a struggling actress, was a frequent date. One night in 1966 she stayed alone at Jay's house. She later claimed that the ghost of Paul Bern appeared before her. While fleeing, she saw another figure—either male or female—with its throat cut. Then the apparition disappeared. This was said to be a vision of her own fate when she would meet her death at the hands of the Charles Manson "Helter Skelter" gang.

***

Howard dropped in to visit the set of the 1931 *Just A Gigolo* to see his friend, Billy Haines, and invite him for an evening on the town that would include dinner and a nightclub. Billy was playing a British nobleman in this little romantic comedy, and introduced Howard to one of the co-stars of the film, the British-born actress, Lilian Bond, cast as Lady Agatha Carrol.

The minor star is remembered today, if at all, for her appearance as Lillie Langtry, the object of Judge Roy Bean's unyielding desire, in the 1940 film *The Westerner.* She lived a long life, dying in 1991, and her name is still romantically linked to Howard's even though their so-called romance was short.

A dark, curvaceous beauty, Lilian was at the peak of her career when she met Howard, having been cast in fifteen movies in only twelve months. She would appear opposite such stars as Loretta Young, Nancy Carroll, Charles Laughton, and Boris Karloff, although she never seemed to catch on with the public.

Howard was impressed with Billy's prediction that she was going to become one of the biggest female stars in pictures. That was her dream, and Howard bought into it.

Decades from the date of their first meeting, Lilian said, "I remember Howard as if it were only yesterday. I thought he was very handsome. Up to then, I had never met any rich man who was handsome."

"I was hoping to make it big in Hollywood, and for a time my dreams were coming true," Lilian said. "I was making films so fast I got dizzy. Of course, on looking back, I realize that none of them was particularly great. Even at the peak of my career, I didn't always get star parts and willingly accepted uncredited roles such as 'actress on a train' or 'girl at the bar.' Some of my characters were a bit outrageous—one I remember, Dolores Divine I was called. Don't you love that?"

"Billy and I went out on the town together, but we were just sisters," Lilian recalled. "I was delighted when Howard joined our party for the evening. And, yes, I went to bed with him on the first date. I don't know what the rules are today. He wasn't a particularly responsive lover. Let's just say he was adequate for the challenge and leave it at that. Billy had told me that Howard had just dumped Billie Dove and was dating Ginger Rogers."

"I guess that determined our choice of a club," she said. "I don't remember the name—something like *The Little Cloud That Cried*. Weird name. I suspected that he didn't want to take me to some important place like the Cocoanut

Grove because Miss Ginger would surely hear about that."

"We had a good evening," she remembered, "and after dinner Billy hastily departed on his nocturnal adventures, leaving Howard and me alone together, which both of us welcomed after the introductions were made."

"The moment Billy left, Howard came on to me like gangbusters," she said. "He told me that he wanted to sign me to a personal contract—God, how many times did he say that to a beautiful woman?—and even suggested that he was lonely and was looking for a new wife."

"I had heard that he was the richest producer in Hollywood—a lot of Texas oil money—and frankly I would have been delighted to become the second Mrs. Howard Hughes. What gal in her right mind wouldn't? Maybe only Katharine Hepburn years from then would say no. But I said 'girl in her right mind' which would exclude Hepburn."

"Before going to bed with me, he insisted that we bathe together," she said, "and he bathed me like I was a baby girl or something. That was one clean man. He wanted to make sure everything was washed. It was years later that I learned that he had previously contacted a venereal disease—I don't think it was syphilis—and was perhaps worried about infecting himself again. I really don't know."

"He was so thorough I made a joke, which seemed to irk him," she said. "I told him that I had heard Charlie Chaplin was so afraid of venereal infection that he coated his penis with iodine before entering a woman. I jokingly suggested that to Howard, but I should have realized that he wouldn't find it funny."

She claimed that Howard dated her for only a few short weeks. "We got together one night a week for our ritual bath. Of course, I was already thoroughly bathed and perfumed before meeting him. He discussed several film projects with me. If I remember, he wanted to make a film about Zeppelins. He was hoping to score a big hit like he did with *Hell's Angels*. He told me that he'd cast me in the female role, and the part would do for me what Jean Harlow's lead did for her in *Hell's Angels*. Fool that I was, I believed him."

She said that at the time she dated him, he was more obsessed with aviation than movies. "I remember once we drove high into the hills above Los Angeles and enjoyed an incredible view. He wasn't paying much attention to me, but kept looking up at the sky. I'll always remember him saying, 'Up there I'm the master of my universe, my own man. Down here I have too many battles to fight with too many shitheads. Of course, being a pilot is great for your love life. If there is anything about a man that a woman goes for, it's learning that he's a pilot. After she hears that, the night is mine.'"

"My great disappointment came when some damn newspaper wrote a story that Howard was finished with films—no more movies," she said. "It was then I knew that all this talk about launching my career would not amount to anything. I had fallen for the old line. Even knowing what I know now, I still would have dated him. It was fun while it lasted. You can write me up as one of his many, many trophies."

"The end came suddenly when two dozen American Beauty roses arrived at my doorstep," she said. "Not only that, but a beautiful brooch. He said that it belonged to his mother, but it looked like something one of his assistants had picked out the week before at Tiffany's. The brooch was eventually stolen from my dressing room, but I at least have my memories of Howard and what might have been."

As a final note, she added, "I bet our Zeppelin film would have cleaned up at the box office. Oh, yes, did I mention it? Howard asked me to marry him, and I accepted. A lot of good that did me!"

***

Both Billy Haines and Ramon Novarro claimed credit for introducing Howard to his short-lived fling with the beautiful southern belle from Tennessee, Dorothy Jordan, who was only a year younger than Howard.

Dorothy had first gained recognition when she'd danced on Broadway with the Astaires in *Funny Face*. Very gay-friendly, before the term was invented, she'd also appeared on stage with the slightly effeminate hoofer, Clifton Webb. Going to Hollywood, she'd become a leading lady in the silents in the late Twenties and in the days of the early Talkies.

She is still seen on the screen today at showings of the famous 1930 film, *Min and Bill*, which starred Marie Dressler. At the time Howard met Dorothy, she was appearing in *Bondage*, playing a resident in a home for unwed mothers.

She had co-starred with Billy in *Tailor Made Man* in 1931, and had appeared opposite Ramon in three films, including *In Gay Madrid* in 1930. Howard had seen only one of her films, *The Lost Squadron*, with Joel McCrea and Richard Dix, and had been impressed with her clean-cut, wholesome beauty.

When Dorothy learned that he hadn't seen her star opposite Bette Davis in *Cabin in the Cotton* ("I'd love to kiss ya but ah just washed ma hair"), she insisted that he drive her to Pasadena where the film was still showing at a small cinema.

"I think he was more taken with Bette in the film that he was with me," Dorothy later said. "But those two were years away from having an affair."

Although he didn't want to be seen in public with Lilian Bond, Howard invited Dorothy to go dancing with him at Cocoanut Grove. Perhaps Ginger Rogers was mad at the time, and he was no longer worried that she'd be jealous. "It started out like a real romantic evening," she said. "Howard looked gorgeous, and I was at my best. But then Jeanette MacDonald entered the room with an entourage. Howard spent most of the evening sending love notes over to her table. Jeanette consistently ignored him, and I thought it served him right the way he was neglecting me."

One morning after Dorothy had spent a night with Howard at Muirfield, he asked her to accompany him on his search for a new wardrobe. She was known for her taste in clothing, and she felt he wanted her to help him select fabrics for his tailor-made suits. During the Twenties, Howard had emulated his father by wearing the best suits from Brook Brothers or Savile Row in London. Howard and his new best friend, Pat DeCicco, were known as two of the smartest dressers in Hollywood.

"To my amazement, he took me to this men's store that looked more like it sold hardware," Dorothy recalled. "It was a place where plumbers and janitors went for their clothes. I remembered he purchased three pairs of khaki work pants. He then drove me to a shoe store where he bought three pairs of white canvas tennis shoes. One night when he took me to a big party Marion Davies was throwing in Santa Monica, he showed up in a well-tailored tuxedo but with one of those pairs of tennis shoes. That soon became his standard outfit for formal occasions. Our shopping spree continued. In the slummy side of Los Angeles, we went to this small department store that catered to low-class workers. He purchased a dozen shirts, mostly white, paying about $1.50 each for them. He said he'd ignore the underwear because he didn't believe in wearing any. Before the afternoon ended, he took me to this resale outlet where he purchased one black suit and one tobacco brown suit off the rack for fifteen odd dollars a piece. No more bespoke tailoring."

Pat DeCicco later recalled his horror at seeing Howard for the first time in what gay men today call "blue collar drag." "How can you dress like that?" he asked Howard.

"Don't worry about it, Pat," Howard said. "You'll be the dude in the expensive clothes, and I'll make the money."

According to Dorothy, the wardrobe incident was only one in a series of irrational acts that Howard would commit in the years ahead. "I remember one night we drove all over Los Angeles looking for a vanilla ice cream that appealed to Howard. We must have gone to more than two dozen outlets before Howard found a vanilla cone that was right in texture and taste. It was a little store called Pat Kelly's Ice Cream. Apparently, there was a Mrs. Kelly in the back room who made the ice cream herself. Howard loved it, ordering four scoops. He then went back and met the wife and ordered three large containers of vanilla ice cream, with the understanding that they'd be delivered to his Muirfield estate. He'd always order some scoops at dinner after he'd finished his steak and petite peas."

Dorothy was too hip to fall for Howard's promise of a big movie contract and starring roles, his usual line with women he was trying to seduce or seducing. "I went along for the party—and for no other reason. Actually, I was looking for a man to marry. My thing with Howard was a passing moment, but fun while it lasted."

284

Cubby Broccoli had his own take on the Hughes/Jordan affair. "Howard was looking for an easy lay, and Jordon was very beautiful. Pat DeCicco called her a southern magnolia."

Once, Howard flew Dorothy to New York, where columnist Walter Winchell spotted them together at the exclusive Stork Club. Back in Los Angeles, he took her three times for dinner at the swanky Perino's. Dorothy remembered that each time he went back into the kitchen to instruct the chef how to prepare his steaks and give him instructions about serving only the smallest peas.

Dorothy's romance with Howard quickly ended when she fell in love with director Merian C. Cooper. At the time, he was in the throes of his big success with *King Kong*, starring Howard's future girlfriend, Fay Wray.

Howard is credited with offering Cooper some advice in cutting *King Kong*. Surprisingly, Howard had gone to a Hollywood theater by himself to see the film. In one clip, four sailors, after King Kong shook them off a log bridge, fall into a ravine where they are eaten alive by hideous giant spiders. The next day Howard called Cooper and told him that many women in the audience screamed and several patrons left the movie palace. "The scene is just too ghastly and takes away from the story."

Cooper agreed with Howard, later saying, "The spider scene stopped the picture cold, so I cut it."

As many Hollywood movie buffs know, Dorothy turned down the role of Honey Dale in *Flying Down to Rio* to go on her honeymoon with Cooper.

In her first role with Fred Astaire, Howard's girlfriend, Ginger Rogers, stepped in to replace Dorothy. The rest is movie history, or so they say.

***

Ginger called Howard and asked him to escort her to a party at the home of Una Merkel, the actress she'd met and befriended on the set of *42nd Street*. Una Merkel is remembered mainly for her no-holds-barred cat fight with Marlene Dietrich in *Destry Rides Again*, and for her ability to always deliver a wise-cracking retort delivered deadpan. In 1932, Merkel had married an aviation designer, Ronald L. Burla, and both of them were hosting the party.

Ginger had gone to Muirfield around two o'clock that afternoon, bringing her evening clothes with her. Howard wanted to spend some quiet time alone with her, and she'd agreed to that. But as she was getting dressed for the party, a call came in for Howard from some distraught woman who had obtained his private number. Normally, he didn't accept such calls, but his housekeeper, Beatrice Dowler, said this one was urgent. "The woman's threatening to kill herself if she doesn't see you at once."

Howard took the call and, when he heard what she had to say, he told the woman to meet him in thirty minutes at the office of his attorney, Neil

McCarthy. Howard then drove, with Ginger at his side, to the attorney's office, where he ordered Ginger to wait in the car until "this nasty business is concluded."

In the lawyer's office Howard confronted a blonde, shapely, and rather attractive would-be actress, Barbara Langford, who, as was later learned, had come to Hollywood two years earlier to make it as a film star. Finding no work, she'd taken a job as a waitress in a diner.

Neither McCarthy nor Howard ever commented on the nature of the threats Langford made that night in the office as an impatient Ginger waited for more than an hour in the car.

All that Howard told Ginger, as she later remembered, was that "I had Neil give the bitch five dollars to get rid of her."

"Is she going to kill herself?" Ginger asked.

"Frankly, as long as she doesn't do it on my property, I don't much care," Ginger remembered Hughes saying as they began their drive toward Una Merkel's party.

Earlier, Una Merkel had been cast opposite Ramon Novarro in the MGM collegiate drama, *Huddle*, and in the process, they had developed a strong friendship. Ramon had very despondent, and Merkel wanted to cheer him up with a party. Ramon had lost almost all his money in the stock market crash of 1929, and had also discovered that his best friend and trusted business manager, Louis Samuel, had been embezzling from him. He had also recently lost his beloved brother, José, to cancer. Worried about his uncertain future in talking pictures, Ramon was depending to an increasing degree on liquor to get him through the night.

When Howard and Ginger arrived late at Merkel's party, Ramon Novarro was already deeply intoxicated. To the party, Merkel had invited cameraman Harold G. Rosson, and the woman he was soon to marry, Jean Harlow, in the wake of the death of her late husband, Paul Bern. Also at the party was William Bakewell, a juvenile actor of the 30s best known for appearing in *All Quiet on the Western Front* with Ginger's next husband, Lew Ayres.

Jean Harlow and Ramon Novarro had little to say to each other. Jean's late husband, Paul Bern, had produced *In Gay Madrid*, starring Ramon and Howard's latest flame, Dorothy Jordan. After Bern's murder, Ramon had told Hollywood gossips that, "I for one am glad to see the little prick go to prick heaven." Word of that had gotten back to Jean, and she didn't want to have anything to do with Ramon. Bern had further infuriated Ramon when he'd gone to Louis B. Mayer and urged the mogul not to renew Ramon's contract. Ramon never spoke to the producer again.

The night of the Merkel party, Howard and Jean had just had another of their big fights, although no one knows for sure just why. It might have been over "the other blonde in your life," Ginger Rogers. Inversely, Ginger was also jealous of Jean because of her success and because of her continuing romantic involvement with Howard.

Bringing together Ramon Novarro, Ginger Rogers, Jean Harlow, and Howard Hughes would have been the nightmare of most hostesses. During the party, Merkel seemed unaware that she had united four people in a potentially explosive situation. But the foursome, as well as Rosson, handled the evening with dignity. Only Ramon misbehaved by continuing to drink heavily.

At one point he disappeared into one of the upstairs bedrooms. A few minutes later, the party was alerted to screams coming from above.

When Merkel and her husband attempted to see what was the matter, Howard jumped up and said, "Let me handle this." Trailed by Ginger, he ascended the steps.

In the master bedroom, Howard was stunned to discover Ramon nude, wearing what looked like a *faux* tiara, jumping up and down on the bed, his cock and balls keeping time with the rhythm.

To everyone's dismay, he kept shouting, "I am Queen Victoria! I am Queen Victoria!"

And thus ended a typical evening in the life of Howard Hughes.

***

One day in 1932, acting on an impulse and unbeknownst to his staff and associates in Los Angeles, Howard rode the train from Los Angeles to Fort Worth, Texas. It would be one among many such disappearances, some of which lasted for weeks and in one instance for months at a time.

He arrived in Fort Worth wearing a newly purchased sky-blue suit from Sears & Roebuck and a pair of two-toned brown and white shoes. Joining other blue-collar workers, he stood in line at the personnel office of American Airlines. He had in his possession a driver's license issued in Texas and an authentic Social Security number. The name on both documents read "Charles Howard."

American Airlines' personnel clerk was impressed with Howard and hired him for a salary of $115 per month as a baggage handler. He was assigned to the daily flight between Fort Worth and Cleveland. He had to report to American every morning at six o'clock to check and stow luggage in the plane, and for some reason, he had to physically accompany the luggage throughout both legs of the flights between the two cities.

On the flight to Cleveland, Howard sat up front with the pilot, observing his every navigational move and absorbing all the dials, switches, buttons, and levers.

He told the pilot, Bruce Dernhill, that he too wanted to become a pilot. Dernhill later recalled that he was impressed with this baggage handler's intricate knowledge of flying.

A district officer for American Airlines, Henry Madsen, just happened to be aboard the flight to Cleveland one morning. By coincidence, he'd met Howard when *Hell's Angels* had premiered in New York. He recognized him at once. "Mr. Hughes, what are you doing working for us?"

To explain his situation, Howard told *The New York Sun* on December 6, 1932, that he was working for American Airlines because he planned to make a film "about commercial aviation" and he wanted to learn the procedural, behind-the-scenes activities as a means of making his movie more authentic.

As for his job, the airline fired him as soon as his identity was exposed. It was against company policy to hire anyone under a false name.

In the aftermath, Howard flew back to Hollywood where he hoped

Howard Hughes Jr. handling baggage

Ginger Rogers still waited for him. It was only then that he became aware, as he later told Noah Dietrich, that he hadn't bothered in advance to tell her about his leaving, and that he hadn't contacted her at any time during his unexplained absence.

After he returned to Muirfield, he made repeated calls to Ginger. She refused to come to the phone, even though he sent her daily flowers and had a diamond brooch delivered to her mother, Lela.

Thwarted and frustrated, Howard came up with an idea. He ordered Noah Dietrich to contact the Rogers household with some very bad news.

"Tell her that I'm dying, and that I have to see her at once!"

CHAPTER TEN

Los Angeles, 1933

Alarmed at the news about Howard's impending death, Ginger Rogers rushed to Muirfield for what she thought might be a final *adieu*. But when she learned that Howard was in fine health, and had only pretended to be ill, she stormed out of the house, tersely informing Noah Dietrich that her romance with Howard had officially ended.

Declaring himself as sick had worked well with Howard's mother, but Ginger was too smart to be fooled a second time. Nonetheless, after her departure, Howard continued to insist that a stroke was imminent. Alarmed, Dietrich rushed him to St. Vincent's Hospital in Los Angeles.

There, one of the nation's top cardiologists put Howard through a battery of tests, the examinations lasting all day. In an early form of a stress test, a monitoring device was attached to his bare chest, and he was instructed to run up and down three flights of steps for a full hour. He performed brilliantly. The cardiologist told Dietrich, "Your boy's as strong as a horse. There's nothing wrong with his heart. I wish mine were as good as his."

Even though Ginger had rejected him, Howard wasn't going to give her up that easily. He hired a pair of private detectives to report all of her activities to him. It was during the course of their sneaky invasion of her privacy that they discovered that she was having a torrid affair with Lew Ayres. Ever since she had seen his handsome, boyish face in the film, *All Quiet on the Western Front*, Ginger had told some friends, "That's my dream man."

Howard already knew that Lew was a bisexual, having learned of the young actor's affair with Spencer Tracy. Howard told Dietrich that he was going to let Ginger go ahead with her plans to marry Lew. "She'll

Hughes Jr. at play

289

find out about him soon enough. Serves her right for walking out on me that way."

Eventually, and in spite of her marriage to Lew Ayres the following year, Ginger would re-enter Howard's life. She would also have affairs with other lovers during the course of her marriage. Not surprisingly, none of this information appears in her sanitized autobiography, *Ginger*, although she warns readers at the beginning that her tome is not a "tell-all" book.

Ginger Rogers, Howard Hughes

***

Scotland, 1933

A week after the fiasco with Ginger, Howard returned East and sailed for Scotland. John Darrow was his bunk mate as he set out for Europe to purchase the *Rover*, the fifth largest yacht in the world. Designed and constructed by Stephens and Company in Glasgow, the *Rover* stretched 320 feet and was manned by a crew of nearly three dozen men under the command of Carl Flynn, whose nickname was "Jock." Jock was a salty Irishman with a fondness for the whiskey of his country—"I can't stand Scotch whisky. The Scots not only don't know how to make whisky, they don't know how to spell it, leaving out the e."

The yacht's asking price was a staggering $850,000, the equivalent of more than 16 million dollars in today's currency. The Scots would not come down on their price, wanting the full amount, forcing Howard to sell the *Hilda* on which he'd sailed with Billie Dove, whom he now referred to as "that tramp."

Since Ella still had a freeze on his assets, he conceived a scheme with Dietrich where the cost of the yacht could be removed discreetly from Toolco royalties paid in London.

Changing its name to the *Southern Cross*, Howard lavished even more money on the vessel after purchasing it. He installed Murano chandeliers imported from Venice and also the largest known bed afloat for the master stateroom. From London, he ordered "the world's largest ermine bedspread."

On the first night, he auditioned the bed with John Darrow. "From the sound of things, it must have been one wild night," Jock later said.

Since booze was still outlawed in America, Howard registered the ship in Panama. He personally supervised the installation of a ten thousand dollar wine cellar from a merchant based in London. That same dealer also secured two dozen bottles of rare 19th-century French brandy that one day would be praised by Sir Winston Churchill.

290

An entire rack of the most expensive perfumes in Paris was also ordered, along with valuable linens created by "nuns going blind somewhere in Flanders." Howard ordered all his linen and towels monogrammed HH.

With John Darrow still at his side, Howard sailed across the Atlantic to Newport.

Jock later reported that Howard was particularly attracted to an extraordinarily handsome, blond-haired, blue-eyed sailor, Ralph Walker, who'd grown up in the slums of Glasgow. Howard first spotted him when Walker was exercising nude on deck. "With a body like he had," Jock recalled, "I think he wanted to show it off. He could also have heard stories about Hughes and was deliberately baiting him."

At any rate the moment the *Southern Cross* reached Newport, John was shipped back to Los Angeles, presumably to resume his film career. The next night, Ralph Walker was sleeping in the master bedroom under that ermine spread.

Howard then launched into what Dietrich would call the *debutante du jour* phase of his life.

***

East Coast, West Coast, 1933

On and off for at least a year, either with or without Pat DeCicco, Howard sailed aboard his "floating palace" into expensive seaports along America's East Coast, especially Newport and Palm Beach.

Many of the young women sailing with him were introduced to him by Pat, who was well connected socially, and who would eventually marry the debutante of the year, Gloria Vanderbilt.

Rich and powerful East Coast families seemed only too willing to entrust their daughters to the two dashing lotharios of the sea. No doubt, the reputation of Howard as the richest man in America was part of the attraction. Pat, on the other hand, was often dismissed as "just a gigolo."

Usually Howard spent no more than a weekend with one of these young beauties. The exception was seventeen-year-old Timmie Landsing, a stunning beauty and Manhattan debutante, who enjoyed a brief but intense romance with Howard. Their inaugural meeting occurred in in Los Angeles. The romance itself was launched in a luxurious suite at the Ambassador Hotel, scene of many of Big Howard's sexual conquests. Howard invited her to sail with him from California to Acapulco, where they spent a "glorious two weeks," as he later told Pat. After that, he sailed with Timmie through the Panama Canal. On shore he would often leave her while he went off with Ralph Walker.

On the East Coast after the cruise, the romance continued. He invited her to come and stay with him at Muirfield where she occupied Ella's old bedroom. During the day, she attended drama classes at Pasadena, as he was holding out the promise to her of a film career. In the afternoon, the Westmore brothers, two famous hairdressers of their day, restyled her image, making her more glamorous than she had been before.

Then Howard, as was typical of him, lost interest. Back at Muirfield, growing lonely and despondent, Timmie threatened suicide. Howard was unmoved. Over the years, many women would threaten suicide when he dumped them. Finally Timmie's parents arrived from the East and removed her "from the clutches of that evil man." The day that happened, Howard was flying over Southern California with William Randolph Hearst, Jr., the handsome, blue-eyed scion of the Hearst empire. He and Howard became almost instant friends and "cruising buddies." Each of them actively pursued a series of lovely young women, few of whom turned down invitations from Howard Hughes Jr. and/or William Randolph Hearst Jr.

Privately, Louella Parsons referred to them as "airborne cocksmen." The two frequently flew their hot dates—a string of starlets, beauty contest winners, and debutantes—to Palm Springs, to Mexico, and sometimes to San Simeon.

Hearst Jr. may have been unaware of Howard's homosexual encounters, which he conducted privately and with an entirely different set of players.

One morning, Howard disappeared. Beatrice Dowler alerted Noah Dietrich but he waited for four days before attempting to find him. He was not on his yacht, and not at his suite at the Ambassador Hotel. He hadn't flown away on one of his planes. Dietrich then called Neil McCarthy, who alerted the police, asking them to be discreet in their search for Howard.

Howard had a morbid fear of being kidnapped, and Dietrich thought that it was entirely possible that he had been abducted, although no ransom note had arrived at Muirfield.

Twice a day Dietrich checked with Leonard Daniel, a Los Angeles detective, but there was still no news of Howard, and still no ransom note. This led Dietrich to speculate that Howard might have been killed accidentally during an abduction, his body dumped somewhere. He ordered a search of the Los Angeles morgues.

Twenty days later, Howard miraculously returned. Beatrice Dowler placed a call to Dietrich. "Mr. Hughes is back, and he's burning all his clothes and all the linens. There's this big bonfire in the garden."

***

Arriving at Muirfield, Noah Dietrich found Howard burning all his clothes and bed linen. It wasn't the clap this time. Somehow, he'd contacted syphilis. In a few months he would enter a phase of the disease called "tertiary syphilis." In this relatively dormant stage, the venereal disease caused damage in various tissues, including his bones, skin, heart, reproductive system, brain functions, and cardiovascular system.

In a pre-penicillin world, Howard had disappeared to begin a risky and rather radical treatment for the disease. The cure involved injecting low dosages of arsenic and mercury in a combination known as "the magic bullet" into the victim's bloodstream. Regrettably, this treatment did not entirely eradicate the disease in Howard's system. His autopsy report in 1976 revealed many signs of tertiary syphilis. The disease, however, did not render him sterile. Pregnancies and abortions lay in his future.

Except for his leather flight jacket, all of his clothes were burned that night at Muirfield. Somehow Ralph Walker had managed to take the jacket as a souvenir. The sailor didn't believe that you could get syphilis from a flight jacket. Of course, he never wore that jacket in Howard's presence.

***

In 1932, Howard had founded Hughes Aircraft Corporation in California for the manufacture of airplanes, and later, through Dietrich, he'd purchased 1,200 acres of land in Culver City for the company's future needs. In the beginning, his aircraft company would comprise a mechanics shop and a dusty office with a set of ledgers. But within the decade it would evolve into one of the country's biggest defense contractors, with demand for its planes fueled by the upcoming world war.

He'd purchased a six-passenger S-43 Sikorsky Amphibian. Accessorized with a red leather sofa positioned on one side of the cabin, it was delivered on January 4, 1933. It was the first of many planes that the newly organized aircraft corporation would purchase. Howard had already leased a hangar for it at the Grand Central Airport in Glendale. He knew "everything" about piloting planes but he admitted that he knew very little about "flying boats."

Immediately he wanted to make the aircraft better and faster. He hired Glenn Odekirk, a handsome and charming young pilot his same age, as a mechanic. Odekirk was relieved to find a job. The Depression had bankrupted his charter plane business that had previously flown high roller gamblers from Los Angeles to the race track at Aquascalientes, Mexico.

Glenn quickly learned what a perfectionist Howard was. At one point he spent three hours arguing with Glenn about the placement of three screws into a sheet of metal.

As part of his new job, Howard ordered Glenn to fly coast-to-coast with him. Dietrich voiced his suspicions about Howard having a secret crush on Glenn but then stated that he was probably too shy to make a pass at him. Glenn was straight and happily married, although those conditions did not always deter Howard.

When Glenn set out with Howard, he told his wife he'd be gone for three months. But as events unfolded, it soon became clear that he'd be away from home much longer than that.

Howard flew Glenn to Phoenix and on to Houston where he visited Toolco for the first time in years, even though it was the source of his fortune. Leaving Houston, the pilots headed for the Mississippi Delta, planning a stopover in New Orleans. As they approached the city, a violent storm erupted, and one of the airplane's twin engines spun to a halt. Not knowing when the storm would end, and with a disabled plane, Howard made a bold decision. Flying over windswept cottonwoods, he landed the amphibian on the Mississippi River, some thirty miles from New Orleans. There they drifted for hours in turbulent waters until they were rescued by the Coast Guard.

Dodging the press, and arriving in town in time for the annual Mardi Gras celebration, he and Glenn checked into a seedy hotel on Bourbon Street under assumed names. They cleared it with the landlady that each of them could bring "friends" back to their room at night. It is believed that Glenn discovered that Howard was a bisexual on this trip when he noted some very beautiful young women and some very handsome young men emerging from his hotel room. It is alleged that at one point Howard "auditioned" a brother and a sister who'd come down from Baton Rouge for the celebration.

Recovering from the party, Howard flew Glenn to Long Island. These two dashing airmen were seen at some of the more glamorous parties that summer season in Southampton. "Everyone wanted to have Howard Hughes as a guest that summer," said Elsa Longworth, a society matron. "The debutantes were crazy about him, and a lot of our dear homosexual young men were always seen fluttering around him. Of course, you must remember it was the Depression, and all of us had heard stories that his Texas oil wells were pumping black gold at the rate of one million dollars a month." Instead of oil wells, Mrs. Longworth meant his drill bit.

Another matron, Betsy Olden, felt that Howard didn't have to pursue any-body. "All he had to do was stand in the corner and nurse one drink all evening. The beauties, both male and female, came to him. Getting a date with Hughes became one of the social coups of that summer season. Hughes engaged in so much debauchery he would put a Roman emperor to shame."

Finally, Howard allowed Glenn to fly back to the west coast with him. Howard had purchased a new toy, a Boeing P-12, a single engine pursuit plane used by the U.S. Army Air Corps. The plane was intended for only military use, but Howard had managed to bribe someone in the Department of Commerce.

He installed the Boeing in one of the Lockheed Aircraft Corporation's hangars in Glendale, and immediately ordered Glenn to "turn this sweet ass prop into the fastest plane on earth."

Howard and Glenn took the revamped Boeing, which had been refitted with a 580 horsepower Wasp engine, on a test flight. The two skilled pilots roared away from Los Angeles and above the San Fernando Valley at 225 miles per hour, an amazing air speed at the time. In Los Angeles after the test flight, Howard informed Glenn that they'd be entering the plane as a contestant in the air show in Miami on the first of the new year.

The only thing that distracted Howard from his latest toy was a new romance. One afternoon while spending the weekend in Palm Springs with Ralph Walker, he spotted a beautiful girl walking with her mother into a restaurant.

It was "love at first sight," as Cubby Broccoli later recalled.

There was a problem. Although she dressed much older and was heavily made up, Ida Lupino was only fifteen years old.

***

Palm Springs and Los Angeles, 1933

A fifty dollar tip to the head waiter, and Howard found himself sitting at a table waiting to be introduced to Ida and her English mother, also an actress, Connie O'Shea Lupino. Eager for her daughter to meet producers and directors in Hollywood, Connie was delighted to have received a spontaneous invitation from such an important—and rich—Hollywood figure as Howard Hughes.

Howard was eager to curry their favor. Wisely, he devoted most of the luncheon to flattering Connie while casting shy glances at Ida, the true object of his affection.

As he would later reveal to Cubby Broccoli, he thought Ida was at least nineteen years old at the time. Since he didn't read the trade papers, he was not aware that the teenager had been brought over from London to test for the lead in *Alice in Wonderland*. At the time of their meeting, she had lost the part to the more wholesome-looking Charlotte Henry.

There was a mischievous glint in Ida's blue eyes that seemed to amuse Howard. Even at her age, she had a brusque quality in her voice that evoked the more mature Ida Lupino that would grace the silver screen in several *noir* films of the Forties. At the time she met Howard, she'd been playing vanilla *ingénue* roles. But, like a horse eager for the race to begin, she wanted to rush forward, in this case to play adult parts. To do so, she started dressing and trying to look far older than her years.

Howard was eager to learn anything he could about the background of his guests. He found out that Connie was married to the well-known British comedian, Stanley Lupino, and that "the theater runs in the blood of all our family."

"I made a real mistake," Connie told him, "by taking my daughter along to an audition. I was trying out for the lead in *Her First Affaire*. That's *affaire* with an e. Regrettably, I introduced Ida to the American director, Allan Dwan. He cast my daughter in the film instead."

Connie told Howard how thrilled she was to have seen *Hell's Angels*. She said that she screamed when she saw the Zeppelin attack London. "Ida here was born under a dining table during a Zeppelin raid on London, so that scene brought back a lot of painful memories for me."

When Connie excused herself to go to the powder room, Howard had the opportunity to do what he'd wanted to do, gaze deeply into Ida's eyes. He took her hand and held it tightly, predicting a dazzling career for her. Ironically, his prediction eventually came true.

Ida Lupino

At that point in her life, Ida had just a glimmer of the hard-boiled broad she was to play in her most memorable films, when she was sometimes identified as "the poor man's Bette Davis."

As she said in an interview granted decades later during her retirement, "I did get star billing over Bogart in *High Sierra*." She seemed rather proud of that accomplishment, but was disdainful of her comparisons to Bette Davis. (The character of the vengeful cockney strumpet she created in *The Light That Failed*, opposite Ronald Colman, did strongly evoke Davis's character of Mildred in *Of Human Bondage*.) Ida was quick to point out that she was offered the roles that Bette turned down, but often refused to accept them, which led to endless battles with Warner Brothers.

When Connie returned to the table, Ida amused Howard by telling him how she first tested herself as an actress. "I rounded up tattered clothing, some of which had been left out on the stoop for the poor. I dressed myself in these rags, smudged a bit of coal on my face, and went from door to door in my neighborhood. I claimed that my father beat me severely if I didn't return home with something to eat. I also told them I was starving to death and hadn't eaten in two days. Apparently I was so convincing that every household gave me a little bit of food to carry away."

Howard's lunch with the Lupinos was a success, and it led to a lavish dinner the following night, again with Connie being invited as guest of honor. Beginning to suspect Howard's motives, Connie warned him that their surname of Lupino comes from the Latin *lupus*. "In Italian it means little wolf," she said. "I can be as ferocious as my name if anybody tries to harm my Ida."

In spite of that threat, Connie began to relax her guard around Howard, especially when he showered expensive presents on her. The full story is not known, but after a week and a half of wooing by Howard, Connie consented to let him go out alone with Ida.

Learning that she had a birthday approaching, he asked what she'd like for a present.

"A pair of the strongest binoculars on earth," she told him.

"Why?"

"To look up at the stars and dream that one day I'll be one of them."

"Why are you so dead-set on becoming an actress?" he asked.

"Because I'm the only woman in Hollywood who can be both fire and ice on the screen," was her enigmatic response.

In the weeks to come, Howard was seen in both Palm Springs and in Los Angeles with Connie and Ida, or else just with Ida. At one point, he flew mother and daughter for a lavish weekend in San Francisco. This would become a standard seduction technique of Howard's.

At her home and in her retirement, Ida refused to reveal any details of her seduction by Howard. In that same interview, Ida showed great interest in both verbally attacking then-President Ronald Reagan, and in denying charges that her former friend, Errol Flynn, was either a Nazi sympathizer or a bisexual, as had been recently alleged in one of his biographies.

Only two sources have claimed knowledge of Howard's seduction of the underaged star. Beatrice Dowler said in later years that "I saw the romance unfold before my eyes." She remembered the night Howard summoned his doctor, Verne Mason, in the early hours of the morning. Beatrice said that she was present when Dr. Mason, after examining and treating Ida, told Howard in the foyer of Muirfield, "Don't get so carried away next time." Cubby Broccoli also claimed that Howard was regularly having sexual intercourse with what came to be known as "jail bait."

Ida spent her days at Paramount Studios. At night, she was eager to share her experiences with Howard. Since he wasn't much of a conversationalist, he was all ears. One of the studio's chiefs, Emmanuel Cohen, had ordered that Ida dye her hair platinum like Jean Harlow. Ida showed up at Muirfield looking like Jean's clone. This must have at least slightly perturbed the man who created the original Jean Harlow.

"I'd much rather be the new Jean Harlow," she told him, "instead of that stupid brat, *Alice in Wonderland*."

One night Howard invited Ida for dinner at the then popular Ship Café, a restaurant that was frequented by such Hollywood greats as Charlie Chaplin. Taking a small clothes bag, Ida disappeared into the women's room. She'd had two alcoholic drinks that night. In a few minutes, she reappeared in red silk pajamas she'd borrowed from Paramount. With the cooperation of the manager and the house band, she got up on a table. Much to the amazement of her fellow patrons, she danced a "snakehips," imitating a scene she'd played that afternoon on the sound stage during the filming of *Search for Beauty*. Howard was not amused.

He much preferred her attempts to entertain him at Muirfield in private. Sometimes she'd do a perfect imitation of one of Stanley Lupino's vaudeville acts. Howard's favorite was when she performed her father's novelty song for him, "I Lift Up My Finger and Say Tweet! Tweet!" He was much amused at this and confided to Dietrich, "This is the most enchanting creature I've ever discovered." Dietrich found that remark unusual, as the words seemed peculiar coming from Howard. It was not typical of his speech pattern.

As the days passed, Howard noticed Ida trying to assume a mask of sophistication she didn't actually possess. She took to wearing high heels and piling her hair higher. He suggested that she cut it shorter and pose for cheesecake to show off her beautiful figure and legs. "That way, the studio will cast you in more mature roles."

One night at Muirfield she asked that he take her to a restaurant patronized by gangsters. She told Howard that she'd seen his movie, *Scarface*, and a number of other films that starred James Cagney and Edward G. Robinson, including *Public Enemy* and *Little Caesar.*

Always willing to please her, he agreed. Since there was no place that really met her criterion, he placed an emergency call to George Raft, explaining his problem. "Could you round up some boys tonight? I'll cover the bill for everyone."

Raft understood his assignment at once. He was eager to curry favor with Howard, feeling that his role in Howard's *Scarface* had jump-started his career. He told Howard to bring Ida to The Blue Iguana in Santa Monica at nine o'clock that evening.

At the appointed time, Howard arrived at the restaurant with Ida to discover some twenty men with their "gun molls," occupying the various tables. Ida was thrilled. As she recalled years later, she whispered to Howard, "I bet they're all from Chicago."

Ida confessed that at the time she believed the men were real gangsters until George Raft told her several years later that it was all a set-up. "Actually, I still believe that Raft rounded up real gangsters," she said. "Those boys weren't just play acting. They were too real."

The following night, Ida returned home breathlessly to tell Howard, "I met Marlene Dietrich, Mae West, Carole Lombard, and Claudette Colbert at a luncheon today."

"I don't want to toot my own horn," he said, "but I've had intimate moments with Lombard and Dietrich."

"What about Colbert and Mae West?" she provocatively asked.

"I hear Colbert is a midget lesbian and that Mae West is really a man all dolled up like a woman," he said. "Not for me."

He wanted to keep Ida a prisoner at Muirfield. Many nights he left her alone to amuse herself, or else he delivered her to Connie's house for dinner while he went off into the night.

Refusing to be confined, Ida began to date other men. She had a fiery temper and a streak of independence, and she grew to hate Howard's attempt to control her life the way Stanley Lupino had done in England.

For a brief time, she fell in love with Buster Crabbe, the handsome Olympic

298

swimmer turned actor. He was her co-star in *Search for Beauty*.

Selected for his physique, Crabbe had won the starring role in the 1933 *Tarzan the Fearless*. All the hottest women in Hollywood were after him. But when *Search for Beauty* opened for its premiere, Ida showed up in white furs and a white satin gown. He escort was neither Crabbe nor Howard but actor Jack La Rue.

Although both Howard and Ida dated other people during the several months of their courtship, their relationship came to an abrupt end in June of 1934. This was a summer of terror in the sweltering heat of Los Angeles. Some four hundred victims had already succumbed to the highly infectious and crippling disease of polio.

After a night on the town, much of it spent tap-dancing with actor Tom Brown, Ida returned to Connie's house in the early morning hours. She was no longer staying at Muirfield.

Two hours later, Connie remembered waking up in fright to see her daughter crawling across the floor trying to summon her to help her. "I found Ida bathed in sweat," Connie said. "She couldn't walk and could hardly talk. She was feverish and kept screaming about the pain in her arms and legs. Placing Ida in her own bed, she immediately called Dr. Percival Gerson to come to her home.

After a thorough examination, Dr. Gerson gave Connie the bad news. More tests would be needed, but it appeared that Ida had come down with polio.

Ida called Howard the next day and informed him of her tragedy, and he immediately promised to secure the best medical attention for her. Germ-obsessed and a hypochondriac himself, he refused to come see her, claiming that he had an emergency at Toolco and must fly to Houston at once. Connie later admitted that Ida seriously contemplated suicide that day.

He had lied, remaining at Muirfield. He feared contamination if he visited Ida. He also stopped going out in public, fearing that he too would contact the polio germ if he frequented restaurants, clubs, or theaters.

As it turned out, Dr. Gerson had delivered a false diagnosis. It is still not clear what overcame Ida but it wasn't polio. The strength gradually returned to her body, and slowly she regained the use of her arms and legs.

She called Howard but he'd left word that he would not be available to take her calls. His housekeeper informed Ida that "Mr. Hughes will be out of town indefinitely."

Having "stared death in the face," as Ida so dramatically put it, she sailed back to England. In a deep depression, she feared that her career as an actress was over. "I failed in Hollywood," she said.

That was not accurate, and soon she'd be back in Hollywood making lackluster B pictures.

At the time that he was seriously dating her, Howard had promised to marry her and "make you a bigger star than Harlow." Upon her return to Hollywood,

Ida had matured and realized that sex was all that Howard wanted from her.

Howard did not abandon her for forever. He would eventually return to her life, but as a producer, not a lover. After he bought RKO in 1948, Ida worked for him as a director. In 1951, he even came up with the title for one of her future films, *Hard, Fast, and Beautiful*. "He helped me a lot," Ida said after her retirement from the screen. "He was willing to take a chance on me, a woman director, when at the time all other studio bosses were horrified at the idea of a woman directing pictures."

But during the intense heat of his affair with Ida in 1933, Howard confided to Cubby Broccoli. "For me, there's nothing finer in all the world than very young teenage pussy. I've become an addict."

***

Los Angeles, 1933

If there was any woman in Hollywood who might have been ideally suited as the second Mrs. Howard Hughes, it was the actress, Corrine Griffith. From the moment he met her, Howard had pursued her, offering her money, a personal and very lucrative contract, and a chance to date Hollywood's most eligible and sought-after bachelor. She had consistently refused. In Ida Lupino, Howard had developed a lifelong taste for teenagers. That made his pursuit of Corrine a bit off course for him. A fellow Texan from Texarkana, she was eleven years older than him.

When Frank Lloyd, who had directed Howard's other love, Billie Dove, in *The Age of Love*, first invited Howard to a private party, he turned him down. But when he learned that Corrine would be the guest of honor, Howard accepted.

He'd heard rumors that her marriage to producer Walter Morosco was starting to unravel after only a few months of unhappiness. Allegedly, she'd told her friend Lloyd, "On my wedding night, I knew it was a mistake." He'd responded, "Men are like cars. You should drive them around the block before making a purchase."

During her heyday, several ladies of the silent screen had competed for the title of the most beautiful, with most film critics giving that honor to Howard's discarded love, Billie Dove. But many writers for pulp magazines stated that Corrine Griffith was the most beautiful woman ever to grace the silver screen, even more stunning than Howard's former girlfriend, Barbara LaMarr. Howard had made the bedroom rounds of all the leading contenders for the title—all except one, that is—Corrine Griffith herself who up until then had been immune to his charms.

Acclaimed as the face "the camera loves in close-up," Corrine was universally disliked by all who worked with her. She was said to look only at her dogs and to ignore fellow actors and crew. When not emoting before the camera, she was speculating on real estate.

As her real-estate holdings grew, her film career declined. Her voice didn't record well. *Time* Magazine claimed that she "talks through her nose," and *The New York Times* call her voice "sad and tired." With the coming of talkies, the career of the "Orchid Lady of the Screen" had come to an end.

Regrettably, what is arguably her best film, *The Divine Lady*, was released in 1929 just as talkies had arrived with a bang. In the role, Corrine appeared as Lady Emma Hamilton, mistress of Admiral Nelson. All the critics felt that Corrine was a suitable choice to play one of history's most fabled beauties. But her acting was judged as wooden.

Although she was moving on in years, she photographed as lovely as ever. At Lloyd's party, the beautifully gowned Corrine entertained the guests by singing "Drink to Me Only With Thine Eyes," accompanying herself on the harp, as she'd done on screen in *The Divine Lady.*

She spent the rest of the evening engaged in conversation with Howard. He later told Pat DeCicco, "I felt I was talking to myself in a woman's body. That lady thinks just like I do. She's a real cash register. She knows more about California real estate and what's going to happen than anybody out here."

From the night of the Lloyd party, Corrine and Howard became friends, but only casual lovers. Corrine later confided to Lloyd that their romance consisted of no more than three weekend romps together. "I think he just wanted to add me to his list of sexual conquests. There was no magic there." Nonetheless, they continued to date occasionally, with no sex involved, until her marriage in 1936 to George Marshall, owner of the Boston Braves.

Howard considered Corrine an astute businesswoman and often called her for advice, especially if it had to do with California real estate. He even stood by like a rock to lean on when she did something stupid like attempt a comeback in 1957 by financing a film, *Stars in the Backyard* starring herself under the direction of Hugo Haas. Howard was rumored to have put up half the money, but Dietrich denied that. When Howard saw the final cut, he wisely advised her not to release it. "It's your version of *Swell Hogan*," he said, referring to his first film which also was so bad it couldn't be released.

One night in 1965 Corrine frantically called Howard, claiming that she had made a dreadful mistake in marrying a young man in his 30s, Danny Scholl. When he asked if she'd ever slept with Scholl, she denied having done so. He advised that she seek a lawyer right away and file for annulment.

Instead of taking immediate action and seeking an annulment, Corrine waited six weeks, and then filed for divorce as part of a process that became the scandal of Hollywood. In court, she stated her age as fifty-one, not her actual age of seventy-one. Many actresses lie about their age, and that wasn't unusual. What was, was that she claimed she was not actually Corrine Griffith.

On May 5, 1966, she testified that the actual Corrine Griffith had died in Mexico during the making of a film. She claimed she was the star's stand-in and had just assumed her identity, which accounted for her being twenty years younger than the age that had been "officially" associated with Corrine. Two stars of the silent screen, Claire Windsor and Betty Blythe, both former friends of the star, were hauled into court. Each of them identified Corrine Griffith as being the friend they had known in the Twenties.

The story was the talk of Hollywood, and became such a popular legend that actor/novelist Tom Tryon used it as the basis for a novella, *Fedora*, which was turned into a movie in 1978 by Billy Wilder, starring William Holden and Marthe Keller.

In granting the divorce with no alimony for Scholl, the judge noted that the marriage was never consummated, according to the testimony, because neither Corrine nor Scholl were "conducive to amorous activities."

As the Fifties deepened, Corrine and Howard met privately from time to time to talk money. Of all the stars of Hollywood, she was the most opposed to Federal income tax. So was Howard. All of her life, she was besieged by charities wanting contributions. She proudly said, "The only contribution I ever made was to send a check for ten thousand dollars in 1972 to George Wallace, governor of Alabama."

Upon her death in Santa Monica of cardiac arrest on July 13, 1979, Corrine left an estate of $150 million, making her one of the wealthiest women in the world at the time.

Of the fifty-eight feature films she made between 1916 and 1932, only ten are known to have survived. One of Howard's Mormon servants later claimed that in his madness in 1974 he watched *The Divine Lady* twenty times in a row.

***

Miami, 1934

A pilot flew Howard's remodeled Boeing pursuit plane to Miami for entry into an air show competition. In a separate and larger plane, Howard and Glenn Odekirk headed to Florida as well.

But first Howard stopped off in Houston for a visit to Toolco and an overdue meeting with his aunt, Annette Lummis, becoming acquainted with Annette's two daughters and two sons. Some biographers claim that Howard had a final reunion with Dudley Sharp and his wife, Tina, during his short stay in Houston, even reporting details of that rendezvous. Dudley himself, however, later claimed that when he called Howard at the Lummis household and asked to speak to his boyhood friend, "He was too busy to come to the phone."

Once in Miami, Howard checked every inch of his Boeing before competing in the All American Air Meet, which he'd entered in the category of "Sportsman Pilot Free-for-All." Then he had Glenn inspect the plane as well. Before Howard had radically adapted the plane into what he defined as a Boeing model 100A, it had been a two-seater with an open cockpit, the civilian version of the Navy's F4B or the Army's P12B. Both the Navy and the Army

302

considered it a sensational performer.

Under Glenn's supervision, Howard's mechanics had improved the plane considerably. It had been turned into a single-seater, and its wing and tail redesigned for greater speed. Purchasing the pursuit plane for $45,000, he'd spent $75,000 on improvements.

Lifting off, Howard achieved an average speed of 185.7 miles per hour for the duration of the twenty-mile contest. The crowd thrilled to his "loop-the-loops" and applauded his spectacular nosedives to within a few yards of the grandstand where the judges sat. All of these aerial tricks, including spins, slow rolls, or snap rolls, Howard had learned from his stunt pilots working on *Hell's Angels*.

The choice of the judges was unanimous. Howard came in with a first prize for his daring feats. Before a crowd of 12,000 spectators, Howard walked to the platform to receive his trophy. Looking tall, handsome, and dashing, he was met with thunderous applause.

On a platform, he accepted a trophy from none other than General Rafael Trujillo, the dictator of the Dominican Republic, called *El Jefe* (the Chief) as a term of deference. (In some circles, and less flatteringly, he was nicknamed "the goat," because of his sexual excessces.) Attired in his full military regalia, he awarded Howard the honor and extended an invitation for him to visit his island.

Obviously Trujillo wanted him to invest some of his vast fortune in his economically depressed nation. Perhaps the dictator was surprised when Howard immediately accepted the invitation, claiming that he'd fly down the following day. But he had one request. He wanted to meet Porfirio Rubirosa, the handsome, dashing playboy who was already on his way to winning his reputation as the "Playboy of the Western World."

If the dictator felt that it was an odd request, he didn't express it. He invited Howard to be his guest of honor at a private dinner in the Dominican Republic. "Rubirosa will definetly be at the dinner--I'll see to that!" Trujillo promised.

***

Dominican Republic, 1934

By the time Howard met Rubirosa, the Dominican playboy was already known for sexual exploits which had earned him the nickname of *Toujours Prêt* ("Always Ready [for sex]"). In time he would marry two of the world's richest and perhaps most temperamental women, Doris Duke and Barbara Hutton, and would seduce literally thousands of women, including Joan Crawford, Veronica Lake, Ava Gardner, Jayne Mansfield, Marilyn Monroe, and debutante Brenda Frazier. Eventually, many of those famous beauties would also be seduced by Howard himself, including Barbara Hutton before her marriage to his longtime lover, Cary Grant.

When Cubby Broccoli once asked Howard about his penchant for mimicking Ruby's sexual exploits, he said, "That's what happens when you fuck in international circles. Ruby got Joan Crawford, and I didn't. But Rubirosa's one coup, which I envied, was getting to screw Evita Peron. I'm sure I could have had her. I just didn't get around to it."

During the private dinner at Trujillo's villa, Howard and Ruby became instant friends. The playboy was known for his ability to instantly bond with men. "He was the ultimate man's man," said Gerard Bonnet, a polo-playing banker friend from Paris. "All the men I know loved Ruby. The ones who didn't were jealous of him. He was indeed the Don Juan or the Casanova of the 20th century."

At Trujillo's dinner, Ruby invited Howard to watch him play polo the following day. His team was competing against a group of visiting athletes from Nicaragua. Ruby introduced Howard to his wife, Flor de Oro ("Flower of Gold"), who just happened to be Trujillo's daughter.

Howard showed no interest in Flor de Oro, although she made it rather clear that she'd be available for sex later in the evening. Both Flor and her husband, Ruby, were sexual carnivores, seducing everyone available. After divorcing Ruby, Flor de Oro would go on to acquire a stable of nine husbands. She was rumored to have "auditioned" most of the Dominican army.

In Rubirosa, Howard found a man who seemed to be everything he wasn't: Articulate with a sensual voice; bright and witty; amusing at social functions; supremely self-confident; debonair; manipulative; well-educated. The list goes on.

After the polo match in which Howard attempted to play, he joined Ruby in the showers. There Howard could see for himself the reason for Ruby's legendary fame as a seducer.

Among the fabled studs of the world, Ruby was endowed with a long, thick penis variously reported to be thirteen or fourteen inches long. By the late Thirties, his endowment became so well-known that male patrons in restaurants, requesting a peppermill, asked the waiter "to bring me a Rubirosa." His *cojones*, as the Spanish say, were almost grapefruit sized, and he had to wear a special jock strap. Howard, particularly as he grew older, was overly concerned with the endowments of his male rivals in bed. Although his reaction is not known, he must have been overwhelmed by a close encounter with Ruby's equipment.

When he met Howard, Ruby was still in training, learning how to be a pilot. For the weekend, Ruby invited Howard to fly over the island of Hispaniola, which the Dominican Republic shares with Haiti.

Ruby in particular wanted to show Howard "the fleshpots" of the city of Port-au-Prince, which was then the bordello of the West Indies.

The details of Howard's secret trip to the Dominican Republic might never have come to light if it were not for Juan Martínez. He was a handsome young

Dominican filmmaker, who never actually made a film but spent most of his life fretting over scripts. He once worked for Ruby as a kind of valet and secretary. He also wrote a sensational tell-all biography of his former employer, but it was never published. His lifelong dream was to make a film about the incredible life of Ruby.

Ironically, one of the century's best-selling novelists, Harold Robbins, would use Howard as the basis of the hero of *The Carpetbaggers*, originally published in 1961, and Ruby himself as a role model for another of his novels, *The Adventurers*, published in 1966. During their trip across Hispaniola, Juan later claimed that Howard and Ruby seduced "any number of beautiful young women, most of them teenagers." He also claimed that he heard Ruby sharing his lovemaking secret with Howard.

Ruby claimed his technique was called *Ismak*, said to be based on an ancient Egyptian principle. The man as the seducer is in complete charge and delays his own climax for hours if necessary, thereby subjecting his female partner to multiple orgasms before his own release. "I am the master of the situation in the boudoir," Rubirosa is alleged to have said. "In complete control at all times."

We can only assume that Howard, who suffered frequent bouts of impotence, must have been impressed.

At one point, and again according to Juan, Howard offered Ruby $15,000 if he would agree to appear in a private stag film with an extraordinarily beautiful young Creole girl of sixteen. Always strapped for cash, Ruby agreed. Juan claimed to have shot the film himself, with Howard directing the action.

This is the first known pornographic movie Howard is believed to have directed. There would be other such films in the future, including one with a starlet who later became one of the biggest legends in film history.

Juan pleaded with Howard to let him keep a copy of the finished film, but Howard refused. He flew the film and its negative back to Florida, where supposedly he took it to Muirfield for his private viewing. It is not known if the film still exists today.

Before leaving the Dominican Republic, as Juan later recalled, Ruby also gave Howard one of his beauty secrets. "Cover your skin in honey at least once or twice a week," Ruby confided, "and keep it on for two or three hours. When it's done its job, invite three or four beautiful young maidens to lick every bit off your body. Make sure beforehand that you've generously coated all appendages and filled all cavities."

According to Juan, on Howard's final morning in Ciudad Trujillo, as his private plane was being readied, a messenger arrived with a single red rose and a note. He smelled the rose and read the note, already knowing who it was from before he opened it.

I still remember your dark brown eyes watching me, wanting me. But you did not touch me. Even so, I felt an incredible tension between us, a tension that was not released. Alas, if you had been born a beautiful woman—

*and not the handsome, charming man that you are—you would be in my
arms right now and I would make love to you like no other man has ever
done before. With me as your lover, there would never be another man who
could satisfy you. But you are who you are, and I am who I am, a hopeless
pursuer of the world's most beautiful ladies.*

Until we meet again.
Your devoted servant,
Don Porfirio Rubirosa.
Minister Penipotentiary of the Dominican Republic."

***

Los Angeles, 1934

En route to California, Howard was seized with a grand ambition. "I want
to fly faster and higher than any man has ever flown before," he told his trusted friend and fellow aviation expert, Glenn Odekirk. The racer he conceived
would soon be called Howard's "mystery ship."

He rented a corner of the Babb Hangar at Grand Central Airport in Glendale
and began designing a racer, the H-1, which would eventually be nicknamed
"The Silver Bullet." Glenn was installed as supervisor of an eighteen man team
of engineers. To assist, Howard hired Richard Palmer, a Cal Tech graduate who
was known for his previous breakthroughs in radical aerodynamics.

Howard's goal was to break the record set by the French pilot, Raymond
Delmonte, who had flown a plane at 314 miles per hour. Howard wanted the
Bullet to go 365 miles per hour.

After much bickering, Howard approved the final plan for the monoplane,
a single-seater with an open cockpit. The craft would be extraordinarily small,
measuring only 25 feet at its wingspan, just 27 feet from its nose to its tail.

The racer would become part of aviation history, as the team developed and
tested the first retractable landing gear. After takeoff, the landing gear would fit
into a cozy compartment under the wings.

A 580-horsepower Pratt & Whitney engine was installed, It was later beefed
up to 1,000 horsepower. The fuel tank held 275 gallons. To make the plane
lighter, Howard ordered that an alloy known as duraluminum be used. At the
time, this was one of the lightest and strongest metals known. And for the aircraft's structural elements, he used specially laminated plywood instead of the
more conventional, and heavier, timbers in widespread use at the time.

Engineer Robert W. Rummel later said that Howard got a lot more credit for
the plane than he deserved. "He wasn't a brilliant engineer, but he was a relent-
less brain-picker. He stole one idea from this one, another idea from that one,
and later claimed all these creative breakthroughs for himself."

Colonel R.C. Kuldell, president and general manager of Toolco, had other concerns. "The fool will kill himself in some test flight. Without a proper will, the Feds will move in on us and absorb most of Toolco for taxes." Kuldell wanted Howard to draw up a will that would leave the assets of Toolco to its trusted employees in the event of his untimely death. Howard sent word to Kuldell that he'd draw up such a will. But he never did.

Privately Howard told Dietrich that he held Kuldell in utter contempt. He dismissed him as "the brewer." In the darkest days of the Depression, when Toolco was losing revenue, Kuldell opened The Gulf Brewing Company on its grounds. Shortly after Prohibition ended, Toolco launched "Grand Prize Beer," which became the best-selling brew in Texas, although it never won a prize. This new source of revenue transferred Toolco from red ink to black ink. When presented with the beer that saved his fortune, Howard refused to taste it.

Acting on orders from Howard, Dietrich managed to undermine Kuldell and forced him out of Toolco within two years.

Howard had little concern with Toolco politics, devoting himself to his love life, his experimental plane, and even to his automobiles.

It was at this stage of life that he began to drive dingy, battered, and aging jalopies destined for the junk heap. No more Rolls Royces and Duesenbergs. He had two reasons for driving around in dilapidated cars—one, he would park a car in some town or city and forget where he left it. "One time, he didn't remember the state he left his vehicle in, much less the town," Dietrich said.

His assistant also claimed that Howard once told him, "If I drive around in an old car, who would think of kidnapping me? No one would go looking for the world's richest man wheezing about town in a jalopy."

In the days leading up to the test flight of "The Silver Bullet," Howard sometimes worked thirty-two hours without sleep, existing on quarts of milk and bacon sandwiches.

As "launch day" grew closer, he talked constantly and obsessively to Glenn and Palmer about piloting his prized toy. Both of them begged him to let some other trained pilot go up in the Bullet.

The suggestion angered Howard. "And deny me my moment in history? Not god damn likely!" He then revealed his ultimate dream in aviation: "One day I'll be the first man to fly to the moon, where I'll walk on its surface."

***

The handsome but tight-lipped actor, Chester Morris, "with the patent leather hair," was startled to receive a phone call from Howard Hughes. Even though he had awarded Chester with a long-ago role in his film, *Cock of the Air*, with Billie Dove, the two men hadn't spoken since. During the shooting of the film, they had not bonded. Howard had also let it be known that he was terribly disappointed at the poor box-office returns of *Cock of the Air*, placing the blame for the picture's failure on Chester and not on his lover at the time, Billie

Dove herself. In fact, however, Howard's picture was so bad that it practically marked the twilight of Billie's film career.

Today, Chester Morris has been almost forgotten, even though he sometimes starred opposite some of Howard's most memorable girlfriends, including Jean Harlow and Carole Lombard. For nostalgic movie buffs, he is remembered mainly as "Boston Blackie," the retired safecracker and amateur detective in more than a dozen 1940s-era B movies. Earlier in his career, Chester had been directed in three separate films (*Alibi* and *Bat Whispers*, both in 1930, and *Corsair* in 1931) by the eccentric and autocratic director, Roland West

Since then, Chester and West had become best friends, often hanging out together at a club that Roland West had established with actress Thelma Todd, who'd had a brief but disappointing encounter with Howard during the casting of *Hell's Angels*. The club, Thelma Todd's Sidewalk Café, evolved into the most popular restaurant and nightclub in Hollywood, regularly attracting such patrons as Clark Gable and Charlie Chaplin.

Since their initial flirtation, Howard had seen Thelma on several occasions since she'd married his friend, Pat DeCicco, in 1932. Howard had never been to her club, however. Suddenly, he wanted to go there with Chester, suggesting that, "We'll arrive stag and pick up some girls once we're there."

At the club both Thelma and West warmly welcomed Howard, although each of them appeared startled to see him show up with Chester. At that point, Pat was not appearing at the club very often, because his marriage to Thelma was on the skids.

After their third visit to the club, Chester figured out Howard's real motives in inviting him. Very casually Howard suggested to Chester that he might like to include the strikingly handsome and rising young actor at MGM, Robert Taylor, at their table. Howard obviously knew that Chester was starring in a film that also featured Robert Taylor and Virginia Bruce .

Eight years before his death in 1970, Chester in an interview said that Robert turned down Howard's first two invitations, claiming "From what I know of Hughes, I find him a bit creepy."

"But Howard could be very persistent, and after badgering us both, Robert finally consented to go to the club," Chester said. "Perhaps for his own protection, he insisted on inviting Virginia Bruce, with whom he was having an affair. Virginia was married to John Gilbert at the time. Her career was on the rise but John's was fading. Sounds like the plot for *A Star is Born*."

Chester revealed that unknown to Virginia, Robert Taylor was having an affair with her husband on the side. "It was hardly any secret in the Hollywood of the Thirties," Chester said. "Both Robert Taylor and John Gilbert were the poster boys, as we call it today, of the bisexual world. Not me. I didn't go that route, though I got a lot of offers back then. I don't think Virginia knew that her husband was sleeping with her lover, Robert. It was very Hollywood. Triangles like that were going on a lot back in those days, and I guess they still are in the

Hollywood of today. Except I'm out of the loop."

"Howard knew that Robert was making only thirty-five dollars a week, and he played up to the actor's ego," Chester said. "He said he had big plans for both of our careers. Personally, I thought it was all bull-shit. He was using the same lines on us that he used on chorines. Once I got Howard launched with Robert, I knew he'd never call me again. I was right. When my career began to slip, I phoned him several times, and the shit never returned one of my calls."

"Robert and Howard had several private talks at Thelma's club, and apparently

Robert Taylor

established some sort of rapport," Chester said. "I think that Robert was not sexually attracted to Howard, but went along for the ride to see what he could get. Call it a form of hustling if you like. I guess Robert figured that if Clark Gable could get his start this way, so could he. Besides, I always knew that money and power are great aphrodisiacs. How else could you explain all those German women throwing themselves at Adolf Hitler. Certainly not for his body!"

The next thing that Chester learned before he'd finished shooting *Society Doctor* was that Robert and Howard were taking weekend trips together. "I even heard they went hunting somewhere," Chester claimed, "and someone told me that Howard hated hunting. I guess to get his man, he'd go to great lengths."

***

Howard was not impressed with Virginia Bruce and accurately predicted that her star, unlike that of Robert Taylor, would not rise over Hollywood. If she's remembered at all today, it is for her eighteen-month marriage to John Gilbert. Movie buffs taking a trivia quiz still recall that in the 1936 film, *Born to Dance,* she introduced the Cole Porter standard, "I've Got You Under My Skin."

In later life, the Minnesota-born, pale-eyed blonde, who often played "the other woman," had become dottily eccentric and tactlessly outspoken from her home at Woodland Hills, a retirement community in California favored by aging movie personnel. She truly detested Howard and didn't mind admitting it. At first, she didn't want to talk about either Robert or Howard, and certain-ly not about John Gilbert.

She was more interested in telling of her appearances in Turkish films, few of which had ever been seen in America. She'd married the Turkish producer,

Ali Ipar, in 1946, divorcing him in 1952. She remarried him in 1952 shortly after the divorce papers were finalized, that bond lasting until 1964 when she divorced him again.

She still seemed proud that she was one of the 20 original Goldwyn Girls that included Betty Grable, Lucille Ball, and two of Howard's former girl-friends, Paulette Goddard and Ann Dvorak.

"I knew Robert was bisexual," she finally admitted when she consented to talk about her former lover. "I was madly in love with him and wanted to marry him as soon as my divorce (from John Gilbert) came through. At one point I had introduced Robert to my husband, John, who was drinking heavily at the time. I didn't know until years later that John was sleeping with Robert on the side. It got very complicated. Robert told me that of all the movie stars in Hollywood, he wanted most to become the next John Gilbert. Maybe, and this is a bit far out, Robert felt that by sleeping with John he could assume his persona. How in hell do I know?"

She claimed that Robert would have married her if Howard hadn't entered the picture. "Between John and Robert, my life was complicated enough. Enter Howard Hughes and that made an already explosive situation become a field of dynamite. As for John, he was still in love with Greta Garbo when he married me, with Marlene Dietrich waiting in the wings. How could I compete with those two?"

"In the years before he married the dyke-bitch, Barbara Stanwyck, Robert was very open with me about his bisexuality," Virginia said. "We often talked about getting married one day. He said he would be true to me, the only woman in his life, but he wanted to be free to have relations with other men. Just so long as another woman wasn't involved, I agreed to that. I was so desperately in love with him, I felt I didn't have much choice."

Suddenly, despite the fact that he was making almost no money at MGM, Robert appeared around Los Angeles in a new car and a new wardrobe. "We had several fights over Hughes," Virginia claimed. "Robert admitted that he didn't like having sex with Hughes. As men go, Hughes was not his type. But he wasn't adverse to accepting gifts from Hughes. Robert had never had money before, and suddenly he was flying in private planes, sailing on one of the world's greatest yachts, and drinking champagne and eating caviar, with a house filled with servants to iron his underwear. One time Hughes presented him with a dozen pair of the most beautiful handmade alligator shoes I'd ever seen in my life. He was also given a pair of diamond cufflinks on one occasion. And he was driving a new Duesenberg. I must say Hughes was very generous to him. He really turned Robert's head. At one point, Robert was convinced that Hughes was going to offer Louis B. Mayer one-hundred thousand dollars to buy out Robert's contract and put him on a salary of five-thousand a week."

"Robert did not conceal his relationship with Hughes from me," Virginia said. "How could he? It was so obvious." Then she leaned back in her bed and

310

hesitated before her next statement. "What really won Robert for Hughes was not the expensive gifts but a common bond they shared. Those two, from all I gathered, spent a lot of time talking about their mothers. Believe it or not, Hughes seduced Robert with all this mother talk!"

***

Because of the way their overly protective mothers had forced them to dress, both Howard and Robert had been taunted as sissies by their boyhood schoolmates. Sam Rudel, a schoolmate, claimed that Robert "looked more like a girl than a boy, especially because of the way his mother combed his curly hair. Actually, we knew him as Spangler Arlington Brugh back then."

Spangler, the future Robert Taylor, was born on August 5, 1911, in Filley, Nebraska. His father, Spangler Andrew Brugh, was a doctor of Pennsylvania Dutch extraction. His mother, Ruth Stanhope Brugh, was descended from Scotch-Irish parents and was a virtual invalid because of a weak heart. Although her illness was real, she was also a hypochondriac like Allene Hughes.

In the prairie environment in which young Robert grew up, his mother dressed him in black velvet knickers and stiffly starched white lace shirts. Like Howard, he was mocked as Little Lord Fauntleroy. School bullies used to knock him down and splatter him with Nebraska mud so that he would go home dirty. When not attending school, the "pretty boy," as his classmates called him, spent long hours practicing the cello. He suffered so much ridicule and taunts from his classmates that he developed a bad speech impediment by the age of eight. He was shy and insecure, just as Howard had been.

After his father's early death in October of 1933, Ruth Brugh became totally dependent on her young son. She obsessed about his every action or movement, even after they moved to California and he started to mature. She selected not only his clothes, but his companions and warned him to stay away from girls "because the hussies can ruin a young man's future." She wanted Robert to spend his nights at home with her. She hand-washed his underwear, even ironing the undergarments. Unlike Allene, however, she did not check his stool daily.

"Ruth Brugh was the biggest mother hen protecting her pretty young chick in Hollywood," said actress Lois Wilson. In 1934 Lois had been cast with Robert in Universal's *There's Always Tomorrow*.

Two years later, Joan Crawford appeared opposite Robert Taylor in *The Gorgeous Hussy*, prompting her to privately tell Billy Haines that "Robert Taylor and Howard Hughes are just two mama's boys." Wags at the time speculated about which star was playing the title role of *The Gorgeous Hussy*: Joan Crawford or Robert Taylor.

Robert told Virginia Bruce that Howard was fascinated to hear stories of his childhood in Nebraska, but he provided few details about the actual romance between the two men.

At Muirfield, housekeeper Beatrice Dowler recalled waking up early one morning and going down to the kitchen to prepare breakfast. Entering the room, she discovered Howard in his underwear reading the morning news. Also in his underwear, Robert was at her stove making pancakes, which he told her was his favorite breakfast food. He claimed that he'd learned to make these pancakes from a former landlady, "Auntie Neuhauser," whose house he had occupied when he was six years old in Nebraska.

Howard invited Beatrice to sit down and have a few pancakes. "They weren't bad," she later said. "Auntie must have had some secret."

On some evenings, she could hear Robert in Howard's library playing his cello. That was followed with Howard presenting a concert on his saxophone. "To my untrained ear," Beatrice said, "both men were lousy musicians."

She later reported a strange happening at Muirfield. As a youth, Robert had wanted to be a doctor like his father and had pursued a career in medicine for a while before switching to acting. "At one point, Mr. Hughes started calling Mr. Taylor, 'Doc,'" Beatrice said. "Mr. Taylor tended to Mr. Hughes's ailments, real or imagined. At one point, six doctor's uniforms arrived for Mr. Taylor. The very next night, Mr. Taylor was seen wandering around Muirfield in one of these uniforms. I assumed he went to Mr. Hughes's room to 'examine' his patient."

Howard told Noah Dietrich that Robert's personality was "prairie style." Since Howard didn't like overly sophisticated men—he hadn't met Cary Grant yet—he found that quality in Robert endearing. When he signed to go to work for MGM, Robert found the film crews calling him a sissy, using the same kinds of taunts that he'd endured as a schoolboy back in Nebraska. The tough, macho crews that Louis B. Mayer employed liked he-men actors like Clark Gable. To most of these crews, Robert was nothing but a pretty boy, an appellation he'd spend years fighting off.

Robert became so disgusted on the set at one point that he ripped open his shirt and yelled, "See here, fellows. I've got hair on my chest! I'm a red-blooded man just like the rest of you."

"Oh, princess," one of the grips yelled at him. "C'mon over here and see the big surprise I've got for you."

"After a tough day's work," Virgina Bruce recalled, "Robert would return to the protective arms of his mother. Later, he might rush over to my protective arms, and, later still, might end the night in Hughes's protective arms. That was a lot of protection!"

Beatrice recalled that very slowly Robert began to move more and more of his clothing and personal goods into Muirfield. "One day he showed up with at least ten quilts. He told me that his mother, Ruth, had made each of them. Mr. Hughes preferred his expensive blankets but gave in to Mr. Taylor's demand that each of them be replaced with his mother's quilts."

"I remember one night Mr. Taylor opened the door to find two of the best tailors in Hollywood," Beatrice said. "Mr. Hughes had summoned them to make Mr. Taylor his first dinner jacket and tails. They also brought ten top hats for him to try on. Mr. Hughes never told me what the occasion was, but it was this big formal affair in San Francisco. I think William Randolph Hearst was throwing a party."

"Mr. Taylor, as I heard later, actually arrived as Mr. Hughes's date," Beatrice said. "That must have started a lot of tongues wagging when the news traveled south to Hollywood."

Although intense, the Taylor/Hughes infatuation eventually flickered and burned out, as was Howard's tendency with both men and women. Getting his racer ready for competition left few nights to spend at Muirfield with Robert. And meanwhile, Robert's romance with Virginia Bruce was unraveling. Complicating matters, the handsome young actor had developed a crush on a twenty-year old extra, whom he'd met on the set of *Society Doctor*, in which he was co-starring with Chester Morris. "He was blond, well built, and very good looking," Chester claimed. "I think his name was Wayne Dedd—close enough. I can't remember. Suddenly, Robert and Dedd were seen everywhere together. I figured that in spite of all his money, Hughes was being pushed aside. What I didn't know until much later was that Hughes had met the true love of his life, a young actor who would eventually evolve into a far bigger star than Taylor himself. When it came to selecting lovers in those days, male or female, Hughes went after the big names. Of course, from what I was told, he still continued to pick up the occasional budding starlet with big knockers or a garage mechanic with a big something else."

In spite of their eventual separation, Robert and Howard remained friends. Even though Howard was no longer sleeping with Robert, he was still interested in news about his love life. To keep him abreast of any new developments, Howard had Robert trailed.

At one point, even though she'd married Lew Ayres, Howard found out that Robert was dating Ginger Rogers secretively. Dietrich later said that Howard found this amusing and wasn't angry at all, even though he was still seeing Ginger secretly himself, but in places far removed from Hollywood so that they would not be seen.

During the filming of *Small Town Girl* for MGM in 1936, the gossip columnists were busy writing about a romance between Robert and his co-star, Janet Gaynor. This was fictional, as Janet was far more interested in members of her own sex than she was in Robert.

Taylor then became momentarily taken with an attractive female extra, Pat Ryan, and started to date her. But for some reason, each of them decided to keep their romance secret.

Years later, as First Lady of the land, Mrs. Patricia Nixon encountered

Robert on a visit to the White House. In front of witnesses, she said, "I had an awful crush on you, Bob Taylor, when I worked on *Small Town Girl*. I had my eye on you all day and dreamed about you at night." Both Mrs. Richard Nixon and Robert Taylor had a public laugh over that.

Howard's detectives had a very different scenario in the 1930s. They were reporting back to Howard that Pat was seen leaving Robert's bungalow around three or four o'clock in the morning.

Later in life, Howard snidely remarked to Dietrich, "I wonder if Dick Nixon ever found out his wife wasn't a virgin when he married her?"

***

It was early afternoon and all the flowers were in bloom at Muirfield as Howard wandered alone in his garden, dreaming dreams known only to himself. Suddenly, he looked up to see Beatrice Dowler leading his on-again, off-again sleeping partner, Randolph Scott, into the garden. He was locked arm in arm with a handsome, debonair looking man that Howard instantly recognized as the dashing Cary Grant. "Mr. Hughes," Randolph said, being rather formal. "May I introduce you to my roommate, Mr. Cary Grant. He's British."

Normally he didn't like to shake hands, but Howard eagerly extended his hand to Cary. "I know who this young man is, and I've been eager to meet you. Call me a fan if you wish."

"To know that Howard Hughes is a fan of mine would make up for a thousand screaming teenage girls," Cary said.

Then Howard said something provocative and uncharacteristic of him. "The whole town's discussing your affair with Mae West. Is it true that she's a hermaphrodite? Or a mere rumor?"

"Mae West," Cary said, flashing a winning smile. "She wishes she could get me. Tallulah tried and failed. In *Blonde Venus*, Marlene didn't even try. She's heard too many stories about me." He turned and hugged Randolph closer to him.

At this point, the interaction between Howard and Cary is lost, because Beatrice was asked to go into the kitchen and prepare some tea for his guests.

Whatever happened on that day in 1934 was the beginning of a lifelong friendship. Beatrice remembered that they went to play a game of golf. Back at Muirfield, Howard told her he'd won the game.

"He seemed so elated," she later recalled, "and it was more than just a game of golf. It was something else. There was a lightness in his step and a bubbly spirit. Very unlike Mr. Hughes." He told her that he'd be having Cary Grant over for dinner that night and that she was to prepare something special.

"Will Mr. Scott be joining you?" she asked.

A frown crossed his face. Without looking at her, he said, "No." He turned and walked toward his library where he locked himself in until eight o'clock that night.

314

***

On the golf course that day, Jack Reeper, a fellow player, had been startled to see Cary Grant, Howard Hughes, and Randolph Scott. "Hughes and Scott were seriously interested in playing golf," Reeper said. "Grant just seemed to tag along. At one point Grant performed a perfect double forward somersault. It was an amazing feat. Involved a roll of his body. His head almost hit the greens. It's a wonder he didn't break his neck." Cary was much more skilled at this than Reeper realized that day, having performed acrobatics on the stage in London.

***

Mexico, 1934

The following weekend, Randolph was left behind in Los Angeles, as Howard took Cary, his new found toy boy (the term had not come into vogue then) for a sail on the *Southern Cross* to Ensenada.

For both the actor and the aviator, it was a voyage of discovery. "From the very beginning, Cary got closer to Howard than any other person he'd ever met," Rupert, his uncle said in the late 30s. "And that included Billie Dove and Ella Rice."

Howard's Uncle Rupert had met Cary during Paramount's 1933 filming of *Woman Accused*, starring Nancy Carroll, "The Candy Doll," so recently tossed aside by Howard. The film had been based on a *Liberty Magazine* serial and promoted as a gimmick since ten celebrated authors had created the story, one of whom had been Rupert himself. "Howard's uncle wasn't needed on the set at all, but when he met Cary he was there all the time," Nancy said. "He practically chased Cary around the set, with tongue panting like that of an overheated dog. Rupert was ugly and out of shape. There was no way that the little troll would have had a chance with Cary. I mean, Cary could have had any beautiful woman in Hollywood if he'd wanted that, and both Howard and Randolph Scott were considered very desirable catches."

Rupert's loss was Howard's gain. What isn't known is what Randolph felt about Howard sailing off with his boyfriend. He must have dealt with it, however, since he would remain friends with Howard until the late 1930s when Howard mysteriously vanished from his life. As a friend to Howard, Cary was alone for the duration of the ride, which would be a lifetime journey. And that ride began with just the two of them—no other invited guests—sailing aboard the *Southern Cross* with an all-male crew.

The only insight that ever surfaced about the secret cruise came from Christian Jacobsen, one of the crew members aboard the *Southern Cross*. Jacobsen had been booted out of the Danish Navy for reasons not known.

315

Leaving Denmark for Los Angeles, he eventually earned his living working on luxury yachts—"but only for the very, very rich." According to his reputation, he made himself available to the owners of these yachts, either male or female or sometimes as a man-and-wife combination for partners who wanted to make it a threesome. It is not clear if he had sex with Howard, but it was assumed that he did because he was known to have visited Howard's stateroom at night.

South of Tijuana, the *Southern Cross* sailed into Bahia Todos Santos (All Saints Bay) at the port of Ensenada. It was a sleepy town in those days, mostly known as a fishing center and a port for the Mexican wine trade.

Jacobsen later claimed that Cary got Howard to abandon his typical steak plate for supper and sample deep-fried tacos cooked fresh by the vendors along the pier. "For Howard, that must have been love," Jacobsen said. "The man was obsessed with germs. But at least for one night, Howard let his hair down and went native. He and Cary even ordered mango on a stick for dessert."

"The next day they sailed over to the uninhabited Todo Santos Island," Jacobsen said. "About five miles offshore. There they wandered around in the nude like Adam and Eve. So did I."

Jacobsen said that Howard hardly touched liquor on the trip but Cary was "into some heavy drinking." The sailor claimed he accompanied Howard and Cary to Hussong's, which is still the most famous drinking establishment in Baja California. The cantina was established by Johan Hussong in 1892, and over the years, its patrons had included Ernest Hemingway and John Steinbeck. Cary and Howard were serenaded that night by Mariachi bands. Cary drank several margaritas, Howard preferring to sip brandy Fundador all night.

Tired of sleeping on the yacht, Howard checked into a suite with Cary at the Playa Ensenada Hotel. This hotel was opened in 1929 by "the champ," Jack Dempsey, with money put up by Al Capone. A young singer, Bing Crosby, backed up by the Xavier Cugat orchestra, had headlined the opening night gala.

But by the time Howard and Cary arrived, the hotel had lost its edge. America was in the midst of a deep economic depression, and the repeal of Prohibition in the States had seriously reduced the hotel's once-fabled popularity.

The following story may be apocryphal because the dates don't quite match up, but Howard, for variety's sake, was said to have picked up a teenage dancer and Baja native, Margarita Carmen Cansino, who at the time was performing at the club. Cary insisted that the story was true, or so he claimed to Raoul Walsh, his one-eyed director on the set of *Big Brown Eyes* in 1936. Whether it was true or not can't be determined at this point. What is better-known is that Howard would later become the dancer's lover in the 1940s after she changed her name to Rita Hayworth.

***

After their sojourn in Ensenada, Howard was due back in Los Angeles. But when it became apparent that Cary had time on his hands between film commitments, Howard called Dietrich, telling him that he would not be stopping off in Los Angeles, but planned instead to continue sailing with Cary all the way north to San Francisco.

"As we headed north," Jacobsen said, "it appeared that Howard and Cary were on their honeymoon. They dined together by candlelight, they strolled the decks together, talked for hours, and spent nights together in Howard's master stateroom."

He recalled coming upon them one sunny afternoon lying nude on the deck with their arms around each other. "They paid no attention to me," Jacobsen said. "It was like I wasn't even there. Neither of them seemed to care what the all-male crew thought. Perhaps I shouldn't say this, but I couldn't help but notice that Howard's endowment looked two and a half times bigger than that of Cary's."

Somewhere during the voyage, Howard discovered that Cary wore women's panties. He always insisted it was a practical matter, finding women's underwear lighter and easier to dry when he was on the road than the heavier men's underwear of the time.

By the time they'd reached San Francisco, both men had also discovered they had a fascination for attending clubs where transvestites performed. Cary may have even told Howard of his days as Archie Leach, and of his first full-blown sexual experience. Cary was sixteen at the time, and his partner was "Francis Renault," a muscular female impersonator in Manhattan.

In San Francisco, Howard purchased beautifully tailored clothes for Cary, even buying very expensive jewelry for him, including a ruby ring. He

Cary Grant

also bought him a set of "the world's most expensive luggage—all matched and monogrammed," according to Dietrich.

The epitome of casual, Howard at the time was traveling around with a few shirts and a pair of baggy trousers stuffed into a cardboard box. Instead of a belt, he often used a discarded necktie to hold up his pants. If he ever had to dress up, he'd borrow clothing from Cary. Fortunately, the two men were about the same size.

At night these two high profile individuals prowled "the pansy clubs" of San Francisco. Word soon reached Hollywood.

Nancy Carroll said she was surprised upon hearing the news. She'd made *Hot Saturday*, which had co-starred both Randolph and Cary. "Those two were cohabitating, and I know this for a fact because I visited the lovers at the time. In private they carried on quite a bit and Cary—not Randolph—sometimes became very effeminate. Poor Virginia Cherrill. Cary put that woman through hell," Nancy claimed.

She was referring to the actress who'd married Cary. Other than for that dubious accomplishment, Virginia Cherrill is remembered today as the female lead in *City Lights*, playing a blind flower girl opposite Charles Chaplin.

Ben Maddox, a writer for *Modern Screen*, had visited the Scott/Grant household and had written an article about them, leaving out his most obvious conclusions. He wrote that as a team, Grant was the "gay, impetuous one," calling Scott more "serious, cautious."

"I thought Howard Hughes just arrived on the scene and lured Grant away with his power and money," Maddox claimed. "Then I saw Scott dating Grant at the Trocadero one night. It was only a week after his cruise with Hughes. I'll tell you what I think, I think Grant, Hughes, and Scott had occasional three-ways. I understand this is a very common practice among homos. Those flighty boys have a lot of orgies."

Director Lowell Sherman died in 1934 of pneumonia in Hollywood and was not privy to the Hughes/Grant romance. A once famous figure, he directed early films for Greta Garbo and Katharine Hepburn and had gone "along for the ride" in 1921 when Fatty Arbuckle took him to San Francisco. That weekend led to the death of starlet Virginia Rappé and charges of manslaughter brought against the popular comedian. Although not convicted, Arbuckle's career was destroyed.

Sherman got to know Randolph—that is "as well as any man could get close to that cold fish" (his words)—when he directed Cary in *She Done Him Wrong,* starring Mae West. "Mae could spot a homo a mile away," Sherman claimed. "And she definitely included Cary and Randy in that category. She was very tolerant of the boys but was not very advanced in her psychological points of view. She claimed that 'all the boys really want to be me. Dress like me and look like me.' Throughout her life she also claimed to have discovered Cary Grant." She would also star opposite Cary in *I'm No Angel*.

318

She once told Tennessee Williams on a visit to her apartment that stories of her romance with Cary Grant were entirely created by the press. "Can you imagine Cary Grant taking me on?" she said to the astonished playwright. "It takes a real man for Mae. Gary Cooper—or so I'm told—could handle me. But he was too busy giving it away to Tallulah. When Cary met Hughes, they'd both already had affairs with Coop. Perhaps that formed some common bond between them. Who knows how these boys operate?"

The director, Sherman, felt that Randolph was deeply disappointed in his relationship with Howard. "He didn't exactly expect Hughes to give him money. But I think he expected tips on the stock market, get-rich schemes. Things like that. He thought Hughes was his key to fortune. I think all that Hughes did was screw around with him and get him some bit parts which launched him into films."

It is not known how the homophobic columnist for the *Hollywood Reporter*, Edyth Gwynne, found out about Howard's mystery voyage to San Francisco with Cary. With her poison pen, she'd been on a campaign to "out" homosexuals, both male and female, in the movie colony long before anyone knew what that word meant. She had already outed Gary Cooper and –surprise of surprises –James Cagney. Her contacts fed her very inside information. She suggested that Greta Garbo's next film might be called *The Son-Daughter*, and that Marlene Deitrich might star in *Male and Female*. Someone had gotten to her with the information that Cary preferred to play the passive role in sodomy. She suggested that his next movie might be titled *One Way Passage*. That 1932 movie, a drama/romance, had already been made starring William Powell and the lesbian actress, Kay Francis.

Cary never publicly talked in any detail about Howard after their return aboard the *Southern Cross* from San Francisco. But throughout his marriages and other lovers, he would become a fixture at Muirfield. He would also be the only movie star, male or female, who remained in touch with Howard until the very end of his life.

One of the few remarks Cary ever made about Howard was to claim, "We were so very different. Opposites attract, I guess. We became such good friends because we were so different."

But were they that different? Many of their friends and associates have claimed that "they were birds of a feather," as Nancy Carroll once put it.

Cary could be charming when he wanted to be, at least on the screen, and he was far more sociable than Howard. Both men were loners, however, and each of them seemed filled with a brooding sense of despair. It is not known if Howard ever attempted suicide like Cary once did. But both men throughout their tortured lives would occasionally collapse into nervous breakdowns.

In the only time Cary ever spoke about Howard to the gossipy Louella Parsons, he said, "I think Howard and I are such great comrades because he doesn't want anything from me, and I don't want anything from him except his friendship and trust. I don't expect him to give me money or push my career forward. He wants a male companion he can sail with, fly with, or just sit silently at dinner together. Sometimes we don't say anything to each other for hours at a time. But it's important to know we're providing comfort and support for each other even if it's not articulated."

That comment was about as much insight as Cary ever provided about his closeted relationship with Howard. Neither man could tolerate too close a scrutiny from the press.

"Cary loved money," Nancy Carroll said. "Not as much as Randolph. No one on God's earth loved money like Randy boy. But it was Cary's love of money that led to his marriage to Miss Moneybags, Barbara Hutton herself. I don't mean he loved money in the sense that he tried to hustle loot from the rich like Randolph did by marrying Marion DuPont. In Cary's case, he liked to be around people with money, namely Howard Hughes and Barbara Hutton. He asked many questions about my relationship with Joe Kennedy. He didn't like Kennedy but admired him for his ability to accumulate millions. Cary had come from a background of poverty, and had broken into show business as a juggler and a song-and-dance man, touring England with an acrobatic troupe. I was told that he'd led a lean and hard life in New York—I should also add a very gay life—and he went to bed many times without even a bowl of Bubble & Squeak. Or should I say Faggots and Pease Pudding?"

After she'd had a drink or two, Nancy could develop a bitchy edge to her comments.

Although Cary became famous for his romantic roles on screen, he was not a romantic at heart and was rather cold and distant with most people. Howard was the same way. "Even in those early days, these two school girls weren't wearing their hearts on their sleeve," said Billy Haines decades later. "They were rather detached in their love affair. From the beginning, Howard and Cary never pledged fidelity to each other and were free to carry on with others. Cary continued to see Randy and also dated other women. Howard also continued to pursue any hot things in pants or a dress. Today we would call their relationship an open one. Yet they did have a commitment. I read somewhere that Queen Elizabeth demanded loyalty but not necessarily fidelity from Prince Philip. The same could be said about Howard and Cary. Among male-male couples, the two buddies remained bonded at the hip almost from the day they met. That doesn't mean they didn't have their troubles, even a little violence on some occasions. But what couple doesn't have that?"

***

Although their friendship would eventually settle into a very peaceful relationship, Cary and Howard had many struggles when they were just getting to know each other. The exact nature of their arguments or fights will perhaps

320

never be known.

Beatrice Dowler reported that one rainy night Cary showed up at Muirfield and virtually stormed into the room where Howard was working on some plans for his next breakthrough in aviation.

"Mr. Grant was drunk and unshaven," Beatrice later said. "Usually he was immaculate. He barged into the library and confronted Mr. Hughes. I've never heard such shouting in all my life. It sounded like Mr. Grant was throwing things and breaking objects."

"About an hour later, I was in the main hallway removing some wilted flowers when Mr. Grant raced out of the library, flinging the door open," Beatrice later claimed. "When he first saw me, he looked distraught and was in tears. 'The bastard doesn't love me,' he shouted, not necessarily to me but to the world in general. 'He loves only himself.'"

"At first I thought he was breaking toward the front door but he ran upstairs to the master bedroom," she said. "I didn't hear anything, and I began to get worried. Finally, I went and knocked on the library door. Mr. Hughes came to the door. I suggested to him that he'd better go upstairs and check on Mr. Grant. He seemed reluctant to do so. Finally, he walked up the steps, taking his own good time."

"I don't know what Mr. Hughes saw in that bedroom," she said. "But he came out in just a minute or two and shouted down the steps for me to call his doctor. I called Dr. Verne Mason, who was accustomed to making midnight house calls at Muirfield. When the doctor arrived, I showed him up the steps and then disappeared, because I felt Mr. Hughes didn't want me to know what was going on."

"I just assumed that Dr. Mason sedated Mr. Grant that night," she said. "When I served breakfast in bed the following morning around ten o'clock, Mr. Hughes and Mr. Grant seemed happy as two love-birds. Later that morning I went into the library. It looked like a bulldozer had been in there. Somebody had been throwing things at somebody."

"When Mr. Hughes walked in on me, he looked around and surveyed the damage but didn't say anything," she said. "Is Mr. Grant all right?" I asked him. "He gets a little carried away from time to time," Howard said. "Nothing that a very intense spanking can't cure." At that point the housekeeper said that Howard turned and headed down the hallway and out the front door, leaving Cary upstairs in the master bedroom.

She said that Cary got up later and demanded endless cups of coffee. "I knew that he was heavily lacing my coffee with bourbon," she said. "All that day he was 'sullen, morose, and quarrelsome,' just like Virginia Cherrill had testified in divorce court against him."

Beatrice claimed that she never liked Cary and always felt uncomfortable as long as he was in the house. "Mr. Hughes was exceedingly kind to him, but I never knew why he put up with what he did. He quickly dismissed most of his lovers who drank heavily. I think he had a double standard, though. He tolerated young men who drank. He couldn't stand women who drank heavily in his presence. Of course, years later he would allow a lush like Ava Gardner to do that, but I think she was an exception."

Cary was not the Mr. Nice Guy that he so often portrayed on screen, Beatrice claimed. As further evidence, she cited his former valet, Dudley Walker, who once said, "He could be a terrible bastard, that one!"

Throughout the early years of their relationship, Beatrice claimed that "frequent outbursts of temper" occurred between Howard and Cary. "Mr. Grant could be very charming at times, and then Mr. Hughes would do something that upset him and there would be shouting matches. Personally, I think Mr. Grant wanted a more serious commitment from Mr. Hughes than he was willing to give him. Mr. Grant could be very jealous and possessive. Yet, almost to contradict what I'm saying, they would sometimes have Mr. Scott over for the weekend. The three of them were very chummy together. I didn't even want to think what went on when all of them retired to the master bedroom upstairs."

Suddenly, without telling Noah Dietrich or Beatrice in advance, Howard and Cary just disappeared for ten days. They were later spotted at the Biltmore Hotel in Phoenix. Howard had flown Cary there in his private plane. A maid walked in on them and reported that she found them lying nude together in bed, locked in an embrace.

From there, they traveled to Tucson and were later seen in Juarez. "Otherwise, no other details of their holiday have ever emerged," Beatrice said. "All I know is that things at Muirfield were a little more peaceful for a few weeks after their return, but Mr. Grant went off the deep edge again, as he so often did in those days. I had a feeling that Mr. Hughes was the forever forgiving father, and Mr. Grant was the forever errant son. Even though it was no doubt a romantic relationship, there was also the element of the father-son in the way they dealt with each other."

Although not knowing the particulars, Beatrice once learned that Howard rescued Cary when he was caught performing fellatio on a handsome young employee in the men's room of a Beverly Hills department store. "I think Mr. Hughes paid a lot of money to hush that up," she claimed. "Following a payoff to the police, Mr. Grant went free. No charges were ever filed, but the story was gossiped about all over Hollywood."

Paying off the police to avoid a homosexual scandal was but a prelude to equivalent circumstances that loomed in Howard's own future.

***

Cary had been cast opposite that fiercely independent New Englander, Katharine Hepburn, in George Cukor's homosexual romp, *Sylvia Scarlett*. It would turn out to be one of the most bizarre films ever made in the 1930s. Kate played the role *en traves-tie.* "I won't be a girl, weak and silly!" she says. "I'll be a boy, rough and hard!"

Sexual ambiguities abound throughout the film, and there are many risqué references to bisexuality, most of which were pitched over the heads of the film's intended audience, just the way its homosexual director, George Cukor, wanted it.

Katharine Hepburn and Cary Grant, the two most closeted bisexuals of Hollywood's Golden Age,

Katharine Hepburn and Brian Aherne in *Sylvia Scarlett*

were ideally cast in their roles.

Starring opposite them was Brian Aherne, who would later marry Joan Fontaine, successfully taking her from Howard himself. Playing an artist in the film, the handsome Aherne says to Kate Hepburn, "I don't know what it is that gives me a queer feeling when I look at you." In the scene she is dressed as a boy.

At one point during the filming, Cary relaxed off-camera with Kate. Looking her over, he said, "I think I like you better as a boy than as a girl. As a girl, you're far too skinny, and I don't like skinny women."

"Do you like women at all?" she provocatively asked him. "Occasionally, but only on that very odd night," he candidly answered. "Randy and Howard have a lot more to play around with." He got up and wandered off as if distracted by something.

Unknown to most of Hollywood, Howard was about to intrude himself into yet another famous homosexual relationship. He was already the third party in the love affair of Randolph Scott and Cary Grant. Now he was about to become another "third wheel" in Kate Hepburn's ongoing affair with the lovely and sophisticated Laura Harding, one of the heiresses to the American Express fortune.

At the time of her first meeting with Howard, Kate had never given any indication that she'd even heard of Howard Hughes, much less cared about him.

But one morning during the shooting of *Sylvia Scarlett,* Kate looked up as a small single engine Boeing Scout was zeroing in on their set. Cukor had arranged part of his filming astride one of the most photogenic strips of beachfront along the Southern California coastline—the rolling dunes of Trancas Beach.

Cukor immediately called for his cinematographer, Joseph August, to stop filming. Hands on his hips in exasperation, Cukor also rubber-necked along with the rest of his crew. "Don't that beat all!" his sound recorder, George D. Ellis, said.

Kate later described the landing of Howard Hughes in a windswept meadow nearby, overlooking the roaring surf below. "His plane just seemed to emerge from the offshore fog. It was about noon. I can still picture the late morning sun glinting off the silver nose of his craft. It was as if Cukor were directing an aerial scene, not the action on the ground. The wings dipped, and the pilot came to a beautiful landing, the small craft gliding gracefully down. At that point, I decided I wanted to be an aviator myself. From the cockpit, the pilot emerged. He was one of the tallest and most boyishly handsome men I'd ever seen—a wondrous sight, really. He wore a brown leather flight jacket, with the sign of an eagle sewn on the left pocket. He also wore elephant-colored jodhpurs and jet-black Cordoban boots with some sort of silver ornamentation on them. The rangy figure came toward us."

In contrast to the dashing aviator, Kate appeared rather plain that day. Her red hair had been closely cropped, and she looked very much like a boy, wearing a nut-brown polo coat she'd borrowed from her makeup artist, Mel Burns. For some unknown reason, she'd splashed rubbing alcohol on her face, which had streaked and partially obliterated her screen mask.

On seeing "the fastest man alive," the fabulously wealthy Howard, coming toward her, she retreated to the safety of her dressing room before Cary could make an introduction.

There she remained for about thirty minutes before emerging again. This time she'd slashed a scarlet mouth on herself and had slipped into a pair of olive green gabardine slacks with a tailored man's white shirt she'd purchased at Brooks Brothers. "With her short hair, she looked like a sodomite's dream," Cukor later said. "Those slacks accentuated her slim hips." Under one arm, she carried a basket of freshly made scones baked by her maid, Johanna Madsen.

Ferocious rivals:
Ginger Rogers and Katharine Hepburn

As part of the picnic setup that Kate often hosted at lunchtime for her friends and invited colleagues on the set, Kate walked over to a blanket that Johanna had spread across a patch of scrub grass. Howard was sitting between Cukor and Cary. Howard rose to greet Kate. What he thought of her appearance is not known.

Other than shaking his hand, Kate didn't seem impressed with the man who had been dubbed by the press, like Rubirosa, as the Playboy of the Western World.

She seemed put off by the high-pitched sound of his voice. "Such a manly looking man should have a deeper, richer voice," she later confided to Cukor.

Ignoring him throughout her picnic lunch, she acted rather arrogantly in his presence. Obviously she didn't want him to think she was impressed with either his wealth or fame.

Howard had so little to say to her that she later told Cary that "he acted like a deaf mute" during the whole picnic, not even complimenting Johanna on her famous fried chicken. Howard was not overly fond of fried foods.

After he had left, flying dramatically away in his aircraft, Cary told her that his friend was really a fascinating fellow but was partially deaf and could not hear much of their conversation. Not only that, but Howard was working on one of his secret airplane projects at the time and found small talk boring.

When Kate later complained that she didn't like the way Howard had barged in, interrupting the filming of the picture, Cary confessed that he'd actually invited the aviator. Each day the stars of the picture, along with Cukor, had been asked to invite the most interesting person in their acquaintance to one of their picnic lunches. Cary had selected Howard.

Throughout the picnic, Kate never made eye contact with Howard. "I never looked at him—not even once after I shook his hand," she told film editor Jane Loring. "He had some nerve flying over us like that. The British would call it cheeky."

The following day, and in spite of Kate's wall of coldness to him, Howard remained intrigued by "that magnificent Yankee." He'd even come up with a nickname for Kate, calling her "Country Mouse." It was a nickname he would use for her during the course of their long relationship, despite its unflattering overtones.

Although he had been cold-shouldered by Kate when they were first introduced, Howard was interested enough to accept another invitation from Cary to fly in the next week for yet another picnic, this one prepared by Cukor's own personal chef. Kate and Brian Aherne were invited as the guests of honor.

It was only later that Kate was to learn that this complicated airborne charade was part of Cary's elaborate plan to bring Kate and the aviator together.

This is how Aherne remembered the second visit: "Without warning, Hughes came back. A biplane roared up and set down on a makeshift landing strip above the dunes. Out stepped Howard Hughes looking like Charles

Lindbergh. At the time, the crew thought that he was already having an affair with Kate. Later we found out that wasn't true. If he was in love with anyone, it was with Cary. Hughes was fascinated by Cary. As I recall, Cary was a bit of a prick-teaser at that picnic. Hughes came over and spoke to Kate and me. He had a high-pitched voice that struck me odd. Kate had told me that he was almost deaf. She seemed to mock his handicap during the picnic. She was playing up to Grant as if he were her lover. She'd lean over to Grant and whisper to him, 'Please, pass me another chicken leg.' It was all innocent enough, but the look on her face was making it seem that she was coming on to Grant. Hughes couldn't understand a word they were saying. He sat there getting angrier by the minute. When he could take Kate's cuddling of Grant no more, he got up and stormed away, heading to his plane. 'I've had enough of this shit!' he shouted back at Kate and Grant. The two doubled over in laughter. Grant promised to explain everything to Hughes later that night. Frankly, I thought it was rather sadistic of Kate to taunt Hughes like that."

Aherne said that after Hughes flew off, Cukor ordered everyone back to the set. The actor overheard Cary tell Kate, "You know what? Howard Hughes would make a perfect new beau for you."

"You must be kidding," she said. "Me and that rich playboy? Could you see me taking that womanizer and 'manizer' home to meet Kit and my father? They'd take a shotgun and run him off the grounds. A romance between Katharine Hepburn and Howard Hughes? Hell will freeze over before that day ever comes."

***

Orange County, California, 1935

Unusual for him, Howard, accompanied by Noah Dietrich, called a press conference on August 10 to announce his intentions to break the world's airspeed record. At that point in his career, most reporters did not take his pursuit of aviation seriously. He was called various names in the press, including the "millionaire playboy flier."

On September 12, at Glendale, the time had come for him to take his mystery ship out of storage and reveal it to the world. During the previous week, he'd ordered his friend and fellow pilot, Glenn Odekirk, to paint it red and silver instead of just silver. He reasoned that the color of silver alone might make his plane invisible in the bright sunshine over southern California.

Since the monoplane was a single-seater, with room only for him, he told Glenn goodbye and agreed to meet him near Santa Ana. Stepping into his cockpit, he made a brisk takeoff. Once airborne, he aimed *The Silver Bullet* toward the Pacific, flying low over the rock-strewn Palos Verdes Peninsula. He was heading for the Eddie Martin Airfield in Orange County. Back then, it was nothing but a strip of tarmac near Santa Ana, at one end of which stood some ramshackle hangers. Today it's the site of the Orange County John Wayne Airport.

By the time Howard landed in his H-1 Racer, the judges were already inspecting their own planes, since all three of them would be airborne to judge Howard's attempt at breaking the world record.

One of those judges was Amelia Earhart, at the time, the country's most celebrated aviatrix. Howard admired Earhart's skill and daring in the air and congratulated her on her record-breaking solo flight from Mexico City to Newark. Advanced for his time, Howard treated women pilots with respect. Many of his fellow pilots felt that only men should be allowed to fly. But Howard had already provided flying lessons to a former girlfriend, Billie Dove, as he would a future girlfriend, Katharine Hepburn.

Earhart would be the sole pilot in the small craft she planned to use to judge Howard's performance. The other two judges would fly together in a shared airplane. Howard shook the hand of Paul Mantz, whom he'd hired as a stunt pilot during the filming of *Hell's Angels.* Mantz was currently employed as a technical advisor to Earhart. The third judge was Lawrence Therkelson of the National Aviation Association.

All three judges found Howard's dress code unusual for a pilot. In a dark blue suit that looked like he was attending a bankers' meeting in Houston, he wore a black tie and a soiled Oxford white shirt. He had donned a leather cap and pair of oversized goggles.

Howard faced a three-kilometer course, with a chronograph installed at each end to take pictures of *The Silver Bullet* as it entered the airspace at the end of the run. For Howard to break the world record, he would have to make a series of four "flypasts," going at a speed that exceeded the 314 miles per hour. The world speed record was held at the time by a French pilot in a plane that had cost the French government, in the mid-1930s, a million U.S. dollars.

As Howard got into the cockpit for his takeoff, one newsman later claimed that *The Silver Bullet* "looked like a spindly legged man-eating insect." Surprisingly, the sun was already beginning its long descent into the Pacific when Howard took off. Glenn wondered it he'd be able to complete all four flypasts before darkness fell over the Santa Ana countryside.

Because of high winds, Howard was able to achieve a speed of only 302 miles per hour even though he took the plane to ten-thousand feet. "Firewalling" the throttle, as pilots say, he made his first flypast at 346 miles per hour. Later, he was seriously pissed off when Lawrence Therkelson of the NAA informed him on his headset that the judges had disqualified his flypast. "When you came into the measured course, you were still pulling out of your dive. You have to be at level flight for cameras to record it."

Angered but more fiercely determined than ever, Howard took off into the skies again. This time he leveled out his plane before executing the flypast at 354 miles per hour. But by then it was too dark for the cameras to record it.

Howard was invited back the next day.

"So that's it!" Howard said in disgust to Dietrich. "I've flown faster than any pilot's ever flown since the airplane was invented. And I'm being sent home to bed until tomorrow."

Friday the 13th of September loomed ominously for superstitious pilots, most of whom didn't like to fly on that day. Howard flew anyway, and the cameras caught the action as the sun was high in the cloudless skies. This time, he did many more flypasts than were required, posting speeds of 355, 339, 351, 340, 350, and 351 miles per hour.

Howard's real aim involved establishing the new world's record at 365 miles per hour. As such, he became impulsive, opting to make an additional run. Waving to Glenn and the ground crew, he took off for one final flypast, piloting *The Silver Bullet* over the brown hills of San Joaquin and making a circle over the turbulent breakers of Corona del Mar. Once *The Silver Bullet* reached its maximum speed, "Hughes just seemed to dive toward the earth," Mantz later said.

"He looked like a bolt of silver lightning coming down," Earhart later told the press. "In one horrifying moment, it dawned on me he was in distress."

Aviation writer Howie Davenport claimed, "To me, his plane looked no more that 1,200 feet above the earth, and he was hurtling to the ground at ferocious speed. Some claimed 100 miles per hour, others 180. It was clear to all of us that he was attempting frantically to pull *The Silver Bullet* up. We later learned that his engine had died when it ran out of fuel. He'd stayed in the air much too long making all those flypasts. He was desperately struggling with the controls. It was later revealed that he was trying to open his emergency gas tank to no avail. It was blocked. He must have known he was going to die."

"I know this sounds weird," Davenport said, "but when *The Silver Bullet* was falling, it gave off a ghostly shriek, almost like a person screaming when he jumps off a high building to a certain death. Earhart and all of us just knew it was curtains for Hughes. I know it wasn't the right thing to think at the time, but I thought that a fool and his money are soon parted."

Suddenly, all that the newsman saw was a dusty red cloud rising over a beetfield. Howard had made landfall. "The migrant workers must have had chopped beets for dinner that night," Davenport said. "I thought Hughes was killed on impact."

Spectators saw Glenn racing across the field, the first to arrive at the downed plane. Amazingly, Howard was emerging unscathed from the cockpit. "I'd never heard him curse like that before," Glenn later said. He rushed to help his boss. "It was son of a bitch this, mother fucker that."

Howard grinned like some fool. "I can fly a lot faster than that," were his first words after his emergency landing.

After finding out he was all right, Glenn asked, "Why didn't you bail out?"

"And throw away the $125,000 I've invested in this beautiful thing?"

Mantz was the second person to reach the plane, telling Howard, "You're the luckiest son-of-a-bitch on the planet. You're the new Lucky Lindy." Howard only frowned at him, as he never liked comparisons to Charles Lindbergh.

He took out a stick of chewing gum and went around to inspect his propeller, finding it damaged. He was at the front of his plane when photographers arrived to snap his picture and flash it around the world. America had created another aviation hero.

Howard had hardly landed on his feet before he was directing Glenn to put the racer on the back of a flatbed truck to be hauled back to Glendale.

"From now on, this baby is going to be called *The Flying Bullet,*" Howard told the press.

The next day at a press conference, Howard modestly downplayed his own achievement. "The day will soon come when commercial airplanes will be flying over the continent of America at the rate of four hundred miles per hour." He turned to some reporters on the side and in a low voice said "and one day man will fly faster than the speed of sound."

***

That same day Howard turned to Glenn and commanded, "Let's go to work." He was determined to find out what had gone wrong, even if it meant dismantling *The Silver Bullet* piece by piece. Since arriving in Glendale, Howard had posted twenty-four hour security guards around the plane. On a Sunday, having worked day and night on the plane's "autopsy" since Thursday, Howard located the problem.

Someone had blocked the pipeline leading from the spare gas tank to the plane's engine with a bunched-up wad of steel wool. That's why Howard had been unable to tap into the emergency fuel source when the plane was going down.

Glenn speculated that the steel wool might have been inserted by accident. "How would a mechanic know that you'd have to use the emergency tank? After all, you told no one that you were planning more than four flypasts."

Glenn had a point, but Howard dismissed it when he discovered that the steel wool was held in place by a tiny lead wire. Howard said that he might idly have told his mechanics that he was going to make a total of eight passes and that his life might depend on accessing the fuel in the second tank. "I was working day and night and half out of my mind," he said to Glenn, "and I just can't remember."

"Someone wanted me to die," Howard said. Through Dietrich he ordered that all the mechanics who worked on the job be interrogated by the toughest police detectives he could find. "Hire only the best. One of them will crack under pressure."

But none did after intensive questioning. And Howard seemed to have sincerely believed that none of the mechanics had harbored a personal grudge against him. Eventually, to an increasing degree, Howard's suspicions became focused on the executives at Toolco.

Howard admitted to Dietrich that he'd made a terrible mistake. When Toolco executives were pressing him to draw up a new will in case he was killed on one of his dangerous missions, he had agreed to their demands. "I did more than that," Howard said. "I actually told them that the will had been signed. They believed that in the event of my death, most of the Toolco assets would go to them. But I lied. I never drew up such a will."

In the months that followed, Howard's relationship with Toolco, the source of his wealth, grew more hostile.

The forced landing and near death at Santa Ana didn't keep Howard out of the air for long. He had far bigger plans than breaking some aerial speed record. In the next few weeks, he would conduct a series of dangerous flights over the bleak Sierra Nevadas. Aviation experts at the time described his flights "like staring Death in the face," or, in the words of one writer, "How to meet the Grim Reaper in one easy lesson."

Through his experimental flights, Howard was proving to skeptics that high altitude flying increased air speed tremendously.

Keeping a careful log, Howard told Glenn, "I'm proving my point. I'm right about this. But I'm doing more than that. I'm becoming the god damn daddy of commercial aviation. The day will soon come when any fool with the price of a ticket can fly across America. Next thing I know, the railroad people will try to have me murdered."

Early one morning, just a few minutes after Glenn reported to work, he called Howard at Muirfield to report a theft at the hangar. "Our papers and records for the *Bullet* have been stolen. Someone broke into our office and made off with them."

Howard was furious at this breakdown in security. But it wouldn't be until years later that he realized who the culprit might be. The first time he saw the dreaded Japanese Zero fighter during the early years of World War II, he knew what had happened. "The Japs have stolen the plans of *The Flying Bullet*," he said. "God knows how many American lives will be lost because of me."

Howard's revolutionary mystery ship now hangs in an alcove at the Smithsonian Air and Space Museum in Washington, D.C.

CHAPTER ELEVEN
Los Angeles, 1935

Having broken one speed record, Howard was determined to go for another. He wanted to break the speed record for a transcontinental flight between the East and the West Coasts. The existing record of ten hours, two minutes, and fifty-seven seconds had been established by Captain Roscoe Turner, who had been one of the stunt pilots during the filming of *Hell's Angels*.

Aware that he'd need an all-new airplane to meet the challenge, and unwilling to wait the full eighteen months that would have been needed to build it, he cast his covetous eye on a state-of-the-art Northrop Gamma owned at the time by Jackie Cochran, a beautiful, blonde, twenty-six year-old aviatrix. Without her knowing it, Howard had secretly spied on Jackie, as her crew put her Northrop Gamma through a battery of fuel-consumption tests at Mines Field.

Although her rival, Amelia Earhart, is a more famous aviatrix today because of her mysterious disappearance, Jacqueline Cochran is actually the greatest woman pilot in aviation history. By the time she'd died in 1980, she held more speed, distance, and altitude records than any other pilot (female or male) in the history of flight.

In stark contrast to Howard, Jackie had been born into poverty, growing up the hard way in a small Florida sawmill town. She was cared for by foster parents who sent her to work full time in the mill at the age of eight. At the age of eleven, she apprenticed herself to a hairdresser. She fled from home after selecting a new name for herself from the phone book. In New York, she became a successful beautician, but she would eventually discover that her true love was in the air.

In time Jackie would marry a multi-millionaire, Floyd Odlum, the founder and chief executive officer of the Atlas Corporation from its beginnings in 1923. But at the time Jackie met Howard, she was strapped for cash.

Their relationship began with a call that came into her hotel room one night at 11:30pm. Sleepy, she picked up the receiver and heard a high-pitched voice with a Texas accent inform her, "Jackie, this is Howard."

At first she didn't know who he was until he clarified it. "Howard Hughes," he said.

"That's nice," she said. "I'm the Queen of Sheba."

"No, it's really me," he insisted. "I want to buy the Northrop Gamma."

She immediately refused, telling him she wanted to fly the plane in the

Bendix Trophy Race, covering the distance between Los Angeles and Cleveland. He told her that he wanted to use her plane to break the existing transcontinental flight record. She startled him by informing him that she wanted to do that as well. But Howard could be very persuasive, and she agreed to see him the next morning if he'd let her get some sleep.

At Mines Field, Howard was fifteen minutes early for their appointment. Usually he was at least an hour late, in some cases four or five hours late. Howard was with his co-pilot, Glenn Odekirk, when he first met Jackie. He would later confide to Glenn that "the dame is a stunner—maybe needs bigger breasts, but so do most women." Glenn found "fire in her eyes and a spine made of steel."

Even though very feminine, Jackie had chosen to enter the tough-talking, hard-driving macho world of the male pilot. Most aviators drank too much at night and took too many risks during the day. "To live without risk, for me, would be tantamount to death," Jackie was fond of saying. She uttered that same sentiment one morning in 1962 when she became the first woman to fly a jet airplane across the Atlantic.

Glenn later recalled that Howard seemed so mesmerized by the charm and beauty of Jackie that at first he forgot to transact business. "My God," he later told Glenn, "her eyes are browner than mine." In the morning sun without her helmet and goggles, her hair was a "shimmering gold" and her skin was "porcelain like," bringing out the poet in Howard. Perhaps Jackie's complexion evoked memories of Billie Dove for him.

He later told Dietrich, "Jackie manages to look like a real woman even when she's dressed up like a pilot. In the same flying togs, Amelia Earhart looks like a transvestite version of Charles Lindbergh."

After Jackie had left for the day, still undecided about what to do with her Northrop Gamma, Howard told Glenn, "I've found Howard Hughes alive and living in a woman's body." In a few short months, he would make the same remark about another "gal pal," Katharine Hepburn.

It took Howard a month to break down Jackie's resistance. Dietrich later claimed that Howard won over Jackie by seducing her. "I know that on two separate occasions he disappeared for a weekend with her in the air—God knows where." Two of his closest male friends, Cubby Broccoli and Pat DeCicco, said they frequently saw Howard during this time—and he never once mentioned Jackie Cochran. Perhaps their testimony could be discounted because he also didn't mention his plans to acquire her plane.

After Howard's seduction of her, Jackie "caved in" (her words), but since she couldn't bring herself to actually sell her plane, she finally agreed to lease it to him instead. He presented her with an offer of $65,000 which "I could not refuse." That figure was more than the total cost of the plane's original construction. "I just couldn't afford to do otherwise," Jackie later said. "He had me." Her last remark, of course, could be taken two different ways.

After Jackie married Floyd Odlum, she no longer desperately needed her lease payments from Howard. But even though Floyd had many reservations about Howard, he became his friend, a relationship that lasted for many years. Howard became a frequent visitor to the couple's California ranch.

When Jackie introduced Howard to Floyd, he later told his friends. "Hughes looks like a suspicious recluse, the kind of guy who might steal something from your house. He even has to borrow a dime to make a phone call or thirty cents to fill up his gas tank. Never has any money on him."

After his seduction of Jackie and right at the time of her marriage, Howard told Billy Haines, "There are three people I want to fuck in this world. "The first, Jackie Cochran. Mission accomplished. The other is Amelia Earhart."

"Pray tell, who is the third?" Billy asked.

"Charles Lindbergh, that son of a bitch!"

One weekend Jackie recalled that Howard arrived at her ranch with a beautiful aspirant young actress. He introduced her to the Odlums as Terry Moore, only fifteen at the time. "He told me he was going to marry Terry," Jackie later said. "On another occasion, he showed up with Rita Hayworth." Jackie claimed that he was growing increasingly paranoid by that time. "He insisted on opening every closet at our ranch before he would talk to us," she said. "He was afraid that spies were hiding in the closets."

In 1960, the relationship soured when Floyd retired early from Atlas to run Toolco for Howard. At the last minute, Howard reneged on his promise without informing Floyd, who then sued him. The lawsuit was settled out of court for an undisclosed amount of money.

Dietrich always claimed that Howard was able to force Floyd into a settlement because Howard's detectives had discovered a startling bit of information about Jackie. It seemed that at some point in her life, she'd had an affair with her friend, Dwight D. Eisenhower.

Aldine Carter, manager of the Odlum ranch, later recalled a midnight call from Howard. "Jackie was asleep when I called Floyd to the phone to take a call from Hughes," Aldine claimed. "Howard was trying to buy a mattress he said he'd slept on at Floyd's ranch. He said the mattress had a hole in it, and he wanted to sleep on it again because he'd come down with a bad case of hemorrhoids."

Floyd denied ever having such a mattress. "If we have a mattress with a hole in it—and we don't—we certainly wouldn't give it to such an honored guest as yourself to sleep on."

Later, when Floyd had hung up, Aldine asked, "Hughes has got all the money in the world. Why doesn't he buy a new mattress and have a hole cut in it?"

"Howard, I fear, has gone into space," Floyd said. "I saw it coming. His mind is now somewhere else—not of this world!"

Cary Grant was still eager for his boyfriend to attach himself to Katharine Hepburn. He told Randolph Scott, director George Cukor, and others that Kate would be the perfect girlfriend for Howard. "The press will go wild about promoting the romance. She'll be the perfect cover. She'll make no sexual demands, and Howard can do pretty much what he likes. And so can Kate." He continued pressing this point of view so frequently he became almost like a stuck record.

Instead of taking Cary's advice, Howard did almost the opposite and, temporarily at least, began to see more and more of Pat DeCicco. Paying him a salary with funds out of who-knows-what cache, Howard chose Pat as his nocturnal associate. If the job description of this hustler/gigolo could be defined at all, it was "an arranger of liaisons."

Pat had begun to date June Knight, a grade B, twenty-two-year-old actress born in Los Angeles. She was not exceptionally pretty but attractive. Pat tantalized Howard with stories of his nighttime activities with her, claiming "we have great sex."

"Better than with Thelma?" Howard asked.

"Much hotter!" Pat said.

Nightclubbers: Pat DeCicco, June Knight, and Howard Hughes

Wilson Heller, the pioneer Hollywood publicist, once said, "Two of his [Howard's] girlfriends told me he wasn't worth a damn as a lover. He was just no good in the sack. They said all he wanted to do was to look and fondle."

That was basically true at the time because Howard was experiencing a prolonged period of impotence with women. From all reports, he performed satisfactorily with men in bed, especially Cary, but could not complete intercourse with women.

Nonetheless, he was more drawn to women than to men and continued to seduce them. "At least he could perform orally," Billy Haines said at the time,

334

"even if he couldn't get it up for the ladies."

As Pat kept boasting about his great sex with June Knight to both Howard and his cousin, Cubby Broccoli, Howard began to invite himself out on late-night dates at nightclubs with the two lovers. As his paid lackey, Pat was not in a position to refuse.

The inevitable finally happened. Howard was becoming more and more the voyeur, and he was growing tired of hearing about the "great sex" his friend was having with June. He wanted to see a demonstration first hand. Pat, from all reports, was very reluctant to grant such a request. But the hustler in him did not want to turn down Howard, as he feared the consequences.

What happened next was reported by Pat DeCicco himself, who relayed it to Cubby Broccoli, who relayed it to, among others, Howard Hawks. More or less simultaneously, the details of the story were independently reconfirmed by June Knight, who relayed the stories to, among others, Una Merkel and Robert Taylor, with whom June was making *Broadway Melody of 1936* at MGM. And somehow, Jack Benny (who was starring in that same film) heard the story too, and relayed it to contacts of his own. As 1935 came to a close, it had blossomed into one of the most oft-repeated raunchy stories in Hollywood.

According to Cubby Broccoli, Pat DeCicco came to him complaining bitterly of "having a sore ass." He felt humiliated and was furious at Howard. Howard had maintained that his impotence would be cured if Pat would let him fuck him while he was fucking June. Although Pat admitted to Cubby that he'd occasionally been on the receiving end of blow-jobs from Hollywood homosexuals, he'd never been "used like a woman before...it's very painful."

Howard may indeed have been correct about the means whereby he could cure himself of his impotence. The bedtime romps with June and Pat seemed to do the trick. In the next few weeks, Howard pronounced himself cured of his sexual underperformance with women. He is said to have made that announcement on the morning after he finally penetrated June directly, supposedly having no further need of using Pat as a surrogate.

Commenting on the situation years later, Una Merkel said, "June had her fifteen minutes of fame in Hollywood underground lore. The Hughes/DeCicco/Knight affair made a great story. And what else was there to talk about? Shirley Temple's triumphs at the box office?"

Another latter-day commentary on the three-way affair was offered many years later by actress Lilian Bond, who maintained that she had heard about it directly from June Knight as well. "June was just one of the two thousand handsome young men and beautiful young women who got dumped by Howard Hughes. Pat DeCicco had promised June that he'd be her agent and make her a bigger star than Ginger Rogers, and Howard had promised to star her in some of his upcoming films."

One dark day, with the gossip probably echoing in her head, June realized that the dreams of 1935 were only to be dreamed. She appeared in four more films, each of them minor, delivering her final performance in 1940 in *The House Across the Bay*, in which she played a supporting role to George Raft and Joan Bennett.

It is entirely possible that Howard wouldn't have even recognized the name of June Knight by 1940. A washed-up and forgotten figure, she died on June 16, 1987 in her native Los Angeles.

***

No longer impotent, at least for the moment, Howard launched the pursuit of one of the most famous blonde bombshells of her era, the beautiful, busty, and provocative Thelma Todd. Sometimes known as "Hot Toddy," she was recently divorced from Pat DeCicco. Thelma might be best known to modern-day readers for her portrayal by the talented actress Loni Anderson in a made-for-TV-movie in 2001.

Howard had already bedded Thelma at least once before. Usually as part of a group of acquaintances, he had been seeing her two or three times a week at Thelma Todd's Sidewalk Café. "Perhaps he likes my sloppy seconds," Pat told Cubby Broccoli. Pat could have been rather ungallantly referring to either June Knight or Thelma Todd. Pat's divorce from Thelma had come through only the year before. Howard had developed a fondness for pursuing divorced actresses, whom he cynically referred to as "wet decks."

As he launched his seduction plans of Thelma Todd, he could not have known that, from the sidelines, he was about to witness the backroom intrigues of one of Hollywood's more sensational murders, a killing that easily matched, and perhaps even surpassed, the speculation surrounding the still-unsolved murder of director William Desmond Taylor in 1922.

***

When he wasn't out with Pat, June, or whomever, Howard was spending time in an airplane hangar with Glenn Odekirk, virtually rebuilding the high-powered Northrop Gamma he'd leased from Jackie Cochran.

Jackie was unaware of what was happening to her plane, which was under heavy security guard. Technically, she still owned the plane, but she wasn't allowed visitation rights. Howard figured he had three months to get the Gamma ready. He planned to fly across the North American continent some time in January of 1936, as soon as he was notified that weather conditions were ideal.

He replaced the plane's original engine, which was less than two years old, with the latest Wright Cyclone R-1820G 850 horsepower engine, a semi-experimental device that wasn't usually available to civilians. To get it, he and his staff weaved their way through a series of intensely private, behind-the-scenes manipulations of the U.S. Army Air Corps. Pilots referred to the installation as "the cyclone engine," because it generated awe-inspiring blasts of power at takeoff. In addition, he installed a Hamilton Standard variable pitch propeller.

To prepare himself for the transcontinental run, Howard made eleven flights as a Douglas DC-2 co-pilot on TWA runs between Los Angeles and New York. Through it all, he still found time for romance.

***

By the time Howard got around to seriously pursuing Thelma Todd, she was a diet pill addict, popping "my little darlings" so fast and so recklessly that she evoked a future Marilyn Monroe. Unknown to him, she'd also become hooked on hard drugs, as supplied to her by her gangster lover, Charles (Lucky) Luciano.

When Billy Haines learned that Howard was dating Thelma, so recently divorced from Pat DeCicco, the actor asked him if he had any guilt about that. "Hell, no!" Howard said. "I've fucked both of them."

He had begun showing up frequently at Thelma Todd's Sidewalk Café, where the actress was in partnership with Roland West, whose career as a director had wound down in 1931. He is known today mainly for his 1926 silent film, *The Bat*, which became the prototype for many of the "scary movie" thrillers that followed.

Thelma had a motive for dating Howard: She wanted him to buy out Roland West, whom she claimed was trying to take control of her life. Complicating matters was the fact that much of the original investment for their restaurant had come not directly from West, but from West's wife, Jewel Carmen, a former beauty queen.

Thelma had been looking puffy-faced and was taking far too many drugs, and consuming too much alcohol until Howard expressed a romantic interest in her. Her new flame seemed to drive her out of her months-long depression. Taking better care of herself, she purchased a new wardrobe and was visited by a hairdresser every day. There was some fantasy spinning through her head that Howard might actually marry her.

Over pillow talk, Thelma told Howard more than he wanted to know about his best friend Pat. She also related this same story to her costar Patsy Kelly, as well as spicy details of her romance with Howard. Pat was known for his violent temper, and in their marriage, he repeatedly beat Thelma and heaped verbal abuse on her. She was as equally hot tempered as her gigolo husband, and their fights, often staged at the café in front of clients, became the gossip of Hollywood.

Much of Howard's affair with Thelma was conducted upstairs over her beachside café. The upstairs had been converted into two apartments, one for West, one for her. West had also been her lover. The building also contained an additional space on the third floor which was usually used for gambling and other illicit encounters. It was this third floor space that became the focus of a battle among Pat DeCicco, Lucky Luciano, and Thelma.

Lucky was eyeing the third floor as a possible site for his own illegal gambling activities in Los Angeles, where he planned to pay off the police. Many of Hollywood's top stars, including Clark Gable, patronized the joint, and Lucky was anxious to separate them from their fat studio paychecks. He also wanted to make Thelma's the hub of his own drug racket.

In addition to being on Howard's payroll, Pat was also a paid frontman for Lucky, who needed someone debonair and charming to represent him. Even though Thelma was divorced, and even though he was having an affair with her himself, Lucky rightly figured that she probably still carried a torch for Pat. He wanted Pat to intercede and get Thelma to grant his request for the clandestine and illegal use of her club. She not only refused Pat, but turned down Lucky to his face, even spitting at him. Pat expressed his concern to Howard. "No dame does that to Lucky Luciano and lives."

***

At first, as Dietrich later reported, Howard seemed unconcerned with the turmoil and drama spinning around Thelma and her club. He viewed her as a "good time gal"—and nothing more. On three different occasions, he took her on his yacht for sails to Catalina Island.

One night at Thelma's Club, and in front of witnesses, Howard said to Pat, "With Thelma, I've had some of the wildest sex in my life. She'll do anything, and I mean anything." One can only imagine what her former husband thought upon hearing that. In the presence of Howard, however, Pat never expressed anger, probably because he wanted to stay on the payroll.

Pat had shared his wife before with other men, and had, in fact, introduced her to Lucky while he was still married to her. In front of both Pat and her partner, Roland West, Lucky's first words to her were, "I love blondes, especially beautiful blondes that get a rise from me. Glad to meet you, babe. My big friend and I would like to get to know you better." It was obvious what he meant by his big friend.

West later claimed that if Pat were jealous, "his face gave not a clue. Pat was a big ball clanker most of the time. But around Howard or Lucky, he became the court eunuch."

Like many movie personalities of his era, Howard seemed enthralled by the idea of Pat introducing him to Lucky Luciano. In time, Howard would become a friend of an even more notorious gangster, Bugsy Siegel. Howard dined with Pat and Lucky on several occasions at Thelma's Club.

"Stars in Hollywood back then, although not necessarily criminals themselves— except in their bedrooms—liked to socialize with cold-blooded killers," Cubby

338

Broccoli once said. "It was a vicarious tingle for them. These guys would show up at A-list parties in those days in their dark suits and their fedoras. Machine gun toting gangsters were fleeing New York and Chicago for the rich pickings in Los Angeles. It was an exciting time. Cousin Pat and Howard were right in the thick of it all."

With both Lucky and Howard taking turns bedding Thelma, Pat launched an affair with the beautiful Iowa-born actress, Margaret Lindsay. No longer the tomboy she was when growing up in Dubuque, she was on the dawn of a career that frequently included roles as "the other woman." She'd had a small but showy part in the Oscar-winning *Cavalcade* in 1933 as a member of the supposedly all-British cast. She'd played a bride honeymooning on the *Titanic*. Today she is known for having appeared opposite Bette Davis in films that included *Bordertown, Dangerous,* and *Jezebel.* In *Jezebel,* she played Henry Fonda's bride from the north and the rival of Bette.

Margaret was to die in Los Angeles in 1981 of emphysema, but in the mid-1970s she spoke about her romance with Pat DeCicco and the weeks leading up to the murder of Thelma Todd.

"Pat, wearing incredibly expensive clothes," Margaret recalled, "took me to all the best places back then. Montmartre. Musso and Frank's. At the Brown Derby, we chatted with Darryl F. Zanuck and waved at Gloria Swanson's table. Sometimes Hughes would show up, but always alone, never with Thelma Todd, although Pat told me they were having a torrid affair at the time."

"Pat was the ultimate hand-kissing hustler and he was fantastic in bed," Margaret said. 'It was obvious why the gals went for him. Frankly, if you ask me, I think he was also putting out for Hughes. He never admitted that, however. There were rumors. Lots of rumors. One night when I casually mentioned them, Pat slapped my face. He was very touchy. He didn't deny the rumors, though."

Both Margaret Lindsay, Pat's girlfriend, and Ida Lupino, Howard's former "jailbait" love, were among the few witnesses to the events that led up to the murder of Thelma Todd, aged thirty, on December 16, 1935.

Ida and Margaret, although not privy to the details of the actual murder, may have been the only ones who ever told the truth.

All the others intimately involved with Thelma at the time, including both Pat and Howard, lied repeatedly over the years. Howard, in fact, claimed that he was not even in town the night Thelma was murdered. Pat dismissed any suspicion of murder, claiming that Thelma accidentally died of carbon monoxide poisoning when she was found in her car parked in a closed garage behind her restaurant.

Despite a "delirious" deathbed confession by Roland West that he murdered Thelma, the truth may never be known.

In lieu of that, rumors—some of them quite well-informed—and speculation remain about exactly what happened to Howard's "Hot Toddy."

Margaret Lindsay recalled the final night of Thelma's life, at least from her long-distance perspective. "The details of that night are absolutely baroque, with everybody playing dangerous games. Perhaps my role was that of the pawn who made Thelma jealous."

The night began with a party at the Trocadero that the Lupino family was throwing in Thelma's honor. Ida's father, Stanley, remembered Thelma fondly for her role in some comedy, *You Made Me Love You*, three years previously, and for the kindness she'd extended frequently to his daughter. This was Stanley's first trip to California since then. To his party, he'd invited some important guests, including Sid Grauman, the owner of Grauman's Chinese Theater.

"Stanley Lupino's wife, Constance, was also there," Margaret claimed. "Unknown to me, Pat DeCicco had also been invited to the Lupino party. I learned about that later. Earlier, he had called Ida and told her that he had a cold and couldn't make it to the party. It all seemed so dumb. Having made such an excuse, how did he dare walk into the same club where the Lupino party was being held? He had to know he'd be spotted by both Ida and Thelma. Something else must have been going on. Perhaps he was ordered to the club on some last-minute mission. After all, he was on Lucky Luciano's payroll at the time. I'll never know the full truth."

"Years later, I learned that Ida herself was having an affair with Pat on the side," Margaret said. "She was only a baby at the time. Pat had met her when she was Hughes's underaged girlfriend. To make matters even more complicated, it seemed that Pat had called Thelma that night, claiming he was back from New York and wanted to get back with her—that he was still in love with her. Of course, I suspect what he really wanted was to take over her sidewalk café and turn it into a nest for that gangster, Lucky. I don't think he ever loved Thelma."

"At the time he started dating me, his divorce from Thelma had only recently come through," Margaret said. "I learned many of the details of that fatal night only later. The plan was, so I gathered, that Pat would break our date early and meet secretly with Thelma to work out a possible reconciliation. I truly don't know how he planned to do that when Thelma was sleeping with each of his bosses: Howard Hughes and Lucky Luciano. But Pat was one crazy, mixed up guy. Always scheming."

Before appearing at the party, Thelma spent a long time in her dressing room, according to the later testimony of her maid. With her heavy use of drugs and alcohol, it was taking her longer and longer to turn herself into the ravishing "Ice Cream Blonde," as the fan magazines called her. "Warpainting" her face in heavy makeup, she put on a shimmering blue gown trimmed in lace and sequins, and "fairy slippers." Around her shoulders she tossed a fabulous brown mink coat to ward off a chilly California night. She also put on nearly $25,000 worth of jewelry—mostly diamonds and gold—including a sardonyx ring Pat had presented to her during their brief engagement.

Years later, Ida herself recalled her last encounter with Thelma. "She was receiving death threats, although I didn't know about it at the time. But when we went together to the ladies room, she was all giggly and girly. She told me she was 'having the greatest romance of her life.' I knew she meant Howard Hughes. But, knowing about our past involvement, she told me that the man in question was a very rich businessman. Instead of saying he was from Houston—too obvious—she lied to me and told me he was from San Francisco. I knew better, of course. I pretended to be happy for her, but I was as jealous as hell."

"She also told me that Pat DeCicco wanted to come back into her life," Ida claimed. "That startled me because I was also seeing Pat on the side. To make both Thelma and me jealous, Pat had arrived at the café with Margaret Lindsay, but they refused to join our table. Frankly, I didn't know how the evening was going to play out. All I know is that Thelma was going to meet Pat at midnight after he sent Margaret home in a taxi. Not only that, but she also had a date with her so-called 'San Francisco businessman' at two o'clock that morning. Such a late hour was not unusual for Howard. He often had his most intense dates at two or three o'clock in the morning in those days. He told me that there weren't too many spies around at that time. I reminded him that the night has a thousand eyes."

"Thelma had a lot on her plate," Ida recalled. "I happen to know that she was also having an affair with one of the guests at father's party, Harvey Priester. I don't know how she juggled all those men and Lucky Luciano, too."

While dancing around the floor with Sid Grauman, Thelma spotted Pat DeCicco and Margaret Lindsay at a table. Breaking from Sid, she walked over to confront her former husband. "On the surface, she was very polite, but the tension in the air could be cut with a fork," Margaret said. "Thelma was very nice to me. With complete insincerity, she suggested we might make a film together one day. She seemed to send some sort of facial signal to Pat. Later I found out that he planned to dump me around midnight and run off with her. To complicate matters, Thelma was officially stationed at the Lupino family table with a guy named Harvey Priester. I guess she planned to dump that lover too. As Thelma left our table, Pat said, 'I'll see you real soon.' He *really* meant that!"

"After Thelma left," Margaret said, "I had lost Pat as my date for the evening. All he did was sit and stare at Ida or Thelma, especially when either of them was dancing with some guy. Thelma got real drunk on champagne and was making a play for every handsome man at the Trocadero. The jealous eyes of Roland West were following her every move. He looked like he could kill her."

"Pat, as I mentioned, was going to cut short our date at midnight and send me home in a taxi," Margaret recalled. "But at 12:15 we were still at table. I remember the time because I looked at my watch when he abruptly got up and said he had to make some urgent phone call. He was gone for about ten minutes. When he returned to table, he was very edgy and short-tempered. He demanded that we leave the club at once. He said he had an urgent business meeting and would call me tomorrow. All my life I've speculated that Pat's mystery call was placed to Lucky Luciano. For all I know, they ironed out the details of how Thelma was going to be murdered later in the night by some hit man."

Margaret left the club shortly before one o'clock, taking a taxi. After seeing her off, Pat called for his own car. Sid Grauman, who'd been dancing with Thelma that evening, said he escorted her to the front of the club where she told him that a car was waiting. "I kissed Thelma good night, and she raced toward a car parked slightly beyond the entrance, near a palm tree," Grauman claimed. "The car was in a night shadow, but it looked like a man behind the wheel. Thelma got in and they drove off to God knows where. That was the last time I saw her alive."

Grauman recalled that he asked the valet who'd retrieved the car, "Who's the mystery man taking Thelma off at this hour?"

"That's Pat DeCicco," the young valet said, holding up a five-dollar bill. "Best tipper at the Troc."

***

The plot thickens.

Except for the sighting by Sid Grauman, Thelma was never seen with Pat again. However, after Thelma's murder, three witnesses came forward to claim that she was seen being driven around Los Angeles in the early hours of Sunday morning with none other than Howard Hughes.

It can be presumed that Pat and Thelma engaged in mutual recriminations about their divorce. Following what was probably a bitter argument, considering their hot tempers, it is also presumed that he drove her to Muirfield for a carefully arranged rendezvous with Howard. A round of sex might have been involved. An autopsy on Thelma's body revealed that she had indeed engaged in sex that night "with an unknown party or parties." That crucial piece of evidence was later suppressed by the crooked district attorney, Buron Fitts.

The first witness was a florist who'd emigrated to Los Angeles from Calabria in Italy ten years before. He said that Hughes and Thelma Todd, both of whom he'd recognized from photographs he'd seen of them previously, came into his all-night shop and bought an orchid corsage for her. Her previous corsage had wilted.

A "soda jerk" at an all-night drugstore reported that Thelma and Howard entered the shop and took stools at the counter where each of them ordered a banana split. Finally, a gasoline attendant reported having spotted them when Howard stopped to refill his tank. The estimated time was around four o'clock that Sunday morning. "The man was definitely Howard Hughes," the young attendant said. "And I know it was Thelma Todd. I was one of her biggest fans."

Noah Dietrich, late in his life, stated that Howard told him that he'd been driving Thelma around Los Angeles on the night of her murder. Why he was driving her around has never been determined. Apparently, she'd told him that she was expected at yet another pre-dawn meeting that night, this one with Lucky Luciano, and one didn't stand up that gangster when he requested a face-to-face.

To get back at Lucky, and fearing for her own life, she'd recklessly gone to the FBI to report everything she knew about Luciano's operations on the West Coast, including gambling, drugs, and prostitution. Apparently, she gave agents a rundown on the gangster's infiltration of several Hollywood nightclubs, and his attempt to take over her own café. She also told what she knew about drug peddling within the Hollywood studios, including MGM, where Luciano's boys were supplying drugs to some of the top stars in Hollywood. She also confessed that Luciano had gotten her "hooked on drugs" and that she'd become an addict.

Howard later told Dietrich that he warned Thelma, "You know what Lucky Luciano does with singing canaries?"

Unknown to Thelma and unknown to most of the FBI, Luciano had planted a "mole" within the FBI's Los Angeles headquarters, who kept him abreast of any informant who came forward.

To make a mysterious night even more mysterious, other witnesses in the wake of Thelma's death came forward to report that she was seen in yet another car with a different man that early Sunday morning in Los Angeles.

This "other man" was described as "foreign looking" with a dark complexion. Various witnesses estimated his age as in his early to mid-forties. Luciano at the time was forty-two years old. He was said to be wearing a dark overcoat and a fedora.

From all reports, Luciano had demanded that Thelma meet with him for "a final showdown." He was reputed to have driven her to Santa Barbara, a two-hour drive back then, and to have ordered his chauffeur to park along the beach. He'd brought several bottles of champagne with him.

Eventually he drove her back to Los Angeles but bypassed her apartment and headed for downtown Los Angeles instead. W.F. Persson, the owner of a local cigar store, reported seeing them around 9 o'clock that Sunday morning. He recognized Thelma but didn't even look to see who she was with. He claimed that she was hysterical and looked like she'd been crying when she entered his store to make an urgent phone call.

"She used the phone," Persson said. "I couldn't hear what she said but I gather that she feared being kidnapped."

Dietrich claimed that phone call was to Howard. Robert Fisher, a customer in the store, also remembered Thelma entering. "She wasn't dressed for church but for a Saturday night on the town. She looked like she was coming from some all-night party."

Apparently, she got no satisfaction from the party she so frantically dialed.

Fisher later claimed that the burly male chauffeur of the car waiting on the curb came into the cigar store and virtually dragged Thelma into the car. Fisher walked out for a final look to see who was in the back seat. "I thought it might be some bigtime movie star like Clark Gable or Gary Cooper. It was some dark man in a black suit," Fisher recalled. "His hand reached out and just seemed to pull her into the back seat with him. It must have been ten minutes after nine when the car pulled away."

The next day A.F. Wagner, the medical examiner for the county of Los Angeles, would report that Thelma had died at two o'clock that Sunday morning. Witnesses knew otherwise.

From this point on, the fate of Thelma becomes pure speculation. Presumably Luciano ordered his driver to take Thelma back to her apartment, upstairs from her famous café. Luciano must have told her goodnight, never to see her again.

All the murder buffs and amateur detectives, who have spent years studying the mysterious death of Thelma Todd, have more or less come to the same conclusion. Luciano brought in a hit man from Chicago to murder Thelma for her defiance of him and her going to the FBI.

The attack came as she was staggering toward her apartment. The hit man came out of the shadows and grabbed her, mauling her, choking her, and knocking her out. When her body was discovered, her nose was broken as were two ribs.

Her unconscious body was placed behind the steering wheel of her chocolate-brown 1934 Lincoln Phaeton convertible. She was still alive, or so it is believed, when the gangster left the garage, after starting her ignition, which would fill the garage and the car with poisonous fumes. He closed the door behind him.

It was there at 10:30am on Monday morning that her maid, Mae Whitehead, discovered the body, the corpse bloody and battered.

Pat DeCicco is believed to have called Howard with news of Thelma's death. Howard was later to confide to Dietrich that he suspected that his friend—Thelma's former husband—was "somehow involved" in her murder. But that day Howard had other more urgent business. "There was no way in hell that Howard wanted to connect himself with Thelma in the hours leading up to her murder," Dietrich said.

Howard immediately swung into action. Dietrich denied any involvement on his part, later claiming "I was not part of any cover-up." Somehow those witnesses who'd seen Howard and Thelma together suddenly didn't remember or weren't sure. All three of them denied accepting a bribe for their silence. But when called in by the police, each of them recanted their former testimony.

According to widely circulated gossip and speculation that month, Howard paid fifty thousand dollars to Buron Fitts, the most notorious and crooked district attorney in the history of Los Angeles County. His name would be linked to various film colony "suicides" or else out-and-out murders, each of which would go unsolved. Neither Howard nor Pat were ever called to testify before the Grand Jury, which was completely in Fitts's pocket anyway. The Thelma Todd cover-up would haunt Fitts for the rest of his life, right up until March 29, 1973, when he killed himself with a .38 caliber pistol at the age of 78.

All the evidence presented to the Grand Jury was either contradictory or perjured. Their final verdict was "Death due to carbon monoxide poisoning."

In her will, Thelma left Pat one dollar. Three pieces of jewelry, in diamonds and gold, given to her by Howard, disappeared shortly after her death. No one knows how they were stolen. No link to Howard was ever proven.

Pat DeCicco continued as Howard's "best pal." When he wasn't with Howard, he began to move into the "fast lane," spending his nights carousing and drinking heavily with Errol Flynn and the always inebriated John Barrymore.

Pat kept urging Howard to join him for one of his all-night orgies with Errol, who kept expressing a desire "to meet this tall Texan, this Mr. Hughes." Howard kept turning down those invitations from Pat.

Howard's sometimes lover, Cary Grant, kept urging him into "the perfect relationship" with Katharine Hepburn. Howard claimed, "I don't think Miss Hepburn is very interested in me. Too many girlfriends."

What Howard didn't tell Pat or his cousin, Cubby Broccoli, or even Dietrich himself, was that he'd become mesmerized by a very handsome young actor.

Richard Cromwell.

***

His youthful looks fading, John Darrow was no longer the blond-haired Adonis he was in *Hell's Angels*. In 1935 he played a minor role in *Annapolis Farewell*, directed by Alexander Hall. During the filming, he'd met and had an affair with one of the other actors, a young, good-looking stud named Richard Cromwell. Knowing of John's link to Howard, Richard urged John for an introduction.

When John mentioned it to Howard, he found that the billionaire was eager to meet Richard. As he would continue to do throughout the rest of his life, Howard screened all the major films, and many minor ones, usually during the dawn hours. He was already familiar with the image and reputation of the boyishly handsome Richard Cromwell.

Howard had been impressed with Richard's appearance when he'd won the coveted role of the kid brother who brings the mail in on time in *Tol'able David* in 1930. After that, Richard was cast in other "sensitive" teenager roles, including the 1933 *This Day and Age*, directed by Cecil B. DeMille himself.

Richard was at the peak of his fame in the mid-1930s when he was brought to Muirfield by John Darrow to meet Howard. Born Roy Radebaugh in Los Angeles in 1910, he was five years younger than Howard.

Richard was obviously impressed with Howard's money and power, although John later claimed that "there was also a powerful sexual attraction between the two of them."

In later years, after his career as an actor had faded, John became a Hollywood agent of the notorious casting couch variety when it came to auditioning handsome young actors. When he was sure that he was speaking off the record, John revealed a genuinely bitchy streak when commenting on his fellow agents or some of the closeted stars of Hollywood's Golden Age. He would even publicly denounce his long time companion, the director Charles Walters, as a "God damn faggot idiot," or "a second rate Vincente Minnelli."

In later years, John recalled that Richard suffered throughout his life from having been a charity case when he was growing up. "He carried that scar with him. For the few brief months that he was the lover of Howard Hughes, he felt empowered. For the first time, he could order anything he wanted in a restaurant. Charge expensive clothing in a fancy men's store in Beverly Hills. Be taken out for ocean voyages on one of the greatest yachts in the world where he'd sleep in the master bedroom of 'the richest man on the planet'—and a good looking one at that. Be flown in a private plane to San Francisco where he'd stay in a lavish suite and accept presents of jewelry. Howard courted Richard as if he were a girl—that's the only way Howard knew how to do it. In Richard's case, Howard's seduction technique worked beautifully."

In Richard, Howard found a man who was "eternally young," but also witty and charming. In some ways, he evoked a young Michael J. Fox. Importantly, Richard had a sense of humor, and he could make Howard laugh.

The first night Howard dated Richard, and looked into his beautiful green eyes, the young actor confided to him that instead of working in films, he'd originally dreamed of becoming an artist and decorator. He also wanted to make ceramics. In fact, he'd started out in Hollywood by creating mask likenesses of celebrities. He knew all the bigtime stars, especially the fading ones such as Gloria Swanson and Norma Talmadge.

He proudly told Howard that both Marie Dressler and Joan Crawford had purchased paintings from him. "At least you've cornered the lesbian market," Howard said. He was still smarting from Crawford's rejection of him.

Midway through a dinner at the Brown Derby, Howard became uncomfortable when Richard, for no apparent reason, burst into tears. As it turned out, Richard was very upset over what the fan magazines had been saying about him.

From the very beginning of his career, the magazines had seemed to question his masculinity. In fact, *Photoplay* had virtually "outed" him (to use a modern-day term) in 1931. The interviewer had written about the "blushes" in Richard's "pink cheeks" and how tears flooded his eyes even when he gazed upon some pretty flowers. "He cried when he thought he'd done something clumsy," the writer said. "He cried when the studio people were kind to him. He cried during the big emotional scene in *Tol'able David*. And lo, and behold, he is a great 'emotional actor.'"

Silver Screen writer Virginia Downs had pointedly asked Richard in an interview, "Are you a shy guy with a too-tender heart and a bawling tendency?"

In 1932 Richard had posed for a pic-

Richard Cromwell

ture in *The Los Angeles Times* with his latest mural in oil. The work depicted a very muscular and erotically posed male nude, his genitals discreetly hidden. Whenever he could manage it, Richard got some of the handsomest young actors in Hollywood to pose nude for him.

During the course of his romance with Richard, the bisexual Howard continued to date Ginger Rogers in private, even though she was married to the very handsome Lew Ayres at the time. Their relationship was strictly on her own terms, as he completely failed to dominate her in any way.

"With Richard, and unlike Ginger, it was a completely different story," John later claimed. "Richard was always there for Howard, even at a moment's notice. He was always willing to do Howard's bidding, even if it humiliated him. If Howard wanted his feet massaged or his big toe licked clean, Richard would be at the bottom of the bed servicing his master."

"Howard told me that Richard would do anything in bed," John said. "Some of Howard's future one-night stands, usually low-rent boys, confided to me that Howard was a sadist. I think that was true. That streak of sadism became more evident as Howard aged. I'm only guessing that he didn't pull that crap with women. Only with young men, and only when he was paying for it. Many of the guys I arranged for Howard to seduce told me that they didn't ever want to see him again."

"Although Howard preferred oral seduction—and, baby, I should know—he was also a top," John claimed. "When he learned that Richard found anal intercourse painful, guess what? Howard insisted on penetrating poor Richard

347

nightly and Howard was overly endowed. Richard confided to me that he was left bleeding on many a night."

As happened to all of Howard's partners, both male and female, Richard learned one night that Howard was kicking him out. Since Richard didn't have a lot of money, Howard gave him ten thousand dollars in cash.

Richard was heartbroken. Only that afternoon, he had told his friend and confidante, the minor Idaho-born actress Clare DuBrey, "I'm going to become the next Mrs. Howard Hughes."

"He nearly committed suicide the night Howard dumped him," John later said. "I may have saved that girl's life. She could carry on so—how she could bawl. The price one paid for getting mixed up with Howard Hughes!"

John said that he managed to stay in Howard's life for a few more years by arranging "tasty morsels" like Richard for him to seduce. "First, Howard dumped me as his lover when I lost my youthful glow. Then I became his pimp. Know what? Eventually the bastard even dumped me as a pimp when he met a guy who could do it better. The creep who replaced me obviously had a better stable of boys. It was Henry Willson, the most vicious queen who ever set foot in Hollywood."

During Richard's cinematic heyday, movie magazines frequently compared him to Errol Flynn. One fan magazine wrote that, "Errol Flynn is the real thing, Richard Cromwell merely the mock." Of course, the comparison was far-fetched. There was no way that Richard Cromwell resembled Errol Flynn in any way except male beauty. Otherwise, they were completely different types.

"Perhaps Howard got tired of mock turtle soup and wanted the real thing," John said rather sarcastically. "If you're Howard Hughes and you desire only the very best—in this case, Flynn himself—you can go and get the real prize."

The agent noted that by the early 1940s, women started turning down Howard. "But in his heyday in the mid-Thirties, he was rich and soon to become a national hero," John said. "All the young, aspirant actors he desired accepted his offers to come to his bed. Of course, his rent boys were always eager for one of his hundred-dollar bills. Most of them were giving it away at the time for ten bucks. The gals paraded in and out of Howard's bedroom as well—except one. Miss Crawford herself. I always found that puzzling, since she fucked everybody else in Hollywood, including both Clark Gable and Barbara Stanwyck. Only Marlene Dietrich had more conquests."

In 1945, Richard Cromwell married the nineteen-year-old actress Angela Lansbury, a relationship that lasted for only nine troubled months. It appears that Angela was unaware that Richard was marrying her in an attempt to go straight. There is no evidence that she knew of his previous entanglement with Howard.

According to Hollywood gossip, Angela came home and found her husband in the arms of another man. (It wasn't Howard.) Angela's only comment, and that came years later, was, "I didn't know until we were separated that he was gay."

It took nearly half a century for the world to learn the secret of Angela's first marriage. A supermarket tabloid on its frontpage blared the news: ANGELA LANSBURY'S GAY HUSBAND REVEALED: TRAGIC SECRET OF *MURDER, SHE WROTE* STAR'S FIRST MARRIAGE.

After an encounter between John Darrow and Howard in 1945, John claimed that Howard spoke briefly of Richard's marriage to Angela Lansbury. Howard was familiar with the actress, having seen her in a film, *The Picture of Dorian Gray*, based on the Oscar Wilde tale.

"She's welcome to him," Howard told John. "But I don't know what use he'll be to her."

Also in 1945, with his career on the skids, Richard called Howard and wrote him repeated letters, asking for his help to get his career jump-started. He also asked Howard if he'd agree to put up the money for an art gallery he wanted to open in Beverly Hills.

When Noah Dietrich asked Howard what he wanted him to do with the letters, Howard said, "Burn them!"

***

Burbank, California, and Newark, New Jersey, 1936

The morning of January 13 dawned bright and clear over Southern California, as Howard sat at his lunch talking business with Noah Dietrich. Wearing sneakers, and dressed in a Palm Beach suit, Howard was halfway through a grilled cheese sandwich when a phone call came in from Glenn Odekirk. Howard was informed that weather conditions across the North American continent were ideal for him to attempt to break the transcontinental record.

On the road, and driving dangerously, with Dietrich pleading for his life, Howard raced across Laurel Canyon Boulevard and headed into the San Fernando Valley, where a slight chill still lingered at noonday.

Arriving at the Union Air Terminal at Burbank, Howard shook the hands of each of his mechanics—something he rarely did as he was germ-obsessed—and embraced Glenn. His number one man told him that Jackie Cochran's much modified Northrop Gamma was loaded with an astonishing 700 gallons of gasoline. Up until then, pilots flying transcontinental had to stop in the Middle West for refueling.

In his haste to get into the cockpit, Howard didn't bother to change his dress clothes. He put on a brown leather flight jacket Glenn held out to him and donned his time-worn goggles and a leather helmet. Once in the cockpit, he put on an oxygen mask and checked his controls for an immediate takeoff. As his ground crew waved him on a *bon voyage*, Howard looked at the time. It was 12:05 in the afternoon as his fuel-laden plane became airborne over the skies of

Los Angeles.

He was ascending to the heavens. No more than three minutes into the flight he realized he'd lost radio contact. His antenna must have snapped off during an otherwise smooth takeoff. At this point in the flight, it would have been easy to turn back, land at Burbank, have his antenna repaired, and then take off again.

Instead, he made a reckless decision. He would fly the Gamma across the continent without radio contact. Boldly, even foolishly, he disappeared into the clouds with an entire continent to cross.

He rose to a cruising altitude of 15,000 feet, which gave him an idea for one of his later achievements in aviation in the months ahead. He'd design and perfect an oxygen feeder system to enhance aviator safety on very high altitude flights.

For more than two hours, he couldn't see the ground as he encountered thick clouds "like rotting buttermilk." He was flying in the direction of Santa Fe, New Mexico.

In a very rough way he was able to estimate his location until he encountered gusty winds north of Wichita, Kansas. There the wind blasts somehow caused the needle of his compass to go off register.

Once again and in a feat of recklessness, he made a decision not to seek a local airport and come in for an emergency landing. He took out a map and placed it across his knees, as he continued eastward on his history-making flight.

He was forced to rely on the moon and the stars for celestial navigation, for which he'd trained himself in case of such an emergency. He spotted what he believed was Columbus, Ohio, and later determined accurately that he was flying over the city of Pittsburgh which appeared below him off his port wing.

As the dark airport at Newark came into view, he realized he'd have to land the Gamma without contact with the tower. His only hope was that there were no other planes in the air at this time of the early morning.

Unlike the mobs waiting to greet Charles Lindbergh in Paris, there was no one on the ground to greet him but a timekeeper, who recorded the details of his epic landing.

He landed his plane at 12:42am, only nine hours, twenty-seven minutes, and ten seconds after becoming airborne over Burbank. Without radio contact or properly functioning navigational equipment, he'd set a new transcontinental record, shaving thirty-six minutes off Colonel Roscoe Turner's time, by flying an average speed of 259.1 miles per hour. But the stunt pilot had stopped on the way to refuel.

Instead of celebrating his heroic achievement, Howard emerged from his cockpit cursing, the timekeeper later told reporters. "God damn it! God damn it! I'm mad as hell!" Those were Howard's angry words as remembered the next morning by the timekeeper.

By dawn reporters for the New York papers had heard of Howard's flight and wanted interviews. In front of newsmen during the days that followed, Howard played down his achievement, telling a reporter for the Associated Press, "I wanted to go to New York anyway, so I tried to see how fast I could get there." He modestly reported, "I just sat in the cockpit. The plane did all the work."

He predicted to newsmen that in the near future, regular airlines would be flying transcontinental in just ten hours from New York to Los Angeles. He even predicted that aircraft would soon be flying at an altitude of thirty-thousand feet.

"Do you think you'll see God if you fly that high?" one reporter asked.

Howard frowned, at first thinking the reporter was suggesting that 30,000 feet would be a suicide mission. "I'm sure of it!" he finally answered.

***

Exhausted from his transcontinental ordeal, Howard checked into Manhattan's Drake Hotel just before three o'clock in the morning after his landing at Newark. The desk clerk startled him by informing him, "Mrs. Hughes is here."

Howard's reaction is not known. He might have suspected that the clerk was making some insulting homophobic remark, because Howard had already sent Richard Cromwell across the United States by train. The handsome and boyish actor was waiting for him upstairs in his suite.

"Exactly what do you mean?" Howard demanded to know.

"Your wife, sir," the clerk said. "Mrs. Ella Rice Hughes. She's in suite eleven. Do you want me to have your luggage sent there?"

"No," he finally said. "I don't want to wake her. I've booked a separate suite." Requesting a notepad, he hastily scribbled a note for her to meet him at eight o'clock that morning in the hotel dining room for breakfast.

The story about the clerk and what later happened at the Drake Hotel was related by Richard Cromwell to both John Darrow and Claire DuBrey.

When Howard came into his suite, Richard rushed into his arms. According to Richard's later reports, Howard resisted his advances. "I've got to take a bath," Howard told his lover. "I must smell like a skunk."

"I like it when you smell like that," Richard said. "The sex is better that way, more exciting. It's like being raped by a beast."

***
New York City, 1936

The next morning, Dietrich called Howard's suite at the Drake Hotel. The woman whose plane he'd flown, Jackie Cochran, had told the press, "I'm happy for Howard but my heart is broken. I wanted to fly my own plane and break that record myself. It's a man's world. Howard had the money and I had the plane. As I've said, I'm happy for him." In an uncharacteristic moment, this brave woman then broke into sobs.

"And you woke me up to tell me this," an angry Howard told Dietrich before slamming down the phone. He turned over in bed and bit into Richard's neck so hard he drew blood. The masochistic actor had known in advance what was coming. As he related to Claire DuBrey upon his return to Los Angeles, "I think Howard learned his seduction techniques by watching roosters in the barnyard."

Howard had to get up anyway to meet his divorced wife Ella, who had agreed to the 8am breakfast meeting. According to an eyewitness reporter, Parley Cooper, who once worked for a newspaper, *The Brooklyn Eagle*, "She appeared in the dining room looking gorgeous. If I had been Hughes, I would never have divorced her in the first place. I was at the hotel that morning wanting some quotes from Hughes about his flight. I'd approached him earlier. He told me that if I would not mention his being with his former wife at breakfast, he'd give me a quote or two after they'd had breakfast. I agreed to that. I only wish I could have eavesdropped on their conversation."

Later, Howard was very vague on the details of that early morning meeting. Back in Los Angeles, he spoke to Dietrich about it and apparently to no one else, unless it was Cary Grant to whom he was confiding almost everything, including details about his indiscretions with other men. Billy Haines, who saw Howard upon his return, said he didn't recall his friend mentioning such an unusual encounter. "Something like that I wouldn't have forgotten," Billy claimed.

At the Drake, Howard encountered a more mature and sophisticated Ella Rice. She had lost none of her original beauty in the wake of her sterile marriage to him.

She later confided to friends, including her paramour, James Overton Winston, that she fully expected the breakfast to be a business meeting about alimony payments. She feared that Howard would be asking for additional extensions in his payments. He didn't. Instead, he impulsively proposed that they get remarried.

She later told her sister, Libby Rice Farish, "He held out every promise in the world to me. He even, if you can believe this, promised to be the ideal husband, forsaking all others for me. He said it'd all be different if I gave him another chance. Of course, I turned him down. But ever so gently." To Libby this was a triumph for Ella and a humiliation for Howard. Violating her sister's confidence, Libby told the story to all of Houston society.

The elegant socialite seated across from Howard at the Drake Hotel had virtually reinvented herself after her disastrous marriage. She'd become a world traveler and a leader in Houston society. What she didn't tell Howard that morning was that her true love, James Overton Winston, was waiting for her in her suite upstairs.

Nearly sixty years after that fateful breakfast, Winston himself spoke publicly for the first time about his ordeal. "Ella was gone for no more than an hour from our suite. It was the longest hour of my life. I'd begged her to turn down Howard's invitation, but she said it was only fair that she hear what he had to say. She thought the talk would be about money. I suspected something was up. When Ella returned to our suite, she confirmed that Hughes had asked her to remarry him and that she'd turned down his proposal. I ran to her and took her in my arms. Although it wasn't a very manly thing to do, I burst into sobs. Ella said she wanted to marry me—not Hughes. She also told me that I was the only man she'd ever loved. Hughes was a total asshole to let a woman as grand as Ella go."

***

After a few days shacked up in New York with Richard, Howard grew bored and sent him packing on a train back to Los Angeles. Howard felt tired and wanted a winter vacation, hoping to go swimming and to soak up some sun. "I'm looking too pale in January," he said. "He also ordered Glenn Odekirk to fly the high-powered Northrop Gamma to Miami. After his rest, Howard planned to break another aviation speed record by flying the craft from Miami back to New York.

Before leaving for Miami, Howard sent a bizarre message to Dietrich. At that time the Hughes Aircraft Company had some fifty-five employees. More than a dozen of them were aviation engineers. Howard told Dietrich that in the future all his male employees would have to submit to being photographed in the nude. Howard cited some vague "security reasons" for making this request. Dietrich at once suspected his motives, having noted that Howard's male workers were getting more and more handsome—"some of them movie star material."

"When he wasn't dating Cary Grant or Richard Cromwell, Howard was growing fonder and fonder of mechanics," Billy Haines claimed. "Especially if they had grease under their fingernails. I guess he didn't want to waste time by auditioning men he wasn't attracted to when the guys took off their pants."

Finding the order repulsive and awkward to manifest, Dietrich nonetheless did his master's bidding. "With very few exceptions, the men agreed to it. I turned the naked photographs over to Howard for him to study in his library at Muirfield."

Dietrich wasn't the only man Howard called in Los Angeles. Another surprising call came in to the home of Howard Hawks. "At first," Hawks later revealed, "I thought Howard was going back into the movie business. I knew he was impressed with my work on *Scarface*. Actually, as it turned out, Howard had a most unusual request. During my long career in Hollywood, I've been asked to do almost everything. But pimp for Howard Hughes! I later learned that Bogie himself had done a little bit of that. I know that Billy Haines had. I went along with his request and conveyed to Tyrone Power an invitation: Howard wanted to fly him down to Miami for an all-expense-paid vacation between pictures."

***

Miami, 1936

When Tyrone Power accepted Howard's unexpected invitation to come to Miami, he was just on the "dawn's early light" of a glorious career that would

Tyrone Power, Loretta Young, Howard Hawks

make him one of the great swashbuckling stars of the mid-20th Century. The Ohio-born actor, a closeted bisexual, was also involved in a torrid affair with Loretta Young at the time. She would become his frequent co-star when she wasn't sleeping with either Spencer Tracy or Clark Gable.

Arriving in Miami, Tyrone appeared like a sun-bronzed god to Howard. Howard later told Billy Haines that "Tyrone is just too good looking to be true." Or, as a fan magazine put it, "Tyrone Power is actually as good looking as Robert Taylor is supposed to be."

As Howard was soon to learn, Tyrone was the fourth in a famous acting dynasty reaching back to the 18th century. Although not personally charming himself, Howard was quick to recognize the trait in other men. As he was driving Tyrone to their suite on Miami Beach, he commented on the actor's bright smile, flashing white teeth, good looks, and overall charm. "I don't know about my looks and all that, but the secret of charm is bullshit," Tyrone said. "Howard thought that over and said, 'My God, I think you're right. You and I are going to hit it off.'"

The early relationship and interchange between Howard and Tyrone would have been lost to Hollywood history were it not for a character actor, Monty

354

Errol Flynn

Woolley, who was also breaking into films that same year.

A notorious homosexual, Monty was also the best friend of Cole Porter. He'd met and "fallen in love with the dear boy" when Tyrone and he had appeared together, along with Loretta Young, in *Ladies in Love* for Twentieth Century Fox. Monty quickly became a confidant of Tyrone's, and seemed to pump indiscreet information from the young actor. "The juicier the details, the better for me," Monty said. "I need stories to dine out on."

On the trip to Miami Beach, Howard—or at least Howard "according to Monty" – asked Tyrone how his love life with Loretta Young was going. Apparently, Tyrone did not answer directly. "Marlene Dietrich, or so I'm told, said that every time Loretta sins, she builds a church. That's why there are so many Catholic churches in Hollywood." Howard found that amusing, as Loretta was definitely not his type.

Having seduced Robert Taylor frequently, Howard was anxious to add Tyrone to his belt, at least according to Howard Hawks, who arranged the off-the-record rendezvous.

Even while he was still a bit player at Twentieth Century Fox, Tyrone had been the subject of several stories in fan magazines, the pulp writers predicting that this beautiful young man was in a neck-to-neck race with another male beauty, Robert Taylor, the "heartthrob" over at MGM. Occasionally, one or another of the magazines gave Errol Flynn the edge. Howard, as he privately confessed to Billy Haines, was anxious to audition all three of these young blades before forming his own judgment.

Howard and Tyrone individually would enjoy affairs with both Robert Taylor and Errol Flynn. Tyrone's explanation? "I wanted to see close-up how my competition stacks up."

"The dirty deed," as Tyrone later reported to Monty, occurred on the night of his arrival on Miami Beach, just prior to his departure with Howard aboard the *Southern Cross* for Nassau.

From all reports, Howard was sometimes a bit shy in his first attempts at seduction of handsome young men, unless he'd paid them. He had no embarrassment about commanding hustlers to do his bidding. But he treated Tyrone with far greater courtesy and sensitivity. It began with a candlelight dinner of champagne and caviar for Tyrone, although Howard preferred a simple steak.

355

Tyrone Power

Tyrone remembered that Howard did consume two glasses of champagne, however.

As a lover, Howard didn't know what to expect from Tyrone. He had a strong masculine appeal, and perhaps Howard anticipated an aggressive, lusty lover. What he got that night was what gay men today refer to as a "dominant bottom."

Before midnight, Howard learned more about Tyrone, who wanted to be deeply penetrated. Again and again. It must have been a very tired Howard who assumed command of the *Southern Cross* the following morning.

"The boy is oversexed," Howard told Billy Haines back in Los Angeles. Upon Tyrone's return to California, he was "de-briefed" by Monty, who wanted to learn "each and every sordid detail" about his friend's lovemaking with Howard.

"I think Ty made Hughes feel more like a man than any woman ever had," Monty claimed. "Many of Ty's male lovers have told me the same story. He whispers incredible flattery into the ear of his top. That gorgeous hunk is an incredible aphrodisiac to a gay male, particularly an insecure one. The poor boy told me that Hughes 'ate me alive.'"

As proof of Howard's attraction to Tyrone, he began to shower the actor with gifts upon his return to Hollywood. "I know for a fact that Hughes paid a lot of Tyrone's bills in the early Thirties," Monty claimed. "He even bought him a car and a new wardrobe."

In the following year, Tyrone became a big star, and Darryl F. Zanuck's favorite boy at Fox, but Howard continued to purchase luxuries for Tyrone, who wasn't getting rich as a contract player. "Both of those living dolls, Ty and Robert Taylor, depended on Hughes's largesse for quite a while," Monty said. "Mr. Moneybags of Texas could afford it."

Unlike Robert Taylor, who desperately wanted to appear macho at all times to compensate for his pretty boy reputation, Tyrone was more connected to his feminine side. In protected company, he could even cry freely and express his humiliations and disappointments. "Although there wasn't that great a difference in their ages," Monty said, "Ty looked upon Hughes as a powerful father figure."

Howard never delivered on any of his promises about making Tyrone a great movie star. Zanuck and Tyrone himself would take care of that.

At the beginning of his affair with Howard, Tyrone was earning only one hundred dollars a week. In contrast, the studio's big money earner, Shirley Temple, was pulling in an annual salary of $300,000.

Despite his physical beauty, life was not easy for Tyrone. When he was cast as a newspaperman in the film, *Sing, Baby, Sing.* Sidney Lanfield, the director, denounced him on the first day of the shoot in front of cast and crew. "You're too much of a pretty boy—too soft like a woman. Your gestures are those of a gal, not a hard-bitten reporter. The trouble with you, Power, is you have no balls to clank!"

Robert Taylor

Monty, who was seeing a lot of Tyrone at the time, claimed that his young friend was so devastated by Lanfield's denunciation that he seriously contemplated suicide.

Alice Faye, the reigning queen of the lot, heard of the director's cruel treatment of the aspirant young actor. She invited him to the Tropics Restaurant in Beverly Hills where all the stars went to dine and get photographed with their dates or escorts for the evening. She assured Tyrone that he had the looks and talent to make it as a big star. "I have faith in you," Alice told him.

She was right. He became the biggest male star on the lot, often appearing at Fox with Alice herself, especially in two hits, *In Old Chicago* and *Alexander's Ragtime Band*, both films released in 1938.

Did they have an affair as was rumored? Years later, Alice denied they had, although admitting that when he kissed her on camera, "I immediately ascended to the heavens, upper balcony seats only. But Loretta got him. I didn't. First, he never asked me, and second, he liked boys too much."

In later years, after Howard had broken off his sexual relationship with Tyrone, but not his friendship, his spies kept him informed of Tyrone's bisexual string of seductions. Howard was especially interested in big names the actor had seduced. "He succeeded in bedding Crawford," Howard told Dietrich, "and I didn't. Of course, we both shared Marlene. Who hasn't? Ty did all right for himself with women: Sonja Henie. Judy Garland. Betty Grable. My God, Evita Peron! At least we got to share two girlfriends, Rita Hayworth and Lana Turner. Lana had it bad for him."

As for Tyrone's ultimate sexual preference, his longtime "trick," hustler Smitty Hanson, summed it up this way: "Ty was basically gay but liked a girl from time to time, occasionally marrying one."

***

Miami and New York, 1936

Late April had come to the Miami airport, a day so hot and muggy it felt like summer. Howard breathed deeply, taking in the faint breezes, blowing across the field before once again climbing into the cockpit of Jackie's much modified Northrop Gamma. He was out to break another record, this time for a flight from Miami to New York.

His departure from Miami went smoothly, and soon he was airborne, anticipating a flight of 1,196 miles.

Even before he'd left Florida airspace, Howard began to encounter difficult crosswinds. Once again and rather disturbingly, he lost radio contact, but instead of attempting a landing at some airfield in the Deep South, he opted to continue his flight. At least this time his compass was working.

Looking down and guided by a map, he determined accurately—as it turned out—that he was flying over Raleigh, North Carolina. After taking an airborne piss in a Mason glass jar, he headed toward the air space over Virginia where he planned to enter a "corridor" that would take him into the Northern states.

He later admitted that he thought about landing in Washington, D.C., to demand an audience with President Franklin D. Roosevelt but then he opted against the idea, dismissing it as impractical.

He began to breathe more rapidly as he saw Coney Island in the distance. He was almost there. The weather was chilly, and the amusement park was still in a lingering slumber from winter.

With no mechanical problems but without radio contact, he landed with a thud at Floyd Bennett Field in Brooklyn.

According to his own calculations, later confirmed, he'd set a record Miami/New York flying time of four hours, twenty-one minutes, and thirty-two seconds.

Only a few airport personnel were on hand to greet him. But four hours later at the Drake Hotel, after radio broadcasts had announced his feat, at least a hundred worshipping fans had gathered outside to cheer his accomplishment.

This was hardly the crowd who'd greeted Lindbergh, but it was a signal to the world that in the not-so-distant-future thousands of New Yorkers would be flying in record time to vacation in Miami Beach. America was giving birth to another genuine aviator hero.

While fans massed outside, Howard was taking a much-needed bubble bath, enjoying a good soak for tired bones. As he was later to tell Pat DeCicco, "I have a taste for debutantes, the younger the better, and I want you to arrange something special." After hanging up on his friend and pimp, Howard called Cary Grant, asking him to come and join him in New York. The actor readily agreed.

While waiting for Cary, Howard was seen about town escorting the beautiful Ruth Moffett, daughter of James Moffett, vice president of Standard Oil of California. That budding debutante was only fifteen years old. Today an older man dating "jail bait" that young might be considered shocking, or even the defendant in a court case involving a child molestation charge. But the mid-Thirties were a different time, even though statutory rape laws were on the books, as Errol Flynn in the years ahead painfully realized.

There were even rumors in the press that "little Miss Moffett" was scheming to marry Howard. After one sail to Long Island aboard the *Southern Cross,* she announced to the press that she was going to redecorate it.

Hoping to escape more press attention, and rather amazingly, Howard appeared at New York restaurants and hot spots in disguise. Having grown a beard, he claimed to be Señor Carlos Gomez, a rich oilman and resident of Mexico City. Columnist Walter Winchell, as well as various headwaiters at exclusive restaurants and nightclubs, quickly saw through the disguise. As one headwaiter quipped, "As long as Hughes paid the bill and tipped me well, I'd pretend he's Greta Garbo if he wants that."

When Cary Grant arrived in New York, Howard resumed what would be his on-again, off-again romance with the actor. Cary arrived with a surprise invitation from Randolph Scott, and he and Howard made plans to join the actor in Virginia.

In the meantime, they sought amusements in New York where Cary, as a former resident, knew places Howard had never been. The actor tantalized his lover with a series of nocturnal adventures. It was reported—but never confirmed—that Howard and Cary appeared one night at a notorious male bordello in Harlem which was flourishing at the time and known for its "exhibitions."

Word of their night in Harlem spread quickly through the grapevine. It was even mentioned in the press, but in the veiled news language of the day. "Cary Grant has been seen in New York with his closest pal, Howard Hughes. The actor and the aviator seemed to have developed an insatiable taste for chocolate, sampling some of New York's biggest éclairs on a visit to Harlem."

***

Virginia, 1936

Having abandoned the foolish notion that Howard would lavish millions on him, and having more or less given up on the idea of a lifetime commitment to Cary Grant, Randolph Scott in a secret ceremony had wed Marion DuPont in Charlotte, North Carolina, on March 23, 1936.

She was not only the heiress to a vast industrial fortune, but a nationally known horsewoman. She lived at Montpelier, an estate in Orange County, Virginia, former home of President

Newlyweds: Randolph Scott and Marion DuPont

James Madison and his wife, Dolly. Cary and Howard had been invited to the Southern estate, where they would spend ten days.

It is believed that Howard got to know Cary better during those ten days at Montpelier than at any other period of his life. Up to then, Cary had been an enigma to him in spite of their long hours spent together. Cary was also an enigma to all his friends or lovers, even to Randolph and perhaps even to himself.

The author, Nigel Cawthorne, once wrote: "Nothing about Cary Grant was quite what it seemed. He was not the Ivy League New Englander he appeared to be on-screen, but a working-class boy from Bristol. His name, of course, was not Cary Grant, but Archibald Alexander Leach. He was not a sophisticated, eligible bachelor, as the woman who succumbed to his charms discovered; he would beat, abuse and sometimes injure them; nor was he a heterosexual."

Howard understood all these contradictions. He himself didn't always live up to his image as the playboy aviator stud.

Mitchell Foster, business partner of Billy Haines and an interior decorator, once moved in with Cary and Randolph in Hollywood. Foster later claimed that Cary once talked to him about his trip to Virginia with Howard.

"First off," Foster said, "Hughes wanted to clear up an issue that had been bothering him. Apparently, he asked Cary point-blank, 'Why are you circumcised?' Cary had never admitted to Hughes that he had been born a Jew, because he was all too aware of his friend's anti-Semitism. Cary lied. He told Hughes that he'd been born with an elongated foreskin, and that the attending doctor suggested that he be circumcised. It was definitely not the custom in those days to circumcise Protestant babies in Bristol, England. Hughes seemed to accept that as an explanation. Even though Cary was his best friend for life, Hughes never knew he was a Jew."

Cary did confess to Foster that at one point he told Howard some of the more tawdry details of his early life, and that Howard found "a certain fascination" there.

Like Gary Cooper, Cary—or rather, Archibald—had been dressed like a girl during his early childhood. Howard could relate to that. Cary also said that, "My greatest humiliation came when I was bathed naked in front of my mother and my grandmother."

Cary spoke of his hard beginnings in New York where he'd had a job carrying an advertising billboard and walking on stilts. To make ends meet, he'd lived as the kept boy of Francis Renault, a muscular drag queen who billed himself as "The Last of the Red Hot Papas." Cary was only sixteen at the time.

When Renault's demands grew impossible, Cary moved in with a chorus boy, an Australian, George Orry-Kelly (called "Jack Kelly"). Handsome, effeminate, hot tempered and stocky, Jack fell in love with Cary, who by then was seventeen. The two young men in the early months of 1921 shared a large, loft-like apartment together in Greenwich Village. Later they opened the door to a third roommate, Charles Spangles, who appeared nightly at the Metropol Club. His act, called *Josephine and Joseph*, called for him to wear a costume that was half-male and half-female. On one side, he was a female complete with lipstick, rice powder, and lots of mascara. The other side of his face was bearded with a moustache. Archie also had an affair with Spangles.

In those early years, Archie met Gracie Allen and George Burns, who introduced him to the rising young comedian, Jack Benny. Cary told Howard that he'd also had an affair with Jack Benny and also a romance with the tall, quietly genteel, well-bred, and witty Moss Hart, the author. Years later, Hart would prepare a script for him, *A Star is Born*, writing the role of a drunken and fading star, Norman Maine, with Cary in mind. Cary, of course, would turn the part down in horror.

As Cary related to Howard, during those early years in New York, Cary fell in love with a young composer, Phil Charig, who brought him to California, where the two of them rented an apartment in West Hollywood.

Until Cary's film career took off, he launched a small men's clothing store with two partners. One, Wright Neale, was an aspiring clothes designer, and the other, Bob Lampe, an interior decorator. Both men called Cary, "Sister," but only in the most affectionate of terms. "All of that led me to Randolph. I met him one day at the studio during a lunch break," Cary told Howard.

"And here we are," Howard said, pulling his car up at the Montpelier estate. In the distance, both men could see Randolph striding forward to greet them.

Neither Howard nor Cary were impressed with Randolph's new wife, the imperious daughter of William DuPont, the industrialist. The tweedy Miss DuPont walked with a manlike stride, with square shoulders, close cropped black hair, and a face that some acquaintances compared to that of a witch. She was rumored to be a lesbian. Actually the opposite was true. She was a heterosexual nymphomaniac.

When the press learned about the Scott/DuPont marriage, the couple were dubbed "The Beauty and the Beast." "Horse-faced Scott marries Miss Horsey herself," quipped Louella Parsons.

On her estate, Marion had installed a private gymnasium and sauna, almost unheard of in those days. The gym's "personal trainer," Ralph Fay, was seemingly hired for his body more than his training in physical education. The young bodybuilder, who evoked a latter day "Mr. America," was handsome and only twenty-two when he'd been hired to work at Montpelier. Miss DuPont had already determined that Fay was a bisexual, and the young man had proven equally adept at satisfying the libido of both herself and her new trinket, the handsome Randolph Scott.

Fay later spoke about some of the private dramas going on within the former home of Dolly Madison. "On several occasions I saw Mr. Hughes, Mr. Scott, and Mr. Grant strip naked and enter the sauna together."

"I was servicing both Mr. Scott and Miss DuPont in those days," he claimed. "But never together. I was a very busy man, but so were two or three other good-looking guys who worked for Miss DuPont. Mr. Scott and Miss DuPont occupied separate bedrooms. It was definitely a non-marriage."

Even so, the arrangement would last until 1939 when Miss DuPont divorced Randolph, settling millions on him. As if seeking revenge against Randolph, or perhaps to show him up, Cary would go on in a few years to marry an even richer heiress, the Woolworth "Poor Little Rich Girl," Barbara Hutton.

It was while visiting Montpelier that Cary arranged for George Cukor to send his most recent film, *Sylvia Scarlett* for a private screening. Although Howard had flown virtually onto the set, disrupting the shooting of one of its scenes, he'd never actually seen the film.

Fay screened it for Howard, Cary, Randolph and Miss DuPont. At the end, Fay heard Howard tell Cary, "You play the part a bit too effeminate. And Kate Hepburn is far too masculine."

At one point Fay said that Howard asked Randolph why he'd married Miss DuPont if they weren't sleeping together. Of course, by this time she'd retired for the evening. "She wanted a beautiful trophy husband," the actor told Howard, "And she got me. I'm just to be brought out like a show hoss. The marriage has not been consummated. Nor will it ever be!"

362

One night after Miss DuPont had retired, Fay was still serving wine to the three male friends. He claimed that Cary with great urgency prevailed upon Howard to start pursuing Katharine Hepburn. "If you think Randolph here has the perfect setup with Marion, you can have the same thing with Kate. If you married her, you could disappear for weeks at a time." He'd already echoed that same theme with Howard several times before. "Unlike Ella Rice, who always wanted to know where you'd been during one of your mysterious disappearances, Kate wouldn't even mention that you'd been gone. The fan magazines would love it. Right now there's too much speculation that Kate likes girls too much and you go in for boys. All that would end with a marriage to Kate. It'd be hailed as the romance of the century!"

"Let me think it over," Howard said. "Her tits look pretty small to me, and you know what a breast man I am."

"Hell with her god damn tits!" Cary said, growing angry in front of Randolph and Fay. "Do you think Marion has ever seen Randolph nude? It'd be the same with you and Kate. You guys would never have to take off your clothes in front of each other. You could sleep in different wings of your house—a perfect Hollywood marriage."

"It sounds better all the time," Fay reported Howard as saying as he rose from the table. "Howard looked first at Mr. Grant, then at Mr. Scott, and then at me."

"I'm going to bed," Howard said. "Which one of you is going to get lucky tonight?"

***

Chicago and Burbank, California, 1936

With Cary Grant safely on the train back to Los Angeles, Howard flew solo to Chicago in Jackie Cochran's radically altered Northrop Gamma. While ordering his lunch at the airport in Chicago, he encountered a heckler, Robert Jamison, who bet him he couldn't fly to Los Angeles in time for dinner.

Jamison claimed he'd pay for Howard's dinner if he'd take the bet. Even though the flight would cost thousands, Howard took the bet, and prepared to leave at once. Facing a distance of some 1,885 miles, he felt time was wasting.

As unbelievable as it sounds, Howard claimed he couldn't find suitable maps in Chicago. He decided to depart on his hazardous gamble without them. The details of his harrowing flight were later told to Noah Dietrich and Glenn Odekirk.

Three hours and fifteen minutes into the flight, Howard said "the shit hit the fan." East of Kansas City, he encountered heavy turbulence. Later, to clear the Rockies, he had to climb to 15,000 feet, then 16,000 feet. Still he felt in danger. He then decided to climb to the then-astonishing altitude of 20,000 feet. He'd never flown this high before.

At that point, his oxygen equipment broke down, and he feared he'd come down with anoxia. He chose to remain aloft instead of attempting to return closer to earth and seek a spot for an emergency landing. Suddenly, he encountered a fierce thunderstorm. Fighting against sleep, he grew dizzy. He claimed that he kept screaming to say awake. The plane grew deadly cold. For the dangerous five subsequent hours, he flew bravely as ice formed on his wings.

Amazingly, he made it to California airspace. Only one hundred miles east of Burbank, his oil pump collapsed, and he was forced to operate it manually for his final descent into his familiar airport. Just fifty miles from the field, his airspeed indicator stopped functioning.

The lights of the city of Los Angeles, a welcome relief, sparkled in the distance. It was at exactly 7:16pm that his Northrop Gamma landed at the Grand Central Air Terminal eight hours, ten minutes, and twenty-five seconds after he became airborne over Chicago. He'd set another world's record, this one from Chicago to Los Angeles.

He'd faced fierce head winds roaring in from the Pacific. "The only god damn thing still working was the engine," he told Glenn once he'd landed. Almost as an afterthought, he added, "As the ace pilot I am, I break flight records like I pierce hymens."

He told reporters, "I've learned more in the past eight hours than I have in a whole decade." During the flight to Burbank he'd proven a theory of his. Flight instruments calibrated at sea level don't work accurately if the pilot flies at high altitudes.

Privately he told Glenn, "I'm through with Jackie's plane. Sell it back to her. I was an idiot not to have put that junkheap down in Kansas City."

He told Glenn that work would begin early tomorrow morning on his *Flying Bullet*. "I'm going to break my own record."

That night, to honor his bet, he had dinner in Los Angeles, ordering a small steak and very small peas, finishing off with a scoop of vanilla ice cream. The total bill came to seventy-eight cents. When he'd finished dinner, he told an astonished waiter, "Send the bill to Robert Jamison in Chicago. I'll give you his address."

***

Santa Barbara and Los Angeles, 1936

Accompanied by three other pilots, including Daniel Montgomery, Hughes flew to Santa Barbara where Howard and Daniel checked into the same suite at a resort. Howard paid for the rooms of the other two pilots, but they were each assigned much smaller single accommodations on the top floor. He liked the area so much that he ordered that the crew of his yacht, *Southern Cross,* head north to Santa Barbara, where he'd meet them for a few days of sailing.

Daniel was an exceedingly handsome, blond, blue-eyed young man who'd won some sort of swimming championship back in his home state of Indiana.

Howard would take up with good-looking men like Daniel, especially if they were pilots or mechanics, and he'd be seen with them for a few days only to grow quickly bored. From all evidence he treated most of his toy boys with far more generosity than he did many of his women companions. Sometimes Howard would bestow as much as ten thousand dollars on one of the men or he'd buy a new car for them. One mechanic claimed that Howard, after spending two weeks with him in Nevada, helped him financially to the point that he was able to open his own service station.

By this time Howard had developed the trait of scanning newspapers and magazines, looking for pictures of beautiful young women. As he and Daniel rested by the pool, a picture of a beautiful local debutante, Nancy Bell Bayly, caught his attention. The twenty-year-old brunette bore a striking resemblance to Ella Rice at the peak of her beauty in Houston.

The following Sunday night at the Montecito Country Club, as Nancy was dancing with her good-looking beau, Ronald Channell, who was still in college, Howard cut in.

Somehow in the days that followed, Howard began a series of dates with Nancy, most of them conducted aboard the *Southern Cross*. Ronald was given an all-expenses-paid trip to Mexico. Nancy later told the press that "Howard was the perfect gentleman. He never even kissed me goodnight, not even a peck on the cheek. We went to the movies twice, and he didn't even hold my hand. In spite of all his money and power, he reminded me of a little lost boy. Women found that quality of vulnerability very appealing."

For Nancy's twenty-first birthday on July 11, 1936, Howard sailed with her to Los Angeles, promising her a lavish evening on the town. Both of them checked into separate suites at the Ambassador Hotel. The night was cloudy with heavy fog rolling off the Pacific. Driving was difficult.

The *faux* Polynesian restaurant, Trader Vic's, was all the rage at the time, and Howard invited her there to celebrate her birthday. No restaurant décor in Los Angeles was more exotic at the time, with an artificial rain forest inhabited by fake "birds of paradise," along with real orchids and an artificial waterfall. The bartender's specialty, called a "Volcano," was an ice-blue drink heavily laced with rum and six tropical juices, including guava and pomegranate. "We got real tipsy," Nancy later recalled, "after ordering three of them." He purchased her a gardenia lei, which he placed around her neck.

After dinner, he drove her to Muirfield, even though he'd booked hotel suites. She thought that he'd invite her to sleep over. While she waited in the living room, Beatrice Dowler made gin martinis for them. She didn't remember if Howard drank his or not but she poured her martini into a potted plant when Beatrice left the room.

Upstairs in his bedroom, Howard changed his clothes. When he came down, he invited her to go dancing at the Cocoanut Grove, with its *papier-maché* palm trees. Once there, Howard encountered Pat DeCicco, who invited them to join his table. His date for the night was the blonde-haired actress, Joan Blondell, who later admitted that she flirted shamelessly with Howard "but it didn't do me any good."

Growing bored with the Cocoanut Grove, Howard invited Nancy to drive west with him to a popular amusement park at the Santa Monica pier. "I want to ride the roller coaster," he announced. Joan was willing to go but Pat turned down the invitation, preferring the more sophisticated pleasures of the nightclub instead.

It was about 10:47pm when Howard's 1929 Duesenberg approached Third Street and Lorraine. The streetlight had burned out, and the night had grown increasingly foggy. "Suddenly, the lights of a streetcar just seemed to emerge out of nowhere," Nancy later recalled. "Howard swerved quickly to avoid a collision with an oncoming big black car. All I remember was this loud thump like someone had thrown a sack of potatoes onto our hood. I screamed when I realized what must have happened. Howard jumped out of the car. To his horror, he discovered that he'd run over and killed a man. In the newspapers the next morning, I read that his name was Gabe Meyer, and that he was fifty-nine years old and a clerk at May Company Department Store."

At that point Nancy had gotten out of the car too. She helped Howard pull the man's body to the curb. By that time a crowd of nearly fifteen rubberneckers had gathered. Most of them were streetcar passengers who'd gotten off at the busy corner of Wilshire and Third. Others were motorists who'd stopped to witness the accident.

"Almost subconsciously I picked up the man's straw hat," Nancy later remembered.

On an impulse, as Nancy later testified, "Howard grabbed me, ripped off my beautiful gardenia lei from Trader Vic's and virtually pushed me onto the next streetcar. 'Get out of here!' he instructed me. 'Go back to the Ambassador. I'll send someone to drive you to Santa Barbara in the morning.' It was only when I boarded the street trolley and had been sitting there for three minutes in shock did I realize that I still held the straw hat of the dead man in my lap."

The details of what happened next are completely obscured. Howard placed an emergency call to his attorney, Neil McCarthy, who immediately took over the case. All eyewitness reports were contradictory. One man claimed that Meyer was "falling down drunk" and "staggered into traffic." Another claimed that Howard was speeding. Yet another witness, a housewife, Florence Smuckler, said she knew for a fact he was going at the rate of fifteen miles per hour.

Someone, not Howard, called the police. C.P. Wallace, a Los Angeles policeman, was first at the scene. Howard said he was a businessman from Houston and gave his address as 3921 Yoakum Boulevard.

When a squad car arrived, Howard was taken to the Hollywood Receiving Hospital where, amazingly, he passed a sobriety test. John Yadkin, who admitted Howard, later told the press that, "Hughes was obviously drunk. I wasn't with him when he was given the sobriety test. There was no way a man in that condition could have passed the test." But by that time, McCarthy had arrived on the scene, and he, not the police, was conducting the show. At Central Jail in Los Angeles, Howard was booked on a charge of "negligent homicide."

Through McCarthy, Howard released a statement to the press. "This is my first accident. I've been driving since I was twelve years old and I've never hit a cat or dog. My father owned the first automobile in the state of Texas and taught me to drive eighteen years ago. I've had a perfect record. I've never even scratched the paint on my Duesenberg in nearly seven years." Released from jail on a writ of Habeas Corpus the following morning, Howard still refused to give the name of his fellow passenger. One Los Angeles newspaper ran this headline: MISSING BEAUTY HOLDS KEY TO DEATH.

Surprisingly, Howard still refused to name his passenger. It was only when a reporter tracked down Pat DeCicco later that day that he identified the woman as Nancy Bell Bayly of Santa Barbara. It is not known if his revealing the identity of Howard's date caused a strain in his relationship with his boss.

Damaging testimony was provided by Walter Scott, a driver for United Parcel Service. He claimed that Gabe Meyer had been standing in the trolley car safety zone. He testified that he saw Howard's car speeding toward the zone, and that he noted at the time that "the driver was real erratic—I thought it was some drunk at the wheel."

At the July 15, 1936 coroner's inquest, Nancy made a stunning appearance. She made eye contact with Howard, who only smiled. No words were exchanged between them. For the occasion, she was chicly dressed in a new black Chanel suit, with a string of white freshwater pearls. She carried a black lizard-skin bag and matching black lizard-skin shoes.

Throughout the inquest, she nervously toyed with a diamond-studded wristwatch that Howard had presented to her in Santa Barbara. She completely backed up his testimony.

Howard's biggest break came from Scott, the United Parcel driver. He recanted his previous testimony claiming that "I was mistaken." In his new version, Meyer was "staggering across the street—obviously drunk when he stepped right in front of the Duesenberg which was traveling at a safe speed." At the end of the inquest, Howard was found not guilty. He later announced to the press that, "I've never been drunk in my life."

There was speculation that Neil McCarthy had bribed the notorious district attorney of Los Angeles, Buron Fitts, who was always willing to take a payoff whenever a celebrity, usually a movie star, ran into trouble.

Howard learned from Dietrich that the members of Gabe Meyer's family were "outraged" at the verdict. The victim left behind one brother, Mendel Meyer, along with married sisters Viola Davis, Stella Carlisle, Rose Schiff, and Laura Loewenthal. Howard ordered Dietrich to "send each of the bereaved a check for five thousand in this their time of need." He never heard from any of the Meyer clan again.

Back in Santa Barbara, Nancy recalled that, "I waited and waited for Howard to call me after the case was settled. He never did. Finally, I made a call to my former beau, Ronald Channell, and he took me back into his good graces. As far as Howard Hughes was concerned, it was CASE CLOSED. I never saw him ever again."

***

Los Angeles, 1936

Under threatening skies, Katharine Hepburn was playing a game of golf at the Bel Air Country Club.

"Hughes landed a Scout on a very narrow expanse of greens," she later told Laura Harding, her longtime companion. "He had to maneuver between two towering pine trees. He had only three feet on either side for his wings to clear. The manager of the club ran out and started to denounce the pilot until he saw it was Howard Hughes. He didn't want to anger Hughes too much, fearing he might buy the golf course and fire the manager."

Kate said that after Howard emerged from the Scout, he played nine holes with her and then she drove him to the Beverly Hills Hotel. Since the plane couldn't take off on the greens, the Scout had to be disassembled and towed back to the hangar in Burbank, all at a cost of ten thousand dollars.

Kate remembered letting Howard off in front of the hotel. Before getting out, he turned to her and said, "Miss Hepburn, I plan to make you my next wife."

"I'll have a lot to say about that!" she said, before shooing him out of her car and driving off into a fading afternoon.

CHAPTER TWELVE
Los Angeles, 1936

Kate Hepburn finally accepted an invitation for a date with Howard, thus launching one of the most publicized romances of the 20th century. Only the best-connected members of the Hollywood community knew how unconventional the relationship would become. After all, Howard and Kate were each among the oddest of the Hollywood oddballs.

When director Howard Hawks first heard about the romance, he quite accurately summed up the attraction. "Howard, in spite of his pursuit of the most glamorous women in Hollywood, was actually looking for a mother. Kate, on the other hand, wanted a golf partner and someone to teach her to fly." Kate revealed the details of her first "date" with Howard to her favorite director, George Cukor, who was a bit gossipy.

Howard instinctively knew that Kate was far too independent a New Englander to be added to his stable of conquests. Throughout the course of their relationship, she'd have a life of her own and never be dependent on him for money, although he would occasionally contribute cash to help her career.

He also sensed that none of the labels placed on him by the press would impress her—moviemaker, matinee idol, handsome playboy, genius inventor, or even billionaire. She would be impressed not by his money or power, but by his daring feats in the air. "He also played a great game of golf," Kate told Cukor, "although not in my league."

When she agreed to get into Howard's car outside Cukor's house after one of the director's Sunday afternoon parties, he immediately delivered the following line. "You'd be ideal as my mate. In you, I could find the perfect woman," he told her. "You're the only woman I've ever met who has the beauty and sensuality of my mother." Those may not be Howard's exact words, but they were later repeated by Kate to Cukor, who then paraphrased them to others.

As Cary Grant had accurately predicted, Kate went for "the mother bait." As Howard drove her to Santa Monica, she wanted to ask many questions about his mother. But first, she complimented him on his choice of vehicle. As everyone knew, Howard could have bought a fleet of the world's most expensive vehicles, including the company that built them. A girlfriend who loomed in Howard's future, Ava Gardner, would sometimes refuse to get inside one of his junky vehicles. In vivid contrast, Kate referred to his jalopy as a "hoot." He explained to her that he'd borrowed the broken-down car from his cook.

It was not only battered, but filthy. The cook apparently didn't like to eat his own food but preferred hamburgers to go, along with bottles of orange juice, all the empty containers thrown haphazardly into the back seat. She was particularly amused that there was no hood to conceal the ferocious-looking, rusty engine, which looked as if it were going to expire before ever reaching the sands of Santa Monica.

"A jalopy without a hood—perfect for me," she exclaimed, or so she later said. "I don't know about you, personally, but I believe that no car should be retired until it gives off its last gasp."

She leaned back and let the breezes blow through her red hair. Here she was, riding with the richest man in the world in a God-awful car. She couldn't have been happier, as she was later to report, and she began to like this unconventional man in spite of his fickle reputation. Sometimes if there was a noise on the road, as from a passing truck, he couldn't hear her exact words, but he always nodded and smiled in agreement regardless of what she said.

When she learned that his plan for the evening involved taking her to a public restaurant, she absolutely refused, claiming she never dined out. "I can't stand to have people watch me eat," she claimed. "It literally makes me faint."

When he pulled the car to a stop at The Rusty Pelican, he turned and faced her squarely. He looked thin and bronzed, with dark, searching eyes that seemed to take in every detail of her own slim frame. "Don't you think I know that already?" he asked. "Cary has told me everything. The restaurant is reserved for just the two of us tonight. I don't like people either. We'll be alone."

Persuaded to go in, she was happily surprised to see that The Rusty Pelican lived up to its promise. An all-male band had been hired for the night, and the eight-man waitstaff existed only for the two of them.

In the restaurant, she appraised his clothes more carefully. He was a towering beanpole in a pair of khaki trousers she knew all too well, as she herself had bought an equivalent pair at a local department store for one dollar and ninety-eight cents. What made his pants intriguing was that they came within six inches of reaching his ankles, and his "time-capsule" old jacket had sleeves that also came within six inches of reaching his wrists. His two-toned shoes in brown and white were scruffed up. What particularly amused her was that instead of a belt, he held up his pants with an old tie with a ragged edge.

If the extensive kitchen staff thought it was going to be an evening of lobster, caviar, and champagne, they were disappointed. Howard, as she was to learn, always ate the same meal every night: a ten-ounce and very lean steak, a small helping of canned—never fresh—peas, and a dessert of one scoop of vanilla ice cream with a caramel topping.

She was appropriately modest in her demands, ordering only a grilled chicken breast and three side dishes followed by instructions not to overcook the vegetables. Unlike Howard's canned peas, she insisted that all her food be fresh.

He figured that since he was paying for the band, he might as well avail himself of its music. He asked her to dance. At RKO she'd never even tried to compete with Ginger Rogers for dancing roles with Fred Astaire. If called upon, Kate could dance a little. Howard also offered Astaire no competition. On the dance floor, he held her so tightly that her feet were hardly touching the floor. She called him "the Bear-Hugger," and was greatly relieved when they could return to table.

Instead of champagne, both of them ordered plain tap water, although a wine steward was standing impatiently by with nothing to do. The bartender hired for the night waited in vain for drink orders that never came. She had had enough to drink that afternoon at Cukor's party.

Before the night was over, Howard won her sympathy by telling her the full story of his relationship with Allene, even describing the masturbation in the pink porcelain bowl. Partly because she had grown up as the daughter of a liberal New England doctor, she was not as shocked as most women would have been. Her family had confronted such matters head-on—birth control, venereal disease. Dr. Thomas Hepburn even told his family at the dinner table, though his children were quite young, about evidence of incest he'd encountered among the cases brought before him.

Cukor later claimed that "Howard won her heart that night. Kate wasn't seeking a stud who'd knock her over the head with a club and drag her back to his cave. She liked people with problems, male or female. Of course, she was a bit cocky—then and now—and always felt she could solve any problem. Her father had wanted her to be a doctor like himself. I always felt she'd have done better as a dictatorial psychiatrist. To me, she seemed to feel that Howard had entrusted her with very secret information."

"None of Howard's close associates, and very few of Kate's friends and confidants really expected the relationship to be very sexual," Cukor claimed. "Kate obviously wasn't Howard's type. If he had a type at the time, it was Ginger Rogers. This gets a little complex here. But I feel that, in Kate, Howard found a playmate. In one person, he'd met the perfect tomboy he'd

The Odd Couple: A Tabloid Romance

always wanted to be with. He also had found the one woman in Hollywood who could mother him, which is what he wanted from Kate all along. I think he was actually looking forward to coming down with his first cold so that Kate could attend to his needs and cook him her own version of chicken soup."

"For sex during his long relationship with Kate, Howard had so many others to turn to," Cukor said. "Ginger Rogers. Fay Wray. Robert Taylor. Tyrone Power. So many others, so very many others, including several New York debutantes. He even went after my two favorite sisters, the very beautiful and talented Joan Fontaine and the equally beautiful and even more talented Olivia de Havilland. My God, I left out Cary Grant. How could I have done that? The big question about Howard's relationship with Kate was when did he find time to see her? Naturally, she wasn't sitting at home knitting by the fireplace, waiting for her man. During their so-called romance, she also had a number of affairs on the side with both men and women, everybody from Leland Hayward to John Ford, from Laura Harding to Claudette Colbert. If any couple in Hollywood pioneered what is called today an open relationship, it was Howard Hughes and Katharine Hepburn. In some ways, Cary Grant was right: they were perfect for each other."

The next morning, in the wake of her bizarre date with Howard, Kate called her closest confidants to report on the evening: George Cukor, as noted above, Kenneth MacKenna, and Anderson Lawler. "Howard is like a little boy, so different from his playboy image," she said. "He doesn't need a woman in the sense that a conventional man needs a female mate. Since I'll never have a son, I might as well adopt him."

When Howard in his private plane flew over Kate's house the morning of the next day, he dipped his wings as if to acknowledge that they had embarked on what might be called a love affair.

It was to become the strangest relationship of Kate's life.

Howard had flown into her life without warning. After their bizarre dinner together, he had flown out just as mysteriously. She had no idea where he'd gone or when—or if—he'd be back.

***

Hartford, 1936

Katharine Hepburn's most recent film, *Quality Street*, had played to practically empty theaters. Dr. Thomas Hepburn, her father, told her to quit making "silly period pictures" and to accept the role of *Jane Eyre*, as a means of reinforcing her reputation as a serious dramatic actress. Apparently he was ignoring the fact that *Jane Eyre* itself was a period piece.

Upon her arrival in Hartford, Kate found one hundred roses—"the most perfect ever grown"—waiting for her along with a diamond bracelet from Howard. She kept the flowers, but returned the diamonds with a note. "Dear

Howard," she wrote, "I've been accused of many things. But a prostitute I'm not. Your bracelet is beautiful, but not my style. Of men, I've never demanded—no ice, no dice. Love, Your Country Mouse."

For some reason known only to himself, Howard had dubbed her "Country Mouse." Whatever she was, Katharine Hepburn was no mouse, country or otherwise.

Jane Eyre opened on December 26, 1936 in New Haven. One thousand long-stemmed roses arrived backstage for Kate. She read the note: "Dear Country Mouse. Become the mouse that roared. Love, Howard."

That night when Kate went on, she felt that the audience didn't respond to her appearance in *Jane Eyre*. With her film career in shambles, she acutely feared failure on the stage. Filled with dread and anxiety, and regretting her decision to go on the road with *Jane Eyre*, she headed for a shaky run in Boston.

***

Boston, 1937

Feeling rather lonely, Kate checked into The Ritz Hotel in Boston. Her only companion was a stout-hearted, no-nonsense Yorkshire woman, Emily Perkins, her secretary. Rather mannish and speaking in a brogue, she had met Kate when she'd served as her wardrobe mistress on the John Ford film, *Mary of Scotland*. Kate had nicknamed her "Em."

As Em slept in an adjoining small maid's room, Kate had gone to bed in the master bedroom at around nine-thirty. At midnight, she heard a door opening. Jumping up, she reached for her gown to investigate who the intruder was.

When she flipped on the lights, she saw Howard standing in the living room of her suite. He'd booked the suite next door and had bribed a hotel clerk to open the locked door to her connecting quarters.

"He looked so helpless and lovesick, I couldn't object," she later told her friends. "I likened him to John the Baptist about to lose his head."

He stayed up talking to her until three o'clock that morning. He even ordered champagne sent up. She joined him for two glasses but that was her limit, although he managed to down three bottles. This was an amazing test for him. He rarely consumed alcohol. But he was filled with a particular excitement on this night and wanted to share a secret with her.

He appeared nervous and apprehensive and used the champagne to steady his nerves. She feared that he might be driving himself toward a nervous breakdown, as he would so often in his future.

As she later told her confidants, including George Cukor, she thought that after all the roses and the diamond bracelet that he was going to declare his undying love for her.

His secret turned out to be quite different, although infinitely more exciting in terms of the world. He revealed that in a few days, when strong winds would be coming in from the Pacific Ocean, blowing behind any airplane headed eastward, he was going to attempt to break his own transcontinental speed record.

Impulsively, she asked if she could fly with him.

He looked amazed at her suggestion. "There's room for only one person—the pilot." Sensing her disappointment, he offered to teach her how to fly.

As she was to tell her pal, Anderson Lawler, upon her return to Hollywood, "Howard didn't even kiss me—not even on the cheek. I'm beginning to think he's more homosexual than bisexual. He shared his great dream with me, but the telling of it seemed to sap all his energy. He fell asleep on my sofa. I got a blanket for him. Don't believe all those stories from maids who were given a hundred dollars to report that they caught us together, going at it like animals in heat. We became great friends on the night he 'broke' into my suite like a rapist. Poor Howard. I doubt if he really knows how to rape a woman. In his heart, he remains mommie's little boy."

***

Chicago, 1937

After their unexpected encounter in Boston, Howard disappeared to "wherever he disappeared to," in Kate's words. Some of his disappearances have been explained; others have not. Billy Haines, who knew about some of them, claimed that Howard would sometimes meet a handsome stranger—male—and lure him away from his job. "None of those hot studs lost financially by going away with Howard," Noah Dietrich claimed. "He could be pursuing a woman on the A-list, such as the Hepburn dame, although I never saw what the attraction was. She was definitely not his type. Then he'd abandon her for an affair of the moment."

Wherever he'd gone, Howard suddenly flew in for Kate's appearance at the opening night of *Jane Eyre* in Chicago. Later, when he was spotted in the theater, the Chicago press went on red alert. "We dealt with the story with the same excitement we'd handle any other, even, say, the assassination of President Roosevelt," claimed Johanton Elder, a reporter at the time. "In other words, 'Second Coming' headlines."

On the second night of *Jane Eyre*, crowds formed around the theater—not just playgoers but thousands of local fans wanting to catch a glimpse of the famous couple. Howard and Kate seemed to enjoy the various ruses they used to escape their fans and the rubberneckers. Once, Kate arrived at the theater in a garbage truck, entering through the back alley.

Almost overnight, Howard Hughes and Katharine Hepburn became the most famous couple in America. There was endless speculation about their possible marriage. Actually, Howard had already proposed to her in the interconnecting suites they shared on the ninth floor of the Ritz Hotel.

Their relationship still hadn't been consummated. "He hadn't even kissed me yet,"

Kate later told Cukor. However, Howard did present her the largest diamond ring she'd ever seen as an engagement ring, perhaps forgetting that she'd rejected his "ice" before. Not only a ring, he also gave her the same diamond bracelet she'd returned to him previously, plus a new diamond tiara.

In essence, Howard had given her a fortune in diamonds during some of the darkest days of the worldwide Depression. Perhaps to show her disdain, she did not wear the ring, which she left, along with the bracelet and tiara, unguarded in her dressing room. When she returned to her dressing room after her third night's performance, she found that the jewelry had been stolen.

Fearing headlines, she never reported the loss to the police, nor did she tell Howard what had happened.

Just as mysteriously as he'd appeared in Chicago, he disappeared again. This time Kate knew where he was heading. Flying to Los Angeles, he arrived at the Hughes Aircraft hanger to prepare for his historic flight across America, hoping to break his own record. He called her every night to keep her abreast of what was happening.

Back in Hollywood, Cary Grant seemed pleased that Howard had taken his advice about pursuing Kate. He told friends, "They've turned into a mutual admiration society, and they have more in common than bad dressing, of which each is the worst in his or her category." In a phone call to Cary and later to Cukor, Kate claimed that she admired Howard's "verve and stamina," although the latter had never been demonstrated in her bed. "He's at the top of the available men in the world, and I of the women," she rather immodestly claimed. "And both of us have a wild desire to be famous."

She had already succeeded in making the world aware of her presence. In a few days, Howard was to become even more celebrated than she was. Howard told Cary and his associates that Kate was a "brilliant woman—totally without pretense, without sham of any kind. She is, in fact, the most totally magnetic woman on the planet."

Actually, it was Howard who was keeping Kate in the headlines. She was on the verge of joining the long list of actors whose careers had soared brilliantly in the Thirties, but which had descended into a kind of twilight on the eve of World War II as new stars, among them Lana Turner and Betty Grable, rose to take their places.

As she faced the possible end of her career, Kate was twenty-eight years old. But Howard, at the age of thirty, was just on the dawn of his greatest acclaim. As a man, he was viewed as the single most desirable catch in the world.

***

Burbank/Newark, 1937

Although the Empire of Japan was plotting to devour China, and Hitler was involved with "the final solution to the Jewish problem," and poised to conquer all of Europe, much of America focused on the exploits of Howard Hughes as he prepared to break his own transcontinental record. Of almost equal interest was the possibility of his marriage to Katharine Hepburn.

It was windy and foggy at 2:14am on January 19, 1937, when Howard in his radically reconfigured *Winged Bullet*, which had cost him $125,000, taxied down the tarmac of the Union Air Terminal in Burbank. For the first time he'd be using his "continuous feed" oxygen mask. Banking his aircraft over the Sierra Nevada mountains, Howard flew into an uncertain voyage in total darkness. Nothing at the time, perhaps, seemed as distant as the East Coast of the United States.

Just before takeoff, Howard had second thoughts about flying across the country, since much of America, especially the Middle West, lay under a heavy cloud cover. The winds were behind him, though, and he carried a potentially dangerous 280 gallons of aviation fuel.

Even at 15,000 feet and above the cloud level, the weather was still rough, the winds choppy. He chose to go even higher, rising at least another 3,000 feet. At this level, he didn't trust his instruments for accurate measurements.

As he entered airspace over Arizona, trouble set in.

"I couldn't breathe," he later related. "I was gasping for air, but my oxygen mask wasn't working properly. I moved my fingers but couldn't feel my right hand on the throttle. I felt my brain swelling like it was going to bust. I was hurtling through space. It was a pit of darkness out there. At the time I was going three-hundred and fifty miles an hour. I desperately pulled on my oxygen mask. No luck! My oxygen had been trapped by an air bubble. I didn't think I could drop altitude in time to save myself. Don't tell anyone, but I was sobbing hysterically. Finally, in a fit of desperation, I actually bit through the rubber hose feeding into the mask. My left arm was numb, and I sucked the air into my lungs just at the moment I felt I was going to pass out. As I sucked in the air, my paralysis receded. As I flew across the country, the throbbing pain in my head was unbearable. All I could do for relief was to scream for periods of about five minutes at a time. Only then could I focus on the dials."

Another astonishing fact emerged. Before take-off, he'd been awake in Los Angeles for a total of thirty hours. Knowing the long and arduous air voyage that lay ahead of him, it is not known why he'd made such a reckless decision and had failed to get the much-needed sleep he'd need before embarking on such a flight.

It was while Howard was flying over Arizona that America, including Kate in Chicago, learned that the aviator had lost radio contact. Announcers speculated that his plane had crashed.

Much of the country was listening to radio sets as an official bulletin from the National Aeronautical Association came over the airwaves. The world was informed that no word had been received from the "millionaire playboy hero of the air"—those were the official words of the NAA—for five hours. It was presumed that the *Winged Bullet* was lost. Search parties were rapidly formed in the Southwest to seek out the wreckage and whatever remained of the pilot's body.

The event was frontpage news around the world. *The Chicago Daily Tribune's* banner headline proclaimed AVIATION HERO LOST!

In reality, Howard was flying over America's vast Middle West, where he'd picked up a tail wind he later described as "lusty." In the foothills of the Appalachian Mountains, the heavy cloud cover began to give way. He could see land, realizing he was flying over the rolling farmlands of Pennsylvania. Suddenly, unknown to Howard, a bulletin came across the Associated Press wires. A pilot coming in for a landing at Army Field in Middleton, Pennsylvania, had spotted *The Bullet*. HOWARD HUGHES ALIVE! screamed a banner newspaper headline in Chicago.

He had begun what was later termed as his "long glide" into Newark, New Jersey. At long last the airport came into view. Without radio contact, he feared he might collide with another plane.

To his horror, he spotted a United Airlines airplane that had been cleared for take-off. Employing what pilots call a *chandelle* maneuver, something he'd learned from Roscoe Turner during the making of *Hell's Angels*, he circled the airport for nearly twenty minutes waiting for the commercial airliner to become airborne.

Once the United flight had cleared his airspace, his silver racer "just seemed to shoot out of the clouds," in the words of one radio announcer. Going at the astonishing rate of three-hundred and eighty miles an hour, it plunged toward the earth in less than a minute, a distance of 12,000 feet. Observers thought the plane was in a tailspin and heading for a crash.

Safely on the ground, Howard emerged from the cockpit looking weary to the point of collapse. Reporters noticed that he was wearing the same double-breasted suit he'd worn on his first record-breaking flight across the continent.

Finally, the news that America had been waiting for came over the air. "Howard Hughes, millionaire aviator and playboy, has landed in Newark at 12:45pm Eastern Standard Time. He left Burbank, California, seven and a half hours ago and has slashed his own speed record for flying across the continent by one hundred and seventeen minutes. Feared lost for five hours, he has emerged as an aviation hero, his fame and achievement topped only by Charles Lindbergh." Even before Howard was on the ground, commercial aviation experts were predicting coast-to-coast flights for everybody at the record-breaking speeds.

The actual record he set was seven hours, twenty-eight minutes, and twenty-five seconds.

Hundreds of people began to descend on Newark Airport, hoping for a glimpse of Howard. After disembarking from the plane, he told the press, "I heard somebody else was going to try and break my record, so I decided to beat him to it." He was referring to aviator Frank Hawks, owner of a racer, *Time Flies*. After hearing about Howard's record-breaking flight, Hawks abandoned his own plan.

From the office of the airport's manager, Howard sent a telegram to Kate: "Am down and safe at Newark, Love, Howard."

No doubt about it. Howard Hughes was the undisputed pilot of the year. "Although known to millions before that flight, his name truly became a household word the moment he stepped onto the tarmac at Newark," Dietrich said in Los Angeles.

When word reached Chicago, where Kate was still appearing in *Jane Eyre,* thousands of fans were waiting, fully anticipating that the wedding of the famous aviator and the fabled actress would take place in the Windy City.

***

Chicago, 1937

Hughes Jr., with Noah Dietrich

With Howard safely on the ground, speculation renewed again over the possibility of an imminent marriage to Kate. Theresa Helburn, a leading spokesperson for the Theater Guild, the outfit that was staging the Chicago production of *Jane Eyre*, was delighted at the box office receipts generated by the alleged Hughes/Hepburn affair. "In America at least, interest was greater than in King Edward VIII's giving up his throne to marry 'the woman I love,'" Helburn claimed.

Howard flew to Chicago, where he booked an adjoining suite to Kate's at her hotel. There he would resume his "hot but chaste romance" (her words).

She was so overjoyed at his safe return and his incredible accomplishment that after her performance in *Jane Eyre* that night, "I got smashed, along with Howard," she revealed to actress Patricia Peardon. "We toasted and toasted, then toasted some more. I told Howard, 'for two people addicted to fame, we have gone beyond our wildest fantasies.'"

He pressed her for an answer to his marriage proposal but she still put him off. That night newspapers broke a story from the Cook County clerk's office. The clerk, Michael J. Flynn, claimed that a "man said to be an agent for Mr. Hughes" had called to inquire about what requirements were necessary to obtain a marriage license in Cook County. The clerk also reported that the manager of Chicago's Ambassador Hotel, where Kate and Howard were staying,

378

had also placed a similar call earlier that day.

The next morning, Kate and Howard awoke in separate beds to read the latest headline proclamations: HUGHES AND HEPBURN TO MARRY TODAY.

An enormous mob of people descended on the theater. Kate wondered if she'd be able to reach the stage door in safety. She later told her beloved "Em": "I feel like a fox cornered by a pack of snarling hounds."

She couldn't be seen anywhere in public without having to face the question, "When's the wedding?" or "How's Howie?"

The following afternoon, a crowd of screaming teenage girls, whose numbers were estimated at three thousand, ignored the recent snowfall and virtually staged a riot as Kate arrived at the theater to rehearse some script changes for *Jane Eyre*.

By the time the curtain went up that night, radio announcers were claiming that some ten thousand spectators—"and not just teenagers"—would be descending on the theater where *Jane Eyre* was playing.

By four o'clock that afternoon, Mr. Flynn, the Cook County clerk, held a press conference. He claimed that he would hold his office open late that night for the arrival of "America's most celebrated lovebirds." Reporters noted that Flynn was wearing a new navy blue pin-striped suit with a maroon-colored carnation with a matching tie.

His gesture was in vain. At 5:15pm that same afternoon, the concierge at the Ambassador Hotel released a message to the press. "Miss Hepburn wishes to announce that she and Mr. Howard Hughes will not marry today."

Enigmatically, headlines in the *Chicago Daily Tribune* the next morning proclaimed: LA HEPBURN'S WEDDING DAY IS REALLY SOMETHING!

Howard told Kate that he had to have an answer to his marriage proposal before curtain time that night. Even as late as fifteen minutes before she was called to the stage, she still hadn't decided what to do.

Because of the thousands of people waiting outside his hotel, Howard dared not risk coming to the actual theater, but remained in his suite.

She delayed her answer until just five minutes before curtain time, as he waited patiently on the phone.

Just as she was heading out of her dressing room, she picked up the receiver, "It's your Country Mouse," she said to him in the presence of "Em." "Yes, God damn it, let's stop all this fuss once and for all. I'm going to become the second Mrs. Howard Hughes, and a hell of a lot better wife to you than Ella Rice."

Before flying out of Chicago, he telegrammed his staff "to get ready for the arrival of one Miss Katharine Hepburn, about to undergo a name change. Muirfield is going to have a new mistress."

***

The Caribbean, 1937

Both Kate and her producer, Theresa Helburn, along with other Theater Guild backers, agreed that *Jane Eyre* was not ready to face the harsh critics of New York. To save face, Helburn announced that the play's Broadway opening had been postponed because of film commitments by Kate. That was a lie. No producer in Hollywood, and Howard was very aware of this, was offering her any role.

The play, however, still had bookings outside of New York, and Kate slogged through previews in cities that included St. Louis, Toledo, Columbus, and Pittsburgh. Her relief from the tedium of these provincial shows revolved around Howard's unexpected arrivals. He would fly in and out of a city where she was appearing. In fact, he was in the theater in Washington, D.C., when this tedious play "mercifully" folded after a road-show run of only fourteen weeks.

She accepted an invitation from her groom-to-be to sail the Caribbean aboard his spectacular yacht, the *Southern Cross*.

On the first day of their sail, Kate was "burning alive with my ambition to fly instead of sail." She told him that the only thing she had waiting for her in Hollywood was the series of flying lessons he'd promised her.

Eager to install her at Muirfield, Howard agreed to take time out from his many business affairs and aviation interests to personally give her the lessons that any trained pilot could have taught instead.

With her acting career advancing sluggishly, at least temporarily, Kate pursued her dreams of carving out a career in aviation. She wrote John Ford, "Soon the world will forget that Charles Lindbergh and Amelia Earhart ever existed. When aviation history is written in the future, it will have chapters devoted to the exploits of Katharine Hepburn and Howard Hughes."

Aboard the *Southern Cross*, sailing first to Nassau, then on to Jamaica, Howard confided to her his most ambitious plan to date. He wanted to fly around the world, breaking all previous records. She was enthralled.

As she would later say, "Right then and there, I knew that I didn't want John Ford, but this great man of vision and dreams, Howard Hughes. John and I were merely making entertainment for the masses—in my case, not even doing that. Howard was writing history with all the daring of a Columbus. I found him absolutely fascinating. In spite of my earlier indecision, I more and more wanted to be less Miss Katharine Hepburn and more Mrs. Howard Hughes, a name I would wear with pride, unlike what I did with my first husband. Of course, even with Howard, a lady is entitled to change her mind."

***

Los Angeles, 1937-1938

Back in Los Angeles, Kate moved into the Muirfield mansion, chasing away the ghosts of Howard's former wife, Ella Rice, and of that great beauty, Billie Dove. It was a beautiful spring day. Only that morning, Kate had read in a Hollywood column that she and Howard had been named "the world's most romantic couple."

She didn't arrive at Muirfield alone. Kate brought some baggage that included, naturally, her personal maid, Johanna Madsen. Although she used to drive herself around Hollywood, Kate had acquired a personal chauffeur, Louis Prysing. Johanna no longer did all the cooking, that assignment going to Ranghild Prysing, Louis's wife. None of this new staff of permanent guests set well with Richard Dreher, Howard's personal valet and *major-domo*. He also wasn't impressed when "Button," Kate's French poodle, immediately bit his ankle. She also brought along two cocker spaniels—one gray, Mica, another black, who answered to the name of Pete.

The *major-domo* assigned Kate "to the bedroom of the first wife," as he put it. He proudly proclaimed it "the master bedroom."

"Where is Mr. Hughes going to sleep?" Kate asked.

She was told that he preferred to sleep in a makeshift bed in his private study, directly above her master bedroom.

"I guess that way I can hear him walking around during his sleepless nights," she said.

Howard's staff also had to make way for a collection of Kate's New England antiques that arrived in a truck the next day, along with her wardrobe—mostly slacks—and a virtual library of books and plays.

To her astonishment, Kate found that many of the rooms at Muirfield were locked. Even some of the rooms that were open were darkened by black velvet draperies. She set out immediately to order some spring cleaning, demanding that the curtains be pulled back and the windows opened to let in the fresh California air. She was truly establishing herself as the *châtelaine* of Muirfield—and not just in name only.

Cary Grant later said that Howard's time with Kate was the most peaceful and stabilizing of his life, even though they were definitely the odd couple. He constantly urged them toward matrimony, although she couldn't help but notice that while she slept alone, it was Cary Grant himself who arrived at least two nights a week to share Howard's bed.

Even so, for a few weeks she genuinely liked her life with Howard. Their two shared passions were not for each other, but for playing golf and flying. Day after day, regardless of how busy he was, he taught her to become an aviator. She seemed to like flying a hell of a lot more than appearing before a movie camera.

Later during her tenure at Muirfield, he placed his most beloved possession on the mantelpiece in his parlor. It was the Harmon International Trophy. (Established in 1926, and administered since 1950 by the Smithsonian Institution, it acknowleges excellence in aviation—particularly flying.) In 1938, the trophy was awarded to Hughes by President Franklin D. Roosevelt himself. Somehow, the president's blessings seemed to be the final endorsement Howard needed to qualify him as a genuine aviation hero.

Nonetheless, Howard assured Kate every night that his greatest achievements were yet to come. He also had something else to be elated about. As the world moved toward war, the American economy was slowly coming out of the Great Depression. That brought resurgence to the Hughes Tool Company. More and more orders were pouring in every day, and he was getting richer and richer.

Muirfield mansion adjoined the Wilshire Country Club. All Kate and Howard had to do was climb over a rather modest fence to play golf, sometimes thirty-six holes a day.

"Even if I talk, which as you know I do all the time," Kate told John Ford, "Howard can't hear half of what I'm saying. His deafness seems to grow worse by the day. I think one day he's going to live alone in darkness and silence—a sad life, really."

Pursued by reporters and photographers, Kate had entered the most ostentatious phase of her life as the so-called mistress of Howard Hughes. It was a world of vast amounts of money, of flying in airplanes he piloted, or sailing yachts down to Mexico or over to Catalina Island. Occasionally they went out to formal affairs, Howard having to rent a tuxedo or she having to borrow a gown, but mostly they avoided such gatherings, preferring to be by themselves or to entertain at home.

"They certainly believed in staying clean," their servant, Richard Dreher, would later say. "Miss Hepburn always took six to eight cold showers a day, and the poor laundress, Florence Foster, was kept busy pressing their table linen and the five or six clean shirts Mr. Hughes insisted on wearing in one day. He was obsessed with germs and would change his underwear eight times a day—that is, on the days he wore underwear. He always insisted that his shorts be carefully pressed. He felt that the heat from the iron destroyed germs."

"Even if he only had to urinate," Dreher claimed, "he always carefully washed his genitals after he was through. If he had a bowel movement, he would insist on a complete bath followed by a shower to rinse off any residual uncleanliness. It was truly amazing. The table would always be set with the best of crystal goblets and Haviland china. Even though sparkling clean, Mr. Hughes would often return to the kitchen to wash his plate, glass, and utensils before he would eat."

Johanna Madsen was always amused when she'd bring Kate some tea in the parlor, Dreher related. Even on the hottest of days, a fire would be roaring in the large colonial-style fireplace. Howard never dressed around the house, but was seen wearing his favorite but tattered old maroon-colored robe and a pair of frayed house slippers. Kate insisted that the windows stay open, and she and Howard always fought over her demand, as he claimed she was letting germs into his house. They had other battles, too, mainly over her smoking. He could not abide tobacco smoke.

382

Sometimes, Kate could be persuaded to go out on the town accompanied by both Howard and Cary Grant. During one of these events, Kate made one of her infrequent appearances at a restaurant, the Cock 'n Bull, and lit up. After she'd taken one puff, Howard leaned over and took the cigarette from her mouth, violently crushing it out in an ashtray. Cary thought that she might put up a fight, but he claimed she said nothing and immediately changed the subject and appeared light and gay for the rest of the evening.

Howard finally won the tobacco war. In time, Kate gave up cigarettes.

One night he came home early. He never told her where he was going or where he'd been. "Tonight I'm going to reveal my greatest dream to you," he claimed. "It's going to make us married before we actually wed."

She misinterpreted what he'd said, thinking that at long last he was going to come to her bed to consummate their relationship.

Instead of coming to her bedroom, he invited her to go for a ride with him. "You're going to see a part of me I've shown to no other woman," he told her. "Only Cary Grant has seen it before you."

"I assume you're talking about your cock," she said flippantly.

Impulsively, he slapped her face.

Before they reached the airfield, he apologized and won her forgiveness for slapping her. To make up, he promised to take her on a glorious trip to San Francisco. In the meantime, he wanted to share his special treasure with her.

He had hired Ralph Langer, a pilot he paid in cash off the books, to work at his hangar a few weeks. The young blond pilot was so startlingly handsome that Kate wondered if Howard wanted him for something other than piloting. Langer's face lit up when he saw Howard drive up, although he showed disappointment—"perhaps jealousy" as she later told Cukor—when he was introduced to Kate.

Langer opened the hangar, and Howard ushered Kate in to see his sparkling Sikorsky S-43. This was a twin-engine amphibian with seating for a crew of six. It could hold enough fuel to fly across the Atlantic Ocean.

He was like a little boy with a treasured toy, showing off his new aircraft to Kate. He invited her aboard, smelling the scent of the new red leather upholstery with her. He pointed out all the features of the plane, even the camel-colored carpeting. "The plane cost half-a-million dollars," he said proudly. "But I can afford it."

He informed her that in this little plane, he was going to encircle the globe. "I won't be some hotshot aviator in some fucking air race. I'll make history. My flight will show the world that the future of commercial aviation is unlimited. Passengers will regularly fly from New York to London or Paris. Commercial aviation will mark the end of the great transatlantic ocean liners."

He filled her with his enthusiasm, and she begged him to let her go with him on the flight. He refused.

"It was that very night, in spite of the jealous eyes of Langer boring in on me, that I knew I was truly in love with Howard Hughes," she later told friend Kenneth MacKenna. "Maybe my love only lasted one week, but it was love for as long as it lasted. I was overwhelmed with his raw courage, his sense of adventure. Actors I had known such as John Barrymore and Van Heflin didn't seem to matter any more. When compared to Howard Hughes, not even directors like George Stevens mattered. Even great writers such as Ernest Hemingway were diminished when compared to Howard. And, yes, my white heat passion for John Ford was mellowing into a friendship. As I became more and more involved with Howard, John seemed less and less real for me. Here I was standing with a man about to circumnavigate the globe and make history, and John didn't even have the balls to leave that shrewish wife of his!"

She claimed that the next few weeks were like bliss for her. Sometimes, with her piloting their small craft, they flew to Catalina and swam nude in the tranquil waters of the lagoon. Although she normally liked to go to bed early, he would keep her up all night with plans for his global flight. She constantly pleaded with him to take her on the flight, but he had many reasons why that would not be possible.

He did fly her to San Francisco and surprised her with the purchase of an astonishing one million dollars worth of jewelry that night. He pressed his desire to marry her. She delayed the marriage date and even returned the jewelry.

Like movie actor George Raft, and like Frank Sinatra in years to come, Howard sometimes socialized with gangsters who included the violent mobster Lucky Luciano, who was widely suspected of ordering the death of Thelma Todd. Kate was astonished one night to learn that she'd be hosting a dinner for the notorious and possibly psychotic gangster, Bugsy Siegel.

She was also surprised to learn from Muirfield's housekeeper, Beatrice Dowler, that Howard used "special dishes" for entertaining his mobster friends. Gone were the Haviland china and the crystal goblets. Out came the cheaper ware. "When the mobsters leave, Mr. Hughes orders me to destroy all the dishes they ate on. He feels their germs won't wash away even if the plates are sterilized."

Viewing it as a challenge and an adventure, Kate gallantly presided over the dinner for Bugsy. As she later told her friend Anderson Lawler, "Each of the rough-and-tumble cohorts he brought with him looked as if they could slit your throat at the slightest provocation. In fact, I'd hazard a guess that they had slit many a throat in their day."

To her surprise, she found the so-called "Casanova of the Mafia" intriguing. She even admitted to Lawler that —"on some other day"—she might have entertained a sexual proposition from him. "I know why women like Jean Harlow were attracted to him." Long before he became a bullet-riddled body in a Mafia slaying, Bugsy was good looking, well-groomed, and wearing smartly tailored clothes when he met Kate. "He was far better dressed than I was," she later said.

384

He might have started out small, stealing cars in Brooklyn, but he was at the height of his power when he was entertained by Howard and Kate. She was startled to learn that the Countess Dorothy di Frasso, the multi-millionaire divorcée, had taken up with Bugsy. The Countess had even taken Bugsy to Italy with her, where she'd introduced him to, among others, Benito Mussolini.

Kate had met the Countess previously through her friend Anderson Lawler when di Frasso became sexually involved with Gary Cooper, thereby infuriating Lawler, who was deeply in love with Cooper at the time.

Bugsy utterly fascinated Kate and Howard with his stories of adventure, including a tale about an expedition with the Countess to the Cocos Islands, a coral-based archipelago, also known as the Keeling Islands, in the Indian Ocean northwest of Australia and south of Sumatra. They'd acquired a rare, supposedly antique map in the hopes that it would guide their way to a vast trove of treasure believed to have been buried in the eighteenth century by the captain of a Spanish galleon. "We used enough dynamite to blow up New York City blasting for that damn treasure, but came up empty-handed."

A pal of George Raft, and a close acquaintance of both Clark Gable and Gary Cooper, Bugsy lived the life of a high-rolling movie star, evocative in some ways of Rudolph Valentino during his heyday. He went on gambling sprees to the French Riviera with Raft, seduced one starlet after another, and even invited Kate and Howard to spend a weekend in one of the illegal gambling houses he operated aboard an offshore casino ship.

Before his departure that evening, Bugsy shared his greatest dream with them. He claimed that "in no time at all," he was going to turn the little desert town of Las Vegas into a gambling mecca.

"I'm going to build a resort hotel out there that all of Hollywood's big shots will flock to," he predicted. He leaned over to Kate. "In fact, pretty lady, I'm going to give you the honor of naming the joint. What's it gonna be called?"

Looking over at a large photograph Howard had taken of bird life in the Florida Everglades, she said, "Oh, I don't know. Flamingo, I suppose. Something as inappropriate to a desert setting as that."

"Okay, pretty lady, you're on," Bugsy said. "Flamingo it will be."

Noah Dietrich always believed that it was at this very dinner that Howard began to think about a future dream—and that was to become the King of Las Vegas one day.

* * *

Kate was with Howard the night he learned that another Sikorsky amphibian had crashed. He was subsequently denied approval by "the Feds," as he called them, to fly an equivalent plane. At first enraged, he was then galvanized into action.

In the days and weeks ahead, he ordered his workers to begin adapting a new Lockheed 14. Unlike the disqualified six-seater Sikorsky, the new craft had room for twelve passengers. Glenn Odekirk worked for two months getting the Lockheed ready to circumnavigate the globe. The craft had to be fitted with new engines and its fuel capacity increased. Howard had purchased and installed the very latest technology and electronic equipment.

Remembering his near-death experience over northern Arizona and his loss of air and radio contact, he ordered a trio of completely independent radio systems in the event one or even two of them shut down. He also arranged for the installation of a self-contained oxygen supply system.

Kate was almost vicariously living Howard's life until the offer of a lead in a film arrived from the offices of Pandro S. Berman, then studio chief of RKO.

It was *Stage Door*.

Howard urged her to take the role, knowing what a juicy part it was. But he had serious misgivings. Kate would be cast opposite Ginger Rogers, who was rapidly toppling Kate from her throne as queen of RKO.

In truth, Howard was unable to commit to Kate, even though he kept urging her to marry him. Unknown to Kate, he continued to see Ginger both in New York and Los Angeles, even in San Francisco. That she was married to the handsome actor, Lew Ayres, at the time didn't seem to bother either Ginger or Howard.

A seventeen-year-old blond-haired Adonis, Robert Stack, quite by accident learned about the Hughes-Rogers affair when he was skeet shooting at his club. He'd just won the National Skeet Championship in St. Louis and practiced daily at the Los Angeles Skeet Shooting Club. At the time, skeet shooting was one of the most popular sports in Hollywood, taken up by such stars as Robert Taylor, Gary Cooper, and Carole Lombard, each of them a former lover of Howard's. Even Clark Gable and Ernest Hemingway were taking skeet shooting lessons.

One day Robert Stack remembered seeing Ginger Rogers in "form-fitting pink slacks," arrive at the club with a "mystery man, a tall, lanky figure with a fedora hat." Robert had been impressed that the club owner, Harry Fleischmann, was so taken with this figure that he carried the man's gun, and he never did that to even the most important of his clients, including Gable himself.

It was a month later that Robert found out that the mystery man who had accompanied Ginger was Howard Hughes himself.

Robert had a way of ingratiating himself with the Hollywood elite, and he desperately wanted to get to know Howard, since he harbored a dream of breaking into movies. He hoped that Howard would be the key to a film career.

Young Robert Stack was familiar with celebrities. His mother was a dazzling California socialite who had attended the wedding of Rudolph Valentino to Natasha Rambova. His father was an advertising executive responsible for such slogans as "the beer that made Milwaukee famous." His family had regularly entertained such celebrities as Will Rogers, Ezio Pinza, Edward G.

Robinson, and Nelson Eddy.

Robert Stack was a very heterosexual young man, and would in time be romantically linked with some of the greatest beauties in Hollywood, as would his best friend, a very young John F. Kennedy.

In 1980, when he published his autobiography, he called it *Straight Shooting*, a reference no doubt to his skeet shooting. But it could also be an indication of his sexual preference.

When he approached Howard one afternoon on the skeet-shooting range, and boldly introduced himself, it cannot be known if Robert were aware of Howard's bisexuality. But if any young man was the ideal type for Howard, it was the strikingly handsome, well-built, clean-cut all-American boy, Robert Stack.

Howard was immediately taken with the young man. In some ways, as Howard later told his associates, Robert Stack reminded him of Robert Taylor. In fact, in his debut film, *First Love*, Stack admitted to "doing a

Robert Stack

Robert Taylor imitation." Released in 1939, this film would make Robert Stack famous. In this Cinderella-like tale, he gave singing sensation, Deanna Durbin, her first on-screen smooch.

Obviously, in his autobiography, Robert didn't go into the extent of his involvement with Howard. He did admit knowing him and seeing him. The full extent of their relationship may never be known at this point.

However, shortly after Howard's initial meeting with Robert, the young man was sailing aboard the *Southern Cross* to Catalina. One of the crew members, Jeffrey Hubbard, recalled seeing Howard and Robert sunbathing in the nude. Although there were guest cabins, Robert shared the master suite with Howard at night.

Robert was flown to Mexico by Howard, and they were spotted together in San Francisco. "Their relationship lasted at least until Robert Stack joined the Navy," Noah Dietrich later claimed. "Although Howard was dressing pretty sloppy himself at the time, he purchased a new wardrobe for the kid. He bought him jewelry too. I should know because I paid the bills. I have no way of knowing if they had sex or not. Stack, I was told, was girl crazy but he spent time with Howard whenever Howard wanted him to. He once told me the kid was like a son to him. If Robert Stack were Howard's son, I think it sure looked like incest to me. During Howard's 'romance of the century,' as the fan magazines called it, with Kate Hepburn, I'd bet my bank account that he slept with the kid more than he did with Hepburn. That is, if he ever slept with Hepburn."

"Around the time he was living at Muirfield with Hepburn, and running around with Tyrone Power, Robert Taylor, and Robert Stack, Howard admitted to me he was experiencing one of his periodic bouts of impotence with women," Dietrich claimed. "He eventually solved that problem, at least temporarily. It was a unique solution."

***

New York/Hollywood, 1937

The newspapers were still filled with stories of the imminent marriage of Kate to Howard. Very few of the reporters, except for the most savvy ones, knew what was really going on. Although in later years press-shy Kate herself suggested that her relationship with Howard was one of the great loves of her life, ranking up there with Spencer Tracy, the evidence suggests otherwise.

At the time when Howard was supposed to be wooing Kate, she was spending many of her nights with film editor Jane Loring, who at least temporarily had replaced the American Express heiress, Laura Harding, in her affection.

Almost as if to humiliate her, Howard continued to date Kate's arch rival at RKO, Ginger Rogers, on the side. Once in New York, during the previous year, their dates even became public when he was seen dancing with the blonde beauty at fashionable nightclubs. One reporter, James Langford, who sometimes wrote articles for *Modern Screen*, said, "I saw Ginger and Hughes dancing together at the St. Regis Roof. I'd never seen two people so much in love. He held her real close. When they sat down at table, he didn't even look up when a waiter came to take their order. He never took his eyes off her."

It's amazing that news of Ginger and Howard didn't make it into the press, even though he continued to date her.

During one of Howard's stays at the Drake Hotel in New York, he'd invited Ginger and her overpowering mother, Lela, to sail with him aboard the *Southern Cross*. They were later spotted together at the estate of industrialist Sherman Fairchild at Lloyd's Neck, near Huntington, Long Island.

Apparently, one of the Fairchild employees, Bertha Milton, reported to Walter Winchell that Howard and Ginger were in residence and sharing the same bedroom. What Ginger's formidable mother had to say about this is not known. In those days the powerful columnist sometimes paid good money for tips like the one from Bertha. But for some reason, he didn't run this very tantalizing item.

Back at Muirfield, Kate—or so the servants and her friends reported—had not heard from Howard in weeks, even though she was living in his house.

Rather brazenly, Howard was spotted by dozens of workers when he took Ginger on a widely publicized visit to the Sikorsky helicopter plant. Surely Lew Ayres, Ginger's husband, must have been informed of these "outings," but by that time the Ayres/Rogers marriage was coming apart, even though she still professed a love for her emotionally troubled and deeply religious bisexual husband.

When Kate, in California, did receive word that Howard was flying back to Los Angeles in his Racer, she sent a message to the Drake Hotel in New York that she'd meet him at the airport. Howard cabled her not to show up. As it turned out, the reason for that was that he was flying Ginger back on that Racer because she had a film commitment at RKO.

Kate got her revenge. When Ginger returned to RKO wearing a mink coat that Howard had bought for her on Fifth Avenue in New York, she called up to the open second floor window of studio chief Pandro S. Berman. Unknown to Ginger, Kate was in the office at the time. Hearing Ginger's voice, Kate took a pitcher of water and tossed its contents down over Ginger's head and her new coat. "If it's real mink," Kate called down provocatively, "it won't shrink."

During the time Kate lived at Muirfield, Howard continued to ask for her to set a date for their marriage. He might do that when they were on the golf course of the Wilshire Country Club. At night in the arms of Ginger Rogers, he also pleaded with her to marry him.

When he experienced serious bouts of impotence in 1937, during preparations for his global flight, he devised "cures." First, he ordered Pat DeCicco to introduce him to only the most glamorous and big-busted of the young starlets arriving by train in Los Angeles from the vast plains of America. When these "luscious babes," as Pat called them, "didn't do the trick," Howard found other means to restore his vigor in the bedroom.

He'd heard that Errol Flynn and other stars, some of them aging, were patronizing a new bordello that was jokingly nicknamed "Tequila Nights." Underaged and sometimes very beautiful Mexican girls were up for grabs. The Madame of the bordello discreetly advertised that "most requests would be considered."

Howard revived a form of sexual activity remembered from his childhood. With him, he carried the pink porcelain bowl that his mother, Allene, had used when she'd gone through a brief period of masturbating her son. Instead of turning to a mother figure, however, Howard took that bowl to Tequila Nights, where he hired young Mexican girls to perform the ritual, with variations, for him.

Howard told Pat about this particular form of amusement, and Pat later reported it to his cousin, Cubby Broccoli. "I thought it was pretty disgusting," Pat claimed. "But who am I to judge? I've done some things in life I'm not proud of."

One night at Muirfield, when Kate was spending the evening with Jane Loring, Howard's housekeeper, Beatrice Dowler, said that he sat in his living room "sobbing his heart out. Here was a man who had everything in the world, or so it seemed, and he was desperately unhappy. I didn't know what to do. I'd never seen him in such despair. I felt he was going to harm himself. I went and called Cary Grant, and asked him to come over right away. In times like this, Mr. Grant seemed to know what to say to make Mr. Hughes come out of these deep, dark moods."

***

Los Angeles/London 1937-38

Howard's major attention in the winter of 1937 and the early spring of 1938 was focused on his upcoming flight around the world. When not otherwise occupied, he devoted some attention to his live-in friend, Kate, joining her whenever he could for a game of golf at the Wilshire Country Club. Somehow he still managed to fit in private rendezvous with Tyrone Power and the very young Robert Stack. "Even so," Cubby Broccoli once said, "Ginger and Cary remain the prized horses in his stable, and forgive me for comparing either of them to a horse."

Katharine Hepburn, Cary Grant

Noah Dietrich, who should know, said that Howard managed to work all these people into his life at the same time "because he saw them in shifts. Hepburn was always in bed by nine o'clock. He often had a late dinner with Ginger before going on a midnight sail with either Power or the young Stack boy."

"Actually, Howard never had to worry about Hepburn," Dietrich claimed. "She was so god damn self-sufficient that I don't think she even noticed if Howard were in residence at Muirfield or not."

Kate had her own problems to think about. In an episode that caused her great humiliation, the Independent Exhibitors of America (theater owners not controlled by the studios) took out full-page advertisements in Hollywood trade papers declaring her "box office poison." Other "poisonalities" included Joan Crawford, Mae West, Greta Garbo, Fred Astaire, and Marlene Dietrich.

At one point during her greatest despair, fearing RKO was planning to dump her, Kate stepped out on the ledge of the two-story makeup building at the studio and threatened to jump. It was Cary Grant who was summoned to talk her into coming back inside. No one knew where Howard was at the time. When Pat DeCicco got in touch with Howard and told him what had happened, his boss issued this not-quite-on-target comment: "Forgive me, but I'm incapable of committing to any one woman."

Kate told George Cukor and her other friends, "I'm madly in love with him and he about me." Cukor, an intimate friend (not a lover) of Cary Grant, knew the inside story but listened patiently to Kate's protestations of love. Privately, he confided to friends such as Joan Crawford, "It's promoted as the Hollywood romance of the century. Non-romance would be a better term." Crawford promulgated gossipy stories about Howard and Kate to half of Hollywood. For some reason, and even though she'd repeatedly turned down Howard, she seemed to take delight in exposing the sham of the widely celebrated Hughes/Hepburn romance.

Ginger's friends, and even her RKO boss, Pandro S. Berman, were told that Howard had personally assured Ginger that he was not sleeping with Kate—and never had. "We're golfing buddies," Howard is reported to have said. "Nothing more. Besides, who could fall in love with a woman who eats kidneys for breakfast? Do you know how many germs reside in the kidney of an animal?"

As Howard labored like a blue-collar mechanic at Burbank, Kate was busy making *Bringing Up Baby*, a comedy in which she was starring opposite Cary Grant. As part of the incestuous Hollywood link, Howard's favorite director, Howard Hawks, was in charge of the picture. During the shoot, Howard Hughes himself visited the set on various occasions. Privately, Hawks said, "I don't know if he's coming to check up on Kate or Cary. He spends equal time in each of their dressing rooms."

During one of his studio visits, Howard received an urgent call from Louis Preyssing at Muirfield. In broad daylight, with the house fully staffed, a thief had broken in and gone directly to Kate's bedroom. There he'd removed all the jewelry, including diamond and ruby bracelets, along with a mink coat, that Howard had given her.

That night, racing back to Muirfield, the engineer in Howard began to design an intricate alarm system. It was jokingly termed a "Rube Goldberg contraption." It was so sensitive—and so loud because of Howard's growing deafness—that even stray animals such as dogs or cats, could set it off in the middle of the night, waking up Hancock Park.

As soon as he'd finished designing it, he rushed back to Union Air Terminal at Burbank. He'd come up with a unique feature for his L-14. He began work on the design for a commode with air suction to install in his plane. Instead of letting human waste collect in the plane, which would cause germs, the airborne toilet would blow the waste into the atmosphere.

His comment, "Birds do this all the time. If someone gets hit in the eye

The Aviator: Howard Hughes Jr.

with a pile of shit, they'll think it's from a very large bird."

He sometimes spent as much as thirty-six hours at a stretch preparing for his around-the-world flight. In New York, Mayor Fiorello La Guardia had asked him to rename his plane, *The 1939 New York World's Fair*, and Howard had agreed.

In Burbank, he faced one delay after another, the main problem centering on the fact that the L-14 Lockheed was simply too small to carry the huge storage tanks of aviation fuel needed. To make matters worse, he'd equipped his plane with extra tanks, running the very grave risk of fatally weighing it down. Some of those tanks had been crowded into the compartment that would be shared by the fliers themselves. In case of an accident, such a move ran the risk of turning the pilots into human torches.

He was bitterly disappointed when U.S. aviation authorities refused to grant him a certificate of air worthiness. That meant he had to fly immediately to Washington where he fully expected to prevail. The refusal of U.S. Aviation Authorities also meant that he would not be allowed to fly over England's air space. That country was vital territory in his global flight plan.

Howard had a strong point to argue. Since he was flying from the East Coast of America over the Atlantic, his heavily loaded plane would not cause any damage to U.S. territory if it exploded, the way a transcontinental flight might do. Also, he argued, by the time he reached the coast of England, his fuel would be low enough so that he would no longer pose a threat. After considerable argument, American authorities granted him the right to fly across their air space upon his return journey. But he still had to convince the stubborn brass in London. He flew to England to persuade authorities to give him permission.

Coming back to his suite at London's Savoy Hotel one afternoon, he was walking across the lobby when he encountered the delicate, almost porcelain beauty of Barbara Hutton, the Woolworth heiress. At the time, she was richer than he was.

Howard greeted her and invited her out to a dinner party. "Mr. Hughes, do you plan to add me to the already notorious list of the world's beauties you've seduced?" she provocatively asked him in front of her two gossipy male escorts, both of whom were homosexuals.

"I may have known some of the world's most glamorous women," he gallantly said, "but the woman of my dreams has always eluded me. That is, until now."

***

In spite of this flirtation, Howard had known Barbara before and had spent several evenings with her, admittedly in a party of other friends. In the early 1930s, he had attended some of her parties at Harlem's Cotton Club, famous for its great jazz bands and dance floor. But until meeting her in London, he'd never shown any romantic interest in her.

Actor David Niven would in a few years join in some of these parties. He once said, "I think Hughes liked to attend because Barbara always picked up the tab." Throughout her life, the heiress paid for thousands of evening festivities. "It's expected of me," she said.

Not wanting Howard to be lonely in London, Cary Grant had arranged for him to meet young Frederick Brisson, the actor's on-again, off-again lover. Even though he was involved with Randolph Scott at the time, Cary had fallen madly in love with the 22-year-old Frederick, who was the son of Carl Brisson, a Danish-born matinee actor and a former professional middleweight prizefighter. Cary had become intrigued with the charming twenty-two-year-old, Frederick, when he was filming *Thirty Day Princess* at Paramount, a movie that was released in 1934, costarring Sylvia Sydney. At the time, Cary was enduring a difficult marriage to actress Virginia Cherrill. Visiting the studio that day, Frederick had approached Cary and asked for his autograph. Apparently, this was one fan with whom Cary became immediately smitten.

Two months later, and it's not known how, Virginia learned of her husband's romantic involvement with Frederick. Dressing for a party, she confronted Cary with what she knew. As she was slipping on a pale blue evening gown, he was so furious at his exposure that he struck her so hard she fell on the floor. Her face hit an iron fender in front of the bedroom fireplace. She later claimed, "I was cut wide open, and blood drenched my face. I lay there in agony, as he stormed out to drive alone to the Brisson party to meet his little Freddie."

Cary's fascination with Frederick would continue for years. In 1939 he made *His Girl Friday* with Rosalind Russell, whom he sometimes dated, although she was no more than a "beard," covering up his own relationship with Randolph Scott, which was receiving far too much press at the time, even though the printed references to the two men were "veiled."

One night Cary invited Frederick to join Rosalind and himself. As it turned out, Frederick was a bisexual, and as a result of that meeting, he fell in love with Rosalind and married her in 1941. Apparently, the very hip future Auntie Mame knew of the young man's other life when she married him. She didn't appear to be threatened by his sexual preference the way Virginia Cherrill had been when confronted with the startling news of Cary's bisexuality. But unlike Cary, Frederick wasn't a wife-beater, and his marriage to Rosalind was successful.

Frederick was in London at the time of Howard's visit to meet with British aviation authorities, and he was also staying at the Savoy. Perhaps wanting "to share the goodies," Cary had arranged for an introduction between Howard and the charming young man. Details are lacking, but Frederick was soon sharing the master bed in Howard's suite. As David Niven would later remark, rather cattily, "Howard was just breaking in Freddie for Rosalind."

On that trip, Howard turned out to be a true bisexual when he'd encountered Barbara whom he hadn't seen in several years. Why this sudden attraction? Maybe it was her new, thinner look, or perhaps her fashionable style in clothing and makeup, or even the vast amounts of press that she received for virtually everything she did, no matter how trivial. (Compared to Barbara Hutton, the amounts of press ink spilled over Paris Hilton's modern-day exploits appear almost inconsequential.)

Howard invited Barbara to join his dinner party which also included Frederick. Frederick was later to recall witnessing both Howard and Barbara "looking very sweet, holding hands, misty-eyed."

Since his arrangement with Howard was strictly sexual—there was no love there at all—Frederick didn't seem jealous. The reason for that became more obvious later. Frederick had developed a fondness for British stage actors, his favorite being Laurence Olivier. When he wasn't with Howard, he was occupied.

When she launched her ten-day affair with Howard, Barbara may or may not have known that Frederick and Howard were also lovers. If she did, it didn't interfere in her fondness for "my darling Freddie," as he soon became in her rich world.

Both Cary Grant and Howard Hughes would rapidly move into Barbara's orbit. And when Frederick married Rosalind Russell, he remained friends with Barbara. And when Cary married Barbara, the two couples often spent evenings together, even sleeping over at each other's homes.

Sometimes Howard would join the foursome as the odd man out. He was to learn that Frederick had enjoyed a brief affair with Barbara before his marriage to Rosalind. "Oh, my God," Billy Haines said. "When all of that gang got together, everybody had slept with everybody else except poor Rosalind, who had enjoyed only the charms of her Freddie. I can assure you it was chaste dating between Cary and Rosalind. If Howard had followed his usual custom, he would have tried to seduce Rosalind, too. For some reason, even though she was attractive, she never appealed to Howard. Personally, I think she was too smart for him, and that was a turn-off."

Back in London during the infamous Hutton encounter, and while Kate occupied her days at Muirfield plotting her Hollywood comeback, Howard divided his time between his own suite with Frederick and the even more lavish Savoy boudoir of Barbara.

Barbara Hutton

The exact details of their liaison would never have been known if Barbara hadn't kept a diary. She also talked candidly about the affair with her friends, especially her notoriously gossipy cousin, Jimmy Donahue. He spread the word about the coupling of his famous cousin and the handsome, super-wealthy aviator. It is not known if Kate Hepburn learned about this affair. Surely she must have, as word spread from London to New York to Hollywood via an electric grapevine.

Apparently, Howard and Frederick were very sexually compatible. Regrettably, Howard and Barbara did not turn out to be ideal sexual partners. He could not bring her to orgasm, which she so desperately wanted. As she was to record in her notebooks: "He sees that I have difficulty reaching orgasm, tries desperately to make me do so the first time, thereafter pleases himself and tells me I won't have one anyway. If I touch myself, he brushes my hand away with an angry snort. He can't take it when a woman loses herself in pleasure. Howard feels he has to be able to control a situation. When he doesn't, panic sets in."

It is not known how such a private, terribly personal, entry in her diary became public, and was published, much to her embarrassment.

In spite of their unsuccessful sessions in bed, Barbara retained a sisterly affection for Howard in the years ahead. She was a most understanding wife in the Forties when her husband, Cary Grant, slept with Howard and not with her. What she didn't understand was Howard's affection for Kate Hepburn. As she told Jimmy Donahue, "A boy would have been a better choice for Howard, instead of a *faux* boy."

After Barbara returned to America, she appraised Howard in her notebooks: "Howard has a talent for making enemies. People think of him as a half-deaf, stuttering billionaire whose only interest in life is money. For myself, I've never met a less materialistic man. He owns two suits and no tuxedo—if he needs one he borrows it. He usually wears tennis sneakers, the result of bad feet, and when he travels he packs a cardboard box with a few shirts and pairs of unmatched socks. He eats nothing but salads and would sooner sleep on a cot than in a comfortable bed. That is, when he sleeps at all. He is an easy person to be with. Doesn't bombard you with a barrage of ideas, doesn't pry, never

395

argues. The charming thing about Howard is that he isn't charming."

***

San Francisco, 1938

The coming together of Howard with Johnny Meyer will forever be cloaked in mystery. Even when Meyer, a few months before his still unexplained death in 1978, made revelations about his connection with Howard, he mixed the truth with lies, preferring the "limited hangout," to quote a future term used in the era of Richard Nixon.

The timing of Howard's first meeting with Meyer is clouded in mist. Some biographers have put it in 1939, others as late as 1943. Noah Dietrich, who should know since he was in charge of issuing Meyer's paycheck, placed it in San Francisco in 1938. Incidentally, Noah Dietrich also noted that "paycheck" wasn't exactly the right word. For virtually anything commissioned by Howard, Meyer demanded to be paid in cash and off the books.

Who was Johnny Meyer? During his notorious career, he was known by many names. Writers Peter Harry Brown and Pat H. Broeske labeled him a "Tinseltown bottom feeder who hustled girls for Charlie Chaplin and Errol Flynn." That was somewhat accurate except in Errol's case, Meyer hustled both girls and boys—more to the point, young girls and boys. This was especially true when Errol went on secret visits to Mexico away from the noisy gossips of Hollywood where some of his nocturnal adventures would have destroyed his career if word had leaked out.

Meyer was a procurer, with ties to the mob. He might have described his occupation as "pimp" on his Internal Revenue tax form—that is, if he bothered to report any of his under-the-table earnings.

It is not known exactly how Howard heard of Johnny Meyer, although by the late Thirties in Hollywood he was already a famous underground figure.

"Any movie star in those days who wanted anything immoral or illegal," Howard Hawks once said, "could count on Johnny Meyer. From what I was told, he didn't actually supply drugs, but he could hook up a star with a dealer. If a dirty old man like Charlie Chaplin wanted to pierce the hymen of a four-teen-year-old virgin, he called Johnny. For a fee, Johnny delivered. He was also known for delivering the best looking and the most well-endowed male hustlers to Hollywood's closeted homosexual stars like Basil Rathbone and James Cagney. His services were eagerly sought out. It was just a matter of time before Hughes himself got interested in what Johnny could supply."

Veteran character actor, Walter Abel, who had appeared with Errol Flynn in *Green Light* in 1937, and knew Johnny Meyer, said at a dinner party in New York in the 1960s: "Meyer's famous boast in Hollywood back in those days was that 'There is no human desire that I can't satisfy through some of my connec-tions.' I cannot vouch for it but word spread in 1938 that Meyer had fulfilled a

396

very special request from this famous producer, whom I will not name even though he's dead. Johnny, if reports are to be believed, secured a beautiful young Mexican girl for this guy. On a boat off the coast of Catalina, the girl's head was forcibly held underwater while she was viciously sodomized so the creep could enjoy the poor thing's death spasms."

Howard was on one of his mysterious trips to San Francisco with a "paid companion" (name and sex unknown) when he heard that Errol Flynn, accompanied by Johnny Meyer, was in town. Howard was staying at the Fairmont, as were Errol and his party. Their suite numbers were not given out, but a ten-dollar bill at the reception desk produced the numbers for Howard.

Howard—and Noah Dietrich is largely guessing at this point—placed a call not to Errol's suite but to Johnny Meyer's quarters. One can only speculate as to what Howard and Johnny discussed during that conversation. Obviously the hustler in Johnny saw creative possibilities with this rich new client.

A relationship between the two men was formed that afternoon at the Fairmont Hotel that would last for many years to come, even becoming the topic of a Senate investigation in 1947. "If Errol Flynn had been Johnny's main source of revenue up to then, before nightfall Howard became Johnny's sugar daddy," Dietrich later claimed.

In the late Thirties, Errol was famous for his nude parties and orgies. Howard was eager to attend one of these parties, wanting to meet this dashing Robin Hood/Captain Blood "who rode into Hollywood like the devil on horseback," as Ida Lupino characterized his arrival.

Meyer arranged for Howard to be invited to a private mansion on Nob Hill, the lair of a multi-millionaire, Philip Mahon, a homosexual who was known for his orgies. To these affairs, he invited gays as well as both straight men and beautiful women because he was more a voyeur than a participant at his parties.

At the time of Howard's meeting with Errol, he was—more so than any other actor in Hollywood—a symbol of masculinity and virility.

"Back in those days all virile red-blooded men and little growing boys who'd learned to masturbate wanted to be like Errol Flynn," his close friend, actor Bruce Cabot, once maintained.

Howard told Meyer that, even though he wanted to attend the Mahon party, he would not appear without his clothes. If Howard wanted to get involved in any of the action, it would have to be conducted in one of the private bedrooms upstairs and not in front of an audience. Errol, even at that time, had no embarrassment about performing sexually in front of an audience. In fact, he often preferred some of these performances more than he did his roles on the screen.

Before meeting him that night in San Francisco, Howard had seen *The Perfect Specimen*, a film in which Errol had co-starred with Joan Blondell under the direction of Michael Curtiz. From the photographs Howard had seen of Errol's physique and his film appearances in green tights, Howard felt that the title of the movie aptly described the Tasmania-born star, whose early life in such places as New Guinea had been filled with more adventure than many of his screen performances.

The party at Mahon's lavishly decorated mansion was in full swing when Meyer and Howard were met in the foyer by a butler and ushered into the sunken living room. It was filled with at least thirty handsome men and women still in evening dress. The night was young. Almost all of the guests, both male and female, had been invited because of their good looks. The only ugly creature in the large room was the host himself, Philip Mahon.

At center stage Errol stood at Mahon's grand piano. Although fully dressed, his trousers were unzipped, and he sported an impressive erection. With his penis, he was playing "You Are My Sunshine" on the piano.

***

Howard must have liked the way Errol played the piano, because the pair became fast friends after their introduction. In later years, Johnny Meyer would give various stories about how he introduced Errol to Howard, but witnesses reported that their first meeting occurred at the Philip Mahon party that night in San Francisco.

Around two o'clock in the morning, Howard and Errol disappeared into one of the upstairs bedrooms at the Mahon mansion. Their host later asserted that the pair didn't emerge until forty-eight hours later. "I sent them room service," Mahon claimed to his gossipy San Francisco clique.

Meyer had told Howard that Errol was a "sexual athlete" with women (or girls) and men (or boys), and Howard seemed eager to sample the handsome actor's already legendary charms. At the time of their inaugural meeting, Errol was known for making such quotes as: "I like my whisky old and my women young." Or, "any man who still has ten grand left when he dies is a failure."

Some biographers have claimed that after meeting Howard and spending time with him, Errol claimed Howard was a "deaf haddock," and didn't want to have anything to do with him. Errol was capable of making such catty remarks, and David Niven once swore that Errol used those exact words in describing Howard.

Even if Errol privately mocked Howard, the star became what is known today as a "toy boy" of the multi-millionaire for a number of months. Howard took Errol on several trips aboard the *Southern Cross* to Mexico, where they pursued various pleasures, and they made frequent weekend trips to San Francisco. Of course, both men had no sexual fidelity to each other and continued to pursue various male and female lovers.

No less than a month into Howard's relationship with Errol, Johnny Meyer went on Howard's payroll, although he continued his association with Errol on some level. Strictly heterosexual himself, Meyer "auditioned" many starlets for Howard, the way Catherine the Great of Russia would order her ladies-in-waiting to sample the charms of her studs at court before actually testing their skills herself. Meyer never auditioned the male hustlers he supplied to Howard, but had them thoroughly "vetted" by his homosexual friends before presenting a young man to his new boss.

When Errol was appearing once again in a film directed by Michael Curtiz,

398

called *Four's a Crowd* for Warner Brothers, he confessed to Howard that he had plans to seduce Olivia de Havilland, his Maid Marion co-star in *The Adventures of Robin Hood*. The actor told David Niven, Bruce Cabot, and others that Olivia "was a tough nut to crack," but he claimed that victory would one day be his. He also had plans, or so he claimed, to seduce Bette Davis as well.

Howard must have silently played a game of one-upmanship with his new-found friend, because he eventually chalked up both Bette and Olivia as conquests for himself.

During the filming of *Four's a Crowd*, Errol invited Howard to become a member of the all-male Olympiads, a small group of fun-loving men consumed with letting the good times roll, no matter what the cost. Howard refused, but not because the club was anti-Semitic. He had no problem with the club's politics, but worried about a possible exposure in the press. Members included the handsome actor, William Lundigan (Errol's sometimes lover), along with Errol's other lovers, Bruce Cabot and Patric Knowles. Even John Barrymore and W.C. Fields were members. Jack Warner and Edward G. Robinson had wanted to join but were turned down because of their Jewish backgrounds.

Members of the Olympiads sometimes sailed aboard Errol's own yacht, *Sirocco*, enjoying an endless supply of young women, liquor, and most definitely cocaine. It was during Howard's courtship of Errol, that the actor taught the aviator to cover the head of his penis with cocaine to obtain greater sexual pleasure.

During his months with Howard, Errol claimed that he more or less had the role of Rhett Butler wrapped up in *Gone With the Wind*. The actor also claimed that Bette Davis "was all but set" for the role of Scarlett O'Hara. Howard, who had not yet met Bette, suggested that Errol fly to New York and make a secret screen test with Kate Hepburn that he would personally finance and send to David O. Selznick. Errol agreed and made the test with Kate, both of them dressed lavishly in costumes appropriate to antebellum plantation life in the Deep South. He also seduced her during their brief time together. That privilege had not been claimed by Howard himself even though the bisexual actress was in residence at Muirfield.

At some point, or so Meyer claimed, Errol confessed to Howard that he preferred sex with girls ages thirteen to sixteen, but he liked his boys older, perhaps seventeen to nineteen. Howard, based on his record of seductions, liked fifteen-year-old girls, although that did not prevent him from seducing A-list female movie stars considerably older. Like Flynn, he preferred his boys a bit older, certainly in their late teens. Most often he requested hustlers in their mid-Twenties "when their bodies are fully formed and they have more experience."

Sexual experience was not something he demanded or even wanted from most of his women—or more accurately, his young girl conquests. "The more innocent the better," Howard told Meyer.

Howard never bothered to clear up his sexual contradictions. He also claimed he still liked recently divorced women, all of whom were much older than fifteen. Finally, when forced to admit the truth, as when confronted by Tyrone Power or others, Howard said that what he was attracted to could change from hour to hour.

In some ways, Errol shared that same changeable nature.

Both men were extremely fond of oral sex, and, according to the crew aboard the *Southern Cross*, indulged themselves freely in fellatio. "Those two spent more time aboard with their clothes off than their clothes on—not that they had anything to be ashamed of," one of the crew members claimed.

Once in Mexico, they visited a millionaire friend of Errol's and spent nearly a week at his estate. Allegedly, the Mexican planned various "exhibitions" in front of the other guests, with young boys and girls. Although Howard watched like a voyeur, he did not participate and kept his clothes on.

Howard later expressed to Dietrich that he valued Errol's companionship and held him in high regard as a "fuck buddy," but he did not approve of the actor's excessive drinking. He particularly infuriated Howard one night in Mexico when he stood up and took Howard's hand, asking, "Wanna poke, sport?"

Howard later told Dietrich that he'd been infuriated at the impression Errol left, clearly suggesting that Howard was on the passive end of sodomy.

Errol promised to cut back on his drinking if Howard would sail with him on a Caribbean cruise in April of 1938, but Howard declined. Errol sailed without him, reaching Port Royal, near Kingston, Jamaica. The actor fell in love with this lush, tropical island and its people. He was especially drawn to the area around Port Antonio on the island's northeast coast.

Leaving Jamaica, Errol sailed his *Sirocco* to Havana where he got involved in a nightclub brawl that made headlines in Hollywood. Claiming he was kicked out of Havana, Errol headed back to Hollywood. Once there, he resumed his friendship with Howard, urging him to go into a partnership with him to purchase huge tracks of virgin land in eastern Jamaica.

Once again Howard refused the offer. However, so as not to alienate Errol completely, he invited him for another cruise down to Mexico.

"I'll have a party favor for you," Howard promised.

"I hope she's gorgeous," Errol reportedly told him.

"I don't know if *she* is the right word," Howard allegedly said, "but gorgeous is certainly the right term."

***

Except for those fans in love with Robert Taylor, much of the movie-going public, at least impressionable women and homosexual men, thought Errol Flynn and

Errol Flynn

400

Tyrone Power were the two best-looking men on the planet. It was called "idol worship." Ever since Tyrone found out that Howard had seduced Errol, he had been urging his friend to arrange a liaison with the star.

Power was around twenty-five when Howard first introduced him to Errol. "Robin Hood" was pushing thirty and still in remarkable physical condition in spite of such bad habits as consuming inordinate amounts of alcohol.

Crew members aboard the *Southern Cross* later reported that Tyrone was on deck in a skimpy bathing suit—unusual for the time—when Errol came aboard with Howard. The two actors had met only casually before and socially at parties thrown by the Hollywood hostess, Jean Howard. Neither man had expressed

Tyrone Power

much interest in the other before, and were actually viewed as rivals, although working for different studios.

With his ethereal beauty, Tyrone seemed to glisten in the golden sunshine, which had bronzed his body. When Errol took in the almost naked man, with his dark hair, brooding eyes, and long, dark lashes, it was as if he were seeing him for the first time. "Thanks for inviting Ty along for the party, sport," Errol said, turning to Howard. Flashing his already world-famous, smirking smile, he added, "I like Mexican types."

That seemed to break the tension in the air. As Howard ordered his crew to set sail for Mexico, the *Southern Cross* carried three of the most desirable and handsomest men in Hollywood to their own private pleasures.

Roddy Johnston, a former Navyman who worked for Howard for two years sailing aboard the *Southern Cross,* later tried to sell the story of his experiences to any newspaper or magazine willing to pay for it. There were no takers because the subject of the homosexuality of Errol, Tyrone, and Howard was still taboo.

However, the Yale-educated gay actor, Vincent Price, recalled that when he first came to Hollywood to appear with Howard's former girlfriend, Constance Bennett, in a light comedy called *Service de Luxe*, the story of the *ménage à trois* of Errol Flynn, Howard Hughes and Tyrone Power was the chief source of gossip on the party circuit.

"Everyone knew about it, but no one wrote about it," Price said.

Roddy was an extremely muscular and handsome sailor. Some of his clients claimed that he was even more "movie star handsome" than the more famous trio sailing aboard the *Southern Cross*. He was not only handsome but was known for his sexual endowment. He called himself a "walking streak of sex." He later claimed, "If I saw a ten-dollar bill, extended by a man or woman, I got an instant hard-on."

If his stories are to be believed, Howard invited both Errol and Tyrone into his master stateroom to share his bed. Privately, Roddy claimed that he serviced all three famous men at various times during their sail to Mexico. He said that both Howard and Errol were "sword swallowers," but he called Tyrone "a brownie queen," meaning the actor preferred to take the passive role in sodomy.

Errol was completely different. Usually he didn't like his male conquests to be of equal rank. He preferred "the young, the beautiful, and the not too bright when it came to boys," Roddy said. "Present company excepted, of course. He went after male teenagers, although he made an exception for me. I was all of twenty-three at the time before I lost my looks and got flabby from too much booze."

"Howard and Errol liked to perform oral sex on each other," Roddy claimed, "but in his developing relationship with Errol, Ty was the woman, Errol strictly the man. I once overheard Errol complaining that Ty was exhausting him because he demanded to be 'poked' so much."

Again, if Roddy is to be believed (and he remains about the only source), Howard often "supervised" the love-making of his two beautiful actor friends. More and more, Howard was moving deeper into voyeurism, and Errol and Tyrone didn't mind putting on a show for him, or even inviting Howard to join them at some point.

But as the Flynn/Power romance progressed, Tyrone rebelled when Errol wanted him to put on a show with just the two of them in front of his Hollywood friends, including actor Bruce Cabot.

"From what I gathered, Tyrone fell in love with Errol in the months ahead, and all Errol wanted was to have a hot piece of ass," Roddy said. "I mean, let's face it. Who wouldn't love to fuck Tyrone Power? Darryl F. Zanuck once reported that, 'The handsome bastard gave me a hard-on when we were in the sauna together, and I'm the only real bona-fide heterosexual in all of Hollywood.'"

When Johnny Meyer first came to work for Howard, he was pleased with the procurer for hooking him into the action that was developing between Errol and Tyrone.

"I thought I'd be hustling far more women for Howard than men," Meyer later confided. "But it wasn't quite like that."

In an interview with biographer Charles Higham, Meyer once assessed his pimping for Howard: "Howard Hughes in my opinion was—and I was close to him as anyone—definitely bisexual. That whole image of his, of having women stashed away in apartments that were set up for him was a lot of baloney. In fact, I deliberately set up these women as a disguise for him. In most cases, he never even went to bed with them. He would go by and discuss the latest events and disappear, in the confident knowledge that the press was following him to the front door and would report on the period he spent there, imagining all kinds of macho events going on inside. The fact of the matter is that I doubt if Howard went to bed with these girls more than once or twice, and then only for a quick fuck and departure. I don't think he could satisfy women, and I very much doubt if he ever had an orgasm with one. On the other hand, he was fascinated by men. In complete secrecy, I would arrange assignations for him with boy hustlers."

Back from his voyage to Mexico with Hollywood's two handsomest actors, Howard decided to turn his attention once again to his upcoming global flight and to revisit the "mistress" he'd installed at Muirfield, who seemed to be doing just fine without him.

"The one good thing about Kate Hepburn," he told Errol, Tyrone, and Roddy, "is that she never asks where you've been when you finally go home."

**

Old Saybrook,Connecticut, 1938

At Fenwick, her family home built on the water's edge of Long Island Sound, Katharine Hepburn awaited the arrival of Howard. To her, Old Saybrook had never looked more beautiful, as the fruit trees had burst into bloom with their snow-white or cherry-pink blossoms. The oaks stood proudly along the coast, overseeing the sand dunes and salt marshes once roamed by Indians.

He had at last agreed to be presented to her family. One of her regrets involved the arrival of Ludlow Ogden Smith, her "beloved" former husband and now a major family friend.

She feared that her bisexual ex-husband nurtured a romantic fixation on Howard, because he collected dozens of photographs of the aviator, which he proudly displayed in his New York townhouse. Luddy had told her that he was not only anxious to take his own pictures of Howard, but had brought along some of his cameras so he could "catch him in action."

She'd warned him that Howard didn't like to be photographed, but Luddy had turned what she called "his deaf ear to me."

Before arriving at Fenwick, Howard had told Cary Grant and others about his three grand plans: To marry Katharine Hepburn "before the frost comes on the pumpkin," to circumnavigate the globe in record-breaking time, and to make Hughes Aircraft the biggest player in the aviation industry.

On the morning of Howard's arrival, Kate had told her family, having previously informed her friends, that "Regardless of what happens, my career must come before love. I must prove myself as an actress before becoming some famous man's playtoy." She seemed to have forgotten that at the very beginning of her career, she'd already won an Oscar.

What she didn't realize that beautiful May morning was that her aviator had plans so big that they would eventually dwarf her own "silly ambitions," as she was later to refer to them.

Before meeting the Hepburn clan, Howard had good news for Kate. Back in California, he had negotiated a deal with Pandro S. Berman, chief of RKO, after Howard had learned about the studio's reluctance to invest more money into the release and distribution of *Bringing Up Baby*, in which Kate had co-starred with Cary Grant. Howard purchased the film himself and would soon be distributing it through the Loew's chain. He'd seen the movie and had told Kate by phone as well as Cary that "my two favorite stars in all the world have a hit on their hands."

Howard was right, but it would take decades for the film to become a classic. Despite rave reviews, moviegoers, for the most part, avoided the film upon its initial release.

Finally, the aviator with his right-wing conservative views arrived to meet the Hepburns, one of the most socially progressive and liberal families in New England.

"It was a disaster waiting to happen," Noah Dietrich claimed.

***

Kate had taken previous "beaux" home to Fenwick in Connecticut to meet her family, including the sometimes sadistic producer Jed Harris, known at the time as "the vampire of Broadway," as well as the hard-drinking and closeted bisexual director, John Ford. The Hepburns tolerated Ford but despised Harris. Dr. Thomas Hepburn said, "If a rattlesnake could inhabit a human body, then it lives within Jed Harris." Ford fared a little better.

Arriving at Fenwick, Howard was distant and remote. He had been going through a particularly difficult time with his hearing, and he complained constantly of "a ringing in my head." In addition to other complications, he'd developed a severe ear infection. Sensing his distress, Dr. Hepburn sent him to an ear specialist the following morning.

Back at Fenwick that night, Kate's mother, Kit, found Howard a rather sullen figure. He sat at their dining table not actually sharing either dinner and certainly not their conversation, even assuming he could hear what was said. Kate spoke directly into his face, theatrically exaggerating her words so that he could almost read her lips.

Howard would go down to the kitchen and cook himself a steak and heat up a small can of peas, which he'd carry back to his room upstairs and eat alone after the Hepburns had retired for the night. Kate slept in her own bedroom, and, from what is known, was never once visited by her suitor.

Dr. Hepburn complained that Howard never joined in any of the family debates. The subject of birth control didn't interest him the way it did Kit. However, one night Howard showed a keen interest in Dr. Hepburn's views of venereal disease, especially the dangers of syphilis and how the disease could eventually cause brain damage. Howard, because of his own health problems, had a very personal interest in listening intently to that lecture.

With his camera, Luddy relentlessly chased after Howard on the golf course, sometimes disrupting his concentration on the game. Howard complained to Dr. Hepburn, who said, "Luddy has been taking pictures of us every day since he first arrived at Fenwick. He'll no doubt be taking them long after you've gone. Now let's get on with the game. Drive. Incidentally, you'll need a seven iron."

Howard followed the doctor's advice. He sunk the shot in two. As Kate remarked, "Cool in a pinch."

The golf game went reasonably well, but Kit that night at dinner remained extremely distant from Howard and never once addressed him. It didn't improve relationships between Kit and Howard when she referred to Luddy as

404

"our dear sweet ex."

In spite of her family's disapproval, Howard continued to plead with Kate to set a date for their wedding. Miracle of miracles, she finally agreed. How serious she was in her agreement is not known. George Cukor, her confidant, later claimed that Kate might have said yes to Howard's proposal merely to stop his annoying requests for her hand in marriage. The director seriously doubted if his friend ever had the slightest intention of marrying Howard. "She knew him too well," Cukor claimed. "Besides, in spite of her disastrous first attempt at marriage, she was just not the marrying kind."

"Kate was more skilled at stealing other women's husbands or other husband's wives than she was in walking down the aisle herself," claimed her gossipy friend, actor Anderson Lawler.

Somehow, word of her upcoming marriage leaked back to Hollywood. On May 28, Louella Parsons in the *Los Angeles Herald*, carried the scoop under the headline: HEPBURN TO WED HUGHES. Believing the marriage would actually take place, Howard ordered Noah Dietrich to redesign the master bedroom aboard the *Southern Cross* for their honeymoon. This was the same bedroom he'd so recently shared with Errol Flynn and Tyrone Power.

With Kate's final reassurance that she'd marry him before the end of that summer, Howard left Fenwick for New York, where he was going to fly back to Los Angeles to continue making plans for his upcoming flight around the world. He seemed as eager to leave Fenwick as the Hepburns were to see him go.

After Howard's departure for New York, Dick Hepburn, Kate's brother, called all the family into the living room to hear his new play, *Sea-Air*. For weeks he'd been typing madly in his bedroom.

As he read deeper and deeper into the play, Kate was shocked that its premise was based on "a handsome, good-looking [a bit redundant] millionaire who comes to visit the New England family of a young woman who is a bigtime Hollywood actress and Oscar winner."

Even before Dick had finished reading his play, Kate was on her feet denouncing it, claiming he had "maliciously and wickedly invaded my privacy—Howard's privacy, too."

Both Dr. Hepburn and Kit agreed, joining Kate in her demand that Dick burn the play in the fireplace page by page.

Dick held his ground and adamantly refused to destroy his work. He claimed that he was going to shop it from Broadway producer to producer.

The history of what happened to *Sea-Air* is not known. The noted writer and friend of Kate's, Garson Kanin, said that he read the play and found it "amusing, insightful, and entertaining." He claimed that the character based on Howard functioned as an unwitting catalyst within the context of a New England family that was evocative of the Hepburn clan, tearing away their pretenses.

On Broadway, rumors abounded that Kate had purchased the rights to the play to keep it from being produced. Kanin speculated that it was Howard himself who bought up all copies of *Sea-Air*. "I heard he sailed on the *Southern Cross*, tossing the pages one by one into the Pacific Ocean."

While at Fenwick, Kate received some distressing news. There was a lot of gossip that as soon as Howard had gotten back to Hollywood, and in spite of her agreement to marry him, he'd taken up again with Ginger Rogers. The second piece of news was that Ginger Rogers had dethroned her as queen of RKO.

The following day, another tantalizing piece of Hollywood gossip reached her when Anderson Lawler called to report on "the latest." Howard was not only "wooing Miss Ginger again," but he was also in ardent pursuit of Luise Rainer, or so it was said.

"You've got to be kidding," Kate said. "I can believe he's taken up with Miss Rogers. After all, she's nothing but a cheap blonde floozie truck-stop cocksucker." When Kate wanted to, she could talk like a drunken sailor. "But the willowy, ethereal Miss Rainer. Hell, she's got even smaller tits that I do. Everyone knows Howard's a breast man!"

***

Los Angeles, 1938

Call it the romance that never was.

The press continued to publish stories about the "greatest romance of the century," the so-called affair of Katharine Hepburn and Howard Hughes.

But insider Hollywood was gossiping about another romance, real or imagined—the "affair" of Luise Rainer and Howard. At the time, Rainer was at the apogee of her celebrity, having won back-to-back Oscars for her performance as the showgirl, Anna Held, in *The Great Ziegfeld* in 1936 (the shortest role ever to win a citation) and for her portrayal of the Chinese peasant woman, O-Lan, in Pearl Buck's *The Good Earth* in 1937.

Dark-eyed, dark-haired, and with a pixyish face and a charming accent, the petite and delicate Viennese beauty was not exactly Howard's type. (In a few months, Jane Russell and her big bosom would be viewed as Howard's ideal woman.) But confidants of both Rainer and Howard have either denied the existence of an affair between this odd couple or else admitted it and contradicted it later. A confused mess.

Howard's close friend, Cubby Broccoli, once suggested that, "Howard may never have met Luise Rainer."

In Los Angeles, Howard learned from Cary that the marriage of Luise Rainer and Clifford Odets, which had occurred in 1937, was unraveling. At the time, Odets was the leading playwright in America.

Cary Grant, meanwhile, had formed an intimate bond with Odets and was frequently seen with him in public. It even appeared to Hollywood insiders that

Luise Rainer

Odets had replaced Randolph Scott in Cary's affections. But in spite of the arrival of Odets in Cary's life, Cary still continued his intimate link with Howard, a bond that would not be broken.

It is entirely believable that Howard might have pursued Rainer, and it's highly likely that if Howard knew her at all, that it was Cary, thanks to his friendship with Odets, who made the introduction. At that point in his life, Howard was on a campaign to seduce female Oscar winners. The list of his Academy Award winning girlfriends over the decades would indeed prove impressive: Katharine Hepburn, Ginger Rogers, Joan Fontaine, Olivia de Havilland, Susan Hayward, and Bette Davis.

Cubby suspected that it might have been Howard himself who fueled the rumors of an affair with Rainer. Although Howard went to great lengths to hide from the press, he was known from time to time to call his old friend, Louella Parsons, with a choice tidbit if it served his purpose.

"I personally think Howard was more impressed with Rainer's two Oscars than the physicality of the actress herself," Cubby claimed. If Rainer and Howard were having a hot affair, they weren't seen dancing cheek-to-cheek at the Cocoanut Grove. If a Hughes/Rainer involvement occurred at all, it must have been the most discreet celebrity affair in Hollywood.

Frederick Brisson once claimed that Cary Grant had admitted that Howard had had a short sexual interlude with Rainer. According to Grant, Howard pursued this affair as a means of distracting his mind from his upcoming global flight. If Cary is to be believed, Howard also wanted a distraction from his troubled, undefined relationship with Kate Hepburn.

Said Brisson, "The full story may never be known about Hughes and Rainer. What I do know for a fact is who Howard really had sex with before flying around the world. Ginger Rogers and Errol Flynn. On separate occasions, of course. I talked with Howard before he left Los Angeles for New York to begin his flight. He said, and I remember his exact words, 'In case I disappear like my buddy, Amelia Earhart, Errol and Ginger might be the final ass that I'll ever know.' Somewhat taken aback by that remark, I then inquired about Kate waiting in New York. 'Yeah, what about her?' Howard said to me before putting down the phone without a good-bye."

***

Burbank, 1938

In Burbank, Howard nervously but meticulously made the final preparations for his around-the-world flight. He and Glenn Odekirk were convinced that his mechanics had created the best possible plane for the mission: a low-wing, sleek silver monoplane, a Lockheed Lodestar, capable of carrying 12 passengers. It had taken two years to prepare the plane for flight. Its pair of 1,200 horsepower Wright engines were the best that money could buy. Weighing close to thirteen tons, it required specially commissioned tires to ensure its ability to land safely. The plane carried 150 gallons of oil and 1,500 gallons of aviation fuel.

Howard had tried to foresee any emergency. He'd equipped it with a pair of high-powered rifles which he might need to fight off bears if the plane was forced to land in the rugged mountains of Siberia. A device had been installed to convert salt water to fresh. Some eighty pounds of Ping Pong balls had been stuffed into the hollow recesses of the wings and fuselage to provide temporary flotation in case the Lockheed, a land plane, was forced to land on water.

Glenn, who had been working night and day for months, had lost 35 pounds. He was far too weak and exhausted to endure a strenuous trip of some 15,000 miles, so Howard found a replacement for him.

For his crew, Howard selected the best technicians in America. Richard Stoddart, age 38, signed on as communications expert. He was a former shipboard radio operator and communications engineer from the National Broadcasting Company. For his co-pilot, Howard hired a skilled navigator, Harry P. McLean Connor, who had flown as co-pilot aboard Captain Erroll Boyd's historic 1930 flight from Montréal to London. At the age of 39, he was the oldest crew member aboard. Also among the team members was Lieutenant Thomas Thurlow, a 33-year-old member of the U.S. Army Air Corps, and an aerial navigator noted for his innovations at Wright Field. Finally, Edward Lund, aged 32, came aboard as Howard's air crew mechanic.

Clearly, he was Howard's favorite. Howard called him "my fellow Westerner," since Ed was born in Montana. He'd proven his skill by working on Howard's Sikorsky and DC-1. There was another reason for hiring him. He was as tall as Howard and bore a physical resemblance to his boss, with his bushy eyebrows and piercing dark eyes. Even their lips and ears resembled each other. If not look-alikes, Ed and Howard could clearly have been brothers. Howard planned to use Ed as a decoy. It was agreed in advance that at refueling stops during the flight, wearing Howard's typical clothing, including his signature Fedora, Ed would get off the plane first. With his hat pulled down over his face, he'd distract the crowds, allowing Howard to slip out of the cockpit and into the privacy of a hangar undetected.

W.C. Rockefeller, a meteorologist, was a member of Howard's ground crew based in New York. His mission involved the creation and the supervision of a 24-hour weather forecast center at the New York World's Fair grounds, monitoring weather conditions along the plane's route and crafting reports for transmission to Howard and his crew. The framework he set up for this became the forerunner of today's Flight Advisory Weather Service.

Before his departure, Howard received a visit in his private office from Noah Dietrich, who interacted with him for more than an hour, reviewing Toolco business that had to be conducted during Howard's absence.

Dietrich noted a picture of the one-eyed pilot, Wiley Post, hanging behind Howard's desk. He'd been impressed with Post's solo flight around the world in 1933 in a single-engine plane, *Winnie Mae*. Howard later told the press,

"That was one of the most remarkable feats of all time. I really don't know how that man could have done it alone." Now, Howard was setting out to break Post's record.

After their business conference, Howard showed Dietrich his Lockheed and explained the new fuel system whereby the tanks had been coated with neoprene to make them self-sealing. His radio transceiver was actually an interconnected series of three separate radio systems. His innovative "Sperry Gyro Pilot" was an automated device that could fly the craft while all the other aviators and technicians snoozed. Howard may have invented the term, "blind flying."

His final visitor was Cary Grant, who'd arrived for a goodbye with his dear friend. Glenn noted that the two men disappeared into Howard's office for only fifteen minutes. Later, only Cary emerged.

Glenn claimed that when he shook the actor's hand goodbye, there were tears in Cary's eyes. Glenn confirmed what Howard had already told Cary. For vast stretches of this dangerous flight, there were no maps. "That mountain that you think is 10,000 feet might actually be 12,000 feet," Glenn said.

***

New York, 1938

When Howard's Lockheed landed at Floyd Bennett Field in Brooklyn, at the time the only airport within the boundaries of New York City, some 10,000 well-wishers turned out to greet him. Surrounding the plane, they were held back by 1,000 policemen. He was shocked at the turn-out. In spite of his efforts to keep his mission secret, word had obviously leaked out. Crewmember Ed Lund later reported that Howard was at first flattered by the welcome but soon dismayed. Disguised as Howard, Ed got off the plane first, hoping to lure the crowds and the press away from the real Howard. "I haven't broken any fucking record yet," Howard had told Ed, "so why are they going crazy?"

Grover Whalen, the head of the 1939 World's Fair, after which Howard had agreed to name his plane, was at first fooled by Ed's disguise. But he soon caught up with the real Howard in Hangar 7, and as New York's official greeter, welcomed him on the dawn of his historic flight.

Everyone expected Howard to stay at Kate's Turtle Bay residence in New York. But to avoid reporters, he was stashed away in the apartment of Laura Harding on East 52nd Street instead. Laura was Kate's longtime lesbian lover and confidante. Not seeing Howard arrive at Turtle Bay, reporters falsely assumed that he was staying at one of the residence halls being readied for the World's Fair of 1939.

That night Kate and Howard talked not of love but of the minute details and challenges of his upcoming flight. He was frank in relating to her the dangers involved, or so she later claimed to her friends. "Other pilots have lost their

409

lives doing exactly what I'm trying to do," he allegedly warned her. She didn't need such warning. Kate had met the doomed pilot, Amelia Earhart, on at least three occasions, and had played a doomed pilot herself in the 1933 film, *Christopher Strong*.

It is also believed that Howard told Kate that before leaving California he'd made a new will which had been placed in a safe deposit box at the First National Bank in Houston. Thirty-eight years later, after Howard died, the will could not be found. Howard told Dietrich and Kate that he'd ordered his executors to establish the Howard R. Hughes Medical Research Laboratories in Houston "to combat the most important and dangerous diseases." It is not known today where the will is, or if it exists at all. Chances are, it was destroyed. But by whom?

Kate later claimed that she didn't know if she'd ever see Howard again, but expressed complete confidence in his Lockheed Lodestar, saying that she "just knew" that he'd beat Wiley Post's trans-global record.

Instead of making love with Howard, Kate insisted on making sandwiches for the crew. Not wanting to take a chance, Howard had tested nearly two dozen different breads for their nutritive value. Deciding on one, he'd purchased several loaves for sandwiches, made with roast beef, ham, and turkey. Kate and Laura wrapped their freshly made sandwiches in brown butcher paper and packed them like carry-out lunches.

Howard had contributed very little to the news frenzy circulating around his flight: In fact, he'd issued a terse "No comment!" to reporters upon his arrival at Floyd Bennett Field, not wanting to reveal any details of his mysterious flight. But that afternoon, one of the New York newspapers had been delivered to Laura's apartment. Its headline screamed: LOOK OUT WORLD—HERE COMES HUGHES!

***

The following morning, Howard climbed into the back seat of Kate's Lincoln, chauffeured by her faithful servant, Charles Newhill, for the drive to Floyd Bennett Field. Howard held her in his arms, hugging and kissing her all the way. He vowed his eternal love for her, promising that he'd dip the wings of his Lockheed Lodestar as he flew over her family home at Fenwick en route to Paris. He also promised to cable her at every stop en route, as well as when he made radio contact with ships traversing the turbulent Atlantic.

Driving far too fast, Charlie heard the sound of a police siren behind him. As her chauffeur pulled over to the side of the road, she cautioned her hot-tempered driver to accept the ticket and not get into an altercation with the traffic policeman. For once, Charlie held his tongue and accepted the ticket with a smile. At no point did the ticketing officer look into the back seat of the Lincoln to discover its two world-famous passengers.

At the airfield, and with one final and passionate kiss for Kate, Howard emerged from the back seat of the Lincoln. He tipped his brown snap-brim felt hat to her. His last words to her, and she feared they might be the last words she'd ever hear from him, were, "You'll be hearing from me, kiddo."

Kate wanted to go into the hangar with him but feared the mob of reporters and well-wishers clustered at the Brooklyn airfield. She ordered Charlie to drive her to Fenwick, in Connecticut, where she'd sit by the radio, listening to news of Howard's flight.

While working on last-minute adjustments, Howard was paid a visit by Sherman Fairchild, whose company, Fairchild Aviation, had installed the Fairchild-Maxon Line-of-Position computer in the Lockheed.

Fairchild's friendship with Howard dated from 1931 when they'd become good friends. Fairchild was rich, good-looking, single, and shared Howard's fascination with beautiful women. With their respective "arm candy," the two men were often photographed together at New York's Stork Club or El Morocco. Their dates often complained that they were left staring into space as Fairfield talked modern aviation or some new aerial navigation concept with Howard.

Because both Howard and Fairchild were interested in so many other things—Howard in movies, Fairchild in photography, boating, tennis—aviation experts tended to dismiss both of them as dilettantes.

Fairchild had arrived at Floyd Bennett Field to adjust the magnetic compass, which he found difficult to do because Howard had insisted on keeping the engines running. "With the damn thing jiggling because of the engines, it's hard to get the compass fitted," Fairchild complained to Howard. "To hell with the compass," Howard told him. "It's more important that the engines run." Fairchild reminded him that when one is flying around the world, often over unchartered terrain, "You need a fucking compass that works." In spite of that protest, Howard demanded that the engines be kept running, and Fairchild had to manage with the calibration of the compass as best as he could.

With Glenn Odekirk and his other mechanics, Howard worked through Saturday, sending word to the reporters and well-wishers outside that there would be no takeoff on Saturday and requesting that they go home. A few hundred did, but many diehards remained, having brought sleeping bags. Dozens of people set up tents and enjoyed packed lunches in a neighboring field. These fans slept in shifts with guards posted. That way, all of them could be awakened in case Howard decided on a surprise takeoff.

All through Saturday night Howard worked with his crew, encountering headaches with the fuselage and the struts. He sent word on Sunday that it appeared that he and his heavily insured crew would take off that afternoon. One newspaper reporter asked Betty Compton, a housewife from Queens, why she'd remained so long at the Brooklyn field. "I want to see Hughes disappear into the sky," she said, "perhaps for the last time."

Hope dimmed in the late afternoon when Glenn discovered a malfunctioning magneto, one of the key elements of the navigation system. Howard demanded that the Wright Aeronautical Company supply one immediately from their warehouse, even though it was closed on Sunday. Arousing the storehouse manager, Howard got his magneto, which he and Glenn installed. After one final and thorough check, Howard at long last announced to his crew, "Let's fly around the world, boys!" He embraced Glenn, holding him for an extra long time, as if this could be their final hug.

The city's official "greeter," Grover Whalen, rushed into the hangar, demanding that Howard say some "final words" to the reporters and assembled mob. He only reluctantly agreed.

On the platform he was greeted by New York Mayor Fiorello La Guardia. After Whalen and the mayor addressed the crowd, Howard, in a strained and high-pitched voice, read a prepared statement. As was obvious to any observer, the world was rapidly drifting to war, but in his prepared statement, Howard said that he hoped his flight would "further international cooperation and friendship." Even as he uttered those words, Hitler was threatening to have his Luftwaffe shoot down Howard's plane if he entered German air space. Before leaving the platform, Howard apologized to newsmen and photographers for having earlier appeared "rude and impolite."

Mrs. Connor, wife of one of the technicians, pasted a thick wad of chewing gum on the tail of the Lockheed Lodestar for good luck. "Be sure and bring it

NYC Mayor Fiorello LaGuardia with Howard Hughes

412

back safe to me—and you with it," she told her husband before kissing him goodbye.

At long last the silver monoplane appeared on the runway, ready for take-off, as the by now exhausted fans cheered its departure. It was exactly thirteen seconds past 7:19 p.m. Howard appeared in no condition to take such a draining flight around the world. At his farewell speech, one reporter noted that his "eyelids were practically closing on him," and that his face was covered in stubble from his overnight mechanical work. One member of the press recalled how romantic and dashing Charles Lindbergh had looked in 1927 when he'd taken off for Paris. "Lindbergh was the movie star portrait of a dashing American aviation hero," Cary Ramsomme wrote in *The Brooklyn Eagle.* "But not Hughes. He looked like a bum who'd fallen off the turnip truck."

One radio announcer, Ralph Saxon, ominously reported that there was speculation that the plane might crash and burn on takeoff because it was "too heavily laden with fuel." Fortunately, Howard and his crew didn't hear that radio bulletin. With all the months of advance planning, one factor had not been figured in. The runway at Floyd Bennett Field was far too short to accommodate the takeoff of the Lockheed Lodestar.

Realizing belatedly the danger, Howard faced an immediate decision, and he was only a minute into the flight. He could either abort the takeoff or else continue down the runway and into a barren field, running the risk of crashing in front of the newsreel cameras and his thousands of admirers. With his stubborn, almost defiant streak, he kept the plane steady on the runway until its pavement ended. Then he continued the final stages of the takeoff from a bumpy stretch of field covered with crabgrass and patches of mud left over from a recent downpour.

Except for the increasingly deaf Howard, every member of the crew heard a loud snapping sound coming from the rear of the craft. Even though the sound presented a potential risk to their own lives, not one member of the crew reported this problem to Howard, fearing it would throw off his concentration on the most difficult takeoff of his aviation career.

Flying over Connecticut, Howard remembered his promise to Kate and dipped his wings as he flew over Fenwick. All the Hepburns were waiting out in their yard to wave hysterically at the plane, perhaps wishing him a *bon voyage*—in their minds, perhaps for the final time.

At this point, before beginning its transit over the vast darkness of the Atlantic Ocean, the progress of the Lockheed was still being measured from the ground. Air controllers in the tower at Boston's airport reported that the craft went over their city at 8:26pm. By 9:55pm, the Lockheed was flying over remote Nova Scotia.

At 10:30pm, the first broadcast ever made from an aircraft in flight was carried by all the nation's radio networks. It was one of the biggest audiences ever reached by a broadcast. The voice of crew member Richard Stoddart, in his well-modulated NBC tones, came across, saying, "The flight is progressing smoothly. The weather is clear, but we cannot see anything below us because of a cloud cover. Mr. Hughes is busy right now, but he will be able to say something a little later."

Stoddart's report to the nation was far too optimistic. Actually, Howard was growing frantic. The Lockheed was gulping down fuel at a rate far greater than his estimates. Facing fierce headwinds, the Lockheed was averaging 175 miles per hour. He knew that by slowing the plane he could conserve fuel yet that would prevent him from breaking the speed record—or so he feared.

Later, when he returned to America, he told Glenn, "I thought somewhere over the Atlantic, long before I reached Europe, the plane would pancake into the ocean. But I could not turn back. I would not turn back!"

After drinking a pint of milk and refusing to join the rest of the crew in a catnap, Howard signaled to Stoddard that he was ready to say just a few words to the nation. His voice was beamed westward. "I hope we can get to Paris before we run out of gas," he told anyone still listening to the radio at that hour. Most definitely the audience at that time consisted of Kate Hepburn, who stayed up long past her bedtime to hear his voice. "But I'm not so sure," he continued. "All I can do is hope that we will get there. I hope that we have enough gas to reach land. I am throttling back the engines as fast as the reducing load permits." In that ominous voice, he signed off. Radio announcers immediately started referring to his mission as "perhaps a doomed flight."

Three New York newspapers prepared EXTRA editions, fearing that Howard and his crew would crash into the murky Atlantic "to join the Titanic," as one commentator put it.

At Fenwick the following morning, Kit Hepburn handed her daughter a cable that Howard had sent before leaving Brooklyn. "See you in three days. Love, Howard." What he told her before leaving was that if he could successfully circumnavigate the globe, setting a world's record, he would be "worthy" of her and that they could wed at the end of the summer.

He had slipped her a note in the back seat of her Lincoln, asking her not to read it until he was somewhere over the Atlantic. At Fenwick that morning, Kate tore open the hand-written note, "On this flight you are my silent partner, my spiritual co-pilot. Love, Howard."

"Who couldn't love a man who'd write a note like that?" Kate asked her family.

Before going to bed in the early dawn, Kate had listened to broadcasts, only to learn that the gambling ships off the coast of Atlantic City, outside U.S. territorial waters, were giving Howard a fifty-fifty chance of survival.

***

Paris, 1938

414

As millions of people around the globe avidly followed the flight of the Lockheed, Howard at midpoint over the dark Atlantic experienced a change of luck. He no longer had to fight the winds. "As if sent by God," Ed Lund later recalled, "a brisk tail wind got on our ass and shot us to the coast of Ireland." That resulted in a massive saving of precious fuel.

With some 100 gallons of aviation fuel aboard, and with the green hills of Ireland visible from his port wing, Howard decided that he had enough fuel to fly across the English Channel to Paris.

Lt. Thomas Thurlow made radio contact with the transatlantic liner, *Ile de France*, requesting a bearing. He asked that the ship's crew radio the control tower at Le Bourget outside Paris, telling of the Lockheed's progress.

Howard sent two messages, one to the ship's captain, boasting that, "We'll see the coast of France before you do." A cable was also sent to Kate at Fenwick: "The Irish coast is breathtaking in its beauty. Will contact you from Paris, Howard."

Some aviation experts had predicted that it would take Howard at least 24 hours to land in Paris, but Howard landed in Paris 16 hours and 38 minutes after leaving Brooklyn. Averaging 219.6 miles per hour, he had cut Charles Lindbergh's historic record in half.

Thousands of jubilant Parisians stormed the airfield at four that afternoon, ignoring the light drizzle raining down from the gray skies that blanketed the city at that historic moment.

Howard was the first to emerge from his plane, looking unshaven, unkempt, and like a man who hadn't slept in countless days and nights.

On the airfield, the first greeter who stormed the plane was William C. Bullitt, the American ambassador to France. "Congratulations," the ambassador said. "Did you have a good trip?"

"We had a good flight," Howard said in a less enthusiastic voice. He turned down the offer to sleep in the luxurious comfort of the ambassador's Parisian townhouse.

Almost immediately, Howard was greeted not only by the well-wishers, but with bad news. That sound his crew had heard at takeoff was that of a rear landing strut that had been damaged.

French mechanics didn't think it could be fixed. The chief mechanic at Le Bourget, Pierre Mazarin, told Howard that, "*Le Lodestar, c'est fini.*"

"Fuck you!" Howard said in anger in front of his crew. "We'll be airborne in an hour!" Determined and very gritty, he ordered an exhausted Ed Lund and others to begin to repair the plane at once. "Precious time is wasting. Let's show these frogs what American ingenuity means."

Howard's boast of one hour proved a false hope. Eight hours later, the Lockheed was towed to the floodlit runway at the same spot where Lindbergh had landed his *Spirit of St. Louis*.

Hundreds of French people still remained on the airfield to wish Howard and his crew *bon voyage*. Despite crossing the darkened Atlantic, the most dangerous part of the flight was yet to come. Trouble began at once, as strong crosswinds were blowing across Le Bourget, making a takeoff in such weather risky.

His face locked in a bitter determination, Howard gave both engines full throttle. The Lockheed became airborne, climbing to sixty feet before it leveled off and dramatically dipped. Screams could be heard from the hundreds of rubberneckers below, some of whom later reported to the French press that they fully expected to see the crash of the Lockheed before their very eyes.

With nerves of steel, Howard fought the winds. His entire aviation career seemed to hinge on this moment being played out in front of the eyes of the world. His hands were locked in an almost death-like grip on the controls. Miraculously and in spite of the winds, the Lockheed began to gain altitude. Within three minutes the craft rose over Paris and disappeared into the eastern skies, "which were black as a funeral cortège," as one member of the French press called them.

Howard was coming into potentially the single most dangerous part of the trip. He had not only uncertain weather to deal with, but danger from enemy aircraft as well.

In London, the BBC reported that, "Luftwaffe pilots were itching to get the famous American aviator, Howard Hughes, in their sights. *The International Herald Tribune* trumpeted this bulletin: STERN WARNINGS FROM HITLER TO HUGHES.

The Nazi dictator had sent ominous word to Howard that his Lockheed would be shot out of the air if it flew over German territory. Hitler apparently feared that the aircraft was actually an American spy plane gathering valuable reconnaissance on the dictator's preparations for a rapidly approaching world war. Howard's response was that his craft would be flying 12,000 feet over Germany, thereby making any aerial reconnaissance impossible with the instruments of that era.

Nonetheless, the moment Howard's Lockheed entered German air space, five fighter planes from the Luftwaffe were ordered into the sky to virtually surround the plane. The leader of the squadron, in making radio contact with Howard, screamed, VERBOTEN! VERBOTEN! into Howard's nearly deaf ears.

Ignoring the warning, Howard stubbornly flew on. The Luftwaffe squadron kept the plane surrounded and kept screaming VERBOTEN! and other German expletives until the Lockheed had flown over Germany and had left its airspace to enter Eastern Europe for the final lap of the flight into Moscow.

The moment Howard cleared German air space, he turned to co-pilot Harry Connor and said, "Now we can breathe again."

***

416

"Hello, America," came the greeting the following morning at 11:15am. "This is Radio Moscow." The Russian announcer said that thousands of well-wishers were storming Howard's *New York World's Fair of 1939.* They ran onto the field at the Civil Air Fleet Aerodrome. The manager of the airport greeted Howard and his crew with a box of Kellogg's Corn Flakes.

A lifelong hater of communism, Howard appeared warm and generous to the people of Russia, even though he loathed Josef Stalin. None of his hostility to the host government was evident in a strained but warm—at least for Howard—speech he delivered to the Muscovites, lauding them for their welcome, and expressing his admiration that the designers of the Aerodrome built it in a location that was convenient to the center of Moscow.

After his speech, Howard excused himself to go to the men's room. A few minutes later, Ed Lund followed him. Ed would later report that he'd noticed that Howard carried a pink porcelain bowl with him on the flight. Not knowing that this bowl was a holdover from his childhood and his incestuous relationship with his mother, Allene, Ed speculated with other crew members that it was some sort of "security blanket" for their boss.

Alone in the men's room with Howard, Ed was astonished to discover Howard masturbating into the bowl. "Relieves tension," was all that Howard said. As Ed relieved himself at the urinal, he couldn't help but notice that Howard continued to masturbate as if he hadn't entered the room. Without saying a word, Ed, according to his later claim, left the men's room as Howard was seen ejaculating into the bowl.

In London, the BBC broadcast the news of Howard's safe arrival, claiming that "the Russians fell in love with the American playboy millionaire who had a patch on the seat of his trousers."

Back at Fenwick, Kate heard Howard's exploits broadcast hourly on the radio. He was clearly the man of the hour. In her narcissistic way, she told family and friends who called, "If Howard and I ever marry, he won't become Mr. Katharine Hepburn but I will definitely become *Mrs. Howard Hughes.*"

Among the Muscovites on hand to greet Howard and his crew were three Russian pilots—Mikhail Gromoff, Georgi Baidukoff, and Andrei Yumasheff—who had pioneered a transpolar flight from Moscow to San Jacinto, California, in the summer of 1937 in sixty-two hours.

Gromoff presented Howard with a container of the rarest of caviar from Stalin himself. Howard was forced to turn it down. "It's much too heavy and on this flight every pound counts."

"Fine," Gromoff said. "I'll take it home to my family tonight. But I'll tell Stalin you thanked him profusely and will be eating it as you fly over Siberia." Before departing, Gromoff warned of potential dangers awaiting Howard as his Lockheed flew over Siberia.

Before reboarding, Howard was handed a cable. Thinking it was from Kate, he discovered it was from silent screen comedian Buster Keaton. BE SURE TO BRING BACK A POT OF CAVIAR, the message urged. Howard merely laughed, crumbled the cable, and tossed it aside as he entered the cockpit for takeoff that afternoon.

In the United States, dozens of boy babies across the land were being named Howard. Even before his flight had been successfully completed, frontpage news and blaring headlines were proclaiming him a genuine aviation hero, the equal of "Charles Lindbergh if not a more daunting achiever." *The New Republic* claimed that he'd "not been spoiled by inherited wealth."

Having braved the murky Atlantic and Hitler's Luftwaffe, Howard and his crew now faced the formidable challenge of the wastelands of Siberia, as his Lockheed flew east into the unknown.

On through the pitch blackness of night, they flew deeper and deeper into central Asia, finally landing at Omsk, an industrial city in the western part of Siberia, lying 1,300 miles east of Moscow. Ed later claimed that the airfield "looked like a cow pasture."

Unlike their arrival at Moscow, the landing of the Lockheed at Omsk was anything but idyllic. Because of inadequate maps, he had to fly blind over much of the bleak and badly charted Siberian landscape. He flew over mammoth rain clouds. Upon his descent he encountered the aftermath of lashing rain, finding the airfield a sea of mud.

Howard had carefully planned to have an English interpreter waiting for him on the ground. But upon landing, barely coming to a halt before running over the too-short runway, he found that the person had come down with the flu. No one else at Omsk spoke English.

The natives were friendly enough, trying to invite him in for a dinner of caviar and champagne. Howard was frantic, wanting it understood that he needed fuel. Finally, in desperation, he drew a diagram of the Lockheed and its empty fuel tanks. An airport crew member was smart enough to understand the problem and ordered the tanks be restocked. To Howard's dismay, he discovered that the fuel did not contain the ethyl he wanted. With a begrudging sigh, he allowed his tanks to be filled with 1,750 gallons of low-grade octane. He was forced to open containers of tetraethyl to add to the low-grade Russian fuel.

Not wanting to immediately face the relatively uncharted mountainous terrain of Siberia that lay before him, Howard and his crew remained on ground for ten and a half hours, losing valuable time for men intent on setting a world record.

After a difficult takeoff because of the poorly maintained runway and the fuel overload, Howard and his crew set out to penetrate deeper into Asia, flying over the steppes of Siberia bound for the town of Yakutsk.

As Howard would later claim, the outpost of Yakutsk in northern Siberia "was a god-forsaken place on the edge of the world suspended somewhere between the sun and the moon." But as foreboding and unwelcoming as it was, Howard and his crew wondered if they'd ever live to see it.

***

Yakutsk, Siberia, 1938

Ten and a half hours after their takeoff from Omsk, the Lockheed approached the runway at the northern Siberian port of Yakutsk. Looking out the plane's window, Ed Lund later claimed that it "did not appear fit for human habitation."

Howard's co-pilot, Harry Connor, had a different view. "There was an air of unreality about it, like we'd left the Earth and were making our descent upon some remote outpost in the universe, perhaps something on Mars." Howard himself found the location of the port city, surrounded by fierce granite mountains, "rather awesome," the austerity relieved by the roaring Lena River.

Once on the ground, Howard and his crew faced the same problem they'd had at Omsk—the need for an English-speaking interpreter. Howard cursed himself for not bringing along a crew member fluent in Russian. Finally, a rotund teacher was summoned. He'd obviously consumed too much vodka early that morning, but he did know the English word for gasoline. Howard gave him the equivalent of one-hundred dollars in U.S. currency, but in Russian rubles. That was enough to get the teacher to instruct the airport crew to refuel the empty tanks. Howard's own crew took over the thorough inspection of the plane to prepare it for its flight to Fairbanks, Alaska.

Locals from the port town began to arrive at the airport in droves. At first Howard thought it was mere curiosity. But the teacher managed to convey to him the superstitions of the Yakutskites. The year was only 1938 but the plane contained "1939" as part of its name. The local rubberneckers thought that Howard's plane was some sort of spaceship that had flown back in time. They felt the Lockheed was an aircraft from the future.

As a final request to the teacher, Howard wrote down a cable for him to send to Kate at Fenwick. "Still safe, HH," was his terse greeting from bleak Siberia.

Bidding the gaping-mouthed people of Yakutsk a final goodbye, Howard and his crew had a beautiful takeoff. But he was extremely nervous, knowing that the maps supplied by the United States Hydrographic Survey were largely speculative in 1938 and had not been carefully plotted. "They were *guesstimates*," Howard later said. To compound his problem, he thought the maps were calibrated in feet. They were actually in meters.

At first the flying had gone smoothly. Something deep within Howard's soul seemed to bring out the poet in him as he later described the adventure to Glenn Odekirk back in New York. "The skies over Siberia were lavender with streaks of magenta. The sky would suddenly be pierced by bolts of the brightest golds and the most fiery reds, like a giant roaring bonfire fueled by kerosene."

Checking his instrument panel, Howard noted that he was flying at 7,500 feet above the earth as they approached a dangerous mountain range. Not knowing exactly how high these mountains were, he nosed the craft up to 8,500 feet. When one mountain came into immediate view, the craft climbed to almost 10,000 feet. Even so, the Lockheed barely cleared the 9,700-foot crest of the jagged mountain, only 25 feet below the plane. Richard Stoddart later said, "I could see every rock up close."

"The mountain was solid granite," Ed Lund later said. "Talk about tombstones!"

Howard had cursed the delay in Paris, but the stopover had saved his life and that of the crew. Without the delay in France, he surely would have been flying over these Siberian mountains in the pitch blackness of night and would no doubt have crashed.

Unnerved by the experiences over Siberia, Howard was eager to return to the North American continent. He pointed his craft in the direction of Fairbanks. "We're going home, fellows," he told his crew. "The worst is over."

***

Fairbanks, Alaska, 1938

It was 3:01pm on the afternoon of Wednesday, July 13th, that Howard's plane touched down on the airport runway at Fairbanks. Waiting to greet him was the widow of Wiley Post. Her husband had been killed instantly in a plane crash with humorist Will Rogers in Point Barrow, Alaska, on August 15, 1935. Mae Post rushed to embrace Howard and kissed him on his cheek, with its three days' growth of beard. Tears were streaming down her face.

The widow talked briefly about Wiley's own successful circling of the globe is 1931. Suddenly, a ground crew member, in attempting to help with the refueling, opened the wrong compartment, releasing thousands of Ping-Pong balls Howard had stored there in case the plane was forced to land on water. Eager souvenir hunters, who had flocked to the Fairbanks airport, fought for the hollow plastic balls, which they rightly perceived would be worth a lot of money one day.

Spending as little time as possible at Fairbanks for refueling, Howard was wished "Godspeed" by Mae Post and waved goodbye as his plane headed south to Canada and ultimately to the United States.

News of Howard's arrival at Alaska was flashed around the world. "We're getting ready to give Hughes and his men a real New York welcome, Grover Whalen, "the greeter," announced to the press.

In New York, at Kate's Turtle Bay residence, reporters, the idle curious, and cameramen (they weren't called paparazzi back then) kept her townhouse under

420

siege. *"Hughes-mania* is sweeping the country," columnist Walter Winchell proclaimed, "to all the ships at sea."

Howard planned another refueling stop in Manitoba. But a violent storm raging over western Canada prevented him from doing that. Changing plans at the last minute, he headed for a "pit stop" in Minneapolis instead.

Only one reporter was there to record the event for a world audience. On ground for only thirty-four minutes for refueling, Howard took off again, heading for his final stop at Floyd Bennett Field in Brooklyn, where it had all begun.

After becoming airborne over Minneapolis, he told his crew, "It's a cakewalk the rest of the way."

Such was not to be the case. Exhausted and so sleepy he could hardly keep his eyes open, Howard insisted on remaining at the controls. Stoddart felt he wanted "all the glory of the flight to belong just to him."

The weather abruptly turned against Howard, as he encountered one cloud bank coming in the wake of another across the Great Lakes. Fierce headwinds bombarded the Lockheed.

At two in the afternoon, the Lockheed passed over Scranton, Pennsylvania. It had begun its descent into Brooklyn.

From Floyd Bennett Field a message arrived for Howard. "You're the toast of New York," a control operator in Brooklyn notified him, as he was about to land. "Get ready to be mobbed!"

***

New York, 1938

From his pilot's seat, Howard could see masses of people "like tiny ants," some thirty thousand of them (estimates varied), converging onto the Brooklyn airfield to cause pandemonium. Although his arrival runway had been designated and a platform of microphones had been set up by New York's "glad-hander," Grover Whalen, Howard made an impulsive decision. He steered his Lodestar to a more isolated strip on the field.

This sudden move completely upset everyone's plans, including Police Commissioner Louis Valentine, who had summoned more that one thousand men in blue from New York's finest to protect Howard, his fellow crewmen, and his plane.

Seeing Howard diverting the Lockheed and not wanting to miss any of the action, the unruly mob broke through police barricades and stormed toward the plane on the more remote airstrip. Howard was the last to emerge from the cockpit. Looking gaunt and with a four-day growth of beard, he stepped down onto the tarmac to the sound of thunderous applause, screaming, sirens, blowing horns, shrill whistles, and loud cheers. His "voyage into history" had taken three days, nineteen hours, eight minutes, and ten seconds.

He and his crew had flown a distance of 14,824 miles, beating the solo

Howard Hughes, Fiorello LaGuardia

flight record of that one-eyed adventurer, Wiley Post, by almost half.

Screaming hysterically, fans, cameramen, and reporters rushed toward Howard and his weary crew. As reported in *The New York Times*, "Microphones were pushed in his face, flashbulbs blinded him throughout the episode, and the crowd became a mob."

Huffing and puffing, Whalen, along with New York's chubby mayor, Fiorello LaGuardia, finally arrived at the remote airstrip. A dozen policemen "cut a pathway" through to Howard.

Still trying to break through, a young staff member from Western Union fought the surging crowd to pierce Howard's inner circle to deliver him a telegram. It was from Kate Hepburn, the first of thousands around the world to congratulate him on his epic voyage.

At the time of the landing and mass hysteria, Kate at her Turtle Bay residence in Manhattan was talking on the phone to Cary Grant who'd called her from Hollywood. He urged her to announce the date of her upcoming marriage to Howard in a hastily called press conference that following morning—"and for God's sake set a date and stick to it." The actor told her that her announcement of her upcoming marriage would be a marvelous way to cash in on all the worldwide publicity generated by Howard's record-breaking flight. "It will revitalize your career," Cary told Kate. Before ringing off, he also claimed that if she'd make an announcement in the press, "It will push David Selznick over the edge in granting you the role of Scarlett."

He was referring, of course, to the role Kate coveted above all others—that of Scarlett O'Hara in the upcoming film version of Margaret Mitchell's *Gone With the Wind*.

At the Brooklyn Field, Whalen practically dragged Howard to a position in front of the microphones, where LaGuardia addressed the nation. "Seven million New Yorkers offer congratulations for the greatest record established in the history of aviation."

In his grating, high-pitched voice, Howard, his eyes sagging in exhaustion, spoke to the nation rather ungracefully. "The flight was wonderful and this is the world's best crew. All I can say is, this crowd frightens me more than anything in the last three days! I'm glad it's over. I expect to get as much sleep this week as possible. I want to bathe and eat, get a massage and a good shave."

Whalen had reserved rooms for Howard and his crew at the Hampshire Hotel on Central Park. But he first invited Howard and his men to be driven by limousine to his house at 48 Washington Mews in Greenwich Village, which originally had been two adjoining stables for horses.

After chatting briefly with LaGuardia and reporters at the mews house, Howard excused himself claiming, "I smell like a skunk." He quickly went upstairs where Whalen's Filipino houseboy, Juan, had prepared a bubble bath for him.

After thirty minutes, Whalen came upstairs to offer Howard a clean white shirt. Howard's already thin and lanky frame had shrunk even more after the flight, and the shirt didn't fit. Whalen quickly summoned Juan to rush over to Wanamaker's and purchase a smaller shirt, size 15 ½.

Howard promised his host he'd be down soon to join the mayor and reporters. When another thirty minutes passed, and no Howard, Whalen went upstairs again to investigate, finding that Howard had flown the coop. He'd crawled through a window, sneaking into the backyard and disappearing through a rose-festooned iron gate onto Eighth Street.

There he hailed a Yellow Cab to take him to Kate's house at Turtle Bay. As the cab approached the house, Howard, to his dismay, saw that the street outside her residence was packed with reporters, photographers and rubberneckers. Each hoped to catch a glimpse of the dashing aviator as he appeared on the doorstep of his lady love.

He ordered the taxi driver to turn back and take him to the Drake Hotel instead. He registered under the name of Howard Alexander.

In his suite, he called Kate and talked for thirty minutes, filling her in on the harrowing details of his around-the-world voyage. Before ringing off, he agreed to meet with her the following day.

There has been much speculation, often in print, about what Howard did on his first night back in New York. Most of these tales are romantic, spinning around the myth that he spent the night in the arms of Kate Hepburn making love. Of course, all these contrived stories fail to take into account that he was too exhausted to make love to anyone, even Cary Grant.

The most fanciful tale of all was written by actress Terry Moore in her tell-all book, *The Passions of Howard Hughes.* Terry was a longtime mistress of Howard's, and, as she claims, one of his wives.

In her tale, Terry has Kate arriving at the Drake Hotel disguised as a bell-hop to avoid reporters. She appears at the door of Howard's suite in a "forest green uniform with gold épaulets on the shoulders, big brass buttons on the front of the jacket, and gold braid running down the sides of her trousers."

Having disguised herself in such a way, we are led to believe, she delivers a bottle of Cristal Rodier, 1931, and sandwiches "for my flyboy."

As if a tape recorder existed within the suite, Terry reports the following dialogue.

HOWARD:	Katie, do it to me.
KATE:	Do what?
HOWARD:	You know what. It's all I could think about.
KATE:	No, I'm not going to do it.
HOWARD:	C'mon Katie, do it.
KATE:	No, you haven't been a good boy.
HOWARD:	I've been a very good boy, in fact, I've been the best.

At this point Terry has Kate unfastening the buckle to Howard's trousers to "feel for him," as his breath becomes spasmodic.

But instead of a night of passion as envisioned by Miss Moore, Howard told Glenn Odekirk the following day that he'd ordered a large piece of pound cake and a quart of cold milk from room service. A bellhop did arrive, a bona-fide man this time, wearing exactly the same uniform as described by Terry.

After consuming the cake and cold milk, Howard claimed that, "I fell into the sleep of the dead."

***

Accompanied by Mayor LaGuardia and Grover Whalen, Howard received the traditional ticker-tape parade that New York awarded during that era to America's heroes. In an open car, he was driven up Broadway through the "Canyon of Heroes," facing a paper snowstorm. At one point a New York telephone directory, weighing two pounds, nearly knocked him unconscious. Later the Sanitation department claimed that some eighteen hundred tons of paper were thrown at Howard, as compared to the sixteen hundred tons which rained down on Charles Lindbergh in 1927 following his solo transatlantic flight to Paris.

"One of the strange customs of New Yorkers is to bombard its heroes with trash," columnist Walter Winchell later remarked. *The New York Times* estimated that a million well-wishers lined the parade route along Broadway. Another eight hundred thousand jammed onto Lower Broadway between the Battery and City Hall.

Finally reaching City Hall in the hot, steamy July weather, Howard had to sit through a barrage of speeches. Mayor LaGuardia made the opening remarks, as Howard sat nervously on the podium, with "the face of a poet and the shyness of a schoolboy," one reporter from *The New York Times* noted.

As he waited to be introduced, Howard kept biting and licking his chapped lips. He took off his hat, only to put it back on again, and he repeated that action endlessly.

In his nervousness, Whalen at long last introduced "the star of the hour," calling Howard "Edward Hughes." Hat in hand, Howard told the adoring throngs that his flight had placed the United States into the number one position in world aviation.

As the day wore on, the acclaim, the speeches, and the adoration began to take a toll on Howard. He was clearly growing impatient, and even bored with his achievement. "I want to move on," he told Ed Lund and Glenn Odekirk.

Eventually, after his return to Burbank, he would tell Lund and Odekirk that he planned another global flight, this time aboard a new Boeing model 307, the *Stratoliner*, the first fully pressurized, high-altitude aircraft. On this upcoming trip, he would fly to the major capitals of the world as part of a goodwill tour. But Hitler's invasion of Poland and the launch of World War II the following year would put an end to Howard's dream.

In New York, it was nearly nine o'clock that evening as Howard's limousine, flanked by a motorcycle escort of two policemen, rode up Fifth Avenue. When it stopped for a red light, Howard suddenly jumped out of the car and ran through the front entrance of a deluxe hotel. Racing through the lobby, he headed toward its side entrance and his escape. On Fifty-Sixth Street, he hailed a taxi and ordered the driver to take him to an official reception that Whalen was staging for him along the Jersey Shore.

Upon reaching the New Jersey coast, he ordered the taxi driver to halt about a block from the reception. Parked on a dark streetcorner was a black Lincoln with its lights off. Howard handed the taxi driver a one hundred dollar bill, although he usually didn't carry cash with him. He waved the driver off and rushed across the street to slip back into the back seat of the darkened Lincoln and into the arms of Kate Hepburn.

Her driver then drove both of them to the entrance of the reception hall, where America's second-most-famous couple, after "Franklin and Eleanor," appeared like a "photographer's dream" as they entered the building. Kate had linked her arm with Howard's.

Back in New York around midnight and on that same evening, the manager of the Drake Hotel personally placed a DO NOT DISTURB sign on the door to the Honeymoon Suite, rented by Howard as a love nest for Kate and himself.

The suite had two bedrooms. After finishing off a bottle of champagne,

Howard retired to his room, after kissing Kate goodbye at the door to hers.

Shortly before two o'clock that morning, if George Cukor's story is to be believed, the tall, lanky frame of Howard appeared at the door to Kate's bedroom. He entered without knocking.

As she would later recall to her confidants in Hollywood, Howard was completely nude except for the felt hat he'd worn on his flight around the world.

In his hand he held the pinkish-red porcelain bowl his mother back in Texas so long ago had repeatedly held up before his genitals.

As he moved toward her bed, she instinctively knew what act he wanted her to perform.

CHAPTER THIRTEEN

New York, 1938

Howard left early the next morning for Washington, D.C., to take part in another parade in his honor. Before checking out of New York's Drake Hotel, he delivered an ultimatum to Kate. She had just three days to set a date for their wedding. After that, he was "withdrawing the offer forever."

She immediately called Cary Grant and burst into tears. "He doesn't want a real woman. He wants me to be his mother. I can't do it. It won't work." Even when he learned more details about the porcelain bowl, Cary still pressed marriage onto Kate. "His demands on you will be few, and you can pursue other affairs." The actor had endlessly repeated this point to her, as if it were the major selling point of a marriage to Howard.

"Sounds like the perfect marriage," she said before ringing off.

She called George Cukor and told him what happened. "I think I love Howard. I think he feels the same way about me. But in the end, both of us want fame more than each other. I fear that ambition has won out over love." She paused. "Or should I say *like?*"

She spent the rest of the day contemplating whether to call Howard and discuss a possible marriage or whether she should let the three-day ultimatum pass without a response.

Finally, she called him, not to discuss a date for their marriage, but to invite him to join her for a weekend at Fenwick where she wanted to spend time with her family. He rather abruptly turned her down.

Unknown to her, he'd already accepted another invitation, planning to visit his friend Sherman Fairchild at Lloyd's Neck. Other than Howard, Fairchild had also invited another guest of honor: Miss Fay Wray, King Kong's would-be mistress (if the ape's plumbing and some fighter planes had not intervened). She was taking time off from films to appear in summer theater in New England, starring in a light comedy, *George and Margaret.*

Ironically, Fay was married at the time to Howard's former friend and cousin by marriage. The writer, John Monk Saunders, had first wed Avis Hughes, Rupert's daughter. Saunders and Howard had several battles over *Hell's Angels*, the writer claiming that Howard had been "much too inspired" by his own script of *Wings* when he began filming *Hell's Angels.*

Saunders and Howard had also tangled over another script he wrote, *The Dawn Patrol*, for Howard Hawks. Howard had actually sued Hawks for *Dawn Patrol*, insisting that much of that film's script was lifted from *Hell's Angels.* The suit was dropped.

Fay Wray

Because of bad blood that existed between Saunders and Howard, he had no qualms about putting the moves on Fay Wray.

"Actually, with Howard, it wouldn't have mattered if Saunders were his best and most loyal friend," Fairchild once confided to a group of men at his club. One of the members, William Lund, reported that Fairchild said that not as a put-down to Howard, but with a certain gleam of satisfaction. "Fairchild did the same thing himself with women, married or not," Lund claimed.

The daughter of a Canadian rancher, Fay was a dark-haired, rather fragile-looking beauty with delicate chalk-white skin. Her father had driven her by stagecoach from Alberta to resettle in Arizona. A fellow Virgo, she was two years older than Howard. He'd seen her on the screen, not only in *King Kong*, but when she'd appeared as a poor Viennese girl, Mitzi, opposite Erich von Stroheim in *The Wedding March* in 1926.

Fay had met Howard on at least three other occasions without arousing any passion in him. On meeting him again on the East Coast, she later said that she'd noticed an enormous change in him. "He'd lost that little boy shyness," she said in a rare 1976 interview she granted. "He was more self-assured. I guess being an aviation hero did that for him."

Both Fay and Howard had been invited as weekend guests at the home of Jock Whitney in Saratoga. Apparently, Howard did not know that Fay would be there until he arrived at the Whitney home. Sportsman and philanthropist, Jock is known today as the last publisher of *The New York Herald Tribune* and the chief financial backer of President Dwight D. Eisenhower.

Jock and Howard had become good friends and often bragged about mutual conquests they'd shared, including Tallulah Bankhead. In spite of Charlie Chaplin, Jock was also having an affair with Paulette Goddard, whom he recommended to Howard "but only after I'm through with her." Jock also kidded Howard, claiming, "Joan Crawford put out for me, but kept her chastity belt locked for you."

Apparently, Jock asked Fay to Saratoga to seduce her, but foolishly he also invited his chief rival in the boudoir, Howard himself.

"When he arrived at Jock's house," Fay said, "Howard paid attention to no one but me. I was extremely flattered. Jock had invited a lot of his society friends to meet the conquering hero of the air. Howard asked me to step out on the terrace for some fresh air. What he wanted was to get away from his adoring fans. Out on the terrace, he took my hand and looked into my eyes. I still remember his comment. He turned to me and said, 'I thought you brought a virginal beauty to the screen.'"

"I'm no virgin, Mr. Hughes,' I told him. I was a bit coy perhaps. Actually, I resented the virginal roles I'd been given. In Hollywood, I was the damsel in distress. Producers called me 'the screamer.' I was also a woman of the world. I'd had affairs with the likes of Gary Cooper, Hoot Gibson, and even Ralph Graves. Decades later, a gossipy friend told me that Howard too had had affairs with Gary and Ralph."

She admitted her surprise that Howard was so obviously in hot pursuit of her because she'd practically read "nothing else in the papers but his passion for Hepburn." She'd been skeptical of "this great romance" between Howard and Kate for some time. Ironically, at the time of her meeting with Howard, Fay's agent was none other than Leland Hayward, with whom she was also having an affair.

Leland had admitted to her that he and Kate were also having an on-again, off-again affair, even though the press had her madly in love with Howard. "What a tangled web we wove with our romantic intrigue back then," Fay said. "At least in Hollywood, we liked to keep our love-making all in the family. I was involved with Leland who was involved with Hepburn who was involved with Howard who was now trying to get involved with me."

While houseguests of Jock, both Fay and Howard met a wealthy Long Island couple, Herbert and Margaret Swope. Assuming that Howard and Fay were "illicit lovers," Herbert invited the couple for a weekend at his own Long Island estate. "You'll escape the reporters there," Herbert promised. Fay admitted her surprise when Howard so readily accepted the invitation. Intrigued by the offer as well, she also accepted.

In her aptly titled memoir, *On the Other Hand,* Fay remembered Howard's arrival at the Swope home. He looked weary "with his shirt rumpled." She recalled that he wore "blue serge trousers held up by a leather belt that was tied in a knot, the buckle missing."

In her 1976 interview, she said, "He didn't look much like America's hero of the decade. But he had an undeniable appeal. My marriage to John Saunders was breaking up, and I was ripe for another affair. Howard appeared in my life just at the right time. I was feeling weak and vulnerable. Of course, women have used that old line for centuries to commit adultery."

After the stay with the Swopes couple, Howard began to show up every night at Fay's dressing room door at a Long Island theater. "He was a real stage door Johnny," she confessed. "After an evening's performance, he would drive me back to the Pierre in New York and gingerly kiss me goodnight—on the cheek no less. Once I invited him up to my room but, like the gentleman that he was, he declined."

"After about eight nights of dating, he asked me to come and spend the weekend with him at Sherman Fairchild's mansion on Long Island," she said. "He tempted me by sending me a hundred blooms of the sweetest smelling gardenias God ever grew on this earth. I'd heard that he'd given the same floral tribute to Hepburn. Foolishly, I agreed to go."

She was to meet him at the train station at Stamford, Connecticut. Arriving at the station, she spotted Howard running toward her. He claimed he couldn't get on the train with her because he was being chased by a "gaggle" of reporters. He feared that both of them would be mobbed by the press, their pictures splashed all over the New York tabloids in the morning.

"Before disappearing again, he then directed me to return to my suite at the Pierre," she said. "I did as he instructed. Once back in my suite, I got a call from him. This time he directed me to meet him at the Thirty Fourth Street Pier on the East River. When I got there, I found him waiting for me in a seaplane, a craft so small it could hardly contain his long, lanky frame."

"We flew under the Fifty-Ninth Street Bridge," she said. "I'd read that he'd pulled the same stunt with Hepburn. The gardenias, the under-the-bridge flight in the seaplane—I was beginning to feel that he was wooing me in the exact same way he'd courted Hepburn."

He steered the plane toward Long Island where he landed on a small lake. From there, he escorted her along the short walk to the Fairchild mansion.

After dinner with Fairchild, she said she turned in early, as Howard remained downstairs to talk to his host. "I dressed for bed and put on a silk nightgown," she said. "In less than an hour, Howard just appeared in my bedroom where I was resting comfortably in a lavish four-poster bed. A door at the far end of the room opened. Naïvely, I was surprised to see him. Realistically and emotionally, I knew I was not going to send him away."

At that point in the saga, Fay in her memoirs dropped the subject. She grew up in an era on the screen when the shades were pulled as a man and woman came together in the boudoir for love-making. In her 1976 interview, she was more candidly revealing.

"Over the years, many other actresses have told me what a disappointing lover Howard was," she said. "I think the word impotent was actually used. That was not the case with Howard and me. I found him a tender, loving male animal, emphasis on the *animal*. He rekindled a passion in me that I thought had been smothered during my difficult marriage to John, who was a notorious womanizer. I think I fell in love with Howard after that first night. Instead of looking upon it as an adulterous affair on my part, I viewed it as my honeymoon night."

"I woke up the next morning looking like Vivien Leigh in *Gone With the Wind*," Fay said. "Of course, the film hadn't been made at the time. You remember the scene where Rhett Butler carries her up those wide stairs and rapes her, and she wakes up the next morning with a cat-swallowed-the-canary smile on her face. That was *moi*. Of course, Howard didn't rape me. I was only too willing. What Kong didn't get from me, Howard did. He did bear some resemblance to Kong, if you get my drift."

She claimed that never once did he mention Kate Hepburn to her. "The papers were full of his upcoming marriage. You couldn't pick up a magazine without seeing those two on the cover. What the world didn't know at the time was that Howard wasn't in Hepburn's arms—that is, if he'd ever been in her arms—but was in mine."

Over the next few days, Howard and Fay were seen everywhere together. For the first time, snippets of gossip about the Wray/Hughes romance began to appear in the newspapers, first in New York and then in Hollywood. Indiscreetly, Fay answered a call from Louella Parsons and confided that Howard had asked her to marry him—and that she had accepted. She said that this tidbit of gossip was off the record, and promised Louella that if she would not print the item now, she'd give her the full scoop of their intended wedding date.

When one reporter spotted Fay and Howard kissing at a Long Island Pier, he asked. "Are you engaged to Hughes?" The couple dashed away from him. Fay turned back coyly and called to the reporter, "Oh, is *this* Mr. Hughes?" Howard rushed her aboard a speedboat and headed back to the Fairchild mansion for privacy.

"By the way, what did those guys pay you for King Kong?" Howard asked Fay one night at dinner. "They made a bundle off of you."

"Ten thousand dollars—that was it," she told him.

"Were you afraid at any time?" he asked her.

"Are you kidding?" she said. "Kong was only eighteen inches tall. Actually, my fear was that I'd slip and fall from his fake arm which was eight feet long. They would bring this fake arm down and tighten it around my waist, then pull me up in the air. Every time I moved, one of the fingers would loosen, so it would look like I was trying to get away. Instead, I was trying not to slip through that hand."

On yet another night, Fay claimed that Howard took her to the 102-story skyscraper, the Empire State Building, where the giant ape had placed her on a ledge before lunging furiously at fighter planes peppering him with bullets before he fell to his death. "If you want to own that building, I'll buy it for you," she claimed that Howard told her that night.

[When Fay Wray died in August of 2004, the Empire State Building dimmed its lights for fifteen minutes in her honor.]

At the time Howard was pursuing Fay, she was also being sought after by author Sinclair Lewis, then at the height of his fame. "Faced with a choice of handsome Howard or ugly Sinclair, it was no contest," Fay said. "To me, Sinclair looked more beastly than Kong." She remembered Sinclair, her stalker, in her memoirs as "unattractive in appearance—tall, gangly, and skeletal, his narrow face pockmarked, his teeth and fingers yellow from smoking. A small amount of hair justified the nickname 'Red.'"

Another writer, Clifford Odets, would succeed with Fay where Sinclair Lewis didn't—that is, when Odets wasn't with Cary Grant who wasn't otherwise engaged with Howard himself.

"It was romance on the air and sea," Fay later claimed. "Howard was picking me up at that East River Pier in New York and flying me to various mansions on Long Island Sound. We were visiting all his rich friends—acquaintances really—that he'd met in summers gone by. The only people we didn't call upon were the Hepburns at Fenwick. He promised to revitalize my career and put me in big and important pictures which would blot out the image of me as the bride of Kong. 'When you see the scripts I've got planned for you, you'll view each one as a potential Oscar winner. No more screams for you. Your vocal chords won't have to work overtime.' I chided him: 'Twas beauty killed the beast,' I said before tumbling into bed with my handsome, rich beau."

After thirty days, Howard abruptly dropped Fay and never called her again. He refused to answer her teary phone calls. "Our affair began like a dream and ended like a nightmare," she said.

After being dumped by Howard, Fay did not repair her marriage to John. Conditions worsened after he injected her with drugs while she slept. He later sold their house and furnishings, keeping all the money for himself. For a time, he kidnapped their daughter, Susan, and disappeared.

John continued to brood about his wife's affair with Howard long after it was over.

"Even when I was no longer seeing Howard, John told everyone I was divorcing him to marry Howard, which wasn't true," she said. "I think John knew it wasn't true. But he still claimed it. It was an excuse for him to keep drinking more and taking more drugs. He was slowly killing himself. Apparently, a slow death was not what he had in mind. He committed suicide in Fort Myers on March 11 in 1940. We'd divorced the year before."

Before his death, Saunders sent Howard a screenplay he'd actually completed in September of 1935. It was entitled *Lawrence of Arabia.* Howard briefly scanned the script and rejected it, finding that the subject of the adventures of Lawrence of Arabia had "no commercial appeal to the general public." The subject of Lawrence would have to wait until 1962 when David Lean came out with his now classic version, much of the action having been preconceived long before by Saunders.

Fay was the final straw for Kate. She never confronted Howard directly but called Cary Grant in Hollywood to tell him, "There will be no marriage! Howard and I were never lovers. We were always good friends, and that's how we'll remain from now on. Our affair is over. Actually, it never began."

Houston, 1938

Like New York, Chicago turned out en masse to greet Howard with a ticker-tape parade along La Salle Street on July 20, 1938. That afternoon he was hailed as "the new king of aviation." *The Chicago Tribune* proclaimed, "As long as America has men like aviator Howard Hughes, Hitler's Luftwaffe doesn't even have a fighting chance." Although the comment smacked of jingoism, Howard lapped it up.

In his silver Lockheed, Howard flew from Chicago for a long overdue appearance in Houston. As his plane landed at the modest airfield—rechristened by city officials as The Howard Hughes Airport—some ten thousand people were on hand to welcome their hometown hero.

As he stepped out of the cockpit, the National Junior Chamber of Commerce had recently proclaimed him as one of the outstanding young men of 1938, along with New York's Thomas E. Dewey, who would run against Franklin D. Roosevelt in 1944 and against Harry Truman in 1948. Not only that, but the National Aeronautics Association had named him Aviator of the Year, and the editorial board at *Colliers* magazine had given him its coveted trophy for aviation achievement of the year. That latter triumph would bring Howard back to the White House where President Roosevelt himself would make the presentation.

Later that afternoon, 350,000 Houstonians—three-fourths of the city's population—lined the streets of Houston to welcome Howard, greeting him with cheers and showers of confetti. He had a reunion with his long-suffering aunt, Annette Lummis, at the old family manse on Yoakum Boulevard, which seemed to stir up bitter childhood memories for Howard.

Even so, some fifty former acquaintances showed up on the back porch to welcome him home. Howard's boyhood friend, Dudley Sharp, had asked to come but Howard turned down the request.

On the back porch, Howard chatted with men and women he'd known, enjoying Houston ice tea punch and slices of watermelon along with Annette's "triple threat" chocolate fudge cake. After the well-wishers had gone, Howard told Annette, "I didn't think any of my friends would speak to me again after I divorced Ella."

That night his aunt accompanied him to a banquet hosted by Texas governor, James V. Allred. Howard appeared uncomfortable, and it became obvious that the constant parades, banquets, and speeches were making him restless.

Even so, he flattered the state of his birth in a speech. "Coming from Texas peculiarly fits a person for flying around the world," he told diners at the banquet. "There's nothing you can see anywhere that you can't see in Texas, and after you've flown across Texas two or three times, the distance around the world doesn't seem so great. Now we'd better sample this ice cream *à la*

Howard on the menu before it melts."

The next day, *Time* magazine referred to him as "the young man who looked like Gary Cooper and flew like Lindbergh." Howard paid a visit to his employees at Toolco, where he was greeted with WELCOME HOWARD signs. At a dinner that night, Howard caught up on his much neglected business affairs with Noah Dietrich. At the time he told Dietrich that he'd already achieved his greatest ambition, which was to become "the world's greatest aviator."

Dietrich confronted him with Toolco business and was dismayed at Howard's lack of attention, even though Toolco remained the source of his wealth. Dietrich quickly brought him up to date on the state of business affairs, even presenting him with evidence that one of his executives was stealing money from Toolco at the rate of $250,000 a year. The executive had been so brazen that he would, for example, charge $25,000 worth of paintings which he would then order delivered to his private home. To Dietrich's surprise, Howard did not immediately order the firing of this official and refused to bring charges. "It'll stir up bad will in Houston if I do because he has powerful friends who will get back at me by taking their business elsewhere." Eventually, Dietrich was able to ease the executive out the Toolco door without charges or a scandal.

Although warm and gracious in public during the banquets, parades, and honors, Howard was "colder than ever, with his arteries pumping ice water," according to Dietrich. He later claimed that Howard had become more ruthless in his sexual use of both handsome young men and beautiful women. "After that flight around the world, he was to launch himself into the most callous period of his life, proceeding without any regard for the feelings of others. He did what he god damn pleased, regardless of how it might have impacted anybody else. He would simply devour people in the future, much like a Roman emperor, summoning them to his court and then discarding them when he grew tired of them like he'd done with Fay Wray. I never knew a man who was so totally devoid of emotion."

That night, Howard told Annette, "There's nothing to come home to when I get back to Muirfield. I don't know what my next career move is going to be. I'm considering big things in aviation because a war's sure to come. Airplanes will decide the ultimate victor."

She inquired about his romance with Kate.

"That's off!" he claimed. "I'm in the market for a new girlfriend."

It was July 31, 1938 at 1:35pm at the Howard Hughes Airport. Toolco employees, Gano cousins from Dallas, Annette, Noah Dietrich and others watched as the *New York's World Fair 1939* was refueled and prepared for take-off.

Howard waved a final goodbye to his well-wishers. He roared down the runway in the Lockheed and disappeared into an ominous gray cloud that had suddenly appeared on the horizon. In its denseness, Houston and its memories

434

were quickly blotted out.

At that very moment, *The Houston Post* was publishing an edition that asserted that Howard had returned to his hometown with "more glory heaped upon his slim shoulders than a dozen men ever know in lifetime." A modest comment, for sure. Instead of dozen men, the Post might have more accurately reported millions of men.

Annette stood for a long moment after the Lockheed had disappeared. She could not have imagined that she would never see her nephew again. Even though he was destined to live for another thirty-eight years, he'd paid his final visit to his hometown and would only return as a corpse flying in on a plane from Mexico.

***

California, 1938-1950s

Even though barely twenty-one, Susan Hayward's granite-hard Brooklynese spirit reminded Howard of Barbara Stanwyck. A sexy, gutsy red-head, she'd been born into poverty, the daughter of a Coney Island carnival barker, Walter Marrener, and his Swedish wife, Ellen. She'd hawked copies of *The Brooklyn Eagle* on street corners before graduating to the stenographer's pool. Eventually she became a photographer's model, which after a few short months landed her photograph on the cover of *The Saturday Evening Post*. There, it was seen by director George Cukor, who brought it to the attention of David O. Selznick, at the time searching for an actress to star as Scarlett O'Hara in *Gone With the Wind*.

Howard, too, had started to scan magazine covers looking for "new talent" to seduce. Like Cukor and Selznick, but unaware of their professional interest, he was struck by Susan's beauty.

Selznick's test of Edythe Marrener (Susan's real name) "was terrible," in the words of her first agent, Ben Medford. "She couldn't act. Nobody liked her. She was a real bitch. But I saw talent there."

Instead of playing Scarlett, Susan ended up in bit parts for Warner Brothers, including the 1938 Grade B flick, *Girls on Probation*. This brought her into contact with another B picture actor, handsome Ronald Reagan from Tampico, Illinois. She fell in love with him at once and began a passionate affair. Trouble was, he also made *Brother Rat* that same year with another rising young star, Jane Wyman, and she fell for Reagan too. At the time Howard met Susan, Jane was winning the race for Reagan.

Howard urged Johnny Meyer to goad Ben Medford to arrange a date between Susan and himself. Howard's pimp made some vague promise that his boss was going back into the movie business, and that he was looking for an unknown to star in a film about Billy the Kid. Of course, the movie would eventually be released as *The Outlaw*, starring not Susan, but a bosomy Jane

Russell.

Learning of his interest, Susan called Howard and invited him to her apartment for "a Brooklyn fried chicken dinner." He readily accepted. "I wouldn't be the first gal from Brooklyn who seduced a tall Texan," she said to Medford.

As Howard later told Noah Dietrich, "I disliked her intensely, and she disliked me. Incidentally, do people in Brooklyn eat their chicken bloody? It was disgusting. She spent the entire evening talking about how crazy she was about Ronald Reagan and what a bitch Jane Wyman was. At least I learned something. She told me that redheads make better actresses than blondes because the emotions of natural redheads are much closer to their face."

Susan Hayward

He quickly dropped Susan from his list, although he continued to watch her career as she won one Oscar nomination after another, appearing in powerful dramas such as *My Foolish Heart, Smash-Up: The Story of a Woman,* and *They Won't Believe Me.* He'd even followed the progress—or lack thereof—of her marriage to Grade B actor, the college-hero-handsome Jess Barker. Howard knew that her marriage had a financial imbalance, with Susan earning $400,000 a year and Jess pulling in only $650.

Howard ordered private screenings of all Susan's films, the good and the bad. Her beauty had captivated him when he'd seen her appear opposite Gregory Peck in *David and Bathsheba* in 1951. He was so intrigued, in fact, that he'd ordered a rough cut of *With A Song in My Heart.* After viewing it, he called Darryl F. Zanuck and told him that he wanted Susan for the female lead role in a property he was developing at RKO called *This Man Is Mine.* A horse trade was in the offing. Zanuck wanted to borrow Jane Russell, still under personal contract to Howard, for *Gentlemen Prefer Blondes* opposite Marilyn Monroe. A deal was worked out, and Zanuck agreed to release Susan to make the film. The title had been changed to *The Lusty Men*, and her co-stars would be Robert Mitchum and Arthur Kennedy. Susan hated the script, rightly perceiving that it was a man's picture. "If anyone goes to see this stinker, it'll be for the rodeo scenes," she said in disgust.

On the set, Susan was warm and cordial to Howard, although there was no immediate romance. She detested Mitchum. "The script calls for me to be antagonistic toward Mitchum," she told Kennedy. "Believe me, that isn't act-

436

ing on my part." Mitchum, Howard's favorite actor, didn't help matters by calling Susan "the old gray mare" every time she walked by. Before intimate on-camera scenes with her, he munched raw cloves of garlic.

Hayward's biographer, Beverly Linet, wrote in *Portrait of a Survivor*, "For all his bizarre behavior and varied sexual exploits, Hughes had an almost prudish morality in some way, which included a self-imposed proviso against bedding another man's wife." Nothing could be more unlike Howard. Although he'd become widely known for preferring recently divorced women—calling them "wet decks"—he liked married women even more. Billie Dove and Ginger Rogers were prime examples of that. In the case of Ginger, it might also be added that Howard liked bedding the husbands of beautiful actresses as well, particularly if they were young and handsome.

Not only was her own marriage to Jess Barker deteriorating, Susan was fascinated with Howard's charm and wealth. She even predicted to Arthur Kennedy that she was going to become the second Mrs. Howard Hughes.

Howard still had an abiding interest in A list actresses, although as the Fifties deepened he was seen more and more with starlets than stars. In the early Fifties, Susan Hayward was the undisputed queen of Twentieth Century Fox. The foreign press had dubbed her "The World's Most Famous Screen Star of 1952." Of course, an Eve Harrington was waiting in the wings to take over for Margo Channing in the film, *All About Eve*. In Susan's case, her dethroning would occur in only two years, when none other than Marilyn Monroe was unofficially crowned queen.

Howard began to pursue Susan with his usual intensity. Every day the most

Jess Barker

beautiful cut flowers in Los Angeles arrived on her doorstep. Even though still married to Barker, but separated, Susan began to date Howard. He'd arrive at her household to pick her up on dates. Her twin sons, Gregory and Timothy, had been born on February 19, 1945, and Susan introduced them to Howard as "Mr. Magic," never giving his real name.

As their affair deepened, a diamond bracelet arrived from Howard. Later, an elephant gray Rolls-Royce. Unknown to Susan at the time, Howard was dating starlet Jean Peters (his future wife) on the side. He was also linked with other starlets, including Debra Paget, who coyly flashed a large diamond ring, "a trinket from Howard," at least according to columnist Walter Winchell.

To camouflage her affair with Howard, Susan went out with other actors, notably cross-dresser Jeff Chandler, an extraordinarily handsome man with premature gray hair. "We're just two kids from Brooklyn," Susan told Louella Parsons, her old friend. Sometimes when Chandler would let Susan off at her doorstep, giving her a chaste kiss on the cheek, Howard would be waiting across the street in his darkened silver Duesenberg to take Susan to Muirfield for an early morning rendezvous.

One evening when Barker had been at Susan's house, after spending a day visiting with his twin boys, a violent fight erupted between the two of them. He pleaded with her to take him back, but she refused. When she denounced him as a failure both as a man and an actor, he struck her in the mouth, knocking her down.

With fierce determination, she picked herself up off the floor and grabbed a heavy vase, throwing it at his face. He ducked in time and punched her in the face again in retaliation. Hitting the floor, she suffered his kicks to her stomach. He then tore off her clothes as she clawed him. Still enraged, he crushed his heel into her face, blooding her nose. He picked her up as she fought like an enraged tiger, and carried her onto the terrace where he tossed her nude body into the pool. When her head emerged, he forced it back down into the water, trying to drown her. He stormed out of the house.

Not knowing where he was, she feared he was going for a gun she kept upstairs in her vanity. Pulling her bloody and bruised body from the pool, she ran nude across the lawn and into a neighbor's backyard, screaming for them to call the police. The news of this blowup would make headlines around the world, and would become part of the testimony at her divorce hearing.

When Susan told Howard about her ordeal, he was furious and totally enraged at Barker, although Howard had slapped a few women in his day. She wanted vengeance, and Howard agreed to help her by setting a trap for Barker. He would arrange a meeting with him, holding out the prospect of a big role to help his stalled career. Secretly, Howard had arranged for two of Johnny Meyer's goons to lay in wait for Barker, with orders to "beat him to a pulp and bash in his face—but not kill him." According to Johnny Meyer, Howard promised Susan that "Jess Barker will never appear in front of a camera again unless he tries out for monster roles."

The rendezvous between Barker and Howard did not go off as Susan or even Howard had intended. He agreed to meet Barker at three o'clock in the morning near the port of Los Angeles. Barker had read in the papers that Howard often conducted business very late at night in parked cars in rough neighborhoods of Los Angeles. Presumably, Barker wasn't too surprised at the circumstances of the invitation.

Meyer never knew exactly what happened on that night the handsome young actor got into the Duesenberg with Howard. All that is known is that

438

when Meyer's toughs came to "rearrange" Barker's face, Howard called off the assault. Instead of giving him a beating, Howard drove Barker to the pier where his *Southern Cross* was waiting. As his crew readied the yacht for a sail to Catalina, Howard invited Barker into his master suite.

"Jess Barker, from all reports, was straight," Meyer later claimed. "But what out-of-work actor would not drop trou for Hughes? All I know is that Howard got to find out what attracted Susan to Barker back in 1944."

Somehow, word of this sail to Catalina got back to Susan. For reasons not known, she decided not to hold this transgression against Howard, but blamed her husband for it instead. Angrily she denounced him and called him "a queer," which he really wasn't.

When that big movie role didn't emerge, and Barker realized he'd been had by Howard, he instructed his attorney to name Howard in his upcoming divorce proceedings against Susan, although not mentioning his homosexual liaison with Howard, which would have destroyed his last chance for a Hollywood career.

At a meeting in her attorney's office, Susan waited impatiently for Jess Barker to show up with his own attorney. Finally, both Barker and the lawyer arrived, deliberately keeping Susan waiting for over an hour. They fought bitterly over the custody of their two boys. She also pleaded with him not to bring up Howard's name in the divorce proceedings. He countered, "I plan to expose your sordid affair in all the papers." At that point, her famous temper flared, and she crushed out her cigarette into his left eyeball. He was rushed to the nearest hospital.

In March of 1954, Howard's name did come up in the divorce proceedings, which horrified him. He told Johnny Meyer that he was going to extricate himself from his affair with Susan.

In her court testimony, Susan claimed that her meetings with Howard were strictly business since she was scheduled to do a film for him. She also falsely claimed that she was trying to "get work from Hughes for my jobless husband."

Howard limped along in his affair with Susan, not breaking it off right away. Actually he was spending more and more time with Jean Peters, other beautiful starlets, and male hustlers supplied by Henry Willson.

In a reckless, impulsive move, Howard on New Year's Eve 1955, booked himself with three dates, all at the same time and on the same night within different areas of the Beverly Hills Hotel. He told Meyer that it was his banana split. "They are the three different scoops of ice cream. I'm the banana."

Each woman—Jean Peters, Susan Hayward, and aspirant singer and starlet, Yvonne Shubert—was placed at a table in a different dining room, with the seemingly amused Howard racing from table to table. To explain his absence, he was summoned by the hotel bellhop, whom he'd already bribed, to take a lot of emergency phone calls.

Many observers of Howard's love life viewed fifteen-year-old Yvonne

Shubert as Howard's "last hurrah." After seeing her picture in a magazine, he'd signed her up and sent her to take vocal, dance, and drama lessons. Howard had promised to marry her, and the young and inexperienced girl had fallen hopelessly in love with the fifty-year-old movie mogul and aviation hero. With increasingly forceful promises of marriage, he'd installed her in a sprawling house in Coldwater Canyon. He'd also "permanently" reserved a suite for her at the Beverly Hills Hotel, where he'd assigned four guards to watch over her. He'd also bugged the phones in both her home and the hotel suite.

In the main salon of the hotel's dining room, Jean Peters sat regally like a queen while waiters brought in chilled bottles of Don Perignon plus dozens of sweet-smelling gardenias.

Thinking she was going to get a proposal of marriage, Jean had never looked more beautiful. She wore a stunning white sequined gown, the creation of Jean Louis. Her brunette hair was piled on top of her head, and a slash of scarlet lipstick effectively set off her porcelain white skin. Howard launched his evening with her with a champagne toast and talk of their upcoming marriage plans when her divorce from Stuart Cramer III came through. When the bellhop arrived with an urgent message from TWA, Howard excused himself, but not before presenting Jean with a diamond-and-sapphire bracelet from Cartier.

Then he was off for a champagne toast with Susan, who had been assigned the best table in the Polo Lounge. Nearing forty, she too looked stunning in mink and a sheer white organdy gown by Edith Head. Upon her arrival in the Polo Lounge, she'd been presented with a nosegay of red roses. Howard delivered a diamond-and-sapphire bracelet from Cartier. Susan later claimed that she fully expected that Howard was going to propose marriage that night.

Excusing himself when the bellhop approached with the urgent call, Howard rushed into the garden to Yvonne's bungalow table. He'd had four guards positioned at the hotel with walkie-talkies to warn him of the approach of either of the other actresses.

A champagne toast with Yvonne, who was technically too young to drink, was followed by the presentation of a diamond-and-sapphire bracelet from Cartier that was nearly identical to the one offered a few moments previously to the other actresses. Yvonne, too, had never looked lovelier in her yellow silk brocaded dress with chiffon accents, the creation of Michael Woulfe, costume designer at MGM. He'd also filled Yvonne's bungalow with "all the yellow roses in Texas."

He pretended to enjoy the beef Stroganoff with her until summoned by an urgent phone call.

From the garden, he practically ran back to the main dining room and the table of Jean Peters.

Of the trio, Susan, the brightest, grew suspicious. She stormed into the main dining room where she caught Howard holding hands with Jean Peters and looking dreamily into her eyes. She came right up to Jean. "Hello, bitch," she said loud enough for the room to hear her. "I'm date number one. I'm a star. You're date number two. Always a starlet. Never a star."

With that remark, Susan raced out of the hotel. Jean, after slapping Howard's face, soon followed, ordering her limousine delivered to the main entrance. Neither woman knew of the presence of Yvonne back in the bungalow.

Yvonne later told writers that the evening was "incredibly romantic."

At the stroke of midnight, it was Yvonne—not Jean or Susan—that Howard was kissing.

Somehow in the days that followed, Howard managed to get back into the good graces of both Susan and Jean. Yvonne still remained clueless. Fearing that Howard would never marry her, Susan grew more and more despondent in the weeks and months ahead. On April 26, 1955, her mother, Ellen Marrener, called the police. Her daughter had taken a near fatal overdose of sleeping pills.

Rushing to the scene, the police broke down her door and hauled her off to the North Hollywood Medical Center where photographers were waiting. A tongue depressor hung from her slack lips. In the emergency room, her stomach was pumped, and she eventually recovered, only to face a film that would become lethal for her. "The sleeping pills didn't do her in," her mother said. "But Hughes's *The Conqueror* did."

Beginning in 1951, the U.S. government had launched nuclear explosions at Yucca Flat, Nevada, under Georgia O'Keefe skies. For background shots in *The Conqueror*, viewed today as "one of the fifty worst films ever made," Howard ordered the crew to St. George, Utah. It was here that radioactive dust had rained down after the nuclear explosions across the border in Nevada. This section of the West was considered the most dangerous ground in the United States.

In sending his crew to such a lethal site, Howard could not totally plead ignorance. He'd produced the film, *Split Second*, with Dick Powell as director. Powell, husband of June Allyson, was also producing *The Conqueror. Split Second* dealt with the danger of radiation in Nevada caused by nuclear testing, so Howard was well versed on the subject.

In perhaps the worst case of miscasting in Hollywood history, John Wayne arrived on the outdoor set in Utah to play Genghis Khan. Susan, "the gal from Brooklyn," was cast as a red-haired Tartar princess. Filming began on what would become a $6 million epic.

Even after filming ended in Utah, several scenes had to be reshot at the RKO sound stages in Hollywood. For authenticity, Howard ordered that sixty tons of the radioactive dust from Utah be shipped to Hollywood. Once the earth arrived, Howard commanded Mexicans to spread it around the studio, hoping to recreate what would appear to be the Gobi Desert.

After the filming of *The Conqueror*, a picture Susan detested, she still continued her pursuit of Howard. Her hopeless quest reminded Louella Parsons of her attempt in the late 1930s to marry Ronald Reagan. When Susan was in Miami at the same time Howard was, she tried to call him at his hotel suite, but he wouldn't return her messages.

Actually, Howard was in Miami with Jean Peters, hoping to establish a residence for her in her upcoming divorce from her husband, Stuart Cramer, whom she'd married in 1954.

Completely rejected by Howard, her dream of becoming Mrs. Howard Hughes a bitter memory, Susan sailed for The Bahamas. In Nassau, to forget Howard, she had an affair with a handsome, tall, and heavily muscled black man, whose appropriate nickname was "Bamboo."

In the months and years ahead, dozens of the cast and crew of *The Conqueror*, including all of the stars, would die of cancer caused by their exposure to the radioactive set. Agnes Moorehead would become a victim of cancer, dying on April 30, 1974. Dick Powell succumbed to the disease on January 3, 1963. When learning he had cancer, Pedro Armdáriz shot himself through the heart with a pistol he'd smuggled into the UCLA Medical Center in June of 1963, after learning that he had lymphatic cancer. Thomas Gomez died on June 18, 1971. Wayne himself fell victim to cancer on June 4, 1979, after a heroic fifteen-year struggle.

Susan would later fall victim to lung cancer, which would ultimately lead to brain tumors.

As she lay on her deathbed on March 14, 1975, she was still denouncing Howard and her other lovers, which included two future presidents, Ronald Reagan and John F. Kennedy. Her final comment on the subject was, "Men, I'd like to fry 'em all in deep fat."

Her last deathbed visitor was a mysterious woman in black who arrived at her doorstep. When Susan's maid learned the woman's identity, she immediately let her in, although Susan at that point was seeing only family members. Without permission, the maid ushered the mysterious woman into Susan's bedroom. She immediately exploded in anger until the guest introduced herself. "Forgive the intrusion, Miss Hayward, but I'm your loyal fan. I'm Greta Garbo."

The one person who did not appear to console Susan was Howard himself. He was almost as close to death as she was, lying in a darkened room, slowing dying with only his memories to keep him company. That and films.

His Mormon staff later reported that Howard ordered the screening of *The Conqueror* at least 150 times during the last years of his life. Critics panned the film, but Howard loved it, considering it his favorite. Eventually he bought back all the prints and withdrew it from circulation.

One of his male staff members reported that originally Howard masturbated as he watched the film until he grew too weak to do even that. Perhaps Howard identified with the role of Genghis Khan, as interpreted by John

Wayne. The barbarian could select any victim in the world he so desired and order the person to submit to his sexual fantasies. Perhaps Howard found the idea of that stimulating now that he'd retired from the actual battleground himself.

***

Los Angeles, 1938

Although Kate Hepburn and Howard would never speak of marriage again, she did call him to solicit his help in jump-starting her career. Playwright Philip Barry had "a work in the oven," a three-act play called *The Philadelphia Story*. Having been labeled as "box office poison" by film exhibitors, she was anxious for a comeback, both on the stage and on the screen.

When she called, Howard agreed to lend her a private plane to fly from Connecticut to Barry's vacation retreat off the coast of Maine. Kate accepted his offer.

When she returned from Maine, she notified Howard that she liked what she'd read of the heroine, Tracy Lord, believing that the role was "the one" for her comeback. She planned to underwrite some of the production costs and needed Howard's help. He told her to accept ten percent of the Broadway gross in lieu of salary and another twelve and a half percent of the road show take. He also advised her to put up twenty-five thousand dollars of her own money to secure the screen rights to *The Philadelphia Story* before it opened on Broadway.

At the time, that was never done. Prospective producers always waited until the play opened on Broadway and was a success, before attempting to purchase the screen rights.

He pledged $30,000 to help her nail down the rights. That move turned out not only to be the greatest advice Kate ever received in her film career, but the money he invested in the play made a profit for him. *The Philadelphia Story*, of course, went on to become a big success for Kate, making her "the comeback kid," both on the stage and in the movies. For the film, she'd wanted Spencer Tracy and Clark Gable, but "settled" for James Stewart and Cary Grant. She followed that role with the highly successful *Woman of the Year* (1942). That would at last bring her together with Spencer Tracy, whom she admired as an actor.

That film became a hit and would jointly launch them as a famous screen couple. Of course, they would be a couple of some sort off the screen as well.

Once she became involved with Tracy, Howard would see very little of Kate in the future. He was contemptuous of Tracy, calling him "the hired hand." That no doubt was a reference to the fact that he'd hired Tracy to star in his film, *Sky Devils*. Howard was none too impressed with the actor, telling Dietrich, "Kate's got herself an old Irish drunk. I give the relationship three months before Tracy goes back to his wife."

Howard was right about *The Philadelphia Story*, wrong about the endurance of the Tracy/Hepburn hookup. The two actors launched a troubled romance—more of a deep and abiding friendship really—that would last until Tracy's death on June 10, 1967. As for Kate, she would "live forever," as she once put it, dying at her beloved Fenwick in 2003.

Back in Connecticut in 1938, Kate was struggling with Philip Barry over rewrites for *The Philadelphia Story* when disaster struck at Fenwick. The hurricane that hit Connecticut in September of 1938 was one of the worst in the history of New England. Striking without warning, it destroyed Kate's family home.

Hearing of her plight, Howard ordered one of his pilots in New York to fly in fresh water and food. When she received Howard's care package, Kate held up a bottle of water. To her mother, Kit, and the rest of the household, she announced, "Water—not wine. Somehow symbolic of what my relationship with Howard has become."

***

Kate Hepburn was hardly on Howard's mind any more. He was involved in too many other love affairs. Since 1937, he'd also been involved in acquiring an airline.

Actually the news had come as a surprise to Noah Dietrich. Without consulting him, Howard had negotiated directly with Jack Frye, the president of Transcontinental and Western Airways, later renamed TransWorld Airlines or TWA. Called "the daredevil of the skies," Frye wanted the check Howard had promised him.

To his shock and dismay, Dietrich learned that Howard had agreed to purchase 100,000 shares of TWA's common stock, held by the Lehman Brothers, at ten dollars a share. (Actually, Howard would have needed only 99,293 shares of common stock for majority control of the airline.) Since Dietrich had told him that Toolco had earned thirteen million dollars in 1937, and that earnings would be even higher in 1938, Howard must have felt he was in the money. Indeed, he was.

Thanks partly to the arrival of World War II, Toolco would be earning $22 million by 1941. Toolco profits would continue to rise throughout the war and into the post-war era. By 1948, Toolco was posting annual profits of fifty-five million dollars.

Before the end of the 1930s, Big Howard's original drill bit had evolved into more than 200 different versions in all shapes and sizes. Whenever Howard heard of a competitor with a better bit, he purchased one of them and ordered his engineers to take it apart to find out what the innovation was. Once he learned what it was, he too went on the market with a new and improved bit.

Often in the redesign of the bit, his engineers would make additional improvements. All this continued to give Toolco the "cutting edge" in the drill bit industry.

From the beginning stages of Howard's acquisition of TWA, the onetime mail pilot, Frye, would be in fierce competition with Dietrich. The relationship between the two warriors got off to a bad start when Dietrich aggressively renegotiated the original agreement that had been struck between Hughes and Frye.

When he learned about TWA's financial troubles, Howard told Dietrich to revise his original offer of ten dollars a share and get him the stock for eight dollars a share. "You be the bad boy," he instructed Dietrich. "I don't want to piss Frye off since I'll be having to work with him."

The new eight-dollar-a-share offer produced a screaming rage in Frye. He told Dietrich that he was "a shitass cocksucker hired to lick Hughes's dingleberries off his crusty asshole." That remark launched Dietrich and Frye into a tumultuous confrontation for the control of TWA that would last for months. After he settled down "and finished off a bottle of bourbon" that night, Frye called Dietrich the next morning, but not with an apology. In a plaintive voice, he asked, "Can I get eight dollars and twenty-five cents a share?"

Dietrich promised to check with the board at Toolco. He waited twenty minutes and amazingly didn't even call Howard. Dialing Frye once again, he falsely claimed, "Toolco approves the deal." Actually, it was Dietrich who'd made the deal, saving Howard $200,000 of the monies he'd originally promised Frye. The ace pilot took the deal but was "forever pissed" at the hard-nosed Dietrich.

As much as Frye hated Dietrich, the former daredevil pilot endlessly admired Howard and his achievements in aviation. Both men shared adventure stories of their exploits in the air during the early days of aviation's barnstorming era. Frye had seen *Hell's Angels* a total of twenty-eight times, flattering Howard by calling it "the greatest movie ever made—and Harlow's tits were easy on the eyes too."

Although unspoken, it was obvious that Howard had a private reason for taking over TWA. He remained just as jealous of Charles Lindbergh in the late 30s as he was when "Lucky Lindy" made his historic flight to Paris. Even though Howard had beaten the aeronautical hero's record, the jealous streak still cut deep into Howard. Lindbergh had founded TWA, and its silver mail planes—a virtual airborne advertisement for the aviator—were known as "The Lindbergh Airline."

By 1940, Howard had acquired seventy-eight percent control of TWA by purchasing stock from all the "big boys" in the airline, including the dreaded Lindbergh himself. Once Howard assumed control, he ordered his maintenance staff to take silver lacquer and paint out the name of Lindbergh wherever it appeared on the planes. At one point Howard was tempted to order his men to paint in his own name, but at the last minute he rescinded the order.

Howard set out to make TWA a serious challenger of Pan American World

Airways and in time American Airlines. In spite of his disappointment at the check for $1.6 million, Frye called Howard "my savior."

Howard would ultimately fail with TWA, as he did in so many other businesses, but initially the airline was a success. By 1941 TWA was transporting 260,000 passengers a year, an increase of nearly sixty percent since Howard's takeover in 1939. He was an active stockholder, taking all the knowledge he'd learned during his record-setting flights and putting them to commercial use.

He installed an advanced hydraulic system in all his planes. Electronic advances included power steering. Cockpits were made larger, more spacious, and much safer. He created the first of the star-studded publicity flights, as when he'd fly movie stars from coast to coast, much to the delight of photographers waiting on the other end.

Writer Robert Sterling proclaimed that, "Howard shaped the line's destiny as one would mold a piece of clay."

After his takeover, Howard placed Dietrich on the board of directors, where almost daily he came into conflict with Frye. TWA boasted as a slogan that it was "An Airline Run by Fliers." Dietrich was contemptuous of that, feeling that businessmen should be running the financially troubled airline.

After two years, Frye "danced in the streets" when he got Howard to agree to remove Dietrich from the TWA board. Even though off the board, Dietrich continued to analyze the airline's finances, sending disturbing reports of mismanagement to Howard, which showed that TWA was overextending itself to fulfill Frye's dream of becoming a global airline. In time, and in fear of losing control if TWA had to go public, Howard was forced to purchase another $1,500,000 worth of TWA stock.

But during the war and its desperate need for air carriers, TWA's fortunes soared. There was such a need for airline transportation that at one point Howard purchased six Boeing Stratoliners right off the assembly line.

The first four-engine, internally pressurized commercial plane, the Stratoliner was better than anything that had ever come on the market up until then. It could carry 40 passengers as compared to about two dozen who could fit into the typical DC-3 at the time. Once America entered the war, the Stratoliner became the commercial equivalent of the Air Force's B-17. At the time, it was the only commercial airplane that could fly nonstop over the Atlantic Ocean.

In the early months of the war, Roosevelt's Secretary of Commerce, Jesse Jones, appealed to Howard to sell or lease his planes at bargain-basement rates to the government.

Jesse Holman Jones, the silver-haired, "Biblically big" Houstonian, had been a friend of Howard Hughes Sr. back in Texas when Howard was just a boy. During Roosevelt's New Deal era, he'd become known as "Emperor Jones," and was regarded as the second most powerful man in Washington.

Howard proposed a deal so advantageous to himself that Jones abruptly cut off negotiations. Then, since it had the power to do so, the government officials merely requisitioned the Stratoliners from Howard, dictating their own terms and refusing to guarantee Howard preferential treatment during TWA's future route applications, as he'd originally wanted. Howard defiantly held back one Stratoliner, claiming it was needed for his aviation research. The government bought that line and let him keep it.

As a footnote, Howard eventually lost his remaining Stratoliner in the 1950s when he sold it to Glenn McCarthy, a millionaire speculator from Houston. Dietrich was sent to collect the funds that had been promised for its purchase, but learned that McCarthy no longer had the money since his reckless investments—Dietrich called them "roller-coaster"—had nose-dived. When Dietrich tried to repossess the plane, he learned that McCarthy had so many liens on it that it would be "a financial disaster" if Howard actually took possession of his plane again. Ironically, he was forced to abandon the Stratoliner to creditors years after he'd stood off the U.S. Department of Commerce with its unlimited requisitioning powers during the world's worst war.

In the middle of Howard's negotiations with TWA, Kate Hepburn continued to call Howard. Initially he'd moved her out of Muirfield and into a cottage on the grounds. As *The Philadelphia Story* had gone from a hit stage play to a hit movie, Kate was gleeful to learn that Howard's initial $30,000 had turned a neat profit of $500,000.

That impressive check didn't impress Howard. Other than acquiring or inventing more airplanes for the war effort, he had yet another driving ambition. He was going to return to making movies as he'd done in the silent era and in the early era of Talkies.

He reopened Caddo Company headquarters on Romaine Street in Hollywood. Then he let word seep out through his oldtime buddy, the increasingly drunk Louella Parsons, that his first film was going "to be a Western masterpiece."

***

Working hand in hand with Robert Gross, CEO of Lockheed, Howard dared to dream impossible dreams.

Gross recalled that one night at Muirfield Howard came into the living room wearing only a frayed robe and battered sandals.

Soon Gross's plans for a radically new series of airplane, the "Constellation," were spread across the living room floor. At one point, Howard found his robe an annoyance and tossed it onto the sofa, revealing to Gross that he wore no underwear. Stark naked, he sat cross-legged on his living room floor, devouring the blueprints and astonishing Gross not only with his unconventional dress code, but with his knowledge of aircraft design. Finally, he stood up. "Give me a price, boy! I want them all."

Gross quoted an inflated estimate of $450,000 per plane, and was prepared for howls of protest from his client. Howard thought it over for a minute and then said, "All right, god damn the shit and fuck and to hell and back." He smiled at Gross. "That's Texas Plains talk for we've made a horse trade. Since my fucking airline doesn't have a pot to piss in, I'll buy the fuckers myself. Just send the bill to Dietrich and listen to him scream. Hold the phone a foot away from your ear when you talk to him."

Putting his robe back on, Howard was dressed when a maid walked in to deliver him a cheese sandwich and a tall glass of cold milk. He turned to Gross for a parting comment. "Don't fuck anybody I wouldn't." Then he tottered off to bed, leaving the Lockheed CEO to crawl across the floor, picking up his blueprints.

The next morning, Gross was eager to share Lockheed's good fortune with the world. Howard had purchased forty planes for a total cost of eighteen million dollars. This was the largest commercial airplane order in the history of aviation.

Gross was getting ready to make the announcement to the press when an urgent call came in from Howard. He did not want an announcement made and demanded that the Lockheed project proceed in utter secrecy. He even demanded that future communications between them be in code. Assigning code names to future communications, Howard designated himself as "God." Gross would be the "Apostle Paul." Jack Frye, over at TWA headquarters, would be referred to as "Jesus Christ."

The Constellations were quickly nicknamed "Connies" by the engineers and mechanics when Howard's planes came off the assembly line.

The Lockheed orders were processed in quick order. The scent of war seemed to pump adrenaline into factories around the world.

Howard himself flew one of the first Constellations, speeding from Los Angeles to Washington, D.C. in just six hours and fifty-six minutes, scheduling that would have been considered impossible just a few months before.

The Washington Post and newspapers throughout the nation hailed this new breakthrough. *The New York Times* announced that Connie is "the outline of things to come in the aviation industry—a great silver bird, shimmering in the noonday sun."

***

In his classic biography of Bette Davis, *Fasten Your Seat Belts*, veteran Hollywood writer, Lawrence J. Quirk, wrote of Howard's "idiosyncrasies, and something else—a homosexual side that filled him with guilt and self-hatred. His tastes ran to handsome airline mechanics and garagemen whom he often took flying—disappearing with them to one of his many retreats for weeks on end. Unable to be faithful to any one young man for long, he would tire of them,

Bette Davis, Howard Hughes (1939)

pay them off, and sometimes set them up in business—then moved on, satisfying his endless curiosity with other males in an endlessly compulsive manner that only added to his guilt, confusion, and self-rage as the years went by." Quirk noted that Howard "also suffered from impotence, especially with women. In forcing himself to live up to what was essentially a false macho image, he tended toward premature ejaculation and was a chronic masturbator, often finding it necessary to masturbate his way through sex with a female partner."

Such was Howard's state of being when Bette Davis sent him an invitation to be the guest of honor at the Tailwaggers Club Ball at the Beverly Hills Hotel. A dog lover, Bette wanted to raise money at the event to help stray canines and to train seeing-eye dogs. Howard sent her a check for $2,500, although he was not a dog lover and didn't even own a pet.

He'd been intrigued by Bette ever since he'd seen her play the bitch, Mildred, in *Of Human Bondage*. Howard felt that she should have won the Oscar for that performance. One reason he wanted to meet her was that he'd been told that she was a virtual shoo-in to win another Oscar in the next few months for her performance in *Jezebel*. She'd won her first for *Dangerous* in 1935. He always liked to seduce Oscar winners.

Bette later said that she was immediately attracted to Howard even though she was married to the failed singer, Harmon Oscar Nelson (Ham), at the time. Her ill-fated, six-year marriage was winding down when she met Howard.

In his rumpled double-breasted tuxedo, Howard was "so debonair and handsome—and so tall, but kind of shy and gangly, not the arrogant prick I'd heard he was," according to Bette.

Although hardly the sexiest actress in movies, Bette had "never looked lovelier," in the words of Louella Parsons, than she did the night she greeted Howard. She was wearing a sexy pink lace dress, evocative of the one she'd worn in *Jezebel*. "I thought Hughes would look at my breasts, since I was showing a bit of cleavage, but he looked into my eyes instead." In later life and after the release of the song, Bette would alter her line, saying, "Instead of looking at my breasts, he looked directly into my Bette Davis eyes, my baby blues." Her hair fell softly around her bare but freckled shoulders in her low-cut and tight-fitting gown. The color pink made her look younger. She had accentuated her beauty with a heavy coating of ruby-red lipstick.

Welcoming him to the ballroom, she'd impulsively stood on her toes and kissed him fully on the lips. He would confide later to Randolph Scott, also at the ball, that he detected a "flicker of tongue—usually I'm the aggressor."

"Davis has bigger balls than you, my good man," Randolph quipped to his former lover.

Howard was seated at the head banquet table next to Bette, who was president of the club. He later told Randolph that at one point Bette reached under the table and gently squeezed his crotch. He would also make this confession to his future mistress, Terry Moore, who would write about it in her memoirs.

In the middle of the banquet, the dethroned queen of Hollywood, Mary Pickford, rose from her seat and walked over to greet Howard and Bette. He hadn't seen Mary in years, not since his relationship had ended with her stepson, Doug Fairbanks Jr. But despite Pickford's very visible presence directly in front of him, Howard pointedly ignored the faded star, giving all his attention to Bette instead. Angered, Mary returned to her seat, perhaps remembering days of greater glory when she was the most famous female face in the world and was treated like royalty.

In a few minutes, Doug Jr. himself came over to greet Howard. Bette sensed tension between the two men but didn't know the reason why. After Doug had greeted both of them and left, she asked, "You know Doug Fairbanks?"

"It was a long time ago," he said, eager to change the subject.

When Bette excused herself and got up to go "powder my nose," the former queen of MGM, Norma Shearer, strode over to his table. Howard acted like he was meeting her for the first time, until she reminded him that they'd already been introduced by William Randolph Hearst, their host at Sam Simeon Castle. In spite of his rebuff, she slipped him her private telephone number and asked him to call her the first night he was free. He took the number and stashed it away.

Norma Shearer

450

Ginger Rogers, Cary Grant

Bette returned to table with a straw basket filled with raffle tickets. He bought every one of them.

Later, when Bette was dancing with Randolph Scott, Howard huddled in the corner with Errol Flynn. Across the room the volatile Lupe Velez, the Mexican spitfire, was standing talking with her handsome, muscular husband, Johnny Weissmuller, who was normally in loincloth making a Tarzan movie. "I could go for that beast of the jungle," Howard whispered to Errol who later told Johnny Meyer. "You went for Lupe's first love, Gary Cooper, so why not her second love?" Errol asked.

Later Errol introduced Howard to his wife, Lili Damita, who had survived a period of her career when she'd been marketed by her studio as "the new Garbo." Born in Bordeaux, France, Lili was a sensual, beautiful woman with a fiery, dynamic personality. She also was a "switch hitter," her affairs ranging from Marlene Dietrich to King Alfonso XIII of Spain.

Lili seemed furious with her husband Errol that night. The couple would soon divorce. She also showed contempt for Howard, no doubt well aware that her husband was having an affair with him. She turned to Howard and said, "From what I gather, Errol will do something to you he won't do to me." "And what might that be?" Howard asked. "He'll go down on you but not on me," she said. "He finds eating out a woman disgusting!" With that remark, she turned her back on both her husband and Howard and headed over to engage Lupe Velez in conversation.

When Lili had gone, Howard turned to Errol to talk about Bette. Errol was also pursuing Bette, but not seriously. "Her breasts are bigger in real life than they photograph on the screen," Howard said. "I wonder if they give milk." Then he added something both bizarre and enigmatic, so much so that Errol at first thought he hadn't understood him: "I bet they're juicier than Clark Gable's breasts," Howard said, leaving open the possibility that he might be jesting. "Sucking his tits is like trying to drain blood from a turnip."

At the door, Howard kissed Bette good-bye, with a promise to meet again. The next morning he ordered that a wreath of flowers be delivered to her home at the rate of one per hour on a 24-hour basis. In the same way he'd romanced Kate, Howard began to fly over Bette's house, buzzing it.

He announced to Dietrich that he was "all but one-hundred certain" that

451

Bette would win the Oscar for *Jezebel*. In February of 1939, Howard's prediction came true. She won with Spencer Tracy, who snared the honor for his portrayal of Father Flanagan in *Boys Town*. Bette later told friends that Tracy propositioned her that night. "We'll have an Academy Award winning fuck," he allegedly promised her.

***

A few nights after the Tailwaggers Ball, Howard finally made contact with Bette after playing phone tag. Her husband, Ham Nelson, was in New York, so she invited Howard to her house at 1700 Coldwater Canyon. Before putting down the phone, Bette warned him, "I kiss on the first date."

"I do more than that!" he assured her.

Details of their first rendezvous and subsequent three weeks of intense romancing would be unknown today if Bette herself hadn't spoken so frequently of her coming together with Howard. She literally dined out on their relationship and continued to tell stories about it long after it had perhaps faded from Howard's memory.

It can only be assumed that Howard's reputation as a Hollywood Lothario had preceded him and that Bette was anticipating a skilled seducer who'd bedded some of the most famous women of the world, including Marlene Dietrich and Tallulah Bankhead. "Those two alone should have entitled Hughes to some sort of merit badge," Bette later quipped.

After her first night in bed with Howard, a shocked Bette discovered a sexually dysfunctional lover who was impotent. Not only that, but if Bette is to be believed, she claimed that Howard confessed his guilt and shame about being a homosexual. Instead of being turned off by Howard, she viewed him as a sexual challenge. Allegedly she told him, "If I could get a chronic masturbator like my husband Ham to perform successfully with a woman, then I can accomplish anything."

From what a drunken Bette often told at parties—usually with a coterie of gay men listening to every nuance of her pronouncements—Howard did not achieve orgasm on the first or even the second night of their coupling. But on the third night, when he was unable to penetrate her, he demanded fellatio. She also learned that "he wanted me to talk scat. He said if I cursed and swore at him, like a sailor, he could shut his eyes and conjure up a vision of me as a handsome young man. He was right. He achieved orgasm that night and for many nights thereafter. Katharine Hepburn couldn't do that for him—and she's a real boy."

All during her daughter's heavy courtship with Howard, her mother, Ruth ("Ruthie") Davis was demanding that Bette manipulate Howard into marrying her as soon as she divorced Ham. When asked why she was encouraging her daughter to marry a man she didn't love, Ruthie said, "It's the money, stupid!

When Bette divorces him, he'll settle so much alimony on her that she'll be fixed for life—and so will I."

During her brief affair, Bette was indiscreet in telling others about it, although Howard wanted to keep it hidden. One reason was that he was seriously dating Ginger Rogers on the side, telling her that "you are the only one for me."

But the romance with Bette became so public that the columnist, Walter Winchell, announced over one of his radio broadcasts that "Bette Davis is about to marry a millionaire as soon as she divorces her present husband." Winchell did not specifically name Howard in his broadcast.

The dynamic within the Davis/Hughes romance changed radically when Ham unexpectedly rushed back from the East Coast to see what was happening to his marriage. Bette denied to Ham that she was having an affair, although he didn't believe her and set out to obtain evidence to use against her in his divorce. He told friends that, "Half of what Bette owns is mine, and I'm entitled to my share."

Ham solicited the aid of his brother-in-law, Robert Pelgram, to audio-record Bette's pillow talk at Coldwater Canyon. Ham drilled a hole in her bedroom's floor, and Pelgram ran a recording wire up a basement wall and along the cciling, channeling it through the hole in the bedroom floor. Ham then attached a small microphone to the wire, nailing it to the baseboard directly beneath the bed. After a test, Pelgram announced that Ham's voice had recorded perfectly during a test. All that remained was to capture the voices of Bette and Howard.

The wires from the bedroom led to a sound truck parked in a secluded spot in the Canyon overlooking the house Ham once shared with Bette.

Now that Howard's impotence was cured, Bette had planned a special evening. She wanted sex in the missionary position. Howard agreed, telling her that he wanted to make a slight change in their plans. He preferred her to be on top. For "my deflowering," as Bette later put it, "I purchased gardenias and personally picked off the petals spreading them across my bed."

On the night of Howard's seduction of Bette—or more accurately her seduction of him—the evening was going perfectly. Bette hoped to achieve orgasm for both Howard and herself.

Perhaps she would have if Ham hadn't used his key to the back door and entered the house. He went right to the bedroom where he caught his wife *in flagrante delicto* with Howard.

Bette quickly removed herself from the bed and desperately reached for her robe. With full erection, Howard too jumped out of the bed and slugged Ham, bloodying his nose.

"I'll destroy both of you!" Ham shouted as he ran toward the door. He paused only momentarily to confront Bette. "You bitch! You fucking whore!"

The next morning, a blackmail note for Howard arrived at Caddo productions. It was from Ham demanding a settlement of $70,000 in cash—or else he'd turn the recording disks over to the media. Howard was fearful that his dialogue with Bette would not only reveal his impotence but also his homosexual leanings. He was also fearful that he could be named correspondent in Bette's upcoming divorce proceedings against Ham.

Without even calling Bette, Howard dialed Johnny Meyer, ordering him to hire a professional killer, and to pay him a thousand dollars to murder Ham.

Later that day, Bette contacted Howard, expressing her concerns that if she were exposed to the public as an adulteress, the Legion of Decency would order a boycott of her films—a censorship which might destroy her career.

"Don't worry," he assured her. "Your boy Ham is being taken care of."

"Don't do it!" she screamed into the phone. "Call off your boys." Her dialogue sounded like something from one of Bette's own bad movies. "He's gone to the police. He told them that if he's found murdered, you're responsible." After hanging up on Bette, Howard called Meyer and rescinded his order just in time.

The next morning, Ham was delivered $70,000 in cash by Meyer. Feeling that he'd been sucked into a trap, Howard abruptly withdrew from his relationship with Bette and refused to take her calls.

Her New England pride took over. Feeling guilty that she'd involved Howard in blackmail, she went to her studio chief, Jack Warner, and borrowed $70,000 from him against her future wages. That very day, she sent Howard a check for $70,000, which he cashed. The discs recording her sexual exploits with Howard were smashed in front of Bette. Ham promised he would not bring up Howard's name in the divorce proceedings.

When Kate Hepburn in Connecticut heard about the caper, she didn't seem jealous at all, calling the episode "a bedroom farce."

Howard would not encounter Bette again until, as head of RKO, he hired her to make a film, *The Story of a Divorce*. This was Bette's first film role after her dramatic exit from Warner Brothers in 1949. It was during the making of the film that she received a phone call from Darryl F. Zanuck, casting her as Margo Channing in *All About Eve*, a role she readily accepted. Bette at the time was having an affair with her co-star, Barry Sullivan. As soon as filming of *All About Eve* began, she'd also launch an affair with her co-star of that picture, Gary Merrill, which would lead to marriage.

The white heat of their romance long cooled, Bette and Howard clashed bitterly in the late 1940s over *The Story of a Divorce*. He demanded that the title be changed to *Payment on Demand*. And after the filming was supposedly wrapped, he also demanded that a new ending be shot. The film finally opened on February 15, 1951 at New York's Radio City Music Hall. Bette later wrote Howard that "the new ending broke my heart. I'm also brokenhearted over the title change." He never responded.

As a sentimental gesture, Howard had been sending her a long gardenia every year on the anniversary of her payment of the $70,000 to him.

454

The volatile actress was not impressed with this cheap show of sentiment and always tossed his flower in the garbage. "The god damn cocksucker's got all the money in the world. He didn't have to cash my fucking check!"

***

When it was clear that his thwarted romance with Kate Hepburn had ended, Howard told Johnny Meyer, "What do I want with the former Queen of RKO? I want the new Queen of RKO."

In earnest, he began to rekindle his romance with Ginger Rogers, Kate's bitter enemy. Kate was excessively jealous of Ginger's recent success with all those musicals with Fred Astaire. Her box office clout had propelled Ginger into a salary of $300,000 a year, which made her the highest paid actress in Hollywood.

Howard ordered that his assistants send five dozen yellow roses—her favorite flower—to her every morning. Delivery was received by Lela Rogers, the star's overly possessive mother, who was Howard's chief ally in romancing her daughter. Lela was strongly urging her daughter to divorce actor Lew Ayres and marry Howard instead "before some cheap little starlet whore—or even Bette Davis—entraps him."

A second floral tribute would arrive every day in the late afternoon. This time it would be purple orchids and white gardenias that smelled so intoxicatingly sweet that Lela suspected that Howard had ordered them perfumed.

He used to address his love notes to Ginger as "My Princess." And after Ginger dethroned Kate at RKO, he began addressing her as "Queen Ginger."

He called Lela every morning and arranged the details of his romantic trysts with her daughter through her, not bothering to check with Ginger directly, which infuriated the star. "Why can't Howard talk to me himself?" Ginger demanded to know of Lela. Her mother replied, "He told me he's afraid you might turn him down."

Some days he'd fly her for lunch to either San Francisco or Lake Tahoe, where they'd pick wildflowers before going for a nude swim. He'd order "champagne and caviar" picnics for consumption on the powdery sands of Coronado Island. Often he took her golfing, complaining later to Johnny Meyer that "her game isn't as good as Kate's." Ginger said that Howard made her game "fifty times better" by teaching her tricks she'd never known before. He even tried to teach her to sail, but she ended up capsizing their little boat. They were rescued by the crew aboard Howard's yacht.

On every date, he pressed marriage on her. She held him off, although at the urging of Lela, she did accept a five-karat, square-cut pink emerald engagement ring.

He kept urging Ginger to go to his lawyer, Neil McCarthy. "Old Neil can get you out of this damn marriage before a mouse can run up a clock."

455

"I've got to think it over," she protested. "Don't rush me." Actually Ginger was having second thoughts about a divorce. She was still in love with her husband, and told friends that if Lew had only called and asked, she would have gone back to him. She also didn't trust Howard or view him as husband material. She'd heard rumors about his recent episode with Bette Davis, but chose not to confront him with any of the details.

Through Noah Dietrich, Howard had purchased one of the most idyllic building sites in the Hollywood Hills. He planned to abandon gloomy Muirfield and erect a mansion on the mountain, somewhat in the style of William Randolph Hearst's San Simeon. He'd already hired an architect to design it.

One moonlit night he drove Ginger up to the mountaintop to share his dream. Later, she told Lela and her friends at RKO, "I think Howard wants to hide me away like a princess in a castle. I'm not the Sleeping Beauty type. If I know Howard, he'll put a moat around the damn castle and stock it with woman-eating alligators so that I can't escape."

During this period, Howard hired private detectives to trail Ginger wherever she went. He'd also ordered that her phone be tapped. That's how he learned that while he was romancing her, she was having a torrid affair with James Stewart, whom she referred to as "my darling Jimmy." Sometimes Ginger and Jimmy would go on double dates with his roommate and rumored lover, Henry Fonda. Fonda was dating Lucille Ball at the time. The two couples were seen dancing at Ciro's or the Trocadero. Both actors were cheap, so instead of supper at the Cocoanut Grove, they'd often end up at a little hole-in-the-wall, Barney's Beanery, on Santa Monica Boulevard. The owner kept a sign behind the counter: FAGOTS (sic) KEEP OUT!

To keep Howard at bay, Ginger kept blaming Lew, using him as the reason she couldn't commit to Howard. She falsely said that he was "putting up barriers" to the divorce and making unreasonable demands.

Taking the bull by the horns, as Howard put it, he personally called the handsome young actor and demanded a meeting at his Caddo offices. To lure Lew over, Howard told him that he was returning to pictures, and he wanted to star him in the first film released by Caddo.

With bait like that, Lew showed up at exactly ten o'clock the next Friday morning. As Meyer would later relate, "I personally ushered Ayres into Howard's office. Even though he'd been married for some time to a woman of the world like Rogers, Ayres still had a soft, delicate look to him. Rather innocent. If I didn't know better, I could swear he was still a virgin."

"When Howard came face to face with his rival for Ginger's hand," Meyer claimed, "I saw that Ayres's virginal look wasn't lost on Howard. It was love at first sight. One handsome bisexual meeting another handsome bisexual. Somehow I just knew that before the stroke of midnight on Saturday, Howard would be in the kid's pants. And I was right, too."

The "romance" of Howard Hughes and Lew Ayres, conducted at one of Howard's off-the-record retreats in western Texas, lasted for three days. Ginger later confessed that she fell in love with Lew's boyishly handsome face on the screen and later married him. Howard, too, watched movies looking for new partners, both male and female, to seduce. He'd been mesmerized by Lew when he'd first seen him on the screen with Greta Garbo in *The Kiss* in 1929.

When Lew had played the role of the innocent Paul Baumer in the anti-war film, *All Quiet on the Western Front*, in 1930, Howard had ordered that the movie be screened for him three times. Howard had been tempted to call his old friend Lewis Milestone, who had directed Lew in the film, to arrange for an introduction, but he'd never gotten around to it.

Meeting Lew for the first time, Howard discovered that he'd lost none of the youthful looks and charm he'd shown in his films. Howard's spies had kept him informed about Lew's private life, his late-night parties, and his homosexual affairs, including discreet dalliances with Spencer Tracy and Joel McCrea.

Howard quickly learned that Lew and Ginger had signed a pre-nuptial agreement, so money wouldn't be the reason to slow down the divorce. When Howard pointedly asked Lew why he wouldn't divorce Ginger, he was stunned to hear the actor tell him, "I'd have no one to cook my breakfast or choose my ties."

It is not clear if Lew knew that Howard was urging an immediate divorce because he had plans to marry Ginger himself. Lew would have had to live in a cave not to know of his wife's romance with Howard. Louella Parsons was practically broadcasting the event.

No one can possibly know at this point what went on in the perverse mind of Howard Hughes. He had learned that Kate Hepburn had tried to seduce Lew when he'd played her drunkard, wastrel brother in *Holiday*, released in 1938. Perhaps Kate was genuinely attracted to the young man. But Howard suspected that she secretly wanted to get back at Ginger by seducing her errant husband. *Holiday* was directed by George Cukor. During the shoot, Cary Grant had chastised Kate, "I, too, have the hots for Lew, and you're completely monopolizing him, leaving nothing for Cukor and me."

In some devious way, Howard presumably felt he'd score some sort of coup by running off with Lew himself. It would be a secret triumph for him, scoring points over both Kate and Ginger. He was not surprised when Lew readily accepted his invitation to fly to a retreat he maintained in western Texas for secret getaways, most often with men since women found such wilderness hideaways too boring.

All that is known about what went on between Howard and Lew that weekend is the gospel according to Johnny Meyer. Apparently, Howard never spoke of his flying away with Lew with anyone else.

What is known is that sometime during their weekend together, Lew confessed to Howard that his real ambition was not to be an actor but to become a Renaissance man with the ability to compose a symphony like Beethoven, to create a sculpture like Michelangelo, and to write a play like Eugene O'Neill.

Apparently, Howard found sex with Lew most satisfactory, telling Meyer that the actor was "properly submissive and did everything I asked." It was only when Lew started to talk that he began to turn off Howard.

The actor told him that he fully expected the United States would soon be at war. If drafted, he said he would claim status as a conscientious objector. Howard took violent exception to this, warning Lew that if word of this got out, movie chains might possibly boycott his films, thereby ending his career. In this respect, Howard turned out to be a prophet. When the war did inevitably arrive, Lew's pacifist stance greatly harmed his career. His studio even replaced him with another actor, Philip Dorn, in Lew's highly successful Dr. Kildare series. As Howard watched from afar in the years ahead, Lew did make a comeback of sorts when he appeared in the 1948 *Johnny Belinda*, playing a sympathetic doctor opposite Jane Wyman's deaf mute. Lew gave the best performance of his career. Off-screen he launched an affair with Wyman. When her husband, Ronald Reagan, heard of it, he said, "Jane's entitled to a good affair from time to time."

By Monday morning, Lew was overcome with guilt for having indulged himself sexually with Howard. It was only then that Howard realized how deeply religious the actor was. He asked Howard to kneel by their bedside and pray for God's forgiveness for the "abomination" they'd committed. Howard, of course, refused, hoping to escape since he'd come to view Lew as some sort of nutbag.

Howard's response was, "I've got more money than God. If you want to worship someone, worship me."

Back in Hollywood after his weekend shack-up with Lew, Howard told Meyer, "The little holy-roller played the banjo for me—in the nude!"

As time went by, religion would consume more and more of Lew's mind. Eventually he'd write a book on the subject, *Altars of the East*. He announced that he was going to make a film of the work. After many years, he contacted Howard, begging him to finance the movie for him. Perhaps to show his contempt for the project, Howard sent Lew a check for just one hundred dollars. To it, he attached a note: "Thanks for the memory."

In 1964 and perhaps to get revenge, Lew agreed to appear in the film, *The Carpetbaggers*, a potboiling novel by Harold Robbins that ripped off Howard's private life. The year 1973 found Lew appearing in simian makeup in *Battle for the Planet of the Apes*. His career long faded, Lew Ayres died on December 30, 1966, confessing that, "I can't endure another year and must go on my way."

There was one artifact left from the ruins of the Hughes/Ayres weekend. On the Sunday afternoon of their weekend together in west Texas, Lew had invited

Howard for a walk along the edge of a lake. Howard only reluctantly agreed. Along the trail, Lew discovered a piece of wood. Picking it up, he said he'd like to whittle it into a piece of sculpture.

Before flying out of Texas the following Monday afternoon, Lew had completed his piece of art. He gave it as a present to Howard. It was an almost perfect rendition of Howard's erect penis.

What became of Lew's artwork? For many years, Liberace in his Palm Beach living room displayed what he claimed was Lew's sculpted penis of Howard. Today, its whereabouts, or even whether it still exists, is unknown. It is not listed within the inventory of exhibits at Liberace's museum in Las Vegas.

* * *

Nassau, 1938

As America prepared for its Thanksgiving holiday, there was one seventeen-year-old girl who had more to be grateful for than most. Canadian-born Brenda Diana Duff Frazier, heiress to a multi-million-dollar fortune, had been named debutante of the year a few months before. Her beautiful face had graced the cover of *Life* magazine, and her fan mail was the equivalent, and sometimes exceeded, what was received by such reigning blonde Hollywood goddesses as Ginger Rogers and Alice Faye. As proof of how famous she was at the time, a letter marked simply, SHE, NEW YORK, was delivered to Brenda's hotel suite. As Tallulah Bankhead remarked, "That snot-nosed Frazier kid is more famous than yours truly, and God knows, I'm the most famous pussy on the planet since Cleo herself."

Throughout the U.S. heartland, teenage girls who didn't want to grow up to be like Joan Crawford wanted to be like Brenda Frazier. She was constantly being written about by reigning columnist Walter Winchell, who was forever interviewing her with her *beau du jour* at the exclusive Stork Club. In spite of her young age, she was often photographed smoking a cigarette held in a long ivory holder.

Following her much ballyhooed debut at the Ritz-Carlton, Brenda, with her Cupid's bow mouth, made headlines just by showing up somewhere. This

Brenda Frazier

459

world-wide celebration of herself, evocative of a latter-day Paris Hilton but on a larger scale, puzzled Brenda. "I don't deserve all this attention. I haven't done anything. I'm just a debutante." Rival heiress Barbara Hutton put it another way. "Brenda is famous just for being famous."

Photographers became intrigued with "the Brenda Frazier look." She was a pioneer of the "white face mask"—in fact, she was said to have invented that much copied look. She overly powdered her already too-white skin before "slashing" her mouth with a lipstick so bright red it would have intimidated even Betty Grable in Technicolor during her WWII musicals.

Brenda's eyebrows were penciled around the corner of her eyes, and her hair was perfectly coiffed and described as "blue-black." She never moved her neck in any direction out of fear of getting one hair out of place. Her appearance at any club, even one filled with celebrities, was usually met with stunning awe as all conversation came to a halt when she entered as a *celebutante*, Winchell's coined word.

In 1938, within only a matter of months, Brenda joined the roster of other "poor little rich girls," who included Woolworth heiress Barbara Hutton, tobacco heiress Doris Duke, and a future girlfriend of Howard's, Gloria Vanderbilt, who would become Brenda's chief rival as the reigning debutante, a title that stuck to both women long after they'd made their actual debuts.

Even before meeting Brenda, Howard had been captivated by her image, not only on the cover of *Life*, but in advertisements for Studebaker cars and Woodbury soap.

Hearing that Brenda would be in Nassau over the holiday, Howard flew there, ordering his crew to pilot the *Southern Cross* into the Nassau Yacht Club so that it would be at his disposal during his stay in The Bahamas.

Howard decided to pursue Brenda, although he knew he had a lot of competition, including every horny young rich boy at Harvard and Yale. Even young John F. Kennedy had expressed an interest in seducing her.

Howard encountered unexpected competition in Joan Crawford, the only A-list movie star he had failed to seduce. Through her good friend, Billy Haines, Howard learned that Joan was in New York sending flowers and expensive perfume every day to Brenda. Soon the two of them were photographed at the Stork Club one night and El Morocco the next night, both of them looking stunning. One entertainment columnist raised the provocative question, "What's wrong with the red-blooded men of New York? Why do two of the town's most glamorous gals, movie star Joan Crawford and debutante Brenda Frazier, have to dine alone two nights in a row?"

Brenda ultimately rejected Joan's sexual advances. In their aftermath, and for years after that, the star referred to the little rich girl as a "debutramp."

In Nassau, Howard accepted an invitation to stay at the mansion of Sir Harry Oakes. At that time, billionaire Oakes was possibly the richest man in the world. A tough old ex-miner, he'd built the largest private home in Nassau.

460

Unlike Howard, he didn't inherit his wealth but discovered it at Kirkland Lake in Canada. There he stumbled upon what became the largest gold mine in Canada and the second biggest gold mine in the world.

To celebrate Howard's arrival in town, Sir Harry threw a lavish dinner-dance at the British Colonial Hotel in Nassau. He invited Brenda, who came accompanied by globe-trotting Elsa Maxwell, the doyenne of society and its biggest sponger.

The stout, pug-nosed American hostess and tattle-tale columnist, the shape of whose body was often compared to a little brown jug, was born in 1881. She aptly described herself as "a short, fat, homely piano player from Keokuk, Iowa, with no money or background, who decided to become a legend—and did just that." The press dubbed her "The Hostess with the Mostest."

In the ballroom of Nassau's British Colonial Hotel, all Howard had to do was slip Maxwell a five-hundred dollar bill.

Within a minute, she had taken Howard's arm and had led him over to Brenda's table. "Brenda, darling, this is the famous—or should I say infamous?—Mr. Howard Hughes. As if you didn't already know and hadn't been spying on him from afar all evening?"

"Your reputation has preceded you," Howard said, bending at the waist and kissing Brenda's extended hand. "Your photographers hardly do you justice."

"Compliments will get you everywhere with me," Brenda said coyly.

For a long moment after the introductions were made, it appeared that Howard had nothing else to say to Brenda. Social butterfly Elsa came to the rescue, as she so often did. "For the sake of Hell or Heaven, whichever it is, ask the fair damsel to dance."

An acceptable ballroom dancer, Howard twirled Brenda around the floor. The body chemistry between them didn't exactly explode, but they came comfortably together.

For the next three months, Howard launched what the press called a "whirlwind romance" with Brenda. Of course, whenever he flew alone to Hollywood, he resumed his "star dates" with the likes of Errol Flynn and Ginger Rogers, among others.

Howard sailed aboard the *Southern Cross* carrying Brenda and her lavish wardrobe. At one point he anchored at Palm Beach, where they were seen together at a series of lavish winter parties thrown by the glittering social elite of the East Coast, each hostess glad to snare such celebrated guests as Howard and Brenda.

At one party, Howard encountered his long-ago nemesis, Joseph Kennedy. Noting Brenda across the room, Kennedy mockingly told Howard, "Bet I could take that filly away from you if I wanted to."

"I've already broken her in, Joe," Howard said cockily. "Constance Bennett told me I have four more inches than you. Why would Brenda settle for a short Mick stub when she can have the Real McCoy?"

461

Angered, Kennedy stormed off.

In her palatial mansion at Newport, Doris Duke entertained the pair. On the first night, the heiress remained alone on her terrace after Brenda had retired for the evening. The interchange between Doris and Howard was later reported by Barbara Hutton, who found the story vastly amusing.

That night Doris proposed that Howard dump Brenda and marry her. If Barbara is to be believed, Doris told Howard, "It will be the wedding of the century. The richest woman in the world marrying its richest man."

He turned her down.

"Then it's true what Barbara says about you?" Doris is alleged to have said.

"Just what does Barbara say?" he asked, no doubt recalling his aborted affair with her at London's Savoy Hotel.

"That you prefer men—take Cary Grant for instance—over women."

"No comment!"

"I could live with your preference," Doris is reported to have said. "When you're out with one of your boyfriends, I'll indulge my lesbian streak. In the world of the very rich, bisexuality is almost mandatory—but you know that, of course."

"Good night, Miss Duke," he said, turning and walking away to join Brenda in a bedroom upstairs. He turned for a parting comment. "We'll leave early in the morning—no need for you to get up and cook our breakfast."

Rebuffed and no doubt feeling humiliated, Doris stood on the terrace watching him go.

Later, in a bit of sweet revenge, she would marry the one man who'd eluded Howard: the super-endowed Porfirio Rubirosa, stud of the Caribbean. Ironically, he would also go on to marry Barbara Hutton after his divorce and settlement from Doris.

While sailing aboard the *Southern Cross* with Howard, Brenda pressed the issue of marriage onto the aviator, who had already extended a standing marriage proposal to Ginger. He refused. Screaming and shouting, and threatening to drown herself, she became hysterical. She took to her bed, locking the door to Howard.

It was that afternoon that he learned that Brenda suffered from a form of edema, sometimes called dropsy. Under stress, it caused her legs and ankles to swell painfully.

After that, Howard never saw Brenda again, ditching her in New York. The edema attacks, and Brenda's propensity for secluding herself, would become a pattern in her future, sometimes lasting for weeks at a time.

With the coming of World War II and other, more compelling headliners, Brenda faded into obscurity. Long forgotten by the press who had made her a media darling, she devoted much of her life to alcohol and pill-popping. Five separate attempts at "slashed wrist suicides," two broken marriages, and her final blow—inoperable bone cancer—led to her demise. Her final comment on

462

her life was, "When I was young, I drove my car in the fast lane but always knew I'd never make it to the finish line. For the entire ride of my life, I experienced engine trouble every mile of the way."

Asked about Howard during her last known interview in 1976, she said, "We broke up—that's all."

"Why?" the reporter asked.

"Because he was a god damn cocksucking faggot!"

* * *

Los Angeles, 1938-39

Reports differ about Howard's next major romantic tryst, and all the key players have told very different versions of what happened. What is known is that as the Thirties came to an end, Howard began to pursue a relationship with Tokyo-born Olivia de Havilland, who had been cast as milky Melanie in David O. Selznick's *Gone With the Wind.*

For months, Howard had been intrigued by Errol Flynn's ongoing attempts to seduce Olivia, stemming from 1935 when they had appeared as co-stars in the highly successful *Captain Blood,* released by Warner Brothers. Frustrated at her constant rejections of his romantic overtures, Errol in exasperation finally told Howard, "I don't think Olivia has a hole between her legs." In contrast, Olivia later wrote, "Errol is the most charming, the most magnetic man I will ever meet."

Perhaps Errol's practical jokes turned off Olivia. He was forever playing tricks on her. One time he put a mammoth dead rattlesnake in her pantaloons. Even more likely, Olivia might have been repulsed by Errol's constant drinking and womanizing. "I think we felt a kind of love for each other, but I also know it could never have come to anything." The handsome actor finally gave up on Olivia, calling her "a professional virgin."

Howard's friend, Louella Parsons, may have launched Olivia's affair with Howard. She wrote that the actress had accepted an engagement ring from Howard, and that the couple was launched "into a whirlwind courtship." The gossip maven got it wrong. Howard had never met Olivia.

Louella had a spy on the set of *Dodge City,* a Warner Brothers' western released in 1939, in which Olivia was co-starring, once again with Errol. One Friday afternoon Howard sent a private plane to the set at barren Modesto, California, to pick up Errol and fly him to Los Angeles. It was understood that at the airport, a limousine would haul Errol to the *Southern Cross* for an off-the-record weekend on Catalina Island. Louella's spy on the set of *Dodge City* mistakenly assumed that Howard had ordered the plane to bring Olivia to him—not Errol.

Louella's mistake may have given Howard an idea. After the wrap of *Dodge City,* he called Olivia. "I read in Louella's column that you and I are engaged.

Ready to get hitched at any moment."

"But I've never met you," she protested.

"I know," he said. "But since we're going to get married—Louella is never wrong about matters of the Hollywood heart—I thought we should get together and check each other out. At least know what the other party looks like in the flesh."

Somewhat reluctant, she agreed to invite him for tea at her home, Nela Vesta, where she lived with her mother, Lilian de Havilland Fontaine, and her beautiful sister, Joan Fontaine, who for a stage name had appropriated the name of her stepfather.

After putting down the phone, Olivia turned to her mother. "Hollywood's most famous wolf—and I don't mean Errol Flynn—just invited me out. He sounded more like a shy little lamb than the big bad wolf. But who knows?"

The next afternoon, Howard showed up for tea. At long last he gazed into Olivia's "aesthetic face," with her brown, melting eyes and Mona Lisa smile. She took him inside and introduced him to Lilian and Joan.

Johnny Meyer had driven Howard to the home and remained in the car outside. "Can you imagine such a thing?" he later said. "Howard Hughes at a ladies tea? I didn't really want to go in—but of course, no one invited me."

Howard's dress shocked the carefully groomed and coiffed ladies. His navy blue yachtman's jacket had been patched several times and was bleached almost white in parts from the fierce sun. He wore ill-fitting, baggy pants that appeared to have been made of sailcloth. For a belt, he used a nautical rope. His famous sneakers were dirty and without laces. Unusual at that time, he wore no socks. His crushed fedora was riddled with holes as if bullets had been fired into it.

Olivia was startled by how highly pitched his voice was. She also later wrote of his "gangly shyness." Of course, he could have been playing country

Olivia de Havilland, Joan Fontaine

boy from Texas, using that hayseed façade to mask his true personality as a skilled seducer. Unlike Errol, Howard immediately brought out the maternal instinct in Olivia.

During the course of the tea, Howard, as was his custom, devoted most of his attention to Lilian. That ploy had worked on Ginger's mother, Lela. As it was later reported, Howard

464

virtually ignored Joan. That, too, as it turned out, was some sort of ploy.

The next evening, Howard arrived for an official date with Olivia. This time he drove himself, showing up at her doorstep in a shabby Chevrolet that was "an unintentional convertible." When it rained that night, water poured in through the rusty roof. In the car with him, she discovered that he wore no deodorant and may have forgotten to bathe in the last few days.

On the way for dinner at the Brown Derby, he made an astonishing statement. "You know, don't you, that I got the role of Melanie for you?" She knew nothing of the sort. Later she heard that Howard, for reasons known only to himself, had called producer David O. Selznick and urged him to cast her in the role. Through an invitation arranged by Cary Grant, Howard drove to director George Cukor's house and also urged him to cast Olivia in the role. He even called his East Coast friend, Jock Whitney, who was putting up a lot of the production money, and urged him to intercede on Olivia's behalf.

She countered by amusing Howard with a story that Joan had also wanted to be in the movie. "Actually, she wanted to play Scarlett. Cukor told her she'd be much more suited for the role of Melanie. That seemed to infuriate Joan. 'If it's a sappy Melanie you want, get Olivia!' Joan told Cukor before storming out of his office. I loved the part of Melanie and went for it right away. If you helped me get the role, I'm grateful."

At the Brown Derby, Olivia told Howard that Errol had taken her here a few months ago. "He's such a Tasmanian Devil," she said. "In the middle of our dinner, he released his pet raccoon. It ran up the legs of Kay Francis."

"I bet that was the first time any male ever got up that one's skirts," he said facetiously.

Over dinner, she took note of his eating eccentricities. He ordered a butterfly steak and some small peas. The waiter brought the steak and Howard pronounced it OK. But there was a scoop of small peas on his plate. He told the waiter to take them back to the kitchen. He wanted only twelve peas. The astonished waiter returned to the kitchen and shortly thereafter came back with Howard's dinner. This time the plate still contained the butterfly steak, but only twelve peas. "You can count them, sir, if you wish," the waiter told Howard.

Olivia may have been astonished when Howard, "the richest man on the planet," asked her to pay for dinner. He informed her, "I never carry money on me."

The whirlwind courtship that Louella had written about came true after all. No one knows how Howard managed to pacify Ginger, but he was "seen everywhere" with Olivia. Even so, he would often mysteriously disappear during their courtship, once for three weeks at a time. Every day that he was gone, three dozen white orchids would appear at Olivia's doorstep. Back in Los Angeles, Howard virtually demanded that Olivia take flying lessons from him. She agreed. Soon he was teaching her to become a lady pilot, as he had with Katharine Hepburn and even earlier with Billie Dove.

It is believed that at some point along the way, Olivia fell in love with Howard. One night he took her dancing at Hugo's Garden Room, a popular spot at the time where Clark Gable might show up with Carole Lombard, or even Ronald Reagan with Jane Wyman. At Hugo's, Olivia learned that Howard could fox-trot "and do a pretty good rumba—no Cesar Romero, of course," Olivia later said.

Once, she dared bring up the subject of love with Howard. "Perhaps we should talk of marriage."

He abruptly told her, "I've got other plans. A lot more to accomplish in aviation before I settle down. When I'm fifty—somewhere about 1955—I'll get married but not before. I'm not ready to give up my wild and wanton ways."

Rebuffed, Olivia informed him that she too had a career and "many, many other things to accomplish." That was true, of course.

In spite of his rejection of a marriage proposal, he would continue to date Olivia for the next few weeks.

But then he made one of those reckless decisions that only Howard in the heady Hollywood days of 1939 could conjure up. While still dating Olivia, while still proposing marriage to Ginger, he told Johnny Meyer that he was going to go after Joan Fontaine. Not only that, and even though he'd rejected Olivia's marriage overtures, he planned to propose marriage to Joan.

Whatever Meyer thought about this, he kept to himself. "You're the boss," was his only comment to Howard.

Meyer later said, "I knew which side of my bread was buttered. Whatever Howard wanted, I tried to get for him."

* * *

Maybe Olivia's romance with Howard would have lasted longer if a party had not been thrown in Joan's honor at the Trocadero. Howard was behind it all, putting up the money, presumably to celebrate Joan's engagement to the dashing British actor, Brian Aherne. Olivia attended the event, escorted by Howard. Joan showed up in pink, looking dazzling, upstaging Olivia's appearance in white organdy.

At one point during the party, Howard asked Joan, as guest of honor, to dance with him. Up close and personal, he whispered into her ear that he'd been in love with her ever since he'd met her at the tea party with Lilian and Olivia. Before the dance ended, he urged her to drop Aherne and marry him instead. "I'll make you forget all about him," was his whispered promise. "I can also do a lot more for you than he can," which was true.

Joan was well aware that her sister was falling in love with Howard. "No one two-times my sister," Joan later told her mother after Howard had slipped her his private telephone number. According to Joan's version, she later called Howard "just to test the waters" to see how far he would go in betraying Olivia.

In the garden of the *faux* Polynesian restaurant, Trader Vic's, Howard asked for Joan's hand in marriage. He urged her to call Aherne that very afternoon and tell him that their engagement was off. Acting coy, she agreed to weigh his offer, having no intention of doing that. Joan was reported to have told friends that she found Howard's high-pitched voice off-putting, making everything he said sound like he was whining. Unlike Olivia, she was not impressed with his shyness and awkwardness, finding it unconvincing in such a man of the world.

Instead of calling off her engagement, she fled that night back into the arms of her handsome, charming, and debonair lover. Joan viewed her engagement to Aherne as some-thing of a coup. After all, she'd rescued him from the arms of an international temptress, Marlene Dietrich. It is not known if Aherne ever told his wife-to-be that he had evidence that Howard was in love with Cary Grant, a dynamic he'd seen up close during the film-ing of *Sylvia Scarlett* with Katharine Hepburn.

When she returned home, Joan informed both her mother and Olivia that Howard had proposed marriage. That must have been scalding water in the face of Olivia, since he'd rejected even casual dialogue about a possible marriage to her.

She was furious at Howard for his proposal to Joan. "Boiling with rage," she rushed to her bedroom and called Howard. After bursting into tears, she told him that their romance was over. "I don't want to see you again," she said. "Please don't call."

He readily let her go. But he persisted in calling Joan, who left instructions with Lilian to tell Howard that "Miss Fontaine is not at home."

The conflict over Howard, and other disagreements, led to Olivia and Joan becoming known as "the feuding sisters." Many of their conflicts were career oriented.

Sometimes directors considered both Olivia and Joan for the same key roles—that is, when they didn't offer the parts first to Ginger Rogers, a long-standing member of the Howard Hughes kennel.

At one point, Ginger exaggerated but claimed that Olivia made a career out of play-ing roles foolishly turned down by her. In 1946, Ginger turned down *To Each His Own*, which brought Olivia her first Oscar. In 1948 Ginger passed on *The Snake Pit* which brought Olivia an Academy Award nomination. "Olivia should thank me for my poor judg-ment," Ginger later said.

The feud between Joan and Olivia wasn't helped when Joan learned that Olivia had originally been offered Daphne du Maurier's classic *Rebecca*, directed by Alfred Hitchcock. After Vivien Leigh and then Loretta Young passed on it, *Rebecca* became one of Joan's most memorable roles. It was Ginger herself who presented Joan with her first Oscar for the 1941 *Suspicion*. As Ginger later said, and photographs at the time prove, "I had my eyes closed at the time so I didn't have to face her."

Ginger falsely assumed that Joan had wanted to marry Howard instead of Aherne. She privately remarked, "Joan, Olivia, and I were at one time or anoth-er Oscar winners. But none of us actually were cast in the role each of us seri-ously considered—that of Mrs. Howard Hughes!"

Howard had made headlines when he'd romanced Billie Dove, "the world's most beautiful woman" at the end of the 1920s. By the end of the 1930s, another sultry actress was being hailed as the world's most beautiful woman.

"I want a piece of the action," he confided to Johnny Meyer.

Forgetting Joan and Olivia, but still keeping a hold on Ginger, Howard set out to seduce Hedy Lamarr.

* * *

As the years went by, and from all reports, Howard didn't bring many women to orgasm. Starlets, call girls, and Las Vegas chorines reported the same sad story. But in 1939 Howard met "the queen of orgasms," as she was called in Hollywood.

In one of her first films, Gustav Machaty's *Extase*, filmed in 1933, Hedy was billed as Hedy Kiesler. (Just before the launch of her film career in Hollywood, she was renamed by Louis B. Mayer as Hedy Lamarr in honor of Barbara LaMarr, one of Howard's early girlfriends, and an actress who seems to have elicited genuine sorrow from Mayer at the time of her early death.) Released in America as *Ecstasy*, the movie had made Hedy a notorious figure in cinema. Howard had screened it ten times and had been fascinated by the scene that depicted her swimming, then running through the woods in the nude. The director had also asked the actress to play a scene in the film in which she simulated orgasm. In real life, Hedy didn't have to fake such passion. It was genuine.

Howard was savvy enough to know that Hedy had little talent as an actress. But she was one of the world's true beauties. "Even if she can't act," he told Dietrich, "I can always look at her."

On a visit to the set of *Lady of the Tropics*, being filmed at Metro-Goldwyn-Mayer, Howard encountered Hedy after she'd just finished playing a love scene with his sometimes boyfriend, Robert Taylor. They shook hands and looked into each other's eyes before the actress retreated to her dressing room.

Later, when they were alone, Robert Taylor revealed to Howard that he was going to marry Barbara Stanwyck sometime in the very near future. He wanted to know if Howard had any objections to his wedding the bisexual star. Howard urged marriage onto the beautiful young man, claiming it would end speculation in Hollywood about Robert's homosexuality. Even though Howard had turned down a "lavender marriage" with Kate Hepburn, he thought it would be right for his friend. "Stanwyck will throw the bloodhounds off your trail," he told Robert. "Fan magazines will be writing about the great Taylor/Stanwyck romance and quit concentrating on what you might really be up to. Besides, it'll take the heat off me."

Before leaving the set that day, Howard knocked on Hedy's door and handed her his private phone number at Muirfield. "Give me a call some night," he suggested to her.

"Mr. Hughes, in Austria, where I come from, it is the gentleman who calls the lady."

"You're in America now," he warned her, "and we have different customs here, especially if we reside in Hollywood." He tipped his fedora to her and walked away.

Later, before its release, he had a copy of *Lady of the Tropics* sent to his home at Muirfield where he screened it in private. He later told Ben Hecht, writer of its screenplay, "Beautiful fuckable Taylor. Beautiful fuckable Lamarr. Beautiful costumes. Exotic story. Lousy picture. But just watching those two on screen will give you something to jerk off to."

In 1966 in New York, agent Jay Garon threw a party for Hedy, celebrating the release of her ghostwritten tell-all autobiography, *Ecstasy and Me*. At the party, she spoke candidly about her aborted affair with Howard. But, first, she showed this author the results of a recent "elbow lift." After an introduction to her latest boyfriend—"he's in porno, darling"—she launched into her tales of Howard. She was goaded on with an extra dry gin martini.

"I made a man out of Howard Hughes," she said, startling her attentive audience. "And on our first date. I met him on the set of *Lady of the Tropics* in which I was appearing with one of his boyfriends. I forget his name."

"Robert Taylor," Garon butted in.

"Yes, *that one*. Remember how Greta Garbo devoured him in *Camille*?"

She leaned back on the sofa and asked her porno star to take off her high heels and massage her feet. "At first I was angry when Howard asked me to call him instead of him calling me. But he was handsome, a little bit sexy, and very, very rich. I finally broke down and made the call. I don't know why. At the time I could have had any other man in Hollywood. All the big stars. Gable. Tracy, James Stewart—they were calling me." She looked with contempt at the young man massaging her shapely feet. "In those days I didn't have to pay for it."

When she reached Howard by phone at Muirfield, he invited her to come over right away. "I had pictured him inviting me to The Cocoanut

Hedy Lamarr

469

Grove and arriving in a big, fat limousine, with sprays of orchids. Nothing like that happened. I put on a simple dirndl I'd purchased in Vienna and drove over to see him. In that garb, I looked like a fourteen-year-old. I'd heard that Howard liked them young. At his home, his housekeeper showed me into his living room. The devil didn't even bother to get up. He was wearing a ratty old bathrobe and some shoddy bedroom slippers. Later that night, I found out he didn't even have on a pair of pajamas under that robe. What a very casual way to receive a lady, I thought."

"He just sat there looking at me," she said. "Didn't even offer me a cocktail. I sat across from him, and we chatted about my life in Austria, my career at MGM. At some point the conversation got personal. I told him that Louis B. Mayer had exposed himself to me in his office and had asked me to perform oral sex on him."

She related that Howard gave her some career advice. "He told me that a big war was coming, and that Hollywood would soon be churning out one war movie after another. He said that I should tell the studio to cast me only as beautiful Nazi spies. He thought I'd gain international fame if I stuck to playing Nazi spies. Later, I would play spies. But that night I thought that Howard was assuming I might have Nazi leanings, because my country was now controlled by Hitler. I informed him that I was a loyal American."

She did admit that at a party she and her husband, munitions king Fritz Mandl, had thrown, Adolf Hitler had kissed her hand. "Obviously he didn't know I was a Jewess."

"Howard seemed eager to learn about my background as Lady Mandl," she claimed. "I told him that I had two bodyguards and twenty servants in those days. Fritz gave me everything. All the jewelry in the world, beautiful gowns, eight cars. But he kept me a virtual prisoner and had me guarded day and night. He loved power and beautiful women. It was said that if he wanted to drum up some business for his munitions, he would merely start a war somewhere."

To assert her patriotism, she claimed that the U.S. Navy practically told her that her invention had won the war for them. A gross exaggeration, but Hedy is credited with inventing a radio-guiding system for torpedoes that indeed turned out to be a useful invention, one on which she took out a patent, although she was never to make any money on it. Supposedly she'd gained knowledge about this system from her Nazi sympathizer husband, Fritz Mandl. Her early version of frequency hopping used a piano roll to change some 88 frequencies. It was intended to make radio-guided torpedoes harder for enemies underwater to detect or jam.

"Considering that Howard was practically ready for bed when he greeted me, I just assumed at one point he'd make a pass at me," she said. "It was growing later and later. He made no move to seduce me. Finally, he asked me rather bluntly, 'Would you like to make ten thousand dollars in cash?'"

"I was insulted," she said. "I informed him that a prominent member of the

Krupp family in Germany had once offered to give me half a million dollars in diamonds, emeralds, and rubies for 'one night of ecstasy' with me. I refused him."

"Sensing that he'd insulted me, Howard apologized," she claimed. "He said I had misunderstood him. For the ten thousand dollars, he wanted me to pose nude for him. From that photograph, he was going to instruct his engineers—if that's what they were—to make a lifesize replica of me in rubber. Realistic down to the last detail. He even wanted my vagina molded from life so that my dummy would have an exact duplicate of my sexual organs. I was horrified at the suggestion."

"He said that the reason for the dummy was that he didn't feel worthy of taking the real me," she claimed. 'You're too much of a goddess,' he told me."

At that point, Hedy's porno boyfriend mocked Howard's comment. "I'll have to use that line on some chick some night. Great seduction technique."

Hedy scolded him for being "a naughty boy," then continued. "I got up from the sofa and stood before Howard. 'You're worthy,' I told him."

"I kneeled down on the carpet and opened his bathrobe," she said. "I told him why bother with some stupid rubber dummy when he could have the real thing. I performed oral sex. Unlike Robert Taylor, I got a rise out of Howard. He took me into his library, and we made love all night. Don't believe all those stories that jealous women spread about Howard being impotent. He was very virile with me."

"Howard bedded me that night, and I think it was more thrilling for him than it was for me," she claimed, "even though I experienced multiple orgasms. He seemed to view this as the greatest accomplishment of his career. I think he considered himself lucky if he gave a woman one orgasm. What he didn't know was that I experienced frequent orgasms when having sex with most men. With some men, I had uncountable orgasms."

She was perhaps the only movie star memoirist who ever wrote publicly of her tendency for multiple orgasms.

On another note, she added, "Men have told me that they can get an orgasm just by looking at me on the screen. I know for a fact that men attended my movies and masturbated under their jackets."

After the night of the orgasms, Hedy claimed that Howard "fell madly in love with me and sent me flowers every day. Our affair lasted for just a few short weeks."

"What went wrong?" she was asked.

"He wanted to marry me and make a prisoner of me," she said. "I wasn't ready for that. I had been married to Fritz when I became Lady Mandl, and he kept me under guard all the time, not wanting another man to look at me. I couldn't go through an experience like that ever again."

She was asked what the jealous Mandl thought of her nudity on the screen in *Ecstasy*. "He tried to purchase all the prints, but never succeeded because of bootleg copies. Benito Mussolini refused to sell Fritz his copy. I know for a fact that Hitler watched the film several times."

"There was no way I could escape from Fritz and plunge into a marriage with yet another man who wanted to imprison me," she said. "Of course Howard was very rich, like Fritz, and I tend to like very rich men. But on my own, I made thirty million dollars. Regrettably, I wasted it all and made many bad decisions. I stupidly turned down the starring role in *Casablanca*, fearing it might be too similar to my role in *Algiers*. The Swedish peasant got it instead. I also turned down *Gaslight* which the bitch also took. I finally told Howard I didn't need him. Later in life, I would need him, but by then it was too late."

She claimed that she repeatedly warned him not to fall in love with her, like so many other unfortunate men had done. She cited the case of Ritter Franz von Hochstatten, who came from one of Germany's most distinguished families. "I wouldn't give up my career to marry him, and he hung himself. I didn't want that to happen to Howard, but I feared he'd do something drastic when I turned him down."

"Had I married Howard," she said, "he would never have had any need for another woman. When you have the world's most beautiful woman in your bed, there is no need for any other."

Before the end of that long-ago party in 1966, the agent, Jay Garon, Hedy's porno boyfriend, and the author of this book assured Hedy that she was the most spectacular creature since God created Eve—and that she ranked up there with Helen of Troy. Even Agnès Sorel in the Middle Ages did not equal her beauty.

"Why else would Cecil B. DeMille cast me as Delilah?" she asked. "The temptress of the ages."

"You sure knew how to deliver a mean haircut," Garon said.

* * *

The day after Hitler ordered the unprovoked attack on Poland, and the world was plunged into World War II, Howard called Noah Dietrich at three o'clock in the morning.

"What's important enough to wake me up," Dietrich demanded of his boss.

"There's a war going on, Noah," he said.

"Don't you think I read the newspapers and listen to the radio?" an impatient Dietrich asked.

"I wanted Hughes Aircraft to become a major player in this war," Howard said. "Douglas, Lockheed, Northrop, Consolidated, even Vultee, are thriving. Why not Hughes Aircraft?"

"Those boys at Wright Field don't trust you," Dietrich said. "They acknowledge you as an aviation hero, but think you're too much of a playboy."

"Let's figure out a way to change that image," Howard ordered.

"Okay, I'll get on it first thing tomorrow. Now, I've got to get some sleep."

472

"One more thing," Howard said, before releasing Noah. "I've decided to go back into the picture business."

"Another *Hell's Angels?*" Dietrich said. "We still have plenty of footage left."

"Something better," he said. "I'm going to make the first sex western ever filmed."

"Westerns aren't about sex," the sleepy Dietrich protested. "They're about shooting Indians. In Westerns, men love their horses, not women."

"My Western is going to change all that," Howard promised. "I'm going to make a Western so sexy that chapters of the Legion of Decency will be howling from coast to coast."

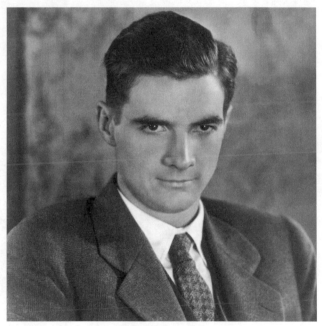

Howard Hughes

CHAPTER FOURTEEN
Los Angeles 1939-40

Howard still didn't like parties unless they served some purpose. When he was invited to the Trocadero in December of 1939, to a post-première celebration of *Gone With the Wind* that David O. Selznick was throwing, he agreed to attend only after he'd obtained a copy of the guest list.

Arriving on the scene, he didn't even pay his respects to the film's co-star and his former girlfriend, Olivia de Havilland. He wanted to meet not a beautiful actress this time, but the film's publicist, Russell Birdwell. Howard had been impressed with the nationwide publicity generated by Birdwell's "Search for Scarlett O'Hara."

One of Selznick's "yes men" pointed out Birdwell to Howard. The publicist was amusing Mary Pickford and Norma Shearer with stories of the filming of *Gone With the Wind*.

As Howard approached, Norma was claiming she turned down the role of Scarlett because her public "didn't want me to play a bitch."

Seeing Howard, Mary made a quick excuse and departed. She no doubt didn't want to face another snub from him, and was still bitter at his insult to her at the Tailwaggers Ball that Bette Davis had thrown. Norma still intended to pursue Howard romantically so she seemed delighted to see him. Merely nodding at her, Howard asked Birdwell if he could see him, privately. "Can't you see I'm talking to Miss Shearer?" Birdwell snapped, not recognizing Howard. Rebuffed, he stalked away.

After Howard had gone, Norma chastised Birdwell. "You're a publicist, for God's sake! How could you not recognize Howard Hughes? He's the second most famous man in America after FDR."

Realizing his mistake, Birdwell excused himself from Norma and searched the room until he found Howard hiding behind a potted palm. He immediately made excuses for his rudeness. Since Birdwell had obviously been told who he was, Howard didn't introduce himself. "I'm going to make a big motion picture. I want it to become more famous than *Gone With the Wind*. I might need your help. Interested?"

"Sounds most intriguing," Birdwell said

"I'll call you," Howard said. "Don't call me." Without a goodbye, he turned and headed across the large dance floor in the direction of the exit.

In the reception area at the coat-check desk, he encountered Norma again.

"Oh, Howard," she said, "I don't have my driver today. He's sick. Would you be a darling and give me a lift home?"

Although he had pointedly ignored Norma up to now, he suddenly seemed to view her in a different light. "For the Queen of Metro-Goldwyn-Mayer, I'd be honored to be her chauffeur."

It was the beginning of a new romance.

Another A-list actress—Hollywood royalty, in fact—had come into his life.

* * *

En route to Norma's elegant home, Howard became intrigued with her patrician profile, her impeccable manners, and her casual grace. A vulgar Jean Harlow she wasn't. Nor a flapper type like Joan Crawford. She'd pushed back her hair into a distinctive coiffure created for her by the effeminate Marty Franks. In a white satin, rather slinky and low-cut gown by Adrian, she looked seductive, very evocative of her role as Irina, the "countess," in *Idiot's Delight*, opposite her former lover, Clark Gable. He'd been astonished to find out that she never wore underwear. "That way, we wolves can better pick up her scent," he jokingly told Victor Fleming, who had directed him in *Gone With the Wind*.

What transpired that night between Howard and Norma would be lost to boudoir history had actress Merle Oberon not talked about it. At the time she was Norma's best friend and confidante, and not known for her discretion, particularly at cocktail parties. Merle, of course, never spoke for publication.

In the late 1940s, Norma also confided certain details about her romance with Howard to her dwindling sets of friends and colleagues. Again, she never spoke on record.

If these sources are to be believed, Howard first asked Norma, "Are you the same in person as you are in the movies?"

She looked flabbergasted, as if not understanding the question. "I don't exactly know what you mean."

"An emancipated woman, one who's been disillusioned by love—maybe marriage, too. One ready to indulge in some hi-jinks with the first good-looking stud from Texas who comes along."

"Mr. Hughes…"

"Call me Howard."

"Howard, that is for you to find out," she said coyly.

"One movie reviewer said you suggest playful eroticism on the screen," he said. "Just how playful and just how erotic?"

"Again a question for the mystery of the night about to unfold," she said, quoting a line from a screenplay, *The Loves of Martha Eggers*, that she'd just turned down.

Before the car pulled into her driveway, she told Howard that his Uncle

Rupert had given a great boost to her career when she'd appeared in his rollicking farce, *Excuse Me*, in 1925. "Rupert went to Louis B. Mayer and told him, 'That little lady can do anything she sets her mind to.'"

"I'm sure my uncle is a man of great judgment when it comes to talent," he said, quickly changing the subject. Talk of Rupert made him uncomfortable. "I saw you in *The Women*. The only lady among the cats in that bitchfest. When it comes to bitches, it was perfect casting for Joan Crawford. As a bitch, she could just play herself."

"Meow!" she said. "You can say that again!" Joan Crawford was Norma's chief rival within MGM. Crawford felt that Norma got all the good roles because she was "sleeping with the boss." Norma had been married to Irving Thalberg, the "boy wonder" or "boy genius" at Metro and the second in command. Before his death of heart failure in 1936, he had been called "the Crown Prince of Hollywood." Once, Crawford sent a message to Norma, "You can tell Miss Shearer I didn't get where I am today on my ass!"

Norma amused Howard by telling him that she had at first mistaken Thalberg for an office boy when they were introduced in 1923.

Montréal-born Norma Shearer was nearing the end of a distinguished career when Howard first drove her to her swanky home. No longer living in a $7.50-a-week room at 8th Avenue and 56th Street in New York City, she was the doyenne of a sumptuously furnished Hollywood mansion. She was surrounded by antiques, paintings, and half of the outstanding stock of MGM, along with eight million dollars, left to her by her late husband. He'd also left her an iron-clad contract to prepare herself for her upcoming battle with the tyrannical Louis B. Mayer.

Even before Howard met her, he was well aware of her reputation as a sexual predator. Thalberg's weak libido and even weaker heart meant Norma had to turn to more virile men to satisfy her strong sexual desires. By the time she'd met Howard at the Trocadero, she'd already had an affair with Mickey Rooney when he was only sixteen, twenty years younger than herself. Of the affair, which was "extinguished" by Mayer, fearing scandal, Rooney later said, "She was hotter than a half-fucked fox in a forest fire."

Howard's homosexual friend, Billy Haines, once confided that Norma "was one of the few women in Hollywood who ever got a rise out of me." Privately, Howard counted at least three actors both Norma and he had bedded, including not only Billy himself, but Clark Gable and cowboy star Johnny Mack Brown.

The man who escaped Norma's clutches was Howard's boyfriend, Tyrone Power. Norma desperately tried to seduce the handsome actor when they had co-starred together in *Marie Antoinette* in 1938. "She invited me frequently to her dressing room and to her home," Tyrone confided to Howard. "But I found her very unsexy. I heard that she was a nymphomaniac. On the set one day, I discovered George Raft banging her against the side of a wall when the crew had broken for lunch. The next week she was entertaining James Stewart in her dressing room. She was also known for having an affair with Robert Montgomery. They starred in some pictures together. I heard that faggot-hating Montgomery is a 'wham, bam, thank you ma'am,' type of lover."

In the comfort of her home, Norma enticed Howard to take two libations, unusual for him. She amused him at her piano, playing songs for him and singing, although she was no Jeanette MacDonald. She told him that at the age of "eight tender years," she had made her living performing in nickelodeons.

It was not Merle Oberon but Billy Haines who later provided details of the Hughes/Shearer romance.

As Howard discovered that first night, Norma spent almost as much time getting ready for bed as she did in the morning when she had to face the cruel lens of the MGM cameras. "I thought I'd wait all night before I got my chance at that honeypot," Howard told Billy. During their romp, she confided that she found sex with Thalberg unsatisfying because she liked it rough and he was just too gentle. "If rough sex is what she wanted, that's what I delivered," Howard said. "Texas style. At one point she wanted me to spank her bottom until it turned a rosy pink. That proved to be a prelude to a type of sex I'd never had with a woman before. She likes to get entered through the rear door. She claims that she prefers that more than entry into that deep passage she has up front."

Howard also told Billy that, "Norma can go all night. You'd have to call out the U.S. Marine Corps to keep that hot hole plugged. Her fingernails dug so deeply into my back I bled."

The next day Howard seemed pleased that, "I've bedded another Oscar winner." Norma had won the Academy Award for her 1930 performance in *The Divorcée* in which she played a young society wife who tired of her husband's indiscretions and set out to beat him at his own game.

Howard would continue to date Norma for only three more weeks, eventually asserting that "the bitch tired me out."

In some far-fetched way, she'd influence his life again, but only indirectly.

Vacationing at the Sugar Bowl Ski Lodge in northern California in the late Forties, and deep into her retirement, Norma was thumbing through a souvenir photo album left on a coffee table. In it she came across a fresh-faced beauty, Jeanette Morrison, posing seductively on the slopes of a snow-covered hill.

Since Norma still retained a financial interest in Metro-Goldwyn-Mayer, she arranged for the young woman to have a screen test. It was successful. With a seven-year contract and a name change to Janet Leigh, the aspiring actress was soon playing opposite Van Johnson in *The Romance of Rosy Ridge*, set in Missouri in the 1860s at the time of the Civil War.

"I'll always be grateful for Norma for jump-starting my career in films," Janet later said. "That was wonderful. What wasn't wonderful was all the attention I was getting. That led me into the clutches of Howard Hughes himself. What a nightmare!"

* * *

Ginger Rogers had endured humiliation in her engagement to Howard, including his absconding with her estranged husband, Lew Ayres, and flying him to a vacation retreat in Texas. "God knows for what purpose Howard flew Lew there," she told her sometimes director, Gregory La Cava.

To divert Ginger, Howard had tried to be clever. While he was involved for a night with Bette Davis or perhaps Olivia de Havilland, and Ginger needed an escort for a lavish party or première, Howard asked Cary Grant to accompany her. Seeing the gorgeous pair together, some of the more foolish members of the press concluded there was romance in the air. As George Cukor impishly remarked, "That was about as likely as Kate Hepburn shacking up with Mussolini." It is not known if Ginger knew how intimate Cary's relationship with Howard was.

She referred to Cary as her "old chum." She also claimed that he was "as dear a gentleman as anyone would ever want." In her memoirs, she wrote, "To be friends with a male who is not your husband is a neat trick that works sometimes!" Privately, she once confessed to Fred Astaire that her so-called romance with Cary never got beyond a polite kiss on the cheek at the door to her Bel Air mansion.

By 1940 Ginger no longer had any intention of marrying Howard, although he was yet to be told that. She told her mother, Lela, and her sometimes lover, director George Stevens, that she was "growing tired and fed up with Howard's attempt to possess her totally, while leading another life as a predatory vulture." More and more, after her divorce from her sexually confused husband, Lew Ayres, became finalized, she was enjoying playing the field, as she could have her pick of the handsomest men in Hollywood. "I wanted a boyfriend, not a policeman," she wrote. "Things between Howard and me were coming to a head." Unknown to her at the time, Howard had tapped her phone and was even monitoring calls to her beloved mother, Lela.

The fuse to the inevitable stick of dynamite was lit by a rather innocent-sounding phone call. Ginger was in the middle of dinner with Lela and director Lewis Milestone, who had also been Howard's director. "The boss man" [Ginger's words] called and asked her if she would go to the dentist with him the following morning at 10:30. "Howard always insisted on calling the shots," she later claimed. "I couldn't believe it when he told me he'd also scheduled a cleaning for me. Howard Hughes telling me when I needed my teeth cleaned. What nerve!"

She refused to go with him, even when he offered to pay the bill. "God damn it, Howard," she shouted into the phone. "I make $300,000 a year. I can afford to pay my own ten dollar dental bill."

"Okay, princess," he said, "you're making a big mistake."

Before she'd finished dinner, another call came in, this time from a writer friend of hers, Alden Nash. Her rather gossipy friend told her, "It's no business of mine, but I don't like to see a friend of mine being two-timed by this big lug Howard Hughes." He may have had another motive for the call. Only that day Caddo Productions had rejected a screenplay of his on which he'd labored for eighteen months.

Nash claimed that for the past ten nights Howard's car had been seen parked in front of the driveway of the residence of Faith Domergue, who lived across the street from him.

"Never heard of her," Ginger said.

"She's just a teenager." After thanking him for the bad news, Ginger hung up the phone and returned to her dinner guests. When Lela and Milestone departed after dinner, she drove over to Faith Domergue's address. She was using a brand new station wagon Howard had presented her. Painted a maroon with lots of wood trim, Howard had ordered the station wagon custom-designed for her with pink leather upholstery, her favorite color.

She immediately recognized Howard's battered old Chevy in front of this unknown teenager's home. Ginger later confessed that she drove all the way back to Bel Air in tears.

Writing in 1991, and after the passage of decades, Ginger still would not reveal Faith's name in her memoirs, preferring to identify her as "the little actress," which had been how Nash had described the starlet.

When Howard called the following morning to urge her—once again—to go to the dentist with him, she shouted, "No! A thousand times no!" She slammed down the phone.

For the rest of the day, she wandered aimlessly around her Bel Air house, "fighting back tears."

Around three o'clock that afternoon, Howard's attorney, Neil McCarthy, called to give her bad news. Howard was in Room 418 of the Hollywood Presbyterian Hospital. On the rain-slick streets of Los Angeles, and en route to the dentist, his Chevy had collided head-on with a black sedan with two passengers—an unknown man and his wife—both of them injured but not killed.

Driving in anger, Howard had forgotten to turn on his windshield wipers. Even so, he was not the cause of the accident. Without warning, the sedan had suddenly veered into his lane, causing the crash. Howard's head was thrown forward, colliding with the windshield as it shattered into jagged pieces. A shard of glass slashed into Howard's head "like deli ham being sliced," as one of the attending motorcycle policemen wrote in his report. That patrolman and his partner found Howard lying unconscious at the wheel, bleeding heavily from a concussion. They didn't know how much blood he'd lost. An ambulance was summoned to rush Howard to the intensive care unit of the hospital.

He didn't regain consciousness for four hours. The moment he did, he stared into the face of Noah Dietrich and Neil McCarthy. Both men were ordered to "Get Ginger! Haul her ass over here!" As Dietrich remembered it, Howard didn't even ask about his medical status.

Alarmed, although still angry at Howard, Ginger asked McCarthy about his condition. "He's badly injured. His face, particularly the area over his left eye, required seventy stitches. He's so bandaged he looks like something from a Boris Karloff movie."

She hesitated about an hour, later stating that she was "at war with myself." Finally, she decided to drive the station wagon to the hospital. "Driving there, I was so mad I almost had an accident myself."

Given special clearance at the hospital—Howard was seeing no visitors— she was allowed into his room. Dietrich had stashed a burly bodyguard outside.

In the room, she was forced to give an autograph to the head nurse, an adoring fan, before she was allowed to be alone with Howard.

"He looked a fright," she later recalled. "All swathed in bandages. His sad brown eyes were at half-mast when they looked up at me. A pitiful look. But I was seething inside and had no pity for him. He told me he was so miserable that he felt he'd 'arrived in Hell or some place even worse.' I got even madder when he blamed the accident on me. He said he was denouncing me in rage on the way to the dentist and wasn't paying attention. 'I'll probably be sued for millions,' he said."

Before leaving her home, she'd put all the jewelry he had given her into a red satin-covered box with a pink ribbon. She tossed the box onto his hospital bed. "Faith Domergue needs these gems more than I do. If you have any left over, you can give them to Bette Davis, Joan Fontaine, Olivia de Havilland, and, yes, Norma Shearer. I know about that bitch too." She headed toward the hospital door. In a parting gesture that befits an actress, she turned to look back at him, staring into his soulful eyes, later comparing them to a bloodhound puppy in her brief account of their breakup in her memoirs. As a final gesture, she took off her emerald engagement ring and tossed that onto the hospital bed. "I am returning everything to you," she said. "We are no longer engaged." She then stormed out of the room, slamming the door behind her.

She was never to see Howard Hughes again.

Fifteen minutes later, Dietrich entered Howard's hospital room to find his boss crying, a very unusual event. "What's the matter?" he asked. "The pain?"

"Ginger's left me!" Howard bellowed.

The next morning after a sleepless night, Ginger rose early to drive herself in her station wagon to the studio for some publicity shots. In her driveway, she frantically looked for her station wagon. It was missing. Fearing it had been stolen, she rushed to call the police. Waiting by the phone, she picked up the receiver an hour later when an officer called her back. He informed her that the station wagon was registered as being owned by the Hughes Tool Company of Houston, Texas. The car had been impounded and was being returned to its officially designated owners.

"That bastard!" Ginger shouted into the phone before slamming down the receiver.

Howard spent little time recovering from the accident and almost no time getting over his heartbreak with Ginger. In the hospital, he was reading a magazine when he discovered a picture of a beautiful seventeen-year-old girl, Gloria Vanderbilt. Like his former flame, Brenda Frazier, the teenager was another widely publicized heiress, and had gained national fame during a bitter custody battle in the 1930s that had occupied the country's headlines for weeks.

The day Dietrich came to the hospital to drive Howard back to Muirfield, he informed his head honcho, "No more slutty Hollywood actresses for me."

That was a promise Howard was not to keep.

"I'm tired of dating Hollywood matrons," Howard informed an astonished Dietrich. "I'm going to New York to bag me some beautiful teenage pussy. Not just any girl. One with a pedigree. I'm about to storm the rarified world of the Vanderbilts."

"But what about Faith Domergue?" Dietrich protested. "If you like them young, she's only fifteen. Two years younger than the Vanderbilt kid."

"Nothing like having a young teenage beauty on each coast. That way you save on having to transport them from the Pacific to the Atlantic."

"Like a girl in every port," Dietrich said.

"Something like that," Howard said, tossing off the hospital bedding, revealing that he was entirely nude. "Now, Noah, get me something to wear so I can cover up my balls and get the hell out of this joint."

* * *

It was Memorial Day, 1940. Howard had just returned to Los Angeles, having sailed the *Southern Cross* to a secret port in western Mexico. As if they already knew that the United States would soon be entering World War II, officials at the War Department were systematically appropriating large vessels like the *Southern Cross* for military use by the Navy. With Errol Flynn, he'd sailed to Mexico to hide the boat at a private marina owned by one of the actor's friends.

Back in Los Angeles, Howard was stalking the deck of his newly rented yacht, *Sea Queen*, impatiently waiting for the Memorial Day sail to begin.

Johnny Meyer had planned a special treat for him. Howard had told his pimp that he was tired of "dating mothers," perhaps a reference to Ginger Rogers and Katharine Hepburn, who were not exactly mothers. "I want to meet babes who are just on the borderline between being a girl and bursting into womanhood—virginal types, completely unspoiled. I'd like to meet a girl who has never even kissed a boy. That way, I can teach her to kiss like I like it."

"Finding a virgin, even a fourteen-year-old virgin, in Los Angeles will be difficult," Meyer said. "But I'll try."

Stated even more graphically, Howard requested a young girl who—unlike Kate or Ginger—"hadn't sucked off James Stewart."

482

Meyer had succeeded beyond his wildest dream, getting Jack Warner to allow several starlets he had under contract to go on this "publicity junket" sponsored by Howard. "If it gets their pictures in the paper, and they're all in bathing suits, it'll be good for the studio," Jack said. "It'll show the world we've got a second act to Bette Davis," and, brother, do we need one for *that one*."

Discreetly, and without a lot of publicity, Howard had been dating nineteen-year-old Susan Peters, a Spokane-born "starlet with promise" at Warners. It was not a very serious romance, but would continue on and off throughout much of World War II.

He'd continue to date "lovely, luminous" Susan even when she married actor Richard Quine. He knew of her dalliance with Howard. But Howard was such a powerful man in Hollywood that the ambitious Quine overlooked his wife's romance, thinking that Howard in some way might advance either of their careers.

She married Quine in November of 1943 when they had appeared in the 1942 Marjorie Main vehicle, *Tish*. Before her tragedy, Susan's career was starting to move, especially after she'd appeared in the 1942 *Random Harvest*, MGM's prestige film for the year. She'd won an Academy Award nomination as best supporting actress. Then tragedy struck.

On New Year's Day, 1945, Quine invited her on a duck-hunting trip outside San Diego. On the hunt, her rifle discharged accidentally, the bullet lodging in her spine, leaving her permanently paralyzed from the waist down. Rumors abounded in Hollywood that Quine had actually shot his wife out of jealousy because of her ongoing fling with Howard. Howard dreaded getting embroiled in another scandal, and quickly dropped Susan after her accident. "I don't make love to quadriplegics," he callously told Meyer.

Susan's marriage to Quine survived for five more years until their divorce. At the age of 31 on October 23, 1952, Susan died. She'd lost her will to live, and had literally starved herself to death, having not eaten in weeks.

Quine went on to enjoy minor renown as a director of such films as *Paris When It Sizzles* in 1964, co-starring William Holden and Audrey Hepburn. On June 10, 1989, Quine also lost his will to live. Using the same shotgun that had misfired into Susan's spine, he fired into his head, blowing his brains out.

"So many people who knew Howard ended tragically," Johnny Meyer said. "I began to think my boss was a jinx." Perhaps Meyer was foreseeing his own tragic early death.

On that bright day in 1940, however, future tragedies were hardly on anyone's mind as Susan and her best friend, Faith Domergue, were driven to Balboa as part of Howard's yachting party for Warner starlets. Howard met Susan and her friend at dockside. He was dressed in white pants tied with a nautical rope and a faded blue yachting jacket that was a cast-off from Cary Grant. Howard's brown eyes, resting under a sea captain's visored hat, lit up when Faith came into his presence. He virtually ignored Susan.

A fresh-faced, raven-haired, Black Irish exotic beauty from the steamy French quarter of New Orleans stood before him. "Bayou baby!" he said. Susan had spoken several times of her friendship with Faith and her Louisiana background while dating Howard. He was immediately captivated by this striking fifteen-year-old and her lustrous eyes and vivid, sensual mouth set off by what was to become known during the war years as "Victory Red " lipstick.

He later told Meyer that he'd never seen such lips on a woman. But Faith would not become known for her mouth. Instead, she would be frequently compared to big-busted Jane Russell, another of Howard's discoveries. At the time Faith was introduced to Howard, her breasts had not yet blossomed into their full mammillary potential.

In spite of all the beautiful young starlets around him, including Susan, Howard never took his eyes off Faith during the sail to Catalina. He noticed that in a certain kind of light, her eyes became a shade of violet, evocative of a future Elizabeth Taylor, another teenager he would pursue.

At the end of the yachting party, Howard dismissed all his other guests, offering to personally drive Faith back to the home of her parents. It was after two o'clock in the morning when he pulled up in front of her doorway. He noticed that there were no lights on in the house, so he assumed the parents were permissive, or else they would be waiting up with a gun for the return of their errant daughter.

In spite of the way it appeared, Faith later claimed that "nothing happened that first night. In fact, when I got to my house in Howard's car, he had to wake me up. I'd fallen asleep. Not only was I tired, but I was bored. All day Howard had kept staring at me. But there was nothing to say to him. He didn't know what to say to me either. So all he did was look. That was okay by me. After all, I was trying to break into pictures and be looked at. So, what the hell!"

"You'll be hearing from me, kiddo," he promised, giving her a kiss on the cheek before driving off. Two months passed, and she'd virtually forgotten about the man old enough to be her father. Then one afternoon he called. But instead of speaking directly to her, he spoke for an hour with her mother and spent half as much time talking to her father.

Faith had only recently learned that she had been adopted shortly after her birth by her adoptive parents, Leo Domergue and Annabella Quimet. They had moved to California in the 1930s, enrolling her at St. Monica's Convent School.

Arriving at the doorstep of the Domergue household, Howard virtually ignored Faith, but began the process of wooing her parents. Learning that Leo was in charge of a car dealership in Los Angeles, Howard asked to be driven there. Once in the showroom, he immediately purchased an emerald green Lincoln from Leo. Weeks later when Faith asked Howard what happened to the Lincoln—he was driving a battered old Buick at the time—he said that he'd parked it outside some airport, but didn't remember which city or even which state.

On the afternoon of his meeting with the Domergues, he hired Leo, giving him a position at Hughes Aviation. Since Mrs. Domergue didn't want to work, he bestowed a gift upon her. Going to his Buick, he returned with his beloved mother's sterling silver tea set from Houston, "worth a king's ransom."

Over dinner that night, he won over the parents, who agreed to let Faith drive to Palm Springs that weekend for a house party. He assured the Domergues that there would be many older women there, including Katharine Hepburn

Robert Mitchum, Faith Domergue

who would chaperone Faith. Kate was actually in New England at the time.

Once they got to Palm Springs, however, Faith learned that there were no other guests. The first night passed uneventfully. On the morning of the second day, he took her from shop to shop in Palm Springs, buying her a new wardrobe which thrilled her.

Around midnight on the second night, he appeared unannounced in her bedroom. He told her that all afternoon he'd been studying her sensuous lips, and had decided she was a perfect candidate for fellatio. She told him that she didn't know what that meant. "I'm here to teach you." Moving toward her bed, he took off his robe, revealing his nudity. She later claimed that she was afraid but he was very gentle with her. "I felt protected when I was with him," she recalled. "Even though I tried, I couldn't bring him to climax. But he didn't seem to be disappointed in me. He masturbated himself in front of me before getting up. He kissed me on the lips. 'Tomorrow is another day,' he said to me. 'With practice, you'll get it right.'"

In the weeks and months to come, Howard got the Domergues to agree not only to the above-mentioned long weekend in Palm Springs, but also to plane trips to Las Vegas and San Francisco, even moonlight sails to Catalina Island. "Day by day I was falling more and more in love with Howard Hughes," Faith later recalled. "And I got better at that other thing he wanted done to him."

He became obsessed with her sensuous lips, almost as much as he was with Jane Russell's breasts. He ordered his studio to endlessly photograph Faith's lipstick-coated mouth—her "luscious kisser" as he called it—and to blow up pictures of only her lips in extreme close-up. He then had about twenty of these pictures plastered across the walls of his library at Muirfield. He later confided to Johnny Meyer that he often masturbated while looking at those lips. "Kinky," Meyer told Dietrich, "considering that if Howard had waited three hours or so, Junior Miss would be home from high school, and he could have the real thing working him over."

Throughout his long relationship with Faith, which would endure for years, Howard preferred the act of fellatio. She claimed that at no time "did Howard and I have sex in the missionary position."

Slowly, and with the parents' permission, he was taking over every aspect of her life. That led to his decision to purchase her contract from Warner Brothers. He promised he was going to "make you the biggest screen attraction of all time. I did it for Harlow, who had no talent. You've got talent. Look what I'll do for you!"

She believed him and arranged for him to meet her agent the following afternoon. She would bring him to Howard's office at 7000 Romaine Street.

Exactly at three o'clock, Henry Willson, along with his discovery, showed up to meet Howard.

Even though both men didn't know it at the time, his meeting with Henry Willson became one of the milestones of Howard's life. It was a relationship that would last for years, yet was so secretive that most of *tout* Hollywood never knew that Howard and Henry were even acquainted.

* * *

Faith Domergue had been discovered by Willson, who at the time was working for the Gummo Marx Agency. Gummo was the only Marx brother who did not appear before the camera, but spent his time instead discovering talent for the movies.

At the time of his meeting with Howard, Willson was already one of the most notorious homosexuals in Hollywood. Pudgy, with a tendency to early baldness, Willson was no beauty. Yet he worshipped beauty. Male beauty, that is. It was said that before his career ended, he'd seduced more beautiful men in Hollywood than any other agent.

He was often compared to John Darrow, the former Adonis of *Hell's Angels*, who'd gone from acting to agenting as his looks faded. As an agent, Darrow had continued to pimp for Howard. But when Willson met Howard, he decided that he wanted to replace Darrow as chief pimp. In the future, it would be Willson, not Darrow, who would arrange for the handsomest men in Hollywood to spend time with Howard. Johnny Meyer was relieved to learn that he would no longer have to recruit young men for Howard's bed, because he found it distasteful. "I'm no pervert," he told Deitrich. Meyer, however, would continue to recruit young starlets for Howard.

To ingratiate himself with Howard, Willson, out of Faith's hearing range,

486

invited him to a poolside party at his house. Through Darrow, Howard had already heard of these pool parties where some of the handsomest and most well-built young men in Hollywood showed up. Most of them were aspirant actors, who seemed only too willing to take off their bathing suits to become part of a "meat market."

Willson invited gay or bisexual producers, directors, cameramen, and other studio executives to these orgies. Various power brokers in Hollywood would then check out the young men before disappearing with one of them into one of Willson's upstairs bedrooms.

Eager to attend one of these events, Howard said that he'd show up, even though he had some concerns about flaunting his homosexuality in such a public way. When Willson told him all the big name stars, producers, and directors who had attended previously, Howard felt more assured that his privacy would be protected. Johnny Meyer said that Howard went over to Willson's house that Sunday afternoon. No details are known about what Howard did or did not do on that day.

In time, however, Willson would introduce Howard to young men who later became big name stars in the late 40s and especially in the 50s. Willson's biggest discovery, whom he pimped only to the Hollywood elite, was Rock Hudson—that is, when the agent himself wasn't enjoying the handsome star's favors.

Howard must have liked what he saw at Willson's pool. After only two weeks of knowing the agent, he ordered Dietrich to pay Willson two hundred dollars a week in cash. Dietrich asked, "What for?" Howard assured his chief honcho that it was "just a finder's fee."

In his capacity as an agent, Willson had negotiated directly with Jack Warner to sign Faith to a seven-year contract at Warner Brothers, where she was paid fifty dollars a week. Taking voice, diction, and drama lessons, she had not yet been cast in a film at the time of her first meeting with Howard.

Howard was determined not only to dominate her life, but her contract as well. Perhaps Willson himself tipped off Jack Warner about Howard's interest. Deciding he could make some extra pocket change, Warner held out for fifty thousand dollars as the price tag on Faith's relatively worthless contract. Determined, Howard paid it, even though he told Willson, "It's highway robbery—just like a damn Jew."

Once he'd secured her contract, Howard demanded that Faith go back to school. "Howard made me finish high school," Faith later recalled. "Or I would have dropped out. Looking back, I'm glad that he did."

When she wasn't in school, he ordered that she take drama lessons at his offices at 7000 Romaine Street. He even hired the best acting coach in the business, Katherine Braden, to personally supervise Faith. Braden had taught many starlets at 20th Century Fox, a number of whom had gone on to become big stars, notably Betty Grable.

At one point, Howard had Faith delivered to the house of the famous lesbian costume designer, Edith Head. He sent a note to Head: "Teach my 'Little Baby' how to dress like a lady. I'm going to make a big star out of her."

Years would go by before Howard actually cast Faith in a movie at RKO. Her only "credit" at the time was "uncredited." In 1941 she appeared in a jitterbug scene in the lackluster film, *Blues in the Night*, which co-starred Priscilla Lane and Betty Field and had been directed by Miriam Hopkins' discarded husband, Anatole Litvak.

Louella Parsons systematically maintained a network of spies who were stationed virtually everywhere, even at an exclusive resort in Phoenix, Arizona, where Howard had taken Faith for an off-the-record weekend. The spy fed Louella some misinformation. In her column the next day, Louella headlined the *faux* scoop: IS SHE MRS. HOWARD HUGHES?. Readers had to dig into the column to learn that SHE referred to the unknown Faith Domergue, not some big name Oscar winner like Howard usually dated. Even though Louella raised a question in the headline, the column actually reported the wedding as already having taken place. "The Gay Illiterate," as she called herself, claimed that Howard had wed Faith in Phoenix "at a very secret and very private civil ceremony."

It wasn't in Phoenix but at the Palm Springs Racquet Club that Howard proposed marriage to her. "It was the greatest thrill of my life," Faith later claimed. "As we stood on the terrace, he slipped the most beautiful emerald engagement ring on my finger, as a harvest Blood Moon shone down on us. I think Howard had ordered God to hang out that incredible moon that night."

Actually the emerald was the one that Ginger Rogers had tossed onto his hospital bed before storming out the door and out of his life forever. As he slipped the ring onto Faith's finger, he said, "You are the baby girl I always wanted and never had. So far, you've known only one man—and that's me. That's the way it's going to be. I don't want you messing around with other boys."

Her fantasy romance got a cold dose of reality when he moved her into Muirfield. For some reason, Howard had ordered his housekeeper, Beatrice Dowler, to put the estate in mothballs. "All the furnishings downstairs had been covered in white sheets as if no one lived there," Faith recalled. "I felt I'd been banished to a lonely castle."

Strangely, there was a scorched airplane propeller displayed in the living room. She asked about the ghoulish artifact, and he explained that this propeller had almost decapitated him during the filming of *Hell's Angels*. "Putting it here means that every night I'll be reminded of Death when I come home."

"Do you really want to be reminded of that?"

"It's not a reminder that I'm going to the grave," he said. "It means I looked Death in the face and cheated the motherfucker!"

All the windows had been shuttered. Evocative of his future as a recluse, he had already begun to withdraw from the world. Packed up and put into storage were the Tiffany lamps, crystal decanters, Venetian chandeliers, and Murano glassware. "I can't bear to look at the stuff any more," he'd told Beatrice Dowler, his housekeeper. Upstairs he'd ordered that the bedrooms once occupied by Kate Hepburn and Billie Dove be "forever locked," the keys thrown away. Once he'd been proud of the trophies he'd garnered as an aviator. But now he ordered that all of them be put in dead storage, even the one personally awarded to him by President Roosevelt himself.

Faith's days were bleak at Muirfield. She discovered that Howard would go away for weeks at a time and not even announce his departure. Most of her meals were taken with her parents, as she could not go out with anyone else. "Even when Howard would return home, he often wouldn't have anything to do with me," she said. "Sometimes we'd pass each other in those gloomy halls at Muirfield, and he wouldn't even speak."

He did let her go out, but only if accompanied by a chauffeur. She felt that the driver was a spy, reporting on all of her activities to Howard. He even insisted that the chauffeur be her escort at her senior high school dance at the end of the school year. "The driver seemed afraid to even speak to me," Faith later said, "much less dance with me." Unknown to her, the driver had been carefully vetted before getting his job as Faith's guardian.

Later in the 1950s, as Howard kept more and more starlets stashed away in apartments or homes in the Hollywood Hills, he demanded that all his drivers and assistants who looked after these girls be homosexual. Meyer said, "It was like eunuchs in the courts of the Sultans of old. Instead of having these guys castrated, Howard demanded they be gay instead. He did that ever since one of his favorite gals ran off and married one of his chauffeurs."

As time went by, Faith came to feel that Howard was becoming increasingly paranoid—that, of course, being her assessment later in her life. "At the time I don't think I knew what paranoia meant," she said. "I'd sit for hours at a time in his battered old Buick while he made all his business calls from pay phones scattered all over Los Angeles. He feared that all his phones at Muirfield and at Caddo were tapped."

Actually, as it was later learned, he was right. Years from that time, it was revealed that J. Edgar Hoover had ordered his FBI agents to tap Howard's lines. Hoover never trusted Howard, especially when his aviation company was doing more and more business with the government.

As the United States progressed through the war years, Howard and some of his associates would give the homosexual FBI director plenty of cause for alarm.

* * *

One week Robert Stack accepted Howard's invitation to go sailing, but asked if he could bring a friend along. Howard reluctantly agreed, thinking it might be one of Robert's young starlet girlfriends. In those days the extraordinarily handsome actor was making the rounds, seducing "a starlet a minute," as he put it. Howard would have preferred to enjoy the actor's charms alone but agreed to play host to whomever Robert brought along for their weekend sail to Catalina.

On the deck of the rented *Sea Queen*, Howard was introduced to the young John F. Kennedy dressed like a sailor, all in whites. "He's Ambassador Kennedy's son," Robert said, introducing the young man who was twenty-three years old and a graduate of Harvard. He'd just published a book, *Why England Slept*, which had been ghost-written for him.

Howard detested the young man's father, Joseph Kennedy, a feud stemming from the time the liquor dealer had been a power broker in Hollywood. On a few occasions, both men had seduced the same women, notably actresses Constance Bennett and Nancy Carroll.

When Howard later thanked Robert for inviting the young man for the weekend, Robert knew Howard was smitten. John soon became "Jack." Howard confided to Robert, "He has the most perfect blue eyes I've ever seen on a man."

The moment Jack flashed his soon-to-be-famous smile at Howard, the tall, thin Texan bonded with the New Englander, with his natural charm and grace. It was as if Howard had waited all his life to meet the perfect Prince Charming. The only problem was that the gleam in this young man's eyes was not for Howard, but for every beautiful woman in Hollywood. Over dinner that night, Jack told Howard that, "I want to fuck every woman in Hollywood." He called it "celebrity poon-tang."

A lifelong lover of gossip, Jack admired Howard and was eager for anything he might reveal about all the legendary stars he'd seduced. For his Hollywood days, Jack wanted to use Howard as his role model. "You're the swordsman out here," Jack told Howard. "No doubt about that. Even dad admits it's true, and he's bedded a few beauties—not just Gloria Swanson. I'm the new boy in town and want to follow in your footsteps."

Robert and Jack had become almost immediate friends the day a mutual friend, Alfredo de la Vega, had introduced them at Robert's studio. Over Howard's champagne and lobster dinner aboard the yacht, Robert told Howard about his secret hideaway, called "the Flag Room."

It was a small flat that lay at the end of a cul-de-sac, Whitley Terrace, between Cahuenga and Highland in the Hollywood Hills. Here stood a jumbled mass of apartments stacked one on top of the other like a set of warped building blocks about to tumble over. The apartments opened onto balconies dripping in wisteria.

At the Flag Room, the name given to their rental, Robert claimed that he learned "about the birds, the bees, the barracudas, and other forms of Hollywood wildlife." Both Robert and Alfredo had convinced their parents that they needed this small hideaway to pursue their studies quietly and without interruption from their families. Their parents fell for this line and agreed to pay the rent. "We studied all right," Robert confessed. "Female anatomy."

In the corner of the apartment was a small bedroom with room for only one double bed, with about two feet on either side of it. Alfredo and Robert turned this into their "chamber of seduction." The ceiling was only five feet high, so both men had to bend over when they came into the room. On the ceiling they plastered flags of various nations, all except Nazi Germany.

When either Robert or Alfredo took a young woman here, they demanded that she memorize the order of the flags for a later quiz—or else she'd have to "Pay the Piper." Since the victim was already spread out horizontally, she was in position to receive her "punishment" for flunking the exam. "All the girls flunked," Robert said. "There were too many flags to remember." One blonde beauty, who looked like a future Marilyn Monroe, was so enticing and alluring to Robert, that he claimed he "penalized" her three times that night.

Many young starlets were repeat visitors to The Flag Room. "Horny bastards that we were," Robert said, "Alfredo and I rearranged the flags every night so that some foxy lady on her fourth or fifth visit would not be able to memorize the order and would flunk one more time."

Robert amused Howard by telling him that Jack, although he'd just arrived in Hollywood, had visited The Flag Room a total of eight times, each time with a different woman. Years later in his memoirs, Robert facetiously claimed that he'd helped Jack in his geopolitical studies by teaching him which flag belonged to which country.

"I've known many of the great Hollywood stars, and only a few of them seemed to hold the attraction for women that JFK did, even then," Robert said. He noted that even before his handsome friend entered politics, he'd just look at a woman and she'd "tumble."

"I had a fixation on Carole Lombard," Robert admitted years later when he agreed to talk candidly about his life with Howard and his friendship with Jack. "Except for posing for some pictures with me, she never gave me the time of day. I guess she was settling for Gable's less than prepossessing inches instead of my fine and noble tool. Actually, Gable became a great friend of mine, and I wouldn't have betrayed him anyway. Nonetheless, in those days I

John F. Kennedy, circa 1940

sought out starlets who looked like Carole Lombard, at least the dime store version."

"Unlike me, Jack had completely versatile taste in women—blondes, brunettes, redheads, young ones, mature ones, gals with large breasts, gals with lemons for breast," Robert said. "Regardless of the girl, he always insisted on shapely legs."

Even in later life, valet George Jacobs in his autobiography, *Mr. S: My Life with Frank Sinatra*, admitted this was true. Jack, by then president, was still fascinated by women with shapely legs, notably dancers Cyd Charisse and Shirley MacLaine. In MacLaine's case, he also wanted to know if "she has a red pussy," according to Jacobs.

Aboard his yacht, Howard seemed eager to learn about young Jack's string of conquests, no doubt planning to conduct raids on the women himself if the seduction sounded enticing enough.

Robert later said that through "the humble portals" of The Flag Room passed a "guest list that ran the gamut from the chorus line to Academy award winners." In his memoirs, the actor claimed that "since I still live in California," suffice it to say that he couldn't "name names."

In private conversations, Robert was much more forthcoming. When pressed, he cited Betty Grable as one of Jack's early conquests. Robert himself had struck out when he'd pursued "America's pinup with the dimples on her knees," but Jack scored big.

Jack claimed that Grable told him that child actor Jackie Coogan had taught her "more tricks than a whore learns in a whorehouse." She also confessed to him that she'd "seduced the unseductive" aspiring young actor Ronald Reagan.

For some reason, known only to himself, Howard didn't pursue Grable himself, even though he'd go after—and win over—all the leading pinup girls of World War II: Lana Turner, Veronica Lake, Rita Hayworth, and Ava Gardner, among others.

Robert amusingly confessed that even though Grable and Howard didn't make it with each other, they shared some of the same lovers, especially Tyrone Power and later Victor Mature. "Even that discovery of Henry Willson, Rory Calhoun, when he wasn't otherwise occupied with Marilyn Monroe and countless others," Robert claimed. "Rory one day told me that the trouble with Hollywood was that there were no good cocksuckers, with the notable exceptions of Betty Grable and Howard Hughes."

Pert young actress Barbara Britton was another conquest for both Jack and Robert. Robert claimed that the actress had "luscious tits." Britton had arrived in Hollywood straight out of college to decorate a Hopalong Cassidy western, *Secrets of the Wasteland*. She is remembered today, if at all, for her dominating image as "the Revlon Lady" on TV.

Margaret Sullavan, the sometimes caustic ex-wife of Henry Fonda, is famous in Hollywood history for her steamy affairs with the likes of James

Stewart and Humphrey Bogart, as well as dozens of handsome young actors and studly men, many of whom she'd pick up in her car while cruising the streets of Los Angeles and Hollywood. Although not admitting to any appearances in The Flag Room, Sullavan later told her biographer, Lawrence J. Quirk, that Jack was "a beautiful, beautiful man. Even in his early twenties, he had all that cocky masculine charm."

Robert claimed that he and Judy Garland were always "great chums," although many insider Hollywood gossips thought this "cute couple" were having an affair on their dates. The actor said they never got around to going to bed. "But when I introduced Judy to Jack, she fell madly in love with him. It was a friendship that would last for all their lives. Even when he was in the White House, the President would call Judy in Hollywood and have her sing 'If birds fly over the rainbow, why, then, oh why can't I?' Those words, and not anything from Camelot, were his favorite lines from any song."

Lana Turner was an emerging blonde bombshell who would share her favors with both Jack and Robert—and later with Howard himself. Robert remembered her as "so vulnerable...so lost!"

"We even bedded Oscar winners," Robert claimed. "Even before they won Oscars." He cited Ingrid Bergman. Even though married to the Swedish doctor, Petter Lindstrom, Ingrid liked to have affairs on the side. In time, her impressive lineup would include her *Casablanca* co-star Humphrey Bogart (in spite of what the biographies say), along with Gregory Peck, Spencer Tracy, Leslie Howard, Yul Brynner, Anthony Quinn, David O. Selznick, Omar Sharif, Joseph Cotton, and Bing Crosby. "She'll do it with doorknobs," said her director, Alfred Hitchcock.

Before they reached Catalina Island, Robert realized that both Howard and Jack were true sailors, "born to ride the waves." "The men quickly bonded," he claimed. Robert said that he never told Jack about Howard's homosexual streak. "I figured Jack could take care of himself. Many gays had come onto him. Besides, Jack told me that his best friend was a devoted cocksucker and always finished him off for the night when he didn't score with a girl."

The reference was to LeMoyne K. Billings, affectionately called "Lem" by Jack. The two men were considered bonded at the hip, and their friendship would endure through his marriage to Jacqueline Bouvier, through countless affairs with such stars as Marilyn Monroe and Gene Tierney, and through the Bay of Pigs, ending only by an assassin's bullet in Dallas.

Somehow Howard and Jack struck a harmonious note with each other in talking about their sexual conquests. Robert later admitted he felt left out. At that point the only woman that both Howard and Jack had each had some form of sexual contact with was Marlene Dietrich. "That didn't surprise me since Marlene did anything in pants or skirts, although she never got around to me," Robert said.

He remembered Jack relating that he'd gone to the south of France when still a teenager as part of a holiday from boarding school. There he'd stayed in Antibes at the ultra-deluxe Hotel du Cap. He was introduced to Marlene Dietrich. "She was fucking my dad at the time," Jack admitted.

He said it wasn't a complete seduction, but he'd gotten intimate with Marlene on the darkened floor of the grand ballroom at the hotel. "We were dancing real close, and she unbuttoned my pants and reached in and stroked my dick. Up and down. The band was playing Cole Porter's *Begin the Beguine*. She smelled like a French whore. I creamed in my tux. Can you imagine what a thrill that was for a teenage boy? To be stroked by Marlene herself."

On Catalina Island, Jack wandered off for about five hours," Robert said, "so Howard and I just assumed he'd gotten lucky. We know for a fact that he boarded another yacht in the harbor. The following Sunday we went for a nude swim. I couldn't help but notice Howard checking out Jack's equipment. Of course, Howard himself had all of us beat."

Robert said that he wasn't surprised when another invitation for another weekend was extended by Howard. "This time I was excluded, and it was all right with me. I got mixed up with Howard in the first place because I thought he was going to advance my career. By 1940 I'd come to realize that Howard wasn't going to do a god damn thing for me. He just wanted Hollywood's hand-somest boy—namely me—to hang out with him."

"Jack told me he was going to Palm Springs for the weekend with Howard," Robert continued. "He said that Howard had promised him 'a pleasant surprise,' whatever that meant. I didn't warn Jack not to go. Why shouldn't he go? He dropped a bomb on me when he told me that Howard had convinced him that he should pursue a career as a motion picture star, even though the ambassador wanted him to go into politics one day. Two days before Jack left to join Howard in Palm Springs, I noticed that he kept looking at himself in every mir-ror he passed. I think every good-looking guy and beautiful gal in the world dreams of becoming a movie star. Why should Jack be an exception? He said, 'I can just hear dad shouting at me: No Kennedy becomes a movie star.'"

Ironically that same line would be uttered years later by Jacqueline Kennedy to her son, John F. Kennedy Jr., when he came to her and told her the startling news that he wanted to be an actor and had actually been offered the starring role in an upcoming movie.

* * *

The details of that weekend in Palm Springs remain sketchy. The only source of what happened was Robert Stack, who wasn't even there. He later reported that he "learned a little bit from Jack and not a lot more from Howard himself."

Howard had obviously set up the weekend to impress Jack. He seemed to bask in the flow of Jack's admiration for him. Jack had been bragging about his conquests to Howard, but the older man wanted to show the younger one that he too could round up two "hot dates" for the weekend.

Howard had flown to Palm Springs with his "two surprises." Jack had not been free to go along with them at the time, so Howard arranged for a long black limousine to pick him up later that day and drive him out to a desert setting where Howard either rented a villa or owned it—no one was ever certain which.

Jack later claimed to Robert that he was completely flabbergasted when he arrived at the villa to learn the identity of the two "dates" Howard had arranged. The young New Englander, it turned out, had been intimate on some level with both of the beautiful foreign-born ladies—one a Swede, the other German. Howard did not need to introduce Jack to Ingrid Bergman and Marlene Dietrich. Robert was asked how Howard had pulled off this coup. He could only speculate. "In Marlene's case, it was no big deal to get her to accept an invitation to Palm Springs," Robert said. Over the years, she became a frequent visitor to Palm Springs. George Jacobs, Sinatra's former valet, reported in his memoirs that he caught Dietrich swimming nude in his boss man's pool, kissing an equally nude Greta Garbo.

"Until Jack that day on the yacht told of his seduction of Ingrid Bergman, Howard had never met the star," Robert said. "I think he wanted to impress Jack that, even though he was an older Lothario, he too could snare that beautiful young Swedish gal for himself."

Robert said that Jack later reported that he was confused at first "about the pair-offs." Had Howard arranged for him to pair off with Ingrid or with Marlene? At first Jack assumed because of the differences in the ages of this quartet, that he and Ingrid would be the young lovers, and that Howard and Marlene would be the more mature romantic duo. But right from the beginning, Howard whispered to him that he planned to seduce Ingrid himself, "since you've already had the pleasure."

Marlene was to be Jack's date. "She was quite a bit older than me but still looked gor-

Ingrid Bergman

geous, and dad said she was great in the sack," Jack later confided to Robert. Jack also said that Marlene's first words to him were "it looks like we've got some unfinished business." No doubt the reference was to her masturbation scene with him on the French Riviera when he was just a teenager.

Robert claimed that Howard's ultimate plan for the weekend had been foiled. What he'd hoped to do on the following night was arrange a four-way with Jack, Ingrid, Marlene, and himself. "I think Howard voyeuristically wanted to see young Jack in action," Robert said. "From what I was told, Jack and Marlene agreed to it."

In later life, Jack as President would become notorious for three-ways. But Ingrid was the lone hold-out that weekend. The woman loved sex, and plenty of it. But, as she told Howard, "I'm not into orgies." Robert also believed that Ingrid did not want to be on the receiving end of Marlene's lesbian affection. "*That one's* [meaning Marlene] reputation has already preceded her," Ingrid told Howard.

Howard may not have been entirely pleased with Ingrid's sexual performance in Palm Springs. He was even less pleased when he learned that their notorious weekend in the desert had become the talk of Hollywood. Nonetheless, he continued to pursue Ingrid for a few weeks, but ever so discreetly. He didn't want any more scandal.

"There must have been something he liked about Ingrid," Robert said, "although he complained to me about her preference for the missionary position. From what I gathered, the Swede refused to indulge Howard in his passion for oral sex."

Even Ingrid's second husband, Roberto Rossellini, the Italian director, complained about this to several of his friends. "She doesn't do the things a whore does," Rossellini claimed, telling his cronies that she always refused to fellate him. For that, he had to go frequently to one of the bordellos of Rome or other cities.

It is not exactly certain how Howard introduced himself to Ingrid, or how he persuaded her to travel that weekend to Palm Springs. Robert didn't know. "I saw his eyes light up when Jack was telling him about his seduction of Ingrid. I knew that Howard had put her at the top of his list. In those days he was going down his list, crossing off one beautiful star after another when he'd had his way with her. I think I know how they met. Howard was a friend of David Selznick and would later try to marry his wife, Irene Mayer Selznick, when she divorced David. I heard that Howard got himself invited to a party at the Selznick home. There Howard met Ingrid who at the time was having an affair with Selznick. He once told me that the reason he liked Ingrid so much was 'because she was the only actress in Hollywood who didn't want to play Scarlett O'Hara.'"

After many years had gone by, Howard would resume seeing Marlene only briefly in 1952. Her longtime friend, director Fritz Lang, had cast her in a

Technicolor western, *Chuck-a-Luck* for Fidelity Pictures. Howard got involved when as chief of RKO he agreed to release the film. He demanded an immediate title change. He told Lang, "What movie-goer in Europe will know what in the fuck *Chuck-a-Luck* means?" Howard's new title was *Rancho Notorious*. His time with Marlene was brief. The star was then aging, although still "a beautiful antique," as Lang told Howard.

After the resumption of his brief affair with Marlene, Howard informed Lang, "The thrill is gone." Their boudoir performance had been lackluster, and so were the box-office receipts on *Rancho Notorious*. Most critics found it a poor man's version of *Destry Rides Again*.

Old friends since the 1930s, Howard would never see Marlene again. "Each of them would watch the other decay from afar," said Orson Welles, who cast Marlene in a guest appearance in his 1958 film, *Touch of Evil*.

After the Palm Springs weekend, Howard continued his hopeless pursuit of Jack, who'd soon be heading back to the East Coast. Howard didn't get to see Jack in action with Ingrid and Marlene, but he did take him to the private studios of a tall Mandingo masseur, who called himself "Nobu." During the war years, Nobu, from some unknown country, was famous in Hollywood for his thorough massages, which involved masturbating his clients, both male and female, to the "mother of all climaxes." His patrons included Errol Flynn, Lana Turner, Paulette Goddard, Joan Crawford, and even Howard himself.

Although it later became fashionable for certain masseurs in New York and California to give massages that involved sexual climaxes, in Nobu's time no one did that except prostitutes hired for that purpose.

Jack told Robert that Howard took him to be worked over by the "magic hands" of Nobu. Both men lay nude on separate beds in Nobu's studio while sensual music played. "I got this big erection," Jack later confided to Robert. "By the time he was finished with me, I was splattering the ceiling. I've never seen anything like it. He really knows how to touch the right spots."

Although Nobu may have been a peak experience in Jack's life, other masseurs have reported that he always got an erection when being massaged, even by a man. Sinatra's valet, George Jacobs, wrote in his memoirs, that he gave Jack a massage in Palm Springs when he was the guest of his boss. "By the time I rolled him [meaning Jack] over to do his trunk and thighs, he had an enormous erection."

From all reports, Howard never got to experience Jack's erection first hand. Robert speculated that Howard made one attempt and failed to win Jack over. Such an occurrence may have happened during Jack's final weekend on the West Coast before his departure back East. This time Jack was picked up and delivered to a beach house in Santa Monica which was owned by Marion Davies.

"I knew Jack was looking forward to it," Robert said. "He thought that Howard, to impress him, would come up with two reigning film queens. How

Howard planned to top Marlene and Ingrid I don't know. But he was an amazing man. I fully anticipated that he'd arranged to have Rita Hayworth, Lana Turner, and Betty Grable there. To Jack's disappointment, when he got to Santa Monica, he found that he was the only invited guest."

"I don't know exactly what happened that weekend because Jack never told me everything." Robert said. "Howard abruptly changed the subject a week later when I inquired."

"The following Monday morning, when I was telling Jack good-bye, he told me that he never wanted 'to see Howard Hughes again—that guy's too much of a creep for me.'"

* * *

Los Angeles 1945-1950

In 1945, Howard once again began his pursuit of Ingrid Bergman, even though she was still married to Petter Lindstrom. In New York to meet with film executives, she renewed her friendship with Cary Grant, which was strictly platonic. Howard wanted in on the action. On several occasions, the three of them were photographed together at a restaurant or a club.

Cary was serving as a chaperone. Actually he was a "beard," concealing the fact that Ingrid was being slipped at night into Howard's suite at the Drake Hotel. When a reporter asked Cary what was going on, perhaps a romance between Ingrid and himself, or between Howard and Ingrid, Cary lied, claiming that Howard was considering casting Ingrid in his next film.

Ever the gallant suitor, Howard came to Ingrid's rescue when she found all flights booked back to Los Angeles. When he learned about her dilemma, he said that he would take care of it. "I'll be your pilot on the flight back to the coast."

The next morning Howard sent a limousine to Ingrid's hotel to deliver her to the airport. Once there and once boarded, she found that she had the plane virtually to herself except for a few passengers, notably Cary Grant. She was introduced to Joseph H. Steele, the son of a missionary in Turkey, who had been hired as a publicist by David O. Selznick. In time he would become her most devoted admirer and defender among the Hollywood hierarchy. The producer's former wife, Irene Mayer Selznick, was aboard. She hardly seemed delighted to see Ingrid. Even though she'd divorced David, Irene was still furious at Ingrid for having had an affair with her husband. Also aboard was Alfred Hitchcock. Ingrid had repeatedly turned down the chubby director's sexual advances, similar to the ones he'd make to Grace Kelly in the future.

En route to Los Angeles, Howard dismissed his co-pilot. He asked Ingrid to fly in the cockpit seat beside him. She slept for most of the way. But he woke her up when he diverted the plane to show her the rim of the Grand Canyon.

Before landing in Los Angeles, Howard said he'd like to throw a party for her at the Beachcomber, inviting all her friends and admirers. She turned down the offer. She was not eager to continue an affair with him. Unknown to him, although his spies would later discover it, she was rushing back not to her husband, but to Gregory Peck. The extraordinarily handsome star had launched a torrid romance with her during the filming of *Spellbound.*

In the next few months, Howard made at least eight calls to Ingrid, asking her to slip away with him. Each time she refused.

In her own autobiography, *Ingrid Bergman My Story*, written with Alan Burgess, Ingrid falsely claimed that she was introduced to Howard by Cary Grant in New York. She completely left out that she'd had a rendezvous with Howard years earlier at a villa in Palm Springs. She also claimed that Cary arranged a "foursome date" with Howard as her escort. The other part of the quartet were Irene Mayer Selznick and Cary himself. Ingrid said they went dancing at El Morocco in New York.

There are problems with that memory. Irene Selznick told her friends, especially Kate Hepburn, that she was furious with Ingrid for contributing to the breakup of her marriage to Selznick. Also, at the time, Howard had a marriage proposal "on the table" to Irene. It seems unlikely that he'd want Irene to see him dating her nemesis while still urging marriage upon her.

Even so, Ingrid maintained that while Howard was dancing with her on the floor of El Morocco, he whispered to her, "I'm so lonely. I'm so terribly lonely. You know I have no friends." Cary later dismissed this as a possibility. "First, it wasn't true. Second, it doesn't sound like something Howard would say."

In her memoirs, Ingrid wrote that she laughed at such statements coming from a rich and famous man. She allegedly scolded him. "It must be your own fault, because you don't go out and look for friends. Anyway, I'm having a good time; you're not lonely tonight, are you?"

It was Ingrid herself who started the widely spread rumor that Howard bought up every available ticket on planes flying from New York to Los Angeles. "If we wanted to fly that day, we had to fly with Howard Hughes."

All he had to do was invite her to fly with him. After all, she'd been sleeping with him. It seems highly doubtful that Howard would have to go to such trouble and expense to get her to fly back with him to Los Angeles, considering how intimate they had been in New York.

Privately, Cary told George Cukor back in Hollywood, "That story about buying up all those seats on every plane was just a conceit on Ingrid's part."

Ingrid claimed that on May 30, 1948, Howard called again. As she was sitting on the floor drying her hair, she picked up the phone to hear the Texan's high-pitched voice. "This is Howard Hughes, and I've just bought a film studio for you," he informed her. "It's yours, my present to you. Are you happy?"

If Ingrid is to be believed, she said, "Well, that's very nice. Thank you!"

"Not only have I bought the god damn place, I'm going to make you Queen of RKO, just like Kate and Ginger, at various times, used to be."

"What actress wouldn't have been impressed to hear that?" Ingrid later said. "Today I would have been very impressed indeed and would have jumped at the offer. But in those days I guess I was a little full of myself. 'Show me a great script and a great director,' I told him, 'and then we'll talk.' Perhaps I said good-bye. Perhaps I said a little more. Who can remember? All I know is that I hung up on him. I must have been the only actress in Hollywood foolish enough to hang up on Howard Hughes when he'd just offered to make me Queen of RKO. Even now, on looking back, I can't believe how arrogant I was."

He did not follow up with any scripts, much less directors. She maintained that, "I had practically forgotten about Howard Hughes when the Italian director, Roberto Rossellini, entered my life." She greatly admired and respected the man and was eager to work with him.

It just so happened that Roberto, like all other directors in the world, had a script in need of financing. It was called *Terra di Dio* (Earth of God), and he claimed that producer Samuel Goldwyn had agreed to put up the financing.

Roberto was not known for submitting a finished script. He always said that, "I carry around the idea for a film in my head." When he finally outlined his bleak, morbid idea to Goldwyn, the outspoken director denounced it as "a piece of shit."

Feeling "depressed and abandoned," Roberto was rescued by Ingrid. She said that she knew a producer who might back the film: His name was Howard Hughes.

To reach Howard, Ingrid claimed that she went to the Beverly Hills Hotel where he was living in a bungalow. She alleged that she found Howard living next door to Arthur Miller and Marilyn Monroe. In 1949 it is highly doubtful if Monroe even knew who Arthur Miller was. She wouldn't marry him until 1956, and they wouldn't appear together at the Beverly Hills Hotel until 1959. Nonetheless, Ingrid managed to reach Howard—probably through Johnny Meyer—as Howard at the time was the most difficult person to contact in all of Hollywood. "You could get Harry Truman on the line a hell of a lot easier than Howard Hughes," Samuel Goldwyn once said.

Regardless of how she managed to pull it off, and there were rumors that she'd slept with Howard at the Beverly Hills Hotel, he agreed to come over to her house the following day to discuss Roberto's latest film idea.

She claimed that during the script conference, Howard never once looked at Roberto and had even failed to shake his hand. Howard said he did not want to hear the plot for the script. "I have just two questions. Are you beautiful in it? Are you going to wear wonderful clothes?"

At this point, she laughed, informing him that she was playing a displaced person in some horrible refugee camp with cheap clothes like prisoners wore in Nazi concentration camps.

"Too bad," he said. "In your next film for me I want you to look like the most beautiful woman on the screen. We'll get Edith Head to design your wardrobe. Maybe I'll design a few gowns myself. After all, I designed a bra for Jane Russell in *The Outlaw*."

Before he left her house, Howard agreed to invest a million dollars to make the film, which was unusually high for a post-war Italian film. In addition to that, he'd pay Ingrid her usual salary of $175,000, plus $150,000 to Roberto as director.

There was one touching moment during Howard's visit to her house. She kept a framed picture of her mother in the living room. Noticing it, he went over and picked it up. His eyes were misty. "My mother died when I was young." He turned and looked into Ingrid's eyes, still ignoring Roberto. "I have completely forgotten what she looked like." He turned and left the living room without a good-bye.

With Howard's advance money, Roberto left with Ingrid for Italy to film *Terra di Dio*. Within weeks, stories began to reach Howard that his star was having a torrid affair, similar to the one she'd had with Gregory Peck. She'd broken with her *Spellbound* co-star because, as she told Cary Grant, she could no longer tolerate Peck's "heavy reliance" on alcohol.

Even though the world was yet to know, Ingrid fell madly in love with Roberto during the filming of their movie, which was set on the island of Stromboli, one of the mythologically rich Aeolian Islands off the coast of northern Sicily. Both Ingrid and Roberto were still married to other people at the time. Not only that, but Roberto had been engaged in a hot affair with Anna Magnani, Italy's leading actress at the time. When he took up with Ingrid, he dropped Magnani.

As if to extract her revenge, the volatile, temptuous Magnani set out to make a rival movie, calling it *Vulcano*. It was released in the United States in 1953 under the title of *Volcano*. Along with Stromboli, Vulcano—known to the ancients as Thermessa—was another one of the Aeolian Islands off the coast of Sicily.

Magnani announced to the press that audiences would flock to see her and not the Bergman/Rossellini film. She told her friend, Tennessee Williams, "I've seen one picture of Bergman's. That's all I could stomach. She's a cow! No emotion whatsoever—a completely blank face. On the other hand, my face can register every known human emotion. That's why my fans call me the new Eleanora Duse."

In the Italian press, the Bergman/Magnani rivalry was referred to as "the duel of titanic actresses, hiding behind volcanoes."

Magnani seemed intent on keeping the feud going, even though Ingrid tried to ignore her. "My Mamma Romma—I play a prostitute—will burn up the screen like an exploding volcano. Besides, William Dieterle, a far greater artist than Rossellini will ever be, is guiding me. Who can forget his *Hunchback of Notre-Dame*. A masterpiece! But we're making an ever better film than *Hunchback*."

501

Roberto's estranged wife, Marcella de Marchis, was rumored to be dealing with Sicilian gangsters in Palermo and was said to have paid them a thousand dollars to see that "the Swede" did not leave Stromboli alive. And for an insight into future upsets that lay in store for Ingrid, Miss America of 1946, Marilyn Buferd, showed up on the island, supposedly to resume her affair with Roberto. If this were true, and it may not have been, Ingrid was perhaps unaware of Buferd's presence on Stromboli.

When the final version of Roberto's film arrived at Caddo Productions, Howard was horrified. He hated the movie, considering it a dismal failure. He immediately set about cutting it, even though he confided to Dietrich that "it appears hopeless." To anyone who wanted to listen, he denounced Roberto "as a WOP son-of-a-bitch." As for Ingrid, he said, "How could any director take one of the world's most beautiful women and photograph her like a hag?"

Back in Italy, Roberto and Ingrid were strapped for cash. In desperation, Ingrid turned to Joe Steele, who then went over to Caddo with some very private information to report to Howard. He presented the plight of the romantic duo to Howard. For the first time, Howard learned that Ingrid was pregnant with Roberto's child. Steele urged Howard to hurry up and release the film. An early release might solve their financial difficulties, but there was another reason. Ingrid feared that when news leaked out about her pregnancy, it would lead to a ban on the film in America.

Howard promised Steele that he'd give the matter his immediate attention. He also informed Steele to tell both Ingrid and Roberto that he was not only cutting *Terra di Dio* "to try to save it," but that he'd retitled it *Stromboli*.

Within the hour, Howard had his old friend Louella Parsons on the phone. He told her that Ingrid was pregnant with Roberto's child. "Louella pissed her pants when I delivered this scoop to her," Howard said to Dietrich.

He also told his honcho "that *Stromboli* stunk." His only hope of saving it was to release news of the scandal, which he felt would lead to thousands of movie-goers flocking to the box office just to get a glimpse of this fallen woman, who no longer was the saintly *Joan of Arc* that she'd portrayed on the screen.

The next morning--thanks to Howard--America learned of Ingrid's affair with Roberto and her pregnancy.

In Los Angeles, the *Herald Express* screamed in two-inch headlines: REPORT INGRID BERGMAN TO HAVE BABY SHOCKS FILMDOM. Knocked down to second place was an announcement by President Harry Truman that America had invented the hydrogen bomb. The news of "the bastard child" was like the dropping of an H-bomb. The Bergman/Rossellini affair—and the subsequent "out of wedlock pregnancy"—became the talk of the world, outdistancing even the late 1930s publicity generated by the Hughes/Hepburn affair.

The public was shocked to learn that Ingrid, still married to her Swedish doctor, was carrying the child of her married director.

Suddenly, Howard became eager to release *Stromboli* at once to take advantage of such worldwide interest. He personally took over the advertising campaign. He designed movie posters to show an erupting volcano in the background. "Get it?" he asked Johnny Meyer. "The volcano will suggest Rossellini's erupting WOP dick, spewing hot come over Ingrid."

Ingrid was denounced by churches throughout America. In Washington, Senator Edwin C. Johnson rose up on the Senate floor and attacked Ingrid as an "influence of evil."

The actress was vilified from coast to coast. When Steele revealed to her that it was Howard "who squealed to Louella," Ingrid vowed never to speak to him again. Roberto shot back that neither he nor Ingrid, or any member of their extended families, would ever fly again on TWA.

Ingrid quickly became an outcast in Hollywood. She'd been transformed, almost overnight, from one of Tinseltown's brightest stars into a pariah. No further roles were offered to her. With one noteworthy exception, her friends dropped her. Cary Grant wrote: "Ingrid, dearest, it would not be possible in a single cablegram to tell you of all your friends who send you love and affection." That was a bit of an overstatement. She had no friends left in Hollywood until, in time, she would make a successful comeback.

The worldwide publicity surrounding Rossellini and Bergman in 1949 rivaled that of the faraway scandal that would one day envelop Elizabeth Taylor, Richard Burton, and *Cleopatra* in 1962. But despite the strenuous efforts of Howard's public relations staff, *Stromboli* bombed at the box office. *Time* magazine reminded its readers that the crater of Stromboli's volcano was once known to the ancients as "the gateway to purgatory."

Ingrid did not become the Queen of RKO, as Howard had promised, and she was never to see him again. In spite of his refusal to fly on TWA, Roberto and Ingrid accepted an invitation from Howard to occupy a suite at the swanky Excelsior Hotel in Rome while she awaited the birth of her child. Ironically, as Anna Magnani's *Vulcano* was having its Roman premiere, Ingrid in another part of town was giving birth to Renato Roberto Giusto Giuseppe. And in yet another part of Rome, *Stromboli* was being screened to a bored audience, many of whom got up and walked out of the theater before the final scenes.

A quarter of a century would pass before Ingrid would make a discovery about Howard. As she was packing to leave her house "forever" at Choisel in France, she discovered an unopened letter dated February 10, 1950, eight days after she'd given birth to her son. It was from Howard himself.

For the first time, she tore open the letter which somehow had remained concealed all these years. His words to her were kind, as he praised her "courage, utter simplicity, and lack of guile or subterfuge." He wrote: "Reality is a matter of intent. It comes from within, not from legislation or legal documents." He assured her that when her son grew into manhood, the attitude of the

503

world might be "a little truer and broader." Her son, he told her, would carry no stigma based of the circumstances of his birth. Instead, he claimed, her child would be imbued with the "heritage of a mother who though she may not have been so terribly clever, shrewd, or wise, is one of the most brilliant and courageous women of our generation."

As she put the letter back into its rotting envelope, she burst into uncontrollable tears.

* * *

London, 1972

Ingrid later claimed that she must have stood for an hour looking up at the façade of London's ultra-deluxe Inn on the Park Hotel. She'd read in the papers that Howard had been taken here, and had secretly entered through the back entrance of the hotel in a hospital stretcher because of his emaciated condition. She was also told that her former lover was being guarded by a phalanx of "fierce aides."

Finally, after one final gaze up at what she thought was his penthouse suite, she entered the lobby of the hotel. She knew that Howard was not looking down at her. From all reports, the windows of his suite had been taped shut and covered by dark velvet blackout curtains of the type Elvis Presley at the time was also ordering in Las Vegas to keep out the sun.

Announcing herself at the reception desk, Ingrid was immediately recognized. One receptionist, Philip David, remembered that he even asked for her autograph, telling her that *Casablanca* was the best movie he'd ever seen. She requested a piece of hotel stationery. On it, she scribbled a quick note to Howard, requesting a meeting.

Philip assured the star that he'd deliver it to Howard's suite personally. After ordering afternoon tea for her, he found a secluded part of the lobby and seated her in its most comfortable armchair. He returned shortly thereafter, assuring her that the message had been delivered.

"I sat in the lobby for at least an hour, maybe two hours," she later said. "I was trapped in my memories of the past, and what might have been if I'd taken Howard's offer and become the Queen of RKO, instead of running off to Italy with Roberto. As time went by, I began to realize that Howard might not have read my message. Maybe his guards didn't even give him my note. Then an even more horrible thought occurred to me. Maybe he was in such a bad condition—so heavily drugged—that he no longer remembered who Ingrid Bergman was."

"The staff was ever so polite to me, but it was so very evident that Howard had not accepted my invitation," she said. "Nor would he ever accept my invitation for a meeting. I was only guessing, but I felt that at this point in his life, Howard would never agree to a private meeting with anyone. Without announcing myself at the reception desk, I got up from their chair and walked as fast as I could to the entrance. I stepped outside and breathed the air. I felt that I was leaving an important part of my past behind me. If I remember, and I do, a light rain was falling over London."

* * *

Los Angeles, 1941

Howard's plan to fly to New York to "bag" Gloria Vanderbilt had to be post-poned. He would not meet her until a few months before the U.S. entry into World War II. And the setting would be Beverly Hills, not New York.

Increasingly, he was absorbed with designing pioneering aircraft that might be of use to the U.S. Air Force once America entered the war. Even as his chief rival, Charles Lindbergh, urged Americans to stay out of "foreign wars," Howard was more realistic. "Any week now we're going to get into the fucking mess," he told Noah Dietrich. "Maybe not this week, but the following week."

When he wasn't at his aircraft factory, Howard spent his nights in the arms of fifteen-year-old Faith Domergue.

Even so, he followed Gloria's progress through key events in her life in the newspapers. In some ways, she evoked debutante Brenda Frazier, with whom she was often confused in the eyes of the American public. Gloria had far bet-ter-developed artistic sensibilities and an even better Social Register pedigree than Brenda, but there were similarities between these two blue-blooded *celebutantes*. Both had porcelain white skin offset by slashes of pomegranate red lipstick that they applied to their succulent mouths. "Gloria Vanderbilt and Brenda Frazier are the two whitest women in America," wrote social commen-tator, Lynn Burlington. Both teenagers had midnight black hair—or, to quote Burlington, "the color the sky becomes on Halloween when the moon goes behind a cloud."

Gloria had first come to Howard's attention when she was only ten years old. The only child of American railroad heir, Reginald Claypoole Vanderbilt (1880-1925), "the poor little rich girl," became the victim of the most famous and the most scandalous custody battle in U.S. legal history. The year was 1934. Testimony at the trial depicted the girl's mother, Gloria Maria Mercedes Morgan (1904-1965), as an unfit parent. At the trial, a Vanderbilt maid testified that the glamorous widow bathed her feet in champagne and gave evidence of a lesbian relationship with a member of the British royal family, Marchioness Milford Haven (Countess Torby), who married a nephew of Queen Mary. Her mother lost the custody battle to Gloria's stern and old-fashioned aunt, Gertrude Vanderbilt Whitney, who would eventually be portrayed on the TV screen by none other than Howard's former girlfriend, Bette Davis. The film was called *Little Gloria...Happy at Last*, a misnomer if there ever was one.

Part of the battle had concerned who would control the four million dollar fortune Gloria had inherited from her father.

Howard anticipated that he'd have to fly East to capture this prize. But one August morning, he read in the paper that Gloria was spending a month in Beverly Hills. At the custody battle, the judge had granted her mother visitation rights for one month a year. He decided to storm the Vanderbilt citadel, which he found easy to do because of his wealth and fame. The Vanderbilt family respected money. Little Gloria's mother, or Gloria Sr. as she was called, had been labeled both a "fortune hunter" and a "gold-digger" in the infamous custody trial.

Howard called Maple Manor, the Beverly Hills villa where the "two Glorias" were staying. He knew that if he wanted to win the heart of this teenager, he would first have to conquer the mother. He'd used the same seduction technique on the mothers of both Ida Lupino and Ginger Rogers.

Speaking to Gloria Sr., he virtually invited himself over for tea at their elegant villa. She eagerly responded, "But, of course, I'd be delighted to meet you, dear Mr. Hughes."

When he arrived the next afternoon at four o'clock, he encountered Gloria Jr. in the hallway. She was dressed in what became known twenty years later as the "Jackie Kennedy look." On her way to an A-list reception at the Beverly Hills Hotel, Gloria awkwardly introduced herself to Howard. "His hat was tilted back on his head, and he was tall—really tall—and his jacket was slung over his shoulder in the most appealing way," she was later to recall. "He couldn't think of anything to say, and I couldn't either."

After Gloria said good-bye, Howard had tea with her mother. He convinced her that he was seriously considering testing her daughter for the lead in his next movie. That was, of course, a complete fabrication but he managed to convince her that it was true anyway. The mother took it upon herself to arrange a date between Howard and her daughter.

When Noah Dietrich heard of this, he claimed, "That Vanderbilt grande dame is pimping her daughter. Gloria is seventeen years old. Howard is thirty-seven, but in some ways at least twenty years older. He could be her grandfather."

The evening of their first date began menacingly. All afternoon, rain clouds had threatened the skies over Los Angeles. Thunder split through the unusual heavy darkness of a California late afternoon. Movie crews filming outdoor scenes were forced to shut down. By eight o'clock, when Howard arrived to retrieve his date, it was raining heavily.

Gloria had spent the better part of the afternoon fretting over her wardrobe, wanting to look her best for the producer, who had claimed that he planned to turn her into a glamorous movie star.

When Austria-born Hedy Lamarr had arrived at Hearst's San Simeon wearing a peasant dress, she'd launched a fad. Gloria had rushed out to buy a similar outfit.

Staring repeatedly at herself in the mirror, she had never looked more radiant. She'd been soaking for an hour in Adena Fluffy Bubble Milk Bath water. Once again, she checked her Austrian skirt and blouse, which made her look like fourteen—not seventeen. To offset the innocent virginal look, she dabbled Schiaparelli Shocking Pink perfume behind her perfectly shaped ears. A black velvet ribbon ran through her ruffled décolletage.

She might have expected him to arrive in a limousine, but Howard showed up in his battered Chevrolet where the raindrops kept falling on his head. Sloppily dressed, he darted across the driveway and up to her doorstep, carrying a recently purchased, big black umbrella, the kind you carry only to the rainiest of funerals. He rang the doorbell and was ush-

Gloria Vanderbilt and her aunt, Mrs. Harry Payne (Gertrude) Whitney, 1939

ered in to see Gloria who was waiting for him in the hallway. Her "shining knight," her "dream lover" was at last standing before her. "Gary Cooper had arrived at my doorstep," she later recalled.

Even though he had nothing to say to her—nor she to him—he drove her to the then-fashionable Sportsman's Lodge in the San Fernando Valley. In the reception area, she excused herself to go powder her nose. He awkwardly encountered an arriving George Raft and his date for the night, Howard's discarded lover, Norma Shearer. The couple only nodded at Howard before passing into the main room.

At dinner, Howard ordered his usual butterfly steak, baked potato, and small green peas. Gloria did likewise and for all her future dates with him, she would always order the same meal that he preferred.

From that night onward, Gloria and Howard began to date seriously. Neither one of them were Noël Coward conversationists, and often they would sit alone for hours at a time. Perhaps they'd lie on the beach at Malibu, watching the turbulent waves roll in from the Pacific. Or else he'd take her to his favorite lookout point high in the Hollywood Hills where he would sit and watch the moon. Sometimes in front of his fireplace at Muirfield, he would hold her in his arms, cradling her like a doting father might his daughter. The sounds of "Moonlight Sonata" drifted in through the open doors of his library.

He'd sail to Catalina Island and have his staff pack a picnic of meatloaf sandwiches—his favorite—along with a baked potato with plenty of catsup. Since it was summer he often had a container of black cherries which both of them would eat, turning their lips blood red and making their mouths sweeter to the taste.

He often flew her in his private plane, and she became familiar with the clouds over the California coast, Las Vegas, and even Arizona. Once he flew her over the Grand Canyon. Sometimes high up in the air, she'd sing to him— "Come, Josephine, in my fly-ing ma-chine"—making her voice very loud for his partially deaf ear.

She wanted to go "higher and higher and faster and faster" into the milky clouds, with her pilot in his masculine leather jacket being the older man to whom she'd given her young heart.

Instead of taking her to the Brown Derby or Ciro's for supper, he often drove her to Elmo's Pancakes House for—guess what?—pancakes for dinner. He'd "drown" his pancakes with lots of maple syrup.

When he learned that she had not seen *Hell's Angels*, he screened it for her. He told her that he'd made a star out of Jean Harlow, and that he'd make an even bigger one out of her. By that time, Gloria realized that Howard was never going to turn her into a star—but it didn't matter any more. She loved the man, not the star-maker.

"All I wanted was for him to love me," she'd write in her memoirs. But that wasn't to be.

One night to Gloria's surprise, Howard abruptly stopped the car to pick up a young male hitchhiker. There must have been something about this forlorn young man that appealed to Howard. He saw beneath the vagrant's shabby clothes and three-day growth of beard to someone who was "actually movie star handsome." He stopped and invited the young man to get into the back seat of his car. He drove the young man, whose name was Terry Dalton, to Bullocks and Robinson's Men Store. There Howard went into the back dressing room with Terry where he demanded that he strip completely naked so that he could be outfitted "for everything," including underwear. Terry emerged wearing an expensive brown suit, leather shoes, and a white shirt with a green tie. As Howard was paying the bill, the young man asked Gloria who Howard was. "Santa Claus," she told him.

Unknown to Gloria, Howard had called Johnny Meyer, ordering him to come to the store to pick up Terry and deliver him to Muirfield. After telling Terry good-bye, Howard resumed his date with Gloria.

Meyer later said that Terry Dalton looked somewhat like the future James Dean—"handsome in a trashy sort of way. By the time Howard arrived home from his date with Gloria, I had Terry all freshly bathed, perfumed, and kissable, waiting in Howard's library. He must have liked having sex with the kid, because Terry stayed on for two weeks before Howard got tired of his latest toy. He sent him on his way with five thousand dollars stuffed in his jeans."

Meyer then made an unusual claim. He said that Howard revealed to him that he and Terry had "done a couple of things together" that he'd never done with any other man." He never explained what that was, Meyer said. "All I know is that he continued to get real kinky with guys. With women, he was a gentleman, at least most times. But he really indulged himself with male hustlers. He was becoming as big a pervert in Hollywood as his uncle, Rupert, and no one topped *that one*. Rupert, or so I was told, had even installed a basement in his house, and had it specially equipped so that he could carry out his 'ultimate fantasies.' Howard found that very amusing when he learned of it. Maybe the sexual streak of weirdness in the Hughes family was genetic."

For reasons not known, Pat DeCicco began to call Gloria and ask her out on dates. Her mother adored this handsome, charming, and debonair hustler, and urged her daughter to date him, too, perhaps to make Howard jealous.

Although he was on Howard's payroll, Pat was defying him behind his back. By becoming part of a triangle with Howard and Gloria, Pat was repeating a pattern established with bit actress June Knight and his former wife, Thelma Todd.

Even when dating Pat, Gloria often saw pictures of him in the newspapers, perhaps a snapshot taken at the Trocadero where he was photographed with the beautiful starlet, Betty Avery, Sometimes he would take Gloria for Sunday brunches poolside at the home of producer Joseph M. Schenck, one of the famous "five moguls" of Hollywood. Pat called Joe "my uncle."

Pat used every occasion he could to warn Gloria that "Howard will dump you like all the others."

Eventually Howard learned of Pat's betrayal. On an ominous note, Howard told Meyer that if Pat "didn't clean up his act, I might start stuffing it up his ass again as punishment. When I used to do that, he squealed like a pig at castration. I might have to show him who's boss."

Instead of a punishing seduction, as threatened, Howard sent Pat "into exile in Siberia," meaning that he flew him to Kansas City where he was put in charge of catering for TWA.

When Gloria's Aunt Gertrude learned that her charge was carrying on "with an older man—and rumored pervert—and a cheap gigolo"—she summoned her niece back to the sanctity of her stern chaperonage.

Disappointed, Howard nonetheless arranged for her to fly back on one of his TWA planes, promising to wing his way to New York "very soon" to resume their romance. In the meantime, he shamelessly promised to be faithful to her. The word *faith*ful ironically contained the name of Faith Domergue, with whom he'd been living during the entire course of his romance with Gloria.

To pass the time on the nine-hour flight to New York, Gloria sipped pink lemonade spiked with pink gin. On the same plane flying to New York, she spotted Kate Hepburn sitting alone with an empty seat beside her. Howard had also arranged for her free passage on the same flight—or rather one of his assistants had done that. Later, Howard was furious when he learned that Kate Hepburn and Gloria Vanderbilt were on the same plane, separated only by two rows of seats.

Kate was a sort of role model for young Gloria. When she'd abandoned her original goal of becoming a nun, she'd decided instead that she wanted to be a star like Kate. "How can I compete with someone like Hepburn?" Gloria asked her traveling companion. She had erroneously heard that Kate and Howard were still carrying on an affair. Brazenly, Gloria rose from her seat and sat down next to Kate. Gloria later admitted that she was so paralyzed with fear that she was too intimidated to speak. Kate ignored her. "Finally, I chickened out and went back to my own seat," Gloria recalled.

Back East with her aunt, Gloria began to receive yellow roses every day from Howard, along with frequent phone calls from him. He lied, claiming that he was "all alone and missing her." Actually, in addition to Faith, Howard was seeing a string of male hustlers that Henry Willson continued to arrange for him.

Suddenly, Pat was back in New York, his exile in Kansas City having ended. Cold shouldering Gloria at first when he encountered her dancing at El Morocco, he was soon smiling at her again. As she later recorded in her memoirs, she was "confused, panicked, and uncertain." Against her better judgment, she launched herself into a serious romance with "the Big Bad Wolf," even though she'd heard that he was a gigolo.

One night at El Morocco, dancing with Pat, Gloria noticed the couple next to her. It was Rita Hayworth and her husband, Edward C. Judson, in town for a publicity junket. Pat whispered in her ear that Howard had a crush on Rita and privately screened her movies for masturbatory purposes. Gloria compared herself unfavorably to the movie goddess, the World War II pinup favorite, along with Betty Grable, of fan magazines. "I just can't be as gorgeous as Rita," Gloria told Pat.

Pat had two unflattering nicknames for Gloria, calling her either "Stupido" or "Fatsy Roo." Gloria had long since lost her baby fat.

In a "fit of madness," Gloria married Pat in 1941, perhaps her main reason being to escape from her Aunt Gertrude. The marriage, up until her divorce in 1945, would be a disaster. Throughout her time with Pat, she suffered mental and physical abuse. He'd often hit her with his fists, but she endured.

Since she would not come into her inheritance until she was twenty-one, she and Pat were often strapped for cash. After his marriage, Pat lost the stipend he'd received from Howard ever since the mid-Thirties. At one point, Pat had to pay off a gambling debt unless he wanted some Brooklyn thugs "to rearrange your face." He repeatedly urged Gloria to call Howard in California and plead with him to send five thousand dollars in cash—"at once."

Resisting at first, Gloria finally gave in to his repeated protests. Nervously she dialed Howard at Caddo Productions. "It was very difficult for me, but I finally stammered out the request for the money. I promised that I would pay him back with interest when I was twenty-one." She was greeted with stone silence on the other end of the phone.

Finally, in a high-pitched and rather soft voice which she had trouble understanding, he told her, "I thought you called to tell me you were coming back to me." He slammed down the phone.

After her divorce from Pat, Gloria married conductor Leopold Stokowsky in 1945 and director Sidney Lumet in 1956. She divorced both of them but found happiness with the Mississippi writer, Wyatt Emory Cooper, whom she married in 1964. She had two sons with him, Carter Vanderbilt Cooper born in 1965, and CNN newsman, Anderson Cooper, born in 1967. In "the tragedy of my life," Carter, only 23 years old, jumped from the terrace of her 14th floor apartment. It was a summer day in 1988.

By the early 80s, the world was wearing "Gloria Vanderbilt designer jeans." She was never to see Howard Hughes again.

* * *

Los Angeles, 1940

Having hired publicist Russell Birdwell, Howard summoned him to spooky Muirfield for a meeting at two o'clock in the morning, standard procedure for Howard, but "bizarre" in Birdwell's view. From the very beginning of their association, the former publicist for *Gone With the Wind* had understood that he was working for an eccentric millionaire. The pay was good. If his boss had no regard for the time of day, so what?

Surprisingly, at Birdwell's first meeting with Howard, he urged him to abandon the theme and persona of *Billy the Kid* and pursue a completely different cinematic vision. "If a bomb exploded in the Hollywood Hills, it would blow out ten-thousand unfilmed scripts. At least one of them might be good."

Through Birdwell, Howard painfully learned that Louis B. Mayer had launched production on a film also called *Billy the Kid*. Howard's sometimes lover, Robert Taylor, had been cast as Billy.

Howard was furious, feeling he'd been betrayed by both Robert and Mayer. He vowed never to speak to Robert again—he would later rescind that—and to threaten the MGM boss with a lawsuit. Birdwell responded by warning Howard about what should have been obvious: The saga of Billy the Kid was in the public domain. He also reminded Howard that MGM had previously cast cowboy star Johnny Mack Brown (another of Howard's former lovers) as Billy in an earlier film, and the Robert Taylor version was a remake of the studio's previous picture. Birdwell also pointed out another obvious fact: the character of Billy the Kid was a standard role in dozens of Grade B westerns, called "oaters."

Growing impatient with Birdwell, Howard stood up. "You don't under-stand. My *Billy the Kid* is going to become the first sex western."

"But, Howard," Birdwell protested, "in westerns men ride off into the sun-set with their horses—not the girl. They don't even kiss the girl."

"They'll do more than kiss in my picture," Howard predicted. "Billy the Kid will actually fuck Rio."

"Who's Rio?"

"The gal. And what a gal! The screen will never have seen anything like her."

"Who's the lucky star?" Birdwell asked. "I know them all."

"Some unknown. There's only one requirement. She doesn't even have to know how to act, but she's got to have the hottest-looking pair of knockers in the history of film. Your job is to launch the search to find her."

* * *

The next day, a sleepy Birdwell wasted no time in launching the search not only for an actress to be cast as Rio, but for some handsome young man to play Billy the Kid. Only hours before, Birdwell had said to his boss, "I understand what you're looking for in the gal. But what about the actor to play Billy the Kid?"

"I want him to look like he's carrying around a ten-inch cock between his legs," Howard said. "And we're talking soft."

The moment the campaign was launched, Howard's office at 7000 Romaine Street was deluged with glossy eight-by-ten photographs of every aspirant young actor or actress in Hollywood. Some were submissions from agents, oth-ers came directly from the hopefuls themselves. "Every handsome gas jockey in Los Angeles, every beautiful gal, sent in their photographs," Birdwell said.

Three weeks later, Howard called Birdwell. "Call off the search for Billy the Kid!" Howard ordered. "I found him last night. Actually, he was sitting alone in the Cock & Bull bar having a drink and looking sad. I came up to him. He knew immediately who I was."

Howard said that the stranger asked him to have a drink with him, and "I accepted his invitation. When I found out he was an actor, I asked him if he'd submitted his picture for *Billy the Kid*. He told me that he didn't see himself playing in a western. He has a Brahmin accent. Very New Englander. I told him that I could hire a diction coach to work on his accent. I also told him that I was signing him to a three-year contract. Yeah, just like that. That's how I do busi-ness. I also told him that I was going to get you, Birdwell, to start the publicity campaign rolling for him. In his case, we're going to bill him as 'the hand-somest man in Hollywood.'"

"Christ, he must really be good looking," Birdwell said.

"He's good looking," Howard said. "In a town known for its male beauties,

512

he's maybe not the handsomest man, although he struck me that night in the bar as real pretty-looking. Anyway, we'll bill him as the handsomest, and the movie-going suckers will fall for it because we said it's so. They'll believe that he's the handsomest. If not, it'll set off a nation-wide debate over just who is the prettiest dick in Hollywood. Errol Flynn? Robert Taylor? Tyrone Power?"

"And who's this new guy about to become immortal?" Birdwell asked. "What's his name? Tell me because I know we'll have to change it. I bet it's Prescott Reginald Percy the Third?"

"Nothing like that," Howard said. "It's David Bacon. We'll keep his name. David will suggest Michelangelo's statue, and Bacon means pork. Not a bad symbol. Haven't you heard of feeding a gal the pork, as we say in Texas?"

* * *

Venice, California 1943

It was September 13, 1943. The wind was blowing in heavily from the Pacific, signaling the end of summer. From that same Pacific came news that the war was going badly. The American soldiers and sailors were meeting a formidable opponent in the Empire of Japan.

Although seemingly a perfect physical specimen, actor David Bacon had used the influence of his politically connected family in Boston to escape the draft.

David Bacon

Back in 1915, he'd been born some 3,000 miles away from Venice, California, in the historic town of Barnstable on Cape Cod. Named Gaspar G. Bacon Jr., he grew up as the son of one of the most prominent and socially connected Brahmin families in all of Massachusetts.

"David's family made Kate Hepburn's family look like white trash," Birdwell later said. David's father, Gaspar G. Bacon Sr., sat on the board of Harvard University and would later be elected lieutenant governor of the state. Backed by the support of his close friend, J.P. Morgan, Bacon Sr. encouraged talk that he might one day make a run for the governorship—"even the White House," he told his son. He never made it to the Oval Office, but he became Secretary of State under Theodore Roosevelt and Ambassador to France under William Howard Taft.

Young David was a disappointment to his father. Instead of becoming an attorney as his father urged, David had "an insane desire" [his

513

father's words] to go to Hollywood and become an actor.

Young David—or Gaspar Jr., as he was called then—managed to irritate his father all the more when he became involved in a homosexual scandal at Harvard that almost got him expelled. David and his roommate were "auditioning" some of the best bodies on the football team when word of this reached the administration. Only through his powerful father's intervention was David allowed to stay on at Harvard and eventually to graduate. His father had promised the board that he would secure psychiatric help for David "to cure my son of certain anti-social tendencies."

In summer, David deserted his family's summer home and appeared on the stage in amateur productions at Woods Hole on the Cape. His first acting role came with the University Players in West Falmouth. He ingratiated himself with two far more talented young actors, James Stewart and Henry Fonda, and "bunked" with the two men for a time. The director, Josh Logan, who knew all three of the actors, once said "when not dating girls, Jimmy, Hank, and David enjoyed the considerable charms of each other." Logan himself was rumored at various times to have had affairs with all three actors.

After Harvard, young Gaspar Jr. became "David Bacon." Fleeing New England, he arrived in New York where he was financially "sponsored" by William Blair, a wealthy Britisher from a prominent family who was spending the war years in New York, fleeing some sort of scandal back in London. According to David, his family had asked William to leave England, promising to support him in "the New World."

Although David's own father had refused to give him even a stipend during his pursuit of a career in the theater, his patron, William, was most generous. The couple were seen at all the New York hot spots together. Although he'd arrived in New York with only two hundred dollars in his wallet, David was soon wearing expensive jewelry and appearing at clubs in bespoke tailored suits.

It is not known exactly what happened to end David's relationship with his sugar daddy. William was a bit corpulent, looking somewhat like a 1940s version of Oscar Wilde. In contrast, David was muscular and handsome, standing six feet tall. On the side, he specialized in equally handsome sailors. Apparently, William returned to his apartment one afternoon to find his pampered Brahmin in bed with one of the more well-endowed members of Uncle Sam's navy.

Within the next two weeks David had taken an overcrowded wartime train to Los Angeles to begin a new life.

A month later, he'd met and married Greta Keller. Glamorous, multi-lingual, blonde, she was Europe's most famous and most celebrated chanteuse and cabaret performer during the 1930s. She had the dubious distinction of being Hitler's favorite singer. It was rumored that she'd had an affair with the Nazi dictator. At the age of eight, she'd studied dancing and acting in Vienna. Some of her greatest concerts were presented to audiences in Vienna, Prague, and

Berlin. Rod McKuen originally wrote the lyrics for "If You Go Away" for her, a song that was later more widely commercialized by Frank Sinatra and Jacques Brel.

Her growing familiarity with members of Hitler's inner circle led to increased scrutiny from SS investigators, which led to the "discovery," as transmitted to Joseph Goebbels, that she was part Jewish.

Fleeing for her life in 1937, and without even returning to her apartment to gather up her wardrobe, she discreetly boarded the next plane out of Berlin, which happened to be headed to Amsterdam. The tip that saved her life, and which started the process by which she escaped from Germany, came from the actor Conrad Veidt, known mainly today as one of the stars of *Casablanca*.

David Bacon

Sailing to the port of New York, she encountered Ernest Hemingway on the transatlantic crossing and had an affair with him, although she later claimed that she believed that the macho writer was a homosexual.

In New York she secured a gig singing at the Algonquin Hotel. There Greta met another Greta: Greta Garbo. Retired from moviemaking, Garbo suddenly began appearing at the club every night. Soon Ms. Garbo was dining privately and frequently with Ms. Keller. New York's lesbian circles started referring to them as "the two Gretas."

But when Garbo grew tired of her Austrian six months later, she rather cruelly and dismissively told her confidantes, "She's just another Marlene."

Following her break-up with Garbo and her gig at the Algonquin, and hoping to break into films on the West Coast, Greta Keller migrated to Hollywood. There she began an affair with former screen vamp, Pola Negri, rumored ex-lover of Valentino. At a party at Pola's house, Greta encountered "a lost and lonely boy," David himself. "He aroused a latent motherly instinct in me," Greta later said. "Even though I knew he had homosexual tendencies, we began to date. Dating led to a quick marriage. I took him under my wing. It was sort of like Barbara Stanwyck's marriage to Robert Taylor. We were beards for each other, and didn't ask each other a lot of questions about private matters. David was a bisexual. We were very much in love when I was with him."

Greta had starred in the stage play, *Broadway*, in Vienna in 1928. She'd had an affair with a member of the cast, Marlene Dietrich. In many ways, Greta became Marlene's role model. Once, when Greta encountered Marlene at the Berlin airport, Marlene said, "Greta, darling, I'm going to sing in my next picture. I've bought all your records." It was Marlene who took Greta's hit record,

515

"Lili Marleen," and made it an even bigger hit as "Lili Marlene."

After she moved to Hollywood, Marlene would not even return Greta's phone calls. Marlene refused to help her break into the movies. Fortunately, Joan Crawford was more understanding, and helped Greta find a role.

Greta had an "understanding" with David, who allowed her to indulge her taste not only in girlfriends but in other men. Some of her young men were shared on the side with David. "He especially liked military men, and there were plenty of those back in Los Angeles in those days," Greta told the author, while dictating her still unpublished memoirs to him at his home in New York in the 1970s.

"Suddenly, Howard Hughes appeared on my doorstep," Greta recalled, referring to the mansion she'd rented in Santa Monica, containing nine bathrooms, twelve bedrooms, and a swimming pool on the second floor. "Without knowing any of the details, I was told that David had signed a three-year contract with Hughes. In addition to the Santa Monica mansion where he 'officially' lived with me, Howard had rented a bungalow in the Hollywood Hills as a love nest where David spent a lot of his time, always in the company of his new boss."

"Even though I didn't think the role of Billy the Kid was right for David, he went ahead with a screen test anyway," Greta said. "I saw the test. It was laughable. David should have been cast in bedroom farces and drawing room comedies like those made in Edwardian England. *I* could have played the merciless William Bonnie better than dear, sweet David. Even though Howard had a powerful crush on my husband, even Mr. Texas Oil had to admit that there was no way in hell that David could be convincing as Billy the Kid."

David's romance with Howard came to an abrupt end when Howard "fell big, and I mean big, for Jack Buetel," Greta said. "As you and everybody else knows, Jack was eventually signed to play Billy the Kid instead of David. Who wouldn't fall for Jack Buetel? I would have divorced David in a minute to get at him. He was the single sexiest man I'd ever met."

Although he was still under contract to Howard, David was offered no parts after his failed screen test.

In time, Howard would become infamous for luring actors (or actresses) into ironclad, "exclusive" long-term contracts and then, to their enormous frustration, letting them "stew" in their semi-enslavement, never offering them a role. That, in fact, became his specialty. Eventually, David did get some parts, playing a good-looking college kid in *Ten Gentlemen from West Point* in 1942. In 1943, he appeared in *Crash Dive* (uncredited), *Gals, Inc.,* and the lackluster *Someone to Remember*.

David's first big break came when he was cast as one of the leads in the serial, *The Masked Marvel*, being shot over at Republic. The film is sometimes shown as *Sakima and the Masked Marvel*. Accurately perceiving the degree to which his career had collapsed, and resentful of having to work for a "Poverty

Row" studio, David grew increasingly furious at Howard and denounced him frequently.

In 1943, he began to write the story of his affair with Howard, knowing that no publisher at the time would touch the material.

"I urged David not to do it," Greta claimed. "But he sat at a typewriter and pounded out almost ten pages a day. I saw some of it. It was very pornographic. There was one very explicit scene where David described in graphic detail just how far Howard would go with him orally."

"My husband never actually planned to offer his manuscript to a publisher," Greta said. "Instead he wanted to show a typewritten copy to Howard Hughes. He said that he was going to demand that his former lover part with forty thousand dollars, which would give Hughes the rights to the manuscript. Of course, Hughes would then burn it."

Through Noah Dietrich, whom David knew, he had what was tantamount to a blackmail threat being delivered directly to Howard. A meeting was arranged between Howard and David.

"I warned David that he was playing with dynamite, making threats to a man as powerful as Howard Hughes," Greta claimed. "But my husband was very stubborn and wouldn't listen. Three days later, he walked out of our house in a white bathing suit and claimed that he was going swimming at Santa Monica beach. I often knew he met his boyfriends there, but nothing was said between us. I knew that he was getting something outside the home that I couldn't give him. He didn't say for certain, but I believed he was meeting Hughes."

Four hours later, a maroon-colored British-made sports car—a gift to David from Howard—was seen moving along Washington Boulevard in Venice. It was a Sunday. The driver was manning the wheel like he'd had two bottles of whiskey. Fortunately, there were no other cars on the road or else he would surely have crashed in a head-on collision.

Suddenly, the driver slammed on the brakes of the small car and rolled to a stop, jumping the curb. Sheila Belkstein was walking her German shepherd that day and later reported what she'd seen to the police. "I was walking my dog near a field of cabbage. At the sound of brakes, I spun around. My dog barked hysterically. From the car emerged a man wearing only a pair of white bathing trunks which showed blood stains. Across the street was a gas station. The attendant there must have seen the man. He called the police, I learned later. I was a little afraid at first, and I was having a hard time restraining my dog. I moved toward the man. I'll always remember the sunken look of despair on his face. 'Help me!' he said in a very plaintive voice. 'Oh, God, please help me. Please help me!' that was all he managed to say. His eyes rolled back in his head, which seemed to loll to the side like it was separating from his body. Then he fell to the ground. A stiletto was lodged in his back."

A coroner later confirmed that the stiletto had pierced his lung, and that David had bled to death. A thorough examination of his body revealed no bruis-

517

es, no signs of struggle. Police surmised that David had known his assailant, and that he had driven the car in a position hunched over the steering wheel.

For weeks to come, his death was the talk of Hollywood. Several years later, the youngest-ever editor of *The Saturday Evening Post*, Cleveland Amory, listed the David Bacon murder among the Top Ten Unsolved Murders of the 20th Century.

Police discovered a leather wallet, soaked with blood, in the pocket of David's bathing trunks. The wallet contained one hundred and fifty dollars, which was remarkable for the time, as few men carried around so much money, especially on a trip to the beach. In the sports car, the police discovered a camera containing a roll of film. The roll was developed by the police. Only one picture had been taken. It depicted David standing happily on a beach completely nude, his white bathing trunks not shown anywhere within the frame. From this, police concluded that David knew the mystery man who stabbed him, and that he posed for his murderer. (The police reports used the word "man" when referring to the unknown murderer. Of course, his murderer could have been a woman, but no one raised that as a possibility.)

After the investigation, the nude photograph and the still blood-stained wallet were returned to Greta Keller, although the case was never officially closed. Today, the wallet and the photograph are the property of the author of this biography.

After David's death, Greta evolved into an internationally celebrated cabaret singer with a sophisticated coterie of devoted fans on both sides of the Atlantic. Movie audiences last heard her singing the song "Married," (*Heirat*) in the 1972 movie, *Cabaret*, which won eight Oscars that year but not for best picture.

Greta Keller died in Vienna in 1977, symbolizing a nostalgic, esoteric, and glamorous figure from a faded golden age. Even until the end of her life, she maintained to anyone interested that she knew who stabbed her husband. "I can't prove it, but Howard Hughes murdered my David."

* * *

Los Angeles, 1940

In the late autumn of 1940, insider Hollywood knew that David Bacon was no longer slated to play Billy the Kid, having lost the role to Jack Buetel, a devilishly handsome, lean but muscular, "walking streak of sex" with a slight leer and a cocky gait.

"He was a homosexual's wet dream," said his agent, Henry Willson, when this darkly good-looking stud was dressed in tight-fitting jeans and buckskins revealing his ample assets. "With that trim waist and those broad shoulders, he was what you wanted Santa Claus to bring you for Christmas. Regrettably, Jack was hopelessly straight. But not so straight he wouldn't drop his jeans for the right producer or agent. That was the limit of it, though. No fucking. And no reciprocation."

There have been many stories spread about how Jack Buetel was cast as Billy the Kid. Director Howard Hawks, who was never one to tell the truth about anything, later claimed that he spotted Jack's picture in a stack of glossy photographs submitted by unknowns or their agents.

Of all the tales spread, Henry Willson, Howard's new pimp, told the most convincing story in later life. Temporarily selling insurance in Hollywood to make ends meet, Jack had been picked up one night at a bar on Hollywood Boulevard by Willson, who promised that he'd help "this physically perfect young man" break into films.

That night Willson learned many things about Jack. "I just assumed he wanted to be an actor. Didn't every handsome young man in Hollywood in those days?" The Dallas-born young man had very limited acting experience, having appeared in only three amateur stage productions. That didn't matter to Willson. "I didn't encounter many male John Barrymores in all my career in the business."

"If getting a blow-job from a guy, something I find a little bit repulsive, is the way to break into movies, then why not play the game?" the already street-smart Jack told Willson. "A guy who looks like me and bums around Hollywood Boulevard for several months either learns the ropes or is a fool."

When Willson eventually extracted his reward from between Jack's legs, he offered to sign him with his talent agency, presided over by Gummo Marx. Jack readily agreed, but he eventually rebelled at the idea of having to travel to Willson's apartment four or five nights a week. Jack privately held Willson in contempt, telling a friend that "the fat queer is insatiable—like a hog slurping at the trough."

In years to come, Willson's future discovery, Rock Hudson, would also endure assaults on his body until he became such a big star that he no longer had to give in to Willson's (or anyone

Jack Buetel

else's) sexual demands.

In the early 1940s, Howard was extremely pleased with the stream of young men Willson supplied to him. He was also grateful that the agent had introduced him to Faith Domergue with whom he was settling into a years-long relationship—romantic but deeply troubled.

Originally, Willson had another young man—more muscular, "more the weightlifter type"—in mind for the role of Billy the Kid. That good-looking aspirant actor was Phil Medina, who grew up on the streets of Trenton, New Jersey, before hitchhiking across the country to the streets of Hollywood. To earn money, he stood on Hollywood Boulevard at night, allowing men, often married, to pick him up for an evening's pleasure, for which he charged ten dollars, even though the going rate on the street at the time was only five dollars.

Willson installed Phil in a sleazy walk-up apartment on Gower Street in Hollywood. The room had two double beds, with rotting, urine-stained mattresses, a gas stove in the corner, a "forever dripping" sink filled with dirty dishes, and a decrepit shower stall and a rusting toilet in the dank hallway. The floor of the small flat was covered with 1920s linoleum, and there was always a bag of garbage infested with roaches in the corner. Willson then moved Jack into this same apartment, for which the agent paid a monthly rent of thirty-five dollars.

Eventually Willson crowded four of his "tricks" into this apartment, two men sharing each of the double beds. "They always slept naked," Willson said. "I brought their breakfast over nearly every morning. The one who woke up with the biggest piss hard-on got an early morning workover from me."

None of the young men was known for his housekeeping, and the bed linens were rarely changed unless Willson sent over his Mexican maid when the joint became uninhabitable.

All of the aspirant actors had been promised movie contracts by Willson, but they were not forthcoming. Along with Jack and Phil, the other two residents of the apartment included Johnny Pearson, a former farm boy from Modesto, California, who was only eighteen, and Charles Reed, twenty-one, an extremely handsome young man from Idaho who drifted back to his native state after only eight months in the Hollywood sleaze factory. "I'd rather plant potatoes for the rest of my life," Charles told Willson, "than do what I've been asked to do in Shittown. What creeps!"

Jack, Johnny, and Phil were more cooperative. When not sleeping with the agent himself, these young men went out on "dates" arranged with producers and directors. "We were the most select choice of Grade A prime in Willson's meat market," Phil later said. "Partly because of us, Willson learned how to be a successful agent. He peddled male flesh to producers and directors like Hughes. By doing so, he eventually went bigtime in the '50s when he launched all those Rocks, Tabs, and Troys. Once, he even named an actor Adonis. Just Adonis. Willson said that with a name like Adonis, you didn't need a last name."

After a weekend at some desert retreat with Phil Medina, Howard agreed with Willson that he'd would be perfect for the role of Billy the Kid.

"I hadn't immediately thought of Jack for the role because he had such a baby face," Willson said. "Even though his body was muscular, it was rather slim. I thought Howard wanted a more rugged, beefy look for Billy the Kid. Not some beautiful kid like Jack, who with the right kind of clothes and makeup could be convincing as a fifteen-year-old in some prep school."

Phil thought he had the role in *The Outlaw* all but locked up until late one Sunday afternoon when Howard drove him back to the apartment on Gower Street. "Howard was aware that I lived there with three other guys," Phil said. "I told him we never had enough beer. That Saturday he bought us three cases. Since I couldn't carry all those suds up the stairs in one trip, he helped me. I thought the boys were out. But as we came into the apartment, Jack was sprawled buck-assed naked on one of the double beds. Howard got an eyeful! When I saw him devouring Jack's body with his eyes, I knew it was curtains for me. Out with Phil Medina and in with the new kid on the block: Jack Buetel."

Howard was reluctant to make his wishes known directly to Jack. But he was delighted to learn that the young Texan was under contract to Willson. The agent told Jack what was needed and wanted, dangling the star-making role of Billy the Kid in front of him if he caved in to Howard's sexual demands. Within a week, Jack had become Howard's new protégé, the equivalent of Faith Domergue on the female side. He signed Jack to an eight-year contract at $75 a week, $25 more per week than he'd later pay Jane Russell. "He kept a lid on Jack's salary all during the years he had him under contract," Willson later said. "It was a form of holding that dear boy under sexual bondage to him."

"When Jack put his name on that contract with Howard, it was like selling himself as a sexual slave to some Caliph of Baghdad centuries ago," Willson said. "Of course, Jack could have broken with Howard, especially when Howard did nothing for his career after *The Outlaw*, but he remained in bondage and did Howard's bidding until the very end of their relationship."

The lowest point came when Howard Hawks was looking for a young actor to play opposite John Wayne in the 1948 *Red River*. Hawks remembered Jack from *The Outlaw* and offered him the part. Although he had no upcoming movie work for his contract player, Howard refused. It would have been easy for Howard to let him go, and it would have represented one of the biggest breaks of Jack's career. But when Jack wasn't available, the part went instead to a handsome young Montgomery Clift. Upon the film's release, his name became a household word. "Jack was crushed beyond belief," Willson said, "and went into a morbid depression."

As if to punish Jack, Howard kept him off the screen between 1940 and 1951, a full eleven years. Jack's "comeback" involved playing Bob Younger in the mediocre 1951 western, *Best of the Badmen*. Then he appeared in *Rose of*

Jack Buetel

Cimarron and the *Half Breed,* both in 1952, and later (1954) as Frank James in *Jesse James' Women.* His final film was the 1959 *Mustang!* He got his greatest exposure playing Jeff Taggert in the 1956 TV series, *Judge Roy Bean.* "But it was a career that never happened, in spite of his initial fame," Willson said.

Yet, in Willson's view, Jack provided Howard with his greatest oral gratification. After a weekend spent at some hideaway with Howard, Jack would be "drained," as he said, and would need two days of sleep just to recover. "Hughes can't get enough of me," Jack told Willson. "It's like he's sucking my life's blood from me."

In a bizarre twist, Howard confessed to Jack one night that he believed by drinking his semen it was rejuvenating him. In an even more bizarre twist, Howard began to prescribe a carefully controlled diet for Jack "to make your semen rejuvenate my dying cells." For some reason not known, Howard focused on the pomegranate as his source of rejuvenation. Instead of eating pomegranates himself, he forced Jack to consume six a day, feeling that this fruit would make the young man's semen more enriched and ultimately more beneficial to Howard. He even selected the exact pomegranates that Jack was to eat. "Here he was," Jack told Willson, "the busiest man on the planet spending time selecting just the ripest and juiciest of pomegranates for me to eat. I hate pomegranates! I would have preferred an apple a day."

For all his life, Jack remained friends with his co-star, Jane Russell, until he died on June 27, 1989 having drifted north to Portland, Oregon. Apparently, he never confided in her what was going on behind the scenes.

He was always concerned that she not find out the exact nature of his relationship with Howard. "She stood up to Howard and demanded her rights, and made something of herself in spite of her contract with Howard," Jack said. "He was a much stronger man than me, and I gave in to him. What did it get me? Money? Never! The bastard was as stingy as hell with me. Fame! Maybe. I guess my name will live forever for that one stinking part. But, even in that, I was a joke. *The Outlaw* made a joke of both Jane and me. She overcame hers. I didn't. I'll always remember that night in San Francisco at the première. That god damn audience laughed at some of my most dramatic scenes. The press still doesn't even how to spell my name. Ninety-nine percent of the time, even in *The New York Times*, it's spelled BEUTEL. I should have kept my real name,

Warren Higgins. Willson thought that sounded like some hayseed farmer and insisted I change it."

Finally, Jack was asked about the rumored nude version of *The Outlaw*.

"That's too sick for words," he said. "My God! I have no comment to make about that. If the true story of that ever gets out, the world will know just how sick Howard Hughes really was."

While most other stars of 1940, except the big names like Katharine Hepburn and Cary Grant, are relatively forgotten, Jack Buetel still has a few dwindling fan clubs left. Mostly his admirers today are composed of an aging homosexual coterie who fell in love with his image in the 1940s and still keep the memory of his appearance as Billy the Kid alive. Even though the group is dying off and memory grows dim, every year "a few old souls" show up at the Portland Memorial Cemetery in Oregon to deliver wreaths of flowers to the baby boy born on one hot summer morning on September 5 back in 1915.

* * *

Of the hundreds of photographs on Howard's desk, submitted by hopeful actresses or else their agents, one stood out. A picture of a five-foot-seven aspiring actress with a thirty-eight-inch bust. With her dark hair and clear complexion, she was about to become the possessor of the world's most famous bust with the exception of Venus de Milo. The picture depicted a very beautiful brunette with a pouty mouth posed in a tight-fitting sweater, which revealed that this teenager was already aware of her chief asset: A large bosom.

"I'm going to turn this gal into a sex symbol," Howard told Birdwell, thus inventing an expression not yet in vogue.

The girl's name was Ernestine Jane Geraldine Russell, and she'd been born in Bemidji, Minnesota on June 21, 1921, the daughter of Roy William Russell and a stage-struck mother, Geraldine Jacobi Russell. A great beauty herself, Geraldine gave elocution lessons and dreamed of seeing her daughter—billed as Jane Russell—in marquee lights.

Jane had moved to Los Angeles in 1932 where she finished high school and took a job as a receptionist in the office of a chiropodist, earning a salary of $27.50 a week. To supplement her income, she occasionally modeled ski clothes, coats, and dresses for a young photographer, Tom Kelley. She'd been reluctant to work for him until he assured her that he did not "do nude calendars." Ironically, and in contrast to what Kelley said, he would one day photograph Jane's future rival, Marilyn Monroe, in the nude, those pictures appearing on history's most famous "girlie calendar."

Like her future co-star, Jack Buetel, Jane had very little theatrical experience when she was ordered to appear at 7000 Romaine Street for a screen test. She'd worked briefly with The Max Reinhardt Theatrical Workshop, but that had been the extent of her training.

Instead of attending classes, Jane remembered that she and a girlfriend, Betty Groblie, skipped the workshop whenever they could and went bowling at an alley on Sunset Boulevard. Instead of becoming stars, Betty and Jane dreamed of dating "handsome hunks," Victor Mature and John Payne, respectively. In Jane's case, her dream would come true.

As a lark, Jane decided to try out for auditions for *Earl Carroll's Most Beautiful Girls in the World Revue.* To her surprise, she was among those chosen. But since she was then being pursued by the rugged football star, Robert Waterfield, whom she'd eventually marry, she turned Carroll down. Besides, she'd decided that she didn't want to be a "cheap showgirl."

At the time she was being considered for the part of Rio, Jane was living with her widowed mother in a ranch-style house in Van Nuys. Every Friday night she had a "gig" playing piano in a band that consisted of her four protective brothers.

Somehow Jane had managed to acquire an agent, Lewis Green, who had submitted her photograph to both Howard and Hawks. Called "The Silver Fox," Green was also the agent for one of Howard's many girlfriends, the ill-fated Susan Peters.

Even though Howard at first thought Jane looked right for the part, he experienced "four o'clock in the morning" doubts as he wandered the lonely halls of Muirfield. In spite of her knockers, he ordered screen tests for four other hopefuls, despite continuing to tell Hawks that Jane had all of them beat in the knockers department.

Jane Russell, Jack Buetel in *The Outlaw*

Unknown to Hawks, Howard had already settled on Jack for the role of Billy the Kid. Jack had passed his auditions—and then some. But "for cosmetic reasons," Howard didn't want Hawks to know about his involvement with the handsome young actor, who had already become Howard's reluctant boyfriend.

Howard informed Hawks that he would personally audition each of the actresses in his bedroom at Muirfield before deeming them worthy of a screen test. Perhaps by instinct, he knew that Jane herself would not submit to such an audition. He'd make a play for her but not until after *The Outlaw* was wrapped.

In spite of her sexy, come-hither look, Jane was actually a highly moral teenager, reared on Christian beliefs, as Howard was about to find out. She was different from the other sex objects he'd pursued, each of whom seemed only too willing to fall into his bed on the first date.

From the first moment she met Howard, Jane was determined not to become one of his "stable of fillies." She wanted to keep their relationship strictly professional.

On the day of her screen test, a nervous and inexperienced Jane appeared at Howard's studio. There, she discovered four other brunettes who had come to test for the role of Rio. For the first time, she spotted Jack, determining at once that there was "no contest" in the looks department when he was stacked against the other cowboy hopefuls.

The scene called for her to be thrown down in hay in a *faux* barn scene after she'd tried to kill Billy the Kid. Jane's test was with one of the other "cowboys," not with Jack. Wearing a voluptuous and revealing peasant-style blouse, she tried to look like the half-Irish, half-Mexican Rio she was supposed to play.

After the test, and hearing nothing for weeks from her agent, she "sweated blood" waiting for the results. She feared she didn't have a chance, although she was almost certain that Jack Buetel would be playing Billy the Kid. When called back to 7000 Romaine Street, she didn't know what to expect. Entering the office of Howard Hawks, she found herself "the only brunette this time."

Jack Buetel was sitting on the sofa with what Hawks later called "a shit-eating grin." When Jane saw the expression on the young actor's face, she knew he was Billy the Kid.

Within minutes, Hawks had told her that after watching all the tests, Howard Hughes himself had selected her to play the lead over all the other unknowns. She burst into tears of gratitude, and thanked cameraman Lucien Ballard for "bringing out something in me." Jack and she would receive standard stock contracts. If *The Outlaw* were a hit, the contracts could be renegotiated at higher salaries. Elated, Jack and she headed out the office door.

In her memoirs, Jane claimed that she spotted Howard for the first time as Jack and she left the director's office. She wrote: "A little way down the hall Jack punched me and we stopped."

"I think that's him," Jack told her.

"Who?" she asked.

"Howard Hughes!" he told her.

She turned and spotted "a tall, lanky man leaning on the wall with his hat on the back of his head, a white shirt open at the neck, and dark trousers."

"Hi," Jack said to Howard with a smile. Jane remembered that the actor even ventured "a little wave" at the strange figure.

Jack had been giving Howard more than "a little wave" at night. Neither Howard nor Jack wanted Jane to learn that each of them "knew each other as David had known Bathsheba," to quote Cubby Broccoli, who had been hired by Hawks as assistant director on *The Outlaw*.

In her role as Rio, Jane before the camera was "busting" out all over. "My boobs were bolting out of my peasant blouse every time I was ordered to bend down and pick up those milk pails," Jane once said. She immediately came to realize that she wasn't being required to act as much as she was putting on a burlesque show. When she complained to Hawks, he told her, "You're a big girl now and you can say a loud 'No!' if you want to." When she took her complaints to Howard, he told her, "That's how we're selling this picture. Sex sells."

In the first week of filming, Hawks went to Howard. "Jane and Jack are nice kids," he told his producer, "but neither one of them can act." "Don't worry about it," Howard assured him. "The horses will do the acting. Besides, if you want acting, I've hired two of the best pros in the business, Thomas Mitchell and Walter Huston."

Watching the rushes, Howard complained to his ace cameraman, cinematographer Gregg Toland, who had filmed *The Grapes of Wrath* and *Citizen Kane*. "We're not getting enough production out of Jane's breasts. I want her knockers to be the real star of the picture."

He was particularly displeased at the way one scene was shot. In this scene, Jane had been tied by leather straps between two trees. The character of Billy the Kid wanted to punish her for putting sand in his water canteens. In the film, he wetted the leather, knowing that as it dried the straps would shrink. With Jane's character of Rio tied up, and supposedly with the leather drying, she'd be like the victim on a torture rack. As she writhed in agony, retake after retake still did not please the boss man.

"Her breasts just kept shooting out in all directions," Howard protested to Toland. "I don't like the way her bosom shifts—it's unnatural and the outline of her bra shows through that flimsy blouse."

Finally, Howard decided that he wanted her "breasts cantilevered like those flying buttresses on the Cathedral of Notre-Dame in Paris."

In a memo to Hawks, dated November 18, 1940, Howard wrote:

I know that you are making every effort to showcase Miss Russell's breasts. But I am just saying that they seem artificial or padded, which I know they are not. I want to see the tops of her breasts as she moves, not be held in place as if they were supported by concrete. This is an engineering prob-

lem, and I will handle it personally.

That night Howard personally designed a brassière for his star. Almost immediately, it became the world's most legendary and celebrated brassière. "It was Howard's version of a medieval chastity belt," Cubby Broccoli later said jokingly. "Except instead of covering Jane's vagina, it held her tits."

"Actually, Howard invented the seamless bra," Jane later recalled. "But since I found it too uncomfortable, I decided to use my regular bra instead. I put tissue over it to conceal the seams. Howard was never the wiser." Filming proceeded, and Howard pronounced to his cameraman Toland that he was pleased by "the movement and rhythm of Jane's large breasts."

"Howard was smart enough to design airplanes," Jane recalled, "but the famous billionaire did not know Victoria's Secret. Believe me, Mr. Playtex he wasn't."

Most of the lists of Howard's lovers, both male and female, includes Jane Russell. If we are to believe this devoted Christian herself, "who found and accepted Jesus at the age of six"—and we do—that was not the case. Howard did try to seduce her—but failed.

Jane remembered that his attempt at seduction followed an all-night party with Faye Emerson, Elliott Roosevelt, Johnny Meyer, Ava Gardner, and a "Brazilian zillionaire," George Guinle. Since it was getting late when the party broke, Howard invited Jane to sleep over in a bedroom next to his. He excused himself to drive a drunken Ava home. Meyer remained at Muirfield.

Jane said that she'd dressed for bed and had fallen into a deep sleep when suddenly she woke up. Meyer had entered her room in what appeared to be an attempt to rape her. He chased her around the bedroom as she ran screaming from his clutches. In the middle of this boudoir farce, Howard in his robe rushed into the bedroom. He immediately ordered the drunken Meyer out of the room. Howard invited Jane into the comfort of his master bedroom where "you'll be safe." Howard told her that she wouldn't be disturbed for the rest of the evening. But an hour later, she woke up again to find him hovering over her. She claimed he said, "I'm freezing. I must have caught cold driving Ava home. Can I get in with you?"

She agreed but warned him, "No funny business. Remember, Howard, I'm married. I'm sleepy, and I've already been disturbed twice."

As she settled down once again for the night, with him curled up beside her, she'd fallen asleep when she was rudely awakened by his hand sliding around her waist. "All right, Howard, that's it. Get out!" He protested, promising that "I'll be a good boy if you let me stay." She finally relented and fell asleep, not to be molested again. When she woke up at ten o'clock the following morning, her boss was gone.

* * *

Hollywood, 1953

Looking back years later, Jane recalled that "Howard and Birdwell tried to sell me like a can of tomatoes." At the time, the world viewed her as a big-time star, one of the sexy bombshells to emerge from the war years. In reality, her life was quite different. She claimed that she had a hard time living and making her auto payments on the fifty dollars a week she was pulling in from Caddo.

She grew increasingly uncomfortable at Howard's ongoing battles with the censors, much of the controversy centering on her bosom. When Howard finally relented and let her see *The Outlaw*, she was disappointed, finding it a "ghastly picture." She also felt that she came across like a "wooden dummy." Many critics agreed with her assessment.

Still under contract to Howard, a link that would last for thirty-five years, Jane moved forward into a famous—perhaps infamous—career. But it wasn't until the filming of *The French Line* in 1953 that her bosom would once again get Howard into "deep do-do," as she called it, with the censors. Jane had been cast in the role of a Texas oil heiress.

Her bosom became the subject of a nationwide scandal even before *The French Line* was released. One solo musical number by Jane was called "Lookin' for Trouble," a four-minute bump-and-grind number. Howard had ordered his costume designer, Michael Woulfe, to create the briefest of bikinis for Jane. At the time no major star had appeared in such a scanty outfit for a top studio. "It was years before actresses started showing everything on camera," said veteran director Lloyd Bacon.

When Jane put on the silver-beaded bikini and appeared on set, she claimed that she felt naked. "In those days no woman in America dressed like that. Bikinis were something a few naughty girls wore in the south of France on a Riviera beach."

This sometimes Sunday school teacher hurried back to her dressing room and took off the costume, returning it to Michael. She told him to tell Howard that she wouldn't appear in it. Eventually, after many angry exchanges, a compromise was reached. Michael would design a revealing one-piece costume with holes above and below the waist. In such an outfit, Jane performed her torrid number, which was choreographed by Billy Daniel, with Hal Schaefer laying out the music.

Even so, when the preview audience at the 5,000-seat Fox Theatre in St. Louis on December 29 in 1953 saw *The French Line*, it caused a nationwide scandal. The Roman Catholic Archdiocese labeled it "a mortal sin" and demanded that the police confiscate all copies.

Ads for *The French Line* were as provocative as they'd been for *The Outlaw*. Billboards proclaimed, JANE RUSSELL IN 3-DIMENSION—AND WHAT DIMENSIONS! Another ad shouted: IT'LL KNOCK *BOTH* YOUR EYES OUT! As if the audience didn't get the point—or "points" as the case may be—the word both was underlined.

Once again, Howard was denied a Seal of Approval for the film. Eventually he lost the battle and cut the controversial number.

In 1955, as Jane's contract was up for renewal, Howard was in the process of winding down his motion picture production at RKO. He didn't have any more film work for the aging star, whom he'd exploited for fifteen years. "I can't let her go like I did Harlow," he said. He offered her, and she accepted, a contract, granting her a thousand dollars a week until 1975.

In the future, her check arrived faithfully. As previously negotiated, payments stopped in 1975, only a year before Howard's death. Despite the ongoing ordeal of long periods without job offers, she once told Dietrich, "I'd still do a picture for Howard—and for nothing."

Jane Russell in *The Outlaw*

Rambling down a dust-covered memory lane, Jane, in her final conclusion about Howard, said, "Ours was truly a platonic love affair."

* * *

Los Angeles, 1940-43

With the lead roles finally cast, director Howard Hawks transported the crew of *The Outlaw* to a remote location eighty miles east of Falstaff, Arizona. He wanted to be far from Hollywood and the interference of Howard. His eccentric boss had given him *carte blanche* during the filming of *Scarface* nearly a decade before, and Hawks was hoping for the same with *The Outlaw*.

"I've got planes to build," Howard told Hawks. "Send me back the undeveloped film. Listen, and listen good, I want to see a great picture up there on the screen." He ordered Hawks to bring in the low-budget western for $250,000. *The Outlaw* would end up costing $3,400,000, a mammoth expense for a film in those days.

Hawks knew from the beginning that the plot for *The Outlaw* had nothing to do with the real life story of Billy the Kid. The script was based on a wild folktale about Billy running off to Mexico, assuming a new identity, and living happily ever after.

Originally Howard had hired Ben Hecht to write the screenplay, considering him the best in the business and having worked with him before. But he found Hecht's script disappointing and hired Jules Furthman instead.

Furthman came up with a sexy script that pleased Howard. His credentials included the screenplay for the Oscar-nominated *Mutiny on the Bounty* that had starred Clark Gable and Charles Laughton. Furthman would later write such scripts as *To Have and Have Not*. Into Lauren Bacall's mouth, he would put her legendary lines to Bogie: "You know how to whistle, don't you, Steve? You just put your lips together…and blow!"

In the desert, Cubby Broccoli, working directly under Hawks, had assembled some 250 actors and technicians, including Jack and Jane. Even though one of Howard's best friends, Cubby had not directly asked him for the job of assistant director. He'd appealed to Hawks directly and had been hired. Howard, in fact, was surprised to find Cubby among the crew. But since he trusted Cubby, he was pleased with the choice. For transport of the cast, crew, and the props needed to stage a western in the desert, Cubby had reserved a specially commissioned eight-car train to haul them out from Los Angeles.

Glenn Odekirk flew to Arizona every few days to retrieve the undeveloped footage, and to fly it back to 7000 Romaine Street in Los Angeles. When the film was developed, Howard, with a very skeptical eye, viewed the rushes.

To the art director, Perry Ferguson, in Arizona, Howard sent this handwritten memo: "More skin, less dust."

At 2:30am one morning in Los Angeles, he summoned a sleepy Birdwell to his screening room. There he showed the publicist the rushes. At first Birdwell praised the performances and Hawk's direction. "What?" Howard asked in astonishment. "You didn't notice? No clouds! Without clouds, the picture looks as naked as a jaybird." It was already part of Hollywood legend that Howard had delayed the production of *Hell's Angels* for weeks and weeks in his search for clouds in the bright California skies.

Fearing the same delay, Birdwell told Howard that the acting and direction alone could carry the picture, even without the clouds.

At seven o'clock the following morning, Howard telephoned Hawks in Arizona. Howard promised Hawks to raise the budget to one million dollars. "But I've got to have clouds. No clouds, no picture!" On that ominous note, he slammed down the phone. Expecting praise and getting this rebuff, Hawks was furious. Even though there were still no clouds in the sky, and with an eye to his budget, he continued his filming anyway, in defiance of Howard's obsession with clouds.

When he saw the next batch of rushes, Howard's temper exploded. He ordered Hawks to stop shooting at once until the clouds rolled into Arizona.

Hawks not only refused, he quit. "Direct the god damn picture yourself." This time it was Hawks who slammed down the phone.

Warner Brothers had just contacted Hawks to direct Gary Cooper in *Sergeant York*. Hawks was eager to accept this prestigious assignment, which would eventually win an Oscar for Cooper, Howard's former lover.

As Hawks told Cubby, "I'm not going to sit around for weeks waiting for some cloud to appear in the sky. I'm also not going to turn this stupid western into some million-dollar extravaganza. Let's face it: *The Outlaw* is a Grade B western. I make Grade A films."

Facing the prospect of a film without a director, Howard called Cubby and ordered him to haul the cast and crew back to Los Angeles, where Howard would assume the director's job. Cubby told him that because the rail line stretching out into the desert had been built without a loop for many miles in either direction, it wouldn't be practical to turn the special eight-car train around.

"Then back the fucking thing into Los Angeles," Howard ordered him.

Back in Hollywood, interior shooting began on *The Outlaw,* but only at night because Howard was never available during the day. Arriving unshaven and without sleep, Howard often slurred his words and appeared drowsy while directing *The Outlaw* at the old Samuel Goldwyn Studios.

By the time Howard arrived on the set every evening, the film's pair of crusty old cowboys, Thomas Mitchell and Walter Huston, were often already drunk. (Huston played Doc Halliday, and hot-tempered veteran actor Mitchell was cast as the sheriff.) For one of the scenes that Howard directed, he ordered a mind-numbing 128 takes. Mitchell, who'd already won an Oscar for his performance in *Stagecoach* as the whiskey-soaked Doc Boone, finally exploded, walking out on "this bastard of a flick." But not before throwing his ten-gallon hat on the floor and stomping on it "like an Apache war dancer," in Cubby's words. In front of the entire cast, with Howard standing in the background, Mitchell shouted, "The cocksucker knows nothing about how to direct a film." He stormed off the set. After a night of boozing with Huston, his old friend persuaded Mitchell to resume shooting the following night.

The endless delays didn't bother Jack and Jane as much. Since neither of these inexperienced actors had ever appeared in a film before, each of them just assumed that this was how movies were made.

During the making of *The Outlaw*, the film was inspiring lots of gossip in Hollywood. The most outrageous tale concerned the allegation that Howard was making a conventional film for presentation to the world at large, but that he was also shooting a version filled with nude scenes for his own private consumption. The inspiration for this gossip derived from a scene that was never included in the final cut of *The Outlaw*. Howard had mysteriously ordered a closed set, consisting of as few members of the crew as possible. Those members included Cubby and cameraman Gregg Toland.

The kind of scene that Howard contemplated now appears frequently in movies. But when Howard conceived his scene, it was both innovative and radical. As a filmmaker, he was a movie pioneer.

In the secret scene, he wanted Jack to pull his pants down as he prepares to hump a Mexican harlot. The camera would focus on Jack's bare buttocks as his pants are lowered. There would be no revelatory frontal view. Even Howard didn't plan to go that far.

Howard himself had laid out the details of the scenario that Cubby had defined as a possibly superfluous "detour" that wasn't essential to the plot of *The Outlaw*. In the scene, Jack would arrive at a saloon of a gambling house. At the bar, he would pick up a Mexican harlot, who would take him to one of the upstairs bedrooms, where the whore earned extra money by seducing horny cowboys who rode in off the plains.

Howard and Jack fought for days over the scene, and at first the actor refused to do it. But, like all his future battles with Jack, Howard prevailed in the end. "Jack was a sweet and loving man," Cubby said. "But Howard was just too powerful. Even though he would resist, Jack would ultimately end up doing Howard's bidding. Howard was truly the boss man, Jack his obedient slave."

Cubby witnessed Howard shooting the scene. Jack had been ordered to wear no underwear. For the girl, whose face was never seen, Howard had secured "a hot Mexican enchilada from a whorehouse in Phoenix," Cubby said. She looked like that Mexican spitfire, Lupe Velez, who'd brought so much pleasure and so many problems to Gary Cooper and, later, to that Tarzan boy."

"Howard hovered over Jack as filming began," Cubby said. "Somewhat embarrassed, Jack lowered his pants. All of his naked ass was revealed, and that boy had some buttocks on him. No wonder Howard was hot for him. Jack had been told to simulate orgasm, and the Mexican spitfire had been told to get an erection out of Jack. Soon, when his big cock was rubbing up against her vagina, the inevitable happened. Jack was young and horny. Howard got what he wanted. Jack penetrated the Mexican whore and rode her to his complete satisfaction. Caught in the throes of orgasm, Jack's moans could be heard across the set. On that shot, Howard asked for only one take."

Within weeks, word got out in Hollywood about this so-called nude version of *The Outlaw*. Instead of the Mexican whore, the gossip mongers had Jack actually penetrating Jane Russell on camera. "Believe me, I was there," Cubby said. "Nothing like that happened."

It was said that Howard "endlessly watched" Jack's scene of seduction with the Mexican prostitute. Howard's frustration, according to Cubby, was that Howard desired Jack's ass. "But the actor would only submit to oral sex regardless of how Howard tried to bribe him," Cubby said.

"I know it sounds far-fetched, but I think Howard punished Jack by sabotaging his career," Cubby claimed. "It was Howard's payback to Jack for not surrendering that beautiful, humpy ass to his boss man."

* * *

All this publicity did not escape the attention of Joseph Breen, who worked directly under the Hays Office, which was assigned the role of censoring films and recommending Seals of Approval—or not. In a warning of trouble to come, Breen wrote Howard: "I see 'by the papers,' as Mr. Dooley used to say, that you have begun shooting your picture. It occurs to me that you ought to let us have a copy of your shooting script, with a view toward examining it, against the possibility that there may be some details in it, which will have to be deleted or changed in the finished picture."

Early in the game, Breen had thrown down the gauntlet, judging the film before it was even made.

He read the script, and, as predicted, Breen objected to page after page of dialogue, finding it "racy" and requesting rewrites. He wrote to Howard that "care must be taken to avoid sexual suggestiveness. Since Howard was making the most sexually suggestive western of all time, Breen's comments might have either angered him or amused him with their silliness. Howard called Breen and agreed to adhere to his demands.

After hanging up on his censor, Howard ordered Hawks, still his director at the time, to go: "Full speed ahead! Fuck Joseph Breen! Fuck the Hays Office! We'll defy them!" Diplomatically, Hawks urged caution but Howard said he wouldn't back down.

When Breen viewed the final version of *The Outlaw*, he exploded in rage. To his bosses at the Hays Office, he wrote: "In more than ten years of critical examination of motion pictures, I have never seen anything quite so unacceptable as the shots of the breasts of the character of Rio. Throughout almost half the picture, the girl's breasts, which are large and prominent, are shockingly uncovered."

The Hays Office demanded 108 cuts which would virtually have narrowed the film down to a running time of 20 minutes. It would have made no sense and would, in fact, make it a mere trailer to some other featured film.

Howard had done all the cutting, scoring, and editing himself, butchering an astonishing "eighty-five miles" of film down to two miles.

He announced to the press that, "I believe filmmakers shouldn't fear the censors, but should fight them." A showdown meeting was called between Howard's representative, including his lawyer, Neil McCarthy, and the Hays Office.

Howard did not attend the meeting but sent Birdwell to supervise what Howard called "a mammalry wall-to-wall display."

When the "blue noses" walked into the meeting to debate *The Outlaw,* they were astonished to see that Birdwell had plastered the walls with large blow-ups of Hollywood goddesses in all their plunging *décolletage*. On the walls hung

533

revealing pictures of Rita Hayworth, Marlene Dietrich, Irene Dunne, Claudette Colbert, Betty Grable, Norma Shearer, Madeleine Carroll, and Loretta Young. There were eight blow-ups alone of Howard's discovery, Jean Harlow, who was never known for keeping her bosom hidden on camera.

With him, Birdwell had brought along Walter S. Slater, one of California's leading mathematicians. In front of the astonished censors, Slater measured the bosoms of the film goddesses with calipers. The conclusion of his "mathematical case" revealed that Jane Russell showed proportionately less bosom than did these leading ladies of the cinema. Slater asserted that each of Harlow's pictures had won the Seal of Approval, in each case with her showing more bosom than Jane.

Later Birdwell said jokingly, "Of course, the point was that there was a great deal more of Jane to photograph than Harlow had. Harlow had modest tits. Jane had 'Hello, officer' kind of tits! The point the censors didn't get is this: ten percent of a hundred is larger than ten percent of one."

Howard went to court and managed to have the 108 objections to *The Outlaw* lowered to three. After seeing the film himself, the presiding judge later said that the breasts of Jane Russell "hung like a thunderstorm over a summer landscape."

Howard had won the first round in his battle with the censors. Birdwell was the first to learn the good news. "It's a victory for us," he gleefully told Howard.

"Like hell!" he countered. "I'll not cut the three scenes. I'll release the god damn picture without a seal."

Birdwell could not believe his ears. It was as if Howard wanted more trouble. The publicist had even managed to get the Legion of Decency to back down, granting the picture a B rating, which meant "morally objectionable in part."

After costly battles, Howard was granted a Seal of Approval on March 23, 1941, providing he would agree to several cuts and changes. Even so, the advertising campaign for *The Outlaw* would bring him into more battles with the censors.

For reasons of his own—Noah Dietrich called it "a rich man's whim"—Howard locked away all copies of *The Outlaw* for two years. Birdwell urged him to release the film at once.

Howard refused. "During the next two years, we'll publicize the hell out of it. Hysteria will mount. Just wait and see!"

* * *

San Francisco, 1943

Since Jane Russell was still under contract to Howard, he wanted to keep her working although he had no more pictures for her. Through Birdwell, he arranged for her to be photographed from one o'clock in the afternoon until around eight in the evening. "Shoot her sitting, standing, rolling around, dancing, smiling, singing, laughing, crying," he told Birdwell. "Shoot! Shoot! From all these photographs, I'll come up with just the right picture to showcase her assets."

Birdwell immediately hired George Hurrell to photograph Jane. He was the leading photographer of Beverly Hills. He was famous for having said: "I can turn any fat, old, ugly producer's wife from the slurping pig she is into Betty Grable."

The photographer came up with a brilliant idea. He ordered five bales of hay for the first shoot. Jane was dressed in a short skirt and peasant blouse and given a six-shooter to hold. Naturally, the blouse would plunge and the skirt would roll high up to her thighs. The picture of Jane rolling in the hay became world famous. Even in the middle of its coverage of World War II, *Life* magazine thought it worthy of a cover. A legend was in the making. Even though the American movie-going public had yet to see Jane in a film, she had become one of the most widely recognized stars of World War II, ranking up there with Rita Hayworth and Lana Turner.

Life was among the first of literally hundreds of magazines and newspapers that would run Hurrell's pictures of Jane. She had become the second most famous pinup of the war, rivaled only by the photograph of Betty Grable wearing a one-piece bathing suit and shot from the rear. (A frontal shot wasn't feasible for Grable at the time because she was pregnant.)

Birdwell had never generated so much publicity before, even during his search for an actress to play Scarlett O'Hara. His "Cleavage-in-a-Haystack" photographs were the biggest publicity triumphs of his career. "Every G.I. in America became familiar with both of them," Birdwell said, referring to Jane's most obvious assets.

After the haystack photographs receded from the public eye, Birdwell conceived another brilliant idea. He found a lonely soldier in San Diego and had him photographed looking wistfully at a large shot of Jane's haystack picture. In an era where women throughout American were knitting sweaters for husbands or lovers, the soldier was photographed knitting a sweater for Jane to cover her ample bosom. Few magazines or newspapers in America resisted running that amusing picture.

During the darkest days of World War II, Howard finally announced that the première of *The Outlaw* would be celebrated on February 5, 1943 in the relatively liberal venue of San Francisco. At the offices of Caddo, nearly 1,200 fan letters a week were arriving for Jane, even more than for other beautiful movie stars who had actually made movies being shown in theaters. Before the San Francisco opening, Birdwell launched a sensational ad campaign, beginning with the slogan: SEX HAS NOT BEEN RATIONED.

Other posters proclaimed in large letters: THE OUTLAW—THE PICTURE

THAT COULDN'T BE STOPPED. Yet another billboard, showing a large blowup of Jane's haystack portrait, provocatively asked: HOW'D YOU LIKE TO TUSSLE WITH RUSSELL?

With Howard as the pilot, some fifty reporters and columnists, along with their spouses, boyfriends, or girlfriends, were flown from Los Angeles to San Francisco at Howard's expense. Jane and Jack, dressed in Billy the Kid and Rio drag from the film, were to make a personal appearance, acting out a scene that never made it to the final cut. It was a night of humiliation for the young actors. The curtain became stuck. All the audience could see were their feet, booted in Jack's case. Howard's invited guests roared with laughter, an ominous sign. Laughter continued when the film was shown.

Even though mocking Howard's movie, the freeloaders accepted an invitation to his celebration party at Bal Tabarin, a San Francisco nightclub. Jack, Jane, and Howard retired to his hotel suite for a private celebration party. En route to the club, Chad Jamison, a reporter, told Birdwell: "In all my forty years of going to theater and movies, this is the worst piece of shit I've ever witnessed. You've got a disaster on your hands!"

In spite of its earlier stand, the Catholic Legion of Decency announced a ban. *Variety* announced that it was going to be kind and not review the film. The newspaper later rescinded itself and reviewed *The Outlaw*, denouncing it as "almost a burlesque of screen westerns." *Time* defined it as "a strong candidate for the flopperoo of all time," giving the acting honors to Red, the movie's horse. Infuriated at the comment, Howard called his attorney to sue *Time*, but Neil McCarthy prevailed on his client to withdraw such a hopeless court action. Although *The Outlaw* is tepid by today's standards, United Artists informed Howard that it would not distribute the film.

Goaded by Howard, Birdwell launched a daring campaign in San Francisco. He hired fifty people, mostly secretaries, to call to stir up protests. These impostors phoned newspapers and magazines, even police stations, ordering them to shut down the showing of *The Outlaw* in San Francisco. Disguising his voice, Birdwell placed some of the more outrageous calls himself.

Birdwell's hired protesters concentrated on churches, women's clubs, and parent-teacher associations. When Birdwell's protesters actually stormed the Geary Theatre, the police moved in and arrested the manager of the movie house for exhibiting "a lewd film." Soon after, for his role in the crafting of the film's allegedly lewd publicity campaigns, Birdwell learned that a warrant had also been issued for his own arrest. Fleeing town without even returning to his hotel to retrieve his luggage, he rushed onto the next plane out of San Francisco. Traveling under the pseudonym "George Hurkos," he found himself in Seattle. Enlisting the aid of Neil McCarthy, Howard won another court battle in San Francisco. The lawyer introduced a statue of Venus de Milo. "A three-dimensional display of the world's perfect bosom won out over a two-dimensional display of another," a reporter claimed. Few judges in the world wanted to issue a ban on the Venus de Milo. Such an argument about a classical statue didn't make a lot of sense, but it won the day, at least in terms of publicity and censorship, for Howard and *The Outlaw*.

Then, Howard took his campaign to the skies: Five times a day Howard's pilots flew above the skies of San Francisco skywriting *"The Outlaw."* The film's name was followed by two giant circles, each dotted in the center. Attention still focused on Jane Russell's breasts, although *Newsweek* called the cheap publicity stunt "a new high in vulgarity." Birdwell commissioned a series of new posters, showing a hot stud of a cowboy dragging Rio with ripped clothes into a barn, with the obvious intent of raping her. Smaller type proclaimed TRIGGER-FAST ACTION!

In the ensuing ten weeks, and in spite of its lackluster opening, *The Outlaw* played to packed houses. The film also opened at select theaters throughout America. Disastrous reviews did not keep audiences from flocking to see the film. Most critics attacked it, one "poison pen" denouncing it as a "shabby, contrived, cornball western, but a marvelous curiosity." No one faulted Birdwell's marketing, however, one of the most brilliant publicity triumphs in the history of cinema.

Howard was disappointed with Jane. He'd raised her salary from $50 to $75 a week. But, tired of promoting *The Outlaw*, she skipped town, marrying her high school sweetheart, football star Robert Waterfield, in April of 1943.

Howard suspended her, a banishment that would last for two years. When she returned to Hollywood after her husband's release from the Army, Howard reinstated his errant star. He lent her to producer Hunt Stromberg so that she could co-star with Louis Hayward in *Young Widow*, a film that was released in 1946. It had been a full six years since Jane, at the height of her beauty and an internationally recognized sex symbol, had appeared before a camera.

After its initial opening in 1943, Howard once again withdrew *The Outlaw* from circulation. Prints of the film would languish in airtight vaults for three more years. In 1946, he decided to reissue the film. In a historical first, the Motion Picture Association of America abruptly withdrew its original seal. Howard immediately sued and lost. He was able to show his controversial film only in theaters that defied the Seal of Approval. He finally made peace with the MPAA and was granted his seal after certain "scenes too vulgar" were cut.

In the reissue of the film, ads asked the question: WHAT ARE THE TWO GREAT REASONS FOR JANE RUSSELL'S RISE TO STARDOM?

Time has been kinder to Howard's attempts to get *The Outlaw* released. In his book, *The Face on the Cutting Room Floor*, Murray Schumach wrote: "Regardless of Hughes's motives, he brought some refreshing honesty to Hollywood's approach to sex. He made the American public laugh a little at its own prudery about the female breasts. If ever a cinematic Rabelais emerges from Hollywood, he will be indebted to this unusual industrialist. Hughes lacked artistry. But he is not afraid to show, on a movie screen, that sex, even without a license, can be fun."

In the 1970s, too weak and too sick to move from his bed, Howard still screened *The Outlaw* at least once a month. Months before he died, it was partially screened for him a final time. A Mormon lackey later reported that his boss did not seem familiar with the film, but vaguely recalled that he might have seen it before. It was apparent that he no longer remembered Jane Russell or even Jack Buetel, his Billy the Kid to whom he'd virtually subjected to bondage during the cream of his youth.

"Jane Russell did all right for herself in spite of Howard," Cubby Broccoli later recalled. "I hear she's going around with some group singing Christian hymns today. But Poor Jack. His life was ruined by Howard. Even so, he came out better than the young man originally slated to be Billy the Kid. Better a ruined career like Jack's than a stiletto in your back like David Bacon."

Jane Russell in *French Line*

CHAPTER FIFTEEN
Los Angeles 1939-41

In 1939, when Hitler's invasion of Poland triggered the beginning of World War II, Howard knew that America's military involvement in the conflict would occur, in his words, "in just a matter of months." In defiant opposition to his pacifist rival, Charles Lindbergh, Howard accurately predicted that what would ultimately win the war would be bombs raining down from airplanes. He even wrote Lindbergh a brief but angry note, attacking him "as a Nazi sympathizer."

Howard also realized, as did many well-placed members of the U.S. military, that America was woefully underequipped with suitable aircraft. Shortly thereafter, Howard announced to his aides and staff that he planned to become the biggest supplier of aircraft to the U.S. government during the war effort.

To achieve his dream, he'd have to design and construct a major industrial compound, create a viable series of assembly lines, and hire and train an army of staff. It was Glenn Odekirk who discovered a tract of about 1,300 acres, bordering the Pacific Ocean at a point near Culver City, site of MGM studios. The land ran perpendicular to the Pacific Coast and paralleled a bluff on which stood the campus of Loyola University.

Howard commanded Dietrich to buy the property. He then began the construction of hangars, a central office building, and a 9,500-foot runway, which, when completed, held the record as the longest privately owned runway in America. Since Toolco was making more money than any other private business in America at the time, Howard probably felt that he could afford these inaugural expenses.

Assembling a qualified staff was more difficult, because "all the good men" were already involved in the war effort. "Form a posse and round 'em up," Howard instructed Dietrich. His chief officer set to work at once, assembling a crew of skilled laborers that consisted, in part, of men deemed unfit for military service because of some disability. Dietrich also scoured the campuses of local colleges and universities, usually hiring students, math and science professors, draftsmen, and engineers—both male and female—right on the spot. It was rumored that Howard himself stood outside the gates of Boeing every evening at closing time, luring workers into his factory at Culver City with promises of bonuses and fatter paychecks.

In spite of the daunting challenges caused by the labor shortage, Howard, through Dietrich and Odekirk, hired five hundred engineers, scientists, draftsmen, and airplane designers. Hughes Aviation was officially launched, but acquiring government contracts would be long and arduous, partly because of Howard's own secrecy and the ill will he'd created in the past by snubbing top Army brass. As it turned out, some of the men who bore the biggest grudges against him would be in positions of power, ruling on his future requests.

Howard's goal involved building the ultimate reconnaissance aircraft. He called it the D-2, short for "Design Number Two." He had originally budgeted two million dollars to develop a prototype. To Dietrich's horror, another four million dollars would eventually get poured into the aircraft's development. Some two million dollars had already been spent building the compound itself.

"Howard was the only one who was convinced that he'd easily win government contracts," Odekirk later said. "He held to that position despite his lack of success in getting the U.S. Army to give him the time of day, much less a contract."

Even though the United States Air Force was not impressed with Howard's vision, Japan and Nazi Germany were. Before the outbreak of war, Japan had ordered their America-based spies to research the technical details of Howard's H-1 and H-2 planes. The Air Force of Japan then used many of Howard's innovations when creating their own highly successful Zero.

Likewise, the Luftwaffe, by means known only to Hitler's Air Force, had successfully employed Howard's Sperry gyroscope, which he had pioneered during his around-the-world flight, during their aerial bombardment of Britain. Even when Howard's innovative designs were pointed out to the U.S. Air Corps, military officials were not moved. Instead they chastised Howard for not maintaining better security at his plant and for allowing valuable technology to fall into the hands of the enemy.

Taking those warnings to heart, Howard ordered strict secrecy and a 24-hour guard to shield the development of his reconnaissance plane, the D-2. It would be piloted by a five-man crew. A twin-engine fighter, with twin fuselages (also known as twin booms) it would carry its crew within a big-windowed oval-shaped pod positioned below the wing, midway between the twin fuselages.

The secret of the plane would be a material called Duramold, developed by Howard's friends at the Fairchild Corporation. Revolutionary and recently patented, it used a system of composite laminate bonding that placed thin veneers of wood, under heat and high pressure, between layers of specially formulated glues. The result might be labeled today as "hi-tech plywood." It was relatively lightweight and stronger, when assembled, than the sum of its individual components. Adaptable into a wide variety of shapes and sizes, it could also be laminated into shapes and surfaces that were curved. Howard's friend, Sherman Fairchild, had convinced him of the merits of Duramold in airplane construction. Steel was in short ration so that the use of wood would remove a major hurdle in the D-2s eventual wartime production.

540

Although Howard was spending as much as thirty-six hours at a time at his aircraft plant, he still managed to find time to produce *The Outlaw* and carry on various affairs. Johnny Meyer said he didn't know if Howard ever slept.

When Dietrich informed him that the Internal Revenue Service was going to tax him as a California resident because of his ownership of Muirfield, he ordered his honcho to sell the property, even at a loss. Dietrich sold the estate, and Howard moved into a bungalow at the Beverly Hills Hotel, the scene of so many of his future romances. "I've become a nomad," he told Cary Grant.

For his jailbait mistress, Faith Domergue, he leased an eighteen-room mansion at 619 Sarbonne Road in the exclusive Bel Air section of Los Angeles. He installed not just Faith but her parents in this French Regency style house set on beautifully landscaped grounds. It was luxury unknown to the Domergues before. Since both her father and her grandfather worked for Howard, their teenage offspring had become their bread ticket. All her family was eager to see her romance with Howard flourish. Once or twice she ran away, but her father always tracked her down and delivered her back to Howard. In almost every case, Mr. Domergue pleaded with Howard to forgive his errant daughter. "Faith will come around," the father said. "Just you wait and see."

She called Howard her "father lover." Her assessment was accurate. Photographs from the early 1940s reveal that he'd lost his movie star handsome looks of the 1920s and early 1930s. His hearing had deteriorated to a point where he missed most of what people said to him. He'd briefly considered joining the Air Force, but he was not physically fit for military service because of his hearing disability. Mainly because of sleepless nights, dark circles—"sometimes tinged with an almost grayish green," in the words of Faith—formed under his eyes. "They were the saddest eyes in the world," she said, "like he could never be happy again." His shoulders had begun to droop into a slouch, a condition that would remain for the rest of his life.

He called her his "perfect lover." She was a virgin when she met him, and he'd trained her to perform sexually as he commanded. "She hasn't been polluted by other men who taught her bad habits," Howard told Dietrich.

"As Howard began a slow withering on the vine," Henry Willson once said, "my former client, Miss Domergue, began to blossom into a hell of a sexy woman. She wasn't Jane Russell, but she was no longer the tender little virgin she was the day I first introduced her to Howard."

It was on the morning of April 8, 1941, that Howard arose from the bed he shared with Faith in their rented home. She was still asleep when he got out of bed and walked nude to the bathroom. He was heading for Hughes Aviation where he'd work until eight in the evening before continuing with his endless and obsessive editing of *The Outlaw*.

As he was soaping his hands, he noticed pus-like blisters on his hands which had seemed to develop overnight. At first he thought this might have been caused by the chemicals used in developing film for his picture. He immediately summoned the ever-faithful Dr. Verne Mason who came at once.

He found Howard sitting entirely nude in his library, demanding a complete body inspection like those his mother used to give him during his childhood in Houston. After a thorough examination, Dr. Mason stood up and faced his nude patient. "It's syphilis! Your old case has come back or else it's a new outbreak."

At first Howard went into a screaming rage. Dr. Mason managed to quiet him down and personally drove him to his medical offices. There Howard was injected with a revolutionary new antibiotic, penicillin. Dr. Mason warned him not to have sex for two months and to not shake hands, fearing that the broken blisters on his hand could also spread syphilis. Not trusting the new miracle drug, Howard also demanded injections of colloidal silver and arsphenamine, an old-fashioned remedy which had been used to treat the disease ever since Howard Hughes Sr. had contacted it during a dalliance with some prostitutes in his private railway car.

For the next two weeks, Howard could barely function. Dr. Mason warned him that "your temperature will reach the moon." Howard also suffered stomach cramps "worse than a woman giving birth to a nineteen-pound baby." With splitting headaches, he was unable to sleep. At times, he became disoriented. At one point Faith grew fearful that he was losing his mind. He sometimes called his factory demanding changes in the design of his D-2 without consulting either his management or his engineering teams. Adding to the confusion was his penchant for issuing orders for complicated design changes through low-ranking mechanics, a trait that usually inaugurated a barrage of heated phone dialogues between virtually everyone involved with the project. At one point he ordered Odekirk to take the D-2 and "push it into the Pacific." His chief pilot sensed that Howard was demented and didn't obey his demand.

When he learned he had syphilis, Howard called Cary Grant and told him. Since he'd had sex with Cary only recently, he feared that the actor might also have contracted the disease. Although Cary had no obvious symptoms, he heeded his friend's warning and went to Dr. Mason for his injections anyway. Without informing her of the reason for the antibiotic being injected into her, Faith too was delivered in a limousine to Dr. Mason for the same treatment.

The first weekend of his cure, Howard demanded the destruction, by fire, of all the bed sheets and all his clothing. He bought the strongest of lye soap, evocative of the type his mother used to scrub him with, and demanded that the house be cleansed with it. Dietrich was asked to send a truck to pick up all the linen and clothing. When he arrived, he supervised the loading but instead of burning the items, he directed the truck to a local branch of the Salvation Army, which was pleased to accept them as a donation. .

Fearing that his cars were also contaminated, Howard ordered Dietrich to destroy his fleet, some of which dated from the 1920s. Instead of demolishing them, Dietrich sold the armada of Packards, Duesenbergs, and Rolls Royces at a hefty profit and pocketed the money. Howard was left with only a 1938

Chevrolet which was in poor condition, the windshield having been cracked in an accident and never repaired. For some odd reason, he believed that his Chevy was not contaminated.

Then, Howard went to Sears & Roebuck and purchased a small and rather modest wardrobe for himself. The only thing left in his original wardrobe was his faithful fedora.

As the weeks went by in his newly sanitized rental home, Howard resumed sexual relations with Faith, never informing her that he'd been suffering the aftermaths of syphilis and its cure. Apparently, she never contracted the disease. The venereal disease left Howard more afraid of germs than ever.

He was at home on the morning of December 7, 1941, when word came over the radio. The Air Force of the Empire of Japan had attacked Pearl Harbor, crippling U.S. naval operations in the Pacific.

"Howard became a madman for the rest of the day," Faith later claimed. "He'd been morose for days. Suddenly, he was goaded into action. I didn't know what he was talking about most of the time. He was using very technical language about all the breakthroughs he was going to make in aviation."

All of this wasn't fantasy. In 1939 he'd perfected power-booster radio receivers and transmitters in airplanes. Between 1941 and 1943 a young engineer in Howard's employ, Claude Slate, would design ammunition feed chutes for fifty-caliber machine guns. This breakthrough doubled the rate of fire that could be used against an enemy. By the end of the war, ninety percent of all American bombardment aircraft carried machine-gun feed chutes manufactured by one of Howard's companies. "We've become a killing machine," Howard told Odekirk at his office at 7000 Romaine Street, which had been converted into a wartime factory. Toolco also won lucrative contracts to manufacture weapons. From the Buffalo Bayou region of Houston, Toolco's Dickson Gun Plant manufactured centrifugally-cast gun barrels in various calibers for several branches of the U.S. military, as well as parts used in the manufacture of the B-25 and B-26 bomber.

Before nightfall on December 7, Howard had convinced himself, if not Faith, that he—and he alone—could design planes that could win the war for the United States. "The Japs have made a terrible mistake," he told her. "In attacking Pearl Harbor, they hadn't reckoned with Howard Hughes."

"In spite of all that big talk," Faith said, "Howard didn't go to the aircraft factory that day, as I was sure he would. Instead he drove over to 7000 Romaine Street where he locked himself away for the next few days. He didn't design aircraft, but spent the hours following Roosevelt's call to arms editing scenes from *The Outlaw*. He'd become obsessed with that film and Jane Russell's bosom."

* * *

Mojave Desert, 1943

In April of 1943, Lockheed notified Howard that the first Constellation had come off the assembly line and was ready to be tested. If it performed well, Howard had plans to make "Connie," his nickname for the craft, the commercial flagship of his emerging Trans World Airlines. After acquiring the airline, he had paid scant attention to it because of other commitments, not only the Spruce Goose, the D-2, but especially *The Outlaw*. Even so, TWA was no longer "Lucky Lindy's Airline." It had become "Howard's Airline."

Over strenuous protests from Lockheed, Howard demanded designation as test pilot for the first Constellation's inaugural flight. Lockheed acquiesced, but insisted that his co-pilot be one of the most skilled aviators in California, Milo Burcham. Kelly Johnson, Lockheed's chief engineer and an experienced test pilot, was also assigned to fly aboard the inaugural flight. Burcham had wanted to be the pilot for the test run but reluctantly gave in to Howard's demands, since he was, in fact, the project's chief investor. Lockheed, however, forced Howard to agree to relinquish control of the vessel at any time during the flight if Burcham decided that he was not piloting it properly.

"Howard resented such "school marm intrusion," but finally gave in to Lockheed's demands. The Mojave Desert was designated as the site of Connie's inaugural flight.

Seated beside Howard, Burcham was armed with the same controls as Howard. At any time he could commandeer the Constellation if he didn't like the way Howard was flying.

Once airborne, and only fifteen minutes into the flight, Howard shouted to Kelly. "What does it take to stall this thing? That's something our pilots must know."

Taking over the controls, Burcham maneuvered the wing flaps slightly, stalling Connie. The aircraft just seemed "to be suspended in midair," but only for a second or so, before its engines started again and the plane continued flying on course.

The suspenseful moment ended, Howard was obviously disappointed. "Fuck, that's not a god damn stall!" he shouted at Burcham.

"Howard's face was lit up like a Christmas tree," Burcham later reported back to his bosses at Lockheed. "That was one determined Texan. I felt he was completely unreasonable in his demands—maybe just a bit mad."

The mammoth craft was going at a speed of 230 miles per hour when Howard, to Burcham's horror, lowered the flaps to their fullest extent. "The Connie shuddered like it was about to break apart on its first flight," Burcham wrote in his report filed with Lockheed. "It was going at zero speed. I couldn't believe it. In all my years of flying, I'd never seen anything like it."

"God damn you, you fool!" Burcham shouted at Howard. "You'll kill us!"

"Fuck off!" Howard shouted back. "I know what I'm doing."

"Raise the flaps, you idiot!" Burcham shouted into Howard's unreliable ears.

Burcham noted a "fierce, almost demonic" look in Howard's eyes. He would later recall that for one moment he felt Howard was committing suicide and taking the Lockheed crew with him. Finally, realizing the danger he'd placed Connie in, he raised the flaps and coaxed the engines back to life, barely in time to prevent a crash landing.

Against his better judgment, Burcham did not commandeer the plane after that recklessness on the part of Howard. As if to restore his image in front of Burcham, Howard went on for a series of four takeoff and landing tests, all successful.

On the fifth pass, he let Connie drift precariously to the left. "It was like a bird flying with one of its wings wounded," Johnson later graphically recalled. "Watch out!" Burcham yelled, having to shout at Howard again for his renewed recklessness. "Steady the fucker, for Christ's sake!"

Determined to retain control of the aircraft, Howard did not listen to these protests shouted from his right. The plane was flying low, and he let it drift so dangerously close that it narrowly missed the desert control tower. "Another twenty-five yards to the left, and we would have crashed into it," Johnson said in his report to Lockheed. Some of the windows in the control tower rattled, and at least two dozen panes went flying into the desert. "The traffic controllers trapped inside were screaming," chief engineer Johnson claimed. "We found this out later. There were several threatened lawsuits against Hughes. Maybe he put up money to settle. We never knew."

"By this time, I had come to realize that Hughes was a crazy fuck," Burcham later told Johnson. In his more formal report to Lockheed, he changed "crazy fuck" to "out-of-control daredevil of the air. His pilot's license should be revoked. He is not fit to pilot a skyliner such as Lockheed's Constellation."

The only problem with that point was that Howard was the aircraft's owner.

Despite Howard's piloting, the Constellation was pronounced a success. It would soon be flying passengers between Los Angeles and New York, sometimes with Howard at the controls, carrying "a bevy of movie stars."

"Howard hauled their spoiled asses for free," Dietrich said. "He got loads of publicity. Pictures of movie stars like Paulette Goddard or Linda Darnell getting off Connie in New York were published in newspapers across the nation."

From his headquarters at Lockheed, Burcham read this publicity with a raised eyebrow. "I think Howard Hughes has an insane streak in him. If that insane streak takes over while he's at the controls of a Constellation, the fool might suddenly decide to nose-dive into the heart of Chicago. If so, Hollywood will have a few less stars in its Heaven."

* * *

Los Angeles, 1943

545

Howard pushed forward with plans to develop the D-2, despite the fact that no one from the Army Air Corps had seen plans for the reconnaissance plane or had been invited to inspect it during its initial construction.

To win government contracts, Howard knew he first had to convince "the boys at Wright Field," outside of Dayton, Ohio, of the merits of his new design. A sprawling compound of runways, airplane hangars, office buildings, and laboratories maintained by the U.S. Air Corps, later called the Air Force, it was charged with the development, testing, and approval of any new aircraft utilized by the U.S. military. The brass at Wright Field awarded Boeing contracts to build the B-17; Lockheed the P-38, and Douglas the A-20. Howard wanted to be a player with his D-2 reconnaissance plane, if only he could get its prototype de-bugged and constructed. Determined, he pressed on with work on the D-2, even though Wright Field had already rejected plans for an earlier prototype, the H-1. He told Dietrich that another name for Wright Field was "The Hate Howard Hughes Club."

Never willing to provide full disclosure, Howard wrote Wright Field hinting that he had a mystery plane under production that "will turn the tide of battle for the Allies." Obviously that was a tantalizing bit of information to "The Boys of Wright Field," launched into a war that they were losing. Typically, Howard provided sparse details about his revolutionary new craft.

On a visit to the West Coast for an inspection of the region's aircraft factories, a tall, gray-haired commander of the Air Force, General H.H. (Hap) Arnold, decided to pay an unannounced visit to Hughes Aviation. Acting under pre-established orders, Howard's security force refused to admit Hap or any of the Air Force brass into the factory. Howard had not been informed in advance of this visit. Hap was furious at Howard's guards. In a temper outburst, he threatened to shoot his way inside. "A war's on, you stupid fuckers! I can go inside any factory in America if I want to." His senior aide finally prevailed upon Hap to leave the entrance, but it was a snub he'd never forget. "For Howard, it was a public relations blunder from which we never recovered," Odekirk claimed.

Finally, Howard was forced to let the government have the plans for the D-2. "Otherwise, how in hell do you expect to win a contract from the Air Corps?" Dietrich asked, pointing out what should have been obvious. Without government interest, Howard had not been able to secure heavily rationed materials, including the right type of resins, woods, and glues needed in the new Duramold process. The Air Corps controlled all such strategic materials, allocating it to companies such as Vultee, which had become the leading aircraft contractor.

Dietrich and eight of Howard's engineers flew for a meeting with Major General Oliver P. Echols, the chief procurement officer for the Air Corps. Like Hap, Echols too had once been snubbed by Howard. In the late 30s, Howard had tried to interest Echols and other Army brass in his *Winged Bullet*. Howard had

546

personally told President Roosevelt that the Army Air Force should manufacture the plane en masse, since, in his view, it would make an idyllic military pursuit plane. Major General Echols and two other Army officials were waiting at Wright Field for Howard to show up in his *Winged Bullet*, as had been arranged.

For reasons known only to himself, and never fully explained, Howard flew over Wright Field, completely snubbing the brass waiting for him below on the tarmac, before finally landing his aircraft at another (unknown) airport. Echols and his staff, on the runway waiting to greet him, were left angered and fuming at Howard. It was a breach of manners which the major general would never forget. Howard had humiliated him.

Now Howard's representatives, led by Dietrich, had come to call on him. Cold and distant with Dietrich and his engineers, Echols informed him that he'd have members of the Air Force in California inspect the D-2. "That is," Echols said with barely concealed hostility, "if your crazy boss will let them in."

Within days after an inspection, Howard had his answer. Echols—perhaps with a certain degree of malice—wrote Howard that the D-2, according to the Army engineers who'd inspected it, was "too heavy for use as a military weapon." In his letter, he attacked the plane's landing gear as being too weak. More importantly, he objected to the use of Duramold. Before signing off, Echols also noted that the D-2 lacked a bullet-resistant windshield and armor plate.

When Dietrich called to protest the decision, Echols shouted into the phone, "Tell that son of a bitch he'll never get a nickel out of this office—not so long as I'm breathing and still in charge."

Echols went a step father. He sent an internal memo to officials at Wright Field, claiming that Hughes Aviation was "a waste of time," and advised that the Air Corps should "discontinue any further aircraft projects with this organization." It was a puzzling memo since there were no aircraft projects to stop.

Learning of the memo and faced with such "stonewalling rejection," Howard told Odekirk, "In Texas, as we say, there are other ways to skin a cat. We'll find a way."

Howard still believed in wood as a material for the construction of his airplanes, even though some of his engineers feared that it would develop cracks, absorb moisture, and shatter under fire.

One U.S. Senator called Howard's D-2 "the playboy's latest fantasy." Angrily, Howard pressed forward with his experimental plane. After spending two million dollars of his own funds, Howard authorized Dietrich to pour yet another four million dollars of corporate funds into the ill-fated plane. He was still determined to build the ultimate reconnaissance aircraft.

Eventually and in spite of the lack of efficiency at Hughes Aviation, the employees came up with a prototype of the D-2 that was ready for a trial run. Howard told his staff that he himself would be the plane's first test pilot.

On June 20, 1943, Howard had flown to a secret location at Harper Dry

Lake in the Mojave Desert, 100 miles north of Culver City, California. He took off in the D-2 on its first run and was airborne for about twenty minutes before he headed back to earth where he made a smooth landing. He later told Stan Bell, one of his chief engineers, that the plane "nibbles," thus coining a word.

His engineers had already been ordered back to the drawing board when Howard, the next day, dictated a twenty-eight page memo outlining what he perceived as design flaws in the aircraft.

"We tried and we tried," Ray Kirkpatrick, a flight engineer, said, "but I think Howard just never liked the D-2. We simply couldn't build the plane that he envisioned."

In spite of his disappointment in the D-2 on its test flight, Howard began to lobby aggressively for it when he learned that the second son of the president, Elliott Roosevelt, was flying to the West Coast. His mission was to find a reconnaissance plane that performed better than the superior German craft in use by the Luftwaffe at the time.

A handsome, dashing playboy type, somewhat like Howard himself, Elliott had been head of the Mediterranean Allied Photo Reconnaissance Command where he'd learned firsthand how inferior American competitive craft was. Called back to Washington by General Hap Arnold, Elliott was assigned the task of locating a better plane by touring the factories of the West Coast.

"There's no need for him to haul ass over to Boeing," Howard said, "Have I got a plane for him!" Odekirk didn't comment, but he knew that Howard had no such plane ready, only a working model that had earned Howard's own condemnation.

As a means of entertaining Elliott, the Air Force, and the Army brass, Howard called in Johnny Meyer. The visiting dignitaries from Washington were to be housed elegantly at Howard's expense. Starlets were to be hired at $100 to $400 a night to entertain them. Howard warned Meyer, "Those $400-a-night broads had better be really good. For that price, we should be able to get Hedy Lamarr herself."

In an impulsive move, Howard ordered Dietrich to deduct the fees paid to each of the call girl bills from his income tax. "It's a legitimate entertainment cost," Howard told Dietrich, who did not agree.

Although planning to arrange "entertainment of a sexual nature" for their men, Howard didn't overlook the wives left back home. He managed to secure beautiful Parisian handbags and black market nylon stockings as gifts to take home to the neglected wives.

On August 8, 1943, in anticipation of Elliott's arrival with his top brass, Meyer appeared at the airport with a flotilla of eight limousines.

"We have to get to Elliott before Lockheed does," Howard instructed Meyer, who had mapped out an entertainment agenda for the men that would "bring a blush to the cheeks of Nero." Through spies, Howard had learned that Elliott was a "devotee of pussy." As Howard told Meyer, "If there's one thing that's not rationed—nor in short supply in Los Angeles—it's pussy. Get him all he wants. I'm paying."

Howard took over much of the wooing of Elliott personally, flying him to the D-2 test ground site at Lake Harper, piloting him on his yacht to Catalina Island, and personally escorting him around the Hughes Aviation plant where he spent hours reviewing plans for his D-2 and touting its "unlimited possibilities" in reconnaissance.

"I think we've got Elliott in our pocket," Howard confided to Odekirk after the first week of entertainment. The deal was cinched not by Howard but by a tawny blonde.

When Meyer arranged a special luncheon for the President's son at the Warner Brother's commissary in Hollywood, he was introduced to a five-foot, four-inch beauty from Louisiana, Faye Emerson, a rising young contract player at Warner Brothers. Each day Meyer arranged "a boob buffet" for Elliott at one of the studios, at which he'd be introduced to some bosomy stars.

At the studio making *Destination Tokyo*, Cary Grant had been asked to join the party. Howard knew that his lover's smooth manners and charm would impress the impressionable Elliott who had a "movie star fixation."

Meyer had pre-tested Faye, relaying to Howard that she "was the fellatio queen of Hollywood." In response, Faye told Howard that Johnny's figure was "less than Greek." Since Howard was an aficionado of the oral arts, he called Faye and asked her to come to his office at 7000 Romaine Street for a demonstration. Kneeling in front of Howard at his desk, the "fiercely ambitious" young woman serviced Howard. Later he told Meyer that, "Faye is the second best cocksucker in Hollywood—only Tyrone Power has a better technique."

Recalling the luncheon at Warners, Meyer later said that "Faye practically fell all over Elliott. She used every excuse she could to touch him." She even got him to order her favorite dish, Brunswick stew, inspired by a recipe she'd picked up in Georgia and had given to the studio chefs to prepare for them.

By nightfall of the same day, she was occupying Elliott's expensive suite that Howard was paying for at the Beverly Hills Hotel. "My boss ordered me to deliver the champagne and caviar personally," Meyer said.

Although Howard would squander millions, he could also threaten to fire an employee for ordering an eighty-five cent subscription to a magazine he deemed unnecessary. But he was delighted with Meyer for linking Faye Emerson with Elliott. "My chief pimp is going to find a five thousand dollar bonus in his next paycheck," he told Meyer.

When he wasn't with Faye, Elliott had his time monopolized by Howard. He boasted to the President's son that his D-2 would be able to fly 433 miles per hour. Commander D.W. Stevenson, who was also being "wined, dined, and fucked," as Odekirk put it, as part of Howard's sales campaign, also praised the D-2. "I have never seen anything more magnificent that could do a better job," Stevenson proclaimed.

Howard's wooing of Elliott continued even after Elliott left California for the East Coast. Within a few days, Howard arranged for Faye to join Elliott in Washington and New York. Soon the actress and the president's son were spotted at El Morocco and the Stork Club in New York. Howard picked up all their bills, as he did their hotel tab at the Waldorf-Astoria.

On August 6, 1944, Elliott and Faye, much to the surprise of Johnny Meyer, got married. Faye immediately became the First Daughter-In-Law. Howard paid for their lavish wedding and their expensive honeymoon. Faye would remain married to Elliott until her divorce from him in 1950. Poised, sophisticated, articulate, and beautiful, she was hardly a bimbo like Meyer's usual starlets. She went on to become the first queen of talk show TV when *The Faye Emerson Show* premiered in October of 1949. One wit claimed that Faye Emerson put the "V" in "TV" because of her designer gowns and plunging necklines. Even, the Emmy Awards, according to some reports, were named for her. (Actually, their name derived from "Immy," a term commonly used for the early orthicon camera tube. The name was later changed to "Emmy," which somehow sounded more appropriate.)

By August 20, Elliott had filed his report with a horrified Hap Arnold. Elliott recommended that plane-building contracts go to Hughes Aviation and not Lockheed. To overcome the Air Force's objections to wood as a major component in their aircraft, Elliott informed Hap that Howard had agreed to make the planes out of steel.

"Hughes is a nutbag," Hap shouted at Elliott. "You've been taken in by this piece of Texas shit. I've heard about what went on out there in Los Angeles. And I just got off the phone with J. Edgar Hoover. Hughes is a homosexual. And his brain is half eaten up with syphilis. Hoover looked at his medical records."

In spite of these warnings, Elliott was not deterred from his recommendation. In his report, he called for mass production on the D-2. Elliott said that Howard had given him his "solemn promise" that delivery of the planes could begin within five months.

Ultimately Elliott prevailed over Hap. It was suspected that Jesse Jones, the Secretary of Commerce, personally got the green light from FDR himself. The end result was that Howard was awarded a $43 million contract for 100 D-2s to be delivered in less than a year. The contract specifically called for nine prototypes and 97 production models.

When they heard the news, the brass at Wright Field was horrified and lobbied to have the contract cancelled. They knew that Hughes Aviation was much too small and too disorganized to build 100 planes, especially on such a tight schedule.

Key figures, including Major General Echols, sided with Hap against Elliott. "There's gonna be an awful smell in Washington," Echols accurately predicted, "when word leaks out about how this contract was won by Hughes.

550

I don't trust the man—I never did."

With great reluctance and a "heavy heart," Hap issued an order on September 1, granting Howard the government's go-ahead for his reconnaissance planes. "Faye's cocksucking really paid off," a gleeful Meyer told Howard.

Even though he'd buckled under pressure from the White House, Hap Arnold still denounced Howard's plane, constantly referring to it as "a piece of shit." He personally flew to Canada where the British were perfecting the Mosquito. "Compared to the Mosquito, Hughes's D-2 sucks," Hap later said. He claimed that the British craft, a twin-engine photo reconnaissance plane, was superior in every way to the D-2 and could fly longer distances and a greater speed.

On the night of November 11, 1943, the fate of the D-2 was decided. The hangar housing the craft caught on fire, and the D-2 proved very flammable indeed. Both the hangar and the D-2 were burned, the prototype remaining only as an ugly skeleton of what might have been.

Lightning was blamed for starting the fire. But there was speculation that Howard deliberately started the blaze himself. "Nothing was ever proven either way," said Howard's chief engineer, Stan Bell. "Maybe it was an act of God— maybe not. Maybe god is Howard Hughes. I've always believed that he was."

A natural disaster or not, Howard had successfully gotten rid of his mistake in the fire, which gave him a new opportunity to design a better reconnaissance plane, the D-5, as a means of fulfilling the government's still-valid contract for 100 airplanes. For his new design, Howard ordered two Pratt and Whitney Wasp Major engines to be installed, in spite of the wartime shortages. This was the most powerful engine on the market. "I want to build a plane that's got the speed of a fighter but the long range of a bomber—we'll give 'em hell. Wait till the Krauts have to deal with my motherfucker."

Hap Arnold's hostility toward the D-2 spilled over onto the new D-5. "It's just a reworked D-2 with a little change here, a little change there," Hap wrote in a report to Wright Field. "The D-2 performed like shit in the Mojave Desert, according to a confidential report I've secured. Hughes tried to cover up that little fact. What an asshole!" Hap didn't edit his memos but wrote them like he spoke.

In spite of Hap's objections, and the protests of the brass at Wright Field, Howard plunged ahead with the D-5, which the Air Force had designated as the XF-11.

His production department—"too many chiefs, too few Indians," Dietrich said—immediately began to lag behind in production of the XF-11s. Several times Hap sent threatening memos to Howard, warning him that the government might cancel its contract for the 100 planes. Other airline officials in California jokingly referred to Hughes Aviation as the "Howard Hughes Country Club."

Hoping to save the day, Howard lured "the boy wonder of the aircraft industry," Charles W. Perelle, from Howard's rival, Vultee. Howard raised his salary to $75,000. At the time, in all of California, no other aircraft officer made that kind of money. To sweeten the deal, Howard threw in an option for Perelle to purchase 10,000 shares of TWA from company reserves at market price, a deal he was making with no one else at the time. At Vultee, Perelle had been in charge of production and was turning out airplanes faster than any other factory on the West Coast.

But even a hotshot like Perelle found Howard impossible to work with. During his seventeen month tenure, Perelle did what Dietrich called the impossible. He brought the XF-11 and Howard's "wild dream" of the Spruce Goose close to completion. But even he could not tolerate Howard's indecision, his sudden disappearances, and his boss's constant rescinding of his orders. Having been promised "complete and unrestricted" control at Hughes Aviation, Perelle got neither. He was forced to resign.

As it happened, during World War II, Hughes Aviation never evolved into a major-league airplane manufacturer. With the dropping of the atomic bombs on Japan in 1945, World War II came to an end. The Allies won without benefit of Howard's XF-11s, which were never delivered.

Dietrich, ironically, without too much personal meddling from Howard, had been far more successful in helping the Hughes Empire evolve into a supplier of spare parts. Instead of airplanes, Toolco and Hughes Aviation had supplied such war matériel as 14,766 landing gear struts, 18,733 aircraft seats, 5,576 aircraft wings, 6,370 fuselages, 939,320 artillery shells, and 16,958 cannon barrels. As Dietrich later said, "Howard was intent in becoming to America what the Krupp family was in munitions to Nazi Germany."

Howard seemed almost disappointed at the victory celebrations. "We've missed the god damn war," Howard told Odekirk. But he was among the first to recognize the immediate threat of the Soviet Union, and the commercial potential of that threat, during the Post-War Era. "More and more," Howard accurately predicted, "the United States is going to need reconnaissance planes to fly over Soviet territory to see what the fucking Communists are up to."

* * *

Lake Mead, 1943

Howard's S-43, his Sikorsky, had been resting in mothballs until the Air Corps requisitioned it for the war effort. The Army Corps of Engineers, in dire need of amphibian craft, wanted the plane for use in Iceland.

He could have turned over the plane to them as it was, but he impulsively decided that he needed to prove that it was "still air worthy" to the government.

On May 16, 1943, Army Air Corps engineers agreed to fly to Lake Mead, Nevada, to put the Sikorsky through a series of tests, with Howard as the pilot. Before flying here, Howard, in spite of other more pressing problems, diverted some of his top engineers to get the Sikorsky in running condition.

The Civil Aeronautics Administration had assigned a fellow Texan, Charles W. Von Rosenberg, to fly with Howard during the test. Accompanying Howard and Von Rosenberg were Gene Blandford, Howard's own flight test engineer; Richard Felt, one of Howard's mechanics, and William M. Cline, known as "Ceco," another CAA inspector.

Odekirk was assigned the duty of filming the landing of the Sikorsky on water. "I urged Howard not to go up," he later said. "Any test pilot could have done it. With millions riding on Howard's back—all those war contracts—it was just too risky."

Howard took off over the 1.9 million acre lake. After flying without incident, he steered the craft toward a murky section of the lake known as the "Vegas Gulch." He brought the Sikorsky in for a perfect landing on tranquil waters. Even though Von Rosenberg had been slightly apprehensive when the Sikorsky pitched forward, Howard as pilot managed to straighten it out.

Plowing into the lake at eighty miles an hour, the plane made a perfect touchdown, as the Sikorsky's pontoons stirred up churns of water shooting up from the lake, a perfect photo opportunity for Odekirk.

All of a sudden, the airplane lunged forward, its nose tilting down as it careened sharply to the right. "As if acrobatic, the craft plunged into the water and began playing skip rope sideways on Lake Mead," Von Rosenberg later recalled. "I thought it was curtains for all of us. I even remember my exact words, 'Oh, shit!' I yelled."

His eyes darting back and forth, like a man facing a beheading, Howard clung desperately to the controls, but his Sikorsky would no longer obey him. It was as if the plane had taken over its own command.

The impact of hitting the lake cracked the propeller which became detached from the plane. Like a dangerous slicer, it flew through the air, hitting the main body of the Sikorsky, slicing a mammoth hole.

Howard had lost control of ten tons of metal that had assumed a life of its own as it slammed against the water "with the power of a hurricane." Pieces of the wing broke loose and flew through the air like deadly missiles. The tail was ripped off, "sounding like a million screeching seagulls," Von Rosenberg said. "The doomed plane finally came to a halt like a marathon racer having a heart attack at the finish line."

Perhaps, and this is only speculation, Howard had forgotten to tell his ground mechanics to place weighty ballast in the tail, which would be needed for any safe water landing.

"The pain in my back was unbearable," Von Rosenberg recalled. "I'd never known so much pain. I wanted to die." As he was to learn later that day, two of his vertebrae had been crushed. "Doctors later informed me that all the muscles in my back had been ripped loose."

Water was rapidly pouring into the cockpit. In his agony Von Rosenberg looked at Howard slumped over the wheel. Blood was rushing from a deep gash in his forehead. "I shook him," Von Rosenberg said. "There was no movement. I knew that he was dead. At that point I felt I'd die either of pain or else I'd drown. Suddenly, I noticed movement in Howard's body. He was coming to."

In an almost impossible feat of human endurance, considering his injuries, Von Rosenberg managed to open the pilot's window on Howard's left and pushed him through. "Thank God he was slender or he'd never have made it," Von Rosenberg said. He opened the escape hatch in the cockpit and crawled out himself. Mercifully, one of the other crew members had inflated a life raft. With Blandford's help, Von Rosenberg was able to get both Howard and himself aboard the life-saving raft.

Blandford was hardly injured. He was initially knocked out but he revived when water began to flood into the plane through its gaping hole. He was the one who'd set up the life raft. He shouted at Von Rosenberg that Ceco had been sucked from the plane. Upon impact, he'd gone flying through the air, seat and all, plunging into the murky depths of Lake Mead, which would never give up his body to the divers sent to search for it.

Von Rosenberg saw Blandford lower Richard Felt into the raft. "It looked like his head had met an ax murderer," Von Rosenberg said. "He was still alive but I had little hope for him."

Von Rosenberg looked back as the Sikorsky sank into the deep lake. "Hughes was coming in and out of consciousness," Von Rosenberg said. "He was mumbling something about his having to get to Faith. I thought a woman was the last thing he needed at a time like this."

Suddenly, Howard sat up. Even though bleeding profusely, he seemed very alert. As Von Rosenberg was to discover later, Howard was looking for landmarks on shore so that he would be able to pinpoint the spot where the Sikorsky went down.

By the time the crew reached land, Odekirk had already summoned an ambulance to rush the men to the Boulder City (Nevada) Hospital. Even before the wounded men arrived, Dr. Lawrence Chaffin was already airborne, flying to Boulder City from Los Angeles to attend to Howard's wounds personally. When Dr. Chaffin arrived, he closed Howard's head wound with skin clips.

Howard had been in the emergency room for two hours, being checked and observed, before Odekirk came in to inform him that Felt had died. He'd arrived alive at the hospital but had died twenty minutes after admittance.

Amazingly, Howard spent only one night in the hospital. Since all his clothes were blood soaked, he had Odekirk drive him to the nearest J.C. Penney's in Boulder City. There, he horrified customers by walking in bloody clothes through the store. He purchased a new wardrobe for himself. "I remember he bought a pair of baby blue pants that were at least six inches too short in the leg," Odekirk said." The world's richest man wore those damn pants for the next three years, much to the horror of future girlfriends such as Ava Gardner."

The crashing of the Sikorsky had caused Howard's seventh major head injury, garnered during either plane crashes or car accidents. Yet he'd refused to allow doctors at the hospital to take an X-ray. He didn't trust X-ray machines. The head injury on Lake Mead, it is believed, had major implications for his mental state in the years to come.

The following morning the empty seat that had held Ceco was found floating bodiless on the surface of the lake.

Since the CAA was involved, an investigation was launched. At first, pilot error was blamed. It was later learned that the craft had been improperly loaded. "Its center of gravity had been dangerously altered, unknown to us," Von Rosenberg said. "When it hit the water at a high speed, the Sikorsky was thrown off balance."

When Howard was able to fly again, Odekirk piloted his boss over Lake Mead to the site where he pinpointed that his craft had gone down. To Odekirk's horror, Howard ordered him to dredge up the plane from the lake's depth. "Haul its ass back to Glendale!" Howard shouted at him. "That motherfucker will fly again with me steering it. It won't kill me!"

After landing the small craft, Odekirk suggested that Howard pay a final visit to Von Rosenberg's hospital bed before flying back to Los Angeles. "Like hell I will!" Howard told him.

Von Rosenberg spent the rest of his life in agonizing pain. When reporters tried to interview him, he told them, "I never want to hear the name Howard Hughes ever again."

Back at Lake Mead, Odekirk faced a daunting challenge in raising the Sikorsky. Through an ingenious method, he used a metal detector with a special phone cable rigged to it. After arduous days, he managed to locate the plane at the bottom of the lake right at the spot where Howard had told him he could find it. An ordinary doorbell had been attached to the metal detector. When the downed plane was located, the doorbell rang.

From the lake's floor at two-hundred feet below sea level, the plane was dredged up. Photographers were waiting on shore to take pictures. Muddy and mutilated, it was then loaded onto a flatbed truck for delivery back to Glendale.

Howard paid $100,000 to have the Sikorsky dredged up. It would cost him another $600,000 for the craft to be put back in mint condition.

"Want to fly with me and take her up again?" Odekirk asked Howard, showing off the restored Sikorsky which looked shiny new within a few weeks.

"Not now," Howard said. "Leave her in the hangar. When I take off with her again, it'll be a mystery flight. No one will know where I'm going."

* * *

Washington, 1942

When Noah Dietrich first heard of Howard's involvement with a mammoth flying ship—the size of the *Queen Mary*—he called it "a colossal boondoggle that would never fly." He was almost right. Dietrich's appraisal referred to what became the notorious "Spruce Goose." The aircraft's original name was the Hercules, or HK-1 (Hughes-Kaiser One).

But the derogatory nickname, Spruce Goose, ultimately prevailed over earlier and also derisive names for the flying boat. It was first called "The Flying Lumberyard" and later "The Jesus Christ."

The nickname Spruce Goose spread across the country because this massive aircraft's "skin" and its structural parts were composed of thin sheets of spruce plywood, the layers held together by waterproof glues.

Howard had to be talked into the idea of the flying boat, although the percentage of the world that's familiar with the Spruce Goose still thinks it was the aviator's dream and creation. The idea had originated as the "half-baked dream"—Dietrich's words—of Henry J. Kaiser, the multi-millionaire tycoon, one of the world's richest men.

In 1942, Kaiser was a man to be reckoned with, even by President Roosevelt himself, because of his past achievements. A great builder, he would eventually own an astonishing 105 companies, including Kaiser Aluminum and Kaiser-Frazer Automobiles. His name was a household word throughout America. He'd built the San Francisco-Oakland Bridge, as well as the Grand Coulee, Bonneville, and Hoover Dams.

But mainly he was known for his revolutionary Liberty Ships. In Kaiser's view, he was "single-handedly winning the war for the Allies." His Liberty Ships rolled off assembly lines faster than any heretofore known production schedule. Thanks to prefabricated parts and highly motivated assembly crews, a ten thousand ton ship could be built in 48 days instead of the usual 355.

Regrettably, though, there was trouble over the North Atlantic. The Liberty Ships were falling victim to Nazi submarine attacks. German subs were sinking Liberty Ships at an alarming rate, some of the attacks occurring only an hour or so after a vessel had disembarked from an East Coast port. In March of 1942, sixty Liberty Ships had been sunk, each carrying desperately needed cargos to a beleaguered Britain. It was estimated that in July of that same year, more than 100,000 tons of supplies ended up, like the *Titanic*, at the bottom of the ocean.

Kaiser's grandiose plan involved the construction of a flying boat so massive that it could transport hundreds of men and tons of equipment to war-torn Europe. "Such a craft would simply fly over Hitler's subs and get the material to where it's needed," Kaiser claimed. Had such a wild proposal originated from Howard, it would surely have been dismissed as a "crackpot scheme." But coming from a man with Kaiser's past achievements in wartime production, the idea, as preposterous as it was, had to be seriously considered. Kaiser had not inspired confidence within the War Department by announcing to the press that his proposed flying ship "would go beyond anything Jules Verne might conjure up."

Even before Kaiser flew to Washington to promote his plan, newspapers throughout American endorsed the idea. In one case, *The Philadelphia Inquirer* heaped praise on his fleet of flying boats even before the first prototype had made it to the drawing board. Unlike Howard, who was called "the most secretive man in California," when Kaiser had an idea, he didn't want to keep quiet about it.

Arriving in Washington "like Diamond Jim Brady and Billy Sunday," as one reporter noted, Kaiser was filled with Messianic fervor. At one point he claimed "divine inspiration" for his idea of the flying cargo boat.

Donald Marr Nelson, a pipe-smoking, professorial type in a tweed jacket, had agreed to hear Kaiser's plan. Nelson was the chief honcho for the War Production Board. Novel ideas such as the flying boat had to clear him before moving on to higher authorities for ultimate approval. At first, Kaiser had been contemptuous of Nelson. Before joining the war effort, Nelson had been head of Sears & Roebuck Co. "I've got to go in and toss my idea at a man whose main concern heretofore was seeing that he ordered enough long johns to keep redneck America from freezing its crusty ass off."

Nelson lent Kaiser an attentive ear and "was mesmerized" at the prospect of the flying boat. After four hours of talks, Kaiser left Nelson's office with a tentative green-light for his project. Of course, more powerful authorities in the War Department, and eventually President Roosevelt himself, would have to okay such a massive undertaking in the middle of a war.

Elated, Kaiser flew back across America. By the time he was flying over the Rocky Mountain states, reality dawned. All the major aircraft companies in California, such as Lockheed or Boeing, were far too busy to undertake such a massive project, even assuming they would consider it. Before going to Washington, he had tentatively approached the head of both aircraft companies, only to be told that Hercules "was impossible to build—much less fly."

Kaiser needed a visionary in aviation. To him, there seemed only one man who met that criterion.

Howard Hughes.

"Nowhere else could Kaiser find such a daring fool—and with money to make up for the inevitable deficit as well," Dietrich later recalled with a certain bitterness.

***

Los Angeles, 1943-45

Back in Los Angeles, Kaiser found that locating Howard Hughes was a daunting challenge.

Howard's absence and refusal to return phone calls angered Kaiser. "I can get FDR on the phone any time I want him. Even Adolf Hitler, I am certain, will return my calls. But not the grand and almighty Howard Hughes."

Since Kaiser had as much money and even more influence than Howard, he merely called J. Edgar Hoover at the FBI. Perhaps Kaiser was aware that Hoover's G-men had already been trailing Howard.

Within forty-eight hours after launching his search for Howard, the FBI notified Kaiser that he was checked into a suite at the Fairmont Hotel in San Francisco. He'd been recently released from a hospital in the Bay Area, where he'd been registered under the name of Frank Lamorose. In the hospital, he'd been treated for a life-threatening case of pneumonia. The accumulated strains on his body had led to his collapse.

In spite of this, and even though some of his staff warned Kaiser that Howard "was a time bomb waiting to go off," he turned a deaf ear to their protests.

Finally contacted, Howard agreed to a meeting with Kaiser, as he admired his production of those Liberty Ships. Flying from Los Angeles to San Francisco, Kaiser studied the FBI's report more closely. There was a tantalizing bit of information at the end. Checked into an adjoining suite with Howard was an underage teenage actress, Faith Domergue. Howard was risking arrest, according to the report, by having sexual intercourse with this actress. Should she turn on him, Howard could be brought up on statutory rape charges like his sometimes lover, Errol Flynn, had been.

The coming together of the great Henry J. Kaiser and the potentially great Howard Hughes was a case of strange bedfellows from the very beginning.

When the sixty-year-old Kaiser barged into Howard's suite at the Fairmont, after finally setting up a meeting, he found him lying on a sofa. He was slumped over, his only suit, in funeral black, covered "in some sort of pink fuzz," as Kaiser recalled.

It was later revealed that Howard had just received his first blow-job in six weeks from his sixteen-year-old so-called fiancée, Faith Domergue. Both she and Howard had remained partially dressed for the act. She even kept her pink angora sweater on. After the act of fellatio, Howard took her in his arms and deeply kissed her, as she lay flat against his body. By so doing, he got pink angora all over his undertaker's suit. Since Kaiser had heard that Howard was an eccentric, he later told his aides, "I thought it was some kind of new fabric, all black but with tufts of pink angora—some awful style of men's clothing created by some faggot back in Los Angeles."

Not knowing that Howard was recovering from both a bout of pneumonia and fellatio, Kaiser, in his booming voice, shouted at him. "Get off your arse, my good man. There's a war to win. With your help, we'll win it together."

As a grand schemer himself, Howard might have been susceptible to Kaiser's *grandioso* scheme. To Howard's astonishment, Kaiser informed him that he'd promised the War Department that he'd deliver the first flying cargo ship in ten months. "That's too ambitious," Howard wisely cautioned the enthusiastic Kaiser. "It just can't be done."

One might have thought that Howard would be the dreamer, and that the producer of the Liberty Ships would be the more practical of the two men, but that was not the case. At one point, Howard bluntly told Kaiser, "You're a lunatic. Forgive me, but I don't know how to say that like a diplomat."

Perhaps Howard was simply too weak to resist that day. In spite of his better judgment, he began to warm to Kaiser's scheme. The tycoon's case was bolstered by a call from Odekirk at Hughes Aviation at Culver City. Kaiser had left his plans for Hercules with Odekirk and Howard's chief engineers. "I'm all for it!" Odekirk shouted into Howard's semi-deaf ears. "You and Kaiser were destined to meet. The two of you will make aviation history."

That last line must have appealed to Howard. More than anything, he wanted to be immortalized in the history of aviation. Before nightfall fell over wartime San Francisco, Howard agreed to design and build the Hercules' first prototype.

The next day, Howard's publicist, Russell Birdwell, made the astonishing announcement to the press that "500 flying boats will be launched, the most ambitious project ever undertaken in the history of aviation."

Dietrich was skeptical. "We'd have to take over a whole county in California just to build hangars," he said. "Then we'd have to cut down every tree in Canada."

Regrettably, the 500 Hercules flying boats winging supplies and personnel to Europe were but dreams to be dreamed.

When he returned with Faith to Los Angeles, he was driven immediately to Hughes Aviation. There in his offices, meeting with Odekirk and his engineers, he confronted the reality of what he had agreed to. When faced with the plans for Hercules, Howard almost had a nervous breakdown, according to Dietrich. Seeing the designs for Hercules for the first time made him realize that there was no way he'd ever be able to have the prototype ready in only ten months. Recalling the event years later, Faith maintained that at one point, Howard was seriously contemplating suicide.

"Why he ever signed a deal with Kaiser, and later with the War Department, to produce Hercules, I will never know," Dietrich said. "Up until he put ink to paper, I warned him that he was making the biggest mistake of his career— something that would tarnish his reputation forever."

Hercules would weigh 200 tons, making it three times heavier than "anything that had ever flown through the air, including a flotilla of flying dinosaurs." It would be capable of transporting 400,000 pounds of cargo as well as 700 fighting men and their equipment. Measuring 200 feet long, its wingspan would be longer than a football field. Its hull alone would be taller than a three-story building. This gigantic seaplane would be fitted with eight 3,000 horsepower engines. Since steel and aluminum were in short supply, Howard planned to make the controversial Hercules from the also controversial Duramold, as he had his D-2 prototype.

Howard was forced to build a mammoth hangar north of his existing plant to accommodate this flying ship. It towered 100 feet high, measuring 250 feet wide and 800 feet long, the largest wooden structure ever built. Dietrich was ordered to provide $1,750,000 of Toolco monies to pay for the construction cost.

Almost from the first week, Howard and Kaiser clashed over the design of Hercules. It quickly reached a point where neither man was speaking to the other, but exchanging messages through their assistants. Howard appointed Odekirk as his emissary to "The Kaiser's Henchmen," as he called them.

In Dietrich's words, in "a move bordering on insanity," Howard named his attorney, Neil McCarthy, as Hercules' Project Chief. "If you murdered someone, you called Neil," Dietrich said. "You didn't put him in charge of building the most preposterous aircraft ever conceived." Hoover's spies never found out that the project's chief executive had a fear of flying.

McCarthy spent far more time at the race track than he did at project headquarters in Culver City. Privately, he told Odekirk that the "Spruce Goose will fly when pigs have wings."

Both Odekirk and McCarthy were careful not to refer to the Hercules as the Spruce Goose. When one of his engineers did that in front of Howard, he fired him on the spot.

In his new post, McCarthy's chief value was to work out an agreement between Howard and Kaiser. Under the terms, Howard would have total authority over the design of the Hercules without interference from Kaiser. Once the prototype had been finalized and tested, Kaiser would be charged with production of the 500 flying boats.

In Washington, J. Edgar Hoover, through information gained from his spies within Hughes Aviation, kept Donald Nelson and the War Department informed of the ongoing chaos in Culver City. In a call to Nelson, Hoover claimed that the Hercules had run into serious trouble even before it got off the ground.

Coming to Howard's defense was Jesse Jones, head of the Reconstruction Finance Corporation. As a former close friend of Howard Sr., he had forgiven Howard Jr. for upsets he'd caused during his acquisition of the Constellation Stratoliners. In the middle of the war, he had more important matters to deal with—namely, overseeing the spending of government money on defense. Hearing of the difficulty Howard was experiencing from Kaiser, Jones fired off a warning note: "Hughes is a genius," he wrote the tycoon. "Let him alone to do his work. Would you stand over the shoulder of Leonardo da Vinci telling him how to paint the *Mona Lisa*?"

On November 16, 1942, a check for $18 million arrived at Hughes Aviation. Under the government's final dictate, three different prototypes of Hercules—not just one—were ordered, each for delivery within ten months.

In retrospect, it is amazing that the War Department would believe that such a commitment could ever be carried out. "Boeing, Lockheed, and Hughes with combined forces couldn't have supplied that god damn order," Odekirk said. "It made me feel that those folks at the War Department were so stupid they would lose the war for us."

The day the contract arrived, instead of ordering that production be speeded up, Howard retreated, as he did in time of emergencies, to 7000 Romaine Street. There in the privacy of his locked offices, he continued to edit *The Outlaw*, never quite satisfied with his work of the day before.

At Hughes Aviation, the ten month deadline for the delivery of three Hercules prototypes was rapidly approaching. Howard didn't even have one prototype of the vessel. Six million dollars of the allocated $9.8 million budget for the first prototype had already been spent, but the Spruce Goose was only a skeleton.

"I told Howard that we should count our blessings if we got the god damn Hercules delivered by Christmas of 1946, not 1944," Odekirk said. "He looked at me with glassy eyes. He didn't address our dilemma but informed me that he had a date that night with Ava Gardner. 'She's still getting the short stick from that runt, Mickey Rooney, even though they're divorced,' Howard told me. 'About time that bitch learns how a plowboy from Texas fucks. Down dirty and deep like my oil drill.'"

As months went by and it appeared obvious that Hughes Aviation was incapable of even manufacturing one prototype of Hercules, serious lobbying against Howard was going on in Washington. Pressure was being put on Donald Nelson, among others in the War Department, to cancel the contract granted to Kaiser and Howard.

According to his agreement with the War Department, Howard was "not to make one cent" from the Hercules until his design went into mass production.

The pressure from Wright Field in Ohio, and others, finally grew so intense that Howard's enemies in Washington prevailed. On February 16, 1944, H. Robert Edwards, the Defense Plant Corporation's resident engineer at Culver City, received an urgent message from the War Department. "All work as of five o'clock today, on Project Hercules, is to stop at once." Howard wasn't even notified. Neither was Kaiser.

When he heard the news, Howard immediately flew to Washington to lobby for Hercules. "Those assholes are making one shitty mistake—a big pile of it," he told Odekirk, who flew with him.

Arriving at the Washington airport, Howard was driven to the Carlton Hotel where he checked into the best suite. Instead of assigning assistants to save the Hercules, he planned to do the lobbying himself. First, he wanted to find someone to bribe. Neil McCarthy had come up with the name of Bennett E. Meyers. He was a balding, cigar-smoking executive in the Hollywood tradition of Darryl F. Zanuck. But as a major general, he had been placed as second in command of the War Department's Matériel Command Center.

"Meyers is your guy," McCarthy told Howard. "He's not against gratuities."

Over dinner at Meyers's apartment, the major general outlined a plan of attack whereby Howard could save Hercules. Only later did Howard learn that Meyers was one of the major figures who had initially blocked the government's purchase of his reconnaissance planes, which were also seriously behind in their production deadlines at Hughes Aviation.

Before dinner ended with brandy, Meyers told Hughes that "this war ain't gonna last forever." There was a slight suggestion that at war's end, he would "not object to being made head of Hughes Aviation." Raising an eyebrow, Meyers added, "If the price is right, of course."

Meyers intervened with Jesse Jones, who once again went to President Roosevelt to save Hercules. FDR didn't think that Hercules would be completed in time to be of use in winning the war. After all, he personally knew that Eisenhower was going to launch D-Day "at any minute" on the beaches of Normandy. Nevertheless, he thought that such a heavy craft might be of use in post-war America. He ordered Jones to see to it that the project was not canceled.

Meyers's intervention via Jones had saved the day. In 1945, as the war was ending, Meyers contacted Hughes for his reward. He wanted a three-year contract at $100,000 annually to run Hughes Aviation. Howard turned him down. But he didn't want to make an enemy out of Meyers, who still had enough influence to harm him. He instructed McCarthy to fly to Washington "to smooth things over with Meyers."

The meeting between McCarthy and Meyers was a disaster. In lieu of a job, Meyers wanted to borrow $2 million at no interest to purchase Liberty Bonds on a margin—"and maybe make millions." When Howard turned that counter offer down as absurd, Meyers lowered his request for a loan to just $200,000. Howard also turned that down.

Meyers was furious and threatened to expose Howard in a Senate investigation that he could personally launch, or so he claimed. Indeed, such an investigation would occur in a matter of months.

Howard blamed McCarthy "for fucking up the deal." Having worked against impossible odds in Washington and facing Howard's refusals at every attempt at compromise, McCarthy was deeply disappointed when Howard abruptly fired him. Howard blamed him for turning Meyers against him.

After "keeping Howard out of jail countless times," McCarthy was forced to submit his resignation on August 12, 1944. Meyers himself eventually ended up in prison for five years. He was charged with evading $61,000 in income taxes during the war and in enticing an employee to lie to a Senate Committee about Meyers's own involvement in defense contracts.

With the war coming to an end, Howard had spent all $18 million of the government's money, plus an additional $13 million out of his own pocket. Hercules was only half completed, and there was no guarantee that even when finished it could fly. Nonetheless, Howard ordered "full steam ahead on Hercules."

An investigation later revealed that Howard's project manager had been fired. Howard hadn't even bothered to replace him. Without a boss to supervise them, twenty-three of his engineers resigned, seeking more lucrative posts. Their quitting was a vote of "no confidence" for the much ridiculed Spruce Goose.

Finally, Howard hired a competent general manager, Edward G. Bern, who looked like a Presbyterian deacon about to attend the hanging of a witch. He'd been a former vice president of American Airlines and was all business. From the first, he was shocked at the lax management at Hughes Aviation. He immediately set about to "right all wrongs."

Within weeks he had the plant operating more efficiently. Even so, behind Howard's back, he fired off a letter to Donald Nelson in Washington. In it, he claimed that the engineers and mechanics at Hughes Aviation were "like a bunch of school kids doing business." He gave it to Nelson straight. "In my opinion, the Spruce Goose is doomed."

Learning of the letter, Howard bitterly denounced Bern. On the day of Bern's resignation, he told Howard, "Might as well use the Spruce Goose for firewood."

***

Los Angeles, 1942-43

On tobacco road in Brogden, North Carolina, the future "Barefoot Contessa," Ava Gardner, had walked the lonely red dirt paths of the poverty-laden South, watching out for rattlesnakes. Even at fourteen, her breasts had fully developed. She was ashamed of them and tried to conceal them behind a loose-fitting feedsack dress.

Soon those breasts would be partially responsible for launching her into a famous marriage with the puckish MGM star, Mickey Rooney, and into an infamous relationship with Howard Hughes that would sprawl messily across two decades.

But, first, she had to be discovered.

Her career was launched by an eight-by-ten glossy taken by her brother-in-law and placed in the window of a Fifth Avenue portrait studio in Manhattan. That photograph attracted hundreds of admirers, including a talent scout for MGM, who sent Ava and her sister, Beatrice ("Bappie") to Hollywood for a screen test.

In Hollywood, Ava's Tarheel drawl was so pronounced that her screen test was silent. Upon seeing it, Louis B. Mayer accurately summed up the starlet. "She can't act. She can't talk. She's terrific!"

The studio's reigning star, pint-sized Mickey Rooney, soon took notice of her and was impressed. When she first met him on a sound stage, she mistook him for Carmen Miranda, a natural mistake as he was in drag impersonating the flamboyant star from Brazil "where the nuts come from."

Four inches shorter than Ava, Mickey married her on January 10, 1942 when he discovered that he couldn't get into her pants by any other means. Later, he boasted that he was the man who took Ava's virginity. Early in their dysfunctional marriage, she revealed a violent streak. When Rooney would stay out drinking at night with his cronies—perhaps womanizing—Ava might be home slashing the furniture or draperies with a knife. In months to come, Howard himself would become a victim of her violence. When Rooney suggested raising a family, she told him, "If you get me pregnant, so help me God I'll kill you."

When not dreaming of aerial conquests, Howard still looked over the latest glossies of Hollywood starlets, an endless supply of pictures provided by Johnny Meyer. He stopped when he came across a sexy picture of Ava. This green-eyed beauty of feline grace and passionate intensity was not the love goddess that she was to become, but he saw something in her face and figure. She was fresh, an original.

Hollywood's leading "breast man," Howard himself, had been captivated by what he called her big tits. "Her knockers are right up there with the best of them," he told Meyer, "but not, of course, in the same league as Jane Russell's."

Ava's breasts had already been praised by Rooney himself, who proclaimed, "She has big brown nipples, which, when aroused, stand out like double-long, golden California raisins."

In addition to being an aficionado of 15-year-old virgins, Howard had an appreciation of "wet decks," his so often expressed appraisal of recently divorced women. In Ava's case, he didn't bother to wait for her divorce from Rooney to come through. With Linda Darnell, Gene Tierney, Lana Turner, and countless others already within his orbit, he didn't need another starlet in his harem. But no one could ever convince Howard of that.

Getting to Ava was easy. After firing Neil McCarthy, Howard had hired the handsome, dashing, and very masculine Greg Bautzer to replace him. At the time, Greg was the most brilliant and fast-rising lawyer in Hollywood. But he was known more for his action in the bedroom than in the courtroom. Joan Crawford, with whom he had the longest and most enduring relationship, remembered his "flashing smile that showed perfect teeth." A world-class connoisseur of men, Noël Coward, disagreed with her, claiming that Greg had too many teeth. Sultry Rita Hayworth claimed that Greg gave her "the most exciting sexual experience of my life." Merle Oberon, stealing a line from gay actor Billy Haines, said that Greg was a "combination of bull and butler," the latter a reference to how solicitous he was around women. Ginger Rogers found him "the perfect gentleman—and, unlike Howard, sane and logical when you're in legal trouble, but wild and passionate when the lights go out."

Greg lives today in Hollywood legend as the man who "deflowered" seventeen-year-old Lana Turner. She confessed, "I didn't enjoy it at all." She would later learn to enjoy it…again and again. Of Lana, Greg later told Howard, "I was breaking her in for you."

The attorney's latest conquest was Ava herself. When Howard expressed an interest in the starlet, Greg said he believed "in sharing the wealth." Those monthly paychecks from Howard meant he couldn't easily afford to say no to his boss. He arranged a meeting. In her memoirs, Ava claimed that a woman friend set up her first date with Howard. But that was not the case. It was her boyfriend, Greg. Ava wanted to be revelatory, but only to a point.

From the ruins of her marriage to Mickey, Ava had acquired $25,000 and a car. Meyer later said that that was the most money she'd ever had in her life, and "she felt rich as an heiress when I came to call on her."

At first Ava didn't understand why Howard himself hadn't shown up for their date. "I opened the door to find this ugly little toad, Johnny Meyer," she recalled. Meyer told her that Howard had to work late, but wanted her to have the flowers and candies he had resting in the back seat of his car. "Did you bring any booze, honey chile?" she asked.

As Tallulah Bankhead called everybody "dah-ling," Ava called everybody "chile."

Although he was not attractive, she found Meyer charming, and they "drank the night away," laughing and talking. She had no idea that Meyer's mission was to appraise her like a cow on the auction block. Faye Emerson had allowed her sexual techniques to be tested by Meyer, and by Howard himself, before her introduction to Elliott Roosevelt. That was not the case with Ava. "From the moment I first met her, I knew that sex was out of the question with her," Meyer said.

"That runt, Rooney, could never satisfy a statuesque beauty like Ava," Howard told Meyer the next day. "She'll be easy pickings."

How wrong he was. Ava would share her charms with countless actors and matadors, "but Howard Hughes never got my honeypot, chile" she once said.

The following night, Howard himself showed up. He was sloppily dressed, as was his custom. In contrast, Ava had both the makeup and wardrobe department at MGM prepare her for the evening. She looked more glamorous than she'd ever looked in a black strapless party dress that clung to her shapely figure. She wore a mink wrap, a gift from Rooney, and "just cuddled" into that fur when she went out with Howard.

At the time, she was the most minor of stars. Rooney had helped her get bit parts in films, but up to then she'd mostly been a decorative screen presence, getting mauled by the East Side Kids or ogled by Bela Lugosi. At MGM, she lived in the long shadows cast by Lana Turner, Hedy Lamarr, and Greer Garson.

Howard was immediately captivated by Ava's beauty, although she was years away from being voted "The Most Beautiful Woman in the World."

He found her voice "smoky and soothing but with a tongue so tart she sounds like a drunken sailor." He also didn't like that she'd obviously had several drinks before opening the door to him. Even so, he decided that to win a prize like Ava he could put up with a potty mouth and a potential alcoholic.

Over dinner on their first date, Ava thought that Howard was actually Howard Hawks, the director. Throughout half the dinner she referred to Howard as "Mr. Hawks."

Ava Gardner

Finally, he corrected her. "I'm Howard Hughes, not Howard Hawks."

She'd never heard of him. He told her that, like Hawks, he was a film director, too, and had directed *Hell's Angels*.

She claimed that she'd heard of the film but had never seen it. He invited her to 7000 Romaine Street the following evening where he said he'd screen it for her.

Since Howard was a director, she asked him if he'd cast her as the lead in one of his pictures. He promised her that he would. What he didn't tell her was that nearly a decade would go by before he'd cast her in the 1951 *My Forbidden Past* with Robert Mitchum.

As Ava launched herself into what evolved into virtually a platonic relationship with Howard, she knew from the beginning that he was bisexual. Perhaps Mickey Rooney had told her. He knew every Hollywood secret worth knowing. If not Rooney, then the handsome MGM actor, Peter Lawford, told her. While Rooney had been out with other starlets during the course of their marriage, Lawford had been secretly dating Ava. He once told her that Howard had made a pass at him but had been turned down.

In the days and weeks ahead, and much to the annoyance of Rooney and Faith Domergue, Howard and Ava were seen everywhere together. They showed up at formal dinners at the homes of producers such as Darryl F. Zanuck and Samuel Goldwyn. He drove her to a rented villa in Palm Springs; he took her on a shopping expedition to Mexico; he invited her dancing at Hollywood's Mocambo, and he flew her to the Plaza Hotel in Manhattan where they checked into separate suites. "After all that, and still no nooky," Howard told Meyer. "She does let me fondle her breasts while I jerk off, though."

Howard wanted to go everywhere with Ava. It was later revealed that she and her sister, Bappie, had been staying with him at the Desert Inn in Las Vegas the day he crashed his Sikorsky on Lake Mead. But most Hollywood gossips were unaware of that, having assumed that Howard hadn't met Ava until a year later.

Howard had little in common with Ava and nothing to talk about. "Neither one of them was what you'd call an intellectual," Dietrich said. "Ava had big boobies, and my boss was obsessed with big boobies. To my surprise, and I heard this from Howard himself, he never penetrated Ava. She wouldn't allow it. Why, I don't know. She let half the matadors in Spain stick their swords into her, and maybe a hundred actors in Hollywood. But not Howard."

Ava claimed that she was never sexually attracted to Howard, and that he "reminded me of my father." She found him a "no bull Texan. I was dating other guys on the side like Peter Lawford who was sexy, handsome, and debonair. In time, I took up with that Argentine Latin lover, Fernando Lamas. He was very well endowed. For a roll in the hay, honey chile, I preferred men like Lamas or Lawford—not skinny Howard."

She admitted that she was impressed with Howard's power "and he could get things done." When she and her sister, Bappie, wanted to fly to North Carolina to attend the funeral of their mother, Howard bumped two four-star generals off a TWA plane to make room for them. Before that, he'd obtained the services of the best cancer specialist in America to help her bed-ridden mother.

If Ava wanted to fly down to Mexico, a plane was put at her disposal. If she wanted a hotel suite, it miraculously appeared. If she wanted to go somewhere, a limousine was waiting at her door.

"Everyone in Hollywood just assumed that Howard was fucking Ava," Meyer said. "But Howard was getting it elsewhere."

Ava later revealed that after their tenth date, Howard had given her a light peck on the cheek. "He proposed marriage, but I told him I wasn't interested," she said. "He even told me he loved me. I told him I didn't love him. He said that he was a patient man and would wait for me to fall in love with him. He said it was inevitable that I would fall for him. I must say, Howard Hughes was one persistent man."

Howard's dating of Ava brought on an inevitable conflict with Faith. One morning as she was passing by his half-opened bedroom door, she heard him talking to someone on the phone. He was calling the other party, "Little Baby," a name Faith thought was reserved for her and her alone.

Over breakfast she confronted him. At first he was furious to learn she'd been eavesdropping on his private conversations. He lied, telling her that he'd been talking on the phone with Errol Flynn, advising him about legal and financial problems.

"Do you call Flynn, Little Baby?" she asked, bursting into tears. Blinded with rage, she ran from the room and into the rose garden out back.

Like Joan Crawford in another part of town, she attacked the rose garden with a vengeance. Instead of shears, she tore into the thorny bushes with her bare hands. In moments, her hands were bleeding profusely. Rushing out the back door, he found her in the garden, bleeding and screaming hysterically. "There's no one but you," he assured her as he wiped the blood off her hands with the long tails of his white shirt.

That night Howard excused himself to go work in the offices of 7000 Romaine Street, or so he said. Actually, he was escorting Ava to the night club opening of singer Frances Langford at the Cocoanut Grove. An hour later a call came into Muirfield for Faith. The name of the gossipy person who called her is not known.

Faith was told where Howard was and that he was escorting Ava. After having calmed down, she rose from her bed blazing with anger all over again. She raced for the garage. With bandaged hands, she got behind the wheel of an emerald green Cadillac that belonged to Toolco and drove all the way to the Cocoanut Grove Club. She waited across the street until the end of the Langford performance.

About fifteen minutes after the show, Howard emerged with Ava on his arm. A valet brought around his battered Chevy.

Faith trailed Howard's car as he drove away. By the time he'd reached Fairfax Avenue, he seemed to be aware that someone was following. Ava later revealed that he thought "it must be Hoover's men." Hoping to shake them, he speeded up. Seeing that, Faith floored the gas petal and stayed only feet from his car. When he stopped abruptly for a red light, she piled into the back of his Chevy.

She heard Ava scream. Putting the Cadillac in reverse, Faith backed up ten feet, then floored the gas pedal again, ramming into Howard's vehicle again. At that point, he jumped out of the car and ran toward the driver. Reaching into the car, he opened the door with one hand and yanked her from the vehicle with the other. Now she was the one screaming, as he slapped her violently and repeatedly, bloodying her nose.

At that moment, Sherman Fairchild, Howard's old friend, appeared in a Cadillac of his own. It was later learned that he was also following Howard. Fairchild and his date were going to join Ava and Howard for a late night of dancing at a club in Santa Monica.

Fairchild slammed on the brakes and jumped out of his car. Rushing up to Howard, he exchanged some words heard neither by Ava nor Faith. Fairchild quickly raced over to the Chevy's right side and door and rescued Ava. Shielding her, he put her into the back seat of his own vehicle and drove away into the night.

Holding a white handkerchief to Faith's nose to stop the bleeding, Howard then managed to get her inside the green Cadillac. She was sobbing hysterically. The hood of the car had been battered, but the sturdy vehicle was still in working order.

On the way home, Howard lied again, claiming that Ava meant nothing to him. "I'm going to cast her in a movie—that's all."

Still in love with Howard, Faith wanted to forgive him. Her career and the welfare of her family depended on that.

Her forgiveness would come at a price.

Later that night, after Howard had bathed the teenager and put her to bed, she sat up after he'd kissed her on the forehead.

"Go to bed," he cautioned her. "You've had enough excitement for one day."

As he headed out of her bedroom, she called to him. "I'm tired of all this shit talk about what a big star you're going to make out of me. Like buying me a studio and making me its queen—all that crap!" She sat up even higher in the bed. "I want to be a star. Now! Now! Now! Do you hear me? *Now!*"

* * *

Through Johnny Meyer, Howard had hired spies to keep tabs on his lovers, both male and female. But in matters associated with Ava, the security became so tight that his coterie of men became known as the "Howard Hughes Secret Police."

Frank Angell, a private dick like the type Humphrey Bogart used to play in 1940s movies, and an expert at photo surveillance and electronic bugging, was made personally responsible for checking on the whereabouts and activities of Ava. "No one gets fucked in this town but what Frank knows about it," Meyer said in recommending Angell to Howard.

Howard secured a house on Nicholas Canyon for Ava and her sister, Bappie Before they moved in, Meyer and Angell bugged the house. Howard ordered 24-hour security guards to stake out the property once Ava was in residence.

Even during the months of their stormy relationship when they were apart or angrily separated, Howard still wanted to know "who Ava is fucking." Over the years his spies delivered a long list of men, including such diverse personalities as Howard Duff, bullfighter Luis Miguel Dominguin, producer Robert Evans, David Niven, Porfirio Rubirosa, Omar Sharif, Robert Taylor, Robert Walker, Richard Burton, Clark Gable, Farley Granger, and Turkish actor Turhan Bey. Howard continued to have her trailed during her ill-fated marriages to bandleader Artie Shaw and especially to Frank Sinatra, whom Howard loathed. The feeling was reciprocal.

Slipping out the back door of her house one night disguised as a maid, Ava later changed into slinky night club clothing. She danced the night away at the Mocambo with a twenty-eight-year-old Mexican bullfighter, Lopez Rubio. "Lopez shared something in common with the bull," Ava later told her girlfriend, Lana Turner.

Tipped off by Angell, Howard arrived unexpectedly at Ava's house. He barged upstairs to find Rubio humping his prize, a pleasure that had been denied Howard himself. Fully erect, the bullfighter jumped from the bed. Having caught them, Howard was not prepared to take on such a muscular and impetuous young man.

He hurried down the steps to summon help from Angell and his men. Later, when they tried to enter Ava's bedroom, it was bolted. The matador had fled nude through Ava's backyard and onto a neighbor's grounds. "I'm sure the way that bull looked, he found another hot bed that night and proceeded to do what we were trying to do," Ava said. "After that incident, Howard went a week without calling. That suited me just fine. He still had me staked out, though. Sometimes I'd put on my nightgown and walk out in the middle of the night to confront Angell's boys. I'd make outrageous requests, like a demand to bring me a tub of orange ice cream. Do you know how hard it was to get orange ice cream in wartime Los Angeles? Angell's boys always delivered. They were good boys. It was just a job to them. They didn't like spying on me."

Home on Army leave, Rooney found Howard's battered old Chevrolet parked in front of Ava's newly rented house. As she later remembered it," a very tall and very lanky Howard exchanged fisticuffs that night with a very short Mickey jealously defending my honor. I forgot who pulled them apart. Somebody in the household. I would have let them fight and the best man win."

Ever since that night, Howard referred to Rooney as "a pygmy."

When Rooney later returned from military service, he secretly resumed dating Ava again, even though their divorce had been finalized. She went to great lengths to avoid Howard finding that out. It was Angell who discovered that Rooney was slipping in and out of Ava's back window, eluding detection by Howard's bodyguards.

One night she received a call from Meyer, informing her that Howard was arriving at the airport and wanted both of them to meet him. She told Meyer, "I'm busy!" She slammed down the phone. Actually she had a date with Rooney that night. Both had early calls the following morning at their studios. After dinner, each of them kissed at the restaurant and went back to their respective residences.

As she remembered it, it was about three or four o'clock in the morning when she woke up to find Howard towering over her bed. She flipped on a bedside lamp and "stared into the angriest face I'd ever seen on a beau." He'd let himself in with his passkey.

He was not only angry, but unfuriatingly jealous. Perhaps a little disappointed. He fully expected to catch her in the bed with Rooney making mad, passionate love. She ordered him from her bedroom, and told him she'd meet him downstairs when she was dressed.

About five minutes later, she discovered him sitting in an armchair looking like "he'd contracted a severe form of leprosy."

As she went to pour herself a drink, he grabbed her and spun her around, pushing her down in a hard wooden chair.

Like an out-of-control police sergeant drilling a murder suspect, he grabbed one of her wrists and held it down. With his right hand, he slapped her face, each blow growing harder and harder. She later said that it was "like he was trying to destroy my beauty." The blows continued to rain down on her, as she struggled to free herself. He held her in a tight grip. "I saw stars," she recalled. Her face was already swelling. She claimed that "my right eye felt permanently closed."

Although she would be beaten up by future lovers, such as George C. Scott, Ava at that point in her young life had never been attacked by a man. Finally, the blows from Howard stopped, as he seemed to get a grip on himself.

He walked away from her, heading for the door. Springing to her feet and "blind with rage," she picked up a mammoth, heavy bronze bell, an 18th-century antique imported from England. With all the power and fury a victim can sometimes summon, she hurled the bell at him.

He turned around just in time to feel the full impact of the bronze missile. It struck his face, digging a wound that spurted blood. The bell cut a zigzag slash from his right forehead to his lower lip, splintering his jaw. He stumbled backward and fell over an armchair before hitting the floor on his back. Prone, and in a helpless position, he was moaning from his wound like some beaten hound.

Even though she saw that she had inflicted what might have been a life-threatening injury, she was still not satisfied. She grabbed the wooden chair in which she'd been held during the beating. Picking it up with a strength she didn't know she had left in her, she moved menacingly toward him.

"Like Howard during his beating of me," she recalled, "I too lost self-control. In fact, I was fucking insane! In all my life, I've never been this mad, even during my marriage to Frank, and we had some knock-out fights. As I approached Howard, I planned to kill him. I wanted him not injured, but dead. A demonic side, one I didn't know I had in me, took over. I couldn't help myself. The Devil in me was driving me to murder. Tomorrow's headlines flashed before me: AVA GARDNER KILLS HOWARD HUGHES. What a field day that would be for the Hollywood jackals."

Just as she was ready to beat his bleeding, semi-conscious head into pulp, Bappie, her lover Charlie Guest, and her black maid, Sadie, ran into the room. Each of them had been awakened from their beds by the noise.

Sadie reached Ava first. "Ava! Ava! Ava! Drop it!"

"I was taken aback," Ava later said. "I know it seems absolutely ridiculous now. I was about to murder a man. But I suddenly developed a new anger directed not at Howard—but Sadie. She'd never called me Ava before. It was always Miss Gardner, or Miss Gardner ma'am. This momentary pause over this show of disrespect from Sadie was all the time that hefty gal needed to grab the chair from my arms."

"All I can remember at that point is looking down at the bastard writhing on the floor in all his pain," she said. "The white carpet around his head was covered in blood. I remember hearing Bappie in the hallway calling for an ambulance and Dr. Verne Mason. 'Howard Hughes is dying!' I heard her shout.

"Fuck you, bastard!" I said, looking down for one final time at Howard. His eyes were shut, and he wasn't moving. I thought he was dead. If he was dead, it wouldn't hurt him. With my one black eye and my bruised face, I kicked the fucker in the balls with a pair of my high heels. Then I turned and stormed from the room. Just as I was leaving, I turned and confronted Sadie. 'Don't you dare call me Ava again!'"

"Yes, ma'am," she said.

"With that grand exit," Ava claimed, "I left the woman-beater dead on the floor and headed upstairs to my bedroom. There I would spend the rest of the night inspecting my face. After all, it was my meal ticket, and Howard had tried to ruin it for me. When the ambulance came for him, it was determined that he was still alive. Bappie came to tell me the news. I didn't much care at that point."

The story never made the press. Howard told his "Little Baby," Faith Domergue, that he'd been in another car accident. She didn't believe him. "Get me that starring role in that god damn film, and get it now!" she shouted at him on the day of his release from the hospital.

He was not as concerned with her movie debut as he was with the partial dentures he'd have to wear for the rest of his life.

At the hospital where the ambulance had taken Howard, Dr. Mason had come to his rescue once again, sewing up his face. But he was growing increasingly disturbed about his famous patient. "Howard's going to get himself killed," he told "Dietrich. "I'm not a psychiatrist, but I'd say Howard is an addict."

"Is he on drugs?" a concerned Dietrich asked.

"No, he's addicted to psycho-drama," the doctor said. That was a new word to Dietrich's ears.

"He likes to tempt fate," Dr. Mason said. "Put himself in harm's way. Just how many times has he come almost close to dying? This is a strange thing for a doctor to say, but even a cat has only nine lives."

* * *

The violence ended Ava's relationship with Howard only temporarily. She fully expected to be dropped by him after she put him in the hospital. "I felt no remorse," she said.

Two months later, after his wounds had healed, he called her. She was shocked to be talking to him. "He asked me out on a date. I said, 'Didn't you get enough last time?'"

"Up to that night, I always thought of myself as a bit of a sadist like my Uncle Rupert," he said. "But you convinced me that around women I'm a masochist. Let's try it again—what fun!"

"After that, Howard and I became the longest running serial in town," she said.

In a few weeks, as if nothing had happened, Ava was dating Howard again, although "still not putting out," as he confided to Meyer.

To make amends for his fight with her, he flew Ava and Bappie in a private plane to Mexico for a holiday. At times he impulsively arranged to have the entire contents of a Beverly Hills florist shop delivered to her doorstep. Sometimes, he'd take her to a beach restaurant in Santa Monica, having hired a band and reserving every table for the night so they would have the dining room to themselves.

If she decided she wanted to go to Palm Springs, always bringing Bappie along, he arranged for a limousine to pick them up, drive them around the resort, and deposit them back at their doorstep in Los Angeles when they were ready to come home.

On more than one occasion, he reserved an entire TWA Constellation for her. When Ava landed in New York, a limousine was waiting to take her to an expensive suite at the Waldorf-Astoria. He opened charge accounts for her at all the leading department stores along Fifth Avenue, including one at Tiffany's.

When Bappie inquired about the propriety of all this, especially in lieu of her continuing refusal to sleep with him, Ava said: "He can afford it, honey chile. He owns all those oilfields in Texas that keep pumping, pumping."

After their brutal fight, Howard showed up one night with $250,000 in cash concealed in a shoe box from Sears & Roebuck. He offered her the money if she'd marry him. "You can't buy me, you bastard!" she shouted at him. She grabbed the shoebox from his hands and tossed the hundred-dollar bills around the living room. Angered, he stormed out. But she noticed that before she got out of the bed the next morning, he had sent Johnny Meyer over to retrieve the cash loot.

She later confessed, "I was never in love with Howard. Nor did I fancy him sexually. Not my cup of tea, honey chile. I knew about all those other girl-friends. It didn't bother me at all. Howard had to get it from somebody. He sure wasn't getting it from me."

She claimed that at the time Howard was dating her, he was keeping at least five other starlets stashed away in the Hollywood Hills. "Often Howard didn't even visit these lonely damsels," she said. "Most of his so-called romances took place in his mind. His sexual ambitions were always greater than his prowess."

Meyer was too busy to arrange housing for all these starlets. Howard hired the soft-spoken Charlie Guest as his "concierge." Guest immediately took a liking to Ava, but in the wake of his recent divorce, he fell in love with Bappie. Soon he was living with Ava and Bappie.

Ava later recalled him as a "sweet-natured alcoholic." Sometimes the two of them, much to the annoyance of Bappie, would go on drinking binges together. It was during one of those confessional drinking bouts that Guest revealed to Ava the story of what he called "Howard's stashes."

Unlike most of Howard's bimbo girlfriends, Ava was no longer "the cute little bitch who fell off the turnip truck from North Carolina." She knew that Meyer haunted Union Station during the day looking for the prettiest girl who got off the train, arriving in Hollywood and dreaming of stardom. Ava estimated that at any given time Howard had "five beauties stashed away in a house Guest rented." But, she noted, "many of those starlets never got movie contracts or Howard's dick. He fancied himself Casanova or the Sultan of Zanzibar, but he was far from that."

Guest might have told Ava that there were five beauties, but Dietrich disputed that. "At any given time Howard had at least ten starlets stashed away. I should know, because I was paying the rent for all of them. At Howard's peak capacity, he had twelve starlets on the leash. Of course, getting around to bed all these gals was another matter. No woman ever called Howard a good cocksman."

"Ava was a prick teaser," Meyer later claimed. "She kept accepting things from Howard like free rent and free airline tickets, but she continued not to put out. Howard was determined to change that. He had to go to San Francisco to meet Henry Kaiser about the Spruce Goose, and he planned to take Ava with him. Up in San Francisco, he planned to force her to marry him, although he didn't tell me how he'd do that. I remember his exact words, 'I want a taste of that Tarheel pussy, and I'm gonna get it.'"

Ava accepted his invitation and departed with Howard aboard the *Santa Fe*. For some reason, he chose to take a train instead of flying.

Ava later admitted she had no idea what Howard was up to. Before boarding the train, Bappie had suspected that Howard was going to ask Ava for her hand in marriage. Bappie's parting words to Ava were, "Marry him, honey. He's the richest man in the world. He'll give us anything." Ava noted that her sister said "us" and not "you."

On the *Santa Fe*, he'd booked two adjacent cabins. When he tried Ava's door, and couldn't get in, he complained, "I'm a Southern gentleman. You don't have to lock me out."

She agreed to meet him in the bar where iced French champagne, a great luxury for a nation at war, arrived unexpectedly in an ugly wrapper. Ava believed she'd never looked more glamorous. "Irene," the doyenne of couture at Metro, had "turned me into a vision of loveliness." Her smartly tailored navy suit was trimmed in black mink. She even wore embroidered black hosiery, almost unavailable because of wartime shortages.

"Suddenly, Howard appeared in the bar of the rail car, and I almost died," she claimed.

He was dressed in an ice cream suit, evocative of one of those Princeton boys depicted in the literature of F. Scott Fitzgerald in the early 1920s. She called his outfit "frat boy pants," held up by a paisley tie in eight shades of pink and red.

To her continuing embarrassment, he pirouetted around the center of the bar in front of everybody "like a god damn mannequin," she recalled. "The passengers must have thought he was a homosexual beanpole. I had to finish off the rest of that champagne to brace myself for that ordeal. I'd heard stories about Howard and the boys. Now I saw in front of my eyes that he had a side to him I'd never seen before. He was a fucking dancing faggot."

What she didn't know at the time was that her suitor was beginning to show serious signs of a major nervous breakdown, as his hearing waned and "dark clouds (as Dietrich claimed) hovered in his brain."

Too drunk to care any more about Howard's dress or gay antics on the train, Ava arrived in San Francisco where she found that Howard had booked them in the most lavish suite in town. She'd been assigned the master bedroom, and he had a small maid's room across the hall. "I felt like the queen of Nob Hill," she said.

Later that afternoon he took her on a shopping binge, delivering her to the city's most elegant store with instructions "to buy it out if you want to. I'll be back later to settle the bill."

She remembered being tempted by a sable coat and especially by some expensive jade, a gem she adored, but she decided not to take advantage of him.

Waiting outside the store for an hour, she spotted him walking toward her with an ugly cardboard box wrapped in a red ribbon.

Back in the hotel suite, he left the box sitting in the living room as he went and dressed in his one dark suit for dinner at an elegant restaurant. She wore a dress that had originally been tailored for Lana Turner at MGM. At the restaurant, he ordered his typical butterfly steak, Ava preferring Southern fried chicken. Later he "bear hugged" her across the dance floor before inviting her to attend a transvestite show where he often took Cary Grant when they descended together on San Francisco.

She had never seen men dressed in drag before. She was mesmerized, but not as much as Howard. He was as addicted to drag shows back then as he would be to morphine later in life.

At the gay club, the star of the show as a very attractive young blonde who called himself (herself?) "Pussy-Katt." Recognizing her famous guests, she came over at the end of her performance. Right in front of Ava, she plopped down on germ-obsessed Howard's lap and gave him a "sloppy wet kiss on his mouth," Ava claimed. "Later on I hung out with half the gay men in the world, but back then I was still a little girl from Tobacco Road. I was somewhat taken aback. When Howard first took me into the club—it was called Finocchio's—I at first thought all the beautiful performers were real women."

At some point Howard went backstage, where Ava assumed he exchanged contact numbers with Pussy-Katt. "The drag bitch was prettier than me," Ava said, "and I was the beauty of MGM."

Back at the Fairmont, it was four o'clock in the morning, and the staff had delivered the Sunday papers to their suite. News of the war didn't interest Ava. She picked up the funnies instead and began to read on the sofa.

He wanted to lure her with champagne and romance, but she preferred to find out what Brenda Starr was doing. Suddenly, he ripped the funnies from her hands, stomping on them.

"You fucking asshole!" she shouted at him. Fearing another fight and more violence, she ran to the master bedroom and bolted the door. He did not try to break it down. Ominously, there was no sound coming from the living room of the suite at all.

It was about ten o'clock Sunday morning when she heard a loud pounding on her door. Thinking at first it was Howard trying to get in, she heard Bappie calling to her. It turned out that Howard, in anger, had flown back to Los Angeles and had put Bappie on a plane to San Francisco to retrieve her.

She urged Ava to get dressed, claiming that he had a private plane waiting to take them back to Los Angeles.

Once dressed, Ava came into the living room to find Bappie opening the mysterious cardboard box. "You were a fool," Bappie told her. "Howard went to Tiffany's. There is exactly one-million dollars worth of jewelry in this box. He was going to give you this stupendous gift and ask you to marry him last night before you acted up."

"I want to be in love," Ava shouted at Bappie. "I can't be bought for a box of jewelry."

Bappie held up gem after gem with awe. Rubies, diamonds, emeralds. One diamond-studded gold bracelet that she dangled before Ava "weighed a ton" in her sister's words. Instead of accepting the box, Ava left the gems in the hotel safe marked HOWARD HUGHES.

She penned a quick note to Howard. "You can take your gems and shove them where the sun don't shine!"

In London, years later, Ava recalled that "my young, stubborn Tarheel temper came out. I was a fool. There was a king's ransom Howard was offering me. That jewelry could have kept me for the rest of my life."

Without the gift, and with no money left from her Hollywood earnings, Ava would, much later in her life, be forced to accept at least a million dollars in charity from Frank Sinatra, her former husband.

"Marriage to Howard would never have worked," she recalled. "The sight of all those pretty boys at Finocchio's in San Francisco got to him like no mere woman ever could. He wanted the mock—not the real thing. He told me that

Pussy-Katt, the star of the show, looked good enough to fuck. I assume a pussy-cat lay in Howard's future. That's *lay*, honey chile."

* * *

Mexico City, 1940

From Mexico City, Tyrone Power called Howard and invited him to fly down to join him for a few days during his remake of the bullfight melodrama, *Blood and Sand*, by Blasco Ibáñez, that had brought such fame to Rudolph Valentino as a silent film star.

In spite of his wartime aviation production, Howard dropped everything and flew to meet with Tyrone, who was in Mexico City with his wife, the French actress, Annabella, whom he'd married in 1939. Theirs was a lavender marriage of convenience, evocative of Barbara Stanwyck's bond to Howard's other lover, Robert Taylor.

Howard had already had several talks with studio chief Darryl F. Zanuck about *Blood and Sand*. The cigar-smoking producer had wanted to borrow "your big tit broad," a reference to Jane Russell, to play the female lead, the Spanish beauty, Doña Sol, in the film. To get Russell to portray the temptress, Zanuck at one point offered Howard $35,000 a week for her services. Since he was paying his star only $50 a week, that would have been a tidy profit for Howard. But he still turned down the offer, since he wanted to control Jane's career personally. He also wanted the American public to see her on the screen for the first time as Rio in *The Outlaw* and not in some Zanuck production which Howard couldn't control.

After losing Jane, director Rouben Mamoulian was forced to test three dozen actresses before settling on Rita Hayworth, whom he'd borrowed from Harry Cohn at Columbia. Howard may or may not have known Rita when she was Margarita Cansino dancing in border towns with her incestuous father, Eduardo. Rumors still persist that Howard seduced Rita in Mexico when she was only a teenager.

Flying to the set of *Blood and Sand* in Mexico City with Johnny Meyer, Howard hired a Mexican chauffeur to drive him to the film's location. He was ushered into Tyrone's dressing room where the two sometimes lovers warmly embraced. When he broke away from Tyrone, Howard carefully checked out the actor's matador costume. In the film, he'd been cast as Juan Gallardo, the bull-fighter.

Howard appraised the costume as carefully as he'd evaluated Jane Russell's breasts through his camera lens. "Bullfighters are supposed to show their cock and balls," he told Tyrone. "You're showing a concave down there."

"I'm wearing a jock strap," Tyrone protested. "Orders of Zanuck personally."

"Valentino showed basket in *Blood and Sand*," Howard reminded him.

"For me, it's a no, no." Tyrone said. "Besides, from what I hear, I don't have as much as Valentino."

Howard kissed Tyrone again. "Sweet bottoms don't need big dicks."

He was very disappointed with his friend's *traje de luces*, claiming that all that embroidery and beading made Tyrone look fifty pounds heavier. "You'll photograph paunchy." Devastated by the critique, Tyrone feared Howard was right. To save the day, Howard and his chauffeur drove Tyrone and him to the best maker of bullfight costumes in the city. There, at his own expense, Howard ordered the designer to come up with a more flattering *traje de luces* for the star.

Howard was right in ordering new costumes for Tyrone. In New York months later, the film critic of *The Herald Tribune* wrote that Tyrone's "fans will become delirious with pleasure at the figure he cuts with his hosts of costumes."

Another male critic, perhaps gay, got even more carried away with Tyrone's handsome, dashing appearance in the films. "In spite of the charms of Miss Hayworth and Miss Darnell," he wrote, "their beauty pales the moment Tyrone Power in toreador pants comes onto the screen. He's not a serious threat to the bulls but a menace to the ladies in the audience."

A tender moment between Howard and one of the supporting players came the following morning. Howard walked over to knock on the door of Nazimova, the former queen of MGM. In *Blood and Sand*, the once grand diva of Hollywood had been cast as Tyrone's scrubwoman mother. Howard knew of the involvement, perhaps romantic, between his father and Nazimova in the heady days of Hollywood in the early 1920s. To honor that long-ago friendship, he presented the faded star with a gold bracelet studded with diamonds and rubies. She burst into tears of gratitude.

The next afternoon, Howard ordered his pimp, Johnny Meyer, to accompany him on a cruise of Mexico City. "I might find some new talent to audition," he told Meyer. "After Tyrone last night, I want something young and virginal." At a private club where Meyer had taken his boss to watch "exhibitions," Howard confided to

Tyrone Power

578

him that "the sex was better than ever. Errol's taught him a lot. Tyrone is the only man I've ever known who can reach a climax while you're chomping down on his nipples. Clark Gable can't do that."

"So, at last, I know what went wrong in the sack between Gable and you," Meyer said. "The King didn't like you working on his nipples."

Tyrone's wife, Annabella, though staying with him in Mexico City, was never introduced to Howard. Meyer suggested that Annabella must be pursuing her own pleasures with some señorita, while her husband shot his movie.

Howard learned that Tyrone hadn't been lonely before Howard's visit. The bisexual actor was carrying on a torrid affair with his co-star, Rita Hayworth. "It won't last beyond the picture," Tyrone told Howard and Meyer. "I've already got Betty Grable in my sights when I go back to film *A Yank in the R.A.F.* with her."

"What about Linda Darnell?" Howard asked. "She's a beauty and only nineteen, I hear."

"Funny you should ask," Tyrone said. "Just yesterday she was asking me if she could meet *the* Howard Hughes."

"Arrange it!" he commanded Tyrone, as if the actor were part of his hired help like Meyer.

Howard would not meet Linda until the following evening. A previous invitation came from a bullfighter known only as Armillita. Mexico's leading matador at the time, he'd been hired by Zanuck to perform the bullfighting scenes for Tyrone in *Blood and Sand*.

The matador had invited both Howard and Tyrone to watch his dressage ceremony. Arriving in his dressing room, Armillita confronted them stark naked. Glancing down at his nudity, he asked, "Do you think my fans will be able to distinguish between me and the real bull?"

Both men laughed nervously as they watched the heavily endowed matador stuff himself into his "suit of lights." His dresser carefully arranged the bullfighter's genitals. "It's their job," he said, winking at Howard and Tyrone. Looking down at the dresser, he said, "That's why *mariposas* are always attracted to the job of dresser."

That afternoon, at Mexico City's Plaza de Toros, some 30,000 spectators turned out to watch Armillita fight the bull in front of Zanuck's cameramen. That was the largest crowd ever assembled to watch a movie scene being shot.

Hours later Tyrone invited Linda Darnell to join Howard, Meyer, and himself for dinner at the city's most exclusive Mexican restaurant. There, Howard had arranged to have a private band serenade them—"only love songs," he'd instructed the musicians.

Wearing a black lace gown with plunging *décolletage* and a mantilla from Seville that showed off her creamy breasts, the sultry nineteen-year-old brunette, Linda Darnell, walked into the dining room on the arm of Tyrone Power. All heads turned to look at these dazzling young stars of 20th Century

Fox. Tyrone led her over to the table where Howard and Meyer stood up to greet her.

"At long last we meet," Linda said, extending her hand to Howard and ignoring Meyer.

"My pleasure has long been overdue," he said. "Your costume is beautiful."

She glanced down at the exposed part of her breasts. "I haven't seen *The Outlaw* yet, but from what I've seen of those publicity stills for Russell, I don't think I can compete."

"You're a worthy contender," he assured her before inviting her to take the seat of honor at his table.

* * *

Born in Dallas, Texas, in 1921, Linda was already being hailed as the "Glory Girl" of Hollywood when she was introduced to Howard. At 20th Century Fox, she was known for her beauty, not her acting skills. Her life as a teenager read like a cliché-ridden, ghost-written, movie star autobiography.

Born to a postal clerk of pioneering stock, she'd been pushed into show business through her ambitious, stage-struck mother. At the age of five, she was sent to learn tap dancing. "I never mastered it like my future best friend, Ann Miller," Linda recalled, "but I could have given that little bitch, Shirley Temple, competition if given a chance."

At 14, she was a photographer's model, and a hatted photograph of her at the age of 15 reveals looks that were mature for her age. Winning a "Gateway to Hollywood" contest at the age of 16 led to a screen test at RKO in 1937. That didn't work out, but Darryl F. Zanuck "saw something" in Linda. By 1939 he'd cast her as the lead in *Hotel for Women*, which gave her star billing over such established stars as Ann Sothern, Lynn Bari, Jean Rogers, Joyce Compton, and even the doyenne of the social world, Elsa Maxwell.

Before meeting Linda, Howard, based solely on her photographs, told Meyer that Linda had "dark, lustrous hair just like I like it. Blondes are a some-times thing. Blondes are like eating rattlesnake in Texas. You don't do it every day."

As the dinner progressed, Howard began to realize that Linda wasn't the inexperienced virgin he'd at first assumed. Nor was she the bitter, disillusioned alcoholic she would become. In later years, she was given to making pro-nouncements like, "I've got more balls than most men do. If there's anything I hate, it's a weak man."

Her director, Henry Hathaway, who'd guided her through *Brigham Young—Frontiersman*, in 1940, also starring Tyrone Power, had found her the "sweetest gal who ever lived."

Howard also found her sweet but not virginal like his own discovery, Faith Domergue—nor as young as Faith who had been only fifteen as opposed to

580

Linda's "more mature" nineteen.

Before Linda came to the table, Meyer, who knew every sordid detail about Hollywood, told his boss that she was "sleeping with that chicken farmer, Mr. Marlene Dietrich." He was referring, of course, to Marlene's much neglected husband, Rudolph Sieber. "Marlene's a tough act to follow," Howard said in response.

When the waiter served Linda a platter of beef with too many fiery red peppers, she yelled "Fiddledeedee" when tasting it.

"You must have learned that from Scarlett O'Hara," Tyrone said.

"It's my favorite cussword," she said.

By the time she was eating her second order of flan, and was deep into her third margarita, she pointedly asked Howard, "All evening you've been looking at my eyes, although I dressed to display my breasts which I thought you'd be devouring with your eyes. Did you get tired of breasts while editing *The Outlaw*?"

"I'll never tire of them," he said. "But I find your eyes liquid. Like those of a fawn. I noticed last week that Louella Parsons called you an American Cinderella. That true?"

Linda Darnell

"If it is," she said, sliding over on the red leather banquette to get closer to him, "I've met my Prince Charming."

"After that little bit of dialogue," Meyer later said, "Linda was practically all over Howard. Touching him everywhere. Putting sugar in his coffee. She wanted my boss, and I knew before the night was over she was gonna get him too."

Over coffee, Linda confessed that in the Thirties Tyrone had been her favorite movie star. "I had a crush on him. Wrote him fan letters. Collected all his pictures in newspapers and magazines. Stole publicity shots of him from displays at the movie theater."

In his usual undiplomatic way, Howard asked: "You two making it in the sack?"

"Not at all," she said. "I made a pass at him when we made *Daytime Wife* for Fox last year. Tyrone told me, 'I'm a married man.'"

"Since when did that stop Ty?" a drunken Meyer asked. Looking at the actor, he said, "I hear you give it away to anybody who asks."

"Why not?" Tyrone said defensively. "They're curious. They want to see what I'm like in bed. When their curiosity is satisfied, we can be friends."

Quickly changing the subject, Howard said, "I think Zanuck is right to keep teaming you two, referring to Linda and Tyrone. "You're the perfect complement to each other. With that dark hair, sex appeal, beauty, and a certain sultry quality, you're evenly matched. I saw you in *The Mark of Zorro*. You two photograph beautifully together."

Linda amused the men at her table by telling how she was called into Zanuck's office her first day on the lot. "He talked to me for ten minutes about my career and its possibilities. Then he called me over to his desk. He pushed his chair away and exposed himself to me. He must have been playing with himself. 'How's that?' he asked me. 'The biggest whopper in a town of whoppers.' I told him that I was impressed, thanked him for the preview, and asked him to put it away."

Howard took Linda away for the weekend. He never told Meyer or Tyrone where because he wanted to shake them. But he was rhapsodic when reporting later to both Meyer and Tyrone about Linda's charms. He said that he planned to add her to "his stable of fillies."

He claimed that he'd taken a bath with her. "I feasted on her melons before tasting juices a little farther down. Thick, sweet nectar as only teenage pussy can be. Just a slight hint of apricot of all flavors. I went down and deep until I found just what I was looking for."

"What, pray tell, was that?" Tyrone asked.

"You stick to cocksucking," he told him. "You never did like to eat pussy. But I do. I call myself *Surelick* Holmes. I fanned that kid's fires. We spent the rest of the weekend heaving and gyrating."

In the future, other lovers would not give as flattering a report about Linda in the boudoir. Joseph Mankiewicz, who directed her in the memorable 1949 *A Letter to Three Wives*, once said, "I don't even think she knew who was on top of her."

Howard reiterated his view that Linda and Tyrone might become the most celebrated screen team of the 1940s. "Two dark-haired beauties," he said. "Sexy with lush contours. Where either of you need curves, you've got them in lush dimension. Although the camera regrettably can't show it—maybe one day— you've got a beautiful cock. She's got beautiful breasts. Both of you have silky pubic hair in the exact same shade. It's as if you were twins."

* * *

Bel Air, 1944

Nadine Henley had become Howard's private secretary in October of 1944. A few weeks after she was hired, he called her into his library where he was staring into the dying ashes of his fireplace. He had not shaven in days. "There was a wild look about him," she later said. "I was a little bit afraid of him. I'd

582

heard so many stories about how eccentric he was."

Noah Dietrich had called that morning, a really urgent call, and had demanded to speak to Howard. He refused to take the call, and he always took Dietrich's calls. "Mr. Dietrich was infuriated," Nadine said. "After getting him on the phone for decades—at any time of the day or night—Mr. Dietrich wasn't allowed to speak to Mr. Hughes."

Nadine claimed that she sat there in the library for almost thirty minutes with her pad in hand to take dictation. Not a sound came from him. His eyes never left that fireplace. "At one point, I asked him if he wanted me to put on another log."

"No," he finally said. "I want to see the last dying ember burn out."

"And that's what we did," she said. "We sat there without speaking until the fireplace had turned cold. Then he told me that he'd brought me into the library to dictate his last Will & Testament. My first suspicion was that he was going to commit suicide."

When he started to dictate, she was astonished at his words. It sounded like no Last Will & Testament she'd ever typed.

"It has suddenly come to my attention," he said in his soft but high-pitched voice, "that I am being treated unfairly by the War Department, by the executives of the Hughes Tool Company in Houston, by Ava Gardner, by Faith Domergue, and by Noah Dietrich. Therefore, as a final gesture to them, I choose to grant each of them a final bequest of one U.S. dollar."

To her astonishment, he repeated these exact words to her four times.

Very gently, she said, "Mr. Hughes, you are repeating yourself."

He looked up at her. "It cannot be," he said. "I never repeat myself." As if realizing that he was repeating himself, he broke into uncontrollable sobbing and demanded that she leave the library.

In the hallway, she called Dr. Verne Mason, hoping he could inject her boss with something to make him feel better.

It took about half an hour for Dr. Mason to drive to Bel Air. She took his arm and directed him to the library. Once there, she knocked on the door. No answer. She tried the knob, finding the door locked. Repeated knocks and calls to Howard produced no result.

Going around to the back of the house, Dr. Mason, with Nadine looking on, found a window open. He crawled inside the library.

Howard was nowhere to be seen.

"For eleven months, Mr. Hughes just disappeared from the planet," Nadine claimed.

CHAPTER SIXTEEN
Las Vegas, 1944-45

Although World War II was still raging in both Europe and the Pacific, Howard was convinced that the Allies would ultimately triumph over Germany and Japan. During sleepless nights, he became obsessed with the vision of his flying cargo boats as key elements in the war effort, hauling a vast tonnage of personnel and supplies across the Atlantic to the battlefields of Europe. His reconnaissance planes, as he once boasted to Glenn Odekirk, would keep America informed "every time Hitler went to take a piss." Regrettably, production was chronically slow at Hughes Aviation, and the prototypes for both the flying cargo boat and the D-2 reconnaissance plane were far from ready even for test flights. As a faint light appeared at the end of the wartime tunnel, Howard was haunted with the realization that he'd lost an amazing opportunity to become a key industrial player in the greatest drama in the history of the world.

He feared failure. More than that, he lived in daily dread that he'd become the laughing stock of America, a disgraced aviation hero once worshipped by millions of adoring fans.

"He developed the worst case of the shakes I've ever seen," Dietrich said. "He couldn't control his hands. Not wanting people to see that he was coming apart, he hid his hands in his pockets."

That didn't solve the problem. He developed a plainly visible nervous tick. He couldn't keep food down, not even his favorite butterfly steak and peas. If he managed to force food down his throat, he'd vomit shortly thereafter.

His trusted friend, Glenn Odekirk, had began to doubt that Howard could continue to direct Hughes Aviation. His decisions became so erratic and preposterous that behind his back, Odekirk sometimes rescinded his orders after Howard had issued them.

He began plotting a move to take a plane into the air and literally disappear from the face of the earth. "A flight to nowhere," he eerily told Odekirk. The low point came when Howard asked Odekirk to fly with him in a plane out into the Pacific. Howard wanted to nose-dive the plane into the ocean, disappearing into the murky depths.

"But I want to live," Odekirk protested. "I enjoy my life. My work. My family. You should find yourself some beautiful gal. Make her your wife. Settle down. Quit taking on jobs like these impossible orders from the War Department. You've got money. Everything. You shouldn't be experiencing this kind of living Hell!"

Odekirk reported that when he said that, Howard broke down in front of him. Sobbing, he held his friend in a tight grip, begging him to escape with him. "We'll disappear into the desert together, instead of the ocean."

"Howard, I don't want to run away to the desert," Odekirk said. "I'm needed here. There's a war on. You're needed too. This is no time for a vacation."

Suddenly Howard turned vicious, perhaps out of fear that he'd shown weakness. "Fuck you!" he said. "I don't need you. I've got friends who are more loyal than you. Joe Petrali, for instance. He'd do anything for me, go anywhere I tell him to. You've let me down." He stormed out of Odekirk's office. Odekirk became afraid that Howard was going to fire him that day, but he didn't. Instead, Howard just disappeared, without a word, even to Noah Dietrich, about where he was going and when he planned to return.

When Dietrich heard that Howard was missing, he at first assumed that one of Howard's worst ongoing fears had been realized: he'd been kidnapped.

Confusingly, the rebuilt Sikorsky, the one Howard had salvaged from the bottom of Lake Mead, was not in its hangar, and could not be accounted for, having disappeared during the early hours of the morning before the workers showed up for the day. Upon further investigation, Dietrich then learned that two of the staff members at Hughes Aviation had also disappeared: Joseph (Joe) Petrali and Richard (Dick) Beatie.

Finally, a guard at Hughes Aviation revealed that he had spotted Howard, accompanied by Beatie and Petrali, climbing into the cockpit and flying into the early dawn, heading eastward toward the rising sun.

Thus began one of the strangest chapters in Howard's life, and it's still relatively unexplained today.

The gossip at the time involved the theory that Howard had embarked on a secret mission for the U.S. Government, and that he'd been entrusted with some dark plan that might win the war for the Allies. In later years, after atomic bombs had been dropped on Japan, hastening the end of the war, the rumor emerged that Howard was heroically testing the planes that would carry the deadly bombs into Japanese airspace.

That false rumor still persists in some quarters. The truth is much different and far less dramatic.

Odekirk later admitted, "Howard had become completely unglued. He couldn't stay in California any more. He didn't want people to see him getting crazier by the minute. He feared he'd be committed to some asylum. He told me he was having nightmares about getting locked up. All night he claimed he heard the sound of cell doors banging shut. In one of his worst scenarios, he said that he'd dreamed that J. Edgar Hoover had him locked up in a cage like you'd find in a circus holding some dangerous animal. In this dream, Howard said he was stripped of all his clothes, put in that cage, and driven through the streets of all the major cities of America so people could mock him and toss rotten, germ-infested food at his cage. My boss was in real bad shape."

Faith Domergue later expressed her belief. "He didn't tell me where he was going or when he'd come back—or even *if* he'd come back. I cried my eyes out night after night. Finally, I became convinced that Howard had to leave the world temporarily—all that wartime production, all those lawsuits, even those who loved him. I guess you'd call it 'finding yourself.' No one will ever really know how tormented he was during that period. By the third month, I came to believe he was dead somewhere. I pictured his corpse lying in some Nevada desert, the buzzards having devoured the flesh before it rotted!"

***

Howard never formed any particularly close bond with Dick Beatie. It's believed that he was chosen to fly away with Howard only because a third man was needed.

In contrast, a strong bond had formed between Howard and Joe Petrali, most of it forged during the long months it took to rebuild the Sikorsky after its retrieval from its grave at the bottom of Lake Mead. Joe had spearheaded its reconstruction. Sometimes he'd be with Howard in one of the hangars at Culver City, accompanied only by a security guard, until three or four o'clock in the morning. Joe never revealed the degree to which a sense of intimacy had formed between the two men at that time. But Dietrich observed that Joe, at least temporarily, had replaced Glenn Odekirk as an emotional anchor in Howard's life.

Joe Petrali, or "Smokin' Joe" as his friends called him, did not have a pretty face. Errol Flynn, who had met him briefly, called him "a dime-store version of Humphrey Bogart."

Howard, along with many other men of his era, had been fascinated by Smokin' Joe's exploits. From around 1925 until deep into the 1930s, he was respected as America's finest motorcycle racer. You name it—board track racing, hillclimbs, speed records, dirt track—Joe was the champ. When he first met Howard, he was a genuine hero, having won a highly impressive total of 49 AMA national championship races. Today, Joe's name also continues as a footnote in the history of aviation, as he was the flight engineer during the infamous only take-off of the Spruce Goose in 1947.

Joe was a year older than Howard, although his birth certificate had been lost in the 1906 San Francisco earthquake. That presented a problem for Hughes Aviation, since it would have helped in the procurement of Joe's security clearances.

Later, Odekirk offered some of his own theories about what had motivated

Howard. "I believe that somehow he had connected the restoration of the Sikorsky to his own rejuvenation. Maybe he figured that in the same way that Joe Petrali had restored the ruined airplane, he could also restore life and vigor to Howard. I know that doesn't make sense, but that was my belief at the time."

Howard's decision to spirit himself into oblivion aboard the Sikorsky was not as spontaneous as it might have seemed. Some of the details about his escape from Culver City were revealed in an article written by Joe Petrali and published posthumously in *True* magazine in 1975. (Joe died of a heart attack in Arizona on November 10, 1973.) In the article, Joe stated that every day, during the course of at least a month, Howard had ordered him to roll the Sikorsky out onto the tarmac at Culver City and prepare it for takeoff. Joe did this morning after morning, and then routinely rolled it, after a few hours, back into the hangar. On the morning when Howard actually showed up for the flight, Joe came close to not rolling the Sikorsky onto the runway. "I figured it'd be a waste of time and Howard would never show. How wrong I was. Howard showed up with only a few possessions stuffed into a cardboard box. 'The Lone Wolf is ready to fly,' he announced to Dick and me." A few months earlier, Errol Flynn had dubbed Howard "The Lone Wolf."

On the morning of his disappearance, Howard looked at both Dick and Joe. "You lucky guys are coming with me."

At the time, they later revealed, both of them thought Howard was going to fly them to San Francisco, or perhaps Mexico City. Joe never realized that this flight would stretch into a journey that lasted a full eleven months.

"We didn't even bring a change of underwear," Dick later said.

Piloting the Sikorsky himself, Howard flew over the beautiful but barren Sierra Nevada Mountains, heading toward Las Vegas. He didn't say a word to his two-man crew. Both Joe and Dick were apprehensive about where their boss was taking them. "It even occurred to me that he might be kidnapping us," Dick later said.

In those days, photographers routinely hung out at the Las Vegas airport, hoping to snap celebrities arriving for an off-the-record weekend at the still emerging resort. Aware of this, and to avoid publicity, Howard piloted the Sikorsky to an obscure and unpaved landing strip in mesquite bush country, twenty-five miles from the center of Las Vegas.

That morning, a sand storm was raging across the desert, blowing sagebrush and tumbleweeds across the makeshift runway. During his landing, sand pelted the aircraft, and gusts of gale-like winds bombarded it. In his deteriorating emotional condition, with his nerves shattered, Howard did not appear to Joe and Dick that he was capable of making the landing. He bumped the ground five times, hard, before the tires stuck to the dirt runway.

Suddenly, he overshot the runway and hit sand dunes. In the mesquite bushes, wild rabbits scampered for safety. The wheel that guided the plane's direction struck an obstacle and tore loose from its strut, spinning high into the air before crashing into the scrub. Unsupported by its front wheel, the fuselage scraped against the jagged and arid terrain as the ruined plane came to a thumping halt.

Despite the violence of the landing, the three men disembarked from the craft without any injuries and immediately surveyed the damage. "After all our work, and after spending $600,000 on its reconstruction, the Sikorsky was a lame duck once again—and after only one flight," Joe lamented. He told Howard that it would take a month of hard, sweaty labor to repair the craft.

"Howard was devastated," Joe later said. "He'd come to identify with that Sikorsky as an extension of himself. He sometimes referred to it as his death-trap. He said that if he could pull the Sikorsky together again, he could pull himself together again. I know this gets complicated, but the Sikorsky was the metal embodiment of Howard himself. He was sobbing when we drove him away. For the first time in my life, I felt sorry for Howard Hughes, a man who had everything."

As their temporary home, Howard selected El Rancho, a bungalow cluster bordering what eventually became known as the Vegas strip. "Howard ordered us to get blankets and nail them over his two windows," Dick said. "He wanted to blanket out the daylight." This blotting out the sun would become a pattern that would last until the end of Howard's life.

In total seclusion, he lived for five weeks in a dark room at El Rancho. "Dick and I knew that he was going through a period of recovery. He didn't read any newspapers, and he didn't have a radio. He didn't want the outside world to intrude. Every day I brought him a box of chocolate chip cookies, a quart of milk, and three candy bars—and that's all he ate to survive."

During those five weeks, Joe and Dick, in a rented plane, made frequent trips back to Culver City to secure parts and to fly Hughes Aviation mechanics back to the barren airfield outside Las Vegas to work on the damaged Sikorsky. Although he'd been (and would continue to be) a "pinch-penny" about many money matters, Howard told Joe that regarding the costs of repairing the damaged aircraft, "the sky's the limit."

"While we were working on the Sikorsky, Howard couldn't bring himself to even go and look at it," Joe said. "In his mind, at least, the damage caused to the Sikorsky became more important than his subsequent failures to deliver the Spruce Goose or the D-2 reconnaissance plane. He began to feel that everything he touched was doomed to failure. Sometimes, late at night, he'd summon me to his bungalow and tell me that he wished he'd never gone into aviation. 'Planes tried to kill me,' he told me one night. 'I've devoted my life to them, and they want me dead. I should never fly again. I'll take the train for the rest of my life.' Yet on other occasions, Howard seemed fanatically interested in the resurrection of the Sikorsky, debating the location and position of every bolt. "Sometimes," Joe said, he'd ask me the same question five—even ten—times. I was very patient with him. I knew I had to get that plane ready to fly again. It was as if Howard's very life depended on it."

Both Joe and Dick were under gag orders, imposed by Howard, not to reveal Howard's whereabouts to any of his colleagues in Culver City. When interrogated by Dietrich during some of his supply runs, Joe, on Howard's orders, told him that Howard had abandoned the Sikorsky, rented a private plane, and had flown toward Mexico.

As Christmas of 1944 approached, both Joe and Dick pleaded with Howard to let them fly back to Los Angeles to be with their families for the holidays. He adamantly refused, telling them that he might need them "at any moment—and you're to stand by. Besides, Christmas Eve is my birthday, and I thought the three of us might have a little party together." At that point in his life, Howard still believed the fiction that his mother had created— that he was born on Christmas Eve and not in the late summer of 1905.

Disappointed, Dick and Joe spent many hours sitting around El Rancho playing cards. Howard didn't want either of them to go out at night in case he needed their services. Finally, depressed and rebellious, Dick came up with a mutinous idea. He urged Joe to fly with him on a private plane for a short holiday visit to Los Angeles, arranging for a note to be delivered to Howard's room after they were airborne.

Grateful for the respite from too much desert, too much Sikorsky, and too much Howard, the men did just that, flying back to El Rancho and their problems the day after New Year's. They feared Howard's reprisals for their "betrayal." But to their surprise, after their return to the desert, they discovered that Howard, after paying a month's advance rent on his bungalow, had mysteriously disappeared. Driving in a rented car to the barren airfield, they also found out that the Sikorsky was missing. There was no note from Howard— nothing.

At first both men feared that they'd been fired for defying their boss. Joe decided to stay and wait for Howard, but Dick would have "none of that." The next morning he was a passenger aboard a commercial flight back to Los Angeles. Reporting for duty at Culver City the following day, he expected to receive notification that he'd been fired, only to find that his old job was still open, his desk piled high with paper work.

Spending each lonely day and night alone at El Rancho, Joe maintained the vigil for Howard's return. It was three o'clock on the afternoon of February 2, 1945 when Howard suddenly opened the unlocked door to Joe's bungalow and barged in. "After all those weeks where Howard had looked like he was withering on the vine, he appeared invigorated and raring for action," Joe later said. "Apparently, he'd begun reading the newspapers again. All he said to me was, 'Any day now, our boys are gonna cut off Hitler's balls and feed them to his German shepherds.'"

He didn't chastise Joe for disobeying him and flying back to Los Angeles for Christmas. Nor did he confide the whereabouts or the condition of the

Sikorsky. As for Dick, he made no inquiries at all, never even mentioning him, almost as if he didn't exist.

Joe went to his grave never telling the truth about his relationship with Howard. But from Johnny Meyer, Noah Dietrich, and Howard's chance encounters along the way, details of Howard's eleven-month disappearance have trickled out, although not in the lush details that Hughes watchers would prefer.

Johnny Meyer remains the only source for the claim that Howard forced Joe to submit to oral sex during their long disappearance.

When Howard reappeared after his mystery trip, the nature of his relationship with Joe changed considerably, at least according to Meyer, admittedly a second-hand source of information. Howard's pimp later claimed that Howard lay on the bed in the bungalow room at El Rancho, listening to the radio. Surprisingly, he asked Joe to take a shower.

Joe later confided to Meyer that he didn't really need a shower, having taken one that morning, but Howard insisted. He told Joe that he planned to take him to the hot spots of Vegas that night, and he wanted him very clean and smelling nice before introducing him to any woman.

No one ever considered Joe Petrali as handsome in the style of some of Howard's sex partners, notably Errol Flynn, Robert Taylor, and Tyrone Power, but Joe must have been a dazzler when he pulled off his clothes. Judging from second-hand reports, Howard was intrigued with the sight. Meyer later stated that Joe told him this: While showering, Howard came into the bathroom and pulled back the curtain. Fully clothed, he bent down on his knees and fellated him under the running water. Joe, a heterosexual, submitted to Howard's demands. He was probably more shocked than he was sexually aroused. But he must have satisfied Howard, who would continue to fellate Joe when not otherwise engaged with strangers he picked up.

Later Joe's talents as a sex object would be verified by both Lana Turner and Ava Gardner. Each of them met Joe on separate occasions. "He was always hanging out with Howard," Ava said. "How could you not meet him?" Meyer maintained that Lana was the first of the actresses to sample his charms.

"After a while, I passed him on to Ava," a drunken Lana confessed one night at the Beverly Hills Hotel. "Then, Joe got involved with Joan Crawford, who never wanted to miss out on *anything*. Smokin' Joe was sure passed around from bed to bed in those days, but darling Howard got there first. But not before Joe's wife, of course. If he had one. I never knew. Never cared."

For his night on the town with Joe, Howard steered his rented car to a ranch-style house on the outskirts of Las Vegas. A private club, open to outsiders only by special invitation, it was amusingly named the Prickly Cactus. Howard's gangster friend, Bugsy Siegel, was said to have put up the money for this house of prostitution and had granted Howard free membership as one of its inaugural members. Howard had been a frequent customer at this club since its opening.

The madam of the house called herself "Belle Watling," taking her name from the bordello keeper in *Gone With the Wind*, as memorably portrayed by actress Ona Munson. Belle introduced Joe and Howard to her latest batch of girls, most of whom had, sometime in their pasts, arrived as show-business hopefuls at Union Station in Los Angeles. As the reality of their dim chances for stardom became more obvious, some of them, at least, opted for a relatively lucrative sojourn at the Prickly Cactus.

For Howard and Joe, "Belle" had reserved four of the most popular girls in the house. Each had been picked because of their resemblance to one of the era's reigning beauty queens. Joe later told Johnny Meyer that he and Howard faced a choice of "Lana Turner," "Rita Hayworth," "Betty Grable," and/or "Ava Gardner."

Supposedly, since Howard had never bedded Ava Gardner in real life, he decided to spend a few hours with her dead-ringer. Joe claimed that selecting his partner presented a difficult choice for him, but he eventually settled on Betty Grable "because every GI in World War II wanted to screw her." He said he would have gone for both "Rita" and "Lana," too, but that earlier, Howard "had drained me dry."

Joe was exhausted when Howard drove him back to his bungalow at El Rancho and then announced, "We're leaving at five o'clock sharp!"

"But, boss," Joe protested. "I'm beat."

"That's five o'clock sharp!" Howard said. "Not 4:59, not 5:01. Five o'clock sharp!"

"Can you at least tell me where we're going?" Joe asked.

"When you get to where we're going," he said, "you can ask somebody on the ground where you are. If they don't know, they're pretty stupid, wouldn't you say?" With that remark, Howard walked toward his own bungalow for one hour of sleep.

In the Sikorsky that Joe had rebuilt, Howard interchanged his pilot duties with Joe. Together, they flew across the West. From Las Vegas, they flew to Reno until Howard tired of that town. From Reno, they flew to Palm Springs, hiding out in secluded motorcourt bungalows, never in a star-studded resort where Howard might be recognized.

In a few weeks, it was on to Mexico City. When he grew bored South of the Border, he flew north to Arizona, where he often retreated.

"It was back and forth, wandering aimlessly from desert to desert," Joe later recalled. "Dreary motel after dreary motel. Howard didn't know where he wanted to go. In any place we landed, he grew restless."

Aboard the Sikorsky, Joe's final flight with him was east to Louisiana.

* * *

Details of Howard's whereabouts in late December of 1944 and January of 1945, just after having fled from Las Vegas in the Sikorsky, alone and without Joe or Dick, emerged from an unlikely source. It came from the drag artist, "Pussy-Katt," whom Howard had first encountered in San Francisco when he took Ava Gardner to Finocchio's to be entertained by a transvestite revue.

He'd made contact with "her"—actually a him who demanded to be called her—with the promise of a future date. Howard was true to his word, returning to Finocchio's again for a meeting with the seventeen-year-old pretty boy who'd been born in Dayton, Ohio in 1929. Pussy-Katt's real name was Steve Clayton (she'd taken the name of a stepfather).

Breaking into the world of show-business drag in San Francisco and lying about her age, Pussy-Katt in her publicity claimed that, "I'm too pretty to be a boy—and much, much too pretty to be a mere gal."

Before meeting Howard, Pussy-Katt had been involved in a scandalous chain of events that had even reached the ears of both Howard Hughes and Louella Parsons. The gossip maven couldn't print it, of course—"it's too scandalous." During the course of a night on the town, a group of friends who included Errol Flynn, William Lundigan, Bruce Cabot, and David Niven were rumored to have invited Pussy-Katt and some of her associates back to their hotel suite at the Fairmont for "a night of debauchery evoking the Roman Empire." According to the rumor, Howard had been tantalized by that story and wanted to duplicate some aspects of it, privately, with Pussy-Katt.

Pussy-Katt later claimed that Howard repeatedly sodomized her when he invited her back to his suite at the Fairmont after her show.

According to the wild stories Pussy-Katt told her cronies at Finocchio's, Howard became mesmerized by a book on eunuchs that he partially read while waiting for her to get dressed one afternoon in her apartment. In this book of sexual practices of ancient Egypt, Howard supposedly read that the most beautiful boys in the land—each of them highly prized as sexual objects—were subjected to the brutal practice of having their penises, testicles, and scrotums removed.

Many of the other eunuchs at court had to suffer removal of only their testicles and scrotums. According to the theory, sodomites of that era claimed that young boys who had suffered the removal of all of their genitalia were more sexually satisfying because they had only one way to receive sexual pleasure—and that was from being penetrated rectally.

If Pussy-Katt is to be believed, she claimed that Howard persuaded her to fly with him to Mexico City where she underwent sexual mutilation. "There wasn't that much to cut off anyway, honey," she later said. "Besides, $50,000 turned my head."

After she recovered in a clinic in Mexico City, Howard flew her to Acapulco—a sleepy town then, just emerging as a resort. There he installed her in a rented villa, promising to return when she'd recovered from her surgery, to test the theory of the ancient Egyptian sodomites.

Howard, and again only Pussy-Katt's word is the source of this, continued to fly to Acapulco for oft-repeated visits over a period of nearly two years. When he grew bored with her, he left her enough money to open up a local transvestite club—Finocchio's South—which flourished for three years in Acapulco, often attracting celebrities from Hollywood.

Eventually, because of alleged prostitution on the premises, both male and female, and illegal drug use, the club was shut down by the local police.

After her club was closed, Pussy-Katt just faded from the radar screen. She was once reported to be a performer at Madame Arthur's, a transvestite revue in Paris that was originally established in the 1930s. But no one is sure what became of her.

What is known is that after his sojourn in Acapulco in January of 1945, allegedly leaving Pussy-Katt to recover from surgery in the villa he'd arranged for her, he flew to Phoenix, again without alerting Joe, Dick, Noah Dietrich, or anyone else about where he was.

Joe Petrali, during most of January of 1945, was still stuck in the Las Vegas desert at El Rancho, and wouldn't be aware of Howard's whereabouts until his reappearance in early February. "As our trip progressed," Joe later recalled, "Howard was showing more and more of his paranoia. I can understand why Howard wanted to get away from Toolco and from the boys at Culver City, including Noah Dietrich. All of Howard's companies were in turmoil, and things were hysterical all the time. But Dick and I were his flyboys. It was just crazy to keep secrets from us. We hadn't betrayed him. Dietrich always suspected that we knew where Howard was at all times. Actually, Dietrich was wrong. We knew where Howard was when we saw him. Where Howard flew without us, we haven't a clue."

As it was revealed many years later, one of the things he did during his long disappearance involved a secret rendezvous with Cary Grant.

* * *

Nogales, Arizona, 1945

In most cases, whenever Howard called Cary Grant, the actor came running if his film commitments allowed him to do so. Knowing that Howard had disappeared from both Toolco and Hughes Aviation, and not having heard from his friend in weeks, Cary was concerned for Howard's safety. It was a relief to the actor when a call came in from Howard, asking him to fly at once to Arizona to be with him. Free to go, and without any ironclad film commitments at the time, Cary left at once without telling anybody where he was going.

594

Arriving in Nogales, Cary went immediately to a mysterious hotel room, R-3, to which no maid had been allowed entrance since Howard's check-in. What he found inside sickened the fastidious Cary. Disheveled, Howard was sprawled nude in the center of a smelly bed rank with rotting semen, as if he'd been lying there masturbating for days.

His normally skeletal frame had lost an additional thirty-five pounds. Cary was shocked at the deterioration. Candy wrappers and empty milk bottles were scattered around the room. It turned out that he'd been surviving on a quart of milk at breakfast, one at lunch, and another at dinner. In the corner of the room was a large cardboard box half filled with almond-studded Hershey bars, Howard's only food source other than the milk.

Much more alarming, feces and urine covered newspapers strewn across the tiled floor. Although the hotel accommodation included a bathroom, he had used the newspapers to relieve himself, like a cat or dog, not bothering to actually walk as far as the toilet.

Like a protective wife, Cary set about organizing and making things right. First, he called management and demanded that Howard be transferred to another suite. Then he paid a maid two hundred dollars to have Howard's former suite cleaned and sanitized.

In a new suite, Cary carefully bathed Howard and cut his long, greasy hair after washing it. He also trimmed his toenails and fingernails before giving him a close shave. Cary called room service and ordered a butterfly steak and small green peas sent to the suite.

Cary had to spoon feed Howard, cutting the meat into very small pieces so that he wouldn't choke. Very slowly, Howard managed to eat the food. Pushing his plate away before he was finished, he broke into uncontrollable sobbing. For the first time, Cary saw firsthand the toll that his friend had paid for the failure of the Spruce Goose and the D-2 reconnaissance plane.

When he returned to Hollywood, Cary confided to director George Cukor his belief that all those plane and car crashes had caused some sort of brain damage. How else to explain Howard's derelict state and his abandonment of Culver City and millions of dollars worth of unfilled government contracts?

When he stopped sobbing, Howard told Cary that he'd continue wandering across the American landscape "like a vagabond until I find myself."

If George Cukor got it right, Howard told Cary that, "I can't commit to anyone except you. You're my only friend. All the others are using me for my money, the women to advance their careers, the boys to get a hundred-dollar bill or much more. With you, it's unconditional love." Even if those weren't the exact words, as recalled by a second-hand source, it is believed that they mirrored Howard's sentiments at the time.

It will never be known in any detail what Howard and Cary talked about during those precious days they spent together in Nogales in 1945. Cary was also emotionally disturbed that his "loveless marriage" to Barbara Hutton was coming to an end.

Cary often turned to Howard for advice, especially in financial matters. But he hadn't listened to Howard three years previously. Then, on July 4, 1942, at Lake Arrowhead, in the mountains of southern California, he'd taken the Woolworth heiress as his bride. At the time, Howard had been horrified that his best friend and sometimes lover was marrying his former girlfriend, one he'd known during their mismatch at the Savoy Hotel in London. Howard had turned down Cary's request to attend the wedding and be his best man. Newspapers around the world published the Hutton/Grant wedding picture under the caption CASH 'N CARY.

At the time of his meeting with Howard in Arizona in 1945, Hutton was only months away (July 15) from filing for divorce, charging Cary with "grievous mental distress, suffering and anguish," which was certainly true. Unlike Hutton's future husbands—often homosexual—Cary did not seek alimony. In Nogales, knowing that the divorce was imminent, Howard urged Cary "to go for the big bucks." Cary refused.

Hutton, speaking to her homosexual cousin, Jimmy Donahue, said, "During my marriage to Cary, I don't remember seeing him. He got up at five o'clock to leave for the studio. I woke up at two in the afternoon. He came home at seven and went to bed. By that time, I was fully dressed and ready for an evening on the town. While I was out, he slept. By the time I got home at dawn, he was already dressing for the studio. I do recall passing him in the hall one morning. During my marriage to Cary, Howard Hughes saw far more of him than I did."

Throughout a lifetime of broken friendships, Howard's bond with Cary would always be strong, enduring for almost half a century, long after sexual passions had ended. Lovers, both male and female, would come and go from the lives of these two closeted bisexuals. But Cary and Howard would be "lovers for life," as Barbara Hutton told Jimmy Donahue. "I guess my husband loves Howard," she claimed. "He certainly never had any love for me. We've slept in separate bedrooms ever since our wedding day. Long after Cary has dumped me, he'll still be carrying on his relationship with Howard. But, if truth be told, I think the love of Cary Grant's life is Cary Grant. Ditto for Howard."

Information about Cary's secret visit with Howard during his long disappearance would not be unearthed by the press of that day. However, a second secret rendezvous between the two men became publicized around the world.

* * *

Early in 1947, long after pulling himself together and making his whereabouts known to his colleagues at Toolco and Hughes Aviation, Howard flew Cary from Los Angeles to New York "for business and pleasure." Howard personally piloted his friend in a converted B-23 bomber left over from reconnaissance duties during World War II. The custom-retrofitted aircraft was called

"The Flying Penthouse." Extravagant amenities included a lavish bedroom, a bathroom with a custom-made bathtub, and a wet bar stocked with rare whiskies and vintage French champagne.

In New York, at an emergency board meeting of TWA, Howard agreed to lend the financially troubled airline ten million dollars. TWA was suffering from a too rapid expansion and a disastrous pilots's strike that had lasted for more than two weeks.

After a brief sojourn for business matters in Washington, D.C., Howard invited Cary for a quick vacation in Mexico. Cary had time because finishing touches were being made on the script of his next picture, *The Bishop's Wife*, in which he was slated to star at RKO opposite Loretta Young.

On his flight from Washington to the Southwest, Howard's last radio contact was at the control tower at the Indianapolis airport. For the holiday in Mexico, Johnny Meyer was already waiting for Cary and Howard on land. "I'd arranged only the finest in boy ass for my two airborne queers," he later revealed.

Flying south into air space above Texas, Howard planned a refueling stop in Amarillo, and alerted the control tower there that he planned to land his bomber there to refuel. En route, he encountered a violent storm roaring across much of the state. To avoid the fury of the storm, Howard directed his plane to El Paso instead, where weather conditions were judged as safe for landing, and where, evidently, there was plenty of fuel.

Several hours had passed since his last known radio contact in Indianapolis, and no one at the Amarillo airport had heard from him. Local aviation authorities grew apprehensive that the plane carrying two of the world's most famous men had gone down somewhere in the hills. After the violent storm, small search planes took off to scout for wreckage.

Radio bulletins were issued across America. Two of America's most celebrated men were believed to have died in a plane crash. Newspaper offices were alerted for "the biggest double obituary of the century." One frontpage of a Chicago paper printed a mock blowup of its special edition: HUGHES AND GRANT DIE IN PLANE CRASH.

From El Paso, Howard flew Cary to Guadalajara, Mexico, where he and Cary checked into El Reforma Hotel. It is not known, but it is believed that Howard was aware of the furor surrounding his so-called disappearance. He seemed determined to let the world speculate whether he were dead or alive. Dietrich later claimed that the refusal to make contact with aviation authorities was "Howard's fuck you to the world."

When they arrived at the lobby of El Reforma, checking in under assumed names, Howard and Cary were greeted with a blazing newspaper headline: SEÑORS GRANT AND HUGHES BELIEVED DEAD IN AIR CRASH. Selfishly, after learning about the furor associated with the misconception, neither of them alerted friends or associates that they were alive. Arrogantly,

Howard and Cary continued to stay at the hotel incognito, despite the frantic headlines.

Thinking they were not in their room, the hotel's housekeeper, Consuelo Marijan, who just happened to be a movie buff, used her passkey to enter their suite. She screamed at the sight of the two naked men asleep in each other's arms. An alert business manager of the hotel, hoping for publicity for his under-booked resort, immediately alerted the local press. Soon bulletins were coming into news rooms all over the world. Wire services in Mexico City proclaimed that Howard and Cary were no longer *presumidos muerto* (presumed dead).

One radio newsman in Mexico claimed that "like Jesus, Señor Hughes and Señor Grant have risen from the dead." Faced with a media storm, Cary flew back to Los Angeles on the next available plane. Arriving there, he told the press that reports of his death had been "greatly exaggerated," ripping off a line from Mark Twain. Howard, however, stayed in Guadalajara where he welcomed the latest girlfriend in his life, the beautiful actress and his future wife, Jean Peters.

* * *

Louisiana, 1945

Joe Petrali never learned where Howard had disappeared to after Petrali had rebelliously flown back to Los Angeles for his Christmas holiday in 1945. It was only later revealed to him that Howard had flown himself to San Francisco, Mexico City, and Nogales, Arizona. When Petrali reunited with Howard in February of 1945 in Las Vegas, his boss told him that he wanted to continue their travels in America. This time, only the two of them would be flying, without Dick Beatie.

Without knowing the day's flight plan, Petrali showed up at the landing strip outside Las Vegas at three o'clock in the morning to ensure that the Sikorsky was in tiptop shape for flying. Two hours later a battered car pulled up near the plane. Attired in a raccoon coat—the type frat boys wore in the early 1920s—Howard emerged from the vehicle. "Let's fly," he called to Petrali.

Piloting the plane himself, Howard refused to divulge his flight plan to the Las Vegas control tower. "We're flying East, boys," he said over his radio. "East."

This was a dangerous defiance of authority over the wartime skies of America. The control tower could have called the Air Force and asked them to intervene, even shoot down the Sikorsky if it did not properly identify itself. But nothing like that happened. Someone alerted the control tower that the plane was being piloted by "none other than Howard Hughes on very secret government business."

Petrali never wrote about this, but later confessed to friends, as well as to Noah Dietrich, that when Howard flew over Texas, he was crying. "That state held some sort of bitter memories for him that he must have dredged up." His co-pilot recalled that in an impetuous move Howard seemed to nose-dive the plane toward the earth as if he were going to crash it on his home state. After Petrali started screaming, Howard came to as if aware of his impulsive act for the first time. He suddenly righted the plane and flew out of Texas into Oklahoma.

It was not until Howard was flying over Oklahoma that Howard finally revealed to his co-pilot their destination: Shreveport, Louisiana.

Petrali later claimed that he never figured out why Howard landed in Shreveport. "He had no business there at all. Since he had to land someplace, I think he chose Shreveport as one of the least likely places for Toolco executives in Houston to come looking for him."

A thunderstorm blackened the skies over Louisiana as Howard landed his Sikorsky at Shreveport. He selected the most battered car he could rent at the airport and drove to the most rundown hotel he could find, The Shreveport Inn, which usually housed vagrants and drunks. "For a week, he stayed in that lonely room," Petrali said. "I brought him milk and cookies—that's all he wanted."

Every night Petrali went out to a bar or a movie. He recalled that after sitting through some Betty Grable movie, he came back to the hotel to find that Howard had disappeared from his room.

As it turned out, Marvin K. Ezell, a patrolman for the local police, spotted what he later described "as a derelict, probably from up north, sitting on a curbside drinking a quart of milk, which he probably stole from some store." In his report, he claimed that the "stranger wore dirty clothes, torn in places, and had at least a week's growth of beard." He also reported that he was wearing a beaten-up fedora. When O.C. Merritt, another officer was called to the scene in a squad car, he demanded that Howard produce identification. When Howard refused to show any identification and would not even tell the officers his name, he was hustled into the squad car and driven to police headquarters.

Before the chief of police, he admitted that his name was Howard Hughes. He produced a room key for his hotel to show them he was no vagrant. At first the chief didn't believe "this obvious looking bum." But when Howard produced $3,500 from his pockets—"nobody in Louisiana except Huey Long carried around that kind of dough," the chief later said—the officers began to believe Howard. Nonetheless, they called the local manager of Toolco, which had an office in Shreveport. Although he'd never met Howard, he'd seen thousands of pictures of him. He rushed down and identified Howard.

Howard showed up at the Toolco plant the following morning, asking for fifty-thousand dollars in cash. A quick call to Noah Dietrich in Hollywood got an okay to release that kind of money. Dietrich demanded to speak to Howard but he refused. While authorizing the cash, Dietrich asked the manager of the plant to figure out how to detain Howard for the day—"but no force"—until executives from Toolco in Houston could fly to meet him. "Desperate business" awaited Howard's decisions, Dietrich told the plant manager.

By the time the officials had flown in from Houston, Howard had disappeared again. This time he instructed Petrali to fly back to Los Angeles as an ordinary passenger aboard a commercial airplane flight. He said that he'd have no more need of his services and that "the folks" at Hughes Aviation "need you more than I do."

It was later learned that for the next leg of his mysterious odyssey in 1945, Howard had selected two flight engineers from Hughes Aviation, Ray Kirkpatrick and Robert Martin, and without Petrali's knowledge, had them secretly flown in from Culver City.

In control of his Sikorsky again, this time with Kirkpatrick and Martin on board, Howard headed for Orlando, Florida. Once in Florida, he rented a car and drove both men to Orlando's Greyhound Bus Station. He'd stuffed all his possessions into a cardboard box. To their astonishment, he then boarded the bus heading for Miami, ordering them to fly the Sikorsky without him back to Culver City. Bewildered, they watched helplessly as he took a seat near the back of the bus as it headed south.

No one in either California or Texas would hear of him again for three months.

With his obligations and his defense contracts collapsing, with urgent business needing attention, Howard set out on yet another leg of his midlife odyssey, the exact details of which may never be known.

In Houston, his aunt, Annette Lummis, hired her own private detectives to search the country for Howard. She called Dietrich daily, and soon began accusing him of conspiring with Toolco executives in Houston to "have Howard done in—you've murdered him and I just know that!" She told Houston friends that her nephew one day would be discovered "in a block of ice in a warehouse somewhere."

Only a glimmer of light has been shed on what Howard was doing in Miami. In October of 1959, a waitress came into the old offices of *The Miami Herald*, asking to sell a story. In those days, *The Herald* rarely bought stories. It assigned George S. Mills, a former reporter for the defunct *Brooklyn Eagle*, to see what the woman wanted. An aging bleached blonde at the time, she identified herself as Lulubelle Hayes. She claimed that for one month in 1945 Howard Hughes had lived with her in a small apartment she occupied on South Flagler Street.

Not only that, but she had photographs. George examined the photographs and decided that they did indeed look like Howard Hughes, although the subject in the photographs was unshaven and always wore a fedora. Since George was a copy editor, he turned the pictures and the woman over to Jane Wood Reno, a doggedly reliable staff reporter. The late Mrs. Reno was the mother of Janet Reno, who became Attorney General of the United States during the Clinton administration.

With the approval of *The Miami Herald's* managing editor, George Beebe,

Mrs. Reno set out to investigate the mysterious disappearance of Howard Hughes and what he was doing in Miami in 1945 and later in The Bahamas.

Her investigation would never turn up anything conclusive but it would produce some powerful hearsay.

* * *

Miami/The Bahamas/Mexico, 1945

The Miami Herald never published Mrs. Reno's revelations because they could not be verified as authentic. Even so, her managing editor, George Beebe, believed that her investigation had turned up accurate information but had not produced what Beebe called "the smoking gun." Nonetheless, the editor wanted to go ahead with a three-part series revealing the details of Howard's infamous disappearance during the final days of World War II. But his powerful publisher, John Knight, pulled the plug.

The world press did not know that Howard had mysteriously descended on South Florida. One night the police in Fort Lauderdale received a report that a strange-looking man was on the beach completely naked and making a bonfire of his clothing. Had Howard's syphilis reoccurred? A squad car was dispatched, and Howard was arrested.

There is no record of this arrest in Broward County files. Although it could never be proven, Mrs. Reno believed that Howard "bribed his way out of that jam." Not wanting more trouble from what appeared to be an out-of-control tycoon, two policemen drove Howard to the Broward-Dade County line and released him. He was left alone to make his way on foot down the coastal strip to Miami Beach and, ultimately, to Miami itself.

In 1959, Lulubelle Hayes reported to *Herald* editor George Mills that she met Howard in a bar and took him home with her. He'd introduced himself as "Robard Lummis." Making thirty-five dollars a week as a waitress, the Georgia-born blonde said that she supported him on her meager salary. Each night she brought him a plate of food from the diner where she worked for quarter tips pushing blue-plate specials.

One night, as Lulubelle claimed, she came home from work to find a rather lavish man's wardrobe spread out on the bed in her small apartment, including a tuxedo and at least three dress suits, along with new shoes, ties, and some shiny white shirts. She was astonished that Howard had acquired such expensive finery, thinking he was a "down-and-out snowbird." He never told her how he acquired all this clothing. When she got off work the following night and rushed home, her lover and the clothing had disappeared.

She never saw him again.

From the Port of Miami, Howard rented a manned private yacht and sailed for a secret rendezvous in The Bahamas. From Miami, he had arranged a private meeting with the Swedish multimillionaire, Axel Wenner-Gren.

With his mop of white hair, and with a figure described as "robust," Wenner-Gren struck many people who met him as the "reincarnation of a Viking." The Duchess of Windsor, his friend, called him "the pinkest man I've ever met," a reference to his skin color.

Like Howard, Wenner-Gren was one of the richest men on the planet. The Swedish-born industrialist had invented both the refrigerator and the vacuum cleaner, and he controlled Electrolux, one of the world's most powerful companies. When he first met Howard in Nassau in 1938, the two tycoons had jointly established a corporation known as the Rover Steamship Company. Its headquarters were in Panama City where you could register any vessel or company if you paid off the right people. During the war, supposedly because of Panama's close connections to the United States, Wenner-Gren had been forced to transfer the company's headquarters from Panama to Stockholm (Sweden was officially neutral throughout the course of World War II) "where it'll be out of harm's way for the duration."

The Rover Steamship Company was ostensibly devoted mainly to exploiting business opportunities in the West Indies, ranging from sugarcane to weaponry. The exact nature of Howard's business dealings with Wenner-Gren may never be known. Noah Dietrich was not a party to these secret dealings. Supplying weapons made in Europe, notably in Sweden, to Banana Republics plotting various revolutions seems to be at the crux of Howard's dealings with the Nazi sympathizer. There were also legitimate shipping interests involved, as in the transport of tobacco from Cuba, sugarcane from the Dominican Republic, and even large shipments of fresh fruit to U.S. markets. Dietrich never knew from what hidden stash of funds Howard got the money to invest in the Swede's enterprises, both legitimate and nefarious. A lot of the company's business involved customers and suppliers in Cuba, then controlled by the corrupt dictator, Fulgencio Batista, or in the Dominican Republic, then under the iron fist of General Rafael Trujillo. Like Hitler himself, although not on such a grand monster scale, both Batista and Trujillo were Fascist dictators. This presented no problem to a Nazi collaborator like Wenner-Gren or an ultra right-wing American patriot like Howard himself.

Mrs. Reno discovered that there were several eyewitnesses who had spotted Howard in The Bahamas, mainly servants. Upon arriving in Nassau, Howard was transported to Wenner-Gren's mansion, Shangri-La on Hog Island (later renamed Paradise Island). Some of their meetings occurred aboard the *Southern Cross*, which Howard had previously sold to the Swedish industrialist for two million dollars.

Since he had acquired the vessel, Wenner-Gren had hauled the Duke and Duchess of Windsor, then stationed in Nassau as Britain's official representatives, aboard the *Southern Cross* to Miami when she was suffering "the worst toothache in the history of the world."

Unlike his sometime lover, Errol Flynn, or his rival, Charles Lindbergh, Howard was never suspected of being a Nazi sympathizer, much less a collaborator. His ties to Wenner-Gren were based more on financial advantages than on any support for Wenner-Gren's politics. Like most of the informed world at the time, Howard was well aware of his friend's involvements in the Krupp industries, his role in supplying munitions to the Third Reich, and the close bond the Swede had established with Nazi Field Marshal Hermann Göring.

Six years previously, in 1939, Wenner-Gren had met with Göring in Germany and had then flown to London. There he convened with Prime Minister Neville Chamberlain to try to broker some "permanent peace" between Nazi Germany and the British Empire.

Hitler's unprovoked attack on Poland abruptly ended Neville Chamberlain's dream of appeasement. Howard—and this is not known for certain—may have been aware that Wenner-Gren was supplying munitions from his Swedish company, Borfors, to the Third Reich. In 1939 he'd also founded The Bank of The Bahamas when he'd purchased Hog Island. Through its affiliation with the Stein Bank of Cologne, Wenner-Gren was helping finance Gestapo activities.

Technically, the Swedish tycoon had been barred from entry into The Bahamas at the time of his secret meetings there with Howard in 1945. He'd been "blacklisted."

Since August 17, 1940, the Duke of Windsor had been the governor of The Bahamas, then a colony within the British Empire. As King Edward VIII, he'd abdicated his throne to "marry the woman I love," the scandal-soaked American divorcée, Wallis Simpson.

Bowing to pressure from both Whitewall and Washington, the Duke of Windsor, as governor, signed a document declaring his dear friend, Wenner-Gren, *persona non grata* in The Bahamas. Wenner-Gren was ordered to leave The Bahamas at once, just as Howard himself would eventually be told the same thing. The Swede then sailed aboard the *Southern Cross* to Mexico, where he acquired a mansion in Cuernavaca. There he lived for the duration of the war, venturing out only rarely, and only under the cloak of extreme secrecy. Some of those visits were to The Bahamas, where he met discreetly with the Windsors. Norman Island in the Exumas was believed to have been the island where Wenner-Gren had a rendezvous with the Windsors.

In 1943, it was the Duke himself who invited Wenner-Gren to a secret meeting in The Bahamas despite his having blacklisted him. The Duke had been informed of an imminent plot wherein he'd be kidnapped from his low-security "tour of duty" in The Bahamas and imprisoned by the Nazis. Hitler would then try to arrange a prisoner's exchange with Britain, their former king returned if they'd free Hitler's former deputy, Rudolf Hess, then a prisoner in Britain. Apparently, the Duke believed at the time that he desperately needed the industrialist's support to avoid such a fate. Apparently, in the wake of his face-to-face dialogues with the Duke, Wenner-Gren intervened with his friend, Field Marshal Göring, and the Nazi plan to kidnap the Duke was cancelled.

At some point, probably in 1942, the darkest year for the Allies in World War II, Howard flew to Mexico to meet with Wenner-Gren to discuss the Rover Steamship Company and other mutual business interests. Johnny Meyer was aboard Howard's flight to Mexico where part of his job would be the arrangement of sexual liaisons for his boss. Meyer accompanied Howard to at least two dinner parties at the Cuernavaca mansion of Wenner-Gren.

Meyer claimed that the Swede was in an ebullient mood, predicting that Hitler would "outdistance" Britain in the war and eventually defeat the United States in a carefully orchestrated series of invasions.

Also according to Meyer, during his dinner parties in Cuernavaca, Wenner-Gren revealed to Howard Hitler's plans, as transmitted to him through Field Marshal Göring, for a post-war America. Göring was convinced that as storm troopers marched through the streets of Boston and New York, as they'd done in Paris, millions of German-Americans would rise up for the Fatherland, rebelling against U.S. government oppression. Instead of defending their adopted country, they'd help in its subjugation. Within that scenario, the dictator would install the Duke of Windsor as viceroy, with the assumption that Americans would consequently embrace and endorse his American-born "queen." Meyer recalled that at Cuernavaca "Howard found the plan laughable."

Roughly three years later, during their Bahamian rendezvous of 1945, Wenner-Gren presented a radically different scenario to Howard. At that point, with Russian and American forces zeroing in on a full-scale invasion of Berlin, an astute and worldly man like the Swede had to admit that the Nazi regime was close to the point of collapse.

Wenner-Gren, therefore, sought Howard's support in his plan for profit-making in a post-war world. Wenner-Gren needed a massive infusion of cash and influence, preferably from American sources, if his scheme to become "the major player" in the development of post-war Europe were to be realized.

In advance of Howard's arrival, Wenner-Gren had already secured, privately, the cooperation of the Duke and Duchess of Windsor.

During previous visits to Nassau, Howard had met the royal pair before. But the Windsors, eccentrics themselves, found Howard much too eccentric for their refined tastes. On Howard's second night on Hog Island, Wenner-Gren threw a private dinner party for Howard, the Duke and his Duchess, and three or four trusted friends, whose names are not known.

Amos Symonette, a Bahamian aide to the Duke, later reported to Mrs. Reno at *The Miami Herald* some "tidbits" of conversation that he'd overheard on the night that the Duke and Duchess, along with Howard, were entertained by Wenner-Gren. The Duke startled his fellow guests by reporting that he planned to resign as governor on March 15, 1945.

Symonette told Mrs. Reno that the Duke seemed disappointed that the war might be concluded. At one point, if Symonette is to be believed, the Duke actually blamed "Roosevelt and the Jews" for America's entry into the war, leaving out the Japanese attack on Pearl Harbor. The aide to the Duke claimed that Howard remained silent throughout the recitation, although it was known that both Howard and Wenner-Gren shared the governor's anti-Semitic views.

The Duchess cited several financial worries and shared her disappointment that drillers did not strike oil on their vast tracts of land in Alberta, Canada.

Wenner-Gren was more reassuring about the future. Now that it appeared that the Third Reich was losing, he was rapidly switching his loyalties over to the Allies since he knew that they would be the source of his future earnings in the post-war era.

There will be money to make—"big, big money"—he assured Howard, the Duke, and the Duchess, after the war. "More money than has been made at any time in the history of the world. There is a daunting fortune to be made just in rebuilding a devastated Europe."

Although his grand scheme was never activated, it seemed that Wenner-Gren was advocating some sort of capitalistic and profit-making venture that eerily evoked some of the tenets of the U.S. financed Marshall Plan for the recovery of a war-torn Europe.

At the dinner, citing the bombs that had devastated parts of England, he said he'd need the Duke's political influence in "the resurrection of London." The Swede was hoping for millions of pounds in government-sponsored contracts, and he was just assuming that the Duke still had political influence in Britain.

After the dinner, and on the following day, Wenner-Gren, along with his alcoholic American wife, the singer, Marguerite Ligget, sailed to the Bahamian Out Islands with Howard. He even let Howard command the *Southern Cross* again. At the time, the yacht was staffed by former officers of the Swedish Navy, each of whom were alleged to have pro-Nazi sentiments.

Since Wenner-Gren was known for having zero tolerance for bad dress, both among his guests and crew, Howard dressed nightly for dinner in the wardrobe he'd acquired in Miami.

Although details were lacking in Mrs. Reno's report to *The Miami Herald*, Howard's erratic behavior on the cruise shocked and profoundly upset Wenner-Gren. The industrialist finally concluded that Howard had become "a wreck of a human being" on the verge of a total breakdown. He urged Howard to spent time at a retreat in Mexico that could restore him physically and mentally. At one point, Howard is alleged to have stood up at the dinner table and urinated into a bowl of food. He could be heard sobbing deep into the night, and he also frequently appeared nude on the deck.

Howard kept repeating simple phrases over and over again. He'd do irrational things such as ordering bottles and bottles of water delivered to his cabin until he'd depleted the supply on board. At one point, after a visit to Norman

Island, Howard jumped overboard and began swimming away from the ship to the point where he had to be rescued by the crew, all skilled swimmers.

By the end of their cruise through the Out Islands, Wenner-Gren had obviously concluded that Howard in his condition was too reckless to take on as a business partner in any capacity.

At Howard's request, the *Southern Cross* sailed on to Cat Island in The Bahamas, a sybaritic retreat both then and now. Once there, the yacht picked up Errol Flynn, who was not only Howard's sometimes lover but a close friend of Wenner-Gren himself. After bringing Errol aboard, the *Southern Cross* sailed back to Mexico.

Arriving at port, Howard was invited to stay in Cuernavaca with Wenner-Gren, but Errol had made other plans. Howard and Errol told Wenner-Gren good-bye and were driven to the Cuernavaca home of a notorious homosexual, Harry Carstairs, who was believed to have been a Nazi collaborator.

Carstairs was famous in Mexico at the time for securing "the world's most beautiful boys," all male prostitutes. He constantly demanded a fresh supply, dismissing those young men of whom he'd grown tired. As a special treat for guests such as Errol (a frequent visitor) or Howard, he had the young men lie nude all day around his Olympic-size pool. His guests were invited to stroll among the young men and make a selection, taking any of the hustlers upstairs for seduction in one of the lavishly decorated bedrooms.

After two weeks of that, Howard had had his fill. Renting a private plane, he flew Errol back with him to Los Angeles where Howard wanted to resume his life.

Errol later told such friends as Bruce Cabot and David Niven that during their time together in Cuernavaca, perhaps inspired by the dialogues with Wenner-Gren, Howard had revealed a permutation of two of his long-standing dreams. He hoped to develop the greatest reconnaissance plane in the history of aviation. It would fly over Communist-held territories after the war. He also he wanted to pilot the Hercules cargo plane on its inaugural flight.

Not only that, but Howard had also vowed to buy one of Hollywood's major film studios, promising Errol that he'd make him king of the studio.

"And for my Queen?" Errol asked.

"Rita Hayworth."

* * *

Los Angeles, 1942-1964

Passing through the outer offices of Samuel Goldwyn, Howard stole a copy of *Life* magazine. Two months before, he'd told Noah Dietrich that he could no longer afford to subscribe to the magazine. Therefore, whenever he wanted to read it, he was forced to lift a copy from a subscriber.

606

The date on the cover was June 8, 1942. Jane Greer, then known by the ingenuous name of Bettejane, was modeling a newly created uniform for the Women's Army Auxiliary Corps, which later became the Women's Army Corps (WAC). Howard was immediately captivated by this teenager's picture. She was eighteen at the time. "She's sloe-eyed," he told Johnny Meyer. "With a Mona Lisa smile. Get me this girl. Track her down. Put her under personal contract to me."

Howard wasn't the only man reading that issue of *Life* magazine. Beating Howard to Bettejane, Rudy Vallee called her mother, claiming that her daughter should be in pictures, and that he was the man to help make it happen. A movie fan like Mrs. Greer already knew of the crooner's reputation as a womanizer. She accurately determined that Rudy wanted into "my daughter's pants more than he wanted to make her a movie star."

Mrs. Greer refused to let Rudy date her daughter, even though she'd been a fan of this wavy-haired singer with the quivery vocals. He had been a sensation in the 1920s, as famous in his heyday with screaming fans as were Elvis Presley, Frank Sinatra, and the Beatles. To get to Jane, *The Vagabond Lover* would have to wait his turn.

But when Howard called Mrs. Greer expressing interest in the movie star potential of her daughter, things were different. Even though he had a far more extensive reputation as a womanizer than Rudy, Mrs. Greer, for some reason never explained, accepted his offer of rail tickets to Hollywood and—with a promise of future stardom—a possible movie contract for her daughter.

Jane later recalled that "Howard Hughes was just a name in the newspapers to me—an aviator, and the producer of a very controversial movie, *The Outlaw*."

The five-foot, five-inch beauty with dark brown hair and haunting brown eyes had a deep-toned voice and perfectly chiseled features. Her look, especially her enigmatic smile, was the result of her struggle with Bell's palsy, a form of partial paralysis which struck her at the age of fifteen. The muscles of her face were temporarily immobilized, and she practiced for hours in front of the mirror "to return expression to my face."

Her only professional training had been as a model and as a "girl singer" with Enric Madriguera's band at The Latin Club Del Rio in Washington, D.C. Her contralto voice was pleasant enough for audiences that weren't particularly demanding, but, as Jane later admitted, "I was no Dinah Shore."

After only a week in Hollywood, Jane found herself under "virtual house arrest" in an apartment that Johnny Meyer had secured for Jane and her mother. Jane was told that she was never to leave the house, that all supplies and foodstuff would be brought in for her. She was to wait by the phone for Howard to contact her. "Imagine me, a young girl, arriving in glamorous Hollywood and sitting by the radio every night waiting for a phone call. Mother was nearby with her knitting. After a few months of this, I couldn't take it anymore. I started to slip out at night. Actually Rudy Vallee obtained my phone number, and I began to date him. Soon I was the girl singer with his Coast Guard band. Howard's spies soon found out."

She remembered that it was three o'clock in the morning when she woke up to find Johnny Meyer and his cohort, Charlie Guest, standing over her bed. Guest was an assistant of Howard's, and had once been his golf instructor. "At first I thought rapists had broken in on me," Jane said. "I screamed."

Since Howard was her landlord, and had a passkey to her apartment, Meyer had let himself in, along with Guest.

"Meyer ordered me to get up and leave immediately to see Howard," Jane later recalled. "I was wearing a nightgown but there was no time to get dressed, not even to refresh my makeup and put on a dress. I was told that Howard often interviewed members of his staff at three o'clock in the morning. 'He never sleeps and never pays attention to time,' Guest told me. I slipped a trenchcoat over my nightgown and was driven to 7000 Romaine Street."

She was ushered into the studio's theater-like screening room. Only the first row was illuminated. Looking around, she saw that all the seats were empty, with no one in sight.

"I was there for a long time," she said, "and suddenly I heard footsteps. Then I saw a shadowy figure, tall and lanky. I just knew it was Howard Hughes. He stood near the light, but only his feet were illuminated. He was wearing tennis shoes. He took a seat in the front row, and called for me to come and sit beside him. I was scared."

Jane reported that for a few minutes Howard just stared at her, not saying a word. "I was far too terrified to speak," she said. "Here I was, sitting with the richest man in the world—me, little Bettejane. All I could think about was that my mother used to give Donne—that was my twin brother—and me two cents on some nights to go to the store to buy lemon-flavored hard candy. We had no food in the house. Penny hard candy was an old timey remedy to stave off hunger in a kid when the pantry was bare."

"You look like my mother," he said. "I don't remember her name, but you remind me of her."

"I don't know if it's a compliment for a young woman to be told by a man that she looks like his mother," Jane said.

"I've learned some very bad news," he said, "and I want you to tell me it isn't true. Are you dating Rudy Vallee?"

"He's a nice man."

"No, he's not," he said. "Vallee is a pervert. Besides, I didn't ask if he's a nice man. I asked you if you were dating him."

"I've been singing with his band—I wouldn't call it dating."

"You were instructed never to leave the apartment," he told her. "You disobeyed me. You are never to see Vallee again."

"He's been very nice to mother and me."

"It's over between you! Never, never see him again!"

"I have a contract with you," she said, standing up and exploding in anger. "That is for appearances on the screen, of which there have been none. What I do with my private life is no god damn business of yours. Do you think you own me?"

"I see," he said. He stood up, towering over her. "I have to teach you a lesson. You're from back East. But you're in California now. I run this town. No one defies me without paying a price." He walked away, turning to look back at her. "Good night."

"What kind of price are you talking about?" she demanded to know.

He glanced at her ominously. "You'll find out."

In time, she learned that that price meant no screen roles for her.

On December 2, 1943, Jane impulsively married Rudy Vallee, mainly to escape from Howard's iron thumb. At the Hollywood-Westwood Community Chapel, a band from the Coast Guard arrived for the ceremony, and the wedded pair passed beneath an arch of crossed sabers. Rudy took her to live in a 22-room mansion in the San Fernando Valley that had once been occupied by the fading star, Ann Harding.

Howard had warned Jane that Rudy was a pervert. After a month of marriage, she began paying closer attention to Howard's assessment. Vallee insisted on dressing her in "a whore's underwear," including black stockings and black spike heels—"real Joan Crawford fuck me shoes," Jane said. He also dyed her hair jet black and insisted that she paint her face a chalky white. After her costume met with his approval, he demanded that she whip his buttocks with a leather belt until they were raw. Only then, would he have sex with her.

Vallee urged her to buy out her contract with Howard, which she eventually succeeded in doing. The contract was settled for $7,575, with Jane agreeing to pay him back at the rate of $25 a week. After two checks, she stopped payment, and he never insisted.

Much to Howard's delight, her marriage to Rudy was rocky from the beginning. Rudy was even more of a pervert than Howard had told her. Thinking he'd gone back to womanizing, after only two months of marriage, she eavesdropped on him, only to discover that her husband employed a "madame." The madame was male, and he arranged for well-built hustlers to accommodate her husband.

In March of 1944, she separated from Rudy. Although they got back together temporarily, they parted for the final time in June of that year.

Even before their divorce was final, Howard had come back into her life. Although she had secretly been dating Howard, Jane told the press, "Rudy is the only man for me. Our divorce has brought us closer together. This time our marriage will last forever." At the very least, these remarks were disingenuous, as she hoped to shield her true affair with Howard from the press.

By August of 1944, she was appearing before RKO cameras making her debut in *Two O'Clock Courage*.

In later life, Jane refused to discuss the intimate details of her life with Howard, but she did talk about him. Johnny Meyer was more forthcoming, claiming that Howard's seduction of the young starlet occurred in his suite at the Town House Hotel. He was so pleased with her as a sexual partner that he later rented her a private apartment overlooking Sunset Boulevard. There he could rendezvous with her away from her mother.

Jane recalled her immediate weeks with Howard, "post Rudy," as happy ones. "It was like Howard was denied a proper childhood because of his mother. He wanted to be a boy again with me. Actually, I was still a girl myself in those days. I felt that Howard, already in middle age, was trying to recapture some lost youth with me."

"He loved throwing baseballs at milk bottles in the amusement arcades," she said. "He had a charming little boy quality that I found endearing. I think he won every Kewpie doll in Santa Monica for me. My apartment soon filled up with Kewpie dolls. He liked magic mirrors, haunted houses, games of chance."

"I got the full treatment from him," Jane said. "I got to see his charming side. He was taking me everywhere. The Cocoanut Grove. El Mocambo. Walks along the Santa Monica Pier. We ate pink cotton candy and rode the carousel. He sent roses to my mother, white gardenias to me."

Reunited with Howard, she would eventually sign a seven-year exclusive contract with him at RKO, although he would lend her out. Her paycheck was $2,500 a week, very good terms since some major stars in those days were pulling in only $750 a week.

She didn't suspect his growing mental deterioration until he took her to the Chi Chi Club in Palm Springs one Saturday night for dinner. Sitting at distant tables were two of Howard's former girlfriends, Ida Lupino and Norma Shearer, each with her immaculately dressed suitors. Each of them would later corroborate the details of the ensuing drama.

Doctors in later life would diagnose Howard's condition as OCD (Obsessive Compulsive Disorder).

Howard's behavior became visibly irrational at Chi-Chi's when he ordered three chocolate chip cookies for dessert. When the cookies were served, he tried to count the chocolate chips in each cookie. Startling to her, he maintained that each cookie was short three chocolate chips. He summoned the chef

Jane Greer

610

to his table and demanded that he rebake the cookies. "I want there to be fifteen chocolate chips in each cookie," Howard told the chef. "Not fourteen, not sixteen, but fifteen."

Since it was Howard Hughes, the chef agreed to bake new cookies, each with fifteen chocolate chips. While the chef was doing that, Howard excused himself and headed for the men's room.

Jane dreaded whenever Howard rose to go to the men's room. Often she was left a wallflower at table. He conducted most of his business during his dates with her, calling associates from pay phones. That night in Palm Springs he was gone for so long that Jane slipped a waiter a five-dollar bill to go to the toilet to find what was keeping him. In the bathroom, the waiter discovered Howard compulsively washing his hands until they were red and raw. After much struggle, the waiter was able to break Howard out of "some trance." Later Howard explained that he was "washing away deadly germs."

On several occasions, she noticed that he'd stand in front of doors waiting for someone to leave or come in so he wouldn't have to touch a doorknob. At night she often wore gloves and would open doors for him.

Later, in a restaurant in Los Angeles, Howard once again disappeared into the men's room. Another five-dollar bill, and a waiter emerged later to tell her that her date was standing naked in the men's room washing his white shirt in the sink. He hadn't worn any underwear that night. Jane managed to enlist the help of the manager, who secured a freshly laundered white shirt which he kept on hand in case one of his waiters spilled something on himself. The waiter was able to get Howard into the shirt. With Jane's assistance, he was led out the back entrance. In his battered Chevy, Jane drove him home that night.

Her worst memory was when he drove her in that same decrepit Chevy to a deserted beach north of Malibu. She was dressed in a beautiful satin gown for an evening on the town and objected to where he'd taken her. "I want to go dancing," she said, "Not for a swim."

He asked her to sing two songs for him, both from a picture where she'd played a "nitery canary," *The Falcon's Alibi*, in 1946. The songs were, "How Do You Fall in Love?" and "Come Out—Wherever You Are." When she'd finished singing, he got out of the car and pulled off all his clothes.

"Howard, I told you, I'm not going swimming," she protested.

"I'm not going for a swim," he told her. "I'm going to go into the water and float out as far as I can into the sea, deeper and deeper. I plan to kill myself." He stalked his way toward the water. She ran after him, trying to force him to come back. He whirled around and slugged her in the mouth, knocking her down on the sands. Her nose was bleeding.

Frantic, and not knowing at first what to do, she ran back to the car where he'd left the keys. Starting the motor, she drove to the nearest motor court and phoned Johnny Meyer. She was afraid to call the police.

Breaking speed limits, Meyer and what Jane called "three of his goons" arrived at Malibu in half an hour. If Howard had meant to kill himself, he would have done so by now. As the men searched the beach for Howard's body, she sat in the car, nervously smoking one cigarette after another. In what for her was an eternity, but was more likely forty minutes, the "goons" returned, walking slowly up from the beach with Howard.

One of Meyer's men had taken his jacket and placed it around Howard's nude, skeletal frame. The men put Howard in the back seat of his Chevy, with Meyer taking the wheel. Without being allowed to speak to Howard, Jane was driven home by one of Meyer's men in a separate car.

She asked her driver to stop at a filling station so she could go into the women's room and wipe the blood from her face.

When she got home, she found her mother sitting by the radio knitting. "Did you and Howard have a nice evening?" her mother asked.

As Jane remembered, she raced up the steps and bolted the door to her bedroom and didn't emerge again until the weekend had come and gone.

Gradually, Howard's fixation on Jane waned. She married Edward Lasker, a rich producer and attorney, in 1947.

Although Howard had derailed Jane's career, he didn't block it completely. She went on to become a Queen of Film Noir, along with Barbara Stanwyck, and he watched her achieve screen immortality when she appeared opposite sleepy-eyed Robert Mitchum and Kirk Douglas in *Out of the Past* in 1947. Jane played the sleek, charming, and baby-faced killer, Kathie Moffett. She was an icy *femme fatale*, one of the great manipulative temptresses of 40s noir. In the film, Robert Mitchum delivers his most famous line to Jane, "Baby, I don't care."

Once her control freak, Howard became less and less interested in Jane's career. His only instructions to his executives at RKO were to "keep Jane bad— no good gal roles for her."

She recalled a final phone call from Howard in 1964—"or maybe in 1963." She was making a film called *Where Love Has Gone*. "What an appropriate title for the story of Howard Hughes and me," she said.

Despite their long-time estrangement, Jane believed at the time that Howard would definitely arrange a screening of *Where Love Has Gone,* purely for nostalgic purposes. It starred three of his former girlfriends: Jane Greer herself as well as Bette Davis and Susan Hayward. It had been based on a novel by Harold Robbins, who had caricatured Howard in another novel, *The Carpetbaggers*. Further, the plot for *Where Love Has Gone* was based on the murder of gangster Johnny Stompanato, Lana Turner's former boyfriend, allegedly stabbed by the star's daughter, Cheryl.

In the 1970s, as Howard lay dying in darkened hotel rooms in various parts of the world, he often watched *Out of the Past*. He'd lived long enough to see it become a film noir cult classic.

"Howard's voice sounded choked, as if he'd been crying," Jane said. I'll always remember his final words to me."

"How could you, Jane, how could you do this to me?" he asked her. "How could you hurt the only person in the whole world who has ever loved you."

"I didn't really know what he was talking about," she later said. "I hadn't seen him in years. 'What have I done to you?' he asked me. "Tell me, for god's sake, what have I done?'"

"You know," he told her. "You've always known how you've hurt me. It was no accident. From the very beginning, you've plotted to destroy me. You and all the others. I know that the people plotting against me had to have a ring-leader. Tonight watching *Out of the Past* I came to realize for the first time that that ringleader is you. I saw how you manipulated Robert Mitchum and Kirk Douglas—just like you tried to do to me. But I outsmarted you."

"I've never plotted against you," she protested.

"I watched you tonight on TV," he said. "You are the ice goddess herself. You were put on this earth to lure men to their deaths."

"Howard, you're talking nonsense!"

"So, now you want the world to think I'm crazy," he said. "You'll pay for this. If it's the last thing I do, I'll see that you pay...." His voice drifted off.

"Howard, Howard, I shouted into the phone," she said. "It was like I was speaking into outer space. I never heard from Howard again—it's a bit sad, real-ly."

* * *

Los Angeles, 1945-47

When Guy Madison, one of the handsomest men ever to grace the silver screen, took off his shirt for the camera, and posed wearing rolled-up Navy dunga-rees, he looked like one of the exaggerated male body sketches drawn by Tom of Finland.

In contrast, Gail Russell was called "angelically beautiful." Her big, sad, haunted eyes brought a kind of poetic melancholia to the screen, the camera capturing a deeper sadness that pervaded her real life and ultimately destroyed her.

This young man and this young woman would unite into a disastrous mar-riage in 1949. Fan magazines went wild, proclaiming the pair "the most gor-geous couple in Hollywood."

But long before that event, Howard, in the words of Johnny Meyer, "sucked both Gail and Guy dry."

Ever on the lookout for male beauties, some of whom he'd obtain studio contracts for, Henry Willson was cruising the beaches of Santa Monica one hot afternoon when he spotted Robert Ozell Moseley in a pair of white bathing trunks. On temporary leave from the Coast Guard, Moseley was "the most gor-geous thing I'd ever seen in Hollywood, even with hair on his chest," Willson claimed. "He had naturally tousled blond hair. There was a soft cleft in his stiff-jawed chin. Playing volleyball in the sands with a pack of sailors, he had the sweetest smile in the history of the world. When he smiled, it brought out his dimples."

When Willson pitched his new discovery to his boss, David O. Selznick, accompanied with a lavish description of his attributes, the producer barked: "Drop these homosexual fantasies. Can this guy act?"

"With looks like I've described, you want Sarah Bernhardt too?"

"Okay, but the name's got to go," Selznick said. "Robert Ozell Moseley sounds too much like a Presbyterian deacon."

Willson claimed later that he selected the name of "Guy" because the young man was the kind of "guy" every girl wanted for her own. He took the surname of Madison from a Dolly Madison cake truck rolling past him. Originally Willson wanted to call Guy "Rock

Guy Madison

Madison," but the agent decided to save the name "Rock" for one of his future discoveries.

Guy was about as straight as any other handsome actor in Hollywood. When fat, pudgy Willson picked him up that day on the beach, he wasn't adverse to returning to the agent's home and even taking off those white bathing trunks and posing nude for Willson's private collection of male pornography. When Willson tired of "flaccid shots," Guy produced an erection for the agent, which was later sampled in the privacy of the agent's boudoir. That boudoir in those days was busier than any male gym in Hollywood.

Often Willson seduced young men and never did anything for their careers. In Guy's case, he actually got him a job. Appearing before the cameras for the first time, Guy, with no acting training or talent, did a bit part in Claudette Colbert's homefront tearjerker, *Since You Went Away*, released in 1944. He appeared in a scene with Jennifer Jones and Robert Walker, the latter playing a milquetoast, insecure soldier. In the film, Walker actually faints when meeting this "pretty boy" sailor. Since it was 1944, no homosexual subplot was intended. Perhaps it was shortness of breath on Walker's part.

When *Since You Went Away* opened across America, this cute-as-a-button sailor, Guy himself, caused young girls "to fall out of the balconies," the press proclaimed. A career was born, and filmdom's future Wild Bill Hickok was on his way.

614

In post-war Hollywood, Guy Madison became a pinup, the male version of Betty Grable during the war years. Willson had scored big with Howard by signing Jack Buetel, and the agent was eager to show off his discovery, first with a set of nude photographs and later with a private screening of *Since You Went Away* at Howard's offices at 7000 Romaine Street. Howard was smitten, ordering Willson to arrange a private meeting with the film's handsomest actor.

When Howard took Guy to dinner, an agent from the FBI was listening behind a banana palm. When Howard invited Guy back to a bungalow at the Beverly Hills Hotel, another agent was reporting on their movements. Back in Washington, J. Edgar Hoover devoured these reports, which he later destroyed. One night in Hollywood, Willson jokingly claimed that he suspected "Nelly Hoover" was using the reports on Guy and Howard "for masturbatory purposes."

During the so-called romance between Howard and Guy, the actor had been cast in the 1946 soldiers-come-home drama, *Till the End of Time*. Guy appeared opposite another handsome young actor, Robert Mitchum. In time Robert, not Guy, would become Howard's all-time favorite star. In the film, which Howard reportedly saw three times, one of the plot sequences involves Guy taking Robert in his arms. Gay America swooned when the picture was released.

One day when Guy drove up to Willson's home, the agent was startled by a change in his appearance. "Not bad for a former telephone lineman making thirty five dollars a week," Guy said.

"He had a beautiful new car, very luxurious," Willson said. "I forgot the make. He was wearing a suit that only the King of England could have afforded. He wore a gold bracelet watch from Tiffany. He even wore a pair of gold

Gail Russell

cufflinks studded with diamonds. Not only that, he had a new apartment with the rent fully paid a year in advance. That weekend he was sailing on a luxury yacht to Catalina. In a few weeks, he'd be flying with Howard to San Francisco, Nevada, or Arizona. If he had to go somewhere, Howard would order that a TWA plane be held for his boy. It was quite a life as long as it lasted."

Guy was born in Bakersfield in 1922, and had some old-fashioned California sense that hospitality had to be returned. He decided to invite Howard over for a July 4 cookout in his backyard where the temperature hovered at 88° F.

615

Willson claimed that Howard would never eat ground beef. But for Guy, he did. Of course, Howard insisted on going to his trusted butcher and ordering the beef—only the choicest cut—ground in front of him and only after the grinder had been sterilized. He even drove over to Donna's Burgers in San Fernando Valley. Donna weighed at least 300 pounds but made the best hamburger buns in Los Angeles at the time. She even made the catsup herself from tomatoes grown in her own garden. Armed with some of her supplies, Howard arrived for a burger cookout in Guy's backyard at his barbecue grill, perhaps a first for America's hero.

Howard continued to dress sloppily, but for some reason he wanted Guy to be the best dressed man in Hollywood. In spite of his busy schedule, he would often take his boyfriend to Bernie Frome, the best men's tailor in the Los Angeles area. Brooklyn-born Bernie supervised the fittings himself in front of Howard's critical eyes. It was rumored that Howard's purchase of a wardrobe for Guy inspired Billy Wilder to write a scene into *Sunset Boulevard*. In that now classic clip, Gloria Swanson, cast as the faded silent screen star, Norma Desmond, purchases an expensive, tailor-made wardrobe for her gigolo, as portrayed by William Holden.

Sometimes Howard would take Guy to the tarmac at Culver City for flying lessons. On some weekends he would often "disappear" with Guy.

Both Willson and Guy were well aware of Howard's fondness for women with big breasts. "That's not the whole story," Guy confided to Willson one afternoon. He unbuttoned his custom-made shirt to reveal the evidence. "After a night with Howard, I can't take off my shirt for a week. Hickey city. Until I met Howard, I never knew I had breasts."

But there was trouble in paradise, and Willson saw it coming. The agent later claimed, "There were things Guy just wouldn't do in spite of how demanding Howard was. Guy was a top. He never let anyone fuck him. He'd submit to blow-jobs but wouldn't give them. I guess Howard got tired of trying to beat down Guy's barriers. I found too many other hot guys willing to do anything Howard wanted. At least he didn't leave Guy without a little token of his appreciation. Often he'd just dump them."

Greg Bautzer had replaced Neil McCarthy as Howard's attorney. The handsome lawyer king of the boudoir was successfully coping with Howard's jilted lovers and helping Howard avoid process servers. "As a parting token of Howard's affection," Bautzer settled fifty thousand dollars of Howard's money on Guy.

Ironically, Howard was dating Guy at the same time he was seducing Gail Russell. "For all I know, Guy was leaving Howard's bungalow as Gail was on her way in," Willson said with a certain wry amusement. "Maybe the two met that way. Who knows? I never asked. Howard must have been greatly amused when his two former lovers—one male, the other female—eventually tied the knot. I never knew if he sent them a wedding present."

Since the end of World War I, the word "bimbo" had been used to describe both dim-witted men and good-looking but dumb women, often blondes.

For Guy Madison, Howard coined the word "himbo."

When the author encountered a shirtless Guy Madison mowing his lawn at Thousand Oaks in 1992, he no longer looked like the actor labeled by Hedda Hopper as "the prettiest boy to ever set foot in Hollywood. Newer male pinups had risen to replace him. Even the gladiator movies he'd made in Europe had dried up. He was last seen on the screen in 1976 in *Won Ton Ton, the Dog Who Saved Hollywood.*

When confronted with questions about Howard Hughes, Guy at first cited him as "a distant memory."

As the night wore on, and over drinks, he became more revelatory, although requesting that his role in the life of Howard Hughes never be publicly revealed. He was filled with stories that included everybody from Robert Mitchum to Shirley Temple to Jean Simmons (Howard's unrequited love). He even asked the author to write his memoirs.

Those memoirs never materialized, mostly because Guy made it clear that he didn't want any intimate details revealed about such key forces in his life as Howard Hughes, Henry Willson, or his former wife, Gail Russell.

Guy Madison did not survive *Till the End of Time*, the title of his 1946 movie. He died on February 6, 1996.

* * *

"Arthur Miller once wrote a screenplay called *The Misfits*," Johnny Meyer said. "It was the last picture that each of its stars, Marilyn Monroe, Clark Gable, and Montgomery Clift, ever made. Each of them was doomed almost from the start of that picture. If some screenwriter ever wrote the story of Howard Hughes and Gail Russell, it would have to be called *The Misfits* as well. No two people were as ill matched as Howard and Gail. In some ways, I blame myself. I brought this odd couple together."

Gail had attended Van Nuys High School with Howard's big-bosom discovery, Jane Russell. Gail had sparkling blue eyes—"bluer than Frank Sinatra's"—and a dark, haunting, almost exotic beauty that caused her to be compared frequently to Howard's former lover, the orgasmic Hedy Lamarr.

Unlike most girls who attended Van Nuys, Gail, who had come from Chicago, wasn't dreaming of stardom in the movies. In spite of her angelic beauty, she was dreadfully shy and terrified of the camera.

Nonetheless, she was "shoved" into motion pictures when she was only 19, appearing briefly in *Henry Aldrich Gets Glamour* in 1943 before securing a better part in *The Uninvited* in 1944 with Ray Milland. If Gail Russell is remembered at all today, it is because of this picture. In the movie, she played Stella Meredith. The hit song from the film, *Stella by Starlight*, is forever associated with Gail.

It was on the set of *The Uninvited*, that Gail began to drink vodka to steady her nerves as part of a trend that would steadily increase.

When Gail was introduced to Howard by Meyer, the actress had scored her first hit, *Our Hearts Were Young and Gay*, in 1944.

From the first night he spent with Gail in his bungalow in Beverly Hills, he was captivated by this doe-eyed beauty. He told Meyer that he found her "dusky." Unlike her future husband, Guy Madison, Gail was a compliant lover, giving in to Howard's demands. She was later to tell Meyer that Howard made her "do demeaning things," although she never explained what that meant. He found her weak but also malleable, and he felt he was in total control of her, unlike his other teenager, Faith Domergue, who frequently defied him, and who occasionally ran away from him.

The more he got to know Gail, the more he realized that she was relying on vodka to get her through a day at the studio and a night with him. He did everything in his power to wean her from the bottle. He went so far as to remove all liquor in her surroundings. For dinner, he always took her to places that didn't serve alcohol.

In spite of this, she managed to sneak around and find a bottle somewhere. He accurately warned her that drinking will "destroy your beauty and wreck your career." But she didn't listen. At the time he was dating Gail, he was also issuing the same warning to Ava Gardner. She didn't listen either.

Unlike many of his mistresses, whom he'd use and dump, Howard for months and even years had a "soft spot in his heart for Gail," in the words of Johnny Meyer. "Gail would get in one jam with the police after another, often because she liked to drive while completely polluted. She got arrested many times. Every time that happened, Howard would call Greg Bautzer, who got her off."

Howard continued to see her for two years. Even after he stopped dating her, he accepted her calls. Whenever he learned about another of her run-ins with the police, he'd call Greg to discreetly post bail and get her released from jail.

By 1950 Paramount decided that it would not renew her contract after she'd made *The Lawless,* the final picture called for in her contract. Howard's warning had come true. In spite of her very limited talent, it was believed that she could have been a major star if not for her drinking.

Although Howard was in control of RKO, he did not use his power and influence to get Gail cast in one of his pictures. On the set of *My Forbidden Past* in 1951, he told Robert Mitchum: "We've got work for Jane Russell, maybe even Rosalind Russell, but no Gail Russell."

Meyer believed that Howard gave Gail "a few infusions of cash" post-1950 but his patience with her was wearing thin. His spies kept Howard abreast of her affairs, notably with John Wayne when he helped her win the lead in *Angel and the Badman* in 1947. But after Paramount dropped her, the parts dried up at other studios except for an occasional role.

In November of 1953, when Howard learned via Greg Bautzer that Gail had been arrested once again for drunk driving, he refused to listen to her call for help or post bond. "Enough is enough."

He'd learn that Gail had pulled up behind a police car and had persisted in honking her horn at the officer, who eventually arrested her. Photographers were waiting at the station. A photograph of her being restrained by her jailer, Robert Mildrew, made frontpages of newspapers around the nation.

Gail once tried to explain to Howard and others, even her husband Guy Madison, why she drank. "I was possessed with an agonizing kind of self-consciousness where I felt my sides tightening in a knot, where my face and hands grew clammy, where I couldn't open my mouth, where I felt compelled to turn and run if I had to meet new people. When my parents had guests, I would run, get under the piano and hide there. Everything happened so fast in my life. I was a sad character. I was sad because of myself. I didn't have any self-confidence, I didn't believe I had any talent. I didn't know how to have fun. I was afraid. The bottle made me believe in myself. It gave me the self-confidence men had taken from me. What was I afraid of? Guy used to ask me that. Howard asked me that too. But he too was haunted by his demons. I used to tell them that I didn't exactly know what I was afraid of—of life, I guess. Isn't life something to be frightened of?"

When Jane Fonda made *The Morning After*, released in 1986, she studied Gail's life as a means of convincingly playing an alcoholic.

Although a few minor roles awaited her, her career was all but over after that final arrest. "Demon rum had her in its grasp," Meyer once commented. She was found dead on August 26, 1961, in her tiny studio apartment in West Hollywood. She was only 36 years old. Her corpse was surrounded by empty vodka bottles and tubes of barbiturates. Her death was attributed to acute alcoholism which had induced a heart attack.

Gail Russell and her jailer, 1953

* * *
Vancouver/Las Vegas/Los Angeles, 1945-47

As regards men, Yvonne de Carlo had nowhere to go but up after an elderly boarder in her grandfather's house walked into her bedroom nude one morning and urinated on her as she slept. Rudely awakened to life and its vagaries, Yvonne was sixteen years old at the time. From there she would go, after many a detour, to having sex with humpy Burt Lancaster (her costar in the 1947 *Brute Force*) on a black mink coat under an oleander bush in her back yard.

Her path would inevitably lead to Howard. Historically, over a period of several decades, his bed partners and her lovers would sometimes overlap: Robert Stack, Robert Taylor, and Clark Cable. Like Howard, the megaphoned crooner, Rudy Vallee would not only be attracted to Jane Greer, but to Yvonne as well. A different type of millionaire playboy, Prince Aly Khan (son of the Aga Khan) would often fall for the same women Howard did, especially Gene Tierney and Rita Hayworth (whom he married). The Prince would also pursue Yvonne.

A native of Vancouver, and a former dancer, Yvonne rose very slowly in show business after an unpromising start filled with many disappointments. When she was appearing in bit parts, Howard took no notice of her. Costarring in *The Road to Morocco*, with Bob Hope and Bing Crosby, actor Anthony Quinn was enraptured by Yvonne in her small part as a harem dancer. "I want to place you on a pedestal where I can worship you hour after hour. With your goddess-like figure, you should never wear clothes."

By 1945, Yvonne was cast in her first starring role in *Salome, Where She Danced.* In it, she played a Mata Hari type spy. Howard finally took notice of her. Ironically, the role had originally been intended for his girlfriend, Jane Greer.

Even before its release, Howard had seen Yvonne shimmy her way through Salome five times. "He seemed crazed by Yvonne," Meyer said. At the time, Yvonne was billed as "The Most Beautiful Girl in the World." That may be hard for television viewers to believe, as she is best remembered today for her most famous role, that of Lily Munster in the 1963 CBS-TV series, *The Munsters*.

As a film, *Salome*, a Technicolor fluff, was dismissed as a "fantastic horse-opera" by *The New York Times*. Howard wasn't interested in either the picture or the story—only Yvonne. "She's pulchritudinous," he told Meyer.

"I don't even know what that means," his pimp said.

"A looker with tits."

Immediately after his long film session with Salome, Howard demanded that Meyer set up a rendezvous between him and its star. Within hours, Meyer learned that Yvonne had returned to Vancouver to celebrate Yvonne de Carlo

Yvonne De Carlo

Week, the hometown girl who had made good in Hollywood. On hearing this, Howard demanded that Meyer fly immediately to Vancouver to arrange a date for him.

In Canada, Meyer encountered Yvonne at a gala dinner thrown in her behalf. She readily agreed to meet Howard.

Taking off on September 5, 1945 in his D-23, Howard violated wartime regulations and flew across the Canadian border into British Columbia. To gain clearance during those closing days of World War II, he falsely claimed he was conducting top-secret government business. In spite of the rationing that was stringently enforced at the time, he tapped into a supply of emergency army fuel. At the Canadian border, authorities noticed the Army Air Corps's star emblazoned on the fuselage of his B-23, and quickly cleared him.

In Washington, J. Edgar Hoover heard about this impulsive flight. He immediately assigned two of his agents in Vancouver to follow Howard's trail. He was mystified why the aviator would be making this sudden and mysterious flight to Canada. Hoover's initial fear was that Howard was going to turn over secret plans to Canadian aviation authorities, or cut a separate deal with them to build aircraft superior to anything the United States was flying at the time.

Left behind in Los Angeles were Lana Turner, Linda Darnell, Ava Gardner, and a "poor and lonely" Faith Domergue.

The next evening in Vancouver, Howard showed up at yet another dinner honoring Yvonne, "the conquering heroine." She vividly recalled her first sight of him in her memoirs, *Yvonne* published in 1987 and dedicated to everybody "from kings and princes to truck drivers." She found him "lanky, underfed, and remarkably sad. I immediately felt my maternal instincts coming out. Not that I was attracted to him in any way; I just felt kind of sorry for him."

The next day he met her family, grandmother and all, and took her to the best golf course in Vancouver where he tried to teach her the game. That sport was followed by a sightseeing flight over Vancouver and, later, a shopping expedition. He even remembered to purchase a leather purse for grandmother.

After his first date with Yvonne, Howard told Meyer that the actress resembled his mother, but he'd said that about many women—true or not.

In Washington, Hoover assigned two of his agents in Vancouver to trail both

621

Yvonne and Howard. A journalist was also on their trail. He called his scoop into *The New York Post*, whose headline the next day proclaimed: HUGHES CHASES DE CARLO TO CANADA.

Action was immediate at the War Materiél Command in Washington. Officials there stripped Howard of military privileges for his personal fleet of airplanes and also cancelled his fuel priority.

Even a maid was hired at Howard's hotel suite to search for "rubbers" from Howard's nightly lovemaking with Yvonne. When one was found, it was dispatched to Washington where Hoover had his laboratory test Howard's semen.

Hoover's wiretaps revealed many of Howard's plans, including his plans to extend TWA routes across the Pacific, an expansion that would position his airline into direct competition with Pan American.

Later, an FBI report (#62-2682), wrongly concluded that by October 2, 1945, Yvonne De Carlo had succeeded Ava Gardner as the primary consort of Howard Hughes.

When it was time to leave Vancouver, Howard threw a big party for Yvonne, her family, and friends, bringing in an orchestra for the occasion. Yvonne recalled that "I felt like a queen."

She remembered more, finding that his seduction of her "wasn't bad— maybe a little too much on the clinical side." At that point in his life, he'd been studying medical books on sexual intercourse—"you know," he told Yvonne, "the kind that's delivered in plain brown paper."

She felt that his lovemaking grew better in time—"maybe all that reading paid off." In her view he was more an "expert" lover than a "passionate" one. In her memoirs, she claimed that Howard would go into the differences between male and female orgasm, calling the female climax "an implosion, a reaction to the male explosion." At times she found his clinical sex talk boring.

She was among the first to notice that he had stopped cutting his toenails. "He had long, curling toenails that nearly wrapped themselves around his toes," she said.

He was growing increasingly obsessed with the penis size of men who had made love to women he was also seducing. This began to manifest itself with Yvonne, as he demanded details about past lovers—"right down to dimensions."

She did not have to report to the studio right away, so he flew her to Reno and on to Las Vegas where he checked her into El Rancho with himself. There she remembered his bathing of her. He always liked his women very clean before he performed oral sex on them. Soaping her breasts, he said, "There is nothing quite so appealing on a woman as a nice set of lavalières." Years later, when Yvonne was "comparing notes" about men with Ava Gardner, she told her that Howard was something of a "lavalière man." Ava laughed but already knew that.

In Las Vegas, Howard was not secretive in his courtship of Yvonne, appearing at such clubs and resorts as the Flamingo with her. She wondered why their names weren't getting into the press. Later, she found out that Meyer was bribing columnists with whiskey, French perfumes, and even gold watches to keep their romance out of print.

Howard wooed her between phone calls. "He was always taking a call or making one," she said. At a stopover at a small airport, as she was coming out of the women's room, she overheard him angrily talking to someone on the phone. "Is this your final answer?" Howard asked this unknown person. "You just plain don't give a damn, do you? You never cared at all, did you?"

Yvonne didn't know who he was talking to and "tippy-toed" back to the plane without his discovering her.

When he'd joined her in the cockpit, he grabbed her by the shoulders. "Are you serious about me?" he asked.

She stuttered through her reply. "Why…uh, yes…yes, I am."

All he did was nod at her answer, as he prepared his private plane for take-off.

Once in Vegas he presented her with a tiny watch with a black ribbon strap. "A watch that one could find for ten dollars at a corner drugstore," Yvonne said. In contrast, he'd presented Ava Gardner a cardboard box filled with a million dollars worth of jewelry from Tiffany's. Yvonne would have preferred an engagement ring like he'd presented to Ginger Rogers.

From Vegas, he flew her to Pebble Beach for three days, checking her into a lavish suite adjoining his at the Del Monte Lodge. He confided in her that he hadn't been here since the late 20s when he'd arrived with Billie Dove and had proposed marriage to her, only to be rejected.

Yvonne later admitted that she fully expected a marriage proposal from him as well, but none was forthcoming. "He probably knew I wouldn't have turned him down," she later wrote in her memoirs.

Before flying back to Los Angeles with Howard, Yvonne said that she was "seriously in love." Back at work at her studio, she continued to see Howard at his suite at the Town House Hotel where they spent many a beautiful evening making love. They were often spotted about town, perhaps at a dinner at Perino's, where that well-dressed couple sitting at the next table might well have been FBI agents.

Her rival at Universal was a beauty from the Dominican Republic, Maria Montez. Today, one of the reigning figures of cinematic camp, Maria Montez is known as "Cobra Woman." Even though they were rivals at the studio, Maria and Yvonne became friends off-screen. Yvonne remembered meeting her for lunch at the Brown Derby. Accompanying Maria was none other than Pat DeCicco, her agent. "Thees Howard Hughes," Maria said. "He ees not for you."

"Don't you know about all the other girls in his life?" DeCicco asked. "Don't overlook Linda Darnell and countless others, a whole stable of chicks stashed away."

Yvonne recalled that she "felt sick" at hearing these revelations, although knowing they were true.

She said that she wanted to announce to the world: "Hey, folks, he's mine." She kept waiting and waiting for a marriage proposal that never came. Finally, she decided to confront him. "Will we ever be married?" she asked him one night at the Town House. "No!" came his instant reply.

Three years went by before she heard from him again. One night he showed up unannounced at her home with a script under his arm. She was shocked by his appearance. As if sensing that, he kept asking her how he looked. She told him he looked fine.

"I lied," she later wrote. "He looked dreadful—like a caricature of his former self. His face seemed drawn, there was a pronounced stoop to his shoulders, and he walked with a slight limp. He had aged at least twenty years and had become a shell of the man I had known and loved."

In front of him, she read the script he'd brought along, claiming it had two great female parts—one for Ava Gardner, another for her. After putting down the script, she told him that the part would be wrong for her.

That was the last time she ever saw him. Years later, she said she didn't even get to keep the cheap watch. One night a robber broke into her house, stealing not only the watch but all of her other jewelry as well.

As the years went by, an aging Yvonne spoke kindly of Howard, calling him "one of the most important loves of my life."

* * *

Los Angeles, 1946

Over a period of six years, beginning in 1940, Howard pursued Linda Darnell on and off, sometimes going for months without calling, and then just showing up. She'd married her cameraman and "father figure," J. Peverell Marley in 1943, but a wedding ring didn't deter Howard in his pursuit of her.

Originally in 1939, Marley had fallen for Linda while she was still underaged, or, as he preferred to say, "jailbait," or "San Quentin quail." She was appearing opposite Tyrone Power in *Daytime Wife* when she caught Marley's attention. At the time, "Pev," as he was nicknamed, was the best friend of Tyrone. The two men spent so much time together in Tyrone's dressing room and in the Fox sauna that Darryl F. Zanuck warned his chief male star "to cut out this faggot stuff!"

The cameraman, who'd photographed such stars as Pola Negri and Gloria Swanson, rival silent screen vamps, was not handsome like Tyrone but exceedingly charming.

Linda said that on the set of *Daytime Wife*, she'd kiss Tyrone and could feel his hard-on rising. "After a take, I'd go and sit on Pev's lap. I'd get him aroused as well. It was like a game with me. But I always lost. Hot and bothered, Pev would go and give his noon-day fuck to Ty—not me. He said I was too young, and Ty was too willing. Pev worshipped beauty: beautiful Ty or beautiful Linda. I guess he liked fucking me better because he married me."

Throughout the war years, Linda and Howard were so secretive about their relationship that her own agent, a generally trusted friend, William Schiffrin, didn't know about it. The only person Linda trusted with her secret was her best friend, Ann Miller. Like Howard, Miller was born in Houston. A leggy brunette with a mile-wide smile, she was known at MGM for her gun-fast tap dancing and breathtaking spins. She and Linda remained close friends until Linda's tragic death.

After both Linda and Howard had died, Ann spoke somewhat candidly about their secret relationship, and her own role in it.

Linda called her agent, William Schiffrin, one April day in 1946. She told him that Howard Hughes had phoned her and had invited her for lunch. Over the phone, she asked Schiffrin to come along as a chaperone. She also lied to him, claiming that she'd never met Howard before and was afraid that he'd put the make on her unless she was accompanied by her agent.

"You don't need a chaperone," Schiffrin chided her. "You're a big girl now!" Nonetheless, he agreed to accompany her to this luncheon. He mistakenly thought his client would be meeting Howard for the first time.

A limousine arrived to drive them to the airport. "Oh, my God," Linda said, "he's going to fly us to New York for lunch—I just know it."

"You wouldn't expect the great Howard Hughes to invite us to lunch at Barney's Beanery, now would you?" he asked her.

"Stick with me at every minute," Linda pleaded. "I hear he's the biggest wolf in Hollywood and he might take advantage of me."

At the airport, an attendant greeted the agent and his star and directed them aboard a TWA *Constellation*. On board, they were startled to find that they were the only passengers, and that the plane's destination was San Francisco. As the large and virtually empty plane taxied down the runway, that same attendant served both of them champagne, pouring it from a rare bottle of Dom Perignon from Howard's pre-war stash of liquor.

Once airborne, Linda was directed to the front of "Connie" where she found Howard in the pilot's seat. She hadn't seen him in more than a year. He invited her to be seated as his co-pilot.

"I don't know what happened in the cockpit," Schiffrin later said. "All I know is I hadn't drunk French champagne since the war, and I was going to get my fill." By the time Connie reached the Bay area, Schiffrin was drunk. He did remember Howard and Linda getting off the plane, hand in hand, and walking across the runway as he staggered behind them.

Howard had booked the entire top floor of the Fairmont Hotel just for the three of them. He'd even hired a small private orchestra to play for them. An elegant champagne buffet of lobster and caviar had been laid out. "The bastard even knew Linda's favorite flower," Schiffrin said. "Yellow tulips. Those flowers were everywhere." The agent/chaperone claimed he had to excuse himself to retreat to his own bedroom because he was about to puke from all that champagne consumed on an empty stomach.

"After San Francisco, Howard wooed Linda with a vengeance," Ann Miller said, "in spite of my warnings that he would use her and then drop her. I also warned her about other women. I knew Lana in those days too." She was referring, of course, to Lana Turner at MGM. "Lana told me that she was going to become the next Mrs. Howard Hughes. I also knew Gene Tierney, who, in spite of Oleg Cassini, was also considering walking down the aisle with Hughes. Even Paulette Goddard hoped that she might marry Howard, that he'd jump-start her career the way Chaplin had done."

Howard hadn't thought much of Linda's last film for Fox, *Centennial Summer*, in which she'd co-starred with Jeanne Crain and Cornel Wilde. He viewed it as a rip-off of Judy Garland's *Meet Me in St. Louis*.

He did accept her invitation to fly for a visit to the set of her next film, *My Darling Clementine*, later described by *Time* magazine as a "horse opera for the carriage trade." Linda, playing an earthy mistress, Chihuahua, was co-starring with Henry Fonda and Victor Mature, directed by John Ford.

Howard flew to Monument Valley, California, for the outdoor scenes.

* * *

Monument Valley, 1946

On the set of the film, Howard spent more time with Ford, Mature, and a rising young actor, John Ireland, than he did with Linda. "Howard said they were just playing cards," Linda later told Ann. The tap-dancer wondered if that were "all those boys were doing. I've heard stories," the much more sophisticated Miller told Linda.

The exact details of what happened on the set of *My Darling Clementine* may never be known. It became the subject of a whisper campaign in Hollywood, gossipy entertainment for many a late-night party.

Howard came to the set and virtually ignored Henry Fonda, but he bonded with Victor Mature, who was playing the role of Doc Halliday. Howard also related to the film's director, John Ford, and spent considerable time with a young actor, John Ireland, playing Billy Clanton. At that time, Ireland was attracting more interest for his exploits in the boudoir than he was on the screen.

One actress facetiously claimed that she had to be taken to the hospital and "sewed up again" after having intercourse with the massively endowed Ireland. Joan Crawford once confided to Billy Haines that Ireland "went where no man has ever gone before—except Porfirio Rubirosa."

Mature resented hearing stories about Ireland's endowment. Before Ireland hit Hollywood, Mature was the cock of the roost. When serving as a petty officer in the Coast Guard in 1943, he was photographed lying "buck ass naked" on an army cot reading a book. A private took that later-to-be-infamous snapshot of Mature. Somehow the picture made it back to Hollywood where it was widely reprinted and distributed, especially to gay America. Gore Vidal once wrote that if Nazi soldiers had seen that picture of Mature's endowment, they would have surrendered immediately.

A close friend of John Wayne's, character actor Ward Bond, was also appearing in the picture. He once said that he and John Wayne had long known that Ford was a closeted bisexual. Bond suspected that the director was servicing both Ireland and Mature during the shooting of the film. "He was fond of saying that 'all actors are crap,'" Bond claimed, "but he could easily succumb to a handsome actor if he packed the right pistol."

Born of Austrian immigrant parents in Kentucky, Mature had virtually invent-

Victor Mature

ed the word "beefcake." In spite of his wooden performances on the screen, Mature was extroverted and gregarious in private. Howard had been impressed with the actor's physique ever since he'd seen him as a fur-clad caveman opposite Carole Landis in *One Million B.C.* in 1940.

Like Ford, Mature was another closeted bisexual, preferring anonymous homosexual encounters in parks, toilets, at beach clubs, and in the back seat of cars in parking lots. Theater ushers were a specialty. In contrast, the women he seduced over the years were A-list beauties—notably Gene Tierney, Veronica Lake, Lana Turner, and Rita Hayworth, each of whom would also be seduced by Howard.

"I can't act," Mature told Howard, "but what I've got that the other competition doesn't is this." Drying off in front of Howard after a shower, he gave him a front-row overview of his beefy charms. Howard later told Johnny Meyer, "I wasn't sure if Victor were talking about his muscular body or his genitals—both mighty impressive."

Over dinner on his first night in Monument Valley, Howard ate with Mature, leaving Linda to sit it out in her hotel room. Mature confided in Howard: "I can't help it if I've got a good set of muscles. But I want to prove

627

I've got something more. I'm tired of being nothing but a male striptease artist."

At that point, and hoping to seduce Mature later that night, Howard promised him the lead in a future picture. Before turning in, Ford invited Mature and Howard to join him in his bungalow. Arriving there, Howard found that Ford had already polished off a bottle. Sitting next to him on the bed, with his shirt off, Howard spotted the young actor, John Ireland.

The next morning the set of *My Darling Clementine* was buzzing with the news of what had happened the previous night in Ford's bungalow. Apparently, if Ward Bond is to be believed, the drunken night turned into a cock-measuring contest. Both Howard and Ford agreed to put up a thousand dollars each if the two young actors would "get it hard" and allow them to take measurements.

Over breakfast the next morning, Johnny Meyer, who had flown to Monument Valley with Howard, asked his boss, "Who won?"

"It was too close to call," Howard informed his pimp. "Besides, I think that son of a bitch, John Ford, was too drunk to take accurate measurements. All I know is that there were two feet of cock exposed in that bungalow last night, more or less equally distributed. Those boys even have me beat, and my ladies tell me I'm the greatest."

"Hell with Mature and Ireland," Meyer said, sucking up to his boss. "You'll always be the champ in my book."

"I'm no god damn champ," Howard responded in anger, rising from the table. "My old problem has returned." He walked away.

Meyer knew that his boss was referring to another of his bouts of impotence. Meyer paid the check and rushed to catch up with Howard. "It's a problem I don't think I'm gonna get over," Howard said. "I just can't count on Old Faithful any more. Sometimes it's there for me. Sometimes in front of the most beautiful women, it lets me down." He looked up at the western sky. "I'm just going to disappear one day and find that Fountain of Youth that Ponce de Leon was searching for in Florida and The Bahamas."

When Howard became chief at RKO, he remembered his long-ago promise to his sexual partner in Monument Valley. He borrowed Mature from 20th Century Fox and cast him to play an Italian-born gambler in *Gambling House*, released in 1951. Mature starred opposite Howard's young mistress, Terry Moore, in this lackluster film.

Impressed with Mature's performance in the bedroom—not on the screen— Howard also cast him in *His Kind of Woman* the same year. That film starred Jane Russsell, still under personal contract to Howard. In 1952, he cast Mature once again in *The Las Vegas Story*, in which he also appeared opposite Jane.

That picture is known mainly today because of a lawsuit brought by its scriptwriter, Paul Jarrico. Jarrico had written a pro-Communist propaganda picture, *Song of Russia*, for MGM. In April of 1951, when Jarrico refused to admit if he were a Communist in front of the House Committee on Un-American Activities, Howard fired him. By that time, Howard had become a violent anti-

Communist. He also removed Jarrico's name from the screen credits and black-listed him. Refusing arbitration with the Screen Writers Guild, Howard was sued for $350,000. But the complaint was dismissed by a judge.

Howard later told Meyer, "I could have Mature any time I wanted him, and I wanted him frequently. But my favorite male star is Robert Mitchum. That handsome devil, however, has always eluded me. Maybe one day!"

* * *

Los Angeles/Chicago, 1946-65

After visiting Linda on the set of *My Darling Clementine*, Howard flew to New York on a business trip. What Linda didn't know was that he was escorting Lana Turner to Manhattan. Unaware of the two-timing going on, Linda became convinced that Howard was going to marry her. She absolutely refused to listen to the warnings issued by Ann Miller. In fact, she became so convinced that they'd eventually marry that she called her producer at Fox, Darryl F. Zanuck, to tell him that she was quitting pictures to become the full-time wife of Howard Hughes. "I'm giving up my career for him."

"You're out of your fucking mind!" Zanuck shouted at her. "That horny bastard doesn't need a wife. He needs a harem and a few shirtless teenage boys on the side."

Linda was rearranging her life to marry Howard. She knew that her marriage to Marley was "all but over—just waiting for the burial." But when Howard flew back to the West Coast, he didn't even call her. Instead he phoned Ann Miller.

"At first I thought Howard Hughes was calling me for a date," Ann said, "and I didn't want to betray Linda. But I thought I'd better go out with him without telling Linda. I figured I'd at least learn what he was up to. After all, he was Howard Hughes!"

Over dinner with Howard, he told her what he hadn't told Linda. Their relationship was over. "There will be no marriage," he said to Ann, who wasn't at all surprised. She'd been warning Linda of that all along. "Tell her to call off those god damn wedding plans. I'm going to marry Lana."

Ann later claimed that she spent ten days and ten nights with Linda, fearing that she might take her own life. "I told her that it was all over between Howard and her," Ann said, "and she took it real bad. She was on the verge of a nervous breakdown. I don't think she really loved Howard. Who could love that one? She just wanted to be Mrs. Howard Hughes. But what gal didn't?"

What Ann admitted only years later was that she went out on four dates with Howard, after she'd delivered the bad news to Linda. "The way I figured it, he didn't want Linda but he might want me. What a fool I was. I gave him what he wanted, but he told me I was too flashy—that he preferred a more natural look in a woman. I placed several calls to him over the next few months after he broke with Linda. He never returned my calls. I was never around long enough to be called one of the gals in his harem."

When many of his former mistresses fell on bad days and pleaded with Howard to come to their rescue, if only with a small loan, he turned both a figurative and literal deaf ear to them. On other occasions, he could be generous, as he was with Linda. Even though he'd broken with her, he still regarded her with a certain affection.

When he read that her home had been broken into and all her clothing stolen, he asked Meyer to hire a couple of private dicks to investigate. These detectives tracked down the robber. It turned out to be John Spainhour, an out-of-work gay actor who had worked briefly for Linda as her unpaid secretary, answering fan mail.

Spainhour had been having a torrid affair with song-and-dance man, Dan Dailey, a married homosexual. The talented hoofer had appeared in some of Fox's major musicals, playing opposite Betty Grable. Dailey was the most likely suspect.

A cross-dresser, he'd stolen dresses or gowns worn by either Betty Grable or Linda during his raids of Fox's wardrobe. Both Grable and Linda had complained to Zanuck about these thefts. "Dan had made several midnight raids on my wardrobe before," Linda told Ann Miller. "But never anything so daring as to get his gay friend to steal from me."

On learning the details, Howard righted all wrongs. No stranger to cross dressing himself, he ordered Dailey to return Linda's wardrobe—"every stitch of her clothing; and, yes, even the panties." To compensate, Howard gave Dailey a gift certificate worth five thousand dollars at one of the leading department stores of Beverly Hills.

"Howard always had a soft spot in his heart for drag queens," Meyer once said.

Howard entered Linda's life once again when he cast her in *Second Chance* in 1953. He starred her opposite his favorite male star, Robert Mitchum. Howard had discovered 3-D and wanted to be a pioneer in the new medium, although he would soon drop it. At the time he cast her in the film, Linda's career was on the skids as she moved deeper and deeper into "that certain age" and alcoholism, two lethal combinations in Hollywood.

After *Second Chance*, he would see her only one more time.

In April of 1965, her career virtually over, her finances in disastrous shape, Linda visited her close friend, Jeanne Curtis, in her new home in Glenview, Illinois, a suburb of Chicago. She had first met Jeanne on the set of *Unfaithfully Yours* in which she'd co-starred with Rex Harrison in 1948.

Linda had stayed up late that night, drinking and smoking, to watch *Star Dust* on television. She'd made the film in 1940, the year she'd met Howard.

Peverell Marley had been the cameraman. But at the time Linda was not sleeping with Marley but with two actors in the film, co-stars John Payne and George Montgomery. Louella Parsons had called them "the two handsomest men in Hollywood."

At some point during that night in Glenview Linda fell asleep with a cigarette in her hand. The room caught on fire. Delivered in an ambulance to the Skokie Valley Community Hospital, she was in tragic shape upon arrival. The intense heat had fused fragments of her pajamas to her skin. In surgery for three hours, much of the burnt tissue was cut from her body. Nearly ninety percent of her body was "turned into a smoky fossil," said Dr. Peter Verges. "There's not a lot we can do to save her." A tracheotomy was performed so that she could breathe. Fluids were fed intravenously into her charred body.

Motivated by some mysterious business, Howard was in Chicago at the time. His aides drove him to the hospital. One of his Mormon guards went inside and bribed a hospital official, allowing Howard to come in dressed as a doctor.

As such, he was allowed to enter Linda's private room where she was guarded 24 hours a day. Thinking he was a doctor, a nurse, Sarah Beevil, told him, "I don't think Miss Darnell is in any pain—she has no nerve endings left."

Howard stood looking down at what was virtually a corpse. Linda's eyes were swollen shut, and she'd slipped into a dreamy state of unconsciousness. The nurse told Howard that about an hour ago, she'd heard Linda speak. She said, "I'm not going to die. Who says I'm going to die?"

"To hear her voice I had to put my finger over her tracheotomy," Sarah said.

There was an eerie, almost creepy quality in the "doctor," Howard himself, standing and looking down at this burnt-out shell of a once beautiful woman to whom he'd made love so frequently. It was as if he had to see for himself that she was rapidly fading from life.

"It wasn't that he was in love with Linda," Johnny Meyer later said. "Who knows what really went on in the head of Howard Hughes, but I think he wanted to see what a burn victim looks like when it survives a fire. Howard often told me that he feared he'd die in a fiery plane crash. He dreaded living after the crash more than he did dying in the crash. He didn't want to hold onto life when life meant nothing but pain and agony. I think he really wanted to see Linda before she went. In some voyeuristic, obsessional way, he was seeing his own future corpse. He always told me that he knew he'd die while airborne. In that, his vision was prophetic."

The nurse, Sarah, intruded on Howard, bringing him back to reality. "What more can I do to help you, doctor?"

When he heard that, he said nothing but quickly left the hospital room and headed rapidly down the corridor before he could be exposed.

Mercifully, Linda never woke up and went peacefully to her death. A memorial service was held on May 8 at a private chapel in Burbank, but

Howard did not attend. Neither did he send flowers.

One of his Mormon guards later revealed that Howard watched *Blood and Sand* nearly every month for years. "Over and over again," the aide claimed.

The movie had starred three of his former lovers, all in their prime. In order of his seduction of them, they were Tyrone Power, Linda Darnell, and Rita Hayworth.

* * *

Los Angeles/New York, 1940-1946

Most tales about the life and loves of Lana Turner, MGM's icy blonde sex goddess of alluring sensuality, claim that she met Howard after the war. Lana, in later life, had a different version. She maintained that she met Howard in 1940 and was introduced to him by her friend, Johnny Meyer, who made a career of knowing all the up-and-coming screen goddesses of his day.

At the time Meyer arranged for Lana to have a date with Howard, she was also being pursued by Clark Gable, who was supposed to be madly in love with Carole Lombard, and by Spencer Tracy, who was supposed to be madly in love with Howard's ex, Katharine Hepburn.

According to Lana, during one of the many drunken evenings she used to spend at the deluxe bar of the Bel Air Hotel in the 1960s, she gave Meyer her private phone number and told him that Howard could call her. Greg Bautzer, Howard's attorney who had already taken Lana's virginity, had sung her praises to Howard. The fact that Lana was married at the time to bandleader Artie Shaw didn't bother Howard in the least. It can be assumed that whenever Howard started dating Lana, Artie was out of town.

Lana "was about twenty," as she recalled, when Howard first came to call on her, wearing a battered fedora and a dirty white shirt, arriving in an even more battered Chevrolet. Although she claimed that she didn't really care for sex that much, the list of her lovers seemed to prove otherwise. That roster would be long and notable, including Desi Arnaz and Richard Burton, with supporting roles played by Sean Connery, Kirk Douglas, Victor Mature, Robert Stack, Frank Sinatra, President John F. Kennedy, and countless pick-ups, including several (known) gas station attendants.

A jealous screen vamp, the aging Gloria Swanson, dismissed Lana with a stinging comment: "She is not even an actress...only a trollop." Robert Taylor, her co-star in the 1941 film *Johnny Eager*, had a different view: "Lana is the type of woman a guy would risk five years in jail for rape."

Her boss, Louis B. Mayer, did not believe Lana's oft-stated comment that she wasn't interested in sex. "She was completely amoral," he once said. "If she saw a stagehand with tight pants and a muscular build, she'd invite him to her dressing room."

After Johnny Meyer's pre-arranged dinner date with Lana, and two other nights on the town set up by Howard himself, she had a complaint. At the time, she was also secretly dating Robert Stack, "but that was more of a friendship than a romance," she later claimed.

Lana's complaint was that on all three dates, Howard hadn't even made a pass at her—"not even a kiss on the cheek." Robert said that he told Lana that she could get Howard in bed if she acted more alluring. "I must have been a fool to have said that," Robert recalled years later. "Imagine me telling the blonde sex goddess of MGM—Hollywood's original 'Sweater Girl'—to act more alluring."

Robert gave a pool party at his family home at Rossmore and invited both Lana and Howard, each of whom arrived separately. Lana was already in a bikini-like two-piece bathing suit when Howard pulled up in his battered Chevy two hours late. He was attired in a dirty white shirt,

Lana Turner

baggy trousers, and a fedora. He refused Robert's offer to don a pair of bathing trunks, presumably because he was embarrassed to show off his skinny frame.

Perhaps Lana had decided to take Robert's advice and make herself more alluring. "I'd told her that Howard was a boob boy, and if there's one thing Lana had, it was boobs, as every movie fan who'd seen those bouncy tits in *They Won't Forget* could testify."

"I remember it like it was only yesterday," Robert later recalled. "Lana took a running dive into my pool. As she did, her strap broke loose and just floated away. She swam around a bit. It was hard for her to swim and cover her boobs at the same time. Finally, she emerged like Venus from the pool, modestly trying to conceal herself and deliberately not doing a good job of it. Ever the gallant gentleman, Howard was waiting at poolside with a large pink bath towel."

"That seemed to do the trick," Robert said. "When Lana called me the next morning, she claimed that she'd gone to bed with Howard but had found sex with him unsatisfactory. She said that he'd gone down on her but she'd refused to return the favor. 'I don't like it that way, as you know,' she said. 'We finally ended up in the missionary position,' she claimed."

For oral gratification at the time, Howard still had easy availability to the greatest female beauties of the 1940s along with a series of aspiring and extraordinarily handsome young actors supplied by Henry Willson, *agent extraordinaire*.

If Lana is to be believed, her affair with Howard, at least during most of the war, was "a casual thing." Considering that she had two husbands during this period, Artie Shaw and Stephen Crane, her word sounds genuine.

In fact, she later claimed that it was Johnny Meyer who invited her to a dinner where she met husband number two, the handsome young Crane who told her he was in the tobacco business. With Crane, Lana would have a daughter, Cheryl Christine, born July 25, 1943. Howard sent Lana a diamond bracelet to mark the occasion. World headlines and one of the greatest scandals in Hollywood history would await Lana and Cheryl.

Lana remembered that after she'd filmed *Johnny Eager* with Robert Taylor in 1941, she arrived home from the studio to find Howard sitting only in a bath towel in the living room. Her mother, Mildred, was sewing up a tear in his trousers. "Why the towel, Howard?" Lana inquired. "Are you embarrassed for us to see you in your shorts?"

"Not wearing any," he told her, as Mildred laughed.

"What?" Lana howled. "You go around with those dirty slacks next to your body…with no shorts?"

"That was all the sewing that went on for Howard in the Turner household," Lana later said. "Don't believe all that bullshit in the press, especially Louella's column, that I had all my towels embroidered with the initials of LH in anticipation of a marriage to Howard. Besides, I hate embroidered towels."

Once between pictures when Lana remembered that she was "growing restless," she called Howard and asked him if he'd teach her to fly. She'd read that he'd taught former lovers like Billie Dove and Katharine Hepburn how to fly. Dropping work on his new version of the XF-11, he readily agreed. "He picked me up in his battered car, drove me to Culver City, and the next thing I knew we were on our way to Nevada. After another missionary position night of sex, he took me to what looked like an abandoned airfield. There he taught me to fly day after day. He told me that one day I might play a lady pilot in a film."

Although Howard neglected the much-married Lana for months at a time during the war years, he was there for her when she needed assistance. On one frantic morning she called him to tell him that she'd come down with a bad case of syphilis, and she feared that she might have infected him. It was never proven but Lana—perhaps erroneously—felt that she'd contracted the venereal disease from her lover, the Turkish actor, Turhan Bey. Howard didn't want to tell her that he might have given her the disease himself. Nonetheless, he arranged for her to get the best of medical treatment.

Before he resumed a sexual relationship with her months later, he sent Dr. Verne Mason to examine her to make sure she was completely cured.

Lana called Howard two more times during the war with medical emergencies. In each case she was pregnant. Instead of thinking one of her husbands was the father, she cited on separate occasions both Mickey Rooney and later Desi Arnaz. Each time Howard generously flew her to Mexico City where she checked into a private and very discreet clinic, as he'd arranged, to have abortions.

It wasn't until February 14, 1946, on Valentine's Day, that a proposal of marriage came in from Howard. At a cost of $250,000, he invited some Hollywood stars to fly with him to New York. He would be piloting TWA's "Connie" himself.

For ten days, he'd booked the stars into the exclusive Sherry-Netherland Hotel in Manhattan. Aboard the plane was the blonde bombshell, Virginia Mayo, the Samuel Goldwyn star, in whom Howard had expressed some sexual interest until she got airsick.

Other notables aboard this publicity junket were Paulette Goddard, the faithful Johnny Meyer, gangster Bugsy Siegel, William Powell, Edward G. Robinson, Myrna Loy, Walter Pidgeon, Jack Warner, Jack Carson, Tyrone Power, Frank Morgan, David O. Selznick, Randolph Scott, Harry Cohn, and Celeste Holm. Also on board was Lana herself, Howard's "official" date. She was flying with her daughter, Cheryl, and Cheryl's governess. In spite of having Lana aboard, Howard had privately instructed Meyer to arrange dates with both Veronica and Paulette during their ten-day stay in Manhattan, with Howard paying all the expenses. Even so, both Paulette and Veronica were ignored during the cross-country flight. Only Howard's lover, Cary Grant, was allowed to sit in the co-pilot's seat next to him.

Constance Moore, the musical star, was also on board with her husband, Johnny Maschio, the Hollywood agent who had laboriously arranged the nuts-and-bolts details of the celebrity trip as a means of building publicity for Howard's struggling TWA. Constance remembered that restaurateur Dave Chasen back in Los Angeles had supplied the food—"everything from the best Beluga caviar in tins to bottles of Dom Perignon in ice buckets. Even baked Alaska for everybody was airborne. But we encountered what seemed like dangerous turbulence. Perhaps we were flying over Colorado. Howard came back into the cabin and removed a quart of Russian vodka. Cary Grant later told me that Howard had soaked a towel in the vodka and was de-icing the plane's windshield. At first I thought he was going to drink the liquor because he knew that all of us were going to crash over the Rocky Mountains."

Unknown to Howard, one of the attendants serving his guests was an agent for the FBI sent by J. Edgar Hoover as a spy. By the time Howard's party reached the Sherry-Netherland, Hoover's men had also bugged the suites Howard had rented: one for Lana, another for himself, one for Johnny Meyer, and yet another for young Cheryl and her governess.

Also bugged by the closeted Hoover, the final suite was reserved for Cary. During the stopover in New York, Howard was a frequent visitor to Cary's suite. Hoover, a closeted homosexual himself, later joked to friends, "From the tape,

I learned that Hughes is the husband, Grant the wife."

When the bellhop opened the door to Lana's suite, she was dazzled to find it filled with ivory-colored roses, her favorite flower, and dozens of gardenias and purple and white orchids. The next morning, he took her on a shopping expedition to the boutiques along Fifth Avenue, with a final stopover at Tiffany's. Unlike her friend, Ava Gardner, Lana was not adverse to accepting expensive jewelry from rich sugar daddies.

On the third night, at El Morocco, Howard proposed marriage to Lana. She was at the peak of her career, having triumphed in a big box office success, *Weekend at the Waldorf*, in which she'd played a stenographer in an updated version of *Grand Hotel*. Joan Crawford had played the original role. Howard had already seen her upcoming triumph, *The Postman Always Rings Twice*, which would become her most memorable role in her most enduring film. From MGM she was pulling in a salary of $250,000 a year, making her one of the ten most highly paid women in America.

Lana recalled that she'd retired about one o'clock that evening after more missionary position sex with Howard. Unknown to her at the time, Howard called her friend, Linda Darnell, and proposed marriage to her on the same night. He told her, "You're the only woman I've ever loved. All the others were mere window dressing until you came along." When she heard that, Linda accepted. She eagerly listened to his next words. "Ava and Lana are all about fake glamour. You're the real thing, a true beauty."

In her autobiography, modestly called *Lana: The Lady, The Legend, The Truth*, published by E.P. Dutton in 1982, Lana, for reasons of her own, minimized her affair with Howard. That was understandable because the last thing she wanted the public to know was "the naked, intimate truth," as the jacket of the paperback promised but didn't deliver. "Touted as a tell-all," wrote one reviewer, "it's more of a tell something."

Back in Los Angeles, Howard agreed to marry Lana in a secret ceremony scheduled for May 10. She'd even gone to "Irene," the MGM designer, and had ordered a special wedding gown. Johnny Meyer showed up as Howard's best man. Lana hadn't even told her mother, Mildred, that she was marrying Howard, who had remained the favorite suitor among her daughter's beaus.

The flowers, the pianist, and even the minister were on time, arriving at the chapel at nine o'clock that morning. No Howard.

"Where is he?" Lana implored Meyer to tell her. He honestly didn't know. "It was a nightmare that featured an uncontrollable Lana who grew more hysterical as the day grew old. She called Noah Dietrich's office every thirty minutes. But Dietrich didn't know where Howard was either. He assured Lana that his boss "often disappears at the oddest times."

"That was not very reassuring to Lana," Meyer later said. "By four she practically had to be carried out of the chapel and sedated by Dr. Mason. She wasn't in love with Howard, but she sure wanted that god damn wedding ring on her finger. I think she was in love with the idea of being married to Howard Hughes. Being Mrs. Howard Hughes in 1946 would have been a very big deal, a very big deal indeed."

Lana quickly recovered from being jilted at the altar. In time, she would forgive Howard and perhaps seek a bit of revenge as well. Within weeks, she told Meyer that she'd fallen in love with Howard's lover.

Tyrone Power himself.

Maybe Lana shouldn't have been so gleeful in reporting the news. The idea of his two former lovers, two incredible beauties, making love together excited Howard. "Somehow he planned to get in on that action too," Meyer claimed.

* * *

Actress Paulette Goddard died in 1990 at her villa in Porto Ronco, a small resort village on the Swiss side of Lake Maggiore. In declining health and believed to have been eighty-five years old at the time, she was examining her decaying teeth in a mirror after having carefully inspected a catalogue of her jewelry being auctioned off that week at Sotheby's. Not many obituaries of film actresses are announced on the frontpage of *The Wall Street Journal*. But Paulette was "known in the best of banks," to paraphrase the song from *Gentlemen Prefer Blondes*. She was one of the richest women Hollywood ever called its own, and the biggest gold-digger of the town's Golden Age.

Daring to offer advice to Marlene Dietrich, she once said: "Never, ever sleep with a man until he gives you a pure white stone of at least ten carats. Every woman needs jewels. They're small, easy to carry—easy to hide, in case the woman has a falling out with the man whom she regards as a keystone in her life."

When she seduced men, she liked to date from the A-list. Her aim was always high. Having married (presumably) the biggest name in Hollywood, Charlie Chaplin, she continued a roster of conquests which was not always limited to actors: Aldous Huxley, producer Sir Alexander Korda, Aristotle Onassis, the Mexican painter Diego Rivera, producer Joseph Schneck, socialite and multimillionaire Jock Whitney, and even author H.G. Welles. She even married one of her author lovers, wealthy Erich Maria Remarque. She didn't neglect seducing actors either: Clark Gable, Gary Cooper, Spencer Tracy, and John Wayne, to name only a few.

A former Ziegfeld Girl and later a Goldwyn Girl, Paulette had been signed by David O. Selznick to play Scarlett O'Hara in *Gone With the Wind*. She lost the part, of course. Selznick privately said he suspected that Chaplin and Paulette weren't really married, and the producer feared some "moral backlash" against the film if this secret were revealed. To compensate for her loss of the role, Chaplin presented Paulette with a gold Cabochon emerald and diamond bangle-bracelet.

Meyer claimed that Howard never bought her jewelry, but he did purchase a most unusual gift for her: two original portraits of Mickey Mouse and Donald Duck, each signed by Walt Disney. At the time, Paulette was disappointed with "such a cheesy gift," although the portraits in time were valued at a "small fortune" by collectors. Meyer jokingly said that the Disney art might have inspired Paulette to become a connoisseur of the arts, herself. In time, she amassed a multimillion-dollar art collection of her own, including paintings by her lover Rivera, such works as "Flower Vendor" and "Young Woman With Sunflowers." On her own, she acquired art by Dalí, Baumier, Degas, Cézanne, Monet, Renoir, Pissarro, and Modigliani.

Johnny Meyer is the only one who ever seemed to know about the brief Goddard/Hughes affair. "Sexually, I think Howard's coming together with Goddard…" He paused. "Forgive the Freudian slip. I think they made it in the sack. Before Howard, I used to pimp young girls for both Chaplin and Errol Flynn. The Little Tramp told me that Paulette was a great fellator—right up there with the best of them."

She even received a kind of screen immortality for this sexual skill. One night all of Hollywood learned that Paulette had disappeared under the table at Ciro's nightclub, performing her specialty on Anatole Litvak, former husband of Miriam Hopkins and lover of Bette Davis. When shooting *Shampoo* in 1975, Warren Beatty included this under-the-table fellatio scene inspired by Paulette.

Even though married at the time to one of her poorer husbands, actor

Paulette Goddard

Burgess Meredith, Paulette was eager to entertain Howard after he'd flown her across the continent and installed her in the Sherry-Netherland. In fact, she'd confided in her new girlfriend, Veronica Lake, that she planned to become the second Mrs. Howard Hughes. "Of course, I'll have to dump Burgess." Paulette and Veronica had bonded ever since they'd starred together in the 1943 *So Proudly We Hail!* "Hughes is the only man in America rich enough for me," Paulette told Veronica.

"What turned Howard off was the gold-digging side of Goddard," Meyer claimed. "Paulette wanted to get her hooks into Howard so bad that she tried too hard to please. She made her intentions too obvious, and that frightened Howard. After the third night with Goddard, he went back to the arms of

Lana, Cary, or whomever. That "whomever" turned out to be Veronica.

"Howard's romantic link with Veronica was different from that with Goddard, which was all about sex," Meyer said. "People accused Howard of being a nutbag. When he took up with Veronica, he met his match in the nuts department!"

Unknown to Paulette, Veronica also had designs on Howard. He'd installed her in an accommodation two floors below Paulette. Above both of them were other lovers, Lana Turner and Cary Grant, installed in suites of their own at the Sherry-Netherland. Instead of having to cross town, all Howard had to do to visit these various lovers was to take the hotel elevator.

Thinking her relationship with him was going successfully, Paulette made plans to continue her affair when both of them returned to the West Coast. She invited him to go sailing with her aboard "Charlie's yacht—I got that in the divorce settlement along with a million dollars." Meyer claimed that Howard later said, "She got a million from Chaplin. I bet she'd want ten million from me."

Although most of Paulette's movies are forgotten today, except by die-hard fans, she lives on in screen history for having appeared opposite Chaplin as the gamine in *Modern Times* in 1936 and again with her then-husband, Chaplin, in the 1940 *The Great Dictator*.

Her relationship with Howard, in spite of Paulette's attempts to make it otherwise, remains a mere footnote.

* * *

"When Howard came together with that hot tomato, Veronica Lake, he finally met somebody as crazy as he was," Johnny Meyer claimed.

Her fame forever rooted in the war years of the 1940s, Brooklyn-born Veronica Lake was most often referred to either as "sexy" or "sultry"—or both. She claimed that, "I wasn't a sex symbol, I was a sex zombie."

With her peek-a-boo bang that dropped down the right side of her face, she became one of the most celebrated blondes of her day, with news of her four separate marriages making headlines across the entertainment media.

At the time Howard met her, Veronica no longer had her trademark peek-a-boo. The War Department had requested that she change her hairdo. Too many factory women, working in defense plants, were imitating her hair style and getting their low-hanging bangs caught, sometimes tragically, in machinery on assembly lines. Like the Biblical Samson, the cutting of her hair seemed to diminish Veronica's standing at the box office. Her popularity was on the wane. She'd never recover her glory days as a leading box office attraction of World War II.

Through Johnny Meyer, Howard had learned about Veronica's infamous sex-and-booze orgies at her home. Not all of her parties were orgies. She was also known for her relatively wholesome monthly kitchen parties. Many Hollywood stars showed up, the female beauties donning aprons to cook "for the men folk." In time, Howard himself would be a guest too. But Veronica was always careful not to invite him when she asked Paulette Goddard.

It was at one of these kitchen parties that Veronica would later make the claim that Howard was not really deaf but was only pretending. "I know for a fact that he could hear a pin drop in the next room. His deafness is just a ploy he uses to trick people he's doing business with. He can hear every whispered secret during a business meeting." Although that was her impression, she was mistaken.

In New York, Howard landed his Connie at La Guardia. Veronica recalled that the booze, even champagne, had flowed throughout the plane's transit across the continent. Not only the stars were sated, but the press members he'd invited along on the junket arrived drunk.

"When the plane landed," she said, "Howard got real stingy. He even chased one reporter across the tarmac, the guy was making off with a half empty bottle of booze. Here he was, the richest man in the world, standing in front of half of Hollywood raging until he got the whiskey bottle back."

In her vanilla autobiography, *Veronica*, published in 1971, she claimed that she'd never had an affair with Howard. That was not quite true. On the set of *Slattery's Hurricane*, released in 1949, in which she'd co-starred with Linda Darnell and Richard Widmark, she confided to Linda that she did go to bed with Howard, but that it hadn't worked out. "The plumbing was there, but it was out of order." She was no doubt referring to Howard's impotence.

She later admitted that she'd been less than candid in her autobiography. "If I had written everything I know about this town, there'd be a rash of divorces and at least a hundred people would die of apoplexy."

Without actually admitting that he'd failed sexually with Veronica, Howard once told Meyer: "I'm sorry she didn't get to sample my big surprise. I would like to have known how I measured up to the competition." Presumably, Howard was referring to Veronica's other lovers, four heavily endowed men: Milton Berle, Gary Cooper, Victor Mature, and Porfirio Rubirosa.

In spite of their not making it together in the sack, Veronica and Howard became friends. He affectionately called her "Ronni."

He was attracted by her rebellious streak, and she liked the way he flaunted authority, be it the War Department or movie censors. "It's you and me against the wind, kid," he once told her.

Veronica later had kind words for Howard. "He was a strange man, which comes as no surprise to anyone—so aloof and detached but with a trace of warmth for those fortunate enough to be touched by it."

She might have viewed him as strange, but that was how much of Hollywood regarded her. As a teenager, she had been diagnosed as a schizophrenic. Her mother refused to have her committed or treated for her illness,

Veronica Lake

and as Veronica grew older, her schizophrenia deepened. This was reflected by her heavy boozing and the abuse of her first child. Her orgies were another manifestation of her deeply rooted problems. At one time, she called Hollywood "one giant, self-contained orgy farm, the inhabitants dedicated to crawling into every pair of pants they can find." She also began picking up strange men randomly encountered. Sometimes she'd pick up men on the street, pulling up to the curb in her car and calling to them. "Hi, I'm Veronica Lake. Get in if you'd like to fuck a movie star. I'll let you play with my peek-a-boo if you'll let me play with yours."

In the years ahead, as Veronica's financial situation worsened, Howard could have helped her but he didn't. Through Johnny Meyer, he learned that she'd been evicted from her apartment and was living with Rita Beery, the lesbian ex-wife of actor Wallace Beery, who had once been married to Gloria Swanson. Meyer said that Veronica was having an affair with the ex-Mrs. Beery and was also "getting drunk and fucking Gary Cooper on the side." Howard's only response was, "Ronni always did go for the big ones."

Veronica claimed that the last time she spoke to Howard was in late August of 1948. She called to offer him a suggestion for TWA.

"What is it, Ronni?" she quotes him as saying.

She revealed that on August 11, she'd flown in a 90-ton giant aircraft, the *Constitution*, a plane with a rocket take-off assist that was the largest craft of its type in service anywhere in the world. She said that the U.S. Navy had been proud of the way it had been depicted in *Slattery's Hurricane*, which was about the Navy's hurricane reconnaissance research in Miami. Navy brass invited 86 members of the press aboard the aircraft to view the picture.

During the three hours the *Constitution* circled over New York, the press corps was treated to a lavish lunch served by an armada of attendants. A temporary projection system was installed so they could view *Slattery's Hurricane* while airborne.

641

"Howard, the greatest thing you can do for TWA is to offer in-flight movies," Veronica urged him. "It's the coming thing."

"Thanks for the idea," he told her. "Bye, Ronni."

She was never to hear from him again. He never took another one of her calls. Nor did he answer any of her written pleadings to 7000 Romaine Street when she became completely broke and had to go into bankruptcy court. Later, she was forced to work as a barmaid in a New York hotel and as a factory worker pasting felt flowers onto lingerie hangers.

She died bitter, broke, and disappointed on July 7, 1973, three years before Howard's own death.

"As for Howard and Veronica," Meyer later said, "their love affair never even got airborne. But they must have sensed some kindred spirit in each other. Otherwise, their friendship would not have endured for as long as it did."

* * *

Los Angeles, 1941-1946

Born in Brooklyn, the daughter of a wealthy stockbroker, the sultry actress, Gene Tierney, spelled sex in any language. On the screen she'd portray characters who were Chinese, Polynesian, Eurasian, Arab, Sicilian, and even American, but she was always sexy. She told friends that her full name was Gene Eliza Tierney, forming the initials of GET. "I'm going to live up to my name, and GET what I want in Hollywood."

Tyrone Power had met her on the lot of 20th Century Fox. Later they would appear together in 1942 in *Son of Fury*, which was followed by the far more memorable *The Razor's Edge* in 1946, based on the famous novel by W. Somerset Maugham.

Howard and Tyrone had seen *Tobacco Road* together in 1941. In the film, Gene played a trashy character called Ellie May. In spite of her convincing on-screen performance, Tyrone assured Howard that Gene had more breeding than Katharine Hepburn. "The gal's got class," he told Howard. He was more intrigued with her sexy overbite. "A man can do a lot of things with an overbite like that," he enigmatically told Tyrone.

On their first date, Gene invited him for dinner but warned him "I can't boil water." She did know how to drop two four-pound lobsters into a pot, and cook them for Howard. It was her favorite food, although he would have preferred a butterfly steak as he viewed lobsters as unclean. Nonetheless, he was smitten by Gene herself, not her cooking. She was a beauty, standing 5 feet, 5 ½ inches, weighing 122 pounds, and having brownish hair with reddish tints. He usually went for brunettes.

He was startled by how Gene, in the middle of a subdued conversation, would suddenly burst out with something, speaking at the top of her voice. At first this characteristic amused Howard, who was partially deaf anyway. But later it became an annoyance, because he preferred discretion.

He had become social friends of Constance Moore, and her husband, the agent Johnny Maschio. He was often seen at their house, perhaps thinking he would meet some beautiful starlet there, which he often did. He called them "killer tomatoes."

One night Gene phoned him and asked him to escort her to a party at the Maschio home. He was flying to San Francisco that night and had to turn her down. Later, Gene showed up alone. It was to be one of the most important nights of her life.

At the party she met a Russian count, Oleg Cassini, who was working for $200 a week as a costume designer at Paramount. Gene later recalled that he was "the most dangerous looking character I had ever seen," with his thin lips, wavy hair, and mustache. At the time, Gene was the star, Cassini a lowly member of the wardrobe department.

Neither could have known that Cassini's career would one day outdazzle Gene's, as he went on to become the premier fashion designer for the jet set. In time he'd be engaged to Grace Kelly and would eventually design a wardrobe for Jacqueline Kennedy during her tenure in the White House.

From the night of her first meeting with Cassini, which would lead to marriage on June 1, 1941, Gene would have two men in her life throughout the war years and beyond. Those two men, of course, would be her husband, Oleg Cassini, and Howard Hughes.

Long before he knew of his wife's involvement with Howard, Cassini had learned much about Howard's private life from a close friend the two rivals mutually shared—Pat DeCicco. DeCicco, then known as "Mr. Gloria Vanderbilt," revealed to Cassini that Howard kept "a stable of thirty-six girls at all times, all under contract to him, although none of them ever appeared in a movie. They are on call like a stewardess working for an airline. They wait until midnight for a call to come in from Howard. That call from their boss rarely comes. Howard

Gene Tierney

643

operates what is perhaps the first great American harem."

For a while, Howard dropped out of Gene's life after her marriage. In time, she became an Army wife, living at Junction City, Kansas, near Fort Riley, when Cassini went into military service. Through his spies, Howard kept tabs on her, wanting to know if she were secretly having affairs with any of the Army officers at Fort Riley. Apparently, she was not.

Gene's troubles were compounded throughout her husband's posting to Fort Riley. Although she was pregnant at the time, Gene agreed one night to appear as part of an entertainment review at the local Hollywood Canteen. A young female WAC heard about her inclusion in the show. Even though the woman was stricken with German measles, she rose from her sick bed to go to the Canteen to meet her favorite star.

Gene came down with the disease, which was disastrous for her unborn baby. The child, eventually named Daria, was born blind, deaf, and severely retarded. Months later, at a tennis match, Gene encountered the fan who told her what had happened. "I'm so sorry," the young woman said. "My family warned me not to go. But I just had to see you. You've always been my favorite actress." Gene slapped her face.

By this time, Cassini had been informed of Gene's earlier involvement with Howard. When Howard tried to come back into her life, Cassini suspected that his rival was just using the Daria situation as an excuse to get close to Gene again. Nonetheless, Howard flew the best specialist from New York aboard TWA to examine Daria. After two weeks of extensive testing, he told Gene that her daughter's condition was "incurable," recommending that both Cassini and Gene put the pretty little girl in an institution that would provide for her care. Howard picked up the specialist's $15,000 tab.

Touched by Howard's kindness, Gene began dating him again. In some way, she was doing this to get revenge on Cassini, whom she'd discovered was also having affairs on the side. At one time she suspected that he was having an affair with a beautiful blonde, whom Gene called "a cheap floozy." Cassini did not deny the affair but claimed that "Marilyn Monroe is no cheap floozy. One day she may be as important as you are."

Meyer later claimed that his boss fell in love with Gene all over again when he saw her in her most memorable and haunting film, the classic noir, *Laura*, released in 1944. "I couldn't tell if Howard were in love with Gene or with Laura."

One day Cassini learned that Howard had been leaving "urgent, urgent messages" with his wife's "harsh Prussian caricature" [Cassini's words] of a secretary.

Gene wasn't very revealing (what actress is?) about her involvement with Howard in her highly sanitized autobiography, *Self-Portrait*. But details of her troubled relationships with both Howard and Cassini have been revealed over the years, notably in autobiographies of Cassini himself as well as of his brother, Igor Cassini. Other sources—including Jack Benny—have also revealed the conflicts within this famous trio.

In the 40s, it was customary for Cassini, usually on Tuesday nights, to go with his pal, Roger Valmy, to the boxing matches in Santa Monica. Cassini later recalled that during one of these matches, he "had a sense that something was wrong at his household." Excusing himself from Valmy, he drove back to his home. There he forced the Prussian secretary to admit that his wife had gone out to dinner with Howard.

With him, Howard had brought a cardboard box rescued from the safe of the Fairmont Hotel in San Francisco. The box contained one million dollars worth of jewelry he'd purchased at Tiffany's in San Francisco. During their disastrous weekend together at the Fairmont, Ava Gardner had refused to accept it. That night with Gene, he urged her to divorce Cassini and marry him. "I'll give you everything on earth—and, yes, heaven too," Gene remembered Howard as promising. He opened the box of gems and generously offered, "Take what you want." Unknown to Gene, Howard had once offered the entire box to Ava. With the genders switched, the offer was similar to what Barbara Hutton would present to Cassini, following her divorce from Cary Grant.

Furious at his wife's infidelity, Cassini decided to hide in his garage and wait for the return of the illicit lovers. He suspected that Gene would want to be delivered back home before his own expected return from the boxing matches. Cassini later remembered that he must have waited in that garage two or even three hours, his fury mounting. To clobber Howard, he looked through piles of junk, finally deciding on a two-by-four piece of lumber.

Finally, Cassini's long wait paid off. Howard pulled up in front of the house in a battered Buick. Cassini could see and hear what was going on. "You've got to marry me and leave him!" Cassini heard Howard tell his wife. Jumping out of the car, she protested. "No, it's not possible—it's not right. I'm already married." She fled toward her house, opening, then slamming the front door. Howard had gotten out of the car to follow her inside.

From the shadows, an irate Cassini emerged. "I could have killed that bastard," he recalled. "I meant to beat him over the head until he was dead. Instead I did something silly. I took the two-by-four and whacked his skinny ass. Howard, America's great hero, leaped back into his Buick and sped away into the night."

Getting into his own Buick, Cassini pressed the accelerator to the floor and roared up Wilshire Boulevard hot in pursuit of Howard. He beat Cassini to the Town House Hotel where he was staying. Having eluded Cassini, Howard ran inside.

Slamming on the brakes, Cassini stopped right at the entrance to the hotel and barged into the lobby. "Where's Hughes?" he shouted at the reception desk. Howard had already taken the elevator to the penthouse.

Getting off a separate elevator were three beefy bodyguards, each hand-picked by Johnny Meyer, to remove Cassini from the lobby of the hotel. The muscle-bound men picked the thin Cassini up and dumped him out on the street. Cassini yelled back at them: "Tell your yellowbelly boss never to walk alone in this town again."

Not knowing of this incident, Constance Moore and Johnny Maschio invited Gene and Cassini to their home for a party. A separate invitation was sent to Howard, who showed up alone, unaware that both Gene and Cassini had also been invited.

Howard was standing in the middle of the living room talking to Constance and her husband, when Cassini entered. On his arm was a beautifully gowned Gene in an outfit designed by her husband.

Cassini moved menacingly to confront Howard again. "You yellow coward!" Cassini called out in front of the startled guests. Immediately Howard turned and ran up the steps to the master bedroom where he barricaded himself inside.

Cassini chased after him, pounding on the door and calling him names. Finally, he gave up and went back downstairs to join his embarrassed hosts.

In about twenty minutes "a dozen of Johnny Meyer's best gorillas" [Cassini's words] arrived to escort Howard from the Maschio household. Howard, flanked by his musclemen, rushed down the steps and disappeared out the door. Knowing he was outnumbered, Cassini did not give chase this time.

This would not be the last encounter between these two jealous rivals. Their last confrontation occurred at a lavish party thrown by Jack Benny, in a setting that included a white tent in a manicured garden, masses of flowers, food by Chasen, and a private orchestra hired for the night.

Howard seemed in a more defiant mood on this evening, daringly taking Gene by the hand and leading her to a secluded part of the garden.

With a drink in hand, Cassini stood for half an hour watching his wife in animated conversation with Howard. Finally, he could take it no more. In a more conciliatory way, he walked over and asked Gene if she'd excuse them while he talked privately to Howard. Without saying a word, she left to rejoin the Benny party.

Sitting down next to Howard in the seat just vacated by Gene, Cassini told him, "You're really bad news! I don't believe your intentions toward my wife are honorable. I think you're a bullshit artist! If you really want my wife, I'll step aside. But only if you publicly announce that you're going to marry her instead of offering her these insulting baubles and making a nuisance of yourself. I also want you to deposit a million dollars in her bank account as proof of your good intentions."

"There's no need for that," Howard said calmly. "I'm a Texas gentleman. A man of my word."

"Bullshit!" Cassini said. "I should beat the shit out of you right now in front of *tout* Hollywood. You need to be taught a lesson."

646

To avoid a fight, Howard got up and walked immediately out of the party without bidding his host a good night. The next day, he penned a note and had it delivered by Johnny Meyer to Gene's studio. "You're married to a god damn, fucking off-the-wall madman!"

Meyer claimed that Howard did not completely "give up on Gene" after the Benny party but saw her very infrequently after that. The competition for Gene's charms heated up. Gene and Howard even shared two boyfriends in common: Tyrone Power and Victor Mature. In time actor Kirk Douglas was climbing a ladder to her window at night. Prince Aly Khan would become one of her biggest catches. Even an aging Spencer Tracy, when they made the 1952 *Plymouth Adventure*, went for Gene.

"What would you expect from a woman who started out by fucking the head of the studio?" Meyer once asked. He was referring, of course, to Darryl F. Zanuck.

Even though he was no longer seeing her, Howard's spies continued to keep tabs on Gene. He was among the first to find out that she was having an affair with John F. Kennedy. That must have caused Howard a certain pang, since he too had once wanted the handsome and charming young man for himself.

Like all sirens of the 40s, the career of Gene Tierney died down to only a burning ember. Her sudden disappearance in the late 1950s caused much speculation. It was later revealed that she'd suffered a nervous breakdown and had been temporarily committed to the Menninger Psychiatric Clinic in Houston, Texas to recuperate. Gene later claimed that "a curtain had been drawn over my mind," as she had trouble distinguishing between illusion and reality.

Like so many of her contemporaries, including Veronica Lake, she did not end up in poverty. Gene married into great wealth. On July 11, 1960, she wed the Texas oil executive, W. Howard Lee, and moved with her husband to Houston, which ironically was Howard's home town.

Her last known comment about Howard Hughes was a lament. "If I had known what bad shape he was in, perhaps I could have helped him—or maybe he could have helped me."

She died on November 6, 1991.

As other, more voluptuous creatures entered Howard's life, he was no longer obsessed by Gene Tierney.

A new and far more alluring creature had appeared to him in her films.

Miss Rita Hayworth.

CHAPTER SEVENTEEN
Beverly Hills, 1946

It was a Sunday morning on July 7, 1946. The war was over except for some Japanese soldiers still fighting on remote islands in the Pacific, having no idea that their country had surrendered.

In California, the sun had sent its rays to light the bullet-nosed XF-11, Howard's reconnaissance plane, which had originated years before as the D-1, but which had not been readied in time to assist America at war. "We missed out," said Glenn Odekirk.

As the sun rose higher, it fully exposed what Howard called "the most beautiful plane ever built."

For its test run that morning, it had been moved out onto the tarmac at five o'clock, since Odekirk wasn't certain when Howard would show up. Measuring 66 feet long, with a wing span of 100 feet, the twin-tailed craft weighed 47,000 pounds. Howard called its graceful lines and streamlined elegance "lean and mean."

Arriving at Culver City at 9:30am, Howard conducted a series of tests on the plane from the safety and privacy of Hughes Aviation's private runway, accompanied by Gene Blandford, his flight engineer. The tests went beautifully, though Joe Petrali wondered how the FX-11 would perform at 5,000 feet racing through the air at 400 miles per hour.

Petrali had learned that Howard planned to fly the plane by himself, and that he was going to kick Blandford out of the cockpit before becoming airborne. "Howard wanted all the glory for himself," Petrali later said. "I'd argued for days with him, even calling him a fool. I told him that it took two pilots to operate the XF-11. He wouldn't listen to me. Finally, I told him it was a suicide mission and walked away."

At the controls, before taking off, Howard got out of the plane and walked over to greet a beautiful young starlet, Jean Peters, whom he had taken an interest in ever since she'd signed to play opposite his friend, Tyrone Power, in the swashbuckling *Captain from Castile*. He'd asked Johnny Meyer to bring her to Culver City to watch the test run. Meyer rounded up some chilled bottles of wine and some southern fried chicken. What Howard didn't expect was that

Jean would show up with her boyfriend, Audie Murphy, the most decorated American soldier of WWII.

If Howard were jealous of Audie that day, he tried not to show it. Shaking hands with Audie and giving Jean a light peck on the cheek, he headed toward the XF-11 for takeoff. Wearing a white sports shirt and wrinkled russet-brown slacks, he'd crowned his head with his lucky but floppy fedora.

Discussing his final flight plan with Odekirk, he climbed into the cockpit and buckled up for the test flight. Condemned by much of the War Department, Howard was determined to show the brass in Washington that he'd designed the world's most successful reconnaissance plane. He'd adorned the silvery wings of his Bullet with blue and white U.S. Air Force insignia.

The day was his. Or so it seemed. Before takeoff, he'd made a big mistake by ordering the plane filled with 1,200 gallons of high-octane fuel in violation of Army regulations that called for only half that amount. Telling only Odekirk, he planned to fly the plane for at least two hours, although regulations called for test flights to be no longer than forty-five minutes.

"Hell, this baby will fly all the way to New York if I want it to," Howard boasted.

Howard Hughes

After taxiing to the end of the runway, he revved his engines, noting that it was already five o'clock. The sun had begun its gradual descent over the Pacific.

It was a tense moment for Howard. A successful flight meant vindication for him. The War Department had reduced their orders for the reconnaissance plane from one hundred to only three aircraft. His engineers had developed a new technique for the craft's propellers. They'd installed two sets of double counter-rotating propellers with four blades on each. "It was thought that the plane could obtain greater speed with eight blades on each side of the craft," Odekirk claimed. Howard was convinced that these new blades "could chew the air" better than conventional three-blade propellers.

The government had protested his testing the plane over the heavily popu-lated area of West Los Angeles. The brass had wanted the craft test-flown at the Army Test Flight Base (later renamed Edwards Air Force Base) in the heart of the Mojave Desert, near Muroc, California. But Howard had prevailed.

He was too impatient to take the plane to the desert, and had been eager to test it at once after his engineers told him the craft was flight ready. He'd already waited too long for this day, having spent millions of dollars of govern-ment money and millions of other dollars from his own pocket on the XF-11. "I want my brightest dream to come true," he told Odekirk. "Finally," he said, "enough of this waiting and testing. I'm taking her up. That's the only way we'll know if shit happens."

Opening the throttle as wide as it would go, he gave complete power to his Pratt & Whitney engines, the largest piston-drive engines in existence, each delivering 3,000 horsepower.

Signaling to his ground crew and waving good-bye to Jean Peters, he also communicated to an observation aircraft circling overhead that he was ready for takeoff. Pulling back on the stick, he lifted the XF-11 skyward. Even to his par-tially deaf ears, he heard the sound of his landing gear retract.

The moment he was airborne, trouble set in. Something was wrong, as a red light on his instrument panels indicated. Some of the gears of his landing mech-anism were malfunctioning, even though he'd heard the landing struts thump into their bays. Nervously he lowered and retracted the landing gear. Everything seemed all right, but that red light ominously stayed on. Then he came up with an idea. He lowered the landing gear once more, then retracted it. As he did, he pushed forward on the plane's control yoke, adding G-force to the wheels, as they folded into their bays. That seemed to do the trick, as that red warning light clicked off.

He blamed the light on the newness of the plane, later claiming it was "like a baby emerging from its mama's womb—I expected birthin' pains, as we say in Texas."

No longer earthbound, he would later tell Odekirk that, "I felt free at last," Gaining speed, he accelerated to his desired speed of 400 miles per hour, defy-ing regulations. "I was going like a bullet shot through the air," he later said.

He headed westward toward the ocean, as the midsummer sun began its death into the Pacific. The XF-11's path was shaped like a half-moon, roaring first over Venice Beach, then over Beverly Hills before returning to the tarmac at Culver City. He had boasted that "all the doubting Thomases in the War Department will be eating crow for breakfast tomorrow morning." In total com-mand of his "flying wonder," he turned his powerful new machine back in the direction of Culver City.

At 6:48pm, serious trouble set in. Without warning, the craft pitched vio-lently to starboard. Within less than a minute, the airspeed menacingly dropped one hundred miles per hour. The plane was literally "falling out of the sky," he'd later say. His instrument panel gave no warning of any malfunctioning, and his powerful engines still functioned at their maximum speed.

Uncontrollably, the plane was pulling dangerously to the right. At first Howard feared that the right wing might be tearing itself loose from the plane. He stood up in the cockpit, knocking the lucky fedora off his head. Thinking the problem was being caused by his landing gear, he raised and lowered it twice, but it seemed to be functioning properly. What was wrong? Was this flight doomed? Was its pilot doomed as well?

Continuing to lose speed and "falling like a skier from an alpine peak," the XF-11 pitched badly. Sudden wind gusts blowing in from the Pacific only made flying conditions worse, shaking the plane with blasts.

"This mysterious pressure continued to be exerted on the right wing, and I didn't have a clue as to what was wrong," Howard later said. "It felt like someone had chained the heaviest Army tank to the wing. The god damn thing had this drag—no lift at all!"

He later told Odekirk that he had two thoughts—one of his mother, Allene, giving him a bath when he was a child, and the other that his estate would battle for years after his death.

In desperation, he contemplated bailing out, but determined that he had already lost so much altitude that that option was no longer viable. He adjusted the spoilers, the rudder, and the ailerons, but nothing worked. The plane continued to lose altitude. By the time he crossed Pico Boulevard, heading directly for the heart of Beverly Hills, he knew the time had passed for him to rescue the doomed craft.

At Santa Monica Boulevard, he was only five-hundred feet above the ground. Pedestrians on their way to dinner screamed. But their cries were obscured by "a death screech" coming from the plane itself. It was in a spiral dive.

"I'm going to die!" he shouted to the emptiness of the cockpit. But the plane in its own dying throes even drowned out that lament from a man facing death.

* * *

Howard was flying into a posh residential section of Beverly Hills on a quiet Sunday at twilight. Movie stars, producers, directors, their spouses, boyfriends, or girlfriends, had come in for the evening from their swimming pools. As he looked down, facing the inevitable, he felt that if he crashed into one of these deluxe homes, death would be instant.

"I knew I was going to die," he later told Glenn Odekirk. "But a kind of euphoria came over me. I didn't have to struggle with the plane anymore. It was fulfilling its own death wish. The fight was no longer in me. I surrendered myself to the power of the XF-11. It wasn't like I had much choice. I'd always feared a fiery death."

Making landfall at 160 miles an hour, the XF-11 plowed into the red-tiled roof of Jules Zimmerman, "dentist to the stars," at 802 North Linden Drive. "It was as if a giant razor had shaved off my roof and sent it crashing into my garden," Zimmerman later told the press. The endangered right wing was the first to break off, shearing a telephone line.

The impact slowed down the plane as it lunged forward, its wing slicing through the bedroom of Rosemary DeCamp, who was resting in the room at the time. She was a famous movie star of her day. Emerging from the bathroom, her husband, Municipal Justice John Ashton Shidler, was just walking into the bedroom at the time, a towel around his nude body. Both of them ran screaming from their bedroom, as the doomed craft piled into their garage, destroying it, before mowing down a row of poplar trees.

This unexpected rampage from the sky ended as the plane crashed through a brick wall on the back side of 808 North Whittier, the home of Lt. Colonel Charles A. Meyer. Saturated with fuel from the plane, it burst into an inferno of flames, but Meyer wasn't in it. He was working as an interpreter at the Nürnberg war trials, laboriously extracting as much information as he could out of bitter and vindictive men like Field Marshal Herman Göring.

Dismembered from most of the airplane's wings, the fuselage and the cockpit, with Howard trapped in it, made their final impact in an alleyway. The damaged fuel tanks exploded, as black smoke rose as if a bomb had hit Beverly Hills. The deafening blast could be heard for miles around, as a ball of orange-red flames shot into the air.

Howard later recalled being on fire, his leather jacket burning. Blood spurted from his nose, mouth, and even his ears. He screamed as he looked down. The high-octane aviation fuel had ignited his left hand. He slapped it against his pants to put out the blaze.

Ripping off his burning leather jacket, he tried to escape, finding his left foot "hopelessly trapped" in the wreckage. He freed himself by slipping his foot out of its boot. "I remember vomiting," he later said. "The smoke was nauseating."

The plane had become an inferno. His burnt hand dripping with blood, he opened the trap door of the Plexiglas canopy. As he remembered, "I summoned strength that wasn't in my body. It came from God knows where. I would have burned alive if I hadn't escaped." Amazingly, he hoisted himself out of the cockpit.

William Lloyd Durkin, a marine sergeant, was visiting James Guston, the son of the Swedish industrialist, Gosta B. Guston. To his astonishment, he witnessed one of the XF-11's engines crash into the front lawn of his hosts. Although Durkin was certain that no one could have survived the crash, he rushed over to search for survivors. On his hands and knees, he crawled under the flames to reach what remained of the plane.

At first his search was in vain. He could find no one. He was about to flee to save his own life. "Suddenly, I heard this loud thud," he recalled. "I looked over and saw the downed pilot struggling to free himself from the wreckage of the shattered fuselage. Howard collapsed into unconsciousness onto what remained of the broken left wing of the XF-11.

Suddenly, Durkin found that his own shirt was on fire. He ripped it from his body before wrapping his arms around Howard to pull him to safety.

"When I got him to safety," Durkin later told reporters, "I looked down at him. I hadn't a clue as to who he was. I only found out later that I had saved the life of Howard Hughes. Actually, at the time there wasn't much life to save. A hundred people in Beverly Hills had called the police and ambulances. But as I looked at this helpless creature I was holding in my arms, I thought that all the medical corps in the world wouldn't piece this tall guy back together again."

A Beverly Hills fireman was one of the first to arrive on the scene. He pushed Durkin aside and examined the body himself. Howard regained consciousness for a moment. "Did I kill anyone?" he asked before fading into unconsciousness again.

Throughout Beverly Hills, people were rushing from their houses into the streets to see what had happened. In a surprising twist, a local resident, Lewis Milestone, one of Howard's first film directors, lived a block away. He was the first of the "rubberneckers" to reach the scene. Looking down at the pilot, he exclaimed, "My God! Do you know who this man is? It's Howard Hughes. Or what's left of him." He looked at the shirtless marine. "Did you pull him from the cockpit?"

"No," Durkin said, "he'd already freed himself."

"Then he'll live," Milestone predicted. "He's got a history of walking away from airplane crashes and surviving. He's God!"

Wreckage of Hughes' XF-11, 1946.

* * *

Los Angeles, 1946

On Thursday before the crash of the XF-11, Howard had made a false promise to Lana Turner. He told her that he would not test the spy plane alone but would take along Gene Blandford as his co-pilot.

"I always had this incredible intuition," she later recalled. "I smell trouble before it's about to happen to me. I just knew that that damn XF-11 was heading for disaster. When I heard the news over the radio, broadcast as a bulletin out of Hollywood, I knew my nightmare had come true."

Howard didn't even tell another of his mistresses, Yvonne De Carlo, about the test flight. But she later said that she felt "that something bad was about to happen to Howard."

At the Beverly Hills Emergency Ward, a gurney carrying the world-famous aviator rushed down the halls, heading for the operating room. Two tourists from Indiana, William Blakewell and Sally Jeffers, were moved aside to make way for this more important patient. Earlier, the car of these two sightseers, cruising around looking at homes of movie stars in Beverly Hills, had been struck by a speeding hit-and-run van and were seriously injured.

A blood transfusion was administered only ten minutes after Howard was admitted. The first of the attending physicians articulated the obvious. The patient was "in severe shock." His heart had been "pushed" to one side of his chest cavity.

Applying his stethoscope to Howard's damaged chest, the attending doctor felt that his patient's lungs were rapidly filling with fluid. It was as if Howard were drowning in his own blood. "He had hours to live, if that," the doctor told his medics. He ordered that the patient be transferred at once to the Good Samaritan Hospital which had a burn unit.

Its siren wailing, its red dome light flashing, Howard was rushed to the Good Samaritan Hospital on Wilshire Boulevard in downtown Los Angeles. He later told Odekirk that all he remembered was "a sea of white lights" and some medic speculating that the patient would arrive at the hospital as a DOA. Dr. Verne Mason had also arrived at the hospital in time to administer Howard's second blood transfusion.

Delivered to the hospital on a stretcher, Howard regained consciousness for about twenty seconds—just enough time to tell the admitting nurse, "I'm Howard Hughes. You know, *The Aviator*!"

Dr. Mason spent four hours at Howard's bed before taking a break. In the corridor he told Odekirk, "It's doubtful if Howard will make it through the night."

The medical report was grim: nine broken ribs—two to the right, seven to the left; a broken left collarbone; third-degree burns on his left hand; his lung punctured in six places; a broken nose; a fractured skull; bad burns on his chest and left buttock. One medic claimed that "Hughes looked like he'd been French fried." There was a severe and deep gash on the left side of his face. Since the collapse of his left lung, which had filled with blood, 3,400 ccs. of fluid had to be drained from his chest cavity. His body was covered from head to toe with deep cuts and bruises. The bones protecting his lungs had been splintered. First damaged in a plane crash on the set of *Hell's Angels*, his chin had been splintered once again. An attending doctor compared it to "a bowl of jelly." When Dr. Mason was not in attendance with Howard, Dr. Lawrence Chaffin took over.

"All I could do," Dr. Mason said, at the end of the first day, "was to set his bones and shoot him with morphine. It was clear to me as I watched him being wheeled away that he was being sent back to his room to die."

Radio bulletins broadcast from Los Angeles alerted the world that one of its fabled figures might be dying. The Monday papers from coast to coast led off with Howard's plight. HOWARD HUGHES GRAVELY INJURED IN CRASH, announced the staid *New York Times*. In Los Angeles, the *Times* headlined its edition: MULTIMILLIONAIRE FLYER GIVEN 50-50 CHANCE. In the days and weeks ahead, newspapers carried follow-up stories, as the world waited to see if a genuine hero was going to make it.

In Houston the editors of both the *Post* and the *Chronicle* were preparing obituaries on their hometown boy. The *Chronicle* was planning to run its largest headline in type so bold and big that it was reserved only for the announcement of the "Second Coming." Even in London, *The Times* was preparing an edition usually reserved for the death of a king of the British empire. During the first forty hours after the accident, radio stations throughout America issued bulletins almost every hour. Police in Houston made plans for what they envisioned as the largest funeral ever held in the State of Texas.

As the deathwatch for Howard began, thousands of letters of condolence poured in from around the world, even from the king of England and the newly installed man in the White House, Harry S. Truman, who as vice president had assumed power following the death of Franklin D. Roosevelt. Truman also shipped him a Congressional medal that the Senate and House had previously awarded Howard for his around-the-world flight. He'd refused to go to the White House to accept it from Roosevelt. The new President told reporters that he thought the medal "would cheer Hughes up."

The mayor of New York, William O'Dwyer, sent Howard a telegram: "Give 'em hell!"

More than fifty cameramen and news reporters milled about the hospital lobby day and night, each eager to be the first to report to the world the death of one of the most famous men ever to grace the 20th century with his presence.

Odekirk recalled Howard's first night in the hospital. He'd taken the room to the immediate left of Howard, and his personal secretary "and guardian at the palace door," Nadine Henley, occupied the room on the right. Against doctor's orders, Odekirk slipped into Howard's bedroom because the door between their rooms was left unlocked. "I remember holding his hand and weeping for about an hour, as Howard silently slept in an oxygen tent. He'd been more than my boss for fifteen years, my comrade in flight. I loved Howard, and if I didn't know that before, I knew it then. Ours was not a sexual relationship, although once or twice on some lonely nights we spent together it almost came to that. Ours was a love affair stronger than any bond he ever had with Katharine Hepburn or Ava Gardner." He confessed that he would have spent the night if the attending nurse hadn't come in and demanded that he return to his own bed next door.

To relieve Howard of his suffering and excruciating pain, Dr. Mason, along with the attending doctor, Lawrence Chaffin, made a decision that would affect Howard for the rest of his life. At any sign of discomfort, he would inject him with morphine.

Glenn Odekirk later said, "Howard and morphine began an affair that would last until the end of his days."

Later, to wean him from morphine, Dr. Mason switched the drug to codeine. In time, Howard would consume both morphine and codeine as fast as his sometimes girlfriend, Marilyn Monroe, swallowed pills.

Hundreds of autograph collectors congregated at the entrance to the hospital and had to be restrained by the police. Lana Turner and Linda Darnell were recognized, of course. Of those visitors whose identities were uncertain, autograph hounds held out notepads asking, "Are you somebody?"

Arriving at the hospital was a parade of international film celebrities of the 1940s. These included Jane Russell, a legitimate friend, but also Joan Crawford, attired in mink and wearing wide sunglasses, presumably to mask her tear-streaked eyes. This was only a show for the press. In private she denounced Howard, claiming to her friend, Billy Haines, that "Howard Hughes would fuck a tree."

Errol Flynn showed up at the hospital but was turned away by Odekirk. Even Ginger Rogers, from whom Howard was estranged, made an appearance at the hospital, as did former girlfriend, Olivia de Havilland. Such unlikely figures showed up as James Cagney, David O. Selznick, and Danny Kaye. Lana Turner came dressed in black, as did Jean Peters, his future wife.

It was Linda Darnell who garnered the most press. In a black mourning dress, she was photographed fingering her rosary. The next morning, the *Hollywood Citizen-News* ran this blaring headline: LINDA DARNELL REFUSED PERMISSION TO SEE HUGHES.

Odekirk had instructions to turn all these notables away, especially acquaintances such as comedian Harold Lloyd and Captain Eddie Rickenbacker, the country's leading fighter pilot of World War I. "Actually, I think Eddie showed up only to see if Howard were really dying," Odekirk claimed. "After all, he was the chief of Eastern Airlines."

Katharine Hepburn arrived and created such loud noise when refused entrance that the director of the hospital had to come down and threaten to call the police if she didn't leave the premises at once.

One of the most desperate-looking visitors was Jack Frye, president of TWA. He was obviously more in fear for the future of his airline than he was troubled by Howard's physical condition. Frye had plenty of reason for distress: TWA stock had slipped from $71 a share to just $2 following the loss of a "Connie" over Reading, Pennsylvania. After the Constellation went down, the airline's entire fleet of Constellations had been grounded by the FAA until the cause of the crash could be determined. TWA was losing $16 million a year. Not only that, but the airline also faced a mounting debt of $40 million, with interest rising daily. Frye desperately wanted to talk to Howard, seeking permission to issue two million additional shares of TWA stock—"that is," he added, "if there are any suckers out there who want to buy it." Odekirk refused to let him go in to talk business with Howard.

The glamour girls would have to wait. The only person Howard agreed to see was Cary Grant, who caused a flutter among female staff members at the hospital. Attired in a black suit, he was allowed to come in and hold Howard's hand. Still in the oxygen tent, Howard asked his longtime lover, "Do I look gorgeous?" Cary told him, "You're looking great considering the alternative."

By July 10, Howard's crushed left lung began to function properly again. That gave Dr. Mason enough courage to face the flashbulbs and the reporters. Surprisingly for a doctor's statement, he claimed, "Howard Hughes is a man of steel. He has literally defied death. In my opinion, no normal man could have survived a crash like that."

By July 11, the patient was able to sit up and eat solid food—a graham cracker. But on July 12 at 10:30pm, he suffered a relapse as his lung refilled with fluid for the third time.

Dr. Mason was forced to change his words. At three o'clock that afternoon he announced that Howard had gone into "profound shock," which was another way of saying that he'd entered into a deep coma. Dr. Mason was forced to say that Howard's condition was no longer critical, but "severely critical."

That night, he called Dietrich at home. "He's not going to make it, Noah, and you should be the first to know. It'll be hell when Howard dies. You and Greg can expect millions of dollars of lawsuits." Dr. Mason was referring to Greg Bautzer, Howard's attorney.

Once again, Howard miraculously rebounded on the morning of July 13. After the latest relapse, he was out of the oxygen tent in twenty-four hours. But over the course of the stay, he had to undergo eight different blood transfusions.

To the amazement of, and later, despite the protests of the hospital staff,

Howard began to conduct business again.

Odekirk told him that the first order of business involved dealing with his aunt, Annette Lummis, who'd arrived by train from Houston with her husband, Dr. Fred Lummis, a well-known physician in Texas. Annette was demanding to see her nephew at once, and Dr. Lummis wanted to personally examine the patient. Dietrich accompanied them to the hospital but was turned away himself. Howard had already sent his chief a note instructing him "to carry on—business as usual."

At the hospital, Dietrich wrote a note to Howard, pleading with him to give Dr. and Mrs. Lummis an audience. Almost immediately Odekirk delivered the note back to Dietrich with a large "NO!" written across it. Before departing on the train back to Houston that day, Annette blamed Dietrich "for coming between Howard and his family." The charge was false.

While in Los Angeles, Annette had demanded to see a copy of Howard's will. She did not believe Dietrich when he said he couldn't produce one. Over the years Howard had attempted to dictate several wills but had never completed or signed one. His last known will was from 1938, but no copy of it had turned up in months. Dietrich suspected that Howard might have destroyed the will.

If he died without a will, Annette knew that the bulk of his estate might go to her, along with her sister and Howard's other aunt, Martha Gano Houstoun. Martha too had rushed to be at Howard's side, but had also been refused admittance. "When a rich man dies," Howard told Odekirk, "all the vultures fly in, even from as faraway as Texas, or especially from as faraway as Texas."

Howard issued another resounding "NO!" to his doctors, who wanted him to submit to surgery to correct the web-shaped scars caused by the severe burns on his left hand. Because of his refusal, he would never fully regain the use of his hand and would be forced to give up one of his most cherished passions—golf.

Since the slightest shift in his movement caused excruciating pain, Howard even designed a special bed for himself. He gave the plans to Odekirk, instructing the engineers at Hughes Aviation to come up with a bed, which was never used because he'd checked out of the hospital before it could be designed and manufactured. His motorized hospital bed had push buttons and even hot and cold running water with a toilet that could be flushed. He hated the ritual of the dreaded bedpan brought to him throughout the day, considering it undignified for a man of his stature.

For his second order of business, Howard ordered Odekirk to find his fedora if it still existed. "Put ten men on the job, twelve even, maybe a hundred," Howard instructed. "Cost is no object." Directing a crew of men at the site of the wreckage, Odekirk had the men search through debris and mud. Surprisingly, in five hours they located the battered fedora. Howard's "good luck piece" had survived the crash of the XF-11. The *Hollywood Citizen-News* ran the banner headline: FLYING FEDORA RECOVERED AT CRASH SITE. It identified the hat as of the snap-brim type, made of gray-brown felt, and measuring a size of 7 ½. On hearing the news, Howard ordered the hat reblocked. He feared if he couldn't wear it out of the hospital, he'd never get out alive.

Near the end of his hospital stay, when he finally allowed Jean Peters to come into his room, he told her, "If I'd been wearing my fedora at the time, all this wouldn't have happened to me."

Jean Peters

The next morning, he summoned Nadine Henley to his bed. Still in his oxygen tent, he dictated a memo to her. He wanted to leave written testimony for the army about why the XF-11 failed. Above all, he told Nadine, he didn't want the world to think the plane crashed because of pilot error.

Dr. Mason later read his memo to reporters assembled outside the hospital:

"The four front blades of the propeller were trying to pull the airplane ahead while the rear four blades were trying equally as hard to pull it backward. To make matters worse, these eight large propeller blades fighting one another created a dead drag on the right-hand side of the plane equal to that of a steel disc, seventeen feet in diameter, turned broadside to the wind at several hundred miles an hour. This disc destroyed the flow of air over the right wing and created a tremendous loss of lift. It felt as if some giant had the right wing in his hand and was pushing it back and down."

Unknown to the press, Howard underwent plastic surgery while in the hospital. When the bandages came off, he allowed Cary Grant to witness the unveiling, claiming that he was the only friend he could trust for an honest opinion. Howard was mortified when Cary held up a mirror to his face. "I've become James Whale's Frankenstein…a monster!" The ugly scar on his upper lip could not be erased. Cary suggested that from now on, he wear a mustache.

During the final days of Howard's stay, Cary

660

dropped in for one of his many visits. Cary had left the room for no more than ten minutes before Ava Gardner barged in. She'd been denied access long enough and was determined to see Howard.

Her pathway was blocked by Nadine Henley, whom Ava suspected was secretly in love with Howard. "There is no way, Miss Gardner, that Mr. Hughes can see you now—doctor's orders."

Ava shoved her out of her way and entered Howard's room anyway. Seeing who it was, he called out to Nadine to let her in.

Unlike all his friends who had been showing up in black, once he'd agreed to have Odekirk admit them, Ava chose a sexy, low-cut dress in toreador red, with black hosiery and high heels.

By his bedside, he reached out to her with his good hand. She gently rubbed his wounded face, perhaps noticing the enormous change in his looks. But she said nothing. As Howard later confided to Odekirk, "God damn it, the Tarheel bitch was giving me a hard-on. I thought I was too medicated, maybe impotent for life."

As Nadine later claimed, and as future mistress Terry Moore reported in her memoirs, Ava was discovered going down on Howard. She'd lowered the top of her dress so he could see and fondle her breasts. Alerted by the noises emanating from the room next door, like a lioness protecting her cub, Nadine screamed at Ava, shouting, "You brazen whore, you. You'll kill him."

It was too late. He was already experiencing his climax as Nadine entered the room to "kick out that little hussy." With an effect that was equivalent to a flood of icy water on a frigid morning in the Arctic, Nadine stridently summoned the doctor to see if Howard had suffered a heart attack from this exertion. Pulling up her dress, Ava stormed out of the hospital room. She later told friends, including Lana Turner, "that was the first time that Howard and I had a scene together that might actually be called a sex act. Before that, it had been just heavy petting. But I felt he deserved some sort of reward for having survived that plane crash."

Ava claimed that, in spite of Howard's pleadings in the future, she would never perform fellatio on him ever again or give in to his demands for sexual intercourse.

But it was to Jean Peters—not Ava—to whom he was giving his heart. He'd liked the way she attended to him in the hospital, telling Odekirk that Jean reminded him of his mother. He also claimed that he found "something virginal" about her, and had practically demanded a signed affidavit from her that she'd never gone to bed with Audie Murphy, who would soon emerge as an action hero in films.

On August 12, 1946, Howard checked himself out of the hospital and went to recover at the home of his beloved Cary. Dr. Mason pleaded with him to remain in the hospital for another six months.

Howard told Odekirk that "fresh orange juice did the trick." He had demanded that succulent blood-red oranges be squeezed into juice right in front of him three times a day. He felt that if the juice were allowed to sit, all its nutrients would vanish into the air. "If they don't do it my way, it'd be about as beneficial as drinking a glass of piss."

In his memoirs, Dietrich wrote that Howard passed through this critical stage of recovery "the hard way—no sleeping pills, no opiates of any kind." In direct contradiction, Cary noted that from the premises of his rented villa, Howard was continuing to take both morphine and codeine.

To Cary, Howard complained of "a constant ringing inside my head." Only the drugs could cure that. Otherwise, he expressed a fear that he might be driven crazy. Within six months, he'd developed a deep and ongoing addiction.

Despite his weakened condition, Howard began to contemplate his next sexual conquest, interpreting his renewed sexual fantasies as a symbol of his return to life. He ordered Johhny Meyer to buy an emerald engagement ring, supposedly to present to Jean Peters on her twenty-first birthday on October 12, 1946. It wasn't clear to Meyer that Howard actually planned to marry Jean.

Simultaneous with his demand for the ring, Howard told Meyer to arrange a rendezvous with what Howard defined as "the reigning goddess of Hollywood—more beautiful than Ava Gardner and Lana Turner combined."

Meyer knew that his boss could be talking about only one woman: Rita Hayworth.

Howard also called Henry Willson, telling him how pleased he was with Guy Madison, whom he'd continued to see. "When I'm well again, I want to meet more guys from your stable. But only the best and the hottest. I've got no more time in my life for runners-up. I want the next Guy Madison, stuff like that."

"Your wish, my command," Willson told his boss.

Cary was usually indulgent about Howard's outside sexual activities. He was more concerned about Howard's health. "Will you ever fly again?" he asked one night.

"In Texas, when you're teaching a boy to ride a horse and he falls off, you pick him up and put him back on again. In no time at all, I'm going to be flying all over this country. For starters, I'm taking you on a vacation to Mexico. And, yes, I'll be your pilot. I've paid my dues to Lady Luck. Now the skies belong to me."

Cary gleefully reported this news to his friends and associates. "He's a new man," Cary told Kate Hepburn, George Cukor, and others. "Except don't be surprised when you see him again. He looks a little different."

* * *

Los Angeles, 1962

Whatever became of the marine sergeant, William Lloyd Durkin?

Ever since 1946, when this temporary national hero pulled Howard to safety from the burning wreckage of the XF-11, he'd continued to serve in the

Marine Corps. Howard had specifically urged him to complete his tour of duty. Only then, he promised, would he set him up in a business that would give him a trouble-free retirement.

Eighteen years after his rescue of Howard back in 1946, he had drawn $200 a month from Toolco as compensation for saving the aviator's life. In addition, during his hospital convalescence, Howard had "guaranteed" that he would provide the funding for any line of business that Durkin wanted to launch.

In 1962, in Los Angeles after his retirement from the Marine Corps, Durkin called on an aging Noah Dietrich to remind him of that long-ago oral agreement. He told Dietrich that the $200 a month "had been just great," but that the money had been spent and that he now needed to discuss setting up that business.

The sergeant informed Dietrich that he'd already made several attempts to get in touch with Howard, but that each of his attempts to speak to Howard had been rejected by some secretary.

In his memoirs, in which Dietrich called the marine "Durkan," he describes his meeting with the troubled sergeant. He later said in an interview, "if it weren't for Durkin, Howard wouldn't be on this earth. It would have been so easy for Howard to settle fifty thousand on the marine to help him set up a business somewhere. But there was nothing I could do for the bewildered man. I had to tell Durkin the painful truth: I no longer worked for Howard Hughes."

On May 12, 1957, over a battle about stock options, Howard had fired "his most faithful servant."

Durkin, alas, never received the funding for his business. And shortly thereafter, his monthly stipend dried up as well.

* * *

Los Angeles/Ohio/Washington, 1946-47

By the third week of his convalescence in Cary's rented villa, Howard was growing restless. It was time to relaunch himself into the business world. Without Cary's permission, he ordered the installation of extra telephone lines and asked Nadine Henley to hire three extra women—"brunettes only"—for secretarial services.

"I protested," Dr. Mason said. "He had not recovered and needed rest. But it was very hard for a mere doctor to stand up to Howard Hughes." Dr. Mason had cut off his supply of codeine and morphine after he left the hospital, but he knew that Howard was getting drugs through some other source, no doubt Johnny Meyer, whose contacts for anything illegal were virtually unlimited.

Barred from seeing Howard in the hospital, Dietrich made daily visits to the villa. At one point he told Howard that "your fortune has gone beyond the half billion dollar mark—it's hard to quote exact figures."

Lying on the sofa, Howard frowned but didn't say anything for a long while, as if mulling over something. Finally he told Dietrich, "Make it an even billion, Noah, and be quick about it, you hear now?"

He had no other instructions that day, but continued to listen to Dinah Shore on the radio and to drink freshly squeezed juice from blood-red oranges. Dietrich also noted a dozen oatmeal cookies on an adjoining table. During his recuperation, Howard had decided that oatmeal cookies would be his only food source.

Night after night Howard was troubled by the crash of the XF-11, considering his own role in it "blameless." Summoning Greg Bautzer to the villa, he ordered his attorney to file a lawsuit against Hamilton-Standard Division, the manufacturers of the malfunctioning right-wing propeller. Within two weeks, and fearing a public scandal and loss of confidence in their products, the company settled out of court for a reported $200,000, though that amount might have been slightly less. The settlement was for personal injury to Howard, not a reimbursement to Hughes Aviation. Howard was delighted that he could pocket the money himself. He also felt that Hamilton-Standard, by admitting its error, had absolved him of blame as the pilot.

When Howard crashed the XF-11, he was technically on government business. All crashes of government planes mandated an investigation by the Air Force. While Howard recovered at Cary's house, the military conducted a thorough probe of the downed XF-11, concluding that the plane crashed "because of pilot error."

The report was severely critical of Howard's test flight, noting, among other attacks, that he'd failed to use a special radio frequency assigned to the craft. He'd also violated several other regulations, including those for retracting the landing gear. The board further concluded that Howard had waited too long to make an emergency landing. Not only that, but he'd violated the time limit for test flights, which was forty-five minutes. Air Force investigators concluded that there would have been no crash if Howard had landed within the proper time frame. The conclusion was that, "Hughes not only risked his own life, but endangered a heavily populated residential community by flying over it instead of using testing grounds in the Mojave Desert."

Getting it completely wrong in his dubious memoirs, Dietrich claimed that the personal injury settlement "ended Howard's interest in the XF-11... I never heard him mention the XF-11 ever again."

In truth, Howard, as part of his compulsive disorder obsession, focused almost entirely on launching a new version of the XF-11. "It became his passion—day and night," Odekirk said. "Those calls at four o'clock in the morning!"

On one of his frantic early morning calls to Odekirk, Howard decided that for the new XF-11 prototype, he would no longer use the innovative conter-rotating props. "I can't trust 'em," he told Odekirk. "The fucking things nearly killed me. As it is, I'll suffer for the rest of my life with ailments stemming out of that crash." He ordered single props on each of the XF-11's two engines.

Even before he'd fully recovered, Howard was eager to fly again. He flew his converted B-23 bomber to Ohio where he met with the Air Force brass at Wright Field. Officials there had contacted Hughes Aviation in Culver City, asking them to "furnish the name of a test pilot other than Mr. H.R. Hughes."

Howard protested their decision, demanding that he be the pilot of the next prototype of the XF-11. He was brutally rejected.

Not taking defeat easily, he flew at once to Washington for a private meeting at the home of Lt. General Ira C. Eaker, Deputy Commanding General of the U.S. Air Force. On that wintry Sunday early in 1947, he made an astonishing offer. He agreed to sign an affidavit to reimburse the government to the tune of five million dollars if the new XF-11 crashed when he was its pilot.

Eaker felt he didn't have the authority to make such a decision and summoned General Carl Spaatz to his home to discuss the matter with Howard. Spaatz was the new Commanding General of the Air Force. After hearing Howard's plea, and being somewhat awed by one of America's genuine aviation heroes—and a rich one at that—Spaatz was easily won over by Howard's facile charm. He said that the five million dollar guarantee would not be necessary and that he'd order Wright Field to rescind its order against Howard being the test pilot. Howard was elated as he flew his bomber back to the tarmac at Culver City.

On the morning of April 5, 1947, Howard, in spite of protests from Odekirk, once again stepped into the cockpit of an XF-11 for its maiden run. "The kinks are worked out," he told Odekirk, promising to adhere strictly to Air Force regulations on this flight.

True to his word, Howard was airborne for only ninety minutes. Nothing went wrong this time. The XF-11 tested perfectly, all its equipment functioning properly. At long last and after a bitter five-year struggle and millions of dollars spent, the government-financed reconnaissance plane was ready.

Landing at Culver City, Howard emerged in his Texas boots, brown leather jacket, and lucky fedora to receive the applause of all 500 employees of Hughes Aviation.

"Today," he boasted to Odekirk, "we have made a major breakthrough in aviation. We're ready to manufacture those one hundred reconnaissance planes for the good ol' U.S. of A."

"Howard," a puzzled Odekirk protested. "Have you forgotten? The government long ago canceled its orders for the XF-11s. The war's been over for nearly two years."

* * *

Los Angeles, 1946

Before the crash, Howard's old friend, the columnist, Louella Parsons, had written that "Howard Hughes is the most glamorous man in the world."

That was no longer true. In the hospital, he'd lost thirty pounds and was skeletally thin.

Continuing to ignore Faith Domergue, Howard had Johnny Meyer drive Linda Darnell over to Cary's villa when he felt he could resume his seduction of beautiful women. But as Linda later recalled, it was not a romantic evening. She found her sometimes lover morbidly depressed.

"The first time I looked into a mirror after leaving the hospital, a stranger was staring back at me," he told her. "It involves more than becoming middle aged. Life has drained from my face. My eyes are dead. There's a look in them I haven't seen before. It's one of fear. Ball-busting fear, the kind that grabs a man in his gut. My gut feels like a giant fist is twisting my bowels. Squeezing the life force out of me." He looked again in the mirror to study his face with its new mustache. "The press used to call me handsome. I don't think they'll be using that word for me any more."

The next day he lamented to Meyer, "In the future it just won't be Henry Willson's hustlers demanding money from me. Beautiful women will also want cash up front. There might even come a day when cash won't buy me what I want."

"I assure you, boss," Meyer said, "that day will never come no matter how old you get."

When he finally got around to calling on her, Lana Turner also noted the remarkable change in Howard. "For starters, I hated his mustache, but I guess it was covering up something worse. After he got out of the hospital, he visited my house only once. I must admit that in those days I had a lot of mirrors. My fortune depended on my face, and I checked it frequently, maybe to see if it were still there and in working order. When he came to visit me, he was so thin and hadn't purchased a new wardrobe. His neck seemed to have gotten lost somewhere in his collar. He'd rescued his old fedora, and the stinking thing was resting jauntily on his battered head. Before the evening was over, I felt that the old Howard Hughes had died. I wasn't sure I liked the present reincarnation. Sitting across from me on my sofa was a tired old man. He could have been my father. But, even so, he was still *the* Howard Hughes. In those days, no one kicked *him* out!"

The reports of other girlfriends were equally damning. Gene Tierney felt that Howard's once penetrating brown eyes "looked beady somehow—gray instead of brown. His face was a mask of anger. He seemed to want to get even with the world. Plastic surgery had altered his once perfect features."

Having brought a potted plant to him at the hospital, Jane Greer was at first glad to see him until he came from the darkness of her foyer into the light of her living room. "He looked like an older man who'd just gotten off the train back from Hell," she later said. "He looked like he'd also run a marathon race across

666

continents. I felt he was on the verge of a total physical collapse. I told him that he should go and readmit himself into that hospital. His cheeks looked sunken, like they'd somehow caved in. It was only later that I learned he was massively consuming drugs."

The still very young Faith Domergue, who'd been neglected by Howard so much, suddenly didn't mind all the nights and even weeks he'd left her alone. "I still loved him…I guess. Sorta loved him. But I came to feel that a night with him was like visiting my grandfather. His attempt at lovemaking…well, let me put it this way. It was an attempt, and I'll say no more."

* * *

Los Angeles, 1946-51

Noah Dietrich once said, "*The Outlaw* should have been Howard's last film. He was involved in nightmarish problems in 1946, mainly with undelivered aircraft and TWA financial woes. He really didn't need to buy RKO two years later, turn it into a whorehouse for himself, and make all those horrible movies that tarnished his reputation. His descent began with that turkey, *Vendetta*."

For years, teenage Faith Domergue had been nagging Howard to launch her film career as an actress. "His little cutie wanted to be a fucking movie star," Johnny Meyer said, "and Little Miss got her wish. After all, she'd been sharing her pussy and those luscious lips with Howard for years. I guess she was entitled. Preston Sturges himself admitted to me, she couldn't act her way out of a paper bag. But that didn't seem to matter. Besides, how does one act one's way out of a paper bag?"

Howard had turned to Preston Sturges to adapt Prosper Mérimée's novel, *Colomba*, for the screen. This murky yarn about revenge in 19th-century Corsica was immediately retitled *Vendetta* by Sturges.

Eager to relaunch himself into films after the long wartime years that followed the making of *The Outlaw*, Howard teamed up with this talented writer and director. He'd been impressed with his film scripts in the 1930s. He was even more impressed with films he'd directed in the 1940s.

Preston had become a master of screwball comedies: *The Lady Eve*, from 1941, with Barbara Stanwyck and Henry Fonda; *Sullivan's Travels* with Joel McCrea and Veronica Lake, also from 1941; and the charming and funny *The Miracle of Morgan's Creek*, (1944) with Eddie Bracken and Betty Hutton.

The end of the war found Preston sitting on top of the heap in Hollywood. In 1944 Paramount had offered him a guaranteed one million dollars to renew his contract. He turned the studio down, saying he wanted to produce his own films independently of any studio. He claimed, "I'm a One Man Band. I became an independent producer to get away from supervision."

667

"For a director of such cockiness, teaming up with a control freak like Howard was a big mistake," Dietrich claimed.

Reared amid wealth and social prestige in Chicago in 1898, and spending most of his teenaged years in Europe (his mother was an inseparable friend of the high priestess of modern dance, Isadora Duncan), Preston was not a typical studio hired hand. Although he would eventually lose them as part of a life fraught with epic melodrama, during the postwar years he owned two yachts—more than Howard—and a dinner theater, The Players, in Los Angeles. He also lived in a large mansion, had a brief marriage to one of the daughters of Marjorie Merriweather Post, and even owned a factory, Sturges Engineering Company, producing diesel engines for the War Department.

Having much in common, Howard and Preston initially bonded. "In short time, the mixture of those two proved as harmonious as blending oil with water," Dietrich said. Nonetheless, over his chief's protests, Howard forged

Preston Sturges (center) with Henry Fonda and Barbara Stanwyck

ahead and formed a new film studio with Preston. Launched in 1944 as California Pictures Corporation, its papers of incorporation left Howard in control of the majority of the shares, as Preston would soon painfully realize.

Before the filming of *Vendetta* was launched, however, Howard allowed Preston to talk him into bringing Harold Lloyd back to the screen for a nostalgic bout with the cinematic past. The silent screen star, during his heyday in the 1920s, had been one of the three great comedians of the Silent Era, ranking up there with Charlie Chaplin and Buster Keaton.

Entitled *The Sin of Harold Diddlebock*, and envisioned as a quick way to occupy California Pictures Corporation until the inaugural preparations for other, more important movies were finished, filming was launched late in 1945, with shooting continuing until March of 1946. After seeing Preston's edited version of the corporation's first film, Howard ordered it shelved for years, pending his input for a reedited final cut. But by the time he got around to reediting it, his partnership with Preston Sturges had collapsed. Retitled *Mad Wednesday*, the film was finally released in 1950, finding no real audience. By then, Harold Lloyd's heyday was a distant memory of the past.

But before his partnership with Preston collapsed completely, Howard tried to bring what energy and enthusiasm he could to the launch of Faith Domergue's career, but his heart clearly wasn't in it. He believed that *Vendetta* would be the right property to showcase her talents—"or lack thereof," as bitchy critics later wrote. At one point, he planned to bill her as "the next Jane Russell." Preston pointed out that the first Jane Russell hadn't yet been established as a film star.

Facing the cameras for the first time in a starring role, Faith had barely gotten over her lisp after endless diction lessons. Suddenly, the weight of this ill-fated melodrama rested on her creamy shoulders.

During the first six weeks of shooting, Preston either showed up in a drunken stupor on the set or else went horseback riding with his mistress. After those six weeks, one million dollars of Howard's money had been spent with nothing to show for it.

In his weakened condition, Howard learned what was happening. "Instead of viewing it as the unsalvageable mess it was," Dietrich said, "Howard forged ahead to save the picture from becoming a disaster. The task proved overwhelming even for him."

His partnership with Preston collapsed. "When Mr. Hughes made suggestions with which I disagreed, as he has a perfect right to do, I rejected them. When I rejected the last one, he remembered that he had an option to take control of the company. He took over. I left!"

Howard even tried to direct the picture himself, after W.R. Burnett had been brought in as a rewrite man. He named a new director, Stuart Heisler, but was dissatisfied with his work. Howard finally settled on a thirty-year-old actor, Mel Ferrer, who had no experience as a director. By 1954, Mel would be known as "Mr. Audrey Hepburn."

The film faced endless delays, just like *The Outlaw*. Years later, Faith recalled that making *Vendetta* was a "tortured, horrible experience. I once made 95 takes for one little short scene."

Meyer later reported that "Howard seemed to be more turned on by one of the male costars of the film, Donald Buka, than he was with Faith. The extraordinarily handsome actor was playing Padrino the Bandit opposite Faith. Possessed of male charm and beauty, Buka thrilled Howard when he watched the rushes. Meyer warned him, however, that Buka was a bonafide heterosexual and wouldn't be interested in any overtures from Howard.

"That's what you said about Jack Buetel," Howard pointed out to him. "And I had him for years." Meyer remembered Howard sighing, eventually deciding that it might be humiliating to pursue Buka. "Maybe some dreams are best if only dreamed."

Responding to Howard's lack of interest, Faith married a musician, Teddy Stauffer in 1947. Stauffer would later marry one of Howard's former girlfriends, Hedy Lamarr.

Donald Buka and Faith Domergue in *Vendetta*

At the finish of *Vendetta* in 1948, Howard delayed its release, but continued to publicize the film. Faith was promoted as "one of the most exciting personalities to reach the screen." She wasn't.

Howard hoped that by holding back the release date, in a way that had worked successfully with *The Outlaw, Vendetta* would generate public anticipation. Its release eventually came in 1950 as an RKO film. Critics immediately dismissed it as a "costume bore," and audiences stayed away in droves.

In spite of his disappointment in Faith as an actress, Howard cast her in another film, *Where Danger Lives*, in 1950. He felt that its star, Robert Mitchum, could carry the picture, even if Faith delivered a weak performance. That film in time would become somewhat of a *noir* classic. Even so, when filming ended, Howard did not renew Faith's contract, letting it expire in 1951.

"Faith Domergue is history," he told his friend, Robert Mitchum. "I've found someone better and more talented. Only thing is, she's got a handsome boyfriend she's going to marry."

"And who is this talented beauty?" the laconic Mitchum asked. "And how do you propose to get rid of the boyfriend?"

"I can only answer the first question," Howard said. "Eliminating the jock will take some thought. She's British. It's Jean Simmons."

* * *

Los Angeles/Paris, 1947-49

Former husband Orson Welles once remarked: "Rita Hayworth one day may be remembered for only two things: the margarita cocktail and the fact that her face was glued onto the atomic bomb that devastated Hiroshima." Before changing her name to Rita Hayworth, the screen goddess was known as Margarita Carmen Cansino when she danced in Tijuana night clubs with her father.

670

Following the worldwide success of *Gilda*, released in 1946 and co-starring Glenn Ford, Rita had become America's love goddess long before Marilyn Monroe grabbed the title from her.

In his weakened condition following his plane crash, Howard revealed to Johnny Meyer that he planned to launch a campaign to seduce Rita, but not immediately. At no point did he reveal to his pimp whether or not he'd seduced a teenage Rita in Mexico years many years previously. Rita had been devastatingly beautiful and buxom since she was thirteen, and she was bound to catch Howard's attention, looking as she did in all those Technicolor movies he'd seen of her.

Like Howard, Rita had had an incestuous relationship with a parent. In her case, it was her Spanish father, Eduardo Cansino, a vaudeville dancer from Seville. Rita later confided that her father repeatedly had had sex with her. Eduardo was always flattered when members of the audience thought that he was the brother—not the father—of Rita when they danced as a team in night clubs.

Before calling on Rita, Howard had seen *Gilda* a total of ten times. He told Meyer that he found Rita vivacious, sexy, and desirable, and was especially attracted to that come-hither glint in her eyes. Long before Meyer actually arranged a rendezvous between the pair, Howard had begun his campaign to seduce Rita.

He'd followed details of her marriage to Edward C. Judson, which lasted from May 29, 1937 to May 24, 1943. Judson was more than just her husband: he was also her pimp. He arranged assignations where he forced his wife to sleep with any producer or director, even leading actor, who might advance her career.

Rita performed her duties as a prostitute at Judson's urging. But she also showed a rebellious streak, refusing to sleep with two of the most powerful studio chiefs in Hollywood. She turned down Darryl F. Zanuck at Fox. She also refused to go to bed with Harry Cohn, who eventually became her boss at Columbia. He had developed an obsession for her and would unsuccessfully pursue his glamorous movie queen for years.

Rita's only comment to the press about the breakup of her first marriage was, "Basically, I'm a good and gentle person. But I'm attracted to mean personalities."

The divorce between Judson and Rita was bitter. She was his meal ticket, and he didn't want her to get away from him. He had stolen various copies of letters that his wife had foolishly written to her lovers. In these letters, the candid and outspoken Rita had revealed intimate sexual details of her affairs. He threatened to make them public unless she gave him all her money and possessions except for her car. So as not to destroy the career of his major star, Cohn paid $30,000 to Rita's "hustler husband." She also agreed to pay her estranged husband $12,000 in monthly installments of $500. When she married Welles on

September 7, 1943, she was bankrupt.

Through Johnny Meyer, Howard sent his pimp to approach Judson. He agreed to sell Howard copies of Rita's letters for ten thousand dollars. For his voyeuristic pleasure, Howard delighted in reading these sexually charged letters.

Normally a breast man, Howard was fascinated by her luscious auburn mane, finding it thick and silky. He liked the way it cascaded down over her creamy shoulders. He'd rerun *Gilda's* sexy and coquettish song and dance number, "Put the Blame on Mame" a total of fifty times. Meyer sat in on one of these screenings. He later claimed that Howard started to sing along with Rita on the screen. "You haven't lived until you've heard my boss sing. Like no sound I've ever heard." Meyer didn't want to spoil Howard's illusion by telling him that Rita's voice had been dubbed. He was actually listening to singer Anita Ellis.

Howard had initially been excited by Rita from tales told by Tyrone Power, who'd seduced her during their remake of *Blood and Sand*, the bullfight picture in which she'd played an exotic and erotic *femme fatale*.

He also learned of her other lovers and was especially disturbed to learn of her affair with Victor Mature. By that time in his life, he'd become particularly concerned with the penis sizes of his boudoir competitors. Having sampled Mature's legendary endowment himself, he was at first shy about presenting himself to Rita. "Victor is a tough act to follow," he told Meyer.

At first Howard launched his campaign to seduce Rita anonymously. He began by having Meyer send dozens of "California's most beautiful roses" every day to her home in Brentwood. Maybe she suspected who her secret admirer was—that's not known.

In Meyer's facetious words, "When Howard denuded Southern California of all its roses," he sent Rita, again anonymously, the most luxurious watch he could find at Cartier's. It was studded with diamonds. Meyer first called Rita and asked if it'd be all right if Howard called her. "I accepted that diamond watch," she told Meyer. "And all those roses. The least I can do is listen to what the man has to say." Granted that go-ahead sign, Howard began to bombard her with phone calls, sometimes at three o'clock in the morning. Finally, he told her, "I'm the man to fill the void in your life left by Orson Welles."

At the time, Rita's marriage to Orson was on the rocks. They were living apart and potentially heading for the divorce courts, even though they'd had a daughter, Rebecca Welles.

Howard told Rita that he'd watched her "Put the Blame on Mame" number fifty times. "But there's nothing like seeing the real thing," she responded. She agreed to meet him at her Brentwood home at one o'clock in the morning. She said that she'd borrow the Gilda gown from wardrobe at Columbia and would greet him at the door in it. He promised to bring along "some surprises, including a big surprise."

Before visiting Rita, Howard contacted Jean Louis, the famous couturier who'd designed Rita's black strapless gown and long gloves as worn in the film. For a hefty price, he ordered the designer to create twelve versions of the same gown, all in different colors.

In the back of his Chevy en route to Brentwood, Howard carried the gowns in colors that included lemon yellow, ivory white, emerald green, shocking pink, tulip red, sky blue, midnight blue, lavender, fuschia, royal purple, butterscotch, and russet. He also carried along two bottles of 1938 Dom Perignon in silver buckets purchased at Tiffany's in New York and flown to Los Angeles aboard a TWA plane. He also brought along a 78 rpm recording of "Put the Blame on Mame."

Laden down, he was nervous as he approached the front door of Rita's home. When she threw open the door, one of his wildest fantasies came true. Gilda herself was standing before him, looking exactly like she did in the 1946 film.

Unknown to him at the time, Rita had emerged only that afternoon from the bed of actor David Niven. As she later told her friend, Marlene Dietrich, she was "trying to comfort David" following the tragic death of his young wife.

Pouring the first of the champagne, Howard toasted her. "To Gilda."

"I'm not Gilda, Howard. I'm Rita. Let me make the toast. To Rita and Howard." After the toast, she gently kissed his scarred lips.

After the first bottle of champagne, even though Howard wasn't much of a drinker, he presented the gowns to Rita and made a strange request. He wanted her to put on each gown and perform the Mame number for him twelve times. Only then, he claimed, could he decide which gown showcased her body most flatteringly and sexily.

A bit tipsy, Rita gave in to this demand, although finding all those wardrobe changes annoying and exhausting. Nonetheless, she agreed to it. As Anita's voice came on in the recording, Rita disappeared behind a

Rita Hayworth, Marlene Dietrich

673

Rita Hayworth as Gilda

screen and slipped on each gown and performed the number for him. Surprisingly, he found that despite the staggering expense of the dozen Jean Louis gowns, he liked the original gown, borrowed from the wardrobe department at Columbia, best.

On the final number, Howard, as he confided in Meyer, "became so hot I whipped it out and showed it to her hard." At the end of her number, she pulled off one long glove and tossed it at his cock. Then she took off the other glove and tossed it at the same target. Within moments, that beautiful mane of auburn hair was bobbing up and down on Howard. "Her father, Judson, Welles, Mature, Spencer Tracy, James Stewart, Glenn Ford, Tony Martin, and Gilbert Roland had taught her well," Howard later told Meyer.

"Only actor Peter Lawford had been displeased with her charms: "The worst lay in the world. She was always drunk and never stopped eating."

When she'd swallowed Howard's offering, she stood up in front of him, striking a pose from *Gilda* and borrowing a line from the movie: "I'm not very good with zippers. Could somebody help me?"

Howard immediately came to her rescue with shaky fingers. As he was to report to Meyer, "it was a night of bliss. My greatest moment was when the gown fell to the floor. She was wearing Juel Parks lingerie." He later described the lingerie to Meyer as "gossamer."

As he recalled to his trusted pimp, "I've seen bigger breasts but none as splendid as the pair on her. I couldn't control myself. She screamed and tried to fight me off. But I bit into those nipples real hard. Her screams only goaded me on. I don't know what came over me. I couldn't control myself." He also revealed that with his fingers in her and his teeth on her nipples, she experienced the first of several orgasms that night, in a style that evoked the self-described sexual receptiveness of Hedy Lamarr.

674

The next morning, Rita was relatively demure in her assessment, telling close friend Marlene Dietrich, "Howard went to bed with Gilda and woke up with me."

In spite of his assault on her nipples, she continued to date him. At least part of their affair was conducted within the 64-room beachfront mansion of the fading screen diva, Marion Davies, in Santa Monica. The aging mistress of William Randolph Hearst and Howard's long-time friend since his days as a teenager, she even redecorated Greta Garbo's old suite for the illicit lovers. Chilled champagne always rested in a silver bucket. On chilly nights, logs burned in the marble fireplace that the press baron had imported from the châteaux country of France's Loire Valley.

Recognizing the couple's need for privacy, Marion instructed her servants never to intrude. One night a new male attendant, who had not been informed, walked in on the couple with a stack of fluffy white towels. He found them lying nude on top of the quilts in a lavish four-poster bed that allegedly had once belonged to the estate of Queen Elizabeth I. Marion always claimed that "Sir Walter Raleigh fucked the good Queen Bess right in this bed." Seeing the intruder, Howard grabbed Rita's long hair and attempted to conceal her breasts, leaving her genitals exposed. "Don't look, you idiot!" he shouted at the startled servant. "Get out!"

Rita and Howard launched themselves into a tempestuous affair that was played out like a 1940s movie drama. One night as he confided to Meyer, Rita became hysterical at his refusal to commit to her. She raced from her Brentwood home, got into her car, and went on a dangerous drive along the curving roads of the Hollywood Hills. Before leaving, she threatened that she was going to kill herself.

In his battered Chevy, he chased after her. He finally caught up with her on a mountain summit. When she came to a screeching halt, he slammed on his brakes so as not to pile into her. He jumped out of his car and raced to hers, where he yanked her from behind the wheel. "You little fool!" He slapped her repeatedly until she fell on the ground at his feet—just like a Lana Turner movie. Picking her up, he forced her into the Chevy and drove her back to Brentwood, as she sobbed.

In a few months, she confronted him with some painful news. She was pregnant with his child, and wanted him to marry her as soon as her divorce from Welles came through.

"I detest kids!" he told her. "Harlow wanted to have my kid. We had it aborted. I don't want some boy coming out of your womb that will replace me. If I had a son, he'd inherit my fortune. He'd probably live every day wanting me to die young so he could take over. I've had those same feelings about my own father."

"But you'd have an heir," she said. "A fucking heir to your fortune. Howard Hughes III. He'd carry on your legacy."

Meyer later claimed this confrontation occurred in front of him at her Brentwood home. He interjected, "I bet the kid would look great. Howard Hughes for a daddy, Rita Hayworth for a mother. The prettiest baby on the planet."

"He'd probably turn out to be the biggest faggot on the planet," Howard said.

"How can you say that?" she protested. "Besides, it might be a girl."

"Then she'd be the biggest whore on the planet."

"You mean, just like her mother?" she shouted at him. "You bastard!" She ran from her living room and up the steps, bolting herself in.

The next day when she confronted Harry Cohn at Columbia with the bad news, he shouted at her. When he cooled down, he urged her to take Howard's advice and abort the child. "Send the rich Texas fucker the bill. He can afford it!" As a parting gesture, he told her, "If you'd given your pussy to me, you wouldn't have gotten pregnant. I know how to take precautions." He couldn't let her leave his office without warning her that if news of her pregnancy leaked out, the Legion of Decency and Women's Clubs all over America would boycott her films. "Your career will be over!"

It was a great dilemma for her. Her Catholic upbringing told her not to have an abortion. She truly wanted Howard's kid, even though he didn't want it.

Fearing her pregnancy might start to show, Howard urged her to take a four-month trip at his expense with a paid companion. She sailed for France. After her third night at the Hotel Crillon in Paris, she complained of severe pains in her abdomen. Rushed by ambulance to the American Hospital at Neuilly, she was extensively examined. Doctors told her that she was experiencing an ectopic pregnancy, meaning that a fertilized egg had been implanted outside the uterus and had settled into her fallopian tubes. The fetus had grown until it was pressing against her fallopian tubes. She was warned that the organ would burst if the child wasn't aborted immediately.

At that point there was no more debate within herself, as she knew that nature had decided the abortion issue for her. She underwent a surgical procedure.

Howard Hughes III would never enter the world to face a lavish life as the son of two of the 20th century's most gilded people.

Some reports claimed that Howard refused to pay any of her medical bills. But Noah Dietrich later said that he transferred $15,000 of Howard's money to Rita in Paris.

Returning to Hollywood to resume her career, Rita learned that Orson Welles was having an affair with a beautiful blonde starlet. The same starlet was also having an affair with Howard. "Who's the competition?" Rita asked Marlene, who managed to keep up with such boudoir affairs. "A little tramp," Dietrich told her. "She'll never amount to...how do you Americans say it?...a hill of beans?"

"Who's the bimbo?" Rita asked.

"Marilyn Monroe."

Welles was having his spies report on Rita's affairs. Harry Cohn was still obsessed with her and had her bedroom bugged as well as her dressing room at Columbia. Unknown to Rita, Howard was also having her spied upon and her phone tapped. "She was the most bugged woman in Hollywood," Meyer later said.

It's been reported that Cohn wanted to obtain incriminating evidence against Rita, so he could evoke the morals clause in her contract. That is highly unlikely. Why would a studio boss want to suspend his chief money-maker?

Howard's sheer curiosity demanded that he be kept informed of Rita's affairs in the wake of her abortion. Although he didn't want her any more for himself, he was still fascinated by her nocturnal adventures. To his dismay, he learned that he'd been replaced by the international playboy, Prince Aly Khan, son of the Aga Khan, "direct descendant of the Prophet Mohammed" and hereditary Imam of the Shi'a Imami Ismaili community comprising 15 million cult followers in Asia and Africa. Apparently to judge from the bugging, the handsome, charming prince had learned the ancient art of *Imsak*, indefinite postponement of ejaculation *(coitus reservatus)*, as an enhancement of sexual pleasure. It was later learned that the prince had been sent as a teenager to the bordellos of Cairo to develop his sexual technique.

To Howard's further surprise, he learned that Rita was also having an affair with Mahmud Pahlavi, the brother of the Shah of Iran. Later, to his increased dismay, he found out that she was also having an affair with the actual Shah of Iran, not just his brother. King Farouk, the fat and notoriously decadent king of Egypt, was also pursuing Rita, but to no avail.

Eventually it was Prince Aly Khan who won her hand, beating out the competition. As Cary Grant later said, "People forget that Rita, a Hollywood goddess, became a princess long before Grace Kelly."

Howard soon learned that Rita was pregnant again. The presumed father was Prince Aly Khan. Through foreign agents arranged by Meyer, Howard went so far as to compile a dossier on the Prince's sexual entanglements. He then flew this data to her before her marriage.

With the evidence he'd accumulated, he wrote a note, "You're marrying the most promiscuous man on the planet." Not that Howard could afford to talk. Ignoring his warning, Rita married her prince on May 27, 1949 on the French Riviera. The world press treated it like another "Second Coming."

Even though he'd let her go, and urged her to abort their child, Howard seemed insulted that the playboy prince had upstaged him with Rita. He bitterly remarked to Meyer, "Rita's famous red hair is known by everybody, I guess. But I happen to know for a fact that it's just as black as her pussy!"

* * *

Los Angeles, 1946-52

At Cary Grant's rented villa, Howard continued his recovery in the wake of his plane crash over Beverly Hills. He didn't like to read books, so Cary brought him the latest magazines every day.

Flipping through the magazines, the cover photograph of a young girl on *Laff* caught his attention. He noted her breasts, golden hair falling to her shoulders, and what he later told Johnny Meyer was "the smile of an innocent child." The picture had been snapped by David Conover, an army photographer who sold pictures to men's magazines. Howard immediately called Meyer and ordered him to contact Conover. Perhaps he still knew the girl's address. "Get to her at once and sign her up to an exclusive seven-year contract. We've got to get her before some other jackal does."

The girl's name was Norma Jeane Dougherty. She'd changed the name "Jean" to "Jeane" because she thought it was sexier. Fortunately, she hadn't changed her address since the shoot, and Meyer was able to locate her.

He found her living "below the poverty level," with a handsome but struggling actor, Ted Jordan, who was talked about as "the next Tyrone Power." From what he gathered, Norma Jeane worked as a prostitute during long intervals between modeling assignments. A date was arranged. Without Howard's knowledge, Meyer employed Norma Jeane in her role as a prostitute. "I wanted to test her skills in bed before wasting my boss's time," Meyer said. "She was a great cocksucker even then. She left me so drained I never got around to number two. I set up a date with Howard and her, even though I didn't think he was in any condition to take on a vixen like Norma Jeane."

Over the course of many years, Norma Jeane told friends and confidants about her early days in Hollywood. She revealed to author Truman Capote that she did not take money for her favors when she was a streetwalker prowling the side streets off Sunset Boulevard. "Depending on the time of day, I'd negotiate for breakfast, lunch, or dinner. Anyone who knows me knows how I love to eat."

Her first agent, Harry Lipton, warned her that Howard was notorious for signing starlets and then "letting them dangle on the vine." He also said that Howard had signed Harlow and did nothing for her after *Hell's Angels*. Instead of immediately signing with Howard, he said he could use the producer's interest in her to drum up excitement at other studios such as Fox.

Norma Jeane knew who Howard Hughes was, but wasn't certain as to his status, other than being aware he was some very big and important person in Hollywood. She was eager to meet him when Meyer presented the deal and told her of Howard's interest. "I think Norma Jeane assumed from the very first that she'd be sleeping with Howard as part of the deal," Meyer said. "From the look of things, she didn't have the slightest objection to that."

Even before her meeting with Howard, Lipton planted an item which ran on July 29, 1946 in Hedda Hopper's syndicated column: *Howard Hughes is on the mend. Picking up a magazine, he was attracted by the cover girl and promptly instructed an aide to sign her for pictures. She's Norma Jeane Dougherty, a model.*

Lipton then used this bait to get Norma Jeane a meeting with Ben Lyon, then working as casting director at Fox. He called Ben and announced, "I've found the next Jean Harlow. She has a fantastic quality—it's an electricity she turns on. She brings out the desire in people to help her, to protect her, to mother and father her. It's not a sex thing at all. She's playing a role—this sex thing."

It was Hollywood irony that Ben, Howard's former lover and the star of *Hell's Angels*, thought of himself as the discoverer of the original Jean Harlow. He seemed anxious to become the discoverer of the next Jean Harlow. He ordered Lipton to bring her over that very afternoon. "The name's got to go, however," he said. "I can't see Dougherty on a theater marquee."

Upon meeting Norma Jeane for the first time, Ben was impressed. Every day beautiful girls hoping to get a Fox contract were paraded before him. None had impressed him like Norma Jeane. He immediately decided she wasn't a Harlow, though, but someone else, someone original. Without getting studio chief Zanuck's permission, he ordered a screen test, hoping to come up with a new discovery to enhance his position at Fox.

He ordered cameraman Leon Shamroy to conduct the test, the same man who'd photograph her in the 1954 *There's No Business Like Show Business*. He remembered Norma Jeane showing up in a gold sequined gown and Joan Crawford fuck-me high heels. He assured Ben that "Norma Jeane projects sex on the screen just like Harlow did."

Upon seeing her test, Zanuck signed her on as a contract player for $75 a week. Howard was furious at Meyer for not moving faster to sign her up with him.

Not liking her name, Ben changed it to Carole Lind. One night he took her out on a secret date when his wife, Bebe Daniels, was out of town. He suddenly came up with an idea. "You're Marilyn!" He practically shouted the name at her, which he'd stolen from another beautiful actress, Marilyn Miller. Norma Jeane—rechristened Marilyn—suggested the Monroe, borrowing the name from her grandmother.

"That's it!" Ben said. "It'll look great on a marquée. To Miss Marilyn Monroe!"

Arriving at Cary's villa the following night, Marilyn was dressed in a skintight cotton dress and high heels. Howard looked enchanted to see her in the flesh.

"Oh, Mr. Hughes," she said to him. "I'm a little sticky. Been posing for a photographer all day. Hot lights, you know. Do you mind if I borrow your shower."

Howard required a moment to take in this young girl with the dyed pale yellow hair and the sexy petulant mouth. "She looked like a tramp," he later told Meyer.

Clad in a bathrobe and lying on the sofa in the living room, he ordered the maid to show her to his bedroom upstairs. Normally, he would never have let anyone use his bathroom, but for her he agreed. He could tell through her thin dress that she wasn't wearing a bra. He suspected she wasn't wearing any other underwear either. Still in those high heels, Marilyn giggled as she followed the maid upstairs.

She must have been in that bathroom for an hour. Growing impatient, he rose from the sofa. It was difficult for him to walk, but even so he climbed the stairs. Without knocking at his bathroom door, he entered.

Once inside the steamy room, he found Marilyn floating around in a bubble bath. Suddenly, she sat up, revealing near perfect breasts. "May I make a request, Mr. Hughes?" she asked. "I noticed that Mr. Grant's bath towels are white. Could you call down to your maid and have her bring me pink towels. I know there must be pink towels somewhere in the linen closet. I like to dry myself only with pink towels, never white."

Perhaps he was taken back by her request, but he quickly called down for pink towels. Marilyn was right. There were pink towels in the linen closet.

Standing up, she showed off her nude figure and showered before him, washing the soap off her luscious body. When she finished, she turned to him and giggled. "Mr. Hughes, I like a man to dry me off all over. Don't miss any spot." As he moved toward her, she coyly stepped back. "I have to warn you. When I feel masculine hands on any part of my body, I'm quickly aroused."

He related the events of the previous night to Meyer. Howard found Marilyn "an excellent cocksucker—a really incredible mouth." Meyer later said that he felt Howard was too weak at the time to engage in regular intercourse—"he was still pretty beat up."

In the days and weeks ahead, Howard saw Marilyn on a number of occasions, at least according to Meyer. He remembered Howard taking her on his plane to some unknown destination. The two lovers had a picnic somewhere. Howard mentioned to Meyer that he'd been charmed by Marilyn without make-up lying in a field of grass with wildflowers growing around her. "She looked like a fresh-faced schoolgirl," he said. "She could pass for fourteen. I didn't eat much picnic that day but I found plenty to devour."

No longer the sexual athlete that he was, Howard engaged in oral sex with Marilyn, according to Meyer. "I think Marilyn was the first woman who'd ever gone around the world with Howard. My boss man loved that. He'd tried to get other women to do that to him. Some of them would refuse. But he'd always find a willing prostitute."

It was late in 1946 that Howard wanted to make a pornographic film with Marilyn, similar to the one he'd made with Porfirio Rubirosa in Santo Domingo years earlier. He didn't think he'd have trouble convincing her. He had already learned that she'd posed nude for the lens of her lover, Ted Jordan. Howard wanted to write and direct the script himself. Meyer "under secret oath" arranged it.

At first Marilyn refused, Meyer later claimed. She feared that her appearance in a blue movie would wreck her career. "When Howard promised that he would not allow her face to be revealed, she readily agreed, especially when she learned that the work in the film, which would be shot in only one night, carried a pay check of ten thousand dollars.

For the male lead, Howard wanted Jack Buetel. Although he'd agreed to allow Howard to film his nude buttocks during sexual intercourse on the set of *The Outlaw*, he absolutely refused to allow his erection to be depicted, even with Howard's guarantee that his face would not be shown in the blue movie.

Rejecting Buetel as a candidate, Howard then turned to another lover, Guy Madison. Henry Willson made the deal. At first Guy refused until he learned that his face wouldn't be shown. "If that's the case," Guy told Willson, "I'd love to get paid ten thousand dollars to fuck Marilyn Monroe. I've seen pictures of her."

Meyer was on the set when the film was shot one night at 7000 Romaine. "Howard's script for the shoot went out the window when Guy and Marilyn got together," Meyer said. "Completely nude, she looked like the most beautiful creature I'd ever seen. Those soon-to-be-famous breasts were plump and firm. Ripe fruit. My boss had picked the right tomato. If anyone thought Guy had a gay streak in him, he didn't show it that night. He was really turned on by Marilyn. When Guy stripped off his pants and presented Marilyn with a long, straight, thick tool, she squealed with delight and went to work polishing it. Even better than Faye Emerson. Her darting tongue continued to lubricate it. Those two turned me on. Guy banged the hell out of her. They were sucking, lapping, kissing, stroking each other. It was like they were worshipping each other's bodies."

"I had to practically pull Guy off her when Howard called cut," Meyer said. "I think that sailor boy wanted to go for his third climax without taking it out of her."

Meyer said that he never saw the developed film. There were rumors that it was shown at Hollywood smokers in the late 1940s, some of which were attended by women.

If a copy exists today, it can be presumed to rest somewhere in a hidden vault. Meyer revealed another tantalizing note. For the shoot, Howard had demanded that Marilyn dye her "black pussy platinum—just like Harlow's." She willingly obliged.

She'd spend the rest of her life dyeing down below, and it would be blonde hairs on the vagina that she'd present to a future U.S. president and his attorney general.

* * *

Howard would go for months without seeing Marilyn. Sometimes he'd be in the mood for that breathy little girl voice, that exaggerated sexuality she put on for him, and he'd call her. Often he didn't even bother to take her to his living quarters, wherever they were at the time, but drove her high into the Hollywood Hills. "Mainly Howard wanted blow-jobs from Marilyn," Johnny Meyer claimed. "At least that's what he told me. I don't know if he ever did it with her in the missionary position."

Sometimes Howard would drive her to a scenic outlook. While he took in the view of Los Angeles at night, Marilyn expertly worked him over. One of those blow-jobs was related to his mistress at the time, actress Terry Moore. She provided descriptive details in her book, *The Passions of Howard Hughes.*

Ms. Moore wrote this:

Unbuckling his belt and unzipping his pants, she let out a squeal when she saw he wasn't wearing any underwear. Taking his cock in her hand, she slowly stroked it up and down, making it even harder than he thought was possible. With his legs extended up onto the dashboard of the Chevy, Howard felt like a contortionist trying to reach for her breasts as she moved her face between his legs. Looking directly up at him, she kept her eyes locked on his as she guided him expertly into her mouth. Howard felt himself start to tremble and then, suddenly, in less than ten seconds, he exploded.

Even when he wasn't with Marilyn, he still monitored her nocturnal activities. Over the years, he tape-recorded many of her scenes of passion with a sometimes startling parade of figures: two of the world's most super endowed personalities, Milton Berle and Porfirio Rubirosa, plus a host of others—George Sanders, Bugsy Siegel, Frank Sinatra, Franchot Tone, Orson Welles, Darryl F. Zanuck, Walter Winchell, Damon Runyon, Dean Martin, Clifford Odets, Mickey Rooney, Tony Curtis, George Jessel, John Huston, Sammy Davis Jr., Harry Cohn, Yul Brynner, Marlon Brando, and, yes, even Albert Einstein.

Howard also learned that Marilyn was having affairs with women, including Joan Crawford. Instead of being jealous, he found that amusing. During the time Marilyn was living and having an affair with her Russian-born drama coach, Natasha Lytees, Howard often invited both of them out for dinner. But he took them to remote, out-of-the-way bistros so they'd be relatively protected from the press.

Natasha once claimed that she was having her morning coffee when Marilyn arrived from an all-night rendezvous with Howard. "Her pink face looked raw, like she'd developed a rash," Natasha said. "Marilyn just looked at me with that bubble-headed innocent gaze. 'Mr. Hughes hasn't shaved in three days,' she said before wiggling off to bed like the Serpent of the Nile."

One time, according to Natasha, Marilyn showed her a pin Howard had presented to her. The next day she took it to have it appraised at a pawnshop on Hollywood Boulevard, where she was told that the value of the gem was five-hundred dollars. "I had expected something much more valuable," a disappointed Marilyn told Natasha. Even more helpful than jewelry, Howard paid for Marilyn's acting lessons with Natasha.

Marilyn used a battered car to drive around from studio to studio, hoping to be cast in any film. In 1949 when Howard hadn't called for a long time, her car was in danger of being repossessed. For some time, Tom Kelley, who had once photographed Jane Russell, had been begging her to pose in the nude for a calendar. In desperation she called him and agreed to the session for fifty dollars. He posed her naked and stretched out on rumpled red velvet which evoked the inside of a Tiffany jewel box.

Kelley took the pictures on May 25, 1949 at his studio at 736 North Seward in Los Angeles. The photographer sold the rights for $500 to the Baumgarth Calendar Company. When Howard learned of the calendar, he lamented to Noah Dietrich that he should have acquired the rights to the calendar. "I bet it'll sell fifteen million copies." He had a different question for Meyer. "Get me a copy of that god damn calendar—and does Marilyn show pubic hair?"

When Meyer delivered a copy of the calendar to Howard, he studied it very carefully. "Now I know why it's called the Calendar of Golden Dreams."

Keith Andes and Marilyn Monroe in *Clash by Night*

When Howard was in charge at RKO in 1952, he wanted to cast Marilyn as the fourth lead in *Clash by Night*, an adaptation of the play by Clifford Odets, the sometimes lover of his sometimes lover, Cary Grant. Howard demanded an all-star cast: Barbara Stanwyck, Paul Douglas, and Robert Ryan. Also cast was male heartthrob Keith Andes, playing a minor role in the film as Marilyn's young husband. Regarding Marilyn, Jerry Wald, then RKO assistant production chief, warned, "She's a cross between an antelope and a cobra."

As director, Howard hired the famous Viennese eccentric Fritz Lang, who habitually wore a monocle. As part of the deal Lang agreed to direct a second film as well, *Rancho Notorious* with Marlene Dietrich.

In the middle of shooting *Clash by Night*, Fritz Lang accidentally walked into Barbara Stanwyck's dressing room, catching Robert Taylor's former wife enjoying

683

the sexual charms of Marilyn. As Marilyn later told Lang, "I let Joan Crawford. Why not Barbara Stanwyck?"

Lang enjoyed sharing this tidbit of gossip with another switch-hitter star, Marlene Dietrich. Howard found the news "delectable," as he told Lang.

In an impulsive move, and as a means of gaining publicity for *Clash by Night*, Howard called Meyer, a pimp who was now categorized as one of the film's publicists, into his office. Howard had decided to break the story to the news media that Marilyn was the model who had posed nude for what had already become a famous calendar. Aficionados of "Golden Dreams" had not yet associated the voluptuous nude in the calendar with the rising young star.

Months before, Howard had been impressed with a story that Aline Mosby, at the time a reporter for the United Press Wire Service, had written about Marilyn and her troubled childhood. "Mosby is a bitch," Howard told Meyer, "but she was nice to Marilyn in print."

Meyer was ordered to contact Mosby and relay the information, as an exclusive scoop, that Marilyn had posed for the nude calendar.

When the story broke, it became frontpage news across the country. Harry Brand, head of publicity at Fox, angrily confronted Marilyn. "This could ruin your career before it even gets started," he told her. He also called her "a little fool." He urged her to deny the story. At Howard's urging, she refused, agreeing to "tell the truth" instead.

Howard was right. The public remained loyal to her. As *Clash by Night* opened across the nation, theater owners, hoping to cash in on the publicity, often billed it as "starring Marilyn Monroe" instead of Barbara Stanwyck. Back in Hollywood, Barbara was in a rage, denouncing Marilyn as a "cheap tramp," even though at one time she'd befriended her co-star and had even made love to her.

Zanuck threatened to exercise the morals clause in Marilyn's contract until he saw the receipts piling up for Howard's *Clash by Night*. Instead of firing Marilyn, he went on to cast her in *Gentlemen Prefer Blondes*, borrowing Jane Russell from Howard to play Marilyn's "sidekick."

Marilyn was hailed as "The Naked Venus," receiving additional exposure in the first-ever issue of Hugh Hefner's *Playboy*.

Howard is credited with inventing the expression "celebrity skin." He told Meyer: "Soon well-stacked actresses in Hollywood will routinely be taking off all their clothes before the camera. That day will come, Johnny. Mark my words."

* * *

Los Angeles, 1946

Elizabeth Jean Peters—later shortened to Jean Peters for movie marquees—would have been a forgotten or obscure film figure of the late 40s and early 50s were it not for one fact: she became the second Mrs. Howard Hughes.

Born in Canton, Ohio, on October 15, 1926, Jean grew up with a dream of becoming an English teacher and in later life would try to revive that long-ago schoolgirl hope. Her roommate, Arlen Hurwitz, shelled out four dollars and sent Jean's picture, taken by a campus photographer, to the Miss Ohio State beauty contest.

Although at the time she thought that it was a waste of money, Jean emerged as the contest's winner. Part of the prize was a Hollywood screen test. Jean, only at the urging of Arlen, headed for Hollywood, protesting, "I can't act." Nonetheless, she was picked out of 13,000 competitors by the head of the agency himself to become a John Powers model.

Before she could be signed on, however, an agent for 20th Century Fox spotted her and was attracted by her charm and fresh-faced beauty. After some tests at Fox, she was signed to a six-month contract at $150 a week. By the early 1950s that figure would be raised to $6,000 a week.

One day on the set of Fox, Darryl F. Zanuck, the studio's chief, spotted Jean posing for some Fourth of July publicity pictures. He told his aides that he thought she could be turned into a sex symbol. More tests led to her being cast as the co-star in *Captain from Castile*, opposite Tyrone Power, who still maintained strong emotional links to Howard Hughes.

The first mention of Jean in Louella Parsons's column was not flattering. The gossip maven claimed that she's "not a beauty at all" and that she "was much like an average co-ed in appearance, with greenish-gray eyes." Louella got it wrong.

Virtually no other member of the press agreed with Louella about the twenty-one-year-old beauty contest winner. One columnist wrote of her "flawless and creamy skin," and still others compared her figure to that of a Greek goddess. One reporter claimed that "God designed Jean Peters to wear revealing bathing suits."

Although she didn't think of herself as the "sex symbol" envisioned by her boss Zanuck, she was a stunning natural beauty. Unpretentious and low-key, she often went out onto the streets of Los Angeles without makeup, wearing blue jeans, a cotton blouse she'd made herself, and sandals. Zanuck ordered her to stop doing this, since some tourist was likely to take her picture.

In spite of Louella's unflattering appraisal, young men of Hollywood took notice of the "new girl on the block," some of them hoping to be among the first to seduce her. As rumor had it, Jean was "the only virgin in Hollywood."

The honor of deflowering the Ohio-born beauty eventually went to Audie Murphy, who was the first to call her for a date.

The most decorated GI of World War II, Audie (pronounced *AW-dee*) Leon Murphy, born near Greenville, Texas, in 1924, was the widely publicized recipient of twenty-four medals for valor from the U.S., three from France, and one from Belgium.

During World War II, Audie had fought bravely (some say obsessively) in North Africa and Sicily before invading the beaches of Anzio. Fighting on the

685

outskirts of Rome, he pushed his way into France and across the border into Nazi Germany itself. He was most famous for an episode near Colmar, France, in January of 1945, when Nazi forces attacked his unit. Jumping atop a burning tank destroyer, he used his machine gun to kill about 50 enemy troops. In another exploit, he single-handedly destroyed a German tank and held off a fleet of six others in a gun battle. Before V-E day, he'd killed maybe as many as 250 Nazi soldiers (he wasn't sure).

At the time, Audie was living in a guest cottage on the grounds of the house inhabited by James Cagney. The screen's tough guy had taken such a personal interest in the war hero that Hollywood gossips claimed that the relationship bordered on the homosexual.

Don Graham, Audie's biographer, claimed that Audie would have made Rambo look like a "pumped up, aerobicized celluloid palooka," and that Audie would have had Sylvester Stallone for breakfast. In military uniform, and wearing some of his decorations, Audie had appeared on the cover of *Life* magazine on July 16, 1945. After that, he'd been lured to Hollywood by James Cagney, who felt Audie might break into pictures. "Every little gal in America wanted that doughboy from Texas," Cagney said.

A sinewy and somewhat small man, the young warrior was eagerly sought out by starlets as well as by Hollywood moguls eager to cash in on

Audie Murphy, 1946

his status as a war hero. He'd met Jean while being shown around Fox studios, and he decided he wanted her.

Audie had become close pals of William (Bill) Cagney, brother of James Cagney. Audie told his friend that he'd climaxed in Jean a total of nine times on their first date.

Howard, too, was aware of the charms of Jean Peters. Meyer related to Howard the story that Audie was spreading about Jean.

"Nine times?" Howard looked both puzzled and skeptical. "Do you think that's humanly possible?"

"I've heard of such things," Meyer said, not wanting to offend a boss known for periodic bouts of impotence.

"These days," Howard confided, "I'm having a hard enough time getting it up for one fuck a night."

686

Howard asked Meyer to arrange an invitation to any social gathering where he might meet Jean casually. Such an occasion occurred when Bill Cagney gave a boating party that began at his brother's house in Newport Beach. The guests were to assemble at the Cagneys, then sail by yacht to Catalina. Meyer called Bill, who was only too happy to include an illustrious guest like Howard Hughes, even though he'd brutally rejected his brother for the role of *Scarface* back in the 1930s.

He concealed it, but Howard was contemptuous of (and perhaps threatened by) Audie the first moment he spoke to the boyishly handsome twenty-two-year-old, a Texan like himself. Privately, and with sarcasm, Howard said to Bill, "I'm surprised Murphy isn't wearing his Congressional Medal of Honor. I have honors myself."

In his attempts to get close to Jean Peters, Audie seemed to be guarding her, territorially, as if he anticipated another Nazi attack. Eventually Howard decided that if he wanted to break through to Jean, he first had to win Audie over to his side. He spent more than an hour talking about the hero's wartime exploits. "If you could imagine such a thing, Howard was listening like a lovesick schoolgirl to Audie's heroic exploits," Bill Cagney later claimed. "That conquering hero was one cocky little kid in those days."

After the cruise, despite his basic mistrust and perhaps a sense of competition, Audie reluctantly agreed to let Howard fly Jean and him back to the California mainland from Catalina Island. As pilot, Howard asked Jean to sit with him in the cockpit. Audie was relegated to a rear seat with Johnny Meyer.

Taking advantage of his proximity to Jean, Howard deliberately extended the flight time, taking them on a scenic aerial tour over Southern California and the Palos Verdes peninsula, and asking questions about the progress of her career.

When he suggested the possibility of a personal contract, she said that Zanuck was on the verge of signing her to a seven-year contract at Fox. Howard frowned. "Every day around one o'clock that horny bastard orders a starlet to come to his office so he can fuck her. Fox practically shuts down at that time every day. Watch out that that doesn't happen to you."

She assured him that she could take care of herself.

As a means of luring Jean away from Audie, Howard adopted the persona of a sympathetic, well-intentioned father to the both of them. That's why he invited both Audie and Jean to watch his ill-fated test of the XF-11 that fateful Sunday morning on July 7, 1946.

Unknown to Audie, Jean was one of the first women allowed to visit Howard in the hospital during his recovery from the Beverly Hills crash. "He turned down Linda Darnell and Lana Turner," Meyer said, "but he let Jean in and he hardly knew her." One day, Jean encountered Cary Grant, who was just leaving the hospital room as she was coming in. She was impressed at meeting the handsome, big-time star.

When she'd left that day, Howard summoned Johnny Meyer. "I think I'm in love with the girl," he claimed. "That Jean Peters—she's amazing. She's a combination of my mother and Ella Rice. Looks just like them."

When Dietrich was finally allowed to visit Howard, he told his chief, "I've found the girl of my dreams."

Dietrich said that if that were so, then Howard should marry her and settle down. "It'll be a lot cheaper keeping one woman instead of fifty."

"I won't get married until I'm fifty," Howard said.

"Why fifty? If you're crazy about her, marry her now before Audie Murphy gets her."

"I can't bring myself to marry," Howard said. "I just can't. I have to share myself with others. I'm split into too many different pieces to share all of those parts with just one woman."

Howard literally swept Jean off her feet, according to Meyer, although he was dating Terry Moore and others at the time. "He promised Jean all the money, glitter, and glamour in the world," Meyer later said. "Even big movie stardom. It was too much for a little farm gal from Ohio who still walked around in cotton dresses she'd sewed herself. What could Audie offer her? War medals?"

Until the end of her life, Jean Peters tended to be secretive about her relationship with Howard. Her only known confidante was fellow actress Jeanne Crain. Much of what is known today about the strange Hughes/Peters liaison comes from Fox's "sweet young thing," Jeanne Crain. The actress is remembered for such memorable roles as *A Letter to Three Wives* and *Pinky*, the latter casting her as a light-skinned black girl passing for white.

"Jean dreaded confronting Audie to tell him that she was leaving him," Jeanne Crain recalled. "She'd already experienced his horrible temper. Audie throughout his life was such a hothead. When Jean finally told him it was all over between them, he struck her, knocking her to the floor. He claimed that if she left him, he was going to kill her."

Jean immediately called Howard, who ordered a 24-hour security guard for the starlet. Somehow, and only the war hero knows for sure and he never told, Audie decided that Jean was "all greed and ambition" and that she wasn't to blame for their breakup. He placed all the blame on Howard Hughes.

Bill Cagney didn't learn until later what Audie planned to do. He borrowed $2,500 from his patron, James Cagney, claiming that he wanted to buy himself a good car and promising to pay Cagney back at one-hundred dollars per month.

With that money, Audie planned to bribe the Mormon guards surrounding Howard at the Town House Hotel where he occupied the top-floor suite. Concealing an army rifle he'd brought back from Germany, Audie drove to the Town House.

The story will never be clear, and there are conflicting versions. But Audie, in a surprise move, managed to bribe at least four of the guards, giving each of them a five-hundred dollar bill. He wanted to gain entrance to Howard's suite and "mow him down," like he'd done the Nazis.

The underpaid guards foolishly accepted the money from Audie and let him pass. The only guard who balked was the one who stood right outside Howard's door. The guard immediately pressed a button alerting the security force's head-quarters. He then stalled Audie, pretending to engage him in negotiations, dur-ing the time it took for three of the house detectives to arrive and subdue the ex-soldier.

This loyal guard then alerted Howard about what Audie had attempted to do and asked if he could call the police. Fearing headlines, Howard refused to allow that. He immediately fired his other guards and called for reinforcements. He was very concerned that his security shield had not proven effective against a bribe, and immediately inaugurated a plan that would discourage an equiva-lent incident in the future.

He called Noah Dietrich and woke him up at four o'clock in the morning. Dietrich promised to double the security guards and get rid of all Mormons on the staff.

"No, keep the Mormons!" Howard commanded. "Just throw out the bad apples."

"I know I urged you to marry Jean, but after this incident I'm not so sure," Dietrich said. "Murphy may start stalking her. He might even lay in wait for you on the rooftop of a building, and gun you down as you're coming and going."

"I know a way to stop that," Howard said. Every man has deep secrets. I'm going to find out what Murphy's are. I've heard rumors. If those secrets are deep and dark enough, and if he wants a career in Hollywood, I think I can blackmail him into staying out of my way."

"What if he's just a good, clean-living boy from Texas?" Dietrich asked.

"I already know he isn't," Howard said. "I have my spies out there. Murphy would kill himself if word leaks out that I know what really goes on when he disappears on weekends and isn't chasing after pussy."

"You mean...."

"Let's not talk about it over the phone," Howard cautioned. "J. Edgar Hoover is probably listening right now."

"Audie Murphy? Dietrich sounded puzzled. I'd never thought it of him."

"Would you have thought it of Robert Taylor, Cary Grant, Errol Flynn, and Tyrone Power?" Howard asked.

"In those cases, my answer is yes," Dietrich said.

"Let's drop the subject," Howard said, growing impatient. "But after I tell Jean what Audie tried to do to me, she's all but mine!" He put down the phone.

Later in his tragic life, Audie called himself "the poor man's Howard Hughes." The soldier/movie star's biographer, Don Graham, speculated as to the nature of that comparison—"insomniac, secretive, suspicious, paranoid, a tireless pursuer of women, a man in touch with the dark side of America."

While still living with Cary Grant in his rented villa, Howard also moved in with Jean, sharing a king-sized bed placed in the master bedroom at her house on Veteran Drive in Westwood. He commuted back and forth between his two lovers. Details about the strange goings-on within this living arrangement were later articulated by Jean's maid, Mary Todd.

Mary claimed that Howard always arrived at Jean's back door, hoping to avoid photographers. "He was still limping from his plane crash." She said that he would usually spend the night and stay until after lunch on the afternoon of the following day. Then he'd return to Cary's rented villa.

Mary quickly grew resentful of Howard's bossing her around, even giving her elaborate instructions how she was to clean the telephone. If he wanted a door opened, he'd call for Mary. If she were not available, he'd place Kleenex over the doorknob and open it that way.

She didn't like Howard's "strange ways," but since the money was good she agreed to houseclean at Cary's house four days a week, and then spend the other three days housecleaning for Jean. She confirmed the fact that Howard slept in the same bed with Cary. Cary always appeared either in a bathrobe or fully dressed. But she was startled to learn soon after her debut on the job that Howard usually walked around nude all day. Sometimes when she came into a room where he was sitting in a chair, he covered his genitals with a Kleenex.

To carry on his other affairs, he continued to maintain two bungalows at the Beverly Hills Hotel, plus two separate apartments in the Town House in Los Angeles. He also had a secret apartment at 10000 Sunset Boulevard plus a hideaway in the San Fernando Valley. He could also retreat to a rented villa in Palm Springs and a relatively modest house in Las Vegas.

Some of the scenes from *Captain from Castile*, Jean's first starring picture, released in 1947, were shot outside Mexico City. Howard flew there to join Jean on the set and to have a reunion with Tyrone Power. Meyer went with him.

His pimp claimed that his boss divided his time at El Reforma Hotel between visitations to Tyrone's suite and other nights spent with Jean.

Even at this early stage of their relationship, he brought up the subject of marriage, claiming that he'd leave Jean a vast fortune upon his death. He warned her that if she didn't agree to marry him, he'd give his millions to medical research. She told him, perhaps inaccurately, that she wasn't interested in his money but in himself as a lover and a future husband—"that is, Howard when you become old enough." She was mocking his oft- stated vow that he'd never marry until he was fifty.

He made his intent to marry her much more obvious in Palm Springs in 1949 when he offered her a large sapphire-and-diamond engagement ring. Jeanne Crain later described the ring as "too splendid even for the Queen of England."

Jean agreed to marry Howard, but noted that no date was set for the wedding. In her embarrassment, she tried to explain it: "We're serious about one another, but we want to be sure before we actually get married," she told best pal Crain. "Howard says that when he marries for the second time, it will be forever."

By the early 50s, Jean Peters became a household word in America. She'd be cast as the star of several CinemaScope hits. By 1952 *Viva Zapata!* was playing on movie screens across the nation. Jean had moved into the big-time, co-starring on that film opposite A-list star Marlon Brando.

As supervisor of his private security force, Howard hired Jeff Chouinard, a former private eye and ex-fighter pilot, allocating an annual budget of two million dollars. Among a long list of other duties, Chouinard was assigned the task of spying on Jean 24 hours a day.

Fearing sexual competition from Brando, Chouinard paid some of the extras on the set of *Viva Zapata!* to report on Jean's activities, especially as they regarded her relationship with Brando.

Within his first dossier, the security chief wrote that, "Brando has the sweet mind of a four-year-old and has no interest in chasing women." But despite Chouinard's report, the much neglected Jean was indeed having a torrid but brief affair with Brando, a liaison that ended before the completion of the film.

When Jean was cast in *Niagara* with Joseph Cotten in 1953, Howard was much more intrigued with Jean's co-star, Marilyn Monroe, than with Jean herself. He confided to Johnny Meyer that "my all time sexual fantasy involves crawling into bed with both Jean and Marilyn at the same time."

By 1954, Jean called Jeanne Crain to say that "forever is just too long to wait for Howard." She announced her upcoming marriage to the very handsome Stuart Cramer III, a Lockheed executive and grandson of the legendary industrialist, Stuart Warren Cramer (1868-1940), founder of eleven textile mills. She'd met Cramer in Rome while filming *Three Coins in the Fountain.*

Catching Howard by surprise, Louella Parsons called him for his reaction to her bombshell about

Newlyweds: Jean Peters and Stuart Cramer

691

Jean's upcoming marriage.

Howard's chief aide at the time, the Mormon, Bill Gay, claimed that his boss's reaction to the news was subdued. That evening he drove over to the Tudor-style home of Kathryn Grayson, MGM's singing sensation. There he formally proposed to her in her rose garden, and she accepted. Their marriage was to take place on the Memorial Day weekend in Las Vegas. "This was Howard's way of getting back at Jean," Gay claimed.

Howard had been secretly dating Kathryn Grayson for some months before his proposal of marriage. Apparently, he planned to go through with this wedding. Unexpectedly, it was Grayson who balked at the last minute. Howard was already at Culver City preparing a private plane to fly the singing star to Las Vegas for the wedding.

Frantically, she called him, claiming that she couldn't marry him because she'd had a premonition that morning that something tragic was about to unfold. She feared it might concern her daughter. A spiritualist, she firmly believed in premonitions.

He tried to dismiss her concerns, claiming that it was "just the jitters before a wedding." But she held firm to her position, saying that there was no way she was going to marry him. He was forced to give up after a long argument. Later that day, she learned that her nephew, Timmy, while playing in her brother's pool, had drowned.

She would never marry Howard.

Jean, however, on May 29, 1954, in Washington, D.C., followed through on her plans to marry Cramer. Jean walked to the altar on the same golden carpet where Queen Elizabeth II's feet had trod on her Coronation Day.

From the beginning of their marriage, Howard ordered spies to report on the

Howard Hughes, 1952. Last Known Picture.

activities of the newlyweds. After their wedding, Cramer and his new bride settled in Washington, where they quickly became part of that city's social scene.

Demanding the hottest private eye in the business, Howard was led to FBI veteran Robert A. Maheu, who supervised Jean's physical surveillance in the wake of Howard's instructions to dig up all the dirt. Howard particularly wanted to know if Cramer had been a CIA operative. In time, Maheu would take over the role of Noah Dietrich in Howard's life.

Within ten days, Maheu submitted a detailed dossier on Cramer, including his links to the CIA as a Lockheed executive.

Maheu had even spied on Cramer as he stripped down to seduce Jean on the living room floor of their townhouse in Washington.

Back in Los Angeles, Howard found that story especially compelling. He wanted to know everything about Cramer's love-making, including his sexual dimensions. He also wanted to know if Jean appeared to have experienced an orgasm during their sex act. Maheu reported that it "seemed that she did."

So impressed was Howard with the dossier that he formed a fifteen-year business relationship with Maheu, thereby filling the void that would appear after he fired Noah Dietrich. The Maheu/Hughes liaison would eventually end in bitterness and lawsuits, however.

Unknown to Cramer, Howard was in constant touch with Jean. It is not known what exactly happened, but suddenly Jean turned up in Miami, discreetly filing for a divorce from Cramer, although there would be delays and complications. Howard was also reported to be in Miami at the time, assisting Jean in her divorce. Simultaneously, but unknown to Jean, Howard was paying for a suite for Ava Gardner in another part of town, still obsessed with the idea of seducing her. The more Ava fended him off, the more he desired her.

Howard summoned Cramer to Beverly Hills, arranging for his transport to California from Washington in a private plane. Picked up by Johnny Meyer at the Los Angeles airport, Cramer was delivered immediately to Howard's offices at 7000 Romaine Street. "At first I thought I was being kidnapped. There were two Mormon guards in the back seat," Cramer later said.

Brought face to face with Howard, Cramer quoted him as saying, "I'm in love with your wife and have been for so many, many years. And she is completely in love with me. Now, if she'll confirm this, will you give her an uncontested divorce?"

Cramer protested, claiming that he was devoted to his wife. He begged Howard not to interfere in their marriage.

The scenario grows thin here. Apparently, Jean received a "marital promissory note," from Howard. With that paper in hand, she agreed to divorce her husband and marry Howard.

There was a final ironic twist in the life of Stuart Cramer. Having allowed Jean Peters to divorce him, he went on in 1959 to marry Howard's longtime mistress: Terry Moore.

Reconciled with Howard in Los Angeles, and now more or less engaged to marry him, Jean was moved into a bungalow near his at the Beverly Hills Hotel. In her divorce petition against Cramer, she charged him with mental cruelty, claiming that their marriage was short lived, although admittedly consummated. Howard at first had wanted her to testify that there had never been any sexual intercourse between Jean and her husband, but she refused.

In the weeks leading up to his marriage to Jean, Howard continued to have affairs with Susan Hayward, Kathryn Grayson (even though she'd refused to marry him), Terry Moore, Debra Paget, Mitzi Gaynor, and starlet Yvonne Shubert, among others.

* * *

Los Angeles, 1956

Regardless of whether Dietrich was plotting against him, Howard thought that he was—and that was what mattered. By 1956 their business relationship had deteriorated to such a point that Howard was hardly talking to his chief officer.

On May 12, 1957, when Dietrich pressed for long overdue stock options in a telephone exchange from room to room at the Beverly Hills Hotel, Howard balked. He was already paying Dietrich half-a-million dollars a year, and apparently he felt that that was enough. "You're holding a gun to my head, Noah," he said.

Dietrich held his ground, demanding the stock options. Both men hung up the phone at the same time. Within minutes, Howard called Bill Gay to go at once to 7000 Romaine Street and padlock the doors to Dietrich. A thirty-two year relationship had abruptly ended.

The Mormon, Bill Gay, had become an increasingly important figure in Howard's life. Originally, he'd plan to teach at a university until hired by Howard as his Administrative Equipment Assistant. Rather good looking and somewhat lanky like Gary Cooper, or even Howard himself, Gay was instructed to hire only Mormons as Howard's assistants. The new recruits servicing Howard were forbidden to smoke or drink. Privately Howard told Gay that he preferred the men on his staff to dislike "kikes and niggers."

Designated for many years as a trusted keeper of the secrets, Dietrich in later years spoke bitterly about Howard and recalled the night he was fired. "I never saw Howard Hughes again. I was free to live my life—no more calls at three o'clock in the morning. I should define that better. I was prepared to live my life—what was left of it after he'd sucked it dry."

Dietrich later speculated about the real reason Howard married Jean Peters. "She may have loved him, but he was in love with Howard Hughes, not Jean Peters. It wasn't true, but Howard began suspecting that I was in cohoots with the boys in Houston. He felt that we were plotting to have him declared mentally incompetent, sent away to an asylum, while we took over his empire and divided the loot among ourselves. Howard knew that if he had a legitimate wife, she would have to commit him. He'd secured Jean's promise that she would never do that to him, and he believed her. Allegedly she'd told Howard, 'I will never be a party to any betrayal of you.' Love or not, I always felt it was a marriage of convenience on Howard's part."

Dietrich might have been lying about his role in a potential palace coup. There was indeed a plot afoot to have Howard declared mentally incompetent. Prompted by Toolco, lawyers in Houston were already working on such a possibility, and Dietrich had been informed of what was happening. Perhaps he lent his cooperation. He was accused of at least discussing the possibility with attorney Raymond Cook. He also conferred with Howard's doctor, Verne Mason, on his boss's mental condition.

Dietrich once tried to explain Howard's fascination for Jean. "She was the first one who wasn't interested in him for his status, his money, and his fame." He was perhaps overlooking Ava Gardner in this assessment.

Dietrich continued, "She [meaning Jean] saw him as an average man, an average man she fell in love with. It was as if all that other stuff never existed. But I also feel that his confrontation with death after the XF-11 made him take stock of his life. And when he did, he was amazed by its emptiness."

* * *

Tonopah, Nevada/Beverly Hills, 1957

At the dawn of the 20th century, Tonopah, Nevada, a dusty and makeshift desert outpost strung along the road between Las Vegas and Reno, was known as the Silver Queen of the West. During its heyday, its mines produced $200 million of silver.

Decades before Howard Hughes, Jr. arrived there in January of 1957 with his bride-to-be, Tonopah had attracted young schemers like Howard Hughes Sr. Long before his drill bit made him a fortune, he had hoped to strike it rich in the silver mines here. That dream never happened.

Where his father had failed, Howard Jr. hoped to succeed. He'd heard rumors that although most of the mines had already been shut down, there were still mother lodes of silver waiting to be discovered. Perhaps haunted by an ongoing competitiveness with his long-dead father, he wanted to tap into these unexcavated riches to become the "Silver King of America."

It's ironic that Howard, who could have afforded a wedding in any of the most ostentatious and glamorous spots in the world, chose such a forbidding landscape, and such unromantic circumstances, for his second marriage. And it's perhaps a sign of his basic alienation that during the days preceding his wedding, when a more conventional man might have been at least trying to relate to his young bride-to-be, he super-charged his schedule with business meetings associated with his growing investments there. As it turned out, the circumstances and logistics associated with the Hughes-Peters union turned out to be almost surreal.

In January of 1957, from Los Angeles, after a sweaty transfer in Las Vegas, Howard flew Jean to an abandoned U.S. Army air base outside Tonopah. In this remote outpost, he was met by James Arditto, an attorney from Los Angeles who had been his advance man, arranging the wedding. In this barren desert, Howard hoped to escape the media frenzy that his marriage would set off. Through a landscape believed to have been radioactively polluted by nuclear testing in the area, Arditto drove the about-to-be-married couple to the dilapidated Mizpah Hotel.

There they were introduced to the Nye County judge, William (Bill) Beko, who married them in a brief civil ceremony on January 12, 1957, thereby ending three decades of bachelorhood for Howard.

In those days, Nevada law allowed couples to wed under assumed names. Jean opted for the pseudonym of Marian Evans, Howard selecting the name G.A. Johnson. He was 51 years old, but listed his age at 46. A voluptuous 30, she claimed to be 29.

The newlyweds remained in Tonopah for only three hours before flying back to Las Vegas, where they boarded a larger plane for the flight back to Los Angeles. Before leaving Tonopah, in a way that seemed to redefine the trip as one primarily concerned with business, Howard ordered Arditto to acquire 750 more deeds to abandoned silver mines. At the time, he already owned 100 such deeds. Before his pursuit of mother lodes of silver ended, he would shell out twelve million dollars, which he would never recoup. In all, he would purchase as much as 14,500 acres of land in Nye County, some of the barren tracts spilling over into other counties.

The townspeople of Tonopah were thrilled to have Howard buying up deserted mines. A barmaid, Patricia Naylor, summed up the local feeling. "With a man like Hughes behind us, we could be put on the map again." But like the dream of a successful marriage to Jean Peters, it was not to be realized.

Flying back to Los Angeles, Howard slept with his bride a total of five nights before insisting that he needed privacy. At the Beverly Hills Hotel, he remained in his "bachelor quarters" at bungalow 4, ordering that she be evicted into a separate bungalow, #19.

The world didn't learn of the Hughes/Peters marriage until March 15, 1957 when columnist Florabel Muir announced that Jean and Howard had been wed on March 12, 1957. That false date still appears in biographies and other articles about the life of Howard Hughes, and is directly attributed to the misinformation once printed in the *Los Angeles Herald & Express*.

Exiled within just a few days of her marriage to a lonely bungalow for one,

Jean called her best friend Jeanne Crain to report, "I've been banished from his bed. Welcome to marriage to Howard Hughes."

Days and nights that were much worse were yet to come.

CHAPTER EIGHTEEN
Washington, 1947

The year had begun badly.

Francis D. Flanagan, the chief investigator for a U.S. Senate probe and a former administrative assistant to FBI chief J. Edgar Hoover, accompanied with six highly aggressive auditors, had arrived at 7000 Romaine Street in Hollywood to seize the accounting records of Hughes Aviation. The investigators were reviewing the company's up-to-now secret books, on a mission to prove that Howard had squandered millions of taxpayers' dollars in his ill-fated development of reconnaissance planes and the Spruce Goose during World War II. The erroneous accusation was that Howard had transferred a huge slush fund of government money into his personal bank accounts.

It wasn't true: Howard had actually invested twelve million dollars of his own money into financing the prototypes for both the Hercules and the XF-11 reconnaissance plane. In addition, he had collected only $40 million of the $90 million that had originally been proposed during wartime for his aircraft development. Regrettably, and much to his and everyone else's chagrin, none of his widely publicized prototype planes had been successfully tested. As a result, the investigating committee sent to his offices in California was instructed to find "financial irregularities."

Even before the arrival of the government auditors in Los Angeles, Howard had been tipped off by Elliott Roosevelt that the probe was underway. (One can only wonder about the records that Howard might have ordered destroyed in the immediate wake of Elliott's warning.) Elliott, who had been deeply

Senator Ferguson (seated, left, gesticulating with his hands); Senator Brewster (standing in background, with open jacket), and Howard Hughes (standing, right).

involved in influence-peddling during his father's wartime regime in the White House, had been specifically targeted for investigation by members of the now-hostile Republican-dominated Senate. With an eye toward winning the upcoming 1948 elections, the Republican party was aggressively working to discredit the Democratic regime of the late Franklin D. Roosevelt, who had died in April of 1945, about 18 months previously. Many of the Republicans's accusations were based on the involvement of Elliott in the controversial assignment to Howard of several multi-million dollar defense contracts for airplanes that literally never got off the ground.

Flying Lumberyard: Spruce Goose under construction.

To complicate matters, the committee looking into Howard's government contracts was headed by the arch conservative senator from Maine, Ralph Owen Brewster, and the equally conservative senator from Michigan, Homer Ferguson. Howard's own spies had already learned that Brewster was "in the pocket" of Juan Trippe, president of Pan American Airways, TWA's major rival.

Juan Trippe had been born on June 27, 1899 in Sea Bright, New Jersey, and entered Yale University in 1917. Although he never saw combat, he became a Navy pilot after America entered World War I. Graduating from Yale, he worked briefly on Wall Street as a bond salesman, soonafter realizing that it was aviation that genuinely interested him. By 1927, he had launched Pan American, almost single handedly building it into a world class airline. As the pioneer and advocate of an inaugural class of efficient and large-scale "flying boats," the Pan Am Flying Clippers, he opened up dozens of global routes across both the Pacific and the Atlantic. Believing that "the average man," and not just the wealthy, should be allowed to fly at affordable prices, he virtually invented the concept of the airline industry's "tourist class."

Independent of his friendship with Trippe, Brewster had his own, highly subjective and ambitious, political agenda. He wanted to be the Republican nominee for vice president in 1948. He already functioned as the powerful chairman of the Special Committee to Investigate the National Defense Program. That office already held many important precedents: During the FDR regime, when Harry Truman had held that job, he had been propelled to national prominence, opening doors that eventually led to Truman's designation as Vice President and, after the untimely death of FDR in April of 1945, to his role as President of the United States. Brewster felt he too could use the post as a stepping stone to greater political power, especially if he could bag "big game" like Howard Hughes.

Hoping to block the Senate probe, Howard had traveled to Washington for a private meeting with Brewster in February of 1947. Meeting in the senator's suite at the Mayflower Hotel, Howard came face to face with his archenemy. Writer Charles Barton once described Brewster as "not a handsome man. The forepart of his head was billiard-bald. His meaty upper lip protruded slightly as though stuffed with chewing tobacco."

Brewster didn't like wasting time in small talk. Over lunch, he got quickly to the point. His words were blunt. He told Howard that there would be no Senate investigation if he would relinquish the coveted transatlantic air routes that the Civil Aeronautics Board had granted to TWA in the spring of 1945. TWA had begun flying between the US and Europe in 1946.

The senator went one step further, informing Howard that it would be in his best interest if TWA actually merged with Pan Am. "It'll be a sweeter deal for all of us," the senator said. "Cash money in all our bank accounts, including yours." Brewster went on to say that if Howard would cooperate with Congress's designation of Pan Am as the exclusive and official national airline of the United States, "You'll be out of the stew pot."

Drew Pearson was the most famous political columnist of his day. His muckraking column, *Washington Merry-Go-Around*, which appeared in newspapers that included *The Washington Post* and *The Miami Herald*, was read each morning by the President of the United States and millions of others. The columnist detested both Senator Brewster and Juan Trippe of Pan Am. In one column, siding with Howard, Pearson called Brewster "the kept boy of Pan Am."

Before his lunch with Howard at the Mayflower, Brewster had introduced the Community Airline Bill, which would, if passed through Congress, grant Pan Am exclusive dominance of the air routes between North America and Europe, cutting out TWA. A roughly equivalent bill, introduced earlier, had already failed in the Senate. Prior to their luncheon, Howard had already publicly denounced Brewster's latest bill "as the same baby in a different set of diapers."

Adding to Howard's contempt and fury was a fact unearthed by his spies: Attorneys for Pan Am had crafted the actual wording and phraseology of the Senate bill as sponsored by Brewster.

Although he'd remained calm throughout the luncheon, neither accepting nor rejecting Brewster's deal, Howard called Noah Dietrich when he'd returned to his hotel. "His fury was equivalent to the dropping of the atomic bomb on Hiroshima," Dietrich later said.

Howard ordered Dietrich to launch, through Johnny Meyer, investigations of both Juan Trippe and Senator Brewster. "Money is no object," he assured Dietrich. "These shitasses are trying to destroy me." Charles Lindbergh had been replaced in the ranks of Howard's leading rivals: Clearly, Juan Trippe was now the enemy seeking to destroy Howard.

Meyer was sent to South America to investigate Brewster's "freeloading" and his acceptance of frequent and lush Pan Am "hospitality" offered by Trippe.

By July of 1947 a particularly muggy summer had descended over the Potomac. The Senate probe of Howard was scheduled to open later that month. In front of Dietrich, Howard had threatened to "take on the entire fucking government if I have to." But first Howard had to be served with a subpoena, and no server could find him.

The "super snooper," George Rossinni, a Federal marshal, had been sent to Los Angeles to serve Howard with a warrant. Facing the press at the Los Angeles airport, Rossinni assured journalists that he'd track Howard down—and soon. "After all," he boasted, "I'm the man who brought in Al Capone."

Unknown to the Senate-appointed investigators hot on his trail, Howard was hiding out at Cary Grant's private villa. When not with Cary, he was housed by Jean Peters in a small apartment in the western section of Los Angeles. When not with Peters, he was slipping around in his battered car on rendezvous with Cyd Charisse, the lovely dancing star at MGM. Although Howard proposed marriage to her, almost simultaneously with his proposals of marriage to Jean Peters, Cyd ultimately gave her heart to singer Tony Martin.

One afternoon as Rossinni and his men were enjoying lunch at Hughes Aviation, Howard, Cary Grant, and co-pilot Earl Martyn slipped onto the tarmac at Culver City and boarded Howard's converted B-23 bomber. The plane was airborne before Rossinni and his men discovered what was happening. The process server ran out of the main building at Hughes Aviation and onto the tarmac, shaking his fist at the departing Howard in the sky.

Only the night before, he'd made the decision that he could not evade the Federal marshals indefinitely. But he didn't want to face the humiliation of being served papers by Rossinni. He thought it would look better if he arrived in Washington in his own plane. He planned to immediately announce that he'd willingly flown in and had freely volunteered to appear before the Senate committee as if he had nothing to hide.

Weeks before his arrival at the hearings, he and Senator Brewster had been waging their battle in the press. Threatening Howard, and in reference to the fact that none of his Senate emissaries had yet been able to serve him with a subpoena, the senator told the press that, "I'll personally drag this millionaire playboy by the ear across the entire continental United States if

Cyd Charisse

702

that's the only way I'll get him to Washington." Smiling with an ominous leer, he said, "I want to see the whites of his lies."

Even though Howard had managed to evade U.S. marshals for more than a month, he, too, privately contacted the press. "I'm a loyal American," he protested. "I'm getting screwed by special interest groups on the payroll of Pan Am." He also

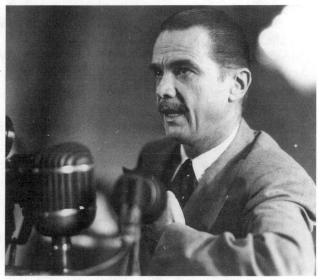
Howard Hughes at the Senate Testimony

claimed that Juan Trippe, "working through crooked senators," was trying to destroy TWA as a means of giving Pan Am "ownership of the skies and no one owns the skies but God himself."

Ironically, Howard was one of the richest men in the world at the time, with Toolco profits "reaching celestial figures," in the words of Dietrich. Even so, Howard managed to portray himself as "a little dog" (TWA), fighting "a big dog" (Pan Am).

Howard's old friend, William Randolph Hearst, had opened the columns of his newspapers for Howard's counterattack against Senator Brewster and Juan Trippe.

Other representatives of the press were not always favorable, however. Another popular columnist of his day, Westbrook Pegler, claimed that Howard had given parties for Elliott Roosevelt in which "semi-nude lovelies swam in a mirrored pool at the Hughes mansion."

In anticipation of their grilling of Howard in front of their committee in Washington, the FBI and investigators commissioned by the Senate had prepared a 2,000-page dossier. But despite its ongoing probes, the dossier contained many false accusations. One report claimed that Elliott had accepted a $75,000 bribe from Howard to win his approval of government contracts. Privately, Brewster read a long and detailed report of Howard's love life, much of which was wrong, superficial, or misguided.

Agents, for example, did not uncover any of Howard's homosexual activities and also mistakenly assumed that he was having a hot, torrid romance with Ava Gardner, the kind of affair she'd ultimately have with another famous man: Frank Sinatra.

They did uncover some incriminating evidence, as documented in their report #62-3541. Howard had hired Hollywood starlets to entertain and/or seduce military brass, who were at the time responsible for eventually awarding government contracts to Hughes Aviation.

Just prior to his appearance in front of the committee, Howard arranged bookings for himself and for Cary Grant within different suites at Washington, D.C.'s Carlton Hotel. When they arrived, and throughout the course of the hearings, they slipped in and out through the hotel's back entrance. Noah Dietrich was housed at the Mayfair Hotel across from the Carlton.

Howard suspected, and rightly so, that his suite had been bugged. Both of the suites on either side of his housed FBI agents listening in on his private conversations. "They could hear every time I went to take a piss," he told Dietrich. The surveillance of Howard was carried out by Lt. Joseph W.W. Shimon, who was hailed as the FBI's greatest eavesdropper.

By this time in his life, Howard was something of a master "bugger" himself. He ordered men from the Schindler Detective Agency to bug Senator Brewster's room at the Mayflower Hotel.

Members of the 80th Congress smelled blood when they called Howard to appear before them. The Republicans, who had been exiled, figuratively speaking, to Siberia during the four terms of the Roosevelt presidency, were eager for power again. Members of the Republican-dominated Senate probe planned to use Howard to discredit the Roosevelts, especially Elliott.

Just before the hearings, Cary commissioned some of the best stylists and tailors in Hollywood for Howard's complete cosmetic makeover. The immaculately groomed actor ordered that two hair stylists give Howard "the latest CEO look" in hair cuts. Two tailors were summoned to outfit Howard with double-breasted dove gray suits with black and blue pinstripes.

In Washington, Howard was coached by Jack Anderson, at the time a "leg man" for the columnist Drew Pearson. With Cary Grant sitting in on the "rehearsals," Howard was repeatedly tossed the kinds of hostile questions likely to be asked by his interrogators. Cary rehearsed him in body posture and what the world media would one day call "sound bites."

But before facing the senators, Howard had to sit glued to his radio, listening to Johnny Meyer's Senate testimony being broadcast across the nation: "He's the greatest pimp in Hollywood, but I don't know if he can hold up under the heat," he told Dietrich.

Nervous, but concealing it from Howard, Dietrich had spent many weeks personally coaching Meyer. The practice sessions had not gone well—despite Dietrich's prolonged coaching, Meyer did not make a convincing witness.

"Do you think Johnny's going to come through this?" Howard asked. "Or will he fuck this up royally?"

"We'll have to wait and see," Dietrich told his boss. "Johnny operates behind the scenes. He's not used to having his fat ass hauled out before movie

704

cameras."

***

Facing what Dietrich called "head-hunters after Howard," Johnny Meyer made his appearance on the world stage. Up to then, most of his life had been spent in the back alleys and parking lots of Hollywood. Although he was inordinately skilled at arranging liaisons in the boudoirs of Hollywood, he'd prove disastrous within a Senate caucus room. Pale, pallid, and fidgety, the pudgy pimp made an unprepossessing witness amid the glare of klieg lights and microphones.

During his interrogation, Senators Ferguson and Brewster took delight in going over a ledger where Meyer had written off about $170,000 in expenses charged to Hughes Aviation. A number of often incongruous items were grouped under the general heading of "entertainment." Probers were especially intrigued as to why the name of Colonel Elliott Roosevelt appeared so frequently, along with that of the then-starlet, Faye Emerson, whom the president's son later married.

Meyer had to face questions as to why $132 worth of hard-to-get nylon stockings were written off as an expense, though presented as a gift to Emerson. He was also quizzed about twenty dollars provided to her and also written off. He claimed that the twenty dollars was for her "to travel home."

The questions were probing, his answers vague and unconvincing.

Brewster: Can you tell me why you were charging up to Hughes Aircraft Company $132 for nylon hose for Miss Emerson and $20 to go home?
Meyer: Because she had been very charming.
Brewster: Very charming?
Meyer: Girls are very pleasant.
Brewster: What has that to do with aircraft production?
Meyer: They just went along. Every company in the business did it. We were no different.

The hearings were going badly for Howard. Millions of Americans were getting the impression that Hughes Aviation was just a sleazy Hollywood operation which used call girls and in some cases, movie stars, to seduce contracts out of military officers.

Meyer was questioned about $220 worth of champagne spent on the wedding party when Elliott married Faye Emerson. Foolishly, Meyer had charged expenses to Hughes Aviation that raised eyebrows, including car rentals and tips to policemen for security for three of FDR's daughters-in-law who attended the president's funeral on April 13, 1945.

Under threat of perjury, Meyer continued to deliver incriminating testimony against Howard.

Eventually, Elliott himself was called before the committee. To save himself, he attacked Meyer. In a loud and angry voice, Elliott claimed, "I deny with all my heart and soul that Johnny Meyer ever got me a girl!"

Not only that, he claimed that Meyer's expense accounts were "very largely inaccurate," citing examples that he was out of the country when many expenses written off for his entertainment were levied by Meyer.

At the end of Meyer's appearance, Senator Ferguson denounced him as "diabolical, an influence peddler the likes of which the world has never seen." Even Howard's enemies had to admit that that was gross exaggeration. The world had witnessed far greater influence peddlers than Howard's private pimp.

At one point Senator Brewster proposed calling to the witness stand some of the greatest beauties of Hollywood in the 40s, secretly telling members of the press "to get your pads ready and get film in your cameras." He claimed he was considering summoning "at least fifty Hollywood stars." Among those listed as potential witnesses were Rita Hayworth, Faith Domergue, Jane Russell, Lana Turner, Ava Gardner, Jane Greer, Jean Peters, Susan Hayward, Katharine Hepburn, Ginger Rogers, Fay Wray, and Bette Davis. Brewster said that he also planned to call Errol Flynn and Cary Grant.

Then, in one of the great mysteries surrounding this Senate probe, both Ferguson and Brewster received phone calls.

It was from some power figure in the Republican Party, warning them not to pursue the above-mentioned plan.

Speculation continues to this day about who that figure was. To his dying day, Noah Dietrich claimed that it was New York State Governor and Presidential hopeful Thomas Dewey, who at the time was planning a second attempt to win back the White House from the Democrats. He'd run unsuccessfully on the Republican ticket against Franklin Roosevelt in 1944 And as events turned out, he'd eventually be nominated to run against Democratic candidate President Truman, again unsuccessfully, in 1948.

When Dietrich told Howard that he thought it was Dewey who called off "the witch hunt," presumably as a means of avoiding a major public circus and scandal, Howard had an unusual reaction.

"Guess I'll owe one to this guy who resembles the figure of the groom placed on top of a wedding cake."

In his later years, Dietrich speculated that Howard had blackmail evidence on the three-time governor of New York (1943-55). Speculation in some quarters today claims that insofar as the Howard Hughes investigation went, Dewey switched "from racketbuster to racketbacker."

Gangster Lucky Luciano maintained in *The Last Testament of Lucky Luciano* that Dewey was "a man on the take," demanding "big bucks as campaign contributions."

Dietrich always suspected that Howard through his gangster connections, including both Luciano and Bugsy Siegel, somehow got to Dewey and demanded that, in reference to Ferguson and Brewster, "cut off their balls."

At this point it's unlikely if the truth will ever be known.

***

July 28, 1947 dawned hotter than most summer days in the Old Senate Office Building,　selected as the venue of the hearings. In the future, this caucus room would also be the site of the McCarthy-Army hearings in 1954 and the Senate Watergate investigation in 1973 that would lead to the downfall of then-President Richard Nixon.

Howard kept the senators waiting nearly an hour before making his appearance at 2:42pm. Already an American legend, his striking appearance before an estimated 1,500 spectators was greeted with loud applause. Writing in *Look* magazine, reporter Stephen White said that Howard was treated "like a dreamboat film star."

The Republican senator, Homer Ferguson, of Michigan, pounded the gavel to restore order in the senatorial hearing room. In his confrontation of powerful government interests, Howard struck many as evocative of the hero of *Mr. Smith Goes to Washington*, that Frank Capra movie from 1939 that had starred James Stewart as a lone voice standing up to powerful senators.

"I think everyone in America had turned on their radio, even President Truman, to hear Howard face the nation," Dietrich said. He accompanied Howard to the hearings, along with one of Howard's personal lawyers, Thomas A. Slack.

After being sworn in, Howard took the defensive, denouncing the committee as "illegitimate." Even so, he was forced to sit through questions that suggested that he'd "squandered" millions of dollars of government money through his gross mismanagement of Hughes Aviation.

Spruce Goose Ready for Assembly

As the hearings progressed, Howard turned the tables on his inquisitors. He traded insults with Senator Brewster, charging him with accepting bribes from Pan Am. Despite the pounding of the gavel by Senator Ferguson, Howard was putting Brewster on trial. One Washington reporter wrote that the hearings had "turned into a lie-passing contest."

On the second day of the hearings, Howard called Brewster "one of the greatest trick-shot artists in Washington." He later said, "I have been called capricious, a playboy, an eccentric, but I don't believe I have the reputation of a liar."

Carefully observing the hearing, perhaps soaking up precedents for anti-Communist Senate investigations that he would spearhead less than five years later, was a little-known and newly elected senator from Wisconsin, Republican Joseph R. McCarthy.

Shortly after the debut of the hearings, the custodian of Howard's wardrobe, Cary Grant, had to fly to New York. Without his taste-setting friend, Howard appeared in court on the third day less well dressed than he had been on the previous days. A reporter for *Fortune* magazine described his appearance as "an enormously rich Huckleberry Finn, tie-less and hatless, in a soiled shirt and rumpled sports jacket borrowed from his butler-valet, with his long, thin wrists protruding from sleeves that were inches too short."

Howard vigorously defended the Hercules (Spruce Goose), admitting that his only mistake had been in supervising "each portion of it in too much detail." He also maintained that the Hercules project had "broken me down physically—I do not know how anybody could have worked harder than I did." He did not mention his mysterious and months-long disappearance and abandonment of the project midway through its development.

Before millions of Americans out there in radio land, Howard made an astonishing vow. He claimed that if the Hercules didn't fly, "I will probably leave this country and never come back."

At the conclusion of the hearing that day, Howard faced a barrage of reporters. He predicted, "The Hercules will fly by the end of the year, and the XF-11 reconnaissance plane is the finest ever built."

In defiance of the Senate committee, and in an amazing show of strength, Howard refused to bring Meyer back for more questions. After Meyer's damaging testimony, Howard had shipped his pimp off to Europe, although he maintained before the Senate committee that he didn't know where his assistant was. When Ferguson demanded that Howard produce Meyer by two o'clock that afternoon, Howard arrogantly countered, and at the risk of going to jail, "No, I don't think I will." The spectators were stunned.

Under pressure from other Republicans, Ferguson was forced to recess the hearings. Howard was clearly winning the day. The probe so far had been a fiasco for the Republicans.

Howard immediately flew back to Culver City, announcing that he'd been vindicated, his reputation emerging intact after the "vicious smear campaign."

Pan Am, under the leadership of Juan Trippe, had been painted as an evil and corrupted manipulator. In the months ahead, TWA planes would continue to fly to Europe, offering Americans a choice of two different competitors for passage across the Atlantic.

Senate hearings would resume on November 5. By that time, Howard had successfully flown the Spruce Goose. The committee had failed to "destroy Howard Hughes," as he put it. The final session that autumn was anticlimactic.

After the first Senate hearing on August 6, 1947, Hughes for President Clubs had had been established across the nation, beginning with a Brooklyn branch that eventually attracted five hundred members. After the second hearing in November, the number of such clubs increased, many backers wanting him as the Democratic nominee during the upcoming Presidential elections of 1948.

Senator Ferguson closed the second batch of hearings on November 22, 1947. In its aftermath, the Republican members of the probe issued a highly critical report of both Howard and Hughes Aviation. But their charges fell on deaf ears to a nation who viewed Howard as a genuine aviation hero in the tradition of Charles Lindbergh.

Spruce Goose in Drydock at Long Beach

Despite speculation in some quarters that a mortal blow had been struck to both his reputation and to Hughes Aviation, Howard clearly emerged from the hearings as the triumphant winner. Hughes Aviation survived as well, going on to become the major supplier of electronic products to the U.S. Air Force as the Cold War deepened.

Howard had to wait patiently for five years before inflicting his revenge upon Senator Brewster. In 1952, when Brewster ran again for the Senate as the Republican nominee from Maine, Howard put up "whatever money it takes" to back Brewster's rival, Frederick Payne, a local newspaper publisher. Since Maine had such a small population at the time, it took only $60,000 to defeat Brewster. Radio commercials and billboards throughout the state, many of them funded by Howard, relentlessly promoted Payne.

As time went by, Brewster lamented the "poisoned arrows shot at me," blaming Howard for all his setbacks in the years following the Senate hearings. The ambitious politician who had dreamed of higher office went down in flames on Election Day.

As Howard later told Dietrich, "Brewster, with all his power, had made himself out to be a giant. He turned out to be a pygmy."

***

Long Beach, California, 1947

In June of 1946, Howard had determined that his flying boat was ready to be moved from its cradle in Culver City to Terminal Island in Long Beach Harbor. It was a massive undertaking. Instead of barging it by sea, Howard ordered an overland trucking. The Star House Movers of Long Beach took on the project for $80,000.

It was a daunting challenge, as 2,300 overhead electrical and telephone wires would have to be cut. These wires belonged to twenty-one separate utility companies of Southern California. Each would have to be negotiated with and paid off.

Schools were let out that day so children could view "history in the making." Some 100,000 spectators lined the route as the Hercules made its 28-mile journey. Prior to the move, the plane had to be disassembled. Riding motorcycles, dozens of police officers from ten different municipalities helped escort the fuselage along city streets, as rubberneckers looked at the mammoth craft— the largest ever made—with awe. A workforce of one hundred and fifty tree trimmers had already helped cleared the route of potentially problematical trees and tree limbs.

Terminal Island, immediately adjacent to the vast but sheltered expanses of Long Beach Harbor, had been selected as the launching pad for the Hercules. At Terminal Island, crews worked night and day reassembling the "giant bird" into which Howard had, in his own words, "put the sweat of my life."

Stung by the accusations that had been thrown at him during the first Senate probe, Howard was determined to prove that the Hercules could fly.

He paid around-the-clock engineering crews to get the Hercules ready for its test run. High winds and rough seas hit the coast of Long Beach on Saturday morning, November 1, 1947, the day Howard had publicly scheduled for the plane's "taxi tests," giving no indication that the notorious Spruce Goose would actually become airborne. In fact, Howard had pointedly told the press that "no flight test will be attempted until April" (of 1948.) Ominously, strong winds had already begun whipping up whitecaps in Long Beach's harbor.

Despite Howard's statement about this being merely a "taxi run," reporters had flocked to Long Beach, many of them flown in at Howard's expense, and many of them stationed aboard a luxurious private yacht, *Vanities,* which

710

Hughes Aviation had rented from showman Earl Carroll. With a looming Senate investigation scheduled to reopen in fewer than five months, the press suspected that Howard might be planning some public displays of the Hercules's airworthiness. As the world looked on, ready and waiting for a show, Howard carefully assessed the weather and his chances of a test run, finally deciding that preparations for the launch would continue.

Cary Grant had driven down from Hollywood to witness the event from the decks of a separate private yacht that tossed its passengers and crew from side to side on the choppy waters. Beside him, at Howard's request, was Jean Peters.

In nervous anticipation of an improvement in the weather, Howard ordered the activation of the initial steps for freeing the Hercules from its drydock. Inlet valves were opened in the drydock structure, flooding its ballast tanks with seawater and lowering its bulk to the point where the Hercules could be, pending an improvement in the weather, maneuvered into open water. But after the inaugural fuss, it was determined that the flight would have to be postponed until weather conditions improved.

The press was hugely disappointed, but decided to hang out in Long Beach anyway, drinking in the taverns all Saturday night, hoping for some action as Sunday morning dawned on November 2.

Glenn Odekirk assured Howard, as he drove him to Terminal Island on that fateful morning, that the weather had improved, "It's not good, but it's better."

In front of cameras and a gaggle of reporters, Howard strode onto the tarmac. Looking tired and a bit nervous, he was photographed wearing his trademark lucky fedora. Heading for the Hercules, he quickly disappeared into its vast bowels like Jonah getting lost in the belly of a whale.

Already aboard were eighteen crewmen, nine invited guests, mostly from the press, and Joe Petrali, with whom Howard had disappeared for many months three years previously. Invitations to journalists had been based on the results of a lottery. Howard denied requests from both Jean Peters and Cary Grant to fly aboard the maiden flight, asserting that he was concerned for their safety.

In the cockpit, balanced about thirty feet above the water, Howard placed

Spruce Goose Before Launch of First Taxi Run

711

his fedora by his side and put on his earphones to make final checks of the aircraft. One by one he fired up each of the eight mammoth engines, very gradually opening the throttles. The Hercules taxied slowly across the surface of the harbor, skimming on its pontoons at a leisurely thirty-five miles per hour before Howard brought it back to its point of origin for some adjustments to the hydropneumatic throttle linkage.

Once that was done, Howard returned to the cockpit and the pilot's seat. He taxied off again, picking up speed. Soon, the pontoons supporting the largest aircraft in the history of aviation were slicing neatly through the surface of the waves lashing in from the Pacific. After a few moments, Howard eased back on the throttles of the giant boat-plane, settling its enormous bulk back into the water. When it came to a complete stop, he went back to greet the reporters as they disembarked. After assuring them that the Hercules would not fly that day, he bid them good-bye. Most of them were eager to file their stories in time to meet their deadlines. He had arranged for a P.T. boat to pick them up and ferry them back to shore.

Remaining behind were six reporters from magazines that didn't have imminent deadlines. One of these journalists was about to become famous: James C. McNamara from radio station KLAC in Los Angeles.

Asserting to the crew and to the remaining members of the press that he wanted to attempt a final test run of the plane's taxiing abilities, Howard returned to the cockpit. After fidgeting with the controls, he then fired each of the eight 3,000 horsepower Pratt and Whitney engines once again. Sitting beside him, David Grant knew better, especially when his boss called for "fifteen degrees flap."

Although he occupied the co-pilot's seat, Grant was not a pilot but a hydraulic engineer. Joe Petrali later speculated that Howard wanted the world to know that he—and he alone—piloted the giant craft. That's why, according to Joe, he didn't want another pilot in the cockpit with him at the time, fearing that he might get some of the credit.

Straining beneath his heavy recording devices, McNamara was allowed to stand behind Howard in the cockpit to broadcast the news to the anxiously awaiting world. As the flaps were lowered, Howard steered the mammoth bird toward the western end of the harbor, pointing it in the direction of San Pedro and opening the throttles as he did so.

The radio announcer's broadcast would later be played across the world. "This is James McNamara speaking to you from aboard the Howard Hughes two-hundred ton flying boat, the world's largest aircraft. At this moment as we speak to you from the spacious flight deck, this mighty monster of the skies is slowly cruising along a northwest course in the outer Los Angeles harbor."

In his broadcast, McNamara referred to Howard as "The Thin Man from Culver City." He even got Howard to speak into the microphone. Rather anticlimactically, Howard told the radio audience, "The wind is changeable. It's

Spruce Goose Airborne

been changing all day. But it's not too serious."

From the rear, Joe Petrali notified Howard that the Hercules was "All set!"

Glancing over his shoulder at McNamara, Howard shouted over the noise: "Hang on!"

At that moment a powerboat filled with drunken, waving well-wishers raced across the path of the Hercules, forcing Howard to swerve dangerously. He cursed the revelers, as he began to accelerate.

For his listeners, McNamara called out the rising speeds. "It's fifty! It's fifty over a choppy sea! It's fifty-five! It's fifty-five—more throttle! Now it's sixty— about sixty five! It's seventy!" Before he could announce a speed of seventy-five, the plane seemed to take off, seemingly on its own volition, and became airborne. "It's off!" shouted McNamara into his mike. "We are airborne," he shouted. "We are airborne, ladies and gentlemen. I don't believe that Howard Hughes meant for this to be."

At that very moment, aviation history was being made. No aircraft of this size had ever left the surface of the earth before.

Denounced as a "flying lumberyard" by Senator Brewster, the Spruce Goose flew smoothly for one mile, reaching a maximum speed of ninety miles per hour at an altitude of only seventy feet. The historic multimillion-dollar flight—the most expensive in the history of the world—lasted for only one minute.

Taxiing the craft back to its home berth at Terminal Island, Howard came to a smooth stop. The much ridiculed Spruce Goose had proven it could fly. Even before he could disembark, the world was once again hailing Howard as a true aviation hero.

After landing the plane, Howard was greeted first by Joe Petrali, who had emerged from the rear of the craft. Petrali later recalled that his pilot "was grinning, talking a lot—almost jumping up and down like a little kid."

McNamara concluded his broadcast. "At one time, Hughes said that if this big ship didn't fly he'd leave the country. Well, it certainly looks at this moment that Howard Hughes will be around the United States for quite some time to come."

Before disembarking, Howard, once again wearing his lucky fedora, told the crew, "She sure jumped off easy." With that remark, he was lowered by cable into a waiting P.T. boat.

Only McNamara rode with Howard aboard the first of the P.T. boat's runs to shore. Asking if the broadcaster were hungry and being told that he was, Howard opened a brown paper bag and handed him his sandwich. Biting into it, McNamara discovered it was just peanut butter—nothing more.

On shore before disappearing, Howard told reporters, "I think the airplane is going to be fairly successful. I sort of hoped it would fly but didn't want to predict it would and make people disappointed."

Earlier, Howard had turned down an invitation for dinner at the Beverly Hills Hotel with Jean Peters and Cary Grant. Howard left his two lovers to fend for themselves.

Driving away alone in an old Chevy, he headed for a secret dinner date in the remote hinterlands of the San Fernando Valley.

Once he got there, he discovered one of the leading love goddesses of the modern age waiting for him. Behind dark sunglasses, and elegantly dressed in tones of midnight blue and black, Ava Gardner was already into her third drink as Howard came in the door, seeking her out at the back of a darkened room at the most remote table.

***

Los Angeles, 1947-53

Although Howard had announced to the press that he would retest his flying cargo boat at an undetermined date in the springtime, the day would never come. The spring of 1948 turned into December and 1949 passed by as a war-torn decade came to an end. During this time dozens of highly skilled and paid engineers struggled to make the Spruce Goose airworthy. Almost every week Howard sent in new changes and suggestions. He often visited the Hercules at Long Beach, sometimes in the company of Jean Peters, and would spend hours going over blueprints for a project that had become a dinosaur amid the rapid technological developments of the post-war era.

Hughes Aviation invested nearly two million dollars on the construction of a climate-controlled hangar, nestled within the confines of a drydock, several feet below sea level, at Long Beach for this giant bird. Hercules was kept on a thirty-day standby alert for its test run by Howard. But he never showed up for any of these test flights.

He tried to interest the Air Force in buying Hercules, but was meet with total indifference. The Air Force brass knew that the Spruce Goose was hopelessly obsolete. Yet Howard stubbornly kept the plane in mint condition, spending more than a million and a half dollars annually to preserve and maintain it.

Howard Hughes in Spruce Goose Cockpit

At one point, he even ordered his engineers to design an even more grandiose HFB-2, a metal flying cargo boat larger than the Hercules that would be powered by turbo-prop engines. There was no market for such a mammoth aircraft.

Finally, faced with mounting expenses, Dietrich had to go to Howard for a confrontation with reality. "Let's face it!" Dietrich told his boss. "Hercules is history. Have it dismantled and hauled away. Or clsc turn it into a museum of your achievement."

Howard was so angered by Dietrich's suggestions that he didn't speak to his chief officer for the next five weeks. Dietrich had confronted him at a bad time. Howard had learned that his other grand dream of the war, the XF-11, was about to be "authorized for reclamation." That meant it was going to be cut up for scrap. He had turned the prototype of his reconnaissance plane over to the Air Force late in 1947, but the military had little use for the plane. "Other craft have been designed superior to this one, and the XF-11 came to us too late," an official at Wright Field told Dietrich, who was already well aware of that fact.

Always contemptuous of the Hercules, Dietrich dismissed it as a "plywood white elephant." As time went by, he watched its maintenance bills mount to three million dollars a year. By that time he was comparing the Spruce Goose to a "leviathan Model T Ford."

On September 17, 1953, Dietrich saw a face-saving way out of this costly dilemma. A barge being pulled past the drydock that held the Spruce Goose broke loose, smashed down part of the drydock, and seawater poured in, severely—perhaps fatally—damaging Hercules. The supervisor of the hangar called Dietrich with the bad news. "The hull, the stabilizers, the ailerons, the wings, and the tail are crushed." He also reported that the hangar had been flooded, and that mud was now standing five feet deep. Headlines the next day screamed: GIANT HUGHES PLANE TOTAL LOSS.

Once again, Dietrich urged Howard to junk the Spruce Goose. Stubbornly, Howard refused and ordered that it be repaired and returned to mint condition. He claimed that his beloved Hercules was "a milestone" in aircraft design, and that future generations would acknowledge that.

The press speculated that Howard was going to use the Spruce Goose in some film he was producing for RKO.

During the Senate investigation, Senator Brewster had asked Howard, "Have you contemplated using Hercules in your movie production business?" Responding with anger, Howard countered, "Senator, that is rather an absurd suggestion."

Actually the Senator was on to something. It was later revealed that Howard had indeed discussed with Cary Grant the idea of casting him in a movie where he would play a suave and debonair secret British agent in the tradition of James Bond. Flying the mammoth aircraft around the world, the Hercules would be transport used by the agent—similar to 007—"to make wrong right again."

In his memoirs, Dietrich indulged in some speculation, writing that Howard "was so frightened that the plane was so unsafe that it would prove to be his own coffin. So he kept the whole thing in limbo, neither terminating the project—which would have been an admission of defeat and denial of his vow to leave the country—nor trying to complete it—which might mean his own demise."

***

Los Angeles/Mexico, 1946-59

In September of 1946, Howard was stunned when Johnny Meyer reported to him that two of his sometimes lovers, Lana Turner and Tyrone Power, had fallen in love. Howard ordered that both of the stunningly beautiful stars be put under 24-hour surveillance. "I want to know everything," he instructed Meyer.

At the time, Tyrone was still married to French actress Annabella. They were separated but not divorced. The Lana Turner/Tyrone Power romance would become a national event, evocative of the interest that once swirled around the heads of Katharine Hepburn and Howard Hughes.

"From the very beginning, Howard wanted in on the affair," Meyer claimed. "He felt left out. He wanted to be a part of the action too. It was almost like, 'How dare you fall in love without getting my permission first?'"

In Mexico, Tyrone was filming *Captain from Castile* which, coincidentally, starred Jean Peters. Howard had already warned Tyrone to stay away from Jean. Apparently, however, Howard had issued no such warning to stay away from Lana. Impetuously Lana flew to Mexico for a secret rendezvous with Tyrone. Because of bad weather, she couldn't get back to Los Angeles in time, causing thousands of dollars worth of delays on her production of *Green Dolphin Street*, which earned her the ire of Louis B. Mayer.

In spite of the difficulties of travel, both Lana and Tyrone fell madly in love with Mexico. "The next time," Howard assured each of them, "let *me* make the travel arrangements."

And so he did, flying both lovebirds to Acapulco in the spring of 1947. When they got there, their designated host was Teddy Stauffer, a visionary Swiss-born big band leader whose tireless promotion of the emerging resort had earned him the name "Mr. Acapulco." Fleeing from the Nazis in the 1940s, and having settled in Mexico, he had been a successful leader of a big band that had introduced American-style Swing music to pre-War Europe, a hotelier, a night club owner, a sometimes actor, and something of a playboy. Even though Teddy was a world-class seducer, Howard apparently wasn't jealous, and they'd become friends. Sometimes they shared the same lovers. Howard only had affairs with Hedy Lamarr and Faith Domergue. Teddy actually married each of these actresses at various times.

Howard had shared other lovers with Teddy, notably Rita Hayworth and Barbara Hutton. When Howard, Lana, and Tyrone arrived at a luxurious villa Teddy had arranged for them, they were greeted with the sounds of his 1937 hit recording of "Goody-goody."

In Acapulco, Howard took Lana and Tyrone on a sailing expedition aboard a luxury yacht he'd rented through Teddy. The press was unaware of the trip. Later, Lana displayed a 210-pound swordfish over the mantel of her Beverly Hills home. "Ty and I caught it together," she told her friends, not mentioning Howard.

In a private interview in 1985 Teddy revealed, "I was in on Howard's plan from the beginning. He wanted a three-way with Lana and Tyrone. I set the whole thing up for him. Howard planned to make a grand entrance in the nude when Lana and Ty were already in bed together and also nude. I told him I thought Ty would be very accommodating. Seducing him in those days was as easy as pie. I warned Howard that Lana might hesitate. Even though sleeping with every Tom, Dick, and Harry, she made cooing sounds from time to time that she was still a lady."

"Howard left the lovebirds alone for their first night in

Lana Turner and Tyrone Power

717

Acapulco," Teddy claimed. "On the second night he made his move. Stripping down in front of me, he headed for their suite. I stayed nearby in case there was any trouble. Like he said he would, Howard went inside their room, taking the lovers by surprise. I heard loud voices at first, then everything seemed to quiet down. I realized Howard's dream had come true. He'd come between the two lovers, and they went along with it."

"The next morning over breakfast, I personally squeezed Howard's drink from blood-red oranges," Stauffer said. "He always insisted it be done in front of him. He reported to me that the night had been a success, claiming that he'd gone down on both Lana and Ty. He also said that before the rooster crowed, he'd fucked Ty while the actor was fucking Lana. In other words, Ty was Lucky Pierre in the middle of the sandwich. 'It was one of the best orgasms I've ever had,' Howard told me."

In her memoirs, *Lana: The Lady, The Legend, The Truth*, she admitted that she'd heard rumors of a homosexual element in Tyrone's nature, "but I never saw it." When Teddy Stauffer read that, he said, "Oh, that Lana!"

After the Acapulco trip, Howard told Johnny Meyer that he didn't think the love affair between Lana and Tyrone would last. "Lana's too possessive of him, and Ty's a real flirt," Howard said. "He doesn't like to be owned by anyone, but likes to share his charms. I don't think Lana's in love with him anyway—she just thinks she is. She's fallen for a male version of herself." Many other Hollywood insiders shared Howard's point of view about the lovers.

Their affair survived until August of 1947. For about a week, Howard disappeared with Tyrone to an undisclosed location. The actor didn't tell Lana where he was going. Johnny Meyer knew nearly all of Howard's movements, but this time Howard didn't even inform his pimp where he was. Meyer suspected that the two illicit lovers were in a villa somewhere in Malibu.

Apparently over "pillow talk," Tyrone informed Howard that he was going on a three-month good will tour, arranged by his studio. The jaunt would take him to Africa, South America, and some European capitals such as Paris and London. Meyer suspected that Tyrone told Howard that he was doing this just as a means of breaking up with Lana. Instead of an outright break, Tyrone was going to let time and distance work to end the relationship.

During the course of Tyrone's absence, as the weeks went by, Lana grew more and more anxious to hear from him. Communications between them were few and far between, and then not very satisfying to Lana.

One night at his Beverly Hills bungalow, after Jean Peters had left his bedroom, Howard received a desperate call from Lana. "I'm pregnant!" she blurted out.

"Is it Ty?" he asked. "Or someone else. Some others?"

"It's Ty's kid," Lana claimed. "The only *other* would be Howard Hughes himself."

Lana feared scandal. Even though Tyrone was separated from Annabella, they were still married. As Lana would later write, "In those days you didn't make babies just because you were deeply in love." She also said, "I'd be publicly branded a whore, and I'd probably never work again."

When Tyrone learned of the pregnancy, he said that he was going to leave the decision up to Lana. Howard made that decision for Lana. Although she claimed in her memoirs that she went alone to a woman doctor—"not to a butcher"—she was actually driven there by her longtime friend, Johnny Meyer. Howard had ordered Meyer to tend to Lana's every need and to stick with her in case something went wrong. Nothing did go wrong. The son or daughter of two of the world's most beautiful people was successfully aborted.

Lana later confessed that "the abortion took more than a fetus from me. It took some part of my heart, a living symbol of the happiest time of my life."

Tyrone would return to Hollywood after his goodwill tour but not to Lana. She was heartbroken. In Rome he had met bit actress Linda Christian and planned to marry her after the finalization of his divorce from Annabella. Ironically, Linda had played a maid in Lana's *Green Dolphin Street*. Errol Flynn's reaction to the marriage was one of wonder, surprise, and dismay. All he said was, "Ty married *her*?"

By December of 1947, a publicist at MGM released the news that "Lana Turner and Tyrone Power have called it quits."

After their breakup, it is believed that Howard never came together intimately with either of the two lovers ever again. "By that time, Howard had other fish to fry," Meyer later said. "Lana resumed her feverish lifestyle, giving her charms away to many men. Ty, as was his way, also continued to give his charms away to many men and women in spite of his marriage to the Christian dame. He was ever so versatile. He even seduced both stars of *Pillow Talk*: Rock Hudson and Doris Day."

Although his involvement with Lana and Tyrone ended, Howard ordered Meyer to continue to have them spied upon.

"I remember when Lana got involved with the Argentine actor, Fernando Lamas," Meyer said. "Howard wanted to know how Lamas was hung. He wanted exact measurements and details, even demanding to know how long Lamas remained in the saddle. For some bizarre reason, he also wanted to know if Lamas were cut or uncut. Since Lamas was screwing dozens of women in Hollywood—not just Lana—it was easy for me to come up with pretty accurate measurements for my boss man. And, yes, before you even ask me the next question, Lamas was very well endowed."

On the night of April 4, 1958, in his bungalow at the Beverly Hills Hotel, Howard received an urgent phone call from Johnny Meyer. In blunt language, Meyer told his boss that Lana's gangster lover, Johnny Stompanato, had been stabbed at her Beverly Hills mansion, following a violent quarrel, and that he was dead.

Although often stingy, Howard ordered Meyer and his squadron of spies to find out all the details of what really happened. Meyer later estimated that Howard spent nearly fifty thousand dollars to learn what happened on that infamous night.

Angered that Lana had not invited him to accompany her to the Oscar presentations, Stompanato had threatened to "carve up" Lana's beautiful face if she ever left him out again. In a "state of madness," she ran down to the kitchen and picked up an eight-inch knife. Returning to her pink satin bedroom, she stabbed Stompanato in his stomach. He lived for another fifteen minutes. Also in the house that fatal night was fourteen-year-old Cheryl Crane, Lana's daughter with husband Stephen Crane.

In typical Hollywood fashion, everybody was called except the police. Even Lana's mother, Mildred, was summoned. A private physician, "Dr. McDonald," arrived at the scene. Remaining remarkably cool, Lana also called Howard's friend, attorney Jerry Geisler, who had defended Errol Flynn during his trial on a charge of statutory rape.

If a star wanted off on a murder rap in those days, the call went out: "Get Jerry Geisler."

In two hours—some reports claimed five hours—a plan was concocted. To avoid Lana having to go to jail, Geisler decided to claim that Cheryl went to the kitchen, got the butcher knife, entered the upstairs bedroom, and stabbed Stompanato.

The belief was that Cheryl as a juvenile would get a light sentence, if one at all, whereas a jury might "throw the book at Lana." Frank Sinatra was also said to have arrived at the scene, and the singer agreed that Geisler's plan was the way to go. "Let Cheryl take the fall."

At long last the police were called after all the participants had been rehearsed in their respective stories. By that time, Stompanato was long dead. Clinton B. Anderson, police chief of Beverly Hills, arrived at the scene of the crime and began to question Lana and her daughter in separate rooms. Both of their stories, in the policeman's words, "were a perfect match." The killing was later ruled as "justifiable homicide."

"In the Johnny Stompanato murder case," Meyer later said, "Lana gave the greatest performance of her career."

In the wake of the gigolo's murder, Lana feared for her safety and not only welcomed but accepted Howard's offer of a 24-hour security guard. Both Howard and Lana felt that the mob would seek revenge on Lana for killing one of its own. Stompanato's friend, gangster Mickey Cohen, was known to take revenge when angered.

During what became Hollywood's most notorious scandal of the 1950s, Howard generously had Lana guarded for eight months until fear of mob reprisal died down.

The following year, in 1959, Tyrone flew to Spain to film *Solomon and Sheba*. Concurrently, in Acapulco, Lana launched a torrid affair with Teddy

Stauffer. "Mr. Acapulco" was in his hotel bar when the news came over the radio. Tyrone had been the victim of a sudden heart attack and was dead. On hearing the news back in Hollywood, Henry Fonda cynically remarked, "The death was caused by Ty's co-star, George Sanders. George probably wore him out in the sack." Like Tyrone, George was a notorious bisexual.

Teddy called Lana's villa with the news. "Oh, my God, you don't know," he said to her. "Oh, God, that I should have to be the one to tell you. Ty is dead!"

She later recalled that the "news shocked my very soul." She claimed that she nearly fainted, her body having gone numb all over. "I realized that the man who broke my heart was dead, and there was no more hope we'd ever get back together. My dream of Ty was all over!"

There was nothing that Lana could do at this point. But at 7000 Romaine Street, there was something that Howard could do. As a final gesture to a long-ago lover, he ordered that a special TWA plane be sent to Barajas Airport in Madrid. The plane was made available to fly the body of the dead actor back to Hollywood.

On reflection, Howard told Meyer, "Of all the men I've known—Errol, Robert, Guy, Jack—Ty was the kindest and the most accommodating in bed. Whatever my request, regardless of how bizarre, he always came through for me. I felt I owed him his final plane ride."

***

Hollywood, 1949-55

In 1948, Howard summoned Noah Dietrich from Houston to Hollywood to tell him what Dietrich considered some very bad news: Howard wanted to purchase a major film studio. Since MGM and 20th Century Fox weren't for sale, Howard had focused on RKO, which Dietrich regarded as "the sickest of all the big studios." At the time Howard was trying to buy into RKO, the film studio's profits had been shrinking and expenses doubling.

For many years, Howard had maintained an on-again, off-again friendship and business relationship with Floyd Odlum, CEO of the $70 million Atlas Corporation, an investment firm and conglomerate. Years before, Odlum had married Jacqueline Cochran, the century's greatest female aviator, with whom Howard (prior to her marriage with Odlum) had had a brief affair and whose airplane he had leased and then rebuilt during one of his youthful aviation adventures.

Since 1935, Atlas had exercised controlling interest over RKO thanks to its ownership of 929,000 of RKO's four million outstanding shares. A businessman, Odlum was neither star struck nor had any interest in movie-making. Sensing that the Golden Age of Hollywood was coming to an end, Odlum was eager to sell his company's ownership of RKO.

Unknown to Dietrich, as part of his negotiations, Howard had flown on five different occasions to the Odlums's sprawling ranch in the Coachella Desert, outside Indio, near Palm Springs. Odlum never got the price he wanted. He wanted $10½ per share, but Howard was willing to pay only $9½ per share. In the end, Howard purchased all the Atlas shares for $8,825,000. Overnight, as its major stockholder, he'd become the head of RKO. With characteristic lack of charm, he informed Dietrich, "I'll be the only non-kike running a studio in Hollywood."

Facing Dietrich fresh off the plane from Houston, Howard told his chief of operations that he needed to borrow ten million dollars from a bank, since he didn't want to use Toolco money. Dietrich immediately contacted the Mellon Bank of Pittsburgh, of which Toolco was the major depositor. The ten million loan was granted that very day.

News of the sale of RKO spread rapidly through the 24 sound stages of RKO between Hollywood and Culver City.

Howard's penchant for delaying production and interfering in every aspect of film-making were all too well known in Hollywood. "He had a reputation for firing anybody who disagreed with him," said N. Peter Rathvon, president of RKO. With the purchase of the studio, Howard also acquired 124 movie theaters across the nation.

At the time of the takeover, Howard's business prospects drew mixed reviews. Toolco had increased its net worth to two hundred million dollars. In contrast, TWA had lost eight million dollars in 1947. To save his troubled airline, Howard had borrowed ten million dollars from the Reconstruction Finance Corporation, using the money to purchase a dozen Lockheed Constellations. With these Connies, he was able to add more attractive routes, picking up new customers.

Howard chose a difficult moment to take over RKO. The anti-Communist scare hung over Hollywood like a poisonous cloud. A congressional committee had already labeled RKO "a hotbed of Red subversion."

Not only that, but government anti-trust laws were forcing studios to give up their profitable theater chains. Television loomed as an ever-growing threat to the future of all film studios.

The most valuable property RKO owned was its backlog of about a thousand films, including such classics as *Citizen Kane* and *King Kong*. RKO also owned the Ginger Rogers and Fred Astaire musicals of the 1930s. In the 1930s, Katharine Hepburn had also worked for RKO, which owned an impressive collection of her films as well. Howard found himself in possession of such films as *Bringing Up Baby* starring his two lovers of yesterday, Cary and Katharine.

An inevitable clash was predicted between Howard and Dore Schary, who was in charge of production at RKO. Howard liked "tits and action" movies, the more liberal Schary preferring pictures with a message. Schary was also a Jew, and Howard was notorious for his anti-Semitism. To highlight the differences between the two men, Schary had made *Crossfire* in 1947, a film dealing with anti-Semitism. The film starred "the three Roberts": Young, Mitchum, and Ryan.

For some time, Howard had been suspicious of Schary. He told Dietrich, "I think Schary's a Commie."

The first encounter between Schary and Howard took place at Rathvon's home. *Fortune* magazine later reported their get-acquainted dialogue.

Howard: I hear you don't like me.
Schary: Well, I hear you don't like me, either. We can either talk in terms of gossip or talk business.
Howard: You can run the studio. I don't have any time.

Schary later claimed that Howard evoked "Gary Cooper in a western." He noted that his new boss did not shake his hand but stepped back two paces when Schary extended his own palm.

When Schary told Dietrich of Howard's promises not to interfere, Dietrich was skeptical. "It was like turning a boy loose in a candystore and expecting him not to touch the merchandise."

From the moment he took over, Howard began to interfere. The first film Schary pitched to Howard was *Battleground*, starring Van Johnson. "The public's fed up with war," he told an infuriated Schary." They'd much rather see a romantic comedy. Drop it!"

Schary had great faith in *Battleground*. He would eventually take the film with him to MGM when he resigned from RKO and went to replace Louis B. Mayer as head of MGM. *Battleground* became MGM's biggest hit in 1950, the studio having acquired the rights from Howard for only $20,000.

Schary and Howard also conflicted over rising star Barbara Bel Geddes, a talented New York actress who was being acclaimed for her role in the 1948 film, *I Remember Mama*, for which she was nominated for an Academy Award. Schary had filmed *Caught* in 1949 with the star, but Howard saw it and was horrified, "Fire her!" he ordered Schary. "She's not my type." The producer later released the Bel Geddes film through MGM. Howard told Schary that the star of the film, James Mason, "was a sissy—no doubt a fag," but he was impressed with the masculine charm of Robert Ryan and would use the actor again.

Bel Geddes was about to go before the cameras on a film called *Bed of Roses*. Schary was forced to cancel it.

The second meeting between Schary and Howard took place at Cary Grant's villa. The actor was in Europe at the time. Ushered into the living room, Schary could see a nude Howard through an open door to a bedroom. He was helping a starlet put on her brassiere. "After that, I knew it was all over between Hughes and me."

"Such contempt for convention," Schary later said. "It was his fuck you to me." Schary later told his friends that after the woman left, Howard invited him in to continue negotiations about the future of RKO while he sat for two hours on a toilet, complaining of constipation.

During that toilet meeting Howard also "pulled the plug" on *Malaya*, which starred James Stewart and Spencer Tracy. Howard claimed that he detested Tracy, blaming him for the breakup of his relationship with Kate Hepburn. To an astonished Schary, Howard said, "Did you know that when Tracy isn't with Kate, he's out sucking off teenage hustlers secured for him by George Cukor?" Schary later acquired *Malaya* for MGM, which released it in 1949.

Dietrich recalled that "Howard went into orbit" when he saw the final cut of the RKO film *The Boy With the Green Hair*, a film which Schary had produced. Howard said that the picture "is Commie inspired," and ordered that many of its scenes be reshot. In Howard's revised version, Dean Stockwell, aged twelve at the time, was instructed to utter a declaration of anti-Communist rhetoric personally written by Howard.

So much for not interfering in studio productions. Howard called a halt to production on more than three dozen films during the first three months of his dictatorship of RKO.

He didn't, however, halt the release of *Every Girl Should Be Married*. It starred best friend Cary Grant appearing opposite Betsy Drake in a romantic comedy. The film was released in 1948, although Howard personally disliked Drake. Even so, he agreed to be best man when Cary married her on Christmas Day in 1949 in Phoenix, Arizona.

Even though Cary and Howard were still close, Cary did not remain at RKO to make pictures exclusively for Howard, although he was strongly encouraged to do so. Beginning in 1949, Cary freelanced his way through future films, beginning with *I Was a Male War Bride* in 1949, which was eventually released through 20th Century Fox. In it, Cary was directed by Howard Hawks, who had become a bitter enemy of Howard's. Hawks later privately speculated that Cary "did not want to be under Hughes's thumb."

Schary left RKO on July 31, 1948. Peter Rathvon resigned shortly thereafter when Howard asked him to fire 700 employees and he refused. Although he had no knowledge of film production, Dietrich was put in charge as chairman of the RKO board.

Taking over after booting Schary, Howard ordered Dietrich to "send pink slips to everybody." Dietrich finally persuaded him not to fire everybody but retain at least a skeletal crew.

The Hollywood Reporter claimed that after Howard's takeover, "RKO became a ghost town." The remaining staff at RKO came under heavy suspicion because of alleged Communist links. Howard hired a squadron of men, mostly ex-policemen, to investigate and spy on the studio's staff. "My God," Schary said when he learned of this, "Hughes is paranoid. He thinks he's J. Edgar Hoover."

"With Schary and Rathvon out of the way," Johnny Meyer said, "the boss

724

immediately set about using RKO as a giant casting couch. RKO became his personal harem. But, to be honest, he never fucked—or even saw—most of the starlet bimbos he had his boy, Walter Kane, put under contract. Just knowing that all those hot pussies were waiting out there for him, if he wanted them, seemed titillation enough for Howard."

In 1948, the year Howard assumed control of RKO, twenty-eight films—most of them already completed or nearing completion by the time of his takeover—were released to the movie-going public. By 1949, production had slowed to a snail's pace. Only one picture, *It's Only Money*, was set for release. Howard never liked the titles studio writers came up with, finding his creations "better box office." He changed *It's Only Money* to *Double Dynamite*, which called attention to the two major assets of its star, Jane Russell. The film was advertised as "double delicious, double delightful, and double delirious." The other star was Groucho Marx. Howard assigned Frank Sinatra third billing. Howard and Sinatra already hated each other because of their romantic conflict over Ava Gardner.

Howard never visited RKO during his entire tenure over the studio. He feared that with all the studio hands milling about, the place was germ-laden. He operated RKO from his rented offices at the Goldwyn Studio, two miles away. However, rumors in Hollywood persisted that Howard once walked through the studio without a word. At the conclusion of his tour, he allegedly said, "Paint it!" before getting into a battered Chevy and driving away.

Although Howard "had more starlets than a Roman emperor at his command," he focused on an actress who proved unobtainable.

California-born Janet Leigh was blonde, bright, pretty, pert, and curvaceous. She won over American audiences as Meg in the 1949 version of *Little Women*.

He borrowed her from MGM for *Two Tickets to Broadway*, even though she wasn't a dancer. The film was finally released in 1951.

Howard demanded that Janet's dance rehearsals be staged at the Goldwyn Studios. He'd hired two of the most skilled experts in the musical theater business, Gower Champion (later choreographer of both *42nd Street* and *Hello, Dolly*) and Marge Champion, to teach Janet to dance. Studio hands reported that Howard would sit for hours at a time watching Janet rehearse in her leotards. "He was mesmer-

Janet Leigh

725

ized by her," Meyer later claimed.

Many books and articles have claimed that Howard and Janet were a romantic duo. Until the day she died, Janet denied this. "I had absolutely no romantic inclination toward Howard—none—not even a flicker," she once wrote. "In my eyes, he belonged more with my parents than he did with me."

Janet was falling in love with an actor from New York, Tony Curtis. She found him "an irresistible personality with black unruly hair, large sensitive eyes fringed by long dark lashes, and a full sensuous mouth." By 1951 she would marry him. Fan magazines would proclaim them as "Hollywood's Perfect Young Couple," even though they weren't. Their troubled marriage would end in 1962.

Before Howard finally gave up his pursuit of Janet, surrendering her to Curtis, he cast her badly as the female co-star in *Jet Pilot*, playing the improbable role of a Russian spy whose seductive techniques were inspired by Mata Hari. Cary Grant had been Howard's first choice for the male lead, but his friend turned him down because of other commitments. Howard cast John Wayne instead. That actor's right-wing politics and anti-Communist stances appealed to Howard.

During the filming, Janet learned that Jules Furthman, her producer, had been instructed by Howard to urge her "to marry the boss." Motivated by a sense of personal discretion, Furthman never carried out that command.

Howard wanted to create "a *Hell's Angels* for the Jet Age." But time and indecision would bog him down. *Jet Pilot*, on which he'd lose millions of dollars, would not be released until 1957 when movie audiences were stunned at how young John Wayne looked, and how old-fashioned the aircraft looked. Innovations in jet aircraft had made *Jet Pilot* "a historical document of aviation," as one critic put it.

On a sad note, Howard had originally hired an aging Josef von Sternberg as director when actual production on *Jet Pilot* had begun right before Christmas in 1949. At the twilight of his career, von Sternberg was still famous for having directed Marlene Dietrich in *The Blue Angel*, but that film had entered the archives of Hollywood history. In a few short weeks, after endless conflicts with Howard, von Sternberg was off the picture. "What does he know about jet planes?" Marlene Dietrich, also working for Howard on *Rancho Notorious*, asked. "He knows about German decadence, cabarets, black hosiery—how to make me more beautiful than I already am."

As another sad footnote, *Jet Pilot* would be the last film to bear the credit HOWARD HUGHES PRESENTS.

After manifesting his rights as the major stockholder of RKO for only two years, Howard told Dietrich, "I need RKO like I need to come down with the black plague." On September 23, 1952, he sold it to a Chicago syndicate headed by financier Ralph Stolkin, who made a $1,250,000 down payment on a projected total price of $7,345,940, which it had been agreed would be due when

726

the deal was finalized. Exposed by *The Wall Street Journal* for its links to organized crime, Stolkin's financial cabal collapsed. Howard's RKO stock was returned to him on February 10, 1953.

To save RKO, Howard brought in two top-flight producers, Jerry Wald and Norman Krasna, promising them fifty million dollars of seed money to launch various films of their own selection. One of these became highly successful. Released in 1951, the "weeper," *The Blue Veil* starred Jane Wyman. Along with Wald and Krasna, Howard watched the film in which Jane played a children's nurse. At the end of the screening, Howard stood up and confronted the producers. "I loathe it. Besides, I hate children. And who would want to fuck Jane Wyman? Maybe Ronald Reagan at one time, but he's always been a nerd when it comes to women." With those comments, he headed out of the studio.

The final showdown between the producers and Howard occurred when they were summoned to his bungalow at the Beverly Hills Hotel at three o'clock in the morning. After keeping them waiting for thirty minutes, Howard came out of the adjoining bedroom wearing only a pair of tennis shoes.

Embarrassed, all Wald could manage to say was, "Tennis, anyone?"

Without any negotiation, Howard welcomed them but excused himself, claiming that he had to make an urgent phone call. Neither Wald nor Krasna ever heard from him again. Through their attorneys the next day, they quickly sought their release from RKO, which Howard granted.

Under Howard's direction, RKO continued to decline. Movie theaters were closing all over America. RKO's misfortunes were also caused by problems other than Howard's gross mismanagement. America's tastes in media were changing, as television took over. Instead of going to the movies two or three nights a week, America was staying home and watching TV.

RKO stockholders filed countless lawsuits against Howard, charging him with mismanagement. At the time, Howard had contracted with actor Dick Powell to direct pictures for the studio. Confronting the press, Powell said, "RKO's contract roster is down to three actors and 127 lawyers."

Dietrich, by now, had been subjected to months of Howard's complaints about the corrosive and ongoing effect of investor lawsuits. But despite Howard's urging to dump RKO, Dietrich couldn't find a buyer for Howard's stock. On February 8, 1954, Howard impulsively purchased all the remaining RKO stock at $6 per share, twice the market value. This maneuver left Howard in total charge of the studio, with no more stockholder lawsuits. To pay for it, through Dietrich, he had to raise $23,489,478 in cash.

He would not retain ownership of the studio for long. On July 19, 1955, he'd sell all his shares to General Teleradio, a subsidiary of General Tire Company, for $25 million. *The Hollywood Reporter* hailed this deal as "the largest cash transaction in film history." As it turned out, General Teleradio was far more interested in acquiring the studio's film library than the studio itself. The library of Golden Age films could be rented at a profit to television stations across the country.

Two years later, in 1957, Howard learned that the new owners of RKO had sold the studio to Desilu, which was jointly owned by Lucille Ball and Desi Arnaz, who were growing rich on the *I Love Lucy* TV series.

"Fitting justice," Howard told Johnny Meyer. "In the '30s RKO used Ball to entertain rich investors from back East. So, she ends up owning the joint. As for Desi, I agree with him. He once told Cesar Romero that men are better cock-suckers than women."

"During his tenure at RKO, Howard had been, in the word of Johnny Meyer, "mesmerized" by yet another performer. He was the broad-shouldered and droopy-eyed Robert Mitchum "with the bourbon voice." Howard had ordered the 1947 *Out of the Past* screened for him a dozen times. "He had developed a secret crush on the super cool actor," Meyer later claimed, "and it was going nowhere except driving boss man crazy with desire."

***

Los Angeles, 1946-1997

In spite of what one reviewer called his "lizard eyes and anteater nose," Robert Mitchum replaced Victor Mature as Howard's favorite actor. Ava Gardner remained his favorite actress, the North Carolina beauty having long ago replaced his former favorite, Katharine Hepburn. Now that an aging Kate was making films with Spencer Tracy, Howard could no longer tolerate looking at any of the films in which they appeared jointly.

Robert's costar from *Out of the Past*, and Howard's sometimes girlfriend Jane Greer, once speculated that the tall, broad-chested Mr. Robert Mitchum possessed the image of what Howard himself wanted to look like. "I think Bob was a fantasy alter ego for Howard. Howard always doubted his own masculinity, whereas Bob seemed completely assured of his. He could get women without buying them. They gravitated to him like bees to the sweet nectar of an aromatic flower. Deep down, Howard suspected that women came to him only because of his power and money, which was so often the case."

Actor Jim Backus shared somewhat the same sentiments as Jane. "Even though Hughes pretended to be upset by Robert's wild streak, it also appealed to him. It was as if Hughes were living vicariously through his biggest male star. Hughes used money as bait for women. Mitchum could have been a bum, and beautiful women would still have fallen head over heels in love with him. Hughes knew that. He admired Mitchum's super cool attitude toward women. I think Hughes was a bit jealous of Mitchum's power over women. Take Ava Gardner, for instance. Hughes had spent a fortune wooing her, offering her everything—gems, cars, trips around the world. All Mitchum had to do was appear on the scene, snap his fingers, and Ava came running."

728

Robert Mitchum

A Yankee from Bridgeport, Connecticut, Robert had been a shoe clerk, a studio writer, an aircraft factory worker, professional boxer, and had even served time in jail as part of a Georgia chain gang, from which he'd escaped.

At the time he met Howard, his bad boy reputation was already established. Before anyone ever heard of Marlon Brando, he was filmdom's first hipster antihero. Once, on a job application, he'd listed his former profession as "petty criminal." Robert had been nominated as best supporting actor for his role in United Artists's *The Story of G.I. Joe.*, but had lost. That would be the only time he'd be nominated to receive an Oscar.

"There was something about Robert's gypsy-like childhood that appealed to Howard," Jane said. "As a hobo, Bob had hopped trains during the worst days of the depression. Howard dreamed of that kind of freedom. Bob had led a life fueled by liquor and drugs. As Howard himself faced life, which he was able to live only with the aid of drugs, he was drawn to Bob's existential detachment from this earth. Aware of Howard's dependence on drugs, Bob told his boss, 'We all need to live on Cloud 9. That way, we don't feel the pain of life.'"

From the beginning of his takeover of RKO, Howard planned to make Robert the studio's biggest star. But Robert remained indifferent to the roles Howard assigned him. "I was just a horseshit salesman to Howard," Robert said years later about his career at RKO.

Almost before any of Howard's big plans for Robert could be realized, the actor's career was almost derailed, and might have been if such a powerful figure as Howard had not intervened. Johnny Meyer called Howard on September 1, 1948 to tell his boss that Robert had been arrested by the police on a drug raid at a private home on Ridpath Drive in Laurel Canyon. Robert had been arrested with friends, including actress Lila Leeds, described by columnist James Bacon as "one of the most beautiful women who ever landed in Hollywood— looks like Lana Turner, but cuter."

"Get him out of jail!" Howard shouted into the phone at Meyer. "Don't let him talk to anyone. And for god's sake, get Jerry Giesler." At the time Giesler was known his ability, as proven by his involvement with Lana Turner in the Johnny Stompanato affair, for helping any celebrity "beat the rap."

But Robert could not be rescued. The case had become too public for Howard's usual bribes. The news was already being carried on the wire services. The next day, headlines all over the nation were revealing the story. A typical banner proclaimed, BOB MITCHUM, 3 OTHERS JAILED AFTER DOPE RAID.

Even though he hardly knew Robert at the time, Howard stood by the star throughout his arrest, imprisonment, and release. The rest of savvy Hollywood was predicting the demise of the actor's career, which had just started to bloom. "It's just the beginning for Bob," Howard told Meyer.

As proof of his belief in the actor, he purchased the remaining half of Robert's contract from David O. Selznick for $400,000. By standing by Robert, Howard snubbed his nose at the Hollywood elite.

Robert was sentenced to serve sixty days at the Wayside Honor Farm in Castaic, California, which was about 42 miles north of Los Angeles.

In a beat-up old sedan, Howard drove up to meet Robert at the prison farm, and even got the warden to vacate his office for this private session with one of his inmates. The warden later said that "Hughes, in spite of his money, looked like one of those bums routinely arrested on the streets for vagrancy."

Arriving at the prison farm with Johnny Meyer, Howard was horrified at "all the riff-raff he saw walking," Meyer said. "The ethnic mixture, especially the number of blacks, distressed Howard greatly. He feared he'd come down with something just by breathing the air." Howard also learned that day that several child molesters were serving time, including "Big Bill" Tilden, the century's most famous tennis player, who'd been convicted of molesting a sixteen-year-old boy.

Howard often expressed his loathing for child molesters. "My boss just didn't get it," Meyer later recalled. "He never saw himself that way, even though he'd seduced fifteen-year-olds like Ida Lupino and Faith Domergue."

Arriving with a bag containing both Hershey bars and vitamin pills, Howard warned Robert not to eat the prison food. He said that he was going to arrange for one big meal a day prepared by Dave Chasen, the famous Los Angeles restaurateur. During Robert's stay in prison, that meal would be personally delivered to him from Chasen's swank restaurant. Howard had hired a driver to make the daily deliveries during Robert's time at the prison farm.

During his talk with Robert, Howard assured the star that "the studio is in back of you one-hundred percent. You're going to emerge from this a bigger star than when you went in." To show his support, Howard informed Robert that he was rushing up the release of *Rachel and the Stranger*, in which the actor had appeared opposite Loretta Young. What Howard didn't say was that he wanted to capitalize off the publicity generated by Robert's imprisonment.

When Howard asked if he could do anything for Robert, the actor requested a loan of $50,000 to help him pay his attorney and to buy a modest house for his family. Howard quickly agreed, saying he would charge only five percent interest. He also told Robert that he would continue to draw his $3,500-a-week salary during his jail term.

Once released from prison, Robert was assigned a "babysitter," actually ex-policeman Kemp Niver. Howard wanted the actor trailed so that he wouldn't get into any more trouble. Robert resented being spied by "this ex-fuzz." He also knew that Howard had bugged his new home and also his dressing room at RKO. Robert bitterly resented that, his anger boiling over one day at the studio. Thinking there was a hidden microphone in the wall, Robert shouted up close into it. "Did you hear what I just said, Mr. Thin Man, you deaf fucker you!"

Howard conducted his future business with Robert as in a *film noir* spy drama. Meyer would pick up Robert at two or three o'clock in the morning and would drive him to some seedy motel in south Los Angeles. There Robert would wait for Howard to show up.

"Robert was too hip not to know that Howard was attracted to him," Meyer later claimed. "He took perverse pleasure in taunting Howard—call it prick-teasing. I remember one night at some sleazy motel, Howard came into the bedroom to find Robert buck-assed naked on the bed smoking a marijuana cigarette. He had this big erection, which he didn't bother to cover up when Howard walked in. 'Sorry, Mr. Phantom,' Robert said to Howard. 'But Old Faithful just does this from time to time.'"

Because of his mysterious appearances and disappearances, Howard was referred to as "Mr. Phantom" by Robert

"Seeing Robert naked on the bed, Howard looked at him like he could eat him for dinner," Meyer claimed. "But instead of doing that, Howard sat down in a chair near the bed and pitched a new film script to Robert. He just lay there taunting Howard, who was really uncomfortable. Robert was perverse in the way he teased the boss man."

Howard, according to Meyer, attempted to conceal his attraction to Robert by feigning indifference or delivering a put-down. "You're just like a pay toilet," he told Robert. "You don't give a shit for nothing."

Even though Meyer felt that Howard desired Robert, the agent also believed that at no point in his relationship with the actor did Howard ever "put the make on Robert." However, he continued to taunt Howard, parading around naked in front of him, especially when they took saunas together at a private health club both men used to frequent.

Robert remained eternally grateful to Howard for standing by him and saving his career, although he was also very realistic in his appraisal of his studio boss. He'd been delighted when Howard immediately cast him in the 1949 *The Big Steal*. No major actress wanted to risk her reputation by appearing opposite "a jailbird." Jane Greer, however, seemed delighted to costar with her *Out of the Past* comrade.

"Howard could have thrown me to the bloodhounds," Robert later said, "but he proved to be a loyal friend." Even so, Robert was smart enough to know how inadequate Howard was in his management of RKO. "The studio became some perverse pleasure palace for Howard, even if he weren't fucking one-quarter of the gals he had under contract. Howard was no great producer like Louis B. Mayer. We turned out a lot of pulp trash in those days. Frankly, I didn't give a damn. I never pretended to be Marlon Brando."

"Mr. Phantom wanted cleavage in his films, especially Jane's breasts." He was, of course, referring to his sometimes costar, Jane Russell. "Howard also liked fistfights where two guys beat the shit out of each other," Robert also claimed. "Many RKO films at the time were just extensions of Howard's sexual fantasies. Maybe I was one of his sexual fantasies—who knows for sure?"

Even though Robert wasn't putting out for Howard, Meyer claimed that the two friends talked more about sex than RKO film scripts when they met. Howard wanted to know the most minute details about Robert's sex life. That became especially true when Howard cast his two favorite stars, Robert and Ava, in *My Forbidden Past*, released in 1951. Filming actually began in the closing weeks of 1949.

Robert was well aware that Howard lusted after Ava, who miraculously managed to keep him at a distance, though continuing the stormy relationship. After the first week of filming, Robert called Howard. "Ava has the hots for me—shall I fuck her or not? Or is she still your exclusive property?"

"She never let me get into her, but you might as well go for it," Howard advised Robert. "Otherwise, the guys at the studio will think you're a fag!"

Ava fell big for Robert. At one point, a drunken Ava even called Robert's wife, Dorothy, begging her to release her husband. "You've had the big fucker for a decade, bitch," Ava shouted. "Give the guy a chance to sample some other pussy." Dorothy slammed down the phone on Ava.

Meyer claimed that Robert took delight in revealing to Howard the most intimate details of his love-making with Ava. "In front of me one day, Robert told Howard that Ava liked to get into a bathtub and have me piss all over her, aiming my dick at her beautiful face. Howard got particularly excited hearing this."

But when Howard cast Robert in 1950 in *Where Danger Lives*, with Faith Domergue, he warned the actor, "Don't move in on her!"

When Howard pitched the script to Robert, he told Howard that he didn't have time to read the script. He wanted Howard to explain it to him.

It's about the price you pay for sexual obsession…and lust," Howard said.

Ava Gardner and Robert Mitchum

732

"You mean, what you have for Ava Gardner?"

"The greatest tension between Robert and Howard was generated over a film script, not over women. Howard adamantly refused to lend Robert to Harry Cohn at Columbia to play the lead in *From Here to Eternity*. The part later went to Burt Lancaster. Howard tried to pacify an angered Robert. "You don't want to go over there and work for all those Jews, do you?" Howard asked.

Robert's exit from RKO was not glorious. His farewell appearance was in an alleged comedy called *She Couldn't Say No*, released in 1954. Co-starring the beautiful and talented Jean Simmons, the film was a dud at the box office. Taking note of the two leads, Meyer later said with a sigh, "Jean Simmons and Robert Mitchum. Two stars Howard lusted for and never got into his bed."

Robert recalled his last meeting with Howard. It occurred some time in the late 60s, although the actor was uncertain of the exact year. In Las Vegas to gamble and see some shows at Howard's Desert Inn, Robert was tapped on the shoulder by one of Howard's white-gloved Mormon guards. The attendant told Robert that Howard was in residence on the top floor of the Desert Inn and would like to see him. Robert readily agreed to the unexpected meeting.

Taking a private elevator up, Robert was ushered immediately into Howard's closely guarded suite. When Howard came into the living room of his suite, Robert was shocked at the appearance of his former boss. "He looked real emaciated and at least twenty-five years older than he actually was."

"What's up, Mr. Phantom?" Robert asked. "Ready to do another picture together? Ava and Jane are still around. This time Jane might actually wear the bra you designed for her."

Robert claimed he was just blabbering to fill in the void since Howard didn't say anything but kept looking at him very intently. "I got this strange feeling that he didn't exactly know who I was, but my face must have looked familiar. I know I'd changed but I still looked a bit like my old self."

Without greeting Robert, Howard finally spoke.

"I would have recognized that high-pitched voice anywhere. But it was weaker and much more frail than it had been. I feared Mr. Phantom was suffering some illness."

"Would you excuse me?" Howard finally said to Robert. "I've got to make an urgent phone call."

Robert remembered that Howard then disappeared into the bedroom. "I waited in the living room for over an hour for Howard to return, but he never came back. A guard tapped me on the shoulder and requested that I leave the suite. Maybe Howard wanted to see my ugly mug for one final time. I never saw him again."

Robert confessed that years later, he was watching a TV show broadcast by NBC when a bulletin came across the screen, announcing that Howard Hughes had died on a plane flying him back to Houston from somewhere in Mexico. "I cried," Robert said. "Bawled like a baby, and I'm not known for crying. It was a rough road Mr. Phantom and I traveled. We each had our demons. But there was some sort of love there that each of us had for the other. That love never really got acted upon, but it was there anyway. What the hell! I'll soon be dying myself."

Actually Robert would go on living until July 1, 1997. He would finally succumb to the cancer eating away at his body. The disease had long ago destroyed his good looks and macho charm.

***

Los Angeles, 1948/1952

Raised as a strict Mormon in Glendale, California, Terry Moore—born Helen Luella Koford—would, by the 1950s, find herself locked into a battle with Marilyn Monroe as to who was the sexiest Hollywood star. In that bout, Marilyn won the supernova crown, but Terry's sexiness endured. In 1984, at the age of fifty-five, she became the oldest woman in history to pose nude for *Playboy.*

One *Celebrity* magazine columnist described Moore as having "a schoolgirl face mounted on an atomic chassis." Such publicity inevitably attracted Howard's attention. "He was always a sucker for some gal with big tits and a schoolgirl face," Johnny Meyer said.

It wasn't Meyer who brought Howard together with Terry but another Johnny, his agent friend, Maschio. At the time, Terry was dating the handsome juvenile actor, Jerome Courtland (nicknamed "Cojo"). If Courtland is remembered at all today, it's for giving Shirley Temple her first screen kiss in *Kiss and Tell*, released in 1945.

In Meyer's view, "Howard set out to recapture his already lost youth when he launched his seduction scheme for Terry Moore, whom he always called by her original name of Helen. Throughout their entire relationship, he would have to maintain a delicate balance between Jean Peters and Terry and many others—both male and female."

Her critics called Terry "the perpetual starlet," but all that Howard could see was that the young star of Swedish ancestry "was beautifully stacked." Meyer later said, "Howard went for King Kong's love interest," a reference to Fay Wray, "why not a gorilla's?" In 1949 Terry starred in "the gorilla movie," *Mighty Joe Young.*

Like Faith Domergue, Terry was only fifteen years old when she caught Howard's interest based on a photograph of her in a bathing suit that had appeared in *Look* magazine. But before he could sign her for RKO, she'd been offered a contract at Columbia.

Lecherous Harry Cohn signed her to play opposite Glenn Ford in a film called *The Return of October*. Terry played an innocent, naïve girl who thought that her uncle had come back as a horse. Howard owned a copy of the film and watched it often.

According to Meyer, Howard became obsessed with Terry and ordered her stalked both day and night, especially during her dates with Cojo. Since Meyer didn't know this emerging starlet, Howard ordered his agent friend, Johnny Maschio, to show up at virtually every gathering where Terry went, especially if Cojo were her escort. Cojo towered six feet, five inches—taller even than Howard himself—so he was hard to miss.

Terry Moore

Invited for drinks with Maschio at the Beverly Wilshire Hotel, presumably to discuss business pertaining to her career, Terry finally met "a tall, slender man sitting alone against the wall" of the hotel's dining room. Maschio summoned the strange man over and introduced him first to Terry and then to Cojo as Howard Hughes. Maschio presented Terry as "Terrible Terry, the terror of Columbia." She found Howard's eyes haunting. He never took them off her, for the most part ignoring Cojo. In her view, Howard was "utterly repulsive."

A budding pilot, Cojo had avidly followed Howard's career. Even though Terry objected, Cojo accepted an invitation for the both of them to fly with Howard the next day to Palm Springs. In her memoirs, Terry remembered that Howard had practically undressed her with his eyes, and she "felt like I wanted to take a bath and rub myself with disinfectant."

Terry and Cojo flew on several flights with Howard before the aviator came up with a scheme. Devising yet another airborne jaunt for the three of them, he called Cojo and told the actor to meet him at the Glendale Airport. He then called Terry, informing her that the flight would depart from the airport at Burbank.

At the Burbank airport, pretending that Cojo had stood them up, Howard flew Terry to Palm Springs and took her to a party at the desert vacation retreat of Darryl F. Zanuck. Beside his pool, the studio chief appeared in a tight-fitting bikini that deliberately revealed the outlines of his proudest achievement: his large penis. Clifton Webb was also there, hot in pursuit of Louis Jourdan, hailed at the time "as the world's handsomest man."

The French actor, also in a bikini, appeared to be extremely well hung.

Fleeing the party with Howard, Terry ended her evening with Howard at the Doll House Restaurant. A handsome young actor, Dale Robertson, came up to Howard and requested permission to "dance with your daughter." Howard was furious, ordering Robertson to "beat it!"

Terry's romance with Howard began as he stalked her, following her on a publicity tour for *The Return of October*, which took her to twenty-six cities. Sometimes he would just show up at an airport, perhaps in Indianapolis, and smile smugly at her from a distance, although not coming over to speak to her. He approached her unexpectedly, showing up in resort clothing in the chilling Arctic blasts of a Buffalo, New York, winter.

Finally, Howard wore her down, filling her house with fresh flowers day after day. She invited him to a family dinner to meet her parents, Mr. and Mrs. Koford. Terry's mother, Luella, was called "Mama Blue." She was known for cooking with garlic and onions, and Howard was known for dropping women from his stable if they even walked past an onion, much less consumed a clove of garlic. "It oozes out of their skin for months," he once told Meyer.

Howard never bonded with Terry's father, Mr. Koford, but found an ally in Mama Blue in spite of her cooking.

Eventually he started dating Terry, sometimes renting an entire restaurant just for the two of them. For entertainment, he hired out-of-work musicians who otherwise played for the studios.

Terry later admitted that it was a mere kiss on the hand from Howard that led to her becoming sexually aroused for the first time in her young life. Cojo had already faded into the background—their relationship had never gone beyond the heavy kissing stage. Like a teenage girl with a schoolgirl crush, Terry came to realize that she was "hopelessly in love" with a man old enough to be her father.

Right at the beginning of their relationship, Terry faced two jolting truths about Howard. Cojo cited a long list of stars and starlets with whom Howard was supposed to be romantically involved. When she accidentally ran into Cojo one day in Hollywood, and Howard knew all about it within an hour, she knew that he was having her tailed. That would begin a pattern of private detectives stalking her day and night, even boarding the same plane carrying her to various destinations around the world, including Istanbul.

In the late summer of 1949, Howard entered into the first of his "marriages" to Terry. It was "under the stars" on top of Mulholland Drive where he'd taken other stars, including Jean Peters, to "marry" them as well.

Howard took Terry by the hand and knelt down with her to be married in the eyes of God. They exchanged vows, and he slipped an owl-shaped ring on her finger, studded with sapphires, rubies, and diamonds. Later that night when he tried to take her to the Beverly Hills Hotel—"a woman's place is in bed with her husband"—she refused, and said that wouldn't happen until they were legally married in a ceremony endorsed by the state. "It's Mormon law, too," she told him.

Instead of a night of bliss and the relinquishment of her virginity, Howard had to drive her back to Glendale where she insisted he sleep on the sofa in her parents' living room so she could keep an eye on him.

Their so-called real marriage took place right before Thanksgiving in 1949. Flying her to San Diego, Howard boarded the yacht, *Hilda*, with her. The captain was Carl Flynn, who had previously commanded Howard's yacht, the *Southern Cross*, before he sold it.

Privately he ordered Captain Flynn to take them beyond the five mile limit where another marriage ceremony between Terry and Howard took place. Like the first one, this ceremony wasn't legal either. The "wedding" was followed by the opening of two dozen bottles of French champagne, which the crew and party consumed while surrounded by bushels of white gardenias which had been brought aboard.

Flynn himself performed the ceremony, which was followed by a wedding banquet of hot dogs flown in from Coney Island.

Around Terry's beautiful neck, Howard placed a string of valuable pearls, claiming that they had belonged to his mother. Actually Johnny Meyer had purchased them at Cartier's.

That night, in bed aboard the yacht, Howard claimed his prize.

Before dawn, Terry was a virgin no more.

***

The very day after his "marriage at sea," Howard once again proposed marriage to Jean Peters. On the same afternoon, he called director Jules Furthman, once again urging him to get starlet Janet Leigh to marry him.

He also decided that he wanted Joan Fontaine after his failed attempt to win her years before. Hoping to entrap her at RKO, he offered her husband, producer William Dozier, the position of production chief at RKO if he'd agree to sign Joan to an exclusive contract with RKO. Recognizing what Howard had in mind, Dozier refused, although he later became head of production at RKO anyway, winning the job in spite of Howard.

When not wooing these stars, Howard was flying to San Francisco for rendezvous with a handsome young stockbroker by day, dancer by night. He was William Stoffler, once described as "more beautiful than Tyrone Power, more dashing than Errol Flynn." Stoffler was also married to a very suspicious wife, Helen. Unknown to her, Stoffler tossed his business suit for the day in the closet and donned drag to appear as a dancer at the transvestite club, Finocchio's. This was the same club where Howard had once taken Ava Gardner and where he had met Pussy-Katt, with whom he'd had a torrid affair following an operation that had removed her male genitals.

Stoffler's wife followed her husband one night, thinking that he was seeing another woman. When she learned what he was really up to, she filed for divorce. In the following weeks, she hired a private investigator who had learned that Stoffler had a male lover and "patron," who turned out to be Howard himself. She planned to name Howard in her divorce suit.

When Greg Bautzer in Hollywood learned of that, he flew at once to San Francisco where he settled fifteen-thousand dollars on Helen, getting her to change her charge against her husband to "mental cruelty." Greg also met with the young man, learning that Howard had sodomized him on several occasions while he was still in heavy woman's makeup.

To prevent Stoffler from selling his story to a magazine, Greg settled fifty thousand dollars on the handsome young man, which bought his silence. After that, fearing a possible involvement in scandal, Howard abruptly dropped Stoffler, returning to Jean Peters and Terry Moore, among others.

"That urge for a man kept cropping up from time to time," Johnny Meyer claimed. "But Henry Willson knew far more about those dalliances that I did. I never liked to arrange boys for Howard or anyone else, and that included Chaplin and Errol Flynn. I disapproved of all this gay stuff, but did what I was called upon to do—it was just part of my job description."

***

Terry lived for a time in a bungalow with Howard at the Beverly Hills Hotel. It was here that she learned from Mama Blue, who'd heard it from a close friend, that Howard might be taking heavy drugs. Mama Blue instructed her daughter to check Howard's arms for any signs of needle marks.

Terry grew restless that Howard wouldn't let her announce their marriage to the world, claiming it would harm both of their careers. She understood why being single would make her "available" in the eyes of thousands of her male fans but she didn't understand what harm marriage would do to his career.

She was also hearing rumors almost daily about Howard's involvement with other women, even reading items in gossip columns. To clear her mind, she moved back to her parents' home to Glendale to try to make sense of her life. Meyer claimed that he felt Howard "was driving Terry crazy with his refusal to really commit to her. It was a sham of a marriage right from the beginning."

Terry inadvertently provoked Howard's seething jealousy when she was sent on location to Silver Springs, Florida, to appear in *The Barefoot Mailman*, which brought her together again with Cojo on an alligator farm. Jerome Courtland ("Cojo") had been cast as her co-star.

While shooting the picture and swimming in a river with real 'gators—their snouts wired shut—Terry became fascinated by these reptiles.

Ross Allen, owner of the farm and a wildlife expert, offered her a copy of his book, *The Sex Life of the Alligator*, and taught her to mimic the wheezing low roar that alligators make during their mating rituals. She perfected this call of the wild, and in time, in a spirit of fun, she taught Howard how to imitate one of the ferocious male reptiles at mating season. During her tenure in Florida, Howard telephoned her at least once a night, sometimes talking for two or three hours. Within a few weeks, sounding off their prolonged dialogues with reciprocated "alligator love calls" became part of their nightly ritual.

Back in Hollywood, Terry moved back into a separate bungalow at the Beverly Hills Hotel, close to Howard's own bungalow. One evening Howard called her at her bungalow, telling her that he might be tied up for a week in Culver City, working on the Hercules. "We have a glue problem," he said.

After signing off with her sweetest ever alligator love call, she dropped the cradle of the phone. When she picked it up, she heard the operator say, "Are you through, Las Vegas?" She knew then that Howard wasn't in Culver City but was calling her from Nevada.

Accompanied by her parents, supposedly for moral support, Terry flew to Las Vegas, where she learned that Howard was staying at the Desert Inn. Informed that he was due for lunch, she asked to be seated at a table in the corner as a means of spying on him, hiding behind a newspaper.

She remembered Howard coming into the dining room as if he owned the place. In a twist of irony, he would own the Desert Inn by March 31 of 1967, acquiring control as the first step of the building up of his Nevada empire.

Terry spotted Howard joining a table where RKO's casting director, Walter Kane, was entertaining an eighteen-year-old starlet, whose name is not known, and her mother. Terry defined Howard's latest attraction as "a tall string bean with an unhealthy pallor." Rising to her feet, Terry crashed Howard's table, much to his embarrassment. She was all charm and grace as she chatted with her rival. After a grandstand performance, Terry departed, not to see Howard for a very long time in spite of his repeated calls and the constant arrival of long-stemmed roses and white gardenias with their intoxicating smell.

For Terry, her love affair with her "husband," whom she'd called "the most exciting man of the century," had come to an end.

***

The gifted athlete Glenn Davis was the most famous football player in America, having won the Heisman Trophy in 1946. Unlike "Granddaddy Hughes," his name for Howard, Glenn was handsome and athletic, a very virile young man and a highly visible member of the Los Angeles Rams.

Terry had known Glenn previous to her involvement with Howard, and had actually double-dated with him when he was escorting

Elizabeth Taylor

739

Elizabeth Taylor.

Beginning with a date where he escorted her to the Rose Bowl, Glenn pursued her like he played a football game—that is, with a determination to win. One date led to another, and soon Terry and Glenn were linked together as an item in the gossip columns, much to Howard's displeasure.

He called Terry frequently and urged her to return to him, reminding her of their marriage at sea. Constant dating, however, led to her acceptance of a proposal of marriage from Glenn. Terry later felt that she "just stumbled" into the engagement and subsequent marriage.

Despite repeated calls from Howard, she refused to see him, calling him "a cheat, a liar, and an adulterer."

Finally, she agreed to meet him one final time at his bungalow at the Beverly Hills Hotel. Once there, she expected him to reclaim her. Instead he presented her with tubes of vaginal jelly. He warned her that she could have her fling but cautioned against getting pregnant. "If you do," he told her, "your nipples will get all brown instead of pretty pink and you'll get stretch marks, and then I could never take you back."

In her memoirs, Terry wrote: "Dr. Hughes had gone out and bought dozens of diaphragms in all sizes and spent an entire afternoon fitting me."

Leaving the Beverly Hills Hotel in tears, Terry walked down the aisle of the Mormon Church in Glendale on February 9, 1951 to become the bride of a football hero who was hailed as "the greatest catch in America." Even at the last minute, she expected to hear Howard's familiar plane overhead, as he circled the chapel, landing on the lawn, and rushed into the church to object to the marriage. That fantasy never came true, and Terry found herself a reluctant bride.

If Terry had legally been married to Howard, then her subsequent marriage to Glenn would have made her a bigamist.

After the ceremony, she headed off on a honeymoon to Acapulco with two dozen diaphragms, each of them previously fitted onto her by "Dr. Hughes."

After the honeymoon in Acapulco, Terry was dumped in Lubbock, Texas, where the movie star ended up scrubbing and baking. Their apartment had a Murphy bed and a Pullman kitchen.

Wanting her again, Howard called her and urged her to visit him at his office at Goldwyn Studios, telling her that he'd acquired the rights to a picture, *High Heels*, and that he wanted her to star in it. Glenn urged her to go because he'd come up with some get-rich-scheme in the oil business and needed Howard's influence with Toolco to pitch his idea.

Terry flew back to Hollywood and appeared in a dress that Howard had designed himself. The sheer black matte jersey was so thin and revealing it might have been created by Howard for Jean Harlow. Terry remembered it as if "I were wearing nothing but a veil of water after a skinny dip."

Meeting Howard for the first time after her marriage, he almost immediately determined that her nipples were still pink. Stripping her down, he made love to her on top of his desk. Their romance was quickly rekindled, something that Glenn soon discovered when Terry called him in Lubbock, asking for a divorce.

Glenn boarded the next plane to Los Angeles, arriving at the home of Terry's parents in Glendale. The next day Howard also arrived at the Kuford home for a showdown, man-to-man talk with Glenn. Almost from the beginning, the confrontation turned into a disaster, with Glenn pleading with Howard not to take "my wife from me—she belongs back in Lubbock with her real husband."

From that point on, accounts differ. In her memoirs, Terry claimed that Glenn appeared as if he were about to shake Howard's hand, but didn't. The athlete took Howard's hand and shoved it backward, causing Howard to fall over an ottoman. Mama Blue, it was alleged, threw herself over Howard's body to prevent Glenn from kicking him once he'd fallen.

Jeff Couinard, the chief of Howard's spy network, recalled it quite differently. He claimed that the husky footballer "beat the shit out of Howard." In the aftermath, according to Chouinard, Howard was flown in a private plane to a hospital in San Francisco as a means of avoiding reporters in Los Angeles. Once there, it was discovered that each of the ribs injured in the Beverly Hills plane crash had been rebroken. His left eye was puffy and swollen shut, and his much-battered chin was shattered for the third time in his life.

From his hospital bed in San Francisco, Howard called Louella Parson and Hedda Hopper, urging them to keep the story out of their columns. Reporters for *Confidential* magazine, however, learned of the incident, and their subsequent revelations were widely read and gossiped about throughout America.

As a result, Jean Peters learned that Howard was involved with Terry Moore once again. How Howard talked his way out of that dilemma with her isn't known.

Dietrich later recalled encountering Howard when he looked like he'd been severely beaten.

Even though he claimed he had at last learned "what type of woman I married," Glenn still stalled the divorce, demanding money. Terry borrowed seven thousand dollars from Howard, which he insisted that she pay back, and sent that to Glenn. He took the money but continued to delay the divorce.

Howard and Terry went into hiding. Members of the Los Angeles Rams were looking all over Los Angeles for Howard, planning "to beat the bastard to pulp."

In hiding himself, Howard sent Terry, along with her close friend and stand-in, Mary Jane Carey, for a discreet, unpublicized holiday at a dude ranch in Nevada.

It was during this period that Howard took Terry on a nighttime ride aboard a TWA Constellation. At one point, overcome with passion, he put the Connie on automatic pilot and carried Terry to the rear of the plane where he seduced her on a pile of mink coats.

"It was Terry's first airborne fuck," Meyer later recalled.

After a stay of several weeks at the ranch, Howard flew Terry and Mary Jane back to Los Angeles where he installed them in a house that felt like a mausoleum to Terry. Howard said it was "the house where Judy Garland slit her throat."

On some evenings in Garland's old mansion, Howard entertained Terry by showing her copies of the "blue movies" that Joan Crawford had made in New York in the mid-1920s.

At one point Howard came up with a scheme to get Glenn to grant the divorce and call off the hunt from the Los Angeles Rams. He had Cubby Broccoli fly to Utah with a script in hand. Glenn was in training there with the Rams. The script had been gathering dust on RKO shelves for years, but Cubby claimed that it was a hot property, eagerly sought by both Tony Curtis and Marlon Brando.

He pitched a contract to Glenn, claiming that Howard wanted to make him a movie star. "But you've got to grant Terry a divorce because Howard wants to turn you into a sex symbol. All the girls in America will dream of going to bed with you every night, but only if you're a bachelor—not a married man."

Surprisingly, Glenn fell for this, signing the divorce papers. To his dismay, neither the movie contract—nor the picture—ever came through. He'd been tricked.

Terry had also been tricked, learning later that Howard had sold the script for *High Heels*. He had merely used it as bait to get her back to Hollywood.

With no help from Howard, Hal Wallis wanted Terry for a key role in *Come Back, Little Sheba*, starring Burt Lancaster and veteran actress Shirley Booth. Marilyn Monroe had been tested for the role and was rejected. The part of the sexy teenager who drives Lancaster to distraction eventually won for Terry an Oscar nomination as Best Supporting Actress of 1952.

Howard assured her she'd win—she didn't—but wouldn't escort her to the awards presentation because of the publicity it would generate for their relationship.

After her divorce from Glenn was finalized, Terry discovered that Howard had been pursuing both Elizabeth Taylor and Jean Simmons at the same time. On learning that, Terry once again moved her things out of the Beverly Hills Hotel and went back to Glendale with her parents. To win her back, Howard, in the presence of Noah Dietrich, handed Terry a million-dollar check. She tore it up and threw it into Howard's face. She stormed out of his office.

Later she learned that Howard had tried to buy both Elizabeth Taylor and Ava Gardner with million-dollar checks and had in both cases been refused.

Terry began dating again. First, singer Johnnie Ray, even though he was gay. Then, Robert Evans, who would in time become head of Paramount. But her favorite was Nicky Hilton, son of hotel magnate Conrad Hilton. Nicky had survived a disastrous marriage to Elizabeth Taylor. Terry liked him the best, finding him "tall and gorgeous." He was "the kindest, sweetest human being I've ever known," she later wrote in her memoirs, leaving out the fact that he was a mean drunk.

When news of Terry's romance with Nicky Hilton reached Howard, he was furious. Both Nicky and Howard competed for the reputation of Leading Playboy of the Western World. Both had looks, money, and charm. And both of them had big dicks. But Nicky had something Howard no longer possessed: "the sweet bird of youth."

"I never knew what was happening back then," Meyer said. "First, I heard the boss man was back with Terry. Then they were apart. Then they were back with each other living together. It was important that I keep everything straight in my head because I often had to babysit with Jean Peters while Howard was pursuing Terry and so many others. I continued to keep Howard in women, and Henry Willson continued to supply the boys, even offering Howard Rock Hudson and Troy Donahue."

When he wasn't with Terry, Howard kept her under constant surveillance. He was particularly enraged when he discovered that in addition to her ongoing dates with Nicky Hilton, she was also seeing his own attorney, Greg Bautzer, as well. "I don't know why Howard didn't fire Greg for this betrayal, but he didn't," Meyer claimed. "I think Greg had too much shit on Howard to ever get fired. There had been too many cover-ups, and Greg knew where all the bodies were buried."

When an offer came in from director Elia Kazan for Terry to fly to Germany to film *Man on a Tightrope*, starring Fredric March and an aging Adolphe Menjou, Terry was bubbling with enthusiasm. Howard didn't want her to go, but she told him she wasn't going to miss out on an opportunity to "work with Gadge," Kazan's nickname.

Somehow Terry had managed to convince the director that she was a "female Brando." At the time Kazan was celebrated for having directed Brando in *A Streetcar Named Desire*.

On her flight to Germany, Terry did not know at the time that there was another passenger on board traveling with her: Howard's child.

***

Munich, 1952

When she arrived in Munich to claim her baggage, Terry was greeted with bad news. Her pet boa constrictor, Midnight, which Elia Kazan had requested as a prop within the film he was making with Terry in Munich, had died en route, presumably because of the sudden changes in climate and altitude between California and Germany. Terry had fallen in love with this large boa constrictor during the filming of *The Barefoot Mailman* in Silver Springs, Florida, and considered it a treasured pet.

More bad news was on the way.

Back on the West Coast, Howard had profited from Terry's absence to launch an abortive affair with the Paris-born star ballerina, Zizi Jeanmaire, a former figurehead at Les Ballets des Champs Elysées.

Her phenomenal success in *Carmen* led to a brief Hollywood career. Her musicals were choreographed by Roland Petit, who became her husband in 1954. Her long legs, brunette locks, and athletic body captivated Howard. Since the star did not speak English at the time, Howard asked his chef, Robert Poussin, to serve as an interpreter.

The so-called Hughes/Jeanmaire affair died a short death. In testimony he gave in 1977 during the battle over Howard's estate, Poussin stated for the courts: "For him [a reference to Howard], sex was mostly to dance with his head on a star's shoulder. He tried to have sex with Zizi Jeanmaire. She told me he was impotent with her."

In Munich, Terry was deep into filming *Tightrope*, a psychological thriller.

Terry and her mother lodged in the Hotel Vier Jahreszeiten, which was only half functioning, as much of it had been bombed during the war. Next door resided Mrs. Herman Göring. Terry noted that the staff treated her like she was the Queen of Germany.

Filming went relatively well, with Fredric March making a grab for Terry's breasts, as he did with many of his female stars.

As Munich deepened into September of 1952, Howard's alligator love call was transmitted nightly over the transatlantic wires.

Although she was the victim of frequent dizzy spells, Terry insisted on doing her own stunts. She was repeatedly thrown from her pony in the circus act she was performing.

Her condition worsened as the crew moved from Munich to a former bordello in the Bavarian Alps close to the Austrian border. She wanted to keep her illness secret, fearing she might be replaced in the picture if word about it got out.

She noticed a weight gain of ten pounds as she went from a 32C to a 36D cup. From his location on America's West Coast, Howard blamed it on German potatoes and told her to cut them out lest she turn into a "plump Fräulein."

One late afternoon, after several days spent filming in the Alps, Terry

Zizi Jeanmaire

traveled back to downtown Munich. She had taken a bad spill from her pony earlier in the day. Back at the Hotel Vier Jahreszeiten, she went to take a long, hot bath. She was gone for so long that Mama Blue went in to check on her. Seeing her daughter, she let out a blood-curdling scream heard down the corridor. Terry was unconscious, lying in a tub of blood-red water.

As Terry was rushed to the hospital, her water broke. Up to that point, she didn't know she was pregnant. Mama Blue had gotten through on the phone to Howard, who was horrified at the news, dispatching Dr. Verne Mason on the next plane to Munich.

By the time Howard's doctor arrived, Terry still hadn't given birth. Instead of comforting her, Dr. Mason told her that "Mr. Hughes doesn't want you to have the child. You'll have to abort it."

Terry became hysterical, refusing the abortion. After that, she seemed to have fainted. The next thing she remembered was the cry of a baby and then oblivion.

When she finally woke up, after a coma-like sleep, she didn't know how many hours she had passed out. Dr. Mason was by her side, informing her that she'd given birth to a little baby girl—no larger than the size of a small rat. Since it was born prematurely, the doctor told her that her child with Howard lived for only twelve hours, dying of septicemia. "It was born too soon to live," Dr. Mason told her.

Terry screamed for Howard. She was furious that he hadn't flown to Munich to be with her. When he called that night, he warned her that news of this scandal would destroy her career if she didn't quiet down.

"It was your child, too," she said to him, hanging up before she'd done her alligator love call.

The next few days passed as if in a coma for her.

Conspiring with Darryl F. Zanuck, Terry's boss, the matter of the dead baby did not become known to the press.

Later, Terry became suspicious that the baby hadn't died, and confronted Howard with her suspicions that their lovechild was still alive. When she revealed her fears, he told her, "I don't want to discuss it."

The rumor still persists that somewhere walking the globe is a woman who bears an amazing resemblance to both her father, Howard Hughes, and her mother, Terry Moore.

***

Los Angeles/Las Vegas, 1954

The tortured, troubled relationship between Howard and Terry continued. She was seen at Ciro's with gay actor Laurence Harvey, and attending the opening of *Call Me Madam* with Nicky Hilton. The hotel heir seemed to be a special favorite. She was rumored to be planning to marry handsome young actor,

Robert Wagner, after he broke off with the much older Barbara Stanwyck, but by Christmas of 1953 Terry and Robert had called it quits.

In 1954 she was escorted to premieres by the likes of Rock Hudson and James Dean. She opened as the headliner in a show at the Flamingo Hotel in Las Vegas, but was billed $15,000 by Howard for her costumes, which was her entire profit on the live show.

After he cashed that check—she didn't think he would—she announced to her parents, "It's all over between Howard and me."

He had promised to be with her during her Vegas performance, but he'd stashed both Ava Gardner and Jean Peters at Lake Tahoe, so he spent many evenings there instead. Both women were waiting out their mandatory residencies, required as a precondition to divorces in Nevada: Ava from Frank Sinatra ("the love of my life"), and Jean Peters from Stuart Warren Cramer III, who, ironically, would eventually wed Terry in June of 1959.

While Howard chased Ava from Nevada to Florida, from Mexico to Cuba, Terry fell ill and was admitted to the Good Samaritan Hospital in Los Angeles. Dr. Verne Mason was once again sent to examine her. Howard also came to her bedside, agreeing to pay all of her medical expenses and to arrange the best medical care. As she lay in her hospital bed, he promised her "a real marriage this time, one that won't be in legal dispute."

She didn't learn that she was pregnant until she'd checked out of the hospital. Howard instructed her to fly from Los Angeles to Las Vegas, where he would meet her, and then fly with her to Tucson for the wedding.

But before leaving Los Angeles, she accepted a final date with Nicky Hilton for a meal at Trader Vic's in the Beverly Hilton, which was owned by his father. Over dinner, she broke the sad news to the hotel heir that she planned to marry Howard. The rich playboy told her that he had thought that the two of them would eventually marry instead. But even though Terry admitted that she loved Nicky dearly, she had to let him go to marry Howard…again.

The next day, with her parents, she flew to Las Vegas, where Howard greeted them at the airport which was caught up in a dust storm. Even so, Howard attempted to fly them to Arizona but the control tower warned that all flights had been grounded. Driving them back into town, he checked them into the Desert Inn.

At dinner that night, an angry Howard confronted Terry, informing her that Nicky Hilton had arrived in Las Vegas and was making threats against his life.

Howard stormed off toward the casino. When Terry went looking for him, she stumbled not upon Howard but a drunken Nicky. "I'll kill him!" Nicky called out to her. "Time for the bastard to die. He's ruined enough lives!"

He then delivered a bombshell. On the plane to Las Vegas, he'd sat next to the mother of actress Debra Paget. Unaware of Howard's involvement with Terry, the mother of the actress informed him rather proudly that her daughter was in Vegas and that Howard had proposed marriage to her.

746

The Colorado-born Debra, another of Howard's brunette beauties, had been used by 20th-Century Fox as an "all-purpose ingénue." Ironically, Debra had been cast as the wife of Louis Jourdan in *Anne of the Indies*, where she is kidnapped by none other than Jean Peters, playing a lady pirate.

That wasn't all. Nicky told Terry that Howard also had actress Mitzi Gaynor stashed away in an accommodation at the nearby Sands Hotel, and that he had learned that he was flying in Jean Peters the following evening.

Terry quoted Nicky as shouting: "I'll kill the son of a bitch, I swear, I'm gonna kill him!"

She informed her jilted lover that that pleasure belonged to her. At that point her parents entered the casino.

Howard also entered the room shortly

Mitzi Gaynor

thereafter and attempted to escort Terry out of the casino, telling her that the storm had subsided and planes were taking off again.

He grabbed her and tried to force her from the room until he was confronted by a drunken Nicky, who revealed that he knew about Debra and Mitzi.

Howard tried to talk him out of his anger, noting that he was drunk and should go to his suite to sober up. Nicky struck him in the face. Not fighting back, Howard shielded himself from the blows. Once again, Mama Blue hurled herself in front of Howard to protect him, as Terry's father attempted to restrain Nicky and cool his violent rage.

Terry left the casino on Nicky's arm. Howard called out to her, "if you leave with that drunken bastard, you'll never work in Hollywood ever again. I'll see to that!"

On the plane back to Los Angeles, Terry told Nicky that she was pregnant with Howard's child. He offered to marry her and give the baby the Hilton name.

Soon after her return to Hollywood, she was rehearsing for *Daddy Long Legs* with Fred Astaire and Leslie Caron. She suddenly came down with cramps. She was rushed to the hospital where Dr. Mason came to her rescue once again. The doctor had informed Howard of her condition, and he too flew in from Vegas, leaving his paramours, to join her.

Fearing that her condition was life-threatening, Dr. Mason advised that the child be aborted. Later, she learned that the aborted fetus was malformed. "The baby might have saved our marriage," Terry later said. "But it was not to be."

Two weeks later, Terry encountered Mitzi Gaynor, a singer dancer from Chicago who'd made *The I Don't Care Girl*, a bio picture of entertainer Eva Tanguay. Even then, Fox doubted if its dream for Mitzi would ever come true—that is, her transformation into a updated, 1950s version of Betty Grable.

Mitzi confessed to Terry that she thought, "I was Howard's only girl until I read about it in the newspapers." She also told Terry that Howard had told her that if she ever encountered Terry that, "You'd beat me up."

Over lunch the next day, the two stars talked about Howard, Mitzi promising that she never planned to see her errant lover ever again.

"If only I could say that with some conviction," Terry said with a certain sadness in her voice. "If only I could say that."

***

Los Angeles/Houston, 1970-1984

It was the night of March 7, 1970, when the phone rang at Terry's home. It was three o'clock in the morning. In her memoirs, Terry reports on the dialogue:

Terry:	Hello.
Howard:	Hello, Helen.
Terry:	What? Who?
Howard:	Hello, Helen.
Terry:	Howard?
Howard:	Yes, baby it's me.
Terry:	Howard, Howard, is it really you?"

The phone went dead.

That was the last she ever heard of him, in spite of her attempts to get in touch with him, including a later episode at the Inn on the Park in London.

Still looking lovely after the passage of many years, Terry became embroiled in 1977 in the long and drawn-out legal battle waged over Howard's estate. The Internal Revenue Service had computed it to be worth $460 million, of which $274,714,977 were due in Federal estate taxes.

Terry never pressed her claim of marriage in the Supreme Court of Texas. But once the heirs to the Hughes estate were legally established, they decided in essence to buy off the 54-year-old star in 1984.

The actual amount of the settlement was never announced. The actress later told the press that it was "not more than eight figures." Reports claimed it was as low as $250,000 but may have been as much as $350,000.

***

748

Although he'd never seen one of her movies, Howard had been obsessed with Elizabeth Taylor ever since he'd noticed her on the cover of *Time* in 1949. He was forty-five years old at the time, Elizabeth a tender seventeen. When a beautiful actress was very young, Howard first wooed the parents before going after the real prey.

Elizabeth's father, Francis Taylor, owned an exclusive art gallery in Beverly Hills. Looking like an unshaven bum, Howard drove to the gallery and introduced himself to Francis. Before he left an hour later, Howard had purchased eight very costly and overpriced paintings which he lost before six o'clock that evening. After leaving the gallery, he'd driven to the apartment of some unknown starlet, spending two hours with her. He'd left his Chevy parked in front of the apartment building with the car windows open. By the time he emerged from her home, all the paintings had been stolen. He didn't seem to care, as he hadn't wanted the art anyway.

Before leaving the gallery, he'd invited Francis to fly with him that weekend to a vacation retreat in Reno. His wife, Sara, was also invited. As an afterthought, Howard added, "Oh, don't forget to bring your daughter."

Before flying to Reno, Howard called Louis B. Mayer and attempted to purchase Elizabeth's contract. In the waning months of his powerful rule over the studio, the gruff Mayer informed him that the contract wasn't for sale. "You'll have to find another way to seduce her, Hughes," Mayer said before putting down the phone.

When Howard met Elizabeth at the airport, he was stunned by her beauty, he later reported to Johnny Meyer. "A real looker with tits," he told his pimp. "I wish I had some way of finding out if she's a virgin."

"Have Dr. Mason examine her," Meyer said.

"Don't be an ass!" Howard snapped at him. "What am I going to do? Call her up and say I've made an appointment for my doctor to examine your hymen to see if it's been pierced."

At the resort in Reno, Howard met privately with Sara and Francis, telling them that he was prepared to put up a dowry of one million dollars if they would let Elizabeth marry him. Always ambitious for the advancement of her daughter, Sara promised her cooperation. She didn't seem bothered by the difference in their ages. Francis, however, urged caution. "Elizabeth's a very independent girl. She'll have to make up her own mind. But I'd love to have an art patron like you in the family."

Goaded on by the encouragement of Sara, Howard approached Elizabeth later that afternoon. She was lying in a white bathing suit by the hotel pool. A fully dressed Howard came up to her. In the same type of cardboard box he'd carried gems for Ava Gardner, he brought a similar unprepossessing package to present to Elizabeth. Opening the box, he dazzled her with rubies, diamonds, and emeralds. He turned up the box and let the stones fall on her sexy stomach. "C'mon," he said. "I'm taking you to get married. I've had someone make the arrangements. We can be married tonight. The chapel's already reserved."

Astonished, she rejected both the stones and the proposal. Jumping up and scattering the stones on the pool tiles, she raced back to her bedroom.

That night over champagne and crêpes suzette, with Sara and Francis listening, Howard more formally proposed marriage. Saying nothing, Elizabeth excused herself and left the table, heading back to her bedroom.

The next day, Howard sent Meyer to apologize. "Howard gets carried away sometimes," Meyer told the star. "He didn't mean to insult you, certainly not rush you into marriage."

"Tell that fucking madman to stay away from me," she shouted at Meyer. "Your boss bores me, flaunting his money. For god's sake, he reminds me of Louis B. Mayer, and I have no intention of marrying that monster. Or your monster either!" She slammed the door in Meyer's face.

Nonetheless, Howard was persistent and continued to pursue her once he'd flown the Taylors back to Hollywood. At her home, Elizabeth called her friend, actor Roddy McDowall, with whom she'd starred in the 1943 *Lassie Come Home*. "I know what I want, and I don't want Howard Hughes. A man can hit on me if he wants, but when I'm not interested, the word is no. I don't give a Flying Fuck who they are."

In spite of her protestations, Elizabeth reluctantly agreed to go out with Howard on three more dates against her better judgment.

Years later, she recalled, "Hughes was such an out-and-out bore, I wouldn't have married him for all his money. The few times I went out with him, he stared into space and never answered any of my questions. That was because he was deaf and wouldn't wear a hearing aid. He smelled like he needed a bath. His pants were wrinkled and hung on him like that of a scarecrow. He wore dirty sneakers with no socks. His left toe stuck out of one of them."

To Howard's disappointment, Elizabeth married Nicky Hilton that same year (1949). By that time, Howard had spies trailing both the hotel heir and Elizabeth herself. The spies learned that after only two weeks of marriage, Nicky was cheating on his wife. Even though Elizabeth remained faithful to Nicky during their short marriage, Howard suspected otherwise. He later said, "Every man should have the opportunity of sleeping with Elizabeth Taylor. At the rate she's going, every man will."

Even before the widely predicted divorce became final, Howard began to woo Elizabeth again. But instead of showing up at her door, he tried to court her through subordinates. She accepted an invitation to fly to Palm Springs with the handsome, dashing attorney, Greg Bautzer, who worked for Howard.

Once installed in a villa there, Elizabeth prepared herself to go to dinner with Greg. When the doorbell rang, she opened it only to find Howard standing on the doorstep, looking his usual bedraggled self.

"I have something to show you," he said, insisting that she walk out to his old battered Chevy. "It's a big surprise." It is not known if Elizabeth had heard about "the big surprise" Howard had shown other starlets.

In the front seat, he held up a red bandana like the kind Aunt Jemima might wear. He opened it to reveal a queen's ransom in jewelry purchased at Tiffany and Cartier. She didn't know if it were the same cache of jewelry presented to her in Reno. "Come with me," he told her, "and this is all yours."

Racing back to the house, she slammed the door on Howard. Packing hurriedly, she fled Palm Springs and returned to Hollywood on her own. On the phone to Roddy again, she told him, "Who does Hughes think I am? One of his bimbo starlets at RKO?"

In a surprise move, Elizabeth agreed to attend a party hosted by Howard in her honor at the Beverly Hills Hotel where he was staying in a bungalow. He pointedly did not ask Jean Peters to the affair, even though she, too, was living in a nearby bungalow. Then, as part of some game he was playing, Howard did not show up himself.

His marriage to Gloria Vanderbilt long dissolved, Pat DeCicco was back in Los Angeles working for Howard again. He was assigned to be Elizabeth's escort at the party. Over champagne, Pat pitched his client, promising Elizabeth that if she would marry Howard, he'd make her the biggest star in Hollywood.

"I'm already on my way to becoming the biggest star in Hollywood, with no help from Hughes," she told Pat. "I prefer to do it on my own." Trying to shake Pat, she told him, "and you can tell Mr. Hughes that I'm flying to London to marry Michael Wilding."

The next day, Pat called on Elizabeth and presented evidence to her that her future husband was a bisexual. Among others, he'd carried on a wartime affair with the handsome London-born actor, Stewart Granger. She refused to look at the evidence and dismissed Pat.

The next day, Hedda Hopper came to call on Elizabeth. Unknown to the star, Hedda had been sent by Howard himself. She, too, told Elizabeth that the man she was about to marry was a homosexual. At least Pat had given Wilding the benefit of being bisexual—but not Hedda. She was a homophobe and deeply distressed that her own son, William Hopper, was also gay. Elizabeth turned a deaf ear to Hedda's pleadings.

On the plane to London to marry Wilding, Elizabeth was startled to find that the seat next to hers was occupied by Pat DeCicco. Howard had obviously arranged for that. All across the Atlantic, Pat pleaded with her not to marry the British actor. The year was 1952. As she cleared customs, she told Pat, "Tell Mr. Hughes he can dream on and present all the evidence he wants against Michael. I'm still going to marry him." As a parting word to Pat, she told him, "I'm sure there are a thousand stars in Hollywood who would jump at Mr. Hughes's offer. Tell your boss to chase after one of those pussycats."

In spite of such rejections, Howard still planned to seduce Elizabeth. "I'll

751

have to wait and play my hand again when the right time comes." He still spied on her during her marriage to Wilding, which lasted until 1957. He made attempts to get in touch with her after the divorce, as she'd become what he still liked to call "a wet deck." She consistently turned him down.

His spies informed him that she was dating showman Mike Todd, whom she married in 1957. When he died in a plane crash the following year, Howard planned to move in on her again after a decent interval had passed.

At the time of Todd's death, Howard swung into action, placing a TWA Constellation at Elizabeth's disposal to fly her to Todd's funeral at the Jewish Waldheim Cemetery in Zurich, Illinois, outside Chicago. Under heavy sedation of morphine and phenobarbitol, Elizabeth was helped aboard the plane, having accepted Howard's generous offer.

Before Howard could make a move toward Elizabeth, his spies brought some startling news. He was told that "the corpse hasn't even cooled yet, and Taylor's shacking up with singer Eddie Fisher." Fisher had been Todd's best friend and had flown with Elizabeth to comfort her in her grief. At the time he was married to Debbie Reynolds in what fan magazines called "a storybook romance."

"That fucking slut!" Howard shouted at Pat, angered at him for not securing Elizabeth's promise of a marriage. "As I figure it, she must be addicted to cut Jewish dick—first Mike Todd, now Eddie Fisher."

As headlines erupted over Elizabeth's scandalous affair and eventual marriage to Fisher, Howard finally gave up the chase. He would make no attempt to contact her in the future. As he told Pat DeCicco, "Future historians of Howard Hughes will record that only two big stars in Hollywood turned me down—namely Joan Crawford and Elizabeth Taylor."

***

Los Angeles/New York, 1950-1989

Even though he was in hot pursuit of Elizabeth Taylor, Howard also launched a campaign to seduce her "look-alike," Jean Simmons. Visitors to his office at 7000 Romaine Street noticed that he'd tacked up several pictures of Jean on his wall behind his desk.

At the time of Howard's growing interest in Jean, she was deep into a seven-year contract with British producer, J. Arthur Rank. Earlier in her career, she'd been called a "Vivien Leigh look-alike," and had actually played a harpist in Cleopatra's court in the 1945 film, *Caesar and Cleopatra*, which, coincidentally, had starred the real Vivien Leigh.

Jean shot to fame playing Ophelia in the screen version of *Hamlet*, with Laurence Olivier in the starring role. At the age of nineteen, she'd received a best supporting Oscar nomination for her performance in Shakespeare's most shameless tear-jerker. That landmark in her career landed her on the cover of *Life* magazine on October 9, 1950. Howard no doubt had stolen a copy of *Life* from some office, having long ago canceled his subscription.

Elizabeth Taylor had several men come between Howard and herself—namely, Nicky Hilton, Michael Wilding, Mike Todd, and Eddie Fisher. Jean

Stewart Granger and Jean Simmons

Simmons had but one man. Also London-born, like herself, he was the handsome, suave, and debonair actor, Stewart Granger, whose real name was James Stewart but that name was already taken. He would have been the ideal star to play James Bond in a tuxedo. Instead he ended up in costume romps and adventure films.

Fighting with British forces during World War II, he was severely wounded. Discharged, he was free to make British films until the end of the year and the post-war years thereafter. Most of these were florid melodramas or light comedies.

In 1949 he had co-starred with the beautiful Jean Simmons in *Adam and Evelyne*. The lovers arrived in Hollywood the following year, as Stewart was set to play the lead in MGM's big adventure film, *King Solomon's Mines*. The movie would go on to receive an Oscar nomination as best picture of the year.

Stewart, in New York City in 1989, revealed that no sooner had he arrived in Hollywood, than he began to receive phone calls from Cary Grant. "I don't know how else to describe these meetings I had with Cary other than a date. I knew he had a crush on me. His excuse was that he wanted 'to catch up on England,' but I knew otherwise. He took me to the Farmers' Market. He took me to the beach, always managing to come into the changing room as I was taking off my underwear. He asked me out for dinner. I had heard rumors that Cary and Howard Hughes were lovers, but I guess that didn't stop Cary from wanting to sample the latest piece of meat arriving from London. In fact, during the first months in Hollywood I was seeing more of Cary than my wife. She grew jealous, but I assured her that the relationship was platonic."

In spite of Cary's advances toward him, Stewart informed the actor that he wanted to wed Jean in a secret ceremony so the press wouldn't find out. Cary claimed that he knew just the man to arrange that. "Howard Hughes!" Cary told him. "I'm sure he'll help you two."

At long last Stewart and Jean got to meet the mysterious Howard Hughes. "A chauffeur arrived for us one day and drove us to an airfield where Cary welcomed us," Stewart said. "He took us over to meet Howard who looked rather unassuming, not like the richest man on the earth. His wardrobe must have cost him all of ten dollars."

Inviting them to fly away with him, Howard asked Stewart to join him in the front seat, with Jean and Cary in the rear. Howard flew them to the Grand

Canyon and installed them in a clifftop hotel overlooking the giant chasm. Howard and Cary occupied one suite, Stewart and Jean the adjoining suite, which was even larger.

At some point Stewart, who was suffering "from the runs," as he called it, had to go to the downstairs men's toilet at the lodge "to take care of urgent business." He entered a stall with a door that had a clear view of the room, thanks to gaps on either side of its swinging door.

While the actor was seated on the toilet, he saw Howard and Cary come in to take a leak. In his memoirs, *Sparks Fly Upward*, Stewart reported on the dialogue between the two friends:

Cary   Well, what do you think of her?
Howard   I'd sure like to get my teeth into that. He's a goddamned lucky
            son of a bitch, that Granger.

            There was a long silence.

Howard   Oh, shit, I've got my cock caught in my zipper.

Asked years later to elaborate on what happened next, which he left out of his memoirs, Stewart said that Howard turned sideways to face Cary. "I had a clear view of his big cock. Without being asked, Cary kneeled down in front of Hughes and took his cock in his hand and very lovingly freed it from the zipper, planting a kiss on the head of it."

"I don't care what latter day biographers have written about Hughes and Cary," Stewart said. "I saw before my own eyes the intimacy between those two. All the claims that those two were straight are bullshit. They were definitely lovers. I knew Cary was after me, and I think at one point Hughes also wanted me. Of course, in Hughes's case, he also wanted every other beautiful brunette woman in Hollywood as well."

Howard agreed to have Stewart and Jean flown to Tucson, Arizona, for a secret wedding, away from the prying eyes of the press. Michael Wilding would be flown in as Stewart's best man.

To plan the wedding, Howard was invited over for an evening with Jean and Stewart at their home. Ironically, both Wilding and Elizabeth Taylor were living with the other British couple until their own home became available.

Stewart recalled that both Jean and Elizabeth, who had become close friends, wore low-cut gowns that night. Howard seemed mesmerized to come face to face with the two beauties he'd been pursuing. "His eyes bugged out of his head," Stewart later claimed. "He literally drooled as he stood looking down at them sitting demurely side by side on a couch. He practically overbalanced trying to look down their cleavages, both of them being well endowed in that department. I'd heard the rumor before but now I was certain. Hughes was a tit man."

Finally, Stewart asked him, "Which do you prefer?"

"Goddamn, I can't make up my mind," Howard said.

"Well, hard cheese, old boy. You're not going to get either of them, so up yours!"

Stewart has gone on record as reporting that much of a more extended conversation. In the 1980s he filled in more details as to how the conversation concluded.

"I was just teasing a deaf mute at our little party," Stewart recalled. "What Michael Wilding and I didn't know at the time was that we were playing with a cobra."

Stewart later recalled that Howard looked at him ominously when told he could have neither Elizabeth nor Jean. Standing real close to Stewart, Howard said, "In that case, I'll just have to take you."

"Dream on, you bugger!" Stewart said. "I've sworn off gay sex."

"That's not what Cary tells me!"

In trying to amass a dossier on Wilding to present to Elizabeth, Howard had learned that the actor had had an affair in London with Stewart when they'd shared a flat during the war. Granger later dismissed the seriousness of this affair.

"People will say Mike and I were both queer. But we weren't, really. It was just something men did during the war."

"Howard hadn't played his hand with Jean, and he was still after Elizabeth for years," Stewart later said. He recalled an incident where "the dirty, double-crossing Machiavellian son of a bitch" invited Jean and me, along with Elizabeth and Michael, to Lake Tahoe for a weekend. Stewart said that he was suffering from a severe cold, but agreed to go along.

Howard took both couples on a flight in a converted airplane, a PBY. He flew real high before taking the plane into a nose-dive. As the plane swooped to earth as if it were crashing, Stewart felt this dreadful pressure in his ear. In agonizing pain, he returned to his hotel room where a doctor confirmed that his eardrum had burst. Alone in bed, he had to lie there in his suffering as Howard "filled in for me," taking Jean, along with Elizabeth and Wilding, to the hottest shows in Lake Tahoe, including performances by Frank Sinatra and Sammy Davis Jr.

At three or four o'clock in the morning, Jean would return to their shared suite, joining her stricken husband in bed. Wilding and Elizabeth would go into another bedroom, and Howard would sleep alone in his bedroom, all of the accommodations opening onto a mutually shared living room.

From the moment he took over her career, Howard disappointed Jean, refusing to let William Wyler cast her in *Roman Holiday*, a role she coveted. She coveted it even more when Audrey Hepburn won the part and also was awarded an Oscar for her portrayal of the runaway princess with Gregory Peck.

Instead, Jean was cast as Lavinia in *Androcles and the Lion*, released in 1952.

Howard continued to pursue Jean, sometimes demanding meetings with her in his car at three o'clock in the morning. Naturally, Stewart's suspicions were aroused. At one point Howard called Jean at her home and asked, "When are you going to get away from that goddamned husband of yours?" Standing nearby, Stewart grabbed the phone from his wife. "Listen, Mr. Howard Bloody Hughes, you'll be sorry if you don't leave my wife alone!" He slammed down the phone.

Angered, Howard threatened that for the remainder of his contract with Jean, he was going to cast her in movies so horrible that they would destroy her career.

With only eighteen days remaining in his contract with Jean, Howard hired director Otto Preminger to shoot *Angel Face*, a black and white *noir* film starring Robert Mitchum. Critics called it the "last of Hughes's tributes to homicidal females."

Howard had decided that Preminger was just the director "to punish Jean." He'd been impressed with Preminger's portrayals of Nazis on the screen. Driving the Viennese-born Jewish director around the deserted streets of Hollywood at three o'clock in the morning, Howard confided, "I want to get even with that bitch."

His final instructions to the director were, "Do your fucking nasty best with her. Make the bitch pay for what's she's put me through."

As Jean later recalled, Preminger "absolutely destroyed me." In one scene he kept ordering Robert to slap her again and again, "harder and harder until you get it right."

"*Vunce* more! Preminger shouted at Robert. Finally, when the actor could take it no more, he slapped the director's face with all his muscular fury. Preminger ended up printing the final take.

Before filming began, Howard had issued several memos about Jean's hair. Stewart later said that "He'd developed a fetish about my wife's hair, the same type he'd hankered for with Jane Russell's breasts."

To defy him, Jean took a pair of shears and hacked off her long locks, which horrified Howard. He called it "butchery," and was furious.

Even after Jean's contract ran out, Howard still exerted power over her. He called every major studio in Hollywood, warning them not to hire her, claiming he had a verbal contract with her for the next seven years. No roles were forthcoming, because every major studio head knew that Howard could tie them up in multi-million dollar lawsuits if they signed even a one-time film contract with Jean.

As Stewart later confessed, "I decided then and there to murder Howard Hughes." He lived with Jean in a cliffside house. At the time, Howard had their home under a 24-hour "spy watch." According to Stewart's plan, he was going to slip out of the house, driving slowly to the airport where he could be easily trailed by his stalkers. Once at the airport, he was going to board a plane for Las Vegas, but slip off at the last moment and drive himself back home, slipping in through a secret entrance only he and Jean knew about. The plan was for Jean to call Howard and tell him that she was reconsidering his previous offers and would like to meet with him in private after all.

In his scheme, Jean would call Howard over for drinks on the terrace, overlooking a deep ravine. Stewart then told his wife that he wanted her to start screaming so loudly that all the neighbors would hear. At that moment, he planned to rush out and push Howard over the railing and into the ravine. Later in life, Stewart recalled, "I woke up in the morning and came to my senses. I decided a shit like Hughes wasn't worth a seat in the gas chamber."

Instead of murdering Howard, Stewart and Jean sued. On hearing the news, Louis B. Mayer called him to his office. "Hollywood is a company town," Mayer told Stewart. "If you sue, you'll destroy Jean's career for good. She'll have to go back to London to look for work. But you'll also destroy your career too. You won't work another day in this town. I'll see to that personally."

Ignoring advice from many of his friends not to take on Howard, Stewart continued the lawsuit. Halfway through the case, Greg Bautzer called to tell him that Howard wanted them to drop the suit, claiming that he would make no more demands on Jean or try to tie her up if other studios hired her. Jean and Stewart, against all advice, decided not to seek damages from Howard, but settled for just their legal expenses.

Howard feared that more court testimony would be damaging to him. At one point Stewart had told the world, "Hughes doesn't want my wife to make films for RKO, he just wants to screw her."

Nearing the end of his life in 1989, Stewart made his Broadway debut in *The Circle*, co-starring his friend, Rex Harrison, along with Glynis Johns. At that point in his life, having long ago been cast aside by Hollywood, he was very outspoken and candid in his comments.

"I still regret that I didn't go through with my plan to murder Hughes," he said over a dinner table at Sardi's. "It would have been so much better for Hollywood—even the world—if I had done that foul act. Somebody should have killed Hughes. Instead I let the bastard live to ruin even more lives.

***

Los Angeles, 1950-1967

"What in hell did bossman ever want to hook up with Barbara Payton for?" Johnny Meyer once asked. "I mean, she was a gorgeous dame at the time before she turned herself into chopped liver. But that was one sicko. Howard wasn't a temple of mental health himself. He didn't need to get involved with this brassy blonde, with her black, whoring heart. Even though for one brief second a movie star, the bitch was Hollywood's number one trollop. Bob Hope and Gregory Peck should have had it cut off for getting involved in the tawdry little world of Payton. No pussy is worth what she put bossman through."

Twenty-three years old at the time she met Howard, Payton had come from the cold winds of Cloquet, Minnesota, to the hot beds of Hollywood. A woman of considerable beauty, she was blessed with blue eyes and a fair complexion that revealed her Norwegian ancestry.

Payton was passed on to Howard by his attorney, Greg Bautzer, who told his male friends, "You have never been given a blow-job until you've been on the receiving end of Barbara's skilled mouth and tongue. I've been blown by the best of them, even Joan Crawford, but Barbara takes top prize."

Intrigued, Howard called Payton for a date, and she readily accepted. "Bossman never minded taking Greg's sloppy seconds," Meyer maintained.

The next morning, Howard phoned Meyer to tell him, "The bitch will do anything in bed—and I mean anything. If you want to piss in her mouth, that's okay with blondie."

"Did you, bossman?" Meyer asked.

"Some secrets I don't even share with you," he said, dismissing further questioning.

Even though Greg warned Howard that Payton "was a stick of dynamite waiting to explode," Howard continued to date her from 1950 to 1952. "Back in those days, Payton was the Queen of the Tabloids," Meyer said. "Howard risked exposure by getting involved in some of her big, headline-making brawls. He came pretty close time and time again of landing on the front page. Fortunately, he had money—and plenty of it—and money talks. Bossman truly believed he could buy himself out of anything, and I guess he could."

Dumping her husband, Payton arrived in Hollywood in the late 40s, with determination like thousands of other beautiful young women, to become a big-time Hollywood star. "If a blonde with absolutely no talent like Lana Turner can become a movie star, then I know I can do it too," she announced to anyone she was introduced to. When her test at RKO didn't work out, she ended up as a carhop at Stan's Drive-In at the corner of Sunset Boulevard and Highland Avenue. Hustling tips while peddling chocolate milkshakes and juicy hamburgers, she also did another type of hustling on the side.

The riches from her nocturnal activities allowed her to buy an expensive wardrobe. Soon she was seen at all the

Barbara Payton

posh clubs, including the Trocadero, Ciro's, and El Mocambo. She was hailed as "the Queen of the Night."

Her love nest on Cheremoya Avenue was paid for in 1949 by none other than the much-married Bob Hope. When the comedian refused to give her $5,000 a week in "spending money," she threatened to blackmail him for her silence. Hope settled what was later called "a huge sum of money" on her, but she went through all her new loot in just three months, claiming, "I have expensive tastes."

"I told Howard all about the shit Hope got himself in," Meyer said. "I told him to drop Payton at once. She was a hot potato looking for trouble. Even though he knew all about the blackmail attempt on Hope, Howard continued to date Payton. He just wouldn't listen to me."

Occasionally Meyer would encounter Payton. "She even offered to have sex with me, but I found her too much of a brazen hussy. She also had a foul mouth and could drink all night. She was such a nympho she would spot a hot hunk and practically rape him before she could take him back to her apartment. I think she had sex in cars more than in her bed."

"One night she told me that actor, John Ireland, had the biggest cock in Hollywood, and she was the only woman who would swallow it to its root," Meyer said. "The next night I saw her hugging and kissing gangster Mickey Cohen in a nightclub booth. The next night she showed up at El Mocambo with bossman himself. Payton was a hot-to-trot hoyden who wanted to be seen in all the fancy spots. Howard couldn't stash her away in some bungalow in Beverly Hills like he did Jean Peters."

A.C. Lyles, the movie producer, once claimed that "Payton never had an itch she didn't scratch." Minor actor Mickey Knox recalled that she'd kept him in bed for three days and nights, all at one stretch. "I had to crawl out of that dump on my hands and knees. What a workout! What a pussy! She sucked you dry. Never left a drop."

She even got involved with James Cagney, who secured her a contract at Warner Brothers for $5,000 a week," Meyer said. "He put her in *Kiss Tomorrow Goodbye*. That film had hardly been released before she was fucking Gary Cooper on the sound stages of *Dallas* and taking in $10,000 a week. On the same picture, she was also fucking that humpy Steve Cochran after Joan Crawford kicked him out of her bed. The next thing I know she was shacked up with Guy Madison, Howard's former lover." They appeared together in a Civil War drama called *Drums in the Deep South*.

Suddenly, when Howard disappeared from Payton's life for three weeks, she was seen around town with the classy New York actor, Franchot Tone, who had been married to Joan Crawford in the 30s. Tone was twenty-two years older than Payton, and he lavished expensive gifts on her, including jewelry.

Somehow Tone found out that Howard was secretly dating Payton, whom he planned to marry. The actor hired a private detective to spy on who was coming and going from Payton's apartment. To set his trap, Tone announced to his errant lover that he was flying to San Francisco on a three-day business trip.

Receiving a call from the detective that Howard had arrived at his girlfriend's apartment, Tone drove over in the middle of the night. Since he paid the rent on the apartment and held a key, he let himself in to discover Howard in bed with Payton, being the beneficiary of her expertise in fellatio.

Meyer said he is not exactly sure of what happened that evening, because Howard, out of embarrassment no doubt, didn't want to provide him with complete details. As Joan Crawford could have told Howard, her former husband had an extreme violent streak in him. Though normally an educated, cultured man, if provoked, he could become "a raging monster" in Crawford's view. She often went to her studio with her face so damaged that makeup could not conceal the bruises or a black eye.

Tone was known for "exploding" if he'd had enough to drink, and he drank all the time, leading columnist Ed Sullivan to call him a "vodka zombie."

"I saw Howard the next day following his fight with that hot-tempered Tone," Meyer said. "I knew that Howard ran from fistfights, and I'm sure Tone struck all the blows. He must have gotten in some good punches, because Howard was badly beaten, with two front teeth missing. They were false teeth, Ava Gardner having knocked out the originals. I drove him to a private clinic where Dr. Verne Mason attended to the bruises. In private, Howard was taken to a dentist who put in new teeth. Howard didn't show his face around town for the next two weeks."

"The worst was yet to come," Meyer revealed. "Tone must have really been crazy about this Payton dame. He sent Howard a death threat. Dietrich urged Howard to go to the police, as this sounded serious. Howard refused. We learned that Tone had purchased a revolver and planned to gun down Howard, perhaps lying in wait for him in a parking lot. Howard doubled his Mormon guards. Already paranoid, he took the threat very, very seriously."

Meyer said that Howard ordered detectives to keep tabs on both Tone and Payton day and night. "Howard even drove over unannounced to Joan Crawford's house one night and asked her to get involved. He pleaded with her to go and talk to Tone and get him to back down from his death threat. Crawford years before had turned down sex with Howard. She also turned down getting involved in all the Tone and Barbara Payton mess, not that I blame her. She had enough bad headlines of her own and didn't need any more."

According to Meyer, Howard decided to probe Tone's background and come up with damaging information that would destroy the actor's career, if he continued to make death threats. "That way, he thought he could blackmail Tone into submission. My boys went to work."

A violent anti-Communist himself, Howard dug up information that Tone had been a Communist when he was involved in the Group Theatre in New York in the 1930s. Tone was also an alcoholic and had been guilty of spousal abuse, especially during his ill-fated marriage to actress Jean Wallace, to whom he was married between 1941 and 1948. She had twice attempted suicide, once with sleeping pills in 1946 and again with a self-inflicted knife wound in 1949 following her divorce from her errant spouse.

Meyer's men found something far more damaging. In 1946, while drinking in the Formosa Café in Hollywood, Tone spotted a stunning, twenty-two-year-old, raven-haired beauty, Elizabeth Short. She wanted to be an actress. Finding no work, she'd become a prostitute instead. For some reason, her steady customers called her "The Black Dahlia."

In spite of his marriage to Jean Wallace, Tone became romantically involved with the beauty for three weeks.

Tone once told his friend, Burgess Meredith, "I always had this uneasy feeling about Elizabeth. When I first met her, she'd been ill and claimed she'd had some operation in her chest. During our entire relationship, I suspected something. Finally, I decided to drop her. Even after she was gone, this eerie feeling stayed with me. It was almost as if I had experienced fear with her. I felt she was going to do me harm."

The actor's intuition had been right. Dumped by Tone, Elizabeth began to stalk him. Wherever he went, he found her lurking in the shadows. He didn't want to go to the police, fearing exposure and feeling that his involvement with a prostitute, while being married to Jean Wallace, would destroy his career.

During their times together, Elizabeth had accumulated blackmail evidence on him. She also had nude pictures of him, apparently taken while he had passed out drunk on her bed. Confronting Tone when he dropped into the Formosa Café, she demanded that he pay her $100,000 in cash or else she was going to turn over her blackmail evidence to the press. He refused to give in to her demands. She didn't carry through on her threat to expose him but continued to stalk him and harass him.

Meyer's men turned up evidence that Tone had ordered her killed to get rid of her. "He knew Mickey Cohen, and we turned up evidence that Tone had gone to Cohen and paid him twenty-five thousand dollars to have Elizabeth murdered," Meyer claimed.

On January 15, 1947, The Black Dahlia's nude and mutilated body was found in a back alley near the Formosa Café. After being brutally tortured, she was cut into two pieces. Investigating the murder, the police found a small cardboard box in Elizabeth's apartment containing blackmail evidence on Tone. Although he was questioned by the police, he was let go and never charged with a crime. The Black Dahlia entered the realm of another one of the famous and unsolved Hollywood murders.

With the evidence he'd accumulated on Tone, Howard ordered Meyer to approach the actor, present the evidence to him, and get his agreement to call off his murder threat.

"With all this going on, Howard was still slipping around and seeing

Payton," Meyer said. "By then, I think Howard's head was seriously on his way to Disneyland. He wasn't thinking right. He began to see Payton as forbidden fruit, and didn't want some two-bit New York actor ordering him around."

Howard was among the first to learn that Payton had fallen for rock-jawed actor Tom Neal, a sort of dime-store John Garfield. She'd met him at a Hollywood pool party. As recorded by *Exposed* magazine at the time, the handsome, macho Neal stood by the pool "displaying his masculinity via a brief pair of bathing panties." Although showgirls at the time laughingly referred to Tone as "jawbreaker," Payton obviously found the much younger Neal's "conspicuous bulge" even more enticing. They began a torrid affair. Almost sadistically, Payton played one man against the other and would in fact marry each of them, thereby creating two of the shortest marriages ever recorded in Hollywood history.

To get even with Tone for his attack and those lost teeth, Howard sent Meyer to Neal, an ex-college boxer. Meyer provided all the details of Tone's love affair with Payton and offered Neal ten thousand dollars if he'd stake out the 46-year-old actor and "beat the shit out of him."

Always broke, the B movie actor readily agreed. Actually, even prior to the offer from Meyer, he had planned to attack Tone anyway.

On September 13, 1951, Payton dined with Tone at Ciro's. Later that night, Neal followed them back to her apartment. Coming out of the bushes, he attacked Tone, smashing his nose and breaking one of his cheekbones. Tone was rushed to the hospital with a brain concussion and remained in a coma for eighteen hours. The morning newspapers headlined this "Love Brawl" across the country.

"Howard's involvement in all this mess was never revealed," Meyer later said. "I think bossman paid out a total of $300,000 before he finally extricated himself from Payton's pile of manure. She got most of it but Neal was paid off too, a lot more than the original ten thousand offered."

After he came so close to making headlines, Howard had finally learned his lesson. He dropped Payton and never saw her again. That was just as well. Deep into her heroin addiction, Payton was headed for skid row. She went from a $10,000-a-week movie star to a broken down and snaggle-toothed whore on Santa Monica Boulevard, jumping inside the cars of strangers and giving fast blow-jobs while they kept the motor running.

In February of 1967 Payton, unconscious, was found in the parking of Thrifty's Drug Store in Hollywood. At first, sanitation workers thought that her reclining body was a bag of trash. She'd been living on the streets for the past three months. She was rushed to Los Angeles County General Hospital.

Rescued by her parents, who were also alcoholics, the former movie star was not long for this world. She soon died in the bathroom of her parents. They found her dead and slumped over a toilet. On the morning of May 8, 1967, an autopsy revealed that she'd died of a heart attack and liver failure.

She was six months shy of her 40th birthday.

"Thus, ended the most tawdry affair bossman ever got involved in," Meyer claimed.

***

Los Angeles/Mexico, 1954

Terry Moore's first meeting with James Dean was auspicious. It took place in her agent's office when she'd discovered, not her agent, but a young slovenly dressed actor asleep on a window seat. Tickling his nose with a Venetian blind cord, she woke him up. Tackling her, he rolled her over and over time and again on the floor. Or so Terry remembered in her memoirs.

Both stars had only one thing in common: Terry had worked for Elia Kazan and Dean had just completed *East of Eden* for the same director. Adapted from the John Steinbeck novel, it would be released in 1955 and would bring instant fame to this handsome, nonconformist Indiana-born actor.

Dean's romance with Terry never really got off the ground. She characterized him more as a "buddy" who followed her around to her various commitments, such as her ballet exercises at Goldwyn Studios or her singing lessons. He even took her to the premiere of *Red Garters*, starring Rosemary Clooney, which was one of the few occasions when he wore a tuxedo. Photographs of Terry and Dean at the time show just how uncomfortable he was and perhaps how ill mated he was with the ebullient Terry.

No sooner did Dean start appearing with Terry than the young actor—soon to be famous—attracted Howard's attention. He ordered Dean trailed day and night, even though from the beginning he was informed that there was no sexual liaison between Dean and his mistress.

Howard immediately learned that Dean was leading a bisexual life,

James Dean

enjoying women but more frequently men. He was lusting for Marlon Brando but ended up with Rock Hudson, with whom he'd make his last picture, *Giant*, in 1956. By that time, Rock and James had soured on each other. Initially they had been attracted to each other when Dean had been cast as a youth in the Rock Hudson/Piper Laurie comedy, *Has Anybody Seen My Gal?* in 1952.

On the night Dean brought Terry back to Glendale from the premiere of *Red Garters*, Howard was waiting in the shadows in a battered Chevy. He followed Dean's car for four blocks until the actor was forced to stop for a red light. Howard deliberately rammed into the rear of the actor's car, but not seriously enough to do any damage.

What happened at this point is not known.

763

Johnny Meyer was told the following day that Howard was flying Dean to Acapulco and that he was to babysit for various mistresses, including Jean Peters, while Howard was away. "His cover story was that he had been called to Washington on urgent business that involved TWA," Meyer said.

In Mexico, Howard's playboy and musician friend, Terry Stauffer, had arranged a luxurious villa for "The New Discovery." Stauffer later became the only source and eyewitness for the off-the-record weekend of what in time became two American legends, Howard Hughes and James Dean.

"The first day I came to call, I found Howard fully dressed and talking on the phone by the pool," Stauffer said. "That young Dean boy was buck-assed naked lounging by the pool wearing only a pair of sunglasses. There were three bedrooms in the villa. Only one bed had been used. The other two were still freshly made. So, I just assumed they connected, although I don't know for sure since I wasn't there with my camera. Oh, how I wish I had been!"

Stauffer claimed that Howard was supposed to stay only through Sunday night, but after the second day he extended his stay with Dean until Thursday night.

"In my opinion, Howard was very attracted to the young boy, who was a bit unconventional for Howard's tastes," Stauffer said. "It was pretty evident to me that Howard liked to devour Dean in bed. The problem came every time Dean opened his mouth and delivered some opinion that made Howard wince. No two men could have been more ill matched. I'm talking personality-wise. To make matters worse, there was a big age barrier between them. Dean, I found out, had been born in 1931. Howard was born years and years before World War I. I'm not sure of the year. There was no doubt about it. Howard could definitely have been Dean's father. It was also evident that Dean had no real interest in Howard. He was just prostituting himself in front of Howard."

"I later learned that Dean had let many bigwigs in Hollywood use his body," Stauffer said. "From what friends told me, he would drop his pants for almost anyone. But with men he rarely reciprocated unless he was attracted to them— or so I was told. Frankly, and I'm not sure, but I think the 'romance' between Howard and Dean consisted of several blow-jobs, and rather frequent ones at that. From what I gathered, Dean just lay on his pillow with his eyes shut imagining god only knows what while Howard did all the dirty work. A sort of rough trade type of thing."

During his stay at Stauffer's villa, Howard and Dean dined with their host only once. One day Howard took Dean flying along the western coast of Mexico. On another day he rented a luxury yacht and took him sailing, landing in some small port somewhere. "Frankly, I think Dean was just going along for the ride, enjoying a Mexican vacation paid for by some rich man," Stauffer claimed.

Howard at one point tried to talk to Dean about flying, perhaps hoping to find some common ground. But Dean, in front of Stauffer, informed Howard that "the open road is what it's about. I like to feel the tires of my car hitting the asphalt."

"I'll always remember the way the evening ended," Stauffer said. "Back at the villa, Dean was trying to polish off a bottle of Tequila, much to Howard's annoyance. At one point, a drunken Dean pulled off all his clothes and danced nude for us. Later I learned that he had briefly studied dance with Katherine Dunham and had, at least somewhat seriously, considered a career in dance. Frankly, he was a lousy dancer, but I think Howard enjoyed watching his cock bounce up and down."

Before finishing off the evening, Dean told Stauffer and Howard, "Dream like you'll live forever but live like you'll die today."

"Later on, I learned he used that line on dozens of people, and for this tragic boy it was a true statement," Stauffer said.

After completing *Giant* for George Stevens in 1956, Dean was killed in a car crash while driving his Porsche Spider to Salinas, California. He was twenty-four years old.

It was Johnny Meyer who brought news of Dean's death to Howard.

"My bossman looked at me with a confused expression," Meyer later recalled. "For a moment, I thought he wasn't sure who Jimmy Dean was. Then he said something enigmatic."

"We'll never know what Jimmy saw when he looked into a mirror—that is, if he ever looked into a mirror. Case closed. Let's not talk about this again."

***

Los Angeles, 1955

Robert Francis was introduced to Howard at a private party hosted by agent Henry Willson in Howard's honor. Howard was already familiar with the rising young star from having seen him appear as a ranking officer in *The Caine Mutiny* the previous year, starring with such formidable talent as Jose Ferrer, Humphrey Bogart, Fred MacMurray, and Van Johnson. Clean cut and All-American looking, Robert had a trim swimmer's build and a fashionable '50s brushcut.

Willson had told Howard that Robert was going to become "the next big male star." The agent's point of view was that long-established stars such as Errol Flynn, Tyrone Power, Robert Taylor, and especially Bogart, were getting "a little long in the tooth," and would soon be replaced by his own discovery, Rock Hudson, and a host of others. Only the year before Robert had been voted one of Screen World's "Promising Personalities of 1954."

Willson later reported that Howard was immensely intrigued with Robert, and was especially captivated to learn of his experiences with Spencer Tracy during the aborted attempt to film *Tribute to a Bad Man*, in June of that year.

"Howard was always a sucker for gossip about Spencer Tracy, whom he still loathed for becoming 'the man' in Katharine Hepburn's life," Willson said. "Howard didn't really want to have sex with Kate, he just wanted to control her. In Kate's case, that was impossible, of course."

With the Greek actress, Irene Papas, Robert Francis had flown to the Rockies, near Montrose, Colorado, to begin filming *Tribute to a Bad Man*.

Much to the fury of director Robert Wise, Tracy arrived in the Rockies five days late, with no excuse for his tardiness. Almost from the first moment they met, Tracy had been enormously attracted to Robert Francis. "Tracy liked that butch military look that Robert had," Willson claimed. "He pursued him with panting tongue. Only problem was, Robert was repulsed by Tracy who was already aging and fat, with the stench of liquor on his breath even in the early morning. When Tracy invited Robert to his motel suite, allegedly to rehearse a scene with him, Robert was apprehensive. He had reason to be. Instead of a rehearsal, Tracy crudely propositioned him by grabbing his crotch. Backing away, Robert fled from the room."

The next day, Robert encountered a hostile Tracy who disrupted filming when he appeared in a scene with Robert. Furious that he was rejected, he began to taunt Robert and make fun of his acting. In one scene when the two men were to ride together, Tracy raced ahead, cutting Robert out of the frame.

Tracy and Wise were at each other's throat, Robert later claimed. "They were heading for a showdown. Wise wanted to get rid of Tracy, and Tracy wanted to get rid of Wise."

Eventually, MGM sent publicity chief Howard Strickling to Colorado. Tracy was fired from MGM, the very studio he'd helped build.

James Cagney was signed to replace Tracy in the movie, but was committed for the next month.

During the month he had off, waiting for Cagney to become free, Robert decided to take up flying lessons. Meeting Howard at Willson's party, Robert said he was shocked when Howard volunteered to personally teach him how to become a pilot.

"With all he had going on in his life," Robert later confided to Willson, "I couldn't believe he'd take the time to teach me to fly. Of course, I knew what was coming, and I didn't mind that at all. I figured there were a lot of things worse in Hollywood than becoming the boy of Howard Hughes. He promised me he was going to make me the biggest male star of Sixties. I believed him."

What Spencer Tracy didn't get to enjoy,

Robert Francis

766

Howard did. "He practically devoured me," Robert later confided to Willson. "Couldn't get enough of me. I think there was no part of my body, even my big toe, that didn't get taken care of—that and a lot more!"

While waiting for *Tribute to a Bad Man* to resume filming, Howard saw Robert every day. A fast learner, Robert was becoming a pilot almost overnight. After only four days of lessons, Howard let Robert assume the controls of his private plane.

It was the last day of July, 1955. Howard had some emergency at 7000 Romaine Street and couldn't accompany Robert that day. Even though Howard warned him not to, a cocky Robert said he wanted to take a plane up on his own, with a male friend as copilot. Howard told him not to. Robert agreed to stay on the ground that day. At the end of the phone call, Robert decided to fly anyway, figuring that Howard would never find out and chastise him.

Up in the air something went wrong with the plane's single engine. Along with his friend, Robert—trapped in the doomed plane—hurtled to his death. Both young men were killed instantly when the plane crashed and exploded.

Willson called Howard with the sad news. "He was devastated," the agent said. "Robert had quickly become what Jack Buetel and Guy Madison once were: one of Howard's greatest physical attractions. After Robert died, Howard began to take reckless chances. I could have arranged to hook him up with some of the hottest guys in Hollywood. The sex could have been carried out discreetly at my home. But Howard didn't want that. It seemed like he wanted more dangerous liaisons—more thrills. I warned him he was headed for trouble. If you're Howard Hughes, you didn't go to bordellos or pick up good-looking young men on Santa Monica Boulevard who just might rob you and cut your throat."

Willson claimed that Howard abruptly dispensed with his services and began turning to a notorious male madam, who was known only as "Mr. Kenneth." A part-time drag queen, Kenneth specialized in arranging private parties for rich producers, directors, or even male movie stars themselves. He found young, well-built, and attractive out-of-work actors who looked like some major star of the time, handsome men like Rock Hudson or Troy Donahue. For one hundred dollars a night, clients could rent "Rock" or "Troy" for an entire evening.

Meyer said that Howard also patronized several of the female bordellos of the time. Like Mr. Kenneth, these houses of prostitution also promoted a night with look-alikes—"Ava," "Lana," or "Marilyn." "What was a bit ironic was that bossman had had the real Ava, Lana, or Marilyn—and not merely the mock," Meyer said. "It's true that Howard wasn't attracting the A-list beauties of his heyday. He was gaunt, dangerously thin, and looked twenty years older than he was. But I think I know why he turned to prostitutes. He could function sexually with only a select few as he got older. But with many partners, both female and male, he was often impotent. A big star might judge him too harshly and gossip about his sexual performance. He knew that Ava and Lana, for instance, often compared their various lovers's performances in bed. Howard couldn't stand that. He once told me, 'With a whore, it doesn't matter whether you get it up or not. They want their money and are probably relieved when you're not too demanding. Also there's a written law that a whore is hired to satisfy you. You don't have to satisfy the whore.'"

As long as Howard stuck to bordellos, he was relatively safe, although he risked possible blackmail or even a police raid if the madam hadn't paid off the cops regularly.

"Bordellos weren't enough to satisfy Howard," Meyer said. "Not dangerous enough. He did what many closeted gay men of the Fifties did. He started picking up handsome young boy prostitutes on the boulevard and demanded that they go down on him while he was still behind the wheel of a battered old Chevy."

One night on Santa Monica Boulevard, something went wrong. Howard had picked up a handsome young prostitute wearing only a white T-shirt, tight jeans, and boots. Once in the car, Howard had requested that the young hustler fellate him. In the midst of this act—evocative of an event in the life of the latter day British actor, Hugh Grant—a policeman unexpectedly came upon the car and shined a flashlight inside. He demanded that Howard and the hustler get out of the car. Howard adjusted his trousers and got out from behind the wheel.

At this point the story grows vague. Apparently, the hustler either was let go by the policeman or else he ran away and wasn't pursued. The policeman wanted his "big game" of the evening, Howard Hughes.

It may never be known what happened on the way to the police station. Howard never made it to the precinct. His name unknown, the arresting officer was hired to become assistant chief of Howard's security forces at $100,000 a year salary, with a guarantee of ten years employment. Greg Bautzer himself drew up the contract. Hughes's biographer Charles Higham got wind of this story, and revelations of the arrest appear in his pioneering book on Howard's sexuality, *The Secret Life*.

Higham claimed that Howard on the night of his arrest wrote a check for one million dollars and signed it "Howard Hughes." Meyer's story of the hiring of the policeman at $100,000 has more creditability. At any rate, both Higham's claim and Meyer's claim still added up to a total of one million dollars.

As Meyer later said jokingly, "Bossman was administered the most expensive blow-job in the history of the world, but was interrupted before he got his rocks off."

Meyer claimed that there was a final irony to the story. The police officer, whose name can't be ascertained, later had special duties to perform at night for Howard. A tall, muscular, and very handsome cop, Mr. Unknown was apparently straight, as Meyer thought, but "didn't mind dropping trousers for bossman from time to time. Do you realize what a $100,000 salary was back in the '50s?

Even CEOs of some big companies weren't hauling in that kind of dough. A man would do a lot for $100,000 a year. I should know better than anyone. For the kind of money I was raking in from Howard, I would have run nude down Hollywood Boulevard if he commanded me to do so."

"The gay streak in Howard eventually tapered off, from what I heard, except for an occasional bout with one of his Mormon guards called in for servicing from time to time when Howard got hungry," Meyer said. "It was an inglorious ending and quite a comedown for a man who had known intimately some of the most celebrated male and female beauties of the 20th Century."

***

Los Angeles/Las Vegas/London, 1945-1990

Ever since her marriage to bandleader Artie Shaw on October 17, 1945, Howard's spies had reported to him the most intimate details of the Ava Gardner marriage. By midsummer of the following year, he noted with a certain glee that Ava was sleeping on a couch in her living room. Often Artie didn't come home to use the lone bedroom. Ava's telephone was bugged, and Howard heard the beautiful young star tell Lana Turner that she hadn't slept with Artie in months. "I had that problem with him too," Lana confessed to Ava, referring to her previous marriage.

Howard learned that Artie had fallen for author Kathleen Winsor weeks before Ava heard the news. Ironically, only months before, Artie had caught Ava reading Winsor's bestseller, *Forever Amber*, the potboiling saga of a buxom beauty's saga through Restoration-era England, and had knocked the book from her hands, denouncing it as trash. At the time, two of Howard's girlfriends, Linda Darnell and Lana herself, were vying to play Amber in the film version, with the part finally going to Linda. No one was more surprised than Ava when Artie announced his marriage to Winsor, following his divorce from Ava. "He wouldn't let me read the trash but he married the trash," Ava told Lana.

After her marriage to Artie, Ava had become another "wet deck" for Howard. He still preferred recently divorced women when not in pursuit of virginal teenagers. She resumed dating him, though "still denying him my honeypot," as she confided to Lana.

With every other actress in Hollywood willing to go to bed with Howard, insiders wondered why he continued to chase after the elusive Ava, who didn't mind sharing her charms with any number of other men, including actors Howard Duff, Peter Lawford, Robert Taylor, and attorney Greg Bautzer, along with gangster Johnny Stompanato who would eventually be killed by Lana herself.

Johnny Meyer once attempted to explain Howard's seemingly eternal attraction to Ava. "In Ava's case, it was the chase that mattered to Howard—he never really wanted to catch her. He pursued her more avidly than all the other gals who got away: Joan Crawford, Elizabeth Taylor, and Jean Simmons. Except for those holdouts, all the other stars and starlets in Hollywood put out for Howard. He knew he'd never conquer Ava. He'd never be able to dominate her, and he certainly couldn't buy her, although he tried to do that repeatedly. He loved the challenge that Ava provided. She was like no other woman he'd ever known."

"One thing that she didn't want was to become Mrs. Howard Hughes, in spite of his repeated proposals of marriage," Meyer said. "Ava was never in love with Howard. She once told Lana that she had to get drunk before she'd even allow him to put his hands on her tits. But when Frank Sinatra came along, that little Hoboken bastard could have tits, ass, and everything else Ava had to offer, including that so-called honeypot of hers that she kept locked away from Howard with a chastity belt."

Howard had managed to endure Ava's marriages to Mickey Rooney and Artie Shaw. What he couldn't endure was her burgeoning romance with the already married Frank Sinatra. "Howard positively hated Sinatra, and wanted him out of the picture. To erase Sinatra from Ava's life, Howard was willing to walk the final mile."

She later claimed that she'd encountered Sinatra a number of times in the late 40s, finding him a "conceited and arrogant son of a bitch." In New York in 1950, at opening night of the stage play, *Gentlemen Prefer Blondes*, she became more intrigued. But she still refused to go out with him.

Encountering him three weeks later at a party in Palm Springs, she said yes. Taking her for a ride in his car, he amused her by pulling out his revolver and shooting out the windows of various darkened but inhabited suburban homes.

That seemed to turn Ava on, and she invited him into her bed that night. On the phone to Lana the next morning, she reported intimate details of the previous night. Lana didn't really need to be told, as Sinatra had seduced her many times in the past. "Frank's not very muscular," Ava told Lana. "All his growth has gone into his cock."

Later Lana jokingly reported the remark to Johnny Meyer, who proceeded to tell Howard. "Bossman became furious," Meyer later said. "He demanded that my boys investigate to find out the exact measurements of Sinatra's dick. It took us only two weeks to round up more than a dozen prostitutes among the Las Vegas showgals who'd slept with the singer. We vetted them and more or less came up with the same story over and over again. That skinny little runt was hung. A full report was given to Howard, who wanted to find out how he stacked up against Sinatra. I don't recall exactly the final results, but I think Sinatra had bossman beat by an inch—maybe an inch and a half."

"My God, he's got a goddamned hollow chest," Howard told Meyer. "A stringbean with no lines. His legs are scrawny. He wears padded shoulders on zoot suits from Hoboken. Instead of hair, he's got patent leather. How could his cock be so big? Not only that, he's a has-been with no money. His career is over, and he's no comeback kid."

Howard even attacked Sinatra's physicality in front of Ava, who reminded him that, "Some gals call you a scarecrow as well, honey chile."

Sinatra divorced his wife, Nancy, and married Ava on November 7, 1951, in Philadelphia. One hour before the wedding, Howard called Ava, begging her to jilt Sinatra at the altar and "marry me." She refused this last-minute proposal, perhaps wondering how serious Howard really was, as she already knew about Susan Hayward, Jean Peters, and Terry Moore. Defeated, Howard told Johnny Meyer that he was "giving the marriage only two months."

Howard's hatred of Sinatra continued, and he even barred him from the RKO lot when Ava was shooting *My Forbidden Past* and having an affair with her costar Robert Mitchum. For reasons of his own, Howard kept knowledge of that affair from Sinatra. However, when Sinatra was out of town on a singing engagement, Howard secretly dated Ava, presenting her detailed reports on the women the singer was seducing on the road. After Sinatra's marriage to Ava, Howard had ordered that the singer be trailed 24 hours a day.

Raging with jealousy, Sinatra accurately accused Ava of secretly dating Howard every time he left town on an engagement. Once at the Hampshire House in New York, Ava tossed a Tiffany gold-and-diamond bracelet—"worth a fortune"—out the window. She did this to prove that "Hughes doesn't mean a god damn hill of beans to me."

Howard had been enraged when he learned that Ava had been cast opposite "his other girlfriend," Kathryn Grayson in MGM's big blockbuster musical of 1951, *Showboat*. The extravaganza also starred Howard Keel, a dashing, tall, and handsome baritone of the time.

Grayson remembered Ava "shooting daggers at me during the filming." Although Ava had repeatedly turned down proposals of marriage from Howard, she apparently was jealous of those same offers made to other actresses. She was also furious to learn that Howard had offered Grayson two million dollars worth of precious gems, whereas he'd once offered her only one million dollars in stones.

One scene in *Showboat* called for a wedding shot that included Grayson and costar Howard Keel. She later said that "the other Howard" (Hughes in this case) in a noisy amphibian swept down over the *Showboat* outdoor set, ruining take after take. He'd become jealous of the younger and more virile Keel.

"Howard knew every time Frank Sinatra and Ava had a knock-out, drag-

Kathryn Grayson

out," Meyer later claimed. "There were a lot of slugfests in those days between this stormy pair. Ava arrived in Las Vegas two days before anticipated, and walked in on Sinatra, catching him in bed with blonde starlet, Barbara Payton. That led to Sinatra's biggest brawl with Ava. She was punched in the face and knocked on the floor, where Sinatra repeatedly kicked her.

Fleeing from the Flamingo, she arrived at the Desert Inn where Howard was staying on the top floor. Allowed entrance to Howard's suite, Ava shocked him with her appearance. He ordered two doctors from the Las Vegas Hospital to come over and treat Ava privately, so as to avoid press coverage.

At about four o'clock in the morning, there was a knock on Meyer's door in the adjoining suite. A sleepy Meyer confronted his bossman in bathrobe and slippers. "I'd never seen Howard this agitated before. He brought me up to date on all that had happened. Inside my suite and in very hushed tones, he told me he wanted two or three of my boys to wipe out Sinatra while he was sleeping at the Flamingo. Somehow Howard had already arranged for my boys to be admitted to Sinatra's private quarters. I was given a passkey to his suite. Howard said that he didn't want Sinatra shot but beaten to death the way he'd attacked Ava. I thought bossman had lost it. In fact, he looked like he'd gone completely bonkers. I listened to his intricate instructions. He had everything mapped out. I think Howard would have made a brilliant bank robber. He wanted me to offer each of my men fifty thousand dollars to do the dirty deed. I didn't want to tell my bossman but I could have gotten the guys for five hundred dollars each."

Meyer later recalled that he'd listened repeatedly as Howard told him in minute detail the exact way that Sinatra was to be bludgeoned to death. "I agreed to carry out his plan. Howard claimed that Sinatra was having a raging dispute with some gang members over an alleged $100,000 gambling debt. The singer was refusing to pay because he claimed that the dice were crooked. Howard believed that Sinatra's death would be blamed on a fallout with the mob. In those days, Sinatra was keeping company with some very dangerous characters. 'No one will ever connect us with Sinatra's murder,' my bossman told me. 'No one will even think we're remotely involved. Sinatra has more dangerous enemies than us.'"

Years later, Meyer claimed that he never made the call to his boys to wipe out Sinatra. He waited in his suite until Howard summoned him next door around noon of the following day. "I got this distress call from Howard and rushed next door. He looked like hell. He as all alone in his suite. Ava had obviously left some time that morning when Howard had finally gone to sleep. He had learned that she'd taken the first available flight back to Los Angeles, wearing huge sunglasses to conceal a black eye."

"To my complete surprise, bossman never mentioned his order to kill Sinatra," Meyer claimed. "I was expecting to be fired on the spot. It was the strangest feeling I had, but I honestly believed—and I still do today—that Howard was so demented the night before that he had completely forgotten issuing Sinatra's death warrant. Lucky for me that Howard was that forgetful. It was even luckier for Sinatra!"

By the time Ava agreed to appear in *The Barefoot Contessa*, to be directed by Joseph L. Mankiewicz, Sinatra was admitting to the press that their marriage "was all washed up." There had been published reports that he'd attempted to commit suicide over a marriage gone sour. Privately, Hedda Hopper and Louella Parsons were claiming that Sinatra's suicide attempt was because of jealousy over Howard.

The Barefoot Contessa was a case of art imitating life. Ava claimed, "I knew I was playing Rita Hayworth and that Humphrey Bogart was playing Howard Hughes."

In Spain, Ava had a scandalous affair with Luis Miguel Dominguin, the country's greatest bullfighter of the time. Back in America, Howard was the first on the tarmac to greet Ava upon her arrival from Madrid. He found her more evasive than ever. Once again she turned down a marriage proposal from him, even though he promised to "make you the greatest movie star the world has ever known."

Not only would there be no marriage, but she also refused to go to bed with him. He had only the memory of that "mercy blow-job," as he called it, that she'd delivered as his reward for surviving the crash of the XF-11 in Beverly Hills.

To Howard's continuing distress, Dominguin arrived in Los Angeles in hot pursuit of Ava. Howard still had her house bugged so he could hear every detail of this burgeoning romance.

For the first three days, according to Meyer, Dominguin never left Ava's bed. The trouble began when Ava, with her attention deficient syndrome, threw a party and invited Duke Ellington and his band. Meyer later claimed that the bullfighter caught a drunken Ava going down on the black musician in the bushes of her garden. She ran upstairs and tried to bolt herself inside her bedroom. But Dominguin was too quick for her. He slapped her face repeatedly and dragged her body from the room. Holding a screaming Ava by the hairs of her head, he tossed her down the steps of her house.

She ended up with no broken bones but a severely sprained ankle and lots of bruises. Rushing into the room, her sister, Bappie, screamed when she saw Ava sprawled on the floor. Bappie rushed to call an ambulance to have her taken to the hospital. Even before Ava arrived at the hospital, Howard with Dr. Verne Mason was waiting in a private room he'd already arranged for her. The next morning, Meyer put Dominguin on a flight back to Madrid.

Howard was "the most delighted man on the planet" when Ava announced her intention to divorce Sinatra in 1957. Howard moved her to the Cal-Neva Lodge on Lake Tahoe to establish residency for her divorce. He also ordered his spy brigade to monitor her activities 24 hours a day in case Sinatra showed up to try to win her back.

For this important mission, Howard entrusted the assignment to Robert Maheu, who later claimed that Howard was more interested in controlling Ava than in romancing her.

As predicted, Sinatra, still madly in love with Ava, did show up at the lodge in Lake Tahoe, hoping for a reconciliation. Ava agreed to go out in a private craft with him on the lake.

In another boat, Maheu followed them. The ever-alert Sinatra quickly realized what was happening. Furious and seething with anger, he piloted his boat toward Maheu's craft, heading for a crash as Ava screamed. Maheu managed to zoom away in time to prevent a head-on collision.

Ava sent Sinatra away that night. On the following evening, Howard showed up at her doorstep, presenting her with a flashy and hugely valuable ring, composed of a Kashmiri sapphire and diamonds. He proposed marriage once again. This time she promised that she'd think it over.

After her stay in Nevada, Howard flew Ava to Miami, installing her in a private villa with her maid, Reenie Jordan. Unknown to Ava, he also flew Jean Peters down, renting a home for her on the Intracoastal Waterway. He was in Miami negotiating with Floyd Odlum, hoping that Odlum would buy back RKO. Under Odlum, the studio had made money. Under Howard's baton, it was "bleeding red," in the words of Noah Dietrich. Odlum turned down Howard's offer. "I'll practically give you back RKO." Even with such generous terms, Odlum still wasn't interested.

In Miami Howard had presented a pearl and diamond necklace to Ava—claiming that it had once belonged to Catherine the Great of Russia—valued at $20,000, it had actually been purchased at Tiffany's in New York.

Growing restless and wanting to escape Howard's attentions, Ava flew to Havana where she was driven to Ernest Hemingway's house to hide out. "Since I didn't see any of his wives around," Ava later recalled to Johnny Meyer, "I fucked Papa. I figured Marlene didn't give him any, so I might as well."

"When Howard learned that she was in the bed with Hemingway, I think he more or less gave up on Ava," Meyer claimed.

"The bloom is off the flower," Howard told Meyer. Howard continued to have Ava spied on, especially when she flew to Spain to play Lady Brett Ashley in Hemingway's *The Sun Also Rises*, released in 1957.

The film starred not only Ava, but two of Howard's former lovers, Tyrone Power and Errol Flynn. "I hope those guys don't get together to compare notes with Ava," Howard told Meyer.

"When Howard sat for a private screening of *The Sun Also Rises*, he was shocked at how Ava had aged on the screen," Meyer said. "I thought she was still beautiful but all that alcohol and all those men—there were even rumors of lesbian affairs—had taken a toll on her once fabulous face. But what really shocked Howard was to see how Ty and Errol had aged. He just couldn't get over it. Unknown to Howard, both actors were close to death at the time. I think bossman wondered what he'd ever seen in them, forgetting what gorgeous guys they'd been in the Thirties."

As was inevitable, Howard and Ava drifted apart, although they occasionally spoke on the phone. Each year on their "mutual birthday" on December 24, he sent her long-stemmed red roses. Living in London's Kensington district in 1972, Ava was astonished to receive roses from Howard, as she'd heard that "he'd gone bonkers," and hadn't remembered her last five birthdays." A florist delivered fifty of the reddest and sweetest smelling roses on God's earth."

"Oh, honey chile," she later said. "What a bastard that Hughes was. He could have been enough of a Texas gentleman to send thirty roses instead of fifty. The sucker likes to rub it in that I'm growing old."

Prematurely aged by a dissipated life, Ava would make her final screen appearance in the film, *Regina*, opening in 1982, although it wasn't released in the United States.

Having watched lines and wrinkles appear on "the most fabulous face ever to grace the screens of the 1940s," Ava died in London on January 25, 1990. A new generation of movie-goers didn't even know who she was.

In one of her last known and flippant remarks to a London reporter, she said, "Honey chile, I was just some poor Tarheel pussy who gave a lot of famous men hard-ons when I was young and beautiful."

***

Los Angeles, 1957-1970

From afar, while ensconced in Bungalow 19 at the Beverly Hills Hotel, Jean Peters watched in horror as Howard descended deeper and deeper into drugs. She learned from a Mormon guard that he was injecting codeine into his arms and swallowing dangerous dosages of Demerol and Valium. Mormon aides called Howard's ten-milligram Valium tablets "blue bombers" because of their color. In time he would pill-pop Seconal and Librium as well.

As Jean confided to Jeanne Crain, "I can't stop him! He orders his guards to remove me from his bungalow any time I mention drugs to him."

Her visits to Howard became severely regulated. A Mormon guard allowed her to visit her husband at 9:15 every morning. Because she always showed up on time at her studio, her nickname was "Punctual Pete." She was also allowed a second visit in the evening. He commanded that it be exactly at 7:31—"and not 7:30." If she were a minute early or a minute late, the visit would be cancelled. At no time was she allowed to go into his bedroom. She was forced to stand in the doorway to his bedroom, talking loudly to him, projecting her voice to his increasingly deaf ears.

In her bungalow, Jean was kept a virtual prisoner under 24-hour security guard. He would go for weeks at a time without seeing her, although he talked to her daily on the phone, inquiring about the most minute details of her life.

Jean once confided in Jeanne Crain that Howard even went so far as to draw up an elaborate memo as to how she was to wash her vagina so as to prevent it from becoming infected. He promised that he'd have a child with her one day, because she was eager to produce a male heir for his empire. What he didn't let her know was that in 1955 he'd checked into a hospital and had a vasectomy performed on himself. Upon leaving the hospital, he told Meyer, "There will never be a Howard Hughes III. The name ends with yours truly." Even before the surgical procedure, his sperm had already been severely weakened by an early case of the mumps.

Howard demanded that his guards clock Jean's every move. He even wanted to read what she ordered from room service to eat or else store in the refrigerator in her bungalow. A memo, dated December 9, 1958 revealed: "6 containers of milk, sweet rolls, toast, 2 baked eggs, 3 raw eggs, cheddar cheese, orange juice, coffee, papers, and 6 bottles of Poland Spring water."

He even refused to let Jean go shopping, claiming that if she wanted something one of his Mormon security guards would go and purchase it for her. Although he failed to prevent her from smoking, he limited her intake of alcohol, refusing to allow room service to bring her any liquor. She was given only half a bottle of champagne every October 15 on her birthday—"and that's it!" he commanded. To pass the time of day, she took up embroidery and later the creation of metal sculptures. Instead of being with her husband, Jean spent many a night reading Plato, Nietzsche, or Aristotle. She would sometimes pass lonely hours listening to recordings of classical music.

Jean loved movies but was not allowed to go with her few remaining friends such as Jeanne Crain to see one. Howard demanded that his Mormon guards escort her to private screenings on the Goldwyn lot and not to a public movie palace. He dictated a memo to Bill Gay: "When escorting Jean Peters to the movies, if it is necessary to open the doors entering the theater, do so with the feet and not the hands. If you need to lower the seat for her, do so with Kleenex."

One day Howard woke up and summoned Gay with an instruction. He claimed that even if Jean were discovered dying, an ambulance was not to be called unless he was consulted first. He also issued instructions that he was not to be awakened even in an emergency. "I will deal with Jean's emergency only when I wake up."

"But she could be dead by then," Gay protested in a rare defiance of Howard.

"You heard me!" he shouted. "Get out!"

Later he backed down from this draconian position. He dictated another memo, claiming that, "If the situation is critical enough, then it's permissible to let a doctor call her on the telephone—but not see her."

He refused to celebrate Christmas with Jean, in 1957, even his alleged birthday which he still believed occurred on Christmas Eve. He always sent her flowers, but only after each petal had been washed in Poland Spring water. He feared that flowers contained germ-carrying insects.

Trapped in the bungalow, Jean would sometimes be allowed to roam the gardens at night. One night she encountered Marilyn Monroe, her neighbor, who told her that she was having an affair with French actor Yves Montand, even though his wife, Simone Signoret, was living next door.

Jean later confided in Jeanne Crain that she had also learned that singer Ethel Merman was a lesbian and actually hired call girls to come to her neighboring bungalow to service her. On one occasion, Jean ran into Elizabeth Taylor, whom Howard secretly lusted for, and the Duke and Duchess of Windsor who told Jean that they'd seen Howard in The Bahamas. The former King of England requested an audience with Howard, via Jean. She was forced to deliver a note to the former monarch the next day, claiming that Howard was too ill to receive visitors.

Insights into Howard's darkening world of 1958 came from security guard Ron Kistler, who published *I Caught Flies for Howard Hughes* in 1976, the year of the tycoon's death. Part of his job was to stand at the door to Howard's bungalow at the Beverly Hills Hotel, waving a newspaper to prevent any insect, especially a fly, from entering. But he said that flies often made "kamikaze dives" to get into the draped darkness of Bungalow 4.

If a fly got in, and Ron killed it, Howard insisted on examining it personally. At no time was Ron supposed to speak to Howard. He found this the most boring assignment in the world.

Other drivers for Howard had more enticing jobs such as hauling around starlets under contract to Hughes Productions. Dozens of beautiful young women had been acquired through Walter Kane, Howard's personal talent scout. Howard issued specific instructions to the drivers. As Ron relates in his memoirs, he cited Howard as saying: "When you're driving a vehicle with one of the female parties as a passenger, do not, at any time, drive over a dip, swale, undulation, or other uneven surface at a speed greater than two miles an hour." One of the employees told Ron "the reasoning" behind this mandate.

"Hughes is a tit man," he said. "You will notice that all the gals you haul around are rather amply endowed. Hughes has a theory that sudden bumps, such as the ones you get when you hit a dip in the road, will cause a girl's tits to bounce. This will inevitably cause a minor breakdown in the tissue, which will lead to sagging tits."

Jean also learned that for a time, Howard was afraid to use the toilet, even if to stand before it to urinate. He began to urinate on the tiles of the bathroom. Then, in contrast, he became fascinated with the toilet. After having it sterilized, he would sit on it for long stretches at a time, once for twenty-seven hours straight, a guard later reported.

Years later he became fascinated with his own urine. Instead of "wasting" it on the tile floors, he began to save it. Milk was his only food source for weeks at a time. After emptying a milk bottle, he'd urinate in it and store it away.

Jean hated living in a hotel bungalow and pleaded with Howard to move out of the Beverly Hills Hotel and into a proper home for the two of them. To pacify her, he purchased the mammoth Major A. Riddle estate in Los Angeles for $950,000, inviting her to move in, presumably without him. She refused to go.

As a means of tempting Jean further, he bought an even more elaborate estate, paying $1.2 million in June of 1961. This 520-acre spread ("Spring Mountain Ranch") outside Las Vegas had been placed on the market by German-born actress Vera Krupp, ex-wife of the Nazi munitions heir, Alfried Krupp. Seeking isolation and anonymity, the Baroness had bought the ranch after her divorce from the industrialist, who had been a major supplier of munitions to the Nazi war machine. With her, she brought the 33.3-carat Krupp diamond, a gift from her husband which she'd retained as part of her divorce settlement. When robbers broke into her home, tied her up, and made off with the diamond, she never felt safe there again—hence, her decision to sell the property. Rediscovered by law enforcement officers in New Jersey, the diamond, worth $250,000 when she owned it, was later returned to her. After passing through several other owners, it was acquired in 1968 by Richard Burton, who paid $305,000 for it and presented it to Elizabeth Taylor.

Jean also refused to move into the Krupp estate, preferring to remain "at my husband's side." Actually, she was not at his side. Their relationship had reached the point where he no longer wanted her to touch him, fearing that she would contaminate him.

Finally, to save what was left of their marriage, he agreed to move to Rancho Santa Fe, an exclusive residential compound in San Diego County, on December 24, 1960, which he was still claiming was his birthday. He lied to her and told her that he'd bought it as a home for her. Actually, he only rented the property.

Away from the hotel, his condition worsened. Fueled by Ritalin, and beset with TWA's financial problems, he slipped deeper and deeper into the lonely world of a drug addict.

When dust balls accumulated in his bedroom where he slept alone, and Howard refused to allow a maid to clean it, his living quarters became filthy. Fecal matter blended with cookie crumbs on the white tile floors.

At one point he reluctantly consented to let Jean vacuum the floor herself, providing she'd enter the room only with the vacuum hose and leave the dirty bag filled with "dangerous germs" outside.

At one point he became hysterical and started to scream. Mormon guards, fearing he might injure himself, strapped him into his bed until a doctor with a needle could arrive to subdue him.

When the pipes broke at the rented house in November of 1961, Howard ordered his guards to pack up and flee the premises. He feared that the entire house had been contaminated with sewage and that inhaling the air would lead to his death.

By November 23, 1961, he'd moved to another deluxe rental property at 1001 Bel Air Road, in the swanky Bel Air section of Los Angeles.

Walking the grounds of the Bel Air estate, Jean pointed out the panoramic views to Howard, including vistas of the distant Santa Monica Mountains. He immediately went inside and ordered black velvet draperies to blot out the view. The property was fenced in and guarded 24 hours a day. For himself, Howard took "the monk's quarters," demanding that only a double bed, a small writing table with a stiff-backed chair, a television set, and one armchair be placed in the room.

The house at Bel Air was owned by John Zurlo, the Los Angeles financier. Howard refused to allow his real estate agent, Virginia Tremaine, to reveal his identity to Zurlo, who obviously found out since both *Life* and *The Saturday Evening Post* ran pictures of the mansion, identifying it as the home of Mr. and Mrs. Howard Hughes.

After the first month in Bel Air, Jean grew alarmed at her husband's weakening physical condition and urged that he be thoroughly examined by Dr. Verne Mason. Howard refused, telling her that never again in his life would he ever submit to a complete physical examination.

He informed her that he needed doctors "only to supply me with drugs for my pain." The Beverly Hills internist, Dr. Norman F. Crane, began to tend to Howard as he'd done in the past.

Jean was also appalled at Howard's grooming, as he refused to cut his hair, letting it grow down to the tip of his buttocks. A long beard trailed onto his chest. He insisted on remaining naked, saying that he could not stand the touch of clothing against his skin.

To get rid of his foul breath, she begged him to brush his teeth but he stubbornly refused. His teeth continued to rot. He'd go so long without bathing that incrustations of dirt formed on his body. After pleading for weeks, he finally gave in to her demands to take a bath. But he let the water overflow in the bathtub, flooding the house.

She told Jeanne Crain that the last time she slept with her husband, his toenails were so long that they clicked whenever he wiggled his toes, keeping her awake. She put tissue between his toes so that the clicking sound couldn't be heard.

Except for speculation, the outside world knew little of this marriage. Even as late as September of 1962, *Life* magazine reported, "Despite his strange ways, theirs is a good marriage."

As weeks gave way to months, Jean watched from afar as Howard's condition grew worse, and her husband retreated more and more into a cocoon. To her horror, she learned that he occupied his mind plotting schemes. Since he was Howard Hughes, he could get some of the most powerful people in the world to indulge him in these fanciful plots.

With his new chief honcho, Robert Maheu, he plotted to have Cuban leader, Fidel Castro, assassinated. For this scheme, Howard—temporarily at least—secured the cooperation of the CIA. He even leased a deserted island, Cay Sal, in The Bahamas, which he planned to make available to anti-Communist military troops who would be trained to invade Cuba. That scheme, like so many others, never got off the ground.

It has been reported that the Bel Air house turned into a divided camp, with Jean fighting against the Mormon guards. In time—specifically on June 10, 1966—she knew she'd lost the battle. Howard moved out, with vague promises to go and live with her on some farm back in the East. He took his phone amplifier and his old lounge chair with him, along with what few possessions, especially clothing, he had. Putting on his lucky fedora, he departed from their last home together. He would never return.

Pouring out her rage that night, she threatened suicide. Jeanne, taking her seriously, called Howard's doctors, who sedated Jean and stationed a 24-hour guard over her to prevent her from committing suicide.

She later learned that Howard had gone by private train to Boston and was staying at a suite at the Ritz-Carlton Hotel. Records show him registering on July 17, 1966.

Growing discontented there, he left Boston on November 25, 1966, again by private train, arriving in Las Vegas, where he'd booked the entire top floor of the Desert Inn.

Jean's marriage to Howard was in name only.

In 1965 an eagle-eyed reporter spotted Jean, using the alias of "Jane Smith," reading to Sunday school classes for blind children sponsored by the Braille Institute of Los Angeles.

Finally, despairing of ever having a reconciliation with Howard, Jean desperately called Jeanne Crain. "Howard has gone to a far and distant place," Jean confided. "A place where I cannot travel."

In Las Vegas, Jean feared that Howard's Mormon guards were holding him a virtual prisoner. She was no longer allowed to speak with him on the phone.

He penned her a desperate note:

Dearest,
I'm ill but very, very ill yet confident I'll feel better soon. You will hear from me the minute I feel even a little better. My very most love."

Her last attempt to see her husband occurred in March of 1967. It was at the Desert Inn. Howard, in his drugged state, refused to see her.

Unknown to Jean at the time, J. Edgar Hoover's FBI agents were trying to determine if Howard were even alive—or if he might have been murdered. The FBI report concluded that it could "not guarantee that Howard Hughes is alive or that he is the man on the ninth floor of the Desert Inn."

That left open the possibility that the man pretending to be Howard Hughes might be an impostor, that the real Howard Hughes was dead, and that a cabal of persons was secretly conducting the Hughes operations and siphoning off the money.

With all hope for her marriage lost, Jean filed for divorce in 1970. She'd grown tired of a telephone marriage, which wasn't even that any more. She asked for $70,000 a year in alimony, which might rise to as much as $140,000, depending on inflation. Howard was shocked at how low the demand was. He even offered to settle millions on her. She refused, claiming that she could live quite well on the amount requested. Columnist Sidney Skolsky reported that the settlement was for $120,000,000. Howard's friend, Louella Parsons, claimed that this figure was "pathologically absurd," but didn't print her rebuttal to Skolsky.

Howard never blamed himself for the failure of the marriage, but placed the responsibility for its failure squarely on one of his most important subordinates, Bill Gay. He told his new chief, Robert Maheu, that, "Bill's total indifference to my pleas for help in my marriage—urgently voiced by me week by week over the past seven years—has resulted in a complete, irrevocable loss of my wife. I blame Bill completely for this unnecessary debacle. I feel he let me down—utterly, totally, completely!"

Maheu claimed that it wasn't the starlets who destroyed the marriage of Howard and Jean. "It was his sickness and pathological fear of personal contact," Maheu wrote in his memoirs. "As time went on, they spent more and more of their time apart."

Her divorce from Howard became final on June 18, 1971 in Hawthorne, Nevada. She was granted a house at 507 North Palm Drive in Beverly Hills.

Wasting no time, she married Stanley Hough, an executive with 20th Century Fox, in the summer of 1971. She was still married to him when he died in 1996.

Still keeping Howard's secrets long after his death, Jean herself died at her home in Carlsbad, California on October 13, 2000. She was suffering from leukemia. At the age of 73, her body was interred at Holy Cross Cemetery at Culver City, the same place she'd watched Howard take off on that fateful Sunday morning test flight in his doomed XF-11.

***

Los Angeles/Washington, DC, 1963-64

A blaze of gunfire on November 22, 1963 in Dallas, Texas, Howard's home state, ended the reign of Camelot. Howard was sitting with Johnny Meyer discussing plans when the news came over his television set that President John F. Kennedy had been shot in a motorcade in that city. The extent of his wounds was not immediately known. According to Meyer, Howard dropped all plans that day and stayed glued to the television set for the next eighteen hours without sleep.

"I knew that bossman had known young Jack Kennedy years ago," Meyer later said. "I also knew that Howard hated old man Kennedy and wasn't a particular admirer of the 'left wing' politics of his son. Yet he stayed glued to that set like he'd lost his best friend. I just didn't get it. It was weeks later before I learned the full extent of bossman's scheme. He wasn't mourning the slain president. He was planning to replace him!"

In the year of Kennedy's death, Howard refused to face business emergencies. He postponed decisions or else ignored them completely. "There were more than brush fires to put out," Meyer said. "There were bonfires. Everybody on the planet was suing Howard, sometimes successfully."

The spring of 1963 had gone badly for Howard. On February 11, 1963, he had refused to appear for deposition in a TWA lawsuit. On May 13 of that same year, a Federal judge in New York had awarded TWA a default judgment for Howard's refusal to show up. He was ordered to pay his own airline $135,000,000 in damages and sell his own stock. "That was a bitter pill for Howard to swallow," Meyer said.

"I think Howard was lusting for other worlds to conquer, but he hadn't made up his mind what those worlds were to be," Meyer said. "By 1967 he would channel his fading energy into acquiring the Desert Inn Hotel and Casino in Las Vegas, the first step on the road to building an empire in Las Vegas and becoming King of the Desert."

In the aftermath of Kennedy's assassination, Howard began to develop a dream that was far greater than Las Vegas. In September of 1960, he'd turned fifty-five and with his gray hair and declining health had begun to refer to himself as middle aged, even though he hated the term. "Who in the fuck decided that a man in his fifties is middle aged?" he once asked Meyer. "How many men do you know who are a hundred years old?"

As November faded into a bleak Christmas of 1963, Howard began to take stock of himself. He'd conquered many fields—more or less well—including aviation and motion pictures. Satellites his company made were orbiting the planet, bringing *I Love Lucy* into homes in Bombay and Sydney. TWA was flying passengers across the globe. But only three years before Kennedy's assassination, Howard had lost control of TWA.

"One time he turned to me and I'd never seen such a pathetic look on his face," Meyer said. "Normally when I looked into his eyes, I saw a feudal baron of immense power staring back at me. Even though we'd been asshole buddies for years, and I knew all his secrets, those blazing eyes of his sent shivers through me. Howard scared the shit out of me he was so vindictive. I never wanted to cross him. I like eating too well, as one look at me will quickly reveal. He'd already turned on Noah Dietrich and made him the enemy. I knew he could do that to me as well."

"He seemed obsessed with Kennedy's assassination and couldn't wipe it from his mind," Meyer claimed. "I don't know how he got it, but he'd obtained a copy of the Zapruder film which he watched endlessly. He must have seen it a thousand times. He wasn't watching a home movie, but studying it with the eyes of a cobra."

A Dallas manufacturer of women's garments, Abraham Zapruder just happened to be shooting a home movie of Kennedy's Dallas motorcade at the precise moment of the assassination. Had he not done so, the actual assassination would not have been captured on film. Zapruder sold this historic film to *Time-Life* for $50,000, although Howard thought that it was worth at least two million—"maybe more"—he confided to Meyer.

"He was watching it for some clue, although I didn't know what at the time," Meyer said. "At first I thought he was seeking some clue as to who shot Kennedy. But he had something else on his mind."

"Mrs. Kennedy is being portrayed in the press as the grieving widow," Howard told Meyer one day after viewing the Zapruder film for at least three playbacks in a row. "But I see something else there. This woman is a me-first type gal. She's a survivor."

The Zapruder film did, in fact, contradict Mrs. Kenendy's future testimony in front of the Warren Commission. As all the world now knows, the Texas governor, John Connally and his wife, Nellie, were riding in the motorcade with the Kennedys. At the first sound of gunfire, Nellie pulled her wounded husband into her lap and out of the line of fire. She even bent over him with her own body. Before the Warren Commission, Mrs. Kennedy testified, "If only I had been looking to the right, I would have seen the first shot that hit him," she said, referring to her own husband. "Then I could have pulled him down, and then the second shot would not have hit him."

With his endless watching of the Zapruder film, Howard came up with another conclusion. Mrs. Kennedy *was* looking to the right. When the first bullet hit, she was riveted to her seat. It appeared that she stared for at least seven seconds at her husband after he'd taken the first bullet. But unlike Nellie Connally, she didn't reach to aid him.

In the film, she appeared shocked and stunned. Instead of coming to the aid of her husband, she jumped up and scrambled out of her seat and onto the trunk of the moving convertible. As she did, the heel of her shoe accidentally kicked her husband in the head. Howard felt that she was probably trying to reach a mounted rubber handgrip at the rear of the trunk. This handgrip could be a way of egress from the limousine, which at that point had begun to accelerate.

Later, Mrs. Kennedy had tried to put a better spin on her attempt to flee the vehicle, claiming that she was trying to retrieve a piece of her husband's head.

"That's one bitch who had survival on the brain," Howard told Meyer. "My kind of woman! I admire that. She probably concluded that Jack was dead and there was nothing she could do for him at that point. She didn't want to be the next victim of a bullet. But in her panic she was also stupid. She should have buried herself on the floorboard of the car and pulled Jack's body down on top of her to serve as her human shield. By trying to crawl across that trunk in that very visible pink dress, she made herself more vulnerable to a potential assassin's bullet."

In the weeks to come, Howard ordered Meyer to gather up all the information he could about those HUGHES FOR PRESIDENT clubs that had once sprang up across the country in the wake of his testimony in front of Senator Brewster's committee after the war. Although they had long dried up, Howard instructed Meyer to "reactivate them—money is no object."

In the weeks ahead, Howard's plan began to reveal itself to Meyer more fully. Howard had more or less assumed that Lyndon B. Johnson, a fellow Texan, would seek and win the presidency in 1964. "Howard announced to me that he was going to run for president in 1968 on the Democratic ticket even though he was an arch-conservative," Meyer said. "He wasn't a Democrat. Neither was he a Republican. Politically, Howard lived in limbo land."

The way Howard saw it, his chief competitors for the 1968 Democratic Presidential nomination would include Lyndon Johnson and Robert Kennedy. Richard Nixon, he surmised, would seek the nomination on the Republican ticket.

"Howard felt he could eliminate Nixon by offering him bribes," Meyer said. "He believed that Nixon was such a crook that he'd accept any bribe. Once Howard had him where he wanted him, he'd release news of Nixon's dirty deeds to the press, which would destroy his political career and cost him the election."

"How do you plan to knock out Bobby Kennedy and LBJ?" Meyer asked Howard. "He looked at me for an astonishing moment, then said, 'I plan to marry Mrs. Kennedy!' You could have knocked me over with a feather. At first I thought he was joking, but when I saw that steely look in his eyes, I knew he was determined."

"My surprise wasn't over," Meyer claimed. "Later that day he told me that I was to be the go-between in negotiating a marriage between Mrs. Kennedy and himself. It was to be a marriage of convenience. I was to contact Mrs. Kennedy and offer her ten million dollars if she'd marry Howard and campaign for him in the 1968 election. For her cooperation, he would also set up separate trust funds for her children, John Kennedy Jr. and Caroline Kennedy."

"Tell Mrs. Kennedy that I'll reinstate her in the White House," Howard said. "She can return in triumph, and I'll promise to give her unlimited power for a First Lady. I understand that dame loves power."

"I'll pay for the next goddamn redecoration of the White House—if that's what it takes to please her," Howard told Meyer. "That's not all. I'll even call that shithead Oleg Cassini, whom I hate, and tell him that Mrs. Kennedy will

Jacqueline Kennedy

have *carte blanche* to order clothes from him, as many outfits as she wants even if it's three gowns a day. Tell her I'll also open charge accounts—the ceiling's the limit—at both Tiffany's and Cartier. I'll also provide 24-hour-a-day security guards for her and her kids."

Meyer said that he made at least eight attempts to get in touch with Mrs. Kennedy, both through hand-delivered courier and by telephone, as he'd easily obtained her private number. "She would not answer my letters nor take my calls," Meyer said. "Someone else always answered the phone at her house. Sometimes it was a man, but more often a woman. One time the voice on the other end sounded like Bobby Kennedy."

"It must have been three o'clock in the morning in Washington, D.C., when Mrs. Kennedy finally returned my call," Meyer said. "I was in bed with, of all people, Ann Miller. I had lured Ann to my bed with three pieces of incredibly expensive jewelry that Howard had originally given Ava Gardner and that she'd thrown back at me, telling me to return the jewelry to Howard. I never did. I presented the gems to Ann, who seemed willing to give me a night of pleasure for the stones. I don't mean to imply that Ann was a hooker. But, unlike Ava, she respected the value of Howard's baubles."

"Mrs. Kennedy's voice came over the phone wires," Meyer said. "I would have recognized that little girl voice anywhere. 'Mr. Meyer,' she said. 'This is Jacqueline Kennedy. I've received your latest letter and would like for you to fly to Washington Tuesday night to meet with me. I'm at least willing to hear what Mr. Hughes has to say.' She proceeded to give me instructions on how to reach her. After doing that, she gently put down the phone."

"I could swear she was drunk," Meyer told Ann. The next morning, he informed Howard of the news, and "bossman seemed elated. His plan to take over the White House, and ultimately the nation—maybe the world—was about to be launched. I'm not exaggerating when I say world. Howard believed that the man who controlled the White House in 1968 could ultimately control the world. He even had a plan to wipe out the Soviet Union in a sudden, unexpected missile attack. 'With Russia out of the way, no one will stop me,' he told me."

Meyer flew to Washington and at the appointed time called on Mrs. Kennedy, finding her alone in her house. "She even answered the door herself," Meyer said. "She asked me if I wanted tea but I requested a drink instead. I was trembling all over. I mean, here I was in the presence of the most famous woman on the planet. In terms of fame, she ranked up there with Helen of Troy,

785

Catherine the Great, and Cleopatra."

Meyer recalled that he sat on a sofa facing Mrs. Kennedy, who occupied a winged armchair, placing her legs in a typical "debutante pose—all prim and proper."

"I tossed out Howard's offer to her even though I knew I was treating her like a hooker," Meyer said. "She didn't seem shocked—nor even surprised."

"In that little girl voice, almost a whisper, she finally said, 'I thought it was something like that.' I remember her leaning back in her chair and saying, 'You go back to your Mr. Hughes and tell him I'll accept his proposal of marriage, but not for ten million. I put a higher price tag on myself than that. Tell him my price tag is fifty million. Also my attorneys will set up trust funds for each of my children. Enough money to give each of them a lavish lifestyle, if that's what they want, for the rest of their lives. I like the offer of 24-hour security protection. But the Hughes Tool Company will have to agree in contract to offer that protection not only for the rest of my life but for the rest of the lives of both John and Caroline.'"

"Of course, Mrs. Kennedy," Meyer said, "I'll take that counter-offer back to Mr. Hughes."

He then remembered Mrs. Kennedy leaning forward in her chair. In almost a whisper she said, "There is one final thing, Mr. Meyer. A delicate issue. Mr. Hughes will have to agree, and put it in contract form, that marriage to me will not entail conjugal visits."

"That hit me like a lead balloon," Meyer claimed. "But I told her I'd also convey that request to Howard. Frankly, I think Howard would have accepted the offer. He wanted to marry Mrs. Kennedy to gain political power unlike anything he'd ever known. He wasn't marrying her to get some pussy, although with her brunette hair and good looks, I think she could have gotten a rise out of bossman. But his libido was pretty much shut down by 1964."

Meyer flew back to the West Coast, conveying the astonishing news to Howard. "The financial terms didn't bother him at all," Meyer claimed. "Bossman knew he'd have to pay many more millions to get into the White House, and he seemed prepared to do that. He said he was going to delay for three weeks a formal response to Mrs. Kennedy, which he was going to deliver in person, meeting her at a secluded cottage on Martha's Vineyard, which I was to rent and secure for him. I went ahead with plans for the Martha's Vineyard rendezvous, but it never came off."

At this point, Meyer hesitated in his remembrance, claiming that what he was about to reveal was so shocking that "it defies believability."

"Howard delivered his answer to me in about three weeks, more or less, but it wasn't the message that Mrs. Kennedy was waiting to hear," Meyer said.

"He had concluded that he could not run for president because of one thing: He'd have to shake the hands of half the male and female population of America, if not the world."

"In the years to come, I'll have to shake all those slimy paws," he said, "some of whom will have just emerged from the toilet after wiping their ass and not washing their hands. The germs will surely kill me. I can't make the run. You have to thank Mrs. Kennedy for her acceptance, but withdraw the offer. I can't go through with it!"

"Frankly," Meyer said, "even though bossman instructed me to, I didn't have the balls to write or call Mrs. Kennedy with the turndown. It was too god-damn embarrassing. But perhaps my visit to Mrs. Kennedy jarred her into a new reality. I'd heard that she'd been drinking heavily, was in a deep depression, and was carrying on an affair with her brother-in-law after her husband's assassination. At least, I got her thinking in the right direction. Another rich man, but not Howard Hughes, lay in that gal's future."

***

Las Vegas/Nassau/London 1959-72

As the late 40s deepened into the 1950s, Howard and Cary Grant would meet rarely and then only for brief interludes. The sexual passion between them had cooled, as both of them had aged and moved on to other affairs with both men and women. As the years went by, their friendship would mostly be conducted on the telephone. The relationship would last until the final months of Howard's life, when he no longer knew who Cary Grant was.

A rare insight into the friendship of these two famous figures was offered by Ray Austin, Cary's chauffeur, assistant, and "all around best friend" for years. In the early autumn of 1959, Austin was at the site of the last known meeting between Cary and Howard. It took place in the parking lot of the Desert Inn in Las Vegas.

On the plane ride to Nevada, Cary had refused to tell Austin why he was flying to Las Vegas. His assistant assumed that the two of them would go to see a number of shows.

Arriving in Las Vegas, Cary prepared to leave his hotel room at around nine o'clock that night, having ordered Austin to rent an inconspicuous Chevy. Once in the car, Cary instructed Austin to drive to the parking lot of the Desert Inn where they waited for an hour. Finally, Austin spotted a tall, lanky figure emerging through the staff entrance at the rear of the hotel. Instructing Austin to stay in the car, Cary got up and walked toward the mysterious figure.

Only when the figure appeared under a security light did Austin recognize who it was. "It was Howard Hughes," he later recalled. "Most of his face was covered by his fedora, and he wore a long trenchcoat, even though the night was hot."

The parking lot was sufficiently lit for Austin to make out the figures of Howard and Cary who must have met for only five minutes before Cary returned to the Chevy, and Howard went back inside the Desert Inn. "Those two guys didn't seem to have much to say to each other," Austin said. "They mainly just stood there looking into each other's eyes. It was like they didn't need words for communication."

Cary would play a final pivotal role in Howard's life during the notorious Clifford Irving affair spinning around a fake "autobiography."

In 1971, McGraw-Hill announced to the world that it was publishing *The Memoirs of Howard Hughes: His True Life Story as Told to Clifford Irving.* From its beginning, the book had been a hoax. Its author, Irving, had never met Howard. Nevertheless, he claimed to have conducted lengthy interviews with him at mysterious locations, and had forged samples of his handwriting.

Throughout the ordeal, wherein the media demanded Howard's reaction to the fraudulent texts, Howard, although heavily drugged, remained in close phone contact with the media-savvy Cary. Finally, Howard took Cary's advice and agreed to be interviewed on the air.

Negotiations in advance of the broadcast were prolonged and laborious. Eventually, it was agreed that TV cameras would have visual access to a panel of well-respected journalists, each of them listening to an audio link hooked up directly to Howard's hotel suite in The Bahamas. At no time, according to the agreement, would TV cameras have access to either Howard, his living quarters, or members of his immediate entourage. The purpose of the communal interview involved verifying that, indeed, the voice at the end of the sound hookup was that of Howard Hughes, and that Howard Hughes, once authenticated, would deny any association, real or implied, with either Clifford Irving or his alleged "autobiography."

At the time, Howard was living in seclusion on Paradise Island, a separate island across from Nassau, in The Bahamas.

On January 7, 1972, listeners around the world heard what was believed to be the voice of Howard as it was transmitted thousands of miles away to seven veteran newsmen. One of them was Hollywood reporter Jim Bacon, who had known Howard in previous years. The press corps members were seated in a studio at the Sheraton-Universal Hotel in Los Angeles.

Cary's advice worked. During the broadcast, despite a very frail voice and an occasional breakdown in memory, the person at the other end of the audio link convinced the reporters that they were indeed talking to the *real* Howard Hughes, and that he'd been the victim of a literary hoax. Irving was exposed for having committed "the literary heist of the decade." *Time* magazine went on to dub him "Con Man of the Year." Later convicted for fraud, his reputation in shambles, Irving went to prison.

The TV broadcast had a negative reaction in Nassau. Howard's residency permit had expired, and the notoriety surrounding the Hughes/Irving affair convinced Bahamian officials that Howard was having a bad effect on their vital tourism industry. Police were dispatched to Paradise Island to remove Howard by force if necessary from his penthouse suite.

A paid tipster in the Bahamian government alerted Howard's guards of this action. Fleeing the hotel dressed only in a bathrobe, and carried on a stretcher, Howard was taken to a private yacht, *Cygnus*. Trying to reach the Florida coast at Key Biscayne, the vessel had to battle twenty-five foot waves. Howard became desperately ill and was given an overdose of Dramamine.

The *Cygnus'* captain, Rob Rehak, later reported that when Howard arrived in Florida he didn't know where he was. Allowed to sleep for eight hours, he made an amazing recovery. Before leaving Florida, he penned a brief note to Cary in Hollywood, thanking him for his advice and help during the Irving affair.

In a leased jet, Howard flew to check into the top floor of the Intercontinental Hotel in Managua, Nicaragua. There he stayed until 12:30am on December 23, 1972. He was watching a James Bond thriller, *Goldfinger*, when a devastating earthquake struck the Central American country.

Starvation-thin, with long, greasy hair and untrimmed toenails and fingernails, an emaciated Howard set out for his next sanctuary: the deluxe Inn on the Park in the heart of London. It was said that from the window of his suite, he could look down and spot the Queen in her dressing room at Buckingham Palace, provided that he'd been given a pair of binoculars. He never tested that rumor, as all of his windows, which otherwise would have provided panoramic views over one of the most sought-after neighborhoods of London, were shrouded in heavy black draperies. "I never want to see daylight again," he told his staff.

In London at the Inn on the Park in 1973, Cary would go by the hotel, hoping to gain admittance to Howard's suite to check on his condition. By that time, Bill Gay had become Howard's chief honcho, having replaced Noah Dietrich and superceding Robert Maheu. Cary was turned away. He later told friends that he suspected that the guards didn't let Howard know that he was in the lobby of the hotel wanting to come up to see him.

Cary never spoke publicly about his longtime companion, except on one occasion. After being refused access by Howard's guards, he told a reporter for the *Times of London*, when asked about Howard's condition: "The soul and the mind are dead."

***

Acapulco, April 5, 1976

A feeble old man, his skeletal body marred by needle tracks and riddled with bedsores, lay dying. His six feet, four inch frame had shrunk two inches, and his frail body weighed only ninety-three pounds. Dirt encrusted the pores of his skin. His fingernails and toenails were eerily yellowed, curved, and impossibly long. And his yellow-gray beard and his long, oily, and stringy hair were in dire need of a shampoo.

It was Howard Hughes, the former Playboy of the Western World and one of the richest men on the planet. He was dying of dehydration and malnutrition. Despite the fact that he was surrounded with attendants, he desperately needed a glass of water and a plate of food.

He was occupying a barren-looking room in the $2,000-a-night penthouse at the Acapulco Princess Hotel, where he'd flown in a chartered British-built BAC II from Freeport, The Bahamas, on the night of February 10. He'd checked into the hotel under heavy security guard and was wheeled to his suite in a stretcher, his face covered with a blanket as if he were already dead.

His eyes, formerly a shade of dark brown, had turned a ghostly, pale yellow. One of the Mormon guards, Gordon Margulis, felt that Howard could no longer see the world. Not that there was much world to see. The gardens of the hotel were lush and filled with flamboyant colors from various flowers. But Howard had ordered sheets of plywood and heavy black velvet curtains placed over all the windows. He no longer wanted to see the world. Nor did he want the world to look and see him in his devastation.

Had he been able to see the hotel he'd checked into, he would have noted that its shape was that of a pyramid, structures that functioned as tombs for some of the ancient rulers of Egypt. Would this hotel also be his graveyard?

Once, an airplane had taken him around the world, setting a historic record in aviation. Piloting other airplanes, he had broken speed records. Now, as he lay nude in his orthopedic bed, an electric-powered wheelchair provided his sole means of transportation.

His bedside table was gaudy, covered with *faux* mosaics depicting golden stars. There was a large crystal bowl filled with Valium tablets along with codeine pills and Librium.

He could no longer speak to anyone. Aides, such as his most trusted, George Francom, remembered him repeatedly calling out the name of Allene. After knowing some of the most celebrated women of the 20th century, his fading memory seemed to be able to recall only his mother who had doted on him back in Houston. He drifted deeper and deeper into a coma, and as the hours passed, no more sound came from his lips.

Before fading into oblivion, Francom heard him utter the name of Allene once more, but it came out as a whisper, barely audible.

His last known command was to tell his guard and aide, Gordon Margulis, to send a message to Jean Peters. It was to read: "You are the only woman I've ever loved." That wasn't really true. Perhaps he'd never really loved any woman. Maybe he hadn't even loved himself. But he wanted that message sent anyway.

His last known coherent conversation was with his old friend, Jack Real, the aviation industrialist. Howard voiced concern about how he'd live in history. He feared future biographers would concentrate on his women and his movies, especially *Hell's Angels* and *The Outlaw*. "God forbid they write a chapter about me and Jane Russell's breasts," he told Real. He wanted biographers to write only about his contribution to aviation, but he knew he could no longer control and manipulate the media as he once had. What he feared the most, but couldn't convey to his macho friend, was that writers of the future might discover his secret life, known only to trusted friends like Cary Grant or to hired pimps such as Johnny Meyer and Henry Willson.

Dr. Lawrence Chaffin, who had helped Howard survive the almost fatal plane crash over Beverly Hills in 1946, was at his bedside in Acapulco. But he was almost powerless to help his fading patient.

Feeling there was very little he could do to save Howard's life, he summoned Dr. Victor Montemayor, who enjoyed a reputation as the best doctor in Acapulco. Answering the summons, Dr. Montemayor rushed to the Acapulco Princess where Mormon guards were waiting to deliver him via private elevator to the 20th floor of the deluxe hotel.

According to a log, the doctor had arrived at the hotel at 5:58am on the morning of April 5.

He was immediately ushered into Howard's suite by Dr. Chaffin. What Montemayor discovered in a head-to-toe examination of the patient horrified him. In spite of all the Mormon guards and the around-the-clock medical care, the patient appeared to be dying of neglect. The Mexican doctor could feel fragments of hypodermic needles broken off in his arms and still imbedded there.

"Those arms looked like rail-thin bamboo shoots," Montemayor later said. "Not arms at all." He was not certain of Howard's age, but guessed him to be "around eighty-eight years old."

His skin was like parchment found in some ancient tomb. It was of a greenish-yellow pallor and seemed to hang from his body in folds.

There was a hideous, bloody gash on Howard's head, like an open sore. It appeared to be a cancerous tumor. The last time Howard had attempted to rise from his hospital bed, he'd fallen, hitting the fleshy growth on his head and bursting it. Even so, he refused to have it stitched back together again or operated on.

Montemayor also noticed that Howard was virtually toothless. He asked if he'd had his teeth pulled. Dr. Chaffin told him that his teeth had apparently fallen out one by one and that Howard presumably had swallowed them since none of the teeth had ever been found in or around his bed.

"I've examined dying vagrants off the street who were cared for better than Mr. Hughes," the doctor later said.

Montemayor expressed his concerns about administering to a man in his condition. He feared that Howard's body showed such neglect and abuse that it might invite a lawsuit under Mexican law. The possible charge? Manslaughter.

As if he could help, Dr. Wilbur Thain, Howard's chief physician, residing in The Bahamas, had been summoned the day before. Thain was asked to fly at once to Acapulco to administer to Howard. Dr. Thain was the brother-in-law of

Bill Gay, Howard's chief Mormon honcho at the time.

Dr. Montemayor had already left Howard's suite before Dr. Thain arrived. Before leaving, Dr. Montemayor had ordered that the patient be flown "at once" to the United States, as he did not feel the hospital in Acapulco was adequate to save him.

Dr. Thain arrived about an hour later, after Montemayor had departed, but he did not immediately enter Howard's suite to examine the patient. One of Howard's Mormon guards, Chuck Waldron, caught the doctor packing up Howard's medical records and stuffing them into his briefcase.

Dr. Thain finally entered the suite and administered two shots of Solu-Cortel, which he hoped would prevent a serious attack of dropsy.

Here the mystery deepens. In all the confusion, some unknown person, who was either in the suite as a member of the staff or else someone who slipped in unnoticed, approached Howard's bed.

Even though he was in a coma and in no conscious pain, a lethal dose of codeine was injected into Howard's blood stream by his unknown man.

When Howard's body was later examined, the high amount of codeine in his bloodstream was considered "a lethal dose."

Wrapped in heavy blankets in spite of the sticky, humid April weather in Mexico, Howard was taken on a stretcher from his bedroom where he'd lain for weeks and slipped out of the hotel through the service elevator. An ambulance was waiting at the rear of the hotel. With sirens wailing, the white limousine headed for the local airport.

On the way there, a plastic oxygen mask covered Howard's face. In the words of aide John Holmes, Howard's "eyes had sunken deep into his head."

Holmes had placed an emergency call to Dr. Henry D. McIntosh, chairman of the Department of Internal Medicine at the Methodist Hospital in Houston. His call came in as a "red alert" for the hospital, although Holmes refused to divulge the name of his famous patient, suggesting that a pseudonym of "J.T. Conover" be used. The Mormon guard requested that the hospital be prepared to receive the patient "as if he's the President of Mexico." Intrigued, Dr. McIntosh agreed to this unusual request.

In Houston, word quickly spread through the hospital that the stricken President of Mexico was flying in for emergency surgery. The best room was prepared for the arrival of this patient, and the finest doctors in the city summoned.

The hospital staff could only wait and wonder.

One doctor is reported to have said, "If the life of this VIP can be saved, we're prepared to do it!"

***

Houston, 1976

Both Dr. Chaffin and Dr. Thain were crowded uncomfortably into the small, specially chartered jet aircraft, since Howard's stretcher occupied most of the

792

space. It was later reported that at 1:27pm, the moment the pilot of the aircraft, Robert Sutton, flew across the Mexican border into Texas airspace, Howard Hughes died.

Sutton later wondered if that were true. Did Howard really die at that exact moment, as was reported. Even on the day of Howard's death, speculation began to rage that he was actually dead when his body was placed aboard that chartered jet. The claim was made that the two doctors were not administering to a dying man but to a corpse.

When Sutton was helping load Howard's stretcher onto his plane, his left arm fell out from under the blankets. When the pilot reached for Howard's arm and tried to put it back under the blankets, he later reported that "It felt as cold as an Arctic night."

Not sworn to secrecy like the Mormon guards, Sutton notified the control tower at the Houston International Airport that he was landing and that he had a dead passenger aboard—"and his name is Howard Hughes!" Sutton requested that the airport have an ambulance waiting.

Obviously someone overheard this announcement from the chartered jet from Mexico. Within twelve minutes, some unknown party placed a call to Associated Press. Unaware of the details, the Associated Press sent out an immediate bulletin to all its affiliated newsrooms around the globe. Editors were advised to stand by for late-breaking news. It was suggested that the story be accorded the same status as the death of a sitting U.S. president or a declaration of war. Newspapers going to bed around the world were told to save their frontpages for an "epic" news event.

The jet from Mexico touched down at the Houston Airport at 1:50pm. A green-and-white ambulance was waiting to take Howard to the Methodist Hospital, which was twenty-seven miles south of the airport. Instead of trying to save Howard's life, doctors at the hospital would now be ordered to perform an autopsy.

Just as Howard's dead body was being wheeled across the tarmac of the Houston airport, the news of his death was flashed around the world. Lacking details, many newspapers went to press immediately with Second Coming banner headlines: HOWARD HUGHES DIES.

Arriving at the hospital at 2:51pm, Howard's body was delivered to the morgue in the basement. Once there, Dr. Jack L. Titus, chief pathologist, conducted a preliminary examination. His finding discovered that Howard may have been dead for three hours. The cadaver was placed in a cooler at the morgue with 24-hour security guards posted nearby.

After the autopsy, a Cadillac hearse, "black as death" in the words of John Holmes, arrived at the hospital to claim the cadaver. What was left of Howard was taken to the George Lewis & Sons Funeral Home for embalming. A security force was hired to guard the corpse from "countless visitors and who knows how many rubberneckers."

In a surprise, the funeral home later reported that there was not one visitor. "Not one person came to pay their final respects to Howard," one of the directors claimed. "All the reporters assigned to the case weren't badgering us but were seeking information from live sources. Only one call came in inquiring about Hughes's body. The caller identified herself as Jean Peters Hughes."

With no known will, Howard's long-suffering aunt, Annette Gano Lummis, now eighty-five years old, and the younger sister of Allene, was the chief heir apparent. Too weak to oversee the chaos following Howard's death, she immediately asked her son, William Rice Lummis, to make the funeral arrangements.

Annette had not seen Howard since his triumphant return to Houston in 1938. On learning of his death, she raised several provocative issues, claiming that she did not believe that the cadaver flown in from Mexico was actually the body of her nephew.

She ordered that an autopsy be performed. However, she balked when J. Edgar Hoover sent in a request to allow FBI agents to enter the morgue and take fingerprints of the cadaver.

In Washington, D.C., the chief of the FBI also didn't believe that the cadaver was actually the body of Howard Hughes. Without recording it to paper, Hoover had even told such cohorts as Richard Nixon that he believed that Howard Hughes had been murdered and that the man pretending to be Howard was actually an impostor, a puppet being manipulated by powerful interests who were in charge of the vast empire.

The FBI had determined that the man who had met on March 13, 1972 with Nicaraguan President Anastasio Somoza in Managua, along with U.S. Ambassador Turner Shelton, "was not Hughes, but someone else."

The real Howard Hughes had allegedly signed papers on September 25, 1972, authorizing the sale of the oil-tool division of Toolco in Houston. By December of that same year, the division was auctioned off to the public for $150 million. Howard's holding company was renamed the Summa Corporation.

Hoover's agents secured copies of Howard's authorization for this. After FBI experts examined the papers, they reported their suspicions that Howard's signature was a very skilled forgery.

Hoover was also convinced that the reason for a burglary of Howard's offices at 7000 Romaine Street in Hollywood on June 5, 1974, involved the removal of private papers revealing the details of Howard's murder.

When Hoover learned that Annette Lummis was objecting to the FBI taking Howard's fingerprints, he felt that he'd not only proven his theory, but that Howard's aunt was part of the conspiracy to defraud. "Why would she not want us to take fingerprints?" he asked associates. "I'll tell you why. The bitch is part of the cover-up!"

Howard was a mystery in life and remained an even bigger mystery in death.

Evocative of the aftermath of the assassination of President Kennedy, tantalizing questions—still unanswered—remain to this day. Many questions were never resolved by the autopsy performed on Howard Hughes in the Houston hospital.

With Howard's doctors, Titus and Chaffin, looking on, medical examiner Dr. Joseph A. Jachimczyk, performed an autopsy on Howard's body. Dr. Ted Bowen, president of the Methodist Hospital, announced to reporters that Howard had died of "chronic renal disease," or kidney failure. Dr. Jachimczyk also maintained that Howard had cancer, as diagnosed in both the ruptured tumor on his head and in his prostate.

The report also concluded that as a result of tertiary syphilis and more than a dozen plane and car crashes, Howard's brain cells had "dangerously deteriorated." The results of Howard's autopsy and the circumstances of his death would be investigated and disputed for years to come.

A Swiss doctor, Bernhardt Geber, who examined the evidence on a visit to Houston, concluded years later that Howard died of AIDS.

In 1976 the HIV virus had not been isolated, and the fatal disease was not referred to as AIDS at that time. Nonetheless, the doctor cited the widely publicized case of a British sailor who had died of a mysterious illness in 1959. A blood sample taken from the stricken man was frozen and later exhumed for examination when more sophisticated medical practices were in use. In the '90s, it was determined that the sailor had died of AIDS.

Dr. Geber concluded that Howard's last known symptoms, including kidney failure, were indicative of AIDS.

Even more provocative were two still unanswered questions: Was Howard Hughes murdered? Was the cadaver that was flown north from Acapulco actually the body of Howard or that of an impostor?

As 1979 rolled around, it appeared that no law enforcement agency planned to investigate rumors that Howard (or his impostor) had been murdered just prior to leaving Acapulco. Likewise, no law enforcement agency showed any real interest in pursuing the possibility that Howard Hughes had been murdered years before, and his empire commandeered by unknown forces. A reporter making an inquiry in Houston in 1981 was bluntly told by the police: "Case closed!"

Dr. John Chappel, who extensively probed the circumstances of Howard's death, issued a conclusion that the body put on the chartered plane in Mexico was already dead. The attorney general of Mexico, who ordered an investigation of Howard's death, announced his conclusion: "Howard Hughes died at 10 o'clock on the morning of April 5, 1976. His dead body was then put on a plane and flown to Houston."

Someone in the attorney general's office later secretly told reporters that Mexican authorities, had they known that Hughes had died in Acapulco, would have sent police officers rushing in squad cars to the Acapulco Airport. They would have seized the body, examined it, and held it as evidence in "what was obviously a murder case occurring on Mexican soil, giving us complete juris-diction over the corpse."

Conspiracy theories proliferated throughout the 1970s. They continue, unresolved, even today.

On a final tantalizing note, one of Howard's Mormon bodyguards, who refused to identify himself, sent a note to Annette Lummis after her nephew's death. "You were right in your suspicions," he wrote. "That was not Howard Hughes we were looking after and protecting all these years. Your nephew was murdered in 1968 in Las Vegas. I personally saw his body wheeled out and an impostor arrive. The man who went on the air to conduct an interview on January 7, 1972, with newsmen in Los Angeles to refute the so-called Clifford Irving autobiography of Howard Hughes was not your nephew but someone else."

It was reported that Annette Lummis debated sending the note to the police, but decided to destroy it. Her final conclusion, as related to her friends, was, "I want to let Howard rest in peace. That was some precious commodity he never got to know in life. God bless his eternal soul!"

***

On a bright sunny day on April 7, 1976, one of the 20th century's most fabled figures was laid to rest in the family plot at the Glenwood Cemetery, uniting Howard with his doting mother and his distant father.

In casinos throughout Las Vegas, public address systems called for a minute of silence.

At the Desert Inn, the head croupier glanced nervously at his wristwatch, waiting impatiently for the minute to tick away. Turning to a cocktail waitress, he whispered, "Let's give the fucker his minute!"

When the minute had passed, he called out to his table, "Let's roll the dice! Lady Luck will surely shine on you today like it did on Howard Hughes. Win a billion!"

In Houston, under the moss-draped oak trees at the Glenwood Cemetery, only twenty-one mourners showed up. Except for Annette, none of them had known Howard personally.

The Reverend Robert Gibson, pastor of Christ Episcopal Church, where Howard had been baptized as a small child, presided. His final blessing, as Howard's coffin was lowered into the ground, was a rewrite of a passage from *The Book of Common Prayer*. "He brought nothing into this world, and it is certain that he will take nothing out of it."

Even as gravediggers were shoveling the final dirt over the body of a man who had wanted to be cremated, anyone with even the remotest claim to Howard's estate was meeting with their attorneys for legal challenges. Howard had been sued ever since the 1920s. In death, he would face an avalanche of lawsuits, many of which were frivolous or fabricated.

Annette lamented to friends, "I thought death would bring peace to my nephew. It has brought peace to none of us."

Howard's coffin was almost covered with red dirt when one final funeral bouquet arrived late. Annette remembered it as filled with three dozen of "the world's most beautiful roses," the type that Howard himself used to send to the likes of Ava Gardner or Katharine Hepburn.

The roses were so stunningly beautiful and had such a tantalizing aroma, that Annette remembered looking at a handwritten message on the card.

Dear Friend,

Until we meet again in Heaven, or some lesser address.
Love Eternal,

C.G.

INDEX

1939 World's Fair, The 392
24th Infantry Division of the Third Battalion 27, 28
Abel, Walter 396
Adorée, Renée 166, 167
Adventurers, The 305
Age for Love, The 234
Aherne, Brian 323, 325, 466, 467
Alexander, J.B. 127, 237
Alfonso XIII, King of Spain 451
All About Eve 454
All Quiet on the Western Front 457
Allen, Gracie 361
Alloy Steel Corporation 165
Allyson, June 441
Altars of the East 458
Amory, Cleveland 518
Annabella 716
Anderson, Jack 704
Anderson, Loni 336
Anderson, Police Chief Clinton B. 720
Andrews, Frank 94-96, 103, 105, 107
Androcles and the Lion 756
Angel and the Badman 619
Angel Face 756
Angel, Joe 200
Angell, Frank 569, 570
Arbuckle, Fatty 46, 192, 318
Archbald, Judge Henry R. 224
Arditto, James 696
Arlen, Richard 147
Armdariz, Pedro 442
Armillita 579
Armstedt, Karl 162
Army Surgeon 246
Arnaz, Desi 635, 728
Arnold, General H.H. ("Hap") 546, 548, 550-551
Arthur, Phil 33
Astaire, Fred 455
Asther, Nils 198
Astor, Mary 151-154
Austin, Ray 787, 788
Aves, Dr. C.M. 93, 94

Axt, William 166
Ayres, Lew 239, 245-246, 262, 286, 289, 313, 386, 389, 455-458
Back Street 261
Bacon, David (Gaspar Bacon Jr.) 513, 514, 515, 516, 517, 518, 538
Bacon, Gaspar G. Sr. 513
Bacon, Jim 788
Baidukoff, Georgi 417
Bakewell, William 286
Ball, Lucille 456, 728
Ballard, Lucien 525
Baltimore, Cpl. Charles 28
Bankhead, Tallulah 235, 251, 270-272, 452, 459
Banky, Vilma 141
Barefoot Contessa, The 773
Barefoot Mailman, The 738
Barker, Jess 436, 438, 439
Barrett, Wilton A. 273
Barry, Philip 443
Barrymore, Ethel 251, 252, 258, 271
Barrymore, John 138, 197, 399
Barthelmess, Richard 186
Barton, Charles 701
Batista, Fulgencio 602
Battle for the Planet of the Apes 458
Battleground 723
Baumgarth Calendar Company, The 683
Bautzer, Greg 564, 616, 618, 632, 658, 664, 738, 743, 750, 757, 758, 768
Bayley, Nancy Bell 365, 366, 367, 368
Beach, Rex 166
Beaconfield Apartments 24
Beard, Daniel Carter 17, 19, 30
Beatie, Richard (Dick) 586-587, 598
Beauties and the Beasts, The 280
Beauty and the Billionaire, The 191
Bed of Roses 723
Beebe, George 600
Beery, Rita 641
Beevil, Sarah 631
Behn, Harry 161
Beko, William (Bill) 696

Bel Geddes, Barbara 723
Belkstein, Sheila 517
Bell, Stan 548
Bellamy, Madge 130-132
Belle of the Nineties 266
Bello, Marino 245
Benchley, Robert 246
Bennett, Constance 133-401
Bennett, Joan 134
Bennett, Richard 134
Benny, Jack 335, 361, 646
Bergman, Ingrid 493-504
Berle, Milton 640, 682
Berman, Bobby Burns (B.B.B.) 250
Berman, Pandro S. 389, 391, 403
Bern, Edward G. 563
Bern, Paul 82, 230, 245, 275-280, 286
Bernhardt, Sarah 614
Bey, Turhan 634
Bickford, Charles 226
Billings, LeMoyne K. ("Lem") 493
Billings, William J. 110
Billy the Kid 265, 511
Birdwell, Russell 475, 511-512, 530, 534-536, 559
Bishop's Wife, The 597
Bissell, Adelaide Manola 43
Black, Caroline 213
Blair, William 514
Blakewell, William 655
Blandford, Gene 553-554, 649, 655
Blondell, Joan 366
Blondie of the Follies 243
Blood and Sand 577-578, 632, 672
Blue Iguana, The 298
Blue Veil, The 727
Blues in the Night 488
Blythe, Betty 302
Boardman, Eleanor 20-22, 31, 47, 55-56, 58, 68, 73, 75-77, 87
Bogart, Humphrey 154, 205, 218-220, 224-225, 238, 240-241, 250-252, 264, 493
Boldt, Hilda 209
Bond, Lilian 281-282
Bond, Ward 627-628
Borzage, Frank 151

Bow, Clara 148-149, 159, 206
Bowen, Dr. Ted 795
Boy With the Green Hair, The 724
Boyd, William ("Stage" Boyd) 246
Boyd, William (Hopalong Cassidy) 150, 153-155, 246
Brand, Harry 684
Brando, Marlon 682, 691, 729
Breen, Joseph 533
Brent, Evelyn 166, 168-169
Brewster, Senator Ralph Owen 700-702, 706-707, 709, 716
Brian, Mary 254
Bringing Up Baby 391, 403
Brisson, Frederick 393
Britton, Barbara 492
Broccoli, Albert ("Cubby") 248, 270, 285, 295, 297, 300, 304-335, 339, 345, 389, 406-407, 530-532, 742
Broeske, Pat H. 203, 396
Bronson, Betty 140
Brooklyn Eagle, The 600
Brother Rat 435
Brown, Johnny Mack 239, 246, 252, 256, 264-266, 477, 511
Brown, Peter Harry 203, 396
Brown, S.T. 93
Bruce, Virginia 308-310, 312
Brugh, Ruth Stanhope 311
Brugh, Spangler Andrew 311
Bruner, Dr. Karl 232
Brynner, Yul 682
Bryant, Charles 4
Buetel, Jack 516, 518, 521-522, 525-526, 532, 538, 615, 681
Buferd, Marilyn 502
Buka, Donald 669
Bullitt, William C. 415
Burcham, Milo 545
Burgess, Alan 499
Burnett, W.R. 669
Burns, George 361
Burton, Richard 778
Busch, Mae 73
Bushman, Francis X. 118
Cabot, Bruce 397, 399, 402, 593, 606
Caddo Productions 130

Caesar and Cleopatra 752
Cagney, James 258, 268, 396, 657, 686-688, 759, 766
Cagney, William (Bill) 687-688
Calhoun, Rory 492
California Pictures Corp. 668
Callaway, Kitty 73
Callow, Reginald 173, 179, 188-189, 202
Camp Teedyuskung 17-18, 20, 30
Campbell, Dr. Monroe 174
Campbell, James 249
Cansino, Eduardo 671
Capone, Al 267, 269, 316, 702
Captain from Castile 685, 690, 716
Carey, Mary Jane 741
Carmen, Jewel 337
Carmichael, John 275
Carpetbaggers, The 305, 458, 612
Carroll, Nancy 248, 258, 259-260, 318
Carson, Jack 635
Carstairs, Harry 606
Carter, Aldine 333
Cassini, Daria 644
Cassini, Igor 645
Cassini, Oleg 643, 645-646, 784
Castro, Fidel 780
Cawthorne, Nigel 360
Chaffin, Dr. Lawrence 554, 656-657, 791-792, 795
Chamberlain, Neville 603
Champion, Gower and Marge 725
Chandler, Jeff 438
Channell, Ronald 365
Chaplin, Charles 63, 73-74, 84, 116-120, 168, 396, 637
Chappel, Dr. John 795
Charig, Phil 361
Charisse, Cyd 702
Chasen, David 635, 730
Cherrill, Virginia 318, 321, 394
Chevalier, Maurice 239
Chickering, Dr. H. T. 32-34, 55
Chorus Line, A 159
Chouinard, Jeff 691, 741
Christ Church Cathedral (Houston) 14
Christian, Linda 719
Citizen Kane 166, 168

Clarke, Frank 172-173, 179
Clarke, Mae 254-255
Clash by Night 683-684
Clayton, Steve 593
Clift, Montgomery 521, 617
Cline, William M.("Ceco") 553, 555
Club Cameleon 99
Cochran, Jacqueline ("Jackie") 331, 336, 349, 351, 358, 363, 721
Cochran, Steve 759
Cock of the Air 242, 307
Cohen, Emmanuel 297
Cohen, Mickey 720, 759, 761
Cohn, Harry 125, 577, 635, 671, 676-677, 682
Colbert, Claudette 263, 372, 614
Collyer, June 189-190, 234
Colman, Ronald 153
Come Back, Little Sheba 742
Compton, Betty 411
Connally, John 783
Connally, Nellie 783
Connon, Hal 122-123
Connor, Harry P. McLean 408, 419
Conover, David 678
Conquerer, The 441-442
Conrad, Dorothy 170
Considine, John W. 152
Constitution, The 641
Cook, Raymond 695
Cooper, Anderson 511
Cooper, Carter Vanderbilt 511
Cooper, Gary 141-144, 147-149, 158-159, 186, 198, 251, 265, 270, 385, 637, 640-641, 759
Cooper, Harry 195
Cooper, Merian C. 285
Cooper, Parley 352
Cooper, Wyatt Emory 511
Cormack, Bartlett 253
Corsair 193
Courtland, Jerome ("Cojo") 734, 736
Coward, Noel 126, 564
Crabbe, Buster 298
Crain, Jeanne 688, 691, 697, 775
Cramer, Stuart III 440, 442, 691, 693
Crane, Cheryl Christine 634-635, 720

Crane, Dr. Norman F. 779-780
Crane, Stephen 634
Crawford, Joan 134, 191, 203, 246-247, 264, 303, 348, 391, 460, 477, 516, 591, 609, 626, 657, 682, 684, 752, 759-760
Cromwell, Richard 345, 346-348, 351
Crosby, Bing 316
Crossfire 722
Cruze, James 165
Cukor, George 257, 362, 369, 371, 391, 405, 426-427, 435, 595, 724
Cullinan, Margaret 13
Curtis, Benjamin 57
Curtis, Jeanne 630
Curtis, Tony 682, 726
D-2, The 546-547, 549, 551
Dailey, Dan 630
Dalton, Terry 508
Damita, Lili 451
Dana, Viola 45
Dancing Town, The 218
Dangerous 449
Daniel, Leonard 292
Daniels, Bebe 146, 163, 213, 679
D'Arcy, Alexander 249
Darnell, Linda 579-582, 624, 626-627, 629-632, 636, 657, 666, 769
Darrow, John 159, 161-162, 164, 172, 175-176, 213, 216, 218, 230, 290-291, 345-346, 348, 351
Davenport, Howie 328
Davies, Marion 119-120, 157, 196, 205, 208, 264, 675
Davis, Bette 296, 399, 448, 451-455, 612, 638
Davis, Glenn 739-742
Davis, Ruth ("Ruthie") 452
Davis, Sammy Jr. 682
Dawn Patrol, The 186-188, 267, 427
Day, Doris 719
Daytime Wife 624
De Carlo, Yvonne 620, 622, 624, 655
De Havilland, Olivia 399, 463, 465-466, 467, 475, 657
De la Vega, Alfredo 490
De Marchis, Marcella 502
Dean, James 763, 764, 765

DeCicco, Pat 248, 249, 291, 308, 334, 335, 338, 341, 342, 344, 365, 366, 367, 389, 509, 510, 643, 751
Dedd, Wayne 313
Delmonte, Raymond 306
DeMille, Cecil B. 46, 60, 154, 237
Dempsey, Jack 199, 316
Dempster, Carol 208
Desert Inn, The 739
Devil's Holiday 259
Divine Lady, The 301, 302
Dewey, Governor Thomas 706
Di Frasso, Countess Dorothy 385
Dial, Elizabeth 89, 105
Dickson Gun Plant 543
Dieterle, William 501
Dietrich, Maria 271
Dietrich, Marlene 270, 271, 285, 451, 452, 493, 495, 497, 515, 637, 675, 676, 726
Dietrich, Noah 15, 107, 108, 114, 115, 121, 123, 132, 145, 150, 158, 160, 162, 171, 175, 183, 204, 210, 211, 212, 213, 216, 222, 227, 228, 231, 232, 243, 292, 343, 344, 349, 374, 390, 396, 408, 434, 445, 446, 480, 541, 556, 559, 560, 574, 583, 585, 590, 591, 594, 597, 598, 599, 602, 606, 659, 662, 663, 664, 667, 669, 676, 688, 689, 693, 694, 695, 701, 715, 721, 727, 789
Disney, Walt 638
Dix, Richard 236, 238
Dodge City 463
Dom, Philip 458
Domergue, Faith 480-489, 505, 510, 520, 541, 543, 558, 567-569, 572, 583, 587, 618, 666-667, 669-670, 717, 732
Domergue, Leo 484
Dominguin, Luis Miguel 773
Donahue, Jimmy 395, 596
Donahue, Troy 743
Donna's Burgers 616
Double Dynamite (It's Only Money) 725
Douglas, Donald 167
Douglas, Kirk 612-613, 647
Douglas, Paul 683
Dove, Billie 108, 128, 164, 205-206,

208-210, 212, 214-219, 222-225, 230-231, 233, 237, 239, 241-243, 260, 264, 308, 437

Dowler, Beatrice 212, 222, 226-227, 265-266, 277, 292, 297, 312, 384, 390, 488

Downs, Virginia 347

Dozier, William 737

Dragnet 169

Drake, Betsy 724

Dreher, Richard 381-382

DuBrey, Claire 348, 351

Duke, Doris 303, 460, 462

Duncan, Isadora 668

DuPont, Marion 320, 360, 362

Durbin, Deanna 387

Durkin, Marine Sgt. William Lloyd 653-654, 662-663

Dvorak, Ann 246,-248, 268

Dwan, Allan 295

Dyer, Elmer 186

Eaker, General Ira C. 665

Earhart, Amelia 327, 331

East Side, West Side 189

Echols, Major General Oliver P. 546-547

Ecstacy (Extase) 468

Ecstacy and Me (autobiography of Hedy Lamarr) 469

Edwards, H. Robert 561

Einstein, Albert 682

Eisenhower, Dwight D. 333, 428

Ellington, Duke 773

Ellis, Anita 672-673

Emerson, Faye 549-550, 565, 705

Estabrook, Howard 161

Every Girl Should be Married 724

Everybody's Acting 102, 139

Ezell, K. Marvin 599

Fairbanks, Douglas Jr. 84, 115-116, 127-129, 186, 191, 450

Fairbanks, Douglas Sr. 45, 115-116

Fairchild, Sherman 411, 427, 430, 540, 568

Fairmont, "Toffee" 122, 123

Falaise de la Coudray, Le Marquis de la 139

Falcon's Alibi, The 611

Farish, Libby Rice 109-110, 132, 156,

174, 352

Farish, William S. 110, 233

Farouk, King 677

Fasten Your Seat Belts 448

Fay, Frank 230

Fay, Ralph 362

Faye, Alice 357

Fedora 302

Felt, Richard 553-554

Ferguson, Governor James 28

Ferguson, Perry 530

Ferguson, Senator Homer 700, 707-709

Ferrer, Mel 669

Fessenden School 35, 37-38, 40

Fessenden, F.J. 38

Fields, W. C. 399

Finocchio's 593-594

Fisher, Eddie 752

Fisher, Robert 344

Fitts, Buron 279, 342, 345

Fitzgerald, F. Scott 77

Flamingo, The (Las Vegas) 385

Flanaghan, Francis 699

Fleischmann, Harry 386

Fleming, Victor 150, 257

Flexner, Dr. Simon 32

Flying Down to Rio 285

Flynn , Michael J. 378

Flynn, Captain Carl 737

Flynn, Carl, ("Jock") 290

Flynn, Errol 355, 389, 396-401, 407, 451, 463, 588, 591, 593, 603, 606, 657, 774

Folies Bergère 99

Follow Thru 258

Fonda, Henry 456, 492, 514, 721

Fonda, Jane 619

Fontaine, Joan 464, 466-467, 737

Fontaine, Lilian de Havilland 464

Ford, John 372, 404, 626, 628

Forever Amber 769

42nd Street 261, 263

Foster, Florence 382

Foster, Mitchell 360

Four's a Crowd 399

Fowler, Dr. Raymond 10

Francis, Kay 225, 465

Francis, Robert 765-767

Frazier, Brenda Diana Duff 303, 459-460, 462, 505

French Line, The 528

From Here to Eternity 733

Frome, Bernie 616

Front Page, The 253, 255

Fruitfly 51

Frye, Jack 444-446, 658

Fudger, Eva K.J. 145

Furthman, Jules 530, 726, 737

Gable, Clark 153, 195, 206, 239, 245, 255-257, 268, 276, 477, 579, 617, 620, 637

Gambling House 628

Gannon, Thomas 250

Gano, Annette (a.k.a. Annette Lummis) 67, 70, 73, 87, 93-94, 103, 108, 302, 433, 600, 659, 794, 796

Garbo, Greta 206, 442, 515

Gardner, Ava 153, 303, 322, 369, 561, 563-569, 571-576, 583, 591-592, 645, 657, 661, 693, 695, 703, 714, 725, 728, 732, 760, 768-774, 785

Gardner, Beatrice ("Bappie") 563, 567, 569, 571, 573-574, 773

Gargan, Frank 20

Garland, Judy 493, 742

Garon, Jay 469, 472

Gay, Bill 692, 694, 776, 781, 789

Gaynor, Mitzi 694, 747-748

Geisler, Jerry 720, 729

General Teleradio 727

Gentlemen Prefer Blondes 684

George and Margaret 427

Gerber, Dr. Bernhardt 795

Gerson, Dr. Percival 299

Gibson, Rev. Robert 796

Gilbert, John 144, 160, 199, 308

Gilda 671

Ginger (autobiography of Ginger Rogers) 290

Girls on Probation 435

Gleason, Russell 175, 177, 185

Goddard, Paulette 428, 635, 637-639

Goebbels, Joseph 515

Gold Diggers of 1933 263

Goldwyn, Samuel 46, 142, 240, 500, 566, 606

Gomez, Thomas 442

Gone With the Wind 243, 399, 423, 435, 475, 592

Göring, Mrs. Hermann 744

Goulding, Edmund 134, 137-138

Grable, Betty 492, 535, 592, 615, 630

Grace, Dick 179

Graham, Carroll & Garrett 226, 246

Graham, Don 686, 689

Granger, Stewart 751, 753-757

Grant, Cary 78, 198, 237, 254, 259, 304, 314-315, 319, 321-322, 325, 334, 345, 359, 361-363, 375, 383, 390-391, 393, 395, 403, 409, 427, 432, 479, 542, 549, 594-595, 597, 635, 658, 660-661, 683, 690, 702, 704, 708, 711, 714, 716, 754, 787-789, 797

Grauman, Sid 229, 340-342

Graves, Ralph 124-127, 286

Grayson, Kathryn 692, 694, 771

Great Dictator, The 639

Green Dolphin Street 717

Green, Lewis 524

Greer, Jane 607, 609, 611-612, 666, 728, 731

Griffith, Corrine 205-206, 208, 300-301

Griffith, D.W. 101, 126

Groblie, Betty 524

Gromoff, Mikhail 417

Gross, Robert 447

Guest, Charlie 571, 573, 608

Guston, Gosta B. 653

Guston, James 653

Gwynne, Edyth 319

Haggart, Stanley 259-260

Haines, William ("Billy") 74, 76, 78, 82, 105, 113, 121, 134, 198, 204, 207, 226-227, 242, 248, 255, 257, 265-266, 272, 275, 281, 320, 353, 477, 657

Hall, James 162, 199

Hall, Mordaunt 230

Hamilton, Dr. Gavin 68

Hamilton, Neil 187

Hamilton-Standard Division 664

Hanson, Smitty 358

Harding, Ann 184, 609

Harding, Laura 323, 372, 388, 409-410
Harlow, Jean 154, 196, 199-205, 208, 223, 227-230, 233, 234, 238-245, 264, 275-278, 286
Harmon International Trophy 381
Harris, Jed 404
Harrison, Alfred 203
Harron, Bobby 126
Hart, Moss 361
Hart, William S. 265
Hathaway, Henry 580
Haven, Marchioness Milford 505
Hawks, Frank 378
Hawks, Howard 153, 186-189, 196, 245, 255, 260, 267, 269, 273, 335, 353, 369, 391, 396, 519, 525, 529, 531, 533, 566, 724
Hayes, Lulubelle 600-601
Hays Office, The 533
Hays, Will 273
Hayward, Leland 372, 429
Hayward, Susan 435-440, 612, 694
Hayworth, Rita 235, 333, 510, 577, 592, 662, 670-671, 673, 675-677, 717
Head, Edith 440
Hearst, William Randolph 63-64, 119, 157, 166, 168, 204, 243, 265, 273, 292, 313, 450, 675, 703
Hecht, Ben 151, 253, 267, 280, 469, 530
Hefner, Hugh 684
Heisler, Stuart 669
Helburn, Theresa 378, 380
Heller, William 203
Heller, Wilson 334
Hell's Angels 149, 152, 158, 162, 172, 174, 177, 183, 186-187, 191-193, 196, 203, 209, 227, 229, 231-232, 238, 242, 267, 295, 377, 427, 445
Hemingway, Ernest 77, 515, 774
Henderson, Cliff 185
Hendry, Whitey 275
Henley, Nadine 582, 657, 660-661, 663
Henry Aldrich Gets Glamour 617
Henry, Charlotte 295
Henry, Vida 28
Hepburn, Dick 405
Hepburn, Dr. Thomas 372, 404-405

Hepburn, Katharine 38, 246, 282, 322, 325-326, 334, 363, 368-369, 371-374, 376, 379-380, 382, 384, 389-391, 395, 399, 403, 405, 410, 414, 422-423, 426-427, 431, 443, 447, 452, 510, 657-658, 724, 728
Hepburn, Kit 404-405
Her First Affaire 295
Hess, Rudolf 603
Hesser, Edwin Bower 227
High Heels 742
Higham, Charles 402, 768
Hilda, The (a.k.a. The Rodeo) 209, 214-215, 290
Hilton, Nicky 742, 746-747, 750
Hilton, Paris 460
His Girl Friday 255, 393
His Kind of Woman 628
Hitler, Adolf 472, 603
Hollywood Revue of 1929 247
Holm, Celeste 635
Holmes, John 792
Hoover, J. Edgar 489, 550, 558, 560, 586, 621-622, 635, 699, 780, 794
Hope, Bob 758-759
Hopkins, Miriam 196, 235, 638
Hopper, Hedda 149, 751
Horner, Jack 31
Hot Saturday 259
Hough, Stanley 781
House of a Thousand and One Delights (Maude's House) 136
Houston's Race Riot of 1917 27
Houstoun, Martha Gano 659
Howard: The Amazing Mr. Hughes 107
Huddle 286
Hudson, Captain Horace 40
Hudson, Rock 487, 519, 719, 743, 763
Hughes Aviation 552, 562-563
Hughes Tool Company 12
Hughes, Allene Gano 1, 8-11, 14, 17-18, 21, 24-25, 29-31, 41, 67-68, 98, 100, 688
Hughes, Avis 427
Hughes, Ella Rice 13, 88-89, 95, 107-109, 111, 113-114, 121, 129, 132-133, 137, 145, 156-157, 172, 174, 180-182, 211-212, 215-217, 232-233, 290, 351-

353, 363, 688
Hughes, Felix Jr. 37-38, 104-106
Hughes, Felix Sr. 36, 94, 103-104, 110
Hughes, Howard Sr. 7, 10, 17, 20-24, 27, 29-30, 34, 37, 40, 48, 55-56, 60, 65, 68, 70-71, 77, 87, 91-95, 124, 695
Hughes, Jean (Mimi) 42, 94, 103-106, 110
Hughes, Rupert 12, 21, 23-24, 37-38, 42-43, 45, 56, 60-61, 63, 69, 71, 76, 104-106, 125, 140, 151, 183, 267, 315, 477, 509
Hurrell, George 535
Hurwitz, Arlen 685
Huston, John 682
Huston, Walter 531
Hutton, Barbara 303, 320, 362, 392, 394-395, 460, 462, 595, 717
Huxley, Aldous 637
I Was a Male War Bride 724
Independent Exhibitors of America 390
Ingrid Bergman: My Story 499
Ipar, Ali 310
Ireland, John 626, 628
Irving, Clifford 788
Jachimczyk, Dr. Joseph A. 795
Jacobs, George 492, 495, 497
Jacobsen, Christian 315
Jamison, Robert 363-364
Jane Eyre 372, 378
Jarrico, Paul 628
Jazz Singer, The 183
Jean Louis 672
Jeanmaire, Zizi 744
Jeffers, Sally 655
Jessel, George 682
Jet Pilot 726
Jezebel 449
Jimmy the Greek 122
Johnny Belinda 458
Johnson, Al 180
Johnson, Kelly 544
Johnson, Lyndon B. 784
Johnson, Senator Edwin C. 503
Johnston, Roddy 401-402
Jones, Jennifer 614
Jones, Jesse 446, 560, 562

Jones, Phil 179
Jordan, Dorothy 283-286
Jordan, Reenie 774
Jordan, Ted 677-680
Jourdan, Louis 735
Judson, Edward C. 510, 671-672
Just a Gigolo 281
Kaiser, Henry J. 556-558, 560-561
Kane, Walter 725, 739, 777
Kanin, Garson 405
Karloff, Boris 151, 268
Kaufman, George S. 153
Kaye, Danny 657
Keaton, Buster 418
Keel, Howard 771
Keller, Greta 514-515, 517-518
Kelley, Tom 523, 683
Kelly, Jack (a.k.a. George Orry-Kelly) 361
Kelly, Patsy 191, 337
Kenaston, Bob 243
Kennedy, Caroline 784
Kennedy, Edward Moore (Teddy) 262
Kennedy, Jacqueline 494, 783-787
Kennedy, John F. 387, 442, 460, 490, 493-494, 496-498, 781
Kennedy, John F. Jr. 494
Kennedy, John Jr. 784
Kennedy, Joseph 139, 227, 259, 261, 320, 461, 782
Kennedy, Robert 784-785
Kerry, Norman 117
Khan, Prince Aly 620, 677
King Kong 285, 428, 431
King, Martin Luther Jr. 30
Kinnecot, Robert 279
Kirkpatrick, Ray 548, 600
Kirkwood, James 159
Kistler, Ron 777
KLAC Radio 712
Knight, John 601
Knight, June 334-335
Knowles, Patric 399
Knox, Mickey 759
Korda, Sir Alexander 637
Krasna, Norman 727
Krupp, Alfried 778

Krupp, Vera 778
Kuldell, Colonel R.C. 92, 306
La Guardia, Mayor Fiorello 392, 412, 422
La Rocque, Rod 142-143
Lady of the Tropics 468
Lahn, Ilse 276, 279
Lake, Veronica 303, 638-639, 641-642
LaMarr, Barbara 74, 78, 80-81, 83-84, 277, 468
Lamarr, Hedy 84, 468-469, 471, 506, 670, 717
Lamas, Fernando 719
Lampe, Bob 361
Lana: The Lady, The Legend, The Truth (Memoirs of Lana Turner) 636, 718
Landau, Arthur 201
Landsing, Timmie 291
Lanfield, Sidney 357
Lang, Fritz 683
Lang, June 250
Langer, Ralph 383
Langford, Barbara 286
Lansbury, Angela 348-349
Larsen, Edwin S 208
Las Vegas Story, The 628
Lasker, Edward 612
Laura 644
Lawford, Peter 566, 674
Lawler, Anderson 372, 385, 405
Lawless, The 618
Lawlow, James 8
Lawrence of Arabia 432
Lederer, Charles 253
Lee, Lila 159-160
Lee, W. Howard 647
Leeds, Lila 729
Leigh, Janet 478, 725-726
Leigh, Vivien 254
LeRoy, Mervyn 261-263
Lewis, Sinclair 431
Liberace 459
Liberty Ships 556
Life Magazine 606
Life Story of Charles Chaplin, The 168
Ligget, Marguerite 605
Lindbergh, Charles 127, 156-158, 270,

333, 377, 413, 415, 418, 424, 445, 505, 603
Lindsay, Cynthia 176
Lindsay, Margaret 339-341
Lindstrom, Petter 493
Linet, Beverly 437
Lipton, Harry 678
Litvak, Anatole 638
Lloyd, Frank 234, 300
Lloyd, Gaylord 269
Lloyd, Harold 269, 657, 668-669
Logan, Josh 514
Lombard, Carole 194-196, 201-202, 225, 491
Lonedale Operator, The 47
Longworth, Elsa 294
Loos, Anita 204
Loring, Jane 388
Los Angeles Rams 739
Lowe, Edmund 250
Lowe, Nick 161
Loy, Myrna 635
Luciano, Lucky 338, 340-343, 384, 706
Lumet, Sidney 511
Lummis, Dr. Frederick Rice 32, 36, 67, 87, 89, 94, 96, 659
Lummis, William Rice 794
Lund, Edward 408-409, 415, 417, 419
Lund, William 428
Lundigan, William 399, 593
Lupino, Connie O'Shea 295, 299
Lupino, Ida 295-299, 339, 341, 397, 610
Lupino, Stanley 295, 297, 340
Lyles, A.C. 759
Lyon, Ben 146, 162-163, 172, 195, 198, 202, 207, 213-214, 226
Lytees, Natasha 682-683
MacDonald, Jeanette 225, 283
Mackaill, Dorothy 163
MacKenna, Kenneth 220, 224-225, 372
Mackinac Island 33
Mad Wednesday (a.k.a. Sin of Harold Diddlebock, The) 668
Maddox, Ben 318
Madison, Guy 613, 615-618, 662, 681, 759
Madriguera, Enric 607

807

Madsen, Johanna 324, 381-382
Magnani, Anna 501, 503
Maheu, Robert 693, 774, 781, 789
Mahon, Philip 397-398
Malaya 724
Mamoulian, Rouben 577
Man on a Tightrope 743
Mandl, Fritz 470
Mankiewicz, Herman J. 166, 168
Mankiewicz, Joseph 582
Manola, Adelaide 21
Mansfield, Jayne 303
Manson, Charles 281
Mantz, Paul 170, 173, 327
March, Fredric 744
March, Joseph Moncure 184, 188-189, 200
Margulis, Gordon 790
Marie Antoinette 477
Marion, Frances 142
Marley, J. Peverell 624-625, 629
Marrener, Walter & Ellen 435, 441
Marsh, Marian 185, 250
Marshall, George 301
Martin, Dean 682
Martin, Glenn 59
Martin, Mart 105
Martin, Robert 600
Martin, Tony 702
Martinez, Juan 304-305
Martyn, Earl 702
Marx, David 200
Marx, Gummo 486, 519
Maschio, Johnny 203, 248, 635, 643, 646, 735
Mason, Dr. Verne 210-211, 222, 241, 244, 321, 542, 572, 583, 655, 658, 660, 663, 695, 747, 760, 779
Mason, James 723
Mattes, Police Captain Joseph 28
Mature, Victor 626-628, 640, 647, 672
Maugham, W. Somerset 126
Maxwell, Elsa 461
Mayer, Louis B. 120, 140, 164, 227, 240, 244, 266, 275-276, 286, 468, 470, 564, 632, 717, 723, 749
Mayfield, Betty 98, 107

Mayo, Virginia 635
Mazarin, Pierre 415
McArthur, Charles 253
McBride, Owen 71
McCarthy, Glenn 447
McCarthy, Joseph R. 708
McCarthy, Neil 130, 189, 198, 217, 228, 233, 243, 268, 286, 366, 455, 480, 533, 536, 560, 562, 616
McCloud, Michael 211
McCrea, Joel 198, 457
McDowall, Roddy 750
McIntosh, Dr. Henry D. 792
McKuen, Rod 515
McNamara, James C. 712
Medford, Ben 435
Medina, Phil 520-521
Meighan, Thomas 166
Men Who Have Made Love to Me 126
Mendoza, David 166
Menjou, Adolphe 253, 255
Menken, Helen 225, 251
Meredith, Burgess 638, 761
Merkel, Una 285-286, 335
Merman, Ethel 777
Merrill, Gary 454
Merrit, O.C. 599
Messick, Hank 280
Meyer, Gabe 366-367
Meyer, Johnny 396-397, 402, 439, 454, 464, 482, 508, 527, 548, 565, 570, 573, 591-592, 597, 604, 607, 610-611, 613, 621, 623, 628, 635, 638, 662-663, 666, 667, 672, 686, 704-708, 718-719, 734, 759, 762, 768, 772, 782, 785-786
Meyer, Lt. Col. Charles A. 653
Meyers, Major General Bennett E. 562
Miami Herald, The 600, 604-605
Mildrew, Robert 619
Milestone, Lewis (Milly) 150-151, 158, 253, 255, 457, 654
Miller, Ann 625, 629, 785
Miller, Arthur 617
Miller, Marilyn 163
Millette, Dorothy 278-279
Mills, George 600-601
Milton, Bertha 388

Min and Bill 283
Minter, Mary Miles 50, 65-66
Misfits, The 617
Mitchell, Thomas 531
Mitchum, Dorothy 732
Mitchum, Robert 436, 566, 612-613, 615, 629-630, 670, 728, 730-733, 756
Modern Times 639
Moffat, James 359
Moffat, Ruth 359
Monroe, Marilyn 228, 303, 437, 617, 644, 680-681, 684, 691, 777
Montand, Yves 777
Montemayor, Dr. Victor 791-792
Montez, Maria 623
Montgomery, Daniel 364
Montgomery, Robert 243, 478
Montieth, Sup. Court Judge Walter 87, 93, 96, 103, 107
Montrose School 23
Moore, "Mama Blue" 738, 741, 745
Moore, Colleen 206
Moore, Constance 635, 643, 646
Moore, Terry 191, 209-210, 333, 424, 450, 628, 661, 682, 693-694, 734-736, 739-741, 743-746, 748, 763
Moore, Tom 167
Moorehead, Agnes 442
Moreno, Antonio 57-58, 61, 64-66, 75, 224
Morgan, Frank 635
Morgan, Gloria Maria Mercedes 505
Morning After, The 619
Morosco, Walter 300
Morris, Chester ("Boston Blackie") 242, 307
Moseley, Ozell Robert 613
Mountbattan, Lady 116
"Mr. Kenneth" 767
Mr. S: My Life with Frank Sinatra 492
Mueller, Dr. Herbert 244
Muni, Paul 268
Munson, Ona 592
Munsters, The 620
Murphy, A. Sanford 132
Murphy, Audie 650, 661, 685-689
Murray, Mae 6, 7, 47

Mussolini, Benito 472
My Darling Clementine 628
My Forbidden Past 566, 618, 732
Nash, Alden 479
Naylor, Patricia 696
Nazimova, Alla 3, 4, 578
Neal, Tom 762
Neale, Wright 361
Negri, Pola 515
Neilan, Marshall ("Mickey") 47, 61, 100-101, 138, 140, 161-162, 171, 177
Nelson, Donald Marr 557, 561, 563
Nelson, Harmon Oscar ("Ham") 449, 452-454
New York World's Fair 1939 434
Newhill, Charles 410
Niagara 691
Nissen, Greta 163, 184
Niven, David 394, 593, 606, 673, 688
Niver, Kemp 731
Nixon, Patricia (a.k.a. Pat Ryan) 313
Nixon, Richard 314, 784, 794
Nobu 497
Normand, Mabel 65, 66
Norsworthy, Dr. Oscar 9
Novarro, Ramon 58, 65, 75, 138, 164, 198, 286-287
Oakes, Sir Harry 460
O'Banion, Deanie 267
Oberon, Merle 476
O'Brien, George 189, 221, 224-225, 246, 251, 266
O'Brien, Pat 254
O'Casey, Pat 207, 210, 216
Odekirk, Glenn 293-294, 306, 353, 386, 407-408, 411, 419, 424, 530, 539, 555, 559-560, 585-587, 650, 657, 659, 664-665, 711
Odets, Clifford 406, 432, 682-683
Odlum, Floyd 331, 721, 774
O'Dwyer, William 656
Of Human Bondage 449
Olden, Betsy 294
Olivier, Laurence 394
Olympiads, The 399
On the Other Hand (autoboigraphy of Fay Wray) 429

Onassis, Aristotle 637
Our Dancing Daughters 264
Our Hearts Were Young and Gay 618
Out of the Past 612, 728
Outlaw, The 435, 526, 528-529, 531, 533-537, 561, 607, 667, 681
Paget, Debra 437, 694, 746
Pahlavi, Mahmud 677
Papas. Irene 766
Paris When it Sizzles 483
Parkinson, H.B. 168
Parsons, Louella 72, 125, 167, 171, 174, 210, 223, 226, 237, 240, 258, 263, 292, 319, 405, 407, 431, 438, 442, 447, 449, 457, 463-465, 488, 502, 581, 593, 666, 691, 781
Pascal, Ernest 234
Passions of Howard Hughes, The 209, 682
Patriot, The 152
Payment on Demand (a.k.a. Story of a Divorce, The) 454
Payne, Frederick 709
Payton, Barbara 757-760, 762
Peardon, Patricia 378
Pearson, Drew 701, 704
Pearson, Johnny 520
Peck, Gregory 499, 501, 758
Pegler, Westbrook 703
Pelgram, Robert 453
Perelle, Charles W. 552
Perfect Specimen 397
Perkins, Emily 373
Peron, Evita 304
Perry, Harry 173
Persson, W.F. 343
Peters, Jean 437, 439, 441-442, 598, 649, 657, 660-662, 684-688, 690-696, 702, 714, 716, 737, 764, 775-776, 778-781, 790, 793
Peters, Susan 483
Petrali, Joe 586-588, 594, 598, 600, 711
Philadelphia Story, The 443, 447
Philips, C.K. 180
Philips, Mary 225
Picasso, Pablo 77
Pickford, Jack 163

Pickford, Mary 44, 65, 74, 80, 101, 116, 131, 167, 206, 450, 475
Pidgeon, Walter 635
Pillow Talk 719
Plant, Philip 139
Plantation Cafe 192
Playboy 684
Plymouth Adventure 647
Polanski, Roman 280
Portrait of a Survivor 437
Post, Mae 420
Post, Marjorie Merriweather 668
Post, Wiley 408, 422
Postman Always Rings Twice, The 636
Poussin, Robert 744
Powell, Dick 442, 727
Powell, William 225, 245, 635
Power, Tyrone 354-355, 358, 390, 401, 477, 577-578, 581-582, 591, 624, 635, 637, 642, 647, 672, 685, 690, 716-719, 721, 774
Prather, Edward 12, 16
Preminger, Otto 756
Prevost, Marie 159-160
Preyssing, Louis 381, 391
Price, Vincent 401
Priester, Harvey 341
Pringle, Aileen 61
Prosso School, The 13
Prysing, Ranghild 381
Pussy-Katt 575-576
Put the Blame on Mame 672-673
Quality Street 372
Quantrill, Robert 156-157
Queer People 226-227
Quimet, Annabella 484
Quine, Richard 483
Quinn, Anthony 620
Quirk, Lawrence J. 448
Rachel and the Stranger 730
Raft, George 219, 232, 260, 268, 298, 507
Rainer, Luise 406-407
Rambova, Natasha 386
Ramsomme, Cary 413
Rancho Notorious (Chuck-a-Luck) 497
Rand, Sally 277

Rappe, Virginia 318
Rathbone, Basil 396
Rathvon, N. Peter 722, 724
Reagan, Ronald 435, 442, 458, 492, 727
Real, Jack 790
Reed, Charles 520
Reed, Luther 162
Reeper, Jack 315
Rehak, Rob 789
Remarque, Erich Maria 637
Renault, Francis 317, 361
Reno, Wood Jane 600, 602, 604-605
Return of October, The 734
Reynolds, Debbie 752
Rice, Mattie 109
Rice, William Marsh 88
Richards, Glenn 234
Richardson, Dr. James 13
Rickenbacker, Captain Eddie 657
Rio, Frank 268
Rivera, Diego 637
RKO Studios 667, 721-722, 724-725,
727, 729, 737, 758
Roach, Hal 192-193
Road to Morocco, The 620
Robbins, Harold 305, 612
Robinson, Edward G. 268, 399, 635
Rockefeller, W.C. 408
Rogers, Charles (Buddy) 147
Rogers, Ginger 160, 196, 248, 261-264,
285, 289, 313, 347, 386, 388-391, 406-
407, 437, 453, 455, 467, 479-481, 488,
657
Rogers, Lela 263, 388, 455, 479
Rollerbit 18
Roman Holiday 755
Romance of Rosy Ridge, The 478
Rooney, Mickey 477, 561, 563-564, 570,
635, 682
Roosevelt, Elliott 548-550, 565, 699,
703-706
Roosevelt, Franklin Delano 433, 656,
700, 703, 705-706
Rose de France, La 101
Roselli, Johnny 250
Rosen, Al 268
Rossellini, Roberto 496, 500, 503

Rossinni, George 702
Rosson, Harold G. 245, 286
Rubio, Lopez 570
Rubirosa (*née* Trujillo), Flor de Oro 304
Rubirosa, Porfirio 303-304, 306, 462,
626, 640, 682
Rudel, Sam 311
Rummel, Robert W. 306
Runyon, Damon 682
Russell, Gail 613, 616-619
Russell, Jane 436, 522-523, 525-527,
529, 534-535, 537-538, 577, 617, 657,
725, 732
Russell, Rosalind 393-394
Ryan, Robert 683, 723
Sachel, Victor 39
Sadie (Ava Gardner's maid) 571-572
Salome 5
Salome, Where She Danced 620
Samuel, Louis 286
Sanders, George 682, 721
Saunders, John Monk 427, 429, 432
Saxon, Ralph 413
Scarface 264, 273-274
Schary, Dore 722-724
Schenck, Joe 180, 192, 227
Scherer, Dr. Walter 15
Schiffrin, William 625
Schindler Detective Agency, the 704
Scholl, Danny 301
Scott, Randolph 197-199, 205, 208, 213,
216, 218, 226, 259, 314, 319, 359-360,
450, 635
Scott, Walter 367
Sea Queen, The 482
Sea-Air 405
Search for Beauty 297
Sears, The Rev. Peter Gray 95, 110
Sebring, Jay 280
Secrets of the Wasteland, 492
Seiter, Ralph 58
Self-Portrait (autobiograpy of Gene
Tierney) 644
Selznick, David O. 243, 275, 435, 465,
496, 614, 635, 657, 730
Selznick, Irene Mayer 496, 498-499
Sennett, Mack 126

Service de Luxe 401
Shah of Iran, The 677
Shampoo 638
Shamroy, Leon 679
Sharp, Dudley 12, 14-15, 18, 23-24, 27, 29, 33, 35, 41, 67, 69, 87, 96-98, 100, 107-109, 164-165, 302, 433
Sharp, Estelle (Mrs. Walter Sharp) 12, 16, 96-98, 165
Sharp, Walter 12, 16
Shaw, Artie 632, 769
She Couldn't Say No 733
Shearer, Norma 450, 475-478, 507, 610
Shelby, Charlotte 50, 65-66
Sherman, Lowell 318
Sherwood, Robert E. 231, 234, 242
Shields, Jimmie 76
Shimon, Lt. Joseph W.W. 704
Short, Elizabeth (Black Dahlia) 761
Showboat 771
Shubert, Yvonne 439-441, 694
Shulman, Irving 277
Sieber, Rudolph 581
Siegel, Benjamin (Bugsy) 245, 250, 338, 384, 591, 635, 682, 707
Signoret, Simone 777
Sikorsky S-43 Amphibian 552-555
Sikorsky, The 586, 588-590, 592-593, 598, 600
Silver Bullet, The 306, 326-327
Simmons, Jean 670, 733, 752, 754-757
Sinatra, Frank 571, 682, 720, 725, 770-772, 774
Since You Went Away 614-615
Singer from Seville, The 167
Sirocco 399
Skolsky, Sidney 781
Sky Devils 245, 443
Slack, Thomas A. 707
Slate, Claude 543
Slater, Walter S. 534
Slattery's Hurricane 641
Slide, Kelly, Slide 265
Small Town Girl 314
Smith, Ludlow Ogden 403-404
Smuckler, Florence 366
Somborn, Herbert K. 61

Somoza, Anastasio 794
Song of Russia 628
Southern Cross, The 290, 356, 380, 387, 400, 405, 439, 461, 463, 482, 602-603, 605-606
Spaatz, General Carl 665
Spainhour, John 630
Spangles, Charles 361
Spirit of St. Louis 158
Split Second 441
Spoilers, The 166
Spruce Goose ("Hercules" or the HK-1), The 552, 556, 560-561, 563, 708, 711, 713, 715
St. Johns, Adela Rogers 139, 199, 204, 277
St. Just, Rod 49, 50-51, 65, 141, 143, 189, 218
Stack, Robert 386-388, 390, 489, 491, 493, 620, 633
Stallone, Sylvester 686
Stanwyck, Barbara 247, 255, 468, 612, 683-684
Starrett, Charles 234-236
Stars in the Backyard 301
Stauffer, Teddy 670, 717-718, 721, 764
Steele, Joseph H. 498, 502
Steele, Sheryl 90-92, 96
Stella by Starlight 617
Sterling, Robert 446
Stevens, George 479
Stewart, James 245, 456, 477, 514, 724
Stockdale, Carl 66
Stockwell, Dean 724
Stoddart, Richard 408, 413, 420-421
Stoffler, Helen 738
Stoffler, William 737
Stokowsky, Leopold 511
Stolkin, Ralph 726
Stompanato, Johnny 612, 719-720, 769
Story of G.I. Joe 729
Straight Shooting (autobiography of Robert Stack) 387
Strickling, Howard 275-276, 278, 766
Stromboli (Terra di Dio) 500-501, 503
Struck, Floyd & Arlene 217
Sturges, Preston 667-669
Sullavan, Margaret 492-493

Sullivan, Barry 454
Sullivan, Ed 760
Summerlin, Jean Amelia 36
Sun Also Rises, The 774
Sutherland, Edward 246
Sutton, Robert 793
Swanson, Gloria 60, 72, 87, 100-101, 120, 181, 206, 259, 632
Sweet, Blanche 46-49, 56-57, 59, 64-66, 100-101, 181
Swell Hogan 124-127, 183, 301
Swope, Herbert & Margaret 429
Sylvia Scarlett 322
Symonette, Amos 604
Talmadge, Norma 139, 208
Tarnished Lady 271
Tashman, Lilyan 250
Tate, Sharon 280
Taylor, Elizabeth 749-752, 777, 778
Taylor, Francis 749
Taylor, Robert 308, 310-313, 335, 355, 356, 468-469, 471, 591, 620, 632
Taylor, Sara 749
Taylor, William Desmond 46, 49-52, 56, 62, 64-67, 336
Temple, Shirley 357
Tequila Nights 389
Tess of the d'Urbervilles 140
Thacher School, the 42, 55, 71
Thacher, Sherman Day 55, 69
Thain, Dr. Wilbur 791-792
Thalberg, Irving 82, 268, 275, 477
The Mating Call 165
Thelma Todd's Sidewalk Cafe 336-337
Therkelson 327
They Won't Forget 633
Thirty Day Princess 393
Thurlow, Lt. Thomas 408, 415
Tierney, Gene 642, 644-647, 666
Tilden, Bill 115-116
Till the End of Time 615
Titus, Dr. Jack L. 793, 795
Todd, Mary 690
Todd, Mike 752
Todd, Thelma 187, 191-192, 249-250, 336-340, 343-344
Toland, Gregg 526, 531

Tomick, Frank 170
Tone, Franchot 682, 759-762
Toolco 444, 722
Tracy, Spencer 225, 246, 265, 444, 452, 457, 637, 647, 724, 728, 766
Tremaine, Virginia 779
Tribute to a Bad Man 767
Trippe, Juan 700-701, 703, 708
Trujillo, General Rafael 303, 602
Truman, Harry S. 502, 656, 700, 706
Tryon, Tom 302
Turner, Captain Roscoe 170, 179, 230, 331, 377
Turner, Lana 493, 591, 592, 612, 629, 632-636, 655, 657, 661, 666, 716-719, 758, 768-769
TWA 444, 446, 597, 658, 667
Twain, Mark 598
Twentieth Century 197
Two Arabian Knights 152-153
Two O'Clock Courage 609
Udell, Ernst 127
Underworld 169
Uninvited, The 617
Unpardonable Sin, The 48
Valentine, Police Commissioner Louis 421
Valentino, Rudolph 224, 386
Vallee, Rudy 607-609, 620
Valmy, Roger 645
Vanderbilt, Gloria 249, 291, 460, 482, 505-511
Vavitch, Michael 151
Veidt, Conrad 515
Velez, Lupe 451
Vendetta 667, 669-670
Verges, Dr. Peter 631
Vernon, Alice 230
Veronica (autobiography of Veronica Lake) 640
Vidal, Gore 627
Vidor, King 77
Viva Zapata! 691
Von Höchstatten, Ritter Franz 472
Von Roserberg, Charles W. 553-555
Von Sternberg, Josef 726
Von Stroheim, Erich 428

Vulcano (Volcano) 501
Wagner, A.F. 344
Wald, Jerry 683, 727
Waldron, Chuck 792
Walker, Dudley 322
Walker, Ralph 291, 293
Walker, Robert 614
Wallace, George 302
Wallace, Jean 761
Walsh, Raoul 316
Walters, Charles 346
Warner, Doris 263
Warner, Jack 399, 454, 635
Waterfield, Robert 524, 537
Way of All Flesh, The 152
Wayne, John 266, 441-443, 637
Webb, Clifton 735
Webb, Maybelle 110
Weekend at the Waldorf 636
Weissmuller, Johnny 199, 451
Welles, H.G. 637
Welles, Orson 166, 168, 497, 670-671,
675-676, 682
Welles, Rebecca 672
Wellman, William ("Wild Bill") 147-149,
172, 178-179
Wenner-Gren, Axel 602-605
West, Mae 266, 314, 318
West, Roland 192-193, 337-338
Whale, James 163-164, 176, 178, 190,
194, 198, 202
Whalen, Grover 409, 412, 420, 423
Where Danger Lives 670
Where Love Has Gone 612
White Sister, The 246
White, Stephen 707
Whitehead, Mae 344
Whitney, Gertrude Vanderbilt 505, 509
Whitney, Jock 428, 637
Wilcox, Horace Henderson 117
Wilde, Roy 237, 242
Wilder, Billy 616
Wilding, Michael 751, 754
Willat, Irwin 128, 205, 207, 208, 210,
214-218, 223-225, 234, 237, 241
Williams, Tennessee 235, 319, 501
Willson, Henry 348, 486-487, 518-521,
541, 613, 615-616, 634, 662, 666, 738,
743, 765-767
Wilson, Al 179-180
Wilson, Lois 236-238
Winchell, Walter 273, 285, 359, 388, 421,
424, 453, 459-460, 682
Windsor, Claire 302
Windsor, Duchess of (Wallis Warfield
Simpson) 602-604
Windsor, Duke of 603, 777
Winged Bullet, The 376-377
Wings 147, 150
Winning of Barbara Worth, The 140
Winsor, Kathleen 769
Winston, James Overton 88, 95, 107-108,
352-353
Wise, Robert 766
Wolfe, Thomas 245
Wolheim, Louis 151, 158, 253
Woman of the Year 443
*Won Ton Ton, the Dog who Saved
Hollywood* 617
Woolley, Monty 355-356
Woulfe, Michael 440
Wray, Fay 427-432
Wright, Harold Bell 140
Wyler, William 755
Wyman, Jane 435, 458, 727
XF-11, The (a.k.a. The D-5) 551, 649-
652, 654-655, 660, 664-665, 687, 695,
708, 715
Young Man of Manhattan 263
Young Widow 537
Young, Loretta 355, 597
Yumasheff, Andrei 417
Yvonne (Memoirs of Yvonne de Carlo)
621
Zantetti, Enrique de Cruzat 57
Zanuck, Darryl F. 356, 402, 566, 577,
629, 671, 679, 684-685, 687, 735, 745
Zapruder, Abraham 783
Zurlo, John 779
Zwillman, Abner ("Longy") 228, 280

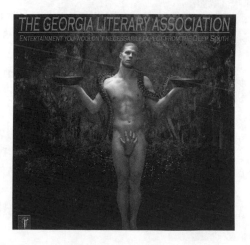

The Secret Life of HUMPHREY BOGART

The Early Years (1899-1931)

by Darwin Porter

When it was released in June of 2003, this book ignited a firestorm of media controversy that spilled immediately from the tabloids into mainstream newspapers, magazines, and talk shows.

This is one of the best, most controversial, and most revealing books ever written about the movie stars of the Golden Age.

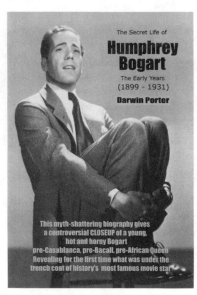

The Secret Life of
Humphrey Bogart
The Early Years
(1899 - 1931)
Darwin Porter

This myth-shattering biography gives a controversial CLOSEUP of a young, hot and horny Bogart pre-Casablanca, pre-Bacall, pre-African Queen Revealing for the first time what was under the trench coat of history's most famous movie star

"Humphrey Bogart was one of Hollywood's most celebrated lovers, his romance with Lauren Bacall hailed as one of the greatest love stories of the 20th century. But before they met, he was a drug-taking womanizer, racking up a string of failed marriages and broken relationships with some of the world's most beautiful women. In this extraordinary biography, drawing on a wealth of previously unseen material, veteran showbusiness writer Darwin Porter, author of *Hollywood's Silent Closet,* reveals the truth about Bogart's shady past."

As reported by London's *Mail on Sunday* in June of 2003

From The Georgia Literary Association
ISBN 0966-8030-5-1
528 pages, plus 64 photos. $16.95

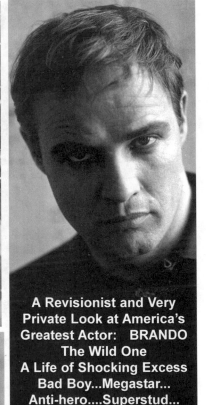